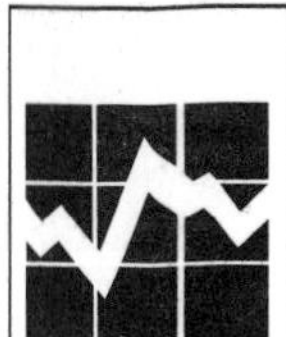

Statistics Canada

Profile of Census Tracts in Toronto

Volume III

Statistique Canada

Profil des secteurs de recensement de Toronto

Volume III

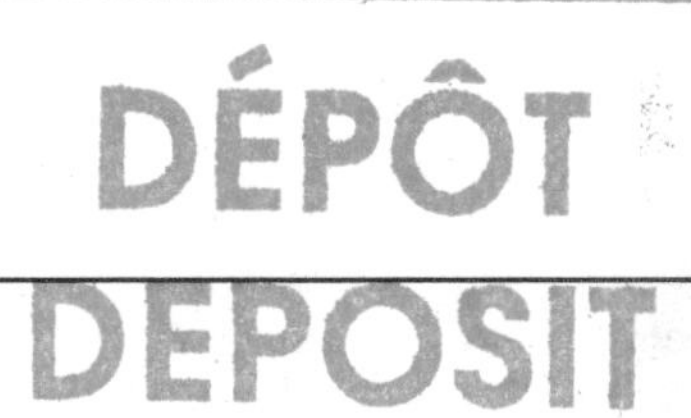

Published by authority of the Minister responsible for Statistics Canada

February 2004

Catalogue No. 95-240-XPB

ISBN 0-660-61905-9

Ottawa

Publication autorisée par le ministre responsable de Statistique Canada

Février 2004

N° 95-240-XPB au catalogue

ISBN 0-660-61905-9

Ottawa

Note of Appreciation

Canada owes the success of its statistical system to a long-standing partnership between Statistics Canada, the citizens of Canada, its businesses, governments and other institutions. Accurate and timely statistical information could not be produced without their continued co-operation and goodwill.

Note de reconnaissance

Le succès du système statistique du Canada repose sur un partenariat bien établi entre Statistique Canada et la population, les entreprises, les administrations et les autres organismes du Canada. Sans cette collaboration et cette bonne volonté, il serait impossible de produire des statistiques précises et actuelles.

National Library of Canada Cataloguing in Publication Data

Profile of census tracts in Toronto = Profil des secteurs de recensement de Toronto

Published in 3 v.
Text in English and French.

ISBN 0-660-61905-9
CS95-240-XPB

1. Toronto (Ont.) - Population - Statistics.
2. Census districts - Ontario - Toronto - Statistics.
3. Toronto (Ont.) - Census, 2001. 4. Canada - Census, 2001. I. Statistics Canada. II. Title: Profil des secteurs de recensement de Toronto.

HA741.5.2001 304.6'09713'541021
C2003-988024-9E

Données de catalogage avant publication de la Bibliothèque nationale du Canada

Profile of census tracts in Toronto = Profil des secteurs de recensement de Toronto

Publié en 3 vol.
Texte en anglais et en français.

ISBN 0-660-61905-9
CS95-240-XPB

1. Toronto (Ont.) - Population - Statistiques démographiques. 2. Secteurs de recensement - Ontario - Toronto - Statistiques. 3. Toronto (Ont.) - Recensement, 2001. 4. Canada - Recensement, 2001. I. Statistique Canada. II. Titre : Profil des secteurs de recensement de Toronto.

HA741.5.2001 304.6'09713'541021
C2003-988024-9F

How to Cite this Document

Statistics Canada. Profile of Census Tracts. Ottawa: Industry Canada, 2004. 2001 Census of Canada. Catalogue number 95-240-XPB.

Pour citer ce document

Statistique Canada. Profil des secteurs de recensement. Ottawa : Industrie Canada, 2004. Recensement du Canada de 2001. Numéro 95-240-XPB au catalogue.

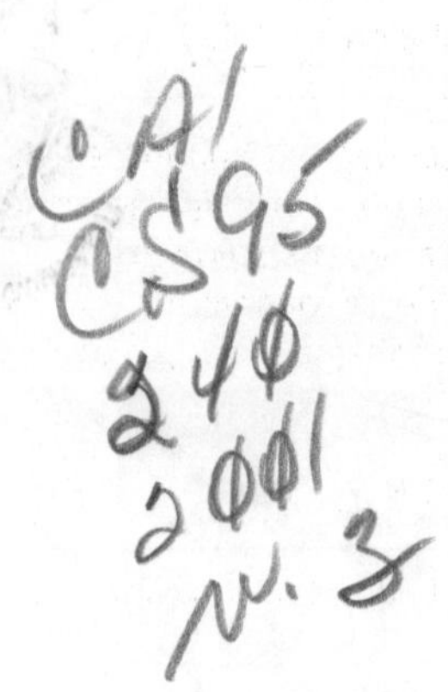

The paper used in this publication meets the minimum requirements of American National Standard for Information Sciences – Permanence of Paper for Printed Library Materials, ANSI Z39.48-1984.

∞

Le papier utilisé dans la présente publication répond aux exigences minimales de l'American National Standard for Information Sciences – Permanence of Paper for Printed Library Materials, ANSI Z39.48-1984.

∞

Table of Contents

Page

Introductory Material

Introduction 1221
Symbols 1222
Abbreviations 1223
Census Subdivision Types 1223
Geographic Index 1224
Constituent Census Tracts for Census Subdivisions 1234
Conversion Table 1235

Table

Table 1. Selected Characteristics for Census Tracts, 2001 Census – 100% Data and 20% Sample Data

Toronto CMA 1242

Reference Material

Footnotes 1723
Definitions 1729
Data Quality 1738
Special Notes 1741
Appendix 1. Incompletely Enumerated Indian Reserves and Indian Settlements, 1996 and 1991 Population Counts 1745
Appendix 2. Suppressed Census Tracts Showing Population Counts by Census Metropolitan Area and Census Agglomeration, 2001 Census 1746

How To Get Help

Regional Reference Centres 1747

Maps

Table des matières

Page

Documents d'introduction

Introduction 1221
Signes conventionnels 1222
Abréviations 1223
Genres de subdivisions de recensement 1223
Index géographique 1224
Secteurs de recensement constituant les subdivisions de recensement 1234
Table de conversion 1235

Tableau

Tableau 1. Certaines caractéristiques des secteurs de recensement, recensement de 2001 – Données intégrales et données-échantillon (20 %)
Toronto RMR 1242

Documents de référence

Renvois 1723
Définitions 1749
Qualité des données 1759
Notes spéciales 1763
Annexe 1. Réserves indiennes et établissements indiens partiellement dénombrés, chiffres de population de 1996 et de 1991 1768
Annexe 2. Secteurs de recensement supprimés par chiffres de population selon la région métropolitaine de recensement et l'agglomération de recensement, recensement de 2001 1769

Comment trouver de l'aide

Centres régionaux de consultation 1770

Cartes

Introduction

The 2001 Census Area Profiles are designed to provide a statistical overview, or profile, for lower levels of geography. Each publication in this series provides a profile of census tracts (CTs) in a census metropolitan area (CMA) or a census agglomeration (CA). The Area Profiles are based on data collected by the 2001 Census of Canada from all households.

In response to client needs, variables from the 20% database are available sooner than ever before. The 2001 Census Area Profiles contain population counts for characteristics from both 100% data and 20% sample data, in each publication. New for 2001 are data on language used at work, generation status, and religion, the latter being reported every 10 years. This series also contains incidence reporting for single- or multiple-response variables. Incidence reporting will display specific categories based on the most frequently reported responses in a CMA or CA. The variables affected by incidence reporting are mother tongue, home language, knowledge of non-official languages, language used at work, and ethnic origin. On the whole, searching for 2001 Census information on your community can now be done sooner and at a greater level of detail.

Each publication in this series consists of a single table displaying the data for geographic areas in a columnar format. The data variables, also referred to as "stubs", are displayed in English on the left side of the table and in French on the right side. With the combination of variables from the 100% and 20% databases, the stubset covers 10 pages. Characteristics of the data have been grouped into blocks by theme, or universe (i.e. population, dwelling and household, family and income). Within each theme, the data are displayed showing different characteristics such as marital status, ethnic origin and census family structure and size.

The geographic headings run across the top of the page. The CTs are sequenced by numerical order within the CMAs and CAs. Reference maps showing CT boundaries are included at the back of each publication.

Definitions of the geographic areas and variables displayed in each publication can be found in the Reference Material section. Also provided at the end of each publication are data quality notes and special notes.

Introduction

Les Profils des secteurs du recensement de 2001 sont conçus de façon à fournir un aperçu statistique, ou profil, de petites régions géographiques. Chaque publication de cette série fournit un profil des secteurs de recensement (SR) d'une région métropolitaine de recensement (RMR) ou d'une agglomération de recensement (AR). Les Profils des secteurs sont fondés sur les données du Recensement du Canada de 2001 pour tous les ménages.

En réponse aux besoins des clients, les variables de la base de données-échantillon (20 %) sont disponibles plus tôt qu'elles ne l'ont jamais été. Les Profils des secteurs du recensement de 2001 contiennent les chiffres de la population selon des caractéristiques des données intégrales (100 %) et des données-échantillon (20 %), réunies dans chaque publication. Du nouveau pour 2001 : il y a des données portant sur la langue utilisée au travail, le statut des générations et la religion, cette dernière étant déclarée tous les 10 ans. Cette série comprend également des fréquences de déclaration pour les variables à réponses uniques et à réponses multiples. La fréquence de déclaration verra certaines catégories présentées selon les réponses le plus souvent déclarées dans une RMR ou une AR. Les variables touchées par la fréquence de déclaration sont la langue maternelle, la langue parlée à la maison, la connaissance des langues non officielles, la langue utilisée au travail et l'origine ethnique. En somme, vous pouvez dorénavant rechercher les informations du recensement de 2001 portant sur votre communauté plus tôt qu'auparavant, et à un niveau plus détaillé.

Chaque publication de cette série consiste en un seul tableau auquel figurent, sous forme de colonnes, les données pour les régions géographiques. Les variables de données, ou « titres », sont affichées en anglais du côté gauche du tableau et en français du côté droit. L'ensemble de titres résultant de la combinaison des variables provenant de la base de données intégrales (100 %) et de la base de données-échantillon (20 %) compte 10 pages. Les caractéristiques des données ont été regroupées en blocs, selon des thèmes ou univers (par exemple, la population, les logements et les ménages, les familles et le revenu). À partir de chacun de ces thèmes, les données sont affichées de façon à souligner les diverses caractéristiques telles l'état matrimonial, l'origine ethnique et la structure et la taille de la famille de recensement.

Les en-têtes géographiques figurent d'un côté à l'autre du haut de la page. Les SR s'enchaînent en suivant un ordre numérique à partir des RMR et des AR. Les cartes de référence démontrant les limites des SR figurent à la fin de chaque publication.

Les définitions des régions géographiques et des variables comprises dans chaque publication apparaissent dans la section sur les documents de référence. On retrouve aussi les notes sur la qualité des données et les notes spéciales à la fin de chaque publication.

Symbols

The following standard symbols are found in this publication.

... Figures not appropriate or not applicable.

– Nil or zero.

XXX Figures suppressed to protect confidentiality.

A 1996 adjusted count; most of these are the result of boundary changes.

¶ Incompletely enumerated Indian reserve or Indian settlement (suppressed).

† Excludes census data for one or more incompletely enumerated Indian reserves or Indian settlements.

◆ Data quality index showing, for the short census questionnaire (100% data), a global non-response rate higher than or equal to 5% but lower than 10%.

◆◆ Data quality index showing, for the short census questionnaire (100% data), a global non-response rate higher than or equal to 10% but lower than 25%.

◆◆◆ Data quality index showing, for the short census questionnaire (100% data), a global non-response rate higher than or equal to 25% (suppressed).

■ An error exists in the 2001 population and dwelling counts for this area. For further information, refer to the "Special Notes" section.

◇ Data quality index showing, for the long census questionnaire (20% sample data), a global non-response rate higher than or equal to 5% but lower than 10%.

◇◇ Data quality index showing, for the long census questionnaire (20% sample data), a global non-response rate higher than or equal to 10% but lower than 25%.

◇◇◇ Data quality index showing, for the long census questionnaire (20% sample data) or the short census questionnaire (100% data), a global non-response rate higher than or equal to 25% (suppressed).

• Part of a census tract.

Signes conventionnels

Les signes conventionnels suivants sont retrouvés dans cette publication.

... N'ayant pas lieu de figurer.

– Néant ou zéro.

XXX Nombres supprimés afin de protéger la confidentialité.

A Chiffre de 1996 rajusté; la plupart de ces rajustements sont le résultat de modifications des limites.

¶ Réserve indienne ou établissement indien partiellement dénombré (supprimées).

† Ne comprend pas les données du recensement pour une ou plusieurs réserves indiennes ou établissements indiens partiellement dénombrés.

◆ Indice de la qualité des données indiquant, pour le questionnaire de recensement abrégé (données intégrales [100 %]), un taux global de non-réponse supérieur ou égal à 5 %, mais inférieur à 10 %.

◆◆ Indice de la qualité des données indiquant, pour le questionnaire de recensement abrégé (données intégrales [100 %]), un taux global de non-réponse supérieur ou égal à 10 %, mais inférieur à 25 %.

◆◆◆ Indice de la qualité des données indiquant, pour le questionnaire de recensement abrégé (données intégrales [100 %]), un taux global de non-réponse supérieur ou égal à 25 % (supprimées).

■ Il y a une erreur dans les chiffres de population et des logements de 2001 pour cette région. Pour de plus amples renseignements, veuillez consulter la section « Notes spéciales ».

◇ Indice de la qualité des données indiquant, pour le questionnaire de recensement complet (données-échantillon [20 %]), un taux global de non-réponse supérieur ou égal à 5 %, mais inférieur à 10 %.

◇◇ Indice de la qualité des données indiquant, pour le questionnaire de recensement complet (données-échantillon [20 %]), un taux global de non-réponse supérieur ou égal à 10 %, mais inférieur à 25 %.

◇◇◇ Indice de la qualité des données indiquant, pour le questionnaire de recensement complet (données-échantillon [20 %]) ou pour le questionnaire de recensement abrégé (données intégrales [100 %]), un taux global de non-réponse supérieur ou égal à 25 % (supprimées).

• Partie de secteur de recensement.

Abbreviations

1997 NAICS = 1997 North American Industry Classification System

2001 NOC–S = 2001 National Occupational Classification for Statistics

n.e.c. = not elsewhere classified

n.i.e. = not included elsewhere

n.o.s. = not otherwise specified

Abréviations

SCIAN de 1997 = Système de classification des industries de l'Amérique du Nord de 1997

CNP–S de 2001 = Classification nationale des professions pour statistiques de 2001

n.c.a. = non classé ailleurs

n.i.a = non inclus ailleurs

n.d.a. = non déclaré ailleurs

Census Subdivision Types – Genres de subdivisions de recensement

C City – Cité
CC Chartered Community
CM County (Municipality)
COM Community
CT Canton (Municipalité de)
CU Cantons unis (Municipalité de)
DM District Municipality
HAM Hamlet
ID Improvement District
IGD Indian Government District
IM Island Municipality
LGD Local Government District
LOT Township and Royalty
M Municipalité
MD Municipal District
NH Northern Hamlet
NL Nisga'a Land
NV Northern Village
NVL Nisga'a Village
P Paroisse (Municipalité de)
PAR Parish
R Indian Reserve – Réserve indienne
RC Rural Community

RDA Regional District Electoral Area
RG Region
RGM Regional Municipality
RM Rural Municipality
RV Resort Village
S–E Indian Settlement – Établissement indien
SA Special Area
SCM Subdivision of County Municipality
SET Settlement
SM Specialized Municipality
SUN Subdivision of Unorganized
SV Summer Village
T Town
TI Terre inuite
TL Teslin Land
TP Township
TR Terres réservées
UNO Unorganized – Non organisé
V Ville
VC Village cri
VK Village naskapi
VL Village
VN Village nordique

Geographic Index

Census Metropolitan Areas, Census Agglomerations and Census Tracts

Index géographique

Régions métropolitaines de recensement, agglomérations de recensement et secteurs de recensement

Toronto CMA/RMR

Volume I:	Toronto 0001	to - à	Toronto 0282	Pages: 22 - 561
Volume II:	Toronto 0283.01	to - à	Toronto 0473.02	Pages: 632 - 1171
Volume III:	Toronto 0473.03	to - à	Toronto 0832	Pages: 1242 - 1721

	Page
Toronto CMA/RMR **A**	22
Toronto 0001	22
Toronto 0002	22
Toronto 0004	22
Toronto 0005	22
Toronto 0006	22
Toronto 0007.01	23
Toronto 0007.02	23
Toronto 0008 ◇◇	23
Toronto 0009	23
Toronto 0010 ◇	23
Toronto 0011 ◇	23
Toronto 0012	42
Toronto 0013 ◆◆	42
Toronto 0014	42
Toronto 0015 ◆	42
Toronto 0016 ◆◇◇◇	42
Toronto 0017 ◆	42
Toronto 0018 ◆◇◇	43
Toronto 0019 ◆	43
Toronto 0020	43
Toronto 0021	43
Toronto 0022	43
Toronto 0023	43
Toronto 0024	62
Toronto 0025	62
Toronto 0026 ◆	62
Toronto 0027 ◇	62
Toronto 0028 ◇	62
Toronto 0029 ◆◇	62
Toronto 0030 ◆◇◇	63
Toronto 0031	63
Toronto 0032 ◆◇◇◇	63
Toronto 0033 ◇	63
Toronto 0034 ◆◇◇	63
Toronto 0035 ◆	63
Toronto 0036 ◇	82
Toronto 0037	82
Toronto 0038	82
Toronto 0039	82
Toronto 0040	82
Toronto 0041	82

	Page
Toronto 0042	83
Toronto 0043	83
Toronto 0044 ◆	83
Toronto 0045 ◆◇	83
Toronto 0046 ◆	83
Toronto 0047.01 **A**	83
Toronto 0047.02 **A**	102
Toronto 0048 ◆	102
Toronto 0049	102
Toronto 0050.01	102
Toronto 0050.02 ◆	102
Toronto 0051 ◆	102
Toronto 0052	103
Toronto 0053 ◇	103
Toronto 0054 ◆	103
Toronto 0055 ◇	103
Toronto 0056	103
Toronto 0057 ◇	103
Toronto 0058	122
Toronto 0059 ◇◇	122
Toronto 0060	122
Toronto 0061 ◆◇	122
Toronto 0062.01 **A**	122
Toronto 0062.02 ◆ **A**	122
Toronto 0063.01 ◆	123
Toronto 0063.02 ◆	123
Toronto 0064 ◆	123
Toronto 0065 ◆	123
Toronto 0066	123
Toronto 0067	123
Toronto 0068	142
Toronto 0069	142
Toronto 0070	142
Toronto 0071	142
Toronto 0072.01 ◆ **A**	142
Toronto 0072.02 **A**	142
Toronto 0073	143
Toronto 0074 ◆	143
Toronto 0075 ◆	143
Toronto 0076	143
Toronto 0077	143
Toronto 0078	143

See reference material at the end of the publication. – Voir les documents de référence à la fin de la publication.

Geographic Index

Census Metropolitan Areas, Census Agglomerations and Census Tracts

Index géographique

Régions métropolitaines de recensement, agglomérations de recensement et secteurs de recensement

	Page
Toronto 0079	162
Toronto 0080.01 **A**	162
Toronto 0080.02 ◆ **A**	162
Toronto 0081 ◇	162
Toronto 0082	162
Toronto 0083 ◆	162
Toronto 0084	163
Toronto 0085 ◆	163
Toronto 0086	163
Toronto 0087	163
Toronto 0088	163
Toronto 0089 ◆	163
Toronto 0090 ◆	182
Toronto 0091.01 ◇◇	182
Toronto 0091.02 ◇	182
Toronto 0092	182
Toronto 0093	182
Toronto 0094	182
Toronto 0095	183
Toronto 0096 ◆	183
Toronto 0097.01 ◆◇	183
Toronto 0097.02 ◆◇	183
Toronto 0098 ◆	183
Toronto 0099 ◆	183
Toronto 0100 ◆◇	202
Toronto 0101 ◆	202
Toronto 0102.01 **A**	202
Toronto 0102.02 ◆ **A**	202
Toronto 0102.03 ◆ **A**	202
Toronto 0103	202
Toronto 0104	203
Toronto 0105	203
Toronto 0106 ◆◇	203
Toronto 0107	203
Toronto 0108	203
Toronto 0109	203
Toronto 0110	222
Toronto 0111 ◆◇	222
Toronto 0112	222
Toronto 0113	222
Toronto 0114 ◆	222
Toronto 0115	222
Toronto 0116 ◇	223
Toronto 0117 ◆	223
Toronto 0118	223
Toronto 0119 ◆	223
Toronto 0120 ◆	223
Toronto 0121	223

	Page
Toronto 0122 ◆	242
Toronto 0123 ◆	242
Toronto 0124	242
Toronto 0125 ◆	242
Toronto 0126 ◆	242
Toronto 0127	242
Toronto 0128.01 ◆◇	243
Toronto 0128.02	243
Toronto 0129	243
Toronto 0130	243
Toronto 0131	243
Toronto 0132	243
Toronto 0133	262
Toronto 0134	262
Toronto 0135 ◆	262
Toronto 0136.01 ◆ **A**	262
Toronto 0136.02 ◆ **A**	262
Toronto 0137 ◆	262
Toronto 0138	263
Toronto 0139	263
Toronto 0140 ◆	263
Toronto 0141.01	263
Toronto 0141.02	263
Toronto 0142	263
Toronto 0150	282
Toronto 0151 ◆	282
Toronto 0152	282
Toronto 0153	282
Toronto 0154	282
Toronto 0155 ◆	282
Toronto 0156.01	283
Toronto 0156.02	283
Toronto 0157	283
Toronto 0158	283
Toronto 0159.01 ◇ **A**	283
Toronto 0159.02 **A**	283
Toronto 0160 ◇	302
Toronto 0161	302
Toronto 0162	302
Toronto 0163 ◆	302
Toronto 0164	302
Toronto 0165 ◆	302
Toronto 0166	303
Toronto 0167.01 ◆	303
Toronto 0167.02	303
Toronto 0168 ◆	303
Toronto 0169.01	303
Toronto 0169.02	303

See reference material at the end of the publication. – Voir les documents de référence à la fin de la publication.

Geographic Index

Census Metropolitan Areas, Census Agglomerations and Census Tracts

Index géographique

Régions métropolitaines de recensement, agglomérations de recensement et secteurs de recensement

	Page
Toronto 0170	322
Toronto 0171	322
Toronto 0172 ◆◇	322
Toronto 0173	322
Toronto 0174	322
Toronto 0175.01	322
Toronto 0175.02	323
Toronto 0176	323
Toronto 0180 ◆◇	323
Toronto 0181.01	323
Toronto 0181.02	323
Toronto 0182	323
Toronto 0183	342
Toronto 0184.01 ◆	342
Toronto 0184.02 ◆	342
Toronto 0185.01	342
Toronto 0185.02 ◆	342
Toronto 0186	342
Toronto 0187	343
Toronto 0188	343
Toronto 0189	343
Toronto 0190.01 ◆	343
Toronto 0190.02	343
Toronto 0191	343
Toronto 0192	362
Toronto 0193	362
Toronto 0194.01 ◆ **A**	362
Toronto 0194.02 **A**	362
Toronto 0194.03 **A**	362
Toronto 0194.04 **A**	362
Toronto 0195	363
Toronto 0196	363
Toronto 0200 ◆	363
Toronto 0201 ◆	363
Toronto 0202	363
Toronto 0203 ◆	363
Toronto 0204 ◆	382
Toronto 0205	382
Toronto 0206.01	382
Toronto 0206.02 ◆	382
Toronto 0207 ◆	382
Toronto 0208 ◆	382
Toronto 0209	383
Toronto 0210 ◆	383
Toronto 0211	383
Toronto 0212	383
Toronto 0213 ◆	383
Toronto 0214	383

	Page
Toronto 0215	402
Toronto 0216	402
Toronto 0217 ◆	402
Toronto 0218	402
Toronto 0219	402
Toronto 0220	402
Toronto 0221.01	403
Toronto 0221.02	403
Toronto 0222.01 ◆	403
Toronto 0222.02 ◆	403
Toronto 0223	403
Toronto 0224	403
Toronto 0225.01 **A**	422
Toronto 0225.02 ◆ **A**	422
Toronto 0226	422
Toronto 0227	422
Toronto 0228	422
Toronto 0229	422
Toronto 0230.01	423
Toronto 0230.02	423
Toronto 0231	423
Toronto 0232	423
Toronto 0233	423
Toronto 0234	423
Toronto 0235.01	442
Toronto 0235.02	442
Toronto 0236.01	442
Toronto 0236.02 ◇	442
Toronto 0237.01	442
Toronto 0237.02	442
Toronto 0237.03 ◆	443
Toronto 0238.01	443
Toronto 0238.02	443
Toronto 0239 ◆	443
Toronto 0240.01	443
Toronto 0240.02 ◆	443
Toronto 0241	462
Toronto 0242 ◆	462
Toronto 0243.01 ◆	462
Toronto 0243.02	462
Toronto 0244.01 ◆	462
Toronto 0244.02 ◆	462
Toronto 0245 ◆	463
Toronto 0246	463
Toronto 0247.01 **A**	463
Toronto 0247.02 ◆◇ **A**	463
Toronto 0248.02 ◇	463
Toronto 0248.03 ◆	463

See reference material at the end of the publication. – Voir les documents de référence à la fin de la publication.

Geographic Index

Census Metropolitan Areas, Census Agglomerations and Census Tracts

Index géographique

Régions métropolitaines de recensement, agglomérations de recensement et secteurs de recensement

	Page
Toronto 0248.04 **A**	482
Toronto 0248.05 **A**	482
Toronto 0249.01	482
Toronto 0249.03 ◇	482
Toronto 0249.04 **A**	482
Toronto 0249.05 ◆ **A**	482
Toronto 0250.01 ◆	483
Toronto 0250.02 ◆	483
Toronto 0250.04 ◆ **A**	483
Toronto 0250.05 ◆ **A**	483
Toronto 0260.01 ◆	483
Toronto 0260.03 ◆	483
Toronto 0260.04 **A**	502
Toronto 0260.05 ◆ **A**	502
Toronto 0261	502
Toronto 0262.01	502
Toronto 0262.02	502
Toronto 0263.02 ◆	502
Toronto 0263.03 ◆ **A**	503
Toronto 0263.04 **A**	503
Toronto 0264 ◇	503
Toronto 0265 ◆◆	503
Toronto 0266	503
Toronto 0267	503
Toronto 0268	522
Toronto 0269.01 **A**	522
Toronto 0269.02 **A**	522
Toronto 0270.01	522
Toronto 0270.02	522
Toronto 0271.01	522
Toronto 0271.02	523
Toronto 0272.01	523
Toronto 0272.02	523
Toronto 0273.01	523
Toronto 0273.02	523
Toronto 0274.01 ◆	523
Toronto 0274.02	542
Toronto 0275	542
Toronto 0276.01	542
Toronto 0276.02	542
Toronto 0277 ◇◇	542
Toronto 0278	542
Toronto 0279.01 ◆	543
Toronto 0279.02	543
Toronto 0280	543
Toronto 0281.01 **A**	543
Toronto 0281.02 **A**	543
Toronto 0282	543

	Page
Toronto CMA/RMR **A**	632
Toronto 0283.01	632
Toronto 0283.02	632
Toronto 0284	632
Toronto 0285	632
Toronto 0286 ◆◇	632
Toronto 0287.01 ◆	633
Toronto 0287.02 ◆◇	633
Toronto 0288	633
Toronto 0289	633
Toronto 0290	633
Toronto 0291.01	633
Toronto 0291.02	652
Toronto 0292 ◇	652
Toronto 0293	652
Toronto 0294.01	652
Toronto 0294.02	652
Toronto 0295	652
Toronto 0296	653
Toronto 0297.01	653
Toronto 0297.02	653
Toronto 0298	653
Toronto 0299	653
Toronto 0300	653
Toronto 0301.01	672
Toronto 0301.03 **A**	672
Toronto 0301.04 **A**	672
Toronto 0302.01	672
Toronto 0302.02	672
Toronto 0302.03	672
Toronto 0303	673
Toronto 0304.01	673
Toronto 0304.02	673
Toronto 0304.03	673
Toronto 0304.04	673
Toronto 0304.05	673
Toronto 0304.06	692
Toronto 0305.01 **A**	692
Toronto 0305.02 **A**	692
Toronto 0306.01 **A**	692
Toronto 0306.02 **A**	692
Toronto 0307.01 **A**	692
Toronto 0307.02 **A**	693
Toronto 0308.01	693
Toronto 0308.02	693
Toronto 0309	693
Toronto 0310.01	693
Toronto 0310.02	693

See reference material at the end of the publication. – Voir les documents de référence à la fin de la publication.

Geographic Index
Census Metropolitan Areas, Census Agglomerations and Census Tracts

Index géographique
Régions métropolitaines de recensement, agglomérations de recensement et secteurs de recensement

Page

Toronto 0311.02 712
Toronto 0311.03 712
Toronto 0311.04 ◇ 712
Toronto 0311.05 **A** 712
Toronto 0311.06 **A** 712
Toronto 0312.02 712

Toronto 0312.03 713
Toronto 0312.04 713
Toronto 0312.05 713
Toronto 0312.06 **A** 713
Toronto 0312.07 **A** 713
Toronto 0313 713

Toronto 0314.01 732
Toronto 0314.02 732
Toronto 0315.01 732
Toronto 0315.02 732
Toronto 0315.03 732
Toronto 0316.01 732

Toronto 0316.03 733
Toronto 0316.04 ◇ 733
Toronto 0316.05 **A** 733
Toronto 0316.06 ◆◇ **A** 733
Toronto 0317.02 733
Toronto 0317.03 733

Toronto 0317.04 **A** 752
Toronto 0317.05 **A** 752
Toronto 0318 752
Toronto 0319 752
Toronto 0320.01 752
Toronto 0320.02 752

Toronto 0321.01 **A** 753
Toronto 0321.02 **A** 753
Toronto 0322 753
Toronto 0323.01 753
Toronto 0323.02 753
Toronto 0324.01 753

Toronto 0324.02 772
Toronto 0324.03 772
Toronto 0324.05 **A** 772
Toronto 0324.06 **A** 772
Toronto 0330 772
Toronto 0331.01 772

Toronto 0331.03 ◆ **A** 773
Toronto 0331.04 **A** 773
Toronto 0332 ◆◇ 773
Toronto 0333 ◇ 773
Toronto 0334 773
Toronto 0335 773

Page

Toronto 0336 792
Toronto 0337 792
Toronto 0338 ◆ 792
Toronto 0339 792
Toronto 0340 792
Toronto 0341.02 792

Toronto 0341.03 ◆ **A** 793
Toronto 0341.04 ◆ **A** 793
Toronto 0342 793
Toronto 0343 793
Toronto 0344.01 **A** 793
Toronto 0344.02 ◆ **A** 793

Toronto 0345 ◆◇ 812
Toronto 0346.01 ◇ 812
Toronto 0346.02 ◆ 812
Toronto 0347 ◇ 812
Toronto 0348 812
Toronto 0349 ◆◇ 812

Toronto 0350 813
Toronto 0351.01 **A** 813
Toronto 0351.02 **A** 813
Toronto 0352 813
Toronto 0353.02 813
Toronto 0353.03 ◆ **A** 813

Toronto 0353.04 ◆ **A** 832
Toronto 0354 832
Toronto 0355.02 832
Toronto 0355.03 **A** 832
Toronto 0355.04 **A** 832
Toronto 0356 ◆ 832

Toronto 0357.01 833
Toronto 0357.02 833
Toronto 0358.01 833
Toronto 0358.02 ◆ 833
Toronto 0358.03 ◆◇◇ 833
Toronto 0359 833

Toronto 0360 ◆◇◇ 852
Toronto 0361.01 ◇ 852
Toronto 0361.02 852
Toronto 0362.01 852
Toronto 0362.02 852
Toronto 0362.03 852

Toronto 0362.04 ◆ 853
Toronto 0363.02 853
Toronto 0363.03 853
Toronto 0363.04 **A** 853
Toronto 0363.05 ◆ **A** 853
Toronto 0364.01 853

See reference material at the end of the publication. – Voir les documents de référence à la fin de la publication.

Geographic Index

Census Metropolitan Areas, Census Agglomerations and Census Tracts

Index géographique

Régions métropolitaines de recensement, agglomérations de recensement et secteurs de recensement

	Page
Toronto 0364.02	872
Toronto 0365	872
Toronto 0366 ◆	872
Toronto 0367.01	872
Toronto 0367.02	872
Toronto 0368	872
Toronto 0369 ◇	873
Toronto 0370.01 ◆	873
Toronto 0370.02	873
Toronto 0370.03	873
Toronto 0371	873
Toronto 0372	873
Toronto 0373	892
Toronto 0374.01	892
Toronto 0374.02	892
Toronto 0374.03	892
Toronto 0375.01	892
Toronto 0375.02	892
Toronto 0375.03	893
Toronto 0375.04	893
Toronto 0375.05	893
Toronto 0376.01	893
Toronto 0376.02	893
Toronto 0376.04	893
Toronto 0376.05	912
Toronto 0376.07	912
Toronto 0376.08	912
Toronto 0376.09	912
Toronto 0376.11 **A**	912
Toronto 0376.12 **A**	912
Toronto 0376.13 **A**	913
Toronto 0376.14 **A**	913
Toronto 0377.01	913
Toronto 0377.02	913
Toronto 0377.03	913
Toronto 0377.04	913
Toronto 0377.06 **A**	932
Toronto 0377.07 **A**	932
Toronto 0378.01	932
Toronto 0378.02	932
Toronto 0378.03	932
Toronto 0378.04	932
Toronto 0378.05	933
Toronto 0378.06 ◆	933
Toronto 0378.07	933
Toronto 0378.08	933
Toronto 0378.10	933
Toronto 0378.11	933

	Page
Toronto 0378.12 ◇	952
Toronto 0378.14	952
Toronto 0378.16 ◆ **A**	952
Toronto 0378.17 ◇ **A**	952
Toronto 0378.18 **A**	952
Toronto 0378.19 **A**	952
Toronto 0378.20 **A**	953
Toronto 0378.21 **A**	953
Toronto 0378.22 **A**	953
Toronto 0400.01	953
Toronto 0400.02	953
Toronto 0400.03	953
Toronto 0400.04 ◆	972
Toronto 0400.05	972
Toronto 0400.06	972
Toronto 0400.07	972
Toronto 0400.08 ◆	972
Toronto 0400.09	972
Toronto 0400.10	973
Toronto 0400.11	973
Toronto 0400.12	973
Toronto 0401.01	973
Toronto 0401.03	973
Toronto 0401.04	973
Toronto 0401.06	992
Toronto 0401.07	992
Toronto 0401.08	992
Toronto 0401.09	992
Toronto 0401.10	992
Toronto 0401.11	992
Toronto 0401.12	993
Toronto 0401.13	993
Toronto 0401.14 **A**	993
Toronto 0401.15 **A**	993
Toronto 0402.01	993
Toronto 0402.02	993
Toronto 0402.03	1012
Toronto 0402.04	1012
Toronto 0402.05	1012
Toronto 0402.06	1012
Toronto 0402.07	1012
Toronto 0402.08	1012
Toronto 0402.09	1013
Toronto 0402.10	1013
Toronto 0402.11	1013
Toronto 0403.01 **A**	1013
Toronto 0403.02 **A**	1013
Toronto 0410.02	1013

See reference material at the end of the publication. – Voir les documents de référence à la fin de la publication.

Geographic Index
Census Metropolitan Areas, Census Agglomerations and Census Tracts

Index géographique
Régions métropolitaines de recensement, agglomérations de recensement et secteurs de recensement

Page

Toronto 0410.03 1032
Toronto 0410.04 1032
Toronto 0410.05 1032
Toronto 0410.07 1032
Toronto 0410.09 ◆ **A** 1032
Toronto 0410.10 **A** 1032

Toronto 0410.11 **A** 1033
Toronto 0410.12 ◆ **A** 1033
Toronto 0410.13 **A** 1033
Toronto 0410.14 **A** 1033
Toronto 0410.15 **A** 1033
Toronto 0411.01 1033

Toronto 0411.02 1052
Toronto 0411.03 1052
Toronto 0411.04 1052
Toronto 0411.05 1052
Toronto 0412.01 1052
Toronto 0412.02 1052

Toronto 0412.03 1053
Toronto 0412.04 1053
Toronto 0412.05 1053
Toronto 0412.06 ◆◆ 1053
Toronto 0412.07 1053
Toronto 0412.08 1053

Toronto 0412.10 ◇ **A** 1072
Toronto 0412.11 **A** 1072
Toronto 0413 1072
Toronto 0420.03 1072
Toronto 0420.05 **A** 1072
Toronto 0420.06 **A** 1072

Toronto 0420.07 **A** 1073
Toronto 0420.08 ◆ **A** 1073
Toronto 0420.09 **A** 1073
Toronto 0420.10 **A** 1073
Toronto 0420.11 **A** 1073
Toronto 0421.01 1073

Toronto 0421.04 **A** 1092
Toronto 0421.05 **A** 1092
Toronto 0421.06 **A** 1092
Toronto 0421.07 **A** 1092
Toronto 0422.01 1092
Toronto 0422.02 1092

Toronto 0423.01 1093
Toronto 0423.02 1093
Toronto 0424.02 1093
Toronto 0424.03 1093
Toronto 0424.04 **A** 1093
Toronto 0424.05 **A** 1093

Page

Toronto 0424.06 **A** 1112
Toronto 0430.01 1112
Toronto 0430.02 1112
Toronto 0431.01 1112
Toronto 0431.02 1112
Toronto 0440 1112

Toronto 0441.02 1113
Toronto 0441.03 **A** 1113
Toronto 0441.04 **A** 1113
Toronto 0442.01 1113
Toronto 0442.02 1113
Toronto 0442.03 1113

Toronto 0450.02 1132
Toronto 0450.03 **A** 1132
Toronto 0450.04 **A** 1132
Toronto 0451.01 1132
Toronto 0451.02 1132
Toronto 0451.03 1132

Toronto 0451.04 1133
Toronto 0452.01 1133
Toronto 0452.02 1133
Toronto 0452.03 1133
Toronto 0452.04 1133
Toronto 0455 1133

Toronto 0456.01 1152
Toronto 0456.02 1152
Toronto 0456.03 1152
Toronto 0460.01 1152
Toronto 0460.02 1152
Toronto 0461.01 1152

Toronto 0461.02 1153
Toronto 0470 1153
Toronto 0471 1153
Toronto 0472 1153
Toronto 0473.01 **A** 1153
Toronto 0473.02 **A** 1153

Toronto CMA/RMR **A** 1242
Toronto 0473.03 **A** 1242
Toronto 0474 1242
Toronto 0475 1242
Toronto 0476 ◆◇◇ 1242
Toronto 0480.01 **A** 1242

Toronto 0480.02 **A** 1243
Toronto 0481 1243
Toronto 0482 1243
Toronto 0483 1243
Toronto 0484 1243
Toronto 0485.01 **A** 1243

See reference material at the end of the publication. – Voir les documents de référence à la fin de la publication.

Geographic Index
Census Metropolitan Areas, Census Agglomerations and Census Tracts

Index géographique
Régions métropolitaines de recensement, agglomérations de recensement et secteurs de recensement

	Page
Toronto 0485.02 **A**	1262
Toronto 0500.01	1262
Toronto 0500.02	1262
Toronto 0501.01	1262
Toronto 0501.02	1262
Toronto 0502.01	1262
Toronto 0502.02	1263
Toronto 0503	1263
Toronto 0504	1263
Toronto 0505.01	1263
Toronto 0505.02	1263
Toronto 0506	1263
Toronto 0507	1282
Toronto 0508	1282
Toronto 0509.01	1282
Toronto 0509.02	1282
Toronto 0510	1282
Toronto 0511.01	1282
Toronto 0511.02	1283
Toronto 0512 ◆	1283
Toronto 0513.01 ◆	1283
Toronto 0513.02	1283
Toronto 0513.03	1283
Toronto 0513.04	1283
Toronto 0514.01 **A**	1302
Toronto 0514.02 **A**	1302
Toronto 0515.01	1302
Toronto 0515.02	1302
Toronto 0516.01	1302
Toronto 0516.02	1302
Toronto 0516.03	1303
Toronto 0516.04	1303
Toronto 0516.05	1303
Toronto 0516.06	1303
Toronto 0516.08	1303
Toronto 0516.09	1303
Toronto 0516.10	1322
Toronto 0516.11	1322
Toronto 0516.14 ◆	1322
Toronto 0516.16 ◆◇	1322
Toronto 0516.17 **A**	1322
Toronto 0516.18 **A**	1322
Toronto 0516.19 **A**	1323
Toronto 0516.20 **A**	1323
Toronto 0516.21 **A**	1323
Toronto 0516.22 **A**	1323
Toronto 0516.23 **A**	1323
Toronto 0516.24 **A**	1323

	Page
Toronto 0516.25 **A**	1342
Toronto 0516.26 **A**	1342
Toronto 0516.27 **A**	1342
Toronto 0516.28 **A**	1342
Toronto 0516.29 **A**	1342
Toronto 0517	1342
Toronto 0518 ◆	1343
Toronto 0519	1343
Toronto 0520.01 ◆	1343
Toronto 0520.02	1343
Toronto 0520.04	1343
Toronto 0520.05 **A**	1343
Toronto 0520.06 **A**	1362
Toronto 0521.01 ◆	1362
Toronto 0521.02 ◆	1362
Toronto 0521.03	1362
Toronto 0521.04	1362
Toronto 0521.05 ◆	1362
Toronto 0521.06 ◆	1363
Toronto 0522 ◆	1363
Toronto 0523 ◆	1363
Toronto 0524.01 ◆◇	1363
Toronto 0524.02 ◆	1363
Toronto 0525.01 ◆	1363
Toronto 0525.02 ◆	1382
Toronto 0526.01	1382
Toronto 0526.02 ◆◇	1382
Toronto 0527.01	1382
Toronto 0527.02	1382
Toronto 0527.03	1382
Toronto 0527.04	1383
Toronto 0527.05	1383
Toronto 0527.06 ◇	1383
Toronto 0527.07	1383
Toronto 0527.08	1383
Toronto 0527.09	1383
Toronto 0528.01	1402
Toronto 0528.02	1402
Toronto 0528.04	1402
Toronto 0528.10 ◆ **A**	1402
Toronto 0528.11 **A**	1402
Toronto 0528.12 **A**	1402
Toronto 0528.13 **A**	1403
Toronto 0528.14 **A**	1403
Toronto 0528.15 **A**	1403
Toronto 0528.16 **A**	1403
Toronto 0528.17 **A**	1403
Toronto 0528.18 **A**	1403

See reference material at the end of the publication. – Voir les documents de référence à la fin de la publication.

Geographic Index
Census Metropolitan Areas, Census Agglomerations and Census Tracts

Index géographique
Régions métropolitaines de recensement, agglomérations de recensement et secteurs de recensement

	Page
Toronto 0528.19 ◆◇ **A**	1422
Toronto 0528.20 **A**	1422
Toronto 0528.21 ◆ **A**	1422
Toronto 0528.22 ◆ **A**	1422
Toronto 0528.23 ◆ **A**	1422
Toronto 0528.24 **A**	1422
Toronto 0528.25 ◆ **A**	1423
Toronto 0528.26 **A**	1423
Toronto 0528.27 **A**	1423
Toronto 0528.28 **A**	1423
Toronto 0528.29 ◆ **A**	1423
Toronto 0528.30 **A**	1423
Toronto 0528.31 **A**	1442
Toronto 0529.01 ◆	1442
Toronto 0529.02 ◆◇	1442
Toronto 0530 ◆	1442
Toronto 0531.01	1442
Toronto 0531.02 ◆◇ **A**	1442
Toronto 0532.01 ◆◇	1443
Toronto 0532.02 ◆◇	1443
Toronto 0540.01	1443
Toronto 0540.02	1443
Toronto 0550.01	1443
Toronto 0550.02	1443
Toronto 0560 **A**	1462
Toronto 0561 **A**	1462
Toronto 0562.01 ◆ **A**	1462
Toronto 0562.02	1462
Toronto 0562.03	1462
Toronto 0562.04 ◇	1462
Toronto 0562.05	1463
Toronto 0562.06	1463
Toronto 0562.07	1463
Toronto 0562.08	1463
Toronto 0562.09	1463
Toronto 0562.10	1463
Toronto 0562.11	1482
Toronto 0563.01	1482
Toronto 0563.02	1482
Toronto 0564.01	1482
Toronto 0564.02 ◆	1482
Toronto 0570.01 ◆	1482
Toronto 0570.02	1483
Toronto 0571.01	1483
Toronto 0571.02	1483
Toronto 0572.01	1483
Toronto 0572.04 **A**	1483
Toronto 0572.05 ◆ **A**	1483

	Page
Toronto 0572.06 **A**	1502
Toronto 0572.07 **A**	1502
Toronto 0572.08 **A**	1502
Toronto 0573.02	1502
Toronto 0573.03	1502
Toronto 0573.04 **A**	1502
Toronto 0573.05 **A**	1503
Toronto 0574	1503
Toronto 0575.01	1503
Toronto 0575.02	1503
Toronto 0575.03	1503
Toronto 0575.04	1503
Toronto 0575.05	1522
Toronto 0575.06	1522
Toronto 0576.01	1522
Toronto 0576.04	1522
Toronto 0576.05	1522
Toronto 0576.06	1522
Toronto 0576.07	1523
Toronto 0576.08 **A**	1523
Toronto 0576.09 **A**	1523
Toronto 0576.10 **A**	1523
Toronto 0576.11 **A**	1523
Toronto 0576.12 **A**	1523
Toronto 0576.13 **A**	1542
Toronto 0585.02	1542
Toronto 0585.03	1542
Toronto 0585.05 **A**	1542
Toronto 0585.06 **A**	1542
Toronto 0585.07 **A**	1542
Toronto 0585.08 **A**	1543
Toronto 0586 **A**	1543
Toronto 0587.01	1543
Toronto 0587.02	1543
Toronto 0590	1543
Toronto 0591	1543
Toronto 0592.01 **A**	1562
Toronto 0592.02 **A**	1562
Toronto 0593	1562
Toronto 0600.01	1562
Toronto 0600.02	1562
Toronto 0601	1562
Toronto 0602	1563
Toronto 0603	1563
Toronto 0604	1563
Toronto 0605	1563
Toronto 0606	1563
Toronto 0607	1563

See reference material at the end of the publication. – Voir les documents de référence à la fin de la publication.

Geographic Index

Census Metropolitan Areas, Census Agglomerations and Census Tracts

Index géographique

Régions métropolitaines de recensement, agglomérations de recensement et secteurs de recensement

Page

Toronto 0608 1582
Toronto 0609 1582
Toronto 0610.02 1582
Toronto 0610.03 **A** 1582
Toronto 0610.04 **A** 1582
Toronto 0611 1582

Toronto 0612.01 1583
Toronto 0612.02 1583
Toronto 0612.03 1583
Toronto 0612.05 1583
Toronto 0612.07 1583
Toronto 0612.08 1583

Toronto 0612.09 1602
Toronto 0612.10 ◆ 1602
Toronto 0612.11 **A** 1602
Toronto 0612.12 **A** 1602
Toronto 0612.13 **A** 1602
Toronto 0612.14 **A** 1602

Toronto 0613.01 1603
Toronto 0613.03 **A** 1603
Toronto 0613.04 **A** 1603
Toronto 0614.01 **A** 1603
Toronto 0614.02 **A** 1603
Toronto 0615 1603

Toronto 0620 1622
Toronto 0621 1622
Toronto 0622 1622
Toronto 0623 1622
Toronto 0624 1622
Toronto 0625 1622

Toronto 0626 1623
Toronto 0630 1623
Toronto 0631 1623
Toronto 0632 1623
Toronto 0633 1623
Toronto 0634 1623

Toronto 0635 1642
Toronto 0636 1642
Toronto 0637 1642
Toronto 0638 1642
Toronto 0639 1642
Toronto 0800.01 1642

Page

Toronto 0800.02 1643
Toronto 0801.01 1643
Toronto 0801.02 1643
Toronto 0802.01 **A** 1643
Toronto 0802.02 **A** 1643
Toronto 0803.03 **A** 1643

Toronto 0803.04 **A** 1662
Toronto 0803.05 **A** 1662
Toronto 0803.06 **A** 1662
Toronto 0804.01 1662
Toronto 0804.02 **A** 1662
Toronto 0804.05 1662

Toronto 0804.06 **A** 1663
Toronto 0804.07 **A** 1663
Toronto 0804.08 **A** 1663
Toronto 0804.09 **A** 1663
Toronto 0805.02 1663
Toronto 0805.03 **A** 1663

Toronto 0805.04 **A** 1682
Toronto 0805.05 **A** 1682
Toronto 0805.06 **A** 1682
Toronto 0805.07 **A** 1682
Toronto 0806 **A** 1682
Toronto 0807 1682

Toronto 0810.01 1683
Toronto 0810.02 1683
Toronto 0810.03 1683
Toronto 0810.04 1683
Toronto 0810.05 1683
Toronto 0811 1683

Toronto 0812 1702
Toronto 0820.01 ◆ **A** 1702
Toronto 0820.02 **A** 1702
Toronto 0820.03 **A** 1702
Toronto 0830 1702
Toronto 0831.01 **A** 1702

Toronto 0831.02 **A** 1703
Toronto 0832 1703

See reference material at the end of the publication. – Voir les documents de référence à la fin de la publication.

Constituent Census Tracts for Census Subdivisions

Secteurs de recensement constituant les subdivisions de recensement

Census Subdivisions Subdivisions de recensement	Census Tracts Secteurs de recensement
Toronto CMA/RMR	
Ajax, T	0805.02-0805.07, 0810.01-0820.03
Aurora, T	0440-0442.03
Bradford West Gwillimbury, T	0480.01-0482
Brampton, C	0528.20-0528.22, 0528.29, 0528.31, 0560-0576.13
Caledon, T	0585.02-0587.02
Chippewas of Georgina Island First Nation, R	0474•, 0476•
East Gwillimbury, T	0455-0456.03
Georgina, T	0470-0473.03, 0474•, 0475, 0476•
Halton Hills, T	0630-0639
King, TP	0460.01-0461.02
Markham, T	0400.01-0403.02
Milton, T	0620-0626
Mississauga, C	0500.01-0528.19, 0528.23-0528.28, 0528.30, 0529.01-0550.02
Mono, T	0593
New Tecumseth, T	0483-0485.02
Newmarket, T	0450.02-0452.04
Oakville, T	0600.01-0615
Orangeville, T	0590-0592.02
Pickering, C	0800.01-0801.02, 0803.03-0804.09, 0806, 0807
Richmond Hill, T	0420.03-0424.06
Toronto, C	0001-0378.22, 0802.01, 0802.02
Uxbridge, TP	0830-0832
Vaughan, C	0410.02-0413
Whitchurch-Stouffville, T	0430.01-0431.02

See reference material at the end of the publication. – Voir les documents de référence à la fin de la publication.

Conversion Table – Table de conversion

Census tract numbers in 2001 with numbers for corresponding census tracts in 1996.

Numéros des secteurs de recensement en 2001 et numéros des secteurs de recensement correspondants en 1996.

Toronto

2001	1996
0047.01	0047•
0047.02	0047•
0062.01	0062•
0062.02	0062•
0072.01	0072•
0072.02	0072•
0080.01	0080•
0080.02	0080•
0102.01	0102•
0102.02	0102•
0102.03	0102•
0136.01	0136•
0136.02	0136•
0159.01	0159•
0159.02	0159•
0194.01	0194•
0194.02	0194•
0194.03	0194•
0194.04	0194•
0225.01	0225•
0225.02	0225•
0247.01	0247•
0247.02	0247•
0248.04	0248.01•
0248.05	0248.01•
0249.04	0249.02•
0249.05	0249.02•
0250.04	0250.03•
0250.05	0250.03•
0260.04	0260.02•
0260.05	0260.02•
0263.03	0263.01•
0263.04	0263.01•
0269.01	0269•
0269.02	0269•
0281.01	0281•
0281.02	0281•
0301.03	0301.02•
0301.04	0301.02•
0305.01	0305•
0305.02	0305•

See reference material at the end of the publication. – Voir les documents de référence à la fin de la publication.

Conversion Table – Table de conversion

Census tract numbers in 2001 with numbers for corresponding census tracts in 1996.

Numéros des secteurs de recensement en 2001 et numéros des secteurs de recensement correspondants en 1996.

Toronto

2001	1996
0306.01	0306•
0306.02	0306•
0307.01	0307•
0307.02	0307•
0311.05	0311.01•
0311.06	0311.01•
0312.06	0312.01•
0312.07	0312.01•
0316.05	0316.02•
0316.06	0316.02•
0317.04	0317.01•
0317.05	0317.01•
0321.01	0321•
0321.02	0321•
0324.05	0324.04•
0324.06	0324.04•
0331.03	0331.02•
0331.04	0331.02•
0341.03	0341.01•
0341.04	0341.01•
0344.01	0344•
0344.02	0344•
0351.01	0351•
0351.02	0351•
0353.03	0353.01•
0353.04	0353.01•
0355.03	0355.01•
0355.04	0355.01•
0363.04	0363.01•
0363.05	0363.01•
0376.11	0376.03•
0376.12	0376.03•
0376.13	0376.10•
0376.14	0376.10•
0377.06	0377.05•
0377.07	0377.05•
0378.16	0378.13•
0378.17	0378.13•
0378.18	0378.09•
0378.19	0378.09•
0378.20	0378.15•

See reference material at the end of the publication. – Voir les documents de référence à la fin de la publication.

Conversion Table – Table de conversion

Census tract numbers in 2001 with numbers for corresponding census tracts in 1996.

Numéros des secteurs de recensement en 2001 et numéros des secteurs de recensement correspondants en 1996.

Toronto

2001	1996
0378.21	0378.15•
0378.22	0378.15•
0401.14	0401.02•
0401.15	0401.02•
0403.01	0403•
0403.02	0403•
0410.09	0410.01•
0410.10	0410.01•
0410.11	0410.01•
0410.12	0410.06•
0410.13	0410.06•
0410.14	0410.08•
0410.15	0410.08•
0412.10	0412.09•
0412.11	0412.09•
0420.05	0420.01•
0420.06	0420.01•
0420.07	0420.01•
0420.08	0420.02•
0420.09	0420.02•
0420.10	0420.04•
0420.11	0420.04•
0421.04	0421.02•
0421.05	0421.02•
0421.06	0421.03•
0421.07	0421.03•
0424.04	0424.01•
0424.05	0424.01•
0424.06	0424.01•
0441.03	0441.01•
0441.04	0441.01•
0450.03	0450.01•
0450.04	0450.01•
0473.01	0473•
0473.02	0473•
0473.03	0473•
0480.01	0480•
0480.02	0480•
0485.01	0485•
0485.02	0485•, 0000
0514.01	0514•

See reference material at the end of the publication. – Voir les documents de référence à la fin de la publication.

Conversion Table – Table de conversion

Census tract numbers in 2001 with numbers for corresponding census tracts in 1996.

Numéros des secteurs de recensement en 2001 et numéros des secteurs de recensement correspondants en 1996.

Toronto

2001	1996
0514.02	0514•
0516.17	0516.07•
0516.18	0516.07•
0516.19	0516.12•
0516.20	0516.12•
0516.21	0516.12•
0516.22	0516.12•
0516.23	0516.12•
0516.24	0516.13•
0516.25	0516.13•
0516.26	0516.13•
0516.27	0516.15•
0516.28	0516.15•
0516.29	0516.15•
0520.05	0520.03•
0520.06	0520.03•
0528.10	0528.03•
0528.11	0528.03•
0528.12	0528.05•
0528.13	0528.05•
0528.14	0528.06•
0528.15	0528.06•
0528.16	0528.06•
0528.17	0528.06•, 0528.19•
0528.18	0528.06•
0528.19	0528.06•, 0528.19•
0528.20	0528.08•
0528.21	0528.08•
0528.22	0528.08•
0528.23	0528.09•
0528.24	0528.09•
0528.25	0528.09•
0528.26	0528.09•
0528.27	0528.09•
0528.28	0528.09•, 0528.28•, 0528.30•
0528.29	0528.07•
0528.30	0528.07•, 0528.30•
0528.31	0528.07•
0531.02	0531.02•
0532.02	0532.02•
0560	0528.28•, 0560

See reference material at the end of the publication. – Voir les documents de référence à la fin de la publication.

Conversion Table – Table de conversion

Census tract numbers in 2001 with numbers for corresponding census tracts in 1996.

Numéros des secteurs de recensement en 2001 et numéros des secteurs de recensement correspondants en 1996.

Toronto

2001	1996
0561	0561, 0528.28•
0562.01	0562.01, 0528.28•
0570.01	0570.01, 0528.28•
0572.04	0572.02•
0572.05	0572.02•
0572.06	0528.03•
0572.07	0572.03•
0572.08	0572.03•
0573.04	0573.01•
0573.05	0573.01•
0576.08	0576.02•, 0586•
0576.09	0576.02•
0576.10	0576.03•
0576.11	0576.03•
0576.12	0576.03•
0576.13	0576.03•, 0528.28•, 0531.02•, 0532.02•
0585.05	0585.04•
0585.06	0585.04•
0585.07	0585.01•
0585.08	0585.01•
0586	0586•
0592.01	0592•
0592.02	0592•
0610.03	0610.01•
0610.04	0610.01•
0612.11	0612.06•, 0612.11•
0612.12	0612.06•, 0612.11•
0612.13	0612.04•
0612.14	0612.04•
0613.03	0613.02•
0613.04	0613.02•
0614.01	0614•
0614.02	0614•
0802.01	0802•
0802.02	0802•
0803.03	0803.01•
0803.04	0803.01•
0803.05	0803.02•
0803.06	0803.02•
0804.02	0804.02, 0820.02•
0804.06	0804.03•

See reference material at the end of the publication. – Voir les documents de référence à la fin de la publication.

Conversion Table – Table de conversion

Census tract numbers in 2001 with numbers for corresponding census tracts in 1996.

Numéros des secteurs de recensement en 2001 et numéros des secteurs de recensement correspondants en 1996.

Toronto

2001	1996
0804.07	0804.03•
0804.08	0804.04•
0804.09	0804.04•, 0805.03•, 0820.01•, 0820.02•
0805.03	0805.03•, 0806•
0805.04	0805.01•
0805.05	0805.01•
0805.06	0805.01•
0805.07	0805.01•
0806	0806•
0820.01	0820•, 0820.01•
0820.02	0820•, 0820.02•
0820.03	0820•
0831.01	0831•
0831.02	0831•

See reference material at the end of the publication. – Voir les documents de référence à la fin de la publication.

Table
–
Tableau

Table 1. Selected Characteristics for Census Tracts, 2001 Census – 100% Data and 20% Sample Data

No.	Characteristics	Toronto A CMA/RMR	Toronto 0473.03 A	Toronto 0474	Toronto 0475	Toronto 0476 ◆◇◇	Toronto 0480.01 A
	POPULATION CHARACTERISTICS						
1	**Population, 1996 (1)**	**4,263,759**	**3,681**	**3,458**	**5,978**	**2,170**	**4,334**
2	**Population, 2001 (2)**	**4,682,897**	**3,884**	**4,141**	**6,366**	**2,469**	**4,443**
3	Population percentage change, 1996-2001	9.8	5.5	19.8	6.5	13.8	2.5
4	Land area in square kilometres, 2001	5,902.74	2.08	31.93	13.17	32.92	3.46
5	**Total population - 100% Data (3)**	**4,682,895**	**3,880**	**4,140**	**6,370**	**2,470**	**4,445**
	by sex and age groups						
6	Male	2,282,665	1,900	2,105	3,080	1,255	2,245
7	0-4 years	148,010	140	95	170	80	170
8	5-9 years	163,370	190	165	205	110	185
9	10-14 years	159,360	170	185	245	90	170
10	15-19 years	156,355	115	145	225	80	150
11	20-24 years	152,420	70	75	170	50	170
12	25-29 years	161,270	100	110	120	55	160
13	30-34 years	185,295	140	145	180	80	205
14	35-39 years	212,215	205	210	250	140	225
15	40-44 years	197,685	215	240	275	115	175
16	45-49 years	169,510	125	160	265	100	175
17	50-54 years	152,290	115	165	195	85	140
18	55-59 years	110,355	85	110	145	70	100
19	60-64 years	87,955	65	90	110	60	65
20	65-69 years	76,220	55	90	140	50	50
21	70-74 years	63,560	45	60	140	45	40
22	75-79 years	45,610	30	35	115	25	35
23	80-84 years	24,930	25	20	75	15	15
24	85 years and over	16,255	15	10	60	5	5
25	Female	2,400,230	1,980	2,030	3,290	1,215	2,195
26	0-4 years	140,650	120	140	175	50	155
27	5-9 years	154,175	185	140	175	85	180
28	10-14 years	150,590	195	165	225	100	140
29	15-19 years	147,580	130	115	220	85	140
30	20-24 years	154,190	100	80	155	50	140
31	25-29 years	173,420	80	105	135	50	165
32	30-34 years	198,160	155	165	180	80	200
33	35-39 years	218,570	240	215	305	135	225
34	40-44 years	207,070	185	220	305	125	180
35	45-49 years	182,220	125	145	260	85	155
36	50-54 years	160,690	120	140	195	80	125
37	55-59 years	115,200	85	110	145	80	90
38	60-64 years	95,605	65	90	135	60	75
39	65-69 years	84,655	60	60	140	45	55
40	70-74 years	76,525	55	55	165	45	60
41	75-79 years	64,955	40	50	170	25	55
42	80-84 years	39,710	25	20	105	15	35
43	85 years and over	36,275	25	15	105	15	25
44	**Total population 15 years and over**	**3,766,745**	**2,885**	**3,240**	**5,175**	**1,945**	**3,440**
	by legal marital status						
45	Never married (single)	1,225,500	745	910	1,480	580	1,015
46	Legally married (and not separated)	1,994,235	1,580	1,685	2,415	975	1,870
47	Separated, but still legally married	117,840	165	190	285	95	165
48	Divorced	220,760	245	295	485	185	220
49	Widowed	208,410	145	165	510	110	170
	by common-law status						
50	Not in a common-law relationship	3,579,710	2,565	2,835	4,675	1,665	3,130
51	In a common-law relationship	187,030	320	405	500	280	315
52	**Total population - 20% Sample Data (4)**	**4,647,955**	**3,885**	**4,115**	**6,150**	**2,470**	**4,445**
	by mother tongue						
53	Single responses	4,556,475	3,860	4,085	6,140	2,465	4,375
54	English	2,684,200	3,575	3,620	5,680	2,335	3,285
55	French	57,485	45	45	95	20	50
56	Non-official languages (5)	1,814,795	240	420	360	105	1,035
57	Italian	195,960	40	65	45	20	100
58	Chinese, n.o.s.	165,125	-	-	15	-	-
59	Cantonese	145,490	-	15	-	-	-
60	Portuguese	108,935	20	45	40	-	480
61	Punjabi	95,945	-	-	-	-	-
62	Other languages (6)	1,103,335	180	300	260	85	450
63	Multiple responses	91,480	25	30	10	-	75
64	English and French	7,810	20	10	-	-	40
65	English and non-official language	77,430	-	15	-	10	30
66	French and non-official language	4,590	-	10	-	10	-
67	English, French and non-official language	1,655	-	-	-	-	-

See reference material at the end of the publication. – Voir les documents de référence à la fin de la publication.

Tableau 1. Certaines caractéristiques des secteurs de recensement, recensement de 2001 – Données intégrales et données-échantillon (20 %)

Toronto 0480.02 A	Toronto 0481	Toronto 0482	Toronto 0483	Toronto 0484	Toronto 0485.01 A	Caractéristiques	N°
						CARACTÉRISTIQUES DE LA POPULATION	
3,497	**7,168**	**5,214**	**7,092**	**7,126**	**3,496**	**Population, 1996 (1)**	1
3,524	**9,113**	**5,148**	**7,764**	**8,696**	**3,712**	**Population, 2001 (2)**	2
0.8	27.1	-1.3	9.5	22.0	6.2	Variation en pourcentage de la population, 1996-2001	3
3.56	7.01	187.00	75.12	183.83	8.68	Superficie des terres en kilomètres carrés, 2001	4
3,525	**9,110**	**5,145**	**7,765**	**8,700**	**3,710**	**Population totale – Données intégrales (3)**	5
						selon le sexe et les groupes d'âge	
1,745	4,535	2,625	3,870	4,310	1,800	Sexe masculin	6
100	350	145	285	270	125	0-4 ans	7
170	395	180	315	335	150	5-9 ans	8
190	405	215	300	315	155	10-14 ans	9
175	335	205	300	260	130	15-19 ans	10
105	280	160	190	175	95	20-24 ans	11
75	320	130	210	205	100	25-29 ans	12
100	390	170	295	285	135	30-34 ans	13
180	495	210	395	420	175	35-39 ans	14
210	465	225	325	380	165	40-44 ans	15
160	305	225	285	295	125	45-49 ans	16
85	265	190	250	280	115	50-54 ans	17
65	175	185	210	225	65	55-59 ans	18
45	105	135	165	195	50	60-64 ans	19
35	90	100	105	210	60	65-69 ans	20
25	70	70	95	215	55	70-74 ans	21
20	45	50	95	155	55	75-79 ans	22
15	25	30	40	65	20	80-84 ans	23
5	20	10	25	40	25	85 ans et plus	24
1,780	4,580	2,520	3,895	4,385	1,910	Sexe féminin	25
95	345	150	270	275	115	0-4 ans	26
160	425	165	280	305	135	5-9 ans	27
180	365	205	270	290	175	10-14 ans	28
150	315	185	240	280	110	15-19 ans	29
105	260	135	175	175	115	20-24 ans	30
70	380	125	250	200	80	25-29 ans	31
105	380	180	295	280	140	30-34 ans	32
230	530	210	380	405	200	35-39 ans	33
210	420	235	370	365	170	40-44 ans	34
145	305	185	285	275	120	45-49 ans	35
90	260	205	240	295	105	50-54 ans	36
60	170	180	230	215	70	55-59 ans	37
40	90	110	145	215	65	60-64 ans	38
45	100	80	125	215	70	65-69 ans	39
35	80	70	125	215	65	70-74 ans	40
30	75	60	105	175	60	75-79 ans	41
10	40	30	70	105	55	80-84 ans	42
10	40	25	40	100	55	85 ans et plus	43
2,630	**6,830**	**4,080**	**6,040**	**6,915**	**2,850**	**Population totale de 15 ans et plus**	44
						selon l'état matrimonial légal	
725	1,835	1,095	1,540	1,550	755	Célibataire (jamais marié(e))	45
1,575	4,145	2,535	3,640	4,360	1,530	Légalement marié(e) (et non séparé(e))	46
90	235	100	225	210	125	Séparé(e), mais toujours légalement marié(e)	47
145	345	195	350	355	190	Divorcé(e)	48
95	270	155	290	445	255	Veuf ou veuve	49
						selon l'union libre	
2,485	6,370	3,835	5,555	6,420	2,675	Ne vivant pas en union libre	50
145	455	250	485	500	175	Vivant en union libre	51
3,525	**9,030**	**5,145**	**7,765**	**8,560**	**3,600**	**Population totale – Données-échantillon (20 %) (4)**	52
						selon la langue maternelle	
3,485	8,935	5,090	7,710	8,530	3,590	Réponses uniques	53
2,740	6,770	4,325	6,945	7,615	3,350	Anglais	54
45	190	45	100	100	60	Français	55
705	1,980	715	665	815	175	Langues non officielles (5)	56
120	225	145	140	185	15	Italien	57
10	30	-	-	10	-	Chinois, n.d.a.	58
-	30	-	20	10	-	Cantonais	59
265	755	105	30	40	-	Portugais	60
40	30	-	-	-	-	Pendjabi	61
275	910	470	475	575	160	Autres langues (6)	62
40	95	60	50	30	10	Réponses multiples	63
-	10	30	20	15	10	Anglais et français	64
35	75	25	30	-	-	Anglais et langue non officielle	65
-	15	-	-	-	-	Français et langue non officielle	66
-	-	-	-	-	-	Anglais, français et langue non officielle	67

See reference material at the end of the publication. – Voir les documents de référence à la fin de la publication.

Table 1. Selected Characteristics for Census Tracts, 2001 Census – 100% Data and 20% Sample Data

No.	Characteristics	Toronto A CMA/RMR	Toronto 0473.03 A	Toronto 0474	Toronto 0475	Toronto 0476 ◆◇◇	Toronto 0480.01 A
	POPULATION CHARACTERISTICS						
	by home language						
68	Single responses	3,605,875	3,725	3,930	6,005	2,400	3,895
69	English	2,902,975	3,720	3,865	5,925	2,390	3,520
70	French	9,875	-	-	10	-	-
71	Non-official languages (5)	693,025	-	65	75	10	375
72	Cantonese	88,970	-	-	-	-	-
73	Chinese, n.o.s.	81,940	-	-	20	-	-
74	Italian	51,800	-	45	10	-	30
75	Punjabi	49,180	-	-	-	-	-
76	Portuguese	37,055	-	15	15	-	200
77	Other languages (6)	384,075	-	-	30	10	145
78	Multiple responses	1,042,080	160	190	140	70	555
79	English and French	49,550	55	30	50	20	-
80	English and non-official language	970,100	110	155	85	50	540
81	French and non-official language	4,780	-	-	-	-	-
82	English, French and non-official language	17,655	-	-	-	10	10
	by knowledge of official languages						
83	English only	4,069,010	3,625	3,860	5,845	2,360	4,135
84	French only	4,070	-	-	10	-	-
85	English and French	393,415	255	240	280	110	180
86	Neither English nor French	181,455	-	15	30	-	125
	by knowledge of non-official languages (5) (7)						
87	Italian	277,560	45	100	60	40	160
88	Cantonese	178,675	-	15	-	-	-
89	Chinese, n.o.s.	161,150	-	-	20	-	-
90	Spanish	142,635	35	25	20	10	50
91	Portuguese	129,945	30	45	25	10	550
92	Punjabi	125,475	-	-	-	-	15
93	Tagalog (Pilipino)	106,590	-	-	-	-	-
	by first official language spoken						
94	English	4,366,370	3,835	4,055	6,040	2,445	4,250
95	French	61,075	50	40	80	25	60
96	English and French	43,460	-	10	-	-	15
97	Neither English nor French	177,055	-	15	25	-	120
98	Official language minority - (number) (8)	82,800	50	45	85	25	65
99	Official language minority - (percentage) (8)	1.8	1.3	1.1	1.4	1.0	1.5
	by ethnic origin (9)						
100	Canadian	861,945	1,445	1,780	2,430	1,090	1,615
101	English	783,770	1,760	1,375	2,405	745	1,080
102	Scottish	517,115	1,000	1,085	1,650	450	735
103	Irish	487,215	1,175	760	1,290	480	600
104	Chinese	435,690	-	35	20	-	10
105	Italian	429,385	190	190	220	190	395
106	East Indian	345,855	10	-	20	10	35
107	French	220,540	410	425	650	140	410
108	German	220,140	290	305	445	180	245
109	Portuguese	171,545	60	40	75	-	570
110	Polish	166,695	75	65	55	15	185
111	Jewish	161,215	50	30	-	25	25
112	Jamaican	150,840	-	10	25	25	30
113	Filipino	140,405	20	-	-	-	-
114	Ukrainian	104,490	200	120	70	40	125
	by Aboriginal identity						
115	Total Aboriginal identity population (10)	20,305	45	50	160	295	50
116	Total non-Aboriginal population	4,627,655	3,835	4,065	5,990	2,175	4,400
	by Aboriginal origin						
117	Total Aboriginal origins population (11)	44,400	160	75	275	325	190
118	Total non-Aboriginal population	4,603,555	3,725	4,035	5,875	2,145	4,255
	by Registered Indian status						
119	Registered Indian (12)	8,705	10	15	60	260	25
120	Not a Registered Indian	4,639,250	3,875	4,100	6,085	2,210	4,420

Tableau 1. Certaines caractéristiques des secteurs de recensement, recensement de 2001 – Données intégrales et données-échantillon (20 %)

Toronto 0480.02 A	Toronto 0481	Toronto 0482	Toronto 0483	Toronto 0484	Toronto 0485.01 A	Caractéristiques	N°
						CARACTÉRISTIQUES DE LA POPULATION	
						selon la langue parlée à la maison	
3,045	7,955	4,780	7,415	8,075	3,500	Réponses uniques	68
2,895	7,240	4,685	7,345	8,040	3,470	Anglais	69
-	20	-	-	-	-	Français	70
150	700	95	70	35	30	Langues non officielles (5)	71
-	-	-	10	-	-	Cantonais	72
-	10	-	-	-	-	Chinois, n.d.a.	73
-	45	45	15	10	-	Italien	74
20	20	-	-	-	-	Pendjabi	75
55	310	35	10	-	-	Portugais	76
75	315	20	40	35	30	Autres langues (6)	77
480	1,075	370	345	480	100	Réponses multiples	78
25	120	30	60	80	20	Anglais et français	79
455	915	335	280	385	80	Anglais et langue non officielle	80
-	10	-	-	15	-	Français et langue non officielle	81
-	30	-	10	-	-	Anglais, français et langue non officielle	82
						selon la connaissance des langues officielles	
3,265	8,170	4,810	7,345	8,055	3,435	Anglais seulement	83
-	15	-	-	-	-	Français seulement	84
190	650	300	405	495	150	Anglais et français	85
70	190	35	15	10	15	Ni l'anglais ni le français	86
						selon la connaissance des langues non officielles (5) (7)	
150	330	225	235	255	35	Italien	87
-	25	-	20	-	-	Cantonais	88
-	55	-	-	10	-	Chinois, n.d.a.	89
10	185	50	115	105	30	Espagnol	90
330	815	110	40	40	10	Portugais	91
45	25	-	-	-	-	Pendjabi	92
-	-	-	10	10	10	Tagalog (pilipino)	93
						selon la première langue officielle parlée	
3,400	8,585	5,050	7,660	8,455	3,530	Anglais	94
40	195	45	80	100	45	Français	95
15	70	20	10	-	10	Anglais et français	96
70	185	35	15	10	15	Ni l'anglais ni le français	97
45	230	55	85	100	50	Minorité de langue officielle - (nombre) (8)	98
1.3	2.5	1.1	1.1	1.2	1.4	Minorité de langue officielle - (pourcentage) (8)	99
						selon l'origine ethnique (9)	
1,145	3,350	1,630	3,030	3,415	1,460	Canadien	100
1,200	2,315	1,450	2,860	3,035	1,385	Anglais	101
650	1,670	1,045	1,920	2,025	875	Écossais	102
730	1,670	895	2,035	2,115	945	Irlandais	103
15	125	35	75	50	-	Chinois	104
365	855	415	410	655	200	Italien	105
55	90	45	-	40	-	Indien de l'Inde	106
345	800	300	755	625	350	Français	107
335	625	585	610	560	365	Allemand	108
350	990	140	65	100	20	Portugais	109
130	260	120	215	390	80	Polonais	110
45	20	40	35	10	-	Juif	111
90	105	50	65	50	10	Jamaïquain	112
-	20	-	15	35	-	Philippin	113
95	255	270	235	225	70	Ukrainien	114
						selon l'identité autochtone	
20	45	10	70	70	20	Total de la population ayant une identité autochtone (10)	115
3,505	8,980	5,140	7,695	8,485	3,575	Total de la population non autochtone	116
						selon l'origine autochtone	
75	160	45	160	175	100	Total de la population ayant une origine autochtone (11)	117
3,450	8,870	5,105	7,600	8,385	3,500	Total de la population non autochtone	118
						selon le statut d'Indien inscrit	
10	20	-	10	35	10	Oui, Indien inscrit (12)	119
3,515	9,005	5,145	7,755	8,525	3,590	Non, pas un Indien inscrit	120

Table 1. Selected Characteristics for Census Tracts, 2001 Census – 100% Data and 20% Sample Data

No.	Characteristics	Toronto A CMA/RMR	Toronto 0473.03 A	Toronto 0474	Toronto 0475	Toronto 0476 ◆◇◇	Toronto 0480.01 A
	POPULATION CHARACTERISTICS						
	by visible minority groups						
121	Total visible minority population	1,712,530	55	85	75	20	295
122	Chinese	409,530	-	30	25	-	20
123	South Asian	473,805	15	-	10	15	75
124	Black	310,500	-	25	-	-	35
125	Filipino	133,675	15	-	-	-	-
126	Latin American	75,910	-	-	15	-	25
127	Southeast Asian	53,565	-	-	-	-	75
128	Arab	42,830	-	10	-	-	20
129	West Asian	52,985	-	-	-	-	-
130	Korean	42,620	-	10	-	-	-
131	Japanese	17,420	10	-	-	-	-
132	Visible minority, n.i.e. (13)	66,450	-	10	25	-	45
133	Multiple visible minorities (14)	33,245	-	-	-	-	-
	by citizenship						
134	Canadian citizenship (15)	4,036,445	3,800	3,955	5,975	2,425	4,115
135	Citizenship other than Canadian	611,510	85	165	180	50	330
	by place of birth of respondent						
136	Non-immigrant population	2,556,860	3,495	3,455	5,335	2,235	3,315
137	Born in province of residence	2,224,905	3,115	3,095	4,810	2,085	2,975
138	Immigrant population (16)	2,032,960	380	660	810	225	1,110
139	United States	37,795	20	30	50	-	20
140	Central and South America	135,720	20	-	15	-	70
141	Caribbean and Bermuda	167,420	10	20	30	-	25
142	United Kingdom	142,985	155	205	340	90	140
143	Other Europe (17)	573,255	165	305	340	120	685
144	Africa	98,975	-	35	-	10	-
145	Asia and the Middle East	869,515	10	50	30	10	150
146	Oceania and other (18)	7,295	-	10	-	-	10
147	Non-permanent residents (19)	58,140	15	-	-	10	25
148	**Total immigrant population**	**2,032,960**	**380**	**665**	**810**	**230**	**1,110**
	by period of immigration						
149	Before 1961	223,520	125	200	400	100	230
150	1961-1970	251,390	135	150	220	60	140
151	1971-1980	343,130	55	120	85	35	285
152	1981-1990	422,890	30	60	60	20	230
153	1991-2001 (20)	792,030	40	130	45	-	220
154	1991-1995	376,530	30	45	10	-	115
155	1996-2001 (20)	415,505	15	85	40	10	105
	by age at immigration						
156	0-4 years	163,310	20	100	65	25	115
157	5-19 years	556,015	180	120	290	55	315
158	20 years and over	1,313,635	175	440	455	145	675
159	**Total population**	**4,647,960**	**3,880**	**4,115**	**6,145**	**2,470**	**4,445**
	by religion						
160	Catholic (21)	1,578,875	880	905	1,340	475	1,925
161	Protestant	1,131,055	1,710	1,770	3,145	1,245	1,525
162	Christian Orthodox	178,695	10	50	55	20	20
163	Christian, n.i.e. (22)	160,420	125	70	45	95	120
164	Muslim	254,115	10	-	-	10	85
165	Jewish	164,510	10	15	-	20	30
166	Buddhist	97,165	-	-	20	-	30
167	Hindu	191,305	-	10	-	-	45
168	Sikh	90,595	-	-	-	-	-
169	Eastern religions (23)	10,990	-	-	-	-	-
170	Other religions (24)	5,540	-	-	10	15	-
171	No religious affiliation (25)	784,695	1,140	1,295	1,540	580	670
172	**Total population 15 years and over**	**3,728,985**	**2,885**	**3,220**	**4,960**	**1,940**	**3,400**
	by generation status						
173	1st generation (26)	1,964,320	380	645	800	235	1,110
174	2nd generation (27)	806,625	660	675	1,065	440	730
175	3rd generation and over (28)	958,035	1,850	1,895	3,095	1,270	1,555
176	**Total population 1 year and over (29)**	**4,590,795**	**3,830**	**4,075**	**6,070**	**2,450**	**4,380**
	by place of residence 1 year ago (mobility)						
177	Non-movers	3,942,615	3,360	3,595	5,175	2,180	3,460
178	Movers	648,180	465	480	895	265	920
179	Non-migrants	368,055	235	225	535	135	445
180	Migrants	280,130	230	255	360	130	470
181	Internal migrants	176,490	205	240	360	130	465
182	Intraprovincial migrants	152,265	190	220	350	125	460
183	Interprovincial migrants	24,220	15	15	-	10	-
184	External migrants	103,640	25	10	10	-	-

Tableau 1. Certaines caractéristiques des secteurs de recensement, recensement de 2001 – Données intégrales et données-échantillon (20 %)

Toronto 0480.02 A	Toronto 0481	Toronto 0482	Toronto 0483	Toronto 0484	Toronto 0485.01 A	Caractéristiques	N°
						CARACTÉRISTIQUES DE LA POPULATION	
						selon les groupes de minorités visibles	
265	800	85	245	215	140	Total de la population des minorités visibles	121
10	60	10	70	30	-	Chinois	122
40	120	15	15	25	-	Sud-Asiatique	123
55	115	15	40	35	70	Noir	124
-	-	-	15	10	-	Philippin	125
-	25	10	50	15	-	Latino-Américain	126
70	365	-	15	20	40	Asiatique du Sud-Est	127
-	40	-	-	10	-	Arabe	128
-	-	-	-	10	-	Asiatique occidental	129
-	-	-	-	-	10	Coréen	130
35	-	-	10	-	20	Japonais	131
30	25	40	20	-	-	Minorité visible, n.i.a. (13)	132
15	50	10	10	65	-	Minorités visibles multiples (14)	133
						selon la citoyenneté	
3,350	8,680	4,870	7,555	8,210	3,515	Citoyenneté canadienne (15)	134
180	350	280	205	350	85	Citoyenneté autre que canadienne	135
						selon le lieu de naissance du répondant	
2,755	7,075	4,280	6,740	7,290	3,235	Population non immigrante	136
2,450	6,360	3,945	6,100	6,580	2,975	Née dans la province de résidence	137
735	1,910	830	1,025	1,255	345	Population immigrante (16)	138
-	30	30	50	180	-	États-Unis	139
15	45	20	70	10	-	Amérique centrale et du Sud	140
40	35	10	45	25	15	Caraïbes et Bermudes	141
125	245	205	375	475	135	Royaume-Uni	142
415	1,065	565	455	475	120	Autre Europe (17)	143
20	25	-	10	10	-	Afrique	144
115	470	10	25	70	60	Asie et Moyen-Orient	145
-	-	10	-	10	-	Océanie et autre (18)	146
35	35	35	-	15	20	Résidents non permanents (19)	147
730	**1,915**	**830**	**1,025**	**1,255**	**340**	**Population immigrante totale**	148
						selon la période d'immigration	
145	290	435	430	465	135	Avant 1961	149
165	370	120	275	405	85	1961-1970	150
115	345	170	120	135	40	1971-1980	151
195	525	45	110	90	30	1981-1990	152
110	380	55	85	165	55	1991-2001 (20)	153
45	290	20	60	45	40	1991-1995	154
65	95	35	20	120	15	1996-2001 (20)	155
						selon l'âge à l'immigration	
95	230	125	110	150	40	0-4 ans	156
225	560	270	350	395	85	5-19 ans	157
415	1,125	435	560	715	220	20 ans et plus	158
3,525	**9,030**	**5,150**	**7,765**	**8,560**	**3,600**	**Population totale**	159
						selon la religion	
1,325	3,540	1,305	2,500	2,160	1,045	Catholique (21)	160
1,405	3,140	2,625	3,855	4,440	1,815	Protestante	161
55	55	70	10	110	10	Orthodoxe chrétienne	162
105	230	140	90	120	65	Chrétiennes, n.i.a. (22)	163
25	20	-	-	15	-	Musulmane	164
-	-	30	20	25	-	Juive	165
55	235	-	35	-	20	Bouddhiste	166
-	70	40	-	10	-	Hindoue	167
45	25	-	-	-	-	Sikh	168
-	-	-	-	-	-	Religions orientales (23)	169
-	15	10	-	35	-	Autres religions (24)	170
510	1,700	935	1,250	1,640	635	Aucune appartenance religieuse (25)	171
2,675	**6,735**	**4,080**	**6,040**	**6,780**	**2,735**	**Population totale de 15 ans et plus**	172
						selon le statut des générations	
730	1,885	875	1,030	1,190	360	1re génération (26)	173
610	1,560	1,065	1,450	1,620	600	2e génération (27)	174
1,335	3,300	2,140	3,565	3,965	1,775	3e génération et plus (28)	175
3,480	**8,905**	**5,070**	**7,645**	**8,455**	**3,560**	**Population totale de 1 an et plus (29)**	176
						selon le lieu de résidence 1 an auparavant (mobilité)	
3,170	7,850	4,625	6,955	7,470	2,890	Personnes n'ayant pas déménagé	177
305	1,050	445	695	980	665	Personnes ayant déménagé	178
110	470	185	250	415	270	Non-migrants	179
200	580	260	450	565	400	Migrants	180
200	555	245	420	560	395	Migrants internes	181
185	510	245	410	540	390	Migrants infraprovinciaux	182
15	45	-	10	25	10	Migrants interprovinciaux	183
-	25	15	30	10	-	Migrants externes	184

Table 1. Selected Characteristics for Census Tracts, 2001 Census – 100% Data and 20% Sample Data

No.	Characteristics	Toronto A CMA/RMR	Toronto 0473.03 A	Toronto 0474	Toronto 0475	Toronto 0476 ◆◇◇	Toronto 0480.01 A
	POPULATION CHARACTERISTICS						
185	**Total population 5 years and over (30)**	**4,356,845**	**3,625**	**3,915**	**5,800**	**2,330**	**4,110**
	by place of residence 5 years ago (mobility)						
186	Non-movers	2,377,470	1,935	2,205	3,010	1,505	2,090
187	Movers	1,979,375	1,690	1,715	2,790	835	2,025
188	Non-migrants	1,051,720	905	885	1,335	460	855
189	Migrants	927,655	790	825	1,455	375	1,165
190	Internal migrants	553,470	740	785	1,420	360	1,080
191	Intraprovincial migrants	466,970	670	735	1,370	345	1,030
192	Interprovincial migrants	86,500	65	45	45	10	50
193	External migrants	374,185	50	45	35	10	85
194	**Total population 15 to 24 years**	**607,665**	**410**	**385**	**770**	**215**	**610**
	by school attendance						
195	Not attending school	195,360	185	200	395	110	300
196	Attending school full time	379,000	185	170	345	100	280
197	Attending school part time	33,300	40	20	25	-	35
198	**Total population 15 years and over**	**3,728,980**	**2,885**	**3,215**	**4,955**	**1,940**	**3,400**
	by highest level of schooling						
199	Less than grade 9 (31)	319,055	135	160	315	150	465
200	Grades 9-13 without high school graduation certificate	693,720	785	925	1,535	595	905
201	Grades 9-13 with high school graduation certificate	494,990	445	520	930	430	535
202	Some postsecondary without degree, certificate or diploma (32)	442,275	270	300	555	145	375
203	Trades certificate or diploma (33)	278,975	400	425	575	280	380
204	College certificate or diploma (34)	542,090	545	535	675	240	510
205	University certificate below bachelor's degree	103,845	35	55	45	35	-
206	University with bachelor's degree or higher	854,035	285	300	335	70	225
	by combinations of unpaid work						
207	Males 15 years and over	1,797,065	1,410	1,640	2,365	960	1,675
208	Reported unpaid work (35)	1,569,655	1,255	1,535	2,055	845	1,500
209	Housework and child care and care or assistance to seniors	137,620	50	105	170	90	65
210	Housework and child care only	455,250	495	520	700	230	585
211	Housework and care or assistance to seniors only	114,105	65	95	135	90	75
212	Child care and care or assistance to seniors only	3,675	-	-	-	-	-
213	Housework only	826,680	635	805	1,025	440	750
214	Child care only	23,555	10	10	15	-	20
215	Care or assistance to seniors only	8,780	-	-	-	-	-
216	Females 15 years and over	1,931,915	1,480	1,580	2,595	980	1,720
217	Reported unpaid work (35)	1,778,265	1,405	1,490	2,375	895	1,665
218	Housework and child care and care or assistance to seniors	209,100	160	175	325	115	140
219	Housework and child care only	574,090	550	585	780	280	720
220	Housework and care or assistance to seniors only	149,040	80	120	195	105	85
221	Child care and care or assistance to seniors only	2,220	-	-	-	-	10
222	Housework only	823,945	615	615	1,050	385	690
223	Child care only	13,345	-	-	-	-	15
224	Care or assistance to seniors only	6,520	-	-	25	10	-
	by labour force activity						
225	Males 15 years and over	1,797,065	1,405	1,640	2,365	965	1,675
226	In the labour force	1,344,785	1,080	1,245	1,630	700	1,440
227	Employed	1,272,115	1,040	1,170	1,525	675	1,375
228	Unemployed	72,665	45	75	105	20	70
229	Not in the labour force	452,285	325	390	735	265	235
230	Participation rate	74.8	76.9	75.9	68.9	72.5	86.0
231	Employment rate	70.8	74.0	71.3	64.5	69.9	82.1
232	Unemployment rate	5.4	4.2	6.0	6.4	2.9	4.9
233	Females 15 years and over	1,931,915	1,480	1,580	2,595	980	1,725
234	In the labour force	1,219,805	935	1,085	1,435	600	1,155
235	Employed	1,140,985	900	1,030	1,340	555	1,120
236	Unemployed	78,820	35	55	95	45	35
237	Not in the labour force	712,110	545	495	1,160	380	565
238	Participation rate	63.1	63.2	68.7	55.3	61.2	67.0
239	Employment rate	59.1	60.8	65.2	51.6	56.6	64.9
240	Unemployment rate	6.5	3.7	5.1	6.6	7.5	3.0

Tableau 1. Certaines caractéristiques des secteurs de recensement, recensement de 2001 – Données intégrales et données-échantillon (20 %)

Toronto 0480.02 A	Toronto 0481	Toronto 0482	Toronto 0483	Toronto 0484	Toronto 0485.01 A	Caractéristiques	N°
						CARACTÉRISTIQUES DE LA POPULATION	
3,335	**8,335**	**4,850**	**7,210**	**8,025**	**3,360**	**Population totale de 5 ans et plus (30)**	185
						selon le lieu de résidence 5 ans auparavant (mobilité)	
2,280	4,395	3,350	4,675	4,370	1,935	Personnes n'ayant pas déménagé	186
1,055	3,945	1,500	2,535	3,655	1,425	Personnes ayant déménagé	187
300	1,600	595	810	1,105	525	Non-migrants	188
750	2,340	910	1,720	2,550	905	Migrants	189
680	2,210	860	1,655	2,400	860	Migrants internes	190
655	2,030	840	1,605	2,325	835	Migrants infraprovinciaux	191
25	180	20	45	80	30	Migrants interprovinciaux	192
75	125	50	70	145	40	Migrants externes	193
530	**1,185**	**695**	**895**	**945**	**435**	**Population totale de 15 à 24 ans**	194
						selon la fréquentation scolaire	
150	560	260	360	360	230	Ne fréquentant pas l'école	195
345	560	400	520	560	205	Fréquentant l'école à plein temps	196
30	65	35	15	25	-	Fréquentant l'école à temps partiel	197
2,675	**6,735**	**4,080**	**6,040**	**6,780**	**2,735**	**Population totale de 15 ans et plus**	198
						selon le plus haut niveau de scolarité atteint	
210	565	235	210	260	185	Niveau inférieur à la 9e année (31)	199
600	1,670	1,010	1,540	1,810	750	De la 9e à la 13e année sans certificat d'études secondaires	200
430	1,145	550	995	1,185	605	De la 9e à la 13e année avec certificat d'études secondaires	201
310	600	415	675	700	265	Études postsecondaires partielles sans grade, certificat ou diplôme (32)	202
310	725	500	725	710	255	Certificat ou diplôme d'une école de métiers (33)	203
515	1,270	840	1,145	1,165	355	Certificat ou diplôme collégial (34)	204
50	115	100	85	125	40	Certificat universitaire inférieur au baccalauréat	205
255	650	415	665	815	285	Études universitaires avec baccalauréat ou diplôme supérieur	206
						selon les combinaisons de travail non rémunéré	
1,320	3,345	2,085	2,985	3,390	1,320	Hommes de 15 ans et plus	207
1,230	3,050	1,905	2,760	3,080	1,145	Travail non rémunéré déclaré (35)	208
130	255	180	245	195	55	Travaux ménagers et soins aux enfants et soins ou aide aux personnes âgées	209
380	1,180	590	930	990	420	Travaux ménagers et soins aux enfants seulement	210
35	160	100	215	270	65	Travaux ménagers et soins ou aide aux personnes âgées seulement	211
25	-	10	-	-	-	Soins aux enfants et soins ou aide aux personnes âgées seulement	212
640	1,405	1,010	1,335	1,585	595	Travaux ménagers seulement	213
15	25	15	25	20	-	Soins aux enfants seulement	214
-	30	10	10	25	-	Soins ou aide aux personnes âgées seulement	215
1,355	3,390	1,990	3,055	3,395	1,410	Femmes de 15 ans et plus	216
1,330	3,195	1,905	2,950	3,215	1,260	Travail non rémunéré déclaré (35)	217
215	335	310	345	295	145	Travaux ménagers et soins aux enfants et soins ou aide aux personnes âgées	218
475	1,360	600	1,040	1,145	510	Travaux ménagers et soins aux enfants seulement	219
55	190	170	295	290	80	Travaux ménagers et soins ou aide aux personnes âgées seulement	220
-	-	-	-	10	-	Soins aux enfants et soins ou aide aux personnes âgées seulement	221
590	1,260	820	1,255	1,485	535	Travaux ménagers seulement	222
-	25	-	10	-	-	Soins aux enfants seulement	223
-	15	-	-	-	-	Soins ou aide aux personnes âgées seulement	224
						selon l'activité	
1,325	3,345	2,090	2,990	3,385	1,320	Hommes de 15 ans et plus	225
1,065	2,785	1,715	2,305	2,460	1,055	Population active	226
1,045	2,740	1,675	2,265	2,405	1,025	Personnes occupées	227
25	45	40	45	50	25	Chômeurs	228
260	560	375	680	930	270	Inactifs	229
80.4	83.3	82.1	77.1	72.7	79.9	Taux d'activité	230
78.9	81.9	80.1	75.8	71.0	77.7	Taux d'emploi	231
2.3	1.6	2.3	2.0	2.0	2.4	Taux de chômage	232
1,355	3,390	1,995	3,060	3,395	1,410	Femmes de 15 ans et plus	233
910	2,470	1,345	2,005	1,960	930	Population active	234
875	2,330	1,275	1,920	1,865	875	Personnes occupées	235
30	145	70	85	100	50	Chômeuses	236
445	915	645	1,055	1,430	485	Inactives	237
67.2	72.9	67.4	65.5	57.7	66.0	Taux d'activité	238
64.6	68.7	63.9	62.7	54.9	62.1	Taux d'emploi	239
3.3	5.9	5.2	4.2	5.1	5.4	Taux de chômage	240

Table 1. Selected Characteristics for Census Tracts, 2001 Census – 100% Data and 20% Sample Data

No.	Characteristics	Toronto A CMA/RMR	Toronto 0473.03 A	Toronto 0474	Toronto 0475	Toronto 0476 ◆◇◇	Toronto 0480.01 A
	POPULATION CHARACTERISTICS						
	by labour force activity – concluded						
241	Both sexes - Participation rate	68.8	69.8	72.5	61.8	67.0	76.4
242	15-24 years	62.1	63.4	66.2	73.9	70.5	76.2
243	25 years and over	70.1	70.9	73.5	59.5	66.5	76.5
244	Both sexes - Employment rate	64.7	67.2	68.3	57.7	63.7	73.4
245	15-24 years	54.6	56.1	58.4	65.4	60.5	68.0
246	25 years and over	66.7	69.1	69.6	56.4	63.6	74.6
247	Both sexes - Unemployment rate	5.9	4.0	5.6	6.5	5.0	3.8
248	15-24 years	12.0	11.8	9.8	12.4	13.3	10.8
249	25 years and over	4.9	2.8	5.1	5.2	3.9	2.3
250	**Total labour force 15 years and over**	**2,564,590**	**2,015**	**2,330**	**3,060**	**1,300**	**2,595**
	by industry based on the 1997 NAICS						
251	Industry - Not applicable (36)	42,565	10	35	45	20	25
252	All industries (37)	2,522,025	2,005	2,295	3,015	1,275	2,570
253	11 Agriculture, forestry, fishing and hunting	9,425	10	20	25	10	155
254	21 Mining and oil and gas extraction	2,665	-	-	10	10	-
255	22 Utilities	15,765	10	25	25	-	20
256	23 Construction	124,395	200	245	255	220	310
257	31-33 Manufacturing	395,975	345	375	470	210	655
258	41 Wholesale trade	151,870	75	110	85	55	130
259	44-45 Retail trade	272,680	255	200	405	105	270
260	48-49 Transportation and warehousing	123,135	120	155	205	90	125
261	51 Information and cultural industries	100,755	85	35	65	35	50
262	52 Finance and insurance	177,210	45	80	55	25	40
263	53 Real estate and rental and leasing	56,890	35	45	80	20	30
264	54 Professional, scientific and technical services	246,655	130	165	135	55	115
265	55 Management of companies and enterprises	4,840	-	-	-	-	-
266	56 Administrative and support, waste management and remediation services	121,490	90	170	160	75	75
267	61 Educational services	143,990	105	165	165	65	60
268	62 Health care and social assistance	189,450	185	170	270	100	130
269	71 Arts, entertainment and recreation	47,875	20	20	55	-	20
270	72 Accommodation and food services	141,560	50	85	270	75	155
271	81 Other services (except public administration)	110,750	130	95	170	80	130
272	91 Public administration	84,660	120	140	125	55	100
	by class of worker						
273	Class of worker - Not applicable (36)	42,560	10	35	45	25	25
274	All classes of worker (37)	2,522,020	2,005	2,290	3,015	1,275	2,570
275	Paid workers	2,324,255	1,825	2,000	2,775	1,105	2,405
276	Employees	2,220,370	1,765	1,845	2,680	1,070	2,345
277	Self-employed (incorporated)	103,885	65	155	95	35	60
278	Self-employed (unincorporated)	191,105	165	290	240	165	160
279	Unpaid family workers	6,670	15	-	-	10	10
	by occupation based on the 2001 NOC-S						
280	Male labour force 15 years and over	1,344,785	1,080	1,245	1,630	700	1,445
281	Occupation - Not applicable (36)	18,665	10	10	25	-	15
282	All occupations (37)	1,326,120	1,075	1,235	1,600	695	1,430
283	A Management occupations	207,875	145	140	185	95	100
284	B Business, finance and administration occupations	171,540	80	90	80	30	70
285	C Natural and applied sciences and related occupations	158,545	50	90	135	60	85
286	D Health occupations	25,560	20	-	25	-	-
287	E Occupations in social science, education, government service and religion	63,035	30	45	65	15	15
288	F Occupations in art, culture, recreation and sport	45,715	-	35	25	-	30
289	G Sales and service occupations	251,335	235	185	300	95	210
290	H Trades, transport and equipment operators and related occupations	269,765	405	460	610	335	575
291	I Occupations unique to primary industry	17,430	25	45	50	30	105
292	J Occupations unique to processing, manufacturing and utilities	115,320	90	140	130	25	235
293	Female labour force 15 years and over	1,219,805	935	1,080	1,430	600	1,155
294	Occupation - Not applicable (36)	23,900	-	30	20	20	10
295	All occupations (37)	1,195,910	930	1,055	1,415	575	1,145
296	A Management occupations	120,415	50	70	180	30	100
297	B Business, finance and administration occupations	376,190	300	310	305	195	335
298	C Natural and applied sciences and related occupations	48,725	55	40	30	10	30
299	D Health occupations	78,460	100	75	75	45	45

Tableau 1. Certaines caractéristiques des secteurs de recensement, recensement de 2001 – Données intégrales et données-échantillon (20 %)

Toronto 0480.02 A	Toronto 0481	Toronto 0482	Toronto 0483	Toronto 0484	Toronto 0485.01 A	Caractéristiques	N°
						CARACTÉRISTIQUES DE LA POPULATION	
						selon l'activité – fin	
73.6	78.0	75.1	71.3	65.3	72.4	Les deux sexes - Taux d'activité	241
64.8	74.3	72.9	69.4	62.8	73.6	15-24 ans	242
76.2	78.8	75.3	71.6	65.7	72.2	25 ans et plus	243
71.8	75.2	72.3	69.2	63.0	69.7	Les deux sexes - Taux d'emploi	244
61.3	67.9	68.6	65.6	59.8	65.5	15-24 ans	245
74.6	76.7	73.0	69.9	63.4	70.2	25 ans et plus	246
2.5	3.5	3.6	3.0	3.5	4.0	Les deux sexes - Taux de chômage	247
5.9	9.1	5.9	5.6	4.3	10.9	15-24 ans	248
2.1	2.5	3.1	2.4	3.3	2.7	25 ans et plus	249
1,970	**5,255**	**3,065**	**4,305**	**4,425**	**1,980**	**Population active totale de 15 ans et plus**	250
						selon l'industrie basée sur le SCIAN de 1997	
10	35	-	35	35	15	Industrie - Sans objet (36)	251
1,965	5,220	3,065	4,270	4,385	1,965	Toutes les industries (37)	252
90	105	395	55	240	40	11 Agriculture, foresterie, pêche et chasse	253
-	-	-	10	-	-	21 Extraction minière et extraction de pétrole et de gaz	254
10	30	10	20	30	25	22 Services publics	255
190	440	340	385	360	95	23 Construction	256
370	1,275	490	890	755	610	31-33 Fabrication	257
95	295	135	360	305	100	41 Commerce de gros	258
280	595	325	400	355	230	44-45 Commerce de détail	259
70	215	120	300	420	140	48-49 Transport et entreposage	260
75	125	60	60	65	15	51 Industrie de l'information et industrie culturelle	261
45	160	100	100	85	25	52 Finance et assurances	262
40	70	30	70	110	45	53 Services immobiliers et services de location et de location à bail	263
70	265	185	210	275	100	54 Services professionnels, scientifiques et techniques	264
-	-	10	-	-	-	55 Gestion de sociétés et d'entreprises	265
110	190	105	170	190	110	56 Services administratifs, services de soutien, services de gestion des déchets et services d'assainissement	266
130	240	175	255	230	55	61 Services d'enseignement	267
160	385	180	295	235	120	62 Soins de santé et assistance sociale	268
15	105	85	65	75	25	71 Arts, spectacles et loisirs	269
95	260	80	220	280	125	72 Hébergement et services de restauration	270
35	245	145	285	170	60	81 Autres services, sauf les administrations publiques	271
75	230	100	115	195	60	91 Administrations publiques	272
						selon la catégorie de travailleurs	
10	35	-	35	35	20	Catégorie de travailleurs - Sans objet (36)	273
1,965	5,220	3,065	4,270	4,385	1,960	Toutes les catégories de travailleurs (37)	274
1,830	4,860	2,700	3,885	3,855	1,815	Travailleurs rémunérés	275
1,740	4,755	2,430	3,705	3,620	1,780	Employés	276
90	105	270	185	240	40	Travailleurs autonomes (entreprise constituée en société)	277
130	345	330	380	490	140	Travailleurs autonomes (entreprise non constituée en société)	278
-	20	40	10	45	10	Travailleurs familiaux non rémunérés	279
						selon la profession basée sur la CNP-S de 2001	
1,070	2,785	1,715	2,305	2,455	1,050	Hommes actifs de 15 ans et plus	280
10	15	-	15	-	10	Profession - Sans objet (36)	281
1,065	2,770	1,715	2,290	2,455	1,045	Toutes les professions (37)	282
175	440	235	460	345	190	A Gestion	283
85	205	105	170	165	60	B Affaires, finance et administration	284
95	230	130	165	225	30	C Sciences naturelles et appliquées et professions apparentées	285
-	25	15	20	25	20	D Secteur de la santé	286
40	80	30	105	80	25	E Sciences sociales, enseignement, administration publique et religion	287
10	45	35	45	20	10	F Arts, culture, sports et loisirs	288
215	475	230	315	425	165	G Ventes et services	289
270	860	550	715	775	340	H Métiers, transport et machinerie	290
65	50	260	80	225	40	I Professions propres au secteur primaire	291
105	365	135	230	175	170	J Transformation, fabrication et services d'utilité publique	292
905	2,470	1,345	2,005	1,965	930	Femmes actives de 15 ans et plus	293
10	20	-	25	35	10	Profession - Sans objet (36)	294
905	2,455	1,350	1,980	1,930	915	Toutes les professions (37)	295
95	205	155	160	140	70	A Gestion	296
210	715	385	600	615	240	B Affaires, finance et administration	297
-	50	20	65	20	25	C Sciences naturelles et appliquées et professions apparentées	298
90	160	75	160	125	35	D Secteur de la santé	299

Table 1. Selected Characteristics for Census Tracts, 2001 Census – 100% Data and 20% Sample Data

No.	Characteristics	Toronto A CMA/RMR	Toronto 0473.03 A	Toronto 0474	Toronto 0475	Toronto 0476 ◆◇◇	Toronto 0480.01 A
	POPULATION CHARACTERISTICS						
	by occupation based on the 2001 NOC-S – concluded						
300	E Occupations in social science, education, government service and religion	126,225	85	115	150	40	75
301	F Occupations in art, culture, recreation and sport	47,445	35	25	15	30	25
302	G Sales and service occupations	285,645	215	300	485	165	310
303	H Trades, transport and equipment operators and related occupations	24,940	20	45	45	15	35
304	I Occupations unique to primary industry	4,615	-	10	20	15	45
305	J Occupations unique to processing, manufacturing and utilities	83,245	65	70	105	50	145
306	**Total employed labour force 15 years and over**	**2,413,100**	**1,935**	**2,200**	**2,860**	**1,230**	**2,495**
	by place of work						
307	Males	1,272,115	1,040	1,175	1,525	680	1,375
308	Usual place of work	1,038,285	795	845	1,135	465	1,050
309	At home	74,105	65	85	45	20	65
310	Outside Canada	8,985	-	10	10	10	-
311	No fixed workplace address	150,740	175	230	340	190	260
312	Females	1,140,985	900	1,030	1,335	555	1,120
313	Usual place of work	1,008,320	755	845	1,205	490	1,015
314	At home	78,185	70	85	60	40	75
315	Outside Canada	3,770	-	-	-	-	-
316	No fixed workplace address	50,715	75	105	75	25	35
317	**Total employed labour force 15 years and over with usual place of work or no fixed workplace address**	**2,248,060**	**1,805**	**2,030**	**2,750**	**1,170**	**2,355**
	by mode of transportation						
318	Males	1,189,025	975	1,080	1,470	655	1,310
319	Car, truck, van, as driver	873,095	870	1,010	1,250	575	1,065
320	Car, truck, van, as passenger	50,270	65	35	125	50	175
321	Public transit	201,505	15	15	-	10	30
322	Walked	43,300	10	10	50	15	30
323	Other method	20,845	15	-	40	10	10
324	Females	1,059,035	830	945	1,280	515	1,050
325	Car, truck, van, as driver	591,845	690	790	1,060	445	790
326	Car, truck, van, as passenger	90,585	60	95	70	30	100
327	Public transit	302,290	40	40	35	-	30
328	Walked	59,065	25	-	100	15	115
329	Other method	15,250	10	20	-	25	10
330	**Total population 15 years and over who worked since January 1, 2000**	**2,741,935**	**2,180**	**2,470**	**3,240**	**1,360**	**2,740**
	by language used at work						
331	Single responses	2,462,700	2,100	2,405	3,170	1,325	2,470
332	English	2,413,940	2,100	2,395	3,170	1,325	2,415
333	French	2,650	-	10	-	-	-
334	Non-official languages (5)	46,105	-	-	-	-	60
335	Chinese, n.o.s.	12,940	-	-	-	-	-
336	Cantonese	10,490	-	-	-	-	-
337	Other languages (6)	22,670	-	-	-	-	55
338	Multiple responses	279,235	90	70	70	35	265
339	English and French	59,330	45	25	40	15	20
340	English and non-official language	211,735	30	35	30	20	245
341	French and non-official language	295	-	-	-	-	-
342	English, French and non-official language	7,880	10	-	-	-	-
	DWELLING AND HOUSEHOLD CHARACTERISTICS						
343	**Total number of occupied private dwellings**	**1,634,755**	**1,365**	**1,535**	**2,440**	**960**	**1,570**
	by tenure						
344	Owned	1,033,465	1,115	1,290	1,800	850	930
345	Rented	601,280	250	240	640	100	640
346	Band housing	10	-	-	-	10	-
	by structural type of dwelling						
347	Single-detached house	737,325	1,160	1,405	1,895	945	875
348	Semi-detached house	147,985	15	15	30	-	130
349	Row house	124,640	60	15	105	-	10
350	Apartment, detached duplex	31,865	25	50	10	-	165
351	Apartment, building that has five or more storeys	447,245	-	-	-	-	255
352	Apartment, building that has fewer than five storeys (38)	141,040	105	40	355	10	135
353	Other single-attached house	3,890	10	-	35	-	-
354	Movable dwelling (39)	775	-	-	10	-	-

Tableau 1. Certaines caractéristiques des secteurs de recensement, recensement de 2001 – Données intégrales et données-échantillon (20 %)

Toronto 0480.02 A	Toronto 0481	Toronto 0482	Toronto 0483	Toronto 0484	Toronto 0485.01 A	Caractéristiques	N°
						CARACTÉRISTIQUES DE LA POPULATION	
						selon la profession basée sur la CNP-S de 2001 - fin	
85	235	110	185	215	85	E Sciences sociales, enseignement, administration publique et religion	300
25	70	55	45	90	15	F Arts, culture, sports et loisirs	301
255	585	315	485	515	280	G Ventes et services	302
20	85	40	95	40	55	H Métiers, transport et machinerie	303
30	50	150	45	60	10	I Professions propres au secteur primaire	304
85	295	45	145	100	95	J Transformation, fabrication et services d'utilité publique	305
1,920	**5,070**	**2,950**	**4,180**	**4,270**	**1,900**	**Population active occupée totale de 15 ans et plus**	306
						selon le lieu de travail	
1,045	2,740	1,675	2,260	2,405	1,025	Hommes	307
860	2,215	1,190	1,860	1,755	810	Lieu habituel de travail	308
40	95	215	100	300	40	À domicile	309
-	-	-	-	25	10	En dehors du Canada	310
145	435	270	290	325	170	Sans adresse de travail fixe	311
880	2,325	1,275	1,920	1,860	870	Femmes	312
825	2,030	1,025	1,680	1,565	750	Lieu habituel de travail	313
45	190	190	150	210	65	À domicile	314
-	-	-	-	-	-	En dehors du Canada	315
10	115	65	90	85	65	Sans adresse de travail fixe	316
1,845	**4,790**	**2,550**	**3,920**	**3,735**	**1,790**	**Population active occupée totale de 15 ans et plus ayant un lieu habituel de travail ou sans adresse de travail fixe**	317
						selon le mode de transport	
1,010	2,650	1,465	2,150	2,080	980	Hommes	318
875	2,305	1,345	1,915	1,885	840	Automobile, camion ou fourgonnette, en tant que conducteur	319
100	180	65	130	75	55	Automobile, camion ou fourgonnette, en tant que passager	320
10	55	20	25	15	-	Transport en commun	321
15	85	20	65	90	60	À pied	322
10	20	15	15	20	35	Autre moyen	323
840	2,140	1,090	1,770	1,650	810	Femmes	324
645	1,735	965	1,415	1,295	615	Automobile, camion ou fourgonnette, en tant que conductrice	325
120	190	95	170	175	120	Automobile, camion ou fourgonnette, en tant que passagère	326
35	60	15	50	30	-	Transport en commun	327
30	120	-	105	110	65	À pied	328
-	35	10	20	35	10	Autre moyen	329
2,125	**5,565**	**3,335**	**4,665**	**4,840**	**2,080**	**Population totale de 15 ans et plus ayant travaillé depuis le 1er janvier 2000**	330
						selon la langue utilisée au travail	
1,950	5,135	3,200	4,525	4,755	2,040	Réponses uniques	331
1,930	5,035	3,185	4,520	4,750	2,035	Anglais	332
-	20	-	10	10	-	Français	333
15	75	10	-	-	10	Langues non officielles (5)	334
-	-	-	-	-	-	Chinois, n.d.a.	335
-	-	-	-	-	-	Cantonais	336
15	70	15	-	-	-	Autres langues (6)	337
175	435	135	140	85	40	Réponses multiples	338
20	105	20	40	55	20	Anglais et français	339
150	310	110	95	30	20	Anglais et langue non officielle	340
-	-	-	-	-	-	Français et langue non officielle	341
-	20	10	10	-	-	Anglais, français et langue non officielle	342
						CARACTÉRISTIQUES DES LOGEMENTS ET DES MÉNAGES	
1,075	**2,820**	**1,665**	**2,680**	**3,105**	**1,295**	**Nombre total de logements privés occupés**	343
						selon le mode d'occupation	
915	2,390	1,440	2,380	2,740	1,025	Possédé	344
160	425	230	300	360	270	Loué	345
-	-	-	-	-	-	Logement de bande	346
						selon le type de construction résidentielle	
740	2,150	1,630	2,115	2,475	920	Maison individuelle non attenante	347
90	255	10	140	275	30	Maison jumelée	348
100	35	-	255	70	45	Maison en rangée	349
10	180	10	45	70	40	Appartement, duplex non attenant	350
70	-	-	-	35	-	Appartement, immeuble de cinq étages ou plus	351
70	190	15	115	140	260	Appartement, immeuble de moins de cinq étages (38)	352
-	-	-	10	-	10	Autre maison individuelle attenante	353
-	-	15	-	35	-	Logement mobile (39)	354

Table 1. Selected Characteristics for Census Tracts, 2001 Census – 100% Data and 20% Sample Data

No.	Characteristics	Toronto A CMA/RMR	Toronto 0473.03 A	Toronto 0474	Toronto 0475	Toronto 0476 ◆◇◇	Toronto 0480.01 A
	DWELLING AND HOUSEHOLD CHARACTERISTICS						
	by condition of dwelling						
355	Regular maintenance only	1,116,105	705	870	1,520	555	1,030
356	Minor repairs	402,760	450	420	705	295	440
357	Major repairs	115,890	210	245	215	110	100
	by period of construction						
358	Before 1946	213,350	180	285	505	95	75
359	1946-1960	264,760	300	340	350	215	105
360	1961-1970	287,340	180	260	340	255	285
361	1971-1980	304,020	85	210	420	180	525
362	1981-1990	312,650	385	190	620	110	415
363	1991-2001 (20)	252,635	225	245	210	105	165
364	Average number of rooms per dwelling	6.1	6.6	6.6	6.4	6.6	6.4
365	Average number of bedrooms per dwelling	2.6	2.9	2.9	2.7	2.9	2.8
366	Average value of dwelling $	273,397	165,265	184,636	165,672	179,552	174,758
367	**Total number of private households**	**1,634,755**	**1,365**	**1,530**	**2,440**	**960**	**1,570**
	by household size						
368	1 person	359,595	230	285	645	195	300
369	2 persons	448,195	425	515	815	350	435
370	3 persons	287,690	250	310	380	165	325
371	4-5 persons	452,500	425	390	540	220	440
372	6 or more persons	86,775	35	30	65	25	75
	by household type						
373	One-family households	1,141,790	1,105	1,175	1,645	740	1,200
374	Multiple-family households	66,930	20	55	50	10	35
375	Non-family households	426,035	245	300	745	215	330
376	Number of persons in private households	4,637,215	3,880	4,115	6,120	2,470	4,440
377	Average number of persons in private households	2.8	2.8	2.7	2.5	2.6	2.8
378	Average number of persons per room	0.5	0.4	0.4	0.4	0.4	0.4
379	Tenant households in non-farm, non-reserve private dwellings (40)	595,320	250	230	640	90	635
380	Average gross rent $ (40)	870	777	739	734	811	849
381	Tenant households spending 30% or more of household income on gross rent (40) (41)	251,100	105	90	355	45	255
382	Tenant households spending from 30% to 99% of household income on gross rent (40) (41)	201,620	80	70	315	30	240
383	Owner households in non-farm, non-reserve private dwellings (42)	1,030,660	1,115	1,295	1,800	765	935
384	Average owner's major payments $ (42)	1,171	1,075	1,047	889	965	1,144
385	Owner households spending 30% or more of household income on owner's major payments (41) (42)	221,790	245	320	370	165	180
386	Owner households spending from 30% to 99% of household income on owner's major payments (41) (42)	193,340	210	280	330	150	170
	CENSUS FAMILY CHARACTERISTICS						
387	**Total number of census families in private households**	**1,280,955**	**1,145**	**1,280**	**1,745**	**755**	**1,270**
	by census family structure and size						
388	Total couple families	1,070,960	985	1,035	1,455	640	1,105
389	Total families of married couples	974,350	780	830	1,185	490	930
390	Without children at home	320,725	290	310	575	260	295
391	With children at home	653,620	490	520	615	230	640
392	1 child	227,680	135	225	230	70	240
393	2 children	292,915	230	220	285	120	285
394	3 or more children	133,025	130	75	90	40	110
395	Total families of common-law couples	96,610	205	205	265	145	175
396	Without children at home	60,985	95	130	120	45	70
397	With children at home	35,630	105	75	145	105	105
398	1 child	17,995	60	35	50	45	50
399	2 children	12,445	30	30	60	50	35
400	3 or more children	5,190	10	-	30	10	20
401	Total lone-parent families	210,000	160	250	290	120	170
402	Female parent	175,650	130	190	230	85	115
403	1 child	102,455	75	120	70	50	60
404	2 children	51,510	45	50	115	20	45
405	3 or more children	21,685	15	15	35	10	10

Tableau 1. Certaines caractéristiques des secteurs de recensement, recensement de 2001 – Données intégrales et données-échantillon (20 %)

Toronto 0480.02 A	Toronto 0481	Toronto 0482	Toronto 0483	Toronto 0484	Toronto 0485.01 A	Caractéristiques	N°
						CARACTÉRISTIQUES DES LOGEMENTS ET DES MÉNAGES	
						selon l'état du logement	
780	2,090	880	1,765	2,290	925	Entretien régulier seulement	355
250	575	575	820	660	300	Réparations mineures	356
50	155	215	95	150	75	Réparations majeures	357
						selon la période de construction	
10	160	335	325	410	130	Avant 1946	358
25	185	110	75	135	170	1946-1960	359
25	205	350	420	160	170	1961-1970	360
200	535	355	685	675	95	1971-1980	361
680	690	350	665	665	335	1981-1990	362
140	1,035	165	515	1,060	385	1991-2001 (20)	363
7.6	7.2	7.9	7.3	7.0	7.0	Nombre moyen de pièces par logement	364
3.2	3.1	3.3	3.1	2.9	2.9	Nombre moyen de chambres à coucher par logement	365
210,570	198,024	274,612	212,054	218,133	179,897	Valeur moyenne du logement $	366
1,075	**2,815**	**1,665**	**2,680**	**3,100**	**1,295**	**Nombre total de logements privés**	367
						selon la taille du ménage	
125	295	185	365	485	255	1 personne	368
260	710	540	915	1,210	405	2 personnes	369
185	570	300	495	445	210	3 personnes	370
460	1,110	540	820	850	390	4-5 personnes	371
50	135	100	85	120	40	6 personnes ou plus	372
						selon le genre de ménage	
875	2,360	1,385	2,195	2,515	1,005	Ménages unifamiliaux	373
50	100	60	65	40	-	Ménages multifamiliaux	374
150	360	225	410	540	285	Ménages non familiaux	375
3,525	9,030	5,145	7,760	8,550	3,595	Nombre de personnes dans les ménages privés	376
3.3	3.2	3.1	2.9	2.8	2.8	Nombre moyen de personnes dans les ménages privés	377
0.4	0.4	0.4	0.4	0.4	0.4	Nombre moyen de personnes par pièce	378
165	425	210	300	360	265	Ménages locataires dans les logements privés non agricoles hors réserve (40)	379
653	861	709	782	801	673	Loyer brut moyen $ (40)	380
75	155	40	115	130	110	Ménages locataires consacrant 30 % ou plus du revenu du ménage au loyer brut (40) (41)	381
55	100	30	100	110	70	Ménages locataires consacrant de 30 % à 99 % du revenu du ménage au loyer brut (40) (41)	382
910	2,390	1,340	2,355	2,645	1,025	Ménages propriétaires dans les logements privés non agricoles hors réserve (42)	383
1,114	1,157	1,086	1,036	1,052	1,026	Principales dépenses de propriété moyennes $ (42)	384
165	465	240	405	405	155	Ménages propriétaires consacrant 30 % ou plus du revenu du ménage aux principales dépenses de propriété (41) (42)	385
135	415	230	360	370	130	Ménages propriétaires consacrant de 30 % à 99 % du revenu du ménage aux principales dépenses de propriété (41) (42)	386
						CARACTÉRISTIQUES DES FAMILLES DE RECENSEMENT	
980	**2,565**	**1,500**	**2,340**	**2,600**	**1,020**	**Total des familles de recensement dans les ménages privés**	387
						selon la structure et la taille de la famille de recensement	
865	2,275	1,400	2,055	2,345	845	Total des familles avec conjoints	388
780	2,040	1,270	1,810	2,150	755	Total des familles avec couples mariés	389
200	540	470	660	1,015	275	Sans enfants à la maison	390
575	1,500	795	1,150	1,140	480	Avec enfants à la maison	391
150	450	240	410	350	125	1 enfant	392
275	775	345	495	560	260	2 enfants	393
155	275	210	250	225	95	3 enfants ou plus	394
85	235	135	245	190	95	Total des familles en union libre	395
45	115	95	160	105	35	Sans enfants à la maison	396
35	115	35	90	90	55	Avec enfants à la maison	397
20	50	-	65	15	35	1 enfant	398
10	55	20	10	60	10	2 enfants	399
10	10	10	20	20	15	3 enfants ou plus	400
115	290	100	280	255	175	Total des familles monoparentales	401
90	240	55	220	200	160	Parent de sexe féminin	402
45	160	40	130	125	80	1 enfant	403
30	60	15	60	55	60	2 enfants	404
10	25	-	30	20	10	3 enfants ou plus	405

Table 1. Selected Characteristics for Census Tracts, 2001 Census – 100% Data and 20% Sample Data

No.	Characteristics	Toronto A CMA/RMR	Toronto 0473.03 A	Toronto 0474	Toronto 0475	Toronto 0476 ◆◇◇	Toronto 0480.01 A
	CENSUS FAMILY CHARACTERISTICS						
	by census family structure and size – concluded						
406	Male parent	34,350	25	55	65	35	55
407	1 child	21,665	25	45	40	20	40
408	2 children	9,410	10	10	15	10	10
409	3 or more children	3,275	-	-	-	10	-
410	**Total number of children at home**	**1,641,660**	**1,385**	**1,375**	**1,935**	**805**	**1,605**
	by age groups						
411	Under 6 years	351,595	305	290	430	170	400
412	6-14 years	560,230	670	610	760	355	625
413	15-17 years	178,705	140	150	320	75	180
414	18-24 years	326,785	180	170	290	115	315
415	25 years and over	224,345	90	155	140	85	85
416	Average number of children at home per census family (43)	1.3	1.2	1.1	1.1	1.1	1.3
417	**Total number of persons in private households**	**4,637,215**	**3,885**	**4,115**	**6,125**	**2,470**	**4,435**
	by census family status and living arrangements						
418	Number of non-family persons	643,640	370	425	985	270	455
419	Living with relatives (44)	128,310	45	60	155	45	70
420	Living with non-relatives only	155,730	95	75	185	30	85
421	Living alone	359,595	235	285	645	195	300
422	Number of family persons	3,993,575	3,515	3,695	5,135	2,200	3,985
423	Average number of persons per census family	3.1	3.1	2.9	2.9	2.9	3.1
424	**Total number of persons 65 years and over**	**502,575**	**370**	**365**	**1,095**	**285**	**335**
425	Number of non-family persons 65 years and over	173,655	105	120	430	105	165
426	Living with relatives (44)	47,575	30	30	75	25	45
427	Living with non-relatives only	8,510	10	15	10	-	10
428	Living alone	117,570	70	75	340	75	120
429	Number of family persons 65 years and over	328,930	265	245	665	180	175
	ECONOMIC FAMILY CHARACTERISTICS						
430	**Total number of economic families in private households**	**1,231,225**	**1,125**	**1,250**	**1,725**	**755**	**1,255**
	by size of family						
431	2 persons	429,865	440	560	755	350	425
432	3 persons	278,900	240	290	395	160	335
433	4 persons	307,715	290	275	365	175	320
434	5 or more persons	214,740	155	130	215	60	165
435	Total number of persons in economic families	4,121,890	3,560	3,755	5,290	2,240	4,050
436	Average number of persons per economic family	3.3	3.2	3.0	3.1	3.0	3.2
437	Total number of unattached individuals	515,320	325	360	830	230	380
	2000 INCOME CHARACTERISTICS						
	Population 15 years and over by sex and total income groups in 2000						
438	Total - Both sexes	3,728,980	2,885	3,220	4,955	1,940	3,400
439	Without income	214,230	150	145	180	90	160
440	With income	3,514,750	2,735	3,070	4,770	1,860	3,240
441	Under $1,000 (45)	168,025	50	140	170	75	105
442	$ 1,000 - $ 2,999	159,170	110	125	210	100	140
443	$ 3,000 - $ 4,999	132,710	115	80	175	105	110
444	$ 5,000 - $ 6,999	136,835	70	90	210	45	125
445	$ 7,000 - $ 9,999	188,715	125	160	345	100	110
446	$10,000 - $11,999	142,605	80	130	200	80	115
447	$12,000 - $14,999	223,650	170	210	410	135	190
448	$15,000 - $19,999	288,290	250	285	535	100	285
449	$20,000 - $24,999	262,390	275	210	450	220	310
450	$25,000 - $29,999	247,090	235	220	280	165	160
451	$30,000 - $34,999	267,745	250	305	440	135	320
452	$35,000 - $39,999	217,705	175	215	235	100	310
453	$40,000 - $44,999	198,250	170	170	230	150	295
454	$45,000 - $49,999	141,795	140	145	165	95	170
455	$50,000 - $59,999	228,750	235	185	355	95	200
456	$60,000 and over	511,015	280	385	375	155	300
457	Average income $ (46)	35,618	31,315	31,978	27,492	27,980	29,621
458	Median income $ (46)	25,593	27,537	27,170	20,548	24,166	28,787
459	Standard error of average income $ (46)	84	969	1,352	815	865	726

Tableau 1. Certaines caractéristiques des secteurs de recensement, recensement de 2001 – Données intégrales et données-échantillon (20 %)

Toronto 0480.02 A	Toronto 0481	Toronto 0482	Toronto 0483	Toronto 0484	Toronto 0485.01 A	Caractéristiques	N°
						CARACTÉRISTIQUES DES FAMILLES DE RECENSEMENT	
						selon la structure et la taille de la famille de recensement – fin	
25	40	45	65	55	20	Parent de sexe masculin	406
20	30	35	30	15	20	1 enfant	407
10	15	-	30	20	-	2 enfants	408
-	-	-	-	20	-	3 enfants ou plus	409
1,420	**3,500**	**1,860**	**2,765**	**2,830**	**1,310**	**Nombre total d'enfants à la maison**	410
						selon les groupes d'âge	
230	850	380	695	645	290	Moins de 6 ans	411
620	1,425	680	1,025	1,140	575	6-14 ans	412
210	375	245	360	415	155	15-17 ans	413
280	590	380	440	410	190	18-24 ans	414
80	260	175	245	235	100	25 ans et plus	415
1.4	1.4	1.2	1.2	1.1	1.3	Nombre moyen d'enfants à la maison par famille de recensement (43)	416
3,525	**9,030**	**5,150**	**7,760**	**8,555**	**3,600**	**Nombre total de personnes dans les ménages privés**	417
						selon la situation des particuliers dans la famille de recensement et des particuliers dans le ménage	
260	695	380	605	770	425	Nombre de personnes hors famille de recensement	418
55	220	80	125	115	70	Vivant avec des personnes apparentées (44)	419
75	180	115	110	175	100	Vivant avec des personnes non apparentées uniquement	420
130	295	185	365	490	255	Vivant seules	421
3,270	8,335	4,760	7,160	7,780	3,180	Nombre de personnes membres d'une famille	422
3.3	3.3	3.2	3.1	3.0	3.1	Nombre moyen de personnes par famille de recensement	423
265	**515**	**510**	**820**	**1,360**	**435**	**Nombre total de personnes de 65 ans et plus**	424
80	175	130	220	345	170	Nombre de personnes hors famille de recensement de 65 ans et plus	425
15	50	35	40	60	45	Vivant avec des personnes apparentées (44)	426
-	-	-	-	10	-	Vivant avec des personnes non apparentées uniquement	427
60	125	95	175	270	120	Vivant seules	428
185	340	380	595	1,015	265	Nombre de personnes membres d'une famille de 65 ans et plus	429
						CARACTÉRISTIQUES DES FAMILLES ÉCONOMIQUES	
940	**2,490**	**1,460**	**2,280**	**2,580**	**1,010**	**Nombre total de familles économiques dans les ménages privés**	430
						selon la taille de la famille	
255	710	560	895	1,210	385	2 personnes	431
190	565	285	510	440	210	3 personnes	432
280	810	350	535	620	275	4 personnes	433
215	400	265	340	310	135	5 personnes ou plus	434
3,320	8,555	4,845	7,290	7,895	3,245	Nombre total de personnes dans les familles économiques	435
3.6	3.4	3.3	3.2	3.1	3.2	Nombre moyen de personnes par famille économique	436
200	475	305	480	660	350	Nombre total de personnes hors famille économique	437
						CARACTÉRISTIQUES DU REVENU DE 2000	
						Population de 15 ans et plus selon le sexe et les tranches de revenu total en 2000	
2,675	6,735	4,080	6,040	6,780	2,735	Total - Les deux sexes	438
175	315	145	205	320	105	Sans revenu	439
2,505	6,425	3,930	5,840	6,460	2,635	Avec un revenu	440
115	195	100	220	140	60	Moins de 1 000 $ (45)	441
150	360	175	270	320	120	1 000 $ - 2 999 $	442
75	250	160	255	215	110	3 000 $ - 4 999 $	443
80	255	180	165	235	110	5 000 $ - 6 999 $	444
145	280	195	200	360	90	7 000 $ - 9 999 $	445
45	225	145	185	215	75	10 000 $ - 11 999 $	446
205	235	185	210	355	125	12 000 $ - 14 999 $	447
160	470	300	425	460	280	15 000 $ - 19 999 $	448
165	520	355	555	420	205	20 000 $ - 24 999 $	449
90	405	290	400	395	170	25 000 $ - 29 999 $	450
175	640	315	460	520	225	30 000 $ - 34 999 $	451
210	495	200	405	395	220	35 000 $ - 39 999 $	452
160	425	330	435	350	205	40 000 $ - 44 999 $	453
155	315	190	205	280	110	45 000 $ - 49 999 $	454
215	545	225	490	595	165	50 000 $ - 59 999 $	455
365	810	590	955	1,190	370	60 000 $ et plus	456
33,889	31,990	35,345	35,209	36,494	34,067	Revenu moyen $ (46)	457
30,044	29,976	27,913	30,000	30,226	28,663	Revenu médian $ (46)	458
1,308	639	1,259	922	832	2,174	Erreur type de revenu moyen $ (46)	459

Table 1. Selected Characteristics for Census Tracts, 2001 Census – 100% Data and 20% Sample Data

No.	Characteristics	Toronto A CMA/RMR	Toronto 0473.03 A	Toronto 0474	Toronto 0475	Toronto 0476 ◆◇◇	Toronto 0480.01 A
	2000 INCOME CHARACTERISTICS						
	Population 15 years and over by sex and total income groups in 2000 – concluded						
460	Total - Males	1,797,065	1,405	1,640	2,365	965	1,680
461	Without income	80,800	60	60	60	10	55
462	With income	1,716,260	1,350	1,580	2,300	955	1,625
463	Under $1,000 (45)	77,370	20	40	50	25	30
464	$ 1,000 - $ 2,999	63,825	10	40	75	30	55
465	$ 3,000 - $ 4,999	50,025	50	25	65	35	20
466	$ 5,000 - $ 6,999	51,105	45	40	80	25	55
467	$ 7,000 - $ 9,999	69,220	35	35	70	35	40
468	$10,000 - $11,999	61,600	45	30	110	40	40
469	$12,000 - $14,999	78,540	50	85	110	60	40
470	$15,000 - $19,999	119,150	105	125	205	40	80
471	$20,000 - $24,999	117,635	85	85	240	85	150
472	$25,000 - $29,999	112,675	125	155	135	80	75
473	$30,000 - $34,999	127,815	125	180	185	65	105
474	$35,000 - $39,999	108,245	100	130	145	55	185
475	$40,000 - $44,999	108,095	75	90	175	110	210
476	$45,000 - $49,999	80,050	110	70	135	55	145
477	$50,000 - $59,999	139,440	170	140	255	75	150
478	$60,000 and over	351,475	190	305	275	130	245
479	Average income $ (46)	44,126	37,043	39,798	34,517	34,651	36,752
480	Median income $ (46)	31,160	33,018	32,842	30,019	30,250	38,000
481	Standard error of average income $ (46)	162	1,502	2,194	1,420	1,349	1,069
482	Total - Females	1,931,915	1,480	1,580	2,590	980	1,720
483	Without income	133,430	90	85	125	75	105
484	With income	1,798,485	1,385	1,495	2,470	905	1,620
485	Under $1,000 (45)	90,650	30	105	115	45	75
486	$ 1,000 - $ 2,999	95,350	95	90	140	75	90
487	$ 3,000 - $ 4,999	82,685	60	60	105	65	85
488	$ 5,000 - $ 6,999	85,730	25	50	130	25	70
489	$ 7,000 - $ 9,999	119,490	90	120	270	60	75
490	$10,000 - $11,999	81,010	35	100	90	40	75
491	$12,000 - $14,999	145,115	120	125	300	80	145
492	$15,000 - $19,999	169,135	145	165	330	60	200
493	$20,000 - $24,999	144,755	195	120	210	135	155
494	$25,000 - $29,999	134,420	115	70	140	85	85
495	$30,000 - $34,999	139,930	130	125	255	70	210
496	$35,000 - $39,999	109,465	70	85	85	45	130
497	$40,000 - $44,999	90,155	100	80	55	40	85
498	$45,000 - $49,999	61,745	35	75	30	40	25
499	$50,000 - $59,999	89,315	60	45	100	20	50
500	$60,000 and over	159,540	90	80	105	25	55
501	Average income $ (46)	27,498	25,755	23,713	20,941	20,976	22,461
502	Median income $ (46)	20,523	22,502	17,636	15,651	20,011	19,416
503	Standard error of average income $ (46)	53	1,148	1,406	768	893	841
	by composition of total income						
504	Total - Composition of income in 2000 % (47)	100.0	100.0	100.0	100.0	100.0	100.0
505	Employment income %	82.0	84.2	81.9	71.6	76.1	87.2
506	Government transfer payments %	7.9	9.6	9.3	14.9	11.8	8.1
507	Other %	10.1	6.2	8.7	13.4	12.1	4.7
	Population 15 years and over with employment income in 2000 by sex and work activity						
508	Both sexes with employment income (48)	2,659,220	2,140	2,360	3,160	1,275	2,680
509	Average employment income $	38,598	33,721	34,090	29,701	30,917	31,201
510	Standard error of average employment income $	95	1,162	1,436	1,074	1,059	807
511	Worked full year, full time (49)	1,508,125	1,315	1,360	1,770	750	1,560
512	Average employment income $	51,112	41,731	40,859	39,332	39,680	40,176
513	Standard error of average employment income $	145	1,331	1,726	1,584	1,502	945
514	Worked part year or part time (50)	1,083,230	790	980	1,335	515	1,100
515	Average employment income $	22,655	21,489	24,906	17,935	18,966	19,035
516	Standard error of average employment income $	106	1,833	2,368	1,082	1,082	1,020
517	Males with employment income (48)	1,382,055	1,120	1,285	1,660	715	1,475
518	Average employment income $	46,613	39,426	41,101	36,283	37,761	37,094
519	Standard error of average employment income $	172	1,705	2,184	1,720	1,623	1,123
520	Worked full year, full time (49)	857,885	775	800	1,065	470	940
521	Average employment income $	58,789	47,012	46,796	44,467	45,780	44,749
522	Standard error of average employment income $	242	1,831	2,615	2,316	2,191	1,216
523	Worked part year or part time (50)	494,115	325	470	570	235	530
524	Average employment income $	27,287	23,427	31,945	22,047	22,849	23,955
525	Standard error of average employment income $	218	3,024	3,834	2,000	1,715	1,688

Tableau 1. Certaines caractéristiques des secteurs de recensement, recensement de 2001 – Données intégrales et données-échantillon (20 %)

Toronto 0480.02 A	Toronto 0481	Toronto 0482	Toronto 0483	Toronto 0484	Toronto 0485.01 A	Caractéristiques	Nº
						CARACTÉRISTIQUES DU REVENU DE 2000	
						Population de 15 ans et plus selon le sexe et les tranches de revenu total en 2000 – fin	
1,325	3,345	2,090	2,985	3,390	1,320	Total - Hommes	460
90	115	55	95	100	35	Sans revenu	461
1,235	3,235	2,040	2,890	3,290	1,290	Avec un revenu	462
50	70	40	105	40	35	Moins de 1 000 $ (45)	463
60	110	65	115	85	50	1 000 $ - 2 999 $	464
30	80	55	70	85	25	3 000 $ - 4 999 $	465
30	75	65	65	70	50	5 000 $ - 6 999 $	466
40	75	75	75	80	35	7 000 $ - 9 999 $	467
-	75	35	75	65	15	10 000 $ - 11 999 $	468
65	75	75	60	90	35	12 000 $ - 14 999 $	469
50	180	145	115	165	60	15 000 $ - 19 999 $	470
65	255	205	210	125	90	20 000 $ - 24 999 $	471
20	200	120	145	220	100	25 000 $ - 29 999 $	472
60	295	140	165	295	90	30 000 $ - 34 999 $	473
100	270	110	190	210	140	35 000 $ - 39 999 $	474
100	230	200	250	250	100	40 000 $ - 44 999 $	475
110	210	105	120	175	80	45 000 $ - 49 999 $	476
165	350	170	365	410	100	50 000 $ - 59 999 $	477
285	690	430	770	925	285	60 000 $ et plus	478
43,717	39,750	42,210	44,237	47,058	43,210	Revenu moyen $ (46)	479
42,183	36,441	34,435	40,148	41,134	36,290	Revenu médian $ (46)	480
2,258	982	1,924	1,526	1,310	4,239	Erreur type de revenu moyen $ (46)	481
1,350	3,395	1,995	3,060	3,395	1,415	Total - Femmes	482
90	200	95	110	225	70	Sans revenu	483
1,265	3,190	1,895	2,950	3,170	1,345	Avec un revenu	484
65	120	55	115	105	25	Moins de 1 000 $ (45)	485
85	245	110	155	235	70	1 000 $ - 2 999 $	486
45	170	100	185	130	85	3 000 $ - 4 999 $	487
45	185	115	100	160	60	5 000 $ - 6 999 $	488
105	205	115	125	280	55	7 000 $ - 9 999 $	489
45	150	105	105	150	55	10 000 $ - 11 999 $	490
140	165	115	160	265	90	12 000 $ - 14 999 $	491
110	285	155	315	295	225	15 000 $ - 19 999 $	492
100	270	150	350	300	110	20 000 $ - 24 999 $	493
70	205	165	250	175	70	25 000 $ - 29 999 $	494
110	340	175	295	230	130	30 000 $ - 34 999 $	495
105	225	95	215	185	85	35 000 $ - 39 999 $	496
60	195	135	180	105	105	40 000 $ - 44 999 $	497
45	100	85	80	105	35	45 000 $ - 49 999 $	498
45	195	60	130	190	60	50 000 $ - 59 999 $	499
80	125	160	185	265	85	60 000 $ et plus	500
24,283	24,123	27,970	26,348	25,547	25,279	Revenu moyen $ (46)	501
18,938	20,861	22,418	22,330	19,166	20,025	Revenu médian $ (46)	502
1,139	715	1,520	943	844	1,066	Erreur type de revenu moyen $ (46)	503
						selon la composition du revenu total	
100.0	100.0	100.0	100.0	100.0	100.0	Total - Composition du revenu en 2000 % (47)	504
89.4	88.8	84.9	83.5	74.1	77.0	Revenu d'emploi %	505
6.8	6.6	6.8	7.4	9.0	9.0	Transferts gouvernementaux %	506
3.8	4.6	8.3	9.2	16.9	14.0	Autre %	507
						Population de 15 ans et plus ayant un revenu d'emploi en 2000 selon le sexe et le travail	
2,060	5,385	3,190	4,580	4,660	2,045	Les deux sexes ayant un revenu d'emploi (48)	508
36,746	33,895	36,979	37,460	37,454	33,794	Revenu moyen d'emploi $	509
1,470	700	1,344	1,111	1,016	2,383	Erreur type de revenu moyen d'emploi $	510
1,215	3,295	1,965	2,825	2,780	1,235	Ayant travaillé toute l'année à plein temps (49)	511
48,085	42,440	46,165	49,225	49,464	46,400	Revenu moyen d'emploi $	512
2,010	866	1,794	1,531	1,334	3,627	Erreur type de revenu moyen d'emploi $	513
830	2,020	1,185	1,645	1,805	730	Ayant travaillé une partie de l'année ou à temps partiel (50)	514
20,769	20,141	22,619	18,904	20,318	15,962	Revenu moyen d'emploi $	515
1,586	888	1,741	1,026	1,153	1,317	Erreur type de revenu moyen d'emploi $	516
1,095	2,820	1,710	2,420	2,560	1,105	Hommes ayant un revenu d'emploi (48)	517
45,797	41,214	43,470	46,008	46,409	41,909	Revenu moyen d'emploi $	518
2,396	1,040	1,957	1,741	1,510	4,210	Erreur type de revenu moyen d'emploi $	519
740	1,990	1,195	1,760	1,820	740	Ayant travaillé toute l'année à plein temps (49)	520
54,927	47,227	50,246	55,786	54,318	53,627	Revenu moyen d'emploi $	521
3,028	1,184	2,288	2,127	1,795	5,867	Erreur type de revenu moyen d'emploi $	522
355	810	500	620	710	320	Ayant travaillé une partie de l'année ou à temps partiel (50)	523
27,358	26,579	28,818	21,329	27,890	20,262	Revenu moyen d'emploi $	524
3,121	1,719	3,452	1,746	2,244	2,330	Erreur type de revenu moyen d'emploi $	525

Table 1. Selected Characteristics for Census Tracts, 2001 Census – 100% Data and 20% Sample Data

No.	Characteristics	Toronto A CMA/RMR	Toronto 0473.03 A	Toronto 0474	Toronto 0475	Toronto 0476 ◆◇◇	Toronto 0480.01 A
	2000 INCOME CHARACTERISTICS						
	Population 15 years and over with employment income in 2000 by sex and work activity – concluded						
526	Females with employment income (48)	1,277,170	1,020	1,075	1,505	570	1,210
527	Average employment income $	29,924	27,468	25,695	22,440	22,318	23,991
528	Standard error of average employment income $	64	1,449	1,600	1,110	1,001	1,007
529	Worked full year, full time (49)	650,240	545	565	705	280	620
530	Average employment income $	40,984	34,269	32,421	31,550	29,471	33,280
531	Standard error of average employment income $	100	1,670	1,639	1,778	1,286	1,308
532	Worked part year or part time (50)	589,125	465	505	770	280	565
533	Average employment income $	18,769	20,115	18,403	14,905	15,679	14,413
534	Standard error of average employment income $	69	2,272	2,704	1,097	1,251	1,071
	Census families by structure and family income groups in 2000						
535	Total - All census families	1,280,955	1,145	1,280	1,745	755	1,270
536	Under $10,000	64,185	15	35	50	25	30
537	$ 10,000 - $19,999	66,640	20	70	95	55	35
538	$ 20,000 - $29,999	112,350	95	115	220	65	100
539	$ 30,000 - $39,999	120,075	160	130	250	65	120
540	$ 40,000 - $49,999	118,995	145	215	195	130	130
541	$ 50,000 - $59,999	113,210	145	150	140	100	130
542	$ 60,000 - $69,999	111,850	145	115	205	100	175
543	$ 70,000 - $79,999	100,165	105	155	175	60	130
544	$ 80,000 - $89,999	86,695	90	55	175	25	165
545	$ 90,000 - $99,999	73,065	95	90	55	45	85
546	$100,000 and over	313,720	140	160	190	70	175
547	Average family income $	81,245	66,380	65,838	59,904	57,319	65,118
548	Median family income $	63,700	59,683	54,307	55,481	50,799	64,139
549	Standard error of average family income $	232	2,412	3,727	1,964	1,988	1,735
550	Total - All couple census families (51)	1,070,955	985	1,035	1,455	635	1,105
551	Under $10,000	38,815	10	15	15	15	30
552	$ 10,000 - $19,999	36,860	15	-	65	35	10
553	$ 20,000 - $29,999	83,410	65	75	180	40	80
554	$ 30,000 - $39,999	88,295	110	105	160	55	85
555	$ 40,000 - $49,999	93,430	105	180	175	115	105
556	$ 50,000 - $59,999	94,805	145	130	125	95	120
557	$ 60,000 - $69,999	97,425	115	110	165	95	150
558	$ 70,000 - $79,999	89,905	95	135	155	65	130
559	$ 80,000 - $89,999	79,590	90	45	165	25	145
560	$ 90,000 - $99,999	67,900	95	75	55	35	85
561	$100,000 and over	300,530	140	165	185	65	170
562	Average family income $	88,436	70,467	72,923	63,944	60,839	67,937
563	Median family income $	70,079	64,217	61,964	60,467	55,863	65,984
564	Standard error of average family income $	271	2,623	4,330	2,223	2,239	1,820
	Incidence of low income in 2000						
565	Total - Economic families	1,231,145	1,125	1,250	1,730	675	1,250
566	Low income	176,710	105	60	140	50	75
567	Incidence of low income in 2000 % (52)	14.4	9.2	5.0	8.1	7.6	5.7
568	Total - Unattached individuals 15 years and over	511,770	300	360	830	200	370
569	Low income	179,840	115	80	245	30	60
570	Incidence of low income in 2000 % (52)	35.1	38.2	22.3	30.2	14.9	15.9
571	Total - Population in private households	4,633,415	3,860	4,115	6,120	2,195	4,425
572	Low income	771,535	435	250	700	180	300
573	Incidence of low income in 2000 % (52)	16.7	11.2	6.1	11.4	8.2	6.7
	Private households by household income groups in 2000						
574	Total - All private households	1,634,755	1,365	1,530	2,440	960	1,570
575	Under $10,000	87,030	50	65	70	40	30
576	$ 10,000 - $19,999	145,415	60	100	340	100	120
577	$ 20,000 - $29,999	146,420	115	125	370	90	155
578	$ 30,000 - $39,999	155,395	180	170	325	80	135
579	$ 40,000 - $49,999	150,040	185	180	225	170	210
580	$ 50,000 - $59,999	138,200	170	200	185	115	130
581	$ 60,000 - $69,999	133,130	135	185	210	135	195
582	$ 70,000 - $79,999	117,065	90	145	235	65	140
583	$ 80,000 - $89,999	100,945	125	65	170	30	155
584	$ 90,000 - $99,999	84,700	80	110	65	40	90
585	$100,000 and over	376,420	170	195	245	90	200
586	Average household income $	76,454	62,621	64,161	53,591	54,114	61,071
587	Median household income $	59,502	55,319	54,852	44,313	49,493	58,595
588	Standard error of average household income $	192	2,164	3,203	1,643	1,749	1,733

Tableau 1. Certaines caractéristiques des secteurs de recensement, recensement de 2001 – Données intégrales et données-échantillon (20 %)

Toronto 0480.02 A	Toronto 0481	Toronto 0482	Toronto 0483	Toronto 0484	Toronto 0485.01 A	Caractéristiques	N°
						CARACTÉRISTIQUES DU REVENU DE 2000	
						Population de 15 ans et plus ayant un revenu d'emploi en 2000 selon le sexe et le travail – fin	
965	2,560	1,480	2,165	2,110	940	Femmes ayant un revenu d'emploi (48)	526
26,452	25,837	29,465	27,896	26,583	24,231	Revenu moyen d'emploi $	527
1,293	811	1,720	1,202	1,117	1,275	Erreur type de revenu moyen d'emploi $	528
480	1,305	770	1,070	960	495	Ayant travaillé toute l'année à plein temps (49)	529
37,543	35,150	39,866	38,425	40,288	35,563	Revenu moyen d'emploi $	530
1,752	1,125	2,826	1,873	1,685	1,419	Erreur type de revenu moyen d'emploi $	531
470	1,210	685	1,025	1,090	410	Ayant travaillé une partie de l'année ou à temps partiel (50)	532
15,809	15,808	18,085	17,437	15,383	12,589	Revenu moyen d'emploi $	533
1,302	848	1,538	1,255	1,093	1,405	Erreur type de revenu moyen d'emploi $	534
						Familles de recensement selon la structure et les tranches de revenu de la famille en 2000	
980	2,565	1,500	2,335	2,605	1,020	Total - Toutes les familles de recensement	535
35	85	45	45	45	20	Moins de 10 000 $	536
35	55	-	45	110	40	10 000 $ - 19 999 $	537
75	135	130	105	85	90	20 000 $ - 29 999 $	538
25	235	140	200	200	90	30 000 $ - 39 999 $	539
85	215	170	230	155	110	40 000 $ - 49 999 $	540
75	270	125	190	320	75	50 000 $ - 59 999 $	541
120	295	105	255	305	110	60 000 $ - 69 999 $	542
95	265	155	295	345	110	70 000 $ - 79 999 $	543
110	270	140	225	250	115	80 000 $ - 89 999 $	544
45	210	70	215	115	60	90 000 $ - 99 999 $	545
285	520	410	540	680	195	100 000 $ et plus	546
79,923	72,301	83,387	79,566	79,503	73,398	Revenu moyen des familles $	547
74,309	69,479	72,098	72,798	71,992	66,473	Revenu médian des familles $	548
3,202	1,484	3,987	2,306	1,858	5,325	Erreur type de revenu moyen des familles $	549
865	2,275	1,400	2,055	2,350	845	Total - Toutes les familles de recensement comptant un couple (51)	550
25	45	20	35	20	10	Moins de 10 000 $	551
15	30	-	10	55	10	10 000 $ - 19 999 $	552
70	115	110	65	70	65	20 000 $ - 29 999 $	553
10	150	120	160	165	65	30 000 $ - 39 999 $	554
55	185	145	175	130	65	40 000 $ - 49 999 $	555
70	245	125	165	280	60	50 000 $ - 59 999 $	556
115	260	110	235	285	100	60 000 $ - 69 999 $	557
75	265	150	280	315	100	70 000 $ - 79 999 $	558
110	270	140	200	235	110	80 000 $ - 89 999 $	559
50	205	70	210	115	60	90 000 $ - 99 999 $	560
270	505	405	520	670	195	100 000 $ et plus	561
83,970	76,386	86,743	83,946	83,452	80,967	Revenu moyen des familles $	562
78,070	74,070	73,721	75,021	74,544	72,878	Revenu médian des familles $	563
3,464	1,526	4,153	2,498	1,957	6,351	Erreur type de revenu moyen des familles $	564
						Fréquence des unités à faible revenu en 2000	
940	2,490	1,460	2,280	2,580	1,010	Total - Familles économiques	565
60	95	45	75	115	80	Faible revenu	566
6.2	3.7	3.1	3.4	4.3	7.9	Fréquence des unités à faible revenu en 2000 % (52)	567
200	465	295	480	665	350	Total - Personnes hors famille économique de 15 ans et plus	568
85	100	35	115	60	55	Faible revenu	569
41.9	22.2	12.1	24.1	8.7	16.2	Fréquence des unités à faible revenu en 2000 % (52)	570
3,525	9,020	5,140	7,765	8,555	3,600	Total - Population dans les ménages privés	571
245	430	200	360	395	290	Faible revenu	572
7.0	4.8	3.9	4.7	4.6	8.0	Fréquence des unités à faible revenu en 2000 % (52)	573
						Ménages privés selon les tranches de revenu du ménage en 2000	
1,075	2,815	1,670	2,680	3,105	1,295	Total - Tous les ménages privés	574
50	95	30	60	35	35	Moins de 10 000 $	575
60	115	60	140	175	100	10 000 $ - 19 999 $	576
85	155	140	160	200	115	20 000 $ - 29 999 $	577
25	260	140	240	260	145	30 000 $ - 39 999 $	578
90	235	175	240	165	105	40 000 $ - 49 999 $	579
90	290	125	225	360	90	50 000 $ - 59 999 $	580
115	290	120	255	375	140	60 000 $ - 69 999 $	581
95	280	170	280	355	145	70 000 $ - 79 999 $	582
95	275	140	240	290	115	80 000 $ - 89 999 $	583
45	215	90	235	140	70	90 000 $ - 99 999 $	584
310	610	480	610	745	235	100 000 $ et plus	585
78,796	72,920	83,317	76,717	75,863	69,230	Revenu moyen des ménages $	586
71,940	68,623	72,486	70,081	69,480	64,953	Revenu médian des ménages $	587
3,307	1,591	3,669	2,170	1,681	4,405	Erreur type de revenu moyen des ménages $	588

Table 1. Selected Characteristics for Census Tracts, 2001 Census – 100% Data and 20% Sample Data

No.	Characteristics	Toronto 0485.02 A	Toronto 0500.01	Toronto 0500.02	Toronto 0501.01	Toronto 0501.02	Toronto 0502.01
	POPULATION CHARACTERISTICS						
1	**Population, 1996 (1)**	**5,190**	**3,771**	**5,148**	**5,927**	**6,645**	**6,203**
2	**Population, 2001 (2)**	**5,969**	**3,774**	**5,060**	**5,785**	**7,361**	**6,175**
3	Population percentage change, 1996-2001	15.0	0.1	-1.7	-2.4	10.8	-0.5
4	Land area in square kilometres, 2001	6.55	0.82	3.13	8.83	3.99	1.16
5	**Total population - 100% Data (3)**	**5,970**	**3,775**	**5,060**	**5,785**	**7,360**	**6,175**
	by sex and age groups						
6	Male	2,905	1,925	2,510	2,750	3,645	3,045
7	0-4 years	215	130	115	150	240	195
8	5-9 years	205	120	145	180	295	245
9	10-14 years	260	100	140	185	300	235
10	15-19 years	225	105	150	180	315	275
11	20-24 years	155	140	165	170	195	215
12	25-29 years	235	140	145	205	135	230
13	30-34 years	280	210	180	180	190	200
14	35-39 years	295	235	255	215	320	285
15	40-44 years	220	150	255	240	350	285
16	45-49 years	175	160	215	200	325	250
17	50-54 years	170	115	205	190	290	205
18	55-59 years	105	95	140	155	200	155
19	60-64 years	85	75	125	125	165	100
20	65-69 years	90	70	110	110	125	90
21	70-74 years	70	45	70	110	100	40
22	75-79 years	40	20	65	70	55	30
23	80-84 years	45	5	35	50	25	10
24	85 years and over	25	10	10	35	15	10
25	Female	3,065	1,855	2,555	3,035	3,715	3,130
26	0-4 years	200	110	115	140	220	205
27	5-9 years	245	135	125	175	240	265
28	10-14 years	250	115	140	180	280	245
29	15-19 years	215	80	95	160	285	250
30	20-24 years	175	165	165	170	190	170
31	25-29 years	215	175	180	200	135	205
32	30-34 years	225	200	215	180	230	255
33	35-39 years	300	180	230	245	365	305
34	40-44 years	255	145	255	270	405	310
35	45-49 years	200	120	225	225	355	265
36	50-54 years	180	130	175	230	270	210
37	55-59 years	125	80	165	190	210	150
38	60-64 years	85	65	120	145	150	80
39	65-69 years	85	55	115	120	125	90
40	70-74 years	90	35	95	130	100	60
41	75-79 years	100	30	65	115	80	35
42	80-84 years	65	20	30	75	35	15
43	85 years and over	65	10	35	70	25	15
44	**Total population 15 years and over**	**4,595**	**3,065**	**4,280**	**4,770**	**5,785**	**4,790**
	by legal marital status						
45	Never married (single)	1,335	1,090	1,485	1,420	1,555	1,580
46	Legally married (and not separated)	2,355	1,385	1,845	2,380	3,510	2,510
47	Separated, but still legally married	205	165	225	200	160	190
48	Divorced	365	295	480	395	350	335
49	Widowed	330	130	245	375	215	180
	by common-law status						
50	Not in a common-law relationship	4,160	2,765	3,875	4,450	5,540	4,475
51	In a common-law relationship	430	295	405	320	245	310
52	**Total population - 20% Sample Data (4)**	**5,895**	**3,770**	**5,055**	**5,705**	**7,360**	**6,175**
	by mother tongue						
53	Single responses	5,835	3,760	4,935	5,440	7,325	6,025
54	English	5,325	2,145	3,300	4,265	5,485	3,920
55	French	110	60	75	75	80	65
56	Non-official languages (5)	400	1,555	1,555	1,100	1,760	2,040
57	Italian	60	90	105	65	55	40
58	Chinese, n.o.s.	15	25	50	30	70	70
59	Cantonese	-	-	15	10	15	-
60	Portuguese	15	135	185	115	85	125
61	Punjabi	-	-	-	10	15	40
62	Other languages (6)	315	1,310	1,210	860	1,520	1,765
63	Multiple responses	55	15	125	265	35	155
64	English and French	10	-	10	-	-	10
65	English and non-official language	45	10	110	190	20	105
66	French and non-official language	-	-	-	70	10	20
67	English, French and non-official language	-	-	-	-	-	10

See reference material at the end of the publication. – Voir les documents de référence à la fin de la publication.

Tableau 1. Certaines caractéristiques des secteurs de recensement, recensement de 2001 – Données intégrales et données-échantillon (20 %)

Toronto 0502.02	Toronto 0503	Toronto 0504	Toronto 0505.01	Toronto 0505.02	Toronto 0506	Caractéristiques	N°
						CARACTÉRISTIQUES DE LA POPULATION	
2,823	**5,534**	**3,425**	**4,753**	**4,168**	**2,576**	**Population, 1996 (1)**	1
2,733	**5,519**	**3,431**	**4,784**	**4,318**	**2,686**	**Population, 2001 (2)**	2
-3.2	-0.3	0.2	0.7	3.6	4.3	Variation en pourcentage de la population, 1996-2001	3
0.69	1.70	1.38	2.78	3.84	1.87	Superficie des terres en kilomètres carrés, 2001	4
2,730	**5,515**	**3,430**	**4,785**	**4,315**	**2,690**	**Population totale – Données intégrales (3)**	5
						selon le sexe et les groupes d'âge	
1,280	2,725	1,685	2,370	2,180	1,330	Sexe masculin	6
75	155	100	110	115	95	0-4 ans	7
85	200	120	195	150	105	5-9 ans	8
85	225	130	230	215	115	10-14 ans	9
90	190	110	220	185	100	15-19 ans	10
70	190	90	140	135	80	20-24 ans	11
70	185	75	75	75	35	25-29 ans	12
80	215	105	85	50	55	30-34 ans	13
110	255	155	145	130	85	35-39 ans	14
140	250	150	200	190	110	40-44 ans	15
95	205	120	205	195	130	45-49 ans	16
75	180	120	205	190	115	50-54 ans	17
60	120	80	165	140	100	55-59 ans	18
60	105	75	140	110	70	60-64 ans	19
55	90	90	95	100	40	65-69 ans	20
55	90	75	75	80	30	70-74 ans	21
30	45	50	50	65	35	75-79 ans	22
15	15	20	35	30	15	80-84 ans	23
25	10	10	10	20	15	85 ans et plus	24
1,450	2,795	1,745	2,405	2,140	1,355	Sexe féminin	25
75	175	105	105	115	80	0-4 ans	26
75	220	100	160	130	110	5-9 ans	27
70	190	130	210	165	105	10-14 ans	28
75	200	110	215	165	110	15-19 ans	29
70	170	85	160	130	80	20-24 ans	30
70	220	70	90	65	30	25-29 ans	31
90	230	115	80	70	60	30-34 ans	32
105	285	145	155	150	110	35-39 ans	33
115	225	155	235	220	125	40-44 ans	34
100	185	140	220	175	145	45-49 ans	35
70	170	130	215	210	95	50-54 ans	36
70	130	115	165	125	95	55-59 ans	37
65	110	75	120	100	50	60-64 ans	38
90	100	105	90	100	45	65-69 ans	39
75	85	75	70	100	35	70-74 ans	40
70	50	60	55	60	45	75-79 ans	41
70	30	20	45	30	30	80-84 ans	42
100	15	20	20	25	20	85 ans et plus	43
2,265	**4,360**	**2,750**	**3,765**	**3,425**	**2,080**	**Population totale de 15 ans et plus**	44
						selon l'état matrimonial légal	
570	1,425	715	1,005	865	515	Célibataire (jamais marié(e))	45
1,165	2,345	1,635	2,475	2,220	1,365	Légalement marié(e) (et non séparé(e))	46
85	140	90	50	55	35	Séparé(e), mais toujours légalement marié(e)	47
165	265	160	100	115	75	Divorcé(e)	48
285	180	150	135	160	95	Veuf ou veuve	49
						selon l'union libre	
2,125	4,105	2,610	3,700	3,355	2,020	Ne vivant pas en union libre	50
145	255	140	70	70	65	Vivant en union libre	51
2,535	**5,515**	**3,435**	**4,775**	**4,335**	**2,685**	**Population totale – Données-échantillon (20 %) (4)**	52
						selon la langue maternelle	
2,490	5,360	3,380	4,705	4,315	2,675	Réponses uniques	53
1,635	3,730	2,970	3,785	3,180	2,270	Anglais	54
25	65	65	80	105	50	Français	55
825	1,570	350	845	1,035	355	Langues non officielles (5)	56
15	105	50	150	90	90	Italien	57
-	10	-	25	50	10	Chinois, n.d.a.	58
-	-	-	50	-	-	Cantonais	59
35	145	10	145	25	30	Portugais	60
30	30	-	10	-	-	Pendjabi	61
755	1,275	280	465	865	220	Autres langues (6)	62
45	160	50	70	15	10	Réponses multiples	63
-	10	20	35	-	-	Anglais et français	64
40	130	30	40	15	10	Anglais et langue non officielle	65
-	10	-	-	-	-	Français et langue non officielle	66
-	-	-	-	-	-	Anglais, français et langue non officielle	67

See reference material at the end of the publication. – Voir les documents de référence à la fin de la publication.

Table 1. Selected Characteristics for Census Tracts, 2001 Census – 100% Data and 20% Sample Data

No.	Characteristics	Toronto 0485.02 A	Toronto 0500.01	Toronto 0500.02	Toronto 0501.01	Toronto 0501.02	Toronto 0502.01
	POPULATION CHARACTERISTICS						
	by home language						
68	Single responses	5,600	3,060	4,215	4,720	6,175	4,995
69	English	5,505	2,375	3,600	4,555	5,775	4,210
70	French	10	-	-	-	-	-
71	Non-official languages (5)	90	685	615	165	405	780
72	Cantonese	-	-	10	-	15	15
73	Chinese, n.o.s.	-	20	10	-	10	30
74	Italian	10	10	40	10	-	10
75	Punjabi	-	-	-	-	10	15
76	Portuguese	-	55	60	10	10	40
77	Other languages (6)	75	610	495	150	365	670
78	Multiple responses	290	715	840	985	1,180	1,185
79	English and French	65	45	70	90	115	65
80	English and non-official language	220	665	765	810	1,065	1,025
81	French and non-official language	-	-	-	70	-	15
82	English, French and non-official language	10	10	10	15	-	75
	by knowledge of official languages						
83	English only	5,560	3,375	4,640	5,225	6,355	5,570
84	French only	-	-	-	-	-	10
85	English and French	315	290	335	445	900	440
86	Neither English nor French	20	105	85	30	110	160
	by knowledge of non-official languages (5) (7)						
87	Italian	95	155	160	100	135	65
88	Cantonese	15	15	30	15	45	45
89	Chinese, n.o.s.	15	25	30	25	45	30
90	Spanish	30	185	130	150	320	330
91	Portuguese	10	170	275	190	100	170
92	Punjabi	-	20	-	75	25	70
93	Tagalog (Pilipino)	10	85	70	30	60	225
	by first official language spoken						
94	English	5,780	3,565	4,895	5,505	7,105	5,955
95	French	95	55	65	135	90	50
96	English and French	10	50	15	40	75	25
97	Neither English nor French	10	105	85	30	90	145
98	Official language minority - (number) (8)	100	75	75	150	120	65
99	Official language minority - (percentage) (8)	1.7	2.0	1.5	2.6	1.6	1.1
	by ethnic origin (9)						
100	Canadian	2,440	895	1,600	1,495	1,760	1,400
101	English	2,080	590	1,110	1,595	2,065	1,160
102	Scottish	1,270	280	555	970	1,370	770
103	Irish	1,315	415	730	930	1,275	680
104	Chinese	65	115	105	55	185	135
105	Italian	360	220	215	290	445	185
106	East Indian	10	235	115	225	330	320
107	French	530	185	385	525	660	305
108	German	565	180	320	495	645	295
109	Portuguese	45	180	320	245	170	260
110	Polish	195	540	650	385	680	560
111	Jewish	15	35	20	25	30	-
112	Jamaican	25	140	125	80	105	240
113	Filipino	25	90	80	60	90	285
114	Ukrainian	75	145	175	155	285	135
	by Aboriginal identity						
115	Total Aboriginal identity population (10)	60	10	110	45	50	35
116	Total non-Aboriginal population	5,835	3,760	4,950	5,655	7,310	6,145
	by Aboriginal origin						
117	Total Aboriginal origins population (11)	135	85	135	75	110	75
118	Total non-Aboriginal population	5,755	3,690	4,920	5,630	7,255	6,100
	by Registered Indian status						
119	Registered Indian (12)	30	10	50	-	-	15
120	Not a Registered Indian	5,860	3,770	5,005	5,700	7,355	6,160

Tableau 1. Certaines caractéristiques des secteurs de recensement, recensement de 2001 – Données intégrales et données-échantillon (20 %)

Toronto 0502.02	Toronto 0503	Toronto 0504	Toronto 0505.01	Toronto 0505.02	Toronto 0506	Caractéristiques	N°
						CARACTÉRISTIQUES DE LA POPULATION	
						selon la langue parlée à la maison	
2,060	4,440	3,125	4,225	3,690	2,465	Réponses uniques	68
1,975	3,970	3,105	4,120	3,520	2,395	Anglais	69
-	10	-	10	55	10	Français	70
90	460	20	95	120	60	Langues non officielles (5)	71
-	-	-	-	-	-	Cantonais	72
-	-	-	-	-	-	Chinois, n.d.a.	73
-	45	10	-	-	30	Italien	74
10	10	-	10	-	-	Pendjabi	75
10	60	-	30	-	10	Portugais	76
65	350	20	50	110	20	Autres langues (6)	77
470	1,075	305	550	645	225	Réponses multiples	78
10	50	60	65	25	45	Anglais et français	79
455	1,010	225	490	625	180	Anglais et langue non officielle	80
-	-	-	-	-	-	Français et langue non officielle	81
10	20	25	-	-	-	Anglais, français et langue non officielle	82
						selon la connaissance des langues officielles	
2,375	4,925	3,005	3,845	3,880	2,275	Anglais seulement	83
-	10	-	-	-	-	Français seulement	84
120	475	415	910	430	390	Anglais et français	85
35	115	15	25	30	20	Ni l'anglais ni le français	86
						selon la connaissance des langues non officielles (5) (7)	
35	155	70	205	135	135	Italien	87
-	-	-	115	-	-	Cantonais	88
-	10	10	20	35	10	Chinois, n.d.a.	89
20	125	40	115	45	60	Espagnol	90
25	180	-	155	20	25	Portugais	91
30	55	-	10	10	10	Pendjabi	92
65	110	10	10	-	-	Tagalog (pilipino)	93
						selon la première langue officielle parlée	
2,455	5,300	3,350	4,655	4,195	2,605	Anglais	94
25	60	65	75	105	50	Français	95
20	40	-	25	10	10	Anglais et français	96
35	115	15	20	25	20	Ni l'anglais ni le français	97
35	80	65	90	110	55	Minorité de langue officielle - (nombre) (8)	98
1.4	1.5	1.9	1.9	2.5	2.0	Minorité de langue officielle - (pourcentage) (8)	99
						selon l'origine ethnique (9)	
695	1,440	1,210	1,500	1,390	805	Canadien	100
535	1,020	1,220	1,530	1,325	855	Anglais	101
395	715	835	1,125	975	620	Écossais	102
350	830	735	1,105	995	490	Irlandais	103
45	100	20	240	80	55	Chinois	104
75	265	210	430	315	295	Italien	105
145	430	80	155	95	105	Indien de l'Inde	106
180	420	240	355	265	240	Français	107
140	265	385	525	435	285	Allemand	108
70	255	15	170	50	25	Portugais	109
400	365	150	185	445	125	Polonais	110
10	-	40	40	35	40	Juif	111
45	200	75	55	10	35	Jamaïquain	112
115	140	20	20	10	30	Philippin	113
80	100	165	155	295	135	Ukrainien	114
						selon l'identité autochtone	
30	60	20	-	-	-	Total de la population ayant une identité autochtone (10)	115
2,500	5,455	3,420	4,775	4,335	2,685	Total de la population non autochtone	116
						selon l'origine autochtone	
10	90	20	20	-	10	Total de la population ayant une origine autochtone (11)	117
2,525	5,430	3,415	4,755	4,335	2,675	Total de la population non autochtone	118
						selon le statut d'Indien inscrit	
10	10	15	10	-	-	Oui, Indien inscrit (12)	119
2,530	5,510	3,420	4,775	4,335	2,685	Non, pas un Indien inscrit	120

Table 1. Selected Characteristics for Census Tracts, 2001 Census – 100% Data and 20% Sample Data

No.	Characteristics	Toronto 0485.02 A	Toronto 0500.01	Toronto 0500.02	Toronto 0501.01	Toronto 0501.02	Toronto 0502.01
	POPULATION CHARACTERISTICS						
	by visible minority groups						
121	Total visible minority population	275	810	770	1,055	1,255	2,055
122	Chinese	45	115	90	50	155	145
123	South Asian	10	220	135	305	260	440
124	Black	60	235	335	290	215	640
125	Filipino	30	90	80	60	95	280
126	Latin American	10	80	55	65	150	190
127	Southeast Asian	50	15	25	20	40	15
128	Arab	-	10	-	160	65	45
129	West Asian	25	-	-	40	20	40
130	Korean	-	-	10	-	40	25
131	Japanese	10	-	10	40	50	25
132	Visible minority, n.i.e. (13)	-	35	10	10	135	140
133	Multiple visible minorities (14)	40	10	20	25	35	65
	by citizenship						
134	Canadian citizenship (15)	5,740	3,120	4,605	5,175	6,840	5,330
135	Citizenship other than Canadian	150	655	455	530	520	840
	by place of birth of respondent						
136	Non-immigrant population	5,265	2,080	3,245	3,820	4,920	3,465
137	Born in province of residence	4,700	1,745	2,525	3,135	4,020	2,910
138	Immigrant population (16)	625	1,655	1,795	1,865	2,360	2,680
139	United States	10	10	35	65	125	25
140	Central and South America	-	180	150	85	285	265
141	Caribbean and Bermuda	20	155	135	160	125	400
142	United Kingdom	215	100	160	430	370	200
143	Other Europe (17)	245	865	930	630	940	825
144	Africa	-	15	175	95	65	190
145	Asia and the Middle East	130	315	190	385	435	770
146	Oceania and other (18)	-	20	20	15	10	-
147	Non-permanent residents (19)	10	40	15	15	85	30
148	**Total immigrant population**	**620**	**1,650**	**1,795**	**1,870**	**2,360**	**2,680**
	by period of immigration						
149	Before 1961	215	110	215	395	200	170
150	1961-1970	75	165	295	375	305	310
151	1971-1980	130	215	245	280	520	455
152	1981-1990	95	355	480	320	735	645
153	1991-2001 (20)	105	815	555	495	595	1,105
154	1991-1995	50	360	315	200	370	580
155	1996-2001 (20)	55	455	240	295	220	530
	by age at immigration						
156	0-4 years	75	150	185	175	290	255
157	5-19 years	260	465	480	495	630	810
158	20 years and over	285	1,035	1,135	1,195	1,440	1,615
159	**Total population**	**5,895**	**3,775**	**5,055**	**5,705**	**7,360**	**6,175**
	by religion						
160	Catholic (21)	1,515	1,835	2,340	2,170	2,515	2,600
161	Protestant	2,940	790	1,330	1,985	2,800	1,680
162	Christian Orthodox	20	155	210	125	145	200
163	Christian, n.i.e. (22)	185	185	125	75	255	235
164	Muslim	20	125	185	235	160	250
165	Jewish	15	-	25	15	60	-
166	Buddhist	105	-	40	-	55	20
167	Hindu	10	135	55	125	175	260
168	Sikh	-	-	-	65	10	25
169	Eastern religions (23)	10	30	-	-	-	-
170	Other religions (24)	-	-	-	15	25	-
171	No religious affiliation (25)	1,070	510	745	890	1,170	910
172	**Total population 15 years and over**	**4,520**	**3,065**	**4,275**	**4,690**	**5,790**	**4,785**
	by generation status						
173	1st generation (26)	615	1,560	1,725	1,810	2,335	2,505
174	2nd generation (27)	820	580	870	1,055	1,395	875
175	3rd generation and over (28)	3,090	930	1,680	1,825	2,060	1,400
176	**Total population 1 year and over (29)**	**5,765**	**3,730**	**5,040**	**5,675**	**7,260**	**6,090**
	by place of residence 1 year ago (mobility)						
177	Non-movers	5,010	2,975	4,450	4,970	6,400	5,060
178	Movers	755	755	595	705	855	1,030
179	Non-migrants	415	440	380	315	460	660
180	Migrants	345	315	215	390	400	375
181	Internal migrants	325	140	185	270	285	290
182	Intraprovincial migrants	285	115	155	270	220	240
183	Interprovincial migrants	45	30	30	-	70	50
184	External migrants	20	170	35	125	110	85

Tableau 1. Certaines caractéristiques des secteurs de recensement, recensement de 2001 – Données intégrales et données-échantillon (20 %)

Toronto 0502.02	Toronto 0503	Toronto 0504	Toronto 0505.01	Toronto 0505.02	Toronto 0506	Caractéristiques	Nº
						CARACTÉRISTIQUES DE LA POPULATION	
						selon les groupes de minorités visibles	
515	1,460	255	550	400	230	Total de la population des minorités visibles	121
-	60	20	235	100	30	Chinois	122
145	510	90	130	105	105	Sud-Asiatique	123
180	385	80	65	25	20	Noir	124
100	120	20	10	10	-	Philippin	125
-	65	-	20	20	10	Latino-Américain	126
40	40	-	-	10	-	Asiatique du Sud-Est	127
20	65	-	35	75	10	Arabe	128
-	10	-	10	-	-	Asiatique occidental	129
-	75	40	15	10	-	Coréen	130
-	35	-	25	55	20	Japonais	131
15	55	-	10	-	20	Minorité visible, n.i.a. (13)	132
10	50	-	-	-	20	Minorités visibles multiples (14)	133
						selon la citoyenneté	
2,320	4,785	3,235	4,650	4,160	2,575	Citoyenneté canadienne (15)	134
210	735	200	125	175	110	Citoyenneté autre que canadienne	135
						selon le lieu de naissance du répondant	
1,530	3,245	2,680	3,775	3,175	2,185	Population non immigrante	136
1,340	2,735	2,250	3,205	2,735	1,795	Née dans la province de résidence	137
990	2,195	725	995	1,155	490	Population immigrante (16)	138
25	30	20	55	90	35	États-Unis	139
30	120	15	10	30	10	Amérique centrale et du Sud	140
65	160	45	55	-	10	Caraïbes et Bermudes	141
125	245	220	205	200	120	Royaume-Uni	142
415	810	260	385	560	190	Autre Europe (17)	143
120	150	25	70	125	35	Afrique	144
210	635	115	210	145	75	Asie et Moyen-Orient	145
10	45	20	15	-	10	Océanie et autre (18)	146
10	75	35	10	-	10	Résidents non permanents (19)	147
995	**2,195**	**725**	**995**	**1,155**	**490**	**Population immigrante totale**	148
						selon la période d'immigration	
240	235	275	300	355	150	Avant 1961	149
75	320	70	255	220	120	1961-1970	150
165	285	140	225	225	80	1971-1980	151
215	365	165	170	140	40	1981-1990	152
300	1,000	70	35	210	100	1991-2001 (20)	153
145	485	20	15	150	35	1991-1995	154
145	515	45	25	60	60	1996-2001 (20)	155
						selon l'âge à l'immigration	
115	215	80	115	145	35	0-4 ans	156
290	655	185	305	320	140	5-19 ans	157
585	1,330	455	580	690	315	20 ans et plus	158
2,530	**5,515**	**3,435**	**4,775**	**4,335**	**2,685**	**Population totale**	159
						selon la religion	
970	2,325	990	1,535	1,420	945	Catholique (21)	160
915	1,640	1,670	2,070	1,750	1,125	Protestante	161
30	120	60	60	95	10	Orthodoxe chrétienne	162
30	180	75	70	20	60	Chrétiennes, n.i.a. (22)	163
200	295	-	120	90	-	Musulmane	164
10	10	10	40	35	40	Juive	165
10	35	-	10	30	-	Bouddhiste	166
-	230	70	15	10	45	Hindoue	167
25	45	-	-	-	-	Sikh	168
30	-	-	-	-	-	Religions orientales (23)	169
-	20	-	-	15	15	Autres religions (24)	170
310	625	560	850	870	445	Aucune appartenance religieuse (25)	171
2,065	**4,345**	**2,755**	**3,770**	**3,380**	**2,070**	**Population totale de 15 ans et plus**	172
						selon le statut des générations	
915	2,060	725	995	1,100	495	1re génération (26)	173
390	870	715	1,185	970	595	2e génération (27)	174
770	1,410	1,310	1,585	1,310	975	3e génération et plus (28)	175
2,500	**5,470**	**3,405**	**4,755**	**4,285**	**2,670**	**Population totale de 1 an et plus (29)**	176
						selon le lieu de résidence 1 an auparavant (mobilité)	
2,315	4,680	3,245	4,565	4,045	2,395	Personnes n'ayant pas déménagé	177
180	785	165	190	240	270	Personnes ayant déménagé	178
155	325	100	90	120	160	Non-migrants	179
35	460	70	105	115	105	Migrants	180
20	235	55	85	110	45	Migrants internes	181
20	180	50	90	100	45	Migrants infraprovinciaux	182
-	50	10	-	10	10	Migrants interprovinciaux	183
15	225	15	15	10	60	Migrants externes	184

Table 1. Selected Characteristics for Census Tracts, 2001 Census – 100% Data and 20% Sample Data

No.	Characteristics	Toronto 0485.02 A	Toronto 0500.01	Toronto 0500.02	Toronto 0501.01	Toronto 0501.02	Toronto 0502.01
	POPULATION CHARACTERISTICS						
185	**Total population 5 years and over (30)**	**5,480**	**3,530**	**4,825**	**5,410**	**6,905**	**5,775**
	by place of residence 5 years ago (mobility)						
186	Non-movers	2,655	1,550	2,605	3,255	3,990	3,230
187	Movers	2,825	1,980	2,220	2,155	2,920	2,550
188	Non-migrants	1,360	1,035	1,225	1,110	1,550	1,465
189	Migrants	1,470	945	995	1,045	1,370	1,085
190	Internal migrants	1,400	650	860	770	1,125	660
191	Intraprovincial migrants	1,310	475	660	625	920	520
192	Interprovincial migrants	85	175	200	145	205	140
193	External migrants	70	295	135	270	240	425
194	**Total population 15 to 24 years**	**770**	**485**	**570**	**685**	**1,000**	**915**
	by school attendance						
195	Not attending school	380	285	260	305	235	340
196	Attending school full time	360	165	265	335	735	525
197	Attending school part time	30	30	50	45	30	45
198	**Total population 15 years and over**	**4,520**	**3,065**	**4,280**	**4,695**	**5,795**	**4,785**
	by highest level of schooling						
199	Less than grade 9 (31)	250	245	385	125	145	285
200	Grades 9-13 without high school graduation certificate	1,380	735	1,105	865	1,010	995
201	Grades 9-13 with high school graduation certificate	730	500	590	1,000	770	635
202	Some postsecondary without degree, certificate or diploma (32)	475	365	595	550	635	610
203	Trades certificate or diploma (33)	525	340	580	360	465	485
204	College certificate or diploma (34)	730	350	525	740	840	980
205	University certificate below bachelor's degree	65	75	105	75	210	125
206	University with bachelor's degree or higher	365	445	395	980	1,725	660
	by combinations of unpaid work						
207	Males 15 years and over	2,200	1,560	2,110	2,210	2,825	2,355
208	Reported unpaid work (35)	2,050	1,320	1,765	1,955	2,535	2,080
209	Housework and child care and care or assistance to seniors	140	70	90	130	205	220
210	Housework and child care only	695	340	345	535	825	735
211	Housework and care or assistance to seniors only	185	65	175	135	175	85
212	Child care and care or assistance to seniors only	-	-	10	10	-	-
213	Housework only	990	810	1,095	1,140	1,290	1,010
214	Child care only	35	30	35	10	20	25
215	Care or assistance to seniors only	-	-	25	-	10	-
216	Females 15 years and over	2,320	1,505	2,170	2,480	2,970	2,430
217	Reported unpaid work (35)	2,205	1,405	1,965	2,325	2,770	2,270
218	Housework and child care and care or assistance to seniors	265	115	200	250	315	275
219	Housework and child care only	800	470	510	670	1,040	900
220	Housework and care or assistance to seniors only	145	100	230	200	200	140
221	Child care and care or assistance to seniors only	-	-	-	10	-	-
222	Housework only	990	705	985	1,190	1,180	940
223	Child care only	-	15	35	-	25	15
224	Care or assistance to seniors only	-	-	-	-	15	10
	by labour force activity						
225	Males 15 years and over	2,200	1,560	2,110	2,210	2,825	2,355
226	In the labour force	1,720	1,285	1,635	1,720	2,120	1,970
227	Employed	1,660	1,225	1,550	1,610	2,015	1,890
228	Unemployed	60	65	90	110	105	85
229	Not in the labour force	480	275	475	490	705	380
230	Participation rate	78.2	82.4	77.5	77.8	75.0	83.7
231	Employment rate	75.5	78.5	73.5	72.9	71.3	80.3
232	Unemployment rate	3.5	5.1	5.5	6.4	5.0	4.3
233	Females 15 years and over	2,315	1,505	2,170	2,480	2,970	2,425
234	In the labour force	1,565	1,040	1,525	1,615	2,020	1,745
235	Employed	1,465	990	1,440	1,515	1,910	1,640
236	Unemployed	95	50	85	100	115	105
237	Not in the labour force	755	465	640	865	945	685
238	Participation rate	67.6	69.1	70.3	65.1	68.0	72.0
239	Employment rate	63.3	65.8	66.4	61.1	64.3	67.6
240	Unemployment rate	6.1	4.8	5.6	6.2	5.7	6.0

Tableau 1. Certaines caractéristiques des secteurs de recensement, recensement de 2001 – Données intégrales et données-échantillon (20 %)

Toronto 0502.02	Toronto 0503	Toronto 0504	Toronto 0505.01	Toronto 0505.02	Toronto 0506	Caractéristiques	N°
						CARACTÉRISTIQUES DE LA POPULATION	
2,375	**5,195**	**3,235**	**4,560**	**4,080**	**2,485**	**Population totale de 5 ans et plus (30)**	185
						selon le lieu de résidence 5 ans auparavant (mobilité)	
1,550	3,010	2,310	3,385	2,725	1,475	Personnes n'ayant pas déménagé	186
825	2,185	920	1,175	1,350	1,010	Personnes ayant déménagé	187
520	945	600	650	750	590	Non-migrants	188
310	1,235	320	525	600	420	Migrants	189
180	775	270	480	470	335	Migrants internes	190
160	645	245	400	465	285	Migrants infraprovinciaux	191
15	125	20	80	-	50	Migrants interprovinciaux	192
130	460	55	45	130	90	Migrants externes	193
320	**750**	**375**	**730**	**630**	**395**	**Population totale de 15 à 24 ans**	194
						selon la fréquentation scolaire	
85	290	130	115	160	70	Ne fréquentant pas l'école	195
190	415	230	595	450	305	Fréquentant l'école à plein temps	196
40	40	15	20	20	15	Fréquentant l'école à temps partiel	197
2,065	**4,345**	**2,755**	**3,765**	**3,380**	**2,070**	**Population totale de 15 ans et plus**	198
						selon le plus haut niveau de scolarité atteint	
105	280	100	85	80	75	Niveau inférieur à la 9e année (31)	199
425	1,005	575	605	385	235	De la 9e à la 13e année sans certificat d'études secondaires	200
310	625	440	325	320	235	De la 9e à la 13e année avec certificat d'études secondaires	201
240	520	205	480	470	230	Études postsecondaires partielles sans grade, certificat ou diplôme (32)	202
245	345	200	170	260	105	Certificat ou diplôme d'une école de métiers (33)	203
355	785	540	530	605	255	Certificat ou diplôme collégial (34)	204
40	115	55	155	90	110	Certificat universitaire inférieur au baccalauréat	205
350	670	635	1,420	1,165	825	Études universitaires avec baccalauréat ou diplôme supérieur	206
						selon les combinaisons de travail non rémunéré	
1,000	2,130	1,335	1,830	1,680	1,005	Hommes de 15 ans et plus	207
890	1,830	1,165	1,660	1,510	930	Travail non rémunéré déclaré (35)	208
60	140	35	155	165	65	Travaux ménagers et soins aux enfants et soins ou aide aux personnes âgées	209
285	580	385	510	500	350	Travaux ménagers et soins aux enfants seulement	210
85	70	90	105	120	75	Travaux ménagers et soins ou aide aux personnes âgées seulement	211
-	-	-	10	-	-	Soins aux enfants et soins ou aide aux personnes âgées seulement	212
450	1,020	650	875	720	415	Travaux ménagers seulement	213
20	15	10	-	-	15	Soins aux enfants seulement	214
-	15	-	-	-	-	Soins ou aide aux personnes âgées seulement	215
1,070	2,215	1,420	1,940	1,700	1,055	Femmes de 15 ans et plus	216
910	2,090	1,325	1,840	1,595	1,025	Travail non rémunéré déclaré (35)	217
50	235	100	200	235	185	Travaux ménagers et soins aux enfants et soins ou aide aux personnes âgées	218
340	780	505	590	500	305	Travaux ménagers et soins aux enfants seulement	219
90	115	100	155	150	75	Travaux ménagers et soins ou aide aux personnes âgées seulement	220
-	-	-	-	10	-	Soins aux enfants et soins ou aide aux personnes âgées seulement	221
405	935	615	870	700	465	Travaux ménagers seulement	222
15	30	-	15	10	10	Soins aux enfants seulement	223
-	10	10	10	-	-	Soins ou aide aux personnes âgées seulement	224
						selon l'activité	
1,000	2,130	1,335	1,830	1,680	1,010	Hommes de 15 ans et plus	225
755	1,620	1,015	1,405	1,270	765	Population active	226
700	1,535	980	1,355	1,245	745	Personnes occupées	227
60	85	35	45	20	25	Chômeurs	228
245	510	320	425	415	240	Inactifs	229
75.5	76.1	76.0	76.8	75.6	75.7	Taux d'activité	230
70.0	72.1	73.4	74.0	74.1	73.8	Taux d'emploi	231
7.9	5.2	3.4	3.2	1.6	3.3	Taux de chômage	232
1,070	2,215	1,420	1,940	1,700	1,060	Femmes de 15 ans et plus	233
680	1,465	905	1,210	1,070	610	Population active	234
610	1,385	865	1,135	1,010	585	Personnes occupées	235
65	85	35	75	55	30	Chômeuses	236
390	745	520	730	635	450	Inactives	237
63.6	66.1	63.7	62.4	62.9	57.5	Taux d'activité	238
57.0	62.5	60.9	58.5	59.4	55.2	Taux d'emploi	239
9.6	5.8	3.9	6.2	5.1	4.9	Taux de chômage	240

Table 1. Selected Characteristics for Census Tracts, 2001 Census – 100% Data and 20% Sample Data

No.	Characteristics	Toronto 0485.02 A	Toronto 0500.01	Toronto 0500.02	Toronto 0501.01	Toronto 0501.02	Toronto 0502.01
	POPULATION CHARACTERISTICS						
	by labour force activity – concluded						
241	Both sexes - Participation rate	72.8	75.9	73.9	71.0	71.6	77.8
242	15-24 years	83.8	74.0	76.3	67.9	58.8	68.3
243	25 years and over	70.3	76.2	73.7	71.7	74.3	80.1
244	Both sexes - Employment rate	69.2	72.1	69.9	66.6	67.9	73.7
245	15-24 years	77.3	70.1	68.4	56.9	51.0	60.7
246	25 years and over	67.6	72.5	70.0	68.4	71.3	76.8
247	Both sexes - Unemployment rate	4.7	4.7	5.4	6.1	5.3	5.1
248	15-24 years	7.8	4.2	8.1	16.1	12.8	11.2
249	25 years and over	3.8	4.8	4.9	4.5	3.9	3.9
250	**Total labour force 15 years and over**	**3,280**	**2,325**	**3,165**	**3,335**	**4,145**	**3,715**
	by industry based on the 1997 NAICS						
251	Industry - Not applicable (36)	20	30	30	40	15	30
252	All industries (37)	3,260	2,295	3,135	3,300	4,135	3,685
253	11 Agriculture, forestry, fishing and hunting	55	-	-	10	-	10
254	21 Mining and oil and gas extraction	-	-	-	10	10	10
255	22 Utilities	25	-	10	30	25	30
256	23 Construction	155	205	235	100	165	230
257	31-33 Manufacturing	1,075	500	630	515	480	650
258	41 Wholesale trade	190	155	255	240	325	250
259	44-45 Retail trade	260	215	310	300	395	355
260	48-49 Transportation and warehousing	195	235	300	220	215	285
261	51 Information and cultural industries	60	75	95	175	205	105
262	52 Finance and insurance	30	90	115	230	350	245
263	53 Real estate and rental and leasing	25	35	75	80	95	85
264	54 Professional, scientific and technical services	95	55	195	330	485	320
265	55 Management of companies and enterprises	10	-	-	15	-	10
266	56 Administrative and support, waste management and remediation services	145	170	215	170	180	175
267	61 Educational services	140	110	115	130	240	85
268	62 Health care and social assistance	290	110	140	195	370	300
269	71 Arts, entertainment and recreation	45	20	45	75	85	45
270	72 Accommodation and food services	275	145	190	195	175	215
271	81 Other services (except public administration)	135	105	145	140	205	130
272	91 Public administration	60	70	70	145	135	160
	by class of worker						
273	Class of worker - Not applicable (36)	20	30	30	35	15	30
274	All classes of worker (37)	3,265	2,295	3,135	3,300	4,130	3,685
275	Paid workers	3,065	2,140	2,865	3,070	3,720	3,475
276	Employees	3,025	2,095	2,790	2,990	3,420	3,400
277	Self-employed (incorporated)	35	50	75	80	300	80
278	Self-employed (unincorporated)	195	150	270	210	395	200
279	Unpaid family workers	-	-	-	15	15	10
	by occupation based on the 2001 NOC-S						
280	Male labour force 15 years and over	1,720	1,285	1,640	1,725	2,125	1,970
281	Occupation - Not applicable (36)	-	20	-	20	-	10
282	All occupations (37)	1,720	1,265	1,625	1,700	2,125	1,960
283	A Management occupations	165	140	195	315	535	135
284	B Business, finance and administration occupations	175	230	180	215	300	235
285	C Natural and applied sciences and related occupations	115	80	100	235	245	290
286	D Health occupations	-	15	-	20	60	35
287	E Occupations in social science, education, government service and religion	40	30	40	50	95	45
288	F Occupations in art, culture, recreation and sport	35	15	65	35	105	65
289	G Sales and service occupations	220	205	325	275	350	350
290	H Trades, transport and equipment operators and related occupations	490	410	525	410	330	545
291	I Occupations unique to primary industry	75	15	30	25	20	25
292	J Occupations unique to processing, manufacturing and utilities	400	140	180	110	65	240
293	Female labour force 15 years and over	1,565	1,035	1,525	1,615	2,025	1,745
294	Occupation - Not applicable (36)	15	10	20	15	15	15
295	All occupations (37)	1,550	1,030	1,505	1,600	2,010	1,725
296	A Management occupations	70	35	120	180	320	90
297	B Business, finance and administration occupations	330	360	510	570	590	650
298	C Natural and applied sciences and related occupations	25	10	25	45	100	50
299	D Health occupations	75	45	80	110	90	90

Tableau 1. Certaines caractéristiques des secteurs de recensement, recensement de 2001 – Données intégrales et données-échantillon (20 %)

Toronto 0502.02	Toronto 0503	Toronto 0504	Toronto 0505.01	Toronto 0505.02	Toronto 0506	Caractéristiques	N°
						CARACTÉRISTIQUES DE LA POPULATION	
						selon l'activité – fin	
69.5	71.0	69.5	69.4	69.1	66.8	Les deux sexes - Taux d'activité	241
62.5	64.0	69.3	65.1	61.9	55.7	15-24 ans	242
70.3	72.5	69.7	70.5	70.7	69.3	25 ans et plus	243
63.4	67.2	67.0	66.2	66.9	63.8	Les deux sexes - Taux d'emploi	244
50.0	56.7	60.8	54.8	56.3	50.6	15-24 ans	245
65.7	69.4	68.3	68.9	69.1	66.9	25 ans et plus	246
8.7	5.5	3.9	4.6	3.2	4.0	Les deux sexes - Taux de chômage	247
22.0	12.5	13.7	15.8	10.3	6.8	15-24 ans	248
6.5	4.4	2.1	2.1	1.8	3.4	25 ans et plus	249
1,435	**3,085**	**1,915**	**2,615**	**2,335**	**1,375**	**Population active totale de 15 ans et plus selon l'industrie basée sur le SCIAN de 1997**	250
10	30	10	10	15	-	Industrie - Sans objet (36)	251
1,420	3,055	1,905	2,610	2,325	1,375	Toutes les industries (37)	252
-	10	15	10	10	-	11 Agriculture, foresterie, pêche et chasse	253
-	10	-	-	-	-	21 Extraction minière et extraction de pétrole et de gaz	254
10	15	10	25	-	10	22 Services publics	255
80	115	100	85	95	80	23 Construction	256
235	585	205	260	210	80	31-33 Fabrication	257
85	260	105	230	105	65	41 Commerce de gros	258
160	380	205	210	290	130	44-45 Commerce de détail	259
115	220	105	80	75	40	48-49 Transport et entreposage	260
30	55	80	95	110	60	51 Industrie de l'information et industrie culturelle	261
80	160	170	205	180	150	52 Finance et assurances	262
50	85	60	100	135	55	53 Services immobiliers et services de location et de location à bail	263
100	195	155	350	390	230	54 Services professionnels, scientifiques et techniques	264
10	-	-	20	10	10	55 Gestion de sociétés et d'entreprises	265
40	195	80	70	85	40	56 Services administratifs, services de soutien, services de gestion des déchets et services d'assainissement	266
60	130	135	280	175	95	61 Services d'enseignement	267
115	215	120	290	205	155	62 Soins de santé et assistance sociale	268
10	25	75	65	30	25	71 Arts, spectacles et loisirs	269
65	175	45	90	70	55	72 Hébergement et services de restauration	270
70	160	85	55	50	50	81 Autres services, sauf les administrations publiques	271
115	85	135	90	80	60	91 Administrations publiques	272
						selon la catégorie de travailleurs	
15	30	10	-	10	-	Catégorie de travailleurs - Sans objet (36)	273
1,420	3,055	1,905	2,610	2,320	1,380	Toutes les catégories de travailleurs (37)	274
1,360	2,875	1,750	2,370	1,955	1,175	Travailleurs rémunérés	275
1,320	2,855	1,645	2,160	1,760	1,030	Employés	276
40	25	100	210	190	140	Travailleurs autonomes (entreprise constituée en société)	277
55	175	155	230	370	190	Travailleurs autonomes (entreprise non constituée en société)	278
-	10	-	-	-	15	Travailleurs familiaux non rémunérés	279
						selon la profession basée sur la CNP-S de 2001	
755	1,615	1,015	1,405	1,270	765	Hommes actifs de 15 ans et plus	280
10	10	10	10	-	-	Profession - Sans objet (36)	281
745	1,615	1,010	1,395	1,260	765	Toutes les professions (37)	282
75	175	290	310	385	240	A Gestion	283
85	195	140	265	200	145	B Affaires, finance et administration	284
100	240	90	125	105	85	C Sciences naturelles et appliquées et professions apparentées	285
10	10	-	50	80	35	D Secteur de la santé	286
20	35	35	115	85	60	E Sciences sociales, enseignement, administration publique et religion	287
25	25	25	45	30	15	F Arts, culture, sports et loisirs	288
130	305	140	310	225	100	G Ventes et services	289
230	400	240	120	105	75	H Métiers, transport et machinerie	290
10	45	25	25	15	10	I Professions propres au secteur primaire	291
70	195	15	35	25	10	J Transformation, fabrication et services d'utilité publique	292
675	1,465	900	1,210	1,070	610	Femmes actives de 15 ans et plus	293
-	30	10	-	10	-	Profession - Sans objet (36)	294
675	1,440	900	1,210	1,065	610	Toutes les professions (37)	295
75	90	110	215	190	70	A Gestion	296
235	500	245	310	320	160	B Affaires, finance et administration	297
15	50	50	70	25	35	C Sciences naturelles et appliquées et professions apparentées	298
40	70	55	115	95	45	D Secteur de la santé	299

Table 1. Selected Characteristics for Census Tracts, 2001 Census – 100% Data and 20% Sample Data

No.	Characteristics	Toronto 0485.02 A	Toronto 0500.01	Toronto 0500.02	Toronto 0501.01	Toronto 0501.02	Toronto 0502.01
	POPULATION CHARACTERISTICS						
	by occupation based on the 2001 NOC-S – concluded						
300	E Occupations in social science, education, government service and religion	175	90	90	135	280	140
301	F Occupations in art, culture, recreation and sport ...	30	30	50	65	70	45
302	G Sales and service occupations	490	300	360	400	475	515
303	H Trades, transport and equipment operators and related occupations	85	30	90	25	25	15
304	I Occupations unique to primary industry	15	10	10	15	-	10
305	J Occupations unique to processing, manufacturing and utilities	260	130	170	50	65	130
306	**Total employed labour force 15 years and over ....**	**3,125**	**2,210**	**2,995**	**3,130**	**3,925**	**3,525**
	by place of work						
307	Males	1,660	1,225	1,550	1,615	2,020	1,890
308	Usual place of work	1,415	975	1,190	1,320	1,545	1,535
309	At home	70	60	75	115	205	75
310	Outside Canada	-	-	-	15	20	-
311	No fixed workplace address	175	185	290	160	240	280
312	Females	1,465	990	1,440	1,515	1,910	1,640
313	Usual place of work	1,355	825	1,285	1,325	1,560	1,435
314	At home	65	100	75	130	270	145
315	Outside Canada	-	-	-	10	-	10
316	No fixed workplace address	50	55	85	50	80	50
317	**Total employed labour force 15 years and over with usual place of work or no fixed workplace address ....**	**2,995**	**2,040**	**2,845**	**2,855**	**3,430**	**3,300**
	by mode of transportation						
318	Males	1,590	1,155	1,480	1,480	1,790	1,815
319	Car, truck, van, as driver	1,295	940	1,145	1,130	1,420	1,310
320	Car, truck, van, as passenger	140	55	95	55	65	110
321	Public transit	-	120	105	245	280	350
322	Walked	115	20	75	25	10	30
323	Other method	25	30	55	20	25	20
324	Females	1,410	880	1,370	1,375	1,640	1,485
325	Car, truck, van, as driver	1,055	440	750	885	1,115	895
326	Car, truck, van, as passenger	110	155	160	100	140	190
327	Public transit	15	230	310	330	325	330
328	Walked	185	40	90	55	40	75
329	Other method	35	20	55	10	20	-
330	**Total population 15 years and over who worked since January 1, 2000 ....**	**3,550**	**2,405**	**3,265**	**3,535**	**4,420**	**3,930**
	by language used at work						
331	Single responses	3,480	2,110	3,040	3,365	4,110	3,560
332	English	3,475	2,070	2,990	3,340	4,045	3,510
333	French	-	-	-	-	-	-
334	Non-official languages (5)	-	40	45	25	60	50
335	Chinese, n.o.s.	-	10	-	-	-	10
336	Cantonese	-	-	-	-	-	-
337	Other languages (6)	-	30	45	25	65	40
338	Multiple responses	70	300	225	175	315	370
339	English and French	45	35	75	105	80	50
340	English and non-official language	30	250	150	65	210	310
341	French and non-official language	-	-	-	-	-	-
342	English, French and non-official language	-	15	10	-	20	10
	DWELLING AND HOUSEHOLD CHARACTERISTICS						
343	**Total number of occupied private dwellings ....**	**2,200**	**1,570**	**2,135**	**2,255**	**2,405**	**1,970**
	by tenure						
344	Owned	1,610	440	1,240	1,760	2,165	1,425
345	Rented	590	1,135	895	495	240	545
346	Band housing	-	-	-	-	-	-
	by structural type of dwelling						
347	Single-detached house	1,285	380	745	585	1,390	410
348	Semi-detached house	165	-	10	325	160	615
349	Row house	220	-	40	295	725	420
350	Apartment, detached duplex	115	10	10	-	-	-
351	Apartment, building that has five or more storeys	-	1,150	1,090	820	-	155
352	Apartment, building that has fewer than five storeys (38)	410	25	185	225	100	360
353	Other single-attached house	-	-	-	-	30	-
354	Movable dwelling (39)	-	-	45	-	-	-

Tableau 1. Certaines caractéristiques des secteurs de recensement, recensement de 2001 – Données intégrales et données-échantillon (20 %)

Toronto 0502.02	Toronto 0503	Toronto 0504	Toronto 0505.01	Toronto 0505.02	Toronto 0506	Caractéristiques	N°
						CARACTÉRISTIQUES DE LA POPULATION	
						selon la profession basée sur la CNP-S de 2001 - fin	
90	125	130	185	115	110	E Sciences sociales, enseignement, administration publique et religion	300
-	25	45	80	75	20	F Arts, culture, sports et loisirs	301
160	450	220	235	215	160	G Ventes et services	302
10	50	20	-	-	-	H Métiers, transport et machinerie	303
-	-	10	-	-	-	I Professions propres au secteur primaire	304
45	70	15	10	25	10	J Transformation, fabrication et services d'utilité publique	305
1,310	**2,915**	**1,845**	**2,500**	**2,255**	**1,325**	**Population active occupée totale de 15 ans et plus ..... selon le lieu de travail**	306
695	1,535	980	1,355	1,245	740	Hommes	307
540	1,295	740	1,135	980	615	Lieu habituel de travail	308
55	80	90	110	125	90	À domicile	309
-	-	10	10	10	-	En dehors du Canada	310
105	155	140	110	135	40	Sans adresse de travail fixe	311
615	1,385	860	1,140	1,010	585	Femmes	312
580	1,245	705	960	775	470	Lieu habituel de travail	313
20	55	125	150	195	100	À domicile	314
-	-	-	10	-	-	En dehors du Canada	315
10	80	30	20	40	10	Sans adresse de travail fixe	316
1,240	**2,775**	**1,620**	**2,220**	**1,930**	**1,135**	**Population active occupée totale de 15 ans et plus ayant un lieu habituel de travail ou sans adresse de travail fixe.......................... selon le mode de transport**	317
645	1,450	880	1,240	1,115	655	Hommes	318
565	1,185	660	1,000	920	500	Automobile, camion ou fourgonnette, en tant que conducteur	319
10	70	50	65	45	40	Automobile, camion ou fourgonnette, en tant que passager	320
60	125	130	145	105	100	Transport en commun	321
15	70	30	25	35	10	À pied	322
10	-	10	10	-	10	Autre moyen	323
595	1,330	740	975	810	485	Femmes	324
375	830	565	750	645	385	Automobile, camion ou fourgonnette, en tant que conductrice	325
25	160	40	75	70	35	Automobile, camion ou fourgonnette, en tant que passagère	326
160	255	110	135	80	35	Transport en commun	327
20	60	15	15	15	15	À pied	328
10	25	-	10	10	15	Autre moyen	329
1,495	**3,300**	**2,070**	**2,895**	**2,570**	**1,575**	**Population totale de 15 ans et plus ayant travaillé depuis le 1er janvier 2000 .... selon la langue utilisée au travail**	330
1,420	3,105	1,950	2,690	2,340	1,460	Réponses uniques	331
1,415	3,105	1,940	2,685	2,315	1,455	Anglais	332
-	-	-	-	10	-	Français	333
-	-	10	10	15	-	Langues non officielles (5)	334
-	-	-	10	-	-	Chinois, n.d.a.	335
-	-	-	-	-	-	Cantonais	336
-	-	10	-	15	-	Autres langues (6)	337
70	190	120	200	230	120	Réponses multiples	338
30	35	90	55	50	55	Anglais et français	339
45	160	30	140	180	50	Anglais et langue non officielle	340
-	-	-	-	-	-	Français et langue non officielle	341
-	-	-	10	-	15	Anglais, français et langue non officielle	342
						CARACTÉRISTIQUES DES LOGEMENTS ET DES MÉNAGES	
940	**1,870**	**1,205**	**1,450**	**1,385**	**845**	**Nombre total de logements privés occupés .... selon le mode d'occupation**	343
685	1,110	960	1,425	1,340	810	Possédé	344
255	760	245	25	50	35	Loué	345
-	-	-	-	-	-	Logement de bande	346
						selon le type de construction résidentielle	
420	520	970	1,445	1,355	845	Maison individuelle non attenante	347
195	670	-	-	-	-	Maison jumelée	348
200	40	200	-	-	-	Maison en rangée	349
-	15	20	-	-	-	Appartement, duplex non attenant	350
120	540	-	-	-	-	Appartement, immeuble de cinq étages ou plus	351
10	75	10	-	10	-	Appartement, immeuble de moins de cinq étages (38) ...	352
-	-	-	-	-	-	Autre maison individuelle attenante	353
-	-	-	-	-	-	Logement mobile (39)	354

Table 1. Selected Characteristics for Census Tracts, 2001 Census – 100% Data and 20% Sample Data

No.	Characteristics	Toronto 0485.02 A	Toronto 0500.01	Toronto 0500.02	Toronto 0501.01	Toronto 0501.02	Toronto 0502.01
	DWELLING AND HOUSEHOLD CHARACTERISTICS						
	by condition of dwelling						
355	Regular maintenance only	1,545	845	1,455	1,585	1,690	1,185
356	Minor repairs	465	505	365	530	590	615
357	Major repairs	190	220	315	135	130	170
	by period of construction						
358	Before 1946	355	105	215	30	75	40
359	1946-1960	230	385	440	95	320	190
360	1961-1970	255	470	370	405	355	540
361	1971-1980	585	455	490	1,145	675	960
362	1981-1990	410	125	315	450	510	200
363	1991-2001 (20)	365	35	305	125	470	40
364	Average number of rooms per dwelling	6.6	4.6	5.3	6.5	7.9	6.3
365	Average number of bedrooms per dwelling	2.9	1.8	2.3	2.7	3.3	3.0
366	Average value of dwelling $	167,926	206,241	185,288	228,055	358,387	186,763
367	**Total number of private households**	**2,200**	**1,575**	**2,135**	**2,255**	**2,410**	**1,965**
	by household size						
368	1 person	535	470	615	575	300	280
369	2 persons	615	485	730	755	715	485
370	3 persons	385	295	380	360	460	385
371	4-5 persons	610	285	355	505	825	705
372	6 or more persons	55	35	50	65	105	115
	by household type						
373	One-family households	1,595	1,000	1,370	1,515	1,955	1,525
374	Multiple-family households	40	15	50	70	100	125
375	Non-family households	565	550	710	675	355	320
376	Number of persons in private households	5,895	3,770	5,050	5,695	7,360	6,170
377	Average number of persons in private households	2.7	2.4	2.4	2.5	3.1	3.1
378	Average number of persons per room	0.4	0.5	0.4	0.4	0.4	0.5
379	Tenant households in non-farm, non-reserve private dwellings (40)	590	1,105	890	485	240	540
380	Average gross rent $ (40)	764	820	792	956	930	953
381	Tenant households spending 30% or more of household income on gross rent (40) (41)	245	420	365	155	105	205
382	Tenant households spending from 30% to 99% of household income on gross rent (40) (41)	210	370	295	125	100	185
383	Owner households in non-farm, non-reserve private dwellings (42)	1,610	440	1,240	1,755	2,170	1,420
384	Average owner's major payments $ (42)	989	959	1,001	1,083	1,396	1,149
385	Owner households spending 30% or more of household income on owner's major payments (41) (42)	315	130	315	390	460	390
386	Owner households spending from 30% to 99% of household income on owner's major payments (41) (42)	275	130	290	365	415	385
	CENSUS FAMILY CHARACTERISTICS						
387	**Total number of census families in private households**	**1,670**	**1,035**	**1,475**	**1,650**	**2,175**	**1,770**
	by census family structure and size						
388	Total couple families	1,385	825	1,120	1,355	1,865	1,410
389	Total families of married couples	1,170	665	915	1,175	1,745	1,240
390	Without children at home	425	230	445	480	620	305
391	With children at home	740	440	470	695	1,130	930
392	1 child	265	200	180	310	360	300
393	2 children	310	165	220	280	550	430
394	3 or more children	165	70	70	105	215	200
395	Total families of common-law couples	215	160	210	175	120	170
396	Without children at home	95	120	90	120	65	105
397	With children at home	125	45	120	50	55	70
398	1 child	55	20	75	30	15	30
399	2 children	50	15	30	15	40	35
400	3 or more children	20	10	15	-	-	-
401	Total lone-parent families	285	210	355	300	310	360
402	Female parent	200	180	285	265	250	275
403	1 child	110	90	205	175	140	170
404	2 children	60	80	65	40	60	105
405	3 or more children	30	15	15	55	50	-

Tableau 1. Certaines caractéristiques des secteurs de recensement, recensement de 2001 – Données intégrales et données-échantillon (20 %)

Toronto 0502.02	Toronto 0503	Toronto 0504	Toronto 0505.01	Toronto 0505.02	Toronto 0506	Caractéristiques	Nº
						CARACTÉRISTIQUES DES LOGEMENTS ET DES MÉNAGES	
						selon l'état du logement	
635	1,085	790	1,020	955	605	Entretien régulier seulement	355
240	600	325	385	375	165	Réparations mineures	356
60	180	90	40	60	80	Réparations majeures	357
						selon la période de construction	
-	10	30	30	150	150	Avant 1946	358
335	195	390	360	390	355	1946-1960	359
285	855	615	375	405	105	1961-1970	360
185	720	125	405	285	55	1971-1980	361
130	70	15	220	95	95	1981-1990	362
-	10	25	60	60	85	1991-2001 (20)	363
6.3	6.3	7.6	9.2	8.9	9.0	Nombre moyen de pièces par logement	364
2.8	2.8	3.3	3.8	3.6	3.5	Nombre moyen de chambres à coucher par logement	365
194,711	205,984	272,886	442,224	491,466	553,529	Valeur moyenne du logement $	366
935	**1,870**	**1,205**	**1,445**	**1,385**	**845**	**Nombre total de logements privés**	367
						selon la taille du ménage	
210	320	150	110	160	105	1 personne	368
295	525	400	400	415	205	2 personnes	369
160	370	260	250	230	180	3 personnes	370
240	550	370	615	515	320	4-5 personnes	371
35	100	20	80	65	40	6 personnes ou plus	372
						selon le genre de ménage	
700	1,400	1,005	1,280	1,205	735	Ménages unifamiliaux	373
15	75	10	45	10	10	Ménages multifamiliaux	374
225	390	180	125	170	100	Ménages non familiaux	375
2,535	5,520	3,435	4,775	4,335	2,685	Nombre de personnes dans les ménages privés	376
2.7	3.0	2.9	3.3	3.1	3.2	Nombre moyen de personnes dans les ménages privés	377
0.4	0.5	0.4	0.4	0.4	0.4	Nombre moyen de personnes par pièce	378
250	745	245	20	50	35	Ménages locataires dans les logements privés non agricoles hors réserve (40)	379
748	942	1,005	1,381	1,533	1,074	Loyer brut moyen $ (40)	380
100	305	30	-	20	-	Ménages locataires consacrant 30 % ou plus du revenu du ménage au loyer brut (40) (41)	381
80	270	35	-	10	-	Ménages locataires consacrant de 30 % à 99 % du revenu du ménage au loyer brut (40) (41)	382
685	1,110	955	1,430	1,335	810	Ménages propriétaires dans les logements privés non agricoles hors réserve (42)	383
1,061	1,031	1,059	1,362	1,580	1,454	Principales dépenses de propriété moyennes $ (42)	384
130	205	105	150	215	90	Ménages propriétaires consacrant 30 % ou plus du revenu du ménage aux principales dépenses de propriété (41) (42)	385
110	180	90	140	190	80	Ménages propriétaires consacrant de 30 % à 99 % du revenu du ménage aux principales dépenses de propriété (41) (42)	386
						CARACTÉRISTIQUES DES FAMILLES DE RECENSEMENT	
730	**1,550**	**1,050**	**1,370**	**1,225**	**755**	**Total des familles de recensement dans les ménages privés**	387
						selon la structure et la taille de la famille de recensement	
625	1,300	900	1,300	1,155	700	Total des familles avec conjoints	388
550	1,160	820	1,230	1,115	670	Total des familles avec couples mariés	389
220	360	305	390	385	195	Sans enfants à la maison	390
330	800	510	845	735	475	Avec enfants à la maison	391
120	265	185	220	185	140	1 enfant	392
145	335	250	400	335	220	2 enfants	393
70	210	75	220	215	115	3 enfants ou plus	394
70	140	80	70	35	30	Total des familles en union libre	395
45	90	30	25	15	20	Sans enfants à la maison	396
30	45	45	40	20	15	Avec enfants à la maison	397
-	35	30	20	15	10	1 enfant	398
25	15	10	10	-	-	2 enfants	399
-	-	10	10	-	-	3 enfants ou plus	400
105	250	150	70	70	50	Total des familles monoparentales	401
65	205	125	60	50	35	Parent de sexe féminin	402
25	125	85	35	25	15	1 enfant	403
30	40	35	20	20	10	2 enfants	404
10	35	-	-	10	10	3 enfants ou plus	405

Table 1. Selected Characteristics for Census Tracts, 2001 Census – 100% Data and 20% Sample Data

No.	Characteristics	Toronto 0485.02 A	Toronto 0500.01	Toronto 0500.02	Toronto 0501.01	Toronto 0501.02	Toronto 0502.01
	CENSUS FAMILY CHARACTERISTICS						
	by census family structure and size – concluded						
406	Male parent	90	25	65	30	60	85
407	1 child	75	25	45	10	40	55
408	2 children	15	-	15	15	20	15
409	3 or more children	-	-	-	10	-	15
410	**Total number of children at home**	**2,085**	**1,160**	**1,485**	**1,805**	**2,745**	**2,440**
	by age groups						
411	Under 6 years	480	280	270	365	540	515
412	6-14 years	895	430	485	650	1,020	880
413	15-17 years	245	125	135	210	350	320
414	18-24 years	350	180	320	345	570	445
415	25 years and over	115	145	280	240	255	275
416	Average number of children at home per census family (43)	1.2	1.1	1.0	1.1	1.3	1.4
417	**Total number of persons in private households**	**5,895**	**3,770**	**5,050**	**5,695**	**7,360**	**6,170**
	by census family status and living arrangements						
418	Number of non-family persons	750	745	970	885	575	550
419	Living with relatives (44)	100	100	165	100	120	140
420	Living with non-relatives only	125	180	195	215	155	130
421	Living alone	535	465	615	575	300	280
422	Number of family persons	5,140	3,025	4,080	4,810	6,780	5,620
423	Average number of persons per census family	3.1	2.9	2.8	2.9	3.1	3.2
424	**Total number of persons 65 years and over**	**615**	**295**	**615**	**790**	**690**	**400**
425	Number of non-family persons 65 years and over	280	145	190	280	150	125
426	Living with relatives (44)	10	45	50	35	40	65
427	Living with non-relatives only	-	10	25	30	10	-
428	Living alone	275	100	115	220	100	60
429	Number of family persons 65 years and over	335	150	425	515	540	280
	ECONOMIC FAMILY CHARACTERISTICS						
430	**Total number of economic families in private households**	**1,645**	**1,040**	**1,455**	**1,600**	**2,070**	**1,660**
	by size of family						
431	2 persons	645	445	705	705	695	480
432	3 persons	360	285	350	355	475	380
433	4 persons	425	210	265	370	590	485
434	5 or more persons	220	110	135	175	310	315
435	Total number of persons in economic families	5,240	3,125	4,240	4,910	6,905	5,760
436	Average number of persons per economic family	3.2	3.0	2.9	3.1	3.3	3.5
437	Total number of unattached individuals	655	645	810	785	455	410
	2000 INCOME CHARACTERISTICS						
	Population 15 years and over by sex and total income groups in 2000						
438	Total - Both sexes	4,520	3,065	4,280	4,690	5,795	4,785
439	Without income	115	225	165	230	360	220
440	With income	4,405	2,835	4,110	4,465	5,435	4,565
441	Under $1,000 (45)	135	80	185	140	245	155
442	$ 1,000 - $ 2,999	230	105	125	145	255	225
443	$ 3,000 - $ 4,999	100	120	80	150	215	145
444	$ 5,000 - $ 6,999	165	70	135	110	125	195
445	$ 7,000 - $ 9,999	280	145	195	170	315	260
446	$10,000 - $11,999	180	120	175	170	95	160
447	$12,000 - $14,999	290	245	285	210	255	215
448	$15,000 - $19,999	360	300	325	275	355	325
449	$20,000 - $24,999	280	195	370	325	345	375
450	$25,000 - $29,999	380	230	400	375	335	420
451	$30,000 - $34,999	405	305	410	395	280	405
452	$35,000 - $39,999	320	255	275	335	240	380
453	$40,000 - $44,999	345	175	305	305	345	320
454	$45,000 - $49,999	125	185	195	190	200	250
455	$50,000 - $59,999	335	120	215	335	305	315
456	$60,000 and over	470	185	425	830	1,520	420
457	Average income $ (46)	30,307	27,654	37,325	38,533	52,347	29,940
458	Median income $ (46)	26,302	25,321	26,807	31,797	32,081	26,449
459	Standard error of average income $ (46)	758	858	5,455	1,141	2,312	701

Tableau 1. Certaines caractéristiques des secteurs de recensement, recensement de 2001 – Données intégrales et données-échantillon (20 %)

Toronto 0502.02	Toronto 0503	Toronto 0504	Toronto 0505.01	Toronto 0505.02	Toronto 0506	Caractéristiques	N°
						CARACTÉRISTIQUES DES FAMILLES DE RECENSEMENT	
						selon la structure et la taille de la famille de recensement – fin	
40	45	20	10	20	15	Parent de sexe masculin	406
25	40	15	-	-	-	1 enfant	407
10	-	-	10	10	10	2 enfants	408
-	-	-	-	-	-	3 enfants ou plus	409
860	**2,070**	**1,205**	**1,900**	**1,695**	**1,080**	**Nombre total d'enfants à la maison**	410
						selon les groupes d'âge	
165	365	235	270	325	260	Moins de 6 ans	411
300	795	445	735	630	360	6-14 ans	412
75	225	155	280	180	120	15-17 ans	413
210	420	195	410	440	260	18-24 ans	414
110	265	175	205	115	80	25 ans et plus	415
1.2	1.3	1.1	1.4	1.4	1.4	Nombre moyen d'enfants à la maison par famille de recensement (43)	416
2,535	**5,515**	**3,435**	**4,780**	**4,335**	**2,685**	**Nombre total de personnes dans les ménages privés**	417
						selon la situation des particuliers dans la famille de recensement et des particuliers dans le ménage	
320	595	275	210	265	150	Nombre de personnes hors famille de recensement	418
60	95	70	60	80	20	Vivant avec des personnes apparentées (44)	419
50	185	55	45	25	25	Vivant avec des personnes non apparentées uniquement	420
210	315	150	110	160	100	Vivant seules	421
2,210	4,925	3,155	4,565	4,075	2,535	Nombre de personnes membres d'une famille	422
3.1	3.2	3.0	3.3	3.3	3.4	Nombre moyen de personnes par famille de recensement	423
440	**520**	**485**	**550**	**590**	**295**	**Nombre total de personnes de 65 ans et plus**	424
140	140	95	115	155	85	Nombre de personnes hors famille de recensement de 65 ans et plus	425
15	30	35	45	45	10	Vivant avec des personnes apparentées (44)	426
-	10	10	10	10	10	Vivant avec des personnes non apparentées uniquement	427
120	100	50	60	105	70	Vivant seules	428
300	380	385	435	435	205	Nombre de personnes membres d'une famille de 65 ans et plus	429
						CARACTÉRISTIQUES DES FAMILLES ÉCONOMIQUES	
715	**1,490**	**1,030**	**1,325**	**1,220**	**750**	**Nombre total de familles économiques dans les ménages privés**	430
						selon la taille de la famille	
285	515	380	390	410	225	2 personnes	431
160	335	255	255	235	165	3 personnes	432
155	375	290	425	325	215	4 personnes	433
110	260	100	255	255	135	5 personnes ou plus	434
2,275	5,020	3,220	4,620	4,155	2,555	Nombre total de personnes dans les familles économiques	435
3.2	3.4	3.1	3.5	3.4	3.4	Nombre moyen de personnes par famille économique	436
260	500	210	155	180	130	Nombre total de personnes hors famille économique	437
						CARACTÉRISTIQUES DU REVENU DE 2000	
						Population de 15 ans et plus selon le sexe et les tranches de revenu total en 2000	
2,065	4,345	2,750	3,770	3,380	2,070	Total - Les deux sexes	438
70	215	120	190	150	140	Sans revenu	439
1,995	4,125	2,635	3,575	3,230	1,930	Avec un revenu	440
50	155	90	120	105	90	Moins de 1 000 $ (45)	441
75	160	80	190	115	100	1 000 $ - 2 999 $	442
90	160	65	120	105	55	3 000 $ - 4 999 $	443
100	135	85	115	135	80	5 000 $ - 6 999 $	444
80	190	80	180	135	100	7 000 $ - 9 999 $	445
80	175	75	95	60	45	10 000 $ - 11 999 $	446
120	295	125	150	155	60	12 000 $ - 14 999 $	447
180	310	195	150	185	45	15 000 $ - 19 999 $	448
205	385	155	150	175	75	20 000 $ - 24 999 $	449
105	300	195	130	150	60	25 000 $ - 29 999 $	450
140	420	160	175	200	85	30 000 $ - 34 999 $	451
210	310	185	200	75	75	35 000 $ - 39 999 $	452
120	250	200	180	165	105	40 000 $ - 44 999 $	453
75	210	130	95	110	75	45 000 $ - 49 999 $	454
160	225	345	330	240	145	50 000 $ - 59 999 $	455
220	460	465	1,205	1,120	740	60 000 $ et plus	456
30,172	30,050	40,065	73,032	71,600	91,861	Revenu moyen $ (46)	457
26,256	25,599	35,012	40,042	40,010	43,907	Revenu médian $ (46)	458
1,144	759	1,475	4,877	4,116	8,542	Erreur type de revenu moyen $ (46)	459

Table 1. Selected Characteristics for Census Tracts, 2001 Census – 100% Data and 20% Sample Data

No.	Characteristics	Toronto 0485.02 A	Toronto 0500.01	Toronto 0500.02	Toronto 0501.01	Toronto 0501.02	Toronto 0502.01
	2000 INCOME CHARACTERISTICS						
	Population 15 years and over by sex and total income groups in 2000 – concluded						
460	Total - Males	2,200	1,560	2,110	2,215	2,830	2,355
461	Without income	55	100	80	95	160	65
462	With income	2,145	1,460	2,025	2,115	2,660	2,290
463	Under $1,000 (45)	45	25	90	70	120	55
464	$ 1,000 - $ 2,999	75	20	65	50	95	95
465	$ 3,000 - $ 4,999	40	35	30	60	80	65
466	$ 5,000 - $ 6,999	70	20	50	30	30	50
467	$ 7,000 - $ 9,999	85	45	45	55	130	80
468	$10,000 - $11,999	80	45	60	70	35	60
469	$12,000 - $14,999	85	60	115	45	75	95
470	$15,000 - $19,999	140	160	165	75	160	115
471	$20,000 - $24,999	95	105	130	105	150	145
472	$25,000 - $29,999	180	140	160	185	140	205
473	$30,000 - $34,999	180	195	220	170	130	185
474	$35,000 - $39,999	155	160	175	185	85	220
475	$40,000 - $44,999	245	130	180	120	150	195
476	$45,000 - $49,999	65	120	130	140	100	140
477	$50,000 - $59,999	230	95	140	190	170	240
478	$60,000 and over	375	115	265	565	1,015	350
479	Average income $ (46)	37,575	32,459	46,964	48,112	69,021	36,435
480	Median income $ (46)	34,689	30,805	30,314	38,727	42,515	34,681
481	Standard error of average income $ (46)	1,274	1,190	10,932	2,069	4,014	1,115
482	Total - Females	2,320	1,505	2,165	2,480	2,970	2,430
483	Without income	60	130	85	135	200	155
484	With income	2,260	1,375	2,085	2,350	2,770	2,275
485	Under $1,000 (45)	95	55	95	70	125	105
486	$ 1,000 - $ 2,999	155	85	60	95	165	135
487	$ 3,000 - $ 4,999	60	85	45	95	135	80
488	$ 5,000 - $ 6,999	95	50	85	75	95	145
489	$ 7,000 - $ 9,999	195	100	150	120	190	185
490	$10,000 - $11,999	100	70	115	105	60	100
491	$12,000 - $14,999	205	190	175	165	180	120
492	$15,000 - $19,999	220	135	160	205	200	210
493	$20,000 - $24,999	180	95	240	220	195	230
494	$25,000 - $29,999	205	95	235	180	195	210
495	$30,000 - $34,999	225	110	190	220	145	215
496	$35,000 - $39,999	170	90	105	145	155	155
497	$40,000 - $44,999	105	45	125	185	195	125
498	$45,000 - $49,999	55	65	70	55	100	115
499	$50,000 - $59,999	110	30	80	140	140	75
500	$60,000 and over	95	70	160	265	505	70
501	Average income $ (46)	23,395	22,555	27,943	29,888	36,316	23,404
502	Median income $ (46)	20,026	17,317	23,306	25,304	25,584	21,257
503	Standard error of average income $ (46)	753	1,170	1,365	1,012	2,189	761
	by composition of total income						
504	Total - Composition of income in 2000 % (47)	100.0	100.0	100.0	100.0	100.0	100.0
505	Employment income %	81.9	83.3	85.5	81.6	85.7	86.8
506	Government transfer payments %	9.8	9.8	8.1	7.9	4.0	6.5
507	Other %	8.4	6.8	6.4	10.7	10.3	6.6
	Population 15 years and over with employment income in 2000 by sex and work activity						
508	Both sexes with employment income (48)	3,430	2,225	3,135	3,410	4,390	3,890
509	Average employment income $	31,846	29,386	41,851	41,073	55,537	30,532
510	Standard error of average employment income $	873	923	7,059	1,386	2,713	758
511	Worked full year, full time (49)	2,035	1,335	1,900	2,230	2,520	2,275
512	Average employment income $	39,595	36,629	53,199	48,780	70,101	39,799
513	Standard error of average employment income $	968	1,219	11,562	1,728	2,965	977
514	Worked part year or part time (50)	1,325	865	1,170	1,135	1,780	1,560
515	Average employment income $	21,219	18,681	24,678	27,150	35,215	17,893
516	Standard error of average employment income $	1,457	1,045	1,734	2,115	4,940	847
517	Males with employment income (48)	1,805	1,200	1,625	1,735	2,255	2,055
518	Average employment income $	38,762	33,532	52,072	49,962	71,881	35,980
519	Standard error of average employment income $	1,393	1,330	13,493	2,389	4,491	1,183
520	Worked full year, full time (49)	1,190	785	1,080	1,205	1,465	1,330
521	Average employment income $	44,179	40,599	64,823	56,946	84,103	44,613
522	Standard error of average employment income $	1,391	1,587	20,605	2,875	4,722	1,451
523	Worked part year or part time (50)	565	400	515	520	740	695
524	Average employment income $	29,790	20,245	27,129	34,513	47,814	20,902
525	Standard error of average employment income $	3,087	1,675	2,139	4,014	9,357	1,372

Tableau 1. Certaines caractéristiques des secteurs de recensement, recensement de 2001 – Données intégrales et données-échantillon (20 %)

Toronto 0502.02	Toronto 0503	Toronto 0504	Toronto 0505.01	Toronto 0505.02	Toronto 0506	Caractéristiques	N°
						CARACTÉRISTIQUES DU REVENU DE 2000	
						Population de 15 ans et plus selon le sexe et les tranches de revenu total en 2000 – fin	
1,000	2,130	1,335	1,830	1,680	1,005	Total - Hommes	460
30	80	20	75	35	40	Sans revenu	461
975	2,050	1,315	1,755	1,645	965	Avec un revenu	462
20	70	50	30	35	40	Moins de 1 000 $ (45)	463
35	60	40	40	50	25	1 000 $ - 2 999 $	464
25	25	30	60	45	25	3 000 $ - 4 999 $	465
50	60	20	45	70	30	5 000 $ - 6 999 $	466
25	70	10	75	70	30	7 000 $ - 9 999 $	467
30	55	40	45	20	15	10 000 $ - 11 999 $	468
55	70	35	55	70	20	12 000 $ - 14 999 $	469
35	140	65	50	65	20	15 000 $ - 19 999 $	470
110	215	50	55	45	40	20 000 $ - 24 999 $	471
55	150	100	40	65	10	25 000 $ - 29 999 $	472
70	195	60	40	55	20	30 000 $ - 34 999 $	473
85	155	105	75	40	40	35 000 $ - 39 999 $	474
70	140	115	65	50	35	40 000 $ - 44 999 $	475
25	150	95	45	50	25	45 000 $ - 49 999 $	476
105	125	185	165	145	65	50 000 $ - 59 999 $	477
170	365	315	855	775	520	60 000 $ et plus	478
35,643	36,443	48,901	101,664	102,954	139,557	Revenu moyen $ (46)	479
32,420	32,295	42,256	58,066	56,016	64,985	Revenu médian $ (46)	480
1,847	1,239	2,520	8,331	7,576	16,110	Erreur type de revenu moyen $ (46)	481
1,065	2,215	1,415	1,935	1,700	1,060	Total - Femmes	482
45	140	105	115	110	95	Sans revenu	483
1,025	2,080	1,320	1,820	1,590	965	Avec un revenu	484
30	80	35	90	70	50	Moins de 1 000 $ (45)	485
35	100	40	150	70	70	1 000 $ - 2 999 $	486
65	135	35	55	70	25	3 000 $ - 4 999 $	487
50	75	60	70	70	50	5 000 $ - 6 999 $	488
50	120	70	105	65	70	7 000 $ - 9 999 $	489
55	120	35	55	40	30	10 000 $ - 11 999 $	490
70	220	95	100	85	40	12 000 $ - 14 999 $	491
150	170	130	95	115	20	15 000 $ - 19 999 $	492
90	170	105	90	130	45	20 000 $ - 24 999 $	493
45	150	95	85	80	50	25 000 $ - 29 999 $	494
65	225	95	135	145	65	30 000 $ - 34 999 $	495
130	150	75	125	35	35	35 000 $ - 39 999 $	496
45	115	85	115	120	70	40 000 $ - 44 999 $	497
45	55	35	45	60	50	45 000 $ - 49 999 $	498
50	100	160	160	90	75	50 000 $ - 59 999 $	499
55	90	150	350	345	215	60 000 $ et plus	500
24,979	23,730	31,214	45,388	39,109	43,742	Revenu moyen $ (46)	501
20,081	20,253	25,956	30,368	29,955	30,430	Revenu médian $ (46)	502
1,247	799	1,344	4,848	2,081	3,496	Erreur type de revenu moyen $ (46)	503
						selon la composition du revenu total	
100.0	100.0	100.0	100.0	100.0	100.0	Total - Composition du revenu en 2000 % (47)	504
78.7	83.2	79.9	83.8	82.7	86.2	Revenu d'emploi %	505
11.5	9.1	7.5	2.9	3.3	2.3	Transferts gouvernementaux %	506
9.8	7.6	12.6	13.3	14.2	11.2	Autre %	507
						Population de 15 ans et plus ayant un revenu d'emploi en 2000 selon le sexe et le travail	
1,425	3,175	2,020	2,820	2,525	1,530	Les deux sexes ayant un revenu d'emploi (48)	508
33,289	32,534	41,766	77,666	75,645	100,327	Revenu moyen d'emploi $	509
1,442	855	1,796	5,812	4,767	10,556	Erreur type de revenu moyen d'emploi $	510
830	1,900	1,230	1,520	1,380	805	Ayant travaillé toute l'année à plein temps (49)	511
44,069	41,273	55,175	106,278	106,743	137,614	Revenu moyen d'emploi $	512
1,487	1,075	2,543	7,348	7,099	12,653	Erreur type de revenu moyen d'emploi $	513
565	1,175	750	1,260	1,105	705	Ayant travaillé une partie de l'année ou à temps partiel (50)	514
18,329	20,854	21,806	40,802	39,167	60,810	Revenu moyen d'emploi $	515
2,232	1,095	1,492	8,094	5,520	17,302	Erreur type de revenu moyen d'emploi $	516
740	1,660	1,055	1,470	1,360	815	Hommes ayant un revenu d'emploi (48)	517
37,559	38,956	49,328	102,676	107,550	150,727	Revenu moyen d'emploi $	518
2,268	1,316	3,013	9,036	8,337	18,724	Erreur type de revenu moyen d'emploi $	519
475	1,080	675	960	875	535	Ayant travaillé toute l'année à plein temps (49)	520
46,770	46,186	64,391	119,682	135,977	171,611	Revenu moyen d'emploi $	521
2,158	1,589	4,163	9,339	10,518	17,945	Erreur type de revenu moyen d'emploi $	522
245	545	365	490	480	270	Ayant travaillé une partie de l'année ou à temps partiel (50)	523
20,207	26,711	23,279	72,359	57,390	114,325	Revenu moyen d'emploi $	524
4,613	1,917	2,257	19,221	12,491	42,600	Erreur type de revenu moyen d'emploi $	525

Table 1. Selected Characteristics for Census Tracts, 2001 Census – 100% Data and 20% Sample Data

No.	Characteristics	Toronto 0485.02 A	Toronto 0500.01	Toronto 0500.02	Toronto 0501.01	Toronto 0501.02	Toronto 0502.01
	2000 INCOME CHARACTERISTICS						
	Population 15 years and over with employment income in 2000 by sex and work activity – concluded						
526	Females with employment income (48)	1,625	1,025	1,510	1,680	2,130	1,830
527	Average employment income $	24,176	24,525	30,872	31,867	38,246	24,420
528	Standard error of average employment income $	870	1,187	1,541	1,226	2,711	833
529	Worked full year, full time (49)	845	545	820	1,030	1,050	940
530	Average employment income $	33,110	30,919	37,913	39,197	50,563	33,001
531	Standard error of average employment income $	1,123	1,763	1,789	1,470	2,231	1,028
532	Worked part year or part time (50)	760	460	650	615	1,040	865
533	Average employment income $	14,860	17,323	22,723	21,005	26,260	15,490
534	Standard error of average employment income $	976	1,299	2,642	1,860	4,990	1,036
	Census families by structure and family income groups in 2000						
535	Total - All census families	1,670	1,035	1,475	1,650	2,175	1,775
536	Under $10,000	45	65	80	50	65	80
537	$ 10,000 - $19,999	40	50	90	20	40	45
538	$ 20,000 - $29,999	140	110	140	100	125	110
539	$ 30,000 - $39,999	120	220	125	130	140	155
540	$ 40,000 - $49,999	195	155	160	175	135	160
541	$ 50,000 - $59,999	220	95	130	185	135	265
542	$ 60,000 - $69,999	190	75	185	180	160	205
543	$ 70,000 - $79,999	230	85	210	105	135	220
544	$ 80,000 - $89,999	135	45	100	140	135	155
545	$ 90,000 - $99,999	125	50	95	135	110	100
546	$100,000 and over	230	75	150	420	985	285
547	Average family income $	67,286	53,909	60,795	81,405	119,761	67,900
548	Median family income $	63,984	45,512	60,057	66,852	90,025	62,255
549	Standard error of average family income $	1,893	2,622	1,962	3,000	5,332	1,835
550	Total - All couple census families (51)	1,385	825	1,120	1,350	1,865	1,410
551	Under $10,000	35	40	40	45	10	20
552	$ 10,000 - $19,999	25	20	60	10	25	15
553	$ 20,000 - $29,999	85	80	95	75	100	45
554	$ 30,000 - $39,999	70	155	80	70	110	100
555	$ 40,000 - $49,999	155	125	125	110	125	110
556	$ 50,000 - $59,999	165	85	95	145	105	225
557	$ 60,000 - $69,999	170	80	170	140	120	200
558	$ 70,000 - $79,999	210	90	165	80	115	205
559	$ 80,000 - $89,999	125	50	80	130	125	130
560	$ 90,000 - $99,999	120	35	90	120	75	95
561	$100,000 and over	220	70	125	415	955	275
562	Average family income $	71,822	58,328	64,716	88,483	128,637	74,902
563	Median family income $	69,453	49,134	63,365	79,261	100,192	69,390
564	Standard error of average family income $	2,116	3,165	2,268	3,524	5,563	1,937
	Incidence of low income in 2000						
565	Total - Economic families	1,650	1,040	1,455	1,600	2,070	1,655
566	Low income	100	180	210	140	110	130
567	Incidence of low income in 2000 % (52)	6.0	17.2	14.1	8.9	5.2	7.7
568	Total - Unattached individuals 15 years and over	650	645	785	785	460	405
569	Low income	195	190	190	130	170	95
570	Incidence of low income in 2000 % (52)	29.6	29.8	24.0	16.7	37.5	22.9
571	Total - Population in private households	5,885	3,770	5,025	5,695	7,365	6,170
572	Low income	500	770	790	645	505	555
573	Incidence of low income in 2000 % (52)	8.4	20.5	15.8	11.3	6.9	8.9
	Private households by household income groups in 2000						
574	Total - All private households	2,200	1,575	2,135	2,255	2,405	1,965
575	Under $10,000	85	90	135	60	55	40
576	$ 10,000 - $19,999	240	150	205	100	105	70
577	$ 20,000 - $29,999	180	150	220	165	125	140
578	$ 30,000 - $39,999	190	305	225	290	150	215
579	$ 40,000 - $49,999	240	235	210	225	140	180
580	$ 50,000 - $59,999	255	180	160	195	155	230
581	$ 60,000 - $69,999	200	130	225	220	195	240
582	$ 70,000 - $79,999	230	140	215	155	175	240
583	$ 80,000 - $89,999	165	70	135	155	125	145
584	$ 90,000 - $99,999	130	45	135	160	120	100
585	$100,000 and over	290	80	260	515	1,070	360
586	Average household income $	60,670	49,908	71,879	76,219	118,151	69,409
587	Median household income $	55,377	42,810	54,365	62,646	88,971	63,586
588	Standard error of average household income $	1,705	2,082	10,785	2,518	5,138	1,845

Tableau 1. Certaines caractéristiques des secteurs de recensement, recensement de 2001 – Données intégrales et données-échantillon (20 %)

Toronto 0502.02	Toronto 0503	Toronto 0504	Toronto 0505.01	Toronto 0505.02	Toronto 0506	Caractéristiques	N°
						CARACTÉRISTIQUES DU REVENU DE 2000	
						Population de 15 ans et plus ayant un revenu d'emploi en 2000 selon le sexe et le travail – fin	
685	1,520	970	1,350	1,170	710	Femmes ayant un revenu d'emploi (48)	526
28,679	25,504	33,538	50,488	38,503	42,621	Revenu moyen d'emploi $	527
1,589	952	1,615	6,781	2,398	3,833	Erreur type de revenu moyen d'emploi $	528
355	815	555	560	505	260	Ayant travaillé toute l'année à plein temps (49)	529
40,397	34,788	44,016	83,313	56,439	67,867	Revenu moyen d'emploi $	530
1,794	1,221	2,006	11,671	4,134	5,872	Erreur type de revenu moyen d'emploi $	531
315	625	385	760	625	435	Ayant travaillé une partie de l'année ou à temps partiel (50)	532
16,848	15,755	20,403	20,348	25,292	27,823	Revenu moyen d'emploi $	533
1,555	1,060	1,944	1,827	2,405	4,597	Erreur type de revenu moyen d'emploi $	534
						Familles de recensement selon la structure et les tranches de revenu de la famille en 2000	
730	1,550	1,050	1,370	1,225	755	Total - Toutes les familles de recensement	535
15	55	10	-	10	10	Moins de 10 000 $	536
15	55	25	10	-	-	10 000 $ - 19 999 $	537
65	125	60	20	50	10	20 000 $ - 29 999 $	538
55	160	55	55	35	10	30 000 $ - 39 999 $	539
85	210	75	55	60	20	40 000 $ - 49 999 $	540
45	115	95	85	50	35	50 000 $ - 59 999 $	541
130	130	75	60	60	50	60 000 $ - 69 999 $	542
55	180	100	95	45	15	70 000 $ - 79 999 $	543
70	170	85	35	65	50	80 000 $ - 89 999 $	544
25	70	90	100	90	25	90 000 $ - 99 999 $	545
170	280	385	845	765	515	100 000 $ et plus	546
71,822	68,371	90,217	183,901	177,579	227,644	Revenu moyen des familles $	547
67,003	64,869	83,746	129,297	116,514	143,056	Revenu médian des familles $	548
3,069	2,124	3,518	12,420	9,910	20,595	Erreur type de revenu moyen des familles $	549
625	1,305	900	1,295	1,155	700	Total - Toutes les familles de recensement comptant un couple (51)	550
10	35	-	10	-	10	Moins de 10 000 $	551
10	30	-	10	-	-	10 000 $ - 19 999 $	552
60	110	45	20	50	-	20 000 $ - 29 999 $	553
45	120	30	35	25	15	30 000 $ - 39 999 $	554
45	155	60	55	50	20	40 000 $ - 49 999 $	555
40	85	55	80	45	30	50 000 $ - 59 999 $	556
125	105	55	55	65	40	60 000 $ - 69 999 $	557
55	175	90	90	40	15	70 000 $ - 79 999 $	558
75	160	80	30	55	45	80 000 $ - 89 999 $	559
25	70	85	95	75	25	90 000 $ - 99 999 $	560
150	255	375	830	740	495	100 000 $ et plus	561
73,537	72,017	97,014	183,786	183,662	234,977	Revenu moyen des familles $	562
69,164	70,346	92,167	134,209	124,324	149,370	Revenu médian des familles $	563
3,032	2,344	3,803	12,283	10,487	21,886	Erreur type de revenu moyen des familles $	564
						Fréquence des unités à faible revenu en 2000	
715	1,490	1,025	1,325	1,220	750	Total - Familles économiques	565
50	170	45	30	50	-	Faible revenu	566
7.4	11.4	4.7	2.2	4.2	1.1	Fréquence des unités à faible revenu en 2000 % (52)	567
260	485	210	145	180	130	Total - Personnes hors famille économique de 15 ans et plus	568
105	150	45	20	35	30	Faible revenu	569
40.7	30.6	21.2	13.8	19.8	23.5	Fréquence des unités à faible revenu en 2000 % (52)	570
2,530	5,505	3,435	4,770	4,335	2,685	Total - Population dans les ménages privés	571
300	715	180	100	240	45	Faible revenu	572
11.9	12.9	5.2	2.1	5.5	1.8	Fréquence des unités à faible revenu en 2000 % (52)	573
						Ménages privés selon les tranches de revenu du ménage en 2000	
940	1,870	1,205	1,450	1,385	845	Total - Tous les ménages privés	574
20	60	15	10	10	-	Moins de 10 000 $	575
105	120	35	25	40	20	10 000 $ - 19 999 $	576
85	185	65	20	80	25	20 000 $ - 29 999 $	577
65	215	55	55	45	20	30 000 $ - 39 999 $	578
95	220	100	50	80	55	40 000 $ - 49 999 $	579
75	140	135	95	40	45	50 000 $ - 59 999 $	580
130	140	60	70	60	60	60 000 $ - 69 999 $	581
75	165	135	95	40	20	70 000 $ - 79 999 $	582
75	200	85	50	80	60	80 000 $ - 89 999 $	583
50	90	90	100	100	30	90 000 $ - 99 999 $	584
170	325	410	895	810	520	100 000 $ et plus	585
64,162	66,412	87,550	180,449	166,787	209,315	Revenu moyen des ménages $	586
61,517	59,076	78,674	128,975	113,756	117,846	Revenu médian des ménages $	587
2,772	2,065	3,202	11,857	9,124	18,620	Erreur type de revenu moyen des ménages $	588

Table 1. Selected Characteristics for Census Tracts, 2001 Census – 100% Data and 20% Sample Data

No.	Characteristics	Toronto 0507	Toronto 0508	Toronto 0509.01	Toronto 0509.02	Toronto 0510	Toronto 0511.01
	POPULATION CHARACTERISTICS						
1	**Population, 1996 (1)**	**3,650**	**3,501**	**3,974**	**3,058**	**5,774**	**6,058**
2	**Population, 2001 (2)**	**3,665**	**3,314**	**4,749**	**3,109**	**5,735**	**4,935**
3	Population percentage change, 1996-2001	0.4	-5.3	19.5	1.7	-0.7	-18.5
4	Land area in square kilometres, 2001	2.06	1.30	1.96	2.91	6.31	0.47
5	**Total population - 100% Data (3)**	**3,665**	**3,315**	**4,750**	**3,110**	**5,735**	**4,935**
	by sex and age groups						
6	Male	1,795	1,710	2,320	1,540	2,820	2,485
7	0-4 years	95	95	100	85	140	180
8	5-9 years	100	95	160	95	160	145
9	10-14 years	120	115	150	85	185	110
10	15-19 years	100	140	140	80	165	120
11	20-24 years	90	120	130	75	170	180
12	25-29 years	80	90	160	70	155	285
13	30-34 years	100	100	190	85	170	350
14	35-39 years	140	135	225	140	240	320
15	40-44 years	170	180	230	105	210	210
16	45-49 years	145	150	155	125	240	145
17	50-54 years	150	115	155	110	210	135
18	55-59 years	115	80	120	85	145	115
19	60-64 years	100	80	95	80	150	70
20	65-69 years	85	75	110	75	135	45
21	70-74 years	70	70	90	90	165	35
22	75-79 years	60	35	65	80	110	30
23	80-84 years	40	30	30	50	45	10
24	85 years and over	25	10	15	20	25	5
25	Female	1,870	1,605	2,430	1,565	2,915	2,450
26	0-4 years	95	75	135	70	135	190
27	5-9 years	115	85	135	100	180	120
28	10-14 years	125	105	150	75	180	110
29	15-19 years	100	95	150	80	155	90
30	20-24 years	65	85	115	55	145	210
31	25-29 years	90	90	160	60	130	360
32	30-34 years	110	95	185	95	165	320
33	35-39 years	145	140	260	140	220	210
34	40-44 years	190	165	235	130	235	175
35	45-49 years	160	140	190	110	240	155
36	50-54 years	140	120	145	115	220	160
37	55-59 years	120	85	115	90	165	110
38	60-64 years	105	95	110	80	170	75
39	65-69 years	90	65	105	75	160	45
40	70-74 years	75	75	105	105	175	45
41	75-79 years	85	50	80	120	145	35
42	80-84 years	50	40	35	55	65	25
43	85 years and over	30	20	20	30	40	10
44	**Total population 15 years and over**	**3,005**	**2,750**	**3,920**	**2,610**	**4,750**	**4,075**
	by legal marital status						
45	Never married (single)	740	840	1,185	595	1,225	1,490
46	Legally married (and not separated)	1,825	1,535	2,115	1,565	2,935	1,765
47	Separated, but still legally married	75	60	120	70	80	235
48	Divorced	180	135	260	155	205	420
49	Widowed	185	190	245	225	300	160
	by common-law status						
50	Not in a common-law relationship	2,825	2,605	3,645	2,475	4,580	3,610
51	In a common-law relationship	180	145	280	130	170	460
52	**Total population - 20% Sample Data (4)**	**3,660**	**3,315**	**4,710**	**3,150**	**5,735**	**4,935**
	by mother tongue						
53	Single responses	3,605	3,240	4,640	3,090	5,630	4,725
54	English	2,825	2,075	2,835	2,175	3,935	2,315
55	French	40	55	75	45	15	60
56	Non-official languages (5)	740	1,105	1,730	870	1,675	2,350
57	Italian	145	230	150	65	360	40
58	Chinese, n.o.s.	-	15	70	40	25	100
59	Cantonese	-	-	25	-	30	10
60	Portuguese	60	285	320	30	400	45
61	Punjabi	-	15	10	-	-	-
62	Other languages (6)	545	555	1,160	730	855	2,160
63	Multiple responses	55	75	70	55	110	210
64	English and French	10	-	10	-	-	30
65	English and non-official language	40	75	65	50	100	160
66	French and non-official language	-	-	-	10	10	15
67	English, French and non-official language	-	-	-	-	-	-

See reference material at the end of the publication. – Voir les documents de référence à la fin de la publication.

Tableau 1. Certaines caractéristiques des secteurs de recensement, recensement de 2001 – Données intégrales et données-échantillon (20 %)

Toronto 0511.02	Toronto 0512 ◆	Toronto 0513.01 ◆	Toronto 0513.02	Toronto 0513.03	Toronto 0513.04	Caractéristiques	N°
						CARACTÉRISTIQUES DE LA POPULATION	
5,398	**5,805**	**6,951**	**6,638**	**3,691**	**4,209**	**Population, 1996 (1)**	1
5,350	**6,965**	**6,840**	**6,695**	**3,806**	**4,063**	**Population, 2001 (2)**	2
-0.9	20.0	-1.6	0.9	3.1	-3.5	Variation en pourcentage de la population, 1996-2001	3
1.43	1.98	3.51	1.09	1.07	1.36	Superficie des terres en kilomètres carrés, 2001	4
5,350	**6,965**	**6,845**	**6,695**	**3,805**	**4,065**	**Population totale – Données intégrales (3)**	5
						selon le sexe et les groupes d'âge	
2,665	3,475	3,395	3,240	1,775	2,020	Sexe masculin	6
195	240	160	230	135	105	0-4 ans	7
205	250	210	225	125	115	5-9 ans	8
200	200	205	215	100	135	10-14 ans	9
155	200	250	170	180	165	15-19 ans	10
160	210	280	245	110	150	20-24 ans	11
150	250	235	220	115	160	25-29 ans	12
220	290	205	275	145	120	30-34 ans	13
265	400	240	305	155	155	35-39 ans	14
235	310	275	305	150	140	40-44 ans	15
170	225	265	205	105	130	45-49 ans	16
155	205	285	220	85	160	50-54 ans	17
140	165	240	170	80	150	55-59 ans	18
145	135	195	145	75	120	60-64 ans	19
110	120	145	115	45	85	65-69 ans	20
90	90	105	85	50	65	70-74 ans	21
50	95	65	60	45	40	75-79 ans	22
30	35	20	30	40	10	80-84 ans	23
-	45	25	30	40	5	85 ans et plus	24
2,685	3,495	3,445	3,455	2,035	2,040	Sexe féminin	25
200	230	140	210	115	85	0-4 ans	26
215	195	170	210	115	120	5-9 ans	27
170	170	215	215	125	125	10-14 ans	28
160	190	250	220	165	145	15-19 ans	29
165	230	245	230	140	170	20-24 ans	30
175	270	225	265	115	135	25-29 ans	31
210	305	205	270	135	120	30-34 ans	32
240	335	240	300	160	160	35-39 ans	33
205	280	285	265	120	160	40-44 ans	34
200	235	325	260	110	160	45-49 ans	35
170	205	325	230	115	180	50-54 ans	36
160	175	225	165	90	145	55-59 ans	37
150	160	175	155	60	95	60-64 ans	38
100	150	145	150	65	95	65-69 ans	39
75	115	100	100	65	70	70-74 ans	40
55	95	80	95	80	45	75-79 ans	41
20	65	40	45	95	20	80-84 ans	42
15	100	35	80	160	10	85 ans et plus	43
4,165	**5,675**	**5,745**	**5,390**	**3,090**	**3,375**	**Population totale de 15 ans et plus**	44
						selon l'état matrimonial légal	
1,245	1,690	1,750	1,585	990	1,000	Célibataire (jamais marié(e))	45
2,330	3,070	3,290	2,940	1,360	2,055	Légalement marié(e) (et non séparé(e))	46
150	170	145	195	145	60	Séparé(e), mais toujours légalement marié(e)	47
240	350	305	310	180	120	Divorcé(e)	48
190	390	255	360	420	135	Veuf ou veuve	49
						selon l'union libre	
3,925	5,425	5,565	5,210	2,965	3,305	Ne vivant pas en union libre	50
240	255	180	180	130	70	Vivant en union libre	51
5,350	**6,820**	**6,845**	**6,630**	**3,370**	**4,060**	**Population totale – Données-échantillon (20 %) (4)**	52
						selon la langue maternelle	
5,215	6,580	6,710	6,385	3,245	3,900	Réponses uniques	53
2,885	2,590	3,725	2,375	1,515	1,945	Anglais	54
125	50	100	50	30	45	Français	55
2,205	3,945	2,890	3,955	1,705	1,910	Langues non officielles (5)	56
220	320	275	450	55	305	Italien	57
30	85	145	90	105	50	Chinois, n.d.a.	58
-	15	235	50	40	30	Cantonais	59
370	225	315	425	60	560	Portugais	60
50	110	60	135	20	85	Pendjabi	61
1,530	3,190	1,865	2,810	1,430	885	Autres langues (6)	62
130	235	135	250	125	160	Réponses multiples	63
10	-	-	-	15	-	Anglais et français	64
120	240	110	215	100	155	Anglais et langue non officielle	65
-	-	15	25	-	-	Français et langue non officielle	66
-	-	10	10	-	-	Anglais, français et langue non officielle	67

See reference material at the end of the publication. – Voir les documents de référence à la fin de la publication.

Table 1. Selected Characteristics for Census Tracts, 2001 Census – 100% Data and 20% Sample Data

No.	Characteristics	Toronto 0507	Toronto 0508	Toronto 0509.01	Toronto 0509.02	Toronto 0510	Toronto 0511.01
	POPULATION CHARACTERISTICS						
	by home language						
68	Single responses	3,165	2,615	3,595	2,620	4,765	3,595
69	English	3,025	2,265	3,155	2,440	4,305	2,570
70	French	-	-	20	-	-	15
71	Non-official languages (5)	140	350	415	180	460	1,005
72	Cantonese	-	-	25	-	-	-
73	Chinese, n.o.s.	-	15	-	-	10	35
74	Italian	35	65	15	-	75	-
75	Punjabi	-	-	-	-	-	-
76	Portuguese	25	95	60	15	185	10
77	Other languages (6)	65	170	310	165	200	970
78	Multiple responses	495	700	1,115	525	970	1,340
79	English and French	15	35	30	15	15	65
80	English and non-official language	480	655	1,075	495	945	1,195
81	French and non-official language	-	10	-	-	-	45
82	English, French and non-official language	-	-	20	10	20	40
	by knowledge of official languages						
83	English only	3,305	2,990	4,320	2,905	5,325	4,305
84	French only	-	-	-	-	-	-
85	English and French	300	185	285	235	300	460
86	Neither English nor French	55	135	100	-	110	160
	by knowledge of non-official languages (5) (7)						
87	Italian	185	355	235	110	535	80
88	Cantonese	10	-	50	10	30	10
89	Chinese, n.o.s.	-	15	50	40	35	100
90	Spanish	115	75	75	50	60	255
91	Portuguese	65	300	375	35	455	45
92	Punjabi	-	15	10	10	-	75
93	Tagalog (Pilipino)	20	30	20	145	20	65
	by first official language spoken						
94	English	3,540	3,105	4,495	3,055	5,580	4,615
95	French	35	50	70	60	30	105
96	English and French	25	25	55	35	15	60
97	Neither English nor French	55	130	95	-	110	160
98	Official language minority - (number) (8)	50	65	95	75	40	135
99	Official language minority - (percentage) (8)	1.4	2.0	2.0	2.4	0.7	2.7
	by ethnic origin (9)						
100	Canadian	905	735	1,185	855	1,430	850
101	English	1,175	670	935	950	1,470	720
102	Scottish	925	575	565	545	980	515
103	Irish	745	395	590	560	865	450
104	Chinese	35	15	140	90	80	210
105	Italian	320	615	325	135	940	225
106	East Indian	30	90	65	45	90	310
107	French	260	230	295	170	215	250
108	German	290	170	225	215	320	195
109	Portuguese	85	355	460	80	565	65
110	Polish	335	270	615	360	520	585
111	Jewish	25	20	-	35	-	-
112	Jamaican	10	15	60	-	80	190
113	Filipino	20	55	40	140	15	145
114	Ukrainian	180	250	195	185	410	85
	by Aboriginal identity						
115	Total Aboriginal identity population (10)	25	-	40	-	-	30
116	Total non-Aboriginal population	3,640	3,305	4,675	3,145	5,735	4,905
	by Aboriginal origin						
117	Total Aboriginal origins population (11)	40	25	45	30	30	75
118	Total non-Aboriginal population	3,615	3,285	4,670	3,115	5,710	4,865
	by Registered Indian status						
119	Registered Indian (12)	-	-	-	-	-	10
120	Not a Registered Indian	3,660	3,315	4,710	3,145	5,740	4,920

Tableau 1. Certaines caractéristiques des secteurs de recensement, recensement de 2001 – Données intégrales et données-échantillon (20 %)

Toronto 0511.02	Toronto 0512 ◆	Toronto 0513.01 ◆	Toronto 0513.02	Toronto 0513.03	Toronto 0513.04	Caractéristiques	N°
						CARACTÉRISTIQUES DE LA POPULATION	
						selon la langue parlée à la maison	
4,020	4,475	5,025	4,265	2,480	2,710	Réponses uniques	68
3,205	2,665	4,335	2,820	1,735	2,100	Anglais	69
80	30	-	10	15	25	Français	70
730	1,785	695	1,440	730	585	Langues non officielles (5)	71
-	10	75	30	30	-	Cantonais	72
10	65	40	65	65	25	Chinois, n.d.a.	73
55	110	20	155	-	70	Italien	74
15	65	-	85	-	20	Pendjabi	75
75	60	65	125	15	155	Portugais	76
570	1,475	495	980	630	315	Autres langues (6)	77
1,330	2,345	1,815	2,365	890	1,350	Réponses multiples	78
45	20	100	10	35	85	Anglais et français	79
1,285	2,300	1,680	2,315	855	1,255	Anglais et langue non officielle	80
-	10	10	20	-	-	Français et langue non officielle	81
-	20	25	25	-	10	Anglais, français et langue non officielle	82
						selon la connaissance des langues officielles	
4,710	5,900	5,975	5,840	2,960	3,540	Anglais seulement	83
35	10	-	10	-	-	Français seulement	84
405	510	700	455	235	390	Anglais et français	85
190	400	170	330	170	125	Ni l'anglais ni le français	86
						selon la connaissance des langues non officielles (5) (7)	
325	480	400	525	75	400	Italien	87
30	55	190	60	45	35	Cantonais	88
30	80	155	90	125	40	Chinois, n.d.a.	89
105	310	195	250	55	75	Espagnol	90
440	305	355	575	85	705	Portugais	91
120	175	70	180	20	170	Pendjabi	92
105	435	155	195	170	70	Tagalog (pilipino)	93
						selon la première langue officielle parlée	
4,940	6,185	6,520	6,165	3,145	3,855	Anglais	94
140	60	105	55	30	55	Français	95
80	210	50	95	40	35	Anglais et français	96
195	360	170	315	160	120	Ni l'anglais ni le français	97
175	170	125	105	50	70	Minorité de langue officielle - (nombre) (8)	98
3.3	2.5	1.8	1.6	1.5	1.7	Minorité de langue officielle - (pourcentage) (8)	99
						selon l'origine ethnique (9)	
1,090	915	1,540	975	660	505	Canadien	100
740	565	1,020	575	375	485	Anglais	101
395	415	750	380	160	290	Écossais	102
460	375	565	375	135	285	Irlandais	103
65	145	435	195	180	110	Chinois	104
465	670	830	735	125	590	Italien	105
325	445	355	485	195	225	Indien de l'Inde	106
265	125	355	220	125	195	Français	107
220	285	385	215	100	125	Allemand	108
555	335	495	645	80	800	Portugais	109
250	765	800	925	345	335	Polonais	110
45	35	10	20	10	10	Juif	111
135	120	160	175	95	65	Jamaïquain	112
190	505	205	260	240	80	Philippin	113
180	245	285	120	55	115	Ukrainien	114
						selon l'identité autochtone	
40	25	15	20	35	-	Total de la population ayant une identité autochtone (10)	115
5,305	6,795	6,830	6,615	3,335	4,060	Total de la population non autochtone	116
						selon l'origine autochtone	
45	50	40	85	45	10	Total de la population ayant une origine autochtone (11)	117
5,305	6,770	6,805	6,550	3,330	4,045	Total de la population non autochtone	118
						selon le statut d'Indien inscrit	
10	-	15	-	25	-	Oui, Indien inscrit (12)	119
5,340	6,820	6,830	6,630	3,350	4,055	Non, pas un Indien inscrit	120

Table 1. Selected Characteristics for Census Tracts, 2001 Census – 100% Data and 20% Sample Data

No.	Characteristics	Toronto 0507	Toronto 0508	Toronto 0509.01	Toronto 0509.02	Toronto 0510	Toronto 0511.01
	POPULATION CHARACTERISTICS						
	by visible minority groups						
121	Total visible minority population	170	330	555	380	405	1,900
122	Chinese	35	15	80	85	70	155
123	South Asian	35	110	105	65	40	475
124	Black	15	45	115	10	100	340
125	Filipino	25	50	20	135	15	150
126	Latin American	15	35	35	10	25	105
127	Southeast Asian	10	-	30	-	40	25
128	Arab	15	-	105	10	15	210
129	West Asian	25	45	-	10	25	265
130	Korean	-	-	-	25	-	55
131	Japanese	-	25	20	25	-	15
132	Visible minority, n.i.e. (13)	-	-	-	10	60	85
133	Multiple visible minorities (14)	-	-	40	-	10	35
	by citizenship						
134	Canadian citizenship (15)	3,465	3,100	4,550	2,965	5,460	3,640
135	Citizenship other than Canadian	195	215	165	185	275	1,295
	by place of birth of respondent						
136	Non-immigrant population	2,725	2,270	3,140	2,220	4,070	2,315
137	Born in province of residence	2,400	1,995	2,675	2,005	3,675	1,825
138	Immigrant population (16)	900	1,035	1,565	920	1,670	2,475
139	United States	55	15	20	30	30	40
140	Central and South America	20	40	40	30	35	170
141	Caribbean and Bermuda	10	30	80	35	80	200
142	United Kingdom	215	110	160	160	210	70
143	Other Europe (17)	500	680	975	465	1,130	745
144	Africa	40	10	30	25	15	200
145	Asia and the Middle East	70	155	250	180	145	1,040
146	Oceania and other (18)	-	-	15	-	20	10
147	Non-permanent residents (19)	35	-	10	-	-	145
148	**Total immigrant population**	**900**	**1,040**	**1,565**	**925**	**1,670**	**2,475**
	by period of immigration						
149	Before 1961	275	215	325	260	690	75
150	1961-1970	215	240	320	150	440	80
151	1971-1980	190	225	260	165	225	265
152	1981-1990	80	215	360	120	165	445
153	1991-2001 (20)	145	130	300	240	155	1,605
154	1991-1995	95	55	275	165	95	635
155	1996-2001 (20)	50	75	25	75	65	970
	by age at immigration						
156	0-4 years	85	80	125	90	110	185
157	5-19 years	145	250	500	230	530	745
158	20 years and over	675	705	940	600	1,025	1,545
159	**Total population**	**3,660**	**3,315**	**4,710**	**3,145**	**5,735**	**4,935**
	by religion						
160	Catholic (21)	1,340	1,960	2,350	1,465	3,000	1,680
161	Protestant	1,640	755	1,180	1,010	1,790	960
162	Christian Orthodox	50	25	230	80	140	330
163	Christian, n.i.e. (22)	30	80	85	10	95	225
164	Muslim	20	50	110	90	40	715
165	Jewish	25	-	-	10	25	-
166	Buddhist	-	-	95	-	40	15
167	Hindu	-	20	-	15	-	175
168	Sikh	-	15	-	-	-	-
169	Eastern religions (23)	25	-	-	-	-	35
170	Other religions (24)	-	-	-	-	-	-
171	No religious affiliation (25)	530	400	665	465	610	805
172	**Total population 15 years and over**	**3,005**	**2,750**	**3,895**	**2,630**	**4,760**	**4,055**
	by generation status						
173	1st generation (26)	900	1,035	1,555	930	1,660	2,350
174	2nd generation (27)	825	845	940	700	1,425	500
175	3rd generation and over (28)	1,280	875	1,400	995	1,675	1,205
176	**Total population 1 year and over (29)**	**3,635**	**3,290**	**4,675**	**3,110**	**5,675**	**4,805**
	by place of residence 1 year ago (mobility)						
177	Non-movers	3,435	3,035	4,245	2,855	5,515	3,495
178	Movers	200	255	435	260	155	1,305
179	Non-migrants	140	165	230	105	65	515
180	Migrants	60	95	200	150	95	785
181	Internal migrants	45	70	195	130	80	530
182	Intraprovincial migrants	20	55	195	110	80	480
183	Interprovincial migrants	20	15	-	20	-	45
184	External migrants	20	20	10	25	10	260

Tableau 1. Certaines caractéristiques des secteurs de recensement, recensement de 2001 – Données intégrales et données-échantillon (20 %)

Toronto 0511.02	Toronto 0512 ◆	Toronto 0513.01 ◆	Toronto 0513.02	Toronto 0513.03	Toronto 0513.04	Caractéristiques	N°
						CARACTÉRISTIQUES DE LA POPULATION	
						selon les groupes de minorités visibles	
1,515	2,980	1,655	2,190	1,655	1,070	Total de la population des minorités visibles	121
55	115	465	185	180	110	Chinois	122
430	835	350	860	490	385	Sud-Asiatique	123
285	200	155	265	215	285	Noir	124
190	495	150	240	225	80	Philippin	125
50	185	70	125	15	10	Latino-Américain	126
225	665	105	105	85	10	Asiatique du Sud-Est	127
90	235	135	205	195	45	Arabe	128
-	40	-	90	85	-	Asiatique occidental	129
85	75	150	-	10	65	Coréen	130
-	20	50	10	35	40	Japonais	131
80	65	10	100	105	45	Minorité visible, n.i.a. (13)	132
15	50	15	-	20	-	Minorités visibles multiples (14)	133
						selon la citoyenneté	
4,690	5,210	6,310	5,540	2,465	3,760	Citoyenneté canadienne (15)	134
660	1,610	535	1,090	905	300	Citoyenneté autre que canadienne	135
						selon le lieu de naissance du répondant	
3,025	2,685	3,890	2,740	1,425	2,000	Population non immigrante	136
2,635	2,355	3,370	2,410	1,155	1,740	Née dans la province de résidence	137
2,215	4,015	2,950	3,810	1,685	2,035	Population immigrante (16)	138
30	15	85	10	25	10	États-Unis	139
70	210	130	190	75	115	Amérique centrale et du Sud	140
180	165	200	165	175	130	Caraïbes et Bermudes	141
140	100	205	85	90	120	Royaume-Uni	142
950	1,430	1,350	2,045	430	1,145	Autre Europe (17)	143
110	85	95	110	15	40	Afrique	144
735	2,000	885	1,205	890	455	Asie et Moyen-Orient	145
-	10	-	-	-	10	Océanie et autre (18)	146
115	120	-	85	265	25	Résidents non permanents (19)	147
2,215	**4,015**	**2,950**	**3,805**	**1,690**	**2,035**	**Population immigrante totale**	148
						selon la période d'immigration	
370	365	405	310	90	285	Avant 1961	149
360	390	665	510	105	515	1961-1970	150
335	435	505	555	150	455	1971-1980	151
445	765	735	770	365	255	1981-1990	152
705	2,060	640	1,660	980	530	1991-2001 (20)	153
310	790	425	775	410	245	1991-1995	154
395	1,270	215	885	575	285	1996-2001 (20)	155
						selon l'âge à l'immigration	
245	270	230	225	205	175	0-4 ans	156
670	895	935	1,030	465	600	5-19 ans	157
1,305	2,850	1,785	2,550	1,015	1,260	20 ans et plus	158
5,350	**6,820**	**6,840**	**6,635**	**3,370**	**4,060**	**Population totale**	159
						selon la religion	
2,485	3,150	3,580	3,730	1,585	2,570	Catholique (21)	160
1,175	1,070	1,705	870	535	660	Protestante	161
145	260	125	250	70	95	Orthodoxe chrétienne	162
90	175	160	85	110	65	Chrétiennes, n.i.a. (22)	163
310	685	160	560	290	145	Musulmane	164
-	20	15	-	-	10	Juive	165
120	310	55	65	55	15	Bouddhiste	166
210	310	170	350	195	150	Hindoue	167
35	70	35	150	15	95	Sikh	168
10	-	25	40	-	-	Religions orientales (23)	169
-	-	-	-	10	-	Autres religions (24)	170
765	770	805	545	510	255	Aucune appartenance religieuse (25)	171
4,160	**5,520**	**5,715**	**5,300**	**2,595**	**3,445**	**Population totale de 15 ans et plus**	172
						selon le statut des générations	
2,155	3,760	2,865	3,595	1,690	1,950	1re génération (26)	173
965	860	1,275	815	345	1,005	2e génération (27)	174
1,045	905	1,575	885	565	495	3e génération et plus (28)	175
5,295	**6,760**	**6,810**	**6,535**	**3,320**	**4,020**	**Population totale de 1 an et plus (29)**	176
						selon le lieu de résidence 1 an auparavant (mobilité)	
4,450	5,835	6,055	5,815	2,620	3,840	Personnes n'ayant pas déménagé	177
840	925	760	720	695	180	Personnes ayant déménagé	178
525	330	390	450	205	75	Non-migrants	179
325	595	370	270	495	105	Migrants	180
200	245	200	130	160	95	Migrants internes	181
205	210	160	85	140	90	Migrants infraprovinciaux	182
10	40	45	40	20	-	Migrants interprovinciaux	183
115	345	160	140	330	-	Migrants externes	184

Table 1. Selected Characteristics for Census Tracts, 2001 Census – 100% Data and 20% Sample Data

No.	Characteristics	Toronto 0507	Toronto 0508	Toronto 0509.01	Toronto 0509.02	Toronto 0510	Toronto 0511.01
	POPULATION CHARACTERISTICS						
185	**Total population 5 years and over (30)**	**3,485**	**3,125**	**4,480**	**2,980**	**5,465**	**4,545**
	by place of residence 5 years ago (mobility)						
186	Non-movers	2,675	2,235	2,615	2,070	4,265	1,450
187	Movers	810	890	1,870	905	1,205	3,095
188	Non-migrants	525	485	1,010	440	785	1,285
189	Migrants	285	405	855	465	410	1,815
190	Internal migrants	245	335	830	360	385	895
191	Intraprovincial migrants	210	305	755	345	370	745
192	Interprovincial migrants	40	30	75	20	15	150
193	External migrants	35	70	25	100	30	920
194	**Total population 15 to 24 years**	**350**	**440**	**500**	**315**	**630**	**595**
	by school attendance						
195	Not attending school	120	160	205	140	185	220
196	Attending school full time	220	265	270	175	400	310
197	Attending school part time	10	15	35	-	45	55
198	**Total population 15 years and over**	**3,000**	**2,750**	**3,895**	**2,630**	**4,760**	**4,055**
	by highest level of schooling						
199	Less than grade 9 (31)	195	345	420	95	545	120
200	Grades 9-13 without high school graduation certificate	550	555	915	445	865	615
201	Grades 9-13 with high school graduation certificate	400	490	635	355	730	590
202	Some postsecondary without degree, certificate or diploma (32)	265	245	440	290	550	480
203	Trades certificate or diploma (33)	290	275	360	270	385	335
204	College certificate or diploma (34)	350	460	610	450	770	630
205	University certificate below bachelor's degree	115	45	35	75	160	180
206	University with bachelor's degree or higher	845	340	470	640	765	1,090
	by combinations of unpaid work						
207	Males 15 years and over	1,470	1,400	1,890	1,310	2,340	2,050
208	Reported unpaid work (35)	1,330	1,210	1,670	1,085	2,145	1,760
209	Housework and child care and care or assistance to seniors	165	100	110	80	190	120
210	Housework and child care only	370	350	450	270	610	475
211	Housework and care or assistance to seniors only	175	130	95	100	185	115
212	Child care and care or assistance to seniors only	-	-	-	-	-	10
213	Housework only	605	620	980	600	1,135	990
214	Child care only	10	10	30	25	10	45
215	Care or assistance to seniors only	-	-	10	10	20	10
216	Females 15 years and over	1,530	1,355	2,005	1,320	2,420	2,000
217	Reported unpaid work (35)	1,440	1,235	1,800	1,210	2,260	1,890
218	Housework and child care and care or assistance to seniors	165	150	175	135	275	225
219	Housework and child care only	410	415	520	335	650	530
220	Housework and care or assistance to seniors only	185	85	160	80	230	190
221	Child care and care or assistance to seniors only	-	-	-	-	-	-
222	Housework only	665	590	935	640	1,110	930
223	Child care only	15	-	10	20	-	20
224	Care or assistance to seniors only	-	-	10	-	-	-
	by labour force activity						
225	Males 15 years and over	1,470	1,400	1,895	1,310	2,340	2,050
226	In the labour force	1,110	1,080	1,380	870	1,735	1,725
227	Employed	1,065	1,060	1,310	850	1,660	1,670
228	Unemployed	45	15	65	20	75	55
229	Not in the labour force	360	320	515	440	600	325
230	Participation rate	75.5	77.1	72.8	66.4	74.1	84.1
231	Employment rate	72.4	75.7	69.1	64.9	70.9	81.5
232	Unemployment rate	4.1	1.4	4.7	2.3	4.3	3.2
233	Females 15 years and over	1,535	1,355	2,000	1,320	2,425	2,000
234	In the labour force	905	890	1,320	755	1,420	1,450
235	Employed	875	820	1,255	730	1,350	1,330
236	Unemployed	30	70	65	25	65	125
237	Not in the labour force	625	460	680	565	1,010	545
238	Participation rate	59.0	65.7	66.0	57.2	58.6	72.5
239	Employment rate	57.0	60.5	62.8	55.3	55.7	66.5
240	Unemployment rate	3.3	7.9	4.9	3.3	4.6	8.6

Tableau 1. Certaines caractéristiques des secteurs de recensement, recensement de 2001 – Données intégrales et données-échantillon (20 %)

Toronto 0511.02	Toronto 0512 ◆	Toronto 0513.01 ◆	Toronto 0513.02	Toronto 0513.03	Toronto 0513.04	Caractéristiques	N°
						CARACTÉRISTIQUES DE LA POPULATION	
4,945	**6,350**	**6,550**	**6,175**	**3,120**	**3,905**	**Population totale de 5 ans et plus (30)**	185
						selon le lieu de résidence 5 ans auparavant (mobilité)	
3,005	3,205	4,150	3,550	1,385	2,715	Personnes n'ayant pas déménagé	186
1,935	3,145	2,395	2,625	1,735	1,185	Personnes ayant déménagé	187
1,105	1,260	1,370	1,460	780	600	Non-migrants	188
830	1,885	1,020	1,165	955	585	Migrants	189
450	740	800	520	235	320	Migrants internes	190
410	630	740	435	235	265	Migrants infraprovinciaux	191
45	110	55	80	10	55	Migrants interprovinciaux	192
380	1,145	220	645	720	265	Migrants externes	193
635	**830**	**1,020**	**835**	**565**	**635**	**Population totale de 15 à 24 ans**	194
						selon la fréquentation scolaire	
245	360	290	270	145	190	Ne fréquentant pas l'école	195
370	450	665	495	400	420	Fréquentant l'école à plein temps	196
25	20	70	70	20	25	Fréquentant l'école à temps partiel	197
4,160	**5,520**	**5,715**	**5,300**	**2,595**	**3,445**	**Population totale de 15 ans et plus**	198
						selon le plus haut niveau de scolarité atteint	
465	630	390	635	150	515	Niveau inférieur à la 9e année (31)	199
1,015	1,075	730	1,165	630	735	De la 9e à la 13e année sans certificat d'études secondaires	200
645	840	780	655	420	510	De la 9e à la 13e année avec certificat d'études secondaires	201
405	515	695	535	325	325	Études postsecondaires partielles sans grade, certificat ou diplôme (32)	202
405	455	480	505	155	255	Certificat ou diplôme d'une école de métiers (33)	203
525	765	925	915	310	480	Certificat ou diplôme collégial (34)	204
95	190	195	155	40	105	Certificat universitaire inférieur au baccalauréat	205
595	1,055	1,525	730	570	520	Études universitaires avec baccalauréat ou diplôme supérieur	206
						selon les combinaisons de travail non rémunéré	
2,060	2,730	2,790	2,550	1,245	1,705	Hommes de 15 ans et plus	207
1,810	2,335	2,450	2,130	1,035	1,555	Travail non rémunéré déclaré (35)	208
140	235	155	150	65	180	Travaux ménagers et soins aux enfants et soins ou aide aux personnes âgées	209
535	660	665	685	295	410	Travaux ménagers et soins aux enfants seulement	210
95	105	215	65	95	135	Travaux ménagers et soins ou aide aux personnes âgées seulement	211
-	10	-	15	15	-	Soins aux enfants et soins ou aide aux personnes âgées seulement	212
1,000	1,265	1,395	1,160	535	815	Travaux ménagers seulement	213
20	50	20	55	30	15	Soins aux enfants seulement	214
10	10	-	10	-	-	Soins ou aide aux personnes âgées seulement	215
2,105	2,795	2,920	2,750	1,355	1,740	Femmes de 15 ans et plus	216
1,925	2,590	2,665	2,380	1,170	1,575	Travail non rémunéré déclaré (35)	217
210	300	295	220	120	210	Travaux ménagers et soins aux enfants et soins ou aide aux personnes âgées	218
665	715	800	930	410	465	Travaux ménagers et soins aux enfants seulement	219
155	255	275	100	90	145	Travaux ménagers et soins ou aide aux personnes âgées seulement	220
-	-	-	-	-	10	Soins aux enfants et soins ou aide aux personnes âgées seulement	221
885	1,265	1,290	1,115	535	750	Travaux ménagers seulement	222
10	40	15	10	15	-	Soins aux enfants seulement	223
10	10	-	10	-	-	Soins ou aide aux personnes âgées seulement	224
						selon l'activité	
2,055	2,730	2,790	2,550	1,245	1,705	Hommes de 15 ans et plus	225
1,530	2,000	2,165	1,945	880	1,320	Population active	226
1,460	1,905	2,080	1,855	845	1,280	Personnes occupées	227
70	95	85	90	30	35	Chômeurs	228
525	725	625	605	365	390	Inactifs	229
74.5	73.3	77.6	76.3	70.7	77.4	Taux d'activité	230
71.0	69.8	74.6	72.7	67.9	75.1	Taux d'emploi	231
4.6	4.8	3.9	4.6	3.4	2.7	Taux de chômage	232
2,105	2,795	2,920	2,750	1,355	1,740	Femmes de 15 ans et plus	233
1,290	1,670	1,985	1,680	795	1,065	Population active	234
1,200	1,540	1,905	1,560	700	1,000	Personnes occupées	235
95	135	75	120	90	65	Chômeuses	236
815	1,120	935	1,070	555	675	Inactives	237
61.3	59.7	68.0	61.1	58.7	61.2	Taux d'activité	238
57.0	55.1	65.2	56.7	51.7	57.5	Taux d'emploi	239
7.4	8.1	3.8	7.1	11.3	6.1	Taux de chômage	240

Table 1. Selected Characteristics for Census Tracts, 2001 Census – 100% Data and 20% Sample Data

No.	Characteristics	Toronto 0507	Toronto 0508	Toronto 0509.01	Toronto 0509.02	Toronto 0510	Toronto 0511.01
	POPULATION CHARACTERISTICS						
	by labour force activity – concluded						
241	Both sexes - Participation rate	67.1	71.8	69.3	61.7	66.2	78.4
242	15-24 years	60.0	75.0	77.2	67.2	73.8	66.9
243	25 years and over	67.8	71.0	68.0	61.0	65.1	80.3
244	Both sexes - Employment rate	64.4	68.5	65.9	59.9	63.2	74.0
245	15-24 years	50.7	70.5	67.3	64.1	65.9	62.7
246	25 years and over	66.4	68.2	65.5	59.5	62.9	76.1
247	Both sexes - Unemployment rate	4.0	4.3	5.0	2.5	4.5	5.5
248	15-24 years	16.3	4.5	12.8	4.7	9.7	7.5
249	25 years and over	2.5	4.3	3.5	2.1	3.3	5.4
250	**Total labour force 15 years and over**	**2,015**	**1,975**	**2,700**	**1,625**	**3,150**	**3,175**
	by industry based on the 1997 NAICS						
251	Industry - Not applicable (36)	-	10	15	-	15	35
252	All industries (37)	2,010	1,960	2,680	1,620	3,135	3,145
253	11 Agriculture, forestry, fishing and hunting	10	15	-	-	10	-
254	21 Mining and oil and gas extraction	-	-	-	10	-	-
255	22 Utilities	30	20	-	-	10	10
256	23 Construction	135	175	160	125	170	135
257	31-33 Manufacturing	270	300	520	255	460	560
258	41 Wholesale trade	165	80	155	110	245	205
259	44-45 Retail trade	135	285	345	190	420	350
260	48-49 Transportation and warehousing	100	140	245	95	195	260
261	51 Information and cultural industries	40	55	70	55	110	105
262	52 Finance and insurance	135	60	140	65	170	130
263	53 Real estate and rental and leasing	85	40	50	95	150	95
264	54 Professional, scientific and technical services	235	110	210	120	255	320
265	55 Management of companies and enterprises	10	-	-	10	15	10
266	56 Administrative and support, waste management and remediation services	100	140	100	60	110	185
267	61 Educational services	215	165	120	75	195	115
268	62 Health care and social assistance	110	110	220	200	180	205
269	71 Arts, entertainment and recreation	40	50	25	10	50	75
270	72 Accommodation and food services	90	65	115	45	160	180
271	81 Other services (except public administration)	55	80	110	45	115	120
272	91 Public administration	45	75	95	50	105	85
	by class of worker						
273	Class of worker - Not applicable (36)	10	10	15	-	15	35
274	All classes of worker (37)	2,010	1,965	2,680	1,620	3,135	3,145
275	Paid workers	1,790	1,820	2,500	1,460	2,845	2,890
276	Employees	1,645	1,775	2,410	1,350	2,715	2,820
277	Self-employed (incorporated)	145	45	85	105	130	75
278	Self-employed (unincorporated)	220	145	170	145	280	245
279	Unpaid family workers	-	-	10	15	-	-
	by occupation based on the 2001 NOC-S						
280	Male labour force 15 years and over	1,115	1,080	1,375	865	1,730	1,725
281	Occupation - Not applicable (36)	-	-	10	-	20	-
282	All occupations (37)	1,110	1,080	1,370	870	1,720	1,725
283	A Management occupations	210	140	170	160	300	210
284	B Business, finance and administration occupations	135	120	130	100	205	200
285	C Natural and applied sciences and related occupations	140	115	150	90	135	360
286	D Health occupations	30	15	20	40	15	35
287	E Occupations in social science, education, government service and religion	80	40	60	25	40	45
288	F Occupations in art, culture, recreation and sport	45	15	55	20	65	40
289	G Sales and service occupations	180	175	250	135	480	380
290	H Trades, transport and equipment operators and related occupations	245	330	375	225	375	325
291	I Occupations unique to primary industry	15	30	-	10	25	-
292	J Occupations unique to processing, manufacturing and utilities	30	90	145	60	75	130
293	Female labour force 15 years and over	900	895	1,320	755	1,415	1,450
294	Occupation - Not applicable (36)	-	10	10	10	-	35
295	All occupations (37)	900	885	1,310	755	1,415	1,415
296	A Management occupations	165	55	135	95	225	130
297	B Business, finance and administration occupations	260	355	455	220	470	480
298	C Natural and applied sciences and related occupations	20	40	35	50	40	60
299	D Health occupations	30	35	85	75	55	80

Tableau 1. Certaines caractéristiques des secteurs de recensement, recensement de 2001 – Données intégrales et données-échantillon (20 %)

Toronto 0511.02	Toronto 0512 ◆	Toronto 0513.01 ◆	Toronto 0513.02	Toronto 0513.03	Toronto 0513.04	Caractéristiques	N°
						CARACTÉRISTIQUES DE LA POPULATION	
						selon l'activité – fin	
67.8	66.6	72.7	68.4	64.4	69.1	Les deux sexes - Taux d'activité	241
62.5	58.4	72.7	70.2	42.5	65.9	15-24 ans	242
68.8	68.1	72.6	68.1	70.5	69.8	25 ans et plus	243
63.8	62.4	69.7	64.3	59.4	66.2	Les deux sexes - Taux d'emploi	244
55.9	53.0	64.9	59.3	36.3	57.5	15-24 ans	245
65.3	64.1	70.8	65.5	65.8	68.1	25 ans et plus	246
5.7	6.2	4.0	5.8	7.5	4.2	Les deux sexes - Taux de chômage	247
10.0	9.3	10.7	16.9	14.6	13.3	15-24 ans	248
5.0	5.8	2.4	3.6	6.3	2.5	25 ans et plus	249
2,820	**3,675**	**4,150**	**3,625**	**1,675**	**2,380**	**Population active totale de 15 ans et plus**	250
						selon l'industrie basée sur le SCIAN de 1997	
40	50	15	70	45	60	Industrie - Sans objet (36)	251
2,780	3,625	4,135	3,555	1,625	2,315	Toutes les industries (37)	252
10	10	-	-	10	-	11 Agriculture, foresterie, pêche et chasse	253
-	10	10	-	-	10	21 Extraction minière et extraction de pétrole et de gaz	254
45	20	25	-	-	25	22 Services publics	255
165	205	210	225	65	215	23 Construction	256
540	845	515	895	320	420	31-33 Fabrication	257
255	250	245	160	115	145	41 Commerce de gros	258
395	345	490	395	165	245	44-45 Commerce de détail	259
245	240	175	295	135	155	48-49 Transport et entreposage	260
50	100	180	60	30	35	51 Industrie de l'information et industrie culturelle	261
115	170	295	135	40	140	52 Finance et assurances	262
45	75	125	65	25	45	53 Services immobiliers et services de location et de location à bail	263
145	290	505	195	95	165	54 Services professionnels, scientifiques et techniques	264
-	10	15	10	-	-	55 Gestion de sociétés et d'entreprises	265
150	190	135	220	90	110	56 Services administratifs, services de soutien, services de gestion des déchets et services d'assainissement	266
130	165	325	165	120	90	61 Services d'enseignement	267
125	280	335	250	115	245	62 Soins de santé et assistance sociale	268
10	20	95	20	20	15	71 Arts, spectacles et loisirs	269
150	190	160	205	105	105	72 Hébergement et services de restauration	270
110	115	170	195	105	55	81 Autres services, sauf les administrations publiques	271
95	115	140	50	55	100	91 Administrations publiques	272
						selon la catégorie de travailleurs	
45	50	15	70	45	60	Catégorie de travailleurs - Sans objet (36)	273
2,785	3,630	4,135	3,555	1,625	2,315	Toutes les catégories de travailleurs (37)	274
2,625	3,375	3,805	3,305	1,535	2,205	Travailleurs rémunérés	275
2,480	3,260	3,555	3,160	1,490	2,105	Employés	276
140	120	245	150	50	100	Travailleurs autonomes (entreprise constituée en société)	277
155	235	330	245	80	115	Travailleurs autonomes (entreprise non constituée en société)	278
10	15	-	10	-	-	Travailleurs familiaux non rémunérés	279
						selon la profession basée sur la CNP-S de 2001	
1,535	2,000	2,160	1,945	880	1,320	Hommes actifs de 15 ans et plus	280
15	10	10	25	10	25	Profession - Sans objet (36)	281
1,515	1,995	2,155	1,920	865	1,295	Toutes les professions (37)	282
205	235	445	195	120	210	A Gestion	283
135	245	275	250	70	130	B Affaires, finance et administration	284
125	230	320	185	70	165	C Sciences naturelles et appliquées et professions apparentées	285
10	40	80	35	30	40	D Secteur de la santé	286
65	60	120	40	35	30	E Sciences sociales, enseignement, administration publique et religion	287
20	30	40	30	15	10	F Arts, culture, sports et loisirs	288
235	270	375	335	140	185	G Ventes et services	289
510	595	360	565	225	385	H Métiers, transport et machinerie	290
20	10	35	10	15	15	I Professions propres au secteur primaire	291
200	275	105	275	150	120	J Transformation, fabrication et services d'utilité publique	292
1,290	1,670	1,985	1,680	795	1,065	Femmes actives de 15 ans et plus	293
30	40	10	50	35	35	Profession - Sans objet (36)	294
1,265	1,630	1,980	1,635	760	1,025	Toutes les professions (37)	295
85	65	195	100	25	80	A Gestion	296
460	560	775	495	250	300	B Affaires, finance et administration	297
20	45	65	10	25	40	C Sciences naturelles et appliquées et professions apparentées	298
30	155	130	135	40	150	D Secteur de la santé	299

Table 1. Selected Characteristics for Census Tracts, 2001 Census – 100% Data and 20% Sample Data

No.	Characteristics	Toronto 0507	Toronto 0508	Toronto 0509.01	Toronto 0509.02	Toronto 0510	Toronto 0511.01
	POPULATION CHARACTERISTICS						
	by occupation based on the 2001 NOC-S – concluded						
300	E Occupations in social science, education, government service and religion	135	60	140	85	115	145
301	F Occupations in art, culture, recreation and sport	25	45	25	25	50	45
302	G Sales and service occupations	205	250	285	180	375	300
303	H Trades, transport and equipment operators and related occupations	20	20	20	10	25	55
304	I Occupations unique to primary industry	15	10	-	-	-	-
305	J Occupations unique to processing, manufacturing and utilities	35	25	130	10	55	120
306	**Total employed labour force 15 years and over**	**1,935**	**1,885**	**2,560**	**1,580**	**3,010**	**3,000**
	by place of work						
307	Males	1,060	1,065	1,310	850	1,660	1,670
308	Usual place of work	785	875	1,020	675	1,390	1,350
309	At home	130	35	75	40	110	90
310	Outside Canada	-	-	10	-	-	10
311	No fixed workplace address	155	150	200	130	160	220
312	Females	875	820	1,255	730	1,350	1,330
313	Usual place of work	740	710	1,140	640	1,085	1,200
314	At home	85	65	50	65	175	65
315	Outside Canada	-	-	-	-	-	10
316	No fixed workplace address	50	50	65	20	85	65
317	**Total employed labour force 15 years and over with usual place of work or no fixed workplace address**	**1,720**	**1,790**	**2,425**	**1,465**	**2,720**	**2,830**
	by mode of transportation						
318	Males	935	1,030	1,220	810	1,555	1,570
319	Car, truck, van, as driver	780	875	975	685	1,290	1,305
320	Car, truck, van, as passenger	40	45	60	35	80	40
321	Public transit	70	85	120	50	75	145
322	Walked	35	20	20	25	100	70
323	Other method	10	-	45	10	10	15
324	Females	785	760	1,200	660	1,170	1,260
325	Car, truck, van, as driver	605	540	905	490	850	765
326	Car, truck, van, as passenger	60	75	120	65	85	40
327	Public transit	125	95	165	95	155	315
328	Walked	-	50	15	-	80	115
329	Other method	-	10	-	-	-	25
330	**Total population 15 years and over who worked since January 1, 2000**	**2,200**	**2,165**	**2,855**	**1,775**	**3,425**	**3,360**
	by language used at work						
331	Single responses	2,080	2,005	2,630	1,590	3,260	2,985
332	English	2,075	1,980	2,585	1,595	3,240	2,930
333	French	-	-	-	-	-	-
334	Non-official languages (5)	10	25	40	-	20	55
335	Chinese, n.o.s.	-	-	-	-	-	-
336	Cantonese	-	-	-	-	-	-
337	Other languages (6)	10	25	30	-	20	50
338	Multiple responses	120	155	225	185	165	375
339	English and French	25	20	25	30	40	155
340	English and non-official language	95	130	195	155	125	205
341	French and non-official language	-	-	-	-	-	-
342	English, French and non-official language	-	-	-	-	-	15
	DWELLING AND HOUSEHOLD CHARACTERISTICS						
343	**Total number of occupied private dwellings**	**1,335**	**1,090**	**1,675**	**1,220**	**1,960**	**2,255**
	by tenure						
344	Owned	1,210	1,000	1,525	1,115	1,855	250
345	Rented	125	85	150	100	110	2,010
346	Band housing	-	-	-	-	-	-
	by structural type of dwelling						
347	Single-detached house	1,120	930	1,140	900	1,765	20
348	Semi-detached house	-	130	140	20	165	-
349	Row house	175	-	270	70	-	125
350	Apartment, detached duplex	25	10	-	-	-	-
351	Apartment, building that has five or more storeys	-	-	125	220	10	2,110
352	Apartment, building that has fewer than five storeys (38)	10	20	-	-	20	-
353	Other single-attached house	-	-	-	-	10	-
354	Movable dwelling (39)	-	-	-	-	-	-

Tableau 1. Certaines caractéristiques des secteurs de recensement, recensement de 2001 – Données intégrales et données-échantillon (20 %)

Toronto 0511.02	Toronto 0512 ◆	Toronto 0513.01 ◆	Toronto 0513.02	Toronto 0513.03	Toronto 0513.04	Caractéristiques	N°
						CARACTÉRISTIQUES DE LA POPULATION	
						selon la profession basée sur la CNP-S de 2001 - fin	
90	115	235	140	70	80	E Sciences sociales, enseignement, administration publique et religion	300
15	50	105	25	10	30	F Arts, culture, sports et loisirs	301
375	395	375	470	240	250	G Ventes et services	302
55	25	25	35	-	55	H Métiers, transport et machinerie	303
10	10	10	-	-	-	I Professions propres au secteur primaire	304
130	225	75	220	100	45	J Transformation, fabrication et services d'utilité publique	305
2,660	**3,450**	**3,990**	**3,410**	**1,545**	**2,280**	**Population active occupée totale de 15 ans et plus**	306
						selon le lieu de travail	
1,465	1,905	2,080	1,855	850	1,280	Hommes	307
1,150	1,535	1,725	1,470	710	1,040	Lieu habituel de travail	308
90	60	140	65	25	50	À domicile	309
-	10	40	-	10	10	En dehors du Canada	310
225	300	175	320	105	190	Sans adresse de travail fixe	311
1,195	1,540	1,910	1,560	700	1,000	Femmes	312
1,085	1,435	1,605	1,410	640	920	Lieu habituel de travail	313
50	50	220	50	40	45	À domicile	314
-	15	20	10	-	10	En dehors du Canada	315
60	40	55	95	25	25	Sans adresse de travail fixe	316
2,520	**3,310**	**3,565**	**3,290**	**1,480**	**2,165**	**Population active occupée totale de 15 ans et plus ayant un lieu habituel de travail ou sans adresse de travail fixe**	317
						selon le mode de transport	
1,370	1,835	1,905	1,785	815	1,225	Hommes	318
1,150	1,395	1,630	1,455	585	1,060	Automobile, camion ou fourgonnette, en tant que conducteur	319
65	95	60	80	35	45	Automobile, camion ou fourgonnette, en tant que passager	320
90	290	160	205	155	110	Transport en commun	321
30	25	25	35	15	15	À pied	322
35	25	20	10	25	-	Autre moyen	323
1,145	1,470	1,660	1,505	665	945	Femmes	324
800	780	1,155	855	310	700	Automobile, camion ou fourgonnette, en tant que conductrice	325
190	110	165	190	95	75	Automobile, camion ou fourgonnette, en tant que passagère	326
120	465	290	365	175	160	Transport en commun	327
20	85	35	85	60	10	À pied	328
15	30	10	10	20	-	Autre moyen	329
3,085	**4,050**	**4,415**	**3,835**	**1,755**	**2,525**	**Population totale de 15 ans et plus ayant travaillé depuis le 1er janvier 2000**	330
						selon la langue utilisée au travail	
2,790	3,560	3,870	3,305	1,610	2,325	Réponses uniques	331
2,730	3,520	3,835	3,245	1,585	2,305	Anglais	332
10	-	10	-	-	-	Français	333
50	40	30	55	25	20	Langues non officielles (5)	334
-	-	-	-	-	-	Chinois, n.d.a.	335
-	-	15	-	-	-	Cantonais	336
50	40	20	55	25	20	Autres langues (6)	337
295	490	545	530	150	200	Réponses multiples	338
65	45	135	50	25	40	Anglais et français	339
230	430	410	470	125	155	Anglais et langue non officielle	340
-	-	-	-	-	-	Français et langue non officielle	341
-	15	-	10	-	-	Anglais, français et langue non officielle	342
						CARACTÉRISTIQUES DES LOGEMENTS ET DES MÉNAGES	
1,785	**2,480**	**2,285**	**2,335**	**1,140**	**1,160**	**Nombre total de logements privés occupés**	343
						selon le mode d'occupation	
1,075	925	1,850	1,070	370	1,045	Possédé	344
710	1,555	440	1,265	770	110	Loué	345
-	-	-	-	-	-	Logement de bande	346
						selon le type de construction résidentielle	
680	830	1,350	565	265	665	Maison individuelle non attenante	347
345	-	135	305	-	495	Maison jumelée	348
135	-	330	-	-	-	Maison en rangée	349
15	-	-	10	-	-	Appartement, duplex non attenant	350
605	1,460	405	1,385	870	-	Appartement, immeuble de cinq étages ou plus	351
10	185	75	70	-	-	Appartement, immeuble de moins de cinq étages (38)	352
-	-	-	10	-	-	Autre maison individuelle attenante	353
-	-	-	-	-	-	Logement mobile (39)	354

Table 1. Selected Characteristics for Census Tracts, 2001 Census – 100% Data and 20% Sample Data

No.	Characteristics	Toronto 0507	Toronto 0508	Toronto 0509.01	Toronto 0509.02	Toronto 0510	Toronto 0511.01
	DWELLING AND HOUSEHOLD CHARACTERISTICS						
	by condition of dwelling						
355	Regular maintenance only	920	680	1,210	800	1,325	1,445
356	Minor repairs	355	315	360	370	530	615
357	Major repairs	65	100	100	40	110	200
	by period of construction						
358	Before 1946	185	80	80	65	50	15
359	1946-1960	670	615	540	625	925	130
360	1961-1970	205	260	360	85	635	710
361	1971-1980	225	75	190	310	220	850
362	1981-1990	55	70	40	70	90	485
363	1991-2001 (20)	10	-	460	65	40	65
364	Average number of rooms per dwelling	7.4	7.0	6.8	7.0	7.5	4.1
365	Average number of bedrooms per dwelling	3.1	3.1	2.8	2.9	3.2	1.6
366	Average value of dwelling $	309,347	234,458	209,782	267,891	277,790	159,314
367	**Total number of private households**	**1,340**	**1,095**	**1,675**	**1,215**	**1,960**	**2,255**
	by household size						
368	1 person	195	155	315	255	280	785
369	2 persons	490	310	505	460	660	760
370	3 persons	260	210	330	205	360	365
371	4-5 persons	360	360	475	265	580	315
372	6 or more persons	30	55	50	35	90	30
	by household type						
373	One-family households	1,075	850	1,220	900	1,585	1,310
374	Multiple-family households	25	50	90	45	50	25
375	Non-family households	235	185	360	270	330	920
376	Number of persons in private households	3,660	3,315	4,710	3,145	5,735	4,930
377	Average number of persons in private households	2.7	3.0	2.8	2.6	2.9	2.2
378	Average number of persons per room	0.4	0.4	0.4	0.4	0.4	0.5
379	Tenant households in non-farm, non-reserve private dwellings (40)	125	90	150	100	110	1,980
380	Average gross rent $ (40)	1,231	1,045	1,127	1,385	906	951
381	Tenant households spending 30% or more of household income on gross rent (40) (41)	45	50	55	40	40	725
382	Tenant households spending from 30% to 99% of household income on gross rent (40) (41)	45	50	40	40	35	540
383	Owner households in non-farm, non-reserve private dwellings (42)	1,210	1,005	1,525	1,115	1,855	245
384	Average owner's major payments $ (42)	1,110	937	1,042	964	890	1,125
385	Owner households spending 30% or more of household income on owner's major payments (41) (42)	220	115	335	170	245	100
386	Owner households spending from 30% to 99% of household income on owner's major payments (41) (42)	195	90	320	145	245	70
	CENSUS FAMILY CHARACTERISTICS						
387	**Total number of census families in private households**	**1,130**	**955**	**1,400**	**995**	**1,695**	**1,360**
	by census family structure and size						
388	Total couple families	1,005	835	1,190	840	1,540	1,070
389	Total families of married couples	895	770	1,045	765	1,460	860
390	Without children at home	390	255	390	375	560	300
391	With children at home	505	515	655	390	900	555
392	1 child	200	160	315	130	310	280
393	2 children	215	255	215	205	410	230
394	3 or more children	90	105	130	55	180	45
395	Total families of common-law couples	110	65	145	80	85	210
396	Without children at home	40	30	100	40	50	165
397	With children at home	70	35	40	35	30	40
398	1 child	25	35	20	20	10	15
399	2 children	40	-	15	15	20	30
400	3 or more children	-	10	10	-	-	-
401	Total lone-parent families	130	115	215	150	155	290
402	Female parent	120	85	175	110	125	250
403	1 child	90	70	125	85	90	195
404	2 children	30	10	25	20	35	40
405	3 or more children	-	10	20	-	-	10

Tableau 1. Certaines caractéristiques des secteurs de recensement, recensement de 2001 – Données intégrales et données-échantillon (20 %)

Toronto 0511.02	Toronto 0512 ◆	Toronto 0513.01 ◆	Toronto 0513.02	Toronto 0513.03	Toronto 0513.04	Caractéristiques	N°
						CARACTÉRISTIQUES DES LOGEMENTS ET DES MÉNAGES	
						selon l'état du logement	
1,115	1,680	1,700	1,625	720	840	Entretien régulier seulement	355
485	575	455	560	315	285	Réparations mineures	356
185	225	135	150	100	35	Réparations majeures	357
						selon la période de construction	
40	105	40	20	35	10	Avant 1946	358
200	390	105	270	115	35	1946-1960	359
840	1,035	130	475	405	210	1961-1970	360
620	485	905	990	480	770	1971-1980	361
75	290	890	340	95	120	1981-1990	362
10	170	215	230	10	15	1991-2001 (20)	363
6.4	5.3	7.5	5.5	5.3	7.7	Nombre moyen de pièces par logement	364
2.7	2.1	3.2	2.4	2.2	3.4	Nombre moyen de chambres à coucher par logement	365
242,843	267,339	318,840	230,239	358,687	277,376	Valeur moyenne du logement $	366
1,785	**2,480**	**2,290**	**2,335**	**1,140**	**1,155**	**Nombre total de logements privés**	367
						selon la taille du ménage	
250	550	365	525	275	75	1 personne	368
505	720	635	575	330	290	2 personnes	369
400	465	435	445	175	220	3 personnes	370
530	640	720	670	285	445	4-5 personnes	371
95	110	135	120	65	120	6 personnes ou plus	372
						selon le genre de ménage	
1,415	1,760	1,765	1,645	790	925	Ménages unifamiliaux	373
75	60	85	115	60	110	Ménages multifamiliaux	374
290	670	435	575	290	120	Ménages non familiaux	375
5,340	6,815	6,840	6,625	3,145	4,055	Nombre de personnes dans les ménages privés	376
3.0	2.7	3.0	2.8	2.8	3.5	Nombre moyen de personnes dans les ménages privés	377
0.5	0.5	0.4	0.5	0.5	0.5	Nombre moyen de personnes par pièce	378
700	1,545	435	1,260	770	110	Ménages locataires dans les logements privés non agricoles hors réserve (40)	379
853	782	1,056	749	843	810	Loyer brut moyen $ (40)	380
310	535	125	545	350	40	Ménages locataires consacrant 30 % ou plus du revenu du ménage au loyer brut (40) (41)	381
245	385	100	415	265	30	Ménages locataires consacrant de 30 % à 99 % du revenu du ménage au loyer brut (40) (41)	382
1,075	920	1,850	1,070	365	1,050	Ménages propriétaires dans les logements privés non agricoles hors réserve (42)	383
966	1,007	1,219	968	1,183	1,110	Principales dépenses de propriété moyennes $ (42)	384
165	250	360	215	65	170	Ménages propriétaires consacrant 30 % ou plus du revenu du ménage aux principales dépenses de propriété (41) (42)	385
140	210	295	190	55	145	Ménages propriétaires consacrant de 30 % à 99 % du revenu du ménage aux principales dépenses de propriété (41) (42)	386
						CARACTÉRISTIQUES DES FAMILLES DE RECENSEMENT	
1,570	**1,880**	**1,935**	**1,880**	**905**	**1,160**	**Total des familles de recensement dans les ménages privés**	387
						selon la structure et la taille de la famille de recensement	
1,280	1,615	1,735	1,530	710	1,060	Total des familles avec conjoints	388
1,155	1,480	1,640	1,430	630	1,025	Total des familles avec couples mariés	389
405	515	585	410	230	335	Sans enfants à la maison	390
750	965	1,055	1,015	405	690	Avec enfants à la maison	391
300	385	370	385	125	225	1 enfant	392
330	350	440	495	195	315	2 enfants	393
125	235	245	140	85	145	3 enfants ou plus	394
125	135	95	100	75	35	Total des familles en union libre	395
40	80	55	55	55	25	Sans enfants à la maison	396
85	50	40	45	20	15	Avec enfants à la maison	397
35	-	20	30	-	10	1 enfant	398
45	40	10	15	10	-	2 enfants	399
10	10	15	-	10	-	3 enfants ou plus	400
290	260	200	350	195	100	Total des familles monoparentales	401
225	215	155	290	160	80	Parent de sexe féminin	402
130	120	75	205	105	55	1 enfant	403
45	85	50	40	55	20	2 enfants	404
50	10	35	40	-	-	3 enfants ou plus	405

Table 1. Selected Characteristics for Census Tracts, 2001 Census – 100% Data and 20% Sample Data

No.	Characteristics	Toronto 0507	Toronto 0508	Toronto 0509.01	Toronto 0509.02	Toronto 0510	Toronto 0511.01
	CENSUS FAMILY CHARACTERISTICS						
	by census family structure and size - concluded						
406	Male parent	10	25	40	40	35	35
407	1 child	-	25	30	30	30	30
408	2 children	10	10	10	10	-	10
409	3 or more children	-	-	-	-	-	-
410	**Total number of children at home**	**1,200**	**1,190**	**1,550**	**970**	**2,005**	**1,340**
	by age groups						
411	Under 6 years	225	235	255	180	340	465
412	6-14 years	440	330	560	345	635	420
413	15-17 years	130	150	160	100	225	110
414	18-24 years	205	260	275	195	385	255
415	25 years and over	215	210	305	160	420	85
416	Average number of children at home per census family (43)	1.1	1.3	1.1	1.0	1.2	1.0
417	**Total number of persons in private households**	**3,660**	**3,315**	**4,710**	**3,145**	**5,735**	**4,930**
	by census family status and living arrangements						
418	Number of non-family persons	320	330	565	340	495	1,160
419	Living with relatives (44)	75	95	105	55	115	105
420	Living with non-relatives only	45	80	150	35	100	260
421	Living alone	195	155	315	250	275	790
422	Number of family persons	3,340	2,985	4,145	2,805	5,235	3,770
423	Average number of persons per census family	3.0	3.1	3.0	2.8	3.1	2.8
424	**Total number of persons 65 years and over**	**665**	**415**	**655**	**710**	**1,070**	**270**
425	Number of non-family persons 65 years and over	135	120	145	155	265	130
426	Living with relatives (44)	30	30	20	-	70	20
427	Living with non-relatives only	10	20	15	10	10	-
428	Living alone	90	75	110	135	185	110
429	Number of family persons 65 years and over	535	295	515	555	805	145
	ECONOMIC FAMILY CHARACTERISTICS						
430	**Total number of economic families in private households**	**1,130**	**920**	**1,340**	**955**	**1,650**	**1,355**
	by size of family						
431	2 persons	490	325	530	460	640	670
432	3 persons	260	200	315	195	345	340
433	4 persons	260	230	285	210	425	245
434	5 or more persons	120	165	205	85	240	100
435	Total number of persons in economic families	3,415	3,075	4,250	2,855	5,355	3,880
436	Average number of persons per economic family	3.0	3.3	3.2	3.0	3.2	2.9
437	Total number of unattached individuals	250	240	460	285	380	1,050
	2000 INCOME CHARACTERISTICS						
	Population 15 years and over by sex and total income groups in 2000						
438	Total - Both sexes	3,000	2,750	3,895	2,625	4,760	4,055
439	Without income	75	50	120	65	140	250
440	With income	2,925	2,700	3,775	2,560	4,620	3,800
441	Under $1,000 (45)	95	110	50	80	160	195
442	$ 1,000 - $ 2,999	90	115	70	65	135	255
443	$ 3,000 - $ 4,999	65	115	105	105	115	95
444	$ 5,000 - $ 6,999	80	120	150	40	135	80
445	$ 7,000 - $ 9,999	150	150	235	135	240	140
446	$10,000 - $11,999	75	100	205	60	230	180
447	$12,000 - $14,999	230	135	225	155	250	225
448	$15,000 - $19,999	195	200	405	180	430	355
449	$20,000 - $24,999	220	230	285	180	270	355
450	$25,000 - $29,999	155	165	330	160	195	265
451	$30,000 - $34,999	200	245	270	220	385	335
452	$35,000 - $39,999	195	165	270	90	365	240
453	$40,000 - $44,999	135	170	195	150	320	255
454	$45,000 - $49,999	160	90	300	100	265	175
455	$50,000 - $59,999	235	210	330	195	285	340
456	$60,000 and over	640	385	345	635	850	310
457	Average income $ (46)	43,090	31,084	31,675	40,746	39,892	29,334
458	Median income $ (46)	31,203	27,272	27,112	32,078	31,555	25,224
459	Standard error of average income $ (46)	2,218	936	883	1,695	1,544	842

Tableau 1. Certaines caractéristiques des secteurs de recensement, recensement de 2001 – Données intégrales et données-échantillon (20 %)

Toronto 0511.02	Toronto 0512 ◆	Toronto 0513.01 ◆	Toronto 0513.02	Toronto 0513.03	Toronto 0513.04	Caractéristiques	N°
						CARACTÉRISTIQUES DES FAMILLES DE RECENSEMENT	
						selon la structure et la taille de la famille de recensement – fin	
65	50	45	60	35	20	Parent de sexe masculin	406
25	15	20	30	25	10	1 enfant	407
25	35	15	25	-	10	2 enfants	408
20	10	10	10	-	-	3 enfants ou plus	409
2,010	**2,350**	**2,475**	**2,390**	**1,145**	**1,495**	**Nombre total d'enfants à la maison**	410
						selon les groupes d'âge	
470	550	335	545	300	190	Moins de 6 ans	411
715	745	795	785	465	415	6-14 ans	412
165	220	215	235	105	185	15-17 ans	413
380	435	735	495	190	385	18-24 ans	414
275	395	390	335	80	325	25 ans et plus	415
1.3	1.2	1.3	1.3	1.3	1.3	Nombre moyen d'enfants à la maison par famille de recensement (43)	416
5,345	**6,815**	**6,840**	**6,625**	**3,145**	**4,055**	**Nombre total de personnes dans les ménages privés**	417
						selon la situation des particuliers dans la famille de recensement et des particuliers dans le ménage	
480	975	690	825	390	335	Nombre de personnes hors famille de recensement	418
135	250	150	150	95	125	Vivant avec des personnes apparentées (44)	419
95	180	175	150	20	140	Vivant avec des personnes non apparentées uniquement	420
255	550	370	525	275	75	Vivant seules	421
4,860	5,840	6,150	5,800	2,755	3,720	Nombre de personnes membres d'une famille	422
3.1	3.1	3.2	3.1	3.0	3.2	Nombre moyen de personnes par famille de recensement	423
555	**765**	**765**	**725**	**260**	**495**	**Nombre total de personnes de 65 ans et plus**	424
125	220	260	235	95	125	Nombre de personnes hors famille de recensement de 65 ans et plus	425
55	60	90	70	15	85	Vivant avec des personnes apparentées (44)	426
-	10	15	10	-	15	Vivant avec des personnes non apparentées uniquement	427
70	150	155	160	80	25	Vivant seules	428
435	545	510	485	165	370	Nombre de personnes membres d'une famille de 65 ans et plus	429
						CARACTÉRISTIQUES DES FAMILLES ÉCONOMIQUES	
1,505	**1,875**	**1,875**	**1,780**	**855**	**1,040**	**Nombre total de familles économiques dans les ménages privés**	430
						selon la taille de la famille	
510	695	620	575	320	260	2 personnes	431
380	445	420	435	175	230	3 personnes	432
370	430	505	505	190	310	4 personnes	433
245	305	330	265	160	240	5 personnes ou plus	434
4,995	6,090	6,300	5,950	2,845	3,840	Nombre total de personnes dans les familles économiques	435
3.3	3.2	3.4	3.3	3.4	3.7	Nombre moyen de personnes par famille économique	436
350	725	540	675	300	210	Nombre total de personnes hors famille économique	437
						CARACTÉRISTIQUES DU REVENU DE 2000	
						Population de 15 ans et plus selon le sexe et les tranches de revenu total en 2000	
4,160	5,520	5,715	5,300	2,600	3,445	Total - Les deux sexes	438
240	320	245	280	390	185	Sans revenu	439
3,925	5,200	5,470	5,020	2,210	3,260	Avec un revenu	440
215	285	165	270	100	255	Moins de 1 000 $ (45)	441
165	245	250	240	140	115	1 000 $ - 2 999 $	442
145	175	190	260	110	120	3 000 $ - 4 999 $	443
175	285	185	230	110	50	5 000 $ - 6 999 $	444
235	260	310	335	120	155	7 000 $ - 9 999 $	445
165	270	140	195	75	130	10 000 $ - 11 999 $	446
270	340	260	330	100	230	12 000 $ - 14 999 $	447
385	490	430	485	205	335	15 000 $ - 19 999 $	448
300	360	335	410	210	165	20 000 $ - 24 999 $	449
250	540	350	500	205	290	25 000 $ - 29 999 $	450
310	480	455	450	190	220	30 000 $ - 34 999 $	451
275	365	310	340	155	240	35 000 $ - 39 999 $	452
250	270	305	230	70	205	40 000 $ - 44 999 $	453
195	170	205	145	60	80	45 000 $ - 49 999 $	454
260	255	430	270	125	255	50 000 $ - 59 999 $	455
330	395	1,160	325	235	420	60 000 $ et plus	456
28,185	27,459	44,463	27,593	33,411	32,843	Revenu moyen $ (46)	457
22,725	22,855	30,333	21,257	22,837	26,026	Revenu médian $ (46)	458
798	804	1,658	1,486	2,100	1,284	Erreur type de revenu moyen $ (46)	459

Table 1. Selected Characteristics for Census Tracts, 2001 Census – 100% Data and 20% Sample Data

No.	Characteristics	Toronto 0507	Toronto 0508	Toronto 0509.01	Toronto 0509.02	Toronto 0510	Toronto 0511.01
	2000 INCOME CHARACTERISTICS						
	Population 15 years and over by sex and total income groups in 2000 – concluded						
460	Total - Males	1,470	1,400	1,890	1,305	2,335	2,050
461	Without income	40	10	60	15	25	100
462	With income	1,435	1,390	1,835	1,295	2,305	1,955
463	Under $1,000 (45)	45	30	40	40	95	85
464	$ 1,000 - $ 2,999	45	55	10	15	65	105
465	$ 3,000 - $ 4,999	30	40	30	45	35	40
466	$ 5,000 - $ 6,999	20	55	65	-	65	30
467	$ 7,000 - $ 9,999	60	40	80	55	45	40
468	$10,000 - $11,999	30	30	100	15	70	90
469	$12,000 - $14,999	50	50	85	70	60	105
470	$15,000 - $19,999	110	105	155	80	250	150
471	$20,000 - $24,999	70	110	95	100	135	150
472	$25,000 - $29,999	80	60	155	60	55	145
473	$30,000 - $34,999	100	130	130	110	160	195
474	$35,000 - $39,999	105	95	115	40	215	105
475	$40,000 - $44,999	70	100	125	95	235	160
476	$45,000 - $49,999	70	50	185	50	175	110
477	$50,000 - $59,999	110	150	225	115	145	230
478	$60,000 and over	440	285	230	400	505	215
479	Average income $ (46)	51,891	37,338	36,737	46,319	46,236	34,005
480	Median income $ (46)	36,961	34,476	32,461	40,086	36,695	30,108
481	Standard error of average income $ (46)	3,805	1,364	1,453	2,644	2,537	1,350
482	Total - Females	1,530	1,350	2,005	1,320	2,420	2,000
483	Without income	40	40	60	50	115	150
484	With income	1,495	1,310	1,940	1,270	2,310	1,850
485	Under $1,000 (45)	50	75	10	35	65	115
486	$ 1,000 - $ 2,999	50	60	60	50	65	150
487	$ 3,000 - $ 4,999	35	75	70	60	80	55
488	$ 5,000 - $ 6,999	60	65	80	35	75	50
489	$ 7,000 - $ 9,999	90	110	160	80	195	105
490	$10,000 - $11,999	45	65	105	50	160	90
491	$12,000 - $14,999	180	85	140	90	185	120
492	$15,000 - $19,999	90	90	250	100	185	200
493	$20,000 - $24,999	150	120	195	85	135	210
494	$25,000 - $29,999	75	105	175	100	140	120
495	$30,000 - $34,999	100	115	140	110	220	145
496	$35,000 - $39,999	90	70	155	55	150	135
497	$40,000 - $44,999	70	65	70	60	80	100
498	$45,000 - $49,999	90	45	115	50	90	60
499	$50,000 - $59,999	125	60	100	70	135	110
500	$60,000 and over	195	95	120	235	345	95
501	Average income $ (46)	34,636	24,445	26,899	35,072	33,547	24,403
502	Median income $ (46)	24,819	20,217	22,625	26,082	24,993	21,281
503	Standard error of average income $ (46)	2,242	1,166	984	2,073	1,740	951
	by composition of total income						
504	Total - Composition of income in 2000 % (47)	100.0	100.0	100.0	100.0	100.0	100.0
505	Employment income %	77.6	82.7	82.1	68.3	77.6	87.7
506	Government transfer payments %	7.7	9.3	10.6	9.8	8.1	7.5
507	Other %	14.8	8.2	7.2	21.8	14.2	4.7
	Population 15 years and over with employment income in 2000 by sex and work activity						
508	Both sexes with employment income (48)	2,180	2,105	2,850	1,685	3,420	3,130
509	Average employment income $	44,843	32,843	34,452	42,293	41,887	31,257
510	Standard error of average employment income $	2,820	1,069	1,059	2,074	1,816	938
511	Worked full year, full time (49)	1,250	1,230	1,850	940	1,945	1,770
512	Average employment income $	58,329	44,942	42,802	57,745	55,342	39,942
513	Standard error of average employment income $	4,471	1,256	1,297	2,943	2,313	1,144
514	Worked part year or part time (50)	880	845	910	690	1,370	1,290
515	Average employment income $	26,470	16,232	17,834	23,657	24,536	20,261
516	Standard error of average employment income $	2,535	1,172	1,261	2,099	2,785	1,367
517	Males with employment income (48)	1,115	1,155	1,445	885	1,855	1,680
518	Average employment income $	52,241	37,772	38,614	48,431	47,314	35,860
519	Standard error of average employment income $	4,706	1,471	1,663	3,339	3,012	1,466
520	Worked full year, full time (49)	705	730	995	525	1,180	1,020
521	Average employment income $	62,836	48,168	46,664	61,011	59,147	43,405
522	Standard error of average employment income $	6,931	1,592	1,961	4,524	3,415	1,682
523	Worked part year or part time (50)	400	405	400	320	615	645
524	Average employment income $	34,221	20,565	20,547	31,033	27,299	24,425
525	Standard error of average employment income $	4,863	2,040	2,409	4,013	5,921	2,456

Tableau 1. Certaines caractéristiques des secteurs de recensement, recensement de 2001 – Données intégrales et données-échantillon (20 %)

Toronto 0511.02	Toronto 0512 ◆	Toronto 0513.01 ◆	Toronto 0513.02	Toronto 0513.03	Toronto 0513.04	Caractéristiques	N°
						CARACTÉRISTIQUES DU REVENU DE 2000	
						Population de 15 ans et plus selon le sexe et les tranches de revenu total en 2000 – fin	
2,055	2,730	2,795	2,550	1,240	1,705	Total - Hommes	460
80	125	85	115	175	50	Sans revenu	461
1,975	2,610	2,710	2,435	1,070	1,655	Avec un revenu	462
115	90	60	100	65	70	Moins de 1 000 $ (45)	463
60	100	75	50	50	55	1 000 $ - 2 999 $	464
60	70	95	90	40	55	3 000 $ - 4 999 $	465
50	100	60	90	35	20	5 000 $ - 6 999 $	466
80	110	85	135	45	55	7 000 $ - 9 999 $	467
85	125	45	90	25	65	10 000 $ - 11 999 $	468
130	110	110	100	45	95	12 000 $ - 14 999 $	469
155	180	245	170	70	125	15 000 $ - 19 999 $	470
185	150	160	190	70	125	20 000 $ - 24 999 $	471
95	275	110	295	140	100	25 000 $ - 29 999 $	472
110	265	205	205	125	120	30 000 $ - 34 999 $	473
115	220	155	220	75	100	35 000 $ - 39 999 $	474
150	180	140	135	45	140	40 000 $ - 44 999 $	475
140	120	120	110	25	70	45 000 $ - 49 999 $	476
195	205	185	230	70	160	50 000 $ - 59 999 $	477
265	310	865	225	160	305	60 000 $ et plus	478
33,592	34,537	58,624	35,581	42,483	40,800	Revenu moyen $ (46)	479
28,328	29,526	37,117	28,402	28,476	31,806	Revenu médian $ (46)	480
1,273	1,338	2,969	2,852	3,741	2,058	Erreur type de revenu moyen $ (46)	481
2,105	2,790	2,925	2,750	1,355	1,740	Total - Femmes	482
150	195	165	165	215	130	Sans revenu	483
1,955	2,595	2,760	2,585	1,145	1,605	Avec un revenu	484
95	200	105	170	40	185	Moins de 1 000 $ (45)	485
110	145	175	190	90	60	1 000 $ - 2 999 $	486
80	110	95	165	75	70	3 000 $ - 4 999 $	487
125	190	125	135	75	30	5 000 $ - 6 999 $	488
160	155	225	200	75	100	7 000 $ - 9 999 $	489
80	145	100	105	50	60	10 000 $ - 11 999 $	490
140	230	145	230	60	135	12 000 $ - 14 999 $	491
235	310	185	320	140	210	15 000 $ - 19 999 $	492
115	210	175	220	140	40	20 000 $ - 24 999 $	493
155	270	235	205	65	190	25 000 $ - 29 999 $	494
200	210	250	245	60	100	30 000 $ - 34 999 $	495
165	145	150	125	80	140	35 000 $ - 39 999 $	496
100	90	165	100	30	70	40 000 $ - 44 999 $	497
50	55	85	30	35	15	45 000 $ - 49 999 $	498
65	55	245	45	50	95	50 000 $ - 59 999 $	499
65	85	300	100	70	115	60 000 $ et plus	500
22,714	20,342	30,554	20,065	24,900	24,649	Revenu moyen $ (46)	501
18,352	17,081	25,477	16,848	18,602	18,406	Revenu médian $ (46)	502
882	745	1,214	767	1,746	1,306	Erreur type de revenu moyen $ (46)	503
						selon la composition du revenu total	
100.0	100.0	100.0	100.0	100.0	100.0	Total - Composition du revenu en 2000 % (47)	504
82.3	80.3	83.4	77.5	74.1	80.4	Revenu d'emploi %	505
9.5	10.3	5.4	11.0	9.0	9.2	Transferts gouvernementaux %	506
8.2	9.4	11.2	11.5	16.8	10.4	Autre %	507
						Population de 15 ans et plus ayant un revenu d'emploi en 2000 selon le sexe et le travail	
2,910	3,890	4,450	3,725	1,660	2,410	Les deux sexes ayant un revenu d'emploi (48)	508
31,303	29,476	45,591	28,825	33,061	35,661	Revenu moyen d'emploi $	509
956	973	1,759	1,195	2,457	1,529	Erreur type de revenu moyen d'emploi $	510
1,675	2,065	2,380	1,975	900	1,425	Ayant travaillé toute l'année à plein temps (49)	511
40,398	38,988	65,024	39,428	48,550	46,811	Revenu moyen d'emploi $	512
1,291	1,310	2,712	1,977	4,255	2,109	Erreur type de revenu moyen d'emploi $	513
1,185	1,710	1,955	1,685	710	925	Ayant travaillé une partie de l'année ou à temps partiel (50)	514
18,798	18,582	22,808	16,965	14,909	19,689	Revenu moyen d'emploi $	515
1,085	1,123	1,429	857	1,222	1,799	Erreur type de revenu moyen d'emploi $	516
1,605	2,140	2,310	1,995	845	1,305	Hommes ayant un revenu d'emploi (48)	517
35,922	35,202	57,750	34,269	43,089	43,048	Revenu moyen d'emploi $	518
1,435	1,522	3,012	2,019	4,260	2,335	Erreur type de revenu moyen d'emploi $	519
1,010	1,275	1,380	1,195	510	805	Ayant travaillé toute l'année à plein temps (49)	520
44,545	43,789	77,979	43,872	59,837	53,710	Revenu moyen d'emploi $	521
1,860	1,855	4,229	3,093	6,710	3,146	Erreur type de revenu moyen d'emploi $	522
570	825	895	760	325	465	Ayant travaillé une partie de l'année ou à temps partiel (50)	523
21,196	21,436	26,359	19,985	17,624	26,133	Revenu moyen d'emploi $	524
1,655	1,990	2,589	1,370	2,186	3,021	Erreur type de revenu moyen d'emploi $	525

Table 1. Selected Characteristics for Census Tracts, 2001 Census – 100% Data and 20% Sample Data

No.	Characteristics	Toronto 0507	Toronto 0508	Toronto 0509.01	Toronto 0509.02	Toronto 0510	Toronto 0511.01
	2000 INCOME CHARACTERISTICS						
	Population 15 years and over with employment income in 2000 by sex and work activity – concluded						
526	Females with employment income (48)	1,065	955	1,405	805	1,565	1,450
527	Average employment income $	37,154	26,874	30,170	35,571	35,462	25,918
528	Standard error of average employment income $	2,898	1,461	1,247	2,246	1,726	1,052
529	Worked full year, full time (49)	545	500	850	410	770	755
530	Average employment income $	52,553	40,219	38,297	53,601	49,496	35,282
531	Standard error of average employment income $	4,965	1,959	1,551	3,079	2,629	1,379
532	Worked part year or part time (50)	480	445	510	365	760	650
533	Average employment income $	20,032	12,270	15,706	17,172	22,308	16,139
534	Standard error of average employment income $	1,901	1,124	1,231	1,817	1,786	1,252
	Census families by structure and family income groups in 2000						
535	Total - All census families	1,130	955	1,405	995	1,695	1,365
536	Under $10,000	-	15	15	35	15	135
537	$ 10,000 - $19,999	30	35	45	25	45	120
538	$ 20,000 - $29,999	50	75	105	70	80	110
539	$ 30,000 - $39,999	100	80	150	40	105	180
540	$ 40,000 - $49,999	100	80	120	75	135	180
541	$ 50,000 - $59,999	110	70	190	115	100	170
542	$ 60,000 - $69,999	95	70	175	60	235	150
543	$ 70,000 - $79,999	65	105	80	75	170	95
544	$ 80,000 - $89,999	75	80	125	75	100	50
545	$ 90,000 - $99,999	60	105	90	50	105	50
546	$100,000 and over	430	235	315	375	615	120
547	Average family income $	99,559	76,443	70,744	89,656	96,991	50,860
548	Median family income $	79,919	76,481	63,918	79,919	77,681	48,047
549	Standard error of average family income $	5,651	2,628	2,060	4,250	4,225	2,022
550	Total - All couple census families (51)	1,000	840	1,190	845	1,535	1,070
551	Under $10,000	-	-	-	10	-	90
552	$ 10,000 - $19,999	20	25	25	15	20	50
553	$ 20,000 - $29,999	45	70	85	55	75	75
554	$ 30,000 - $39,999	70	65	125	25	80	135
555	$ 40,000 - $49,999	75	70	85	60	120	145
556	$ 50,000 - $59,999	90	50	180	100	90	155
557	$ 60,000 - $69,999	85	60	135	50	225	130
558	$ 70,000 - $79,999	55	90	70	60	145	75
559	$ 80,000 - $89,999	80	70	115	70	95	50
560	$ 90,000 - $99,999	60	110	85	40	95	50
561	$100,000 and over	415	225	285	355	585	115
562	Average family income $	105,787	79,507	73,473	96,459	100,926	56,037
563	Median family income $	83,989	78,606	65,660	86,292	80,247	52,139
564	Standard error of average family income $	6,310	2,840	2,228	4,645	4,667	2,356
	Incidence of low income in 2000						
565	Total - Economic families	1,130	920	1,340	955	1,650	1,355
566	Low income	35	60	75	55	85	305
567	Incidence of low income in 2000 % (52)	2.8	6.7	5.8	5.7	5.1	22.8
568	Total - Unattached individuals 15 years and over	245	235	460	285	375	1,050
569	Low income	70	60	150	45	90	255
570	Incidence of low income in 2000 % (52)	27.3	25.8	31.8	15.3	23.8	24.2
571	Total - Population in private households	3,660	3,310	4,710	3,145	5,735	4,925
572	Low income	155	255	375	195	350	1,245
573	Incidence of low income in 2000 % (52)	4.3	7.7	7.9	6.2	6.1	25.3
	Private households by household income groups in 2000						
574	Total - All private households	1,340	1,090	1,670	1,215	1,960	2,260
575	Under $10,000	10	15	20	15	-	210
576	$ 10,000 - $19,999	70	65	105	55	85	230
577	$ 20,000 - $29,999	85	105	125	85	105	195
578	$ 30,000 - $39,999	105	65	150	80	160	330
579	$ 40,000 - $49,999	110	100	145	105	160	290
580	$ 50,000 - $59,999	120	90	165	135	100	300
581	$ 60,000 - $69,999	120	65	230	80	270	250
582	$ 70,000 - $79,999	85	100	100	110	185	125
583	$ 80,000 - $89,999	105	75	105	75	110	70
584	$ 90,000 - $99,999	65	105	100	55	110	65
585	$100,000 and over	455	300	415	420	675	195
586	Average household income $	94,329	76,927	71,378	85,766	93,741	49,298
587	Median household income $	73,495	75,332	63,792	72,751	74,322	45,100
588	Standard error of average household income $	4,957	2,683	2,120	3,630	3,769	1,492

Tableau 1. Certaines caractéristiques des secteurs de recensement, recensement de 2001 – Données intégrales et données-échantillon (20 %)

Toronto 0511.02	Toronto 0512 ◆	Toronto 0513.01 ◆	Toronto 0513.02	Toronto 0513.03	Toronto 0513.04	Caractéristiques	N°
						CARACTÉRISTIQUES DU REVENU DE 2000	
						Population de 15 ans et plus ayant un revenu d'emploi en 2000 selon le sexe et le travail – fin	
1,310	1,755	2,140	1,730	815	1,110	Femmes ayant un revenu d'emploi (48)	526
25,640	22,490	32,452	22,551	22,628	26,992	Revenu moyen d'emploi $	527
1,110	942	1,401	928	1,878	1,617	Erreur type de revenu moyen d'emploi $	528
660	790	995	780	390	620	Ayant travaillé toute l'année à plein temps (49)	529
34,004	31,242	47,036	32,591	33,850	37,812	Revenu moyen d'emploi $	530
1,477	1,380	2,124	1,271	3,447	2,264	Erreur type de revenu moyen d'emploi $	531
615	885	1,065	930	385	465	Ayant travaillé une partie de l'année ou à temps partiel (50)	532
16,579	15,916	19,822	14,491	12,589	13,280	Revenu moyen d'emploi $	533
1,389	1,079	1,460	1,041	1,184	1,500	Erreur type de revenu moyen d'emploi $	534
						Familles de recensement selon la structure et les tranches de revenu de la famille en 2000	
1,570	1,880	1,935	1,875	900	1,160	Total - Toutes les familles de recensement	535
80	130	45	115	85	20	Moins de 10 000 $	536
95	115	65	140	55	10	10 000 $ - 19 999 $	537
145	165	95	225	135	65	20 000 $ - 29 999 $	538
195	205	145	250	125	105	30 000 $ - 39 999 $	539
120	265	80	220	85	90	40 000 $ - 49 999 $	540
150	235	100	155	100	100	50 000 $ - 59 999 $	541
160	250	175	135	75	155	60 000 $ - 69 999 $	542
180	90	130	145	45	95	70 000 $ - 79 999 $	543
160	85	140	160	20	110	80 000 $ - 89 999 $	544
95	45	100	90	20	45	90 000 $ - 99 999 $	545
190	290	865	245	155	355	100 000 $ et plus	546
62,162	62,272	112,775	62,959	70,520	86,437	Revenu moyen des familles $	547
60,029	52,335	89,512	49,197	47,995	74,861	Revenu médian des familles $	548
2,087	2,333	4,538	4,346	6,024	3,539	Erreur type de revenu moyen des familles $	549
1,285	1,615	1,735	1,530	705	1,060	Total - Toutes les familles de recensement comptant un couple (51)	550
60	100	35	65	40	15	Moins de 10 000 $	551
70	90	40	90	35	10	10 000 $ - 19 999 $	552
125	130	85	140	95	50	20 000 $ - 29 999 $	553
90	160	115	185	95	90	30 000 $ - 39 999 $	554
95	230	70	180	75	90	40 000 $ - 49 999 $	555
140	205	75	140	100	70	50 000 $ - 59 999 $	556
125	225	150	115	50	140	60 000 $ - 69 999 $	557
160	85	105	125	45	90	70 000 $ - 79 999 $	558
145	80	120	160	15	110	80 000 $ - 89 999 $	559
85	40	85	90	15	40	90 000 $ - 99 999 $	560
185	275	860	240	145	360	100 000 $ et plus	561
66,013	65,448	119,352	69,518	78,363	89,745	Revenu moyen des familles $	562
64,913	53,670	99,028	55,679	50,719	77,288	Revenu médian des familles $	563
2,338	2,591	4,864	5,109	7,036	3,722	Erreur type de revenu moyen des familles $	564
						Fréquence des unités à faible revenu en 2000	
1,505	1,875	1,875	1,785	855	1,040	Total - Familles économiques	565
260	330	140	325	220	75	Faible revenu	566
17.5	17.5	7.6	18.2	25.7	7.1	Fréquence des unités à faible revenu en 2000 % (52)	567
345	720	540	675	300	200	Total - Personnes hors famille économique de 15 ans et plus	568
150	290	140	335	70	100	Faible revenu	569
42.9	40.4	25.1	49.3	24.8	49.5	Fréquence des unités à faible revenu en 2000 % (52)	570
5,345	6,815	6,840	6,625	3,145	4,045	Total - Population dans les ménages privés	571
1,040	1,460	635	1,410	875	355	Faible revenu	572
19.5	21.4	9.3	21.3	27.9	8.9	Fréquence des unités à faible revenu en 2000 % (52)	573
						Ménages privés selon les tranches de revenu du ménage en 2000	
1,785	2,480	2,290	2,335	1,140	1,155	Total - Tous les ménages privés	574
80	185	60	160	95	40	Moins de 10 000 $	575
150	275	125	290	115	25	10 000 $ - 19 999 $	576
190	270	110	205	150	50	20 000 $ - 29 999 $	577
165	250	215	320	175	70	30 000 $ - 39 999 $	578
135	315	115	325	100	110	40 000 $ - 49 999 $	579
190	275	125	185	160	100	50 000 $ - 59 999 $	580
205	280	175	145	70	105	60 000 $ - 69 999 $	581
160	130	160	155	25	95	70 000 $ - 79 999 $	582
180	100	125	160	45	70	80 000 $ - 89 999 $	583
90	65	120	95	40	60	90 000 $ - 99 999 $	584
240	325	960	285	155	450	100 000 $ et plus	585
61,930	57,573	106,197	59,244	64,444	92,356	Revenu moyen des ménages $	586
57,969	48,110	84,334	45,744	43,052	79,583	Revenu médian des ménages $	587
2,030	2,061	4,172	3,720	5,020	3,836	Erreur type de revenu moyen des ménages $	588

Table 1. Selected Characteristics for Census Tracts, 2001 Census – 100% Data and 20% Sample Data

No.	Characteristics	Toronto 0514.01 A	Toronto 0514.02 A	Toronto 0515.01	Toronto 0515.02	Toronto 0516.01	Toronto 0516.02
	POPULATION CHARACTERISTICS						
1	**Population, 1996 (1)**	**2,581**	**5,923**	**4,738**	**3,446**	**6,115**	**5,278**
2	**Population, 2001 (2)**	**2,451**	**6,342**	**4,683**	**3,886**	**6,082**	**5,214**
3	Population percentage change, 1996-2001	-5.0	7.1	-1.2	12.8	-0.5	-1.2
4	Land area in square kilometres, 2001	3.32	1.93	2.74	1.40	1.45	1.73
5	**Total population - 100% Data (3)**	**2,450**	**6,345**	**4,685**	**3,885**	**6,080**	**5,210**
	by sex and age groups						
6	Male	1,215	3,135	2,335	1,775	3,035	2,620
7	0-4 years	45	250	130	110	205	205
8	5-9 years	70	325	165	125	280	255
9	10-14 years	75	280	190	115	285	245
10	15-19 years	105	285	210	105	295	210
11	20-24 years	105	190	155	90	190	185
12	25-29 years	60	155	125	110	135	110
13	30-34 years	45	200	130	105	170	180
14	35-39 years	70	275	190	160	290	280
15	40-44 years	75	275	175	130	295	325
16	45-49 years	100	270	185	155	315	215
17	50-54 years	120	180	175	115	255	195
18	55-59 years	110	145	150	100	145	100
19	60-64 years	75	120	135	75	70	50
20	65-69 years	50	80	90	75	45	30
21	70-74 years	50	70	70	80	30	25
22	75-79 years	35	25	35	50	15	15
23	80-84 years	15	10	15	35	15	-
24	85 years and over	10	5	10	35	10	5
25	Female	1,235	3,210	2,350	2,110	3,050	2,590
26	0-4 years	55	235	115	85	195	170
27	5-9 years	60	275	175	115	260	275
28	10-14 years	70	300	160	130	280	210
29	15-19 years	90	240	150	120	265	180
30	20-24 years	95	205	150	110	190	150
31	25-29 years	40	205	125	115	130	115
32	30-34 years	50	230	160	130	190	185
33	35-39 years	85	275	200	165	305	325
34	40-44 years	95	265	215	165	360	310
35	45-49 years	120	235	200	140	295	220
36	50-54 years	135	200	165	155	230	150
37	55-59 years	90	150	150	110	125	115
38	60-64 years	70	110	140	95	50	55
39	65-69 years	50	85	95	95	35	50
40	70-74 years	50	65	75	90	40	35
41	75-79 years	45	50	40	90	45	20
42	80-84 years	10	35	10	70	35	10
43	85 years and over	10	40	10	135	15	10
44	**Total population 15 years and over**	**2,075**	**4,675**	**3,740**	**3,205**	**4,580**	**3,855**
	by legal marital status						
45	Never married (single)	585	1,430	1,095	820	1,275	1,120
46	Legally married (and not separated)	1,285	2,690	2,225	1,685	2,875	2,310
47	Separated, but still legally married	30	150	105	100	115	100
48	Divorced	70	200	170	210	160	225
49	Widowed	105	205	145	390	160	100
	by common-law status						
50	Not in a common-law relationship	2,020	4,530	3,615	3,045	4,435	3,660
51	In a common-law relationship	50	150	130	160	150	195
52	**Total population - 20% Sample Data (4)**	**2,425**	**6,300**	**4,680**	**3,620**	**6,080**	**5,215**
	by mother tongue						
53	Single responses	2,410	6,160	4,655	3,585	6,005	5,140
54	English	1,590	2,705	3,550	2,435	4,655	4,065
55	French	35	85	135	60	150	80
56	Non-official languages (5)	785	3,375	975	1,095	1,200	1,000
57	Italian	30	55	40	70	80	95
58	Chinese, n.o.s.	85	90	35	240	35	10
59	Cantonese	35	80	35	30	50	35
60	Portuguese	20	75	60	75	100	55
61	Punjabi	-	275	30	40	100	50
62	Other languages (6)	625	2,795	770	645	840	760
63	Multiple responses	15	135	25	30	75	75
64	English and French	-	20	-	-	-	10
65	English and non-official language	15	115	15	25	70	45
66	French and non-official language	-	-	10	10	10	10
67	English, French and non-official language	-	-	-	-	-	15

See reference material at the end of the publication. – Voir les documents de référence à la fin de la publication.

Tableau 1. Certaines caractéristiques des secteurs de recensement, recensement de 2001 – Données intégrales et données-échantillon (20 %)

Toronto 0516.03	Toronto 0516.04	Toronto 0516.05	Toronto 0516.06	Toronto 0516.08	Toronto 0516.09	Caractéristiques	N°
						CARACTÉRISTIQUES DE LA POPULATION	
6,174	**5,902**	**7,014**	**5,096**	**6,553**	**7,456**	**Population, 1996 (1)**	1
6,041	**6,376**	**6,957**	**5,177**	**6,535**	**7,399**	**Population, 2001 (2)**	2
-2.2	8.0	-0.8	1.6	-0.3	-0.8	Variation en pourcentage de la population, 1996-2001	3
1.12	1.03	1.16	0.91	1.33	2.37	Superficie des terres en kilomètres carrés, 2001	4
6,040	**6,375**	**6,960**	**5,180**	**6,535**	**7,395**	**Population totale – Données intégrales (3)**	5
						selon le sexe et les groupes d'âge	
2,890	3,175	3,450	2,455	3,130	3,640	Sexe masculin	6
175	200	250	190	195	200	0-4 ans	7
240	225	325	225	280	275	5-9 ans	8
235	220	310	205	275	300	10-14 ans	9
220	210	295	165	290	300	15-19 ans	10
200	230	250	180	260	290	20-24 ans	11
200	355	230	130	200	195	25-29 ans	12
220	375	230	185	185	230	30-34 ans	13
295	330	370	235	210	300	35-39 ans	14
300	310	325	240	255	335	40-44 ans	15
215	230	275	165	280	320	45-49 ans	16
210	185	245	185	215	280	50-54 ans	17
135	120	165	115	175	240	55-59 ans	18
80	60	80	65	100	165	60-64 ans	19
55	35	50	40	65	90	65-69 ans	20
45	40	30	35	50	65	70-74 ans	21
30	20	15	45	40	40	75-79 ans	22
20	20	10	30	35	15	80-84 ans	23
15	15	5	20	20	10	85 ans et plus	24
3,155	3,200	3,505	2,720	3,410	3,755	Sexe féminin	25
180	200	250	160	180	185	0-4 ans	26
230	215	280	210	240	245	5-9 ans	27
225	205	305	215	270	295	10-14 ans	28
185	180	270	185	310	275	15-19 ans	29
195	250	235	165	225	270	20-24 ans	30
210	390	220	165	220	220	25-29 ans	31
260	365	275	190	230	220	30-34 ans	32
335	330	385	280	265	355	35-39 ans	33
315	295	355	230	330	375	40-44 ans	34
255	255	310	215	280	335	45-49 ans	35
240	170	235	205	250	320	50-54 ans	36
185	100	150	100	160	235	55-59 ans	37
85	70	85	70	90	165	60-64 ans	38
85	50	55	50	80	110	65-69 ans	39
70	50	45	65	70	65	70-74 ans	40
40	50	30	80	80	45	75-79 ans	41
35	35	10	55	70	25	80-84 ans	42
25	10	10	75	50	25	85 ans et plus	43
4,750	**5,110**	**5,240**	**3,980**	**5,095**	**5,890**	**Population totale de 15 ans et plus**	44
						selon l'état matrimonial légal	
1,485	1,900	1,695	1,110	1,695	1,810	Célibataire (jamais marié(e))	45
2,430	2,330	2,865	2,105	2,595	3,240	Légalement marié(e) (et non séparé(e))	46
215	320	200	155	170	210	Séparé(e), mais toujours légalement marié(e)	47
415	425	345	335	385	420	Divorcé(e)	48
210	145	130	280	245	210	Veuf ou veuve	49
						selon l'union libre	
4,415	4,545	4,905	3,765	4,830	5,585	Ne vivant pas en union libre	50
335	565	335	215	265	305	Vivant en union libre	51
6,040	**6,375**	**6,955**	**5,180**	**6,535**	**7,395**	**Population totale – Données-échantillon (20 %) (4)**	52
						selon la langue maternelle	
5,975	6,295	6,775	5,060	6,380	7,255	Réponses uniques	53
4,690	4,085	4,905	3,735	4,065	5,320	Anglais	54
105	150	90	80	85	135	Français	55
1,180	2,070	1,780	1,245	2,230	1,800	Langues non officielles (5)	56
40	55	40	45	60	35	Italien	57
65	85	15	40	-	80	Chinois, n.d.a.	58
55	30	40	-	35	10	Cantonais	59
95	60	125	65	60	115	Portugais	60
10	55	40	30	25	255	Pendjabi	61
905	1,780	1,520	1,060	2,040	1,305	Autres langues (6)	62
65	80	190	115	155	145	Réponses multiples	63
30	45	-	25	30	25	Anglais et français	64
25	40	175	90	115	100	Anglais et langue non officielle	65
10	-	-	10	15	15	Français et langue non officielle	66
-	-	-	-	-	-	Anglais, français et langue non officielle	67

See reference material at the end of the publication. – Voir les documents de référence à la fin de la publication.

Table 1. Selected Characteristics for Census Tracts, 2001 Census – 100% Data and 20% Sample Data

No.	Characteristics	Toronto 0514.01 A	Toronto 0514.02 A	Toronto 0515.01	Toronto 0515.02	Toronto 0516.01	Toronto 0516.02
	POPULATION CHARACTERISTICS						
	by home language						
68	Single responses	1,965	4,085	4,025	3,035	5,330	4,635
69	English	1,775	2,975	3,840	2,700	5,040	4,265
70	French	-	-	-	-	60	-
71	Non-official languages (5)	190	1,105	190	330	235	360
72	Cantonese	15	45	20	15	-	-
73	Chinese, n.o.s.	10	35	10	110	-	-
74	Italian	-	-	-	15	-	10
75	Punjabi	-	40	10	-	35	-
76	Portuguese	-	-	30	10	30	-
77	Other languages (6)	165	980	130	190	160	340
78	Multiple responses	460	2,210	655	580	750	585
79	English and French	30	30	80	45	75	60
80	English and non-official language	430	2,110	545	510	655	510
81	French and non-official language	-	-	-	-	-	10
82	English, French and non-official language	-	70	30	25	20	10
	by knowledge of official languages						
83	English only	2,085	5,455	4,115	3,085	5,615	4,660
84	French only	-	15	-	15	45	10
85	English and French	300	520	505	440	385	505
86	Neither English nor French	45	310	55	80	40	40
	by knowledge of non-official languages (5) (7)						
87	Italian	100	80	70	110	120	135
88	Cantonese	65	85	45	35	75	35
89	Chinese, n.o.s.	95	85	40	220	50	15
90	Spanish	95	195	60	55	105	180
91	Portuguese	50	80	65	90	120	80
92	Punjabi	35	545	30	40	130	65
93	Tagalog (Pilipino)	25	75	105	110	85	15
	by first official language spoken						
94	English	2,345	5,815	4,460	3,450	5,885	5,035
95	French	30	80	140	65	155	95
96	English and French	10	115	25	25	-	40
97	Neither English nor French	45	290	55	80	35	40
98	Official language minority - (number) (8)	35	135	150	80	155	115
99	Official language minority - (percentage) (8)	1.4	2.1	3.2	2.2	2.5	2.2
	by ethnic origin (9)						
100	Canadian	510	740	1,595	655	1,750	1,185
101	English	620	840	1,360	1,135	1,470	1,305
102	Scottish	350	350	785	665	1,230	840
103	Irish	430	320	780	545	870	865
104	Chinese	230	305	160	345	210	110
105	Italian	210	195	280	210	465	475
106	East Indian	105	890	180	45	435	315
107	French	165	335	390	230	435	505
108	German	120	250	390	245	455	390
109	Portuguese	110	120	135	145	320	250
110	Polish	225	280	290	200	285	325
111	Jewish	10	30	25	30	60	110
112	Jamaican	20	205	55	85	170	200
113	Filipino	20	95	130	110	180	65
114	Ukrainian	150	110	135	105	205	110
	by Aboriginal identity						
115	Total Aboriginal identity population (10)	10	-	10	-	25	15
116	Total non-Aboriginal population	2,420	6,285	4,675	3,615	6,055	5,195
	by Aboriginal origin						
117	Total Aboriginal origins population (11)	10	50	70	30	110	60
118	Total non-Aboriginal population	2,415	6,245	4,610	3,590	5,975	5,155
	by Registered Indian status						
119	Registered Indian (12)	-	10	-	-	15	10
120	Not a Registered Indian	2,425	6,290	4,685	3,620	6,065	5,210

Tableau 1. Certaines caractéristiques des secteurs de recensement, recensement de 2001 – Données intégrales et données-échantillon (20 %)

Toronto 0516.03	Toronto 0516.04	Toronto 0516.05	Toronto 0516.06	Toronto 0516.08	Toronto 0516.09	Caractéristiques	N°
						CARACTÉRISTIQUES DE LA POPULATION	
						selon la langue parlée à la maison	
5,160	4,970	5,540	4,345	5,085	6,095	Réponses uniques	68
4,945	4,405	5,175	3,940	4,445	5,530	Anglais	69
10	45	10	25	10	-	Français	70
210	520	360	380	640	560	Langues non officielles (5)	71
20	15	-	-	15	10	Cantonais	72
40	15	-	-	10	50	Chinois, n.d.a.	73
-	-	-	20	-	-	Italien	74
-	-	25	15	-	140	Pendjabi	75
20	40	-	-	10	20	Portugais	76
130	450	325	340	615	350	Autres langues (6)	77
875	1,410	1,420	830	1,450	1,300	Réponses multiples	78
110	100	80	75	90	120	Anglais et français	79
745	1,275	1,290	760	1,335	1,145	Anglais et langue non officielle	80
10	10	-	-	-	-	Français et langue non officielle	81
10	20	50	-	15	30	Anglais, français et langue non officielle	82
						selon la connaissance des langues officielles	
5,455	5,550	6,410	4,745	5,880	6,505	Anglais seulement	83
-	-	-	-	10	-	Français seulement	84
525	700	525	345	560	765	Anglais et français	85
55	120	25	85	90	120	Ni l'anglais ni le français	86
						selon la connaissance des langues non officielles (5) (7)	
60	65	85	65	105	60	Italien	87
95	40	40	10	40	20	Cantonais	88
45	80	10	35	10	75	Chinois, n.d.a.	89
135	105	185	155	250	220	Espagnol	90
155	65	150	90	65	145	Portugais	91
30	150	120	40	105	325	Pendjabi	92
95	105	100	90	325	215	Tagalog (pilipino)	93
						selon la première langue officielle parlée	
5,855	6,025	6,780	4,980	6,240	7,085	Anglais	94
110	160	85	85	110	140	Français	95
20	70	65	25	105	60	Anglais et français	96
55	125	20	90	85	105	Ni l'anglais ni le français	97
120	195	125	95	160	170	Minorité de langue officielle - (nombre) (8)	98
2.0	3.1	1.8	1.8	2.4	2.3	Minorité de langue officielle - (pourcentage) (8)	99
						selon l'origine ethnique (9)	
1,630	1,490	1,800	1,235	1,720	1,950	Canadien	100
1,420	1,285	1,500	1,190	1,340	1,785	Anglais	101
1,075	780	1,310	945	865	1,160	Écossais	102
905	825	1,255	790	950	1,115	Irlandais	103
260	195	140	140	100	225	Chinois	104
160	290	240	185	220	420	Italien	105
355	575	460	255	315	610	Indien de l'Inde	106
500	470	515	305	375	525	Français	107
450	520	475	305	310	500	Allemand	108
260	125	255	230	170	275	Portugais	109
185	280	530	360	585	530	Polonais	110
25	90	75	100	30	60	Juif	111
310	215	375	440	170	380	Jamaïquain	112
180	110	130	80	415	310	Philippin	113
150	220	185	110	200	310	Ukrainien	114
						selon l'identité autochtone	
15	55	65	10	50	15	Total de la population ayant une identité autochtone (10)	115
6,025	6,320	6,895	5,175	6,485	7,375	Total de la population non autochtone	116
						selon l'origine autochtone	
75	95	140	30	55	70	Total de la population ayant une origine autochtone (11)	117
5,970	6,280	6,815	5,150	6,480	7,325	Total de la population non autochtone	118
						selon le statut d'Indien inscrit	
10	20	45	-	20	10	Oui, Indien inscrit (12)	119
6,030	6,355	6,910	5,175	6,510	7,390	Non, pas un Indien inscrit	120

Table 1. Selected Characteristics for Census Tracts, 2001 Census – 100% Data and 20% Sample Data

No.	Characteristics	Toronto 0514.01 A	Toronto 0514.02 A	Toronto 0515.01	Toronto 0515.02	Toronto 0516.01	Toronto 0516.02
	POPULATION CHARACTERISTICS						
	by visible minority groups						
121	Total visible minority population	520	3,775	785	950	1,390	1,295
122	Chinese	235	340	130	340	180	70
123	South Asian	140	2,030	160	150	615	500
124	Black	10	410	100	210	175	330
125	Filipino	25	100	125	110	175	65
126	Latin American	-	150	20	30	35	45
127	Southeast Asian	-	20	75	-	-	30
128	Arab	-	130	40	50	15	100
129	West Asian	40	265	-	-	35	-
130	Korean	60	30	-	15	10	-
131	Japanese	-	80	-	-	10	20
132	Visible minority, n.i.e. (13)	-	175	95	10	145	35
133	Multiple visible minorities (14)	-	45	35	50	-	95
	by citizenship						
134	Canadian citizenship (15)	2,305	4,470	4,270	3,440	5,700	4,815
135	Citizenship other than Canadian	125	1,825	410	180	375	400
	by place of birth of respondent						
136	Non-immigrant population	1,535	2,540	3,355	2,325	4,360	3,615
137	Born in province of residence	1,320	2,120	2,740	1,995	3,690	3,080
138	Immigrant population (16)	895	3,605	1,310	1,290	1,725	1,595
139	United States	45	90	30	55	50	35
140	Central and South America	35	200	10	75	90	135
141	Caribbean and Bermuda	15	230	100	125	210	230
142	United Kingdom	110	90	210	185	245	200
143	Other Europe (17)	275	600	500	390	380	470
144	Africa	60	135	80	25	45	55
145	Asia and the Middle East	350	2,260	380	430	690	465
146	Oceania and other (18)	10	-	-	10	15	-
147	Non-permanent residents (19)	-	150	15	-	-	-
148	**Total immigrant population**	**895**	**3,605**	**1,310**	**1,290**	**1,720**	**1,595**
	by period of immigration						
149	Before 1961	155	175	195	150	125	130
150	1961-1970	180	190	245	265	290	130
151	1971-1980	220	470	260	285	410	355
152	1981-1990	155	580	275	265	330	495
153	1991-2001 (20)	185	2,195	335	320	565	485
154	1991-1995	65	490	150	225	275	245
155	1996-2001 (20)	120	1,700	185	95	290	240
	by age at immigration						
156	0-4 years	90	410	145	135	185	185
157	5-19 years	205	1,100	325	350	585	410
158	20 years and over	600	2,100	840	810	955	995
159	**Total population**	**2,425**	**6,295**	**4,685**	**3,615**	**6,085**	**5,215**
	by religion						
160	Catholic (21)	1,195	1,600	1,615	1,200	2,485	2,165
161	Protestant	555	965	1,755	1,330	1,950	1,910
162	Christian Orthodox	90	135	160	60	80	90
163	Christian, n.i.e. (22)	45	285	70	60	170	50
164	Muslim	70	1,860	15	130	340	280
165	Jewish	10	40	15	25	30	15
166	Buddhist	30	35	85	45	55	25
167	Hindu	60	510	25	20	125	95
168	Sikh	-	75	30	10	75	25
169	Eastern religions (23)	65	45	55	-	-	-
170	Other religions (24)	-	-	-	25	-	-
171	No religious affiliation (25)	310	750	860	695	765	545
172	**Total population 15 years and over**	**2,115**	**4,630**	**3,750**	**2,935**	**4,590**	**3,870**
	by generation status						
173	1st generation (26)	895	3,060	1,285	1,220	1,605	1,500
174	2nd generation (27)	675	850	905	760	1,165	910
175	3rd generation and over (28)	550	725	1,560	960	1,825	1,460
176	**Total population 1 year and over (29)**	**2,420**	**6,215**	**4,625**	**3,580**	**6,035**	**5,165**
	by place of residence 1 year ago (mobility)						
177	Non-movers	2,300	4,975	4,220	3,195	5,620	4,590
178	Movers	115	1,235	405	390	415	575
179	Non-migrants	55	535	245	235	250	290
180	Migrants	60	700	160	155	160	285
181	Internal migrants	30	220	140	130	150	230
182	Intraprovincial migrants	20	175	105	120	140	225
183	Interprovincial migrants	10	45	35	-	10	10
184	External migrants	35	480	20	25	15	60

Tableau 1. Certaines caractéristiques des secteurs de recensement, recensement de 2001 – Données intégrales et données-échantillon (20 %)

Toronto 0516.03	Toronto 0516.04	Toronto 0516.05	Toronto 0516.06	Toronto 0516.08	Toronto 0516.09	Caractéristiques	N°
						CARACTÉRISTIQUES DE LA POPULATION	
						selon les groupes de minorités visibles	
1,695	2,135	2,045	1,495	2,000	2,050	Total de la population des minorités visibles	121
220	125	110	105	60	135	Chinois	122
455	920	725	340	620	695	Sud-Asiatique	123
420	470	525	605	460	465	Noir	124
145	110	125	85	405	295	Philippin	125
55	45	145	135	180	145	Latino-Américain	126
-	-	10	-	-	25	Asiatique du Sud-Est	127
90	155	170	45	145	40	Arabe	128
65	80	-	60	15	55	Asiatique occidental	129
10	60	70	-	-	20	Coréen	130
10	15	10	-	40	15	Japonais	131
150	120	160	70	-	140	Minorité visible, n.i.a. (13)	132
85	50	10	35	65	35	Minorités visibles multiples (14)	133
						selon la citoyenneté	
5,465	5,010	5,870	4,705	5,685	6,630	Citoyenneté canadienne (15)	134
575	1,365	1,090	475	845	775	Citoyenneté autre que canadienne	135
						selon le lieu de naissance du répondant	
3,950	3,795	4,350	3,370	3,785	4,655	Population non immigrante	136
3,305	2,800	3,730	2,725	3,060	3,690	Née dans la province de résidence	137
2,090	2,495	2,575	1,800	2,705	2,705	Population immigrante (16)	138
60	75	50	25	45	40	États-Unis	139
140	100	130	140	95	315	Amérique centrale et du Sud	140
275	240	255	325	175	310	Caraïbes et Bermudes	141
330	175	390	220	395	370	Royaume-Uni	142
405	510	595	500	765	705	Autre Europe (17)	143
190	220	270	165	120	85	Afrique	144
675	1,165	875	425	1,110	875	Asie et Moyen-Orient	145
10	10	20	-	-	10	Océanie et autre (18)	146
10	85	35	10	45	40	Résidents non permanents (19)	147
2,085	**2,495**	**2,575**	**1,800**	**2,705**	**2,700**	**Population immigrante totale**	148
						selon la période d'immigration	
165	120	90	160	150	235	Avant 1961	149
270	150	235	185	195	355	1961-1970	150
405	300	575	275	355	485	1971-1980	151
500	415	485	595	610	680	1981-1990	152
750	1,510	1,190	590	1,395	945	1991-2001 (20)	153
385	250	335	275	705	455	1991-1995	154
370	1,260	860	315	690	490	1996-2001 (20)	155
						selon l'âge à l'immigration	
180	300	305	180	240	255	0-4 ans	156
635	755	830	565	870	710	5-19 ans	157
1,280	1,435	1,435	1,055	1,595	1,745	20 ans et plus	158
6,040	**6,375**	**6,955**	**5,180**	**6,535**	**7,395**	**Population totale**	159
						selon la religion	
2,245	2,070	2,575	1,940	2,720	2,930	Catholique (21)	160
2,190	1,985	2,215	1,825	1,835	2,570	Protestante	161
65	245	135	95	225	80	Orthodoxe chrétienne	162
145	200	275	190	195	180	Chrétiennes, n.i.a. (22)	163
255	695	430	360	685	320	Musulmane	164
20	20	75	45	35	40	Juive	165
50	20	-	-	20	30	Bouddhiste	166
100	170	170	10	35	205	Hindoue	167
15	65	45	40	40	235	Sikh	168
-	-	30	-	10	10	Religions orientales (23)	169
-	10	-	-	-	-	Autres religions (24)	170
960	905	1,010	670	735	805	Aucune appartenance religieuse (25)	171
4,755	**5,110**	**5,215**	**3,975**	**5,090**	**5,905**	**Population totale de 15 ans et plus**	172
						selon le statut des générations	
1,950	2,150	2,260	1,690	2,495	2,575	1re génération (26)	173
900	930	1,055	800	885	1,240	2e génération (27)	174
1,900	2,035	1,895	1,480	1,715	2,090	3e génération et plus (28)	175
5,975	**6,305**	**6,875**	**5,100**	**6,445**	**7,310**	**Population totale de 1 an et plus (29)**	176
						selon le lieu de résidence 1 an auparavant (mobilité)	
5,275	4,345	5,870	4,390	5,535	6,195	Personnes n'ayant pas déménagé	177
695	1,960	1,005	710	910	1,115	Personnes ayant déménagé	178
435	895	470	450	375	745	Non-migrants	179
260	1,070	530	255	530	370	Migrants	180
130	750	235	220	390	255	Migrants internes	181
110	560	205	145	370	230	Migrants infraprovinciaux	182
15	195	30	75	20	30	Migrants interprovinciaux	183
135	320	295	40	140	115	Migrants externes	184

Table 1. Selected Characteristics for Census Tracts, 2001 Census – 100% Data and 20% Sample Data

No.	Characteristics	Toronto 0514.01 A	Toronto 0514.02 A	Toronto 0515.01	Toronto 0515.02	Toronto 0516.01	Toronto 0516.02
	POPULATION CHARACTERISTICS						
185	**Total population 5 years and over (30)**	**2,350**	**5,810**	**4,430**	**3,425**	**5,690**	**4,825**
	by place of residence 5 years ago (mobility)						
186	Non-movers	1,815	2,595	2,990	2,110	3,895	3,020
187	Movers	540	3,215	1,435	1,315	1,800	1,805
188	Non-migrants	270	930	875	700	900	940
189	Migrants	265	2,285	560	615	900	865
190	Internal migrants	170	690	410	555	650	680
191	Intraprovincial migrants	130	495	325	520	510	585
192	Interprovincial migrants	35	195	85	35	140	95
193	External migrants	95	1,600	150	60	245	190
194	**Total population 15 to 24 years**	**385**	**935**	**660**	**430**	**945**	**730**
	by school attendance						
195	Not attending school	35	285	200	135	290	215
196	Attending school full time	300	605	420	270	615	485
197	Attending school part time	45	45	45	20	45	40
198	**Total population 15 years and over**	**2,120**	**4,630**	**3,755**	**2,940**	**4,590**	**3,870**
	by highest level of schooling						
199	Less than grade 9 (31)	40	270	95	150	105	120
200	Grades 9-13 without high school graduation certificate	290	785	715	515	805	675
201	Grades 9-13 with high school graduation certificate	310	725	585	345	620	650
202	Some postsecondary without degree, certificate or diploma (32)	295	545	425	385	605	525
203	Trades certificate or diploma (33)	120	235	315	225	415	415
204	College certificate or diploma (34)	265	475	750	535	985	730
205	University certificate below bachelor's degree	40	185	140	125	130	100
206	University with bachelor's degree or higher	750	1,410	725	650	925	670
	by combinations of unpaid work						
207	Males 15 years and over	1,030	2,280	1,865	1,370	2,270	1,930
208	Reported unpaid work (35)	880	1,995	1,655	1,240	2,080	1,655
209	Housework and child care and care or assistance to seniors	95	255	120	100	145	165
210	Housework and child care only	205	630	565	445	800	655
211	Housework and care or assistance to seniors only	65	75	115	45	115	70
212	Child care and care or assistance to seniors only	10	-	-	-	10	-
213	Housework only	475	980	825	620	985	745
214	Child care only	15	30	30	20	15	20
215	Care or assistance to seniors only	20	20	-	10	10	-
216	Females 15 years and over	1,085	2,355	1,890	1,570	2,320	1,940
217	Reported unpaid work (35)	980	2,115	1,795	1,465	2,190	1,840
218	Housework and child care and care or assistance to seniors	120	305	145	205	310	235
219	Housework and child care only	315	770	700	480	815	785
220	Housework and care or assistance to seniors only	135	120	120	105	140	110
221	Child care and care or assistance to seniors only	-	-	-	-	-	-
222	Housework only	405	910	815	665	900	685
223	Child care only	-	10	10	-	10	15
224	Care or assistance to seniors only	10	10	-	-	10	15
	by labour force activity						
225	Males 15 years and over	1,030	2,280	1,860	1,370	2,270	1,930
226	In the labour force	765	1,815	1,400	1,100	1,880	1,690
227	Employed	740	1,710	1,345	1,045	1,830	1,605
228	Unemployed	20	105	55	50	50	85
229	Not in the labour force	270	460	460	275	390	240
230	Participation rate	74.3	79.6	75.3	80.3	82.8	87.6
231	Employment rate	71.8	75.0	72.3	76.3	80.6	83.2
232	Unemployment rate	2.6	5.8	3.9	4.5	2.7	5.0
233	Females 15 years and over	1,090	2,350	1,890	1,565	2,320	1,940
234	In the labour force	580	1,460	1,350	1,000	1,695	1,460
235	Employed	560	1,350	1,305	970	1,630	1,420
236	Unemployed	15	110	50	30	70	40
237	Not in the labour force	505	895	540	565	620	485
238	Participation rate	53.2	62.1	71.4	63.9	73.1	75.3
239	Employment rate	51.4	57.4	69.0	62.0	70.3	73.2
240	Unemployment rate	2.6	7.5	3.7	3.0	4.1	2.7

Tableau 1. Certaines caractéristiques des secteurs de recensement, recensement de 2001 – Données intégrales et données-échantillon (20 %)

Toronto 0516.03	Toronto 0516.04	Toronto 0516.05	Toronto 0516.06	Toronto 0516.08	Toronto 0516.09	Caractéristiques	N°
						CARACTÉRISTIQUES DE LA POPULATION	
5,670	**5,980**	**6,450**	**4,825**	**6,145**	**7,000**	**Population totale de 5 ans et plus (30)**	185
						selon le lieu de résidence 5 ans auparavant (mobilité)	
2,970	1,745	3,670	2,690	3,340	4,420	Personnes n'ayant pas déménagé	186
2,705	4,235	2,780	2,135	2,810	2,585	Personnes ayant déménagé	187
1,840	1,690	1,170	1,255	1,465	1,355	Non-migrants	188
865	2,545	1,610	880	1,345	1,230	Migrants	189
525	1,400	850	690	660	840	Migrants internes	190
480	1,025	750	620	520	710	Migrants infraprovinciaux	191
45	370	100	65	140	130	Migrants interprovinciaux	192
340	1,145	755	195	690	390	Migrants externes	193
795	**865**	**1,035**	**695**	**1,080**	**1,160**	**Population totale de 15 à 24 ans**	194
						selon la fréquentation scolaire	
250	425	380	215	435	375	Ne fréquentant pas l'école	195
505	390	625	440	605	715	Fréquentant l'école à plein temps	196
40	50	35	45	35	70	Fréquentant l'école à temps partiel	197
4,755	**5,115**	**5,215**	**3,975**	**5,090**	**5,910**	**Population totale de 15 ans et plus**	198
						selon le plus haut niveau de scolarité atteint	
160	110	90	160	160	210	Niveau inférieur à la 9e année (31)	199
985	895	1,025	795	1,115	1,270	De la 9e à la 13e année sans certificat d'études secondaires	200
825	690	915	595	740	925	De la 9e à la 13e année avec certificat d'études secondaires	201
515	570	685	565	710	735	Études postsecondaires partielles sans grade, certificat ou diplôme (32)	202
485	365	540	425	425	555	Certificat ou diplôme d'une école de métiers (33)	203
890	890	925	830	765	1,070	Certificat ou diplôme collégial (34)	204
115	90	150	85	150	145	Certificat universitaire inférieur au baccalauréat	205
770	1,500	885	505	1,025	1,000	Études universitaires avec baccalauréat ou diplôme supérieur	206
						selon les combinaisons de travail non rémunéré	
2,215	2,520	2,545	1,845	2,365	2,880	Hommes de 15 ans et plus	207
2,020	2,215	2,255	1,605	2,050	2,565	Travail non rémunéré déclaré (35)	208
160	85	120	75	165	220	Travaux ménagers et soins aux enfants et soins ou aide aux personnes âgées	209
675	695	845	700	760	745	Travaux ménagers et soins aux enfants seulement	210
165	65	105	60	120	105	Travaux ménagers et soins ou aide aux personnes âgées seulement	211
-	-	10	10	-	-	Soins aux enfants et soins ou aide aux personnes âgées seulement	212
1,005	1,335	1,115	720	975	1,420	Travaux ménagers seulement	213
20	30	45	20	30	60	Soins aux enfants seulement	214
-	10	15	20	10	10	Soins ou aide aux personnes âgées seulement	215
2,535	2,590	2,670	2,125	2,720	3,030	Femmes de 15 ans et plus	216
2,435	2,425	2,565	1,930	2,480	2,805	Travail non rémunéré déclaré (35)	217
230	160	210	185	265	350	Travaux ménagers et soins aux enfants et soins ou aide aux personnes âgées	218
735	870	1,055	795	965	950	Travaux ménagers et soins aux enfants seulement	219
145	155	170	125	145	235	Travaux ménagers et soins ou aide aux personnes âgées seulement	220
-	-	10	-	-	10	Soins aux enfants et soins ou aide aux personnes âgées seulement	221
1,295	1,230	1,085	805	1,075	1,235	Travaux ménagers seulement	222
15	-	15	-	30	25	Soins aux enfants seulement	223
20	-	20	15	-	-	Soins ou aide aux personnes âgées seulement	224
						selon l'activité	
2,215	2,525	2,545	1,845	2,365	2,875	Hommes de 15 ans et plus	225
1,810	2,120	2,180	1,515	1,935	2,325	Population active	226
1,740	1,995	2,065	1,470	1,850	2,215	Personnes occupées	227
70	125	110	45	80	105	Chômeurs	228
405	405	365	330	435	550	Inactifs	229
81.7	84.0	85.7	82.1	81.8	80.9	Taux d'activité	230
78.6	79.0	81.1	79.7	78.2	77.0	Taux d'emploi	231
3.9	5.9	5.0	3.0	4.1	4.5	Taux de chômage	232
2,535	2,590	2,670	2,125	2,725	3,030	Femmes de 15 ans et plus	233
1,890	1,925	2,055	1,480	1,865	2,180	Population active	234
1,820	1,810	1,905	1,380	1,745	2,040	Personnes occupées	235
70	115	145	100	115	140	Chômeuses	236
645	660	615	645	860	850	Inactives	237
74.6	74.3	77.0	69.6	68.4	71.9	Taux d'activité	238
71.8	69.9	71.3	64.9	64.0	67.3	Taux d'emploi	239
3.7	6.0	7.1	6.8	6.2	6.4	Taux de chômage	240

Table 1. Selected Characteristics for Census Tracts, 2001 Census – 100% Data and 20% Sample Data

No.	Characteristics	Toronto 0514.01 A	Toronto 0514.02 A	Toronto 0515.01	Toronto 0515.02	Toronto 0516.01	Toronto 0516.02
	POPULATION CHARACTERISTICS						
	by labour force activity – concluded						
241	Both sexes - Participation rate	63.2	70.7	73.2	71.6	78.0	81.3
242	15-24 years	40.3	60.4	65.2	76.5	66.7	70.5
243	25 years and over	68.3	73.2	75.1	70.7	80.8	83.9
244	Both sexes - Employment rate	61.3	66.1	70.4	68.5	75.5	78.2
245	15-24 years	32.5	52.9	59.1	65.1	59.3	64.6
246	25 years and over	67.9	69.3	72.7	69.1	79.4	81.3
247	Both sexes - Unemployment rate	2.6	6.7	4.0	4.3	3.2	3.8
248	15-24 years	19.4	13.3	8.2	13.8	10.3	6.8
249	25 years and over	0.8	5.4	3.2	2.3	1.5	3.0
250	**Total labour force 15 years and over**	**1,340**	**3,280**	**2,755**	**2,100**	**3,575**	**3,145**
	by industry based on the 1997 NAICS						
251	Industry - Not applicable (36)	-	55	15	10	-	40
252	All industries (37)	1,340	3,225	2,740	2,090	3,575	3,105
253	11 Agriculture, forestry, fishing and hunting	30	10	10	-	-	-
254	21 Mining and oil and gas extraction	10	-	-	-	10	-
255	22 Utilities	-	15	25	-	25	-
256	23 Construction	80	65	105	75	130	130
257	31-33 Manufacturing	165	560	330	290	630	500
258	41 Wholesale trade	115	165	190	185	330	385
259	44-45 Retail trade	100	485	360	195	485	305
260	48-49 Transportation and warehousing	15	145	160	140	260	190
261	51 Information and cultural industries	30	175	70	70	95	35
262	52 Finance and insurance	80	170	220	150	270	270
263	53 Real estate and rental and leasing	90	40	50	30	90	70
264	54 Professional, scientific and technical services	125	340	245	205	270	275
265	55 Management of companies and enterprises	-	10	-	-	-	-
266	56 Administrative and support, waste management and remediation services	75	225	130	110	100	110
267	61 Educational services	105	135	160	140	185	175
268	62 Health care and social assistance	170	205	245	150	225	215
269	71 Arts, entertainment and recreation	10	35	60	60	45	15
270	72 Accommodation and food services	55	285	135	135	170	165
271	81 Other services (except public administration)	50	115	100	50	105	135
272	91 Public administration	25	60	140	95	130	125
	by class of worker						
273	Class of worker - Not applicable (36)	-	55	15	10	10	40
274	All classes of worker (37)	1,340	3,220	2,740	2,090	3,575	3,105
275	Paid workers	1,150	2,985	2,540	1,860	3,395	2,880
276	Employees	980	2,835	2,425	1,785	3,245	2,810
277	Self-employed (incorporated)	170	150	115	75	145	65
278	Self-employed (unincorporated)	185	215	205	210	180	215
279	Unpaid family workers	10	25	-	25	-	15
	by occupation based on the 2001 NOC-S						
280	Male labour force 15 years and over	760	1,815	1,400	1,095	1,875	1,690
281	Occupation - Not applicable (36)	-	15	-	10	-	30
282	All occupations (37)	765	1,800	1,395	1,095	1,880	1,655
283	A Management occupations	265	305	255	180	415	230
284	B Business, finance and administration occupations	100	235	205	165	315	225
285	C Natural and applied sciences and related occupations	10	175	120	140	265	220
286	D Health occupations	80	80	20	20	15	-
287	E Occupations in social science, education, government service and religion	35	45	110	25	50	75
288	F Occupations in art, culture, recreation and sport	15	40	30	60	45	25
289	G Sales and service occupations	150	415	300	245	325	345
290	H Trades, transport and equipment operators and related occupations	70	265	290	190	360	355
291	I Occupations unique to primary industry	20	-	10	25	15	25
292	J Occupations unique to processing, manufacturing and utilities	25	245	65	40	75	150
293	Female labour force 15 years and over	580	1,465	1,350	1,005	1,700	1,455
294	Occupation - Not applicable (36)	-	40	10	-	-	10
295	All occupations (37)	580	1,425	1,340	995	1,695	1,445
296	A Management occupations	110	195	210	110	200	200
297	B Business, finance and administration occupations	190	370	405	310	585	480
298	C Natural and applied sciences and related occupations	25	40	40	50	110	50
299	D Health occupations	40	80	110	85	95	75

Tableau 1. Certaines caractéristiques des secteurs de recensement, recensement de 2001 – Données intégrales et données-échantillon (20 %)

Toronto 0516.03	Toronto 0516.04	Toronto 0516.05	Toronto 0516.06	Toronto 0516.08	Toronto 0516.09	Caractéristiques	N°
						CARACTÉRISTIQUES DE LA POPULATION	
						selon l'activité – fin	
77.7	79.2	81.2	75.6	74.4	76.3	Les deux sexes - Taux d'activité	241
67.5	74.6	71.5	77.7	73.6	68.1	15-24 ans	242
79.8	80.2	83.7	75.0	74.7	78.2	25 ans et plus	243
74.9	74.4	76.3	71.7	70.6	72.0	Les deux sexes - Taux d'emploi	244
60.4	64.7	58.5	66.9	69.0	62.5	15-24 ans	245
77.7	76.4	80.7	72.8	71.1	74.4	25 ans et plus	246
3.7	6.0	6.0	5.0	5.1	5.5	Les deux sexes - Taux de chômage	247
10.2	12.5	17.6	14.8	6.3	8.9	15-24 ans	248
2.5	4.7	3.7	2.8	4.8	4.8	25 ans et plus	249
3,695	**4,050**	**4,235**	**2,995**	**3,795**	**4,510**	**Population active totale de 15 ans et plus**	250
						selon l'industrie basée sur le SCIAN de 1997	
30	45	35	45	55	40	Industrie - Sans objet (36)	251
3,665	4,005	4,200	2,950	3,740	4,465	Toutes les industries (37)	252
30	10	-	-	55	10	11 Agriculture, foresterie, pêche et chasse	253
-	-	-	10	-	10	21 Extraction minière et extraction de pétrole et de gaz	254
45	20	15	10	15	20	22 Services publics	255
130	155	170	140	190	225	23 Construction	256
610	640	720	560	500	705	31-33 Fabrication	257
390	400	530	190	280	395	41 Commerce de gros	258
370	495	475	360	575	465	44-45 Commerce de détail	259
330	285	290	175	270	310	48-49 Transport et entreposage	260
110	205	75	75	110	150	51 Industrie de l'information et industrie culturelle	261
270	215	290	155	235	255	52 Finance et assurances	262
90	75	130	55	55	95	53 Services immobiliers et services de location et de location à bail	263
235	410	265	270	280	420	54 Services professionnels, scientifiques et techniques	264
-	-	25	10	-	-	55 Gestion de sociétés et d'entreprises	265
120	185	120	100	175	185	56 Services administratifs, services de soutien, services de gestion des déchets et services d'assainissement	266
180	155	215	155	205	225	61 Services d'enseignement	267
190	245	300	225	285	365	62 Soins de santé et assistance sociale	268
40	70	85	35	50	55	71 Arts, spectacles et loisirs	269
215	200	205	205	235	205	72 Hébergement et services de restauration	270
140	170	155	95	100	175	81 Autres services, sauf les administrations publiques	271
175	60	135	130	115	195	91 Administrations publiques	272
						selon la catégorie de travailleurs	
30	40	35	50	55	40	Catégorie de travailleurs - Sans objet (36)	273
3,670	4,005	4,205	2,950	3,740	4,465	Toutes les catégories de travailleurs (37)	274
3,565	3,770	3,960	2,840	3,500	4,155	Travailleurs rémunérés	275
3,550	3,685	3,855	2,760	3,445	4,070	Employés	276
20	85	105	80	60	90	Travailleurs autonomes (entreprise constituée en société)	277
100	205	245	110	215	310	Travailleurs autonomes (entreprise non constituée en société)	278
-	30	-	-	20	-	Travailleurs familiaux non rémunérés	279
						selon la profession basée sur la CNP-S de 2001	
1,805	2,120	2,180	1,520	1,935	2,325	Hommes actifs de 15 ans et plus	280
20	25	10	10	15	15	Profession - Sans objet (36)	281
1,790	2,095	2,175	1,505	1,920	2,310	Toutes les professions (37)	282
325	230	360	185	300	425	A Gestion	283
235	305	235	235	345	330	B Affaires, finance et administration	284
160	400	265	150	160	165	C Sciences naturelles et appliquées et professions apparentées	285
25	40	40	-	65	25	D Secteur de la santé	286
65	120	50	65	70	65	E Sciences sociales, enseignement, administration publique et religion	287
25	65	60	25	25	35	F Arts, culture, sports et loisirs	288
290	365	500	330	385	425	G Ventes et services	289
470	405	460	360	425	530	H Métiers, transport et machinerie	290
30	50	20	25	45	40	I Professions propres au secteur primaire	291
165	105	190	110	105	270	J Transformation, fabrication et services d'utilité publique	292
1,885	1,925	2,055	1,485	1,865	2,185	Femmes actives de 15 ans et plus	293
10	15	25	40	45	25	Profession - Sans objet (36)	294
1,880	1,910	2,030	1,440	1,820	2,155	Toutes les professions (37)	295
215	210	170	125	175	260	A Gestion	296
750	635	765	550	550	700	B Affaires, finance et administration	297
50	105	60	55	85	85	C Sciences naturelles et appliquées et professions apparentées	298
65	130	100	100	85	195	D Secteur de la santé	299

Table 1. Selected Characteristics for Census Tracts, 2001 Census – 100% Data and 20% Sample Data

No.	Characteristics	Toronto 0514.01 A	Toronto 0514.02 A	Toronto 0515.01	Toronto 0515.02	Toronto 0516.01	Toronto 0516.02
	POPULATION CHARACTERISTICS						
	by occupation based on the 2001 NOC-S – concluded						
300	E Occupations in social science, education, government service and religion	45	90	180	110	140	105
301	F Occupations in art, culture, recreation and sport	20	30	30	40	30	40
302	G Sales and service occupations	125	490	315	240	435	400
303	H Trades, transport and equipment operators and related occupations	10	35	-	25	55	25
304	I Occupations unique to primary industry	15	-	10	-	-	-
305	J Occupations unique to processing, manufacturing and utilities	-	90	45	30	50	70
306	**Total employed labour force 15 years and over**	**1,305**	**3,060**	**2,650**	**2,010**	**3,460**	**3,025**
	by place of work						
307	Males	740	1,710	1,345	1,045	1,830	1,605
308	Usual place of work	600	1,440	1,075	870	1,600	1,360
309	At home	75	80	125	75	80	50
310	Outside Canada	15	-	10	-	10	-
311	No fixed workplace address	50	180	140	105	145	195
312	Females	565	1,350	1,300	970	1,630	1,420
313	Usual place of work	455	1,225	1,105	815	1,395	1,235
314	At home	85	65	110	90	140	120
315	Outside Canada	-	10	10	15	35	-
316	No fixed workplace address	20	40	80	50	55	60
317	**Total employed labour force 15 years and over with usual place of work or no fixed workplace address**	**1,120**	**2,890**	**2,400**	**1,835**	**3,190**	**2,850**
	by mode of transportation						
318	Males	650	1,620	1,210	970	1,740	1,555
319	Car, truck, van, as driver	580	1,205	975	765	1,500	1,335
320	Car, truck, van, as passenger	15	60	25	70	90	105
321	Public transit	30	300	135	80	105	75
322	Walked	10	30	65	40	25	35
323	Other method	10	25	15	10	20	10
324	Females	475	1,270	1,190	865	1,455	1,300
325	Car, truck, van, as driver	375	630	825	615	1,105	960
326	Car, truck, van, as passenger	65	120	90	45	95	100
327	Public transit	20	365	175	160	215	215
328	Walked	10	135	80	30	30	20
329	Other method	-	15	20	10	10	-
330	**Total population 15 years and over who worked since January 1, 2000**	**1,500**	**3,465**	**2,965**	**2,225**	**3,830**	**3,355**
	by language used at work						
331	Single responses	1,215	3,080	2,785	1,995	3,620	3,190
332	English	1,205	3,020	2,755	1,970	3,620	3,180
333	French	-	20	20	-	-	-
334	Non-official languages (5)	15	45	15	20	10	-
335	Chinese, n.o.s.	-	-	-	-	-	-
336	Cantonese	10	-	-	10	-	-
337	Other languages (6)	10	40	10	15	-	10
338	Multiple responses	285	385	175	230	205	170
339	English and French	30	55	65	55	85	85
340	English and non-official language	245	320	85	165	110	80
341	French and non-official language	-	-	-	-	-	-
342	English, French and non-official language	10	10	20	-	10	-
	DWELLING AND HOUSEHOLD CHARACTERISTICS						
343	**Total number of occupied private dwellings**	**780**	**1,825**	**1,510**	**1,340**	**1,780**	**1,550**
	by tenure						
344	Owned	755	895	1,320	830	1,660	1,465
345	Rented	20	930	190	505	120	85
346	Band housing	-	-	-	-	-	-
	by structural type of dwelling						
347	Single-detached house	775	690	795	710	1,665	780
348	Semi-detached house	-	-	370	-	-	305
349	Row house	-	-	245	160	40	375
350	Apartment, detached duplex	-	-	10	-	-	-
351	Apartment, building that has five or more storeys	-	1,135	90	390	-	95
352	Apartment, building that has fewer than five storeys (38)	-	10	-	70	70	-
353	Other single-attached house	-	-	-	-	-	-
354	Movable dwelling (39)	-	-	-	-	-	-

Tableau 1. Certaines caractéristiques des secteurs de recensement, recensement de 2001 – Données intégrales et données-échantillon (20 %)

Caractéristiques	Toronto 0516.03	Toronto 0516.04	Toronto 0516.05	Toronto 0516.06	Toronto 0516.08	Toronto 0516.09	N°
CARACTÉRISTIQUES DE LA POPULATION							
selon la profession basée sur la CNP-S de 2001 – fin							
E Sciences sociales, enseignement, administration publique et religion	130	155	230	140	150	240	300
F Arts, culture, sports et loisirs	35	45	45	25	45	35	301
G Ventes et services	485	530	555	355	565	490	302
H Métiers, transport et machinerie	45	40	20	30	45	45	303
I Professions propres au secteur primaire	-	-	-	-	20	15	304
J Transformation, fabrication et services d'utilité publique	95	75	95	65	110	90	305
Population active occupée totale de 15 ans et plus	**3,560**	**3,805**	**3,980**	**2,850**	**3,600**	**4,255**	306
selon le lieu de travail							
Hommes	1,740	1,995	2,070	1,470	1,855	2,220	307
Lieu habituel de travail	1,540	1,690	1,800	1,285	1,505	1,900	308
À domicile	30	75	105	50	125	120	309
En dehors du Canada	15	10	-	-	10	-	310
Sans adresse de travail fixe	155	220	165	140	210	190	311
Femmes	1,820	1,810	1,910	1,380	1,745	2,040	312
Lieu habituel de travail	1,705	1,640	1,730	1,235	1,560	1,805	313
À domicile	90	100	130	80	145	165	314
En dehors du Canada	-	15	10	-	-	10	315
Sans adresse de travail fixe	25	60	50	60	40	65	316
Population active occupée totale de 15 ans et plus ayant un lieu habituel de travail ou sans adresse de travail fixe	**3,425**	**3,605**	**3,740**	**2,720**	**3,315**	**3,960**	317
selon le mode de transport							
Hommes	1,695	1,915	1,960	1,425	1,715	2,090	318
Automobile, camion ou fourgonnette, en tant que conducteur	1,370	1,505	1,670	1,135	1,260	1,760	319
Automobile, camion ou fourgonnette, en tant que passager	85	70	90	95	110	60	320
Transport en commun	165	240	145	140	285	185	321
À pied	25	30	40	40	55	60	322
Autre moyen	45	60	10	20	-	20	323
Femmes	1,730	1,695	1,780	1,300	1,600	1,865	324
Automobile, camion ou fourgonnette, en tant que conductrice	1,220	1,160	1,265	945	920	1,300	325
Automobile, camion ou fourgonnette, en tant que passagère	125	120	150	100	175	125	326
Transport en commun	300	370	330	200	430	335	327
À pied	90	30	20	50	80	95	328
Autre moyen	-	10	10	10	-	10	329
Population totale de 15 ans et plus ayant travaillé depuis le 1er janvier 2000	**3,950**	**4,285**	**4,530**	**3,125**	**3,995**	**4,890**	330
selon la langue utilisée au travail							
Réponses uniques	3,730	3,935	4,280	2,950	3,725	4,540	331
Anglais	3,720	3,920	4,270	2,925	3,690	4,505	332
Français	-	10	-	-	15	-	333
Langues non officielles (5)	10	20	10	15	15	30	334
Chinois, n.d.a.	-	-	-	-	10	-	335
Cantonais	-	-	-	-	-	-	336
Autres langues (6)	10	20	10	15	10	35	337
Réponses multiples	220	350	255	175	270	355	338
Anglais et français	145	175	80	65	105	130	339
Anglais et langue non officielle	65	160	165	110	165	215	340
Français et langue non officielle	-	-	-	-	-	-	341
Anglais, français et langue non officielle	15	10	10	-	10	-	342
CARACTÉRISTIQUES DES LOGEMENTS ET DES MÉNAGES							
Nombre total de logements privés occupés	**2,195**	**2,620**	**2,140**	**1,780**	**2,180**	**2,395**	343
selon le mode d'occupation							
Possédé	1,675	540	1,545	1,205	935	2,080	344
Loué	520	2,075	595	580	1,240	310	345
Logement de bande	-	-	-	-	-	-	346
selon le type de construction résidentielle							
Maison individuelle non attenante	325	285	440	380	405	470	347
Maison jumelée	420	-	600	335	385	1,050	348
Maison en rangée	875	260	575	580	530	800	349
Appartement, duplex non attenant	-	-	10	-	-	-	350
Appartement, immeuble de cinq étages ou plus	485	1,070	455	405	860	-	351
Appartement, immeuble de moins de cinq étages (38)	80	990	65	80	-	70	352
Autre maison individuelle attenante	-	-	-	-	-	-	353
Logement mobile (39)	-	-	-	-	-	-	354

Table 1. Selected Characteristics for Census Tracts, 2001 Census – 100% Data and 20% Sample Data

No.	Characteristics	Toronto 0514.01 A	Toronto 0514.02 A	Toronto 0515.01	Toronto 0515.02	Toronto 0516.01	Toronto 0516.02
	DWELLING AND HOUSEHOLD CHARACTERISTICS						
	by condition of dwelling						
355	Regular maintenance only	505	1,165	990	930	1,135	1,050
356	Minor repairs	240	425	445	285	585	400
357	Major repairs	30	240	75	120	60	100
	by period of construction						
358	Before 1946	25	10	10	-	-	-
359	1946-1960	95	95	60	85	-	10
360	1961-1970	205	620	800	695	10	45
361	1971-1980	205	625	605	205	330	890
362	1981-1990	215	370	35	170	1,350	310
363	1991-2001 (20)	40	105	-	180	85	300
364	Average number of rooms per dwelling	9.9	6.5	7.6	6.7	7.4	7.1
365	Average number of bedrooms per dwelling	4.0	2.8	3.4	2.9	3.2	3.2
366	Average value of dwelling $	522,830	366,771	227,382	277,011	229,896	205,608
367	**Total number of private households**	**780**	**1,830**	**1,505**	**1,335**	**1,780**	**1,550**
	by household size						
368	1 person	60	190	140	315	155	160
369	2 persons	255	410	470	395	330	330
370	3 persons	130	355	310	215	350	305
371	4-5 persons	295	700	520	360	850	660
372	6 or more persons	30	180	70	50	95	100
	by household type						
373	One-family households	665	1,500	1,300	975	1,550	1,290
374	Multiple-family households	20	75	30	35	30	70
375	Non-family households	90	250	170	330	200	195
376	Number of persons in private households	2,400	6,275	4,680	3,620	6,080	5,215
377	Average number of persons in private households	3.1	3.4	3.1	2.7	3.4	3.4
378	Average number of persons per room	0.3	0.5	0.4	0.4	0.5	0.5
379	Tenant households in non-farm, non-reserve private dwellings (40)	10	915	185	505	120	85
380	Average gross rent $ (40)	-	875	1,072	726	870	1,030
381	Tenant households spending 30% or more of household income on gross rent (40) (41)	-	400	80	160	75	35
382	Tenant households spending from 30% to 99% of household income on gross rent (40) (41)	-	280	55	130	70	35
383	Owner households in non-farm, non-reserve private dwellings (42)	760	900	1,320	830	1,655	1,470
384	Average owner's major payments $ (42)	1,706	1,491	1,059	1,116	1,379	1,383
385	Owner households spending 30% or more of household income on owner's major payments (41) (42)	125	190	190	120	280	225
386	Owner households spending from 30% to 99% of household income on owner's major payments (41) (42)	80	155	170	105	230	210
	CENSUS FAMILY CHARACTERISTICS						
387	**Total number of census families in private households**	**705**	**1,655**	**1,365**	**1,040**	**1,620**	**1,435**
	by census family structure and size						
388	Total couple families	655	1,380	1,170	890	1,500	1,250
389	Total families of married couples	625	1,295	1,100	810	1,430	1,150
390	Without children at home	235	305	375	290	290	265
391	With children at home	395	990	725	520	1,135	880
392	1 child	125	245	255	180	260	255
393	2 children	205	415	330	225	640	390
394	3 or more children	65	330	140	110	240	240
395	Total families of common-law couples	30	80	70	80	75	105
396	Without children at home	15	30	20	55	30	60
397	With children at home	15	50	45	20	40	40
398	1 child	10	25	-	20	25	40
399	2 children	-	25	15	10	15	-
400	3 or more children	-	-	25	-	10	-
401	Total lone-parent families	50	275	195	160	115	180
402	Female parent	45	220	155	130	80	145
403	1 child	10	105	65	65	40	85
404	2 children	30	100	65	45	35	45
405	3 or more children	-	20	25	20	10	15

Tableau 1. Certaines caractéristiques des secteurs de recensement, recensement de 2001 – Données intégrales et données-échantillon (20 %)

Toronto 0516.03	Toronto 0516.04	Toronto 0516.05	Toronto 0516.06	Toronto 0516.08	Toronto 0516.09	Caractéristiques	N°
						CARACTÉRISTIQUES DES LOGEMENTS ET DES MÉNAGES	
						selon l'état du logement	
1,535	2,015	1,535	1,265	1,400	1,730	Entretien régulier seulement	355
585	530	485	420	600	555	Réparations mineures	356
75	70	115	90	180	105	Réparations majeures	357
						selon la période de construction	
15	10	-	-	10	-	Avant 1946	358
10	20	-	10	35	45	1946-1960	359
110	105	55	95	170	235	1961-1970	360
1,535	720	1,600	1,305	1,500	1,440	1971-1980	361
495	1,530	465	365	410	535	1981-1990	362
35	230	15	-	50	135	1991-2001 (20)	363
6.5	4.9	6.7	6.4	6.0	6.9	Nombre moyen de pièces par logement	364
2.8	2.0	3.0	2.8	2.7	3.2	Nombre moyen de chambres à coucher par logement	365
173,048	219,365	202,396	187,853	222,252	200,962	Valeur moyenne du logement $	366
2,195	**2,620**	**2,140**	**1,785**	**2,180**	**2,390**	**Nombre total de logements privés**	367
						selon la taille du ménage	
415	720	235	400	400	315	1 personne	368
640	880	470	405	520	640	2 personnes	369
490	435	500	325	435	505	3 personnes	370
595	510	820	550	695	790	4-5 personnes	371
55	70	115	95	130	150	6 personnes ou plus	372
						selon le genre de ménage	
1,665	1,745	1,790	1,260	1,650	1,900	Ménages unifamiliaux	373
45	25	65	90	50	125	Ménages multifamiliaux	374
485	850	280	430	480	370	Ménages non familiaux	375
6,045	6,375	6,955	5,175	6,535	7,390	Nombre de personnes dans les ménages privés	376
2.8	2.4	3.3	2.9	3.0	3.1	Nombre moyen de personnes dans les ménages privés	377
0.4	0.5	0.5	0.5	0.5	0.4	Nombre moyen de personnes par pièce	378
520	2,030	555	575	1,240	300	Ménages locataires dans les logements privés non agricoles hors réserve (40)	379
1,042	1,073	1,086	959	852	1,050	Loyer brut moyen $ (40)	380
230	680	260	315	490	115	Ménages locataires consacrant 30 % ou plus du revenu du ménage au loyer brut (40) (41)	381
190	555	205	295	420	85	Ménages locataires consacrant de 30 % à 99 % du revenu du ménage au loyer brut (40) (41)	382
1,680	540	1,550	1,210	940	2,080	Ménages propriétaires dans les logements privés non agricoles hors réserve (42)	383
1,160	1,205	1,172	1,238	1,181	1,149	Principales dépenses de propriété moyennes $ (42)	384
365	155	300	245	150	405	Ménages propriétaires consacrant 30 % ou plus du revenu du ménage aux principales dépenses de propriété (41) (42)	385
355	130	290	205	150	380	Ménages propriétaires consacrant de 30 % à 99 % du revenu du ménage aux principales dépenses de propriété (41) (42)	386
						CARACTÉRISTIQUES DES FAMILLES DE RECENSEMENT	
1,755	**1,790**	**1,920**	**1,435**	**1,755**	**2,150**	**Total des familles de recensement dans les ménages privés**	387
						selon la structure et la taille de la famille de recensement	
1,390	1,430	1,595	1,140	1,420	1,760	Total des familles avec conjoints	388
1,205	1,140	1,415	1,040	1,285	1,600	Total des familles avec couples mariés	389
365	365	300	300	340	495	Sans enfants à la maison	390
845	775	1,115	745	940	1,110	Avec enfants à la maison	391
335	310	350	255	285	350	1 enfant	392
365	325	520	340	425	535	2 enfants	393
150	140	240	150	235	225	3 enfants ou plus	394
185	290	175	105	140	160	Total des familles en union libre	395
90	225	85	50	45	80	Sans enfants à la maison	396
95	70	95	50	90	80	Avec enfants à la maison	397
55	45	40	30	40	25	1 enfant	398
20	25	30	15	45	45	2 enfants	399
15	-	25	10	-	15	3 enfants ou plus	400
365	360	325	295	330	385	Total des familles monoparentales	401
320	295	260	235	305	325	Parent de sexe féminin	402
230	200	125	130	150	200	1 enfant	403
95	70	105	85	110	105	2 enfants	404
10	20	35	20	45	25	3 enfants ou plus	405

Table 1. Selected Characteristics for Census Tracts, 2001 Census – 100% Data and 20% Sample Data

No.	Characteristics	Toronto 0514.01 A	Toronto 0514.02 A	Toronto 0515.01	Toronto 0515.02	Toronto 0516.01	Toronto 0516.02
	CENSUS FAMILY CHARACTERISTICS						
	by census family structure and size – concluded						
406	Male parent	10	50	45	25	40	35
407	1 child	10	15	20	20	20	10
408	2 children	-	25	10	10	10	15
409	3 or more children	-	15	15	-	10	15
410	**Total number of children at home**	**855**	**2,740**	**1,845**	**1,280**	**2,585**	**2,145**
	by age groups						
411	Under 6 years	95	585	290	230	490	505
412	6-14 years	215	1,060	615	450	1,005	840
413	15-17 years	135	305	190	130	345	245
414	18-24 years	245	530	450	255	560	430
415	25 years and over	170	260	290	215	185	130
	Average number of children at home per						
416	census family (43)	1.2	1.7	1.3	1.2	1.6	1.5
417	**Total number of persons in private households**	**2,405**	**6,275**	**4,680**	**3,620**	**6,080**	**5,210**
	by census family status and living arrangements						
418	Number of non-family persons	180	505	305	410	370	385
419	Living with relatives (44)	80	215	70	55	120	120
420	Living with non-relatives only	40	100	100	40	100	105
421	Living alone	60	190	140	310	155	160
422	Number of family persons	2,220	5,770	4,370	3,210	5,705	4,825
423	Average number of persons per census family	3.1	3.5	3.2	3.1	3.5	3.4
424	**Total number of persons 65 years and over**	**330**	**420**	**450**	**485**	**285**	**225**
425	Number of non-family persons 65 years and over	105	120	70	195	150	105
426	Living with relatives (44)	65	45	25	50	65	60
427	Living with non-relatives only	20	20	-	-	-	-
428	Living alone	25	50	45	145	80	50
429	Number of family persons 65 years and over	220	305	385	295	140	120
	ECONOMIC FAMILY CHARACTERISTICS						
	Total number of economic families in						
430	**private households**	**700**	**1,605**	**1,340**	**1,010**	**1,600**	**1,370**
	by size of family						
431	2 persons	240	385	460	385	325	315
432	3 persons	140	350	300	215	340	350
433	4 persons	230	435	370	255	635	430
434	5 or more persons	90	435	210	155	305	285
435	Total number of persons in economic families	2,300	5,985	4,440	3,265	5,825	4,950
436	Average number of persons per economic family	3.3	3.7	3.3	3.2	3.6	3.6
437	Total number of unattached individuals	100	290	240	355	255	265
	2000 INCOME CHARACTERISTICS						
	Population 15 years and over by sex and total income groups in 2000						
438	Total - Both sexes	2,115	4,635	3,750	2,935	4,590	3,870
439	Without income	170	395	145	45	255	165
440	With income	1,950	4,235	3,605	2,895	4,335	3,705
441	Under $1,000 (45)	85	195	145	90	290	165
442	$ 1,000 - $ 2,999	70	180	165	90	190	150
443	$ 3,000 - $ 4,999	45	240	130	95	125	155
444	$ 5,000 - $ 6,999	80	310	135	85	160	165
445	$ 7,000 - $ 9,999	110	370	200	155	270	120
446	$10,000 - $11,999	25	180	120	60	155	105
447	$12,000 - $14,999	95	195	110	175	205	130
448	$15,000 - $19,999	95	385	210	295	195	205
449	$20,000 - $24,999	95	360	215	175	195	225
450	$25,000 - $29,999	95	220	275	195	220	150
451	$30,000 - $34,999	140	275	325	245	275	275
452	$35,000 - $39,999	90	165	240	190	305	245
453	$40,000 - $44,999	70	155	205	185	220	225
454	$45,000 - $49,999	50	140	200	170	210	230
455	$50,000 - $59,999	190	195	255	240	365	420
456	$60,000 and over	630	665	670	465	970	740
457	Average income $ (46)	82,629	40,708	38,746	36,555	38,078	38,463
458	Median income $ (46)	37,145	20,413	30,879	30,081	32,837	34,915
459	Standard error of average income $ (46)	10,514	3,394	1,371	1,188	1,151	1,161

Tableau 1. Certaines caractéristiques des secteurs de recensement, recensement de 2001 – Données intégrales et données-échantillon (20 %)

Toronto 0516.03	Toronto 0516.04	Toronto 0516.05	Toronto 0516.06	Toronto 0516.08	Toronto 0516.09	Caractéristiques	N°
						CARACTÉRISTIQUES DES FAMILLES DE RECENSEMENT	
						selon la structure et la taille de la famille de recensement – fin	
40	70	65	60	25	60	Parent de sexe masculin	406
30	50	45	35	15	45	1 enfant	407
15	20	20	10	15	15	2 enfants	408
-	-	-	15	-	-	3 enfants ou plus	409
2,150	**2,025**	**2,905**	**1,970**	**2,645**	**2,855**	**Nombre total d'enfants à la maison**	410
						selon les groupes d'âge	
505	500	610	440	470	475	Moins de 6 ans	411
765	765	1,135	750	970	1,005	6-14 ans	412
195	180	320	200	345	355	15-17 ans	413
480	415	565	390	630	680	18-24 ans	414
200	160	275	190	230	335	25 ans et plus	415
1.2	1.1	1.5	1.4	1.5	1.3	Nombre moyen d'enfants à la maison par famille de recensement (43)	416
6,045	**6,375**	**6,955**	**5,180**	**6,535**	**7,390**	**Nombre total de personnes dans les ménages privés**	417
						selon la situation des particuliers dans la famille de recensement et des particuliers dans le ménage	
750	1,125	525	630	720	625	Nombre de personnes hors famille de recensement	418
170	175	140	145	130	155	Vivant avec des personnes apparentées (44)	419
165	225	150	90	185	155	Vivant avec des personnes non apparentées uniquement	420
415	725	240	400	400	310	Vivant seules	421
5,290	5,250	6,425	4,545	5,815	6,765	Nombre de personnes membres d'une famille	422
3.0	2.9	3.3	3.2	3.3	3.1	Nombre moyen de personnes par famille de recensement	423
425	**315**	**245**	**500**	**550**	**485**	**Nombre total de personnes de 65 ans et plus**	424
215	140	85	250	240	100	Nombre de personnes hors famille de recensement de 65 ans et plus	425
80	45	40	30	50	40	Vivant avec des personnes apparentées (44)	426
15	20	10	-	-	15	Vivant avec des personnes non apparentées uniquement	427
120	75	35	220	190	45	Vivant seules	428
205	180	160	250	310	385	Nombre de personnes membres d'une famille de 65 ans et plus	429
						CARACTÉRISTIQUES DES FAMILLES ÉCONOMIQUES	
1,740	**1,820**	**1,875**	**1,380**	**1,730**	**2,035**	**Nombre total de familles économiques dans les ménages privés**	430
						selon la taille de la famille	
645	845	465	435	485	635	2 personnes	431
480	425	485	310	460	475	3 personnes	432
410	365	560	385	470	560	4 personnes	433
210	185	360	250	315	365	5 personnes ou plus	434
5,455	5,425	6,565	4,690	5,950	6,920	Nombre total de personnes dans les familles économiques	435
3.1	3.0	3.5	3.4	3.4	3.4	Nombre moyen de personnes par famille économique	436
585	950	390	485	585	475	Nombre total de personnes hors famille économique	437
						CARACTÉRISTIQUES DU REVENU DE 2000	
						Population de 15 ans et plus selon le sexe et les tranches de revenu total en 2000	
4,755	5,110	5,210	3,970	5,090	5,910	Total - Les deux sexes	438
220	300	360	150	305	315	Sans revenu	439
4,535	4,810	4,855	3,820	4,785	5,595	Avec un revenu	440
205	145	215	175	255	215	Moins de 1 000 $ (45)	441
120	210	180	130	235	200	1 000 $ - 2 999 $	442
145	205	235	115	155	220	3 000 $ - 4 999 $	443
145	205	220	185	240	240	5 000 $ - 6 999 $	444
190	240	200	160	300	260	7 000 $ - 9 999 $	445
75	130	160	90	125	130	10 000 $ - 11 999 $	446
240	250	205	185	290	335	12 000 $ - 14 999 $	447
330	335	360	280	420	360	15 000 $ - 19 999 $	448
265	240	335	280	295	340	20 000 $ - 24 999 $	449
340	385	310	255	465	460	25 000 $ - 29 999 $	450
440	535	360	400	355	425	30 000 $ - 34 999 $	451
390	370	310	345	355	445	35 000 $ - 39 999 $	452
370	360	315	240	220	400	40 000 $ - 44 999 $	453
250	220	305	185	200	260	45 000 $ - 49 999 $	454
440	430	485	320	270	485	50 000 $ - 59 999 $	455
590	565	655	490	615	825	60 000 $ et plus	456
34,454	32,447	32,597	34,864	30,699	33,896	Revenu moyen $ (46)	457
31,455	30,070	29,924	30,059	25,488	30,025	Revenu médian $ (46)	458
814	813	748	1,331	910	761	Erreur type de revenu moyen $ (46)	459

Table 1. Selected Characteristics for Census Tracts, 2001 Census – 100% Data and 20% Sample Data

No.	Characteristics	Toronto 0514.01 A	Toronto 0514.02 A	Toronto 0515.01	Toronto 0515.02	Toronto 0516.01	Toronto 0516.02
	2000 INCOME CHARACTERISTICS						
	Population 15 years and over by sex and total income groups in 2000 – concluded						
460	Total - Males	1,030	2,280	1,865	1,370	2,270	1,930
461	Without income	55	185	50	30	110	50
462	With income	975	2,090	1,810	1,340	2,155	1,885
463	Under $1,000 (45)	35	110	80	55	105	60
464	$ 1,000 - $ 2,999	60	90	85	40	95	75
465	$ 3,000 - $ 4,999	35	95	50	35	55	80
466	$ 5,000 - $ 6,999	55	70	60	50	30	60
467	$ 7,000 - $ 9,999	30	90	55	60	95	40
468	$10,000 - $11,999	10	85	20	15	75	60
469	$12,000 - $14,999	10	60	45	20	50	35
470	$15,000 - $19,999	30	205	80	95	60	50
471	$20,000 - $24,999	45	210	90	70	65	130
472	$25,000 - $29,999	45	105	105	105	140	50
473	$30,000 - $34,999	40	140	130	80	130	125
474	$35,000 - $39,999	45	110	170	70	120	150
475	$40,000 - $44,999	35	80	145	95	105	125
476	$45,000 - $49,999	15	70	105	120	100	115
477	$50,000 - $59,999	85	95	140	120	185	190
478	$60,000 and over	405	475	460	310	750	545
479	Average income $ (46)	116,851	56,257	45,683	43,370	48,043	45,926
480	Median income $ (46)	49,922	26,950	36,881	36,403	42,100	40,172
481	Standard error of average income $ (46)	21,382	6,705	2,069	1,944	1,928	1,893
482	Total - Females	1,085	2,350	1,890	1,570	2,325	1,940
483	Without income	110	210	95	20	140	120
484	With income	970	2,145	1,795	1,550	2,180	1,820
485	Under $1,000 (45)	45	90	65	35	185	110
486	$ 1,000 - $ 2,999	10	85	80	45	95	75
487	$ 3,000 - $ 4,999	10	145	80	60	75	75
488	$ 5,000 - $ 6,999	30	240	75	30	130	100
489	$ 7,000 - $ 9,999	80	280	145	90	175	85
490	$10,000 - $11,999	15	95	100	45	80	40
491	$12,000 - $14,999	80	140	70	150	155	100
492	$15,000 - $19,999	65	180	125	200	135	160
493	$20,000 - $24,999	45	145	125	110	125	90
494	$25,000 - $29,999	50	115	170	95	75	100
495	$30,000 - $34,999	105	140	195	165	140	155
496	$35,000 - $39,999	45	50	75	120	190	95
497	$40,000 - $44,999	35	75	60	90	110	100
498	$45,000 - $49,999	35	65	100	45	110	115
499	$50,000 - $59,999	105	100	120	120	180	230
500	$60,000 and over	225	190	210	155	225	195
501	Average income $ (46)	48,400	25,519	31,748	30,651	28,214	30,742
502	Median income $ (46)	32,059	14,947	25,439	25,538	22,174	27,862
503	Standard error of average income $ (46)	3,548	1,419	1,735	1,352	1,108	1,160
	by composition of total income						
504	Total - Composition of income in 2000 % (47)	100.0	100.0	100.0	100.0	100.0	100.0
505	Employment income %	78.6	83.0	82.8	77.7	93.0	92.4
506	Government transfer payments %	3.0	6.2	5.6	8.5	3.9	4.2
507	Other %	18.5	10.7	11.4	13.6	3.2	3.4
	Population 15 years and over with employment income in 2000 by sex and work activity						
508	Both sexes with employment income (48)	1,465	3,280	2,940	2,185	3,760	3,270
509	Average employment income $	86,306	43,695	39,378	37,696	40,820	40,238
510	Standard error of average employment income $	11,712	3,808	1,537	1,305	1,269	1,256
511	Worked full year, full time (49)	815	1,625	1,710	1,290	2,355	2,030
512	Average employment income $	126,473	66,233	52,672	49,131	53,667	52,282
513	Standard error of average employment income $	20,228	7,133	2,138	1,682	1,684	1,637
514	Worked part year or part time (50)	570	1,535	1,115	830	1,375	1,195
515	Average employment income $	38,844	21,839	21,438	22,031	19,655	20,429
516	Standard error of average employment income $	6,905	2,665	1,827	1,562	1,182	1,320
517	Males with employment income (48)	795	1,785	1,505	1,080	1,995	1,725
518	Average employment income $	119,915	56,703	44,934	43,615	49,146	47,629
519	Standard error of average employment income $	21,788	6,859	2,213	2,075	2,034	2,013
520	Worked full year, full time (49)	495	1,010	965	685	1,355	1,210
521	Average employment income $	163,143	79,667	57,689	55,058	62,250	58,593
522	Standard error of average employment income $	33,628	11,229	2,664	2,532	2,565	2,498
523	Worked part year or part time (50)	255	710	500	370	625	510
524	Average employment income $	59,454	27,275	23,061	24,670	21,924	21,191
525	Standard error of average employment income $	15,608	5,593	3,361	2,741	1,893	2,060

Tableau 1. Certaines caractéristiques des secteurs de recensement, recensement de 2001 – Données intégrales et données-échantillon (20 %)

Toronto 0516.03	Toronto 0516.04	Toronto 0516.05	Toronto 0516.06	Toronto 0516.08	Toronto 0516.09	Caractéristiques	N°
						CARACTÉRISTIQUES DU REVENU DE 2000	
						Population de 15 ans et plus selon le sexe et les tranches de revenu total en 2000 – fin	
2,215	2,525	2,540	1,845	2,370	2,880	Total - Hommes	460
125	140	125	40	120	145	Sans revenu	461
2,095	2,385	2,415	1,805	2,255	2,730	Avec un revenu	462
95	85	90	65	95	75	Moins de 1 000 $ (45)	463
30	75	60	60	90	65	1 000 $ - 2 999 $	464
45	95	105	45	50	95	3 000 $ - 4 999 $	465
30	65	95	70	80	95	5 000 $ - 6 999 $	466
65	60	90	40	100	115	7 000 $ - 9 999 $	467
25	80	85	25	75	45	10 000 $ - 11 999 $	468
35	85	70	75	110	125	12 000 $ - 14 999 $	469
135	140	140	110	140	80	15 000 $ - 19 999 $	470
90	75	105	85	95	120	20 000 $ - 24 999 $	471
110	170	150	110	235	220	25 000 $ - 29 999 $	472
205	250	145	140	210	230	30 000 $ - 34 999 $	473
180	170	135	175	160	250	35 000 $ - 39 999 $	474
180	180	150	130	165	205	40 000 $ - 44 999 $	475
140	155	195	105	105	150	45 000 $ - 49 999 $	476
305	280	295	180	120	300	50 000 $ - 59 999 $	477
430	400	505	400	435	570	60 000 $ et plus	478
42,790	38,353	38,971	43,338	37,760	40,246	Revenu moyen $ (46)	479
39,978	34,826	36,573	36,982	30,331	36,300	Revenu médian $ (46)	480
1,361	1,337	1,166	2,390	1,606	1,192	Erreur type de revenu moyen $ (46)	481
2,535	2,590	2,670	2,125	2,720	3,030	Total - Femmes	482
90	160	235	110	190	170	Sans revenu	483
2,440	2,430	2,435	2,015	2,530	2,860	Avec un revenu	484
105	65	135	105	165	135	Moins de 1 000 $ (45)	485
85	135	120	75	150	135	1 000 $ - 2 999 $	486
105	105	140	65	105	130	3 000 $ - 4 999 $	487
120	135	120	115	160	150	5 000 $ - 6 999 $	488
130	180	105	120	200	150	7 000 $ - 9 999 $	489
45	50	75	65	50	80	10 000 $ - 11 999 $	490
205	160	140	110	180	210	12 000 $ - 14 999 $	491
200	190	220	170	280	280	15 000 $ - 19 999 $	492
175	160	225	195	205	220	20 000 $ - 24 999 $	493
230	220	160	150	230	240	25 000 $ - 29 999 $	494
230	285	220	265	145	190	30 000 $ - 34 999 $	495
215	200	175	170	200	195	35 000 $ - 39 999 $	496
195	175	165	115	60	185	40 000 $ - 44 999 $	497
110	65	105	80	85	110	45 000 $ - 49 999 $	498
135	150	190	135	150	180	50 000 $ - 59 999 $	499
155	160	145	85	175	255	60 000 $ et plus	500
27,309	26,659	26,275	27,288	24,417	27,827	Revenu moyen $ (46)	501
25,718	25,086	22,330	24,763	18,802	23,814	Revenu médian $ (46)	502
846	856	846	1,259	882	911	Erreur type de revenu moyen $ (46)	503
						selon la composition du revenu total	
100.0	100.0	100.0	100.0	100.0	100.0	Total - Composition du revenu en 2000 % (47)	504
88.6	90.1	91.3	84.0	84.7	87.2	Revenu d'emploi %	505
5.3	5.6	4.8	7.7	8.2	5.5	Transferts gouvernementaux %	506
6.2	4.3	3.8	8.1	7.1	7.2	Autre %	507
						Population de 15 ans et plus ayant un revenu d'emploi en 2000 selon le sexe et le travail	
3,845	4,130	4,355	3,065	3,810	4,760	Les deux sexes ayant un revenu d'emploi (48)	508
35,974	34,054	33,198	36,568	32,626	34,750	Revenu moyen d'emploi $	509
892	848	778	1,379	1,028	801	Erreur type de revenu moyen d'emploi $	510
2,385	2,550	2,670	1,880	2,155	2,565	Ayant travaillé toute l'année à plein temps (49)	511
44,976	42,903	43,174	47,798	44,590	46,657	Revenu moyen d'emploi $	512
1,047	992	920	1,902	1,449	990	Erreur type de revenu moyen d'emploi $	513
1,415	1,530	1,605	1,135	1,590	2,090	Ayant travaillé une partie de l'année ou à temps partiel (50)	514
21,578	20,425	17,922	19,084	17,216	20,952	Revenu moyen d'emploi $	515
1,281	1,208	968	1,293	979	1,027	Erreur type de revenu moyen d'emploi $	516
1,895	2,145	2,260	1,560	1,940	2,405	Hommes ayant un revenu d'emploi (48)	517
43,207	39,280	39,320	44,600	38,644	40,506	Revenu moyen d'emploi $	518
1,445	1,339	1,196	2,445	1,698	1,213	Erreur type de revenu moyen d'emploi $	519
1,300	1,425	1,525	1,065	1,210	1,455	Ayant travaillé toute l'année à plein temps (49)	520
50,966	47,410	48,543	55,749	50,092	52,025	Revenu moyen d'emploi $	521
1,582	1,506	1,343	3,140	2,280	1,455	Erreur type de revenu moyen d'emploi $	522
565	690	695	475	685	910	Ayant travaillé une partie de l'année ou à temps partiel (50)	523
26,888	24,169	20,632	20,860	20,108	22,789	Revenu moyen d'emploi $	524
2,574	2,216	1,721	2,190	1,711	1,483	Erreur type de revenu moyen d'emploi $	525

Table 1. Selected Characteristics for Census Tracts, 2001 Census – 100% Data and 20% Sample Data

No.	Characteristics	Toronto 0514.01 A	Toronto 0514.02 A	Toronto 0515.01	Toronto 0515.02	Toronto 0516.01	Toronto 0516.02
	2000 INCOME CHARACTERISTICS						
	Population 15 years and over with employment income in 2000 by sex and work activity – concluded						
526	Females with employment income (48)	665	1,495	1,440	1,100	1,760	1,545
527	Average employment income $	46,274	28,133	33,563	31,891	31,364	31,975
528	Standard error of average employment income $	3,978	1,624	2,082	1,484	1,266	1,256
529	Worked full year, full time (49)	320	615	750	605	995	825
530	Average employment income $	70,715	44,247	46,246	42,409	42,023	43,010
531	Standard error of average employment income $	6,982	2,992	3,441	1,946	1,623	1,437
532	Worked part year or part time (50)	320	825	615	460	745	685
533	Average employment income $	22,343	17,149	20,128	19,911	17,743	19,860
534	Standard error of average employment income $	2,490	1,449	1,914	1,751	1,465	1,709
	Census families by structure and family income groups in 2000						
535	Total - All census families	710	1,655	1,365	1,045	1,620	1,430
536	Under $10,000	30	150	30	15	30	30
537	$ 10,000 - $19,999	35	90	20	25	20	40
538	$ 20,000 - $29,999	10	195	50	35	80	40
539	$ 30,000 - $39,999	-	160	55	50	75	105
540	$ 40,000 - $49,999	50	195	150	80	55	55
541	$ 50,000 - $59,999	25	120	155	135	90	130
542	$ 60,000 - $69,999	45	130	85	90	185	120
543	$ 70,000 - $79,999	20	85	90	80	135	130
544	$ 80,000 - $89,999	40	45	135	75	130	175
545	$ 90,000 - $99,999	35	20	90	120	140	120
546	$100,000 and over	420	455	515	330	675	495
547	Average family income $	205,840	95,938	95,579	87,463	94,954	86,731
548	Median family income $	118,767	52,078	83,963	81,411	90,059	85,182
549	Standard error of average family income $	31,511	8,914	3,436	2,966	2,701	2,418
550	Total - All couple census families (51)	655	1,380	1,165	885	1,500	1,250
551	Under $10,000	20	95	15	10	35	15
552	$ 10,000 - $19,999	30	75	15	10	10	15
553	$ 20,000 - $29,999	-	140	40	30	50	30
554	$ 30,000 - $39,999	10	130	35	45	35	75
555	$ 40,000 - $49,999	45	135	110	65	50	40
556	$ 50,000 - $59,999	20	110	120	100	90	80
557	$ 60,000 - $69,999	40	115	65	85	175	105
558	$ 70,000 - $79,999	20	85	75	80	130	130
559	$ 80,000 - $89,999	30	40	110	65	125	160
560	$ 90,000 - $99,999	35	10	90	100	135	120
561	$100,000 and over	415	430	490	295	665	485
562	Average family income $	217,776	97,922	99,542	90,481	98,553	92,839
563	Median family income $	122,571	61,812	88,929	83,025	93,697	88,630
564	Standard error of average family income $	34,024	6,799	3,454	3,211	2,812	2,477
	Incidence of low income in 2000						
565	Total - Economic families	700	1,605	1,345	1,005	1,605	1,370
566	Low income	55	395	55	45	100	75
567	Incidence of low income in 2000 % (52)	7.7	24.5	3.9	4.3	6.4	5.4
568	Total - Unattached individuals 15 years and over	105	285	220	350	255	265
569	Low income	10	90	65	120	100	35
570	Incidence of low income in 2000 % (52)	6.0	31.3	29.4	34.4	39.6	14.6
571	Total - Population in private households	2,400	6,275	4,660	3,615	6,075	5,210
572	Low income	235	1,740	260	250	510	355
573	Incidence of low income in 2000 % (52)	9.7	27.7	5.7	6.9	8.5	6.8
	Private households by household income groups in 2000						
574	Total - All private households	775	1,830	1,510	1,340	1,780	1,550
575	Under $10,000	30	130	30	25	35	20
576	$ 10,000 - $19,999	30	125	40	145	90	45
577	$ 20,000 - $29,999	10	205	50	50	65	30
578	$ 30,000 - $39,999	25	185	100	80	75	75
579	$ 40,000 - $49,999	35	185	150	115	55	70
580	$ 50,000 - $59,999	25	145	170	155	90	115
581	$ 60,000 - $69,999	50	170	80	110	190	145
582	$ 70,000 - $79,999	20	110	115	90	160	165
583	$ 80,000 - $89,999	40	60	140	60	155	140
584	$ 90,000 - $99,999	45	30	90	155	160	175
585	$100,000 and over	475	480	550	350	700	565
586	Average household income $	206,721	94,244	92,670	79,153	92,664	91,776
587	Median household income $	120,318	54,017	82,142	67,828	88,644	87,469
588	Standard error of average household income $	29,360	8,247	3,258	2,847	2,655	2,599

Tableau 1. Certaines caractéristiques des secteurs de recensement, recensement de 2001 – Données intégrales et données-échantillon (20 %)

Toronto 0516.03	Toronto 0516.04	Toronto 0516.05	Toronto 0516.06	Toronto 0516.08	Toronto 0516.09	Caractéristiques	N°
						CARACTÉRISTIQUES DU REVENU DE 2000	
						Population de 15 ans et plus ayant un revenu d'emploi en 2000 selon le sexe et le travail – fin	
1,955	1,980	2,095	1,505	1,875	2,360	Femmes ayant un revenu d'emploi (48)	526
28,959	28,387	26,611	28,223	26,412	28,885	Revenu moyen d'emploi $	527
949	928	865	1,054	1,055	994	Erreur type de revenu moyen d'emploi $	528
1,085	1,120	1,150	815	950	1,110	Ayant travaillé toute l'année à plein temps (49)	529
37,805	37,175	36,040	37,399	37,601	39,612	Revenu moyen d'emploi $	530
1,156	1,083	1,024	1,082	1,438	1,160	Erreur type de revenu moyen d'emploi $	531
845	840	905	660	900	1,180	Ayant travaillé une partie de l'année ou à temps partiel (50)	532
18,018	17,341	15,843	17,803	15,018	19,542	Revenu moyen d'emploi $	533
1,192	1,162	1,027	1,574	1,102	1,407	Erreur type de revenu moyen d'emploi $	534
						Familles de recensement selon la structure et les tranches de revenu de la famille en 2000	
1,750	1,790	1,920	1,440	1,750	2,145	Total - Toutes les familles de recensement	535
10	110	85	40	80	70	Moins de 10 000 $	536
40	120	50	60	105	45	10 000 $ - 19 999 $	537
95	145	115	70	105	140	20 000 $ - 29 999 $	538
155	145	105	130	185	95	30 000 $ - 39 999 $	539
210	210	225	95	170	215	40 000 $ - 49 999 $	540
200	200	225	125	140	240	50 000 $ - 59 999 $	541
255	175	160	170	170	170	60 000 $ - 69 999 $	542
150	230	180	145	140	255	70 000 $ - 79 999 $	543
170	75	165	150	130	195	80 000 $ - 89 999 $	544
140	155	110	165	155	235	90 000 $ - 99 999 $	545
325	230	500	275	365	490	100 000 $ et plus	546
74,256	63,575	74,059	78,956	71,376	77,608	Revenu moyen des familles $	547
64,661	57,482	69,165	71,005	64,339	74,049	Revenu médian des familles $	548
2,016	2,144	1,957	3,930	2,381	1,923	Erreur type de revenu moyen des familles $	549
1,390	1,435	1,595	1,145	1,425	1,760	Total - Toutes les familles de recensement comptant un couple (51)	550
10	85	65	25	50	50	Moins de 10 000 $	551
25	70	35	30	75	10	10 000 $ - 19 999 $	552
55	95	70	50	50	90	20 000 $ - 29 999 $	553
80	90	75	85	95	60	30 000 $ - 39 999 $	554
140	145	150	45	125	165	40 000 $ - 49 999 $	555
130	145	175	115	135	170	50 000 $ - 59 999 $	556
210	145	150	140	150	155	60 000 $ - 69 999 $	557
135	230	145	135	130	200	70 000 $ - 79 999 $	558
160	75	145	135	110	165	80 000 $ - 89 999 $	559
140	140	105	140	150	220	90 000 $ - 99 999 $	560
325	210	485	255	355	465	100 000 $ et plus	561
80,902	68,287	79,422	85,501	78,487	82,339	Revenu moyen des familles $	562
74,459	63,932	75,149	77,625	71,370	78,474	Revenu médian des familles $	563
2,237	2,444	2,126	4,859	2,704	2,169	Erreur type de revenu moyen des familles $	564
						Fréquence des unités à faible revenu en 2000	
1,745	1,820	1,875	1,380	1,730	2,035	Total - Familles économiques	565
65	340	240	125	280	120	Faible revenu	566
3.8	18.7	12.6	8.9	16.0	6.0	Fréquence des unités à faible revenu en 2000 % (52)	567
565	950	385	470	580	465	Total - Personnes hors famille économique de 15 ans et plus	568
110	215	80	130	185	115	Faible revenu	569
19.5	22.4	20.6	27.9	31.7	25.2	Fréquence des unités à faible revenu en 2000 % (52)	570
6,025	6,375	6,950	5,165	6,525	7,380	Total - Population dans les ménages privés	571
305	1,390	950	610	1,255	510	Faible revenu	572
5.1	21.8	13.7	11.8	19.2	6.9	Fréquence des unités à faible revenu en 2000 % (52)	573
						Ménages privés selon les tranches de revenu du ménage en 2000	
2,195	2,615	2,140	1,785	2,180	2,390	Total - Tous les ménages privés	574
35	160	80	50	90	50	Moins de 10 000 $	575
95	195	70	165	240	65	10 000 $ - 19 999 $	576
145	205	130	185	155	115	20 000 $ - 29 999 $	577
210	260	175	125	215	170	30 000 $ - 39 999 $	578
245	320	245	115	235	195	40 000 $ - 49 999 $	579
230	345	210	105	185	205	50 000 $ - 59 999 $	580
285	290	200	180	195	270	60 000 $ - 69 999 $	581
185	290	185	145	140	235	70 000 $ - 79 999 $	582
180	110	180	165	140	250	80 000 $ - 89 999 $	583
190	160	115	190	145	245	90 000 $ - 99 999 $	584
380	285	560	355	450	590	100 000 $ et plus	585
71,157	59,654	73,964	74,815	67,414	79,176	Revenu moyen des ménages $	586
63,137	54,029	67,257	67,608	58,465	74,225	Revenu médian des ménages $	587
1,836	1,709	1,909	3,447	2,126	1,785	Erreur type de revenu moyen des ménages $	588

Table 1. Selected Characteristics for Census Tracts, 2001 Census – 100% Data and 20% Sample Data

No.	Characteristics	Toronto 0516.10	Toronto 0516.11	Toronto 0516.14 ◆	Toronto 0516.16 ◆◇	Toronto 0516.17 A	Toronto 0516.18 A
	POPULATION CHARACTERISTICS						
1	**Population, 1996 (1)**	**7,038**	**5,068**	**4,215**	**4,991**	**3,969**	**3,883**
2	**Population, 2001 (2)**	**8,574**	**5,033**	**4,273**	**5,511**	**3,804**	**3,916**
3	Population percentage change, 1996-2001	21.8	-0.7	1.4	10.4	-4.2	0.8
4	Land area in square kilometres, 2001	3.85	2.17	2.65	2.97	1.07	1.15
5	**Total population - 100% Data (3)**	**8,570**	**5,035**	**4,275**	**5,515**	**3,805**	**3,915**
	by sex and age groups						
6	Male	4,255	2,535	2,120	2,700	1,830	1,945
7	0-4 years	220	115	100	130	75	95
8	5-9 years	290	210	165	150	120	145
9	10-14 years	345	235	200	210	170	170
10	15-19 years	405	285	205	265	180	190
11	20-24 years	400	205	155	275	145	175
12	25-29 years	255	95	125	160	95	100
13	30-34 years	215	85	110	160	105	105
14	35-39 years	255	175	150	155	135	145
15	40-44 years	380	205	200	170	190	190
16	45-49 years	380	275	225	185	170	175
17	50-54 years	415	250	170	235	160	210
18	55-59 years	235	180	120	195	105	130
19	60-64 years	185	100	75	125	60	50
20	65-69 years	135	50	35	90	50	30
21	70-74 years	70	35	25	85	30	15
22	75-79 years	40	20	20	65	25	10
23	80-84 years	25	5	15	30	15	-
24	85 years and over	15	5	5	10	5	-
25	Female	4,315	2,495	2,155	2,815	1,975	1,975
26	0-4 years	220	115	95	115	100	95
27	5-9 years	285	160	165	165	120	140
28	10-14 years	350	215	190	170	125	175
29	15-19 years	370	250	200	235	185	180
30	20-24 years	370	200	135	270	140	135
31	25-29 years	245	75	120	155	90	90
32	30-34 years	250	110	125	155	110	135
33	35-39 years	335	210	205	185	180	170
34	40-44 years	405	260	255	220	215	225
35	45-49 years	440	280	225	255	200	175
36	50-54 years	395	280	155	270	170	200
37	55-59 years	220	135	105	175	100	110
38	60-64 years	150	65	55	135	55	65
39	65-69 years	90	55	40	90	55	30
40	70-74 years	80	30	40	100	40	20
41	75-79 years	45	25	30	60	45	15
42	80-84 years	45	10	10	35	25	15
43	85 years and over	30	10	5	15	15	5
44	**Total population 15 years and over**	**6,865**	**3,985**	**3,355**	**4,575**	**3,100**	**3,090**
	by legal marital status						
45	Never married (single)	2,190	1,205	1,050	1,535	1,005	980
46	Legally married (and not separated)	4,210	2,500	1,975	2,490	1,635	1,760
47	Separated, but still legally married	100	55	90	130	115	90
48	Divorced	155	125	150	230	205	160
49	Widowed	210	90	90	200	135	95
	by common-law status						
50	Not in a common-law relationship	6,750	3,885	3,255	4,370	2,935	2,955
51	In a common-law relationship	110	90	105	205	160	135
52	**Total population - 20% Sample Data (4)**	**8,540**	**5,035**	**4,270**	**5,505**	**3,805**	**3,895**
	by mother tongue						
53	Single responses	8,380	5,020	4,190	5,425	3,720	3,875
54	English	4,200	3,675	2,360	3,775	2,665	3,070
55	French	65	70	25	80	65	35
56	Non-official languages (5)	4,115	1,275	1,805	1,570	990	765
57	Italian	165	120	135	110	40	35
58	Chinese, n.o.s.	485	125	190	185	85	25
59	Cantonese	460	180	125	100	60	-
60	Portuguese	200	50	170	35	20	35
61	Punjabi	420	10	135	35	-	-
62	Other languages (6)	2,385	790	1,045	1,110	775	670
63	Multiple responses	160	10	80	80	85	30
64	English and French	20	-	10	20	10	10
65	English and non-official language	140	10	70	55	60	15
66	French and non-official language	-	-	-	-	-	-
67	English, French and non-official language	-	-	-	-	20	10

See reference material at the end of the publication. – Voir les documents de référence à la fin de la publication.

Tableau 1. Certaines caractéristiques des secteurs de recensement, recensement de 2001 – Données intégrales et données-échantillon (20 %)

Toronto 0516.19 A	Toronto 0516.20 A	Toronto 0516.21 A	Toronto 0516.22 A	Toronto 0516.23 A	Toronto 0516.24 A	Caractéristiques	N°
						CARACTÉRISTIQUES DE LA POPULATION	
4,959	**5,426**	**2,591**	**2,913**	**4,774**	**4,397**	**Population, 1996 (1)**	1
9,770	**5,964**	**3,027**	**6,387**	**5,331**	**4,506**	**Population, 2001 (2)**	2
97.0	9.9	16.8	119.3	11.7	2.5	Variation en pourcentage de la population, 1996-2001	3
4.62	1.31	1.07	1.27	1.07	2.56	Superficie des terres en kilomètres carrés, 2001	4
9,770	**5,965**	**3,030**	**6,385**	**5,335**	**4,510**	**Population totale – Données intégrales (3)**	5
						selon le sexe et les groupes d'âge	
4,885	3,000	1,500	3,120	2,680	2,290	Sexe masculin	6
585	225	90	360	215	125	0-4 ans	7
540	270	135	355	295	170	5-9 ans	8
375	285	150	295	260	235	10-14 ans	9
305	265	155	190	200	260	15-19 ans	10
195	190	100	120	150	165	20-24 ans	11
275	130	80	180	110	120	25-29 ans	12
605	195	90	355	180	90	30-34 ans	13
700	345	115	425	285	185	35-39 ans	14
535	340	155	375	340	215	40-44 ans	15
310	265	155	175	220	225	45-49 ans	16
185	215	120	125	180	205	50-54 ans	17
105	125	75	60	100	140	55-59 ans	18
60	55	40	40	60	80	60-64 ans	19
50	45	30	40	40	35	65-69 ans	20
30	25	10	15	20	20	70-74 ans	21
15	10	5	10	15	10	75-79 ans	22
5	10	5	-	10	5	80-84 ans	23
5	5	5	-	-	-	85 ans et plus	24
4,885	2,970	1,525	3,265	2,655	2,215	Sexe féminin	25
595	225	110	365	195	140	0-4 ans	26
510	265	120	345	280	175	5-9 ans	27
370	270	120	295	235	210	10-14 ans	28
255	230	125	185	195	205	15-19 ans	29
175	165	115	135	140	170	20-24 ans	30
335	145	80	240	125	85	25-29 ans	31
715	240	110	415	225	125	30-34 ans	32
685	355	145	460	340	185	35-39 ans	33
470	375	165	320	315	270	40-44 ans	34
275	260	165	160	200	235	45-49 ans	35
180	210	110	115	165	185	50-54 ans	36
95	80	60	65	85	95	55-59 ans	37
80	40	30	50	65	60	60-64 ans	38
65	45	25	45	25	35	65-69 ans	39
45	20	20	35	20	15	70-74 ans	40
25	15	15	15	20	15	75-79 ans	41
10	10	5	10	20	15	80-84 ans	42
5	10	5	5	5	5	85 ans et plus	43
6,805	**4,415**	**2,305**	**4,365**	**3,850**	**3,445**	**Population totale de 15 ans et plus**	44
						selon l'état matrimonial légal	
1,515	1,250	700	975	980	1,050	Célibataire (jamais marié(e))	45
4,735	2,845	1,410	3,035	2,605	2,160	Légalement marié(e) (et non séparé(e))	46
140	80	45	95	85	50	Séparé(e), mais toujours légalement marié(e)	47
255	145	85	160	105	95	Divorcé(e)	48
165	95	65	105	85	85	Veuf ou veuve	49
						selon l'union libre	
6,520	4,220	2,225	4,165	3,745	3,360	Ne vivant pas en union libre	50
285	195	80	200	110	90	Vivant en union libre	51
9,770	**5,965**	**3,025**	**6,385**	**5,330**	**4,525**	**Population totale – Données-échantillon (20 %) (4)**	52
						selon la langue maternelle	
9,550	5,885	2,985	6,280	5,230	4,475	Réponses uniques	53
6,620	4,270	2,145	3,875	3,485	3,190	Anglais	54
145	160	35	165	75	175	Français	55
2,780	1,450	810	2,240	1,670	1,115	Langues non officielles (5)	56
225	85	60	145	155	120	Italien	57
80	110	60	85	110	150	Chinois, n.d.a.	58
165	55	25	45	105	35	Cantonais	59
205	85	75	270	125	75	Portugais	60
100	105	60	85	265	-	Pendjabi	61
2,015	1,005	530	1,610	905	740	Autres langues (6)	62
220	85	45	100	100	45	Réponses multiples	63
25	15	-	-	25	-	Anglais et français	64
190	65	25	75	70	45	Anglais et langue non officielle	65
10	-	15	20	10	-	Français et langue non officielle	66
-	-	-	-	-	-	Anglais, français et langue non officielle	67

See reference material at the end of the publication. – Voir les documents de référence à la fin de la publication.

Table 1. Selected Characteristics for Census Tracts, 2001 Census – 100% Data and 20% Sample Data

No.	Characteristics	Toronto 0516.10	Toronto 0516.11	Toronto 0516.14 ◆	Toronto 0516.16 ◆◇	Toronto 0516.17 A	Toronto 0516.18 A
	POPULATION CHARACTERISTICS						
	by home language						
68	Single responses	5,790	4,330	3,195	4,500	3,135	3,420
69	English	4,670	3,985	2,570	4,120	2,795	3,235
70	French	-	-	-	15	20	-
71	Non-official languages (5)	1,115	340	625	365	315	185
72	Cantonese	290	105	35	50	35	-
73	Chinese, n.o.s.	185	10	100	80	60	20
74	Italian	10	-	10	-	15	-
75	Punjabi	120	-	85	35	-	-
76	Portuguese	30	20	10	-	10	10
77	Other languages (6)	485	190	395	195	205	155
78	Multiple responses	2,750	705	1,080	1,005	670	480
79	English and French	25	75	65	95	30	45
80	English and non-official language	2,665	620	1,000	890	620	405
81	French and non-official language	10	-	-	-	10	-
82	English, French and non-official language	50	10	20	20	15	25
	by knowledge of official languages						
83	English only	7,510	4,465	3,775	4,885	3,245	3,570
84	French only	10	-	-	10	-	-
85	English and French	795	505	370	555	470	305
86	Neither English nor French	220	65	130	65	90	20
	by knowledge of non-official languages (5) (7)						
87	Italian	280	195	215	160	85	45
88	Cantonese	600	195	125	75	85	-
89	Chinese, n.o.s.	445	90	165	210	80	20
90	Spanish	65	155	85	90	90	170
91	Portuguese	255	85	170	40	25	55
92	Punjabi	560	65	235	75	20	-
93	Tagalog (Pilipino)	70	45	110	120	60	120
	by first official language spoken						
94	English	8,110	4,890	4,100	5,310	3,590	3,820
95	French	80	70	15	90	75	40
96	English and French	135	10	30	40	55	15
97	Neither English nor French	210	65	130	65	85	20
98	Official language minority - (number) (8)	145	75	30	110	100	50
99	Official language minority - (percentage) (8)	1.7	1.5	0.7	2.0	2.6	1.3
	by ethnic origin (9)						
100	Canadian	1,035	1,100	740	1,360	805	1,095
101	English	1,015	1,475	515	1,465	795	1,185
102	Scottish	710	835	330	835	605	815
103	Irish	655	755	325	830	635	750
104	Chinese	1,395	360	395	390	260	60
105	Italian	610	510	395	335	235	120
106	East Indian	1,580	295	720	335	265	190
107	French	335	370	140	345	170	235
108	German	320	405	120	365	265	325
109	Portuguese	340	140	245	80	70	85
110	Polish	435	265	145	350	280	280
111	Jewish	70	85	15	15	120	45
112	Jamaican	105	10	115	135	70	60
113	Filipino	110	105	230	160	80	145
114	Ukrainian	195	135	85	170	90	215
	by Aboriginal identity						
115	Total Aboriginal identity population (10)	15	30	-	20	20	10
116	Total non-Aboriginal population	8,525	5,005	4,275	5,485	3,785	3,895
	by Aboriginal origin						
117	Total Aboriginal origins population (11)	45	30	10	80	35	30
118	Total non-Aboriginal population	8,495	5,000	4,265	5,420	3,770	3,870
	by Registered Indian status						
119	Registered Indian (12)	-	-	-	10	15	-
120	Not a Registered Indian	8,535	5,035	4,275	5,495	3,790	3,900

Tableau 1. Certaines caractéristiques des secteurs de recensement, recensement de 2001 – Données intégrales et données-échantillon (20 %)

Toronto 0516.19 A	Toronto 0516.20 A	Toronto 0516.21 A	Toronto 0516.22 A	Toronto 0516.23 A	Toronto 0516.24 A	Caractéristiques	N°
						CARACTÉRISTIQUES DE LA POPULATION	
						selon la langue parlée à la maison	
7,710	4,815	2,505	4,840	4,385	3,645	Réponses uniques	68
6,975	4,540	2,285	4,175	3,855	3,365	Anglais	69
40	15	-	55	15	-	Français	70
695	260	220	615	515	280	Langues non officielles (5)	71
90	35	15	30	50	-	Cantonais	72
-	-	15	70	40	40	Chinois, n.d.a.	73
10	10	-	30	20	10	Italien	74
10	25	20	-	110	-	Pendjabi	75
45	-	15	45	35	10	Portugais	76
550	190	150	430	275	215	Autres langues (6)	77
2,060	1,150	520	1,545	940	885	Réponses multiples	78
235	190	25	125	65	155	Anglais et français	79
1,765	955	495	1,380	875	665	Anglais et langue non officielle	80
-	10	-	15	-	15	Français et langue non officielle	81
55	-	-	25	10	50	Anglais, français et langue non officielle	82
						selon la connaissance des langues officielles	
8,770	5,245	2,780	5,645	4,580	3,890	Anglais seulement	83
-	-	-	10	-	-	Français seulement	84
875	685	210	610	655	560	Anglais et français	85
120	35	35	120	95	75	Ni l'anglais ni le français	86
						selon la connaissance des langues non officielles (5) (7)	
390	190	80	200	275	240	Italien	87
170	110	25	55	120	85	Cantonais	88
90	85	60	100	100	165	Chinois, n.d.a.	89
290	145	110	190	75	90	Espagnol	90
265	90	85	325	125	95	Portugais	91
130	170	120	120	290	20	Pendjabi	92
225	100	65	145	70	65	Tagalog (pilipino)	93
						selon la première langue officielle parlée	
9,415	5,760	2,945	5,995	5,115	4,270	Anglais	94
135	160	50	185	85	160	Français	95
105	10	-	105	35	25	Anglais et français	96
125	30	30	100	95	70	Ni l'anglais ni le français	97
190	170	50	240	100	175	Minorité de langue officielle - (nombre) (8)	98
1.9	2.8	1.7	3.8	1.9	3.9	Minorité de langue officielle - (pourcentage) (8)	99
						selon l'origine ethnique (9)	
2,260	1,545	675	1,500	1,155	1,145	Canadien	100
1,390	1,250	515	965	925	895	Anglais	101
1,170	805	340	600	770	810	Écossais	102
905	725	345	575	650	685	Irlandais	103
430	245	100	310	330	400	Chinois	104
1,005	455	250	525	605	435	Italien	105
945	650	345	810	675	280	Indien de l'Inde	106
570	430	185	360	280	480	Français	107
420	440	160	425	240	205	Allemand	108
580	190	130	580	265	205	Portugais	109
690	415	210	510	335	130	Polonais	110
25	20	10	30	-	10	Juif	111
370	215	60	355	130	95	Jamaïquain	112
355	190	100	205	125	80	Philippin	113
265	255	110	180	75	270	Ukrainien	114
						selon l'identité autochtone	
10	60	-	-	10	10	Total de la population ayant une identité autochtone (10)	115
9,760	5,905	3,030	6,375	5,320	4,520	Total de la population non autochtone	116
						selon l'origine autochtone	
90	40	10	60	20	20	Total de la population ayant une origine autochtone (11)	117
9,680	5,920	3,015	6,325	5,315	4,500	Total de la population non autochtone	118
						selon le statut d'Indien inscrit	
-	-	-	-	10	-	Oui, Indien inscrit (12)	119
9,765	5,965	3,025	6,385	5,320	4,515	Non, pas un Indien inscrit	120

Table 1. Selected Characteristics for Census Tracts, 2001 Census – 100% Data and 20% Sample Data

No.	Characteristics	Toronto 0516.10	Toronto 0516.11	Toronto 0516.14 ◆	Toronto 0516.16 ◆◇	Toronto 0516.17 A	Toronto 0516.18 A
	POPULATION CHARACTERISTICS						
	by visible minority groups						
121	Total visible minority population	4,145	1,200	2,220	1,535	1,150	755
122	Chinese	1,350	365	395	365	240	50
123	South Asian	1,645	345	755	375	280	190
124	Black	115	35	425	260	215	110
125	Filipino	100	105	210	140	110	145
126	Latin American	20	45	45	20	45	135
127	Southeast Asian	115	-	70	25	-	10
128	Arab	400	10	70	125	95	-
129	West Asian	85	35	75	35	55	55
130	Korean	140	90	15	80	45	15
131	Japanese	15	120	65	15	-	30
132	Visible minority, n.i.e. (13)	70	40	70	40	35	10
133	Multiple visible minorities (14)	90	20	30	45	15	-
	by citizenship						
134	Canadian citizenship (15)	7,720	4,680	3,730	5,050	3,505	3,670
135	Citizenship other than Canadian	815	355	545	450	305	230
	by place of birth of respondent						
136	Non-immigrant population	4,245	3,535	2,170	3,510	2,345	2,625
137	Born in province of residence	3,675	3,030	1,815	2,980	1,975	2,135
138	Immigrant population (16)	4,185	1,435	2,005	1,860	1,440	1,280
139	United States	35	35	30	35	65	30
140	Central and South America	110	110	110	50	40	100
141	Caribbean and Bermuda	100	70	120	170	100	90
142	United Kingdom	245	180	140	265	200	320
143	Other Europe (17)	900	370	425	555	340	365
144	Africa	235	60	170	75	75	50
145	Asia and the Middle East	2,545	580	995	715	610	325
146	Oceania and other (18)	10	25	15	-	-	-
147	Non-permanent residents (19)	110	65	100	135	20	-
148	**Total immigrant population**	**4,190**	**1,430**	**2,005**	**1,860**	**1,435**	**1,280**
	by period of immigration						
149	Before 1961	245	180	70	235	150	90
150	1961-1970	520	225	220	400	190	200
151	1971-1980	1,075	370	535	310	315	295
152	1981-1990	810	470	535	425	310	300
153	1991-2001 (20)	1,530	185	650	480	470	385
154	1991-1995	1,085	120	325	265	250	270
155	1996-2001 (20)	445	65	330	210	220	120
	by age at immigration						
156	0-4 years	430	160	150	165	135	150
157	5-19 years	1,140	380	515	560	395	365
158	20 years and over	2,610	890	1,340	1,135	915	760
159	**Total population**	**8,540**	**5,035**	**4,275**	**5,500**	**3,805**	**3,900**
	by religion						
160	Catholic (21)	3,450	2,020	1,535	2,080	1,495	1,495
161	Protestant	1,345	1,445	850	1,810	1,030	1,405
162	Christian Orthodox	245	85	65	125	120	70
163	Christian, n.i.e. (22)	160	100	175	165	95	115
164	Muslim	580	75	385	225	355	60
165	Jewish	45	65	55	20	125	15
166	Buddhist	320	45	85	45	45	-
167	Hindu	680	70	340	90	20	10
168	Sikh	455	110	125	35	15	-
169	Eastern religions (23)	-	130	25	-	-	10
170	Other religions (24)	-	-	-	-	-	10
171	No religious affiliation (25)	1,260	885	635	905	520	705
172	**Total population 15 years and over**	**6,805**	**3,985**	**3,360**	**4,570**	**3,095**	**3,040**
	by generation status						
173	1st generation (26)	4,080	1,445	1,970	1,935	1,365	1,205
174	2nd generation (27)	1,595	1,015	770	1,005	800	705
175	3rd generation and over (28)	1,130	1,520	625	1,630	930	1,130
176	**Total population 1 year and over (29)**	**8,450**	**5,000**	**4,225**	**5,470**	**3,780**	**3,840**
	by place of residence 1 year ago (mobility)						
177	Non-movers	7,710	4,775	3,890	4,695	3,270	3,530
178	Movers	735	225	340	780	510	305
179	Non-migrants	405	145	125	450	275	200
180	Migrants	335	75	215	335	230	105
181	Internal migrants	200	55	140	245	205	110
182	Intraprovincial migrants	155	55	125	185	200	70
183	Interprovincial migrants	45	-	20	60	-	40
184	External migrants	135	25	75	90	30	-

Tableau 1. Certaines caractéristiques des secteurs de recensement, recensement de 2001 – Données intégrales et données-échantillon (20 %)

Toronto 0516.19 A	Toronto 0516.20 A	Toronto 0516.21 A	Toronto 0516.22 A	Toronto 0516.23 A	Toronto 0516.24 A	Caractéristiques	N°
						CARACTÉRISTIQUES DE LA POPULATION	
						selon les groupes de minorités visibles	
3,305	1,690	965	2,330	1,840	1,305	Total de la population des minorités visibles	121
360	230	105	270	290	405	Chinois	122
1,030	625	360	825	735	320	Sud-Asiatique	123
770	355	160	575	350	265	Noir	124
290	155	95	190	75	75	Philippin	125
110	65	120	40	50	10	Latino-Américain	126
100	40	-	65	25	-	Asiatique du Sud-Est	127
160	60	65	50	105	80	Arabe	128
30	-	-	15	20	75	Asiatique occidental	129
75	40	-	30	-	15	Coréen	130
-	15	-	15	10	-	Japonais	131
215	60	55	170	130	50	Minorité visible, n.i.a. (13)	132
155	55	10	80	50	10	Minorités visibles multiples (14)	133
						selon la citoyenneté	
8,895	5,380	2,830	5,605	4,890	4,185	Citoyenneté canadienne (15)	134
870	580	200	785	440	340	Citoyenneté autre que canadienne	135
						selon le lieu de naissance du répondant	
6,175	4,060	1,855	3,665	3,375	3,075	Population non immigrante	136
5,440	3,505	1,590	3,110	2,880	2,505	Née dans la province de résidence	137
3,550	1,890	1,165	2,620	1,895	1,440	Population immigrante (16)	138
100	65	25	60	30	55	États-Unis	139
335	145	165	180	130	40	Amérique centrale et du Sud	140
485	225	80	295	245	145	Caraïbes et Bermudes	141
105	250	110	155	155	125	Royaume-Uni	142
965	445	330	775	485	350	Autre Europe (17)	143
270	135	120	285	140	60	Afrique	144
1,275	605	335	865	690	665	Asie et Moyen-Orient	145
25	20	-	-	20	10	Océanie et autre (18)	146
45	10	-	100	60	10	Résidents non permanents (19)	147
3,550	**1,890**	**1,165**	**2,620**	**1,895**	**1,440**	**Population immigrante totale**	148
						selon la période d'immigration	
95	115	85	45	115	70	Avant 1961	149
405	150	235	280	285	340	1961-1970	150
715	445	255	435	435	400	1971-1980	151
1,015	510	370	780	550	285	1981-1990	152
1,320	675	220	1,080	505	350	1991-2001 (20)	153
810	380	105	480	275	220	1991-1995	154
505	305	115	595	235	130	1996-2001 (20)	155
						selon l'âge à l'immigration	
450	150	145	360	245	130	0-4 ans	156
1,005	570	340	845	435	445	5-19 ans	157
2,100	1,175	675	1,415	1,210	875	20 ans et plus	158
9,770	**5,965**	**3,025**	**6,385**	**5,330**	**4,525**	**Population totale**	159
						selon la religion	
4,845	2,715	1,470	3,140	2,565	2,410	Catholique (21)	160
2,170	1,880	690	1,460	1,240	1,145	Protestante	161
425	85	70	160	225	130	Orthodoxe chrétienne	162
225	115	90	190	50	20	Chrétiennes, n.i.a. (22)	163
440	135	45	255	235	180	Musulmane	164
-	-	15	35	25	-	Juive	165
105	25	10	55	30	40	Bouddhiste	166
400	260	195	280	220	90	Hindoue	167
80	125	85	95	235	35	Sikh	168
10	15	35	55	25	20	Religions orientales (23)	169
-	15	-	-	-	-	Autres religions (24)	170
1,055	600	330	660	480	450	Aucune appartenance religieuse (25)	171
6,780	**4,410**	**2,330**	**4,370**	**3,830**	**3,455**	**Population totale de 15 ans et plus**	172
						selon le statut des générations	
3,325	1,795	1,130	2,370	1,820	1,375	1re génération (26)	173
1,565	1,020	555	995	1,005	830	2e génération (27)	174
1,890	1,595	640	1,010	1,000	1,255	3e génération et plus (28)	175
9,555	**5,890**	**2,985**	**6,180**	**5,255**	**4,495**	**Population totale de 1 an et plus (29)**	176
						selon le lieu de résidence 1 an auparavant (mobilité)	
8,090	5,465	2,740	5,415	4,780	4,105	Personnes n'ayant pas déménagé	177
1,460	425	240	770	475	390	Personnes ayant déménagé	178
1,030	245	100	400	215	165	Non-migrants	179
430	180	140	370	255	225	Migrants	180
320	175	90	290	240	115	Migrants internes	181
255	150	50	225	210	90	Migrants infraprovinciaux	182
65	25	40	60	30	25	Migrants interprovinciaux	183
110	-	55	80	15	115	Migrants externes	184

Table 1. Selected Characteristics for Census Tracts, 2001 Census – 100% Data and 20% Sample Data

No.	Characteristics	Toronto 0516.10	Toronto 0516.11	Toronto 0516.14 ◆	Toronto 0516.16 ◆◇	Toronto 0516.17 A	Toronto 0516.18 A
	POPULATION CHARACTERISTICS						
185	**Total population 5 years and over (30)**	**8,085**	**4,800**	**4,080**	**5,260**	**3,630**	**3,665**
	by place of residence 5 years ago (mobility)						
186	Non-movers	4,760	3,595	2,695	2,915	2,175	2,320
187	Movers	3,325	1,205	1,385	2,350	1,455	1,340
188	Non-migrants	2,025	690	545	1,340	885	850
189	Migrants	1,300	515	840	1,010	570	490
190	Internal migrants	765	365	430	645	415	450
191	Intraprovincial migrants	540	310	340	480	370	310
192	Interprovincial migrants	220	50	85	160	35	140
193	External migrants	540	155	410	365	160	40
194	**Total population 15 to 24 years**	**1,535**	**945**	**700**	**1,010**	**650**	**645**
	by school attendance						
195	Not attending school	320	145	135	240	150	190
196	Attending school full time	1,150	775	550	695	470	425
197	Attending school part time	65	25	15	75	25	30
198	**Total population 15 years and over**	**6,805**	**3,985**	**3,360**	**4,570**	**3,100**	**3,045**
	by highest level of schooling						
199	Less than grade 9 (31)	290	110	115	95	115	40
200	Grades 9-13 without high school graduation certificate	985	595	490	670	555	440
201	Grades 9-13 with high school graduation certificate	680	395	555	525	425	425
202	Some postsecondary without degree, certificate or diploma (32)	1,045	465	415	745	365	435
203	Trades certificate or diploma (33)	440	180	295	295	200	255
204	College certificate or diploma (34)	915	555	445	760	505	595
205	University certificate below bachelor's degree	320	200	110	110	120	45
206	University with bachelor's degree or higher	2,120	1,470	940	1,370	810	805
	by combinations of unpaid work						
207	Males 15 years and over	3,385	1,995	1,650	2,190	1,475	1,545
208	Reported unpaid work (35)	3,015	1,820	1,435	1,910	1,365	1,355
209	Housework and child care and care or assistance to seniors	350	215	165	125	105	95
210	Housework and child care only	920	570	435	535	410	480
211	Housework and care or assistance to seniors only	230	180	130	150	85	115
212	Child care and care or assistance to seniors only	-	-	-	-	15	-
213	Housework only	1,460	805	685	1,080	740	640
214	Child care only	30	30	20	15	10	10
215	Care or assistance to seniors only	20	20	-	15	10	15
216	Females 15 years and over	3,420	1,990	1,710	2,380	1,625	1,500
217	Reported unpaid work (35)	3,090	1,845	1,570	2,155	1,515	1,395
218	Housework and child care and care or assistance to seniors	450	330	270	200	160	110
219	Housework and child care only	1,190	645	590	690	490	595
220	Housework and care or assistance to seniors only	260	165	150	200	150	130
221	Child care and care or assistance to seniors only	-	-	-	-	10	-
222	Housework only	1,155	675	535	1,045	695	555
223	Child care only	20	-	15	15	15	10
224	Care or assistance to seniors only	10	15	10	10	-	-
	by labour force activity						
225	Males 15 years and over	3,385	1,995	1,645	2,195	1,475	1,545
226	In the labour force	2,560	1,565	1,260	1,590	1,065	1,310
227	Employed	2,410	1,515	1,230	1,490	1,045	1,250
228	Unemployed	145	50	35	100	15	55
229	Not in the labour force	830	430	390	600	410	240
230	Participation rate	75.6	78.4	76.6	72.4	72.2	84.8
231	Employment rate	71.2	75.9	74.8	67.9	70.8	80.9
232	Unemployment rate	5.7	3.2	2.8	6.3	1.4	4.2
233	Females 15 years and over	3,415	1,990	1,710	2,380	1,625	1,500
234	In the labour force	2,120	1,395	1,220	1,550	1,115	1,090
235	Employed	2,020	1,345	1,110	1,495	1,040	1,035
236	Unemployed	100	55	115	60	70	60
237	Not in the labour force	1,295	595	495	825	510	405
238	Participation rate	62.1	70.1	71.3	65.1	68.6	72.7
239	Employment rate	59.2	67.6	64.9	62.8	64.0	69.0
240	Unemployment rate	4.7	3.9	9.4	3.9	6.3	5.5

Tableau 1. Certaines caractéristiques des secteurs de recensement, recensement de 2001 – Données intégrales et données-échantillon (20 %)

Toronto 0516.19 A	Toronto 0516.20 A	Toronto 0516.21 A	Toronto 0516.22 A	Toronto 0516.23 A	Toronto 0516.24 A	Caractéristiques	Nº
						CARACTÉRISTIQUES DE LA POPULATION	
8,565	**5,510**	**2,800**	**5,660**	**4,945**	**4,280**	**Population totale de 5 ans et plus (30)**	185
						selon le lieu de résidence 5 ans auparavant (mobilité)	
3,110	3,560	1,545	1,790	2,820	2,965	Personnes n'ayant pas déménagé	186
5,450	1,955	1,255	3,870	2,130	1,310	Personnes ayant déménagé	187
3,435	1,045	725	2,205	1,080	745	Non-migrants	188
2,020	910	530	1,665	1,050	565	Migrants	189
1,605	635	415	1,135	820	390	Migrants internes	190
1,350	585	300	945	620	255	Migrants infraprovinciaux	191
255	55	115	190	200	135	Migrants interprovinciaux	192
415	275	115	530	230	170	Migrants externes	193
930	**860**	**510**	**640**	**680**	**805**	**Population totale de 15 à 24 ans**	194
						selon la fréquentation scolaire	
240	260	190	160	220	165	Ne fréquentant pas l'école	195
655	525	290	460	445	590	Fréquentant l'école à plein temps	196
35	75	25	20	15	55	Fréquentant l'école à temps partiel	197
6,780	**4,415**	**2,330**	**4,370**	**3,825**	**3,455**	**Population totale de 15 ans et plus**	198
						selon le plus haut niveau de scolarité atteint	
200	125	50	170	125	145	Niveau inférieur à la 9e année (31)	199
995	815	400	630	710	545	De la 9e à la 13e année sans certificat d'études secondaires	200
880	635	315	625	575	535	De la 9e à la 13e année avec certificat d'études secondaires	201
790	550	300	430	430	485	Études postsecondaires partielles sans grade, certificat ou diplôme (32)	202
445	315	170	315	355	250	Certificat ou diplôme d'une école de métiers (33)	203
1,445	800	440	935	710	580	Certificat ou diplôme collégial (34)	204
150	110	75	140	95	115	Certificat universitaire inférieur au baccalauréat	205
1,880	1,080	575	1,125	835	790	Études universitaires avec baccalauréat ou diplôme supérieur	206
						selon les combinaisons de travail non rémunéré	
3,365	2,200	1,155	2,110	1,870	1,735	Hommes de 15 ans et plus	207
3,020	2,030	1,035	1,975	1,705	1,645	Travail non rémunéré déclaré (35)	208
290	140	55	185	175	180	Travaux ménagers et soins aux enfants et soins ou aide aux personnes âgées	209
1,455	795	390	905	695	580	Travaux ménagers et soins aux enfants seulement	210
105	120	25	110	100	115	Travaux ménagers et soins ou aide aux personnes âgées seulement	211
10	-	-	10	-	10	Soins aux enfants et soins ou aide aux personnes âgées seulement	212
1,115	940	555	725	685	740	Travaux ménagers seulement	213
30	30	10	50	40	25	Soins aux enfants seulement	214
15	-	-	-	10	-	Soins ou aide aux personnes âgées seulement	215
3,410	2,215	1,175	2,260	1,960	1,720	Femmes de 15 ans et plus	216
3,275	2,090	1,055	2,155	1,850	1,650	Travail non rémunéré déclaré (35)	217
360	270	105	280	320	245	Travaux ménagers et soins aux enfants et soins ou aide aux personnes âgées	218
1,655	875	405	1,090	780	610	Travaux ménagers et soins aux enfants seulement	219
110	150	70	125	95	140	Travaux ménagers et soins ou aide aux personnes âgées seulement	220
-	-	-	10	10	-	Soins aux enfants et soins ou aide aux personnes âgées seulement	221
1,140	785	475	610	625	640	Travaux ménagers seulement	222
10	-	-	40	25	10	Soins aux enfants seulement	223
10	-	-	-	-	-	Soins ou aide aux personnes âgées seulement	224
						selon l'activité	
3,365	2,195	1,155	2,110	1,865	1,740	Hommes de 15 ans et plus	225
2,940	1,925	985	1,840	1,575	1,460	Population active	226
2,835	1,835	970	1,775	1,525	1,400	Personnes occupées	227
105	90	10	70	55	55	Chômeurs	228
430	270	170	265	290	280	Inactifs	229
87.4	87.7	85.3	87.2	84.5	83.9	Taux d'activité	230
84.2	83.6	84.0	84.1	81.8	80.5	Taux d'emploi	231
3.6	4.7	1.0	3.8	3.5	3.8	Taux de chômage	232
3,410	2,215	1,180	2,260	1,960	1,720	Femmes de 15 ans et plus	233
2,500	1,700	920	1,645	1,375	1,230	Population active	234
2,365	1,580	885	1,570	1,325	1,150	Personnes occupées	235
135	115	40	75	50	80	Chômeuses	236
915	515	255	615	585	490	Inactives	237
73.3	76.7	78.0	72.8	70.2	71.5	Taux d'activité	238
69.4	71.3	75.0	69.5	67.6	66.9	Taux d'emploi	239
5.4	6.8	4.3	4.6	3.6	6.5	Taux de chômage	240

Table 1. Selected Characteristics for Census Tracts, 2001 Census – 100% Data and 20% Sample Data

No.	Characteristics	Toronto 0516.10	Toronto 0516.11	Toronto 0516.14 ◆	Toronto 0516.16 ◆◇	Toronto 0516.17 A	Toronto 0516.18 A
	POPULATION CHARACTERISTICS						
	by labour force activity – concluded						
241	Both sexes - Participation rate	68.8	74.3	73.8	68.8	70.3	78.9
242	15-24 years	56.5	59.8	63.1	62.9	59.2	66.2
243	25 years and over	72.5	78.7	76.5	70.4	73.4	82.3
244	Both sexes - Employment rate	65.2	71.9	69.5	65.3	67.5	75.2
245	15-24 years	49.0	55.0	54.6	54.5	55.4	58.9
246	25 years and over	69.9	76.9	73.1	68.3	70.6	79.3
247	Both sexes - Unemployment rate	5.3	3.4	5.8	5.1	4.1	4.8
248	15-24 years	13.3	8.0	13.3	13.4	5.3	10.5
249	25 years and over	3.5	2.3	4.2	2.8	4.2	3.3
250	**Total labour force 15 years and over**	**4,685**	**2,960**	**2,480**	**3,145**	**2,175**	**2,400**
	by industry based on the 1997 NAICS						
251	Industry - Not applicable (36)	80	-	30	45	-	-
252	All industries (37)	4,600	2,950	2,450	3,100	2,170	2,390
253	11 Agriculture, forestry, fishing and hunting	10	15	10	15	-	-
254	21 Mining and oil and gas extraction	-	-	10	15	-	-
255	22 Utilities	25	35	25	10	10	15
256	23 Construction	225	115	60	95	95	110
257	31-33 Manufacturing	640	385	385	310	265	265
258	41 Wholesale trade	500	225	230	240	210	195
259	44-45 Retail trade	415	410	285	450	240	335
260	48-49 Transportation and warehousing	160	115	110	175	110	140
261	51 Information and cultural industries	125	105	70	90	105	135
262	52 Finance and insurance	375	200	200	265	160	205
263	53 Real estate and rental and leasing	145	30	65	135	60	45
264	54 Professional, scientific and technical services	620	350	260	285	245	250
265	55 Management of companies and enterprises	10	-	-	-	-	-
266	56 Administrative and support, waste management and remediation services	205	90	80	130	80	55
267	61 Educational services	245	200	110	225	140	180
268	62 Health care and social assistance	360	300	240	195	145	135
269	71 Arts, entertainment and recreation	35	70	20	70	20	50
270	72 Accommodation and food services	210	125	110	110	80	120
271	81 Other services (except public administration)	210	45	75	130	85	80
272	91 Public administration	85	125	110	150	105	80
	by class of worker						
273	Class of worker - Not applicable (36)	80	10	30	45	10	10
274	All classes of worker (37)	4,605	2,945	2,450	3,100	2,170	2,395
275	Paid workers	4,140	2,690	2,310	2,855	2,045	2,235
276	Employees	3,535	2,450	2,210	2,670	1,945	2,095
277	Self-employed (incorporated)	610	245	100	180	100	140
278	Self-employed (unincorporated)	430	255	135	245	110	155
279	Unpaid family workers	30	-	-	-	20	-
	by occupation based on the 2001 NOC-S						
280	Male labour force 15 years and over	2,560	1,565	1,260	1,590	1,065	1,305
281	Occupation - Not applicable (36)	40	10	-	25	-	-
282	All occupations (37)	2,520	1,555	1,255	1,560	1,065	1,305
283	A Management occupations	765	475	305	425	250	305
284	B Business, finance and administration occupations	405	170	140	235	210	185
285	C Natural and applied sciences and related occupations	380	245	170	225	130	150
286	D Health occupations	120	45	30	55	10	15
287	E Occupations in social science, education, government service and religion	65	50	50	70	45	50
288	F Occupations in art, culture, recreation and sport	35	50	35	20	30	55
289	G Sales and service occupations	315	270	240	290	220	280
290	H Trades, transport and equipment operators and related occupations	290	155	215	155	115	220
291	I Occupations unique to primary industry	15	40	-	15	-	-
292	J Occupations unique to processing, manufacturing and utilities	115	55	60	65	45	35
293	Female labour force 15 years and over	2,125	1,395	1,220	1,550	1,115	1,090
294	Occupation - Not applicable (36)	35	10	30	15	-	-
295	All occupations (37)	2,085	1,390	1,195	1,535	1,110	1,090
296	A Management occupations	335	165	185	165	145	100
297	B Business, finance and administration occupations	720	390	405	490	360	370
298	C Natural and applied sciences and related occupations	110	70	50	25	75	45
299	D Health occupations	185	150	95	85	85	70

Tableau 1. Certaines caractéristiques des secteurs de recensement, recensement de 2001 – Données intégrales et données-échantillon (20 %)

Toronto 0516.19 A	Toronto 0516.20 A	Toronto 0516.21 A	Toronto 0516.22 A	Toronto 0516.23 A	Toronto 0516.24 A	Caractéristiques	N°
						CARACTÉRISTIQUES DE LA POPULATION	
						selon l'activité – fin	
80.2	82.1	81.8	79.7	77.1	77.7	Les deux sexes - Taux d'activité	241
54.3	68.6	71.6	62.2	64.0	65.2	15-24 ans	242
84.3	85.5	84.3	82.8	80.0	81.5	25 ans et plus	243
76.8	77.3	79.8	76.4	74.3	74.0	Les deux sexes - Taux d'emploi	244
46.8	55.2	67.6	54.7	56.3	55.9	15-24 ans	245
81.5	82.6	83.0	80.2	78.1	79.1	25 ans et plus	246
4.4	5.8	2.4	4.2	3.4	4.8	Les deux sexes - Taux de chômage	247
13.9	18.6	6.8	11.4	11.5	14.3	15-24 ans	248
3.4	3.3	1.3	3.2	2.0	2.5	25 ans et plus	249
5,440	**3,625**	**1,905**	**3,485**	**2,945**	**2,685**	**Population active totale de 15 ans et plus**	250
						selon l'industrie basée sur le SCIAN de 1997	
30	55	10	20	10	25	Industrie - Sans objet (36)	251
5,405	3,570	1,890	3,465	2,940	2,655	Toutes les industries (37)	252
20	10	-	-	-	10	11 Agriculture, foresterie, pêche et chasse	253
-	-	10	-	-	-	21 Extraction minière et extraction de pétrole et de gaz	254
30	40	25	10	30	30	22 Services publics	255
185	105	30	165	130	105	23 Construction	256
815	445	215	625	540	325	31-33 Fabrication	257
555	340	225	395	290	280	41 Commerce de gros	258
530	435	190	380	300	405	44-45 Commerce de détail	259
390	240	120	230	195	235	48-49 Transport et entreposage	260
195	145	90	115	60	105	51 Industrie de l'information et industrie culturelle	261
445	335	195	245	200	255	52 Finance et assurances	262
145	70	50	60	65	50	53 Services immobiliers et services de location et de location à bail	263
570	345	160	310	235	260	54 Services professionnels, scientifiques et techniques	264
20	10	-	-	10	10	55 Gestion de sociétés et d'entreprises	265
195	160	110	140	90	55	56 Services administratifs, services de soutien, services de gestion des déchets et services d'assainissement	266
245	140	105	175	175	145	61 Services d'enseignement	267
365	230	125	185	160	165	62 Soins de santé et assistance sociale	268
35	75	35	30	30	45	71 Arts, spectacles et loisirs	269
235	135	90	135	140	55	72 Hébergement et services de restauration	270
200	145	65	155	120	55	81 Autres services, sauf les administrations publiques	271
235	160	60	120	170	60	91 Administrations publiques	272
						selon la catégorie de travailleurs	
30	55	10	15	10	25	Catégorie de travailleurs - Sans objet (36)	273
5,405	3,570	1,890	3,470	2,945	2,660	Toutes les catégories de travailleurs (37)	274
5,080	3,420	1,755	3,220	2,810	2,505	Travailleurs rémunérés	275
4,920	3,275	1,655	3,165	2,710	2,385	Employés	276
155	140	105	55	95	120	Travailleurs autonomes (entreprise constituée en société)	277
325	150	140	225	135	150	Travailleurs autonomes (entreprise non constituée en société)	278
10	-	-	20	-	-	Travailleurs familiaux non rémunérés	279
						selon la profession basée sur la CNP-S de 2001	
2,940	1,925	985	1,845	1,575	1,460	Hommes actifs de 15 ans et plus	280
10	25	-	-	10	10	Profession - Sans objet (36)	281
2,930	1,905	980	1,835	1,570	1,455	Toutes les professions (37)	282
535	395	290	375	260	365	A Gestion	283
440	250	145	200	180	190	B Affaires, finance et administration	284
460	350	135	295	225	140	C Sciences naturelles et appliquées et professions apparentées	285
55	20	10	25	15	10	D Secteur de la santé	286
90	20	30	80	65	60	E Sciences sociales, enseignement, administration publique et religion	287
40	35	20	45	35	50	F Arts, culture, sports et loisirs	288
565	390	165	295	315	290	G Ventes et services	289
530	350	90	390	370	270	H Métiers, transport et machinerie	290
40	30	20	10	20	30	I Professions propres au secteur primaire	291
185	70	75	120	80	55	J Transformation, fabrication et services d'utilité publique	292
2,500	1,695	920	1,645	1,375	1,225	Femmes actives de 15 ans et plus	293
20	25	10	10	-	25	Profession - Sans objet (36)	294
2,480	1,670	910	1,635	1,370	1,205	Toutes les professions (37)	295
370	230	150	200	160	135	A Gestion	296
810	650	285	635	465	475	B Affaires, finance et administration	297
120	75	25	40	70	50	C Sciences naturelles et appliquées et professions apparentées	298
175	95	80	60	80	55	D Secteur de la santé	299

Table 1. Selected Characteristics for Census Tracts, 2001 Census – 100% Data and 20% Sample Data

No.	Characteristics	Toronto 0516.10	Toronto 0516.11	Toronto 0516.14 ◆	Toronto 0516.16 ◆◇	Toronto 0516.17 A	Toronto 0516.18 A
	POPULATION CHARACTERISTICS						
	by occupation based on the 2001 NOC-S – concluded						
	E Occupations in social science, education,						
300	government service and religion	200	195	70	205	140	125
301	F Occupations in art, culture, recreation and sport	65	75	30	60	35	35
302	G Sales and service occupations	350	280	290	435	240	315
	H Trades, transport and equipment						
303	operators and related occupations	45	15	15	15	10	25
304	I Occupations unique to primary industry	10	30	-	10	-	-
	J Occupations unique to processing,						
305	manufacturing and utilities	60	30	45	55	20	-
306	**Total employed labour force 15 years and over**	**4,430**	**2,855**	**2,335**	**2,985**	**2,085**	**2,285**
	by place of work						
307	Males	2,410	1,510	1,225	1,490	1,040	1,255
308	Usual place of work	1,895	1,240	1,060	1,205	860	1,010
309	At home	250	125	55	125	55	95
310	Outside Canada	40	15	10	10	-	10
311	No fixed workplace address	230	130	100	145	130	140
312	Females	2,020	1,340	1,110	1,495	1,045	1,030
313	Usual place of work	1,640	1,105	1,015	1,305	905	885
314	At home	215	135	55	125	65	95
315	Outside Canada	20	-	-	-	-	15
316	No fixed workplace address	145	105	40	60	75	40
	Total employed labour force 15 years and over with usual place of work or no fixed						
317	**workplace address**	**3,905**	**2,585**	**2,215**	**2,715**	**1,965**	**2,070**
	by mode of transportation						
318	Males	2,125	1,370	1,160	1,350	985	1,145
319	Car, truck, van, as driver	1,820	1,180	1,015	1,115	835	1,020
320	Car, truck, van, as passenger	110	85	25	70	30	30
321	Public transit	180	95	80	115	105	100
322	Walked	-	10	30	35	-	-
323	Other method	10	-	15	15	10	-
324	Females	1,785	1,210	1,050	1,370	980	925
325	Car, truck, van, as driver	1,365	960	720	875	710	655
326	Car, truck, van, as passenger	150	105	90	165	70	125
327	Public transit	200	110	155	255	160	115
328	Walked	60	30	70	55	35	10
329	Other method	15	10	20	15	-	15
	Total population 15 years and over who worked						
330	**since January 1, 2000**	**5,165**	**3,280**	**2,645**	**3,440**	**2,395**	**2,640**
	by language used at work						
331	Single responses	4,585	3,015	2,400	3,185	2,210	2,515
332	English	4,525	3,000	2,390	3,155	2,200	2,510
333	French	10	-	-	-	-	-
334	Non-official languages (5)	60	15	10	30	15	-
335	Chinese, n.o.s.	-	-	-	-	10	-
336	Cantonese	10	-	-	-	-	-
337	Other languages (6)	40	-	-	30	10	-
338	Multiple responses	580	270	245	250	185	125
339	English and French	60	75	85	105	65	55
340	English and non-official language	510	190	150	135	110	55
341	French and non-official language	-	-	-	-	-	-
342	English, French and non-official language	15	10	10	10	10	15
	DWELLING AND HOUSEHOLD CHARACTERISTICS						
343	**Total number of occupied private dwellings**	**2,300**	**1,425**	**1,230**	**1,800**	**1,335**	**1,160**
	by tenure						
344	Owned	2,160	1,370	950	1,385	975	1,025
345	Rented	140	65	275	420	355	135
346	Band housing	-	-	-	-	-	-
	by structural type of dwelling						
347	Single-detached house	1,805	1,370	725	555	435	515
348	Semi-detached house	260	20	155	-	95	410
349	Row house	210	35	210	865	375	245
350	Apartment, detached duplex	10	-	-	-	10	-
351	Apartment, building that has five or more storeys	10	-	125	285	430	-
	Apartment, building that has fewer than						
352	five storeys (38)	-	-	10	95	-	-
353	Other single-attached house	-	-	-	-	-	-
354	Movable dwelling (39)	10	-	-	-	-	-

Tableau 1. Certaines caractéristiques des secteurs de recensement, recensement de 2001 – Données intégrales et données-échantillon (20 %)

Toronto 0516.19 A	Toronto 0516.20 A	Toronto 0516.21 A	Toronto 0516.22 A	Toronto 0516.23 A	Toronto 0516.24 A	Caractéristiques	N°
						CARACTÉRISTIQUES DE LA POPULATION	
						selon la profession basée sur la CNP-S de 2001 – fin	
						E Sciences sociales, enseignement,	
260	160	105	180	170	145	administration publique et religion	300
40	40	20	35	10	20	F Arts, culture, sports et loisirs	301
535	360	205	360	350	295	G Ventes et services	302
55	20	15	25	25	10	H Métiers, transport et machinerie	303
10	-	-	10	-	-	I Professions propres au secteur primaire	304
						J Transformation, fabrication et	
105	50	30	90	55	20	services d'utilité publique	305
5,200	**3,410**	**1,855**	**3,345**	**2,845**	**2,550**	**Population active occupée totale de 15 ans et plus .....**	306
						selon le lieu de travail	
2,835	1,835	970	1,770	1,525	1,405	Hommes	307
2,360	1,550	880	1,520	1,335	1,175	Lieu habituel de travail	308
210	55	25	50	40	50	À domicile	309
10	10	10	10	10	-	En dehors du Canada	310
265	220	55	195	140	175	Sans adresse de travail fixe	311
2,365	1,580	880	1,570	1,325	1,150	Femmes	312
2,155	1,440	785	1,425	1,185	1,035	Lieu habituel de travail	313
140	70	75	100	90	90	À domicile	314
10	-	10	-	-	-	En dehors du Canada	315
65	65	20	45	50	30	Sans adresse de travail fixe	316
						Population active occupée totale de 15 ans et	
						plus ayant un lieu habituel de travail ou	
4,840	**3,275**	**1,740**	**3,180**	**2,710**	**2,410**	**sans adresse de travail fixe ....**	317
						selon le mode de transport	
2,620	1,770	940	1,710	1,475	1,350	Hommes	318
						Automobile, camion ou fourgonnette, en tant	
2,320	1,500	810	1,500	1,325	1,135	que conducteur	319
						Automobile, camion ou fourgonnette, en tant	
90	35	40	50	35	45	que passager	320
185	160	60	120	95	140	Transport en commun	321
15	60	10	10	15	10	À pied	322
-	15	25	30	15	20	Autre moyen	323
2,215	1,505	805	1,470	1,235	1,065	Femmes	324
						Automobile, camion ou fourgonnette, en tant	
1,565	1,165	650	1,160	925	720	que conductrice	325
						Automobile, camion ou fourgonnette, en tant	
200	125	70	110	165	135	que passagère	326
375	205	70	165	120	155	Transport en commun	327
70	-	10	15	10	50	À pied	328
10	-	-	20	10	-	Autre moyen	329
						Population totale de 15 ans et plus ayant travaillé	
5,815	**3,770**	**2,005**	**3,740**	**3,145**	**2,925**	**depuis le 1er janvier 2000 ....**	330
						selon la langue utilisée au travail	
5,315	3,470	1,895	3,475	2,900	2,670	Réponses uniques	331
5,280	3,460	1,880	3,450	2,875	2,660	Anglais	332
-	-	-	-	10	-	Français	333
35	10	15	25	20	15	Langues non officielles (5)	334
-	-	-	10	-	-	Chinois, n.d.a.	335
15	-	-	-	-	-	Cantonais	336
25	10	15	10	15	15	Autres langues (6)	337
500	300	105	265	245	255	Réponses multiples	338
170	140	55	115	100	120	Anglais et français	339
330	160	50	140	135	130	Anglais et langue non officielle	340
-	-	-	-	-	-	Français et langue non officielle	341
-	-	-	10	-	-	Anglais, français et langue non officielle	342
						CARACTÉRISTIQUES DES LOGEMENTS ET DES MÉNAGES	
2,850	**1,690**	**825**	**1,790**	**1,470**	**1,225**	**Nombre total de logements privés occupés ....**	343
						selon le mode d'occupation	
2,780	1,660	820	1,700	1,450	1,190	Possédé	344
70	30	-	100	15	35	Loué	345
-	-	-	-	-	-	Logement de bande	346
						selon le type de construction résidentielle	
1,480	1,585	745	1,090	1,230	1,225	Maison individuelle non attenante	347
995	110	30	510	135	-	Maison jumelée	348
370	-	55	175	65	-	Maison en rangée	349
-	-	-	15	40	-	Appartement, duplex non attenant	350
-	-	-	-	-	-	Appartement, immeuble de cinq étages ou plus	351
10	-	-	-	-	-	Appartement, immeuble de moins de cinq étages (38) ...	352
-	-	-	-	-	-	Autre maison individuelle attenante	353
-	-	-	-	-	-	Logement mobile (39)	354

Table 1. Selected Characteristics for Census Tracts, 2001 Census – 100% Data and 20% Sample Data

No.	Characteristics	Toronto 0516.10	Toronto 0516.11	Toronto 0516.14 ◆	Toronto 0516.16 ◆◇	Toronto 0516.17 A	Toronto 0516.18 A
	DWELLING AND HOUSEHOLD CHARACTERISTICS						
	by condition of dwelling						
355	Regular maintenance only	1,925	1,000	935	1,310	1,035	745
356	Minor repairs	340	375	280	420	220	360
357	Major repairs	30	50	10	65	80	55
	by period of construction						
358	Before 1946	15	15	-	10	-	10
359	1946-1960	20	10	-	10	20	-
360	1961-1970	10	20	-	50	25	30
361	1971-1980	10	495	45	500	495	885
362	1981-1990	1,120	850	950	870	615	220
363	1991-2001 (20)	1,140	40	230	365	175	15
364	Average number of rooms per dwelling	8.7	8.5	7.5	7.0	6.6	7.7
365	Average number of bedrooms per dwelling	3.9	3.6	3.4	3.1	2.7	3.3
366	Average value of dwelling $	423,576	341,361	260,761	322,601	239,461	228,453
367	**Total number of private households**	**2,295**	**1,430**	**1,225**	**1,800**	**1,330**	**1,165**
	by household size						
368	1 person	105	80	110	245	280	80
369	2 persons	435	280	255	585	345	250
370	3 persons	385	290	235	350	250	280
371	4-5 persons	1,135	705	535	540	420	500
372	6 or more persons	235	80	100	85	45	55
	by household type						
373	One-family households	2,010	1,295	1,025	1,455	1,020	1,025
374	Multiple-family households	155	40	80	55	10	25
375	Non-family households	130	95	120	290	305	115
376	Number of persons in private households	8,540	5,035	4,275	5,340	3,800	3,900
377	Average number of persons in private households	3.7	3.5	3.5	3.0	2.9	3.3
378	Average number of persons per room	0.4	0.4	0.5	0.4	0.4	0.4
379	Tenant households in non-farm, non-reserve private dwellings (40)	140	60	270	415	350	135
380	Average gross rent $ (40)	1,685	1,546	1,176	1,125	1,125	1,026
381	Tenant households spending 30% or more of household income on gross rent (40) (41)	35	10	95	190	120	45
382	Tenant households spending from 30% to 99% of household income on gross rent (40) (41)	35	10	90	170	100	25
383	Owner households in non-farm, non-reserve private dwellings (42)	2,155	1,365	950	1,385	975	1,025
384	Average owner's major payments $ (42)	1,528	1,260	1,280	1,199	1,187	1,225
385	Owner households spending 30% or more of household income on owner's major payments (41) (42)	495	160	170	240	220	180
386	Owner households spending from 30% to 99% of household income on owner's major payments (41) (42)	415	160	155	225	180	170
	CENSUS FAMILY CHARACTERISTICS						
387	**Total number of census families in private households**	**2,335**	**1,375**	**1,180**	**1,565**	**1,035**	**1,070**
	by census family structure and size						
388	Total couple families	2,140	1,270	1,020	1,335	900	955
389	Total families of married couples	2,090	1,240	970	1,225	815	870
390	Without children at home	495	270	215	490	225	210
391	With children at home	1,600	970	750	730	590	660
392	1 child	415	265	215	225	190	195
393	2 children	770	480	355	320	255	335
394	3 or more children	410	230	180	185	145	130
395	Total families of common-law couples	45	25	50	115	85	85
396	Without children at home	30	10	25	80	40	25
397	With children at home	20	15	25	35	40	60
398	1 child	10	10	10	10	30	-
399	2 children	15	-	15	20	10	25
400	3 or more children	-	-	-	10	-	30
401	Total lone-parent families	200	100	165	230	135	115
402	Female parent	175	80	140	195	120	95
403	1 child	85	45	70	130	55	50
404	2 children	65	25	55	40	30	35
405	3 or more children	25	10	15	15	30	10

Tableau 1. Certaines caractéristiques des secteurs de recensement, recensement de 2001 – Données intégrales et données-échantillon (20 %)

Toronto 0516.19 A	Toronto 0516.20 A	Toronto 0516.21 A	Toronto 0516.22 A	Toronto 0516.23 A	Toronto 0516.24 A	Caractéristiques	N°
						CARACTÉRISTIQUES DES LOGEMENTS ET DES MÉNAGES	
						selon l'état du logement	
2,630	1,235	615	1,610	1,250	900	Entretien régulier seulement	355
200	410	190	185	190	295	Réparations mineures	356
20	45	20	-	30	30	Réparations majeures	357
						selon la période de construction	
10	-	-	-	-	-	Avant 1946	358
-	-	-	-	-	-	1946-1960	359
-	10	-	-	-	-	1961-1970	360
-	15	-	-	20	15	1971-1980	361
45	1,145	380	90	870	1,170	1981-1990	362
2,800	520	445	1,705	575	40	1991-2001 (20)	363
7.2	7.8	8.4	7.1	7.9	8.3	Nombre moyen de pièces par logement	364
3.4	3.5	3.7	3.4	3.6	3.7	Nombre moyen de chambres à coucher par logement	365
249,141	243,806	281,838	247,754	255,540	280,000	Valeur moyenne du logement $	366
2,850	**1,695**	**825**	**1,795**	**1,470**	**1,225**	**Nombre total de logements privés**	367
						selon la taille du ménage	
210	110	30	85	95	45	1 personne	368
560	300	145	335	250	190	2 personnes	369
630	345	155	395	310	245	3 personnes	370
1,270	825	460	870	675	675	4-5 personnes	371
175	110	30	110	145	75	6 personnes ou plus	372
						selon le genre de ménage	
2,430	1,505	765	1,585	1,295	1,105	Ménages unifamiliaux	373
135	45	25	80	80	40	Ménages multifamiliaux	374
285	135	40	130	95	75	Ménages non familiaux	375
9,770	5,965	3,025	6,385	5,330	4,520	Nombre de personnes dans les ménages privés	376
3.4	3.5	3.7	3.6	3.6	3.7	Nombre moyen de personnes dans les ménages privés	377
0.5	0.5	0.4	0.5	0.5	0.4	Nombre moyen de personnes par pièce	378
70	35	10	95	20	35	Ménages locataires dans les logements privés non agricoles hors réserve (40)	379
1,335	1,103	-	1,477	1,156	1,280	Loyer brut moyen $ (40)	380
45	15	-	35	10	-	Ménages locataires consacrant 30 % ou plus du revenu du ménage au loyer brut (40) (41)	381
35	10	-	35	-	-	Ménages locataires consacrant de 30 % à 99 % du revenu du ménage au loyer brut (40) (41)	382
2,775	1,660	825	1,695	1,455	1,190	Ménages propriétaires dans les logements privés non agricoles hors réserve (42)	383
1,533	1,432	1,412	1,532	1,381	1,310	Principales dépenses de propriété moyennes $ (42)	384
655	235	165	325	255	205	Ménages propriétaires consacrant 30 % ou plus du revenu du ménage aux principales dépenses de propriété (41) (42)	385
570	225	150	310	235	190	Ménages propriétaires consacrant de 30 % à 99 % du revenu du ménage aux principales dépenses de propriété (41) (42)	386
						CARACTÉRISTIQUES DES FAMILLES DE RECENSEMENT	
2,720	**1,605**	**810**	**1,750**	**1,455**	**1,190**	**Total des familles de recensement dans les ménages privés**	387
						selon la structure et la taille de la famille de recensement	
2,470	1,505	755	1,595	1,325	1,105	Total des familles avec conjoints	388
2,325	1,410	700	1,490	1,280	1,080	Total des familles avec couples mariés	389
535	260	115	280	260	180	Sans enfants à la maison	390
1,795	1,145	590	1,205	1,020	900	Avec enfants à la maison	391
565	300	145	345	290	230	1 enfant	392
940	610	315	630	470	450	2 enfants	393
285	240	130	230	265	215	3 enfants ou plus	394
150	90	55	105	50	30	Total des familles en union libre	395
45	45	35	50	20	15	Sans enfants à la maison	396
100	50	20	60	30	15	Avec enfants à la maison	397
40	35	-	35	15	15	1 enfant	398
50	15	20	25	10	-	2 enfants	399
10	-	-	10	-	-	3 enfants ou plus	400
255	100	60	155	125	85	Total des familles monoparentales	401
205	85	50	135	115	65	Parent de sexe féminin	402
105	30	-	90	65	45	1 enfant	403
95	50	45	30	45	25	2 enfants	404
10	10	10	15	-	-	3 enfants ou plus	405

Table 1. Selected Characteristics for Census Tracts, 2001 Census – 100% Data and 20% Sample Data

No.	Characteristics	Toronto 0516.10	Toronto 0516.11	Toronto 0516.14 ◆	Toronto 0516.16 ◆◇	Toronto 0516.17 A	Toronto 0516.18 A
	CENSUS FAMILY CHARACTERISTICS						
	by census family structure and size – concluded						
406	Male parent	25	25	20	30	20	25
407	1 child	-	10	10	30	10	10
408	2 children	10	10	10	-	15	15
409	3 or more children	10	-	-	-	-	-
410	**Total number of children at home**	**3,695**	**2,170**	**1,825**	**1,845**	**1,455**	**1,625**
	by age groups						
411	Under 6 years	550	305	220	295	225	260
412	6-14 years	1,185	745	690	630	475	595
413	15-17 years	455	365	210	265	205	230
414	18-24 years	1,030	565	450	445	410	390
415	25 years and over	480	185	250	210	135	155
416	Average number of children at home per census family (43)	1.6	1.6	1.6	1.2	1.4	1.5
417	**Total number of persons in private households**	**8,540**	**5,035**	**4,275**	**5,335**	**3,805**	**3,895**
	by census family status and living arrangements						
418	Number of non-family persons	370	225	245	590	415	250
419	Living with relatives (44)	185	70	105	145	50	80
420	Living with non-relatives only	75	80	35	200	90	85
421	Living alone	105	80	105	245	275	80
422	Number of family persons	8,165	4,805	4,025	4,745	3,390	3,650
423	Average number of persons per census family	3.5	3.5	3.4	3.0	3.3	3.4
424	**Total number of persons 65 years and over**	**540**	**255**	**235**	**575**	**305**	**145**
425	Number of non-family persons 65 years and over	120	55	65	130	105	30
426	Living with relatives (44)	115	35	30	55	30	30
427	Living with non-relatives only	-	-	10	-	-	-
428	Living alone	10	15	25	75	70	10
429	Number of family persons 65 years and over	415	205	165	440	195	115
	ECONOMIC FAMILY CHARACTERISTICS						
430	**Total number of economic families in private households**	**2,175**	**1,330**	**1,110**	**1,515**	**1,025**	**1,065**
	by size of family						
431	2 persons	425	280	240	615	320	260
432	3 persons	405	285	235	300	240	275
433	4 persons	760	475	365	355	305	345
434	5 or more persons	590	295	270	245	160	190
435	Total number of persons in economic families	8,355	4,875	4,130	4,890	3,435	3,730
436	Average number of persons per economic family	3.8	3.7	3.7	3.2	3.3	3.5
437	Total number of unattached individuals	185	155	145	445	370	170
	2000 INCOME CHARACTERISTICS						
	Population 15 years and over by sex and total income groups in 2000						
438	Total - Both sexes	6,805	3,980	3,360	4,570	3,095	3,040
439	Without income	455	215	270	250	270	165
440	With income	6,355	3,765	3,095	4,320	2,830	2,875
441	Under $1,000 (45)	385	265	210	200	130	110
442	$ 1,000 - $ 2,999	350	180	170	225	165	150
443	$ 3,000 - $ 4,999	245	160	90	145	60	90
444	$ 5,000 - $ 6,999	305	195	120	215	145	150
445	$ 7,000 - $ 9,999	310	150	90	185	105	205
446	$10,000 - $11,999	200	110	125	205	90	70
447	$12,000 - $14,999	340	140	190	200	210	160
448	$15,000 - $19,999	340	255	195	310	220	100
449	$20,000 - $24,999	420	100	120	250	195	115
450	$25,000 - $29,999	270	130	225	260	100	195
451	$30,000 - $34,999	310	185	230	295	135	190
452	$35,000 - $39,999	355	120	270	200	155	165
453	$40,000 - $44,999	220	250	150	285	95	105
454	$45,000 - $49,999	205	130	170	145	165	170
455	$50,000 - $59,999	395	285	140	300	220	305
456	$60,000 and over	1,700	1,100	585	900	635	600
457	Average income $ (46)	48,868	49,497	35,632	48,596	38,648	37,611
458	Median income $ (46)	29,986	34,880	29,986	29,320	28,500	32,117
459	Standard error of average income $ (46)	1,944	2,144	1,300	2,946	1,562	1,329

Tableau 1. Certaines caractéristiques des secteurs de recensement, recensement de 2001 – Données intégrales et données-échantillon (20 %)

Toronto 0516.19 A	Toronto 0516.20 A	Toronto 0516.21 A	Toronto 0516.22 A	Toronto 0516.23 A	Toronto 0516.24 A	Caractéristiques	N°
						CARACTÉRISTIQUES DES FAMILLES DE RECENSEMENT	
						selon la structure et la taille de la famille de recensement - fin	
50	15	10	15	10	20	Parent de sexe masculin	406
30	10	10	-	-	10	1 enfant	407
10	-	-	-	10	10	2 enfants	408
10	-	-	10	-	-	3 enfants ou plus	409
3,920	**2,510**	**1,315**	**2,680**	**2,300**	**1,940**	**Nombre total d'enfants à la maison**	410
						selon les groupes d'âge	
1,470	540	260	815	485	300	Moins de 6 ans	411
1,505	1,005	440	1,180	1,020	770	6-14 ans	412
320	320	170	245	270	315	15-17 ans	413
475	485	300	315	360	425	18-24 ans	414
155	155	145	125	165	140	25 ans et plus	415
1.4	1.6	1.6	1.5	1.6	1.6	Nombre moyen d'enfants à la maison par famille de recensement (43)	416
9,770	**5,960**	**3,030**	**6,385**	**5,330**	**4,520**	**Nombre total de personnes dans les ménages privés**	417
						selon la situation des particuliers dans la famille de recensement et des particuliers dans le ménage	
660	345	145	360	250	285	Nombre de personnes hors famille de recensement	418
290	145	80	140	100	165	Vivant avec des personnes apparentées (44)	419
150	95	40	135	55	75	Vivant avec des personnes non apparentées uniquement	420
215	105	30	85	90	45	Vivant seules	421
9,115	5,620	2,880	6,025	5,080	4,235	Nombre de personnes membres d'une famille	422
3.3	3.5	3.6	3.4	3.5	3.6	Nombre moyen de personnes par famille de recensement	423
260	**175**	**105**	**170**	**190**	**145**	**Nombre total de personnes de 65 ans et plus**	424
105	75	40	70	65	65	Nombre de personnes hors famille de recensement de 65 ans et plus	425
80	60	35	65	55	60	Vivant avec des personnes apparentées (44)	426
10	-	-	-	-	-	Vivant avec des personnes non apparentées uniquement	427
10	15	-	10	-	10	Vivant seules	428
155	100	65	100	125	80	Nombre de personnes membres d'une famille de 65 ans et plus	429
						CARACTÉRISTIQUES DES FAMILLES ÉCONOMIQUES	
2,600	**1,570**	**790**	**1,680**	**1,380**	**1,170**	**Nombre total de familles économiques dans les ménages privés**	430
						selon la taille de la famille	
570	300	140	340	260	180	2 personnes	431
620	350	160	370	315	260	3 personnes	432
895	600	285	600	460	455	4 personnes	433
520	320	200	365	350	270	5 personnes ou plus	434
9,405	5,765	2,960	6,165	5,180	4,405	Nombre total de personnes dans les familles économiques	435
3.6	3.7	3.7	3.7	3.8	3.8	Nombre moyen de personnes par famille économique	436
365	200	70	215	150	120	Nombre total de personnes hors famille économique	437
						CARACTÉRISTIQUES DU REVENU DE 2000	
						Population de 15 ans et plus selon le sexe et les tranches de revenu total en 2000	
6,780	4,415	2,330	4,370	3,825	3,460	Total - Les deux sexes	438
345	240	90	220	265	230	Sans revenu	439
6,435	4,170	2,240	4,145	3,560	3,225	Avec un revenu	440
205	215	70	195	130	185	Moins de 1 000 $ (45)	441
335	185	105	135	130	160	1 000 $ - 2 999 $	442
285	125	65	75	165	180	3 000 $ - 4 999 $	443
185	160	95	160	85	115	5 000 $ - 6 999 $	444
190	135	185	210	150	180	7 000 $ - 9 999 $	445
150	85	100	105	110	90	10 000 $ - 11 999 $	446
195	140	120	150	180	160	12 000 $ - 14 999 $	447
365	240	45	175	215	140	15 000 $ - 19 999 $	448
295	200	160	185	180	195	20 000 $ - 24 999 $	449
245	210	130	260	190	130	25 000 $ - 29 999 $	450
555	340	105	325	245	150	30 000 $ - 34 999 $	451
505	275	130	345	240	180	35 000 $ - 39 999 $	452
485	330	155	310	210	225	40 000 $ - 44 999 $	453
390	150	55	270	160	135	45 000 $ - 49 999 $	454
630	405	235	320	360	225	50 000 $ - 59 999 $	455
1,425	975	495	925	800	780	60 000 $ et plus	456
40,779	41,708	42,819	39,464	39,542	40,219	Revenu moyen $ (46)	457
36,220	35,223	30,291	35,897	34,665	31,357	Revenu médian $ (46)	458
970	1,268	2,399	967	1,213	1,659	Erreur type de revenu moyen $ (46)	459

Table 1. Selected Characteristics for Census Tracts, 2001 Census – 100% Data and 20% Sample Data

No.	Characteristics	Toronto 0516.10	Toronto 0516.11	Toronto 0516.14 ◆	Toronto 0516.16 ◆◇	Toronto 0516.17 A	Toronto 0516.18 A
	2000 INCOME CHARACTERISTICS						
	Population 15 years and over by sex and total income groups in 2000 – concluded						
460	Total - Males	3,390	1,995	1,650	2,190	1,475	1,545
461	Without income	145	80	105	70	110	55
462	With income	3,245	1,915	1,545	2,120	1,365	1,490
463	Under $1,000 (45)	195	100	80	105	55	50
464	$ 1,000 - $ 2,999	120	105	80	70	60	60
465	$ 3,000 - $ 4,999	80	75	35	50	30	-
466	$ 5,000 - $ 6,999	130	90	45	105	50	20
467	$ 7,000 - $ 9,999	135	45	45	85	30	115
468	$10,000 - $11,999	90	40	80	65	40	25
469	$12,000 - $14,999	95	55	85	50	90	80
470	$15,000 - $19,999	135	125	80	115	90	35
471	$20,000 - $24,999	220	15	40	105	95	60
472	$25,000 - $29,999	115	55	95	75	40	90
473	$30,000 - $34,999	165	95	85	160	30	70
474	$35,000 - $39,999	135	35	130	95	65	95
475	$40,000 - $44,999	120	120	65	155	35	40
476	$45,000 - $49,999	130	50	100	95	110	110
477	$50,000 - $59,999	215	140	65	145	120	190
478	$60,000 and over	1,165	790	430	650	430	460
479	Average income $ (46)	64,122	65,771	43,034	68,758	48,525	47,446
480	Median income $ (46)	39,976	45,804	35,087	38,694	40,120	45,932
481	Standard error of average income $ (46)	3,454	3,684	2,237	5,920	2,742	2,155
482	Total - Females	3,415	1,985	1,710	2,375	1,625	1,495
483	Without income	310	140	160	175	165	110
484	With income	3,110	1,850	1,550	2,200	1,465	1,390
485	Under $1,000 (45)	195	170	130	95	75	60
486	$ 1,000 - $ 2,999	225	80	85	150	105	90
487	$ 3,000 - $ 4,999	165	85	60	90	30	90
488	$ 5,000 - $ 6,999	175	105	70	105	100	130
489	$ 7,000 - $ 9,999	170	100	45	95	70	95
490	$10,000 - $11,999	110	70	45	140	50	50
491	$12,000 - $14,999	245	90	110	150	120	80
492	$15,000 - $19,999	200	130	115	195	130	60
493	$20,000 - $24,999	205	95	80	145	100	60
494	$25,000 - $29,999	150	75	130	185	65	105
495	$30,000 - $34,999	140	95	145	135	105	115
496	$35,000 - $39,999	220	85	145	100	95	70
497	$40,000 - $44,999	100	130	85	135	55	70
498	$45,000 - $49,999	80	80	75	50	60	65
499	$50,000 - $59,999	180	145	75	160	100	115
500	$60,000 and over	530	310	160	255	205	145
501	Average income $ (46)	32,938	32,616	28,247	29,159	29,431	27,060
502	Median income $ (46)	20,535	24,596	26,095	22,238	22,143	23,968
503	Standard error of average income $ (46)	1,477	1,705	1,225	1,145	1,451	1,278
	by composition of total income						
504	Total - Composition of income in 2000 % (47)	100.0	100.0	100.0	100.0	100.0	100.0
505	Employment income %	86.0	89.6	90.9	78.5	86.8	91.5
506	Government transfer payments %	3.3	2.6	4.9	4.6	5.8	3.4
507	Other %	10.8	7.8	4.2	16.9	7.4	5.1
	Population 15 years and over with employment income in 2000 by sex and work activity						
508	Both sexes with employment income (48)	4,960	3,220	2,575	3,335	2,260	2,610
509	Average employment income $	53,739	51,853	38,980	49,458	41,920	37,952
510	Standard error of average employment income $	2,195	2,355	1,483	3,537	1,779	1,397
511	Worked full year, full time (49)	2,730	1,705	1,555	1,825	1,370	1,455
512	Average employment income $	73,701	73,803	51,842	74,421	57,018	51,525
513	Standard error of average employment income $	3,397	3,425	1,969	6,342	2,366	1,889
514	Worked part year or part time (50)	2,090	1,490	945	1,440	875	1,120
515	Average employment income $	30,171	27,519	19,988	19,299	18,632	21,226
516	Standard error of average employment income $	2,273	2,587	1,570	1,543	1,673	1,510
517	Males with employment income (48)	2,655	1,720	1,350	1,695	1,110	1,375
518	Average employment income $	68,237	66,883	45,840	68,937	52,598	47,401
519	Standard error of average employment income $	3,748	3,935	2,477	6,803	3,031	2,242
520	Worked full year, full time (49)	1,620	1,025	885	1,055	765	905
521	Average employment income $	87,366	88,299	59,047	96,270	66,684	57,206
522	Standard error of average employment income $	5,254	5,176	3,154	10,555	3,691	2,789
523	Worked part year or part time (50)	965	670	430	605	330	455
524	Average employment income $	40,083	36,402	21,285	24,369	21,272	29,048
525	Standard error of average employment income $	4,603	5,176	2,652	3,318	3,394	2,976

Tableau 1. Certaines caractéristiques des secteurs de recensement, recensement de 2001 – Données intégrales et données-échantillon (20 %)

Toronto 0516.19 A	Toronto 0516.20 A	Toronto 0516.21 A	Toronto 0516.22 A	Toronto 0516.23 A	Toronto 0516.24 A	Caractéristiques	N°
						CARACTÉRISTIQUES DU REVENU DE 2000	
						Population de 15 ans et plus selon le sexe et les tranches de revenu total en 2000 – fin	
3,370	2,200	1,155	2,110	1,865	1,735	Total - Hommes	460
140	100	50	65	110	120	Sans revenu	461
3,230	2,100	1,105	2,045	1,760	1,620	Avec un revenu	462
55	115	25	50	25	80	Moins de 1 000 $ (45)	463
100	65	25	45	50	50	1 000 $ - 2 999 $	464
145	40	35	30	45	95	3 000 $ - 4 999 $	465
70	50	30	55	30	60	5 000 $ - 6 999 $	466
70	70	55	65	60	40	7 000 $ - 9 999 $	467
35	50	75	35	35	25	10 000 $ - 11 999 $	468
90	45	40	15	70	45	12 000 $ - 14 999 $	469
185	100	15	60	90	80	15 000 $ - 19 999 $	470
100	65	60	60	60	70	20 000 $ - 24 999 $	471
100	55	40	110	100	25	25 000 $ - 29 999 $	472
290	135	30	160	85	50	30 000 $ - 34 999 $	473
185	125	60	135	105	55	35 000 $ - 39 999 $	474
205	185	90	165	95	105	40 000 $ - 44 999 $	475
180	100	40	120	100	80	45 000 $ - 49 999 $	476
400	200	130	200	210	150	50 000 $ - 59 999 $	477
1,020	690	350	725	605	595	60 000 $ et plus	478
48,865	50,332	56,365	49,985	48,792	51,113	Revenu moyen $ (46)	479
43,939	42,808	42,188	45,036	46,240	45,648	Revenu médian $ (46)	480
1,584	2,055	4,553	1,487	1,828	2,575	Erreur type de revenu moyen $ (46)	481
3,415	2,215	1,175	2,260	1,960	1,720	Total - Femmes	482
210	145	35	155	160	120	Sans revenu	483
3,205	2,070	1,140	2,100	1,800	1,600	Avec un revenu	484
150	105	45	145	105	105	Moins de 1 000 $ (45)	485
240	115	75	95	80	110	1 000 $ - 2 999 $	486
140	85	35	45	125	80	3 000 $ - 4 999 $	487
115	115	65	110	55	50	5 000 $ - 6 999 $	488
120	60	130	150	85	140	7 000 $ - 9 999 $	489
115	30	30	70	80	60	10 000 $ - 11 999 $	490
110	100	75	130	115	110	12 000 $ - 14 999 $	491
175	140	30	110	130	60	15 000 $ - 19 999 $	492
190	135	105	125	120	125	20 000 $ - 24 999 $	493
145	155	85	145	90	105	25 000 $ - 29 999 $	494
265	205	75	165	160	95	30 000 $ - 34 999 $	495
320	145	65	205	130	120	35 000 $ - 39 999 $	496
275	145	65	135	115	120	40 000 $ - 44 999 $	497
215	55	15	150	60	55	45 000 $ - 49 999 $	498
235	200	100	125	150	70	50 000 $ - 59 999 $	499
405	280	145	200	195	180	60 000 $ et plus	500
32,629	32,967	29,700	29,229	30,494	29,200	Revenu moyen $ (46)	501
30,847	29,965	23,438	26,928	24,962	22,102	Revenu médian $ (46)	502
1,037	1,367	1,587	1,064	1,465	1,953	Erreur type de revenu moyen $ (46)	503
						selon la composition du revenu total	
100.0	100.0	100.0	100.0	100.0	100.0	Total - Composition du revenu en 2000 % (47)	504
92.9	92.2	94.0	94.0	92.1	89.4	Revenu d'emploi %	505
3.7	3.7	3.0	3.6	4.1	2.8	Transferts gouvernementaux %	506
3.4	4.0	3.0	2.4	3.8	7.8	Autre %	507
						Population de 15 ans et plus ayant un revenu d'emploi en 2000 selon le sexe et le travail	
5,700	3,675	1,935	3,700	3,085	2,820	Les deux sexes ayant un revenu d'emploi (48)	508
42,710	43,668	46,591	41,591	42,075	41,134	Revenu moyen d'emploi $	509
1,008	1,313	2,656	1,031	1,288	1,408	Erreur type de revenu moyen d'emploi $	510
3,755	2,385	1,135	2,285	1,995	1,675	Ayant travaillé toute l'année à plein temps (49)	511
52,275	54,588	64,293	52,882	52,410	52,849	Revenu moyen d'emploi $	512
1,228	1,578	3,983	1,242	1,474	1,826	Erreur type de revenu moyen d'emploi $	513
1,875	1,275	775	1,345	1,035	1,100	Ayant travaillé une partie de l'année ou à temps partiel (50)	514
24,566	23,357	22,004	23,653	24,183	24,511	Revenu moyen d'emploi $	515
1,379	1,864	1,878	1,327	2,007	1,817	Erreur type de revenu moyen d'emploi $	516
3,050	1,940	1,020	1,940	1,635	1,500	Hommes ayant un revenu d'emploi (48)	517
49,122	51,168	58,907	50,779	49,255	50,423	Revenu moyen d'emploi $	518
1,582	2,055	4,809	1,529	1,860	2,201	Erreur type de revenu moyen d'emploi $	519
2,230	1,370	650	1,360	1,160	980	Ayant travaillé toute l'année à plein temps (49)	520
57,125	60,341	78,780	59,907	58,568	60,766	Revenu moyen d'emploi $	521
1,826	2,238	6,588	1,695	2,093	2,592	Erreur type de revenu moyen d'emploi $	522
805	560	345	545	460	510	Ayant travaillé une partie de l'année ou à temps partiel (50)	523
27,375	28,882	25,103	30,521	27,695	31,380	Revenu moyen d'emploi $	524
2,468	3,826	3,687	2,471	2,883	3,452	Erreur type de revenu moyen d'emploi $	525

Table 1. Selected Characteristics for Census Tracts, 2001 Census – 100% Data and 20% Sample Data

No.	Characteristics	Toronto 0516.10	Toronto 0516.11	Toronto 0516.14 ◆	Toronto 0516.16 ◆◇	Toronto 0516.17 A	Toronto 0516.18 A
	2000 INCOME CHARACTERISTICS						
	Population 15 years and over with employment income in 2000 by sex and work activity – concluded						
526	Females with employment income (48)	2,310	1,500	1,225	1,640	1,150	1,230
527	Average employment income $	37,037	34,654	31,387	29,330	31,612	27,407
528	Standard error of average employment income $	1,711	1,812	1,388	1,391	1,680	1,347
529	Worked full year, full time (49)	1,115	680	670	770	605	545
530	Average employment income $	53,797	52,003	42,298	44,556	44,804	42,064
531	Standard error of average employment income $	2,905	2,833	1,595	2,329	2,294	1,761
532	Worked part year or part time (50)	1,125	815	520	835	540	665
533	Average employment income $	21,668	20,233	18,909	15,611	17,006	15,833
534	Standard error of average employment income $	1,468	1,677	1,866	1,199	1,658	1,367
	Census families by structure and family income groups in 2000						
535	Total - All census families	2,335	1,375	1,180	1,565	1,040	1,070
536	Under $10,000	100	-	35	40	55	30
537	$ 10,000 - $19,999	45	10	50	75	25	10
538	$ 20,000 - $29,999	145	55	40	95	85	50
539	$ 30,000 - $39,999	105	80	145	85	45	40
540	$ 40,000 - $49,999	115	35	100	90	65	45
541	$ 50,000 - $59,999	115	70	55	140	80	100
542	$ 60,000 - $69,999	195	80	105	150	95	90
543	$ 70,000 - $79,999	130	115	115	100	90	125
544	$ 80,000 - $89,999	135	85	65	135	75	120
545	$ 90,000 - $99,999	90	75	95	100	45	85
546	$100,000 and over	1,165	765	375	565	385	375
547	Average family income $	125,991	129,533	84,741	119,645	88,509	91,390
548	Median family income $	99,389	109,793	74,211	80,364	78,038	82,916
549	Standard error of average family income $	5,306	5,556	3,442	8,525	3,870	3,193
550	Total - All couple census families (51)	2,140	1,270	1,020	1,335	900	955
551	Under $10,000	50	-	30	20	35	25
552	$ 10,000 - $19,999	25	-	30	25	15	-
553	$ 20,000 - $29,999	120	55	30	65	70	35
554	$ 30,000 - $39,999	75	55	80	70	35	40
555	$ 40,000 - $49,999	95	25	85	75	35	30
556	$ 50,000 - $59,999	115	65	45	125	55	65
557	$ 60,000 - $69,999	180	65	100	130	90	85
558	$ 70,000 - $79,999	125	90	100	80	80	105
559	$ 80,000 - $89,999	120	70	65	110	60	120
560	$ 90,000 - $99,999	80	70	85	90	50	90
561	$100,000 and over	1,150	765	365	550	380	365
562	Average family income $	133,442	135,089	89,939	132,261	94,145	96,397
563	Median family income $	105,203	112,593	79,992	86,552	86,383	86,948
564	Standard error of average family income $	5,605	5,784	3,686	10,051	4,254	3,404
	Incidence of low income in 2000						
565	Total - Economic families	2,175	1,330	1,110	1,520	1,025	1,065
566	Low income	175	45	100	145	125	60
567	Incidence of low income in 2000 % (52)	8.1	3.5	9.1	9.6	12.2	5.6
568	Total - Unattached individuals 15 years and over	185	160	140	435	365	170
569	Low income	50	40	20	125	90	-
570	Incidence of low income in 2000 % (52)	25.7	25.9	14.2	28.6	24.0	-
571	Total - Population in private households	8,540	5,030	4,275	5,330	3,800	3,895
572	Low income	775	165	375	615	500	240
573	Incidence of low income in 2000 % (52)	9.0	3.3	8.8	11.5	13.2	6.2
	Private households by household income groups in 2000						
574	Total - All private households	2,295	1,425	1,225	1,800	1,335	1,165
575	Under $10,000	65	10	20	40	60	25
576	$ 10,000 - $19,999	40	15	70	75	60	10
577	$ 20,000 - $29,999	100	50	20	135	120	40
578	$ 30,000 - $39,999	105	90	105	105	65	55
579	$ 40,000 - $49,999	110	40	125	100	110	50
580	$ 50,000 - $59,999	125	55	35	180	110	110
581	$ 60,000 - $69,999	155	70	95	140	110	70
582	$ 70,000 - $79,999	140	85	110	90	135	130
583	$ 80,000 - $89,999	140	115	70	165	90	125
584	$ 90,000 - $99,999	90	85	120	140	50	95
585	$100,000 and over	1,230	805	445	640	415	435
586	Average household income $	135,097	130,454	89,895	115,691	81,884	93,091
587	Median household income $	105,320	110,040	81,394	82,466	70,816	85,604
588	Standard error of average household income $	5,592	5,455	3,412	7,575	3,362	3,030

Tableau 1. Certaines caractéristiques des secteurs de recensement, recensement de 2001 – Données intégrales et données-échantillon (20 %)

Toronto 0516.19 A	Toronto 0516.20 A	Toronto 0516.21 A	Toronto 0516.22 A	Toronto 0516.23 A	Toronto 0516.24 A	Caractéristiques	N°
						CARACTÉRISTIQUES DU REVENU DE 2000	
						Population de 15 ans et plus ayant un revenu d'emploi en 2000 selon le sexe et le travail – fin	
2,650	1,740	915	1,755	1,445	1,315	Femmes ayant un revenu d'emploi (48)	526
35,335	35,302	32,876	31,421	33,947	30,507	Revenu moyen d'emploi $	527
1,107	1,465	1,716	1,182	1,655	1,510	Erreur type de revenu moyen d'emploi $	528
1,525	1,010	485	930	835	695	Ayant travaillé toute l'année à plein temps (49)	529
45,181	46,785	44,860	42,619	43,851	41,656	Revenu moyen d'emploi $	530
1,327	2,038	2,333	1,543	1,811	2,202	Erreur type de revenu moyen d'emploi $	531
1,070	715	425	795	580	590	Ayant travaillé une partie de l'année ou à temps partiel (50)	532
22,453	19,017	19,485	18,934	21,399	18,572	Revenu moyen d'emploi $	533
1,553	1,327	1,827	1,378	2,752	1,616	Erreur type de revenu moyen d'emploi $	534
						Familles de recensement selon la structure et les tranches de revenu de la famille en 2000	
2,725	1,605	810	1,750	1,450	1,190	Total - Toutes les familles de recensement	535
115	25	-	25	25	15	Moins de 10 000 $	536
60	10	25	30	20	25	10 000 $ - 19 999 $	537
70	50	40	65	15	30	20 000 $ - 29 999 $	538
145	70	15	90	90	45	30 000 $ - 39 999 $	539
170	60	10	130	80	75	40 000 $ - 49 999 $	540
200	90	40	95	145	70	50 000 $ - 59 999 $	541
225	95	75	175	175	75	60 000 $ - 69 999 $	542
290	165	50	220	125	75	70 000 $ - 79 999 $	543
265	195	125	185	125	150	80 000 $ - 89 999 $	544
280	135	65	150	150	65	90 000 $ - 99 999 $	545
905	715	360	590	500	565	100 000 $ et plus	546
87,855	100,762	112,681	87,376	91,802	102,266	Revenu moyen des familles $	547
84,126	92,974	91,289	82,107	84,198	93,839	Revenu médian des familles $	548
2,110	2,950	6,255	2,044	2,798	4,882	Erreur type de revenu moyen des familles $	549
2,470	1,500	750	1,600	1,330	1,105	Total - Toutes les familles de recensement comptant un couple (51)	550
90	25	-	10	15	15	Moins de 10 000 $	551
35	-	25	20	15	20	10 000 $ - 19 999 $	552
40	50	20	55	15	-	20 000 $ - 29 999 $	553
125	45	15	55	75	35	30 000 $ - 39 999 $	554
140	45	10	115	55	65	40 000 $ - 49 999 $	555
180	70	40	75	125	55	50 000 $ - 59 999 $	556
200	100	80	160	160	70	60 000 $ - 69 999 $	557
290	160	50	215	115	65	70 000 $ - 79 999 $	558
240	175	115	170	125	150	80 000 $ - 89 999 $	559
265	130	60	145	155	65	90 000 $ - 99 999 $	560
855	700	345	575	485	555	100 000 $ et plus	561
90,622	103,523	115,856	90,588	95,464	106,205	Revenu moyen des familles $	562
86,181	96,127	91,929	84,046	87,630	99,992	Revenu médian des familles $	563
2,192	3,063	6,710	2,067	2,923	5,094	Erreur type de revenu moyen des familles $	564
						Fréquence des unités à faible revenu en 2000	
2,605	1,570	790	1,680	1,380	1,165	Total - Familles économiques	565
150	50	50	70	50	60	Faible revenu	566
5.9	3.3	6.3	4.1	3.5	5.1	Fréquence des unités à faible revenu en 2000 % (52)	567
360	200	70	195	150	120	Total - Personnes hors famille économique de 15 ans et plus	568
85	65	15	35	35	75	Faible revenu	569
24.5	30.6	27.8	16.9	22.2	62.2	Fréquence des unités à faible revenu en 2000 % (52)	570
9,765	5,965	3,025	6,360	5,330	4,525	Total - Population dans les ménages privés	571
640	290	210	335	200	345	Faible revenu	572
6.5	4.9	6.8	5.3	3.8	7.7	Fréquence des unités à faible revenu en 2000 % (52)	573
						Ménages privés selon les tranches de revenu du ménage en 2000	
2,850	1,695	825	1,790	1,470	1,225	Total - Tous les ménages privés	574
50	30	15	-	15	-	Moins de 10 000 $	575
70	15	25	10	15	50	10 000 $ - 19 999 $	576
65	40	35	60	35	10	20 000 $ - 29 999 $	577
120	45	15	75	80	40	30 000 $ - 39 999 $	578
185	80	10	145	85	70	40 000 $ - 49 999 $	579
205	100	35	105	120	75	50 000 $ - 59 999 $	580
250	125	70	145	160	75	60 000 $ - 69 999 $	581
260	160	55	205	115	60	70 000 $ - 79 999 $	582
300	185	90	195	130	150	80 000 $ - 89 999 $	583
335	130	70	170	150	70	90 000 $ - 99 999 $	584
995	785	395	675	575	620	100 000 $ et plus	585
91,969	102,804	116,277	91,247	95,767	105,693	Revenu moyen des ménages $	586
87,578	96,236	94,664	85,769	88,372	99,986	Revenu médian des ménages $	587
2,106	2,911	6,285	1,977	2,841	4,814	Erreur type de revenu moyen des ménages $	588

Table 1. Selected Characteristics for Census Tracts, 2001 Census – 100% Data and 20% Sample Data

No.	Characteristics	Toronto 0516.25 A	Toronto 0516.26 A	Toronto 0516.27 A	Toronto 0516.28 A	Toronto 0516.29 A	Toronto 0517
	POPULATION CHARACTERISTICS						
1	**Population, 1996 (1)**	**4,311**	**7,297**	**3,957**	**2,620**	**4,338**	**1,826**
2	**Population, 2001 (2)**	**4,192**	**7,404**	**12,513**	**4,641**	**4,802**	**1,795**
3	Population percentage change, 1996-2001	-2.8	1.5	216.2	77.1	10.7	-1.7
4	Land area in square kilometres, 2001	2.83	1.51	8.65	0.93	0.74	1.23
5	**Total population - 100% Data (3)**	**4,190**	**7,400**	**12,515**	**4,640**	**4,800**	**1,795**
	by sex and age groups						
6	Male	2,065	3,605	6,180	2,280	2,270	875
7	0-4 years	125	215	540	240	225	50
8	5-9 years	180	375	590	240	275	60
9	10-14 years	205	345	490	165	195	55
10	15-19 years	210	370	415	145	140	60
11	20-24 years	170	270	340	115	120	70
12	25-29 years	105	190	465	90	90	55
13	30-34 years	85	170	600	205	165	50
14	35-39 years	135	250	680	290	290	75
15	40-44 years	170	365	605	245	275	55
16	45-49 years	210	310	480	195	175	60
17	50-54 years	185	305	340	125	125	70
18	55-59 years	110	145	220	70	60	55
19	60-64 years	85	115	155	60	50	55
20	65-69 years	40	70	105	50	25	40
21	70-74 years	20	45	80	20	35	35
22	75-79 years	10	30	35	10	20	20
23	80-84 years	-	15	20	10	5	15
24	85 years and over	-	15	5	5	5	5
25	Female	2,125	3,800	6,335	2,365	2,535	920
26	0-4 years	105	205	530	215	195	55
27	5-9 years	170	335	555	215	265	55
28	10-14 years	170	345	480	175	215	60
29	15-19 years	200	320	385	160	190	60
30	20-24 years	155	280	340	115	125	55
31	25-29 years	115	200	530	145	130	45
32	30-34 years	145	245	705	270	230	65
33	35-39 years	175	355	745	305	355	80
34	40-44 years	230	425	660	240	275	65
35	45-49 years	220	335	420	175	180	80
36	50-54 years	180	275	305	120	115	90
37	55-59 years	95	130	205	70	75	55
38	60-64 years	60	85	155	50	50	40
39	65-69 years	40	70	125	40	35	35
40	70-74 years	30	60	95	30	50	30
41	75-79 years	15	55	55	25	30	25
42	80-84 years	15	30	20	10	5	10
43	85 years and over	5	35	20	-	10	10
44	**Total population 15 years and over**	**3,235**	**5,585**	**9,320**	**3,395**	**3,430**	**1,460**
	by legal marital status						
45	Never married (single)	1,075	1,800	2,340	825	980	425
46	Legally married (and not separated)	1,820	3,190	6,210	2,250	2,045	860
47	Separated, but still legally married	85	135	180	95	120	50
48	Divorced	165	235	365	145	160	60
49	Widowed	95	225	230	80	115	60
	by common-law status						
50	Not in a common-law relationship	3,155	5,425	8,910	3,260	3,245	1,390
51	In a common-law relationship	85	160	410	140	180	75
52	**Total population - 20% Sample Data (4)**	**4,195**	**7,340**	**12,510**	**4,640**	**4,800**	**1,795**
	by mother tongue						
53	Single responses	4,115	7,225	12,155	4,565	4,685	1,780
54	English	2,660	3,930	6,395	2,685	2,925	1,310
55	French	65	70	225	80	70	-
56	Non-official languages (5)	1,395	3,230	5,535	1,800	1,685	460
57	Italian	75	140	275	135	80	10
58	Chinese, n.o.s.	110	295	500	155	305	30
59	Cantonese	30	145	305	290	160	-
60	Portuguese	65	205	345	50	95	-
61	Punjabi	200	270	340	45	55	10
62	Other languages (6)	920	2,170	3,755	1,130	990	410
63	Multiple responses	75	110	360	75	120	20
64	English and French	-	15	15	-	-	-
65	English and non-official language	70	75	330	60	80	20
66	French and non-official language	-	20	10	15	35	-
67	English, French and non-official language	-	-	-	-	-	-

See reference material at the end of the publication. – Voir les documents de référence à la fin de la publication.

Tableau 1. Certaines caractéristiques des secteurs de recensement, recensement de 2001 – Données intégrales et données-échantillon (20 %)

Toronto 0518 ◆	Toronto 0519	Toronto 0520.01 ◆	Toronto 0520.02	Toronto 0520.04	Toronto 0520.05 A	Caractéristiques	N°
						CARACTÉRISTIQUES DE LA POPULATION	
4,825	**4,043**	**5,576**	**5,487**	**5,633**	**6,230**	**Population, 1996 (1)**	1
4,834	**3,946**	**5,812**	**6,834**	**8,137**	**3,783**	**Population, 2001 (2)**	2
0.2	-2.4	4.2	24.5	44.5	-39.3	Variation en pourcentage de la population, 1996-2001	3
0.74	1.12	2.63	1.65	1.44	0.56	Superficie des terres en kilomètres carrés, 2001	4
4,835	**3,945**	**5,815**	**6,835**	**8,135**	**3,785**	**Population totale – Données intégrales (3)**	5
						selon le sexe et les groupes d'âge	
2,380	1,950	2,945	3,365	3,920	1,875	Sexe masculin	6
210	130	190	215	325	130	0-4 ans	7
185	130	220	235	270	120	5-9 ans	8
170	130	270	270	255	135	10-14 ans	9
190	125	250	290	225	185	15-19 ans	10
175	145	230	250	240	140	20-24 ans	11
160	125	220	230	415	140	25-29 ans	12
185	160	205	260	485	180	30-34 ans	13
210	165	255	290	445	175	35-39 ans	14
185	170	240	300	355	135	40-44 ans	15
170	145	190	280	255	125	45-49 ans	16
145	135	205	265	200	140	50-54 ans	17
115	95	155	170	125	85	55-59 ans	18
100	75	115	105	110	75	60-64 ans	19
80	85	80	75	85	45	65-69 ans	20
45	65	65	50	70	40	70-74 ans	21
30	40	40	50	50	20	75-79 ans	22
15	20	20	20	30	5	80-84 ans	23
10	5	5	10	10	5	85 ans et plus	24
2,460	2,000	2,870	3,470	4,215	1,910	Sexe féminin	25
195	120	165	180	330	120	0-4 ans	26
155	120	205	215	300	120	5-9 ans	27
160	145	190	250	185	125	10-14 ans	28
165	130	215	300	210	140	15-19 ans	29
185	130	235	265	290	140	20-24 ans	30
170	150	200	275	515	165	25-29 ans	31
190	135	240	290	500	170	30-34 ans	32
220	165	240	305	465	165	35-39 ans	33
205	160	245	305	330	175	40-44 ans	34
180	150	215	330	280	145	45-49 ans	35
150	130	225	235	220	140	50-54 ans	36
120	110	140	165	155	85	55-59 ans	37
110	115	135	115	120	80	60-64 ans	38
85	80	90	85	115	60	65-69 ans	39
65	80	70	65	100	25	70-74 ans	40
50	40	45	55	75	30	75-79 ans	41
25	20	10	25	30	10	80-84 ans	42
25	10	5	15	10	10	85 ans et plus	43
3,760	**3,170**	**4,580**	**5,470**	**6,485**	**3,035**	**Population totale de 15 ans et plus**	44
						selon l'état matrimonial légal	
1,180	935	1,455	1,820	2,040	1,035	Célibataire (jamais marié(e))	45
1,985	1,805	2,625	3,150	3,445	1,610	Légalement marié(e) (et non séparé(e))	46
155	95	120	115	260	100	Séparé(e), mais toujours légalement marié(e)	47
250	150	195	210	455	165	Divorcé(e)	48
195	190	190	185	275	130	Veuf ou veuve	49
						selon l'union libre	
3,580	3,040	4,465	5,340	6,115	2,910	Ne vivant pas en union libre	50
180	130	110	130	370	125	Vivant en union libre	51
4,835	**3,945**	**5,815**	**6,830**	**8,135**	**3,775**	**Population totale – Données-échantillon (20 %) (4)**	52
						selon la langue maternelle	
4,605	3,850	5,635	6,640	7,775	3,685	Réponses uniques	53
2,320	2,125	2,200	2,305	3,260	1,595	Anglais	54
95	10	50	40	90	25	Français	55
2,190	1,715	3,380	4,295	4,430	2,065	Langues non officielles (5)	56
95	80	120	125	130	135	Italien	57
75	55	65	370	260	165	Chinois, n.d.a.	58
30	20	45	440	135	90	Cantonais	59
35	275	500	450	320	140	Portugais	60
230	125	250	300	210	30	Pendjabi	61
1,720	1,165	2,395	2,615	3,380	1,510	Autres langues (6)	62
225	100	180	190	355	90	Réponses multiples	63
-	-	10	10	-	15	Anglais et français	64
205	85	170	180	320	70	Anglais et langue non officielle	65
25	-	-	10	-	-	Français et langue non officielle	66
-	-	-	-	25	-	Anglais, français et langue non officielle	67

See reference material at the end of the publication. – Voir les documents de référence à la fin de la publication.

Table 1. Selected Characteristics for Census Tracts, 2001 Census – 100% Data and 20% Sample Data

No.	Characteristics	Toronto 0516.25 A	Toronto 0516.26 A	Toronto 0516.27 A	Toronto 0516.28 A	Toronto 0516.29 A	Toronto 0517
	POPULATION CHARACTERISTICS						
	by home language						
68	Single responses	3,290	5,425	8,575	3,440	3,430	1,450
69	English	2,890	4,520	7,255	2,980	2,955	1,365
70	French	-	15	40	-	10	-
71	Non-official languages (5)	400	890	1,280	460	460	85
72	Cantonese	15	45	145	85	85	-
73	Chinese, n.o.s.	15	95	295	60	140	10
74	Italian	-	15	15	-	10	-
75	Punjabi	85	125	100	-	10	-
76	Portuguese	10	25	40	-	-	-
77	Other languages (6)	275	580	685	315	215	75
78	Multiple responses	905	1,915	3,935	1,195	1,375	345
79	English and French	80	65	195	85	75	10
80	English and non-official language	825	1,785	3,675	1,075	1,255	335
81	French and non-official language	-	25	15	-	-	-
82	English, French and non-official language	-	40	45	35	45	-
	by knowledge of official languages						
83	English only	3,755	6,595	11,210	4,110	4,310	1,665
84	French only	-	-	-	-	-	-
85	English and French	330	580	1,005	465	405	120
86	Neither English nor French	105	160	285	65	90	10
	by knowledge of non-official languages (5) (7)						
87	Italian	125	220	425	150	125	20
88	Cantonese	35	185	395	320	205	10
89	Chinese, n.o.s.	85	285	540	165	355	30
90	Spanish	50	95	495	120	50	50
91	Portuguese	70	225	405	70	90	-
92	Punjabi	265	380	605	95	110	10
93	Tagalog (Pilipino)	130	145	550	135	75	-
	by first official language spoken						
94	English	4,015	7,020	11,930	4,440	4,610	1,760
95	French	65	80	220	85	70	10
96	English and French	10	80	90	55	30	15
97	Neither English nor French	100	160	275	70	90	10
98	Official language minority - (number) (8)	70	120	265	110	90	15
99	Official language minority - (percentage) (8)	1.7	1.6	2.1	2.4	1.9	0.8
	by ethnic origin (9)						
100	Canadian	700	1,170	1,785	860	1,015	715
101	English	1,045	985	1,355	725	530	465
102	Scottish	495	690	1,060	530	435	345
103	Irish	475	720	1,160	630	410	255
104	Chinese	205	670	1,300	700	655	120
105	Italian	310	415	1,060	385	385	85
106	East Indian	430	1,045	1,440	570	475	30
107	French	280	330	575	330	225	320
108	German	250	190	530	315	205	185
109	Portuguese	95	395	660	115	180	25
110	Polish	310	455	685	310	175	165
111	Jewish	40	35	35	30	40	-
112	Jamaican	200	370	570	90	315	50
113	Filipino	215	180	755	300	95	10
114	Ukrainian	100	210	345	70	110	50
	by Aboriginal identity						
115	Total Aboriginal identity population (10)	15	15	10	60	20	10
116	Total non-Aboriginal population	4,175	7,325	12,505	4,580	4,780	1,785
	by Aboriginal origin						
117	Total Aboriginal origins population (11)	15	40	25	110	30	20
118	Total non-Aboriginal population	4,175	7,295	12,480	4,530	4,770	1,780
	by Registered Indian status						
119	Registered Indian (12)	-	10	-	-	20	-
120	Not a Registered Indian	4,190	7,325	12,505	4,645	4,790	1,795

Tableau 1. Certaines caractéristiques des secteurs de recensement, recensement de 2001 – Données intégrales et données-échantillon (20 %)

Toronto 0518 ◆	Toronto 0519	Toronto 0520.01 ◆	Toronto 0520.02	Toronto 0520.04	Toronto 0520.05 A	Caractéristiques	Nº
						CARACTÉRISTIQUES DE LA POPULATION	
						selon la langue parlée à la maison	
3,560	3,030	4,015	4,385	5,690	2,360	Réponses uniques	68
2,490	2,285	2,650	2,715	3,845	1,840	Anglais	69
85	-	15	10	15	-	Français	70
990	745	1,350	1,660	1,830	520	Langues non officielles (5)	71
15	10	40	195	95	60	Cantonais	72
75	15	35	105	135	30	Chinois, n.d.a.	73
-	10	20	15	25	20	Italien	74
115	40	165	80	140	-	Pendjabi	75
10	105	140	145	35	30	Portugais	76
765	565	945	1,120	1,415	375	Autres langues (6)	77
1,275	915	1,800	2,450	2,445	1,415	Réponses multiples	78
-	-	35	20	115	35	Anglais et français	79
1,250	875	1,740	2,400	2,330	1,335	Anglais et langue non officielle	80
15	15	-	15	-	-	Français et langue non officielle	81
10	25	15	20	-	45	Anglais, français et langue non officielle	82
						selon la connaissance des langues officielles	
4,155	3,605	5,315	6,005	7,375	3,420	Anglais seulement	83
10	-	-	20	20	-	Français seulement	84
335	225	255	410	505	210	Anglais et français	85
330	115	240	400	235	145	Ni l'anglais ni le français	86
						selon la connaissance des langues non officielles (5) (7)	
165	155	205	220	260	230	Italien	87
35	20	55	465	155	105	Cantonais	88
95	70	75	395	260	150	Chinois, n.d.a.	89
125	210	245	180	390	70	Espagnol	90
35	385	540	495	345	140	Portugais	91
420	170	370	415	285	80	Pendjabi	92
225	195	475	445	585	235	Tagalog (pilipino)	93
						selon la première langue officielle parlée	
4,325	3,805	5,475	6,285	7,745	3,605	Anglais	94
110	10	55	65	90	30	Français	95
70	15	45	95	60	25	Anglais et français	96
325	120	240	395	240	125	Ni l'anglais ni le français	97
145	15	75	110	120	40	Minorité de langue officielle - (nombre) (8)	98
3.0	0.4	1.3	1.6	1.5	1.1	Minorité de langue officielle - (pourcentage) (8)	99
						selon l'origine ethnique (9)	
970	695	390	480	970	310	Canadien	100
615	650	345	215	645	260	Anglais	101
325	320	255	140	475	200	Écossais	102
405	235	235	145	470	120	Irlandais	103
200	110	225	1,035	565	325	Chinois	104
270	250	320	390	345	235	Italien	105
580	475	835	1,005	990	400	Indien de l'Inde	106
150	80	75	75	240	115	Français	107
170	140	125	60	275	85	Allemand	108
45	450	675	620	490	240	Portugais	109
490	230	460	660	880	335	Polonais	110
10	-	-	-	30	20	Juif	111
250	200	175	230	380	165	Jamaïquain	112
305	240	605	615	740	355	Philippin	113
130	70	50	145	255	75	Ukrainien	114
						selon l'identité autochtone	
10	-	-	-	55	20	Total de la population ayant une identité autochtone (10)	115
4,825	3,935	5,810	6,830	8,080	3,755	Total de la population non autochtone	116
						selon l'origine autochtone	
35	15	-	-	90	50	Total de la population ayant une origine autochtone (11)	117
4,800	3,925	5,815	6,835	8,045	3,725	Total de la population non autochtone	118
						selon le statut d'Indien inscrit	
10	10	-	-	15	10	Oui, Indien inscrit (12)	119
4,820	3,940	5,810	6,835	8,115	3,770	Non, pas un Indien inscrit	120

Table 1. Selected Characteristics for Census Tracts, 2001 Census – 100% Data and 20% Sample Data

No.	Characteristics	Toronto 0516.25 A	Toronto 0516.26 A	Toronto 0516.27 A	Toronto 0516.28 A	Toronto 0516.29 A	Toronto 0517
	POPULATION CHARACTERISTICS						
	by visible minority groups						
121	Total visible minority population	1,510	3,650	5,840	1,895	2,275	325
122	Chinese	210	580	1,175	620	675	80
123	South Asian	595	1,310	1,940	710	590	50
124	Black	290	595	670	110	465	30
125	Filipino	205	165	665	255	90	-
126	Latin American	15	40	270	40	10	40
127	Southeast Asian	-	70	215	-	95	60
128	Arab	60	250	290	30	70	15
129	West Asian	10	65	105	15	90	10
130	Korean	10	100	85	-	25	10
131	Japanese	10	95	40	40	50	10
132	Visible minority, n.i.e. (13)	90	235	255	65	85	15
133	Multiple visible minorities (14)	15	145	125	10	30	10
	by citizenship						
134	Canadian citizenship (15)	3,825	6,675	10,715	4,070	4,400	1,715
135	Citizenship other than Canadian	365	670	1,800	570	400	80
	by place of birth of respondent						
136	Non-immigrant population	2,565	3,860	6,370	2,600	2,815	1,230
137	Born in province of residence	2,235	3,200	5,430	2,215	2,315	985
138	Immigrant population (16)	1,625	3,435	6,010	2,020	1,985	560
139	United States	80	70	135	30	35	15
140	Central and South America	45	175	300	50	70	30
141	Caribbean and Bermuda	215	410	485	105	200	25
142	United Kingdom	115	140	330	115	80	70
143	Other Europe (17)	395	795	1,270	450	355	180
144	Africa	80	85	275	90	145	30
145	Asia and the Middle East	690	1,770	3,195	1,165	1,110	205
146	Oceania and other (18)	10	-	20	10	-	-
147	Non-permanent residents (19)	-	40	135	15	-	10
148	**Total immigrant population**	**1,625**	**3,440**	**6,010**	**2,020**	**1,990**	**560**
	by period of immigration						
149	Before 1961	110	150	205	125	60	130
150	1961-1970	265	325	500	120	225	85
151	1971-1980	350	700	905	390	310	95
152	1981-1990	345	1,095	1,635	375	600	150
153	1991-2001 (20)	550	1,160	2,770	1,020	790	100
154	1991-1995	320	655	1,360	545	515	70
155	1996-2001 (20)	230	500	1,410	475	280	30
	by age at immigration						
156	0-4 years	170	280	505	225	170	55
157	5-19 years	415	1,050	1,850	615	605	200
158	20 years and over	1,040	2,105	3,655	1,180	1,215	305
159	**Total population**	**4,190**	**7,340**	**12,510**	**4,640**	**4,800**	**1,800**
	by religion						
160	Catholic (21)	1,645	2,870	5,605	2,060	1,715	700
161	Protestant	1,240	1,495	2,130	880	1,080	595
162	Christian Orthodox	105	190	400	130	145	-
163	Christian, n.i.e. (22)	100	170	435	110	185	25
164	Muslim	190	670	1,045	255	365	55
165	Jewish	20	15	20	25	15	10
166	Buddhist	10	155	225	125	170	85
167	Hindu	275	600	535	280	235	20
168	Sikh	120	240	380	90	75	-
169	Eastern religions (23)	-	85	-	-	-	25
170	Other religions (24)	-	-	-	-	-	-
171	No religious affiliation (25)	485	850	1,740	680	825	290
172	**Total population 15 years and over**	**3,245**	**5,505**	**9,310**	**3,380**	**3,425**	**1,515**
	by generation status						
173	1st generation (26)	1,535	3,310	5,605	1,805	1,885	560
174	2nd generation (27)	785	1,110	2,075	690	730	280
175	3rd generation and over (28)	920	1,085	1,635	890	810	670
176	**Total population 1 year and over (29)**	**4,165**	**7,280**	**12,305**	**4,560**	**4,730**	**1,775**
	by place of residence 1 year ago (mobility)						
177	Non-movers	3,820	6,420	7,155	4,190	4,170	1,590
178	Movers	350	860	5,155	370	555	185
179	Non-migrants	140	535	3,675	195	290	130
180	Migrants	205	320	1,480	180	270	55
181	Internal migrants	135	170	1,140	120	195	45
182	Intraprovincial migrants	130	115	1,030	115	170	40
183	Interprovincial migrants	-	50	105	-	25	-
184	External migrants	70	150	340	55	75	15

Tableau 1. Certaines caractéristiques des secteurs de recensement, recensement de 2001 – Données intégrales et données-échantillon (20 %)

Toronto 0518 ◆	Toronto 0519	Toronto 0520.01 ◆	Toronto 0520.02	Toronto 0520.04	Toronto 0520.05 A	Caractéristiques	N°
						CARACTÉRISTIQUES DE LA POPULATION	
						selon les groupes de minorités visibles	
2,415	1,490	3,195	3,970	4,255	2,100	Total de la population des minorités visibles	121
195	90	235	940	530	285	Chinois	122
1,105	485	1,050	1,105	1,310	600	Sud-Asiatique	123
475	265	385	315	570	395	Noir	124
285	215	605	605	735	390	Philippin	125
95	175	125	70	225	60	Latino-Américain	126
40	35	285	340	170	145	Asiatique du Sud-Est	127
60	60	145	280	260	60	Arabe	128
65	30	-	100	40	20	Asiatique occidental	129
10	15	25	85	165	-	Coréen	130
-	-	25	-	10	-	Japonais	131
55	80	295	55	195	120	Minorité visible, n.i.a. (13)	132
30	30	25	75	40	30	Minorités visibles multiples (14)	133
						selon la citoyenneté	
3,825	3,425	4,800	5,805	6,230	3,170	Citoyenneté canadienne (15)	134
1,010	520	1,015	1,030	1,910	610	Citoyenneté autre que canadienne	135
						selon le lieu de naissance du répondant	
2,385	1,885	2,180	2,545	3,095	1,500	Population non immigrante	136
2,050	1,710	2,020	2,260	2,615	1,350	Née dans la province de résidence	137
2,360	2,025	3,625	4,235	4,995	2,255	Population immigrante (16)	138
25	15	30	20	35	25	États-Unis	139
95	165	235	225	355	150	Amérique centrale et du Sud	140
175	215	345	205	420	205	Caraïbes et Bermudes	141
70	145	180	85	185	55	Royaume-Uni	142
660	750	1,000	1,210	1,310	650	Autre Europe (17)	143
60	20	150	110	255	125	Afrique	144
1,280	700	1,655	2,390	2,410	1,015	Asie et Moyen-Orient	145
-	10	35	-	25	20	Océanie et autre (18)	146
85	40	-	50	40	25	Résidents non permanents (19)	147
2,365	**2,020**	**3,630**	**4,235**	**5,000**	**2,255**	**Population immigrante totale**	148
						selon la période d'immigration	
155	270	175	95	150	75	Avant 1961	149
165	305	385	505	325	245	1961-1970	150
285	320	695	855	585	450	1971-1980	151
455	485	945	1,145	1,265	500	1981-1990	152
1,305	645	1,430	1,630	2,675	980	1991-2001 (20)	153
650	400	760	940	1,205	380	1991-1995	154
655	240	670	690	1,465	600	1996-2001 (20)	155
						selon l'âge à l'immigration	
125	200	225	375	380	160	0-4 ans	156
600	650	1,060	1,170	1,385	580	5-19 ans	157
1,635	1,170	2,340	2,695	3,240	1,515	20 ans et plus	158
4,830	**3,945**	**5,810**	**6,835**	**8,135**	**3,780**	**Population totale**	159
						selon la religion	
1,695	1,810	2,790	3,360	3,640	1,730	Catholique (21)	160
1,290	965	675	655	1,260	575	Protestante	161
90	190	135	245	265	125	Orthodoxe chrétienne	162
80	90	120	170	390	115	Chrétiennes, n.i.a. (22)	163
545	160	875	700	750	280	Musulmane	164
-	-	-	10	15	15	Juive	165
15	25	230	355	220	170	Bouddhiste	166
310	175	320	310	540	290	Hindoue	167
210	100	300	270	140	50	Sikh	168
35	-	-	10	-	-	Religions orientales (23)	169
-	-	10	-	-	10	Autres religions (24)	170
560	430	365	750	915	420	Aucune appartenance religieuse (25)	171
3,765	**3,165**	**4,560**	**5,455**	**6,490**	**2,995**	**Population totale de 15 ans et plus**	172
						selon le statut des générations	
2,275	1,940	3,355	3,980	4,700	2,105	1re génération (26)	173
650	615	790	1,055	875	580	2e génération (27)	174
845	615	415	410	920	305	3e génération et plus (28)	175
4,785	**3,910**	**5,775**	**6,755**	**7,990**	**3,705**	**Population totale de 1 an et plus (29)**	176
						selon le lieu de résidence 1 an auparavant (mobilité)	
3,990	3,495	5,110	6,155	6,710	3,170	Personnes n'ayant pas déménagé	177
795	420	665	600	1,275	535	Personnes ayant déménagé	178
475	315	390	325	590	285	Non-migrants	179
320	105	280	275	685	250	Migrants	180
190	75	195	175	405	130	Migrants internes	181
175	70	195	155	375	95	Migrants infraprovinciaux	182
15	-	-	20	30	35	Migrants interprovinciaux	183
125	25	75	100	280	125	Migrants externes	184

Table 1. Selected Characteristics for Census Tracts, 2001 Census – 100% Data and 20% Sample Data

No.	Characteristics	Toronto 0516.25 A	Toronto 0516.26 A	Toronto 0516.27 A	Toronto 0516.28 A	Toronto 0516.29 A	Toronto 0517
	POPULATION CHARACTERISTICS						
185	**Total population 5 years and over (30)**	**3,960**	**6,905**	**11,440**	**4,180**	**4,380**	**1,735**
	by place of residence 5 years ago (mobility)						
186	Non-movers	2,610	4,475	2,825	1,880	2,400	1,125
187	Movers	1,355	2,430	8,610	2,305	1,975	610
188	Non-migrants	815	1,565	5,440	1,105	965	365
189	Migrants	540	865	3,170	1,200	1,005	245
190	Internal migrants	340	465	1,810	735	765	205
191	Intraprovincial migrants	300	360	1,385	615	630	160
192	Interprovincial migrants	40	105	425	115	130	50
193	External migrants	200	405	1,365	465	245	40
194	**Total population 15 to 24 years**	**740**	**1,220**	**1,465**	**520**	**575**	**275**
	by school attendance						
195	Not attending school	255	340	370	140	145	60
196	Attending school full time	450	810	1,055	330	365	200
197	Attending school part time	30	65	45	45	70	15
198	**Total population 15 years and over**	**3,245**	**5,500**	**9,315**	**3,385**	**3,430**	**1,515**
	by highest level of schooling						
199	Less than grade 9 (31)	120	230	370	125	75	20
200	Grades 9-13 without high school graduation certificate	475	1,085	1,175	415	600	310
201	Grades 9-13 with high school graduation certificate	415	805	1,000	360	430	220
202	Some postsecondary without degree, certificate or diploma (32)	425	620	1,195	385	430	180
203	Trades certificate or diploma (33)	230	410	675	135	315	175
204	College certificate or diploma (34)	510	995	1,585	665	480	165
205	University certificate below bachelor's degree	55	190	330	155	110	50
206	University with bachelor's degree or higher	1,010	1,170	2,975	1,140	995	405
	by combinations of unpaid work						
207	Males 15 years and over	1,540	2,650	4,570	1,645	1,575	745
208	Reported unpaid work (35)	1,420	2,325	4,170	1,500	1,380	670
209	Housework and child care and care or assistance to seniors	115	300	425	140	135	70
210	Housework and child care only	435	830	1,685	670	625	170
211	Housework and care or assistance to seniors only	85	125	170	55	25	85
212	Child care and care or assistance to seniors only	-	-	10	-	-	10
213	Housework only	750	985	1,790	605	595	315
214	Child care only	25	65	70	30	-	15
215	Care or assistance to seniors only	10	20	25	-	-	10
216	Females 15 years and over	1,705	2,855	4,740	1,735	1,855	765
217	Reported unpaid work (35)	1,590	2,670	4,485	1,695	1,720	700
218	Housework and child care and care or assistance to seniors	180	465	490	230	220	105
219	Housework and child care only	565	1,095	2,010	785	735	215
220	Housework and care or assistance to seniors only	85	220	235	50	60	70
221	Child care and care or assistance to seniors only	-	-	-	10	-	10
222	Housework only	735	870	1,705	615	670	290
223	Child care only	20	15	45	10	30	15
224	Care or assistance to seniors only	-	15	-	10	10	-
	by labour force activity						
225	Males 15 years and over	1,540	2,650	4,570	1,645	1,570	750
226	In the labour force	1,275	2,095	3,795	1,375	1,270	580
227	Employed	1,210	1,980	3,640	1,335	1,240	560
228	Unemployed	65	115	155	45	30	25
229	Not in the labour force	270	550	775	265	310	165
230	Participation rate	82.8	79.1	83.0	83.6	80.9	77.3
231	Employment rate	78.6	74.7	79.6	81.2	79.0	74.7
232	Unemployment rate	5.1	5.5	4.1	3.3	2.4	4.3
233	Females 15 years and over	1,700	2,860	4,745	1,735	1,855	770
234	In the labour force	1,250	2,030	3,330	1,220	1,365	475
235	Employed	1,135	1,835	3,160	1,145	1,270	450
236	Unemployed	115	190	170	70	95	25
237	Not in the labour force	455	830	1,410	520	490	295
238	Participation rate	73.5	71.0	70.2	70.3	73.6	61.7
239	Employment rate	66.8	64.2	66.6	66.0	68.5	58.4
240	Unemployment rate	9.2	9.4	5.1	5.7	7.0	5.3

Tableau 1. Certaines caractéristiques des secteurs de recensement, recensement de 2001 – Données intégrales et données-échantillon (20 %)

Toronto 0518 ◆	Toronto 0519	Toronto 0520.01 ◆	Toronto 0520.02	Toronto 0520.04	Toronto 0520.05 A	Caractéristiques	N°
						CARACTÉRISTIQUES DE LA POPULATION	
4,435	**3,695**	**5,460**	**6,425**	**7,465**	**3,520**	**Population totale de 5 ans et plus (30)**	185
						selon le lieu de résidence 5 ans auparavant (mobilité)	
2,210	2,275	2,955	2,805	1,860	1,745	Personnes n'ayant pas déménagé	186
2,225	1,410	2,505	3,615	5,605	1,775	Personnes ayant déménagé	187
1,180	815	1,500	2,280	2,650	730	Non-migrants	188
1,050	605	1,005	1,335	2,955	1,045	Migrants	189
415	365	575	725	1,795	540	Migrants internes	190
345	330	530	660	1,570	410	Migrants infraprovinciaux	191
75	35	50	60	225	125	Migrants interprovinciaux	192
635	235	425	615	1,160	505	Migrants externes	193
710	**525**	**930**	**1,090**	**965**	**560**	**Population totale de 15 à 24 ans**	194
						selon la fréquentation scolaire	
225	210	255	355	390	180	Ne fréquentant pas l'école	195
450	300	620	715	505	345	Fréquentant l'école à plein temps	196
35	15	55	25	75	35	Fréquentant l'école à temps partiel	197
3,760	**3,165**	**4,560**	**5,450**	**6,490**	**2,995**	**Population totale de 15 ans et plus**	198
						selon le plus haut niveau de scolarité atteint	
385	285	390	475	475	205	Niveau inférieur à la 9e année (31)	199
725	680	935	1,035	1,030	615	De la 9e à la 13e année sans certificat d'études secondaires	200
525	470	770	610	885	340	De la 9e à la 13e année avec certificat d'études secondaires	201
450	375	740	750	860	380	Études postsecondaires partielles sans grade, certificat ou diplôme (32)	202
355	295	500	355	555	205	Certificat ou diplôme d'une école de métiers (33)	203
550	590	670	870	1,025	520	Certificat ou diplôme collégial (34)	204
140	70	105	265	190	65	Certificat universitaire inférieur au baccalauréat	205
625	400	445	1,095	1,465	660	Études universitaires avec baccalauréat ou diplôme supérieur	206
						selon les combinaisons de travail non rémunéré	
1,815	1,540	2,255	2,625	3,065	1,470	Hommes de 15 ans et plus	207
1,610	1,365	1,800	2,240	2,700	1,290	Travail non rémunéré déclaré (35)	208
160	125	220	265	250	120	Travaux ménagers et soins aux enfants et soins ou aide aux personnes âgées	209
575	460	595	695	745	405	Travaux ménagers et soins aux enfants seulement	210
115	100	80	100	60	30	Travaux ménagers et soins ou aide aux personnes âgées seulement	211
-	-	-	-	20	-	Soins aux enfants et soins ou aide aux personnes âgées seulement	212
725	660	880	1,085	1,590	715	Travaux ménagers seulement	213
35	15	25	55	20	10	Soins aux enfants seulement	214
-	-	-	30	15	10	Soins ou aide aux personnes âgées seulement	215
1,950	1,625	2,305	2,825	3,425	1,525	Femmes de 15 ans et plus	216
1,790	1,495	2,015	2,605	3,205	1,365	Travail non rémunéré déclaré (35)	217
225	185	280	375	315	130	Travaux ménagers et soins aux enfants et soins ou aide aux personnes âgées	218
685	530	740	905	1,080	470	Travaux ménagers et soins aux enfants seulement	219
100	110	100	150	175	75	Travaux ménagers et soins ou aide aux personnes âgées seulement	220
-	-	-	-	-	-	Soins aux enfants et soins ou aide aux personnes âgées seulement	221
770	650	860	1,150	1,610	670	Travaux ménagers seulement	222
10	15	25	20	20	-	Soins aux enfants seulement	223
10	10	-	10	-	15	Soins ou aide aux personnes âgées seulement	224
						selon l'activité	
1,815	1,540	2,250	2,625	3,065	1,475	Hommes de 15 ans et plus	225
1,390	1,135	1,770	1,960	2,395	1,185	Population active	226
1,330	1,040	1,650	1,860	2,200	1,090	Personnes occupées	227
65	95	115	105	195	95	Chômeurs	228
425	405	480	665	670	285	Inactifs	229
76.6	73.7	78.7	74.7	78.1	80.3	Taux d'activité	230
73.3	67.5	73.3	70.9	71.8	73.9	Taux d'emploi	231
4.7	8.4	6.5	5.4	8.1	8.0	Taux de chômage	232
1,950	1,620	2,310	2,825	3,425	1,520	Femmes de 15 ans et plus	233
1,240	1,020	1,545	1,915	2,375	1,050	Population active	234
1,150	950	1,405	1,820	2,160	980	Personnes occupées	235
85	70	140	95	210	70	Chômeuses	236
710	605	765	915	1,050	475	Inactives	237
63.6	63.0	66.9	67.8	69.3	69.1	Taux d'activité	238
59.0	58.6	60.8	64.4	63.1	64.5	Taux d'emploi	239
6.9	6.9	9.1	5.0	8.8	6.7	Taux de chômage	240

Table 1. Selected Characteristics for Census Tracts, 2001 Census – 100% Data and 20% Sample Data

No.	Characteristics	Toronto 0516.25 A	Toronto 0516.26 A	Toronto 0516.27 A	Toronto 0516.28 A	Toronto 0516.29 A	Toronto 0517
	POPULATION CHARACTERISTICS						
	by labour force activity – concluded						
241	Both sexes - Participation rate	78.0	74.9	76.5	76.7	76.8	70.0
242	15-24 years	70.1	63.0	55.1	55.3	65.2	60.0
243	25 years and over	80.4	78.4	80.5	80.5	79.4	72.2
244	Both sexes - Employment rate	72.6	69.5	73.1	73.2	73.1	66.3
245	15-24 years	55.8	52.5	48.0	51.5	58.3	50.9
246	25 years and over	77.4	74.2	77.7	77.3	76.1	69.8
247	Both sexes - Unemployment rate	6.7	7.4	4.5	4.6	4.8	4.7
248	15-24 years	19.6	16.3	13.0	8.6	9.3	12.1
249	25 years and over	3.5	5.4	3.5	4.1	4.0	3.9
250	**Total labour force 15 years and over**	**2,525**	**4,120**	**7,125**	**2,595**	**2,635**	**1,055**
	by industry based on the 1997 NAICS						
251	Industry - Not applicable (36)	60	75	115	25	40	10
252	All industries (37)	2,465	4,050	7,015	2,570	2,595	1,050
253	11 Agriculture, forestry, fishing and hunting	10	-	10	-	-	-
254	21 Mining and oil and gas extraction	-	-	-	-	10	-
255	22 Utilities	30	35	30	30	20	10
256	23 Construction	75	125	290	100	80	45
257	31-33 Manufacturing	470	570	940	395	430	145
258	41 Wholesale trade	225	300	605	200	250	95
259	44-45 Retail trade	280	555	820	280	295	130
260	48-49 Transportation and warehousing	135	225	430	120	180	90
261	51 Information and cultural industries	145	115	280	120	115	45
262	52 Finance and insurance	125	355	635	215	185	10
263	53 Real estate and rental and leasing	25	95	215	85	30	35
264	54 Professional, scientific and technical services	255	365	700	355	310	105
265	55 Management of companies and enterprises	-	10	-	10	-	-
266	56 Administrative and support, waste management and remediation services	80	160	275	65	100	55
267	61 Educational services	170	240	360	175	100	95
268	62 Health care and social assistance	140	260	550	190	180	95
269	71 Arts, entertainment and recreation	20	40	55	25	30	10
270	72 Accommodation and food services	115	285	220	80	110	45
271	81 Other services (except public administration)	100	170	355	65	100	40
272	91 Public administration	60	145	245	70	85	10
	by class of worker						
273	Class of worker - Not applicable (36)	60	75	110	20	40	10
274	All classes of worker (37)	2,470	4,050	7,015	2,570	2,590	1,050
275	Paid workers	2,380	3,700	6,640	2,395	2,430	905
276	Employees	2,290	3,570	6,300	2,290	2,335	860
277	Self-employed (incorporated)	90	130	340	105	90	45
278	Self-employed (unincorporated)	75	325	330	165	160	140
279	Unpaid family workers	10	20	40	15	10	-
	by occupation based on the 2001 NOC-S						
280	Male labour force 15 years and over	1,275	2,095	3,795	1,375	1,265	585
281	Occupation - Not applicable (36)	25	30	55	10	-	10
282	All occupations (37)	1,250	2,070	3,745	1,370	1,260	580
283	A Management occupations	280	385	895	370	210	150
284	B Business, finance and administration occupations	170	260	500	170	185	50
285	C Natural and applied sciences and related occupations	145	270	525	245	230	65
286	D Health occupations	15	10	35	10	30	20
287	E Occupations in social science, education, government service and religion	20	65	190	55	40	20
288	F Occupations in art, culture, recreation and sport	30	30	60	30	15	15
289	G Sales and service occupations	210	425	655	260	250	115
290	H Trades, transport and equipment operators and related occupations	220	455	655	155	230	125
291	I Occupations unique to primary industry	-	10	30	10	10	-
292	J Occupations unique to processing, manufacturing and utilities	155	160	205	55	60	30
293	Female labour force 15 years and over	1,245	2,025	3,330	1,220	1,365	475
294	Occupation - Not applicable (36)	30	50	60	10	35	10
295	All occupations (37)	1,215	1,980	3,270	1,210	1,330	465
296	A Management occupations	110	270	420	225	150	55
297	B Business, finance and administration occupations	505	645	1,260	425	450	100
298	C Natural and applied sciences and related occupations	25	60	175	35	125	25
299	D Health occupations	60	135	220	85	45	25

Tableau 1. Certaines caractéristiques des secteurs de recensement, recensement de 2001 – Données intégrales et données-échantillon (20 %)

Toronto 0518 ◆	Toronto 0519	Toronto 0520.01 ◆	Toronto 0520.02	Toronto 0520.04	Toronto 0520.05 A	Caractéristiques	Nº
						CARACTÉRISTIQUES DE LA POPULATION	
						selon l'activité – fin	
69.9	68.1	72.7	71.1	73.5	74.7	Les deux sexes - Taux d'activité	241
57.7	67.6	67.6	58.7	66.3	58.9	15-24 ans	242
72.5	68.0	74.0	74.2	74.8	78.4	25 ans et plus	243
66.0	63.0	66.9	67.5	67.2	69.4	Les deux sexes - Taux d'emploi	244
51.4	58.1	55.4	55.0	54.9	50.0	15-24 ans	245
69.2	64.0	70.0	70.6	69.3	73.7	25 ans et plus	246
5.7	7.7	7.8	5.2	8.5	7.4	Les deux sexes - Taux de chômage	247
12.2	15.5	18.4	6.2	17.2	15.2	15-24 ans	248
4.7	6.1	5.4	4.8	7.3	5.8	25 ans et plus	249
2,630	**2,155**	**3,315**	**3,880**	**4,770**	**2,235**	**Population active totale de 15 ans et plus**	250
						selon l'industrie basée sur le SCIAN de 1997	
20	15	55	110	110	45	Industrie - Sans objet (36)	251
2,605	2,140	3,260	3,765	4,660	2,190	Toutes les industries (37)	252
10	-	-	-	-	-	11 Agriculture, foresterie, pêche et chasse	253
10	-	10	-	-	-	21 Extraction minière et extraction de pétrole et de gaz	254
20	10	-	35	10	15	22 Services publics	255
125	120	170	145	155	75	23 Construction	256
500	375	865	680	905	470	31-33 Fabrication	257
240	135	210	265	315	120	41 Commerce de gros	258
265	270	415	455	500	230	44-45 Commerce de détail	259
190	150	210	205	355	165	48-49 Transport et entreposage	260
60	100	80	120	210	45	51 Industrie de l'information et industrie culturelle	261
160	100	165	325	350	110	52 Finance et assurances	262
80	65	50	110	80	35	53 Services immobiliers et services de location et de location à bail	263
120	120	145	335	395	190	54 Services professionnels, scientifiques et techniques	264
10	10	-	-	10	-	55 Gestion de sociétés et d'entreprises	265
100	140	185	125	250	150	56 Services administratifs, services de soutien, services de gestion des déchets et services d'assainissement	266
100	80	120	165	140	65	61 Services d'enseignement	267
245	130	270	300	335	220	62 Soins de santé et assistance sociale	268
15	35	10	40	50	10	71 Arts, spectacles et loisirs	269
160	80	125	295	335	130	72 Hébergement et services de restauration	270
155	135	105	110	190	105	81 Autres services, sauf les administrations publiques	271
45	75	115	60	85	50	91 Administrations publiques	272
						selon la catégorie de travailleurs	
20	15	55	110	115	50	Catégorie de travailleurs - Sans objet (36)	273
2,605	2,140	3,260	3,770	4,660	2,190	Toutes les catégories de travailleurs (37)	274
2,450	1,960	3,105	3,395	4,435	2,090	Travailleurs rémunérés	275
2,350	1,920	3,055	3,315	4,335	2,025	Employés	276
95	35	50	85	100	65	Travailleurs autonomes (entreprise constituée en société)	277
130	180	150	335	220	100	Travailleurs autonomes (entreprise non constituée en société)	278
20	-	-	30	-	-	Travailleurs familiaux non rémunérés	279
						selon la profession basée sur la CNP-S de 2001	
1,385	1,135	1,770	1,955	2,395	1,185	Hommes actifs de 15 ans et plus	280
15	15	25	55	50	30	Profession - Sans objet (36)	281
1,370	1,125	1,745	1,900	2,350	1,155	Toutes les professions (37)	282
175	95	155	310	265	115	A Gestion	283
225	100	270	220	310	140	B Affaires, finance et administration	284
160	80	125	285	345	100	C Sciences naturelles et appliquées et professions apparentées	285
40	10	-	50	30	30	D Secteur de la santé	286
25	40	50	20	30	50	E Sciences sociales, enseignement, administration publique et religion	287
10	35	-	20	70	-	F Arts, culture, sports et loisirs	288
215	250	300	430	460	250	G Ventes et services	289
365	380	550	390	510	270	H Métiers, transport et machinerie	290
-	10	10	10	15	-	I Professions propres au secteur primaire	291
160	130	285	165	315	195	J Transformation, fabrication et services d'utilité publique	292
1,240	1,020	1,540	1,920	2,375	1,050	Femmes actives de 15 ans et plus	293
10	-	30	55	65	15	Profession - Sans objet (36)	294
1,235	1,015	1,515	1,860	2,310	1,035	Toutes les professions (37)	295
110	70	50	145	215	100	A Gestion	296
330	325	455	595	800	430	B Affaires, finance et administration	297
30	25	45	130	130	40	C Sciences naturelles et appliquées et professions apparentées	298
100	85	120	120	160	80	D Secteur de la santé	299

Table 1. Selected Characteristics for Census Tracts, 2001 Census – 100% Data and 20% Sample Data

No.	Characteristics	Toronto 0516.25 A	Toronto 0516.26 A	Toronto 0516.27 A	Toronto 0516.28 A	Toronto 0516.29 A	Toronto 0517
	POPULATION CHARACTERISTICS						
	by occupation based on the 2001 NOC-S – concluded						
300	E Occupations in social science, education, government service and religion	180	205	325	165	115	40
301	F Occupations in art, culture, recreation and sport	30	35	85	15	20	20
302	G Sales and service occupations	235	490	610	215	330	175
303	H Trades, transport and equipment operators and related occupations	-	25	70	10	40	15
304	I Occupations unique to primary industry	-	-	-	-	-	-
305	J Occupations unique to processing, manufacturing and utilities	65	110	95	35	60	10
306	**Total employed labour force 15 years and over**	**2,350**	**3,815**	**6,805**	**2,475**	**2,510**	**1,005**
	by place of work						
307	Males	1,215	1,980	3,640	1,330	1,235	560
308	Usual place of work	1,080	1,645	3,095	1,060	1,020	420
309	At home	50	140	155	85	75	70
310	Outside Canada	-	15	40	40	-	10
311	No fixed workplace address	75	180	350	150	140	60
312	Females	1,135	1,840	3,160	1,145	1,270	450
313	Usual place of work	975	1,605	2,845	1,005	1,155	375
314	At home	95	140	180	95	100	75
315	Outside Canada	-	-	20	10	-	-
316	No fixed workplace address	70	90	115	35	15	10
317	**Total employed labour force 15 years and over with usual place of work or no fixed workplace address**	**2,200**	**3,515**	**6,405**	**2,250**	**2,330**	**860**
	by mode of transportation						
318	Males	1,160	1,825	3,445	1,210	1,160	475
319	Car, truck, van, as driver	1,005	1,475	2,940	1,045	935	420
320	Car, truck, van, as passenger	50	60	115	30	80	25
321	Public transit	90	220	300	125	125	20
322	Walked	10	50	40	10	20	15
323	Other method	-	25	45	-	-	-
324	Females	1,045	1,695	2,955	1,040	1,170	380
325	Car, truck, van, as driver	830	1,180	2,155	745	860	260
326	Car, truck, van, as passenger	60	170	275	125	85	30
327	Public transit	150	250	480	145	200	70
328	Walked	10	80	30	30	25	15
329	Other method	-	15	15	-	-	10
330	**Total population 15 years and over who worked since January 1, 2000**	**2,665**	**4,425**	**7,530**	**2,805**	**2,830**	**1,140**
	by language used at work						
331	Single responses	2,475	4,075	6,790	2,545	2,595	1,055
332	English	2,445	4,050	6,710	2,525	2,560	1,055
333	French	-	10	25	10	-	-
334	Non-official languages (5)	25	20	55	10	30	10
335	Chinese, n.o.s.	-	-	25	-	15	-
336	Cantonese	-	-	10	15	10	-
337	Other languages (6)	25	20	25	-	10	-
338	Multiple responses	190	345	740	265	235	85
339	English and French	70	95	220	80	95	15
340	English and non-official language	120	245	520	175	135	70
341	French and non-official language	-	-	-	-	-	-
342	English, French and non-official language	-	10	10	10	10	-
	DWELLING AND HOUSEHOLD CHARACTERISTICS						
343	**Total number of occupied private dwellings**	**1,210**	**1,955**	**3,740**	**1,410**	**1,465**	**580**
	by tenure						
344	Owned	915	1,585	3,560	1,370	1,010	430
345	Rented	290	370	180	45	455	150
346	Band housing	-	-	-	-	-	-
	by structural type of dwelling						
347	Single-detached house	850	1,435	2,030	810	800	430
348	Semi-detached house	-	15	835	-	-	10
349	Row house	105	355	870	605	405	145
350	Apartment, detached duplex	-	20	-	-	-	-
351	Apartment, building that has five or more storeys	245	130	-	-	140	-
352	Apartment, building that has fewer than five storeys (38)	-	10	-	-	125	-
353	Other single-attached house	-	-	-	-	-	-
354	Movable dwelling (39)	-	-	-	-	-	-

Tableau 1. Certaines caractéristiques des secteurs de recensement, recensement de 2001 – Données intégrales et données-échantillon (20 %)

Toronto 0518 ◆	Toronto 0519	Toronto 0520.01 ◆	Toronto 0520.02	Toronto 0520.04	Toronto 0520.05 A	Caractéristiques	Nº
						CARACTÉRISTIQUES DE LA POPULATION	
						selon la profession basée sur la CNP-S de 2001 – fin	
105	55	70	180	170	80	E Sciences sociales, enseignement, administration publique et religion	300
45	35	25	45	40	10	F Arts, culture, sports et loisirs	301
310	325	445	490	520	220	G Ventes et services	302
20	35	50	15	80	25	H Métiers, transport et machinerie	303
-	-	-	-	-	-	I Professions propres au secteur primaire	304
180	60	255	145	200	60	J Transformation, fabrication et services d'utilité publique	305
2,480	**1,990**	**3,060**	**3,680**	**4,365**	**2,075**	**Population active occupée totale de 15 ans et plus**	306
						selon le lieu de travail	
1,325	1,045	1,650	1,860	2,200	1,090	Hommes	307
1,140	845	1,420	1,565	1,865	910	Lieu habituel de travail	308
30	65	45	80	65	85	À domicile	309
15	15	-	10	35	-	En dehors du Canada	310
140	120	180	210	240	100	Sans adresse de travail fixe	311
1,150	950	1,405	1,820	2,165	980	Femmes	312
1,010	900	1,295	1,670	1,990	930	Lieu habituel de travail	313
85	30	65	90	85	35	À domicile	314
-	-	-	-	10	-	En dehors du Canada	315
60	20	40	60	75	15	Sans adresse de travail fixe	316
2,345	**1,875**	**2,940**	**3,500**	**4,165**	**1,955**	**Population active occupée totale de 15 ans et plus ayant un lieu habituel de travail ou sans adresse de travail fixe**	317
						selon le mode de transport	
1,280	960	1,605	1,775	2,100	1,010	Hommes	318
1,040	830	1,320	1,365	1,655	800	Automobile, camion ou fourgonnette, en tant que conducteur	319
35	60	70	110	50	60	Automobile, camion ou fourgonnette, en tant que passager	320
190	65	155	270	325	125	Transport en commun	321
-	10	50	35	45	20	À pied	322
10	-	10	-	30	-	Autre moyen	323
1,065	915	1,340	1,730	2,070	945	Femmes	324
590	610	785	1,205	1,100	575	Automobile, camion ou fourgonnette, en tant que conductrice	325
130	65	170	175	175	45	Automobile, camion ou fourgonnette, en tant que passagère	326
295	210	310	310	665	295	Transport en commun	327
55	25	70	35	95	20	À pied	328
-	-	-	10	35	10	Autre moyen	329
2,865	**2,295**	**3,450**	**4,080**	**5,015**	**2,355**	**Population totale de 15 ans et plus ayant travaillé depuis le 1er janvier 2000**	330
						selon la langue utilisée au travail	
2,590	2,075	3,100	3,410	4,465	2,030	Réponses uniques	331
2,520	2,070	3,070	3,360	4,370	1,990	Anglais	332
-	-	-	-	15	-	Français	333
70	10	25	55	85	35	Langues non officielles (5)	334
10	-	-	15	10	10	Chinois, n.d.a.	335
-	-	-	10	10	-	Cantonais	336
65	-	20	35	65	30	Autres langues (6)	337
275	215	355	665	550	325	Réponses multiples	338
10	25	20	40	90	50	Anglais et français	339
270	175	335	605	445	265	Anglais et langue non officielle	340
-	-	-	-	-	-	Français et langue non officielle	341
-	20	-	15	15	10	Anglais, français et langue non officielle	342
						CARACTÉRISTIQUES DES LOGEMENTS ET DES MÉNAGES	
1,615	**1,255**	**1,585**	**2,015**	**3,180**	**1,210**	**Nombre total de logements privés occupés**	343
						selon le mode d'occupation	
695	1,090	1,290	1,565	1,360	765	Possédé	344
920	165	300	445	1,825	445	Loué	345
-	-	-	-	-	-	Logement de bande	346
						selon le type de construction résidentielle	
450	290	275	1,115	265	370	Maison individuelle non attenante	347
90	965	740	150	525	135	Maison jumelée	348
110	-	360	-	25	190	Maison en rangée	349
-	-	65	50	20	35	Appartement, duplex non attenant	350
935	-	20	690	2,270	460	Appartement, immeuble de cinq étages ou plus	351
40	-	125	-	10	25	Appartement, immeuble de moins de cinq étages (38)	352
-	-	-	-	-	-	Autre maison individuelle attenante	353
-	-	-	-	75	-	Logement mobile (39)	354

Table 1. Selected Characteristics for Census Tracts, 2001 Census – 100% Data and 20% Sample Data

No.	Characteristics	Toronto 0516.25 A	Toronto 0516.26 A	Toronto 0516.27 A	Toronto 0516.28 A	Toronto 0516.29 A	Toronto 0517
	DWELLING AND HOUSEHOLD CHARACTERISTICS						
	by condition of dwelling						
355	Regular maintenance only	915	1,560	3,440	1,325	1,275	400
356	Minor repairs	250	330	255	85	180	130
357	Major repairs	50	65	40	10	15	50
	by period of construction						
358	Before 1946	-	-	10	-	-	10
359	1946-1960	-	-	-	-	-	205
360	1961-1970	15	35	10	-	-	220
361	1971-1980	50	40	10	-	10	115
362	1981-1990	1,010	1,400	280	10	65	20
363	1991-2001 (20)	140	480	3,435	1,405	1,395	20
364	Average number of rooms per dwelling	7.6	7.6	7.3	7.4	6.6	7.8
365	Average number of bedrooms per dwelling	3.4	3.5	3.4	3.4	3.0	3.5
366	Average value of dwelling $	302,039	265,002	265,153	264,492	264,184	339,751
367	**Total number of private households**	**1,210**	**1,955**	**3,740**	**1,415**	**1,465**	**580**
	by household size						
368	1 person	130	105	270	140	155	50
369	2 persons	235	330	940	330	330	200
370	3 persons	220	375	820	300	315	105
371	4-5 persons	545	925	1,455	575	570	200
372	6 or more persons	90	220	255	70	95	30
	by household type						
373	One-family households	1,045	1,695	3,180	1,205	1,215	470
374	Multiple-family households	40	140	210	65	40	50
375	Non-family households	125	120	355	150	210	60
376	Number of persons in private households	4,195	7,335	12,510	4,645	4,800	1,795
377	Average number of persons in private households	3.4	3.8	3.3	3.3	3.3	3.1
378	Average number of persons per room	0.5	0.5	0.5	0.4	0.5	0.4
379	Tenant households in non-farm, non-reserve private dwellings (40)	290	375	180	45	450	150
380	Average gross rent $ (40)	634	874	1,582	1,636	882	1,078
381	Tenant households spending 30% or more of household income on gross rent (40) (41)	105	150	95	35	135	30
382	Tenant households spending from 30% to 99% of household income on gross rent (40) (41)	80	110	60	30	100	25
383	Owner households in non-farm, non-reserve private dwellings (42)	915	1,585	3,545	1,360	1,010	430
384	Average owner's major payments $ (42)	1,386	1,369	1,493	1,439	1,466	1,325
385	Owner households spending 30% or more of household income on owner's major payments (41) (42)	155	285	795	285	185	45
386	Owner households spending from 30% to 99% of household income on owner's major payments (41) (42)	135	230	725	260	165	45
	CENSUS FAMILY CHARACTERISTICS						
387	**Total number of census families in private households**	**1,120**	**1,985**	**3,615**	**1,330**	**1,300**	**570**
	by census family structure and size						
388	Total couple families	940	1,640	3,290	1,185	1,095	475
389	Total families of married couples	895	1,565	3,085	1,115	1,010	430
390	Without children at home	185	280	780	260	235	195
391	With children at home	715	1,290	2,305	855	770	240
392	1 child	155	350	810	295	240	95
393	2 children	365	605	1,095	410	375	105
394	3 or more children	195	330	400	155	160	40
395	Total families of common-law couples	45	75	210	70	95	45
396	Without children at home	15	30	115	45	35	30
397	With children at home	35	50	100	25	50	10
398	1 child	15	25	65	10	15	10
399	2 children	15	20	20	10	15	-
400	3 or more children	-	-	20	10	20	-
401	Total lone-parent families	180	340	315	145	200	100
402	Female parent	170	280	245	115	175	80
403	1 child	90	140	155	55	75	45
404	2 children	65	90	75	60	65	30
405	3 or more children	10	50	20	-	35	-

Tableau 1. Certaines caractéristiques des secteurs de recensement, recensement de 2001 – Données intégrales et données-échantillon (20 %)

Toronto 0518 ◆	Toronto 0519	Toronto 0520.01 ◆	Toronto 0520.02	Toronto 0520.04	Toronto 0520.05 A	Caractéristiques	N°
						CARACTÉRISTIQUES DES LOGEMENTS ET DES MÉNAGES	
						selon l'état du logement	
1,010	780	1,080	1,675	2,760	930	Entretien régulier seulement	355
440	380	440	270	320	245	Réparations mineures	356
165	90	75	65	100	40	Réparations majeures	357
						selon la période de construction	
25	-	-	-	10	10	Avant 1946	358
195	365	25	-	50	50	1946-1960	359
690	710	350	10	205	100	1961-1970	360
650	155	920	15	205	325	1971-1980	361
45	20	125	1,175	615	510	1981-1990	362
15	-	155	815	2,100	230	1991-2001 (20)	363
5.6	6.8	6.6	6.5	4.8	5.8	Nombre moyen de pièces par logement	364
2.4	3.2	3.1	3.0	1.9	2.6	Nombre moyen de chambres à coucher par logement	365
214,843	216,012	194,907	256,342	193,564	224,880	Valeur moyenne du logement $	366
1,620	**1,255**	**1,590**	**2,010**	**3,185**	**1,210**	**Nombre total de logements privés**	367
						selon la taille du ménage	
320	175	150	265	880	170	1 personne	368
400	330	275	435	945	330	2 personnes	369
310	255	315	360	560	255	3 personnes	370
480	365	645	755	665	370	4-5 personnes	371
100	125	200	195	140	80	6 personnes ou plus	372
						selon le genre de ménage	
1,120	975	1,225	1,560	2,145	925	Ménages unifamiliaux	373
105	70	185	135	85	65	Ménages multifamiliaux	374
390	215	180	315	960	220	Ménages non familiaux	375
4,835	3,950	5,815	6,830	8,135	3,775	Nombre de personnes dans les ménages privés	376
3.0	3.1	3.7	3.4	2.6	3.1	Nombre moyen de personnes dans les ménages privés	377
0.5	0.5	0.6	0.5	0.5	0.5	Nombre moyen de personnes par pièce	378
920	165	300	445	1,810	430	Ménages locataires dans les logements privés non agricoles hors réserve (40)	379
747	1,062	955	1,019	936	936	Loyer brut moyen $ (40)	380
365	90	100	180	850	130	Ménages locataires consacrant 30 % ou plus du revenu du ménage au loyer brut (40) (41)	381
280	70	75	130	665	115	Ménages locataires consacrant de 30 % à 99 % du revenu du ménage au loyer brut (40) (41)	382
695	1,080	1,290	1,560	1,340	765	Ménages propriétaires dans les logements privés non agricoles hors réserve (42)	383
1,090	1,071	1,087	1,273	1,214	1,211	Principales dépenses de propriété moyennes $ (42)	384
165	265	235	425	365	230	Ménages propriétaires consacrant 30 % ou plus du revenu du ménage aux principales dépenses de propriété (41) (42)	385
155	215	220	365	335	190	Ménages propriétaires consacrant de 30 % à 99 % du revenu du ménage aux principales dépenses de propriété (41) (42)	386
						CARACTÉRISTIQUES DES FAMILLES DE RECENSEMENT	
1,345	**1,105**	**1,610**	**1,840**	**2,310**	**1,085**	**Total des familles de recensement dans les ménages privés**	387
						selon la structure et la taille de la famille de recensement	
1,060	960	1,345	1,610	1,875	850	Total des familles avec conjoints	388
970	895	1,285	1,545	1,690	780	Total des familles avec couples mariés	389
280	320	320	385	650	210	Sans enfants à la maison	390
685	570	970	1,160	1,040	570	Avec enfants à la maison	391
275	205	290	310	435	205	1 enfant	392
285	255	460	540	430	245	2 enfants	393
125	115	215	315	170	125	3 enfants ou plus	394
90	65	60	70	185	65	Total des familles en union libre	395
55	25	25	40	115	35	Sans enfants à la maison	396
40	45	35	35	75	25	Avec enfants à la maison	397
20	20	25	10	50	20	1 enfant	398
20	15	10	10	25	10	2 enfants	399
-	-	-	10	-	-	3 enfants ou plus	400
285	150	260	225	435	235	Total des familles monoparentales	401
250	120	190	195	405	205	Parent de sexe féminin	402
150	80	85	95	220	145	1 enfant	403
60	25	70	85	135	45	2 enfants	404
45	10	30	15	45	15	3 enfants ou plus	405

Table 1. Selected Characteristics for Census Tracts, 2001 Census – 100% Data and 20% Sample Data

No.	Characteristics	Toronto 0516.25 A	Toronto 0516.26 A	Toronto 0516.27 A	Toronto 0516.28 A	Toronto 0516.29 A	Toronto 0517
	CENSUS FAMILY CHARACTERISTICS						
	by census family structure and size – concluded						
406	Male parent	15	65	70	25	25	20
407	1 child	-	50	55	25	20	10
408	2 children	-	10	10	-	-	10
409	3 or more children	-	10	10	-	-	-
410	**Total number of children at home**	**1,835**	**3,285**	**4,875**	**1,860**	**2,005**	**595**
	by age groups						
411	Under 6 years	320	535	1,320	570	525	70
412	6-14 years	625	1,280	1,875	690	855	210
413	15-17 years	240	405	510	175	235	90
414	18-24 years	460	735	765	295	275	125
415	25 years and over	190	330	405	135	120	100
416	Average number of children at home per census family (43)	1.6	1.7	1.3	1.4	1.5	1.0
417	**Total number of persons in private households**	**4,195**	**7,335**	**12,510**	**4,640**	**4,805**	**1,795**
	by census family status and living arrangements						
418	Number of non-family persons	290	425	725	265	400	150
419	Living with relatives (44)	110	260	315	85	155	65
420	Living with non-relatives only	55	65	140	40	85	40
421	Living alone	125	105	270	140	155	45
422	Number of family persons	3,900	6,910	11,780	4,375	4,405	1,645
423	Average number of persons per census family	3.5	3.5	3.3	3.3	3.4	2.9
424	**Total number of persons 65 years and over**	**190**	**390**	**565**	**185**	**205**	**240**
425	Number of non-family persons 65 years and over	75	135	155	55	60	70
426	Living with relatives (44)	70	115	105	40	50	35
427	Living with non-relatives only	-	-	-	-	-	10
428	Living alone	10	15	40	10	10	30
429	Number of family persons 65 years and over	115	255	410	130	140	170
	ECONOMIC FAMILY CHARACTERISTICS						
430	**Total number of economic families in private households**	**1,085**	**1,850**	**3,455**	**1,265**	**1,280**	**525**
	by size of family						
431	2 persons	245	340	955	325	310	190
432	3 persons	220	370	820	295	300	110
433	4 persons	350	610	1,025	415	405	130
434	5 or more persons	270	530	660	225	255	90
435	Total number of persons in economic families	4,010	7,170	12,095	4,460	4,560	1,710
436	Average number of persons per economic family	3.7	3.9	3.5	3.5	3.6	3.3
437	Total number of unattached individuals	180	165	415	185	245	90
	2000 INCOME CHARACTERISTICS						
	Population 15 years and over by sex and total income groups in 2000						
438	Total - Both sexes	3,240	5,505	9,310	3,380	3,425	1,515
439	Without income	205	390	735	250	190	110
440	With income	3,035	5,115	8,575	3,130	3,240	1,405
441	Under $1,000 (45)	160	280	355	130	145	35
442	$ 1,000 - $ 2,999	165	310	345	120	190	50
443	$ 3,000 - $ 4,999	90	150	295	100	105	45
444	$ 5,000 - $ 6,999	185	150	300	110	80	30
445	$ 7,000 - $ 9,999	110	330	410	120	160	95
446	$10,000 - $11,999	100	225	235	80	115	45
447	$12,000 - $14,999	110	275	350	110	135	80
448	$15,000 - $19,999	140	320	455	165	150	85
449	$20,000 - $24,999	240	440	385	155	255	100
450	$25,000 - $29,999	155	295	430	150	195	95
451	$30,000 - $34,999	190	290	590	230	170	105
452	$35,000 - $39,999	240	270	635	185	250	90
453	$40,000 - $44,999	185	215	665	200	185	95
454	$45,000 - $49,999	110	190	450	180	175	100
455	$50,000 - $59,999	225	305	910	255	305	40
456	$60,000 and over	625	1,075	1,760	850	615	315
457	Average income $ (46)	40,028	36,061	40,369	46,144	38,363	46,516
458	Median income $ (46)	31,647	26,107	35,138	37,025	31,355	31,138
459	Standard error of average income $ (46)	1,782	1,063	1,052	1,881	1,426	3,177

Tableau 1. Certaines caractéristiques des secteurs de recensement, recensement de 2001 – Données intégrales et données-échantillon (20 %)

Toronto 0518 ◆	Toronto 0519	Toronto 0520.01 ◆	Toronto 0520.02	Toronto 0520.04	Toronto 0520.05 A	Caractéristiques	N°
						CARACTÉRISTIQUES DES FAMILLES DE RECENSEMENT	
						selon la structure et la taille de la famille de recensement – fin	
40	25	70	30	30	30	Parent de sexe masculin	406
15	30	20	20	15	15	1 enfant	407
25	-	50	10	20	15	2 enfants	408
-	-	10	-	-	-	3 enfants ou plus	409
1,805	**1,390**	**2,435**	**2,795**	**2,665**	**1,485**	**Nombre total d'enfants à la maison**	410
						selon les groupes d'âge	
460	310	445	510	810	300	Moins de 6 ans	411
605	455	790	855	815	480	6-14 ans	412
255	100	250	350	300	200	15-17 ans	413
310	325	595	670	460	290	18-24 ans	414
175	200	345	405	280	220	25 ans et plus	415
1.3	1.3	1.5	1.5	1.2	1.4	Nombre moyen d'enfants à la maison par famille de recensement (43)	416
4,835	**3,950**	**5,815**	**6,830**	**8,135**	**3,780**	**Nombre total de personnes dans les ménages privés**	417
						selon la situation des particuliers dans la famille de recensement et des particuliers dans le ménage	
625	495	430	580	1,285	360	Nombre de personnes hors famille de recensement	418
135	195	175	155	220	85	Vivant avec des personnes apparentées (44)	419
170	115	100	165	185	100	Vivant avec des personnes non apparentées uniquement	420
320	180	150	260	880	175	Vivant seules	421
4,210	3,455	5,390	6,250	6,855	3,415	Nombre de personnes membres d'une famille	422
3.1	3.1	3.3	3.4	3.0	3.1	Nombre moyen de personnes par famille de recensement	423
435	**460**	**440**	**460**	**580**	**240**	**Nombre total de personnes de 65 ans et plus**	424
175	155	125	105	235	80	Nombre de personnes hors famille de recensement de 65 ans et plus	425
50	75	95	50	80	40	Vivant avec des personnes apparentées (44)	426
35	-	10	15	-	-	Vivant avec des personnes non apparentées uniquement	427
90	75	25	40	165	40	Vivant seules	428
265	305	315	355	340	160	Nombre de personnes membres d'une famille de 65 ans et plus	429
						CARACTÉRISTIQUES DES FAMILLES ÉCONOMIQUES	
1,260	**1,055**	**1,425**	**1,705**	**2,245**	**995**	**Nombre total de familles économiques dans les ménages privés**	430
						selon la taille de la famille	
395	335	270	400	910	310	2 personnes	431
320	260	320	360	560	245	3 personnes	432
305	265	405	495	445	240	4 personnes	433
235	200	425	450	325	200	5 personnes ou plus	434
4,345	3,655	5,560	6,400	7,070	3,505	Nombre total de personnes dans les familles économiques	435
3.4	3.5	3.9	3.8	3.2	3.5	Nombre moyen de personnes par famille économique	436
490	290	250	430	1,065	275	Nombre total de personnes hors famille économique	437
						CARACTÉRISTIQUES DU REVENU DE 2000	
						Population de 15 ans et plus selon le sexe et les tranches de revenu total en 2000	
3,765	3,165	4,560	5,455	6,490	2,990	Total - Les deux sexes	438
275	185	310	385	395	230	Sans revenu	439
3,485	2,980	4,250	5,070	6,095	2,765	Avec un revenu	440
130	145	205	380	335	100	Moins de 1 000 $ (45)	441
150	160	225	180	320	90	1 000 $ - 2 999 $	442
175	80	130	210	170	140	3 000 $ - 4 999 $	443
155	125	200	215	145	110	5 000 $ - 6 999 $	444
240	225	285	330	375	165	7 000 $ - 9 999 $	445
165	160	120	280	260	140	10 000 $ - 11 999 $	446
275	165	285	335	410	215	12 000 $ - 14 999 $	447
370	220	425	360	530	170	15 000 $ - 19 999 $	448
290	225	395	350	515	245	20 000 $ - 24 999 $	449
235	310	430	435	470	320	25 000 $ - 29 999 $	450
340	220	320	335	540	210	30 000 $ - 34 999 $	451
190	220	255	325	465	165	35 000 $ - 39 999 $	452
170	155	260	330	385	215	40 000 $ - 44 999 $	453
105	105	140	205	320	85	45 000 $ - 49 999 $	454
220	225	285	225	375	175	50 000 $ - 59 999 $	455
285	245	290	575	470	210	60 000 $ et plus	456
27,091	27,447	26,363	28,712	28,298	27,375	Revenu moyen $ (46)	457
20,935	24,255	22,157	23,809	24,961	25,005	Revenu médian $ (46)	458
854	844	697	881	684	853	Erreur type de revenu moyen $ (46)	459

Table 1. Selected Characteristics for Census Tracts, 2001 Census – 100% Data and 20% Sample Data

No.	Characteristics	Toronto 0516.25 A	Toronto 0516.26 A	Toronto 0516.27 A	Toronto 0516.28 A	Toronto 0516.29 A	Toronto 0517
	2000 INCOME CHARACTERISTICS						
	Population 15 years and over by sex and total income groups in 2000 – concluded						
460	Total - Males	1,540	2,645	4,570	1,645	1,575	745
461	Without income	70	165	235	75	75	50
462	With income	1,475	2,480	4,335	1,565	1,500	695
463	Under $1,000 (45)	70	140	160	50	65	10
464	$ 1,000 - $ 2,999	65	110	90	40	50	25
465	$ 3,000 - $ 4,999	40	65	160	50	10	15
466	$ 5,000 - $ 6,999	90	90	100	35	30	-
467	$ 7,000 - $ 9,999	45	130	145	25	90	50
468	$10,000 - $11,999	35	80	115	20	55	-
469	$12,000 - $14,999	15	80	115	35	60	-
470	$15,000 - $19,999	30	115	170	60	50	30
471	$20,000 - $24,999	85	230	140	55	60	55
472	$25,000 - $29,999	85	100	175	70	100	25
473	$30,000 - $34,999	40	125	215	90	55	55
474	$35,000 - $39,999	115	115	285	130	105	50
475	$40,000 - $44,999	85	95	355	75	100	45
476	$45,000 - $49,999	60	80	240	75	80	80
477	$50,000 - $59,999	135	190	585	190	180	25
478	$60,000 and over	475	725	1,270	565	405	230
479	Average income $ (46)	52,133	43,284	50,024	58,812	47,569	63,479
480	Median income $ (46)	40,574	33,709	43,848	47,650	40,299	43,481
481	Standard error of average income $ (46)	3,186	1,756	1,886	3,328	2,556	5,429
482	Total - Females	1,700	2,855	4,740	1,735	1,855	770
483	Without income	135	225	500	175	115	65
484	With income	1,570	2,635	4,245	1,565	1,740	705
485	Under $1,000 (45)	95	140	200	80	75	20
486	$ 1,000 - $ 2,999	95	200	255	80	140	25
487	$ 3,000 - $ 4,999	55	80	130	55	90	30
488	$ 5,000 - $ 6,999	95	60	205	70	55	30
489	$ 7,000 - $ 9,999	65	195	265	100	80	45
490	$10,000 - $11,999	65	140	125	60	65	50
491	$12,000 - $14,999	95	195	235	70	80	70
492	$15,000 - $19,999	115	205	285	105	100	60
493	$20,000 - $24,999	155	210	245	100	195	45
494	$25,000 - $29,999	75	190	250	75	90	75
495	$30,000 - $34,999	145	160	375	140	115	50
496	$35,000 - $39,999	135	150	350	55	150	35
497	$40,000 - $44,999	100	120	310	120	85	50
498	$45,000 - $49,999	50	110	210	110	95	20
499	$50,000 - $59,999	90	115	320	65	125	10
500	$60,000 and over	145	350	495	285	210	85
501	Average income $ (46)	28,662	29,253	30,510	33,433	30,445	29,696
502	Median income $ (46)	23,718	21,233	27,387	28,235	24,433	22,016
503	Standard error of average income $ (46)	1,508	1,183	808	1,537	1,380	2,438
	by composition of total income						
504	Total - Composition of income in 2000 % (47)	100.0	100.0	100.0	100.0	100.0	100.0
505	Employment income %	89.8	90.3	91.1	92.7	90.8	80.3
506	Government transfer payments %	3.9	4.9	3.6	3.3	4.8	6.8
507	Other %	6.3	4.8	5.3	4.0	4.3	12.9
	Population 15 years and over with employment income in 2000 by sex and work activity						
508	Both sexes with employment income (48)	2,605	4,225	7,265	2,745	2,715	1,095
509	Average employment income $	41,906	39,410	43,406	48,764	41,568	47,747
510	Standard error of average employment income $	1,820	1,177	1,170	1,776	1,557	3,733
511	Worked full year, full time (49)	1,515	2,435	4,955	1,800	1,765	680
512	Average employment income $	57,514	51,911	52,942	61,574	53,714	64,333
513	Standard error of average employment income $	2,640	1,539	1,544	1,897	2,034	5,472
514	Worked part year or part time (50)	1,030	1,715	2,220	920	925	390
515	Average employment income $	20,803	22,349	23,521	24,815	19,273	21,341
516	Standard error of average employment income $	1,698	1,496	1,138	3,124	1,535	3,312
517	Males with employment income (48)	1,335	2,130	3,850	1,440	1,325	590
518	Average employment income $	52,406	46,762	52,273	59,851	50,052	62,748
519	Standard error of average employment income $	3,020	1,877	2,036	2,952	2,633	6,009
520	Worked full year, full time (49)	890	1,420	2,830	1,090	995	425
521	Average employment income $	66,142	57,055	61,595	68,276	60,239	76,532
522	Standard error of average employment income $	3,984	2,211	2,551	2,782	3,139	7,974
523	Worked part year or part time (50)	430	690	965	345	320	165
524	Average employment income $	26,096	25,517	27,423	34,282	20,191	26,603
525	Standard error of average employment income $	3,449	2,873	2,049	7,798	2,365	5,538

Tableau 1. Certaines caractéristiques des secteurs de recensement, recensement de 2001 – Données intégrales et données-échantillon (20 %)

Toronto 0518 ◆	Toronto 0519	Toronto 0520.01 ◆	Toronto 0520.02	Toronto 0520.04	Toronto 0520.05 A	Caractéristiques	N°
						CARACTÉRISTIQUES DU REVENU DE 2000	
						Population de 15 ans et plus selon le sexe et les tranches de revenu total en 2000 – fin	
1,815	1,540	2,255	2,625	3,065	1,470	Total - Hommes	460
135	35	130	135	150	85	Sans revenu	461
1,685	1,510	2,125	2,485	2,920	1,390	Avec un revenu	462
85	85	90	165	110	70	Moins de 1 000 $ (45)	463
30	60	30	75	150	40	1 000 $ - 2 999 $	464
45	20	65	80	50	65	3 000 $ - 4 999 $	465
40	35	55	90	55	55	5 000 $ - 6 999 $	466
60	80	85	120	135	65	7 000 $ - 9 999 $	467
60	85	55	135	95	60	10 000 $ - 11 999 $	468
70	90	145	140	150	70	12 000 $ - 14 999 $	469
170	80	160	180	195	70	15 000 $ - 19 999 $	470
170	115	145	145	250	125	20 000 $ - 24 999 $	471
140	180	245	190	240	150	25 000 $ - 29 999 $	472
175	95	185	160	245	120	30 000 $ - 34 999 $	473
95	125	120	185	240	65	35 000 $ - 39 999 $	474
125	90	165	160	225	115	40 000 $ - 44 999 $	475
70	30	90	115	200	35	45 000 $ - 49 999 $	476
110	165	215	145	235	135	50 000 $ - 59 999 $	477
230	170	265	395	340	145	60 000 $ et plus	478
33,921	31,223	33,177	33,297	33,582	30,327	Revenu moyen $ (46)	479
29,408	27,930	29,386	27,358	30,036	27,432	Revenu médian $ (46)	480
1,422	1,284	1,142	1,466	1,158	1,345	Erreur type de revenu moyen $ (46)	481
1,950	1,625	2,305	2,825	3,425	1,520	Total - Femmes	482
150	155	180	245	240	145	Sans revenu	483
1,805	1,475	2,125	2,585	3,180	1,375	Avec un revenu	484
50	60	110	215	225	35	Moins de 1 000 $ (45)	485
120	100	190	105	170	55	1 000 $ - 2 999 $	486
130	60	70	130	115	70	3 000 $ - 4 999 $	487
115	90	145	130	85	50	5 000 $ - 6 999 $	488
175	145	200	205	240	100	7 000 $ - 9 999 $	489
105	75	60	140	170	80	10 000 $ - 11 999 $	490
205	80	140	195	260	140	12 000 $ - 14 999 $	491
200	135	270	175	335	100	15 000 $ - 19 999 $	492
120	110	250	205	265	115	20 000 $ - 24 999 $	493
90	135	190	245	230	165	25 000 $ - 29 999 $	494
165	120	135	175	295	90	30 000 $ - 34 999 $	495
90	90	135	135	225	100	35 000 $ - 39 999 $	496
40	65	90	175	160	100	40 000 $ - 44 999 $	497
35	75	50	90	120	55	45 000 $ - 49 999 $	498
110	55	70	85	145	40	50 000 $ - 59 999 $	499
50	70	30	180	130	70	60 000 $ et plus	500
20,722	23,582	19,553	24,303	23,450	24,387	Revenu moyen $ (46)	501
15,057	19,671	17,390	20,019	19,339	21,333	Revenu médian $ (46)	502
876	1,057	679	974	732	1,023	Erreur type de revenu moyen $ (46)	503
						selon la composition du revenu total	
100.0	100.0	100.0	100.0	100.0	100.0	Total - Composition du revenu en 2000 % (47)	504
81.3	79.7	86.3	84.8	88.2	88.2	Revenu d'emploi %	505
10.6	11.4	9.9	7.6	8.1	8.4	Transferts gouvernementaux %	506
8.2	8.9	3.9	7.6	3.8	3.3	Autre %	507
						Population de 15 ans et plus ayant un revenu d'emploi en 2000 selon le sexe et le travail	
2,730	2,255	3,415	3,870	4,845	2,375	Les deux sexes ayant un revenu d'emploi (48)	508
28,100	28,890	28,351	31,891	31,395	28,095	Revenu moyen d'emploi $	509
911	994	778	892	769	930	Erreur type de revenu moyen d'emploi $	510
1,385	1,275	1,775	2,310	2,885	1,220	Ayant travaillé toute l'année à plein temps (49)	511
37,368	38,212	37,194	40,790	39,807	37,798	Revenu moyen d'emploi $	512
1,177	1,306	1,029	1,097	1,005	1,201	Erreur type de revenu moyen d'emploi $	513
1,245	960	1,480	1,490	1,815	1,030	Ayant travaillé une partie de l'année ou à temps partiel (50)	514
19,350	17,006	18,189	18,389	19,869	18,071	Revenu moyen d'emploi $	515
1,242	1,102	961	1,074	918	1,185	Erreur type de revenu moyen d'emploi $	516
1,445	1,165	1,815	1,970	2,445	1,230	Hommes ayant un revenu d'emploi (48)	517
33,940	32,755	34,414	36,131	36,242	30,872	Revenu moyen d'emploi $	518
1,383	1,510	1,226	1,312	1,228	1,413	Erreur type de revenu moyen d'emploi $	519
785	730	1,010	1,245	1,550	645	Ayant travaillé toute l'année à plein temps (49)	520
41,319	40,543	42,680	44,516	43,942	39,937	Revenu moyen d'emploi $	521
1,705	1,872	1,576	1,449	1,547	1,809	Erreur type de revenu moyen d'emploi $	522
590	435	730	690	835	520	Ayant travaillé une partie de l'année ou à temps partiel (50)	523
26,534	20,108	22,846	20,705	24,114	20,509	Revenu moyen d'emploi $	524
2,183	1,911	1,593	1,724	1,618	1,927	Erreur type de revenu moyen d'emploi $	525

Table 1. Selected Characteristics for Census Tracts, 2001 Census – 100% Data and 20% Sample Data

No.	Characteristics	Toronto 0516.25 A	Toronto 0516.26 A	Toronto 0516.27 A	Toronto 0516.28 A	Toronto 0516.29 A	Toronto 0517
	2000 INCOME CHARACTERISTICS						
	Population 15 years and over with employment income in 2000 by sex and work activity – concluded						
526	Females with employment income (48)	1,270	2,100	3,415	1,305	1,390	510
527	Average employment income $	30,856	31,946	33,412	36,579	33,471	30,284
528	Standard error of average employment income $	1,737	1,342	862	1,627	1,589	3,111
529	Worked full year, full time (49)	635	1,015	2,125	710	775	255
530	Average employment income $	45,382	44,727	41,415	51,358	45,327	43,838
531	Standard error of average employment income $	2,774	1,940	1,001	2,067	2,026	4,379
532	Worked part year or part time (50)	595	1,020	1,255	575	600	230
533	Average employment income $	16,964	20,196	20,518	19,156	18,786	17,612
534	Standard error of average employment income $	1,339	1,577	1,242	1,619	1,972	3,901
	Census families by structure and family income groups in 2000						
535	Total - All census families	1,125	1,985	3,610	1,330	1,300	570
536	Under $10,000	50	110	110	45	20	30
537	$ 10,000 - $19,999	10	85	120	30	50	20
538	$ 20,000 - $29,999	85	135	190	65	90	35
539	$ 30,000 - $39,999	70	120	200	70	125	25
540	$ 40,000 - $49,999	90	100	195	65	130	40
541	$ 50,000 - $59,999	55	150	245	85	75	60
542	$ 60,000 - $69,999	85	160	325	105	100	45
543	$ 70,000 - $79,999	70	75	430	105	120	45
544	$ 80,000 - $89,999	85	195	360	110	85	25
545	$ 90,000 - $99,999	80	115	330	140	70	35
546	$100,000 and over	450	730	1,125	510	450	210
547	Average family income $	101,242	88,608	87,591	98,382	84,484	106,936
548	Median family income $	85,411	82,777	80,059	87,194	76,178	77,222
549	Standard error of average family income $	5,062	2,849	2,428	4,216	3,154	8,491
550	Total - All couple census families (51)	940	1,645	3,295	1,185	1,100	475
551	Under $10,000	30	45	100	40	-	10
552	$ 10,000 - $19,999	-	50	90	10	30	-
553	$ 20,000 - $29,999	25	80	150	50	65	20
554	$ 30,000 - $39,999	40	50	140	60	35	25
555	$ 40,000 - $49,999	55	90	150	55	125	30
556	$ 50,000 - $59,999	45	120	200	75	70	55
557	$ 60,000 - $69,999	80	145	300	75	85	40
558	$ 70,000 - $79,999	70	65	400	100	110	45
559	$ 80,000 - $89,999	90	195	355	95	75	30
560	$ 90,000 - $99,999	75	120	315	135	65	35
561	$100,000 and over	435	685	1,090	490	435	185
562	Average family income $	113,022	98,353	90,998	102,550	92,650	117,229
563	Median family income $	93,763	88,566	82,242	90,876	84,803	84,555
564	Standard error of average family income $	5,627	3,122	2,588	4,584	3,380	9,268
	Incidence of low income in 2000						
565	Total - Economic families	1,085	1,850	3,455	1,265	1,275	520
566	Low income	95	195	285	115	145	35
567	Incidence of low income in 2000 % (52)	8.7	10.6	8.2	9.1	11.7	5.9
568	Total - Unattached individuals 15 years and over	180	165	405	185	245	90
569	Low income	50	85	80	25	60	15
570	Incidence of low income in 2000 % (52)	29.3	51.0	20.2	14.1	24.5	18.2
571	Total - Population in private households	4,190	7,335	12,505	4,640	4,800	1,795
572	Low income	315	770	1,190	455	645	105
573	Incidence of low income in 2000 % (52)	7.6	10.5	9.5	9.8	13.5	6.0
	Private households by household income groups in 2000						
574	Total - All private households	1,215	1,955	3,740	1,410	1,465	580
575	Under $10,000	40	65	65	35	50	10
576	$ 10,000 - $19,999	60	115	95	40	50	10
577	$ 20,000 - $29,999	95	75	135	55	85	20
578	$ 30,000 - $39,999	50	85	160	65	130	30
579	$ 40,000 - $49,999	95	85	225	65	145	60
580	$ 50,000 - $59,999	50	180	260	70	90	65
581	$ 60,000 - $69,999	90	150	315	110	105	40
582	$ 70,000 - $79,999	75	100	440	115	105	45
583	$ 80,000 - $89,999	85	200	410	125	80	35
584	$ 90,000 - $99,999	75	120	360	155	105	25
585	$100,000 and over	495	790	1,280	570	515	240
586	Average household income $	100,438	94,197	92,571	102,173	84,645	112,261
587	Median household income $	85,168	86,505	83,621	90,485	77,879	83,222
588	Standard error of average household income $	5,023	2,928	2,327	4,317	3,154	8,099

Tableau 1. Certaines caractéristiques des secteurs de recensement, recensement de 2001 – Données intégrales et données-échantillon (20 %)

Toronto 0518 ◆	Toronto 0519	Toronto 0520.01 ◆	Toronto 0520.02	Toronto 0520.04	Toronto 0520.05 A	Caractéristiques	N°
						CARACTÉRISTIQUES DU REVENU DE 2000	
						Population de 15 ans et plus ayant un revenu d'emploi en 2000 selon le sexe et le travail – fin	
1,285	1,085	1,600	1,900	2,395	1,150	Femmes ayant un revenu d'emploi (48)	526
21,567	24,730	21,471	27,496	26,442	25,112	Revenu moyen d'emploi $	527
1,046	1,235	790	1,167	875	1,165	Erreur type de revenu moyen d'emploi $	528
600	545	760	1,065	1,335	570	Ayant travaillé toute l'année à plein temps (49)	529
32,205	35,090	29,945	36,448	35,023	35,400	Revenu moyen d'emploi $	530
1,442	1,722	963	1,626	1,162	1,526	Erreur type de revenu moyen d'emploi $	531
655	530	750	800	980	500	Ayant travaillé une partie de l'année ou à temps partiel (50)	532
12,840	14,478	13,647	16,384	16,259	15,528	Revenu moyen d'emploi $	533
1,104	1,241	1,005	1,321	959	1,297	Erreur type de revenu moyen d'emploi $	534
						Familles de recensement selon la structure et les tranches de revenu de la famille en 2000	
1,350	1,105	1,610	1,840	2,310	1,080	Total - Toutes les familles de recensement	535
125	65	60	115	175	40	Moins de 10 000 $	536
90	65	70	85	105	75	10 000 $ - 19 999 $	537
155	105	105	170	315	110	20 000 $ - 29 999 $	538
185	130	220	170	225	145	30 000 $ - 39 999 $	539
135	115	175	155	250	110	40 000 $ - 49 999 $	540
115	85	195	130	340	95	50 000 $ - 59 999 $	541
145	95	185	125	235	110	60 000 $ - 69 999 $	542
70	75	125	230	175	105	70 000 $ - 79 999 $	543
45	100	125	165	185	85	80 000 $ - 89 999 $	544
75	90	115	120	110	60	90 000 $ - 99 999 $	545
215	185	225	375	200	145	100 000 $ et plus	546
58,303	63,308	63,761	69,450	55,446	60,368	Revenu moyen des familles $	547
48,626	58,488	59,280	67,548	52,768	54,012	Revenu médian des familles $	548
2,534	2,505	1,939	2,323	1,595	2,345	Erreur type de revenu moyen des familles $	549
1,060	960	1,350	1,615	1,875	850	Total - Toutes les familles de recensement comptant un couple (51)	550
65	45	35	85	90	30	Moins de 10 000 $	551
40	40	25	50	75	60	10 000 $ - 19 999 $	552
120	95	85	160	225	50	20 000 $ - 29 999 $	553
135	95	180	140	185	80	30 000 $ - 39 999 $	554
115	95	150	120	175	95	40 000 $ - 49 999 $	555
100	80	155	110	290	90	50 000 $ - 59 999 $	556
115	100	185	100	205	95	60 000 $ - 69 999 $	557
50	65	115	210	155	85	70 000 $ - 79 999 $	558
40	90	95	160	185	65	80 000 $ - 89 999 $	559
75	85	110	115	110	60	90 000 $ - 99 999 $	560
205	170	215	360	185	140	100 000 $ et plus	561
65,232	66,362	67,128	72,960	60,096	66,036	Revenu moyen des familles $	562
54,158	61,827	62,305	73,069	55,960	62,128	Revenu médian des familles $	563
2,983	2,708	2,089	2,554	1,771	2,702	Erreur type de revenu moyen des familles $	564
						Fréquence des unités à faible revenu en 2000	
1,260	1,055	1,425	1,705	2,240	995	Total - Familles économiques	565
305	200	100	260	450	145	Faible revenu	566
24.2	18.6	7.1	15.2	20.1	14.3	Fréquence des unités à faible revenu en 2000 % (52)	567
490	285	250	425	1,055	270	Total - Personnes hors famille économique de 15 ans et plus	568
195	75	70	155	350	60	Faible revenu	569
39.8	26.2	28.3	36.9	32.9	22.4	Fréquence des unités à faible revenu en 2000 % (52)	570
4,835	3,940	5,815	6,825	8,125	3,775	Total - Population dans les ménages privés	571
1,130	725	455	1,115	1,795	545	Faible revenu	572
23.4	18.3	7.8	16.3	22.1	14.4	Fréquence des unités à faible revenu en 2000 % (52)	573
						Ménages privés selon les tranches de revenu du ménage en 2000	
1,620	1,250	1,590	2,010	3,185	1,210	Total - Tous les ménages privés	574
135	60	50	115	260	45	Moins de 10 000 $	575
130	90	50	125	315	75	10 000 $ - 19 999 $	576
190	135	95	205	310	120	20 000 $ - 29 999 $	577
195	135	180	150	360	165	30 000 $ - 39 999 $	578
185	115	150	155	345	135	40 000 $ - 49 999 $	579
140	100	205	155	400	115	50 000 $ - 59 999 $	580
170	110	180	120	340	120	60 000 $ - 69 999 $	581
75	85	95	190	205	100	70 000 $ - 79 999 $	582
65	85	120	140	210	80	80 000 $ - 89 999 $	583
65	90	135	140	125	65	90 000 $ - 99 999 $	584
260	260	330	510	315	195	100 000 $ et plus	585
58,384	65,153	70,611	72,274	54,188	62,566	Revenu moyen des ménages $	586
48,294	60,902	63,676	68,893	49,595	55,355	Revenu médian des ménages $	587
2,278	2,472	2,149	2,499	1,496	2,412	Erreur type de revenu moyen des ménages $	588

Table 1. Selected Characteristics for Census Tracts, 2001 Census – 100% Data and 20% Sample Data

No.	Characteristics	Toronto 0520.06 A	Toronto 0521.01 ◆	Toronto 0521.02 ◆	Toronto 0521.03	Toronto 0521.04	Toronto 0521.05 ◆
	POPULATION CHARACTERISTICS						
1	**Population, 1996 (1)**	**3,426**	**5,116**	**3,909**	**5,539**	**7,027**	**3,947**
2	**Population, 2001 (2)**	**6,266**	**5,352**	**3,810**	**5,461**	**6,804**	**3,876**
3	Population percentage change, 1996-2001	82.9	4.6	-2.5	-1.4	-3.2	-1.8
4	Land area in square kilometres, 2001	0.74	0.20	0.86	0.64	1.29	0.75
5	**Total population – 100% Data (3)**	**6,265**	**5,350**	**3,810**	**5,460**	**6,805**	**3,875**
	by sex and age groups						
6	Male	3,135	2,580	1,920	2,670	3,355	1,840
7	0-4 years	195	135	95	150	190	90
8	5-9 years	175	110	115	205	275	120
9	10-14 years	145	115	140	215	275	90
10	15-19 years	160	150	145	215	240	110
11	20-24 years	210	165	195	225	245	140
12	25-29 years	300	265	115	195	220	145
13	30-34 years	400	310	95	200	240	160
14	35-39 years	350	245	140	260	305	195
15	40-44 years	280	185	150	230	280	150
16	45-49 years	220	210	165	210	260	155
17	50-54 years	195	145	145	175	220	125
18	55-59 years	140	110	115	125	205	95
19	60-64 years	105	110	105	70	150	75
20	65-69 years	100	95	85	75	105	65
21	70-74 years	65	80	70	45	75	55
22	75-79 years	55	85	30	55	45	45
23	80-84 years	25	45	15	10	15	20
24	85 years and over	15	30	-	10	5	20
25	Female	3,135	2,765	1,890	2,785	3,455	2,040
26	0-4 years	205	155	90	160	215	100
27	5-9 years	170	125	95	230	255	90
28	10-14 years	140	110	115	185	220	90
29	15-19 years	140	130	140	220	235	120
30	20-24 years	190	185	125	215	225	135
31	25-29 years	355	270	105	185	250	175
32	30-34 years	365	295	120	185	270	155
33	35-39 years	340	225	115	235	305	180
34	40-44 years	250	210	190	250	320	170
35	45-49 years	210	180	175	220	265	170
36	50-54 years	200	165	155	180	240	140
37	55-59 years	140	155	120	130	205	115
38	60-64 years	150	100	115	125	185	90
39	65-69 years	105	125	100	85	85	85
40	70-74 years	70	125	70	85	75	75
41	75-79 years	60	110	35	40	60	65
42	80-84 years	35	75	15	30	30	50
43	85 years and over	15	40	10	10	10	35
44	**Total population 15 years and over**	**5,240**	**4,610**	**3,155**	**4,315**	**5,370**	**3,305**
	by legal marital status						
45	Never married (single)	1,775	1,390	965	1,490	1,655	1,130
46	Legally married (and not separated)	2,755	2,365	1,845	2,290	3,035	1,515
47	Separated, but still legally married	195	200	65	105	170	130
48	Divorced	320	340	130	200	290	270
49	Widowed	195	320	145	230	215	255
	by common-law status						
50	Not in a common-law relationship	4,960	4,340	3,085	4,185	5,135	3,110
51	In a common-law relationship	280	270	75	130	235	190
52	**Total population – 20% Sample Data (4)**	**6,265**	**5,350**	**3,810**	**5,470**	**6,805**	**3,875**
	by mother tongue						
53	Single responses	6,010	5,125	3,770	5,370	6,635	3,795
54	English	2,685	2,260	1,730	2,455	3,025	1,690
55	French	110	105	50	75	35	55
56	Non-official languages (5)	3,215	2,760	1,995	2,840	3,570	2,055
57	Italian	120	90	205	45	95	140
58	Chinese, n.o.s.	280	105	40	140	85	30
59	Cantonese	225	105	25	70	45	40
60	Portuguese	155	125	130	140	375	200
61	Punjabi	50	50	-	145	25	20
62	Other languages (6)	2,390	2,285	1,595	2,300	2,945	1,620
63	Multiple responses	255	230	35	95	170	85
64	English and French	-	10	-	-	-	10
65	English and non-official language	235	205	40	100	140	80
66	French and non-official language	15	-	-	-	30	-
67	English, French and non-official language	-	10	-	-	-	-

See reference material at the end of the publication. – Voir les documents de référence à la fin de la publication.

Tableau 1. Certaines caractéristiques des secteurs de recensement, recensement de 2001 – Données intégrales et données-échantillon (20 %)

Toronto 0521.06 ◆	Toronto 0522 ◆	Toronto 0523 ◆	Toronto 0524.01 ◆◇	Toronto 0524.02 ◆	Toronto 0525.01 ◆	Caractéristiques	N°
						CARACTÉRISTIQUES DE LA POPULATION	
4,953	**6,429**	**5,910**	**4,485**	**3,775**	**3,956**	**Population, 1996 (1)**	1
5,316	**6,285**	**6,019**	**4,848**	**3,775**	**3,735**	**Population, 2001 (2)**	2
7.3	-2.2	1.8	8.1	-	-5.6	Variation en pourcentage de la population, 1996-2001	3
0.61	1.74	1.16	0.81	0.63	0.52	Superficie des terres en kilomètres carrés, 2001	4
5,315	**6,285**	**6,020**	**4,850**	**3,775**	**3,735**	**Population totale - Données intégrales (3)**	5
						selon le sexe et les groupes d'âge	
2,525	3,065	2,875	2,365	1,880	1,930	Sexe masculin	6
140	160	140	150	95	120	0-4 ans	7
170	175	165	180	125	150	5-9 ans	8
155	190	165	200	90	160	10-14 ans	9
130	215	165	170	110	140	15-19 ans	10
150	225	180	170	95	145	20-24 ans	11
250	220	240	145	125	125	25-29 ans	12
280	205	235	150	130	150	30-34 ans	13
270	215	255	225	185	180	35-39 ans	14
185	220	220	230	140	150	40-44 ans	15
185	205	190	195	140	150	45-49 ans	16
145	205	175	145	105	120	50-54 ans	17
100	220	155	90	75	75	55-59 ans	18
95	160	150	80	105	75	60-64 ans	19
75	170	155	70	90	65	65-69 ans	20
80	150	130	65	90	55	70-74 ans	21
70	75	85	45	85	30	75-79 ans	22
45	30	50	35	60	15	80-84 ans	23
10	15	30	10	25	10	85 ans et plus	24
2,795	3,220	3,145	2,485	1,895	1,805	Sexe féminin	25
130	170	125	130	90	100	0-4 ans	26
155	180	145	160	100	135	5-9 ans	27
150	175	145	195	80	130	10-14 ans	28
135	150	155	175	70	120	15-19 ans	29
180	250	200	145	95	130	20-24 ans	30
265	205	230	160	125	130	25-29 ans	31
270	225	245	180	150	150	30-34 ans	32
240	235	255	210	165	170	35-39 ans	33
195	220	230	250	130	150	40-44 ans	34
185	255	210	190	105	130	45-49 ans	35
140	240	205	150	110	100	50-54 ans	36
130	220	180	95	105	70	55-59 ans	37
125	220	165	105	100	85	60-64 ans	38
125	175	175	100	110	90	65-69 ans	39
140	140	180	85	115	45	70-74 ans	40
105	95	135	80	125	50	75-79 ans	41
80	35	100	50	80	15	80-84 ans	42
55	30	65	25	40	10	85 ans et plus	43
4,415	**5,235**	**5,135**	**3,830**	**3,190**	**2,930**	**Population totale de 15 ans et plus**	44
						selon l'état matrimonial légal	
1,325	1,580	1,495	1,195	880	930	Célibataire (jamais marié(e))	45
2,235	3,030	2,670	2,010	1,720	1,655	Légalement marié(e) (et non séparé(e))	46
170	115	185	125	115	85	Séparé(e), mais toujours légalement marié(e)	47
340	215	385	270	210	140	Divorcé(e)	48
345	305	405	230	265	125	Veuf ou veuve	49
						selon l'union libre	
4,135	5,115	4,855	3,655	3,030	2,855	Ne vivant pas en union libre	50
275	125	285	175	165	75	Vivant en union libre	51
5,315	**6,285**	**6,015**	**4,850**	**3,775**	**3,735**	**Population totale - Données-échantillon (20 %) (4)**	52
						selon la langue maternelle	
5,260	6,100	5,895	4,730	3,705	3,690	Réponses uniques	53
2,185	2,805	3,325	2,300	2,305	1,400	Anglais	54
65	45	95	60	60	35	Français	55
3,005	3,250	2,470	2,370	1,345	2,250	Langues non officielles (5)	56
90	400	160	20	60	100	Italien	57
70	285	85	225	50	60	Chinois, n.d.a.	58
45	125	25	275	50	20	Cantonais	59
50	330	145	20	75	110	Portugais	60
30	65	-	40	-	130	Pendjabi	61
2,725	2,050	2,050	1,785	1,100	1,830	Autres langues (6)	62
55	185	120	120	70	45	Réponses multiples	63
10	-	-	10	-	-	Anglais et français	64
40	185	120	115	40	50	Anglais et langue non officielle	65
-	-	-	-	-	-	Français et langue non officielle	66
-	-	-	-	25	-	Anglais, français et langue non officielle	67

See reference material at the end of the publication. – Voir les documents de référence à la fin de la publication.

Table 1. Selected Characteristics for Census Tracts, 2001 Census – 100% Data and 20% Sample Data

No.	Characteristics	Toronto 0520.06 A	Toronto 0521.01 ◆	Toronto 0521.02 ◆	Toronto 0521.03	Toronto 0521.04	Toronto 0521.05 ◆
	POPULATION CHARACTERISTICS						
	by home language						
68	Single responses	4,230	3,645	2,600	3,940	4,285	2,710
69	English	3,050	2,610	2,065	2,615	3,185	1,945
70	French	65	20	10	15	-	35
71	Non-official languages (5)	1,115	1,015	520	1,310	1,095	730
72	Cantonese	110	75	-	45	20	20
73	Chinese, n.o.s.	80	35	-	90	40	10
74	Italian	10	-	30	-	15	35
75	Punjabi	25	-	-	80	-	-
76	Portuguese	45	15	50	30	135	75
77	Other languages (6)	850	890	445	1,065	885	590
78	Multiple responses	2,040	1,710	1,205	1,530	2,520	1,165
79	English and French	55	95	20	20	75	10
80	English and non-official language	1,930	1,605	1,150	1,495	2,375	1,110
81	French and non-official language	15	10	-	-	-	-
82	English, French and non-official language	35	-	30	10	80	45
	by knowledge of official languages						
83	English only	5,220	4,790	3,440	4,810	6,055	3,430
84	French only	45	15	-	-	-	-
85	English and French	720	395	270	380	485	300
86	Neither English nor French	280	155	100	270	265	145
	by knowledge of non-official languages (5) (7)						
87	Italian	225	125	280	60	215	235
88	Cantonese	325	125	35	80	55	55
89	Chinese, n.o.s.	205	55	35	175	90	35
90	Spanish	245	225	235	195	305	70
91	Portuguese	190	125	180	150	520	235
92	Punjabi	175	120	25	195	45	50
93	Tagalog (Pilipino)	310	120	115	510	360	160
	by first official language spoken						
94	English	5,710	5,020	3,590	5,060	6,415	3,625
95	French	135	125	45	60	55	45
96	English and French	140	65	75	90	75	60
97	Neither English nor French	280	140	100	255	260	145
98	Official language minority - (number) (8)	205	155	85	110	90	75
99	Official language minority - (percentage) (8)	3.3	2.9	2.2	2.0	1.3	1.9
	by ethnic origin (9)						
100	Canadian	545	685	495	540	795	470
101	English	500	720	300	575	860	585
102	Scottish	315	450	290	290	450	385
103	Irish	265	360	215	305	485	280
104	Chinese	725	330	110	420	315	180
105	Italian	350	175	410	105	270	280
106	East Indian	880	835	170	755	295	155
107	French	280	260	100	230	315	150
108	German	155	240	255	130	240	210
109	Portuguese	230	170	230	195	595	235
110	Polish	185	260	435	165	1,075	555
111	Jewish	45	10	-	-	10	10
112	Jamaican	180	85	120	260	180	125
113	Filipino	370	150	190	625	445	205
114	Ukrainian	155	105	235	55	285	155
	by Aboriginal identity						
115	Total Aboriginal identity population (10)	-	10	-	-	25	10
116	Total non-Aboriginal population	6,270	5,350	3,810	5,465	6,775	3,870
	by Aboriginal origin						
117	Total Aboriginal origins population (11)	-	45	-	30	35	15
118	Total non-Aboriginal population	6,270	5,310	3,805	5,435	6,770	3,860
	by Registered Indian status						
119	Registered Indian (12)	-	-	-	-	-	10
120	Not a Registered Indian	6,265	5,355	3,810	5,465	6,795	3,870

Tableau 1. Certaines caractéristiques des secteurs de recensement, recensement de 2001 – Données intégrales et données-échantillon (20 %)

Toronto 0521.06 ◆	Toronto 0522 ◆	Toronto 0523 ◆	Toronto 0524.01 ◆◇	Toronto 0524.02 ◆	Toronto 0525.01 ◆	Caractéristiques	N°
						CARACTÉRISTIQUES DE LA POPULATION	
						selon la langue parlée à la maison	
3,420	4,335	4,520	3,505	2,915	2,490	Réponses uniques	68
2,460	3,155	3,650	2,395	2,500	1,480	Anglais	69
-	-	-	45	-	20	Français	70
960	1,180	870	1,065	420	990	Langues non officielles (5)	71
-	65	20	120	30	-	Cantonais	72
40	175	15	145	20	40	Chinois, n.d.a.	73
-	125	40	10	10	45	Italien	74
10	55	-	10	-	50	Pendjabi	75
10	115	65	10	-	10	Portugais	76
910	640	735	780	360	845	Autres langues (6)	77
1,895	1,950	1,500	1,340	860	1,240	Réponses multiples	78
135	35	70	10	70	25	Anglais et français	79
1,710	1,830	1,400	1,335	760	1,205	Anglais et langue non officielle	80
-	20	15	-	10	-	Français et langue non officielle	81
50	60	15	-	20	10	Anglais, français et langue non officielle	82
						selon la connaissance des langues officielles	
4,615	5,555	5,385	4,385	3,480	3,285	Anglais seulement	83
-	20	15	35	-	10	Français seulement	84
470	415	465	250	230	245	Anglais et français	85
230	290	155	180	60	190	Ni l'anglais ni le français	86
						selon la connaissance des langues non officielles (5) (7)	
185	535	235	35	90	180	Italien	87
45	135	25	270	45	40	Cantonais	88
70	375	85	230	65	65	Chinois, n.d.a.	89
360	275	150	165	70	50	Espagnol	90
50	365	160	40	75	110	Portugais	91
145	80	10	50	40	205	Pendjabi	92
270	305	45	345	130	95	Tagalog (pilipino)	93
						selon la première langue officielle parlée	
4,940	5,885	5,615	4,560	3,650	3,425	Anglais	94
70	55	105	60	50	60	Français	95
85	60	160	50	15	75	Anglais et français	96
225	285	140	180	65	180	Ni l'anglais ni le français	97
110	85	180	80	60	95	Minorité de langue officielle - (nombre) (8)	98
2.1	1.4	3.0	1.6	1.6	2.5	Minorité de langue officielle - (pourcentage) (8)	99
						selon l'origine ethnique (9)	
605	875	1,195	1,090	805	510	Canadien	100
515	720	1,100	750	760	350	Anglais	101
355	410	785	500	360	140	Écossais	102
300	480	650	475	400	240	Irlandais	103
195	595	280	530	180	230	Chinois	104
230	760	515	150	145	180	Italien	105
535	330	155	135	230	490	Indien de l'Inde	106
355	110	260	125	285	85	Français	107
270	275	375	195	195	145	Allemand	108
120	430	200	65	105	125	Portugais	109
265	540	515	645	330	130	Polonais	110
35	20	40	30	10	10	Juif	111
130	180	75	10	55	75	Jamaïquain	112
325	400	65	435	145	130	Philippin	113
125	300	290	260	135	115	Ukrainien	114
						selon l'identité autochtone	
-	25	15	10	15	-	Total de la population ayant une identité autochtone (10)	115
5,320	6,265	6,005	4,835	3,760	3,730	Total de la population non autochtone	116
						selon l'origine autochtone	
10	25	20	30	25	-	Total de la population ayant une origine autochtone (11)	117
5,310	6,260	5,995	4,815	3,745	3,730	Total de la population non autochtone	118
						selon le statut d'Indien inscrit	
-	15	15	10	10	10	Oui, Indien inscrit (12)	119
5,315	6,270	6,005	4,845	3,770	3,730	Non, pas un Indien inscrit	120

Table 1. Selected Characteristics for Census Tracts, 2001 Census – 100% Data and 20% Sample Data

No.	Characteristics	Toronto 0520.06 A	Toronto 0521.01 ◆	Toronto 0521.02 ◆	Toronto 0521.03	Toronto 0521.04	Toronto 0521.05 ◆
	POPULATION CHARACTERISTICS						
	by visible minority groups						
121	Total visible minority population	3,680	2,870	1,235	3,755	2,195	980
122	Chinese	745	255	110	305	255	110
123	South Asian	1,195	1,175	325	1,240	455	240
124	Black	320	195	235	660	345	175
125	Filipino	370	125	165	630	470	185
126	Latin American	115	160	175	160	170	45
127	Southeast Asian	125	10	45	425	215	105
128	Arab	250	305	95	85	130	40
129	West Asian	115	185	15	-	10	-
130	Korean	235	270	-	50	-	50
131	Japanese	50	30	-	25	-	-
132	Visible minority, n.i.e. (13)	95	120	20	130	105	25
133	Multiple visible minorities (14)	70	35	35	50	45	-
	by citizenship						
134	Canadian citizenship (15)	4,735	3,710	3,380	4,305	5,935	3,385
135	Citizenship other than Canadian	1,530	1,640	430	1,160	865	490
	by place of birth of respondent						
136	Non-immigrant population	2,320	2,055	1,745	2,045	3,100	1,880
137	Born in province of residence	1,845	1,640	1,520	1,850	2,715	1,570
138	Immigrant population (16)	3,785	3,245	2,055	3,370	3,670	1,930
139	United States	55	50	15	30	40	15
140	Central and South America	220	170	200	255	300	90
141	Caribbean and Bermuda	170	215	120	290	150	110
142	United Kingdom	115	100	65	65	165	60
143	Other Europe (17)	655	615	1,040	465	1,830	1,080
144	Africa	285	105	85	85	130	40
145	Asia and the Middle East	2,290	1,985	535	2,170	1,020	530
146	Oceania and other (18)	-	-	-	10	35	-
147	Non-permanent residents (19)	160	50	10	60	35	70
148	**Total immigrant population**	**3,790**	**3,250**	**2,055**	**3,365**	**3,665**	**1,925**
	by period of immigration						
149	Before 1961	90	230	360	105	335	205
150	1961-1970	320	210	255	195	420	290
151	1971-1980	625	315	300	480	365	240
152	1981-1990	865	475	575	805	960	405
153	1991-2001 (20)	1,885	2,015	565	1,775	1,590	790
154	1991-1995	455	540	285	915	1,005	490
155	1996-2001 (20)	1,430	1,475	280	860	585	305
	by age at immigration						
156	0-4 years	320	205	165	200	285	85
157	5-19 years	895	840	690	1,020	1,005	520
158	20 years and over	2,570	2,205	1,205	2,145	2,380	1,320
159	**Total population**	**6,265**	**5,355**	**3,810**	**5,465**	**6,800**	**3,875**
	by religion						
160	Catholic (21)	2,455	1,750	2,140	2,260	3,835	1,880
161	Protestant	935	1,070	730	755	1,055	810
162	Christian Orthodox	285	145	115	120	380	180
163	Christian, n.i.e. (22)	250	180	65	270	170	130
164	Muslim	885	935	275	610	405	105
165	Jewish	30	10	-	-	15	-
166	Buddhist	180	30	50	325	140	115
167	Hindu	340	460	60	410	130	120
168	Sikh	70	55	-	115	-	30
169	Eastern religions (23)	25	15	35	-	-	-
170	Other religions (24)	-	10	-	-	-	15
171	No religious affiliation (25)	815	685	350	595	665	485
172	**Total population 15 years and over**	**5,235**	**4,605**	**3,145**	**4,340**	**5,375**	**3,305**
	by generation status						
173	1st generation (26)	3,520	2,985	1,925	3,140	3,455	1,935
174	2nd generation (27)	950	725	640	665	990	675
175	3rd generation and over (28)	760	895	575	535	940	695
176	**Total population 1 year and over (29)**	**6,160**	**5,305**	**3,780**	**5,420**	**6,750**	**3,840**
	by place of residence 1 year ago (mobility)						
177	Non-movers	4,800	3,720	3,390	4,520	6,005	3,395
178	Movers	1,355	1,580	390	895	745	445
179	Non-migrants	580	550	260	600	360	210
180	Migrants	780	1,025	125	300	390	225
181	Internal migrants	405	465	110	105	295	160
182	Intraprovincial migrants	315	415	105	110	275	155
183	Interprovincial migrants	90	50	10	-	15	-
184	External migrants	375	565	15	195	100	65

Tableau 1. Certaines caractéristiques des secteurs de recensement, recensement de 2001 – Données intégrales et données-échantillon (20 %)

Toronto 0521.06 ◆	Toronto 0522 ◆	Toronto 0523 ◆	Toronto 0524.01 ◆◇	Toronto 0524.02 ◆	Toronto 0525.01 ◆	Caractéristiques	N°
						CARACTÉRISTIQUES DE LA POPULATION	
						selon les groupes de minorités visibles	
2,755	2,175	1,340	2,010	1,085	1,885	Total de la population des minorités visibles	121
165	550	255	435	160	175	Chinois	122
1,035	395	270	320	470	1,025	Sud-Asiatique	123
255	415	180	80	80	210	Noir	124
315	375	65	435	140	120	Philippin	125
235	205	60	135	55	-	Latino-Américain	126
90	45	55	265	50	160	Asiatique du Sud-Est	127
255	10	105	185	55	55	Arabe	128
95	10	10	25	-	15	Asiatique occidental	129
175	55	165	30	-	40	Coréen	130
-	25	15	10	-	15	Japonais	131
80	70	140	-	50	20	Minorité visible, n.i.a. (13)	132
50	25	15	90	15	60	Minorités visibles multiples (14)	133
						selon la citoyenneté	
3,435	5,525	4,970	4,130	3,235	2,775	Citoyenneté canadienne (15)	134
1,885	760	1,045	715	540	960	Citoyenneté autre que canadienne	135
						selon le lieu de naissance du répondant	
1,800	3,025	3,180	2,435	2,185	1,390	Population non immigrante	136
1,385	2,675	2,725	2,170	1,635	1,175	Née dans la province de résidence	137
3,465	3,230	2,825	2,400	1,565	2,260	Population immigrante (16)	138
25	25	55	20	15	15	États-Unis	139
270	165	85	120	70	20	Amérique centrale et du Sud	140
190	235	180	75	110	90	Caraïbes et Bermudes	141
160	150	245	75	150	85	Royaume-Uni	142
720	1,530	1,355	820	535	725	Autre Europe (17)	143
280	150	95	50	40	50	Afrique	144
1,820	970	800	1,240	640	1,230	Asie et Moyen-Orient	145
10	10	-	-	-	30	Océanie et autre (18)	146
45	30	10	10	25	90	Résidents non permanents (19)	147
3,465	**3,230**	**2,830**	**2,400**	**1,565**	**2,260**	**Population immigrante totale**	148
						selon la période d'immigration	
265	485	585	105	250	150	Avant 1961	149
215	640	375	205	215	235	1961-1970	150
455	495	300	225	160	305	1971-1980	151
315	555	360	805	240	330	1981-1990	152
2,215	1,055	1,200	1,060	700	1,240	1991-2001 (20)	153
510	650	440	350	265	360	1991-1995	154
1,705	410	765	710	440	880	1996-2001 (20)	155
						selon l'âge à l'immigration	
280	215	255	160	70	155	0-4 ans	156
730	905	690	660	305	630	5-19 ans	157
2,455	2,115	1,885	1,580	1,190	1,475	20 ans et plus	158
5,320	**6,285**	**6,015**	**4,850**	**3,775**	**3,735**	**Population totale**	159
						selon la religion	
1,995	3,160	2,315	2,380	1,460	1,155	Catholique (21)	160
1,005	1,330	1,655	890	1,155	560	Protestante	161
235	220	340	95	100	315	Orthodoxe chrétienne	162
220	305	240	115	20	125	Chrétiennes, n.i.a. (22)	163
695	200	305	415	240	370	Musulmane	164
45	-	15	15	10	-	Juive	165
45	310	75	210	50	240	Bouddhiste	166
400	135	80	75	295	550	Hindoue	167
15	60	-	45	15	60	Sikh	168
20	-	10	-	15	-	Religions orientales (23)	169
-	10	-	-	-	-	Autres religions (24)	170
640	555	975	610	425	355	Aucune appartenance religieuse (25)	171
4,415	**5,240**	**5,130**	**3,830**	**3,240**	**2,870**	**Population totale de 15 ans et plus**	172
						selon le statut des générations	
3,080	3,145	2,625	2,190	1,535	2,035	1re génération (26)	173
660	1,110	1,125	630	555	345	2e génération (27)	174
675	980	1,385	1,010	1,155	490	3e génération et plus (28)	175
5,250	**6,235**	**5,970**	**4,790**	**3,760**	**3,720**	**Population totale de 1 an et plus (29)**	176
						selon le lieu de résidence 1 an auparavant (mobilité)	
3,960	5,710	5,070	4,295	3,305	3,090	Personnes n'ayant pas déménagé	177
1,290	525	900	495	455	635	Personnes ayant déménagé	178
500	310	385	230	165	255	Non-migrants	179
795	215	515	265	290	380	Migrants	180
380	125	350	95	145	60	Migrants internes	181
300	125	320	95	125	60	Migrants infraprovinciaux	182
75	-	25	-	25	10	Migrants interprovinciaux	183
415	90	170	170	145	320	Migrants externes	184

Table 1. Selected Characteristics for Census Tracts, 2001 Census – 100% Data and 20% Sample Data

No.	Characteristics	Toronto 0520.06 A	Toronto 0521.01 ◆	Toronto 0521.02 ◆	Toronto 0521.03	Toronto 0521.04	Toronto 0521.05 ◆
	POPULATION CHARACTERISTICS						
185	**Total population 5 years and over (30)**	**5,860**	**5,060**	**3,650**	**5,160**	**6,395**	**3,690**
	by place of residence 5 years ago (mobility)						
186	Non-movers	2,070	1,780	2,430	2,605	3,695	1,900
187	Movers	3,790	3,285	1,220	2,555	2,705	1,790
188	Non-migrants	1,315	900	660	1,325	1,515	900
189	Migrants	2,470	2,380	560	1,230	1,190	885
190	Internal migrants	1,105	1,070	405	485	720	675
191	Intraprovincial migrants	825	895	365	445	630	570
192	Interprovincial migrants	280	175	40	35	90	110
193	External migrants	1,365	1,310	155	740	470	210
194	**Total population 15 to 24 years**	**700**	**610**	**615**	**925**	**945**	**505**
	by school attendance						
195	Not attending school	200	200	210	300	325	195
196	Attending school full time	435	345	380	545	555	255
197	Attending school part time	70	65	25	80	60	55
198	**Total population 15 years and over**	**5,235**	**4,610**	**3,145**	**4,340**	**5,375**	**3,305**
	by highest level of schooling						
199	Less than grade 9 (31)	260	290	235	350	465	185
200	Grades 9-13 without high school graduation certificate	505	640	655	925	995	670
201	Grades 9-13 with high school graduation certificate	730	565	445	665	875	535
202	Some postsecondary without degree, certificate or diploma (32)	670	660	380	575	810	335
203	Trades certificate or diploma (33)	320	220	315	305	495	340
204	College certificate or diploma (34)	695	610	555	510	725	690
205	University certificate below bachelor's degree	215	185	130	160	135	60
206	University with bachelor's degree or higher	1,845	1,440	425	855	875	495
	by combinations of unpaid work						
207	Males 15 years and over	2,625	2,150	1,570	2,120	2,615	1,560
208	Reported unpaid work (35)	2,235	1,755	1,435	1,830	2,350	1,325
209	Housework and child care and care or assistance to seniors	160	140	95	195	240	70
210	Housework and child care only	515	450	375	545	725	290
211	Housework and care or assistance to seniors only	130	150	120	85	220	115
212	Child care and care or assistance to seniors only	15	10	-	10	10	10
213	Housework only	1,345	980	815	945	1,125	820
214	Child care only	45	25	20	35	30	15
215	Care or assistance to seniors only	25	-	-	10	-	-
216	Females 15 years and over	2,610	2,460	1,570	2,225	2,760	1,745
217	Reported unpaid work (35)	2,435	2,250	1,500	2,025	2,575	1,635
218	Housework and child care and care or assistance to seniors	205	215	130	265	315	175
219	Housework and child care only	690	565	475	725	900	370
220	Housework and care or assistance to seniors only	155	215	75	95	190	130
221	Child care and care or assistance to seniors only	-	-	10	15	-	-
222	Housework only	1,360	1,225	795	925	1,135	940
223	Child care only	25	20	10	10	25	15
224	Care or assistance to seniors only	-	-	-	10	10	-
	by labour force activity						
225	Males 15 years and over	2,625	2,150	1,570	2,115	2,615	1,555
226	In the labour force	2,055	1,560	1,190	1,630	2,125	1,200
227	Employed	1,935	1,475	1,145	1,515	2,025	1,145
228	Unemployed	120	85	50	115	100	55
229	Not in the labour force	570	590	380	490	490	355
230	Participation rate	78.3	72.6	75.8	77.1	81.3	77.2
231	Employment rate	73.7	68.6	72.9	71.6	77.4	73.6
232	Unemployment rate	5.8	5.4	4.2	7.1	4.7	4.6
233	Females 15 years and over	2,610	2,455	1,570	2,220	2,760	1,745
234	In the labour force	1,575	1,395	1,050	1,505	1,875	1,135
235	Employed	1,520	1,300	980	1,400	1,755	1,085
236	Unemployed	55	90	70	105	115	45
237	Not in the labour force	1,035	1,060	520	715	890	610
238	Participation rate	60.3	56.8	66.9	67.8	67.9	65.0
239	Employment rate	58.2	53.0	62.4	63.1	63.6	62.2
240	Unemployment rate	3.5	6.5	6.7	7.0	6.1	4.0

Tableau 1. Certaines caractéristiques des secteurs de recensement, recensement de 2001 – Données intégrales et données-échantillon (20 %)

Toronto 0521.06 ◆	Toronto 0522 ◆	Toronto 0523 ◆	Toronto 0524.01 ◆◇	Toronto 0524.02 ◆	Toronto 0525.01 ◆	Caractéristiques	N°
						CARACTÉRISTIQUES DE LA POPULATION	
5,050	**5,960**	**5,750**	**4,625**	**3,605**	**3,480**	**Population totale de 5 ans et plus (30)**	185
						selon le lieu de résidence 5 ans auparavant (mobilité)	
1,645	4,230	3,010	2,510	1,905	1,680	Personnes n'ayant pas déménagé	186
3,405	1,725	2,745	2,115	1,700	1,795	Personnes ayant déménagé	187
980	905	1,120	905	775	710	Non-migrants	188
2,425	825	1,625	1,210	925	1,085	Migrants	189
875	535	935	610	470	355	Migrants internes	190
665	510	820	605	390	295	Migrants infraprovinciaux	191
215	25	120	-	85	60	Migrants interprovinciaux	192
1,545	290	685	595	450	725	Migrants externes	193
595	**850**	**695**	**660**	**395**	**500**	**Population totale de 15 à 24 ans**	194
						selon la fréquentation scolaire	
255	305	245	160	165	210	Ne fréquentant pas l'école	195
300	480	415	475	200	270	Fréquentant l'école à plein temps	196
40	65	35	25	35	10	Fréquentant l'école à temps partiel	197
4,415	**5,235**	**5,130**	**3,835**	**3,240**	**2,865**	**Population totale de 15 ans et plus**	198
						selon le plus haut niveau de scolarité atteint	
270	700	335	380	235	430	Niveau inférieur à la 9e année (31)	199
670	825	905	730	705	640	De la 9e à la 13e année sans certificat d'études secondaires	200
455	760	770	690	515	445	De la 9e à la 13e année avec certificat d'études secondaires	201
585	705	500	415	375	245	Études postsecondaires partielles sans grade, certificat ou diplôme (32)	202
250	455	455	290	295	225	Certificat ou diplôme d'une école de métiers (33)	203
630	765	820	520	465	295	Certificat ou diplôme collégial (34)	204
125	160	215	140	80	55	Certificat universitaire inférieur au baccalauréat	205
1,420	875	1,130	670	575	520	Études universitaires avec baccalauréat ou diplôme supérieur	206
						selon les combinaisons de travail non rémunéré	
2,065	2,520	2,400	1,835	1,620	1,440	Hommes de 15 ans et plus	207
1,840	2,240	2,120	1,620	1,360	1,115	Travail non rémunéré déclaré (35)	208
105	210	140	215	115	160	Travaux ménagers et soins aux enfants et soins ou aide aux personnes âgées	209
520	555	545	510	300	340	Travaux ménagers et soins aux enfants seulement	210
120	145	185	105	95	105	Travaux ménagers et soins ou aide aux personnes âgées seulement	211
10	-	10	-	-	-	Soins aux enfants et soins ou aide aux personnes âgées seulement	212
1,055	1,315	1,210	740	815	470	Travaux ménagers seulement	213
35	10	10	20	30	20	Soins aux enfants seulement	214
-	10	25	25	10	15	Soins ou aide aux personnes âgées seulement	215
2,350	2,720	2,730	1,995	1,625	1,430	Femmes de 15 ans et plus	216
2,120	2,530	2,490	1,800	1,470	1,310	Travail non rémunéré déclaré (35)	217
130	285	235	315	155	145	Travaux ménagers et soins aux enfants et soins ou aide aux personnes âgées	218
650	680	775	620	385	500	Travaux ménagers et soins aux enfants seulement	219
160	180	250	105	160	140	Travaux ménagers et soins ou aide aux personnes âgées seulement	220
-	-	-	-	10	-	Soins aux enfants et soins ou aide aux personnes âgées seulement	221
1,160	1,375	1,220	755	760	500	Travaux ménagers seulement	222
10	-	-	10	-	15	Soins aux enfants seulement	223
10	10	10	-	10	-	Soins ou aide aux personnes âgées seulement	224
						selon l'activité	
2,065	2,520	2,405	1,835	1,620	1,440	Hommes de 15 ans et plus	225
1,575	1,825	1,680	1,265	1,080	990	Population active	226
1,460	1,750	1,585	1,170	1,045	925	Personnes occupées	227
120	80	95	95	40	65	Chômeurs	228
490	695	720	570	540	450	Inactifs	229
76.3	72.4	69.9	68.9	66.7	68.8	Taux d'activité	230
70.7	69.4	65.9	63.8	64.5	64.2	Taux d'emploi	231
7.6	4.4	5.7	7.5	3.7	6.6	Taux de chômage	232
2,350	2,715	2,730	1,995	1,620	1,430	Femmes de 15 ans et plus	233
1,255	1,750	1,590	1,255	880	805	Population active	234
1,085	1,615	1,485	1,185	840	735	Personnes occupées	235
170	130	105	75	45	70	Chômeuses	236
1,095	975	1,135	740	740	630	Inactives	237
53.4	64.5	58.2	62.9	54.3	56.3	Taux d'activité	238
46.2	59.5	54.4	59.4	51.9	51.4	Taux d'emploi	239
13.5	7.4	6.6	6.0	5.1	8.7	Taux de chômage	240

Table 1. Selected Characteristics for Census Tracts, 2001 Census – 100% Data and 20% Sample Data

No.	Characteristics	Toronto 0520.06 A	Toronto 0521.01 ◆	Toronto 0521.02 ◆	Toronto 0521.03	Toronto 0521.04	Toronto 0521.05 ◆
	POPULATION CHARACTERISTICS						
	by labour force activity – concluded						
241	Both sexes - Participation rate	69.3	64.2	71.4	72.2	74.3	70.8
242	15-24 years	54.3	55.4	66.9	64.9	66.7	71.0
243	25 years and over	71.7	65.6	72.5	74.2	76.0	70.4
244	Both sexes - Employment rate	66.0	60.3	67.7	67.1	70.2	67.6
245	15-24 years	53.2	53.3	59.3	58.4	57.1	66.0
246	25 years and over	68.0	61.2	69.5	69.4	73.0	68.0
247	Both sexes - Unemployment rate	4.8	6.1	5.3	7.2	5.5	4.5
248	15-24 years	2.6	3.0	10.8	9.2	13.5	6.9
249	25 years and over	5.1	6.7	4.1	6.3	3.9	3.8
250	**Total labour force 15 years and over**	**3,635**	**2,955**	**2,245**	**3,135**	**3,995**	**2,335**
	by industry based on the 1997 NAICS						
251	Industry - Not applicable (36)	35	50	50	75	75	25
252	All industries (37)	3,600	2,905	2,195	3,060	3,920	2,315
253	11 Agriculture, forestry, fishing and hunting	-	-	-	10	10	10
254	21 Mining and oil and gas extraction	-	20	-	-	10	-
255	22 Utilities	15	-	15	-	-	10
256	23 Construction	80	55	100	90	185	170
257	31-33 Manufacturing	585	430	405	720	870	430
258	41 Wholesale trade	205	250	175	215	225	145
259	44-45 Retail trade	465	295	270	270	410	295
260	48-49 Transportation and warehousing	195	200	125	220	430	195
261	51 Information and cultural industries	135	120	85	70	50	75
262	52 Finance and insurance	325	220	130	245	275	145
263	53 Real estate and rental and leasing	70	55	60	65	65	40
264	54 Professional, scientific and technical services	545	425	120	190	240	185
265	55 Management of companies and enterprises	20	10	-	-	-	-
266	56 Administrative and support, waste management and remediation services	190	150	120	190	200	95
267	61 Educational services	120	105	75	60	220	75
268	62 Health care and social assistance	215	160	225	220	240	190
269	71 Arts, entertainment and recreation	70	80	-	25	35	15
270	72 Accommodation and food services	200	150	90	185	210	125
271	81 Other services (except public administration)	110	75	120	200	180	70
272	91 Public administration	60	100	80	75	75	50
	by class of worker						
273	Class of worker - Not applicable (36)	35	50	50	70	70	25
274	All classes of worker (37)	3,600	2,905	2,195	3,065	3,925	2,315
275	Paid workers	3,285	2,745	2,095	2,940	3,665	2,130
276	Employees	3,065	2,590	2,005	2,890	3,535	2,085
277	Self-employed (incorporated)	215	155	90	50	125	55
278	Self-employed (unincorporated)	290	150	95	115	240	170
279	Unpaid family workers	30	10	-	10	20	10
	by occupation based on the 2001 NOC-S						
280	Male labour force 15 years and over	2,055	1,560	1,190	1,630	2,125	1,200
281	Occupation - Not applicable (36)	30	20	10	35	50	10
282	All occupations (37)	2,030	1,540	1,190	1,590	2,075	1,190
283	A Management occupations	345	285	215	100	195	85
284	B Business, finance and administration occupations	280	250	185	235	260	140
285	C Natural and applied sciences and related occupations	480	285	120	180	270	110
286	D Health occupations	50	20	25	15	10	10
287	E Occupations in social science, education, government service and religion	45	30	10	45	65	40
288	F Occupations in art, culture, recreation and sport	35	15	15	35	25	20
289	G Sales and service occupations	425	300	190	290	365	260
290	H Trades, transport and equipment operators and related occupations	255	240	310	405	615	390
291	I Occupations unique to primary industry	-	-	20	10	10	10
292	J Occupations unique to processing, manufacturing and utilities	105	115	100	280	255	140
293	Female labour force 15 years and over	1,580	1,400	1,050	1,500	1,875	1,135
294	Occupation - Not applicable (36)	-	25	40	35	20	15
295	All occupations (37)	1,570	1,370	1,010	1,470	1,850	1,125
296	A Management occupations	175	120	55	75	140	110
297	B Business, finance and administration occupations	520	520	410	575	575	360
298	C Natural and applied sciences and related occupations	125	75	40	20	50	50
299	D Health occupations	155	35	105	80	105	90

Tableau 1. Certaines caractéristiques des secteurs de recensement, recensement de 2001 – Données intégrales et données-échantillon (20 %)

Toronto 0521.06 ◆	Toronto 0522 ◆	Toronto 0523 ◆	Toronto 0524.01 ◆◇	Toronto 0524.02 ◆	Toronto 0525.01 ◆	Caractéristiques	N°
						CARACTÉRISTIQUES DE LA POPULATION	
						selon l'activité – fin	
64.2	68.2	63.8	65.8	60.4	62.4	Les deux sexes - Taux d'activité	241
60.0	64.1	63.8	60.6	60.8	60.0	15-24 ans	242
64.9	69.0	63.9	66.8	60.5	63.1	25 ans et plus	243
57.6	64.3	59.9	61.6	58.0	57.8	Les deux sexes - Taux d'emploi	244
51.7	54.7	60.1	56.1	56.2	51.0	15-24 ans	245
58.5	66.1	59.8	62.8	58.3	59.3	25 ans et plus	246
10.2	5.9	6.1	6.5	4.1	7.5	Les deux sexes - Taux de chômage	247
12.5	14.7	4.5	8.8	8.3	15.0	15-24 ans	248
9.9	4.3	6.3	6.1	3.5	5.7	25 ans et plus	249
2,830	**3,575**	**3,270**	**2,520**	**1,965**	**1,795**	**Population active totale de 15 ans et plus**	250
						selon l'industrie basée sur le SCIAN de 1997	
115	40	40	10	10	50	Industrie - Sans objet (36)	251
2,715	3,535	3,235	2,515	1,950	1,740	Toutes les industries (37)	252
-	10	10	-	-	10	11 Agriculture, foresterie, pêche et chasse	253
-	-	-	-	-	-	21 Extraction minière et extraction de pétrole et de gaz	254
15	15	10	-	15	-	22 Services publics	255
55	165	85	140	115	60	23 Construction	256
520	775	550	525	410	380	31-33 Fabrication	257
210	205	345	145	155	185	41 Commerce de gros	258
225	340	370	350	190	165	44-45 Commerce de détail	259
135	235	295	125	165	130	48-49 Transport et entreposage	260
160	105	160	60	50	30	51 Industrie de l'information et industrie culturelle	261
185	190	150	125	85	70	52 Finance et assurances	262
50	105	70	50	45	45	53 Services immobiliers et services de location et de location à bail	263
315	220	315	210	120	85	54 Services professionnels, scientifiques et techniques	264
10	-	-	-	-	-	55 Gestion de sociétés et d'entreprises	265
155	200	115	140	90	110	56 Services administratifs, services de soutien, services de gestion des déchets et services d'assainissement	266
120	165	150	75	60	80	61 Services d'enseignement	267
135	250	160	140	155	65	62 Soins de santé et assistance sociale	268
50	65	80	55	50	15	71 Arts, spectacles et loisirs	269
190	205	125	190	135	200	72 Hébergement et services de restauration	270
135	165	130	130	65	80	81 Autres services, sauf les administrations publiques	271
65	125	115	60	45	15	91 Administrations publiques	272
						selon la catégorie de travailleurs	
120	40	40	10	15	55	Catégorie de travailleurs - Sans objet (36)	273
2,710	3,535	3,235	2,510	1,950	1,745	Toutes les catégories de travailleurs (37)	274
2,560	3,340	2,985	2,400	1,845	1,635	Travailleurs rémunérés	275
2,535	3,260	2,915	2,360	1,775	1,610	Employés	276
30	80	75	40	70	30	Travailleurs autonomes (entreprise constituée en société)	277
150	175	245	110	85	105	Travailleurs autonomes (entreprise non constituée en société)	278
-	25	-	10	15	-	Travailleurs familiaux non rémunérés	279
						selon la profession basée sur la CNP-S de 2001	
1,575	1,825	1,680	1,265	1,080	990	Hommes actifs de 15 ans et plus	280
15	20	25	-	10	15	Profession - Sans objet (36)	281
1,560	1,800	1,655	1,260	1,075	975	Toutes les professions (37)	282
225	205	265	95	150	75	A Gestion	283
275	230	260	130	135	100	B Affaires, finance et administration	284
360	160	275	170	115	110	C Sciences naturelles et appliquées et professions apparentées	285
20	55	10	-	15	15	D Secteur de la santé	286
55	45	25	30	25	45	E Sciences sociales, enseignement, administration publique et religion	287
25	30	40	25	50	45	F Arts, culture, sports et loisirs	288
260	405	335	335	190	245	G Ventes et services	289
175	455	335	250	260	205	H Métiers, transport et machinerie	290
-	-	-	-	15	-	I Professions propres au secteur primaire	291
165	215	115	225	130	140	J Transformation, fabrication et services d'utilité publique	292
1,255	1,750	1,595	1,260	880	805	Femmes actives de 15 ans et plus	293
100	15	15	-	10	40	Profession - Sans objet (36)	294
1,155	1,730	1,580	1,255	875	765	Toutes les professions (37)	295
135	105	125	40	75	55	A Gestion	296
455	595	535	445	265	255	B Affaires, finance et administration	297
75	70	80	40	30	15	C Sciences naturelles et appliquées et professions apparentées	298
45	100	60	60	80	30	D Secteur de la santé	299

Table 1. Selected Characteristics for Census Tracts, 2001 Census – 100% Data and 20% Sample Data

No.	Characteristics	Toronto 0520.06 A	Toronto 0521.01 ◆	Toronto 0521.02 ◆	Toronto 0521.03	Toronto 0521.04	Toronto 0521.05 ◆
	POPULATION CHARACTERISTICS						
	by occupation based on the 2001 NOC-S – concluded						
300	E Occupations in social science, education, government service and religion	110	140	100	85	145	60
301	F Occupations in art, culture, recreation and sport	40	35	10	30	25	25
302	G Sales and service occupations	380	325	200	355	495	285
303	H Trades, transport and equipment operators and related occupations	-	10	10	50	80	40
304	I Occupations unique to primary industry	-	-	-	-	10	-
305	J Occupations unique to processing, manufacturing and utilities	55	100	85	195	230	110
306	**Total employed labour force 15 years and over**	**3,455**	**2,775**	**2,125**	**2,910**	**3,775**	**2,235**
	by place of work						
307	Males	1,940	1,475	1,145	1,510	2,025	1,150
308	Usual place of work	1,695	1,140	970	1,305	1,700	950
309	At home	105	95	30	70	45	20
310	Outside Canada	35	40	15	15	10	-
311	No fixed workplace address	100	195	130	130	265	175
312	Females	1,520	1,300	980	1,400	1,755	1,090
313	Usual place of work	1,390	1,155	875	1,255	1,590	990
314	At home	65	80	45	60	75	35
315	Outside Canada	10	-	-	-	-	-
316	No fixed workplace address	60	65	60	75	90	55
317	**Total employed labour force 15 years and over with usual place of work or no fixed workplace address**	**3,250**	**2,560**	**2,035**	**2,765**	**3,645**	**2,180**
	by mode of transportation						
318	Males	1,795	1,340	1,095	1,435	1,965	1,125
319	Car, truck, van, as driver	1,445	1,030	950	1,065	1,620	880
320	Car, truck, van, as passenger	45	10	30	45	75	30
321	Public transit	225	260	115	290	250	165
322	Walked	60	30	-	15	15	50
323	Other method	25	-	-	20	-	-
324	Females	1,455	1,215	935	1,330	1,680	1,050
325	Car, truck, van, as driver	770	725	615	685	1,000	670
326	Car, truck, van, as passenger	185	125	125	185	260	70
327	Public transit	360	265	190	405	365	275
328	Walked	130	85	-	50	55	20
329	Other method	15	15	10	10	10	20
330	**Total population 15 years and over who worked since January 1, 2000**	**3,900**	**3,195**	**2,390**	**3,305**	**4,195**	**2,480**
	by language used at work						
331	Single responses	3,540	2,805	2,120	2,965	3,680	2,155
332	English	3,435	2,710	2,075	2,940	3,620	2,120
333	French	15	15	-	-	-	-
334	Non-official languages (5)	100	75	45	20	55	35
335	Chinese, n.o.s.	20	15	-	-	15	-
336	Cantonese	-	-	-	-	-	-
337	Other languages (6)	75	60	45	25	40	35
338	Multiple responses	360	390	275	340	515	325
339	English and French	90	95	40	35	90	40
340	English and non-official language	245	280	230	300	410	255
341	French and non-official language	-	-	-	-	-	-
342	English, French and non-official language	25	15	-	10	20	25
	DWELLING AND HOUSEHOLD CHARACTERISTICS						
343	**Total number of occupied private dwellings**	**2,540**	**2,340**	**1,145**	**1,510**	**2,130**	**1,650**
	by tenure						
344	Owned	1,440	1,100	1,010	1,320	1,515	815
345	Rented	1,100	1,230	135	195	615	830
346	Band housing	-	-	-	-	-	-
	by structural type of dwelling						
347	Single-detached house	265	-	470	85	710	220
348	Semi-detached house	10	-	335	245	355	-
349	Row house	10	10	315	735	440	200
350	Apartment, detached duplex	15	-	-	10	15	-
351	Apartment, building that has five or more storeys	2,245	2,330	-	450	610	975
352	Apartment, building that has fewer than five storeys (38)	-	-	25	-	-	250
353	Other single-attached house	-	-	-	-	-	-
354	Movable dwelling (39)	-	-	-	-	-	-

Tableau 1. Certaines caractéristiques des secteurs de recensement, recensement de 2001 – Données intégrales et données-échantillon (20 %)

Toronto 0521.06 ◆	Toronto 0522 ◆	Toronto 0523 ◆	Toronto 0524.01 ◆◇	Toronto 0524.02 ◆	Toronto 0525.01 ◆	Caractéristiques	N°
						CARACTÉRISTIQUES DE LA POPULATION	
						selon la profession basée sur la CNP-S de 2001 – fin	
105	170	210	95	45	65	E Sciences sociales, enseignement, administration publique et religion	300
10	55	60	20	10	45	F Arts, culture, sports et loisirs	301
250	390	325	360	235	175	G Ventes et services	302
10	30	35	60	15	30	H Métiers, transport et machinerie	303
10	10	20	10	-	-	I Professions propres au secteur primaire	304
65	195	125	120	110	100	J Transformation, fabrication et services d'utilité publique	305
2,540	**3,365**	**3,070**	**2,360**	**1,880**	**1,660**	**Population active occupée totale de 15 ans et plus selon le lieu de travail**	306
1,455	1,750	1,585	1,170	1,045	925	Hommes	307
1,310	1,505	1,390	1,030	860	805	Lieu habituel de travail	308
55	50	90	50	40	30	À domicile	309
15	15	20	10	35	-	En dehors du Canada	310
75	180	85	85	110	80	Sans adresse de travail fixe	311
1,085	1,615	1,490	1,185	835	740	Femmes	312
995	1,475	1,315	1,090	775	675	Lieu habituel de travail	313
60	70	105	40	40	25	À domicile	314
-	15	-	10	-	-	En dehors du Canada	315
25	60	65	40	20	40	Sans adresse de travail fixe	316
2,410	**3,215**	**2,855**	**2,250**	**1,765**	**1,595**	**Population active occupée totale de 15 ans et plus ayant un lieu habituel de travail ou sans adresse de travail fixe selon le mode de transport**	317
1,390	1,685	1,475	1,115	970	885	Hommes	318
1,040	1,410	1,130	855	725	670	Automobile, camion ou fourgonnette, en tant que conducteur	319
60	70	55	75	35	25	Automobile, camion ou fourgonnette, en tant que passager	320
240	185	255	140	150	115	Transport en commun	321
30	20	15	40	40	45	À pied	322
15	10	25	-	15	25	Autre moyen	323
1,020	1,535	1,375	1,130	800	710	Femmes	324
545	845	830	645	440	375	Automobile, camion ou fourgonnette, en tant que conductrice	325
75	200	95	120	110	70	Automobile, camion ou fourgonnette, en tant que passagère	326
340	435	345	280	185	205	Transport en commun	327
40	45	80	75	40	40	À pied	328
15	10	20	10	25	15	Autre moyen	329
3,025	**3,850**	**3,505**	**2,825**	**2,155**	**1,930**	**Population totale de 15 ans et plus ayant travaillé depuis le 1er janvier 2000 selon la langue utilisée au travail**	330
2,710	3,525	3,145	2,510	2,010	1,680	Réponses uniques	331
2,670	3,460	3,115	2,410	2,010	1,630	Anglais	332
-	-	-	15	-	-	Français	333
35	70	30	85	-	45	Langues non officielles (5)	334
-	25	-	30	-	15	Chinois, n.d.a.	335
-	10	-	10	-	-	Cantonais	336
40	35	30	55	-	30	Autres langues (6)	337
320	320	355	320	145	250	Réponses multiples	338
85	50	105	35	25	45	Anglais et français	339
215	265	235	280	120	195	Anglais et langue non officielle	340
-	-	-	-	-	-	Français et langue non officielle	341
25	10	15	-	10	10	Anglais, français et langue non officielle	342
						CARACTÉRISTIQUES DES LOGEMENTS ET DES MÉNAGES	
2,320	**2,025**	**2,485**	**1,580**	**1,575**	**1,115**	**Nombre total de logements privés occupés selon le mode d'occupation**	343
595	1,635	1,115	1,145	970	570	Possédé	344
1,725	390	1,370	435	610	545	Loué	345
-	-	-	-	-	-	Logement de bande	346
						selon le type de construction résidentielle	
10	895	580	405	215	300	Maison individuelle non attenante	347
-	695	130	165	215	95	Maison jumelée	348
240	160	150	430	-	250	Maison en rangée	349
-	-	-	-	-	-	Appartement, duplex non attenant	350
2,070	250	1,615	130	1,145	460	Appartement, immeuble de cinq étages ou plus	351
-	30	15	460	-	-	Appartement, immeuble de moins de cinq étages (38)	352
-	-	-	-	-	-	Autre maison individuelle attenante	353
-	-	-	-	-	-	Logement mobile (39)	354

Table 1. Selected Characteristics for Census Tracts, 2001 Census – 100% Data and 20% Sample Data

No.	Characteristics	Toronto 0520.06 A	Toronto 0521.01 ◆	Toronto 0521.02 ◆	Toronto 0521.03	Toronto 0521.04	Toronto 0521.05 ◆
	DWELLING AND HOUSEHOLD CHARACTERISTICS						
	by condition of dwelling						
355	Regular maintenance only	2,185	1,935	735	975	1,475	1,125
356	Minor repairs	285	300	295	415	515	345
357	Major repairs	75	100	120	125	145	180
	by period of construction						
358	Before 1946	30	-	25	-	-	55
359	1946-1960	40	20	60	25	70	160
360	1961-1970	40	115	310	180	310	435
361	1971-1980	80	1,045	655	990	1,475	755
362	1981-1990	1,895	1,100	85	300	250	235
363	1991-2001 (20)	445	55	-	10	25	10
364	Average number of rooms per dwelling	4.8	4.4	6.9	6.0	6.3	5.1
365	Average number of bedrooms per dwelling	1.9	1.7	3.2	3.0	2.8	2.0
366	Average value of dwelling $	172,798	157,500	221,455	160,783	199,649	183,979
367	**Total number of private households**	**2,535**	**2,340**	**1,150**	**1,510**	**2,130**	**1,645**
	by household size						
368	1 person	705	710	85	185	250	585
369	2 persons	810	860	315	255	515	455
370	3 persons	470	350	225	255	475	250
371	4-5 persons	485	380	440	615	760	310
372	6 or more persons	70	40	85	200	135	50
	by household type						
373	One-family households	1,615	1,475	930	1,155	1,685	985
374	Multiple-family households	55	45	65	125	100	45
375	Non-family households	865	820	150	230	345	615
376	Number of persons in private households	6,265	5,350	3,810	5,465	6,805	3,875
377	Average number of persons in private households	2.5	2.3	3.3	3.6	3.2	2.3
378	Average number of persons per room	0.5	0.5	0.5	0.6	0.5	0.5
379	Tenant households in non-farm, non-reserve private dwellings (40)	1,075	1,225	135	190	605	835
380	Average gross rent $ (40)	1,156	1,078	1,171	834	954	758
381	Tenant households spending 30% or more of household income on gross rent (40) (41)	420	470	25	85	185	235
382	Tenant households spending from 30% to 99% of household income on gross rent (40) (41)	335	360	30	55	180	210
383	Owner households in non-farm, non-reserve private dwellings (42)	1,425	1,105	1,010	1,320	1,515	810
384	Average owner's major payments $ (42)	1,156	974	1,031	1,167	1,036	980
385	Owner households spending 30% or more of household income on owner's major payments (41) (42)	545	390	125	400	400	230
386	Owner households spending from 30% to 99% of household income on owner's major payments (41) (42)	445	325	120	320	350	210
	CENSUS FAMILY CHARACTERISTICS						
387	**Total number of census families in private households**	**1,735**	**1,565**	**1,060**	**1,410**	**1,885**	**1,075**
	by census family structure and size						
388	Total couple families	1,485	1,310	945	1,185	1,595	855
389	Total families of married couples	1,340	1,170	905	1,115	1,470	760
390	Without children at home	515	535	230	220	450	280
391	With children at home	825	635	670	895	1,020	485
392	1 child	415	315	235	290	370	220
393	2 children	275	250	305	345	480	170
394	3 or more children	130	75	125	255	170	95
395	Total families of common-law couples	150	135	45	70	125	95
396	Without children at home	85	110	35	25	50	80
397	With children at home	60	25	15	50	75	20
398	1 child	30	20	-	10	30	10
399	2 children	20	-	10	25	20	-
400	3 or more children	-	-	-	20	30	-
401	Total lone-parent families	255	255	115	225	290	220
402	Female parent	205	245	95	185	255	170
403	1 child	160	155	60	115	150	120
404	2 children	35	65	10	55	70	25
405	3 or more children	10	20	25	10	40	20

Tableau 1. Certaines caractéristiques des secteurs de recensement, recensement de 2001 – Données intégrales et données-échantillon (20 %)

Toronto 0521.06 ◆	Toronto 0522 ◆	Toronto 0523 ◆	Toronto 0524.01 ◆◇	Toronto 0524.02 ◆	Toronto 0525.01 ◆	Caractéristiques	N°
						CARACTÉRISTIQUES DES LOGEMENTS ET DES MÉNAGES	
						selon l'état du logement	
1,930	1,340	1,620	1,055	1,020	670	Entretien régulier seulement	355
320	590	665	455	385	330	Réparations mineures	356
75	100	200	70	170	115	Réparations majeures	357
						selon la période de construction	
-	10	45	20	35	10	Avant 1946	358
35	100	200	170	175	180	1946-1960	359
245	870	1,200	560	595	455	1961-1970	360
1,375	775	885	535	690	410	1971-1980	361
475	250	145	130	90	45	1981-1990	362
190	25	-	165	-	15	1991-2001 (20)	363
4.2	7.1	5.6	6.1	5.3	5.9	Nombre moyen de pièces par logement	364
1.7	3.1	2.3	2.8	2.2	2.6	Nombre moyen de chambres à coucher par logement	365
156,696	244,382	242,182	200,851	200,032	209,938	Valeur moyenne du logement $	366
2,320	**2,025**	**2,480**	**1,580**	**1,575**	**1,110**	**Nombre total de logements privés**	367
						selon la taille du ménage	
810	245	725	265	460	125	1 personne	368
720	600	805	390	530	265	2 personnes	369
335	435	410	310	260	220	3 personnes	370
390	645	485	515	260	390	4-5 personnes	371
60	105	55	100	60	115	6 personnes ou plus	372
						selon le genre de ménage	
1,325	1,615	1,550	1,155	1,020	870	Ménages unifamiliaux	373
60	125	100	120	45	90	Ménages multifamiliaux	374
940	285	835	305	505	155	Ménages non familiaux	375
5,305	6,280	6,020	4,850	3,775	3,730	Nombre de personnes dans les ménages privés	376
2.3	3.1	2.4	3.1	2.4	3.4	Nombre moyen de personnes dans les ménages privés	377
0.5	0.4	0.4	0.5	0.4	0.6	Nombre moyen de personnes par pièce	378
1,700	395	1,345	435	605	520	Ménages locataires dans les logements privés non agricoles hors réserve (40)	379
931	934	1,028	752	837	974	Loyer brut moyen $ (40)	380
810	125	565	185	195	195	Ménages locataires consacrant 30 % ou plus du revenu du ménage au loyer brut (40) (41)	381
680	95	505	155	155	160	Ménages locataires consacrant de 30 % à 99 % du revenu du ménage au loyer brut (40) (41)	382
590	1,630	1,115	1,145	965	565	Ménages propriétaires dans les logements privés non agricoles hors réserve (42)	383
966	995	981	1,008	828	925	Principales dépenses de propriété moyennes $ (42)	384
165	295	290	210	160	160	Ménages propriétaires consacrant 30 % ou plus du revenu du ménage aux principales dépenses de propriété (41) (42)	385
165	230	245	190	150	150	Ménages propriétaires consacrant de 30 % à 99 % du revenu du ménage aux principales dépenses de propriété (41) (42)	386
						CARACTÉRISTIQUES DES FAMILLES DE RECENSEMENT	
1,440	**1,875**	**1,755**	**1,395**	**1,110**	**1,040**	**Total des familles de recensement dans les ménages privés**	387
						selon la structure et la taille de la famille de recensement	
1,230	1,555	1,470	1,075	950	835	Total des familles avec conjoints	388
1,085	1,495	1,320	985	850	805	Total des familles avec couples mariés	389
475	530	575	325	390	255	Sans enfants à la maison	390
610	960	745	665	460	550	Avec enfants à la maison	391
255	350	355	205	205	165	1 enfant	392
240	435	310	340	225	230	2 enfants	393
115	175	80	115	30	150	3 enfants ou plus	394
140	65	145	90	105	25	Total des familles en union libre	395
110	35	90	55	60	-	Sans enfants à la maison	396
35	25	55	30	40	25	Avec enfants à la maison	397
10	15	30	15	30	15	1 enfant	398
15	15	-	10	-	10	2 enfants	399
-	-	15	10	10	-	3 enfants ou plus	400
210	320	285	315	160	205	Total des familles monoparentales	401
180	275	235	225	140	140	Parent de sexe féminin	402
125	170	150	110	100	90	1 enfant	403
35	70	60	55	30	40	2 enfants	404
20	35	20	55	10	10	3 enfants ou plus	405

Table 1. Selected Characteristics for Census Tracts, 2001 Census – 100% Data and 20% Sample Data

No.	Characteristics	Toronto 0520.06 A	Toronto 0521.01 ◆	Toronto 0521.02 ◆	Toronto 0521.03	Toronto 0521.04	Toronto 0521.05 ◆
	CENSUS FAMILY CHARACTERISTICS						
	by census family structure and size – concluded						
406	Male parent	45	10	20	40	30	50
407	1 child	35	-	15	30	15	45
408	2 children	10	10	-	-	15	10
409	3 or more children	-	-	10	10	10	-
410	**Total number of children at home**	**1,840**	**1,445**	**1,470**	**2,280**	**2,540**	**1,195**
	by age groups						
411	Under 6 years	455	355	185	400	525	220
412	6-14 years	565	390	480	715	890	355
413	15-17 years	165	180	170	300	270	130
414	18-24 years	390	250	410	500	545	305
415	25 years and over	270	270	230	370	305	190
416	Average number of children at home per census family (43)	1.1	0.9	1.4	1.6	1.3	1.1
417	**Total number of persons in private households**	**6,270**	**5,350**	**3,810**	**5,470**	**6,800**	**3,875**
	by census family status and living arrangements						
418	Number of non-family persons	1,205	1,035	335	590	790	750
419	Living with relatives (44)	185	125	185	210	260	80
420	Living with non-relatives only	320	205	60	200	280	85
421	Living alone	700	705	90	180	250	585
422	Number of family persons	5,060	4,310	3,475	4,875	6,015	3,130
423	Average number of persons per census family	2.9	2.8	3.3	3.5	3.2	2.9
424	**Total number of persons 65 years and over**	**555**	**815**	**365**	**480**	**505**	**515**
425	Number of non-family persons 65 years and over	165	310	110	145	140	180
426	Living with relatives (44)	65	35	75	65	75	30
427	Living with non-relatives only	25	25	-	15	20	-
428	Living alone	85	260	35	60	45	150
429	Number of family persons 65 years and over	390	500	260	335	360	335
	ECONOMIC FAMILY CHARACTERISTICS						
430	**Total number of economic families in private households**	**1,705**	**1,535**	**1,045**	**1,300**	**1,815**	**1,035**
	by size of family						
431	2 persons	720	770	305	260	500	440
432	3 persons	440	355	225	270	465	245
433	4 persons	340	270	315	375	535	210
434	5 or more persons	205	145	200	395	315	135
435	Total number of persons in economic families	5,250	4,435	3,665	5,080	6,275	3,205
436	Average number of persons per economic family	3.1	2.9	3.5	3.9	3.5	3.1
437	Total number of unattached individuals	1,015	910	145	385	530	670
	2000 INCOME CHARACTERISTICS						
	Population 15 years and over by sex and total income groups in 2000						
438	Total - Both sexes	5,235	4,605	3,145	4,340	5,375	3,305
439	Without income	425	375	135	310	295	130
440	With income	4,810	4,235	3,005	4,030	5,080	3,175
441	Under $1,000 (45)	215	205	85	275	240	115
442	$ 1,000 - $ 2,999	250	170	105	235	190	140
443	$ 3,000 - $ 4,999	215	165	170	175	225	80
444	$ 5,000 - $ 6,999	150	125	85	160	240	100
445	$ 7,000 - $ 9,999	215	215	145	295	140	135
446	$10,000 - $11,999	180	140	130	220	175	155
447	$12,000 - $14,999	320	240	130	235	410	265
448	$15,000 - $19,999	365	360	200	365	465	295
449	$20,000 - $24,999	365	320	235	290	420	290
450	$25,000 - $29,999	265	365	375	360	370	210
451	$30,000 - $34,999	410	360	285	335	500	420
452	$35,000 - $39,999	260	290	205	265	395	225
453	$40,000 - $44,999	370	195	195	305	375	245
454	$45,000 - $49,999	195	190	110	140	195	145
455	$50,000 - $59,999	290	390	205	155	300	155
456	$60,000 and over	750	495	345	225	435	200
457	Average income $ (46)	32,413	31,025	33,433	24,441	28,551	27,105
458	Median income $ (46)	26,639	26,839	27,286	20,387	25,192	25,028
459	Standard error of average income $ (46)	870	774	1,609	693	686	732

Tableau 1. Certaines caractéristiques des secteurs de recensement, recensement de 2001 – Données intégrales et données-échantillon (20 %)

Toronto 0521.06 ◆	Toronto 0522 ◆	Toronto 0523 ◆	Toronto 0524.01 ◆◇	Toronto 0524.02 ◆	Toronto 0525.01 ◆	Caractéristiques	N°
						CARACTÉRISTIQUES DES FAMILLES DE RECENSEMENT	
						selon la structure et la taille de la famille de recensement – fin	
30	50	50	95	25	65	Parent de sexe masculin	406
25	10	25	60	10	40	1 enfant	407
10	35	25	30	10	20	2 enfants	408
-	-	-	-	-	10	3 enfants ou plus	409
1,465	**2,350**	**1,770**	**1,870**	**1,060**	**1,495**	**Nombre total d'enfants à la maison**	410
						selon les groupes d'âge	
325	380	355	265	235	315	Moins de 6 ans	411
575	665	535	750	295	550	6-14 ans	412
150	235	200	190	115	170	15-17 ans	413
275	540	400	410	200	275	18-24 ans	414
135	530	280	255	210	180	25 ans et plus	415
1.0	1.3	1.0	1.3	1.0	1.4	Nombre moyen d'enfants à la maison par famille de recensement (43)	416
5,310	**6,280**	**6,015**	**4,845**	**3,775**	**3,735**	**Nombre total de personnes dans les ménages privés**	417
						selon la situation des particuliers dans la famille de recensement et des particuliers dans le ménage	
1,175	500	1,030	500	650	365	Nombre de personnes hors famille de recensement	418
140	155	90	120	115	145	Vivant avec des personnes apparentées (44)	419
215	100	215	110	80	90	Vivant avec des personnes non apparentées uniquement	420
810	245	725	265	460	125	Vivant seules	421
4,135	5,780	4,985	4,345	3,120	3,370	Nombre de personnes membres d'une famille	422
2.9	3.1	2.9	3.1	2.8	3.2	Nombre moyen de personnes par famille de recensement	423
775	**910**	**1,110**	**560**	**815**	**410**	**Nombre total de personnes de 65 ans et plus**	424
395	185	395	175	250	110	Nombre de personnes hors famille de recensement de 65 ans et plus	425
50	85	25	45	55	60	Vivant avec des personnes apparentées (44)	426
30	10	25	10	-	15	Vivant avec des personnes non apparentées uniquement	427
310	90	345	120	190	40	Vivant seules	428
380	725	715	380	565	300	Nombre de personnes membres d'une famille de 65 ans et plus	429
						CARACTÉRISTIQUES DES FAMILLES ÉCONOMIQUES	
1,430	**1,760**	**1,660**	**1,295**	**1,090**	**965**	**Nombre total de familles économiques dans les ménages privés**	430
						selon la taille de la famille	
680	590	740	405	530	260	2 personnes	431
315	435	385	265	250	220	3 personnes	432
255	440	345	340	205	250	4 personnes	433
175	300	190	275	110	235	5 personnes ou plus	434
4,280	5,940	5,075	4,470	3,230	3,510	Nombre total de personnes dans les familles économiques	435
3.0	3.4	3.0	3.5	3.0	3.6	Nombre moyen de personnes par famille économique	436
1,030	340	945	375	540	215	Nombre total de personnes hors famille économique	437
						CARACTÉRISTIQUES DU REVENU DE 2000	
						Population de 15 ans et plus selon le sexe et les tranches de revenu total en 2000	
4,415	5,240	5,130	3,830	3,245	2,870	Total - Les deux sexes	438
300	275	195	260	160	250	Sans revenu	439
4,110	4,960	4,940	3,570	3,080	2,620	Avec un revenu	440
170	235	230	105	115	195	Moins de 1 000 $ (45)	441
245	235	250	135	135	165	1 000 $ - 2 999 $	442
235	210	110	110	105	65	3 000 $ - 4 999 $	443
120	140	150	120	80	190	5 000 $ - 6 999 $	444
225	180	260	190	175	115	7 000 $ - 9 999 $	445
240	150	225	135	130	100	10 000 $ - 11 999 $	446
375	430	295	260	170	155	12 000 $ - 14 999 $	447
280	425	430	375	240	275	15 000 $ - 19 999 $	448
300	410	450	300	275	245	20 000 $ - 24 999 $	449
320	295	355	335	265	260	25 000 $ - 29 999 $	450
340	395	410	290	330	265	30 000 $ - 34 999 $	451
300	435	345	180	235	175	35 000 $ - 39 999 $	452
205	320	230	220	160	55	40 000 $ - 44 999 $	453
175	270	295	120	135	75	45 000 $ - 49 999 $	454
300	250	315	210	190	110	50 000 $ - 59 999 $	455
280	570	580	470	335	185	60 000 $ et plus	456
27,195	31,021	32,296	30,861	34,273	24,511	Revenu moyen $ (46)	457
22,109	25,855	25,535	26,059	27,159	20,437	Revenu médian $ (46)	458
933	977	1,306	924	3,147	942	Erreur type de revenu moyen $ (46)	459

Table 1. Selected Characteristics for Census Tracts, 2001 Census – 100% Data and 20% Sample Data

No.	Characteristics	Toronto 0520.06 A	Toronto 0521.01 ◆	Toronto 0521.02 ◆	Toronto 0521.03	Toronto 0521.04	Toronto 0521.05 ◆
	2000 INCOME CHARACTERISTICS						
	Population 15 years and over by sex and total income groups in 2000 – concluded						
460	Total - Males	2,620	2,150	1,575	2,115	2,615	1,560
461	Without income	110	160	50	120	140	15
462	With income	2,510	1,995	1,525	1,995	2,475	1,545
463	Under $1,000 (45)	130	65	30	100	65	35
464	$ 1,000 - $ 2,999	100	60	40	125	60	60
465	$ 3,000 - $ 4,999	70	80	60	70	65	35
466	$ 5,000 - $ 6,999	50	55	45	55	110	45
467	$ 7,000 - $ 9,999	75	60	70	120	65	40
468	$10,000 - $11,999	95	45	30	110	75	105
469	$12,000 - $14,999	120	75	35	90	170	105
470	$15,000 - $19,999	180	120	100	135	170	120
471	$20,000 - $24,999	240	135	130	110	190	135
472	$25,000 - $29,999	175	170	140	195	185	100
473	$30,000 - $34,999	215	195	115	155	230	190
474	$35,000 - $39,999	100	140	120	130	215	110
475	$40,000 - $44,999	150	110	115	200	205	160
476	$45,000 - $49,999	100	105	75	125	120	105
477	$50,000 - $59,999	190	240	120	110	220	60
478	$60,000 and over	520	350	295	170	345	140
479	Average income $ (46)	37,016	36,897	38,600	28,870	34,352	29,721
480	Median income $ (46)	30,012	32,284	32,082	27,085	31,819	29,364
481	Standard error of average income $ (46)	1,370	1,232	1,719	1,132	1,062	1,100
482	Total - Females	2,615	2,460	1,575	2,220	2,760	1,750
483	Without income	315	215	85	190	150	115
484	With income	2,295	2,240	1,485	2,035	2,610	1,635
485	Under $1,000 (45)	80	140	55	175	175	85
486	$ 1,000 - $ 2,999	155	110	60	115	130	80
487	$ 3,000 - $ 4,999	145	90	110	105	165	50
488	$ 5,000 - $ 6,999	105	70	35	100	135	55
489	$ 7,000 - $ 9,999	140	155	75	175	75	95
490	$10,000 - $11,999	85	95	95	110	100	50
491	$12,000 - $14,999	200	160	90	145	235	155
492	$15,000 - $19,999	180	240	100	230	295	175
493	$20,000 - $24,999	125	185	115	185	235	150
494	$25,000 - $29,999	90	200	235	165	180	110
495	$30,000 - $34,999	195	175	175	180	270	235
496	$35,000 - $39,999	155	145	85	130	185	110
497	$40,000 - $44,999	220	90	80	105	165	85
498	$45,000 - $49,999	90	85	30	20	80	45
499	$50,000 - $59,999	100	155	85	50	75	95
500	$60,000 and over	230	145	50	55	90	55
501	Average income $ (46)	27,378	25,804	28,139	20,093	23,039	24,637
502	Median income $ (46)	22,133	21,149	25,073	16,844	19,775	21,732
503	Standard error of average income $ (46)	997	916	2,689	754	821	960
	by composition of total income						
504	Total - Composition of income in 2000 % (47)	100.0	100.0	100.0	100.0	100.0	100.0
505	Employment income %	86.8	75.7	79.2	85.6	84.6	80.8
506	Government transfer payments %	7.2	10.7	6.8	9.4	7.6	10.7
507	Other %	6.0	13.5	13.8	4.9	7.8	8.6
	Population 15 years and over with employment income in 2000 by sex and work activity						
508	Both sexes with employment income (48)	3,720	3,045	2,485	3,200	4,045	2,425
509	Average employment income $	36,363	32,647	32,123	26,404	30,308	28,691
510	Standard error of average employment income $	993	922	1,127	793	737	813
511	Worked full year, full time (49)	2,235	1,765	1,395	1,785	2,365	1,455
512	Average employment income $	45,639	41,604	43,429	36,298	39,318	35,211
513	Standard error of average employment income $	1,249	1,186	1,558	1,080	915	943
514	Worked part year or part time (50)	1,400	1,195	935	1,350	1,590	920
515	Average employment income $	23,093	19,731	19,692	14,289	17,653	19,421
516	Standard error of average employment income $	1,380	1,110	1,180	732	903	1,215
517	Males with employment income (48)	2,060	1,600	1,330	1,660	2,130	1,230
518	Average employment income $	39,771	38,711	38,624	31,103	35,356	30,730
519	Standard error of average employment income $	1,505	1,394	1,834	1,249	1,130	1,153
520	Worked full year, full time (49)	1,300	1,005	780	990	1,375	765
521	Average employment income $	48,721	46,476	51,686	41,614	43,968	35,065
522	Standard error of average employment income $	1,899	1,699	2,396	1,637	1,379	1,248
523	Worked part year or part time (50)	750	575	470	650	705	445
524	Average employment income $	24,311	24,660	22,789	16,129	19,331	24,328
525	Standard error of average employment income $	2,008	1,894	1,951	1,123	1,265	2,128

Tableau 1. Certaines caractéristiques des secteurs de recensement, recensement de 2001 – Données intégrales et données-échantillon (20 %)

Toronto 0521.06 ◆	Toronto 0522 ◆	Toronto 0523 ◆	Toronto 0524.01 ◆◇	Toronto 0524.02 ◆	Toronto 0525.01 ◆	Caractéristiques	N[o]
						CARACTÉRISTIQUES DU REVENU DE 2000	
						Population de 15 ans et plus selon le sexe et les tranches de revenu total en 2000 – fin	
2,060	2,520	2,405	1,830	1,620	1,435	Total - Hommes	460
105	105	75	115	45	115	Sans revenu	461
1,960	2,410	2,325	1,720	1,575	1,320	Avec un revenu	462
65	140	110	50	40	90	Moins de 1 000 $ (45)	463
65	85	60	80	80	70	1 000 $ - 2 999 $	464
80	85	55	55	35	45	3 000 $ - 4 999 $	465
50	55	45	40	30	45	5 000 $ - 6 999 $	466
70	45	65	75	60	35	7 000 $ - 9 999 $	467
95	70	120	40	45	40	10 000 $ - 11 999 $	468
85	90	95	45	65	30	12 000 $ - 14 999 $	469
130	205	190	170	70	115	15 000 $ - 19 999 $	470
140	170	165	135	120	140	20 000 $ - 24 999 $	471
165	145	170	120	125	125	25 000 $ - 29 999 $	472
190	210	160	105	235	170	30 000 $ - 34 999 $	473
175	210	235	120	145	110	35 000 $ - 39 999 $	474
100	200	120	105	85	35	40 000 $ - 44 999 $	475
110	160	165	70	90	45	45 000 $ - 49 999 $	476
205	160	165	150	105	90	50 000 $ - 59 999 $	477
230	385	405	360	245	145	60 000 $ et plus	478
34,243	37,305	39,692	36,581	42,401	29,628	Revenu moyen $ (46)	479
30,416	32,049	31,864	32,081	31,586	25,799	Revenu médian $ (46)	480
1,644	1,756	2,568	1,476	6,025	1,562	Erreur type de revenu moyen $ (46)	481
2,345	2,720	2,730	2,000	1,620	1,430	Total - Femmes	482
195	165	115	150	120	135	Sans revenu	483
2,150	2,550	2,615	1,845	1,505	1,300	Avec un revenu	484
100	100	120	60	75	100	Moins de 1 000 $ (45)	485
175	150	190	50	60	90	1 000 $ - 2 999 $	486
160	125	60	55	70	20	3 000 $ - 4 999 $	487
75	85	105	75	50	140	5 000 $ - 6 999 $	488
155	135	200	115	110	80	7 000 $ - 9 999 $	489
145	85	100	95	85	65	10 000 $ - 11 999 $	490
290	340	200	220	105	120	12 000 $ - 14 999 $	491
150	215	250	200	170	155	15 000 $ - 19 999 $	492
155	245	285	165	150	110	20 000 $ - 24 999 $	493
160	160	185	215	140	135	25 000 $ - 29 999 $	494
150	190	245	185	95	95	30 000 $ - 34 999 $	495
125	225	115	65	90	65	35 000 $ - 39 999 $	496
110	125	115	115	75	15	40 000 $ - 44 999 $	497
65	110	120	50	45	35	45 000 $ - 49 999 $	498
95	90	155	60	90	25	50 000 $ - 59 999 $	499
55	185	175	110	90	40	60 000 $ et plus	500
20,777	25,079	25,722	25,531	25,759	19,309	Revenu moyen $ (46)	501
14,280	20,329	20,724	20,941	20,355	15,691	Revenu médian $ (46)	502
878	857	942	1,085	1,570	987	Erreur type de revenu moyen $ (46)	503
						selon la composition du revenu total	
100.0	100.0	100.0	100.0	100.0	100.0	Total - Composition du revenu en 2000 % (47)	504
82.7	81.5	73.9	79.5	68.6	79.4	Revenu d'emploi %	505
11.2	9.8	12.5	10.1	11.3	13.0	Transferts gouvernementaux %	506
6.0	8.6	13.8	10.4	20.2	7.7	Autre %	507
						Population de 15 ans et plus ayant un revenu d'emploi en 2000 selon le sexe et le travail	
2,890	3,725	3,410	2,780	2,110	1,865	Les deux sexes ayant un revenu d'emploi (48)	508
32,015	33,699	34,547	31,525	34,302	27,341	Revenu moyen d'emploi $	509
1,211	1,216	1,796	1,056	3,809	1,120	Erreur type de revenu moyen d'emploi $	510
1,690	2,150	1,915	1,660	1,210	1,095	Ayant travaillé toute l'année à plein temps (49)	511
41,604	43,894	47,247	42,130	39,362	35,086	Revenu moyen d'emploi $	512
1,765	1,817	2,869	1,387	1,614	1,517	Erreur type de revenu moyen d'emploi $	513
						Ayant travaillé une partie de l'année ou	
1,115	1,425	1,435	1,025	840	695	à temps partiel (50)	514
18,955	20,059	18,783	15,953	27,371	16,625	Revenu moyen d'emploi $	515
1,281	1,114	1,208	945	9,369	1,225	Erreur type de revenu moyen d'emploi $	516
1,635	1,865	1,755	1,415	1,170	1,060	Hommes ayant un revenu d'emploi (48)	517
36,828	40,130	41,532	35,945	40,576	30,362	Revenu moyen d'emploi $	518
1,890	2,185	3,297	1,624	6,724	1,697	Erreur type de revenu moyen d'emploi $	519
1,040	1,130	1,130	915	710	675	Ayant travaillé toute l'année à plein temps (49)	520
45,801	52,538	52,587	46,602	43,247	38,328	Revenu moyen d'emploi $	521
2,705	3,157	4,770	1,914	2,072	2,139	Erreur type de revenu moyen d'emploi $	522
						Ayant travaillé une partie de l'année ou	
560	675	580	440	425	360	à temps partiel (50)	523
21,556	20,933	22,448	16,598	35,570	15,485	Revenu moyen d'emploi $	524
1,746	1,870	2,132	1,666	18,058	1,762	Erreur type de revenu moyen d'emploi $	525

Table 1. Selected Characteristics for Census Tracts, 2001 Census – 100% Data and 20% Sample Data

No.	Characteristics	Toronto 0520.06 A	Toronto 0521.01 ◆	Toronto 0521.02 ◆	Toronto 0521.03	Toronto 0521.04	Toronto 0521.05 ◆
	2000 INCOME CHARACTERISTICS						
	Population 15 years and over with employment income in 2000 by sex and work activity – concluded						
526	Females with employment income (48)	1,655	1,445	1,150	1,535	1,920	1,195
527	Average employment income $	32,132	25,938	24,603	21,323	24,710	26,585
528	Standard error of average employment income $	1,180	1,066	1,042	864	851	1,133
529	Worked full year, full time (49)	935	755	610	795	990	690
530	Average employment income $	41,346	35,131	32,870	29,701	32,879	35,374
531	Standard error of average employment income $	1,319	1,457	1,322	1,135	921	1,426
532	Worked part year or part time (50)	650	620	460	695	885	475
533	Average employment income $	21,677	15,158	16,538	12,566	16,312	14,856
534	Standard error of average employment income $	1,861	1,100	1,292	930	1,264	1,155
	Census families by structure and family income groups in 2000						
535	Total - All census families	1,735	1,560	1,060	1,415	1,885	1,075
536	Under $10,000	115	95	10	85	70	40
537	$ 10,000 - $19,999	85	85	30	75	90	10
538	$ 20,000 - $29,999	175	165	65	140	145	100
539	$ 30,000 - $39,999	200	145	65	125	255	135
540	$ 40,000 - $49,999	190	145	80	175	195	190
541	$ 50,000 - $59,999	170	200	125	165	245	140
542	$ 60,000 - $69,999	135	235	105	155	155	120
543	$ 70,000 - $79,999	165	145	105	145	190	125
544	$ 80,000 - $89,999	140	60	110	125	170	85
545	$ 90,000 - $99,999	75	100	75	40	75	20
546	$100,000 and over	280	190	295	175	305	120
547	Average family income $	62,425	58,761	83,689	60,348	65,848	60,150
548	Median family income $	55,600	57,204	72,172	57,294	57,432	54,277
549	Standard error of average family income $	2,124	1,879	4,409	2,014	1,996	2,032
550	Total - All couple census families (51)	1,485	1,305	945	1,180	1,595	860
551	Under $10,000	105	80	-	70	45	30
552	$ 10,000 - $19,999	55	65	20	50	45	-
553	$ 20,000 - $29,999	140	130	60	80	85	75
554	$ 30,000 - $39,999	180	120	45	105	190	95
555	$ 40,000 - $49,999	140	95	75	155	155	145
556	$ 50,000 - $59,999	140	170	120	130	215	100
557	$ 60,000 - $69,999	120	205	85	140	140	90
558	$ 70,000 - $79,999	135	120	85	135	180	105
559	$ 80,000 - $89,999	125	55	110	110	170	80
560	$ 90,000 - $99,999	70	85	65	35	65	20
561	$100,000 and over	270	180	285	170	300	110
562	Average family income $	65,219	60,574	86,728	63,800	70,749	63,522
563	Median family income $	59,092	59,861	75,815	60,762	63,080	57,989
564	Standard error of average family income $	2,388	2,120	4,863	2,235	2,227	2,322
	Incidence of low income in 2000						
565	Total - Economic families	1,710	1,535	1,045	1,300	1,815	1,030
566	Low income	315	270	70	215	215	80
567	Incidence of low income in 2000 % (52)	18.4	17.8	6.7	16.4	11.9	7.9
568	Total - Unattached individuals 15 years and over	1,015	910	145	375	520	670
569	Low income	225	200	15	130	125	220
570	Incidence of low income in 2000 % (52)	22.1	21.8	9.8	34.5	23.7	33.0
571	Total - Population in private households	6,260	5,350	3,810	5,460	6,795	3,875
572	Low income	1,320	1,135	280	955	865	490
573	Incidence of low income in 2000 % (52)	21.1	21.2	7.3	17.5	12.8	12.6
	Private households by household income groups in 2000						
574	Total - All private households	2,540	2,340	1,150	1,515	2,130	1,645
575	Under $10,000	165	140	-	90	55	60
576	$ 10,000 - $19,999	150	175	30	65	115	150
577	$ 20,000 - $29,999	255	245	80	90	105	180
578	$ 30,000 - $39,999	310	300	90	150	285	240
579	$ 40,000 - $49,999	270	220	60	185	235	275
580	$ 50,000 - $59,999	260	270	115	170	285	185
581	$ 60,000 - $69,999	230	290	105	190	195	150
582	$ 70,000 - $79,999	240	200	115	150	195	150
583	$ 80,000 - $89,999	180	135	105	110	185	85
584	$ 90,000 - $99,999	85	125	75	45	100	35
585	$100,000 and over	390	255	375	260	375	140
586	Average household income $	61,420	56,184	87,586	65,136	68,123	52,285
587	Median household income $	54,959	54,185	75,541	60,248	59,791	47,216
588	Standard error of average household income $	1,810	1,517	4,390	2,082	1,918	1,705

Tableau 1. Certaines caractéristiques des secteurs de recensement, recensement de 2001 – Données intégrales et données-échantillon (20 %)

Toronto 0521.06 ◆	Toronto 0522 ◆	Toronto 0523 ◆	Toronto 0524.01 ◆◇	Toronto 0524.02 ◆	Toronto 0525.01 ◆	Caractéristiques	N°
						CARACTÉRISTIQUES DU REVENU DE 2000	
						Population de 15 ans et plus ayant un revenu d'emploi en 2000 selon le sexe et le travail – fin	
1,250	1,855	1,650	1,360	940	800	Femmes ayant un revenu d'emploi (48)	526
25,723	27,241	27,147	26,932	26,494	23,349	Revenu moyen d'emploi $	527
1,247	992	1,247	1,298	1,856	1,321	Erreur type de revenu moyen d'emploi $	528
645	1,025	780	745	500	420	Ayant travaillé toute l'année à plein temps (49)	529
34,861	34,347	39,524	36,634	33,845	29,843	Revenu moyen d'emploi $	530
1,438	1,331	1,678	1,916	2,477	1,858	Erreur type de revenu moyen d'emploi $	531
555	745	855	585	410	335	Ayant travaillé une partie de l'année ou à temps partiel (50)	532
16,325	19,266	16,297	15,467	18,826	17,845	Revenu moyen d'emploi $	533
1,850	1,296	1,399	1,108	2,683	1,695	Erreur type de revenu moyen d'emploi $	534
						Familles de recensement selon la structure et les tranches de revenu de la famille en 2000	
1,440	1,875	1,755	1,395	1,115	1,040	Total - Toutes les familles de recensement	535
100	90	70	45	35	85	Moins de 10 000 $	536
85	25	80	60	45	30	10 000 $ - 19 999 $	537
205	165	155	150	65	150	20 000 $ - 29 999 $	538
175	155	225	100	100	190	30 000 $ - 39 999 $	539
175	195	195	105	230	165	40 000 $ - 49 999 $	540
205	190	140	190	125	95	50 000 $ - 59 999 $	541
160	230	220	155	115	60	60 000 $ - 69 999 $	542
135	155	125	85	125	75	70 000 $ - 79 999 $	543
65	75	130	120	80	50	80 000 $ - 89 999 $	544
35	125	35	100	30	50	90 000 $ - 99 999 $	545
100	465	380	290	165	90	100 000 $ et plus	546
50,029	73,157	70,399	69,695	74,070	52,914	Revenu moyen des familles $	547
49,484	65,499	60,262	62,508	55,936	42,577	Revenu médian des familles $	548
1,654	2,249	3,549	2,449	9,067	2,752	Erreur type de revenu moyen des familles $	549
1,230	1,550	1,465	1,080	950	830	Total - Toutes les familles de recensement comptant un couple (51)	550
85	55	45	30	25	75	Moins de 10 000 $	551
70	-	55	15	40	10	10 000 $ - 19 999 $	552
170	135	95	85	40	110	20 000 $ - 29 999 $	553
145	125	185	70	70	125	30 000 $ - 39 999 $	554
140	150	150	60	190	135	40 000 $ - 49 999 $	555
170	145	130	180	115	80	50 000 $ - 59 999 $	556
150	205	190	120	90	60	60 000 $ - 69 999 $	557
125	110	115	55	120	65	70 000 $ - 79 999 $	558
55	65	120	115	75	40	80 000 $ - 89 999 $	559
30	115	30	80	30	50	90 000 $ - 99 999 $	560
90	445	350	265	155	90	100 000 $ et plus	561
51,065	77,678	74,734	75,617	72,653	56,709	Revenu moyen des familles $	562
50,002	66,519	62,994	68,705	59,542	47,220	Revenu médian des familles $	563
1,802	2,515	4,060	2,774	5,956	3,308	Erreur type de revenu moyen des familles $	564
						Fréquence des unités à faible revenu en 2000	
1,430	1,755	1,665	1,290	1,095	965	Total - Familles économiques	565
325	150	195	185	110	205	Faible revenu	566
22.7	8.8	11.6	14.5	9.9	21.1	Fréquence des unités à faible revenu en 2000 % (52)	567
1,025	340	940	375	545	220	Total - Personnes hors famille économique de 15 ans et plus	568
385	135	230	175	145	55	Faible revenu	569
37.2	40.2	24.9	45.9	26.6	26.7	Fréquence des unités à faible revenu en 2000 % (52)	570
5,305	6,285	6,015	4,845	3,775	3,730	Total - Population dans les ménages privés	571
1,405	590	895	785	445	890	Faible revenu	572
26.5	9.3	14.9	16.2	11.8	23.8	Fréquence des unités à faible revenu en 2000 % (52)	573
						Ménages privés selon les tranches de revenu du ménage en 2000	
2,320	2,025	2,485	1,580	1,580	1,110	Total - Tous les ménages privés	574
180	90	75	50	50	70	Moins de 10 000 $	575
295	100	230	135	110	45	10 000 $ - 19 999 $	576
280	190	295	125	155	115	20 000 $ - 29 999 $	577
310	190	310	125	215	195	30 000 $ - 39 999 $	578
270	160	275	155	270	185	40 000 $ - 49 999 $	579
305	160	200	160	145	115	50 000 $ - 59 999 $	580
200	245	275	165	130	60	60 000 $ - 69 999 $	581
190	150	155	75	120	65	70 000 $ - 79 999 $	582
80	65	165	125	90	55	80 000 $ - 89 999 $	583
35	125	60	115	35	65	90 000 $ - 99 999 $	584
170	550	435	355	245	140	100 000 $ et plus	585
47,995	75,914	64,192	69,743	66,905	57,706	Revenu moyen des ménages $	586
44,358	65,462	53,763	62,620	48,769	47,178	Revenu médian des ménages $	587
1,713	2,778	2,696	2,429	6,454	2,855	Erreur type de revenu moyen des ménages $	588

Table 1. Selected Characteristics for Census Tracts, 2001 Census – 100% Data and 20% Sample Data

No.	Characteristics	Toronto 0525.02 ◆	Toronto 0526.01	Toronto 0526.02 ◆◇	Toronto 0527.01	Toronto 0527.02	Toronto 0527.03
	POPULATION CHARACTERISTICS						
1	**Population, 1996 (1)**	**4,249**	**6,493**	**3,089**	**4,250**	**5,835**	**5,460**
2	**Population, 2001 (2)**	**4,273**	**6,532**	**3,106**	**4,212**	**5,746**	**5,339**
3	Population percentage change, 1996-2001	0.6	0.6	0.6	-0.9	-1.5	-2.2
4	Land area in square kilometres, 2001	1.81	0.76	0.80	2.46	1.16	1.30
5	**Total population - 100% Data (3)**	**4,270**	**6,535**	**3,105**	**4,215**	**5,745**	**5,340**
	by sex and age groups						
6	Male	2,115	3,270	1,600	2,070	2,750	2,675
7	0-4 years	135	290	105	105	130	135
8	5-9 years	135	270	110	130	160	135
9	10-14 years	115	245	105	155	185	165
10	15-19 years	140	245	95	180	205	215
11	20-24 years	135	185	110	180	210	220
12	25-29 years	145	190	125	165	160	225
13	30-34 years	180	285	120	155	170	250
14	35-39 years	225	365	160	170	210	210
15	40-44 years	170	350	130	155	210	205
16	45-49 years	140	220	105	175	220	210
17	50-54 years	115	155	110	165	235	190
18	55-59 years	125	110	95	110	170	175
19	60-64 years	95	115	75	90	130	125
20	65-69 years	110	100	60	55	120	95
21	70-74 years	70	70	45	55	85	50
22	75-79 years	40	50	30	20	55	35
23	80-84 years	30	20	10	5	40	15
24	85 years and over	5	5	-	5	55	10
25	Female	2,160	3,260	1,505	2,140	2,995	2,665
26	0-4 years	135	270	95	105	115	130
27	5-9 years	130	255	70	130	145	140
28	10-14 years	120	220	90	125	190	165
29	15-19 years	115	185	100	190	215	210
30	20-24 years	120	210	110	190	210	220
31	25-29 years	165	255	115	155	175	230
32	30-34 years	180	280	150	165	175	205
33	35-39 years	185	320	130	165	190	200
34	40-44 years	180	315	135	195	240	230
35	45-49 years	125	220	100	200	255	240
36	50-54 years	155	155	115	150	240	210
37	55-59 years	130	145	90	115	165	155
38	60-64 years	110	130	65	80	130	120
39	65-69 years	95	120	55	75	120	85
40	70-74 years	90	80	35	45	90	60
41	75-79 years	65	60	30	20	100	45
42	80-84 years	35	25	10	10	100	15
43	85 years and over	25	15	10	20	145	10
44	**Total population 15 years and over**	**3,500**	**4,980**	**2,530**	**3,460**	**4,820**	**4,460**
	by legal marital status						
45	Never married (single)	1,000	1,515	815	1,190	1,405	1,505
46	Legally married (and not separated)	1,935	2,750	1,310	1,925	2,680	2,460
47	Separated, but still legally married	120	170	115	85	105	130
48	Divorced	220	315	200	140	205	195
49	Widowed	225	235	90	115	435	170
	by common-law status						
50	Not in a common-law relationship	3,360	4,725	2,375	3,365	4,675	4,295
51	In a common-law relationship	140	250	155	100	150	170
52	**Total population - 20% Sample Data (4)**	**4,275**	**6,535**	**3,105**	**4,205**	**5,475**	**5,340**
	by mother tongue						
53	Single responses	4,175	6,405	3,070	4,110	5,315	5,205
54	English	1,675	2,395	1,415	1,565	2,460	2,110
55	French	30	100	50	20	50	35
56	Non-official languages (5)	2,470	3,910	1,600	2,535	2,805	3,055
57	Italian	165	35	75	100	325	250
58	Chinese, n.o.s.	40	65	20	190	290	60
59	Cantonese	10	10	-	195	125	75
60	Portuguese	165	110	35	130	205	440
61	Punjabi	185	165	-	370	50	220
62	Other languages (6)	1,920	3,525	1,470	1,540	1,820	2,005
63	Multiple responses	95	130	35	90	160	140
64	English and French	-	10	10	-	-	-
65	English and non-official language	100	110	25	95	155	140
66	French and non-official language	-	10	-	-	-	-
67	English, French and non-official language	-	-	-	-	-	-

See reference material at the end of the publication. – Voir les documents de référence à la fin de la publication.

Tableau 1. Certaines caractéristiques des secteurs de recensement, recensement de 2001 – Données intégrales et données-échantillon (20 %)

Toronto 0527.04	Toronto 0527.05	Toronto 0527.06 ◇	Toronto 0527.07	Toronto 0527.08	Toronto 0527.09	Caractéristiques	Nº
						CARACTÉRISTIQUES DE LA POPULATION	
6,377	**5,634**	**4,681**	**5,578**	**5,003**	**3,759**	**Population, 1996 (1)**	1
6,212	**5,682**	**4,514**	**5,289**	**4,872**	**3,781**	**Population, 2001 (2)**	2
-2.6	0.9	-3.6	-5.2	-2.6	0.6	Variation en pourcentage de la population, 1996-2001	3
1.67	1.65	1.07	1.32	1.21	1.90	Superficie des terres en kilomètres carrés, 2001	4
6,210	**5,685**	**4,515**	**5,290**	**4,875**	**3,785**	**Population totale – Données intégrales (3)**	5
						selon le sexe et les groupes d'âge	
3,060	2,785	2,130	2,545	2,435	1,865	Sexe masculin	6
145	135	110	145	120	120	0-4 ans	7
185	160	120	180	165	140	5-9 ans	8
210	205	180	195	210	175	10-14 ans	9
240	270	185	190	220	155	15-19 ans	10
235	230	175	225	205	160	20-24 ans	11
225	220	120	195	175	95	25-29 ans	12
235	160	135	185	140	105	30-34 ans	13
250	150	150	230	190	150	35-39 ans	14
245	210	165	200	195	160	40-44 ans	15
240	215	195	205	215	170	45-49 ans	16
240	250	180	175	240	170	50-54 ans	17
225	195	120	120	130	115	55-59 ans	18
165	170	110	115	90	55	60-64 ans	19
100	100	65	75	60	40	65-69 ans	20
65	55	50	45	35	35	70-74 ans	21
40	35	40	40	10	25	75-79 ans	22
15	15	20	15	10	15	80-84 ans	23
10	15	10	10	10	5	85 ans et plus	24
3,150	2,900	2,380	2,745	2,435	1,920	Sexe féminin	25
165	110	95	130	140	90	0-4 ans	26
190	160	165	200	170	140	5-9 ans	27
190	195	150	180	185	140	10-14 ans	28
225	250	180	250	205	170	15-19 ans	29
220	245	200	195	225	145	20-24 ans	30
210	190	125	200	130	100	25-29 ans	31
220	190	125	220	140	120	30-34 ans	32
250	180	185	230	195	160	35-39 ans	33
280	240	190	235	235	205	40-44 ans	34
310	280	235	225	220	190	45-49 ans	35
295	275	200	225	210	150	50-54 ans	36
225	190	130	155	130	100	55-59 ans	37
135	125	100	105	75	45	60-64 ans	38
90	95	60	75	70	60	65-69 ans	39
60	65	80	55	40	40	70-74 ans	40
60	60	60	45	35	25	75-79 ans	41
20	15	65	20	20	20	80-84 ans	42
20	25	30	15	10	10	85 ans et plus	43
5,130	**4,720**	**3,690**	**4,265**	**3,880**	**2,980**	**Population totale de 15 ans et plus**	44
						selon l'état matrimonial légal	
1,655	1,660	1,175	1,420	1,265	930	Célibataire (jamais marié(e))	45
2,765	2,570	2,030	2,305	2,305	1,770	Légalement marié(e) (et non séparé(e))	46
165	110	85	130	60	60	Séparé(e), mais toujours légalement marié(e)	47
350	170	155	240	105	115	Divorcé(e)	48
190	205	245	175	140	105	Veuf ou veuve	49
						selon l'union libre	
4,895	4,600	3,630	4,105	3,830	2,910	Ne vivant pas en union libre	50
235	120	55	165	55	70	Vivant en union libre	51
6,210	**5,680**	**4,515**	**5,290**	**4,870**	**3,775**	**Population totale – Données-échantillon (20 %) (4)**	52
						selon la langue maternelle	
6,090	5,515	4,250	5,140	4,695	3,725	Réponses uniques	53
3,290	2,610	1,955	2,510	2,225	2,175	Anglais	54
50	55	90	40	80	120	Français	55
2,745	2,845	2,210	2,580	2,390	1,425	Langues non officielles (5)	56
185	570	205	370	75	60	Italien	57
170	225	185	45	195	175	Chinois, n.d.a.	58
150	180	105	-	170	120	Cantonais	59
120	340	225	160	230	70	Portugais	60
30	10	70	55	270	15	Pendjabi	61
2,095	1,520	1,420	1,950	1,445	985	Autres langues (6)	62
125	165	260	150	170	50	Réponses multiples	63
10	-	-	10	-	-	Anglais et français	64
110	165	255	140	170	45	Anglais et langue non officielle	65
-	-	-	-	-	-	Français et langue non officielle	66
10	-	-	-	-	-	Anglais, français et langue non officielle	67

See reference material at the end of the publication. – Voir les documents de référence à la fin de la publication.

Table 1. Selected Characteristics for Census Tracts, 2001 Census – 100% Data and 20% Sample Data

No.	Characteristics	Toronto 0525.02 ◆	Toronto 0526.01	Toronto 0526.02 ◆◇	Toronto 0527.01	Toronto 0527.02	Toronto 0527.03
	POPULATION CHARACTERISTICS						
	by home language						
68	Single responses	2,890	4,465	2,270	2,825	3,790	3,160
69	English	1,805	2,555	1,635	1,895	2,955	2,290
70	French	-	25	-	-	-	-
71	Non-official languages (5)	1,080	1,885	640	935	825	875
72	Cantonese	10	10	-	140	50	25
73	Chinese, n.o.s.	20	45	20	155	155	50
74	Italian	60	-	-	10	70	100
75	Punjabi	105	105	-	110	-	35
76	Portuguese	50	25	20	25	10	105
77	Other languages (6)	840	1,710	600	500	540	555
78	Multiple responses	1,385	2,065	835	1,375	1,685	2,175
79	English and French	65	50	30	20	25	35
80	English and non-official language	1,325	1,975	800	1,335	1,630	2,140
81	French and non-official language	-	10	-	-	10	-
82	English, French and non-official language	-	30	-	25	15	-
	by knowledge of official languages						
83	English only	3,725	5,645	2,785	3,780	4,820	4,760
84	French only	-	10	-	-	10	-
85	English and French	225	395	220	215	460	375
86	Neither English nor French	325	480	100	215	190	195
	by knowledge of non-official languages (5) (7)						
87	Italian	175	65	80	115	490	335
88	Cantonese	10	20	-	235	115	95
89	Chinese, n.o.s.	40	135	20	255	320	80
90	Spanish	205	200	85	75	100	200
91	Portuguese	175	130	45	165	260	520
92	Punjabi	225	310	-	435	60	385
93	Tagalog (Pilipino)	120	95	135	265	90	250
	by first official language spoken						
94	English	3,860	5,930	2,875	3,910	5,100	5,020
95	French	35	95	45	20	40	40
96	English and French	65	55	85	60	140	90
97	Neither English nor French	315	450	105	215	190	185
98	Official language minority - (number) (8)	65	120	90	50	115	85
99	Official language minority - (percentage) (8)	1.5	1.8	2.9	1.2	2.1	1.6
	by ethnic origin (9)						
100	Canadian	615	870	395	215	670	465
101	English	520	645	450	190	625	435
102	Scottish	335	320	245	185	335	210
103	Irish	230	310	225	125	475	285
104	Chinese	85	290	35	715	625	300
105	Italian	280	145	185	190	735	535
106	East Indian	485	635	110	650	275	730
107	French	145	220	225	70	170	170
108	German	205	200	150	35	245	120
109	Portuguese	185	300	45	235	355	660
110	Polish	495	515	430	160	445	425
111	Jewish	-	30	10	10	-	85
112	Jamaican	-	55	50	215	45	135
113	Filipino	155	170	205	415	100	420
114	Ukrainian	170	180	60	45	205	140
	by Aboriginal identity						
115	Total Aboriginal identity population (10)	15	30	20	-	25	-
116	Total non-Aboriginal population	4,260	6,505	3,090	4,205	5,450	5,335
	by Aboriginal origin						
117	Total Aboriginal origins population (11)	-	65	40	10	70	10
118	Total non-Aboriginal population	4,265	6,470	3,070	4,200	5,405	5,335
	by Registered Indian status						
119	Registered Indian (12)	-	15	10	-	10	-
120	Not a Registered Indian	4,275	6,515	3,100	4,205	5,465	5,340

Tableau 1. Certaines caractéristiques des secteurs de recensement, recensement de 2001 – Données intégrales et données-échantillon (20 %)

Toronto 0527.04	Toronto 0527.05	Toronto 0527.06 ◇	Toronto 0527.07	Toronto 0527.08	Toronto 0527.09	Caractéristiques	N°
						CARACTÉRISTIQUES DE LA POPULATION	
						selon la langue parlée à la maison	
4,730	3,510	2,985	3,520	3,365	2,770	Réponses uniques	68
3,800	2,805	2,380	2,720	2,540	2,315	Anglais	69
10	-	10	15	45	40	Français	70
915	700	590	790	780	415	Langues non officielles (5)	71
50	70	35	-	130	45	Cantonais	72
50	60	85	30	75	85	Chinois, n.d.a.	73
20	95	15	130	10	-	Italien	74
-	-	-	-	105	-	Pendjabi	75
45	55	30	45	30	20	Portugais	76
745	415	420	575	430	260	Autres langues (6)	77
1,480	2,175	1,530	1,765	1,505	1,005	Réponses multiples	78
40	30	55	30	35	105	Anglais et français	79
1,425	2,125	1,475	1,715	1,445	890	Anglais et langue non officielle	80
10	-	10	-	10	-	Français et langue non officielle	81
15	15	-	20	20	15	Anglais, français et langue non officielle	82
						selon la connaissance des langues officielles	
5,600	5,195	4,045	4,755	4,285	3,310	Anglais seulement	83
10	-	-	10	-	15	Français seulement	84
475	325	345	330	420	390	Anglais et français	85
135	165	125	195	165	75	Ni l'anglais ni le français	86
						selon la connaissance des langues non officielles (5) (7)	
345	750	270	515	105	80	Italien	87
170	190	165	-	205	110	Cantonais	88
185	245	155	55	180	170	Chinois, n.d.a.	89
95	145	60	195	130	90	Espagnol	90
130	520	220	265	250	80	Portugais	91
45	30	110	135	340	55	Pendjabi	92
35	15	305	305	400	230	Tagalog (pilipino)	93
						selon la première langue officielle parlée	
5,975	5,430	4,290	5,000	4,600	3,530	Anglais	94
65	40	65	45	75	120	Français	95
45	50	45	75	35	50	Anglais et français	96
130	160	120	165	165	75	Ni l'anglais ni le français	97
85	65	85	85	90	150	Minorité de langue officielle - (nombre) (8)	98
1.4	1.1	1.9	1.6	1.8	4.0	Minorité de langue officielle - (pourcentage) (8)	99
						selon l'origine ethnique (9)	
1,260	625	355	585	640	505	Canadien	100
840	470	405	370	350	620	Anglais	101
600	285	260	540	220	410	Écossais	102
495	380	290	465	160	410	Irlandais	103
440	530	390	75	475	470	Chinois	104
645	1,210	460	620	170	305	Italien	105
385	255	425	270	995	450	Indien de l'Inde	106
245	165	265	245	110	225	Français	107
270	110	110	140	85	140	Allemand	108
190	600	380	300	395	165	Portugais	109
780	390	610	675	250	155	Polonais	110
25	-	-	-	-	35	Juif	111
70	140	70	375	185	235	Jamaïquain	112
65	15	480	385	520	275	Philippin	113
370	350	160	170	85	55	Ukrainien	114
						selon l'identité autochtone	
45	10	15	-	-	10	Total de la population ayant une identité autochtone (10)	115
6,165	5,675	4,505	5,285	4,865	3,770	Total de la population non autochtone	116
						selon l'origine autochtone	
90	55	45	55	20	35	Total de la population ayant une origine autochtone (11)	117
6,125	5,630	4,470	5,235	4,855	3,740	Total de la population non autochtone	118
						selon le statut d'Indien inscrit	
10	-	10	-	-	10	Oui, Indien inscrit (12)	119
6,205	5,680	4,510	5,285	4,870	3,770	Non, pas un Indien inscrit	120

Table 1. Selected Characteristics for Census Tracts, 2001 Census – 100% Data and 20% Sample Data

No.	Characteristics	Toronto 0525.02 ◆	Toronto 0526.01	Toronto 0526.02 ◆◇	Toronto 0527.01	Toronto 0527.02	Toronto 0527.03
	POPULATION CHARACTERISTICS						
	by visible minority groups						
121	Total visible minority population	1,460	3,485	730	2,835	1,830	2,525
122	Chinese	70	195	35	625	610	200
123	South Asian	590	2,045	195	990	370	950
124	Black	70	195	95	305	180	195
125	Filipino	135	165	150	385	105	455
126	Latin American	145	100	60	35	70	100
127	Southeast Asian	225	595	110	70	60	150
128	Arab	35	10	-	150	285	285
129	West Asian	10	-	40	15	-	100
130	Korean	75	35	25	95	-	30
131	Japanese	-	10	-	25	30	-
132	Visible minority, n.i.e. (13)	65	55	15	65	90	60
133	Multiple visible minorities (14)	30	90	10	65	35	10
	by citizenship						
134	Canadian citizenship (15)	3,230	5,075	2,375	3,655	4,845	4,445
135	Citizenship other than Canadian	1,045	1,455	730	550	630	890
	by place of birth of respondent						
136	Non-immigrant population	1,775	2,560	1,400	1,660	2,690	2,045
137	Born in province of residence	1,485	2,180	1,105	1,525	2,465	1,885
138	Immigrant population (16)	2,445	3,810	1,675	2,475	2,715	3,255
139	United States	15	20	10	30	35	25
140	Central and South America	165	125	100	100	60	135
141	Caribbean and Bermuda	70	75	110	205	170	145
142	United Kingdom	135	120	75	25	95	100
143	Other Europe (17)	1,115	1,100	845	415	1,255	1,145
144	Africa	10	125	55	110	150	170
145	Asia and the Middle East	950	2,240	490	1,580	965	1,515
146	Oceania and other (18)	-	-	-	-	-	20
147	Non-permanent residents (19)	55	160	25	70	70	40
148	**Total immigrant population**	**2,445**	**3,805**	**1,680**	**2,470**	**2,715**	**3,255**
	by period of immigration						
149	Before 1961	235	165	140	30	325	180
150	1961-1970	330	175	155	315	535	505
151	1971-1980	265	380	150	675	570	575
152	1981-1990	355	725	190	565	495	820
153	1991-2001 (20)	1,260	2,365	1,045	890	785	1,180
154	1991-1995	425	1,030	335	515	355	350
155	1996-2001 (20)	840	1,335	710	380	435	825
	by age at immigration						
156	0-4 years	190	235	160	185	250	260
157	5-19 years	660	995	450	580	660	955
158	20 years and over	1,590	2,580	1,075	1,710	1,805	2,040
159	**Total population**	**4,270**	**6,530**	**3,110**	**4,205**	**5,475**	**5,335**
	by religion						
160	Catholic (21)	1,720	2,040	1,305	1,675	2,945	2,840
161	Protestant	830	875	710	570	935	475
162	Christian Orthodox	340	355	185	135	320	170
163	Christian, n.i.e. (22)	105	155	80	165	105	175
164	Muslim	280	660	310	355	200	660
165	Jewish	-	10	-	10	-	20
166	Buddhist	150	410	85	65	115	175
167	Hindu	265	1,160	100	255	250	220
168	Sikh	140	120	-	365	25	175
169	Eastern religions (23)	30	25	-	30	10	10
170	Other religions (24)	-	-	-	10	-	40
171	No religious affiliation (25)	400	710	330	580	575	385
172	**Total population 15 years and over**	**3,490**	**4,965**	**2,515**	**3,470**	**4,555**	**4,460**
	by generation status						
173	1st generation (26)	2,240	3,565	1,500	2,430	2,630	3,015
174	2nd generation (27)	605	615	360	740	1,210	860
175	3rd generation and over (28)	645	780	660	305	710	585
176	**Total population 1 year and over (29)**	**4,200**	**6,415**	**3,075**	**4,155**	**5,445**	**5,305**
	by place of residence 1 year ago (mobility)						
177	Non-movers	3,240	5,230	2,345	3,775	4,865	4,410
178	Movers	960	1,180	735	385	575	890
179	Non-migrants	445	715	385	200	330	400
180	Migrants	515	465	350	185	245	495
181	Internal migrants	195	280	265	95	140	320
182	Intraprovincial migrants	175	245	215	85	130	270
183	Interprovincial migrants	25	40	55	15	10	50
184	External migrants	315	185	90	85	110	175

Tableau 1. Certaines caractéristiques des secteurs de recensement, recensement de 2001 – Données intégrales et données-échantillon (20 %)

Toronto 0527.04	Toronto 0527.05	Toronto 0527.06 ◇	Toronto 0527.07	Toronto 0527.08	Toronto 0527.09	Caractéristiques	N°
						CARACTÉRISTIQUES DE LA POPULATION	
						selon les groupes de minorités visibles	
1,450	1,450	1,740	1,910	2,825	1,960	Total de la population des minorités visibles	121
495	465	390	55	430	360	Chinois	122
455	435	505	475	1,010	720	Sud-Asiatique	123
150	250	145	565	300	330	Noir	124
65	15	425	360	525	260	Philippin	125
35	35	15	95	80	35	Latino-Américain	126
15	20	105	125	155	70	Asiatique du Sud-Est	127
35	65	-	70	10	65	Arabe	128
15	20	-	25	20	-	Asiatique occidental	129
130	40	35	15	80	30	Coréen	130
-	-	40	10	10	-	Japonais	131
40	35	55	90	170	50	Minorité visible, n.i.a. (13)	132
20	70	15	25	50	30	Minorités visibles multiples (14)	133
						selon la citoyenneté	
5,465	5,215	4,145	4,445	4,435	3,460	Citoyenneté canadienne (15)	134
750	465	365	850	430	320	Citoyenneté autre que canadienne	135
						selon le lieu de naissance du répondant	
3,345	2,950	2,075	2,305	2,165	1,915	Population non immigrante	136
2,880	2,815	1,860	2,080	1,975	1,705	Née dans la province de résidence	137
2,800	2,725	2,420	2,895	2,695	1,820	Population immigrante (16)	138
35	10	35	30	15	25	États-Unis	139
55	100	120	165	135	120	Amérique centrale et du Sud	140
100	125	60	355	260	150	Caraïbes et Bermudes	141
140	105	110	210	80	105	Royaume-Uni	142
1,440	1,465	1,035	1,255	730	305	Autre Europe (17)	143
90	100	90	80	140	200	Afrique	144
940	820	960	800	1,340	910	Asie et Moyen-Orient	145
10	-	10	-	-	-	Océanie et autre (18)	146
60	-	20	90	20	45	Résidents non permanents (19)	147
2,800	**2,725**	**2,420**	**2,900**	**2,690**	**1,820**	**Population immigrante totale**	148
						selon la période d'immigration	
415	405	265	245	140	100	Avant 1961	149
450	660	305	585	285	185	1961-1970	150
360	605	545	495	695	360	1971-1980	151
510	435	790	490	735	395	1981-1990	152
1,070	615	515	1,085	835	775	1991-2001 (20)	153
450	330	335	630	670	480	1991-1995	154
620	290	180	455	170	295	1996-2001 (20)	155
						selon l'âge à l'immigration	
175	230	190	225	220	180	0-4 ans	156
965	895	625	880	660	530	5-19 ans	157
1,665	1,605	1,595	1,790	1,810	1,115	20 ans et plus	158
6,210	**5,680**	**4,515**	**5,290**	**4,870**	**3,780**	**Population totale**	159
						selon la religion	
3,200	3,625	2,660	2,930	2,290	1,700	Catholique (21)	160
1,305	665	710	950	695	775	Protestante	161
420	360	180	225	210	140	Orthodoxe chrétienne	162
90	90	125	220	215	70	Chrétiennes, n.i.a. (22)	163
180	300	105	245	265	345	Musulmane	164
20	-	-	-	-	35	Juive	165
105	125	70	125	35	105	Bouddhiste	166
145	150	185	155	340	165	Hindoue	167
30	-	55	50	265	15	Sikh	168
-	-	-	-	-	-	Religions orientales (23)	169
-	10	-	-	-	-	Autres religions (24)	170
705	345	425	390	555	435	Aucune appartenance religieuse (25)	171
5,130	**4,715**	**3,695**	**4,270**	**3,865**	**2,925**	**Population totale de 15 ans et plus**	172
						selon le statut des générations	
2,625	2,615	2,370	2,810	2,590	1,725	1re génération (26)	173
1,270	1,425	840	975	870	575	2e génération (27)	174
1,240	680	480	490	410	630	3e génération et plus (28)	175
6,165	**5,630**	**4,470**	**5,255**	**4,825**	**3,695**	**Population totale de 1 an et plus (29)**	176
						selon le lieu de résidence 1 an auparavant (mobilité)	
5,420	5,325	4,185	4,755	4,455	3,425	Personnes n'ayant pas déménagé	177
745	305	280	505	370	270	Personnes ayant déménagé	178
315	155	150	290	235	140	Non-migrants	179
430	150	135	205	140	130	Migrants	180
250	115	130	120	105	115	Migrants internes	181
220	95	120	105	100	115	Migrants infraprovinciaux	182
30	25	10	15	10	-	Migrants interprovinciaux	183
185	35	10	90	30	15	Migrants externes	184

Table 1. Selected Characteristics for Census Tracts, 2001 Census – 100% Data and 20% Sample Data

No.	Characteristics	Toronto 0525.02 ◆	Toronto 0526.01	Toronto 0526.02 ◆◇	Toronto 0527.01	Toronto 0527.02	Toronto 0527.03
	POPULATION CHARACTERISTICS						
185	**Total population 5 years and over (30)**	**3,970**	**5,980**	**2,910**	**3,995**	**5,235**	**5,080**
	by place of residence 5 years ago (mobility)						
186	Non-movers	2,025	2,600	1,395	2,270	3,750	2,630
187	Movers	1,945	3,380	1,515	1,725	1,480	2,445
188	Non-migrants	740	1,355	565	935	775	1,055
189	Migrants	1,205	2,025	950	785	705	1,390
190	Internal migrants	515	925	395	485	340	665
191	Intraprovincial migrants	395	790	295	365	280	560
192	Interprovincial migrants	120	135	95	115	55	105
193	External migrants	690	1,100	560	305	370	725
194	**Total population 15 to 24 years**	**545**	**830**	**365**	**755**	**840**	**870**
	by school attendance						
195	Not attending school	255	275	150	155	165	290
196	Attending school full time	275	510	215	555	590	520
197	Attending school part time	15	45	-	50	80	60
198	**Total population 15 years and over**	**3,490**	**4,965**	**2,515**	**3,470**	**4,550**	**4,460**
	by highest level of schooling						
199	Less than grade 9 (31)	390	415	110	290	355	550
200	Grades 9-13 without high school graduation certificate	830	1,285	625	545	730	735
201	Grades 9-13 with high school graduation certificate	475	850	490	440	575	440
202	Some postsecondary without degree, certificate or diploma (32)	405	560	225	490	545	580
203	Trades certificate or diploma (33)	300	380	185	265	480	350
204	College certificate or diploma (34)	430	670	365	515	650	685
205	University certificate below bachelor's degree	160	85	60	180	135	150
206	University with bachelor's degree or higher	500	710	455	750	1,085	970
	by combinations of unpaid work						
207	Males 15 years and over	1,720	2,440	1,280	1,685	2,210	2,235
208	Reported unpaid work (35)	1,450	2,145	1,145	1,475	1,905	1,950
209	Housework and child care and care or assistance to seniors	75	270	85	145	135	140
210	Housework and child care only	435	730	315	360	585	520
211	Housework and care or assistance to seniors only	110	135	70	75	165	155
212	Child care and care or assistance to seniors only	-	-	-	-	-	-
213	Housework only	825	960	650	860	995	1,090
214	Child care only	-	35	25	20	10	25
215	Care or assistance to seniors only	-	10	-	15	10	10
216	Females 15 years and over	1,770	2,520	1,235	1,790	2,345	2,220
217	Reported unpaid work (35)	1,580	2,260	1,140	1,595	2,175	2,020
218	Housework and child care and care or assistance to seniors	105	295	80	255	260	185
219	Housework and child care only	565	915	405	550	700	640
220	Housework and care or assistance to seniors only	130	205	110	75	250	165
221	Child care and care or assistance to seniors only	-	15	-	-	10	10
222	Housework only	770	815	540	705	935	990
223	Child care only	15	10	10	-	25	25
224	Care or assistance to seniors only	-	15	10	10	-	-
	by labour force activity						
225	Males 15 years and over	1,720	2,440	1,275	1,685	2,210	2,235
226	In the labour force	1,250	1,925	1,025	1,305	1,675	1,780
227	Employed	1,160	1,805	995	1,245	1,645	1,675
228	Unemployed	95	120	30	50	30	100
229	Not in the labour force	465	510	250	385	535	460
230	Participation rate	72.7	78.9	80.4	77.4	75.8	79.6
231	Employment rate	67.4	74.0	78.0	73.9	74.4	74.9
232	Unemployment rate	7.6	6.2	2.9	3.8	1.8	5.6
233	Females 15 years and over	1,770	2,525	1,235	1,790	2,345	2,220
234	In the labour force	1,045	1,610	905	1,220	1,525	1,555
235	Employed	940	1,435	855	1,170	1,440	1,475
236	Unemployed	110	170	50	50	85	80
237	Not in the labour force	720	915	330	570	820	665
238	Participation rate	59.0	63.8	73.3	68.2	65.0	70.0
239	Employment rate	53.1	56.8	69.2	65.4	61.4	66.4
240	Unemployment rate	10.5	10.6	5.5	4.1	5.6	5.1

Tableau 1. Certaines caractéristiques des secteurs de recensement, recensement de 2001 – Données intégrales et données-échantillon (20 %)

Toronto 0527.04	Toronto 0527.05	Toronto 0527.06 ◇	Toronto 0527.07	Toronto 0527.08	Toronto 0527.09	Caractéristiques	N°
						CARACTÉRISTIQUES DE LA POPULATION	
5,900	**5,445**	**4,315**	**5,000**	**4,600**	**3,540**	**Population totale de 5 ans et plus (30)**	185
						selon le lieu de résidence 5 ans auparavant (mobilité)	
3,485	4,265	3,140	2,835	3,110	2,250	Personnes n'ayant pas déménagé	186
2,420	1,180	1,180	2,165	1,490	1,290	Personnes ayant déménagé	187
955	565	620	1,165	775	535	Non-migrants	188
1,465	615	560	1,000	715	755	Migrants	189
855	340	455	610	580	490	Migrants internes	190
745	315	405	500	505	460	Migrants infraprovinciaux	191
110	30	40	110	80	30	Migrants interprovinciaux	192
610	275	110	390	130	260	Migrants externes	193
925	**995**	**745**	**835**	**845**	**595**	**Population totale de 15 à 24 ans**	194
						selon la fréquentation scolaire	
200	235	210	245	210	125	Ne fréquentant pas l'école	195
645	715	485	535	590	405	Fréquentant l'école à plein temps	196
75	45	50	45	50	60	Fréquentant l'école à temps partiel	197
5,130	**4,715**	**3,695**	**4,270**	**3,865**	**2,925**	**Population totale de 15 ans et plus**	198
						selon le plus haut niveau de scolarité atteint	
295	520	345	435	290	140	Niveau inférieur à la 9e année (31)	199
755	915	660	865	695	390	De la 9e à la 13e année sans certificat d'études secondaires	200
605	590	560	635	530	340	De la 9e à la 13e année avec certificat d'études secondaires	201
725	740	500	480	615	315	Études postsecondaires partielles sans grade, certificat ou diplôme (32)	202
360	430	385	425	285	175	Certificat ou diplôme d'une école de métiers (33)	203
800	565	495	705	570	535	Certificat ou diplôme collégial (34)	204
110	85	125	110	120	80	Certificat universitaire inférieur au baccalauréat	205
1,490	870	615	610	760	955	Études universitaires avec baccalauréat ou diplôme supérieur	206
						selon les combinaisons de travail non rémunéré	
2,510	2,285	1,710	2,030	1,925	1,410	Hommes de 15 ans et plus	207
2,185	1,970	1,460	1,790	1,790	1,280	Travail non rémunéré déclaré (35)	208
155	165	145	135	150	165	Travaux ménagers et soins aux enfants et soins ou aide aux personnes âgées	209
620	595	405	620	640	300	Travaux ménagers et soins aux enfants seulement	210
175	190	115	135	115	65	Travaux ménagers et soins ou aide aux personnes âgées seulement	211
10	-	-	-	-	-	Soins aux enfants et soins ou aide aux personnes âgées seulement	212
1,205	955	795	860	830	715	Travaux ménagers seulement	213
25	55	-	15	45	30	Soins aux enfants seulement	214
-	10	-	20	-	-	Soins ou aide aux personnes âgées seulement	215
2,625	2,430	1,980	2,240	1,940	1,510	Femmes de 15 ans et plus	216
2,415	2,240	1,720	2,135	1,830	1,425	Travail non rémunéré déclaré (35)	217
225	275	260	195	165	225	Travaux ménagers et soins aux enfants et soins ou aide aux personnes âgées	218
765	740	545	730	720	465	Travaux ménagers et soins aux enfants seulement	219
295	175	175	220	190	65	Travaux ménagers et soins ou aide aux personnes âgées seulement	220
-	-	-	-	-	-	Soins aux enfants et soins ou aide aux personnes âgées seulement	221
1,105	985	730	960	720	655	Travaux ménagers seulement	222
30	65	10	-	30	10	Soins aux enfants seulement	223
-	-	10	25	-	-	Soins ou aide aux personnes âgées seulement	224
						selon l'activité	
2,510	2,285	1,715	2,030	1,925	1,415	Hommes de 15 ans et plus	225
1,950	1,660	1,320	1,565	1,575	1,130	Population active	226
1,855	1,620	1,250	1,445	1,480	1,090	Personnes occupées	227
100	40	65	125	95	35	Chômeurs	228
555	630	395	465	355	285	Inactifs	229
77.7	72.6	77.0	77.1	81.8	79.9	Taux d'activité	230
73.9	70.9	72.9	71.2	76.9	77.0	Taux d'emploi	231
5.1	2.4	4.9	8.0	6.0	3.1	Taux de chômage	232
2,625	2,430	1,985	2,240	1,940	1,510	Femmes de 15 ans et plus	233
1,795	1,640	1,190	1,525	1,300	1,060	Population active	234
1,735	1,575	1,145	1,460	1,265	990	Personnes occupées	235
55	60	45	65	35	70	Chômeuses	236
835	790	790	720	640	455	Inactives	237
68.4	67.5	59.9	68.1	67.0	70.2	Taux d'activité	238
66.1	64.8	57.7	65.2	65.2	65.6	Taux d'emploi	239
3.1	3.7	3.8	4.3	2.7	6.6	Taux de chômage	240

Table 1. Selected Characteristics for Census Tracts, 2001 Census – 100% Data and 20% Sample Data

No.	Characteristics	Toronto 0525.02 ◆	Toronto 0526.01	Toronto 0526.02 ◆◇	Toronto 0527.01	Toronto 0527.02	Toronto 0527.03
	POPULATION CHARACTERISTICS						
	by labour force activity – concluded						
241	Both sexes - Participation rate	65.9	71.3	76.5	72.6	70.4	74.7
242	15-24 years	69.7	64.5	75.3	61.8	64.9	67.4
243	25 years and over	65.0	72.6	77.0	75.5	71.7	76.5
244	Both sexes - Employment rate	60.0	65.3	73.6	69.6	67.6	70.6
245	15-24 years	61.5	53.3	74.0	57.9	60.9	60.0
246	25 years and over	59.9	67.7	73.5	72.9	69.3	73.1
247	Both sexes - Unemployment rate	8.9	8.3	4.2	4.2	3.7	5.6
248	15-24 years	11.7	16.8	-	7.4	6.5	10.2
249	25 years and over	8.1	6.8	4.5	3.2	3.4	4.4
250	**Total labour force 15 years and over**	**2,300**	**3,535**	**1,930**	**2,520**	**3,200**	**3,335**
	by industry based on the 1997 NAICS						
251	Industry - Not applicable (36)	55	75	25	20	25	70
252	All industries (37)	2,250	3,460	1,900	2,495	3,175	3,260
253	11 Agriculture, forestry, fishing and hunting	10	20	10	-	-	-
254	21 Mining and oil and gas extraction	-	-	10	-	-	-
255	22 Utilities	10	10	-	15	25	-
256	23 Construction	105	180	120	80	150	170
257	31-33 Manufacturing	470	930	395	510	530	495
258	41 Wholesale trade	205	290	180	110	250	245
259	44-45 Retail trade	230	360	205	325	350	430
260	48-49 Transportation and warehousing	170	255	110	145	220	130
261	51 Information and cultural industries	75	45	75	70	100	95
262	52 Finance and insurance	115	115	65	205	135	175
263	53 Real estate and rental and leasing	30	65	40	15	120	105
264	54 Professional, scientific and technical services	130	220	90	185	340	390
265	55 Management of companies and enterprises	10	10	10	-	-	-
266	56 Administrative and support, waste management and remediation services	135	205	85	140	150	200
267	61 Educational services	75	195	115	105	230	180
268	62 Health care and social assistance	110	140	95	195	190	200
269	71 Arts, entertainment and recreation	25	50	15	45	40	30
270	72 Accommodation and food services	190	210	150	145	135	125
271	81 Other services (except public administration)	100	85	105	95	120	185
272	91 Public administration	60	75	35	100	95	95
	by class of worker						
273	Class of worker - Not applicable (36)	55	75	25	20	20	70
274	All classes of worker (37)	2,250	3,460	1,905	2,495	3,175	3,260
275	Paid workers	2,105	3,270	1,795	2,260	2,920	3,025
276	Employees	2,080	3,235	1,775	2,180	2,735	2,900
277	Self-employed (incorporated)	25	35	15	75	185	125
278	Self-employed (unincorporated)	140	195	100	215	245	225
279	Unpaid family workers	-	-	-	20	15	10
	by occupation based on the 2001 NOC-S						
280	Male labour force 15 years and over	1,250	1,930	1,025	1,300	1,675	1,775
281	Occupation - Not applicable (36)	20	30	10	10	10	35
282	All occupations (37)	1,235	1,900	1,015	1,290	1,675	1,740
283	A Management occupations	80	150	80	180	215	310
284	B Business, finance and administration occupations	165	215	135	165	195	135
285	C Natural and applied sciences and related occupations	160	180	105	130	290	280
286	D Health occupations	20	-	10	75	35	35
287	E Occupations in social science, education, government service and religion	20	55	35	50	40	60
288	F Occupations in art, culture, recreation and sport	20	15	20	30	15	35
289	G Sales and service occupations	285	365	210	250	375	420
290	H Trades, transport and equipment operators and related occupations	320	505	325	285	370	305
291	I Occupations unique to primary industry	10	15	10	10	-	10
292	J Occupations unique to processing, manufacturing and utilities	150	395	80	120	130	135
293	Female labour force 15 years and over	1,050	1,605	905	1,220	1,530	1,555
294	Occupation - Not applicable (36)	35	40	15	15	20	35
295	All occupations (37)	1,015	1,560	885	1,210	1,505	1,520
296	A Management occupations	100	110	95	95	115	175
297	B Business, finance and administration occupations	395	400	250	375	560	465
298	C Natural and applied sciences and related occupations	35	45	25	30	80	35
299	D Health occupations	25	85	35	105	75	65

Tableau 1. Certaines caractéristiques des secteurs de recensement, recensement de 2001 – Données intégrales et données-échantillon (20 %)

Toronto 0527.04	Toronto 0527.05	Toronto 0527.06 ◇	Toronto 0527.07	Toronto 0527.08	Toronto 0527.09	Caractéristiques	N°
						CARACTÉRISTIQUES DE LA POPULATION	
						selon l'activité – fin	
72.9	69.9	67.9	72.2	74.3	74.7	Les deux sexes - Taux d'activité	241
61.1	63.3	64.9	67.7	66.3	66.4	15-24 ans	242
75.5	71.5	68.7	73.4	76.5	76.8	25 ans et plus	243
70.0	67.8	64.8	67.9	71.1	71.1	Les deux sexes - Taux d'emploi	244
52.2	59.8	59.5	59.9	59.2	60.5	15-24 ans	245
73.8	70.2	66.3	69.9	74.3	73.7	25 ans et plus	246
4.3	3.0	4.6	6.2	4.3	4.8	Les deux sexes - Taux de chômage	247
15.0	7.1	8.3	10.7	10.6	10.1	15-24 ans	248
2.4	2.3	3.4	5.0	2.6	3.9	25 ans et plus	249
3,745	**3,295**	**2,510**	**3,085**	**2,870**	**2,185**	**Population active totale de 15 ans et plus**	250
						selon l'industrie basée sur le SCIAN de 1997	
-	-	35	55	40	15	Industrie - Sans objet (36)	251
3,740	3,290	2,475	3,030	2,835	2,175	Toutes les industries (37)	252
-	-	-	-	-	-	11 Agriculture, foresterie, pêche et chasse	253
-	-	-	-	-	10	21 Extraction minière et extraction de pétrole et de gaz	254
10	40	25	20	30	20	22 Services publics	255
280	230	115	160	135	65	23 Construction	256
430	535	545	580	615	325	31-33 Fabrication	257
335	225	140	255	170	150	41 Commerce de gros	258
405	425	250	315	315	245	44-45 Commerce de détail	259
310	225	200	210	200	140	48-49 Transport et entreposage	260
120	90	90	80	120	80	51 Industrie de l'information et industrie culturelle	261
150	235	175	150	220	145	52 Finance et assurances	262
90	60	10	85	50	45	53 Services immobiliers et services de location et de location à bail	263
430	205	185	195	160	205	54 Services professionnels, scientifiques et techniques	264
-	-	10	-	-	10	55 Gestion de sociétés et d'entreprises	265
140	115	100	160	115	110	56 Services administratifs, services de soutien, services de gestion des déchets et services d'assainissement	266
325	210	130	90	105	130	61 Services d'enseignement	267
260	240	135	225	285	205	62 Soins de santé et assistance sociale	268
45	60	20	35	20	25	71 Arts, spectacles et loisirs	269
140	160	130	205	125	40	72 Hébergement et services de restauration	270
135	160	100	185	100	155	81 Autres services, sauf les administrations publiques	271
135	85	115	80	80	85	91 Administrations publiques	272
						selon la catégorie de travailleurs	
10	-	35	55	35	10	Catégorie de travailleurs - Sans objet (36)	273
3,740	3,290	2,475	3,030	2,835	2,175	Toutes les catégories de travailleurs (37)	274
3,450	3,065	2,320	2,880	2,700	2,065	Travailleurs rémunérés	275
3,195	2,910	2,295	2,785	2,600	2,010	Employés	276
255	150	30	95	105	60	Travailleurs autonomes (entreprise constituée en société)	277
260	215	145	130	135	110	Travailleurs autonomes (entreprise non constituée en société)	278
25	15	10	20	-	-	Travailleurs familiaux non rémunérés	279
						selon la profession basée sur la CNP-S de 2001	
1,955	1,660	1,320	1,565	1,575	1,125	Hommes actifs de 15 ans et plus	280
10	-	10	45	30	10	Profession - Sans objet (36)	281
1,950	1,660	1,310	1,520	1,545	1,115	Toutes les professions (37)	282
410	280	190	140	170	245	A Gestion	283
255	175	135	180	285	115	B Affaires, finance et administration	284
290	195	170	145	195	205	C Sciences naturelles et appliquées et professions apparentées	285
15	10	10	25	40	-	D Secteur de la santé	286
105	55	25	30	35	60	E Sciences sociales, enseignement, administration publique et religion	287
45	20	20	20	20	20	F Arts, culture, sports et loisirs	288
320	360	245	325	275	245	G Ventes et services	289
385	380	360	440	375	165	H Métiers, transport et machinerie	290
10	10	-	10	10	-	I Professions propres au secteur primaire	291
110	175	150	215	130	60	J Transformation, fabrication et services d'utilité publique	292
1,795	1,640	1,190	1,525	1,300	1,060	Femmes actives de 15 ans et plus	293
-	10	25	15	10	-	Profession - Sans objet (36)	294
1,790	1,630	1,165	1,510	1,295	1,055	Toutes les professions (37)	295
225	235	80	115	70	105	A Gestion	296
590	550	425	500	475	365	B Affaires, finance et administration	297
65	30	70	45	65	55	C Sciences naturelles et appliquées et professions apparentées	298
125	110	60	90	140	100	D Secteur de la santé	299

Table 1. Selected Characteristics for Census Tracts, 2001 Census – 100% Data and 20% Sample Data

No.	Characteristics	Toronto 0525.02 ◆	Toronto 0526.01	Toronto 0526.02 ◆◇	Toronto 0527.01	Toronto 0527.02	Toronto 0527.03
	POPULATION CHARACTERISTICS						
	by occupation based on the 2001 NOC-S – concluded						
	E Occupations in social science, education,						
300	government service and religion	20	90	95	80	155	165
301	F Occupations in art, culture, recreation and sport ...	30	30	15	40	70	25
302	G Sales and service occupations	245	400	225	305	345	430
	H Trades, transport and equipment						
303	operators and related occupations	40	45	40	35	30	30
304	I Occupations unique to primary industry	-	10	10	-	10	-
	J Occupations unique to processing,						
305	manufacturing and utilities	130	340	100	145	70	140
306	**Total employed labour force 15 years and over ....**	**2,095**	**3,240**	**1,845**	**2,415**	**3,085**	**3,145**
	by place of work						
307	Males	1,160	1,805	990	1,250	1,640	1,675
308	Usual place of work	955	1,520	820	1,065	1,410	1,355
309	At home	35	55	20	40	105	125
310	Outside Canada	-	10	-	10	-	10
311	No fixed workplace address	170	220	150	135	125	190
312	Females	940	1,435	855	1,170	1,440	1,470
313	Usual place of work	850	1,295	800	1,115	1,270	1,345
314	At home	50	60	15	50	95	75
315	Outside Canada	-	-	-	-	-	-
316	No fixed workplace address	35	75	45	-	75	55
	Total employed labour force 15 years and over with usual place of work or no fixed						
317	**workplace address ....**	**2,005**	**3,115**	**1,810**	**2,310**	**2,885**	**2,935**
	by mode of transportation						
318	Males	1,120	1,740	970	1,195	1,540	1,540
319	Car, truck, van, as driver	855	1,330	740	980	1,325	1,230
320	Car, truck, van, as passenger	50	95	40	55	55	40
321	Public transit	195	275	165	125	100	230
322	Walked	10	35	20	15	40	15
323	Other method	-	10	-	25	20	25
324	Females	890	1,370	840	1,110	1,350	1,395
325	Car, truck, van, as driver	485	705	490	735	790	840
326	Car, truck, van, as passenger	95	200	90	110	125	190
327	Public transit	285	390	240	205	350	270
328	Walked	25	70	-	60	70	75
329	Other method	-	-	25	-	10	20
	Total population 15 years and over who worked						
330	**since January 1, 2000 ....**	**2,455**	**3,675**	**1,990**	**2,705**	**3,415**	**3,515**
	by language used at work						
331	Single responses	2,120	3,185	1,730	2,370	3,035	3,115
332	English	2,080	3,155	1,700	2,275	3,010	3,065
333	French	-	-	10	-	-	-
334	Non-official languages (5)	35	30	25	95	20	50
335	Chinese, n.o.s.	-	-	-	-	10	20
336	Cantonese	-	-	-	-	-	-
337	Other languages (6)	35	30	25	95	15	30
338	Multiple responses	335	495	260	335	380	400
339	English and French	50	60	50	10	65	70
340	English and non-official language	285	440	190	310	310	325
341	French and non-official language	-	-	-	-	-	-
342	English, French and non-official language	-	-	15	15	-	-
	DWELLING AND HOUSEHOLD CHARACTERISTICS						
343	**Total number of occupied private dwellings ....**	**1,550**	**1,990**	**1,180**	**1,215**	**1,760**	**1,705**
	by tenure						
344	Owned	645	915	305	990	1,360	1,265
345	Rented	905	1,075	870	225	400	435
346	Band housing	-	-	-	-	-	-
	by structural type of dwelling						
347	Single-detached house	300	235	265	750	950	380
348	Semi-detached house	160	160	55	15	175	540
349	Row house	30	395	90	-	85	70
350	Apartment, detached duplex	-	-	-	70	-	-
351	Apartment, building that has five or more storeys	835	980	750	380	565	715
	Apartment, building that has fewer than						
352	five storeys (38)	-	215	20	10	-	-
353	Other single-attached house	-	-	-	-	-	-
354	Movable dwelling (39)	225	-	-	-	-	-

Tableau 1. Certaines caractéristiques des secteurs de recensement, recensement de 2001 – Données intégrales et données-échantillon (20 %)

Toronto 0527.04	Toronto 0527.05	Toronto 0527.06 ◇	Toronto 0527.07	Toronto 0527.08	Toronto 0527.09	Caractéristiques	N°
						CARACTÉRISTIQUES DE LA POPULATION	
						selon la profession basée sur la CNP-S de 2001 - fin	
235	130	75	100	65	85	E Sciences sociales, enseignement, administration publique et religion	300
30	55	40	35	10	30	F Arts, culture, sports et loisirs	301
390	385	265	445	275	250	G Ventes et services	302
35	25	20	25	50	-	H Métiers, transport et machinerie	303
-	10	-	-	-	-	I Professions propres au secteur primaire	304
90	110	135	150	145	60	J Transformation, fabrication et services d'utilité publique	305
3,585	**3,200**	**2,395**	**2,900**	**2,745**	**2,075**	**Population active occupée totale de 15 ans et plus**	306
						selon le lieu de travail	
1,855	1,620	1,250	1,440	1,480	1,090	Hommes	307
1,510	1,335	1,065	1,240	1,290	905	Lieu habituel de travail	308
135	80	35	65	25	70	À domicile	309
10	-	-	-	45	10	En dehors du Canada	310
195	210	145	135	125	105	Sans adresse de travail fixe	311
1,740	1,580	1,145	1,455	1,265	990	Femmes	312
1,480	1,450	1,050	1,360	1,165	920	Lieu habituel de travail	313
125	70	40	30	60	50	À domicile	314
20	-	-	-	-	-	En dehors du Canada	315
105	55	45	65	35	15	Sans adresse de travail fixe	316
3,295	**3,045**	**2,315**	**2,800**	**2,620**	**1,940**	**Population active occupée totale de 15 ans et plus ayant un lieu habituel de travail ou sans adresse de travail fixe**	317
						selon le mode de transport	
1,705	1,545	1,210	1,380	1,410	1,005	Hommes	318
1,440	1,365	995	1,095	1,210	775	Automobile, camion ou fourgonnette, en tant que conducteur	319
90	65	55	70	60	30	Automobile, camion ou fourgonnette, en tant que passager	320
145	115	145	175	130	185	Transport en commun	321
15	-	-	25	15	-	À pied	322
20	10	15	10	10	10	Autre moyen	323
1,585	1,500	1,100	1,425	1,205	930	Femmes	324
1,145	1,125	740	895	725	560	Automobile, camion ou fourgonnette, en tant que conductrice	325
110	160	155	170	175	125	Automobile, camion ou fourgonnette, en tant que passagère	326
265	200	170	300	250	225	Transport en commun	327
60	10	20	45	40	25	À pied	328
10	10	20	20	15	-	Autre moyen	329
4,075	**3,620**	**2,680**	**3,310**	**3,145**	**2,365**	**Population totale de 15 ans et plus ayant travaillé depuis le 1er janvier 2000**	330
						selon la langue utilisée au travail	
3,620	3,195	2,455	3,005	2,765	2,110	Réponses uniques	331
3,590	3,170	2,425	2,930	2,720	2,080	Anglais	332
-	-	-	10	10	-	Français	333
35	30	30	60	40	30	Langues non officielles (5)	334
-	10	-	-	10	-	Chinois, n.d.a.	335
-	10	-	-	10	10	Cantonais	336
25	20	35	55	20	15	Autres langues (6)	337
455	425	225	300	380	255	Réponses multiples	338
115	60	40	60	50	80	Anglais et français	339
325	355	175	225	320	175	Anglais et langue non officielle	340
-	-	-	-	-	-	Français et langue non officielle	341
15	10	15	15	-	-	Anglais, français et langue non officielle	342
						CARACTÉRISTIQUES DES LOGEMENTS ET DES MÉNAGES	
2,110	**1,675**	**1,410**	**1,620**	**1,270**	**1,080**	**Nombre total de logements privés occupés**	343
						selon le mode d'occupation	
1,515	1,345	1,015	890	1,160	835	Possédé	344
590	330	395	730	115	245	Loué	345
-	-	-	-	-	-	Logement de bande	346
						selon le type de construction résidentielle	
860	1,250	945	445	1,100	835	Maison individuelle non attenante	347
-	40	40	245	125	85	Maison jumelée	348
735	-	60	835	-	20	Maison en rangée	349
-	10	-	-	45	-	Appartement, duplex non attenant	350
510	310	135	90	-	145	Appartement, immeuble de cinq étages ou plus	351
-	65	230	-	-	-	Appartement, immeuble de moins de cinq étages (38)	352
-	-	-	-	-	-	Autre maison individuelle attenante	353
-	-	-	-	-	-	Logement mobile (39)	354

Table 1. Selected Characteristics for Census Tracts, 2001 Census – 100% Data and 20% Sample Data

No.	Characteristics	Toronto 0525.02 ◆	Toronto 0526.01	Toronto 0526.02 ◆◇	Toronto 0527.01	Toronto 0527.02	Toronto 0527.03
	DWELLING AND HOUSEHOLD CHARACTERISTICS						
	by condition of dwelling						
355	Regular maintenance only	915	1,195	665	985	1,220	1,270
356	Minor repairs	445	620	345	220	510	380
357	Major repairs	185	170	170	10	30	60
	by period of construction						
358	Before 1946	30	35	35	-	10	-
359	1946-1960	120	195	90	20	-	-
360	1961-1970	645	870	635	10	80	55
361	1971-1980	425	675	335	125	535	530
362	1981-1990	295	165	70	915	1,060	985
363	1991-2001 (20)	30	45	-	145	65	135
364	Average number of rooms per dwelling	5.2	5.4	5.3	6.7	6.8	6.0
365	Average number of bedrooms per dwelling	2.2	2.4	2.2	3.0	2.9	2.7
366	Average value of dwelling $	187,781	179,768	318,230	231,133	262,472	210,334
367	**Total number of private households**	**1,550**	**1,990**	**1,180**	**1,215**	**1,765**	**1,705**
	by household size						
368	1 person	370	245	275	150	250	280
369	2 persons	435	445	350	265	435	440
370	3 persons	265	420	250	210	335	300
371	4-5 persons	385	715	290	450	680	545
372	6 or more persons	85	170	20	135	65	135
	by household type						
373	One-family households	1,055	1,505	795	920	1,390	1,210
374	Multiple-family households	80	160	25	115	85	125
375	Non-family households	415	325	355	180	290	365
376	Number of persons in private households	4,270	6,530	3,100	4,205	5,475	5,335
377	Average number of persons in private households	2.8	3.3	2.6	3.5	3.1	3.1
378	Average number of persons per room	0.5	0.6	0.5	0.5	0.5	0.5
379	Tenant households in non-farm, non-reserve private dwellings (40)	895	1,070	865	225	400	435
380	Average gross rent $ (40)	884	940	814	1,162	1,085	1,160
381	Tenant households spending 30% or more of household income on gross rent (40) (41)	320	375	275	90	170	190
382	Tenant households spending from 30% to 99% of household income on gross rent (40) (41)	255	340	215	60	130	125
383	Owner households in non-farm, non-reserve private dwellings (42)	645	915	300	990	1,360	1,265
384	Average owner's major payments $ (42)	841	1,031	1,054	1,233	1,009	1,049
385	Owner households spending 30% or more of household income on owner's major payments (41) (42)	95	205	35	235	280	280
386	Owner households spending from 30% to 99% of household income on owner's major payments (41) (42)	90	195	30	205	240	265
	CENSUS FAMILY CHARACTERISTICS						
387	**Total number of census families in private households**	**1,225**	**1,830**	**845**	**1,165**	**1,555**	**1,470**
	by census family structure and size						
388	Total couple families	1,030	1,465	720	990	1,375	1,275
389	Total families of married couples	950	1,335	620	940	1,300	1,185
390	Without children at home	350	365	205	225	400	375
391	With children at home	595	970	415	715	905	810
392	1 child	245	375	195	220	285	295
393	2 children	235	440	170	330	465	305
394	3 or more children	115	155	55	160	155	205
395	Total families of common-law couples	85	135	100	55	70	95
396	Without children at home	45	45	75	30	50	50
397	With children at home	40	90	25	25	20	40
398	1 child	20	40	10	20	10	25
399	2 children	20	30	20	10	10	10
400	3 or more children	-	15	-	-	-	15
401	Total lone-parent families	190	360	125	170	180	195
402	Female parent	160	325	115	160	165	130
403	1 child	95	155	70	95	105	65
404	2 children	40	115	30	40	45	55
405	3 or more children	25	50	15	15	15	15

Tableau 1. Certaines caractéristiques des secteurs de recensement, recensement de 2001 – Données intégrales et données-échantillon (20 %)

Toronto 0527.04	Toronto 0527.05	Toronto 0527.06 ◇	Toronto 0527.07	Toronto 0527.08	Toronto 0527.09	Caractéristiques	N°
						CARACTÉRISTIQUES DES LOGEMENTS ET DES MÉNAGES	
						selon l'état du logement	
1,495	1,120	975	1,170	785	660	Entretien régulier seulement	355
555	450	405	365	425	370	Réparations mineures	356
55	105	35	85	60	55	Réparations majeures	357
						selon la période de construction	
10	-	-	20	-	-	Avant 1946	358
-	45	-	30	-	-	1946-1960	359
205	10	20	145	10	10	1961-1970	360
1,280	395	260	790	175	100	1971-1980	361
595	1,010	1,055	605	1,025	975	1981-1990	362
15	215	75	30	65	-	1991-2001 (20)	363
7.0	7.2	6.4	6.5	7.5	7.2	Nombre moyen de pièces par logement	364
3.1	3.2	2.9	2.9	3.5	3.2	Nombre moyen de chambres à coucher par logement	365
281,548	278,111	257,458	244,385	244,278	255,836	Valeur moyenne du logement $	366
2,110	**1,675**	**1,410**	**1,620**	**1,270**	**1,080**	**Nombre total de logements privés**	367
						selon la taille du ménage	
360	175	235	170	70	90	1 personne	368
555	355	290	385	200	205	2 personnes	369
425	325	255	375	225	245	3 personnes	370
685	675	545	565	590	470	4-5 personnes	371
85	150	85	120	185	80	6 personnes ou plus	372
						selon le genre de ménage	
1,565	1,365	1,065	1,325	1,035	920	Ménages unifamiliaux	373
90	110	70	85	145	50	Ménages multifamiliaux	374
450	200	275	210	90	115	Ménages non familiaux	375
6,205	5,680	4,510	5,285	4,875	3,775	Nombre de personnes dans les ménages privés	376
2.9	3.4	3.2	3.3	3.8	3.5	Nombre moyen de personnes dans les ménages privés	377
0.4	0.5	0.5	0.5	0.5	0.5	Nombre moyen de personnes par pièce	378
590	325	400	730	100	245	Ménages locataires dans les logements privés non agricoles hors réserve (40)	379
1,116	914	700	1,002	1,135	1,019	Loyer brut moyen $ (40)	380
200	140	185	180	40	60	Ménages locataires consacrant 30 % ou plus du revenu du ménage au loyer brut (40) (41)	381
160	95	165	180	35	50	Ménages locataires consacrant de 30 % à 99 % du revenu du ménage au loyer brut (40) (41)	382
1,515	1,345	1,010	890	1,155	835	Ménages propriétaires dans les logements privés non agricoles hors réserve (42)	383
1,178	953	1,073	971	1,204	1,142	Principales dépenses de propriété moyennes $ (42)	384
260	210	185	205	210	80	Ménages propriétaires consacrant 30 % ou plus du revenu du ménage aux principales dépenses de propriété (41) (42)	385
210	195	150	185	190	70	Ménages propriétaires consacrant de 30 % à 99 % du revenu du ménage aux principales dépenses de propriété (41) (42)	386
						CARACTÉRISTIQUES DES FAMILLES DE RECENSEMENT	
1,755	**1,600**	**1,210**	**1,495**	**1,340**	**1,035**	**Total des familles de recensement dans les ménages privés**	387
						selon la structure et la taille de la famille de recensement	
1,490	1,330	1,040	1,225	1,165	905	Total des familles avec conjoints	388
1,365	1,270	1,015	1,150	1,140	870	Total des familles avec couples mariés	389
400	285	230	330	225	200	Sans enfants à la maison	390
965	985	785	820	915	670	Avec enfants à la maison	391
350	325	260	280	285	205	1 enfant	392
455	455	370	345	440	325	2 enfants	393
155	215	150	195	185	145	3 enfants ou plus	394
125	65	25	80	30	40	Total des familles en union libre	395
80	30	-	20	-	15	Sans enfants à la maison	396
40	30	20	50	30	15	Avec enfants à la maison	397
20	10	15	25	-	10	1 enfant	398
20	10	10	30	25	10	2 enfants	399
-	15	-	-	-	-	3 enfants ou plus	400
270	275	170	270	170	130	Total des familles monoparentales	401
230	220	145	225	125	95	Parent de sexe féminin	402
130	140	115	125	90	40	1 enfant	403
60	55	35	75	30	50	2 enfants	404
35	25	10	25	10	10	3 enfants ou plus	405

Table 1. Selected Characteristics for Census Tracts, 2001 Census – 100% Data and 20% Sample Data

No.	Characteristics	Toronto 0525.02 ◆	Toronto 0526.01	Toronto 0526.02 ◆◇	Toronto 0527.01	Toronto 0527.02	Toronto 0527.03
	CENSUS FAMILY CHARACTERISTICS						
	by census family structure and size – concluded						
406	Male parent	30	35	10	10	15	60
407	1 child	20	20	-	15	10	30
408	2 children	10	-	10	-	-	20
409	3 or more children	-	15	-	-	-	10
410	**Total number of children at home**	**1,480**	**2,550**	**995**	**1,695**	**1,995**	**1,965**
	by age groups						
411	Under 6 years	355	655	240	260	285	280
412	6-14 years	430	885	345	470	635	595
413	15-17 years	155	280	95	220	255	265
414	18-24 years	310	385	170	485	510	525
415	25 years and over	230	340	150	260	305	295
416	Average number of children at home per census family (43)	1.2	1.4	1.2	1.5	1.3	1.3
417	**Total number of persons in private households**	**4,270**	**6,530**	**3,100**	**4,205**	**5,475**	**5,335**
	by census family status and living arrangements						
418	Number of non-family persons	535	690	535	355	550	620
419	Living with relatives (44)	60	280	120	130	210	165
420	Living with non-relatives only	100	160	135	70	85	180
421	Living alone	375	250	275	150	250	275
422	Number of family persons	3,730	5,840	2,565	3,850	4,930	4,715
423	Average number of persons per census family	3.1	3.2	3.0	3.3	3.2	3.2
424	**Total number of persons 65 years and over**	**600**	**530**	**255**	**320**	**630**	**420**
425	Number of non-family persons 65 years and over	190	145	75	80	190	115
426	Living with relatives (44)	30	60	10	60	90	50
427	Living with non-relatives only	-	-	-	10	10	10
428	Living alone	160	85	60	15	95	60
429	Number of family persons 65 years and over	405	385	175	235	435	305
	ECONOMIC FAMILY CHARACTERISTICS						
430	**Total number of economic families in private households**	**1,160**	**1,720**	**850**	**1,045**	**1,495**	**1,375**
	by size of family						
431	2 persons	435	460	325	260	430	415
432	3 persons	275	405	225	220	335	300
433	4 persons	260	490	215	260	450	345
434	5 or more persons	185	365	90	310	285	310
435	Total number of persons in economic families	3,790	6,120	2,685	3,990	5,140	4,880
436	Average number of persons per economic family	3.3	3.6	3.2	3.8	3.4	3.5
437	Total number of unattached individuals	475	410	410	220	335	460
	2000 INCOME CHARACTERISTICS						
	Population 15 years and over by sex and total income groups in 2000						
438	Total - Both sexes	3,490	4,960	2,515	3,475	4,550	4,455
439	Without income	250	315	110	225	210	275
440	With income	3,235	4,645	2,400	3,250	4,340	4,185
441	Under $1,000 (45)	125	205	130	185	150	295
442	$ 1,000 - $ 2,999	130	305	85	205	240	220
443	$ 3,000 - $ 4,999	120	165	155	130	180	185
444	$ 5,000 - $ 6,999	155	230	90	130	135	190
445	$ 7,000 - $ 9,999	145	305	125	185	270	135
446	$10,000 - $11,999	200	180	115	175	155	140
447	$12,000 - $14,999	215	350	75	170	320	240
448	$15,000 - $19,999	415	405	260	170	385	305
449	$20,000 - $24,999	280	470	150	200	275	205
450	$25,000 - $29,999	295	380	225	260	270	390
451	$30,000 - $34,999	260	425	200	305	240	475
452	$35,000 - $39,999	220	260	160	250	275	300
453	$40,000 - $44,999	190	225	180	225	290	265
454	$45,000 - $49,999	80	195	90	145	210	165
455	$50,000 - $59,999	170	180	80	190	255	255
456	$60,000 and over	240	370	280	320	695	420
457	Average income $ (46)	26,585	26,065	30,451	28,975	32,993	28,492
458	Median income $ (46)	21,929	21,382	25,049	26,022	25,806	26,182
459	Standard error of average income $ (46)	828	725	1,359	952	982	738

Tableau 1. Certaines caractéristiques des secteurs de recensement, recensement de 2001 – Données intégrales et données-échantillon (20 %)

Toronto 0527.04	Toronto 0527.05	Toronto 0527.06 ◇	Toronto 0527.07	Toronto 0527.08	Toronto 0527.09	Caractéristiques	N°
						CARACTÉRISTIQUES DES FAMILLES DE RECENSEMENT	
						selon la structure et la taille de la famille de recensement - fin	
40	50	25	40	50	35	Parent de sexe masculin	406
30	35	15	30	30	10	1 enfant	407
10	15	10	-	10	15	2 enfants	408
-	-	-	-	-	-	3 enfants ou plus	409
2,230	**2,380**	**1,760**	**2,115**	**2,095**	**1,585**	**Nombre total d'enfants à la maison**	410
						selon les groupes d'âge	
400	295	245	370	335	305	Moins de 6 ans	411
675	665	570	650	670	550	6-14 ans	412
275	305	230	225	245	150	15-17 ans	413
535	655	435	545	525	415	18-24 ans	414
335	460	285	320	315	170	25 ans et plus	415
1.3	1.5	1.5	1.4	1.6	1.5	Nombre moyen d'enfants à la maison par famille de recensement (43)	416
6,210	**5,680**	**4,510**	**5,285**	**4,870**	**3,775**	**Nombre total de personnes dans les ménages privés**	417
						selon la situation des particuliers dans la famille de recensement et des particuliers dans le ménage	
735	365	500	445	270	245	Nombre de personnes hors famille de recensement	418
200	130	145	115	160	80	Vivant avec des personnes apparentées (44)	419
175	60	120	160	40	70	Vivant avec des personnes non apparentées uniquement	420
365	170	235	170	70	90	Vivant seules	421
5,470	5,315	4,010	4,840	4,605	3,535	Nombre de personnes membres d'une famille	422
3.1	3.3	3.3	3.2	3.4	3.4	Nombre moyen de personnes par famille de recensement	423
470	**480**	**490**	**475**	**295**	**255**	**Nombre total de personnes de 65 ans et plus**	424
145	130	275	120	80	55	Nombre de personnes hors famille de recensement de 65 ans et plus	425
75	75	90	75	65	40	Vivant avec des personnes apparentées (44)	426
-	10	15	-	-	10	Vivant avec des personnes non apparentées uniquement	427
60	55	170	45	15	10	Vivant seules	428
335	345	220	350	215	200	Nombre de personnes membres d'une famille de 65 ans et plus	429
						CARACTÉRISTIQUES DES FAMILLES ÉCONOMIQUES	
1,695	**1,485**	**1,145**	**1,425**	**1,205**	**970**	**Nombre total de familles économiques dans les ménages privés**	430
						selon la taille de la famille	
530	355	290	390	210	195	2 personnes	431
405	325	240	360	235	240	3 personnes	432
520	450	365	405	390	335	4 personnes	433
240	360	250	265	370	205	5 personnes ou plus	434
5,675	5,445	4,160	4,955	4,760	3,615	Nombre total de personnes dans les familles économiques	435
3.4	3.7	3.6	3.5	4.0	3.7	Nombre moyen de personnes par famille économique	436
540	235	355	330	115	160	Nombre total de personnes hors famille économique	437
						CARACTÉRISTIQUES DU REVENU DE 2000	
						Population de 15 ans et plus selon le sexe et les tranches de revenu total en 2000	
5,135	4,715	3,695	4,270	3,865	2,925	Total - Les deux sexes	438
255	270	210	315	220	145	Sans revenu	439
4,880	4,445	3,485	3,950	3,650	2,785	Avec un revenu	440
270	210	255	200	155	145	Moins de 1 000 $ (45)	441
185	235	150	245	125	135	1 000 $ - 2 999 $	442
180	150	130	125	210	130	3 000 $ - 4 999 $	443
150	285	155	110	195	70	5 000 $ - 6 999 $	444
260	220	125	260	200	130	7 000 $ - 9 999 $	445
190	200	130	215	80	75	10 000 $ - 11 999 $	446
190	295	205	245	200	140	12 000 $ - 14 999 $	447
260	320	345	375	225	180	15 000 $ - 19 999 $	448
280	305	265	315	255	205	20 000 $ - 24 999 $	449
260	300	250	210	200	200	25 000 $ - 29 999 $	450
360	260	250	295	380	190	30 000 $ - 34 999 $	451
350	290	170	325	275	140	35 000 $ - 39 999 $	452
255	300	275	370	285	205	40 000 $ - 44 999 $	453
305	165	140	140	165	100	45 000 $ - 49 999 $	454
410	295	250	200	270	205	50 000 $ - 59 999 $	455
960	615	390	310	425	535	60 000 $ et plus	456
37,333	31,346	29,747	26,639	31,360	36,675	Revenu moyen $ (46)	457
32,219	24,977	24,114	22,805	28,845	28,967	Revenu médian $ (46)	458
997	932	963	699	969	1,416	Erreur type de revenu moyen $ (46)	459

Table 1. Selected Characteristics for Census Tracts, 2001 Census – 100% Data and 20% Sample Data

No.	Characteristics	Toronto 0525.02 ◆	Toronto 0526.01	Toronto 0526.02 ◆◇	Toronto 0527.01	Toronto 0527.02	Toronto 0527.03
	2000 INCOME CHARACTERISTICS						
	Population 15 years and over by sex and total income groups in 2000 – concluded						
460	Total - Males	1,715	2,440	1,280	1,685	2,210	2,240
461	Without income	95	170	25	95	110	105
462	With income	1,625	2,265	1,250	1,590	2,105	2,135
463	Under $1,000 (45)	70	100	70	40	65	160
464	$ 1,000 - $ 2,999	25	120	45	90	105	75
465	$ 3,000 - $ 4,999	50	50	80	35	90	90
466	$ 5,000 - $ 6,999	50	50	15	70	25	75
467	$ 7,000 - $ 9,999	25	120	50	60	115	60
468	$10,000 - $11,999	110	85	70	60	65	65
469	$12,000 - $14,999	60	130	50	55	110	85
470	$15,000 - $19,999	195	145	140	90	140	115
471	$20,000 - $24,999	120	230	75	95	135	120
472	$25,000 - $29,999	165	195	95	170	120	140
473	$30,000 - $34,999	110	260	115	150	85	215
474	$35,000 - $39,999	130	125	100	95	140	175
475	$40,000 - $44,999	125	155	105	115	155	170
476	$45,000 - $49,999	60	105	50	80	115	105
477	$50,000 - $59,999	120	110	65	125	165	170
478	$60,000 and over	200	300	130	250	470	305
479	Average income $ (46)	32,588	31,072	33,648	35,301	39,209	33,044
480	Median income $ (46)	27,266	28,334	26,065	30,246	33,837	30,316
481	Standard error of average income $ (46)	1,307	1,113	2,152	1,582	1,600	1,172
482	Total - Females	1,770	2,525	1,240	1,785	2,345	2,225
483	Without income	155	145	85	130	105	165
484	With income	1,615	2,380	1,150	1,660	2,240	2,055
485	Under $1,000 (45)	60	105	65	145	85	130
486	$ 1,000 - $ 2,999	105	190	40	115	130	145
487	$ 3,000 - $ 4,999	75	115	75	95	85	95
488	$ 5,000 - $ 6,999	100	175	80	55	110	115
489	$ 7,000 - $ 9,999	125	185	75	125	155	80
490	$10,000 - $11,999	90	95	50	110	90	80
491	$12,000 - $14,999	150	215	25	110	210	160
492	$15,000 - $19,999	220	255	130	80	240	180
493	$20,000 - $24,999	160	245	75	105	135	85
494	$25,000 - $29,999	125	185	125	95	150	245
495	$30,000 - $34,999	145	160	85	160	155	255
496	$35,000 - $39,999	90	135	60	155	140	125
497	$40,000 - $44,999	70	75	70	110	130	95
498	$45,000 - $49,999	20	95	35	60	100	60
499	$50,000 - $59,999	50	65	15	65	90	85
500	$60,000 and over	35	70	145	70	225	115
501	Average income $ (46)	20,537	21,288	26,976	22,919	27,164	23,767
502	Median income $ (46)	17,549	16,649	22,133	19,284	20,063	23,403
503	Standard error of average income $ (46)	874	893	1,590	1,007	1,125	842
	by composition of total income						
504	Total - Composition of income in 2000 % (47)	100.0	100.0	100.0	100.0	100.0	100.0
505	Employment income %	77.6	83.3	80.1	88.8	82.9	87.4
506	Government transfer payments %	13.3	11.0	8.4	6.7	8.6	7.0
507	Other %	9.1	5.7	11.5	4.6	8.5	5.6
	Population 15 years and over with employment income in 2000 by sex and work activity						
508	Both sexes with employment income (48)	2,320	3,575	1,920	2,660	3,325	3,425
509	Average employment income $	28,843	28,217	30,634	31,442	35,698	30,402
510	Standard error of average employment income $	996	835	1,554	1,076	1,038	830
511	Worked full year, full time (49)	1,295	1,850	1,080	1,385	1,890	1,915
512	Average employment income $	36,749	38,645	40,937	42,867	47,712	40,463
513	Standard error of average employment income $	1,272	1,212	2,006	1,451	1,268	998
514	Worked part year or part time (50)	965	1,620	785	1,200	1,340	1,415
515	Average employment income $	18,190	17,336	18,393	18,883	20,829	18,535
516	Standard error of average employment income $	1,111	825	2,086	1,124	1,334	1,096
517	Males with employment income (48)	1,245	1,920	1,025	1,365	1,720	1,825
518	Average employment income $	33,906	31,878	32,990	37,284	41,708	34,712
519	Standard error of average employment income $	1,491	1,173	2,359	1,739	1,600	1,280
520	Worked full year, full time (49)	765	1,115	585	800	1,100	1,105
521	Average employment income $	40,139	39,943	42,550	48,307	53,305	44,427
522	Standard error of average employment income $	1,855	1,544	2,875	2,162	1,848	1,483
523	Worked part year or part time (50)	465	750	425	540	580	665
524	Average employment income $	21,441	21,287	20,574	20,500	22,167	21,093
525	Standard error of average employment income $	1,653	1,436	3,666	1,848	2,118	1,800

Tableau 1. Certaines caractéristiques des secteurs de recensement, recensement de 2001 – Données intégrales et données-échantillon (20 %)

Toronto 0527.04	Toronto 0527.05	Toronto 0527.06 ◇	Toronto 0527.07	Toronto 0527.08	Toronto 0527.09	Caractéristiques	N°
						CARACTÉRISTIQUES DU REVENU DE 2000	
						Population de 15 ans et plus selon le sexe et les tranches de revenu total en 2000 – fin	
2,505	2,285	1,715	2,025	1,930	1,415	Total - Hommes	460
110	110	95	105	75	60	Sans revenu	461
2,400	2,175	1,620	1,920	1,850	1,360	Avec un revenu	462
90	65	105	105	60	50	Moins de 1 000 $ (45)	463
75	125	60	130	70	55	1 000 $ - 2 999 $	464
85	75	35	30	75	55	3 000 $ - 4 999 $	465
60	115	65	35	65	35	5 000 $ - 6 999 $	466
105	80	20	135	80	75	7 000 $ - 9 999 $	467
105	110	45	90	30	25	10 000 $ - 11 999 $	468
65	85	75	60	50	50	12 000 $ - 14 999 $	469
105	155	125	160	85	60	15 000 $ - 19 999 $	470
135	140	105	115	115	70	20 000 $ - 24 999 $	471
130	115	75	110	95	35	25 000 $ - 29 999 $	472
145	120	125	145	165	100	30 000 $ - 34 999 $	473
170	155	110	155	125	90	35 000 $ - 39 999 $	474
145	130	120	220	195	85	40 000 $ - 44 999 $	475
170	95	65	75	115	50	45 000 $ - 49 999 $	476
235	165	170	135	190	125	50 000 $ - 59 999 $	477
580	435	320	230	330	395	60 000 $ et plus	478
43,093	36,736	38,096	30,601	38,188	45,459	Revenu moyen $ (46)	479
37,085	30,013	34,033	29,264	36,100	39,022	Revenu médian $ (46)	480
1,643	1,521	1,624	1,118	1,535	2,445	Erreur type de revenu moyen $ (46)	481
2,625	2,430	1,980	2,240	1,940	1,515	Total - Femmes	482
140	160	115	210	140	85	Sans revenu	483
2,480	2,270	1,865	2,030	1,800	1,430	Avec un revenu	484
185	145	145	90	95	90	Moins de 1 000 $ (45)	485
105	110	90	110	60	80	1 000 $ - 2 999 $	486
95	75	100	95	130	75	3 000 $ - 4 999 $	487
95	170	90	75	125	35	5 000 $ - 6 999 $	488
155	140	105	130	120	60	7 000 $ - 9 999 $	489
80	90	85	130	50	50	10 000 $ - 11 999 $	490
130	210	135	185	145	90	12 000 $ - 14 999 $	491
155	165	220	215	140	125	15 000 $ - 19 999 $	492
145	165	160	205	145	130	20 000 $ - 24 999 $	493
130	185	180	105	105	165	25 000 $ - 29 999 $	494
215	140	125	155	215	90	30 000 $ - 34 999 $	495
180	140	60	165	150	45	35 000 $ - 39 999 $	496
115	170	150	155	85	120	40 000 $ - 44 999 $	497
140	70	70	55	50	45	45 000 $ - 49 999 $	498
180	125	85	60	75	85	50 000 $ - 59 999 $	499
380	180	75	80	95	140	60 000 $ et plus	500
31,762	26,177	22,503	22,892	24,330	28,327	Revenu moyen $ (46)	501
29,262	20,312	18,391	18,593	20,077	24,214	Revenu médian $ (46)	502
1,116	1,046	956	816	1,045	1,341	Erreur type de revenu moyen $ (46)	503
						selon la composition du revenu total	
100.0	100.0	100.0	100.0	100.0	100.0	Total - Composition du revenu en 2000 % (47)	504
85.1	83.8	84.2	86.3	89.1	89.3	Revenu d'emploi %	505
5.8	8.2	9.7	9.0	5.2	4.4	Transferts gouvernementaux %	506
9.1	8.0	6.1	4.7	5.8	6.3	Autre %	507
						Population de 15 ans et plus ayant un revenu d'emploi en 2000 selon le sexe et le travail	
3,995	3,565	2,665	3,185	3,115	2,320	Les deux sexes ayant un revenu d'emploi (48)	508
38,759	32,769	32,761	28,489	32,716	39,323	Revenu moyen d'emploi $	509
1,069	1,043	1,116	793	1,034	1,574	Erreur type de revenu moyen d'emploi $	510
2,400	1,940	1,580	1,705	1,890	1,355	Ayant travaillé toute l'année à plein temps (49)	511
52,115	45,950	42,076	36,905	42,951	51,824	Revenu moyen d'emploi $	512
1,329	1,481	1,367	1,040	1,124	2,280	Erreur type de revenu moyen d'emploi $	513
1,445	1,500	995	1,415	1,140	940	Ayant travaillé une partie de l'année ou à temps partiel (50)	514
19,189	17,304	19,509	18,583	17,383	22,158	Revenu moyen d'emploi $	515
1,162	970	1,618	977	1,611	1,478	Erreur type de revenu moyen d'emploi $	516
2,065	1,820	1,385	1,585	1,695	1,170	Hommes ayant un revenu d'emploi (48)	517
43,804	37,953	39,789	32,523	37,732	47,947	Revenu moyen d'emploi $	518
1,727	1,688	1,779	1,273	1,550	2,628	Erreur type de revenu moyen d'emploi $	519
1,365	1,060	890	930	1,120	760	Ayant travaillé toute l'année à plein temps (49)	520
56,561	51,008	48,731	42,442	46,760	59,125	Revenu moyen d'emploi $	521
2,051	2,309	2,055	1,531	1,530	3,490	Erreur type de revenu moyen d'emploi $	522
670	705	465	625	530	405	Ayant travaillé une partie de l'année ou à temps partiel (50)	523
18,520	19,940	23,212	18,613	20,791	27,415	Revenu moyen d'emploi $	524
1,865	1,555	2,930	1,609	3,003	2,957	Erreur type de revenu moyen d'emploi $	525

Table 1. Selected Characteristics for Census Tracts, 2001 Census – 100% Data and 20% Sample Data

No.	Characteristics	Toronto 0525.02 ◆	Toronto 0526.01	Toronto 0526.02 ◆◇	Toronto 0527.01	Toronto 0527.02	Toronto 0527.03
	2000 INCOME CHARACTERISTICS						
	Population 15 years and over with employment income in 2000 by sex and work activity – concluded						
526	Females with employment income (48)	1,070	1,660	890	1,290	1,605	1,605
527	Average employment income $	22,955	23,987	27,917	25,265	29,277	25,500
528	Standard error of average employment income $	1,140	1,149	1,938	1,148	1,215	972
529	Worked full year, full time (49)	525	740	495	585	790	805
530	Average employment income $	31,845	36,689	39,034	35,354	39,964	35,024
531	Standard error of average employment income $	1,410	1,944	2,726	1,620	1,439	1,100
532	Worked part year or part time (50)	500	875	365	660	755	755
533	Average employment income $	15,185	13,961	15,846	17,551	19,801	16,277
534	Standard error of average employment income $	1,429	857	1,737	1,358	1,704	1,315
	Census families by structure and family income groups in 2000						
535	Total - All census families	1,220	1,825	845	1,165	1,555	1,475
536	Under $10,000	65	65	75	45	80	120
537	$ 10,000 - $19,999	50	135	20	35	35	65
538	$ 20,000 - $29,999	140	200	115	125	85	105
539	$ 30,000 - $39,999	195	325	90	135	190	95
540	$ 40,000 - $49,999	140	235	90	90	140	155
541	$ 50,000 - $59,999	150	180	110	100	120	115
542	$ 60,000 - $69,999	95	200	60	105	165	175
543	$ 70,000 - $79,999	105	125	70	90	85	160
544	$ 80,000 - $89,999	65	60	20	85	130	85
545	$ 90,000 - $99,999	35	80	45	75	80	125
546	$100,000 and over	170	225	160	285	445	260
547	Average family income $	57,745	56,888	65,465	71,289	80,384	65,842
548	Median family income $	51,138	48,644	53,056	63,493	67,714	62,840
549	Standard error of average family income $	2,241	1,945	3,990	2,654	3,053	2,094
550	Total - All couple census families (51)	1,030	1,470	720	995	1,375	1,280
551	Under $10,000	55	45	55	30	65	95
552	$ 10,000 - $19,999	40	85	15	35	25	45
553	$ 20,000 - $29,999	120	165	85	95	80	80
554	$ 30,000 - $39,999	150	215	75	90	135	80
555	$ 40,000 - $49,999	135	185	65	75	115	150
556	$ 50,000 - $59,999	115	160	100	75	95	95
557	$ 60,000 - $69,999	85	190	45	95	130	140
558	$ 70,000 - $79,999	80	110	60	90	80	140
559	$ 80,000 - $89,999	70	50	20	80	120	90
560	$ 90,000 - $99,999	30	55	40	70	85	125
561	$100,000 and over	155	200	155	260	445	250
562	Average family income $	59,486	60,132	70,590	75,339	84,625	67,862
563	Median family income $	52,294	51,358	55,021	70,844	72,954	65,050
564	Standard error of average family income $	2,501	2,256	4,553	2,863	3,416	2,192
	Incidence of low income in 2000						
565	Total - Economic families	1,160	1,720	850	1,045	1,495	1,370
566	Low income	160	300	175	95	185	200
567	Incidence of low income in 2000 % (52)	13.8	17.5	20.9	8.9	12.1	14.4
568	Total - Unattached individuals 15 years and over	475	405	415	220	335	460
569	Low income	205	95	105	50	85	100
570	Incidence of low income in 2000 % (52)	43.3	23.0	24.2	24.1	25.1	21.2
571	Total - Population in private households	4,270	6,525	3,100	4,205	5,475	5,340
572	Low income	790	1,265	610	445	685	820
573	Incidence of low income in 2000 % (52)	18.5	19.4	19.6	10.5	12.5	15.3
	Private households by household income groups in 2000						
574	Total - All private households	1,545	1,990	1,175	1,215	1,760	1,705
575	Under $10,000	65	65	80	30	65	105
576	$ 10,000 - $19,999	210	125	85	35	110	90
577	$ 20,000 - $29,999	165	210	145	90	105	95
578	$ 30,000 - $39,999	210	305	145	70	175	130
579	$ 40,000 - $49,999	205	225	120	110	145	175
580	$ 50,000 - $59,999	135	195	150	125	120	140
581	$ 60,000 - $69,999	120	240	110	125	125	200
582	$ 70,000 - $79,999	120	160	90	105	105	165
583	$ 80,000 - $89,999	65	90	35	120	165	140
584	$ 90,000 - $99,999	35	70	55	70	95	120
585	$100,000 and over	210	300	175	340	545	355
586	Average household income $	55,545	60,879	62,060	77,548	81,274	69,982
587	Median household income $	45,291	51,428	51,935	71,399	72,898	66,265
588	Standard error of average household income $	2,288	1,904	3,308	2,601	2,877	2,140

Tableau 1. Certaines caractéristiques des secteurs de recensement, recensement de 2001 – Données intégrales et données-échantillon (20 %)

Toronto 0527.04	Toronto 0527.05	Toronto 0527.06 ◇	Toronto 0527.07	Toronto 0527.08	Toronto 0527.09	Caractéristiques	N°
						CARACTÉRISTIQUES DU REVENU DE 2000	
						Population de 15 ans et plus ayant un revenu d'emploi en 2000 selon le sexe et le travail – fin	
1,935	1,745	1,280	1,600	1,425	1,145	Femmes ayant un revenu d'emploi (48)	526
33,376	27,357	25,152	24,500	26,744	30,524	Revenu moyen d'emploi $	527
1,189	1,141	1,105	905	1,211	1,530	Erreur type de revenu moyen d'emploi $	528
1,035	880	685	780	770	595	Ayant travaillé toute l'année à plein temps (49)	529
46,261	39,823	33,407	30,293	37,393	42,465	Revenu moyen d'emploi $	530
1,378	1,529	1,374	1,153	1,524	2,373	Erreur type de revenu moyen d'emploi $	531
775	790	535	790	615	540	Ayant travaillé une partie de l'année ou à temps partiel (50)	532
19,767	14,938	16,283	18,559	14,474	18,239	Revenu moyen d'emploi $	533
1,468	1,195	1,436	1,214	1,338	1,247	Erreur type de revenu moyen d'emploi $	534
						Familles de recensement selon la structure et les tranches de revenu de la famille en 2000	
1,755	1,605	1,210	1,495	1,340	1,040	Total - Toutes les familles de recensement	535
60	85	50	35	45	45	Moins de 10 000 $	536
40	40	60	105	45	15	10 000 $ - 19 999 $	537
140	110	85	150	40	65	20 000 $ - 29 999 $	538
85	165	100	165	95	60	30 000 $ - 39 999 $	539
145	165	65	200	130	70	40 000 $ - 49 999 $	540
135	145	160	120	145	80	50 000 $ - 59 999 $	541
155	55	115	155	110	75	60 000 $ - 69 999 $	542
115	140	100	155	115	95	70 000 $ - 79 999 $	543
210	100	95	95	160	90	80 000 $ - 89 999 $	544
85	110	50	70	125	90	90 000 $ - 99 999 $	545
585	485	330	235	340	360	100 000 $ et plus	546
87,709	80,255	75,276	62,648	79,388	88,608	Revenu moyen des familles $	547
79,829	73,220	67,340	57,153	77,867	82,601	Revenu médian des familles $	548
2,978	2,905	2,771	1,967	2,637	3,714	Erreur type de revenu moyen des familles $	549
1,490	1,335	1,040	1,225	1,170	910	Total - Toutes les familles de recensement comptant un couple (51)	550
50	35	35	20	35	25	Moins de 10 000 $	551
25	25	50	65	10	-	10 000 $ - 19 999 $	552
105	90	40	120	15	35	20 000 $ - 29 999 $	553
55	105	55	110	60	50	30 000 $ - 39 999 $	554
100	135	55	160	95	40	40 000 $ - 49 999 $	555
110	95	155	95	135	70	50 000 $ - 59 999 $	556
110	55	105	140	110	65	60 000 $ - 69 999 $	557
110	125	70	135	110	85	70 000 $ - 79 999 $	558
170	90	95	90	160	85	80 000 $ - 89 999 $	559
75	95	50	75	125	90	90 000 $ - 99 999 $	560
570	475	325	210	320	355	100 000 $ et plus	561
93,780	88,173	80,871	66,298	85,240	94,983	Revenu moyen des familles $	562
83,314	80,267	72,582	63,462	80,345	88,871	Revenu médian des familles $	563
3,380	3,140	2,920	2,132	2,708	3,933	Erreur type de revenu moyen des familles $	564
						Fréquence des unités à faible revenu en 2000	
1,695	1,490	1,140	1,420	1,200	965	Total - Familles économiques	565
150	185	110	195	80	80	Faible revenu	566
8.9	12.5	9.6	13.9	6.4	8.3	Fréquence des unités à faible revenu en 2000 % (52)	567
535	235	350	325	110	160	Total - Personnes hors famille économique de 15 ans et plus	568
105	80	155	100	55	20	Faible revenu	569
19.2	36.3	44.6	30.9	47.0	12.9	Fréquence des unités à faible revenu en 2000 % (52)	570
6,205	5,680	4,515	5,285	4,875	3,775	Total - Population dans les ménages privés	571
665	730	585	850	310	335	Faible revenu	572
10.8	12.8	13.0	16.1	6.4	8.9	Fréquence des unités à faible revenu en 2000 % (52)	573
						Ménages privés selon les tranches de revenu du ménage en 2000	
2,110	1,670	1,410	1,620	1,270	1,080	Total - Tous les ménages privés	574
85	50	55	30	30	35	Moins de 10 000 $	575
55	85	160	115	50	10	10 000 $ - 19 999 $	576
100	130	95	140	30	45	20 000 $ - 29 999 $	577
155	145	105	180	65	60	30 000 $ - 39 999 $	578
165	140	100	215	65	65	40 000 $ - 49 999 $	579
220	145	135	135	140	95	50 000 $ - 59 999 $	580
180	75	95	155	115	70	60 000 $ - 69 999 $	581
130	145	90	195	95	75	70 000 $ - 79 999 $	582
240	105	140	100	165	100	80 000 $ - 89 999 $	583
100	120	45	80	95	110	90 000 $ - 99 999 $	584
675	530	395	280	425	420	100 000 $ et plus	585
86,434	83,249	73,470	64,912	89,984	94,334	Revenu moyen des ménages $	586
76,468	74,717	66,724	59,848	83,087	88,601	Revenu médian des ménages $	587
2,702	2,862	2,715	1,969	3,177	3,598	Erreur type de revenu moyen des ménages $	588

Table 1. Selected Characteristics for Census Tracts, 2001 Census – 100% Data and 20% Sample Data

No.	Characteristics	Toronto 0528.01	Toronto 0528.02	Toronto 0528.04	Toronto 0528.10 ◆ A	Toronto 0528.11 A	Toronto 0528.12 A
	POPULATION CHARACTERISTICS						
1	**Population, 1996 (1)**	**4,334**	**5,450**	**5,169**	**6,047**	**3,745**	**5,879**
2	**Population, 2001 (2)**	**5,331**	**6,095**	**5,715**	**6,236**	**4,474**	**5,938**
3	Population percentage change, 1996-2001	23.0	11.8	10.6	3.1	19.5	1.0
4	Land area in square kilometres, 2001	1.34	1.54	1.65	1.53	0.21	1.44
5	**Total population - 100% Data (3)**	**5,330**	**6,095**	**5,715**	**6,240**	**4,475**	**5,935**
	by sex and age groups						
6	Male	2,660	2,995	2,705	3,115	2,250	2,975
7	0-4 years	215	200	190	170	100	160
8	5-9 years	215	285	260	230	85	255
9	10-14 years	195	280	235	275	85	295
10	15-19 years	215	270	215	265	80	305
11	20-24 years	205	210	215	270	130	245
12	25-29 years	155	190	170	230	245	190
13	30-34 years	180	160	160	185	285	170
14	35-39 years	245	255	240	205	245	190
15	40-44 years	255	280	280	240	215	260
16	45-49 years	235	280	225	290	140	255
17	50-54 years	205	215	190	230	165	255
18	55-59 years	120	125	130	190	110	160
19	60-64 years	75	75	75	125	100	85
20	65-69 years	55	70	45	90	80	70
21	70-74 years	35	50	40	75	75	45
22	75-79 years	30	30	20	25	65	20
23	80-84 years	10	10	15	10	30	15
24	85 years and over	10	10	5	10	5	10
25	Female	2,670	3,105	3,010	3,120	2,225	2,960
26	0-4 years	160	175	195	145	95	125
27	5-9 years	205	290	275	215	85	230
28	10-14 years	205	265	255	255	70	260
29	15-19 years	205	205	210	255	85	315
30	20-24 years	180	215	210	265	140	260
31	25-29 years	160	170	205	190	300	160
32	30-34 years	210	230	245	205	260	150
33	35-39 years	290	315	320	255	195	265
34	40-44 years	290	320	300	295	180	310
35	45-49 years	245	280	245	305	150	290
36	50-54 years	185	195	200	225	170	225
37	55-59 years	105	110	125	155	120	115
38	60-64 years	75	85	75	125	115	80
39	65-69 years	55	95	65	90	85	60
40	70-74 years	50	55	30	70	80	45
41	75-79 years	30	55	30	35	55	30
42	80-84 years	20	20	20	25	25	25
43	85 years and over	5	15	-	15	20	20
44	**Total population 15 years and over**	**4,130**	**4,600**	**4,315**	**4,950**	**3,955**	**4,615**
	by legal marital status						
45	Never married (single)	1,265	1,360	1,445	1,610	1,275	1,505
46	Legally married (and not separated)	2,540	2,805	2,395	2,960	2,035	2,820
47	Separated, but still legally married	55	110	120	70	160	60
48	Divorced	130	135	215	140	310	90
49	Widowed	135	195	145	170	180	140
	by common-law status						
50	Not in a common-law relationship	4,035	4,525	4,175	4,850	3,695	4,560
51	In a common-law relationship	90	75	135	100	265	60
52	**Total population - 20% Sample Data (4)**	**5,330**	**6,095**	**5,715**	**6,240**	**4,475**	**5,935**
	by mother tongue						
53	Single responses	5,190	5,905	5,535	6,110	4,410	5,760
54	English	2,620	2,340	2,650	2,930	2,035	3,055
55	French	40	10	45	30	90	115
56	Non-official languages (5)	2,530	3,560	2,840	3,150	2,290	2,590
57	Italian	120	205	255	170	70	215
58	Chinese, n.o.s.	300	350	160	115	190	190
59	Cantonese	270	525	95	245	380	130
60	Portuguese	75	235	205	230	50	260
61	Punjabi	110	405	180	510	45	555
62	Other languages (6)	1,655	1,830	1,940	1,880	1,555	1,225
63	Multiple responses	140	190	180	125	65	180
64	English and French	-	-	-	-	-	10
65	English and non-official language	125	165	185	110	45	175
66	French and non-official language	10	10	-	15	15	-
67	English, French and non-official language	10	20	-	-	-	-

See reference material at the end of the publication. – Voir les documents de référence à la fin de la publication.

Tableau 1. Certaines caractéristiques des secteurs de recensement, recensement de 2001 – Données intégrales et données-échantillon (20 %)

Toronto 0528.13 A	Toronto 0528.14 A	Toronto 0528.15 A	Toronto 0528.16 A	Toronto 0528.17 A	Toronto 0528.18 A	Caractéristiques	N°
						CARACTÉRISTIQUES DE LA POPULATION	
3,356	**2,115**	**2,795**	**3,693**	**2,150**	**4,403**	**Population, 1996 (1)**	1
3,355	**6,913**	**4,354**	**4,902**	**6,180**	**5,975**	**Population, 2001 (2)**	2
-	226.9	55.8	32.7	187.4	35.7	Variation en pourcentage de la population, 1996-2001	3
1.41	2.47	0.84	0.90	1.87	1.54	Superficie des terres en kilomètres carrés, 2001	4
3,355	**6,915**	**4,355**	**4,900**	**6,180**	**5,975**	**Population totale – Données intégrales (3)**	5
						selon le sexe et les groupes d'âge	
1,630	3,355	2,140	2,400	3,065	2,955	Sexe masculin	6
80	335	165	220	275	240	0-4 ans	7
140	330	240	250	260	305	5-9 ans	8
150	290	180	180	270	270	10-14 ans	9
130	265	160	180	210	200	15-19 ans	10
125	200	155	150	190	195	20-24 ans	11
100	225	100	145	195	150	25-29 ans	12
80	340	165	210	315	220	30-34 ans	13
105	360	230	275	355	315	35-39 ans	14
150	330	205	225	300	325	40-44 ans	15
120	220	190	215	245	220	45-49 ans	16
155	155	130	135	160	195	50-54 ans	17
115	95	75	75	100	110	55-59 ans	18
75	80	50	50	55	85	60-64 ans	19
40	50	40	45	55	55	65-69 ans	20
20	35	35	20	35	50	70-74 ans	21
15	25	15	10	20	15	75-79 ans	22
20	10	10	10	10	10	80-84 ans	23
20	-	-	5	5	-	85 ans et plus	24
1,725	3,555	2,215	2,500	3,120	3,020	Sexe féminin	25
80	315	170	230	260	215	0-4 ans	26
125	330	200	240	265	285	5-9 ans	27
130	250	160	185	245	260	10-14 ans	28
150	260	170	165	210	220	15-19 ans	29
135	215	155	150	185	190	20-24 ans	30
95	290	125	175	260	185	25-29 ans	31
85	420	190	240	335	255	30-34 ans	32
120	385	250	325	380	345	35-39 ans	33
170	350	240	220	310	305	40-44 ans	34
135	230	195	185	210	240	45-49 ans	35
160	165	130	135	150	165	50-54 ans	36
85	100	55	85	80	105	55-59 ans	37
50	90	65	50	65	85	60-64 ans	38
40	65	45	45	65	65	65-69 ans	39
25	35	30	40	50	40	70-74 ans	40
35	25	20	20	35	40	75-79 ans	41
40	15	5	10	10	15	80-84 ans	42
50	10	10	10	5	5	85 ans et plus	43
2,650	**5,065**	**3,245**	**3,605**	**4,600**	**4,410**	**Population totale de 15 ans et plus**	44
						selon l'état matrimonial légal	
795	1,475	935	1,015	1,265	1,220	Célibataire (jamais marié(e))	45
1,600	3,110	2,025	2,285	2,865	2,830	Légalement marié(e) (et non séparé(e))	46
40	125	80	75	120	75	Séparé(e), mais toujours légalement marié(e)	47
70	200	115	130	210	145	Divorcé(e)	48
145	150	90	105	145	135	Veuf ou veuve	49
						selon l'union libre	
2,590	4,925	3,170	3,520	4,375	4,290	Ne vivant pas en union libre	50
55	145	70	85	225	115	Vivant en union libre	51
3,230	**6,910**	**4,355**	**4,900**	**6,180**	**5,975**	**Population totale – Données-échantillon (20 %) (4)**	52
						selon la langue maternelle	
3,125	6,655	4,115	4,760	6,000	5,710	Réponses uniques	53
1,760	2,895	1,800	2,005	2,335	2,540	Anglais	54
10	20	45	100	20	90	Français	55
1,350	3,740	2,270	2,655	3,640	3,080	Langues non officielles (5)	56
215	100	120	110	150	215	Italien	57
65	270	290	305	375	215	Chinois, n.d.a.	58
65	320	510	175	465	230	Cantonais	59
145	390	225	205	425	300	Portugais	60
140	275	180	280	210	330	Pendjabi	61
720	2,395	950	1,590	2,010	1,790	Autres langues (6)	62
105	260	240	145	185	270	Réponses multiples	63
10	-	-	-	-	-	Anglais et français	64
80	255	220	140	170	245	Anglais et langue non officielle	65
20	-	20	10	10	10	Français et langue non officielle	66
-	-	-	-	-	10	Anglais, français et langue non officielle	67

See reference material at the end of the publication. – Voir les documents de référence à la fin de la publication.

Table 1. Selected Characteristics for Census Tracts, 2001 Census – 100% Data and 20% Sample Data

No.	Characteristics	Toronto 0528.01	Toronto 0528.02	Toronto 0528.04	Toronto 0528.10 ◆ A	Toronto 0528.11 A	Toronto 0528.12 A
	POPULATION CHARACTERISTICS						
	by home language						
68	Single responses	3,815	4,145	3,835	3,910	3,150	4,300
69	English	3,095	2,690	3,025	3,080	2,270	3,540
70	French	25	-	20	-	40	25
71	Non-official languages (5)	700	1,450	790	830	835	735
72	Cantonese	180	390	85	145	225	85
73	Chinese, n.o.s.	185	130	20	45	115	50
74	Italian	10	20	20	25	25	-
75	Punjabi	-	165	35	190	-	315
76	Portuguese	10	30	45	40	10	35
77	Other languages (6)	315	720	585	390	460	250
78	Multiple responses	1,515	1,955	1,880	2,325	1,325	1,635
79	English and French	-	40	35	35	55	45
80	English and non-official language	1,485	1,875	1,825	2,285	1,250	1,570
81	French and non-official language	-	20	20	10	-	-
82	English, French and non-official language	25	20	-	-	20	20
	by knowledge of official languages						
83	English only	4,900	5,285	5,240	5,490	3,920	5,245
84	French only	-	-	-	-	20	-
85	English and French	280	390	300	555	430	500
86	Neither English nor French	155	425	170	190	105	195
	by knowledge of non-official languages (5) (7)						
87	Italian	210	355	265	315	130	290
88	Cantonese	360	640	255	330	450	190
89	Chinese, n.o.s.	280	350	80	90	190	125
90	Spanish	330	155	85	90	100	80
91	Portuguese	105	265	185	295	55	290
92	Punjabi	190	495	240	685	110	765
93	Tagalog (Pilipino)	125	145	390	220	85	400
	by first official language spoken						
94	English	5,080	5,575	5,440	5,915	4,185	5,600
95	French	40	20	65	25	115	130
96	English and French	55	75	40	105	70	15
97	Neither English nor French	155	425	170	190	105	195
98	Official language minority - (number) (8)	70	55	85	80	150	140
99	Official language minority - (percentage) (8)	1.3	0.9	1.5	1.3	3.4	2.4
	by ethnic origin (9)						
100	Canadian	745	380	570	770	475	725
101	English	565	260	295	330	460	440
102	Scottish	285	120	320	215	310	270
103	Irish	435	170	225	235	310	225
104	Chinese	915	1,375	510	515	725	475
105	Italian	560	640	515	640	260	580
106	East Indian	785	845	650	1,695	455	1,370
107	French	170	85	200	65	140	175
108	German	210	40	150	120	180	105
109	Portuguese	260	400	335	295	60	465
110	Polish	150	195	495	315	120	125
111	Jewish	15	15	10	-	55	65
112	Jamaican	220	290	495	230	100	265
113	Filipino	205	230	510	270	125	650
114	Ukrainian	160	45	185	175	100	120
	by Aboriginal identity						
115	Total Aboriginal identity population (10)	10	10	10	-	-	40
116	Total non-Aboriginal population	5,325	6,090	5,710	6,235	4,475	5,900
	by Aboriginal origin						
117	Total Aboriginal origins population (11)	10	-	65	10	20	45
118	Total non-Aboriginal population	5,325	6,095	5,650	6,235	4,455	5,890
	by Registered Indian status						
119	Registered Indian (12)	-	-	10	-	-	10
120	Not a Registered Indian	5,325	6,095	5,710	6,235	4,470	5,935

Tableau 1. Certaines caractéristiques des secteurs de recensement, recensement de 2001 – Données intégrales et données-échantillon (20 %)

Toronto 0528.13 A	Toronto 0528.14 A	Toronto 0528.15 A	Toronto 0528.16 A	Toronto 0528.17 A	Toronto 0528.18 A	Caractéristiques	Nº
						CARACTÉRISTIQUES DE LA POPULATION	
						selon la langue parlée à la maison	
2,440	4,690	2,835	3,085	4,015	3,850	Réponses uniques	68
2,075	3,385	1,960	2,135	2,725	2,840	Anglais	69
-	10	15	15	-	60	Français	70
365	1,295	870	930	1,290	950	Langues non officielles (5)	71
65	200	380	95	305	135	Cantonais	72
-	145	130	175	155	85	Chinois, n.d.a.	73
30	30	-	10	10	25	Italien	74
45	75	60	75	125	170	Pendjabi	75
-	130	35	55	70	45	Portugais	76
230	705	270	525	630	490	Autres langues (6)	77
790	2,220	1,515	1,820	2,170	2,125	Réponses multiples	78
15	30	30	75	35	55	Anglais et français	79
740	2,175	1,465	1,710	2,060	2,045	Anglais et langue non officielle	80
-	-	-	-	15	20	Français et langue non officielle	81
40	15	20	30	50	-	Anglais, français et langue non officielle	82
						selon la connaissance des langues officielles	
2,975	6,260	3,735	4,340	5,450	5,290	Anglais seulement	83
-	-	-	-	-	-	Français seulement	84
215	320	345	370	390	485	Anglais et français	85
45	330	275	190	345	200	Ni l'anglais ni le français	86
						selon la connaissance des langues non officielles (5) (7)	
315	230	225	175	205	320	Italien	87
80	380	740	200	505	305	Cantonais	88
20	230	260	295	365	215	Chinois, n.d.a.	89
40	200	80	180	230	265	Espagnol	90
155	450	290	255	430	400	Portugais	91
175	400	215	360	295	450	Pendjabi	92
100	390	200	305	440	370	Tagalog (pilipino)	93
						selon la première langue officielle parlée	
3,140	6,540	3,950	4,595	5,740	5,635	Anglais	94
10	25	60	90	25	95	Français	95
30	35	90	30	75	40	Anglais et français	96
40	320	255	190	340	200	Ni l'anglais ni le français	97
30	45	100	105	65	115	Minorité de langue officielle - (nombre) (8)	98
0.9	0.7	2.3	2.1	1.1	1.9	Minorité de langue officielle - (pourcentage) (8)	99
						selon l'origine ethnique (9)	
455	770	545	560	510	770	Canadien	100
465	565	180	260	260	400	Anglais	101
245	285	200	175	165	180	Écossais	102
185	325	155	235	210	185	Irlandais	103
190	795	1,095	760	1,020	610	Chinois	104
590	410	395	370	365	645	Italien	105
325	940	515	680	1,215	1,140	Indien de l'Inde	106
60	165	135	120	60	140	Français	107
140	170	10	110	90	140	Allemand	108
245	575	365	475	570	535	Portugais	109
115	545	185	425	450	260	Polonais	110
10	-	-	-	45	15	Juif	111
120	370	130	210	250	110	Jamaïquain	112
155	570	205	335	585	565	Philippin	113
95	95	60	100	60	55	Ukrainien	114
						selon l'identité autochtone	
-	10	-	-	-	10	Total de la population ayant une identité autochtone (10)	115
3,225	6,900	4,355	4,900	6,180	5,970	Total de la population non autochtone	116
						selon l'origine autochtone	
40	20	10	-	-	15	Total de la population ayant une origine autochtone (11)	117
3,190	6,895	4,350	4,900	6,175	5,965	Total de la population non autochtone	118
						selon le statut d'Indien inscrit	
-	10	-	-	-	10	Oui, Indien inscrit (12)	119
3,230	6,910	4,355	4,900	6,180	5,970	Non, pas un Indien inscrit	120

Table 1. Selected Characteristics for Census Tracts, 2001 Census – 100% Data and 20% Sample Data

No.	Characteristics	Toronto 0528.01	Toronto 0528.02	Toronto 0528.04	Toronto 0528.10 ◆ A	Toronto 0528.11 A	Toronto 0528.12 A
	POPULATION CHARACTERISTICS						
	by visible minority groups						
121	Total visible minority population	2,915	4,040	3,120	3,520	2,340	3,555
122	Chinese	850	1,255	450	485	705	425
123	South Asian	950	1,195	690	2,025	625	1,535
124	Black	305	490	900	300	155	415
125	Filipino	205	210	505	265	90	615
126	Latin American	90	60	50	25	30	30
127	Southeast Asian	145	140	125	135	30	55
128	Arab	130	350	55	145	265	165
129	West Asian	30	-	70	45	190	100
130	Korean	110	110	80	-	100	45
131	Japanese	10	10	25	-	65	85
132	Visible minority, n.i.e. (13)	35	180	90	35	30	25
133	Multiple visible minorities (14)	55	35	85	60	60	55
	by citizenship						
134	Canadian citizenship (15)	4,885	5,290	5,155	5,560	3,575	5,240
135	Citizenship other than Canadian	445	810	555	675	900	695
	by place of birth of respondent						
136	Non-immigrant population	2,585	2,310	2,560	2,940	1,790	3,015
137	Born in province of residence	2,350	2,185	2,395	2,720	1,460	2,680
138	Immigrant population (16)	2,725	3,730	3,135	3,260	2,575	2,920
139	United States	15	35	45	15	75	30
140	Central and South America	190	240	225	170	60	140
141	Caribbean and Bermuda	150	150	375	235	140	210
142	United Kingdom	150	145	75	75	100	60
143	Other Europe (17)	465	675	940	785	525	415
144	Africa	185	510	140	200	145	175
145	Asia and the Middle East	1,560	1,965	1,335	1,780	1,530	1,885
146	Oceania and other (18)	10	-	-	-	10	10
147	Non-permanent residents (19)	15	50	25	35	110	-
148	**Total immigrant population**	**2,725**	**3,735**	**3,135**	**3,260**	**2,580**	**2,925**
	by period of immigration						
149	Before 1961	130	105	95	105	240	70
150	1961-1970	300	335	360	455	225	325
151	1971-1980	860	740	685	1,015	450	840
152	1981-1990	640	940	1,090	860	485	805
153	1991-2001 (20)	795	1,615	900	825	1,170	870
154	1991-1995	485	905	615	385	400	370
155	1996-2001 (20)	310	705	280	445	770	500
	by age at immigration						
156	0-4 years	250	360	325	190	220	235
157	5-19 years	770	1,050	985	945	710	855
158	20 years and over	1,705	2,320	1,820	2,125	1,650	1,835
159	**Total population**	**5,330**	**6,095**	**5,715**	**6,235**	**4,470**	**5,940**
	by religion						
160	Catholic (21)	2,215	2,230	3,005	2,330	1,430	2,625
161	Protestant	810	815	905	870	755	960
162	Christian Orthodox	220	465	125	385	350	160
163	Christian, n.i.e. (22)	180	280	250	140	135	165
164	Muslim	340	490	315	640	620	515
165	Jewish	25	-	10	-	40	15
166	Buddhist	155	170	180	40	120	165
167	Hindu	350	285	230	590	215	375
168	Sikh	175	430	160	645	100	515
169	Eastern religions (23)	-	-	30	65	-	-
170	Other religions (24)	-	-	-	-	-	-
171	No religious affiliation (25)	865	930	510	535	700	435
172	**Total population 15 years and over**	**4,125**	**4,600**	**4,310**	**4,945**	**3,960**	**4,605**
	by generation status						
173	1st generation (26)	2,635	3,470	2,965	3,170	2,505	2,830
174	2nd generation (27)	910	910	925	1,340	800	1,070
175	3rd generation and over (28)	580	220	425	430	660	705
176	**Total population 1 year and over (29)**	**5,260**	**6,045**	**5,630**	**6,180**	**4,425**	**5,895**
	by place of residence 1 year ago (mobility)						
177	Non-movers	4,805	5,520	4,890	5,745	2,960	5,405
178	Movers	450	525	740	435	1,465	495
179	Non-migrants	205	250	420	150	780	340
180	Migrants	240	280	320	285	685	155
181	Internal migrants	225	135	280	145	510	130
182	Intraprovincial migrants	205	90	260	105	485	130
183	Interprovincial migrants	20	40	20	40	25	-
184	External migrants	20	140	40	135	175	25

Tableau 1. Certaines caractéristiques des secteurs de recensement, recensement de 2001 – Données intégrales et données-échantillon (20 %)

Toronto 0528.13 A	Toronto 0528.14 A	Toronto 0528.15 A	Toronto 0528.16 A	Toronto 0528.17 A	Toronto 0528.18 A	Caractéristiques	N°
						CARACTÉRISTIQUES DE LA POPULATION	
						selon les groupes de minorités visibles	
1,115	3,925	2,690	2,915	4,005	3,350	Total de la population des minorités visibles	121
155	750	1,050	690	925	565	Chinois	122
420	1,200	595	945	1,360	1,330	Sud-Asiatique	123
165	680	350	345	470	230	Noir	124
130	550	205	335	580	545	Philippin	125
10	125	35	90	185	150	Latino-Américain	126
-	145	60	150	45	170	Asiatique du Sud-Est	127
70	205	70	100	185	110	Arabe	128
50	35	65	-	35	30	Asiatique occidental	129
40	20	75	20	100	35	Coréen	130
-	10	10	35	10	-	Japonais	131
25	155	120	130	60	160	Minorité visible, n.i.a. (13)	132
45	65	50	60	60	30	Minorités visibles multiples (14)	133
						selon la citoyenneté	
2,965	5,925	3,830	4,165	4,790	5,255	Citoyenneté canadienne (15)	134
265	990	520	735	1,390	720	Citoyenneté autre que canadienne	135
						selon le lieu de naissance du répondant	
1,775	2,955	1,830	2,030	2,230	2,790	Population non immigrante	136
1,605	2,715	1,710	1,840	2,060	2,565	Née dans la province de résidence	137
1,445	3,905	2,475	2,820	3,865	3,135	Population immigrante (16)	138
10	35	10	15	80	25	États-Unis	139
35	230	65	115	235	210	Amérique centrale et du Sud	140
105	205	175	210	275	225	Caraïbes et Bermudes	141
95	90	65	45	120	110	Royaume-Uni	142
510	980	430	630	650	705	Autre Europe (17)	143
65	260	170	230	215	125	Afrique	144
620	2,110	1,565	1,565	2,275	1,735	Asie et Moyen-Orient	145
10	-	-	-	20	-	Océanie et autre (18)	146
10	50	55	50	85	50	Résidents non permanents (19)	147
1,445	**3,905**	**2,475**	**2,825**	**3,865**	**3,135**	**Population immigrante totale**	148
						selon la période d'immigration	
195	55	50	60	45	70	Avant 1961	149
275	245	175	195	200	270	1961-1970	150
370	605	510	460	630	840	1971-1980	151
165	1,320	605	865	885	890	1981-1990	152
435	1,685	1,135	1,250	2,100	1,065	1991-2001 (20)	153
225	805	775	605	1,140	620	1991-1995	154
210	875	360	640	960	450	1996-2001 (20)	155
						selon l'âge à l'immigration	
145	365	185	250	350	260	0-4 ans	156
510	1,175	770	865	1,230	875	5-19 ans	157
795	2,370	1,515	1,710	2,285	2,000	20 ans et plus	158
3,230	**6,910**	**4,350**	**4,900**	**6,180**	**5,975**	**Population totale**	159
						selon la religion	
1,835	3,205	2,010	2,150	2,780	2,830	Catholique (21)	160
560	870	425	690	740	695	Protestante	161
120	295	115	115	50	220	Orthodoxe chrétienne	162
75	180	240	135	295	60	Chrétiennes, n.i.a. (22)	163
180	605	255	455	585	285	Musulmane	164
-	10	-	10	35	15	Juive	165
-	280	240	235	125	265	Bouddhiste	166
125	470	195	235	460	630	Hindoue	167
105	235	190	275	265	455	Sikh	168
-	-	-	-	70	35	Religions orientales (23)	169
-	10	-	-	-	-	Autres religions (24)	170
225	770	680	610	775	490	Aucune appartenance religieuse (25)	171
2,540	**5,070**	**3,205**	**3,605**	**4,610**	**4,400**	**Population totale de 15 ans et plus**	172
						selon le statut des générations	
1,375	3,580	2,350	2,625	3,560	3,045	1re génération (26)	173
750	975	625	600	630	950	2e génération (27)	174
420	510	235	385	410	405	3e génération et plus (28)	175
3,205	**6,765**	**4,295**	**4,800**	**6,095**	**5,875**	**Population totale de 1 an et plus (29)**	176
						selon le lieu de résidence 1 an auparavant (mobilité)	
3,010	5,390	3,900	4,150	4,095	5,325	Personnes n'ayant pas déménagé	177
190	1,375	390	645	2,005	550	Personnes ayant déménagé	178
85	970	215	400	1,400	300	Non-migrants	179
110	400	175	255	600	250	Migrants	180
40	260	130	150	415	170	Migrants internes	181
40	260	110	150	365	165	Migrants infraprovinciaux	182
-	10	15	-	50	-	Migrants interprovinciaux	183
70	140	50	95	185	80	Migrants externes	184

Table 1. Selected Characteristics for Census Tracts, 2001 Census – 100% Data and 20% Sample Data

No.	Characteristics	Toronto 0528.01	Toronto 0528.02	Toronto 0528.04	Toronto 0528.10 ◆ A	Toronto 0528.11 A	Toronto 0528.12 A
	POPULATION CHARACTERISTICS						
185	**Total population 5 years and over (30)**	**4,955**	**5,715**	**5,325**	**5,905**	**4,270**	**5,660**
	by place of residence 5 years ago (mobility)						
186	Non-movers	3,045	3,320	3,105	4,115	1,235	3,885
187	Movers	1,910	2,400	2,220	1,790	3,040	1,770
188	Non-migrants	1,160	1,300	1,455	800	1,280	1,090
189	Migrants	750	1,100	770	995	1,760	675
190	Internal migrants	500	515	530	555	935	310
191	Intraprovincial migrants	390	360	465	450	840	215
192	Interprovincial migrants	105	160	60	105	95	100
193	External migrants	250	585	240	440	820	365
194	**Total population 15 to 24 years**	**795**	**895**	**850**	**1,055**	**435**	**1,110**
	by school attendance						
195	Not attending school	165	260	215	285	165	315
196	Attending school full time	590	590	585	755	225	750
197	Attending school part time	40	50	50	20	45	50
198	**Total population 15 years and over**	**4,120**	**4,600**	**4,310**	**4,940**	**3,960**	**4,605**
	by highest level of schooling						
199	Less than grade 9 (31)	265	395	325	415	180	365
200	Grades 9-13 without high school graduation certificate	630	875	675	805	450	695
201	Grades 9-13 with high school graduation certificate	420	485	595	760	455	605
202	Some postsecondary without degree, certificate or diploma (32)	565	505	610	655	390	735
203	Trades certificate or diploma (33)	310	245	385	385	235	285
204	College certificate or diploma (34)	590	605	730	760	535	765
205	University certificate below bachelor's degree	170	180	130	155	165	150
206	University with bachelor's degree or higher	1,180	1,305	860	1,000	1,545	1,010
	by combinations of unpaid work						
207	Males 15 years and over	2,015	2,225	2,010	2,435	1,980	2,275
208	Reported unpaid work (35)	1,770	1,930	1,815	2,180	1,705	2,035
209	Housework and child care and care or assistance to seniors	185	225	255	250	70	265
210	Housework and child care only	655	700	620	760	405	730
211	Housework and care or assistance to seniors only	60	125	90	220	115	125
212	Child care and care or assistance to seniors only	-	-	25	-	-	10
213	Housework only	865	860	795	935	1,065	890
214	Child care only	-	20	30	20	40	25
215	Care or assistance to seniors only	-	10	-	-	10	-
216	Females 15 years and over	2,105	2,380	2,300	2,510	1,980	2,330
217	Reported unpaid work (35)	2,015	2,150	2,155	2,330	1,860	2,140
218	Housework and child care and care or assistance to seniors	275	330	365	310	165	375
219	Housework and child care only	805	815	915	915	520	750
220	Housework and care or assistance to seniors only	95	170	125	215	165	140
221	Child care and care or assistance to seniors only	-	10	-	-	-	10
222	Housework only	815	805	735	885	995	830
223	Child care only	25	15	15	10	-	25
224	Care or assistance to seniors only	-	-	10	-	-	-
	by labour force activity						
225	Males 15 years and over	2,020	2,225	2,015	2,440	1,980	2,280
226	In the labour force	1,595	1,705	1,700	1,905	1,535	1,700
227	Employed	1,500	1,610	1,625	1,800	1,470	1,625
228	Unemployed	95	95	75	105	70	80
229	Not in the labour force	420	520	310	530	440	575
230	Participation rate	79.0	76.6	84.4	78.1	77.5	74.6
231	Employment rate	74.3	72.4	80.6	73.8	74.2	71.3
232	Unemployment rate	6.0	5.6	4.4	5.5	4.6	4.7
233	Females 15 years and over	2,110	2,375	2,295	2,505	1,980	2,330
234	In the labour force	1,455	1,540	1,710	1,690	1,245	1,610
235	Employed	1,400	1,490	1,630	1,560	1,125	1,490
236	Unemployed	60	45	80	130	120	120
237	Not in the labour force	650	840	590	815	735	720
238	Participation rate	69.0	64.8	74.5	67.5	62.9	69.1
239	Employment rate	66.4	62.7	71.0	62.3	56.8	63.9
240	Unemployment rate	4.1	2.9	4.7	7.7	9.6	7.5

Tableau 1. Certaines caractéristiques des secteurs de recensement, recensement de 2001 – Données intégrales et données-échantillon (20 %)

Toronto 0528.13 A	Toronto 0528.14 A	Toronto 0528.15 A	Toronto 0528.16 A	Toronto 0528.17 A	Toronto 0528.18 A	Caractéristiques	N°
						CARACTÉRISTIQUES DE LA POPULATION	
3,100	**6,255**	**3,990**	**4,455**	**5,655**	**5,515**	**Population totale de 5 ans et plus (30)**	185
						selon le lieu de résidence 5 ans auparavant (mobilité)	
2,220	1,235	1,880	2,145	915	2,910	Personnes n'ayant pas déménagé	186
875	5,020	2,110	2,310	4,735	2,605	Personnes ayant déménagé	187
455	3,205	1,365	980	2,840	1,630	Non-migrants	188
425	1,815	750	1,325	1,895	975	Migrants	189
205	1,085	465	750	1,135	585	Migrants internes	190
175	1,040	400	655	1,030	530	Migrants infraprovinciaux	191
30	50	65	90	100	55	Migrants interprovinciaux	192
215	725	280	575	760	390	Migrants externes	193
565	**945**	**610**	**640**	**790**	**805**	**Population totale de 15 à 24 ans**	194
						selon la fréquentation scolaire	
170	265	170	200	235	200	Ne fréquentant pas l'école	195
385	655	410	425	515	550	Fréquentant l'école à plein temps	196
10	25	35	20	45	50	Fréquentant l'école à temps partiel	197
2,540	**5,070**	**3,210**	**3,605**	**4,605**	**4,395**	**Population totale de 15 ans et plus**	198
						selon le plus haut niveau de scolarité atteint	
155	375	245	210	335	300	Niveau inférieur à la 9e année (31)	199
495	775	515	655	685	685	De la 9e à la 13e année sans certificat d'études secondaires	200
410	655	545	450	630	580	De la 9e à la 13e année avec certificat d'études secondaires	201
265	665	390	460	465	475	Études postsecondaires partielles sans grade, certificat ou diplôme (32)	202
175	465	195	265	370	320	Certificat ou diplôme d'une école de métiers (33)	203
375	735	470	595	770	750	Certificat ou diplôme collégial (34)	204
40	135	150	70	195	155	Certificat universitaire inférieur au baccalauréat	205
615	1,260	695	895	1,155	1,130	Études universitaires avec baccalauréat ou diplôme supérieur	206
						selon les combinaisons de travail non rémunéré	
1,230	2,405	1,555	1,760	2,240	2,135	Hommes de 15 ans et plus	207
1,045	2,120	1,400	1,590	2,030	1,980	Travail non rémunéré déclaré (35)	208
165	220	205	170	180	280	Travaux ménagers et soins aux enfants et soins ou aide aux personnes âgées	209
320	780	640	695	880	765	Travaux ménagers et soins aux enfants seulement	210
65	110	80	80	85	130	Travaux ménagers et soins ou aide aux personnes âgées seulement	211
10	-	25	10	-	-	Soins aux enfants et soins ou aide aux personnes âgées seulement	212
470	945	430	605	835	800	Travaux ménagers seulement	213
15	55	-	30	35	-	Soins aux enfants seulement	214
-	10	10	-	-	-	Soins ou aide aux personnes âgées seulement	215
1,315	2,665	1,655	1,845	2,370	2,265	Femmes de 15 ans et plus	216
1,180	2,485	1,525	1,735	2,205	2,105	Travail non rémunéré déclaré (35)	217
235	280	265	195	220	330	Travaux ménagers et soins aux enfants et soins ou aide aux personnes âgées	218
365	1,085	660	810	995	910	Travaux ménagers et soins aux enfants seulement	219
100	150	85	105	145	145	Travaux ménagers et soins ou aide aux personnes âgées seulement	220
-	-	-	-	-	-	Soins aux enfants et soins ou aide aux personnes âgées seulement	221
445	945	495	605	825	680	Travaux ménagers seulement	222
15	15	15	20	15	20	Soins aux enfants seulement	223
15	15	-	-	-	10	Soins ou aide aux personnes âgées seulement	224
						selon l'activité	
1,225	2,405	1,555	1,760	2,240	2,135	Hommes de 15 ans et plus	225
960	1,935	1,205	1,445	1,760	1,705	Population active	226
895	1,835	1,155	1,375	1,720	1,625	Personnes occupées	227
65	95	45	70	45	80	Chômeurs	228
265	475	355	315	475	435	Inactifs	229
78.4	80.5	77.5	82.1	78.6	79.9	Taux d'activité	230
73.1	76.3	74.3	78.1	76.8	76.1	Taux d'emploi	231
6.8	4.9	3.7	4.8	2.6	4.7	Taux de chômage	232
1,315	2,660	1,655	1,840	2,365	2,265	Femmes de 15 ans et plus	233
835	1,885	1,055	1,250	1,675	1,585	Population active	234
780	1,790	1,005	1,170	1,590	1,465	Personnes occupées	235
60	95	55	80	85	115	Chômeuses	236
475	775	600	595	690	680	Inactives	237
63.5	70.9	63.7	67.9	70.8	70.0	Taux d'activité	238
59.3	67.3	60.7	63.6	67.2	64.7	Taux d'emploi	239
7.2	5.0	5.2	6.4	5.1	7.3	Taux de chômage	240

Table 1. Selected Characteristics for Census Tracts, 2001 Census – 100% Data and 20% Sample Data

No.	Characteristics	Toronto 0528.01	Toronto 0528.02	Toronto 0528.04	Toronto 0528.10 ◆ A	Toronto 0528.11 A	Toronto 0528.12 A
	POPULATION CHARACTERISTICS						
	by labour force activity – concluded						
241	Both sexes - Participation rate	73.9	70.5	79.2	72.7	70.2	71.9
242	15-24 years	57.9	58.1	72.9	59.4	62.1	59.5
243	25 years and over	77.8	73.5	80.6	76.4	71.2	75.7
244	Both sexes - Employment rate	70.3	67.3	75.4	68.0	65.4	67.5
245	15-24 years	50.6	53.6	68.2	51.7	56.3	50.2
246	25 years and over	74.8	70.5	77.2	72.5	66.7	73.0
247	Both sexes - Unemployment rate	4.9	4.5	4.7	6.7	7.0	6.0
248	15-24 years	12.0	6.7	7.3	13.5	9.3	15.9
249	25 years and over	3.7	4.0	4.3	5.2	6.6	3.8
250	**Total labour force 15 years and over**	**3,050**	**3,245**	**3,415**	**3,600**	**2,780**	**3,310**
	by industry based on the 1997 NAICS						
251	Industry - Not applicable (36)	30	40	35	85	35	60
252	All industries (37)	3,020	3,205	3,375	3,515	2,750	3,250
253	11 Agriculture, forestry, fishing and hunting	10	-	-	10	-	10
254	21 Mining and oil and gas extraction	-	-	-	-	10	-
255	22 Utilities	35	15	15	40	10	20
256	23 Construction	130	110	190	90	55	70
257	31-33 Manufacturing	565	525	705	585	475	475
258	41 Wholesale trade	255	215	280	290	235	265
259	44-45 Retail trade	330	445	385	470	275	410
260	48-49 Transportation and warehousing	125	155	190	235	175	225
261	51 Information and cultural industries	95	100	115	175	65	65
262	52 Finance and insurance	195	345	240	280	285	240
263	53 Real estate and rental and leasing	105	55	85	40	65	45
264	54 Professional, scientific and technical services	295	230	170	280	430	355
265	55 Management of companies and enterprises	-	-	-	10	15	-
266	56 Administrative and support, waste management and remediation services	125	120	195	195	75	150
267	61 Educational services	100	165	120	140	140	95
268	62 Health care and social assistance	195	215	235	205	135	285
269	71 Arts, entertainment and recreation	35	-	80	30	20	35
270	72 Accommodation and food services	195	265	195	170	125	235
271	81 Other services (except public administration)	140	135	105	165	85	140
272	91 Public administration	100	95	70	105	75	135
	by class of worker						
273	Class of worker - Not applicable (36)	30	40	35	85	30	60
274	All classes of worker (37)	3,020	3,205	3,380	3,510	2,745	3,250
275	Paid workers	2,800	3,045	3,220	3,265	2,505	3,050
276	Employees	2,625	2,925	3,095	3,040	2,335	2,890
277	Self-employed (incorporated)	175	125	120	220	170	165
278	Self-employed (unincorporated)	215	155	155	235	230	195
279	Unpaid family workers	-	-	10	10	10	-
	by occupation based on the 2001 NOC-S						
280	Male labour force 15 years and over	1,595	1,705	1,705	1,910	1,540	1,700
281	Occupation - Not applicable (36)	25	20	20	45	-	25
282	All occupations (37)	1,570	1,685	1,685	1,860	1,530	1,675
283	A Management occupations	315	265	205	315	390	350
284	B Business, finance and administration occupations	185	210	220	335	275	305
285	C Natural and applied sciences and related occupations	220	240	155	220	350	225
286	D Health occupations	15	40	-	50	25	60
287	E Occupations in social science, education, government service and religion	35	45	20	30	30	55
288	F Occupations in art, culture, recreation and sport	25	20	10	30	15	25
289	G Sales and service occupations	265	355	365	325	215	300
290	H Trades, transport and equipment operators and related occupations	280	345	425	375	180	225
291	I Occupations unique to primary industry	-	-	30	10	-	20
292	J Occupations unique to processing, manufacturing and utilities	225	150	245	175	55	125
293	Female labour force 15 years and over	1,460	1,540	1,710	1,690	1,245	1,610
294	Occupation - Not applicable (36)	10	20	15	40	25	35
295	All occupations (37)	1,445	1,520	1,690	1,655	1,220	1,575
296	A Management occupations	125	135	135	160	115	185
297	B Business, finance and administration occupations	435	530	545	595	400	495
298	C Natural and applied sciences and related occupations	50	60	65	80	70	55
299	D Health occupations	105	110	100	85	65	160

Tableau 1. Certaines caractéristiques des secteurs de recensement, recensement de 2001 – Données intégrales et données-échantillon (20 %)

Toronto 0528.13 A	Toronto 0528.14 A	Toronto 0528.15 A	Toronto 0528.16 A	Toronto 0528.17 A	Toronto 0528.18 A	Caractéristiques	N°
						CARACTÉRISTIQUES DE LA POPULATION	
						selon l'activité – fin	
70.7	75.4	70.5	75.0	74.7	74.7	Les deux sexes - Taux d'activité	241
53.6	57.7	55.3	55.5	49.7	58.4	15-24 ans	242
75.7	79.4	74.0	79.1	79.8	78.4	25 ans et plus	243
65.7	71.6	67.3	70.6	71.8	70.3	Les deux sexes - Taux d'emploi	244
45.5	52.4	50.8	48.1	44.0	47.8	15-24 ans	245
71.7	76.1	71.2	75.5	77.7	75.1	25 ans et plus	246
6.9	5.0	4.4	5.6	3.8	5.9	Les deux sexes - Taux de chômage	247
16.7	10.0	7.4	12.5	11.4	17.0	15-24 ans	248
5.0	4.1	3.6	4.5	2.6	4.1	25 ans et plus	249
1,795	**3,820**	**2,255**	**2,700**	**3,440**	**3,285**	**Population active totale de 15 ans et plus**	250
						selon l'industrie basée sur le SCIAN de 1997	
35	55	35	25	30	40	Industrie - Sans objet (36)	251
1,765	3,765	2,225	2,675	3,405	3,245	Toutes les industries (37)	252
-	-	-	-	-	15	11 Agriculture, foresterie, pêche et chasse	253
-	-	-	-	-	-	21 Extraction minière et extraction de pétrole et de gaz	254
-	15	30	45	10	15	22 Services publics	255
165	175	75	80	220	125	23 Construction	256
275	635	390	515	540	650	31-33 Fabrication	257
110	250	175	145	275	270	41 Commerce de gros	258
130	425	245	290	345	390	44-45 Commerce de détail	259
125	295	100	225	270	295	48-49 Transport et entreposage	260
60	110	70	75	110	70	51 Industrie de l'information et industrie culturelle	261
130	310	165	245	275	250	52 Finance et assurances	262
45	65	65	75	60	35	53 Services immobiliers et services de location et de location à bail	263
165	295	215	165	295	250	54 Services professionnels, scientifiques et techniques	264
-	10	10	-	-	-	55 Gestion de sociétés et d'entreprises	265
40	180	60	195	145	110	56 Services administratifs, services de soutien, services de gestion des déchets et services d'assainissement	266
130	150	105	55	135	145	61 Services d'enseignement	267
145	230	160	120	225	210	62 Soins de santé et assistance sociale	268
25	25	25	35	35	25	71 Arts, spectacles et loisirs	269
80	250	160	175	235	110	72 Hébergement et services de restauration	270
80	185	105	110	145	155	81 Autres services, sauf les administrations publiques	271
65	155	60	120	85	120	91 Administrations publiques	272
						selon la catégorie de travailleurs	
35	55	35	25	30	40	Catégorie de travailleurs - Sans objet (36)	273
1,765	3,760	2,225	2,670	3,410	3,245	Toutes les catégories de travailleurs (37)	274
1,605	3,485	2,065	2,580	3,115	3,035	Travailleurs rémunérés	275
1,410	3,335	1,950	2,475	3,000	2,945	Employés	276
195	155	115	100	120	90	Travailleurs autonomes (entreprise constituée en société)	277
160	245	150	95	260	195	Travailleurs autonomes (entreprise non constituée en société)	278
-	35	10	-	30	15	Travailleurs familiaux non rémunérés	279
						selon la profession basée sur la CNP-S de 2001	
960	1,935	1,205	1,450	1,760	1,705	Hommes actifs de 15 ans et plus	280
20	25	25	20	10	-	Profession - Sans objet (36)	281
940	1,910	1,175	1,425	1,755	1,700	Toutes les professions (37)	282
225	255	255	235	310	310	A Gestion	283
135	250	105	230	225	260	B Affaires, finance et administration	284
125	325	165	205	320	190	C Sciences naturelles et appliquées et professions apparentées	285
-	20	15	10	20	20	D Secteur de la santé	286
55	65	40	35	65	65	E Sciences sociales, enseignement, administration publique et religion	287
20	25	15	20	45	25	F Arts, culture, sports et loisirs	288
130	330	215	260	245	300	G Ventes et services	289
205	480	220	245	345	345	H Métiers, transport et machinerie	290
-	20	10	10	10	10	I Professions propres au secteur primaire	291
40	140	140	170	160	185	J Transformation, fabrication et services d'utilité publique	292
835	1,885	1,060	1,255	1,675	1,585	Femmes actives de 15 ans et plus	293
15	35	10	10	20	40	Profession - Sans objet (36)	294
820	1,855	1,045	1,245	1,650	1,540	Toutes les professions (37)	295
65	145	130	110	150	130	A Gestion	296
290	640	355	525	605	575	B Affaires, finance et administration	297
40	70	50	55	100	60	C Sciences naturelles et appliquées et professions apparentées	298
70	115	80	60	140	70	D Secteur de la santé	299

Table 1. Selected Characteristics for Census Tracts, 2001 Census – 100% Data and 20% Sample Data

No.	Characteristics	Toronto 0528.01	Toronto 0528.02	Toronto 0528.04	Toronto 0528.10 ◆ A	Toronto 0528.11 A	Toronto 0528.12 A
	POPULATION CHARACTERISTICS						
	by occupation based on the 2001 NOC-S – concluded						
300	E Occupations in social science, education, government service and religion	120	120	115	120	160	110
301	F Occupations in art, culture, recreation and sport	35	25	15	35	40	15
302	G Sales and service occupations	435	340	455	390	265	400
303	H Trades, transport and equipment operators and related occupations	30	45	30	30	45	30
304	I Occupations unique to primary industry	-	15	-	-	-	10
305	J Occupations unique to processing, manufacturing and utilities	110	145	230	165	60	115
306	**Total employed labour force 15 years and over**	**2,900**	**3,100**	**3,250**	**3,360**	**2,590**	**3,110**
	by place of work						
307	Males	1,505	1,610	1,625	1,800	1,465	1,620
308	Usual place of work	1,290	1,440	1,380	1,540	1,150	1,345
309	At home	85	35	55	105	120	85
310	Outside Canada	10	20	-	-	65	15
311	No fixed workplace address	115	110	190	155	130	170
312	Females	1,400	1,490	1,630	1,555	1,125	1,490
313	Usual place of work	1,270	1,405	1,490	1,380	995	1,250
314	At home	80	50	80	75	55	115
315	Outside Canada	20	10	-	25	10	-
316	No fixed workplace address	30	30	50	80	55	120
317	**Total employed labour force 15 years and over with usual place of work or no fixed workplace address**	**2,700**	**2,985**	**3,110**	**3,150**	**2,330**	**2,885**
	by mode of transportation						
318	Males	1,405	1,555	1,565	1,690	1,275	1,510
319	Car, truck, van, as driver	1,150	1,260	1,290	1,395	1,085	1,305
320	Car, truck, van, as passenger	85	90	70	80	50	60
321	Public transit	160	180	170	185	120	120
322	Walked	10	10	20	25	10	20
323	Other method	10	-	15	10	10	15
324	Females	1,295	1,430	1,545	1,460	1,055	1,375
325	Car, truck, van, as driver	890	935	950	945	750	860
326	Car, truck, van, as passenger	120	125	170	155	75	160
327	Public transit	250	310	395	315	210	295
328	Walked	40	35	25	30	20	45
329	Other method	-	30	10	25	-	20
330	**Total population 15 years and over who worked since January 1, 2000**	**3,260**	**3,525**	**3,620**	**3,805**	**2,905**	**3,555**
	by language used at work						
331	Single responses	2,900	3,150	3,220	3,470	2,505	3,305
332	English	2,860	3,105	3,205	3,425	2,470	3,260
333	French	-	-	-	-	10	15
334	Non-official languages (5)	35	45	15	45	30	30
335	Chinese, n.o.s.	10	-	10	10	-	-
336	Cantonese	10	15	-	-	20	15
337	Other languages (6)	15	25	10	35	10	20
338	Multiple responses	360	380	395	340	400	245
339	English and French	45	65	60	25	105	60
340	English and non-official language	300	305	320	290	290	190
341	French and non-official language	-	-	10	-	-	-
342	English, French and non-official language	15	15	10	20	-	-
	DWELLING AND HOUSEHOLD CHARACTERISTICS						
343	**Total number of occupied private dwellings**	**1,480**	**1,640**	**1,720**	**1,590**	**2,170**	**1,395**
	by tenure						
344	Owned	1,345	1,160	1,125	1,440	1,580	1,285
345	Rented	135	485	595	150	590	110
346	Band housing	-	-	-	-	-	-
	by structural type of dwelling						
347	Single-detached house	1,155	1,015	935	1,210	-	1,375
348	Semi-detached house	-	85	35	70	-	-
349	Row house	310	115	230	160	-	-
350	Apartment, detached duplex	15	35	-	130	-	15
351	Apartment, building that has five or more storeys	-	385	520	-	2,165	-
352	Apartment, building that has fewer than five storeys (38)	-	-	-	20	-	-
353	Other single-attached house	-	-	-	-	-	-
354	Movable dwelling (39)	-	-	-	-	-	-

Tableau 1. Certaines caractéristiques des secteurs de recensement, recensement de 2001 – Données intégrales et données-échantillon (20 %)

Toronto 0528.13 A	Toronto 0528.14 A	Toronto 0528.15 A	Toronto 0528.16 A	Toronto 0528.17 A	Toronto 0528.18 A	Caractéristiques	N°
						CARACTÉRISTIQUES DE LA POPULATION	
						selon la profession basée sur la CNP-S de 2001 – fin	
125	165	75	65	120	145	E Sciences sociales, enseignement, administration publique et religion	300
20	25	10	10	20	25	F Arts, culture, sports et loisirs	301
145	485	265	330	395	380	G Ventes et services	302
35	40	10	20	10	25	H Métiers, transport et machinerie	303
-	-	-	-	-	-	I Professions propres au secteur primaire	304
30	160	85	75	115	130	J Transformation, fabrication et services d'utilité publique	305
1,675	**3,630**	**2,160**	**2,545**	**3,310**	**3,095**	**Population active occupée totale de 15 ans et plus**	306
						selon le lieu de travail	
900	1,835	1,160	1,380	1,720	1,625	Hommes	307
700	1,455	985	1,125	1,350	1,345	Lieu habituel de travail	308
85	105	40	55	95	40	À domicile	309
15	45	35	10	25	30	En dehors du Canada	310
95	235	100	190	255	200	Sans adresse de travail fixe	311
780	1,795	1,000	1,175	1,590	1,470	Femmes	312
670	1,630	925	1,115	1,405	1,295	Lieu habituel de travail	313
65	80	45	35	100	75	À domicile	314
-	10	-	-	-	-	En dehors du Canada	315
40	70	25	20	85	95	Sans adresse de travail fixe	316
1,505	**3,395**	**2,035**	**2,445**	**3,085**	**2,940**	**Population active occupée totale de 15 ans et plus ayant un lieu habituel de travail ou sans adresse de travail fixe**	317
						selon le mode de transport	
790	1,690	1,080	1,315	1,600	1,555	Hommes	318
690	1,445	945	1,120	1,380	1,355	Automobile, camion ou fourgonnette, en tant que conducteur	319
30	55	60	45	50	75	Automobile, camion ou fourgonnette, en tant que passager	320
65	150	75	130	145	90	Transport en commun	321
15	35	-	15	15	10	À pied	322
-	-	-	10	20	15	Autre moyen	323
710	1,705	955	1,135	1,490	1,390	Femmes	324
580	1,090	710	770	1,050	960	Automobile, camion ou fourgonnette, en tant que conductrice	325
35	270	110	100	175	165	Automobile, camion ou fourgonnette, en tant que passagère	326
70	305	130	235	235	245	Transport en commun	327
20	35	-	25	20	25	À pied	328
-	-	-	-	10	-	Autre moyen	329
1,965	**4,040**	**2,450**	**2,855**	**3,665**	**3,535**	**Population totale de 15 ans et plus ayant travaillé depuis le 1er janvier 2000**	330
						selon la langue utilisée au travail	
1,800	3,590	2,140	2,460	3,085	3,125	Réponses uniques	331
1,775	3,520	2,065	2,450	3,030	3,070	Anglais	332
-	-	-	-	-	10	Français	333
30	70	85	15	60	45	Langues non officielles (5)	334
-	15	20	10	15	-	Chinois, n.d.a.	335
10	25	70	10	20	15	Cantonais	336
20	35	-	-	20	30	Autres langues (6)	337
165	450	310	395	580	410	Réponses multiples	338
25	75	35	95	80	75	Anglais et français	339
140	375	260	285	480	325	Anglais et langue non officielle	340
-	-	-	-	15	-	Français et langue non officielle	341
-	-	10	15	-	10	Anglais, français et langue non officielle	342
						CARACTÉRISTIQUES DES LOGEMENTS ET DES MÉNAGES	
845	**1,915**	**1,165**	**1,330**	**1,705**	**1,525**	**Nombre total de logements privés occupés**	343
						selon le mode d'occupation	
800	1,610	975	1,140	1,555	1,445	Possédé	344
50	300	190	195	150	85	Loué	345
-	-	-	-	-	-	Logement de bande	346
						selon le type de construction résidentielle	
790	1,135	775	765	640	1,140	Maison individuelle non attenante	347
-	330	10	105	475	315	Maison jumelée	348
35	330	375	315	585	75	Maison en rangée	349
25	10	-	-	10	-	Appartement, duplex non attenant	350
-	105	-	100	-	-	Appartement, immeuble de cinq étages ou plus	351
-	-	-	40	-	-	Appartement, immeuble de moins de cinq étages (38)	352
-	-	-	-	-	-	Autre maison individuelle attenante	353
-	-	10	-	-	-	Logement mobile (39)	354

Table 1. Selected Characteristics for Census Tracts, 2001 Census – 100% Data and 20% Sample Data

No.	Characteristics	Toronto 0528.01	Toronto 0528.02	Toronto 0528.04	Toronto 0528.10 ◆ A	Toronto 0528.11 A	Toronto 0528.12 A
	DWELLING AND HOUSEHOLD CHARACTERISTICS						
	by condition of dwelling						
355	Regular maintenance only	1,285	1,425	1,295	1,180	1,960	1,055
356	Minor repairs	170	200	395	385	170	290
357	Major repairs	25	25	30	25	40	55
	by period of construction						
358	Before 1946	-	-	-	-	-	-
359	1946-1960	-	-	-	-	-	-
360	1961-1970	-	-	-	-	-	-
361	1971-1980	10	-	20	65	45	-
362	1981-1990	575	555	1,035	1,400	1,180	1,070
363	1991-2001 (20)	885	1,080	650	135	945	320
364	Average number of rooms per dwelling	7.7	7.2	6.6	7.8	4.6	8.6
365	Average number of bedrooms per dwelling	3.6	3.2	2.9	3.6	1.7	3.9
366	Average value of dwelling $	302,724	287,368	242,447	266,222	196,239	300,147
367	**Total number of private households**	**1,480**	**1,645**	**1,725**	**1,590**	**2,165**	**1,400**
	by household size						
368	1 person	105	120	205	85	810	60
369	2 persons	255	265	350	230	795	145
370	3 persons	290	295	365	305	290	215
371	4-5 persons	695	780	680	760	265	720
372	6 or more persons	125	175	125	220	15	255
	by household type						
373	One-family households	1,270	1,380	1,405	1,335	1,215	1,135
374	Multiple-family households	75	130	85	165	15	185
375	Non-family households	130	125	230	95	945	75
376	Number of persons in private households	5,330	6,095	5,715	6,230	4,470	5,935
377	Average number of persons in private households	3.6	3.7	3.3	3.9	2.1	4.3
378	Average number of persons per room	0.5	0.5	0.5	0.5	0.4	0.5
379	Tenant households in non-farm, non-reserve private dwellings (40)	130	480	595	150	585	115
380	Average gross rent $ (40)	1,330	751	801	1,075	1,215	1,312
381	Tenant households spending 30% or more of household income on gross rent (40) (41)	35	135	225	50	200	35
382	Tenant households spending from 30% to 99% of household income on gross rent (40) (41)	30	115	145	45	140	30
383	Owner households in non-farm, non-reserve private dwellings (42)	1,340	1,160	1,125	1,445	1,580	1,285
384	Average owner's major payments $ (42)	1,380	1,367	1,272	1,134	1,166	1,410
385	Owner households spending 30% or more of household income on owner's major payments (41) (42)	330	255	220	300	610	240
386	Owner households spending from 30% to 99% of household income on owner's major payments (41) (42)	275	230	185	275	490	185
	CENSUS FAMILY CHARACTERISTICS						
387	**Total number of census families in private households**	**1,430**	**1,650**	**1,590**	**1,675**	**1,235**	**1,545**
	by census family structure and size						
388	Total couple families	1,300	1,420	1,225	1,555	1,105	1,395
389	Total families of married couples	1,250	1,375	1,155	1,455	970	1,365
390	Without children at home	275	280	230	295	530	295
391	With children at home	975	1,095	925	1,165	450	1,070
392	1 child	270	275	305	325	215	185
393	2 children	455	580	445	550	185	550
394	3 or more children	255	245	175	285	50	345
395	Total families of common-law couples	55	40	70	95	135	30
396	Without children at home	30	25	45	35	120	15
397	With children at home	20	20	25	60	15	20
398	1 child	-	15	10	15	10	10
399	2 children	15	-	-	30	10	-
400	3 or more children	-	-	10	10	-	10
401	Total lone-parent families	125	235	365	125	130	150
402	Female parent	100	200	315	110	100	130
403	1 child	45	100	175	70	65	80
404	2 children	50	60	90	25	35	40
405	3 or more children	10	40	55	15	-	10

Tableau 1. Certaines caractéristiques des secteurs de recensement, recensement de 2001 – Données intégrales et données-échantillon (20 %)

Toronto 0528.13 A	Toronto 0528.14 A	Toronto 0528.15 A	Toronto 0528.16 A	Toronto 0528.17 A	Toronto 0528.18 A	Caractéristiques	N°
						CARACTÉRISTIQUES DES LOGEMENTS ET DES MÉNAGES	
						selon l'état du logement	
605	1,745	1,030	1,170	1,590	1,360	Entretien régulier seulement	355
225	145	100	145	85	160	Réparations mineures	356
20	15	35	20	25	-	Réparations majeures	357
						selon la période de construction	
-	10	-	-	-	-	Avant 1946	358
20	-	-	-	-	-	1946-1960	359
10	-	-	-	-	-	1961-1970	360
60	10	10	-	-	10	1971-1980	361
640	55	-	60	20	505	1981-1990	362
125	1,850	1,145	1,270	1,685	1,020	1991-2001 (20)	363
8.9	6.7	7.6	7.1	6.7	7.4	Nombre moyen de pièces par logement	364
3.9	3.2	3.6	3.3	3.2	3.5	Nombre moyen de chambres à coucher par logement	365
341,200	249,517	288,590	261,291	242,920	280,589	Valeur moyenne du logement $	366
850	**1,910**	**1,160**	**1,330**	**1,705**	**1,525**	**Nombre total de logements privés**	367
						selon la taille du ménage	
35	135	70	95	125	75	1 personne	368
140	355	175	210	325	230	2 personnes	369
150	425	255	275	355	280	3 personnes	370
445	785	520	620	720	745	4-5 personnes	371
70	200	145	135	180	195	6 personnes ou plus	372
						selon le genre de ménage	
775	1,570	985	1,080	1,410	1,280	Ménages unifamiliaux	373
30	165	95	130	130	160	Ménages multifamiliaux	374
35	175	80	120	160	85	Ménages non familiaux	375
3,230	6,910	4,355	4,895	6,175	5,970	Nombre de personnes dans les ménages privés	376
3.8	3.6	3.7	3.7	3.6	3.9	Nombre moyen de personnes dans les ménages privés	377
0.4	0.5	0.5	0.5	0.5	0.5	Nombre moyen de personnes par pièce	378
50	295	190	185	140	85	Ménages locataires dans les logements privés non agricoles hors réserve (40)	379
1,058	806	1,132	807	1,232	1,073	Loyer brut moyen $ (40)	380
15	110	75	65	65	25	Ménages locataires consacrant 30 % ou plus du revenu du ménage au loyer brut (40) (41)	381
15	80	60	45	55	20	Ménages locataires consacrant de 30 % à 99 % du revenu du ménage au loyer brut (40) (41)	382
800	1,615	975	1,135	1,545	1,445	Ménages propriétaires dans les logements privés non agricoles hors réserve (42)	383
1,299	1,504	1,351	1,483	1,511	1,403	Principales dépenses de propriété moyennes $ (42)	384
150	480	215	290	430	305	Ménages propriétaires consacrant 30 % ou plus du revenu du ménage aux principales dépenses de propriété (41) (42)	385
140	430	200	265	370	265	Ménages propriétaires consacrant de 30 % à 99 % du revenu du ménage aux principales dépenses de propriété (41) (42)	386
						CARACTÉRISTIQUES DES FAMILLES DE RECENSEMENT	
855	**1,915**	**1,180**	**1,355**	**1,680**	**1,615**	**Total des familles de recensement dans les ménages privés**	387
						selon la structure et la taille de la famille de recensement	
810	1,625	1,035	1,150	1,510	1,440	Total des familles avec conjoints	388
790	1,545	955	1,110	1,395	1,370	Total des familles avec couples mariés	389
160	400	180	220	295	240	Sans enfants à la maison	390
630	1,145	775	890	1,095	1,135	Avec enfants à la maison	391
160	375	240	290	360	325	1 enfant	392
290	505	395	420	520	555	2 enfants	393
180	265	135	175	220	255	3 enfants ou plus	394
20	75	75	45	115	60	Total des familles en union libre	395
10	30	25	15	35	20	Sans enfants à la maison	396
10	50	50	30	80	40	Avec enfants à la maison	397
10	20	20	20	30	25	1 enfant	398
10	10	10	10	30	20	2 enfants	399
-	25	25	-	15	-	3 enfants ou plus	400
45	290	145	205	175	180	Total des familles monoparentales	401
40	260	110	170	155	160	Parent de sexe féminin	402
15	125	60	100	115	80	1 enfant	403
15	85	25	65	35	70	2 enfants	404
10	45	20	-	10	10	3 enfants ou plus	405

Table 1. Selected Characteristics for Census Tracts, 2001 Census – 100% Data and 20% Sample Data

No.	Characteristics	Toronto 0528.01	Toronto 0528.02	Toronto 0528.04	Toronto 0528.10 ◆ A	Toronto 0528.11 A	Toronto 0528.12 A
	CENSUS FAMILY CHARACTERISTICS						
	by census family structure and size – concluded						
406	Male parent	25	30	45	15	30	20
407	1 child	-	25	10	-	15	10
408	2 children	20	10	25	20	10	10
409	3 or more children	-	-	15	-	-	-
410	**Total number of children at home**	**2,260**	**2,680**	**2,410**	**2,700**	**940**	**2,700**
	by age groups						
411	Under 6 years	455	455	515	400	225	375
412	6-14 years	730	1,035	890	890	285	955
413	15-17 years	270	345	270	295	90	385
414	18-24 years	480	490	485	700	195	655
415	25 years and over	315	360	250	415	140	330
416	Average number of children at home per census family (43)	1.6	1.6	1.5	1.6	0.8	1.7
417	**Total number of persons in private households**	**5,330**	**6,095**	**5,715**	**6,230**	**4,470**	**5,935**
	by census family status and living arrangements						
418	Number of non-family persons	340	345	480	300	1,185	300
419	Living with relatives (44)	165	160	210	170	195	170
420	Living with non-relatives only	70	65	70	50	185	65
421	Living alone	105	120	205	85	810	60
422	Number of family persons	4,990	5,755	5,235	5,930	3,280	5,640
423	Average number of persons per census family	3.5	3.5	3.3	3.5	2.6	3.7
424	**Total number of persons 65 years and over**	**300**	**420**	**280**	**435**	**525**	**335**
425	Number of non-family persons 65 years and over	90	110	160	105	155	100
426	Living with relatives (44)	85	100	135	100	30	95
427	Living with non-relatives only	-	-	10	10	-	-
428	Living alone	10	10	20	-	135	10
429	Number of family persons 65 years and over	205	310	125	330	365	235
	ECONOMIC FAMILY CHARACTERISTICS						
430	**Total number of economic families in private households**	**1,360**	**1,515**	**1,505**	**1,520**	**1,280**	**1,325**
	by size of family						
431	2 persons	245	280	345	250	730	150
432	3 persons	295	290	370	300	275	200
433	4 persons	465	505	460	495	195	425
434	5 or more persons	350	440	330	475	85	540
435	Total number of persons in economic families	5,155	5,910	5,435	6,100	3,475	5,810
436	Average number of persons per economic family	3.8	3.9	3.6	4.0	2.7	4.4
437	Total number of unattached individuals	180	185	280	130	990	125
	2000 INCOME CHARACTERISTICS						
	Population 15 years and over by sex and total income groups in 2000						
438	Total - Both sexes	4,125	4,605	4,310	4,945	3,960	4,605
439	Without income	255	260	185	290	200	385
440	With income	3,865	4,345	4,130	4,650	3,755	4,220
441	Under $1,000 (45)	315	300	185	225	215	265
442	$ 1,000 - $ 2,999	175	180	200	235	110	205
443	$ 3,000 - $ 4,999	130	190	225	185	145	215
444	$ 5,000 - $ 6,999	145	140	140	250	125	170
445	$ 7,000 - $ 9,999	160	275	210	275	180	310
446	$10,000 - $11,999	165	210	115	230	115	130
447	$12,000 - $14,999	165	320	230	270	155	275
448	$15,000 - $19,999	255	260	295	365	185	215
449	$20,000 - $24,999	200	365	310	370	255	155
450	$25,000 - $29,999	185	250	330	315	240	270
451	$30,000 - $34,999	320	325	365	360	280	280
452	$35,000 - $39,999	270	270	240	230	265	270
453	$40,000 - $44,999	160	140	235	265	290	245
454	$45,000 - $49,999	175	165	170	220	195	230
455	$50,000 - $59,999	330	345	255	215	340	355
456	$60,000 and over	710	600	610	645	650	630
457	Average income $ (46)	38,938	30,346	32,388	30,497	41,046	33,129
458	Median income $ (46)	30,045	23,990	27,165	23,596	31,336	27,512
459	Standard error of average income $ (46)	1,707	851	1,132	924	1,962	1,033

Tableau 1. Certaines caractéristiques des secteurs de recensement, recensement de 2001 – Données intégrales et données-échantillon (20 %)

Toronto 0528.13 A	Toronto 0528.14 A	Toronto 0528.15 A	Toronto 0528.16 A	Toronto 0528.17 A	Toronto 0528.18 A	Caractéristiques	N°
						CARACTÉRISTIQUES DES FAMILLES DE RECENSEMENT	
						selon la structure et la taille de la famille de recensement – fin	
-	35	30	30	20	25	Parent de sexe masculin	406
-	15	10	20	-	10	1 enfant	407
-	15	10	10	15	10	2 enfants	408
-	10	10	-	-	-	3 enfants ou plus	409
1,440	**2,940**	**1,895**	**2,055**	**2,585**	**2,620**	**Nombre total d'enfants à la maison**	410
						selon les groupes d'âge	
200	775	440	570	605	605	Moins de 6 ans	411
490	1,070	700	720	965	965	6-14 ans	412
180	330	145	195	280	245	15-17 ans	413
355	530	390	370	455	515	18-24 ans	414
215	230	215	195	280	285	25 ans et plus	415
1.7	1.5	1.6	1.5	1.5	1.6	Nombre moyen d'enfants à la maison par famille de recensement (43)	416
3,230	**6,910**	**4,355**	**4,895**	**6,175**	**5,975**	**Nombre total de personnes dans les ménages privés**	417
						selon la situation des particuliers dans la famille de recensement et des particuliers dans le ménage	
130	435	245	330	395	305	Nombre de personnes hors famille de recensement	418
70	185	135	155	200	195	Vivant avec des personnes apparentées (44)	419
25	115	40	85	75	35	Vivant avec des personnes non apparentées uniquement	420
35	135	65	95	120	70	Vivant seules	421
3,100	6,480	4,110	4,565	5,775	5,665	Nombre de personnes membres d'une famille	422
3.6	3.4	3.5	3.4	3.4	3.5	Nombre moyen de personnes par famille de recensement	423
165	**275**	**220**	**260**	**290**	**295**	**Nombre total de personnes de 65 ans et plus**	424
45	90	90	80	75	95	Nombre de personnes hors famille de recensement de 65 ans et plus	425
30	80	75	65	75	80	Vivant avec des personnes apparentées (44)	426
-	-	-	-	-	-	Vivant avec des personnes non apparentées uniquement	427
10	15	10	15	10	10	Vivant seules	428
125	185	135	180	210	200	Nombre de personnes membres d'une famille de 65 ans et plus	429
						CARACTÉRISTIQUES DES FAMILLES ÉCONOMIQUES	
810	**1,750**	**1,085**	**1,220**	**1,580**	**1,470**	**Nombre total de familles économiques dans les ménages privés**	430
						selon la taille de la famille	
145	355	175	195	330	245	2 personnes	431
155	425	265	280	390	295	3 personnes	432
285	545	355	415	475	505	4 personnes	433
225	425	300	325	385	425	5 personnes ou plus	434
3,175	6,660	4,245	4,715	5,975	5,865	Nombre total de personnes dans les familles économiques	435
3.9	3.8	3.9	3.9	3.8	4.0	Nombre moyen de personnes par famille économique	436
55	250	110	180	200	105	Nombre total de personnes hors famille économique	437
						CARACTÉRISTIQUES DU REVENU DE 2000	
						Population de 15 ans et plus selon le sexe et les tranches de revenu total en 2000	
2,540	5,065	3,205	3,600	4,610	4,400	Total - Les deux sexes	438
265	460	220	315	345	260	Sans revenu	439
2,275	4,610	2,990	3,290	4,260	4,130	Avec un revenu	440
130	220	175	145	225	175	Moins de 1 000 $ (45)	441
130	190	180	155	205	180	1 000 $ - 2 999 $	442
85	170	110	90	100	165	3 000 $ - 4 999 $	443
120	155	135	120	125	150	5 000 $ - 6 999 $	444
120	290	130	245	235	225	7 000 $ - 9 999 $	445
55	165	120	150	155	155	10 000 $ - 11 999 $	446
110	220	170	150	235	235	12 000 $ - 14 999 $	447
130	260	200	210	235	220	15 000 $ - 19 999 $	448
175	270	250	170	260	275	20 000 $ - 24 999 $	449
155	350	215	255	315	305	25 000 $ - 29 999 $	450
105	465	205	235	440	355	30 000 $ - 34 999 $	451
100	385	195	205	330	250	35 000 $ - 39 999 $	452
180	340	145	255	225	340	40 000 $ - 44 999 $	453
75	225	65	190	190	165	45 000 $ - 49 999 $	454
175	310	270	240	340	295	50 000 $ - 59 999 $	455
435	580	425	475	640	630	60 000 $ et plus	456
41,499	31,999	31,122	33,163	33,085	33,575	Revenu moyen $ (46)	457
27,287	29,964	25,329	28,977	30,034	28,861	Revenu médian $ (46)	458
3,899	817	1,059	1,085	849	944	Erreur type de revenu moyen $ (46)	459

Table 1. Selected Characteristics for Census Tracts, 2001 Census – 100% Data and 20% Sample Data

No.	Characteristics	Toronto 0528.01	Toronto 0528.02	Toronto 0528.04	Toronto 0528.10 ◆ A	Toronto 0528.11 A	Toronto 0528.12 A
	2000 INCOME CHARACTERISTICS						
	Population 15 years and over by sex and total income groups in 2000 – concluded						
460	Total - Males	2,015	2,220	2,015	2,435	1,980	2,280
461	Without income	105	110	80	110	40	160
462	With income	1,910	2,115	1,930	2,325	1,940	2,120
463	Under $1,000 (45)	185	155	60	85	95	150
464	$ 1,000 - $ 2,999	45	70	95	95	45	75
465	$ 3,000 - $ 4,999	80	85	85	70	75	120
466	$ 5,000 - $ 6,999	55	50	70	120	40	85
467	$ 7,000 - $ 9,999	55	115	85	115	65	100
468	$10,000 - $11,999	95	70	20	95	50	65
469	$12,000 - $14,999	50	115	70	85	55	100
470	$15,000 - $19,999	120	145	125	180	40	110
471	$20,000 - $24,999	55	100	100	190	115	85
472	$25,000 - $29,999	55	100	180	155	90	90
473	$30,000 - $34,999	120	150	140	140	145	100
474	$35,000 - $39,999	120	130	85	130	105	160
475	$40,000 - $44,999	95	65	115	150	180	95
476	$45,000 - $49,999	90	85	70	140	100	165
477	$50,000 - $59,999	185	210	195	130	215	155
478	$60,000 and over	495	485	440	445	530	470
479	Average income $ (46)	46,800	37,298	39,508	36,016	54,151	38,897
480	Median income $ (46)	35,937	31,069	31,515	28,307	41,500	31,935
481	Standard error of average income $ (46)	2,767	1,416	2,009	1,490	3,516	1,739
482	Total - Females	2,110	2,380	2,295	2,505	1,980	2,330
483	Without income	155	150	105	180	165	230
484	With income	1,960	2,230	2,195	2,325	1,815	2,100
485	Under $1,000 (45)	130	145	125	145	115	120
486	$ 1,000 - $ 2,999	125	115	105	135	70	130
487	$ 3,000 - $ 4,999	50	110	140	110	75	95
488	$ 5,000 - $ 6,999	85	90	70	130	90	85
489	$ 7,000 - $ 9,999	100	160	125	165	115	215
490	$10,000 - $11,999	70	150	90	135	65	70
491	$12,000 - $14,999	115	205	165	185	100	170
492	$15,000 - $19,999	135	115	170	185	145	105
493	$20,000 - $24,999	140	260	215	180	145	70
494	$25,000 - $29,999	130	155	150	155	155	175
495	$30,000 - $34,999	195	175	230	220	135	180
496	$35,000 - $39,999	150	140	155	95	160	105
497	$40,000 - $44,999	70	80	125	115	110	155
498	$45,000 - $49,999	90	80	100	80	100	65
499	$50,000 - $59,999	145	135	65	90	125	200
500	$60,000 and over	210	115	170	200	120	165
501	Average income $ (46)	31,259	23,767	26,117	24,978	27,054	27,311
502	Median income $ (46)	25,040	20,291	22,281	18,955	24,223	24,457
503	Standard error of average income $ (46)	1,945	886	1,076	1,033	1,131	1,056
	by composition of total income						
504	Total - Composition of income in 2000 % (47)	100.0	100.0	100.0	100.0	100.0	100.0
505	Employment income %	89.7	88.6	91.3	86.2	84.1	90.5
506	Government transfer payments %	4.0	6.8	5.6	6.9	6.2	4.9
507	Other %	6.2	4.6	3.0	6.9	9.8	4.6
	Population 15 years and over with employment income in 2000 by sex and work activity						
508	Both sexes with employment income (48)	3,185	3,435	3,540	3,650	2,780	3,445
509	Average employment income $	42,408	33,960	34,518	33,497	46,618	36,758
510	Standard error of average employment income $	1,935	980	1,114	1,046	2,440	1,181
511	Worked full year, full time (49)	2,000	1,955	2,110	2,125	1,750	1,900
512	Average employment income $	56,213	46,514	43,864	44,819	59,965	49,645
513	Standard error of average employment income $	2,781	1,285	1,537	1,415	3,490	1,598
514	Worked part year or part time (50)	1,095	1,420	1,330	1,435	975	1,385
515	Average employment income $	19,659	17,639	21,548	18,365	24,459	21,531
516	Standard error of average employment income $	1,679	1,007	1,267	1,098	1,926	1,444
517	Males with employment income (48)	1,615	1,790	1,755	1,925	1,535	1,780
518	Average employment income $	50,833	40,466	40,725	37,962	59,086	43,035
519	Standard error of average employment income $	3,010	1,538	1,826	1,595	4,128	1,963
520	Worked full year, full time (49)	1,065	1,120	1,090	1,265	1,045	1,060
521	Average employment income $	65,024	52,586	50,629	48,099	72,683	56,421
522	Standard error of average employment income $	4,048	1,868	2,454	2,015	5,614	2,480
523	Worked part year or part time (50)	535	630	635	600	465	665
524	Average employment income $	22,932	21,026	24,904	19,928	31,362	23,082
525	Standard error of average employment income $	3,029	1,826	2,098	1,804	3,362	2,627

Tableau 1. Certaines caractéristiques des secteurs de recensement, recensement de 2001 – Données intégrales et données-échantillon (20 %)

Toronto 0528.13 A	Toronto 0528.14 A	Toronto 0528.15 A	Toronto 0528.16 A	Toronto 0528.17 A	Toronto 0528.18 A	Caractéristiques	N°
						CARACTÉRISTIQUES DU REVENU DE 2000	
						Population de 15 ans et plus selon le sexe et les tranches de revenu total en 2000 – fin	
1,225	2,405	1,555	1,760	2,245	2,135	Total - Hommes	460
90	215	85	140	150	130	Sans revenu	461
1,135	2,190	1,470	1,620	2,090	2,000	Avec un revenu	462
75	95	75	65	100	60	Moins de 1 000 $ (45)	463
30	40	45	50	65	65	1 000 $ - 2 999 $	464
40	40	35	30	15	40	3 000 $ - 4 999 $	465
45	30	70	55	50	40	5 000 $ - 6 999 $	466
30	150	60	125	105	60	7 000 $ - 9 999 $	467
10	55	45	35	50	95	10 000 $ - 11 999 $	468
45	70	80	35	90	100	12 000 $ - 14 999 $	469
40	120	95	75	110	75	15 000 $ - 19 999 $	470
55	120	125	55	130	80	20 000 $ - 24 999 $	471
75	55	80	70	110	140	25 000 $ - 29 999 $	472
55	210	85	110	205	135	30 000 $ - 34 999 $	473
50	215	85	115	170	140	35 000 $ - 39 999 $	474
110	205	95	155	120	180	40 000 $ - 44 999 $	475
25	130	25	145	130	90	45 000 $ - 49 999 $	476
120	220	170	155	205	215	50 000 $ - 59 999 $	477
330	430	305	345	445	480	60 000 $ et plus	478
57,190	39,378	37,238	40,023	38,789	42,447	Revenu moyen $ (46)	479
40,017	36,226	30,282	38,391	35,066	39,125	Revenu médian $ (46)	480
7,477	1,342	1,674	1,629	1,281	1,600	Erreur type de revenu moyen $ (46)	481
1,310	2,665	1,655	1,840	2,365	2,265	Total - Femmes	482
175	245	135	175	195	130	Sans revenu	483
1,140	2,415	1,520	1,665	2,170	2,135	Avec un revenu	484
50	125	95	80	125	120	Moins de 1 000 $ (45)	485
105	150	130	105	140	115	1 000 $ - 2 999 $	486
55	125	75	60	90	125	3 000 $ - 4 999 $	487
70	130	65	65	70	115	5 000 $ - 6 999 $	488
90	135	70	125	130	170	7 000 $ - 9 999 $	489
45	115	80	110	110	65	10 000 $ - 11 999 $	490
65	155	90	115	145	135	12 000 $ - 14 999 $	491
90	140	105	135	130	150	15 000 $ - 19 999 $	492
115	155	125	110	135	190	20 000 $ - 24 999 $	493
85	285	135	185	205	165	25 000 $ - 29 999 $	494
45	255	120	125	235	215	30 000 $ - 34 999 $	495
50	175	115	90	160	110	35 000 $ - 39 999 $	496
65	135	45	100	100	165	40 000 $ - 44 999 $	497
45	95	45	50	60	75	45 000 $ - 49 999 $	498
55	95	100	85	135	85	50 000 $ - 59 999 $	499
110	150	120	130	200	150	60 000 $ et plus	500
25,917	25,318	25,214	26,503	27,586	25,261	Revenu moyen $ (46)	501
20,017	24,457	21,296	21,276	25,038	21,309	Revenu médian $ (46)	502
1,541	883	1,214	1,345	1,067	928	Erreur type de revenu moyen $ (46)	503
						selon la composition du revenu total	
100.0	100.0	100.0	100.0	100.0	100.0	Total - Composition du revenu en 2000 % (47)	504
88.1	91.4	90.3	91.7	92.3	91.3	Revenu d'emploi %	505
4.9	5.3	6.1	5.3	4.9	5.3	Transferts gouvernementaux %	506
7.0	3.3	3.5	3.1	2.7	3.3	Autre %	507
						Population de 15 ans et plus ayant un revenu d'emploi en 2000 selon le sexe et le travail	
1,860	3,885	2,340	2,740	3,620	3,515	Les deux sexes ayant un revenu d'emploi (48)	508
44,766	34,636	35,949	36,499	35,975	36,094	Revenu moyen d'emploi $	509
3,976	881	1,210	1,160	917	1,026	Erreur type de revenu moyen d'emploi $	510
1,005	2,610	1,380	1,725	2,200	2,125	Ayant travaillé toute l'année à plein temps (49)	511
59,695	42,784	44,966	47,268	46,285	46,873	Revenu moyen d'emploi $	512
4,111	1,069	1,511	1,422	1,151	1,292	Erreur type de revenu moyen d'emploi $	513
830	1,200	915	965	1,315	1,325	Ayant travaillé une partie de l'année ou à temps partiel (50)	514
27,339	18,573	23,601	18,977	20,424	19,380	Revenu moyen d'emploi $	515
7,218	1,071	1,692	1,264	1,054	1,236	Erreur type de revenu moyen d'emploi $	516
925	1,935	1,215	1,415	1,870	1,785	Hommes ayant un revenu d'emploi (48)	517
62,945	41,603	41,846	43,288	40,964	44,161	Revenu moyen d'emploi $	518
7,467	1,403	1,847	1,640	1,351	1,646	Erreur type de revenu moyen d'emploi $	519
580	1,400	750	1,015	1,235	1,160	Ayant travaillé toute l'année à plein temps (49)	520
75,647	48,895	52,051	52,053	50,001	54,175	Revenu moyen d'emploi $	521
6,472	1,671	2,269	1,857	1,610	1,961	Erreur type de revenu moyen d'emploi $	522
335	510	440	385	600	585	Ayant travaillé une partie de l'année ou à temps partiel (50)	523
41,929	23,008	26,089	21,807	23,055	25,154	Revenu moyen d'emploi $	524
16,791	1,779	2,509	2,081	1,733	2,407	Erreur type de revenu moyen d'emploi $	525

Table 1. Selected Characteristics for Census Tracts, 2001 Census – 100% Data and 20% Sample Data

No.	Characteristics	Toronto 0528.01	Toronto 0528.02	Toronto 0528.04	Toronto 0528.10 ◆ A	Toronto 0528.11 A	Toronto 0528.12 A
	2000 INCOME CHARACTERISTICS						
	Population 15 years and over with employment income in 2000 by sex and work activity – concluded						
526	Females with employment income (48)	1,580	1,645	1,785	1,720	1,245	1,665
527	Average employment income $	33,782	26,874	28,411	28,505	31,201	30,057
528	Standard error of average employment income $	2,317	1,081	1,206	1,253	1,423	1,170
529	Worked full year, full time (49)	935	835	1,020	860	705	840
530	Average employment income $	46,141	38,384	36,679	39,976	41,135	41,075
531	Standard error of average employment income $	3,616	1,485	1,640	1,780	1,734	1,601
532	Worked part year or part time (50)	560	795	700	830	510	720
533	Average employment income $	16,536	14,966	18,500	17,234	18,178	20,099
534	Standard error of average employment income $	1,490	1,069	1,460	1,359	1,738	1,388
	Census families by structure and family income groups in 2000						
535	Total - All census families	1,430	1,655	1,595	1,680	1,235	1,545
536	Under $10,000	80	75	95	45	65	55
537	$ 10,000 - $19,999	50	85	85	60	35	75
538	$ 20,000 - $29,999	55	160	105	135	100	120
539	$ 30,000 - $39,999	90	105	155	115	125	85
540	$ 40,000 - $49,999	75	120	140	175	75	100
541	$ 50,000 - $59,999	70	155	95	150	180	150
542	$ 60,000 - $69,999	145	125	155	125	130	100
543	$ 70,000 - $79,999	150	135	185	140	125	130
544	$ 80,000 - $89,999	90	130	70	125	85	110
545	$ 90,000 - $99,999	115	110	130	135	65	110
546	$100,000 and over	505	450	390	465	245	520
547	Average family income $	97,541	74,861	75,198	78,062	78,988	84,715
548	Median family income $	79,978	70,053	68,045	71,405	62,286	76,504
549	Standard error of average family income $	4,478	2,346	3,216	2,532	4,858	2,957
550	Total - All couple census families (51)	1,305	1,415	1,225	1,550	1,105	1,400
551	Under $10,000	65	45	15	30	60	40
552	$ 10,000 - $19,999	45	60	25	55	35	45
553	$ 20,000 - $29,999	45	120	55	105	65	90
554	$ 30,000 - $39,999	75	95	85	110	80	70
555	$ 40,000 - $49,999	65	65	85	160	60	80
556	$ 50,000 - $59,999	70	135	75	145	170	130
557	$ 60,000 - $69,999	130	115	135	130	130	90
558	$ 70,000 - $79,999	120	125	180	125	120	120
559	$ 80,000 - $89,999	85	120	75	125	75	110
560	$ 90,000 - $99,999	110	110	110	135	70	110
561	$100,000 and over	495	430	380	440	240	505
562	Average family income $	100,700	79,473	87,730	80,077	82,755	89,608
563	Median family income $	82,245	74,180	76,810	73,856	65,771	83,339
564	Standard error of average family income $	4,666	2,494	3,568	2,636	5,353	3,147
	Incidence of low income in 2000						
565	Total - Economic families	1,355	1,515	1,505	1,525	1,280	1,325
566	Low income	150	240	245	135	135	120
567	Incidence of low income in 2000 % (52)	11.3	15.9	16.2	9.1	10.6	9.1
568	Total - Unattached individuals 15 years and over	170	180	275	130	990	125
569	Low income	45	100	95	30	215	30
570	Incidence of low income in 2000 % (52)	26.0	57.6	34.5	22.0	21.3	23.5
571	Total - Population in private households	5,320	6,095	5,710	6,230	4,470	5,935
572	Low income	665	875	870	605	630	505
573	Incidence of low income in 2000 % (52)	12.4	14.4	15.2	9.7	14.1	8.5
	Private households by household income groups in 2000						
574	Total - All private households	1,475	1,640	1,720	1,590	2,170	1,395
575	Under $10,000	40	70	100	30	145	25
576	$ 10,000 - $19,999	40	90	100	40	135	30
577	$ 20,000 - $29,999	85	135	110	70	205	65
578	$ 30,000 - $39,999	100	95	170	115	210	70
579	$ 40,000 - $49,999	55	105	140	140	160	60
580	$ 50,000 - $59,999	95	120	80	125	305	115
581	$ 60,000 - $69,999	130	135	160	130	210	90
582	$ 70,000 - $79,999	130	135	190	145	195	115
583	$ 80,000 - $89,999	105	110	95	120	115	105
584	$ 90,000 - $99,999	120	95	110	155	95	110
585	$100,000 and over	565	540	460	535	380	605
586	Average household income $	102,062	80,307	77,460	88,979	71,050	100,171
587	Median household income $	82,431	74,090	70,279	80,128	55,386	92,516
588	Standard error of average household income $	4,503	2,562	3,208	2,946	3,351	3,290

Tableau 1. Certaines caractéristiques des secteurs de recensement, recensement de 2001 – Données intégrales et données-échantillon (20 %)

Toronto 0528.13 A	Toronto 0528.14 A	Toronto 0528.15 A	Toronto 0528.16 A	Toronto 0528.17 A	Toronto 0528.18 A	Caractéristiques	N°
						CARACTÉRISTIQUES DU REVENU DE 2000	
						Population de 15 ans et plus ayant un revenu d'emploi en 2000 selon le sexe et le travail – fin	
930	1,955	1,125	1,320	1,750	1,725	Femmes ayant un revenu d'emploi (48)	526
26,711	27,717	29,594	29,234	30,646	27,732	Revenu moyen d'emploi $	527
1,745	955	1,409	1,528	1,183	1,072	Erreur type de revenu moyen d'emploi $	528
425	1,210	625	710	965	965	Ayant travaillé toute l'année à plein temps (49)	529
37,848	35,721	36,442	40,442	41,529	38,124	Revenu moyen d'emploi $	530
2,757	1,108	1,648	2,107	1,580	1,390	Erreur type de revenu moyen d'emploi $	531
490	690	485	575	715	735	Ayant travaillé une partie de l'année ou à temps partiel (50)	532
17,306	15,307	21,348	17,071	18,226	14,781	Revenu moyen d'emploi $	533
1,846	1,250	2,250	1,542	1,263	1,075	Erreur type de revenu moyen d'emploi $	534
						Familles de recensement selon la structure et les tranches de revenu de la famille en 2000	
855	1,910	1,180	1,355	1,685	1,615	Total - Toutes les familles de recensement	535
20	140	55	75	60	45	Moins de 10 000 $	536
25	65	45	80	75	60	10 000 $ - 19 999 $	537
25	80	75	80	100	105	20 000 $ - 29 999 $	538
70	145	105	65	100	120	30 000 $ - 39 999 $	539
65	190	90	100	155	95	40 000 $ - 49 999 $	540
80	170	135	100	90	115	50 000 $ - 59 999 $	541
80	240	90	140	210	155	60 000 $ - 69 999 $	542
70	185	115	190	205	175	70 000 $ - 79 999 $	543
35	175	65	70	185	160	80 000 $ - 89 999 $	544
50	180	130	110	105	100	90 000 $ - 99 999 $	545
330	345	265	340	405	480	100 000 $ et plus	546
107,014	69,783	73,756	73,673	75,774	80,722	Revenu moyen des familles $	547
76,989	66,696	67,323	70,840	72,311	76,353	Revenu médian des familles $	548
10,546	1,970	2,726	2,688	2,131	2,529	Erreur type de revenu moyen des familles $	549
805	1,625	1,035	1,155	1,510	1,440	Total - Toutes les familles de recensement comptant un couple (51)	550
20	85	35	55	60	25	Moins de 10 000 $	551
20	15	30	55	60	35	10 000 $ - 19 999 $	552
20	45	65	60	75	85	20 000 $ - 29 999 $	553
75	100	95	50	80	100	30 000 $ - 39 999 $	554
55	155	60	65	125	60	40 000 $ - 49 999 $	555
70	150	125	75	70	105	50 000 $ - 59 999 $	556
75	225	80	125	190	135	60 000 $ - 69 999 $	557
60	175	105	160	185	160	70 000 $ - 79 999 $	558
30	170	55	65	170	140	80 000 $ - 89 999 $	559
50	175	120	110	100	100	90 000 $ - 99 999 $	560
330	330	260	330	400	480	100 000 $ et plus	561
110,310	75,838	77,485	78,989	78,671	85,558	Revenu moyen des familles $	562
83,128	70,519	72,322	74,157	75,303	80,145	Revenu médian des familles $	563
11,080	2,118	2,947	2,949	2,289	2,712	Erreur type de revenu moyen des familles $	564
						Fréquence des unités à faible revenu en 2000	
805	1,750	1,085	1,220	1,575	1,470	Total - Familles économiques	565
70	210	125	160	180	135	Faible revenu	566
8.3	11.9	11.8	13.0	11.2	9.1	Fréquence des unités à faible revenu en 2000 % (52)	567
55	250	105	175	195	100	Total - Personnes hors famille économique de 15 ans et plus	568
10	35	15	55	20	20	Faible revenu	569
12.6	12.8	16.4	33.3	10.0	21.2	Fréquence des unités à faible revenu en 2000 % (52)	570
3,230	6,915	4,350	4,890	6,170	5,965	Total - Population dans les ménages privés	571
285	890	510	645	730	550	Faible revenu	572
8.8	12.9	11.7	13.2	11.8	9.3	Fréquence des unités à faible revenu en 2000 % (52)	573
						Ménages privés selon les tranches de revenu du ménage en 2000	
850	1,915	1,165	1,335	1,700	1,525	Total - Tous les ménages privés	574
10	80	25	65	50	20	Moins de 10 000 $	575
20	75	30	70	50	40	10 000 $ - 19 999 $	576
30	70	60	30	90	70	20 000 $ - 29 999 $	577
80	145	105	75	85	90	30 000 $ - 39 999 $	578
60	150	90	80	115	90	40 000 $ - 49 999 $	579
65	165	105	90	100	100	50 000 $ - 59 999 $	580
75	200	85	125	205	125	60 000 $ - 69 999 $	581
55	200	130	175	195	160	70 000 $ - 79 999 $	582
35	155	75	90	190	170	80 000 $ - 89 999 $	583
60	195	150	110	125	80	90 000 $ - 99 999 $	584
360	470	305	425	500	585	100 000 $ et plus	585
111,293	77,096	80,007	81,878	82,656	90,914	Revenu moyen des ménages $	586
87,188	72,772	75,764	77,142	77,462	85,525	Revenu médian des ménages $	587
10,836	2,085	2,693	2,783	2,252	2,784	Erreur type de revenu moyen des ménages $	588

Table 1. Selected Characteristics for Census Tracts, 2001 Census – 100% Data and 20% Sample Data

No.	Characteristics	Toronto 0528.19 ◆◇ A	Toronto 0528.20 A	Toronto 0528.21 ◆ A	Toronto 0528.22 ◆ A	Toronto 0528.23 ◆ A	Toronto 0528.24 A
	POPULATION CHARACTERISTICS						
1	**Population, 1996 (1)**	**4,457**	**5,641**	**3,012**	**5,904**	**5,465**	**5,241**
2	**Population, 2001 (2)**	**5,370**	**6,035**	**3,553**	**6,604**	**9,139**	**5,337**
3	Population percentage change, 1996-2001	20.5	7.0	18.0	11.9	67.2	1.8
4	Land area in square kilometres, 2001	0.78	3.30	1.41	1.43	4.44	4.61
5	**Total population - 100% Data (3)**	**5,370**	**6,035**	**3,550**	**6,605**	**9,135**	**5,335**
	by sex and age groups						
6	Male	2,630	2,995	1,610	3,305	4,630	2,630
7	0-4 years	145	155	125	310	370	145
8	5-9 years	220	215	155	300	515	155
9	10-14 years	220	220	105	265	445	210
10	15-19 years	220	255	125	245	345	280
11	20-24 years	215	275	105	265	280	270
12	25-29 years	165	225	95	240	250	185
13	30-34 years	180	185	115	275	340	155
14	35-39 years	245	175	145	300	465	205
15	40-44 years	235	215	130	235	490	210
16	45-49 years	230	230	105	225	345	205
17	50-54 years	210	235	110	210	270	240
18	55-59 years	105	220	70	145	190	120
19	60-64 years	95	135	60	100	120	100
20	65-69 years	70	100	40	80	100	60
21	70-74 years	40	85	35	50	65	35
22	75-79 years	20	35	25	30	20	20
23	80-84 years	10	25	35	10	15	10
24	85 years and over	5	10	20	10	5	10
25	Female	2,740	3,040	1,940	3,305	4,510	2,705
26	0-4 years	145	165	115	285	355	135
27	5-9 years	205	180	155	275	440	190
28	10-14 years	205	215	130	250	380	210
29	15-19 years	220	250	115	225	305	245
30	20-24 years	195	265	105	265	280	245
31	25-29 years	200	205	145	290	265	195
32	30-34 years	200	175	185	280	410	190
33	35-39 years	280	225	175	300	495	205
34	40-44 years	265	230	120	230	470	240
35	45-49 years	260	285	140	230	345	265
36	50-54 years	190	270	125	175	260	215
37	55-59 years	120	180	80	140	165	115
38	60-64 years	80	135	70	120	125	75
39	65-69 years	70	95	70	80	85	55
40	70-74 years	55	75	55	80	55	35
41	75-79 years	30	45	55	45	30	40
42	80-84 years	20	30	35	30	15	25
43	85 years and over	5	10	55	15	15	15
44	**Total population 15 years and over**	**4,235**	**4,890**	**2,765**	**4,930**	**6,630**	**4,280**
	by legal marital status						
45	Never married (single)	1,335	1,475	820	1,310	1,685	1,485
46	Legally married (and not separated)	2,495	2,935	1,405	3,115	4,490	2,415
47	Separated, but still legally married	90	95	105	115	100	85
48	Divorced	170	180	220	175	175	130
49	Widowed	140	200	220	220	180	165
	by common-law status						
50	Not in a common-law relationship	4,130	4,785	2,645	4,815	6,505	4,190
51	In a common-law relationship	100	105	125	115	120	90
52	**Total population - 20% Sample Data (4)**	**5,370**	**6,035**	**3,455**	**6,605**	**9,140**	**5,335**
	by mother tongue						
53	Single responses	5,180	5,865	3,365	6,405	8,860	5,195
54	English	2,080	2,805	1,480	2,570	4,820	2,235
55	French	55	10	20	10	100	10
56	Non-official languages (5)	3,045	3,055	1,865	3,825	3,945	2,950
57	Italian	145	180	90	-	300	190
58	Chinese, n.o.s.	285	60	20	30	415	195
59	Cantonese	385	45	60	-	230	265
60	Portuguese	140	215	135	350	415	335
61	Punjabi	260	1,515	540	2,565	800	545
62	Other languages (6)	1,835	1,040	1,015	870	1,785	1,420
63	Multiple responses	190	175	85	200	275	145
64	English and French	-	-	-	-	-	10
65	English and non-official language	175	95	80	200	240	130
66	French and non-official language	-	80	-	-	30	-
67	English, French and non-official language	10	-	10	-	-	-

See reference material at the end of the publication. – Voir les documents de référence à la fin de la publication.

Tableau 1. Certaines caractéristiques des secteurs de recensement, recensement de 2001 – Données intégrales et données-échantillon (20 %)

Toronto 0528.25 ◆ A	Toronto 0528.26 A	Toronto 0528.27 A	Toronto 0528.28 A	Toronto 0528.29 ◆ A	Toronto 0528.30 A	Caractéristiques	N°
						CARACTÉRISTIQUES DE LA POPULATION	
5,345	**4,070**	**4,153**	**1,303**	**3,295**	**-**	**Population, 1996 (1)**	1
6,487	**3,979**	**8,578**	**5,523**	**6,362**	**7,685**	**Population, 2001 (2)**	2
21.4	-2.2	106.5	323.9	93.1	-	Variation en pourcentage de la population, 1996-2001	3
1.23	0.62	18.35	59.29	9.89	9.68	Superficie des terres en kilomètres carrés, 2001	4
6,490	**3,975**	**8,580**	**5,525**	**6,360**	**7,685**	**Population totale - Données intégrales (3)**	5
						selon le sexe et les groupes d'âge	
3,210	1,880	4,175	2,715	3,180	3,810	Sexe masculin	6
250	140	395	320	305	470	0-4 ans	7
260	165	390	240	325	325	5-9 ans	8
270	145	290	190	235	230	10-14 ans	9
240	155	265	150	220	150	15-19 ans	10
235	170	235	150	225	135	20-24 ans	11
220	140	235	195	265	365	25-29 ans	12
265	130	405	325	300	560	30-34 ans	13
310	155	520	330	290	575	35-39 ans	14
340	175	450	260	275	370	40-44 ans	15
240	145	340	160	175	185	45-49 ans	16
210	125	240	145	160	160	50-54 ans	17
120	70	135	85	130	110	55-59 ans	18
80	70	80	65	105	70	60-64 ans	19
75	35	80	45	70	45	65-69 ans	20
40	30	45	30	50	35	70-74 ans	21
30	20	25	25	30	15	75-79 ans	22
15	5	15	5	10	10	80-84 ans	23
5	5	20	5	10	5	85 ans et plus	24
3,280	2,100	4,405	2,810	3,180	3,875	Sexe féminin	25
190	140	385	320	305	475	0-4 ans	26
255	180	350	265	290	325	5-9 ans	27
245	160	305	175	245	245	10-14 ans	28
245	140	290	140	215	160	15-19 ans	29
220	155	240	140	255	150	20-24 ans	30
265	155	320	275	305	450	25-29 ans	31
320	170	450	365	295	620	30-34 ans	32
355	210	555	320	280	530	35-39 ans	33
305	195	460	220	235	285	40-44 ans	34
270	180	305	175	175	175	45-49 ans	35
190	135	205	130	165	155	50-54 ans	36
105	70	105	95	140	105	55-59 ans	37
100	75	95	55	110	85	60-64 ans	38
70	40	80	60	70	45	65-69 ans	39
60	50	70	30	45	30	70-74 ans	40
30	25	40	30	25	20	75-79 ans	41
30	15	50	15	10	10	80-84 ans	42
20	15	95	5	10	5	85 ans et plus	43
5,020	**3,050**	**6,455**	**4,020**	**4,665**	**5,610**	**Population totale de 15 ans et plus**	44
						selon l'état matrimonial légal	
1,575	1,065	1,705	985	1,135	1,200	Célibataire (jamais marié(e))	45
2,830	1,595	4,030	2,620	3,160	3,930	Légalement marié(e) (et non séparé(e))	46
140	120	145	115	90	120	Séparé(e), mais toujours légalement marié(e)	47
275	145	260	190	135	235	Divorcé(e)	48
195	120	310	105	150	130	Veuf ou veuve	49
						selon l'union libre	
4,830	2,990	6,240	3,810	4,545	5,230	Ne vivant pas en union libre	50
180	65	215	210	120	380	Vivant en union libre	51
6,430	**3,980**	**8,385**	**5,530**	**6,360**	**7,690**	**Population totale - Données-échantillon (20 %) (4)**	52
						selon la langue maternelle	
6,270	3,855	8,100	5,390	6,250	7,425	Réponses uniques	53
2,830	1,800	3,720	2,630	2,090	4,430	Anglais	54
95	25	90	50	40	155	Français	55
3,350	2,025	4,290	2,720	4,120	2,835	Langues non officielles (5)	56
195	160	225	170	155	215	Italien	57
185	275	420	250	10	155	Chinois, n.d.a.	58
185	195	210	85	-	55	Cantonais	59
195	85	310	140	105	140	Portugais	60
275	255	270	765	3,030	385	Pendjabi	61
2,315	1,055	2,850	1,300	820	1,890	Autres langues (6)	62
160	125	285	135	110	260	Réponses multiples	63
-	-	15	10	15	20	Anglais et français	64
155	100	240	115	80	235	Anglais et langue non officielle	65
-	-	-	-	10	10	Français et langue non officielle	66
-	20	20	10	-	-	Anglais, français et langue non officielle	67

See reference material at the end of the publication. – Voir les documents de référence à la fin de la publication.

Table 1. Selected Characteristics for Census Tracts, 2001 Census – 100% Data and 20% Sample Data

No.	Characteristics	Toronto 0528.19 ◆◇ A	Toronto 0528.20 A	Toronto 0528.21 ◆ A	Toronto 0528.22 ◆ A	Toronto 0528.23 ◆ A	Toronto 0528.24 A
	POPULATION CHARACTERISTICS						
	by home language						
68	Single responses	3,285	4,150	2,350	4,455	6,255	3,340
69	English	2,435	3,030	1,635	2,610	5,240	2,395
70	French	35	-	-	-	-	10
71	Non-official languages (5)	825	1,115	715	1,840	1,015	935
72	Cantonese	230	15	35	-	120	170
73	Chinese, n.o.s.	90	25	-	20	160	70
74	Italian	15	25	-	-	15	15
75	Punjabi	75	645	305	1,485	215	295
76	Portuguese	45	100	75	30	95	65
77	Other languages (6)	365	305	290	310	410	320
78	Multiple responses	2,080	1,885	1,105	2,150	2,885	1,995
79	English and French	-	10	25	40	80	35
80	English and non-official language	1,965	1,750	1,080	2,095	2,750	1,900
81	French and non-official language	55	40	-	10	-	-
82	English, French and non-official language	65	90	-	15	50	55
	by knowledge of official languages						
83	English only	4,830	5,405	3,150	5,965	8,055	4,805
84	French only	-	-	-	-	-	-
85	English and French	340	370	175	210	805	325
86	Neither English nor French	200	260	130	425	270	205
	by knowledge of non-official languages (5) (7)						
87	Italian	215	235	130	35	445	290
88	Cantonese	420	75	60	-	315	295
89	Chinese, n.o.s.	245	75	15	35	480	210
90	Spanish	70	55	115	80	85	165
91	Portuguese	175	230	190	370	510	350
92	Punjabi	490	1,730	660	2,955	960	680
93	Tagalog (Pilipino)	165	160	240	50	270	205
	by first official language spoken						
94	English	5,085	5,720	3,275	6,100	8,650	5,105
95	French	65	10	25	10	115	15
96	English and French	40	60	30	65	105	25
97	Neither English nor French	185	250	125	425	275	190
98	Official language minority - (number) (8)	85	40	35	40	165	25
99	Official language minority - (percentage) (8)	1.6	0.7	1.0	0.6	1.8	0.5
	by ethnic origin (9)						
100	Canadian	415	820	330	600	1,120	295
101	English	335	620	335	225	1,015	165
102	Scottish	175	375	145	140	625	70
103	Irish	110	335	75	160	560	90
104	Chinese	940	310	155	100	1,070	580
105	Italian	240	395	180	75	1,065	505
106	East Indian	1,210	1,875	710	2,910	1,555	1,130
107	French	195	80	45	50	255	90
108	German	115	170	85	155	375	95
109	Portuguese	260	300	195	445	670	450
110	Polish	130	80	60	95	405	180
111	Jewish	80	20	10	-	55	-
112	Jamaican	340	315	400	410	265	240
113	Filipino	250	245	345	65	440	320
114	Ukrainian	65	50	45	50	145	110
	by Aboriginal identity						
115	Total Aboriginal identity population (10)	-	10	-	15	30	25
116	Total non-Aboriginal population	5,370	6,030	3,455	6,585	9,110	5,310
	by Aboriginal origin						
117	Total Aboriginal origins population (11)	15	10	-	35	40	25
118	Total non-Aboriginal population	5,355	6,030	3,455	6,565	9,095	5,315
	by Registered Indian status						
119	Registered Indian (12)	-	-	-	-	20	-
120	Not a Registered Indian	5,370	6,035	3,450	6,605	9,120	5,330

Tableau 1. Certaines caractéristiques des secteurs de recensement, recensement de 2001 – Données intégrales et données-échantillon (20 %)

Toronto 0528.25 ◆ A	Toronto 0528.26 A	Toronto 0528.27 A	Toronto 0528.28 A	Toronto 0528.29 ◆ A	Toronto 0528.30 A	Caractéristiques	N°
						CARACTÉRISTIQUES DE LA POPULATION	
						selon la langue parlée à la maison	
4,305	2,540	5,655	4,005	4,795	5,810	Réponses uniques	68
3,110	1,805	4,255	2,815	2,305	5,080	Anglais	69
15	-	10	-	40	40	Français	70
1,180	730	1,400	1,190	2,445	700	Langues non officielles (5)	71
65	165	150	80	-	15	Cantonais	72
30	135	120	85	-	20	Chinois, n.d.a.	73
25	50	-	10	50	15	Italien	74
150	90	135	450	2,110	115	Pendjabi	75
25	10	80	35	25	15	Portugais	76
890	295	910	530	260	515	Autres langues (6)	77
2,125	1,440	2,730	1,520	1,570	1,870	Réponses multiples	78
30	55	110	85	15	75	Anglais et français	79
2,035	1,380	2,555	1,415	1,515	1,750	Anglais et langue non officielle	80
-	-	20	-	15	-	Français et langue non officielle	81
65	10	45	25	25	50	Anglais, français et langue non officielle	82
						selon la connaissance des langues officielles	
5,745	3,520	7,325	4,765	5,470	6,885	Anglais seulement	83
-	-	10	-	25	20	Français seulement	84
500	260	745	410	230	560	Anglais et français	85
190	195	305	350	635	220	Ni l'anglais ni le français	86
						selon la connaissance des langues non officielles (5) (7)	
290	255	445	300	165	335	Italien	87
235	245	365	120	25	120	Cantonais	88
185	260	360	235	-	115	Chinois, n.d.a.	89
430	285	235	215	100	225	Espagnol	90
285	110	375	215	145	210	Portugais	91
375	315	360	855	3,250	450	Pendjabi	92
320	145	425	190	35	310	Tagalog (pilipino)	93
						selon la première langue officielle parlée	
6,080	3,710	7,825	5,100	5,605	7,265	Anglais	94
85	25	95	45	55	165	Français	95
80	45	160	35	75	50	Anglais et français	96
190	200	310	345	630	200	Ni l'anglais ni le français	97
125	50	170	65	90	190	Minorité de langue officielle - (nombre) (8)	98
1.9	1.3	2.0	1.2	1.4	2.5	Minorité de langue officielle - (pourcentage) (8)	99
						selon l'origine ethnique (9)	
620	425	790	535	605	1,310	Canadien	100
470	275	820	595	255	1,120	Anglais	101
220	90	365	430	155	825	Écossais	102
225	170	290	395	145	750	Irlandais	103
610	555	995	485	20	450	Chinois	104
615	330	850	570	290	805	Italien	105
1,015	695	1,050	1,240	3,065	1,030	Indien de l'Inde	106
190	115	295	160	130	545	Français	107
80	65	145	165	85	455	Allemand	108
390	165	660	365	200	355	Portugais	109
380	165	745	220	105	380	Polonais	110
20	10	25	30	-	25	Juif	111
215	370	180	280	340	345	Jamaïquain	112
475	140	620	300	85	525	Philippin	113
265	45	175	85	20	145	Ukrainien	114
						selon l'identité autochtone	
15	-	20	10	-	-	Total de la population ayant une identité autochtone (10)	115
6,415	3,980	8,360	5,520	6,360	7,685	Total de la population non autochtone	116
						selon l'origine autochtone	
15	-	55	20	20	40	Total de la population ayant une origine autochtone (11)	117
6,415	3,980	8,330	5,505	6,340	7,650	Total de la population non autochtone	118
						selon le statut d'Indien inscrit	
10	-	-	-	-	-	Oui, Indien inscrit (12)	119
6,425	3,980	8,385	5,525	6,360	7,685	Non, pas un Indien inscrit	120

Table 1. Selected Characteristics for Census Tracts, 2001 Census – 100% Data and 20% Sample Data

No.	Characteristics	Toronto 0528.19 ◆◇ A	Toronto 0528.20 A	Toronto 0528.21 ◆ A	Toronto 0528.22 ◆ A	Toronto 0528.23 ◆ A	Toronto 0528.24 A
	POPULATION CHARACTERISTICS						
	by visible minority groups						
121	Total visible minority population	3,750	3,665	2,065	5,110	4,790	3,345
122	Chinese	800	140	90	75	910	590
123	South Asian	1,395	2,285	955	3,835	2,210	1,580
124	Black	355	560	570	785	435	380
125	Filipino	220	185	340	65	380	330
126	Latin American	20	35	35	50	40	90
127	Southeast Asian	175	90	15	95	165	135
128	Arab	270	25	10	10	220	30
129	West Asian	30	-	-	35	10	15
130	Korean	185	-	15	-	90	70
131	Japanese	-	-	10	-	35	-
132	Visible minority, n.i.e. (13)	185	160	15	135	115	70
133	Multiple visible minorities (14)	120	175	10	15	170	65
	by citizenship						
134	Canadian citizenship (15)	4,595	5,285	2,885	5,180	8,210	4,580
135	Citizenship other than Canadian	775	750	565	1,425	930	755
	by place of birth of respondent						
136	Non-immigrant population	2,110	2,975	1,395	2,655	4,825	2,190
137	Born in province of residence	2,010	2,690	1,220	2,465	4,400	2,065
138	Immigrant population (16)	3,205	2,975	2,020	3,920	4,255	3,100
139	United States	10	35	15	15	60	-
140	Central and South America	155	165	85	240	170	130
141	Caribbean and Bermuda	260	300	230	445	230	305
142	United Kingdom	55	180	110	140	265	55
143	Other Europe (17)	555	540	470	420	885	705
144	Africa	220	90	180	75	260	65
145	Asia and the Middle East	1,940	1,665	920	2,525	2,365	1,830
146	Oceania and other (18)	10	10	-	55	15	-
147	Non-permanent residents (19)	55	85	35	25	60	45
148	**Total immigrant population**	**3,205**	**2,975**	**2,020**	**3,920**	**4,255**	**3,100**
	by period of immigration						
149	Before 1961	95	200	70	50	160	135
150	1961-1970	320	450	125	280	475	420
151	1971-1980	740	845	515	810	960	820
152	1981-1990	870	765	510	955	1,330	740
153	1991-2001 (20)	1,175	715	800	1,820	1,325	980
154	1991-1995	485	355	445	1,010	780	575
155	1996-2001 (20)	690	360	355	810	545	410
	by age at immigration						
156	0-4 years	205	155	135	305	530	230
157	5-19 years	935	825	480	900	1,195	985
158	20 years and over	2,065	1,990	1,405	2,710	2,525	1,885
159	**Total population**	**5,370**	**6,035**	**3,455**	**6,605**	**9,140**	**5,335**
	by religion						
160	Catholic (21)	1,680	1,620	1,355	1,235	3,790	2,350
161	Protestant	595	1,175	740	890	1,410	605
162	Christian Orthodox	115	190	30	80	215	220
163	Christian, n.i.e. (22)	340	70	85	265	235	140
164	Muslim	810	360	185	360	645	440
165	Jewish	25	10	-	-	30	10
166	Buddhist	350	150	10	15	345	110
167	Hindu	555	535	240	1,005	375	310
168	Sikh	280	1,510	535	2,360	905	540
169	Eastern religions (23)	20	-	-	-	105	40
170	Other religions (24)	-	25	-	40	-	-
171	No religious affiliation (25)	595	400	280	355	1,085	575
172	**Total population 15 years and over**	**4,230**	**4,895**	**2,710**	**4,930**	**6,620**	**4,275**
	by generation status						
173	1st generation (26)	3,050	2,990	1,950	3,770	4,025	2,990
174	2nd generation (27)	930	1,160	530	840	1,570	1,045
175	3rd generation and over (28)	250	745	235	325	1,025	240
176	**Total population 1 year and over (29)**	**5,345**	**5,990**	**3,410**	**6,505**	**8,990**	**5,255**
	by place of residence 1 year ago (mobility)						
177	Non-movers	4,515	5,400	2,830	5,660	7,770	4,765
178	Movers	830	595	575	850	1,225	490
179	Non-migrants	510	250	260	395	745	360
180	Migrants	320	340	310	450	480	125
181	Internal migrants	145	215	250	320	410	35
182	Intraprovincial migrants	135	125	225	310	400	25
183	Interprovincial migrants	10	90	25	10	10	10
184	External migrants	175	130	65	135	70	95

Tableau 1. Certaines caractéristiques des secteurs de recensement, recensement de 2001 – Données intégrales et données-échantillon (20 %)

Toronto 0528.25 ◆ A	Toronto 0528.26 A	Toronto 0528.27 A	Toronto 0528.28 A	Toronto 0528.29 ◆ A	Toronto 0528.30 A	Caractéristiques	N°
						CARACTÉRISTIQUES DE LA POPULATION	
						selon les groupes de minorités visibles	
3,625	2,580	4,275	3,070	5,000	3,345	Total de la population des minorités visibles	121
530	500	875	425	10	325	Chinois	122
1,275	915	1,390	1,480	3,870	1,285	Sud-Asiatique	123
535	610	415	405	630	430	Noir	124
455	140	580	305	85	520	Philippin	125
240	150	130	150	95	140	Latino-Américain	126
150	95	350	65	110	205	Asiatique du Sud-Est	127
105	20	210	55	30	90	Arabe	128
105	10	45	30	-	20	Asiatique occidental	129
85	35	15	10	25	85	Coréen	130
-	-	10	-	-	15	Japonais	131
130	60	215	70	150	120	Minorité visible, n.i.a. (13)	132
20	50	50	85	10	110	Minorités visibles multiples (14)	133
						selon la citoyenneté	
5,405	3,340	7,510	4,655	4,640	6,775	Citoyenneté canadienne (15)	134
1,030	645	875	870	1,720	915	Citoyenneté autre que canadienne	135
						selon le lieu de naissance du répondant	
2,790	1,670	3,620	2,655	2,425	4,390	Population non immigrante	136
2,480	1,550	3,355	2,440	2,215	3,835	Née dans la province de résidence	137
3,620	2,265	4,735	2,805	3,895	3,270	Population immigrante (16)	138
30	-	65	30	115	70	États-Unis	139
375	200	280	290	205	245	Amérique centrale et du Sud	140
225	245	300	150	335	235	Caraïbes et Bermudes	141
100	65	250	80	90	255	Royaume-Uni	142
770	410	1,260	455	345	670	Autre Europe (17)	143
215	105	165	150	70	145	Afrique	144
1,895	1,235	2,395	1,650	2,720	1,640	Asie et Moyen-Orient	145
10	-	10	10	20	10	Océanie et autre (18)	146
20	45	30	65	40	25	Résidents non permanents (19)	147
3,620	**2,265**	**4,735**	**2,805**	**3,900**	**3,270**	**Population immigrante totale**	148
						selon la période d'immigration	
100	90	90	45	80	90	Avant 1961	149
200	180	305	185	140	275	1961-1970	150
870	400	835	620	690	575	1971-1980	151
960	605	1,460	640	1,000	925	1981-1990	152
1,490	980	2,035	1,315	1,990	1,405	1991-2001 (20)	153
625	480	1,320	525	1,120	810	1991-1995	154
870	500	720	785	865	590	1996-2001 (20)	155
						selon l'âge à l'immigration	
310	120	385	225	195	400	0-4 ans	156
1,050	625	1,450	830	1,095	925	5-19 ans	157
2,260	1,520	2,905	1,750	2,605	1,945	20 ans et plus	158
6,430	**3,980**	**8,385**	**5,525**	**6,365**	**7,685**	**Population totale**	159
						selon la religion	
2,930	1,485	4,010	2,055	1,270	3,595	Catholique (21)	160
850	640	1,000	955	730	1,530	Protestante	161
240	65	330	200	10	170	Orthodoxe chrétienne	162
210	305	240	145	95	195	Chrétiennes, n.i.a. (22)	163
645	405	505	275	355	400	Musulmane	164
25	-	10	-	-	-	Juive	165
75	75	465	245	20	140	Bouddhiste	166
435	230	500	255	370	440	Hindoue	167
320	210	265	800	3,125	405	Sikh	168
-	15	-	-	25	80	Religions orientales (23)	169
-	-	10	10	45	-	Autres religions (24)	170
700	535	1,045	590	310	730	Aucune appartenance religieuse (25)	171
4,950	**3,050**	**6,250**	**4,025**	**4,655**	**5,600**	**Population totale de 15 ans et plus**	172
						selon le statut des générations	
3,330	2,135	4,435	2,680	3,760	3,095	1re génération (26)	173
970	580	1,220	830	550	1,200	2e génération (27)	174
645	335	595	515	345	1,305	3e génération et plus (28)	175
6,340	**3,940**	**8,245**	**5,390**	**6,245**	**7,455**	**Population totale de 1 an et plus (29)**	176
						selon le lieu de résidence 1 an auparavant (mobilité)	
5,610	3,340	7,445	3,560	5,170	5,035	Personnes n'ayant pas déménagé	177
730	600	795	1,825	1,080	2,420	Personnes ayant déménagé	178
405	255	570	1,110	350	1,680	Non-migrants	179
325	345	225	720	730	740	Migrants	180
165	190	175	555	540	625	Migrants internes	181
145	155	175	520	430	615	Migrants infraprovinciaux	182
20	30	-	35	110	15	Migrants interprovinciaux	183
160	155	50	170	190	115	Migrants externes	184

Table 1. Selected Characteristics for Census Tracts, 2001 Census – 100% Data and 20% Sample Data

No.	Characteristics	Toronto 0528.19 ◆◇ A	Toronto 0528.20 A	Toronto 0528.21 ◆ A	Toronto 0528.22 ◆ A	Toronto 0528.23 ◆ A	Toronto 0528.24 A
	POPULATION CHARACTERISTICS						
185	**Total population 5 years and over (30)**	**5,085**	**5,730**	**3,250**	**6,005**	**8,415**	**5,055**
	by place of residence 5 years ago (mobility)						
186	Non-movers	3,010	3,890	1,545	3,255	4,315	3,075
187	Movers	2,075	1,840	1,705	2,760	4,100	1,985
188	Non-migrants	1,070	935	770	1,160	2,380	1,150
189	Migrants	1,005	900	940	1,595	1,720	835
190	Internal migrants	390	615	645	1,020	1,210	480
191	Intraprovincial migrants	315	495	565	960	1,115	430
192	Interprovincial migrants	75	125	85	65	95	50
193	External migrants	615	285	295	570	510	355
194	**Total population 15 to 24 years**	**855**	**1,050**	**460**	**990**	**1,200**	**1,030**
	by school attendance						
195	Not attending school	220	295	190	420	375	230
196	Attending school full time	610	680	230	525	780	760
197	Attending school part time	30	75	40	40	45	35
198	**Total population 15 years and over**	**4,230**	**4,895**	**2,710**	**4,935**	**6,625**	**4,275**
	by highest level of schooling						
199	Less than grade 9 (31)	360	430	405	635	380	370
200	Grades 9-13 without high school graduation certificate	660	1,005	470	1,160	1,070	765
201	Grades 9-13 with high school graduation certificate	580	650	345	950	835	605
202	Some postsecondary without degree, certificate or diploma (32)	520	675	310	585	745	665
203	Trades certificate or diploma (33)	300	460	235	315	410	340
204	College certificate or diploma (34)	565	665	370	440	1,090	550
205	University certificate below bachelor's degree	150	135	80	120	230	115
206	University with bachelor's degree or higher	1,095	870	485	725	1,865	850
	by combinations of unpaid work						
207	Males 15 years and over	2,050	2,415	1,245	2,430	3,300	2,110
208	Reported unpaid work (35)	1,850	2,100	1,025	2,195	2,960	1,825
209	Housework and child care and care or assistance to seniors	305	190	125	430	400	260
210	Housework and child care only	470	555	255	740	1,135	485
211	Housework and care or assistance to seniors only	130	210	105	130	135	115
212	Child care and care or assistance to seniors only	10	-	-	-	10	10
213	Housework only	900	1,075	500	825	1,235	920
214	Child care only	-	65	40	50	45	25
215	Care or assistance to seniors only	20	10	-	15	10	-
216	Females 15 years and over	2,185	2,485	1,465	2,500	3,325	2,160
217	Reported unpaid work (35)	2,045	2,200	1,325	2,295	3,040	1,970
218	Housework and child care and care or assistance to seniors	350	330	180	505	545	320
219	Housework and child care only	605	740	505	950	1,290	620
220	Housework and care or assistance to seniors only	185	185	100	55	165	160
221	Child care and care or assistance to seniors only	-	-	15	-	10	-
222	Housework only	865	900	490	745	1,010	850
223	Child care only	30	45	25	35	30	25
224	Care or assistance to seniors only	10	-	10	-	-	-
	by labour force activity						
225	Males 15 years and over	2,045	2,410	1,245	2,430	3,300	2,110
226	In the labour force	1,525	1,845	940	1,855	2,795	1,625
227	Employed	1,450	1,735	880	1,790	2,720	1,485
228	Unemployed	75	115	55	65	80	140
229	Not in the labour force	520	570	305	580	500	485
230	Participation rate	74.6	76.6	75.5	76.3	84.7	77.0
231	Employment rate	70.9	72.0	70.7	73.7	82.4	70.4
232	Unemployment rate	4.9	6.2	5.9	3.5	2.9	8.6
233	Females 15 years and over	2,185	2,485	1,465	2,505	3,325	2,160
234	In the labour force	1,555	1,560	875	1,655	2,305	1,435
235	Employed	1,455	1,445	805	1,525	2,160	1,380
236	Unemployed	100	115	70	125	145	60
237	Not in the labour force	630	920	585	850	1,015	725
238	Participation rate	71.2	62.8	59.7	66.1	69.3	66.4
239	Employment rate	66.6	58.1	54.9	60.9	65.0	63.9
240	Unemployment rate	6.4	7.4	8.0	7.6	6.3	4.2

Tableau 1. Certaines caractéristiques des secteurs de recensement, recensement de 2001 – Données intégrales et données-échantillon (20 %)

Toronto 0528.25 ◆ A	Toronto 0528.26 A	Toronto 0528.27 A	Toronto 0528.28 A	Toronto 0528.29 ◆ A	Toronto 0528.30 A	Caractéristiques	N°
						CARACTÉRISTIQUES DE LA POPULATION	
5,995	**3,700**	**7,600**	**4,885**	**5,740**	**6,735**	**Population totale de 5 ans et plus (30)**	185
						selon le lieu de résidence 5 ans auparavant (mobilité)	
2,570	1,980	2,300	620	2,065	185	Personnes n'ayant pas déménagé	186
3,425	1,725	5,300	4,265	3,680	6,550	Personnes ayant déménagé	187
1,770	715	3,410	2,180	1,465	4,030	Non-migrants	188
1,655	1,005	1,895	2,085	2,210	2,520	Migrants	189
980	610	1,365	1,480	1,480	2,055	Migrants internes	190
890	575	1,290	1,405	1,255	1,885	Migrants infraprovinciaux	191
90	35	70	75	225	170	Migrants interprovinciaux	192
670	400	525	605	735	455	Migrants externes	193
940	**645**	**1,040**	**585**	**915**	**580**	**Population totale de 15 à 24 ans**	194
						selon la fréquentation scolaire	
255	180	280	205	400	200	Ne fréquentant pas l'école	195
665	425	675	335	415	335	Fréquentant l'école à plein temps	196
25	35	90	45	100	40	Fréquentant l'école à temps partiel	197
4,955	**3,050**	**6,255**	**4,025**	**4,655**	**5,595**	**Population totale de 15 ans et plus**	198
						selon le plus haut niveau de scolarité atteint	
245	335	420	325	645	200	Niveau inférieur à la 9e année (31)	199
835	500	915	825	1,000	570	De la 9e à la 13e année sans certificat d'études secondaires	200
705	390	985	410	805	635	De la 9e à la 13e année avec certificat d'études secondaires	201
685	280	720	515	460	685	Études postsecondaires partielles sans grade, certificat ou diplôme (32)	202
385	290	555	265	360	670	Certificat ou diplôme d'une école de métiers (33)	203
635	515	1,065	685	555	1,090	Certificat ou diplôme collégial (34)	204
175	150	260	135	85	135	Certificat universitaire inférieur au baccalauréat	205
1,275	590	1,340	855	745	1,615	Études universitaires avec baccalauréat ou diplôme supérieur	206
						selon les combinaisons de travail non rémunéré	
2,405	1,425	3,050	1,975	2,300	2,775	Hommes de 15 ans et plus	207
2,135	1,275	2,725	1,795	2,075	2,615	Travail non rémunéré déclaré (35)	208
195	100	360	235	250	180	Travaux ménagers et soins aux enfants et soins ou aide aux personnes âgées	209
740	400	1,055	645	840	1,110	Travaux ménagers et soins aux enfants seulement	210
110	45	145	50	110	155	Travaux ménagers et soins ou aide aux personnes âgées seulement	211
10	-	10	15	-	-	Soins aux enfants et soins ou aide aux personnes âgées seulement	212
1,020	675	1,120	800	795	1,110	Travaux ménagers seulement	213
40	45	20	35	70	50	Soins aux enfants seulement	214
15	10	15	15	-	-	Soins ou aide aux personnes âgées seulement	215
2,545	1,620	3,200	2,055	2,360	2,825	Femmes de 15 ans et plus	216
2,385	1,545	3,045	1,965	2,190	2,655	Travail non rémunéré déclaré (35)	217
320	235	470	330	285	275	Travaux ménagers et soins aux enfants et soins ou aide aux personnes âgées	218
980	565	1,245	805	1,010	1,230	Travaux ménagers et soins aux enfants seulement	219
135	80	145	85	105	145	Travaux ménagers et soins ou aide aux personnes âgées seulement	220
10	-	-	-	-	-	Soins aux enfants et soins ou aide aux personnes âgées seulement	221
900	635	1,140	725	745	995	Travaux ménagers seulement	222
20	25	25	20	35	10	Soins aux enfants seulement	223
15	-	-	-	-	-	Soins ou aide aux personnes âgées seulement	224
						selon l'activité	
2,405	1,425	3,045	1,970	2,300	2,775	Hommes de 15 ans et plus	225
2,000	1,095	2,580	1,645	1,840	2,425	Population active	226
1,885	1,050	2,490	1,565	1,690	2,395	Personnes occupées	227
110	50	85	85	145	30	Chômeurs	228
405	330	470	325	460	355	Inactifs	229
83.2	76.8	84.7	83.5	80.0	87.4	Taux d'activité	230
78.4	73.7	81.8	79.4	73.5	86.3	Taux d'emploi	231
5.5	4.6	3.3	5.2	7.9	1.2	Taux de chômage	232
2,550	1,625	3,205	2,050	2,360	2,825	Femmes de 15 ans et plus	233
1,825	1,000	2,405	1,460	1,540	2,105	Population active	234
1,700	925	2,325	1,370	1,440	2,015	Personnes occupées	235
125	75	80	85	105	90	Chômeuses	236
725	625	805	595	815	715	Inactives	237
71.6	61.5	75.0	71.2	65.3	74.5	Taux d'activité	238
66.7	56.9	72.5	66.8	61.0	71.3	Taux d'emploi	239
6.8	7.5	3.3	5.8	6.8	4.3	Taux de chômage	240

Table 1. Selected Characteristics for Census Tracts, 2001 Census – 100% Data and 20% Sample Data

No.	Characteristics	Toronto 0528.19 ◆◇ A	Toronto 0528.20 A	Toronto 0528.21 ◆ A	Toronto 0528.22 ◆ A	Toronto 0528.23 ◆ A	Toronto 0528.24 A
	POPULATION CHARACTERISTICS						
	by labour force activity – concluded						
241	Both sexes - Participation rate	72.8	69.6	67.2	71.0	77.1	71.6
242	15-24 years	50.9	63.8	72.5	59.6	62.9	57.0
243	25 years and over	78.4	71.3	66.1	74.1	80.2	76.0
244	Both sexes - Employment rate	68.7	65.0	62.2	67.2	73.8	67.0
245	15-24 years	48.0	55.7	67.0	53.5	58.3	49.5
246	25 years and over	73.9	67.5	61.4	70.7	77.2	72.7
247	Both sexes - Unemployment rate	5.7	6.8	7.2	5.4	4.3	6.4
248	15-24 years	5.7	11.9	7.7	9.3	7.3	13.6
249	25 years and over	5.5	5.3	7.0	4.6	3.7	4.5
250	**Total labour force 15 years and over**	**3,080**	**3,400**	**1,815**	**3,510**	**5,105**	**3,060**
	by industry based on the 1997 NAICS						
251	Industry - Not applicable (36)	60	75	15	45	40	50
252	All industries (37)	3,020	3,325	1,800	3,460	5,065	3,010
253	11 Agriculture, forestry, fishing and hunting	-	25	20	10	-	-
254	21 Mining and oil and gas extraction	10	-	-	10	-	-
255	22 Utilities	-	10	-	10	10	20
256	23 Construction	75	90	100	80	175	135
257	31-33 Manufacturing	660	915	500	985	835	650
258	41 Wholesale trade	320	275	105	245	385	180
259	44-45 Retail trade	415	320	205	355	475	430
260	48-49 Transportation and warehousing	215	335	180	490	345	195
261	51 Information and cultural industries	90	45	25	70	230	120
262	52 Finance and insurance	215	165	75	90	435	205
263	53 Real estate and rental and leasing	85	45	30	40	155	40
264	54 Professional, scientific and technical services	190	190	75	100	520	180
265	55 Management of companies and enterprises	10	-	-	-	15	-
266	56 Administrative and support, waste management and remediation services	95	145	110	220	115	105
267	61 Educational services	125	115	65	115	230	165
268	62 Health care and social assistance	100	180	95	185	290	185
269	71 Arts, entertainment and recreation	15	30	10	10	25	30
270	72 Accommodation and food services	165	210	85	190	355	220
271	81 Other services (except public administration)	125	125	45	185	230	90
272	91 Public administration	110	110	75	75	220	65
	by class of worker						
273	Class of worker - Not applicable (36)	60	80	15	45	35	50
274	All classes of worker (37)	3,020	3,325	1,805	3,465	5,065	3,010
275	Paid workers	2,815	3,120	1,695	3,235	4,720	2,835
276	Employees	2,725	3,020	1,670	3,130	4,455	2,680
277	Self-employed (incorporated)	90	100	30	105	265	155
278	Self-employed (unincorporated)	160	195	100	205	345	175
279	Unpaid family workers	45	10	10	20	10	-
	by occupation based on the 2001 NOC-S						
280	Male labour force 15 years and over	1,525	1,845	940	1,850	2,800	1,625
281	Occupation - Not applicable (36)	20	30	-	15	10	40
282	All occupations (37)	1,505	1,810	935	1,840	2,790	1,590
283	A Management occupations	255	295	100	190	590	235
284	B Business, finance and administration occupations	240	200	115	200	430	200
285	C Natural and applied sciences and related occupations	205	215	80	80	390	175
286	D Health occupations	15	30	10	30	50	25
287	E Occupations in social science, education, government service and religion	25	50	35	30	115	65
288	F Occupations in art, culture, recreation and sport	-	30	15	20	65	25
289	G Sales and service occupations	215	285	125	295	450	265
290	H Trades, transport and equipment operators and related occupations	315	440	290	630	490	400
291	I Occupations unique to primary industry	-	10	15	30	20	10
292	J Occupations unique to processing, manufacturing and utilities	225	265	160	330	195	170
293	Female labour force 15 years and over	1,555	1,560	880	1,655	2,305	1,435
294	Occupation - Not applicable (36)	40	45	10	35	30	10
295	All occupations (37)	1,515	1,515	865	1,625	2,275	1,425
296	A Management occupations	200	105	75	85	280	135
297	B Business, finance and administration occupations	465	505	250	445	820	495
298	C Natural and applied sciences and related occupations	70	70	40	20	100	65
299	D Health occupations	75	120	40	100	140	95

Tableau 1. Certaines caractéristiques des secteurs de recensement, recensement de 2001 – Données intégrales et données-échantillon (20 %)

Toronto 0528.25 ◆ A	Toronto 0528.26 A	Toronto 0528.27 A	Toronto 0528.28 A	Toronto 0528.29 ◆ A	Toronto 0528.30 A	Caractéristiques	N°
						CARACTÉRISTIQUES DE LA POPULATION	
						selon l'activité – fin	
77.2	68.7	79.5	77.1	72.6	81.0	Les deux sexes - Taux d'activité	241
66.7	60.9	63.5	66.7	67.8	63.8	15-24 ans	242
79.6	71.0	82.9	78.9	73.8	83.0	25 ans et plus	243
72.4	64.8	77.1	73.0	67.2	78.7	Les deux sexes - Taux d'emploi	244
59.3	52.3	56.7	58.1	55.7	55.2	15-24 ans	245
75.4	68.0	81.0	75.4	70.2	81.6	25 ans et plus	246
6.2	5.7	3.3	5.3	7.4	2.8	Les deux sexes - Taux de chômage	247
11.9	14.1	10.7	12.8	16.9	13.7	15-24 ans	248
5.2	3.8	2.1	4.2	5.1	1.7	25 ans et plus	249
3,820	**2,095**	**4,980**	**3,105**	**3,380**	**4,525**	**Population active totale de 15 ans et plus selon l'industrie basée sur le SCIAN de 1997**	250
50	40	20	30	70	30	Industrie - Sans objet (36)	251
3,775	2,055	4,955	3,065	3,310	4,505	Toutes les industries (37)	252
-	-	10	10	20	10	11 Agriculture, foresterie, pêche et chasse	253
10	-	-	-	-	15	21 Extraction minière et extraction de pétrole et de gaz	254
10	-	15	-	20	20	22 Services publics	255
120	70	195	125	140	195	23 Construction	256
720	380	1,105	695	1,055	870	31-33 Fabrication	257
260	150	375	385	195	480	41 Commerce de gros	258
435	210	585	245	305	340	44-45 Commerce de détail	259
340	90	255	255	405	275	48-49 Transport et entreposage	260
170	75	160	60	40	175	51 Industrie de l'information et industrie culturelle	261
235	200	425	185	130	405	52 Finance et assurances	262
85	60	90	55	40	80	53 Services immobiliers et services de location et de location à bail	263
435	140	425	240	90	435	54 Services professionnels, scientifiques et techniques	264
-	-	15	15	10	15	55 Gestion de sociétés et d'entreprises	265
185	75	210	125	220	190	56 Services administratifs, services de soutien, services de gestion des déchets et services d'assainissement	266
110	85	175	75	75	190	61 Services d'enseignement	267
220	170	280	180	175	270	62 Soins de santé et assistance sociale	268
10	30	50	25	30	55	71 Arts, spectacles et loisirs	269
170	200	345	65	205	195	72 Hébergement et services de restauration	270
165	90	130	210	85	135	81 Autres services, sauf les administrations publiques	271
100	35	110	120	75	155	91 Administrations publiques	272
						selon la catégorie de travailleurs	
50	45	20	35	70	25	Catégorie de travailleurs - Sans objet (36)	273
3,775	2,060	4,955	3,070	3,310	4,505	Toutes les catégories de travailleurs (37)	274
3,505	1,920	4,665	2,970	3,200	4,220	Travailleurs rémunérés	275
3,335	1,820	4,475	2,845	3,080	4,000	Employés	276
175	95	190	120	120	215	Travailleurs autonomes (entreprise constituée en société)	277
255	130	280	95	110	280	Travailleurs autonomes (entreprise non constituée en société)	278
15	10	15	-	-	-	Travailleurs familiaux non rémunérés	279
						selon la profession basée sur la CNP-S de 2001	
2,000	1,095	2,575	1,645	1,840	2,425	Hommes actifs de 15 ans et plus	280
35	-	10	25	30	10	Profession - Sans objet (36)	281
1,965	1,090	2,570	1,620	1,805	2,415	Toutes les professions (37)	282
275	160	450	330	165	460	A Gestion	283
215	170	305	185	125	310	B Affaires, finance et administration	284
365	140	390	235	125	440	C Sciences naturelles et appliquées et professions apparentées	285
10	10	25	25	10	40	D Secteur de la santé	286
55	40	30	50	40	80	E Sciences sociales, enseignement, administration publique et religion	287
35	20	55	20	10	60	F Arts, culture, sports et loisirs	288
395	255	420	175	240	360	G Ventes et services	289
455	200	535	365	665	485	H Métiers, transport et machinerie	290
-	-	10	20	40	-	I Professions propres au secteur primaire	291
150	95	350	205	380	180	J Transformation, fabrication et services d'utilité publique	292
1,825	1,005	2,400	1,460	1,540	2,105	Femmes actives de 15 ans et plus	293
15	35	15	-	40	20	Profession - Sans objet (36)	294
1,810	965	2,385	1,445	1,505	2,090	Toutes les professions (37)	295
220	70	245	175	110	320	A Gestion	296
560	365	860	415	330	675	B Affaires, finance et administration	297
100	30	165	70	35	125	C Sciences naturelles et appliquées et professions apparentées	298
155	80	120	135	80	110	D Secteur de la santé	299

Table 1. Selected Characteristics for Census Tracts, 2001 Census – 100% Data and 20% Sample Data

No.	Characteristics	Toronto 0528.19 ◆◇ A	Toronto 0528.20 A	Toronto 0528.21 ◆ A	Toronto 0528.22 ◆ A	Toronto 0528.23 ◆ A	Toronto 0528.24 A
	POPULATION CHARACTERISTICS						
	by occupation based on the 2001 NOC-S – concluded						
	E Occupations in social science, education,						
300	government service and religion	120	90	75	105	235	125
301	F Occupations in art, culture, recreation and sport	30	30	15	15	40	15
302	G Sales and service occupations	395	295	185	395	510	305
	H Trades, transport and equipment						
303	operators and related occupations	15	60	-	80	30	10
304	I Occupations unique to primary industry	-	10	10	-	-	-
	J Occupations unique to processing,						
305	manufacturing and utilities	135	240	165	375	115	175
306	**Total employed labour force 15 years and over**	**2,910**	**3,180**	**1,685**	**3,315**	**4,885**	**2,860**
	by place of work						
307	Males	1,450	1,730	880	1,790	2,725	1,485
308	Usual place of work	1,295	1,540	730	1,465	2,375	1,325
309	At home	45	55	35	50	160	40
310	Outside Canada	10	20	10	10	-	10
311	No fixed workplace address	110	120	110	280	185	105
312	Females	1,460	1,445	805	1,525	2,160	1,380
313	Usual place of work	1,365	1,345	725	1,255	1,905	1,280
314	At home	45	65	40	90	175	45
315	Outside Canada	-	-	-	-	-	-
316	No fixed workplace address	55	40	45	175	80	50
	Total employed labour force 15 years and over with usual place of work or no fixed						
317	**workplace address**	**2,820**	**3,045**	**1,610**	**3,175**	**4,545**	**2,760**
	by mode of transportation						
318	Males	1,405	1,660	845	1,740	2,560	1,430
319	Car, truck, van, as driver	1,185	1,455	730	1,530	2,280	1,180
320	Car, truck, van, as passenger	65	45	50	50	90	115
321	Public transit	135	120	35	100	125	115
322	Walked	20	25	20	15	50	15
323	Other method	-	20	10	40	15	15
324	Females	1,410	1,380	770	1,435	1,990	1,330
325	Car, truck, van, as driver	935	975	505	985	1,445	985
326	Car, truck, van, as passenger	210	190	60	175	245	150
327	Public transit	225	180	155	195	215	175
328	Walked	45	40	50	55	50	10
329	Other method	-	10	10	15	30	10
	Total population 15 years and over who worked						
330	**since January 1, 2000**	**3,280**	**3,635**	**1,970**	**3,890**	**5,440**	**3,350**
	by language used at work						
331	Single responses	2,885	3,210	1,695	3,290	4,915	2,920
332	English	2,815	3,150	1,675	3,180	4,865	2,880
333	French	-	-	-	-	-	-
334	Non-official languages (5)	60	60	20	110	50	40
335	Chinese, n.o.s.	15	-	-	-	20	-
336	Cantonese	35	-	-	-	10	30
337	Other languages (6)	10	60	10	110	25	10
338	Multiple responses	400	425	280	600	525	430
339	English and French	45	40	35	20	115	40
340	English and non-official language	335	370	240	550	395	380
341	French and non-official language	-	-	-	-	-	-
342	English, French and non-official language	20	15	10	35	10	10
	DWELLING AND HOUSEHOLD CHARACTERISTICS						
343	**Total number of occupied private dwellings**	**1,475**	**1,690**	**1,205**	**1,675**	**2,380**	**1,315**
	by tenure						
344	Owned	1,270	1,455	490	1,375	2,215	1,220
345	Rented	205	235	710	305	160	100
346	Band housing	-	-	-	-	-	-
	by structural type of dwelling						
347	Single-detached house	740	1,160	145	965	2,250	955
348	Semi-detached house	100	-	-	-	20	-
349	Row house	460	180	165	345	35	355
350	Apartment, detached duplex	-	70	15	165	-	-
351	Apartment, building that has five or more storeys	180	200	885	200	-	-
	Apartment, building that has fewer than						
352	five storeys (38)	-	85	-	-	80	-
353	Other single-attached house	-	-	-	-	-	-
354	Movable dwelling (39)	-	-	-	-	-	-

Tableau 1. Certaines caractéristiques des secteurs de recensement, recensement de 2001 – Données intégrales et données-échantillon (20 %)

Toronto 0528.25 ◆ A	Toronto 0528.26 A	Toronto 0528.27 A	Toronto 0528.28 A	Toronto 0528.29 ◆ A	Toronto 0528.30 A	Caractéristiques	N°
						CARACTÉRISTIQUES DE LA POPULATION	
						selon la profession basée sur la CNP-S de 2001 – fin	
100	75	200	65	80	245	E Sciences sociales, enseignement, administration publique et religion	300
45	25	25	30	-	60	F Arts, culture, sports et loisirs	301
390	225	500	280	325	405	G Ventes et services	302
30	10	45	40	70	20	H Métiers, transport et machinerie	303
-	-	-	-	-	-	I Professions propres au secteur primaire	304
210	80	225	240	460	120	J Transformation, fabrication et services d'utilité publique	305
3,585	**1,970**	**4,815**	**2,940**	**3,130**	**4,405**	**Population active occupée totale de 15 ans et plus**	306
						selon le lieu de travail	
1,885	1,050	2,490	1,565	1,695	2,390	Hommes	307
1,610	900	2,000	1,370	1,440	1,980	Lieu habituel de travail	308
75	45	170	35	10	120	À domicile	309
15	-	30	10	10	30	En dehors du Canada	310
180	110	295	150	230	250	Sans adresse de travail fixe	311
1,700	925	2,325	1,375	1,440	2,015	Femmes	312
1,590	790	2,145	1,270	1,355	1,825	Lieu habituel de travail	313
45	65	100	25	30	130	À domicile	314
-	-	-	-	-	15	En dehors du Canada	315
65	75	75	80	50	50	Sans adresse de travail fixe	316
3,445	**1,865**	**4,525**	**2,865**	**3,075**	**4,110**	**Population active occupée totale de 15 ans et plus ayant un lieu habituel de travail ou sans adresse de travail fixe**	317
						selon le mode de transport	
1,790	1,005	2,295	1,520	1,670	2,235	Hommes	318
1,575	775	2,010	1,330	1,430	2,035	Automobile, camion ou fourgonnette, en tant que conducteur	319
95	30	55	50	140	55	Automobile, camion ou fourgonnette, en tant que passager	320
105	145	165	105	75	100	Transport en commun	321
10	50	65	-	15	30	À pied	322
10	-	-	25	10	15	Autre moyen	323
1,650	860	2,225	1,350	1,405	1,875	Femmes	324
1,160	585	1,480	940	1,020	1,450	Automobile, camion ou fourgonnette, en tant que conductrice	325
210	70	245	180	215	180	Automobile, camion ou fourgonnette, en tant que passagère	326
225	170	440	180	160	235	Transport en commun	327
55	30	50	40	-	10	À pied	328
-	-	10	10	-	-	Autre moyen	329
3,980	**2,285**	**5,255**	**3,285**	**3,505**	**4,900**	**Population totale de 15 ans et plus ayant travaillé depuis le 1er janvier 2000**	330
						selon la langue utilisée au travail	
3,665	2,055	4,615	2,905	2,995	4,400	Réponses uniques	331
3,625	1,935	4,540	2,835	2,875	4,365	Anglais	332
-	-	10	-	-	-	Français	333
30	115	70	60	125	25	Langues non officielles (5)	334
-	45	15	-	-	-	Chinois, n.d.a.	335
15	-	10	-	-	-	Cantonais	336
15	70	45	60	120	20	Autres langues (6)	337
315	230	640	380	510	505	Réponses multiples	338
55	35	140	35	65	190	Anglais et français	339
245	185	475	330	435	315	Anglais et langue non officielle	340
-	-	-	-	-	-	Français et langue non officielle	341
15	10	30	15	-	-	Anglais, français et langue non officielle	342
						CARACTÉRISTIQUES DES LOGEMENTS ET DES MÉNAGES	
1,995	**1,240**	**2,455**	**1,595**	**1,445**	**2,380**	**Nombre total de logements privés occupés**	343
						selon le mode d'occupation	
1,435	580	2,325	1,350	1,160	2,325	Possédé	344
555	660	130	240	285	55	Loué	345
-	-	-	-	-	-	Logement de bande	346
						selon le type de construction résidentielle	
790	445	1,115	665	1,030	1,165	Maison individuelle non attenante	347
15	10	625	575	110	870	Maison jumelée	348
525	240	370	130	95	320	Maison en rangée	349
15	-	-	-	210	10	Appartement, duplex non attenant	350
510	545	-	225	-	-	Appartement, immeuble de cinq étages ou plus	351
135	-	345	-	10	10	Appartement, immeuble de moins de cinq étages (38)	352
-	-	-	-	-	-	Autre maison individuelle attenante	353
-	-	-	-	-	-	Logement mobile (39)	354

Table 1. Selected Characteristics for Census Tracts, 2001 Census – 100% Data and 20% Sample Data

No.	Characteristics	Toronto 0528.19 ◆◇ A	Toronto 0528.20 A	Toronto 0528.21 ◆ A	Toronto 0528.22 ◆ A	Toronto 0528.23 ◆ A	Toronto 0528.24 A
	DWELLING AND HOUSEHOLD CHARACTERISTICS						
	by condition of dwelling						
355	Regular maintenance only	1,160	1,340	1,080	1,420	1,980	1,115
356	Minor repairs	275	325	95	245	345	195
357	Major repairs	40	25	35	15	50	-
	by period of construction						
358	Before 1946	-	-	-	-	-	-
359	1946-1960	-	-	10	-	-	10
360	1961-1970	10	10	10	-	-	-
361	1971-1980	15	35	20	35	-	-
362	1981-1990	1,015	1,425	605	1,085	785	790
363	1991-2001 (20)	445	215	560	560	1,580	520
364	Average number of rooms per dwelling	6.8	7.6	5.3	6.9	8.2	7.6
365	Average number of bedrooms per dwelling	3.3	3.4	2.4	3.3	3.8	3.6
366	Average value of dwelling $	244,145	258,633	193,614	219,970	321,757	278,654
367	**Total number of private households**	**1,475**	**1,690**	**1,205**	**1,680**	**2,380**	**1,315**
	by household size						
368	1 person	135	170	305	165	135	65
369	2 persons	260	385	290	265	345	175
370	3 persons	265	260	195	275	435	230
371	4-5 persons	660	655	310	670	1,210	640
372	6 or more persons	160	220	105	295	260	210
	by household type						
373	One-family households	1,195	1,270	785	1,200	2,090	1,075
374	Multiple-family households	110	215	100	295	160	140
375	Non-family households	175	205	325	185	135	95
376	Number of persons in private households	5,365	6,035	3,455	6,600	9,135	5,335
377	Average number of persons in private households	3.6	3.6	2.9	3.9	3.8	4.1
378	Average number of persons per room	0.5	0.5	0.5	0.6	0.5	0.5
379	Tenant households in non-farm, non-reserve private dwellings (40)	205	235	705	300	165	100
380	Average gross rent $ (40)	1,429	780	839	634	1,137	1,329
381	Tenant households spending 30% or more of household income on gross rent (40) (41)	80	65	295	100	40	45
382	Tenant households spending from 30% to 99% of household income on gross rent (40) (41)	50	55	220	85	35	30
383	Owner households in non-farm, non-reserve private dwellings (42)	1,270	1,450	495	1,375	2,220	1,215
384	Average owner's major payments $ (42)	1,378	1,173	1,212	1,346	1,576	1,321
385	Owner households spending 30% or more of household income on owner's major payments (41) (42)	385	210	145	415	550	300
386	Owner households spending from 30% to 99% of household income on owner's major payments (41) (42)	340	175	135	365	490	275
	CENSUS FAMILY CHARACTERISTICS						
387	**Total number of census families in private households**	**1,435**	**1,720**	**995**	**1,845**	**2,425**	**1,380**
	by census family structure and size						
388	Total couple families	1,250	1,490	745	1,555	2,275	1,230
389	Total families of married couples	1,195	1,440	680	1,495	2,200	1,185
390	Without children at home	250	450	235	355	390	270
391	With children at home	945	995	450	1,140	1,815	915
392	1 child	240	270	130	350	465	205
393	2 children	460	500	220	550	915	410
394	3 or more children	250	225	100	235	435	295
395	Total families of common-law couples	55	45	65	60	70	45
396	Without children at home	25	30	35	30	65	15
397	With children at home	30	15	25	25	10	30
398	1 child	20	10	20	-	-	-
399	2 children	10	-	10	-	10	10
400	3 or more children	-	10	-	25	-	25
401	Total lone-parent families	190	235	245	295	150	150
402	Female parent	160	185	210	225	125	130
403	1 child	95	100	95	120	60	65
404	2 children	40	55	90	80	65	30
405	3 or more children	25	25	25	30	-	25

Tableau 1. Certaines caractéristiques des secteurs de recensement, recensement de 2001 – Données intégrales et données-échantillon (20 %)

Toronto 0528.25 ◆ A	Toronto 0528.26 A	Toronto 0528.27 A	Toronto 0528.28 A	Toronto 0528.29 ◆ A	Toronto 0528.30 A	Caractéristiques	N°
						CARACTÉRISTIQUES DES LOGEMENTS ET DES MÉNAGES	
						selon l'état du logement	
1,755	1,030	2,215	1,375	1,205	2,230	Entretien régulier seulement	355
200	170	175	165	195	120	Réparations mineures	356
40	40	65	55	50	30	Réparations majeures	357
						selon la période de construction	
-	-	-	20	40	50	Avant 1946	358
-	-	-	70	40	10	1946-1960	359
-	10	-	20	15	-	1961-1970	360
55	30	10	60	25	-	1971-1980	361
1,120	750	85	10	440	-	1981-1990	362
820	450	2,370	1,415	885	2,315	1991-2001 (20)	363
6.4	5.7	6.4	6.5	7.0	7.1	Nombre moyen de pièces par logement	364
3.0	2.6	3.0	3.0	3.5	3.3	Nombre moyen de chambres à coucher par logement	365
232,944	253,796	242,920	276,745	256,939	271,734	Valeur moyenne du logement $	366
1,995	**1,240**	**2,455**	**1,595**	**1,445**	**2,380**	**Nombre total de logements privés**	367
						selon la taille du ménage	
275	185	275	130	50	175	1 personne	368
440	285	465	375	210	685	2 personnes	369
415	260	515	335	210	565	3 personnes	370
720	395	1,015	605	620	810	4-5 personnes	371
150	110	190	145	355	145	6 personnes ou plus	372
						selon le genre de ménage	
1,585	980	1,960	1,310	1,050	2,030	Ménages unifamiliaux	373
90	60	180	110	320	120	Ménages multifamiliaux	374
320	205	315	170	75	225	Ménages non familiaux	375
6,430	3,975	8,375	5,520	6,360	7,690	Nombre de personnes dans les ménages privés	376
3.2	3.2	3.4	3.5	4.4	3.2	Nombre moyen de personnes dans les ménages privés	377
0.5	0.6	0.5	0.5	0.6	0.5	Nombre moyen de personnes par pièce	378
555	660	130	240	285	60	Ménages locataires dans les logements privés non agricoles hors réserve (40)	379
973	697	1,173	737	881	1,225	Loyer brut moyen $ (40)	380
210	225	45	60	105	25	Ménages locataires consacrant 30 % ou plus du revenu du ménage au loyer brut (40) (41)	381
170	170	40	35	65	15	Ménages locataires consacrant de 30 % à 99 % du revenu du ménage au loyer brut (40) (41)	382
1,430	580	2,325	1,350	1,160	2,320	Ménages propriétaires dans les logements privés non agricoles hors réserve (42)	383
1,350	1,227	1,421	1,524	1,470	1,573	Principales dépenses de propriété moyennes $ (42)	384
375	135	680	310	310	505	Ménages propriétaires consacrant 30 % ou plus du revenu du ménage aux principales dépenses de propriété (41) (42)	385
300	130	620	265	280	450	Ménages propriétaires consacrant de 30 % à 99 % du revenu du ménage aux principales dépenses de propriété (41) (42)	386
						CARACTÉRISTIQUES DES FAMILLES DE RECENSEMENT	
1,765	**1,115**	**2,350**	**1,555**	**1,740**	**2,290**	**Total des familles de recensement dans les ménages privés**	387
						selon la structure et la taille de la famille de recensement	
1,485	810	2,090	1,390	1,550	2,145	Total des familles avec conjoints	388
1,395	765	1,965	1,290	1,495	1,945	Total des familles avec couples mariés	389
330	195	445	300	365	605	Sans enfants à la maison	390
1,065	570	1,520	990	1,135	1,340	Avec enfants à la maison	391
330	135	520	340	365	570	1 enfant	392
505	285	725	475	505	540	2 enfants	393
235	150	275	170	265	225	3 enfants ou plus	394
90	40	125	100	50	200	Total des familles en union libre	395
30	30	75	90	25	135	Sans enfants à la maison	396
65	10	45	10	25	65	Avec enfants à la maison	397
20	-	20	-	10	30	1 enfant	398
35	10	20	10	10	15	2 enfants	399
-	-	-	-	10	20	3 enfants ou plus	400
275	305	255	160	195	145	Total des familles monoparentales	401
230	275	235	135	160	120	Parent de sexe féminin	402
160	190	145	55	90	65	1 enfant	403
50	65	65	55	30	30	2 enfants	404
20	10	25	25	35	25	3 enfants ou plus	405

Table 1. Selected Characteristics for Census Tracts, 2001 Census – 100% Data and 20% Sample Data

No.	Characteristics	Toronto 0528.19 ◆◇ A	Toronto 0528.20 A	Toronto 0528.21 ◆ A	Toronto 0528.22 ◆ A	Toronto 0528.23 ◆ A	Toronto 0528.24 A
	CENSUS FAMILY CHARACTERISTICS						
	by census family structure and size – concluded						
406	Male parent	30	50	40	70	20	25
407	1 child	15	40	30	60	-	15
408	2 children	15	10	10	10	20	-
409	3 or more children	-	-	-	-	10	-
410	**Total number of children at home**	**2,320**	**2,395**	**1,300**	**2,765**	**4,010**	**2,375**
	by age groups						
411	Under 6 years	330	375	285	660	910	335
412	6-14 years	800	765	455	995	1,585	725
413	15-17 years	290	295	115	260	470	310
414	18-24 years	535	630	305	565	610	645
415	25 years and over	365	335	145	280	435	355
416	Average number of children at home per census family (43)	1.6	1.4	1.3	1.5	1.7	1.7
417	**Total number of persons in private households**	**5,365**	**6,040**	**3,455**	**6,595**	**9,135**	**5,335**
	by census family status and living arrangements						
418	Number of non-family persons	360	430	415	440	425	355
419	Living with relatives (44)	140	120	85	205	255	190
420	Living with non-relatives only	80	130	20	65	35	105
421	Living alone	135	170	310	165	135	60
422	Number of family persons	5,010	5,610	3,035	6,160	8,710	4,975
423	Average number of persons per census family	3.5	3.3	3.1	3.3	3.6	3.6
424	**Total number of persons 65 years and over**	**335**	**525**	**365**	**415**	**395**	**320**
425	Number of non-family persons 65 years and over	85	155	135	120	120	75
426	Living with relatives (44)	65	75	40	85	125	55
427	Living with non-relatives only	-	-	-	-	-	-
428	Living alone	20	75	95	30	-	15
429	Number of family persons 65 years and over	250	375	230	295	270	250
	ECONOMIC FAMILY CHARACTERISTICS						
430	**Total number of economic families in private households**	**1,350**	**1,490**	**885**	**1,500**	**2,250**	**1,225**
	by size of family						
431	2 persons	285	360	285	260	350	180
432	3 persons	265	260	190	280	430	200
433	4 persons	435	415	215	410	810	400
434	5 or more persons	360	450	195	550	655	445
435	Total number of persons in economic families	5,145	5,730	3,120	6,365	8,965	5,165
436	Average number of persons per economic family	3.8	3.8	3.5	4.2	4.0	4.2
437	Total number of unattached individuals	225	305	330	230	170	170
	2000 INCOME CHARACTERISTICS						
	Population 15 years and over by sex and total income groups in 2000						
438	Total - Both sexes	4,230	4,895	2,710	4,930	6,620	4,275
439	Without income	310	355	180	375	430	235
440	With income	3,920	4,535	2,530	4,555	6,195	4,035
441	Under $1,000 (45)	220	220	140	265	265	305
442	$ 1,000 - $ 2,999	170	115	105	215	265	215
443	$ 3,000 - $ 4,999	150	180	130	140	190	225
444	$ 5,000 - $ 6,999	215	160	120	225	225	180
445	$ 7,000 - $ 9,999	220	200	155	185	285	230
446	$10,000 - $11,999	125	205	145	140	190	155
447	$12,000 - $14,999	190	265	190	305	355	185
448	$15,000 - $19,999	275	380	200	540	420	285
449	$20,000 - $24,999	305	380	255	485	430	315
450	$25,000 - $29,999	270	275	200	370	330	260
451	$30,000 - $34,999	325	385	125	460	495	375
452	$35,000 - $39,999	280	330	160	315	365	325
453	$40,000 - $44,999	225	280	140	275	315	225
454	$45,000 - $49,999	180	135	105	165	315	205
455	$50,000 - $59,999	275	300	135	200	480	190
456	$60,000 and over	490	730	210	280	1,275	380
457	Average income $ (46)	30,318	35,217	25,762	27,133	39,357	27,605
458	Median income $ (46)	25,323	27,720	21,140	23,081	30,708	24,010
459	Standard error of average income $ (46)	889	1,293	895	1,024	1,331	845

Tableau 1. Certaines caractéristiques des secteurs de recensement, recensement de 2001 – Données intégrales et données-échantillon (20 %)

Toronto 0528.25 ◆ A	Toronto 0528.26 A	Toronto 0528.27 A	Toronto 0528.28 A	Toronto 0528.29 ◆ A	Toronto 0528.30 A	Caractéristiques	N°
						CARACTÉRISTIQUES DES FAMILLES DE RECENSEMENT	
						selon la structure et la taille de la famille de recensement - fin	
40	30	30	25	35	25	Parent de sexe masculin	406
15	20	25	20	15	10	1 enfant	407
20	10	-	10	-	15	2 enfants	408
10	10	-	-	10	-	3 enfants ou plus	409
2,620	**1,665**	**3,300**	**2,175**	**2,675**	**2,780**	**Nombre total d'enfants à la maison**	410
						selon les groupes d'âge	
555	335	940	765	735	1,095	Moins de 6 ans	411
925	590	1,190	735	965	995	6-14 ans	412
280	165	365	150	300	200	15-17 ans	413
550	405	575	335	425	320	18-24 ans	414
310	170	230	190	250	170	25 ans et plus	415
1.5	1.5	1.4	1.4	1.5	1.2	Nombre moyen d'enfants à la maison par famille de recensement (43)	416
6,425	**3,980**	**8,375**	**5,515**	**6,360**	**7,685**	**Nombre total de personnes dans les ménages privés**	417
						selon la situation des particuliers dans la famille de recensement et des particuliers dans le ménage	
560	390	640	395	405	475	Nombre de personnes hors famille de recensement	418
220	165	270	165	250	225	Vivant avec des personnes apparentées (44)	419
65	40	90	100	95	70	Vivant avec des personnes non apparentées uniquement	420
275	190	275	130	55	175	Vivant seules	421
5,870	3,590	7,740	5,120	5,960	7,215	Nombre de personnes membres d'une famille	422
3.3	3.2	3.3	3.3	3.4	3.2	Nombre moyen de personnes par famille de recensement	423
330	**275**	**350**	**250**	**335**	**235**	**Nombre total de personnes de 65 ans et plus**	424
125	110	115	85	105	65	Nombre de personnes hors famille de recensement de 65 ans et plus	425
80	75	90	65	90	55	Vivant avec des personnes apparentées (44)	426
10	-	-	-	-	-	Vivant avec des personnes non apparentées uniquement	427
40	30	25	20	10	10	Vivant seules	428
210	165	240	165	230	170	Nombre de personnes membres d'une famille de 65 ans et plus	429
						CARACTÉRISTIQUES DES FAMILLES ÉCONOMIQUES	
1,700	**1,050**	**2,160**	**1,430**	**1,390**	**2,195**	**Nombre total de familles économiques dans les ménages privés**	430
						selon la taille de la famille	
425	300	455	360	225	680	2 personnes	431
415	260	525	325	215	570	3 personnes	432
520	245	710	425	390	565	4 personnes	433
345	245	470	320	565	380	5 personnes ou plus	434
6,085	3,750	8,010	5,285	6,205	7,445	Nombre total de personnes dans les familles économiques	435
3.6	3.6	3.7	3.7	4.5	3.4	Nombre moyen de personnes par famille économique	436
345	230	365	230	150	245	Nombre total de personnes hors famille économique	437
						CARACTÉRISTIQUES DU REVENU DE 2000	
						Population de 15 ans et plus selon le sexe et les tranches de revenu total en 2000	
4,955	3,050	6,255	4,025	4,655	5,595	Total - Les deux sexes	438
330	245	275	285	400	250	Sans revenu	439
4,625	2,805	5,980	3,740	4,255	5,350	Avec un revenu	440
185	170	225	155	205	135	Moins de 1 000 $ (45)	441
185	190	160	145	185	185	1 000 $ - 2 999 $	442
135	85	210	145	245	100	3 000 $ - 4 999 $	443
160	120	265	120	185	170	5 000 $ - 6 999 $	444
255	175	370	185	210	195	7 000 $ - 9 999 $	445
215	175	230	155	185	140	10 000 $ - 11 999 $	446
255	245	255	160	300	205	12 000 $ - 14 999 $	447
385	235	340	210	375	250	15 000 $ - 19 999 $	448
310	185	410	230	375	355	20 000 $ - 24 999 $	449
415	280	390	240	350	220	25 000 $ - 29 999 $	450
300	255	575	290	305	480	30 000 $ - 34 999 $	451
300	120	490	215	270	420	35 000 $ - 39 999 $	452
395	100	460	240	265	440	40 000 $ - 44 999 $	453
185	80	325	170	140	385	45 000 $ - 49 999 $	454
375	180	495	395	370	590	50 000 $ - 59 999 $	455
560	205	780	695	305	1,055	60 000 $ et plus	456
31,650	25,130	32,984	37,964	27,957	40,985	Revenu moyen $ (46)	457
27,309	19,999	30,257	31,702	22,491	36,473	Revenu médian $ (46)	458
787	912	693	1,379	888	968	Erreur type de revenu moyen $ (46)	459

Table 1. Selected Characteristics for Census Tracts, 2001 Census – 100% Data and 20% Sample Data

No.	Characteristics	Toronto 0528.19 ◆◇ A	Toronto 0528.20 A	Toronto 0528.21 ◆ A	Toronto 0528.22 ◆ A	Toronto 0528.23 ◆ A	Toronto 0528.24 A
	2000 INCOME CHARACTERISTICS						
	Population 15 years and over by sex and total income groups in 2000 – concluded						
460	Total - Males	2,045	2,410	1,245	2,430	3,300	2,110
461	Without income	140	110	65	120	130	85
462	With income	1,905	2,305	1,180	2,315	3,170	2,025
463	Under $1,000 (45)	80	105	55	135	125	160
464	$ 1,000 - $ 2,999	75	60	45	120	105	115
465	$ 3,000 - $ 4,999	55	85	45	40	40	85
466	$ 5,000 - $ 6,999	115	55	40	80	80	75
467	$ 7,000 - $ 9,999	80	65	55	45	75	105
468	$10,000 - $11,999	40	75	70	70	90	35
469	$12,000 - $14,999	85	95	55	115	150	90
470	$15,000 - $19,999	85	200	85	200	190	130
471	$20,000 - $24,999	125	160	105	175	195	145
472	$25,000 - $29,999	125	110	90	175	120	80
473	$30,000 - $34,999	175	180	60	260	210	200
474	$35,000 - $39,999	135	135	65	190	155	140
475	$40,000 - $44,999	110	145	90	175	185	145
476	$45,000 - $49,999	115	80	60	125	190	95
477	$50,000 - $59,999	225	215	95	170	335	130
478	$60,000 and over	295	535	175	225	935	295
479	Average income $ (46)	34,873	42,369	31,785	33,691	49,853	31,629
480	Median income $ (46)	31,590	33,053	27,168	29,955	40,149	28,914
481	Standard error of average income $ (46)	1,308	2,215	1,497	1,898	2,373	1,344
482	Total - Females	2,185	2,480	1,465	2,500	3,320	2,165
483	Without income	175	250	120	260	295	150
484	With income	2,015	2,235	1,345	2,240	3,025	2,015
485	Under $1,000 (45)	145	120	90	125	140	140
486	$ 1,000 - $ 2,999	95	60	65	90	160	95
487	$ 3,000 - $ 4,999	100	100	90	100	150	145
488	$ 5,000 - $ 6,999	100	105	80	140	145	110
489	$ 7,000 - $ 9,999	135	130	95	145	210	130
490	$10,000 - $11,999	85	125	80	70	100	115
491	$12,000 - $14,999	105	175	135	185	205	100
492	$15,000 - $19,999	190	180	115	340	230	155
493	$20,000 - $24,999	180	215	155	310	235	165
494	$25,000 - $29,999	150	165	115	190	205	180
495	$30,000 - $34,999	150	205	60	195	290	175
496	$35,000 - $39,999	145	190	95	120	205	180
497	$40,000 - $44,999	115	135	50	100	140	75
498	$45,000 - $49,999	60	55	50	35	120	110
499	$50,000 - $59,999	50	85	50	30	150	60
500	$60,000 and over	195	190	40	50	345	85
501	Average income $ (46)	26,011	27,841	20,494	20,363	28,358	23,558
502	Median income $ (46)	21,038	21,716	16,415	18,345	23,027	20,284
503	Standard error of average income $ (46)	1,167	1,214	943	652	987	984
	by composition of total income						
504	Total - Composition of income in 2000 % (47)	100.0	100.0	100.0	100.0	100.0	100.0
505	Employment income %	88.7	86.0	84.8	88.2	91.1	89.4
506	Government transfer payments %	7.3	6.9	11.7	7.2	4.1	6.4
507	Other %	3.9	7.1	3.7	4.6	4.8	4.3
	Population 15 years and over with employment income in 2000 by sex and work activity						
508	Both sexes with employment income (48)	3,240	3,585	1,840	3,820	5,350	3,290
509	Average employment income $	32,516	38,270	29,949	28,554	41,533	30,249
510	Standard error of average employment income $	1,007	1,558	1,079	1,180	1,439	966
511	Worked full year, full time (49)	1,775	1,840	970	2,075	3,250	1,790
512	Average employment income $	41,698	52,088	37,012	37,875	55,313	41,525
513	Standard error of average employment income $	1,401	1,890	1,518	1,965	2,109	1,391
514	Worked part year or part time (50)	1,395	1,625	830	1,590	1,970	1,425
515	Average employment income $	20,917	23,928	22,202	17,934	20,865	16,955
516	Standard error of average employment income $	1,162	2,452	1,344	848	1,092	913
517	Males with employment income (48)	1,630	1,875	940	2,020	2,870	1,690
518	Average employment income $	36,756	45,375	35,042	35,285	51,164	34,698
519	Standard error of average employment income $	1,443	2,598	1,740	2,099	2,465	1,495
520	Worked full year, full time (49)	970	1,055	540	1,285	2,000	1,030
521	Average employment income $	45,297	57,576	42,539	44,169	63,531	45,535
522	Standard error of average employment income $	1,877	2,652	2,296	3,065	3,276	2,023
523	Worked part year or part time (50)	635	780	380	695	825	635
524	Average employment income $	24,601	29,578	24,716	20,437	23,357	18,262
525	Standard error of average employment income $	1,907	4,960	2,278	1,591	1,852	1,472

Tableau 1. Certaines caractéristiques des secteurs de recensement, recensement de 2001 – Données intégrales et données-échantillon (20 %)

Toronto 0528.25 ◆ A	Toronto 0528.26 A	Toronto 0528.27 A	Toronto 0528.28 A	Toronto 0528.29 ◆ A	Toronto 0528.30 A	Caractéristiques	N°
						CARACTÉRISTIQUES DU REVENU DE 2000	
						Population de 15 ans et plus selon le sexe et les tranches de revenu total en 2000 - fin	
2,405	1,425	3,050	1,975	2,295	2,780	Total - Hommes	460
105	75	145	90	110	100	Sans revenu	461
2,300	1,355	2,905	1,880	2,185	2,670	Avec un revenu	462
70	90	95	75	135	60	Moins de 1 000 $ (45)	463
85	80	55	55	100	50	1 000 $ - 2 999 $	464
60	15	85	10	90	20	3 000 $ - 4 999 $	465
55	65	70	45	40	40	5 000 $ - 6 999 $	466
75	85	165	70	95	70	7 000 $ - 9 999 $	467
70	120	105	45	75	60	10 000 $ - 11 999 $	468
100	35	110	60	95	55	12 000 $ - 14 999 $	469
195	110	95	95	145	120	15 000 $ - 19 999 $	470
130	70	145	110	155	115	20 000 $ - 24 999 $	471
165	110	140	95	125	65	25 000 $ - 29 999 $	472
185	110	305	120	165	260	30 000 $ - 34 999 $	473
175	60	255	115	180	165	35 000 $ - 39 999 $	474
195	50	245	160	195	215	40 000 $ - 44 999 $	475
95	60	140	95	65	225	45 000 $ - 49 999 $	476
265	130	310	215	275	365	50 000 $ - 59 999 $	477
375	160	580	510	260	785	60 000 $ et plus	478
37,031	29,651	39,019	45,545	33,848	50,437	Revenu moyen $ (46)	479
32,190	25,198	36,198	40,197	30,236	44,977	Revenu médian $ (46)	480
1,200	1,530	1,134	1,986	1,481	1,603	Erreur type de revenu moyen $ (46)	481
2,550	1,625	3,205	2,055	2,360	2,820	Total - Femmes	482
220	170	130	195	290	140	Sans revenu	483
2,325	1,455	3,075	1,860	2,070	2,680	Avec un revenu	484
115	80	130	85	70	80	Moins de 1 000 $ (45)	485
100	110	105	85	85	135	1 000 $ - 2 999 $	486
85	70	120	130	155	75	3 000 $ - 4 999 $	487
110	55	190	75	145	130	5 000 $ - 6 999 $	488
175	90	205	115	120	130	7 000 $ - 9 999 $	489
140	60	130	115	110	90	10 000 $ - 11 999 $	490
160	210	140	100	205	150	12 000 $ - 14 999 $	491
185	130	245	115	235	130	15 000 $ - 19 999 $	492
185	115	265	120	215	240	20 000 $ - 24 999 $	493
250	175	250	145	230	160	25 000 $ - 29 999 $	494
120	145	270	165	140	225	30 000 $ - 34 999 $	495
125	60	240	95	90	260	35 000 $ - 39 999 $	496
200	50	215	85	70	220	40 000 $ - 44 999 $	497
90	20	185	75	65	160	45 000 $ - 49 999 $	498
110	45	180	180	90	220	50 000 $ - 59 999 $	499
180	45	200	180	45	265	60 000 $ et plus	500
26,336	20,928	27,285	30,293	21,739	31,557	Revenu moyen $ (46)	501
22,368	16,610	25,228	24,798	18,039	29,989	Revenu médian $ (46)	502
960	994	769	1,835	857	964	Erreur type de revenu moyen $ (46)	503
						selon la composition du revenu total	
100.0	100.0	100.0	100.0	100.0	100.0	Total - Composition du revenu en 2000 % (47)	504
89.5	87.5	92.4	91.1	87.2	93.9	Revenu d'emploi %	505
6.1	9.2	4.5	4.5	8.0	3.2	Transferts gouvernementaux %	506
4.4	3.2	3.1	4.4	4.8	2.9	Autre %	507
						Population de 15 ans et plus ayant un revenu d'emploi en 2000 selon le sexe et le travail	
3,800	2,175	5,145	3,225	3,445	4,865	Les deux sexes ayant un revenu d'emploi (48)	508
34,438	28,354	35,429	40,147	30,103	42,298	Revenu moyen d'emploi $	509
870	1,076	720	1,502	994	1,016	Erreur type de revenu moyen d'emploi $	510
2,325	1,175	3,365	2,120	1,940	3,315	Ayant travaillé toute l'année à plein temps (49)	511
43,304	40,057	42,754	49,695	38,096	50,296	Revenu moyen d'emploi $	512
1,131	1,469	861	1,943	1,071	1,111	Erreur type de revenu moyen d'emploi $	513
1,410	935	1,700	1,015	1,460	1,470	Ayant travaillé une partie de l'année ou à temps partiel (50)	514
20,366	14,913	22,097	21,347	20,101	25,331	Revenu moyen d'emploi $	515
979	941	1,030	1,907	1,681	1,890	Erreur type de revenu moyen d'emploi $	516
1,960	1,135	2,660	1,690	1,875	2,510	Hommes ayant un revenu d'emploi (48)	517
39,786	32,796	40,284	47,000	35,773	51,082	Revenu moyen d'emploi $	518
1,282	1,696	1,154	2,117	1,588	1,638	Erreur type de revenu moyen d'emploi $	519
1,340	655	1,880	1,220	1,125	1,910	Ayant travaillé toute l'année à plein temps (49)	520
47,631	45,627	48,119	55,783	43,848	56,267	Revenu moyen d'emploi $	521
1,577	2,122	1,314	2,604	1,581	1,608	Erreur type de revenu moyen d'emploi $	522
605	435	745	435	725	570	Ayant travaillé une partie de l'année ou à temps partiel (50)	523
22,766	15,474	21,991	24,186	23,843	35,609	Revenu moyen d'emploi $	524
1,505	1,509	1,668	2,371	2,974	4,446	Erreur type de revenu moyen d'emploi $	525

Table 1. Selected Characteristics for Census Tracts, 2001 Census – 100% Data and 20% Sample Data

No.	Characteristics	Toronto 0528.19 ◆◇ A	Toronto 0528.20 A	Toronto 0528.21 ◆ A	Toronto 0528.22 ◆ A	Toronto 0528.23 ◆ A	Toronto 0528.24 A
	2000 INCOME CHARACTERISTICS						
	Population 15 years and over with employment income in 2000 by sex and work activity – concluded						
526	Females with employment income (48)	1,615	1,710	900	1,795	2,480	1,595
527	Average employment income $	28,239	30,501	24,664	20,951	30,395	25,533
528	Standard error of average employment income $	1,364	1,488	1,144	735	1,098	1,149
529	Worked full year, full time (49)	810	790	430	795	1,250	770
530	Average employment income $	37,413	44,768	30,043	27,693	42,173	36,153
531	Standard error of average employment income $	2,050	2,526	1,595	1,138	1,506	1,716
532	Worked part year or part time (50)	755	850	460	895	1,140	785
533	Average employment income $	17,805	18,754	20,135	15,990	19,054	15,904
534	Standard error of average employment income $	1,355	1,215	1,542	857	1,313	1,137
	Census families by structure and family income groups in 2000						
535	Total - All census families	1,435	1,725	990	1,845	2,420	1,375
536	Under $10,000	55	55	75	130	45	45
537	$ 10,000 - $19,999	65	45	55	90	50	55
538	$ 20,000 - $29,999	80	140	115	130	95	85
539	$ 30,000 - $39,999	115	160	90	205	170	80
540	$ 40,000 - $49,999	160	140	160	285	150	125
541	$ 50,000 - $59,999	130	140	120	195	175	155
542	$ 60,000 - $69,999	130	150	90	225	240	175
543	$ 70,000 - $79,999	140	150	70	150	195	85
544	$ 80,000 - $89,999	125	90	65	110	220	160
545	$ 90,000 - $99,999	100	135	60	130	160	115
546	$100,000 and over	340	515	85	205	925	300
547	Average family income $	73,756	83,179	54,403	62,415	95,097	73,524
548	Median family income $	68,936	72,609	49,924	56,108	84,010	67,510
549	Standard error of average family income $	2,344	3,369	2,245	2,557	3,187	2,321
550	Total - All couple census families (51)	1,245	1,490	745	1,550	2,275	1,225
551	Under $10,000	30	25	70	110	40	35
552	$ 10,000 - $19,999	40	20	40	45	45	35
553	$ 20,000 - $29,999	55	100	90	85	90	80
554	$ 30,000 - $39,999	100	95	45	150	140	60
555	$ 40,000 - $49,999	140	125	85	215	125	120
556	$ 50,000 - $59,999	115	125	100	165	150	145
557	$ 60,000 - $69,999	105	150	70	205	240	165
558	$ 70,000 - $79,999	135	150	55	140	190	65
559	$ 80,000 - $89,999	115	75	70	110	205	135
560	$ 90,000 - $99,999	100	120	50	120	145	110
561	$100,000 and over	320	505	85	205	895	275
562	Average family income $	76,778	90,205	57,648	66,889	96,969	74,971
563	Median family income $	74,753	78,048	54,739	59,383	85,175	67,570
564	Standard error of average family income $	2,455	3,723	2,724	2,933	3,359	2,474
	Incidence of low income in 2000						
565	Total - Economic families	1,345	1,490	885	1,500	2,250	1,225
566	Low income	130	115	155	210	140	90
567	Incidence of low income in 2000 % (52)	9.8	7.7	17.4	13.9	6.2	7.4
568	Total - Unattached individuals 15 years and over	215	300	330	230	155	170
569	Low income	55	100	190	90	20	30
570	Incidence of low income in 2000 % (52)	24.9	32.9	56.8	39.6	12.6	17.8
571	Total - Population in private households	5,360	6,030	3,450	6,595	9,120	5,335
572	Low income	545	520	680	915	630	345
573	Incidence of low income in 2000 % (52)	10.1	8.6	19.7	13.9	6.9	6.5
	Private households by household income groups in 2000						
574	Total - All private households	1,475	1,685	1,205	1,675	2,380	1,315
575	Under $10,000	45	45	120	70	20	20
576	$ 10,000 - $19,999	70	45	165	95	60	35
577	$ 20,000 - $29,999	35	80	125	95	50	70
578	$ 30,000 - $39,999	100	85	95	175	125	60
579	$ 40,000 - $49,999	155	155	125	150	105	95
580	$ 50,000 - $59,999	90	105	125	135	150	130
581	$ 60,000 - $69,999	150	140	110	195	205	160
582	$ 70,000 - $79,999	190	200	75	150	255	95
583	$ 80,000 - $89,999	140	65	70	130	210	110
584	$ 90,000 - $99,999	100	155	50	135	185	100
585	$100,000 and over	405	615	150	350	1,020	435
586	Average household income $	80,467	94,688	53,966	73,637	102,423	84,783
587	Median household income $	76,100	79,367	48,874	65,546	90,857	77,905
588	Standard error of average household income $	2,525	3,627	2,448	2,982	3,310	2,867

Tableau 1. Certaines caractéristiques des secteurs de recensement, recensement de 2001 – Données intégrales et données-échantillon (20 %)

Toronto 0528.25 ◆ A	Toronto 0528.26 A	Toronto 0528.27 A	Toronto 0528.28 A	Toronto 0528.29 ◆ A	Toronto 0528.30 A	Caractéristiques	N°
						CARACTÉRISTIQUES DU REVENU DE 2000	
						Population de 15 ans et plus ayant un revenu d'emploi en 2000 selon le sexe et le travail – fin	
1,840	1,040	2,480	1,530	1,570	2,355	Femmes ayant un revenu d'emploi (48)	526
28,739	23,520	30,221	32,600	23,347	32,937	Revenu moyen d'emploi $	527
1,090	1,231	799	2,046	959	1,041	Erreur type de revenu moyen d'emploi $	528
985	520	1,485	900	815	1,405	Ayant travaillé toute l'année à plein temps (49)	529
37,410	33,039	35,969	41,410	30,144	42,209	Revenu moyen d'emploi $	530
1,489	1,786	918	2,791	1,061	1,327	Erreur type de revenu moyen d'emploi $	531
805	500	955	585	730	900	Ayant travaillé une partie de l'année ou à temps partiel (50)	532
18,558	14,422	22,181	19,229	16,383	18,824	Revenu moyen d'emploi $	533
1,270	1,176	1,301	2,836	1,476	1,162	Erreur type de revenu moyen d'emploi $	534
						Familles de recensement selon la structure et les tranches de revenu de la famille en 2000	
1,760	1,115	2,350	1,555	1,740	2,290	Total - Toutes les familles de recensement	535
75	80	40	60	105	65	Moins de 10 000 $	536
75	60	65	70	115	45	10 000 $ - 19 999 $	537
85	145	145	105	160	70	20 000 $ - 29 999 $	538
105	160	195	75	190	60	30 000 $ - 39 999 $	539
200	135	240	120	200	160	40 000 $ - 49 999 $	540
255	85	210	165	200	205	50 000 $ - 59 999 $	541
175	125	265	135	130	255	60 000 $ - 69 999 $	542
200	80	245	160	135	225	70 000 $ - 79 999 $	543
105	55	195	115	135	245	80 000 $ - 89 999 $	544
120	25	185	95	115	240	90 000 $ - 99 999 $	545
365	150	550	460	250	720	100 000 $ et plus	546
72,284	55,728	75,061	83,151	63,488	88,246	Revenu moyen des familles $	547
65,117	46,088	70,274	74,406	55,916	81,667	Revenu médian des familles $	548
2,206	2,457	1,705	3,265	2,473	2,115	Erreur type de revenu moyen des familles $	549
1,485	810	2,090	1,390	1,545	2,145	Total - Toutes les familles de recensement comptant un couple (51)	550
50	40	40	45	90	50	Moins de 10 000 $	551
30	15	40	50	95	25	10 000 $ - 19 999 $	552
65	80	115	55	145	60	20 000 $ - 29 999 $	553
85	100	135	45	155	50	30 000 $ - 39 999 $	554
125	90	185	105	170	150	40 000 $ - 49 999 $	555
230	75	180	160	190	165	50 000 $ - 59 999 $	556
155	115	245	115	125	230	60 000 $ - 69 999 $	557
180	80	240	155	120	220	70 000 $ - 79 999 $	558
90	40	170	110	130	245	80 000 $ - 89 999 $	559
120	25	190	90	100	235	90 000 $ - 99 999 $	560
355	145	540	455	225	715	100 000 $ et plus	561
77,698	64,479	78,511	88,299	64,151	90,902	Revenu moyen des familles $	562
70,239	59,956	72,328	78,149	57,077	84,866	Revenu médian des familles $	563
2,427	3,018	1,813	3,481	2,611	2,181	Erreur type de revenu moyen des familles $	564
						Fréquence des unités à faible revenu en 2000	
1,705	1,050	2,160	1,435	1,395	2,190	Total - Familles économiques	565
190	240	155	150	175	100	Faible revenu	566
11.1	23.2	7.2	10.4	12.8	4.7	Fréquence des unités à faible revenu en 2000 % (52)	567
345	220	365	230	150	245	Total - Personnes hors famille économique de 15 ans et plus	568
115	105	40	70	35	50	Faible revenu	569
33.8	47.2	11.3	30.5	22.7	20.4	Fréquence des unités à faible revenu en 2000 % (52)	570
6,425	3,975	8,375	5,520	6,360	7,685	Total - Population dans les ménages privés	571
820	895	620	680	710	435	Faible revenu	572
12.8	22.6	7.5	12.4	11.1	5.6	Fréquence des unités à faible revenu en 2000 % (52)	573
						Ménages privés selon les tranches de revenu du ménage en 2000	
1,995	1,240	2,455	1,595	1,445	2,380	Total - Tous les ménages privés	574
85	100	30	55	45	35	Moins de 10 000 $	575
135	110	65	35	45	45	10 000 $ - 19 999 $	576
85	125	105	75	65	50	20 000 $ - 29 999 $	577
100	185	185	85	120	65	30 000 $ - 39 999 $	578
225	135	245	95	130	140	40 000 $ - 49 999 $	579
275	105	225	160	135	200	50 000 $ - 59 999 $	580
185	105	265	120	140	290	60 000 $ - 69 999 $	581
200	75	270	180	110	185	70 000 $ - 79 999 $	582
135	75	230	135	115	280	80 000 $ - 89 999 $	583
120	45	160	85	85	265	90 000 $ - 99 999 $	584
460	185	685	555	450	820	100 000 $ et plus	585
73,226	56,792	80,242	88,798	82,181	92,098	Revenu moyen des ménages $	586
64,230	45,934	73,553	78,822	71,501	85,640	Revenu médian des ménages $	587
2,238	2,427	1,776	3,246	3,007	2,097	Erreur type de revenu moyen des ménages $	588

Table 1. Selected Characteristics for Census Tracts, 2001 Census – 100% Data and 20% Sample Data

No.	Characteristics	Toronto 0528.31 A	Toronto 0529.01 ◆	Toronto 0529.02 ◆◇	Toronto 0530 ◆	Toronto 0531.01	Toronto 0531.02 ◆◇ A
	POPULATION CHARACTERISTICS						
1	**Population, 1996 (1)**	**6,018**	**3,908**	**4,732**	**8,616**	**4,032**	**7,135**
2	**Population, 2001 (2)**	**6,560**	**4,174**	**5,086**	**8,811**	**4,273**	**7,301**
3	Population percentage change, 1996-2001	9.0	6.8	7.5	2.3	6.0	2.3
4	Land area in square kilometres, 2001	0.82	0.99	0.79	1.24	0.67	1.33
5	**Total population - 100% Data (3)**	**6,560**	**4,175**	**5,085**	**8,810**	**4,275**	**7,300**
	by sex and age groups						
6	Male	3,140	2,160	2,605	4,430	2,140	3,665
7	0-4 years	255	175	195	355	195	270
8	5-9 years	275	155	225	375	190	290
9	10-14 years	215	135	205	325	150	240
10	15-19 years	215	135	170	340	205	265
11	20-24 years	265	155	170	330	195	300
12	25-29 years	240	180	215	385	170	305
13	30-34 years	230	195	220	435	160	300
14	35-39 years	235	175	240	380	175	305
15	40-44 years	220	170	180	320	155	230
16	45-49 years	190	155	140	260	125	210
17	50-54 years	195	140	125	225	135	230
18	55-59 years	130	115	125	200	95	215
19	60-64 years	105	105	115	155	80	195
20	65-69 years	60	80	95	160	55	145
21	70-74 years	65	45	90	105	25	80
22	75-79 years	95	25	55	60	20	45
23	80-84 years	65	15	25	20	10	20
24	85 years and over	85	5	15	5	5	10
25	Female	3,420	2,015	2,480	4,385	2,135	3,635
26	0-4 years	210	165	215	335	160	245
27	5-9 years	245	120	145	345	180	260
28	10-14 years	230	125	165	315	150	245
29	15-19 years	225	135	150	260	165	240
30	20-24 years	240	170	185	380	180	310
31	25-29 years	240	170	225	395	195	295
32	30-34 years	235	180	195	370	180	300
33	35-39 years	260	170	210	360	170	265
34	40-44 years	225	130	155	265	145	240
35	45-49 years	205	130	140	280	135	225
36	50-54 years	195	125	130	255	155	265
37	55-59 years	115	115	150	230	110	215
38	60-64 years	85	90	125	190	75	200
39	65-69 years	90	75	105	155	45	130
40	70-74 years	115	40	85	110	40	70
41	75-79 years	155	35	55	80	15	65
42	80-84 years	155	25	25	30	15	15
43	85 years and over	195	5	20	30	10	30
44	**Total population 15 years and over**	**5,130**	**3,295**	**3,935**	**6,760**	**3,240**	**5,755**
	by legal marital status						
45	Never married (single)	1,365	960	1,060	2,035	1,220	1,680
46	Legally married (and not separated)	2,925	1,800	2,405	3,815	1,570	3,500
47	Separated, but still legally married	130	150	120	235	130	135
48	Divorced	180	205	170	325	195	200
49	Widowed	525	175	185	345	135	240
	by common-law status						
50	Not in a common-law relationship	5,030	3,115	3,830	6,490	3,085	5,655
51	In a common-law relationship	100	180	105	265	160	95
52	**Total population - 20% Sample Data (4)**	**6,440**	**4,170**	**5,065**	**8,815**	**4,260**	**7,305**
	by mother tongue						
53	Single responses	6,340	4,070	5,000	8,515	4,185	7,080
54	English	2,295	2,005	2,185	3,955	2,370	3,275
55	French	20	40	20	65	30	35
56	Non-official languages (5)	4,025	2,020	2,790	4,495	1,785	3,780
57	Italian	105	160	440	375	215	900
58	Chinese, n.o.s.	85	-	-	-	10	50
59	Cantonese	20	45	-	30	-	-
60	Portuguese	250	40	55	60	-	75
61	Punjabi	2,060	1,305	1,620	1,885	665	2,040
62	Other languages (6)	1,510	480	685	2,145	890	710
63	Multiple responses	100	105	70	295	70	225
64	English and French	-	-	15	10	-	-
65	English and non-official language	95	100	50	260	70	215
66	French and non-official language	-	-	-	25	-	-
67	English, French and non-official language	-	-	-	-	-	-

See reference material at the end of the publication. – Voir les documents de référence à la fin de la publication.

Tableau 1. Certaines caractéristiques des secteurs de recensement, recensement de 2001 – Données intégrales et données-échantillon (20 %)

Toronto 0532.01 ◆◇	Toronto 0532.02 ◆◇	Toronto 0540.01	Toronto 0540.02	Toronto 0550.01	Toronto 0550.02	Caractéristiques	N°
						CARACTÉRISTIQUES DE LA POPULATION	
4,606	**5,178**	**5,485**	**4,564**	**4,864**	**6,889**	**Population, 1996 (1)**	1
4,765	**5,305**	**5,366**	**4,510**	**4,644**	**7,235**	**Population, 2001 (2)**	2
3.5	2.5	-2.2	-1.2	-4.5	5.0	Variation en pourcentage de la population, 1996-2001	3
0.83	0.69	1.55	1.09	7.52	3.02	Superficie des terres en kilomètres carrés, 2001	4
4,765	**5,305**	**5,365**	**4,510**	**4,645**	**7,235**	**Population totale – Données intégrales (3)**	5
						selon le sexe et les groupes d'âge	
2,470	2,675	2,615	2,115	2,295	3,540	Sexe masculin	6
220	240	125	120	140	170	0-4 ans	7
210	220	145	140	175	235	5-9 ans	8
170	215	125	115	205	225	10-14 ans	9
160	205	100	95	185	255	15-19 ans	10
185	215	150	115	150	240	20-24 ans	11
220	210	220	160	135	225	25-29 ans	12
210	230	255	230	115	265	30-34 ans	13
210	240	325	220	195	330	35-39 ans	14
145	195	245	175	220	295	40-44 ans	15
160	170	220	175	190	295	45-49 ans	16
165	140	195	145	170	295	50-54 ans	17
120	125	150	110	130	190	55-59 ans	18
110	105	105	95	105	140	60-64 ans	19
80	75	90	75	65	130	65-69 ans	20
70	45	65	55	45	110	70-74 ans	21
20	25	50	45	35	85	75-79 ans	22
10	5	40	30	25	30	80-84 ans	23
10	10	20	20	10	20	85 ans et plus	24
2,300	2,625	2,745	2,395	2,350	3,695	Sexe féminin	25
185	215	115	120	150	185	0-4 ans	26
150	240	135	145	160	195	5-9 ans	27
155	190	110	110	160	230	10-14 ans	28
155	175	100	95	155	215	15-19 ans	29
170	195	150	115	130	235	20-24 ans	30
215	235	245	205	140	230	25-29 ans	31
200	225	285	225	150	300	30-34 ans	32
205	220	280	250	235	335	35-39 ans	33
150	165	240	200	235	305	40-44 ans	34
130	155	210	185	210	310	45-49 ans	35
170	180	170	165	185	305	50-54 ans	36
130	135	160	130	145	205	55-59 ans	37
100	130	105	80	110	155	60-64 ans	38
85	65	90	85	60	150	65-69 ans	39
45	45	100	80	40	135	70-74 ans	40
30	25	120	100	55	115	75-79 ans	41
15	15	65	70	15	70	80-84 ans	42
5	5	75	35	15	40	85 ans et plus	43
3,680	**3,980**	**4,620**	**3,765**	**3,655**	**6,000**	**Population totale de 15 ans et plus**	44
						selon l'état matrimonial légal	
1,030	1,190	1,675	1,310	1,055	1,825	Célibataire (jamais marié(e))	45
2,245	2,320	1,770	1,595	2,080	3,190	Légalement marié(e) (et non séparé(e))	46
105	135	245	195	120	200	Séparé(e), mais toujours légalement marié(e)	47
150	170	565	385	260	435	Divorcé(e)	48
150	170	365	280	145	355	Veuf ou veuve	49
						selon l'union libre	
3,600	3,890	4,110	3,415	3,450	5,685	Ne vivant pas en union libre	50
80	90	510	345	205	315	Vivant en union libre	51
4,765	**5,320**	**5,320**	**4,510**	**4,645**	**7,215**	**Population totale – Données-échantillon (20 %) (4)**	52
						selon la langue maternelle	
4,585	5,140	5,260	4,470	4,610	7,080	Réponses uniques	53
1,890	2,345	3,785	3,395	3,595	5,055	Anglais	54
65	15	80	115	120	100	Français	55
2,630	2,780	1,395	965	895	1,925	Langues non officielles (5)	56
295	370	80	75	80	55	Italien	57
10	-	-	10	-	110	Chinois, n.d.a.	58
15	-	-	-	-	95	Cantonais	59
30	190	20	15	120	435	Portugais	60
1,640	1,280	-	25	-	10	Pendjabi	61
630	930	1,285	845	695	1,215	Autres langues (6)	62
175	180	55	40	40	135	Réponses multiples	63
-	-	15	-	15	15	Anglais et français	64
165	170	35	35	15	115	Anglais et langue non officielle	65
15	10	10	-	15	-	Français et langue non officielle	66
-	-	-	-	-	-	Anglais, français et langue non officielle	67

See reference material at the end of the publication. – Voir les documents de référence à la fin de la publication.

Table 1. Selected Characteristics for Census Tracts, 2001 Census – 100% Data and 20% Sample Data

No.	Characteristics	Toronto 0528.31 A	Toronto 0529.01 ◆	Toronto 0529.02 ◆◇	Toronto 0530 ◆	Toronto 0531.01	Toronto 0531.02 ◆◇ A
	POPULATION CHARACTERISTICS						
	by home language						
68	Single responses	4,320	3,305	3,840	6,555	3,480	5,245
69	English	2,725	2,150	2,260	4,200	2,565	3,425
70	French	-	-	-	30	15	-
71	Non-official languages (5)	1,595	1,155	1,575	2,320	900	1,820
72	Cantonese	10	10	-	40	-	-
73	Chinese, n.o.s.	20	-	-	-	-	35
74	Italian	15	65	200	115	30	345
75	Punjabi	1,155	865	990	1,220	545	1,155
76	Portuguese	80	10	15	15	-	35
77	Other languages (6)	325	210	370	940	330	255
78	Multiple responses	2,120	870	1,230	2,255	785	2,055
79	English and French	-	30	-	35	35	80
80	English and non-official language	2,090	825	1,200	2,165	740	1,960
81	French and non-official language	-	-	-	15	-	-
82	English, French and non-official language	20	-	25	40	10	10
	by knowledge of official languages						
83	English only	5,835	3,650	4,365	7,890	3,935	6,580
84	French only	-	-	-	-	-	-
85	English and French	270	200	145	325	150	315
86	Neither English nor French	335	320	560	600	175	405
	by knowledge of non-official languages (5) (7)						
87	Italian	145	200	520	565	250	1,175
88	Cantonese	55	50	-	-	-	-
89	Chinese, n.o.s.	80	-	-	35	10	65
90	Spanish	180	55	90	90	165	115
91	Portuguese	270	40	55	85	20	100
92	Punjabi	2,255	1,460	1,755	2,230	790	2,245
93	Tagalog (Pilipino)	40	10	30	105	85	60
	by first official language spoken						
94	English	6,060	3,810	4,480	8,115	4,050	6,840
95	French	15	35	25	60	35	35
96	English and French	30	20	20	55	15	35
97	Neither English nor French	335	315	550	590	155	395
98	Official language minority - (number) (8)	25	40	30	85	40	50
99	Official language minority - (percentage) (8)	0.4	1.0	0.6	1.0	0.9	0.7
	by ethnic origin (9)						
100	Canadian	490	650	495	775	645	485
101	English	305	610	355	475	340	240
102	Scottish	220	355	295	385	360	160
103	Irish	130	255	235	240	325	105
104	Chinese	195	75	15	105	45	100
105	Italian	235	255	735	725	355	1,520
106	East Indian	2,685	1,365	1,875	2,515	1,230	2,615
107	French	160	125	85	190	125	140
108	German	105	115	135	135	20	20
109	Portuguese	325	75	125	130	70	140
110	Polish	115	35	45	285	15	40
111	Jewish	-	-	20	10	20	-
112	Jamaican	600	200	235	740	570	735
113	Filipino	50	15	30	150	90	65
114	Ukrainian	30	10	65	105	15	55
	by Aboriginal identity						
115	Total Aboriginal identity population (10)	15	50	25	10	15	45
116	Total non-Aboriginal population	6,425	4,130	5,045	8,805	4,245	7,260
	by Aboriginal origin						
117	Total Aboriginal origins population (11)	15	65	60	25	40	45
118	Total non-Aboriginal population	6,425	4,105	5,005	8,790	4,225	7,260
	by Registered Indian status						
119	Registered Indian (12)	-	25	10	-	10	-
120	Not a Registered Indian	6,440	4,150	5,060	8,805	4,255	7,300

Tableau 1. Certaines caractéristiques des secteurs de recensement, recensement de 2001 – Données intégrales et données-échantillon (20 %)

Toronto 0532.01 ◆◇	Toronto 0532.02 ◆◇	Toronto 0540.01	Toronto 0540.02	Toronto 0550.01	Toronto 0550.02	Caractéristiques	N°
						CARACTÉRISTIQUES DE LA POPULATION	
						selon la langue parlée à la maison	
3,415	3,975	4,485	3,905	4,035	5,980	Réponses uniques	68
2,085	2,590	4,130	3,670	3,860	5,385	Anglais	69
-	-	20	-	-	-	Français	70
1,330	1,385	335	230	180	595	Langues non officielles (5)	71
-	-	-	-	-	55	Cantonais	72
-	-	-	10	-	80	Chinois, n.d.a.	73
90	105	10	30	-	-	Italien	74
1,030	850	-	-	-	-	Pendjabi	75
-	30	-	-	10	185	Portugais	76
210	400	325	190	165	275	Autres langues (6)	77
1,350	1,340	830	610	610	1,230	Réponses multiples	78
60	10	75	65	150	135	Anglais et français	79
1,275	1,275	755	535	455	1,100	Anglais et langue non officielle	80
-	50	-	-	-	-	Français et langue non officielle	81
10	10	10	10	-	-	Anglais, français et langue non officielle	82
						selon la connaissance des langues officielles	
4,185	4,725	4,730	3,995	4,055	6,505	Anglais seulement	83
-	-	-	-	-	-	Français seulement	84
285	145	545	480	555	510	Anglais et français	85
290	450	40	30	30	200	Ni l'anglais ni le français	86
						selon la connaissance des langues non officielles (5) (7)	
435	470	110	125	120	105	Italien	87
20	-	15	-	-	50	Cantonais	88
15	-	-	10	-	110	Chinois, n.d.a.	89
45	225	235	55	145	110	Espagnol	90
45	175	30	15	130	495	Portugais	91
1,870	1,465	10	60	-	75	Pendjabi	92
65	15	20	90	20	60	Tagalog (pilipino)	93
						selon la première langue officielle parlée	
4,360	4,800	5,125	4,365	4,470	6,905	Anglais	94
70	20	95	95	115	90	Français	95
40	60	55	20	25	30	Anglais et français	96
295	435	40	35	30	195	Ni l'anglais ni le français	97
90	50	125	105	130	105	Minorité de langue officielle - (nombre) (8)	98
1.9	0.9	2.3	2.3	2.8	1.5	Minorité de langue officielle - (pourcentage) (8)	99
						selon l'origine ethnique (9)	
485	495	1,410	1,280	1,560	1,740	Canadien	100
290	270	1,585	1,470	1,325	1,935	Anglais	101
125	135	1,040	830	945	1,065	Écossais	102
145	90	915	920	880	1,350	Irlandais	103
70	20	55	15	95	195	Chinois	104
560	635	255	235	265	330	Italien	105
1,785	1,950	25	150	55	340	Indien de l'Inde	106
90	20	390	325	340	475	Français	107
80	55	325	340	400	415	Allemand	108
65	145	100	25	275	675	Portugais	109
15	20	510	180	245	295	Polonais	110
-	-	25	25	85	25	Juif	111
235	675	45	20	105	110	Jamaïquain	112
70	25	35	130	45	85	Philippin	113
45	-	145	160	175	240	Ukrainien	114
						selon l'identité autochtone	
-	10	45	75	30	55	Total de la population ayant une identité autochtone (10)	115
4,760	5,315	5,275	4,435	4,620	7,160	Total de la population non autochtone	116
						selon l'origine autochtone	
55	10	115	130	60	120	Total de la population ayant une origine autochtone (11)	117
4,710	5,310	5,200	4,380	4,585	7,095	Total de la population non autochtone	118
						selon le statut d'Indien inscrit	
-	-	25	30	-	40	Oui, Indien inscrit (12)	119
4,765	5,320	5,290	4,480	4,640	7,175	Non, pas un Indien inscrit	120

Table 1. Selected Characteristics for Census Tracts, 2001 Census – 100% Data and 20% Sample Data

No.	Characteristics	Toronto 0528.31 A	Toronto 0529.01 ◆	Toronto 0529.02 ◆◇	Toronto 0530 ◆	Toronto 0531.01	Toronto 0531.02 ◆◇ A
	POPULATION CHARACTERISTICS						
	by visible minority groups						
121	Total visible minority population	4,280	2,635	3,330	6,095	2,980	4,910
122	Chinese	160	55	15	50	40	85
123	South Asian	2,805	1,855	2,340	3,770	1,395	2,900
124	Black	710	435	505	1,345	1,040	1,105
125	Filipino	45	10	30	130	100	65
126	Latin American	145	75	90	190	100	90
127	Southeast Asian	70	70	45	85	70	95
128	Arab	40	-	10	105	-	30
129	West Asian	20	10	80	10	35	-
130	Korean	30	-	-	-	-	-
131	Japanese	-	-	10	-	-	10
132	Visible minority, n.i.e. (13)	235	105	170	310	190	425
133	Multiple visible minorities (14)	-	25	45	100	-	110
	by citizenship						
134	Canadian citizenship (15)	5,265	3,235	3,660	6,365	3,315	6,035
135	Citizenship other than Canadian	1,175	940	1,405	2,445	945	1,265
	by place of birth of respondent						
136	Non-immigrant population	2,290	2,030	1,970	3,295	1,845	3,015
137	Born in province of residence	2,105	1,790	1,820	3,020	1,610	2,775
138	Immigrant population (16)	4,125	2,090	3,000	5,450	2,365	4,245
139	United States	10	25	-	30	40	20
140	Central and South America	255	160	290	385	305	455
141	Caribbean and Bermuda	525	265	365	855	530	630
142	United Kingdom	160	50	180	220	105	125
143	Other Europe (17)	1,090	200	515	1,020	200	870
144	Africa	65	30	60	150	110	90
145	Asia and the Middle East	2,030	1,355	1,585	2,760	1,060	2,025
146	Oceania and other (18)	-	15	10	30	15	35
147	Non-permanent residents (19)	30	50	90	70	50	40
148	**Total immigrant population**	**4,120**	**2,095**	**3,000**	**5,445**	**2,365**	**4,245**
	by period of immigration						
149	Before 1961	710	95	245	255	90	375
150	1961-1970	225	170	370	560	270	525
151	1971-1980	705	350	315	660	285	845
152	1981-1990	935	450	600	1,010	545	1,025
153	1991-2001 (20)	1,550	1,015	1,475	2,960	1,180	1,475
154	1991-1995	975	350	630	1,370	610	715
155	1996-2001 (20)	575	665	845	1,585	570	765
	by age at immigration						
156	0-4 years	245	125	165	380	160	260
157	5-19 years	835	455	625	1,510	690	1,200
158	20 years and over	3,035	1,510	2,210	3,565	1,515	2,795
159	**Total population**	**6,440**	**4,170**	**5,065**	**8,810**	**4,260**	**7,300**
	by religion						
160	Catholic (21)	1,625	980	1,270	2,540	1,185	2,320
161	Protestant	1,305	765	620	1,215	880	1,010
162	Christian Orthodox	10	20	10	180	20	75
163	Christian, n.i.e. (22)	290	120	305	240	260	330
164	Muslim	210	240	370	1,065	415	400
165	Jewish	-	-	10	45	-	10
166	Buddhist	115	110	-	145	20	125
167	Hindu	485	390	620	865	675	740
168	Sikh	2,140	1,330	1,630	1,835	400	1,995
169	Eastern religions (23)	20	-	10	-	-	10
170	Other religions (24)	25	10	10	-	-	-
171	No religious affiliation (25)	210	225	205	675	405	295
172	**Total population 15 years and over**	**5,000**	**3,295**	**3,880**	**6,685**	**3,220**	**5,730**
	by generation status						
173	1st generation (26)	4,015	2,035	2,940	5,035	2,235	4,125
174	2nd generation (27)	730	600	555	1,020	575	1,180
175	3rd generation and over (28)	255	660	375	635	410	420
176	**Total population 1 year and over (29)**	**6,375**	**4,095**	**4,970**	**8,695**	**4,180**	**7,220**
	by place of residence 1 year ago (mobility)						
177	Non-movers	5,535	3,440	4,310	7,375	3,575	6,485
178	Movers	840	655	660	1,330	600	735
179	Non-migrants	400	395	325	690	240	245
180	Migrants	435	255	335	635	360	490
181	Internal migrants	310	150	195	385	275	350
182	Intraprovincial migrants	305	140	145	325	200	340
183	Interprovincial migrants	10	10	50	65	70	10
184	External migrants	120	110	135	250	85	140

Tableau 1. Certaines caractéristiques des secteurs de recensement, recensement de 2001 – Données intégrales et données-échantillon (20 %)

Toronto 0532.01 ◆◇	Toronto 0532.02 ◆◇	Toronto 0540.01	Toronto 0540.02	Toronto 0550.01	Toronto 0550.02	Caractéristiques	N°
						CARACTÉRISTIQUES DE LA POPULATION	
						selon les groupes de minorités visibles	
3,195	4,055	590	585	655	1,185	Total de la population des minorités visibles	121
65	10	50	15	50	195	Chinois	122
2,410	2,280	25	220	50	320	Sud-Asiatique	123
500	1,105	135	60	220	215	Noir	124
60	25	35	125	35	70	Philippin	125
10	90	140	10	95	15	Latino-Américain	126
70	150	-	10	15	-	Asiatique du Sud-Est	127
-	-	70	100	30	125	Arabe	128
-	15	35	35	10	10	Asiatique occidental	129
-	25	70	-	45	45	Coréen	130
-	10	15	10	10	30	Japonais	131
70	290	10	10	40	125	Minorité visible, n.i.a. (13)	132
-	55	10	-	50	45	Minorités visibles multiples (14)	133
						selon la citoyenneté	
3,670	3,785	4,740	4,075	4,245	6,585	Citoyenneté canadienne (15)	134
1,095	1,530	575	435	400	625	Citoyenneté autre que canadienne	135
						selon le lieu de naissance du répondant	
1,830	1,935	3,590	3,190	3,415	4,740	Population non immigrante	136
1,695	1,795	2,945	2,555	2,900	4,015	Née dans la province de résidence	137
2,925	3,235	1,715	1,315	1,230	2,440	Population immigrante (16)	138
30	10	65	25	60	35	États-Unis	139
85	320	120	50	140	100	Amérique centrale et du Sud	140
315	645	45	50	85	180	Caraïbes et Bermudes	141
150	80	375	325	280	420	Royaume-Uni	142
470	420	865	455	460	1,025	Autre Europe (17)	143
30	105	65	25	35	145	Afrique	144
1,845	1,630	185	385	160	510	Asie et Moyen-Orient	145
10	25	-	15	10	30	Océanie et autre (18)	146
10	150	15	10	10	40	Résidents non permanents (19)	147
2,925	**3,235**	**1,715**	**1,315**	**1,230**	**2,440**	**Population immigrante totale**	148
						selon la période d'immigration	
205	150	335	260	210	255	Avant 1961	149
345	325	180	220	280	550	1961-1970	150
330	435	205	130	255	570	1971-1980	151
700	645	360	140	160	430	1981-1990	152
1,350	1,675	630	560	320	630	1991-2001 (20)	153
475	705	205	245	105	365	1991-1995	154
875	970	430	320	220	265	1996-2001 (20)	155
						selon l'âge à l'immigration	
170	230	215	180	105	200	0-4 ans	156
840	830	435	315	425	585	5-19 ans	157
1,915	2,175	1,065	815	695	1,655	20 ans et plus	158
4,765	**5,320**	**5,315**	**4,510**	**4,650**	**7,215**	**Population totale**	159
						selon la religion	
1,615	1,540	1,745	1,375	1,665	2,860	Catholique (21)	160
580	830	1,675	1,580	1,845	2,555	Protestante	161
95	15	205	215	75	170	Orthodoxe chrétienne	162
160	350	185	85	180	240	Chrétiennes, n.i.a. (22)	163
315	345	280	295	20	200	Musulmane	164
-	-	10	40	15	20	Juive	165
40	25	45	15	15	-	Bouddhiste	166
410	810	25	15	-	120	Hindoue	167
1,415	1,215	-	-	-	10	Sikh	168
-	-	15	15	-	55	Religions orientales (23)	169
-	50	-	10	-	10	Autres religions (24)	170
135	145	1,135	870	835	980	Aucune appartenance religieuse (25)	171
3,675	**3,965**	**4,575**	**3,765**	**3,645**	**5,970**	**Population totale de 15 ans et plus**	172
						selon le statut des générations	
2,740	3,090	1,575	1,240	1,155	2,355	1re génération (26)	173
635	670	950	885	810	1,370	2e génération (27)	174
290	210	2,050	1,640	1,675	2,240	3e génération et plus (28)	175
4,710	**5,215**	**5,235**	**4,445**	**4,595**	**7,140**	**Population totale de 1 an et plus (29)**	176
						selon le lieu de résidence 1 an auparavant (mobilité)	
4,095	4,410	4,385	3,790	4,255	6,140	Personnes n'ayant pas déménagé	177
615	805	855	655	340	1,000	Personnes ayant déménagé	178
325	295	435	305	165	660	Non-migrants	179
285	510	415	350	170	340	Migrants	180
165	185	275	265	120	300	Migrants internes	181
155	175	250	165	110	255	Migrants infraprovinciaux	182
10	15	25	95	10	50	Migrants interprovinciaux	183
120	325	140	90	55	40	Migrants externes	184

Table 1. Selected Characteristics for Census Tracts, 2001 Census – 100% Data and 20% Sample Data

No.	Characteristics	Toronto 0528.31 A	Toronto 0529.01 ◆	Toronto 0529.02 ◆◇	Toronto 0530 ◆	Toronto 0531.01	Toronto 0531.02 ◆◇ A
	POPULATION CHARACTERISTICS						
185	**Total population 5 years and over (30)**	**5,965**	**3,825**	**4,650**	**8,065**	**3,905**	**6,775**
	by place of residence 5 years ago (mobility)						
186	Non-movers	3,030	2,190	2,525	3,910	1,715	4,155
187	Movers	2,935	1,630	2,125	4,155	2,190	2,620
188	Non-migrants	1,165	720	985	1,775	885	1,200
189	Migrants	1,765	915	1,140	2,375	1,310	1,425
190	Internal migrants	1,280	390	420	895	935	860
191	Intraprovincial migrants	1,165	340	350	705	795	770
192	Interprovincial migrants	115	50	70	190	140	90
193	External migrants	490	525	720	1,480	375	565
194	**Total population 15 to 24 years**	**945**	**605**	**590**	**1,260**	**690**	**1,105**
	by school attendance						
195	Not attending school	430	295	325	585	340	430
196	Attending school full time	490	295	235	620	320	560
197	Attending school part time	25	20	30	50	30	110
198	**Total population 15 years and over**	**5,005**	**3,295**	**3,875**	**6,685**	**3,220**	**5,730**
	by highest level of schooling						
199	Less than grade 9 (31)	840	460	740	980	250	950
200	Grades 9-13 without high school graduation certificate	1,105	805	940	1,460	945	1,345
201	Grades 9-13 with high school graduation certificate	740	615	680	1,165	470	985
202	Some postsecondary without degree, certificate or diploma (32)	620	315	430	790	395	590
203	Trades certificate or diploma (33)	385	255	340	530	315	435
204	College certificate or diploma (34)	620	360	325	835	505	810
205	University certificate below bachelor's degree	60	55	60	75	25	125
206	University with bachelor's degree or higher	630	430	365	855	315	490
	by combinations of unpaid work						
207	Males 15 years and over	2,345	1,700	1,960	3,330	1,610	2,870
208	Reported unpaid work (35)	1,995	1,495	1,660	2,840	1,290	2,455
209	Housework and child care and care or assistance to seniors	340	215	235	290	155	295
210	Housework and child care only	620	340	515	890	390	660
211	Housework and care or assistance to seniors only	160	80	155	125	80	150
212	Child care and care or assistance to seniors only	-	-	20	10	-	10
213	Housework only	825	805	695	1,395	635	1,250
214	Child care only	20	40	35	105	20	45
215	Care or assistance to seniors only	25	15	-	20	15	45
216	Females 15 years and over	2,650	1,595	1,915	3,355	1,610	2,860
217	Reported unpaid work (35)	2,410	1,540	1,715	3,035	1,455	2,595
218	Housework and child care and care or assistance to seniors	450	260	275	355	200	325
219	Housework and child care only	790	550	610	1,295	570	970
220	Housework and care or assistance to seniors only	310	90	140	145	70	200
221	Child care and care or assistance to seniors only	10	-	-	10	-	-
222	Housework only	825	600	650	1,175	605	1,050
223	Child care only	20	30	35	65	-	25
224	Care or assistance to seniors only	10	10	-	-	-	20
	by labour force activity						
225	Males 15 years and over	2,350	1,700	1,960	3,330	1,615	2,875
226	In the labour force	1,685	1,325	1,335	2,450	1,280	2,160
227	Employed	1,600	1,235	1,280	2,300	1,190	2,070
228	Unemployed	80	90	60	150	85	90
229	Not in the labour force	665	375	625	885	335	710
230	Participation rate	71.7	77.9	68.1	73.6	79.3	75.1
231	Employment rate	68.1	72.6	65.3	69.1	73.7	72.0
232	Unemployment rate	4.7	6.8	4.5	6.1	6.6	4.2
233	Females 15 years and over	2,650	1,595	1,915	3,355	1,605	2,855
234	In the labour force	1,510	955	1,170	2,015	1,085	1,925
235	Employed	1,430	885	1,115	1,915	1,005	1,790
236	Unemployed	80	70	55	95	80	135
237	Not in the labour force	1,140	645	745	1,345	525	930
238	Participation rate	57.0	59.9	61.1	60.1	67.6	67.4
239	Employment rate	54.0	55.5	58.2	57.1	62.6	62.7
240	Unemployment rate	5.3	7.3	4.7	4.7	7.4	7.0

Tableau 1. Certaines caractéristiques des secteurs de recensement, recensement de 2001 – Données intégrales et données-échantillon (20 %)

Toronto 0532.01 ◆◇	Toronto 0532.02 ◆◇	Toronto 0540.01	Toronto 0540.02	Toronto 0550.01	Toronto 0550.02	Caractéristiques	N°
						CARACTÉRISTIQUES DE LA POPULATION	
4,370	**4,835**	**5,080**	**4,270**	**4,355**	**6,845**	**Population totale de 5 ans et plus (30)**	185
						selon le lieu de résidence 5 ans auparavant (mobilité)	
2,560	2,390	2,430	2,315	2,775	3,985	Personnes n'ayant pas déménagé	186
1,810	2,445	2,655	1,950	1,585	2,865	Personnes ayant déménagé	187
1,035	930	1,375	860	995	1,890	Non-migrants	188
775	1,520	1,275	1,090	590	975	Migrants	189
235	725	915	800	420	690	Migrants internes	190
165	660	760	595	375	575	Migrants infraprovinciaux	191
70	60	150	210	45	120	Migrants interprovinciaux	192
540	795	360	290	170	285	Migrants externes	193
680	**815**	**500**	**425**	**605**	**940**	**Population totale de 15 à 24 ans**	194
						selon la fréquentation scolaire	
310	290	295	185	195	330	Ne fréquentant pas l'école	195
355	470	190	220	350	530	Fréquentant l'école à plein temps	196
15	55	15	25	65	85	Fréquentant l'école à temps partiel	197
3,670	**3,970**	**4,575**	**3,765**	**3,645**	**5,965**	**Population totale de 15 ans et plus**	198
						selon le plus haut niveau de scolarité atteint	
475	620	245	195	160	520	Niveau inférieur à la 9e année (31)	199
765	925	895	735	635	1,095	De la 9e à la 13e année sans certificat d'études secondaires	200
880	660	800	600	620	970	De la 9e à la 13e année avec certificat d'études secondaires	201
465	465	540	465	450	670	Études postsecondaires partielles sans grade, certificat ou diplôme (32)	202
180	330	415	250	325	480	Certificat ou diplôme d'une école de métiers (33)	203
365	480	850	635	720	1,115	Certificat ou diplôme collégial (34)	204
60	60	165	100	45	165	Certificat universitaire inférieur au baccalauréat	205
485	420	670	780	690	955	Études universitaires avec baccalauréat ou diplôme supérieur	206
						selon les combinaisons de travail non rémunéré	
1,875	1,940	2,215	1,745	1,775	2,895	Hommes de 15 ans et plus	207
1,610	1,665	1,940	1,595	1,610	2,580	Travail non rémunéré déclaré (35)	208
245	160	115	115	140	205	Travaux ménagers et soins aux enfants et soins ou aide aux personnes âgées	209
515	685	405	315	490	635	Travaux ménagers et soins aux enfants seulement	210
110	95	150	105	150	180	Travaux ménagers et soins ou aide aux personnes âgées seulement	211
10	-	-	-	-	-	Soins aux enfants et soins ou aide aux personnes âgées seulement	212
695	690	1,235	1,050	795	1,530	Travaux ménagers seulement	213
25	35	15	-	35	25	Soins aux enfants seulement	214
10	-	15	10	-	20	Soins ou aide aux personnes âgées seulement	215
1,795	2,025	2,355	2,020	1,875	3,075	Femmes de 15 ans et plus	216
1,665	1,855	2,170	1,885	1,760	2,815	Travail non rémunéré déclaré (35)	217
285	245	190	170	220	330	Travaux ménagers et soins aux enfants et soins ou aide aux personnes âgées	218
695	860	510	525	610	810	Travaux ménagers et soins aux enfants seulement	219
100	85	210	155	165	275	Travaux ménagers et soins ou aide aux personnes âgées seulement	220
-	10	-	-	-	10	Soins aux enfants et soins ou aide aux personnes âgées seulement	221
540	655	1,240	1,030	740	1,360	Travaux ménagers seulement	222
25	10	15	10	10	30	Soins aux enfants seulement	223
20	-	-	-	20	-	Soins ou aide aux personnes âgées seulement	224
						selon l'activité	
1,880	1,940	2,220	1,745	1,770	2,895	Hommes de 15 ans et plus	225
1,405	1,465	1,825	1,395	1,380	2,225	Population active	226
1,305	1,360	1,700	1,365	1,325	2,165	Personnes occupées	227
105	105	125	25	60	60	Chômeurs	228
470	475	400	350	390	675	Inactifs	229
74.7	75.5	82.2	79.9	78.0	76.9	Taux d'activité	230
69.4	70.1	76.6	78.2	74.9	74.8	Taux d'emploi	231
7.5	7.2	6.8	1.8	4.3	2.7	Taux de chômage	232
1,795	2,025	2,355	2,015	1,870	3,075	Femmes de 15 ans et plus	233
1,160	1,340	1,630	1,275	1,290	1,995	Population active	234
1,060	1,195	1,540	1,205	1,185	1,905	Personnes occupées	235
95	140	80	70	105	90	Chômeuses	236
640	690	730	740	585	1,080	Inactives	237
64.6	66.2	69.2	63.3	69.0	64.9	Taux d'activité	238
59.1	59.0	65.4	59.8	63.4	62.0	Taux d'emploi	239
8.2	10.4	4.9	5.5	8.1	4.5	Taux de chômage	240

Table 1. Selected Characteristics for Census Tracts, 2001 Census – 100% Data and 20% Sample Data

No.	Characteristics	Toronto 0528.31 A	Toronto 0529.01 ◆	Toronto 0529.02 ◆◇	Toronto 0530 ◆	Toronto 0531.01	Toronto 0531.02 ◆◇ A
	POPULATION CHARACTERISTICS						
	by labour force activity – concluded						
241	Both sexes - Participation rate	63.9	69.3	64.6	66.7	73.4	71.3
242	15-24 years	69.3	57.9	58.8	63.3	77.5	64.5
243	25 years and over	62.8	71.8	65.7	67.5	72.3	72.9
244	Both sexes - Employment rate	60.5	64.2	61.6	63.1	68.3	67.4
245	15-24 years	65.3	48.3	55.9	57.5	69.6	58.8
246	25 years and over	59.6	67.8	62.8	64.2	68.1	69.3
247	Both sexes - Unemployment rate	5.2	7.4	4.4	5.5	7.0	5.6
248	15-24 years	4.6	17.4	5.7	8.2	10.3	9.2
249	25 years and over	5.1	5.7	4.2	4.9	6.0	5.0
250	**Total labour force 15 years and over**	**3,195**	**2,285**	**2,505**	**4,455**	**2,365**	**4,090**
	by industry based on the 1997 NAICS						
251	Industry - Not applicable (36)	60	80	30	40	50	65
252	All industries (37)	3,130	2,205	2,475	4,420	2,310	4,025
253	11 Agriculture, forestry, fishing and hunting	15	-	-	25	10	10
254	21 Mining and oil and gas extraction	-	-	-	-	-	-
255	22 Utilities	10	-	-	-	-	15
256	23 Construction	155	130	135	215	95	205
257	31-33 Manufacturing	895	615	775	1,230	620	1,190
258	41 Wholesale trade	145	210	115	350	195	235
259	44-45 Retail trade	390	225	220	520	245	400
260	48-49 Transportation and warehousing	395	275	340	470	185	545
261	51 Information and cultural industries	40	45	40	125	45	60
262	52 Finance and insurance	100	10	35	130	55	125
263	53 Real estate and rental and leasing	15	15	15	50	45	45
264	54 Professional, scientific and technical services	105	45	55	220	80	235
265	55 Management of companies and enterprises	10	10	-	10	-	10
266	56 Administrative and support, waste management and remediation services	170	130	170	245	145	195
267	61 Educational services	120	80	40	110	65	120
268	62 Health care and social assistance	160	100	145	225	145	175
269	71 Arts, entertainment and recreation	25	35	45	35	65	55
270	72 Accommodation and food services	205	120	205	255	155	225
271	81 Other services (except public administration)	75	130	105	170	115	155
272	91 Public administration	100	45	20	45	40	30
	by class of worker						
273	Class of worker - Not applicable (36)	60	80	30	35	50	65
274	All classes of worker (37)	3,135	2,205	2,475	4,425	2,310	4,025
275	Paid workers	2,965	2,045	2,340	4,205	2,200	3,855
276	Employees	2,910	1,975	2,300	4,130	2,190	3,760
277	Self-employed (incorporated)	50	70	35	75	15	90
278	Self-employed (unincorporated)	160	155	125	210	105	170
279	Unpaid family workers	15	-	15	-	-	-
	by occupation based on the 2001 NOC-S						
280	Male labour force 15 years and over	1,685	1,325	1,335	2,450	1,280	2,160
281	Occupation - Not applicable (36)	30	45	10	10	20	30
282	All occupations (37)	1,655	1,280	1,325	2,435	1,255	2,125
283	A Management occupations	115	110	65	140	75	165
284	B Business, finance and administration occupations	175	155	115	235	135	185
285	C Natural and applied sciences and related occupations	120	75	65	255	90	180
286	D Health occupations	30	20	-	-	-	20
287	E Occupations in social science, education, government service and religion	45	30	15	55	-	35
288	F Occupations in art, culture, recreation and sport	-	35	25	10	35	15
289	G Sales and service occupations	245	165	185	355	210	310
290	H Trades, transport and equipment operators and related occupations	595	470	560	835	435	830
291	I Occupations unique to primary industry	20	15	10	25	15	30
292	J Occupations unique to processing, manufacturing and utilities	305	205	285	525	245	360
293	Female labour force 15 years and over	1,510	955	1,170	2,010	1,085	1,925
294	Occupation - Not applicable (36)	35	30	20	25	35	35
295	All occupations (37)	1,475	925	1,150	1,990	1,050	1,895
296	A Management occupations	75	30	65	105	55	130
297	B Business, finance and administration occupations	450	245	240	500	255	565
298	C Natural and applied sciences and related occupations	20	10	15	55	35	25
299	D Health occupations	65	10	50	135	75	80

Tableau 1. Certaines caractéristiques des secteurs de recensement, recensement de 2001 – Données intégrales et données-échantillon (20 %)

Toronto 0532.01 ◆◇	Toronto 0532.02 ◆◇	Toronto 0540.01	Toronto 0540.02	Toronto 0550.01	Toronto 0550.02	Caractéristiques	N°
						CARACTÉRISTIQUES DE LA POPULATION	
						selon l'activité – fin	
69.7	70.5	75.3	71.0	73.3	70.7	Les deux sexes - Taux d'activité	241
65.4	68.7	77.0	67.9	58.7	69.3	15-24 ans	242
70.8	71.0	75.2	71.3	76.2	70.9	25 ans et plus	243
64.2	64.2	70.9	68.3	68.7	68.2	Les deux sexes - Taux d'emploi	244
56.6	63.2	71.3	64.7	48.8	64.6	15-24 ans	245
66.3	64.6	70.8	69.0	72.7	68.8	25 ans et plus	246
7.8	8.8	5.9	3.7	6.2	3.4	Les deux sexes - Taux de chômage	247
14.6	8.0	6.5	6.9	16.9	6.1	15-24 ans	248
6.4	8.9	5.9	3.4	4.5	2.9	25 ans et plus	249
2,560	**2,800**	**3,450**	**2,675**	**2,670**	**4,220**	**Population active totale de 15 ans et plus**	250
						selon l'industrie basée sur le SCIAN de 1997	
65	110	35	20	30	15	Industrie - Sans objet (36)	251
2,500	2,695	3,420	2,645	2,640	4,200	Toutes les industries (37)	252
-	-	10	10	20	15	11 Agriculture, foresterie, pêche et chasse	253
-	10	10	10	-	-	21 Extraction minière et extraction de pétrole et de gaz	254
10	-	15	10	35	-	22 Services publics	255
95	100	235	105	100	240	23 Construction	256
760	855	535	345	510	700	31-33 Fabrication	257
165	135	350	175	250	340	41 Commerce de gros	258
260	270	340	220	345	530	44-45 Commerce de détail	259
375	270	325	220	180	285	48-49 Transport et entreposage	260
25	50	105	150	100	115	51 Industrie de l'information et industrie culturelle	261
50	90	95	185	130	340	52 Finance et assurances	262
20	40	85	80	55	90	53 Services immobiliers et services de location et de location à bail	263
65	100	315	310	265	325	54 Services professionnels, scientifiques et techniques	264
-	-	10	-	-	-	55 Gestion de sociétés et d'entreprises	265
145	205	175	130	95	220	56 Services administratifs, services de soutien, services de gestion des déchets et services d'assainissement	266
100	45	170	120	165	260	61 Services d'enseignement	267
95	110	260	160	160	200	62 Soins de santé et assistance sociale	268
20	20	50	65	25	75	71 Arts, spectacles et loisirs	269
230	190	125	160	65	155	72 Hébergement et services de restauration	270
80	130	110	120	85	190	81 Autres services, sauf les administrations publiques	271
20	60	95	85	70	110	91 Administrations publiques	272
						selon la catégorie de travailleurs	
65	110	35	25	30	15	Catégorie de travailleurs - Sans objet (36)	273
2,500	2,695	3,420	2,650	2,640	4,200	Toutes les catégories de travailleurs (37)	274
2,405	2,570	3,115	2,380	2,420	3,880	Travailleurs rémunérés	275
2,350	2,505	3,020	2,295	2,320	3,725	Employés	276
55	65	95	85	105	155	Travailleurs autonomes (entreprise constituée en société)	277
90	120	305	255	220	315	Travailleurs autonomes (entreprise non constituée en société)	278
10	-	-	15	-	-	Travailleurs familiaux non rémunérés	279
						selon la profession basée sur la CNP-S de 2001	
1,405	1,465	1,820	1,390	1,380	2,225	Hommes actifs de 15 ans et plus	280
30	45	10	-	10	10	Profession - Sans objet (36)	281
1,375	1,415	1,810	1,395	1,380	2,220	Toutes les professions (37)	282
110	130	255	210	195	320	A Gestion	283
95	140	255	195	255	270	B Affaires, finance et administration	284
85	85	185	170	165	220	C Sciences naturelles et appliquées et professions apparentées	285
15	10	35	10	35	-	D Secteur de la santé	286
15	10	55	80	50	75	E Sciences sociales, enseignement, administration publique et religion	287
10	30	75	60	45	55	F Arts, culture, sports et loisirs	288
290	250	265	285	225	560	G Ventes et services	289
435	465	535	265	320	490	H Métiers, transport et machinerie	290
-	10	-	10	25	40	I Professions propres au secteur primaire	291
320	290	135	110	70	190	J Transformation, fabrication et services d'utilité publique	292
1,160	1,335	1,630	1,280	1,290	1,990	Femmes actives de 15 ans et plus	293
35	65	20	25	25	10	Profession - Sans objet (36)	294
1,125	1,275	1,605	1,255	1,265	1,980	Toutes les professions (37)	295
25	85	150	175	185	180	A Gestion	296
215	335	560	360	440	715	B Affaires, finance et administration	297
10	30	50	55	35	65	C Sciences naturelles et appliquées et professions apparentées	298
55	90	70	55	50	130	D Secteur de la santé	299

Table 1. Selected Characteristics for Census Tracts, 2001 Census – 100% Data and 20% Sample Data

No.	Characteristics	Toronto 0528.31 A	Toronto 0529.01 ◆	Toronto 0529.02 ◆◇	Toronto 0530 ◆	Toronto 0531.01	Toronto 0531.02 ◆◇ A
	POPULATION CHARACTERISTICS						
	by occupation based on the 2001 NOC-S – concluded						
	E Occupations in social science, education,						
300	government service and religion	120	65	45	70	40	85
301	F Occupations in art, culture, recreation and sport	15	45	10	50	-	10
302	G Sales and service occupations	325	285	320	525	325	510
	H Trades, transport and equipment						
303	operators and related occupations	65	55	120	120	90	75
304	I Occupations unique to primary industry	10	10	10	-	10	-
	J Occupations unique to processing,						
305	manufacturing and utilities	335	175	285	420	190	415
306	**Total employed labour force 15 years and over**	**3,035**	**2,115**	**2,395**	**4,215**	**2,200**	**3,860**
	by place of work						
307	Males	1,600	1,230	1,280	2,300	1,190	2,070
308	Usual place of work	1,345	1,100	1,070	1,865	1,050	1,740
309	At home	25	20	20	45	10	25
310	Outside Canada	-	-	-	35	10	-
311	No fixed workplace address	225	110	190	355	120	300
312	Females	1,430	885	1,115	1,915	1,010	1,790
313	Usual place of work	1,270	785	1,050	1,790	960	1,715
314	At home	55	55	45	85	30	25
315	Outside Canada	-	-	-	-	-	-
316	No fixed workplace address	110	40	20	40	20	50
	Total employed labour force 15 years and over with usual place of work or no fixed						
317	**workplace address**	**2,945**	**2,040**	**2,335**	**4,050**	**2,150**	**3,800**
	by mode of transportation						
318	Males	1,570	1,215	1,260	2,215	1,170	2,040
319	Car, truck, van, as driver	1,360	1,010	955	1,710	895	1,720
320	Car, truck, van, as passenger	85	55	75	140	75	125
321	Public transit	110	100	195	295	180	165
322	Walked	10	35	15	40	10	10
323	Other method	10	15	20	30	20	20
324	Females	1,375	825	1,070	1,830	980	1,760
325	Car, truck, van, as driver	895	530	615	1,020	510	1,220
326	Car, truck, van, as passenger	250	105	150	260	145	240
327	Public transit	170	155	235	435	270	285
328	Walked	30	25	55	80	50	-
329	Other method	30	10	20	35	10	10
	Total population 15 years and over who worked						
330	**since January 1, 2000**	**3,350**	**2,355**	**2,730**	**4,775**	**2,510**	**4,330**
	by language used at work						
331	Single responses	2,920	2,105	2,310	4,175	2,275	3,825
332	English	2,875	2,060	2,215	4,125	2,220	3,775
333	French	-	-	-	-	-	-
334	Non-official languages (5)	50	40	95	50	55	50
335	Chinese, n.o.s.	-	-	-	-	-	-
336	Cantonese	-	-	-	-	-	-
337	Other languages (6)	45	40	95	50	55	50
338	Multiple responses	430	255	425	600	245	505
339	English and French	20	20	30	45	30	25
340	English and non-official language	405	235	380	530	205	465
341	French and non-official language	-	-	-	-	-	-
342	English, French and non-official language	-	-	10	20	10	10
	DWELLING AND HOUSEHOLD CHARACTERISTICS						
343	**Total number of occupied private dwellings**	**2,000**	**1,245**	**1,435**	**2,415**	**1,160**	**1,810**
	by tenure						
344	Owned	1,100	855	870	1,265	675	1,485
345	Rented	910	390	565	1,155	485	325
346	Band housing	-	-	-	-	-	-
	by structural type of dwelling						
347	Single-detached house	1,020	525	515	415	275	840
348	Semi-detached house	55	365	390	510	190	580
349	Row house	240	15	80	235	265	55
350	Apartment, detached duplex	-	115	125	100	40	115
351	Apartment, building that has five or more storeys	690	-	270	460	40	-
	Apartment, building that has fewer than						
352	five storeys (38)	-	205	55	700	305	215
353	Other single-attached house	-	-	-	-	45	10
354	Movable dwelling (39)	-	25	-	-	-	-

Tableau 1. Certaines caractéristiques des secteurs de recensement, recensement de 2001 – Données intégrales et données-échantillon (20 %)

Toronto 0532.01 ◆◇	Toronto 0532.02 ◆◇	Toronto 0540.01	Toronto 0540.02	Toronto 0550.01	Toronto 0550.02	Caractéristiques	Nº
						CARACTÉRISTIQUES DE LA POPULATION	
						selon la profession basée sur la CNP-S de 2001 – fin	
55	70	140	125	135	220	E Sciences sociales, enseignement, administration publique et religion	300
10	-	85	50	35	45	F Arts, culture, sports et loisirs	301
365	310	405	345	275	465	G Ventes et services	302
60	55	65	45	50	20	H Métiers, transport et machinerie	303
-	-	-	15	-	10	I Professions propres au secteur primaire	304
330	305	90	20	70	115	J Transformation, fabrication et services d'utilité publique	305
2,360	**2,555**	**3,245**	**2,575**	**2,505**	**4,070**	**Population active occupée totale de 15 ans et plus**	306
						selon le lieu de travail	
1,305	1,355	1,700	1,365	1,320	2,165	Hommes	307
1,170	1,160	1,335	1,045	1,065	1,870	Lieu habituel de travail	308
30	25	90	115	125	120	À domicile	309
-	-	15	10	-	10	En dehors du Canada	310
105	180	260	210	135	165	Sans adresse de travail fixe	311
1,060	1,195	1,545	1,205	1,180	1,905	Femmes	312
1,015	1,135	1,330	1,000	1,045	1,690	Lieu habituel de travail	313
25	15	115	125	75	155	À domicile	314
-	-	10	-	-	-	En dehors du Canada	315
20	40	100	75	65	55	Sans adresse de travail fixe	316
2,310	**2,510**	**3,015**	**2,330**	**2,310**	**3,780**	**Population active occupée totale de 15 ans et plus ayant un lieu habituel de travail ou sans adresse de travail fixe**	317
						selon le mode de transport	
1,275	1,335	1,590	1,250	1,200	2,035	Hommes	318
1,075	1,030	1,205	825	1,005	1,685	Automobile, camion ou fourgonnette, en tant que conducteur	319
65	105	55	30	55	95	Automobile, camion ou fourgonnette, en tant que passager	320
85	175	270	325	115	150	Transport en commun	321
50	15	50	55	15	85	À pied	322
-	-	15	10	10	25	Autre moyen	323
1,035	1,175	1,425	1,080	1,105	1,745	Femmes	324
680	670	890	610	840	1,260	Automobile, camion ou fourgonnette, en tant que conductrice	325
170	215	100	65	130	120	Automobile, camion ou fourgonnette, en tant que passagère	326
155	245	310	340	100	295	Transport en commun	327
25	45	80	45	35	55	À pied	328
10	-	40	20	-	20	Autre moyen	329
2,705	**2,890**	**3,660**	**2,815**	**2,925**	**4,585**	**Population totale de 15 ans et plus ayant travaillé depuis le 1er janvier 2000**	330
						selon la langue utilisée au travail	
2,290	2,475	3,375	2,680	2,780	4,260	Réponses uniques	331
2,265	2,395	3,325	2,675	2,770	4,210	Anglais	332
-	-	-	-	10	-	Français	333
25	85	45	10	-	50	Langues non officielles (5)	334
-	-	10	10	-	-	Chinois, n.d.a.	335
-	-	-	-	-	10	Cantonais	336
25	80	40	-	-	30	Autres langues (6)	337
415	415	280	135	150	325	Réponses multiples	338
45	35	75	70	85	120	Anglais et français	339
365	375	195	60	60	205	Anglais et langue non officielle	340
-	-	-	-	-	-	Français et langue non officielle	341
-	10	10	10	10	10	Anglais, français et langue non officielle	342
						CARACTÉRISTIQUES DES LOGEMENTS ET DES MÉNAGES	
1,250	**1,290**	**2,695**	**2,150**	**1,555**	**2,720**	**Nombre total de logements privés occupés**	343
						selon le mode d'occupation	
985	910	810	705	1,390	1,870	Possédé	344
270	380	1,885	1,450	170	850	Loué	345
-	-	-	-	-	-	Logement de bande	346
						selon le type de construction résidentielle	
580	220	465	605	705	1,565	Maison individuelle non attenante	347
445	495	10	10	105	245	Maison jumelée	348
45	200	225	10	735	175	Maison en rangée	349
50	40	120	30	-	15	Appartement, duplex non attenant	350
-	125	1,450	985	-	560	Appartement, immeuble de cinq étages ou plus	351
130	215	370	520	15	140	Appartement, immeuble de moins de cinq étages (38)	352
-	-	-	-	-	25	Autre maison individuelle attenante	353
-	-	45	-	-	-	Logement mobile (39)	354

Table 1. Selected Characteristics for Census Tracts, 2001 Census – 100% Data and 20% Sample Data

No.	Characteristics	Toronto 0528.31 A	Toronto 0529.01 ◆	Toronto 0529.02 ◆◇	Toronto 0530 ◆	Toronto 0531.01	Toronto 0531.02 ◆◇ A
	DWELLING AND HOUSEHOLD CHARACTERISTICS						
	by condition of dwelling						
355	Regular maintenance only	1,675	745	1,045	1,730	725	1,310
356	Minor repairs	290	385	265	550	355	380
357	Major repairs	35	115	120	140	80	120
	by period of construction						
358	Before 1946	-	160	25	35	10	-
359	1946-1960	-	340	335	85	20	45
360	1961-1970	45	395	410	960	525	410
361	1971-1980	120	200	465	1,080	455	995
362	1981-1990	1,045	105	125	235	140	305
363	1991-2001 (20)	785	30	75	10	20	50
364	Average number of rooms per dwelling	5.8	6.0	5.5	5.9	6.1	7.0
365	Average number of bedrooms per dwelling	2.7	2.9	2.6	2.8	2.8	3.3
366	Average value of dwelling $	254,441	190,481	201,153	179,467	182,805	213,505
367	**Total number of private households**	**2,000**	**1,245**	**1,435**	**2,420**	**1,160**	**1,810**
	by household size						
368	1 person	475	180	165	250	140	95
369	2 persons	390	295	320	530	215	340
370	3 persons	275	235	255	440	215	335
371	4-5 persons	615	410	490	830	420	690
372	6 or more persons	240	125	205	365	175	350
	by household type						
373	One-family households	1,345	900	1,000	1,830	820	1,380
374	Multiple-family households	185	150	200	255	155	275
375	Non-family households	475	200	230	330	185	150
376	Number of persons in private households	6,430	4,170	5,065	8,810	4,250	7,300
377	Average number of persons in private households	3.2	3.4	3.5	3.6	3.7	4.0
378	Average number of persons per room	0.6	0.6	0.6	0.6	0.6	0.6
379	Tenant households in non-farm, non-reserve private dwellings (40)	905	385	550	1,145	485	325
380	Average gross rent $ (40)	840	752	717	896	897	845
381	Tenant households spending 30% or more of household income on gross rent (40) (41)	545	180	240	420	190	100
382	Tenant households spending from 30% to 99% of household income on gross rent (40) (41)	525	145	165	330	160	65
383	Owner households in non-farm, non-reserve private dwellings (42)	1,085	855	865	1,265	665	1,480
384	Average owner's major payments $ (42)	1,466	1,083	1,047	1,025	1,157	1,123
385	Owner households spending 30% or more of household income on owner's major payments (41) (42)	385	290	235	350	220	330
386	Owner households spending from 30% to 99% of household income on owner's major payments (41) (42)	335	245	200	315	195	305
	CENSUS FAMILY CHARACTERISTICS						
387	**Total number of census families in private households**	**1,725**	**1,215**	**1,455**	**2,400**	**1,155**	**2,010**
	by census family structure and size						
388	Total couple families	1,465	965	1,210	1,925	865	1,740
389	Total families of married couples	1,420	870	1,150	1,785	770	1,690
390	Without children at home	385	250	420	540	240	470
391	With children at home	1,030	620	730	1,240	530	1,220
392	1 child	295	220	275	380	135	390
393	2 children	470	280	295	500	235	535
394	3 or more children	265	120	165	360	155	295
395	Total families of common-law couples	45	90	60	140	100	50
396	Without children at home	25	50	20	50	50	-
397	With children at home	20	45	40	95	50	45
398	1 child	10	10	15	50	25	20
399	2 children	-	20	-	30	15	10
400	3 or more children	-	15	15	15	10	15
401	Total lone-parent families	255	255	245	475	290	270
402	Female parent	205	190	190	395	255	230
403	1 child	90	110	120	230	115	125
404	2 children	90	70	40	115	105	45
405	3 or more children	20	10	25	55	40	65

Tableau 1. Certaines caractéristiques des secteurs de recensement, recensement de 2001 – Données intégrales et données-échantillon (20 %)

Toronto 0532.01 ◆◇	Toronto 0532.02 ◆◇	Toronto 0540.01	Toronto 0540.02	Toronto 0550.01	Toronto 0550.02	Caractéristiques	N°
						CARACTÉRISTIQUES DES LOGEMENTS ET DES MÉNAGES	
						selon l'état du logement	
840	755	1,755	1,220	1,040	1,805	Entretien régulier seulement	355
310	410	705	705	450	740	Réparations mineures	356
100	130	235	225	65	180	Réparations majeures	357
						selon la période de construction	
40	15	330	375	15	160	Avant 1946	358
145	70	600	620	215	750	1946-1960	359
420	415	935	590	230	395	1961-1970	360
515	625	695	485	820	430	1971-1980	361
115	140	85	75	265	570	1981-1990	362
10	25	45	15	10	420	1991-2001 (20)	363
6.4	6.2	4.7	5.1	7.2	6.5	Nombre moyen de pièces par logement	364
3.2	3.2	1.9	2.0	3.2	2.8	Nombre moyen de chambres à coucher par logement	365
211,843	199,053	219,143	294,932	216,058	245,764	Valeur moyenne du logement $	366
1,250	**1,290**	**2,695**	**2,155**	**1,560**	**2,720**	**Nombre total de logements privés**	367
						selon la taille du ménage	
75	65	1,195	870	185	695	1 personne	368
250	185	860	710	455	770	2 personnes	369
240	245	315	255	340	480	3 personnes	370
465	515	315	285	580	665	4-5 personnes	371
215	280	15	40	-	105	6 personnes ou plus	372
						selon le genre de ménage	
950	1,010	1,345	1,190	1,295	1,875	Ménages unifamiliaux	373
195	200	25	10	40	100	Ménages multifamiliaux	374
105	85	1,325	950	220	750	Ménages non familiaux	375
4,765	5,305	5,315	4,510	4,645	7,205	Nombre de personnes dans les ménages privés	376
3.8	4.1	2.0	2.1	3.0	2.6	Nombre moyen de personnes dans les ménages privés	377
0.6	0.7	0.4	0.4	0.4	0.4	Nombre moyen de personnes par pièce	378
270	365	1,885	1,450	170	845	Ménages locataires dans les logements privés non agricoles hors réserve (40)	379
835	897	780	794	1,024	771	Loyer brut moyen $ (40)	380
135	130	705	560	55	275	Ménages locataires consacrant 30 % ou plus du revenu du ménage au loyer brut (40) (41)	381
105	95	590	400	50	255	Ménages locataires consacrant de 30 % à 99 % du revenu du ménage au loyer brut (40) (41)	382
980	910	805	705	1,385	1,870	Ménages propriétaires dans les logements privés non agricoles hors réserve (42)	383
1,073	1,137	1,097	1,043	1,087	1,101	Principales dépenses de propriété moyennes $ (42)	384
260	295	210	120	275	305	Ménages propriétaires consacrant 30 % ou plus du revenu du ménage aux principales dépenses de propriété (41) (42)	385
215	240	175	90	255	270	Ménages propriétaires consacrant de 30 % à 99 % du revenu du ménage aux principales dépenses de propriété (41) (42)	386
						CARACTÉRISTIQUES DES FAMILLES DE RECENSEMENT	
1,365	**1,410**	**1,395**	**1,210**	**1,370**	**2,070**	**Total des familles de recensement dans les ménages privés**	387
						selon la structure et la taille de la famille de recensement	
1,140	1,125	1,100	965	1,155	1,710	Total des familles avec conjoints	388
1,090	1,075	845	790	1,030	1,575	Total des familles avec couples mariés	389
295	245	380	360	325	580	Sans enfants à la maison	390
795	835	460	435	705	990	Avec enfants à la maison	391
240	245	200	170	220	395	1 enfant	392
375	340	190	185	370	450	2 enfants	393
180	250	70	80	110	145	3 enfants ou plus	394
50	50	255	175	120	145	Total des familles en union libre	395
20	20	195	145	65	90	Sans enfants à la maison	396
35	30	60	30	55	55	Avec enfants à la maison	397
30	10	35	20	35	25	1 enfant	398
-	-	20	-	10	20	2 enfants	399
-	20	-	10	15	10	3 enfants ou plus	400
230	285	295	245	220	365	Total des familles monoparentales	401
180	225	250	210	185	320	Parent de sexe féminin	402
135	120	200	150	110	180	1 enfant	403
45	65	45	45	60	105	2 enfants	404
-	50	10	10	15	35	3 enfants ou plus	405

Table 1. Selected Characteristics for Census Tracts, 2001 Census – 100% Data and 20% Sample Data

No.	Characteristics	Toronto 0528.31 A	Toronto 0529.01 ◆	Toronto 0529.02 ◆◇	Toronto 0530 ◆	Toronto 0531.01	Toronto 0531.02 ◆◇ A
	CENSUS FAMILY CHARACTERISTICS						
	by census family structure and size – concluded						
406	Male parent	55	60	55	80	35	40
407	1 child	35	30	25	45	25	15
408	2 children	20	30	20	15	-	15
409	3 or more children	-	-	10	20	-	10
410	**Total number of children at home**	**2,610**	**1,655**	**1,810**	**3,535**	**1,735**	**3,020**
	by age groups						
411	Under 6 years	585	405	495	870	420	650
412	6-14 years	840	470	635	1,235	590	915
413	15-17 years	350	175	120	350	130	250
414	18-24 years	520	325	305	555	355	745
415	25 years and over	310	280	260	525	240	455
416	Average number of children at home per census family (43)	1.5	1.4	1.2	1.5	1.5	1.5
417	**Total number of persons in private households**	**6,435**	**4,175**	**5,065**	**8,810**	**4,250**	**7,295**
	by census family status and living arrangements						
418	Number of non-family persons	630	335	585	950	495	520
419	Living with relatives (44)	120	70	240	370	165	305
420	Living with non-relatives only	30	85	180	335	185	120
421	Living alone	480	180	165	250	135	95
422	Number of family persons	5,805	3,840	4,480	7,860	3,755	6,780
423	Average number of persons per census family	3.4	3.1	3.1	3.3	3.3	3.4
424	**Total number of persons 65 years and over**	**980**	**345**	**650**	**790**	**250**	**595**
425	Number of non-family persons 65 years and over	445	105	170	270	60	180
426	Living with relatives (44)	50	55	55	135	30	145
427	Living with non-relatives only	-	-	20	15	10	10
428	Living alone	390	55	95	115	20	25
429	Number of family persons 65 years and over	535	240	485	520	195	415
	ECONOMIC FAMILY CHARACTERISTICS						
430	**Total number of economic families in private households**	**1,530**	**1,040**	**1,230**	**2,135**	**995**	**1,710**
	by size of family						
431	2 persons	395	270	305	570	235	340
432	3 persons	280	250	235	435	205	325
433	4 persons	400	260	300	470	245	455
434	5 or more persons	445	265	385	660	315	590
435	Total number of persons in economic families	5,925	3,910	4,715	8,230	3,925	7,080
436	Average number of persons per economic family	3.9	3.7	3.8	3.8	3.9	4.1
437	Total number of unattached individuals	510	265	345	580	325	215
	2000 INCOME CHARACTERISTICS						
	Population 15 years and over by sex and total income groups in 2000						
438	Total - Both sexes	5,000	3,295	3,875	6,690	3,220	5,730
439	Without income	370	320	240	530	240	450
440	With income	4,635	2,975	3,635	6,160	2,975	5,285
441	Under $1,000 (45)	265	170	185	330	150	280
442	$ 1,000 - $ 2,999	265	190	225	400	180	240
443	$ 3,000 - $ 4,999	165	200	130	210	95	180
444	$ 5,000 - $ 6,999	185	120	170	245	155	295
445	$ 7,000 - $ 9,999	325	150	290	365	265	230
446	$10,000 - $11,999	190	125	220	330	130	220
447	$12,000 - $14,999	400	215	340	470	225	320
448	$15,000 - $19,999	480	275	440	650	240	500
449	$20,000 - $24,999	385	270	355	595	325	615
450	$25,000 - $29,999	390	330	340	580	225	545
451	$30,000 - $34,999	345	265	325	645	290	535
452	$35,000 - $39,999	340	195	200	375	220	345
453	$40,000 - $44,999	250	110	190	215	175	290
454	$45,000 - $49,999	110	110	50	250	65	180
455	$50,000 - $59,999	240	130	115	235	120	315
456	$60,000 and over	300	115	60	265	125	200
457	Average income $ (46)	24,603	22,663	20,307	23,119	23,204	24,581
458	Median income $ (46)	20,170	20,291	17,607	20,247	20,605	22,381
459	Standard error of average income $ (46)	648	670	519	494	695	521

Tableau 1. Certaines caractéristiques des secteurs de recensement, recensement de 2001 – Données intégrales et données-échantillon (20 %)

Toronto 0532.01 ◆◇	Toronto 0532.02 ◆◇	Toronto 0540.01	Toronto 0540.02	Toronto 0550.01	Toronto 0550.02	Caractéristiques	N°
						CARACTÉRISTIQUES DES FAMILLES DE RECENSEMENT	
						selon la structure et la taille de la famille de recensement – fin	
45	55	50	30	30	45	Parent de sexe masculin	406
30	40	35	20	15	30	1 enfant	407
15	20	10	10	-	15	2 enfants	408
-	-	-	-	15	-	3 enfants ou plus	409
1,940	**2,355**	**1,265**	**1,175**	**1,735**	**2,415**	**Nombre total d'enfants à la maison**	410
						selon les groupes d'âge	
460	585	295	290	370	430	Moins de 6 ans	411
635	760	440	455	630	805	6-14 ans	412
205	225	80	90	220	310	15-17 ans	413
355	435	275	215	340	525	18-24 ans	414
285	340	180	130	175	350	25 ans et plus	415
1.4	1.7	0.9	1.0	1.3	1.2	Nombre moyen d'enfants à la maison par famille de recensement (43)	416
4,765	**5,310**	**5,315**	**4,505**	**4,645**	**7,210**	**Nombre total de personnes dans les ménages privés**	417
						selon la situation des particuliers dans la famille de recensement et des particuliers dans le ménage	
320	415	1,555	1,150	385	1,005	Nombre de personnes hors famille de recensement	418
130	230	80	115	95	125	Vivant avec des personnes apparentées (44)	419
115	125	280	165	110	180	Vivant avec des personnes non apparentées uniquement	420
75	65	1,195	865	185	700	Vivant seules	421
4,440	4,890	3,760	3,355	4,255	6,205	Nombre de personnes membres d'une famille	422
3.3	3.5	2.7	2.8	3.1	3.0	Nombre moyen de personnes par famille de recensement	423
380	**320**	**665**	**590**	**365**	**885**	**Nombre total de personnes de 65 ans et plus**	424
75	80	375	300	90	315	Nombre de personnes hors famille de recensement de 65 ans et plus	425
45	65	20	40	30	60	Vivant avec des personnes apparentées (44)	426
10	10	10	10	-	10	Vivant avec des personnes non apparentées uniquement	427
20	10	345	250	65	240	Vivant seules	428
305	235	285	295	270	570	Nombre de personnes membres d'une famille de 65 ans et plus	429
						CARACTÉRISTIQUES DES FAMILLES ÉCONOMIQUES	
1,150	**1,220**	**1,380**	**1,220**	**1,345**	**1,980**	**Nombre total de familles économiques dans les ménages privés**	430
						selon la taille de la famille	
240	225	750	670	460	760	2 personnes	431
255	225	315	245	305	475	3 personnes	432
280	290	200	195	405	475	4 personnes	433
375	480	115	115	175	275	5 personnes ou plus	434
4,575	5,115	3,840	3,475	4,350	6,330	Nombre total de personnes dans les familles économiques	435
4.0	4.2	2.8	2.8	3.2	3.2	Nombre moyen de personnes par famille économique	436
190	190	1,475	1,035	295	880	Nombre total de personnes hors famille économique	437
						CARACTÉRISTIQUES DU REVENU DE 2000	
						Population de 15 ans et plus selon le sexe et les tranches de revenu total en 2000	
3,675	3,970	4,580	3,765	3,650	5,970	Total - Les deux sexes	438
235	425	140	190	150	240	Sans revenu	439
3,440	3,540	4,440	3,570	3,495	5,730	Avec un revenu	440
215	185	175	155	110	195	Moins de 1 000 $ (45)	441
185	230	165	180	100	225	1 000 $ - 2 999 $	442
210	180	115	115	120	185	3 000 $ - 4 999 $	443
100	135	120	140	110	255	5 000 $ - 6 999 $	444
205	225	180	145	155	220	7 000 $ - 9 999 $	445
215	215	155	80	130	145	10 000 $ - 11 999 $	446
260	295	285	200	150	315	12 000 $ - 14 999 $	447
365	320	350	305	205	420	15 000 $ - 19 999 $	448
295	385	445	295	220	375	20 000 $ - 24 999 $	449
390	320	400	215	240	360	25 000 $ - 29 999 $	450
245	310	380	240	355	630	30 000 $ - 34 999 $	451
150	120	325	275	235	425	35 000 $ - 39 999 $	452
125	255	345	295	305	400	40 000 $ - 44 999 $	453
150	135	270	155	170	280	45 000 $ - 49 999 $	454
210	90	265	260	330	425	50 000 $ - 59 999 $	455
110	140	455	525	560	870	60 000 $ et plus	456
22,662	22,396	32,666	37,969	37,582	35,405	Revenu moyen $ (46)	457
19,426	19,658	26,594	29,183	32,106	30,316	Revenu médian $ (46)	458
671	644	1,285	1,913	1,482	925	Erreur type de revenu moyen $ (46)	459

Table 1. Selected Characteristics for Census Tracts, 2001 Census – 100% Data and 20% Sample Data

No.	Characteristics	Toronto 0528.31 A	Toronto 0529.01 ◆	Toronto 0529.02 ◆◇	Toronto 0530 ◆	Toronto 0531.01	Toronto 0531.02 ◆◇ A
	2000 INCOME CHARACTERISTICS						
	Population 15 years and over by sex and total income groups in 2000 – concluded						
460	Total - Males	2,350	1,700	1,960	3,335	1,615	2,870
461	Without income	130	100	100	205	80	180
462	With income	2,220	1,595	1,865	3,120	1,530	2,695
463	Under $1,000 (45)	160	85	85	135	75	135
464	$ 1,000 - $ 2,999	100	60	100	160	70	120
465	$ 3,000 - $ 4,999	50	45	25	60	35	65
466	$ 5,000 - $ 6,999	70	40	55	75	60	75
467	$ 7,000 - $ 9,999	95	80	100	115	120	100
468	$10,000 - $11,999	60	80	135	160	50	105
469	$12,000 - $14,999	130	60	160	215	90	125
470	$15,000 - $19,999	200	155	255	295	115	255
471	$20,000 - $24,999	180	140	165	280	115	275
472	$25,000 - $29,999	160	170	205	345	100	290
473	$30,000 - $34,999	165	180	175	320	185	255
474	$35,000 - $39,999	210	145	110	265	140	190
475	$40,000 - $44,999	165	70	120	150	125	200
476	$45,000 - $49,999	85	90	40	165	55	140
477	$50,000 - $59,999	145	80	95	170	100	215
478	$60,000 and over	250	100	45	215	100	165
479	Average income $ (46)	29,769	27,015	23,019	27,413	27,892	28,207
480	Median income $ (46)	27,235	25,901	20,302	25,618	27,309	25,472
481	Standard error of average income $ (46)	1,081	950	776	761	1,084	799
482	Total - Females	2,650	1,600	1,910	3,360	1,605	2,860
483	Without income	240	220	140	325	165	270
484	With income	2,415	1,380	1,775	3,035	1,440	2,590
485	Under $1,000 (45)	105	85	100	190	75	150
486	$ 1,000 - $ 2,999	160	130	125	245	110	120
487	$ 3,000 - $ 4,999	115	155	105	155	60	105
488	$ 5,000 - $ 6,999	115	80	115	175	100	220
489	$ 7,000 - $ 9,999	230	70	190	250	145	130
490	$10,000 - $11,999	130	45	85	175	80	115
491	$12,000 - $14,999	270	150	170	255	135	200
492	$15,000 - $19,999	285	120	185	360	130	250
493	$20,000 - $24,999	205	130	195	315	210	340
494	$25,000 - $29,999	235	165	140	235	125	255
495	$30,000 - $34,999	185	85	145	325	105	285
496	$35,000 - $39,999	125	45	90	115	80	160
497	$40,000 - $44,999	85	40	75	70	50	95
498	$45,000 - $49,999	25	20	15	85	-	45
499	$50,000 - $59,999	95	45	20	60	15	95
500	$60,000 and over	45	20	15	50	20	40
501	Average income $ (46)	19,854	17,629	17,456	18,697	18,216	20,815
502	Median income $ (46)	16,496	14,232	14,814	16,043	15,334	19,985
503	Standard error of average income $ (46)	684	858	656	577	756	628
	by composition of total income						
504	Total - Composition of income in 2000 % (47)	100.0	100.0	100.0	100.0	100.0	100.0
505	Employment income %	77.7	84.1	78.3	81.4	83.6	84.4
506	Government transfer payments %	14.5	10.6	16.9	12.2	11.0	10.1
507	Other %	7.8	5.3	4.8	6.5	5.4	5.5
	Population 15 years and over with employment income in 2000 by sex and work activity						
508	Both sexes with employment income (48)	3,305	2,295	2,640	4,570	2,465	4,165
509	Average employment income $	26,816	24,713	21,856	25,348	23,409	26,326
510	Standard error of average employment income $	819	723	631	572	759	580
511	Worked full year, full time (49)	1,750	1,205	1,435	2,550	1,210	2,435
512	Average employment income $	36,110	31,937	27,707	32,146	32,596	32,363
513	Standard error of average employment income $	1,129	942	812	730	994	729
514	Worked part year or part time (50)	1,475	965	1,130	1,870	1,115	1,620
515	Average employment income $	16,680	17,610	15,196	17,211	15,216	18,422
516	Standard error of average employment income $	927	947	840	758	916	792
517	Males with employment income (48)	1,740	1,335	1,450	2,470	1,345	2,185
518	Average employment income $	32,044	28,044	23,653	29,393	27,596	29,769
519	Standard error of average employment income $	1,272	948	935	837	1,137	876
520	Worked full year, full time (49)	1,080	800	785	1,500	735	1,320
521	Average employment income $	39,640	33,703	28,962	35,426	37,007	35,354
522	Standard error of average employment income $	1,635	1,132	1,227	1,019	1,361	1,113
523	Worked part year or part time (50)	650	475	600	920	550	820
524	Average employment income $	19,630	21,021	18,017	20,392	17,503	21,757
525	Standard error of average employment income $	1,593	1,450	1,326	1,216	1,496	1,204

Tableau 1. Certaines caractéristiques des secteurs de recensement, recensement de 2001 – Données intégrales et données-échantillon (20 %)

Toronto 0532.01 ◆◇	Toronto 0532.02 ◆◇	Toronto 0540.01	Toronto 0540.02	Toronto 0550.01	Toronto 0550.02	Caractéristiques	N°
						CARACTÉRISTIQUES DU REVENU DE 2000	
						Population de 15 ans et plus selon le sexe et les tranches de revenu total en 2000 – fin	
1,875	1,940	2,220	1,745	1,770	2,895	Total - Hommes	460
115	155	55	30	30	115	Sans revenu	461
1,760	1,790	2,165	1,720	1,740	2,780	Avec un revenu	462
105	115	25	85	45	70	Moins de 1 000 $ (45)	463
80	120	60	50	40	90	1 000 $ - 2 999 $	464
105	65	60	35	50	85	3 000 $ - 4 999 $	465
20	35	55	70	50	90	5 000 $ - 6 999 $	466
75	90	80	60	70	70	7 000 $ - 9 999 $	467
65	90	65	20	50	55	10 000 $ - 11 999 $	468
105	90	85	60	40	110	12 000 $ - 14 999 $	469
155	120	160	115	80	190	15 000 $ - 19 999 $	470
135	225	220	110	120	160	20 000 $ - 24 999 $	471
200	140	180	105	125	85	25 000 $ - 29 999 $	472
160	220	160	160	140	355	30 000 $ - 34 999 $	473
90	70	180	165	125	115	35 000 $ - 39 999 $	474
80	165	255	140	165	220	40 000 $ - 44 999 $	475
115	85	130	65	70	155	45 000 $ - 49 999 $	476
170	70	140	160	195	270	50 000 $ - 59 999 $	477
100	105	310	325	375	655	60 000 $ et plus	478
27,147	25,602	39,038	45,918	43,987	43,146	Revenu moyen $ (46)	479
25,158	23,417	32,114	34,426	36,989	35,740	Revenu médian $ (46)	480
1,075	1,003	2,448	3,432	2,754	1,552	Erreur type de revenu moyen $ (46)	481
1,795	2,025	2,355	2,015	1,875	3,075	Total - Femmes	482
120	275	90	170	120	120	Sans revenu	483
1,680	1,750	2,270	1,855	1,750	2,950	Avec un revenu	484
115	75	145	70	70	125	Moins de 1 000 $ (45)	485
110	110	110	130	60	130	1 000 $ - 2 999 $	486
100	120	55	80	70	100	3 000 $ - 4 999 $	487
85	90	60	70	60	165	5 000 $ - 6 999 $	488
135	130	105	85	80	140	7 000 $ - 9 999 $	489
145	125	95	60	80	95	10 000 $ - 11 999 $	490
155	205	200	140	110	205	12 000 $ - 14 999 $	491
210	195	190	190	120	235	15 000 $ - 19 999 $	492
160	165	220	180	100	215	20 000 $ - 24 999 $	493
190	185	220	105	115	275	25 000 $ - 29 999 $	494
85	95	220	80	215	270	30 000 $ - 34 999 $	495
60	55	150	115	110	305	35 000 $ - 39 999 $	496
45	85	95	150	145	185	40 000 $ - 44 999 $	497
35	55	140	90	105	130	45 000 $ - 49 999 $	498
40	20	125	105	135	155	50 000 $ - 59 999 $	499
15	40	140	195	180	210	60 000 $ et plus	500
17,948	19,118	26,580	30,596	31,212	28,112	Revenu moyen $ (46)	501
15,019	15,166	23,353	21,976	30,016	25,462	Revenu médian $ (46)	502
733	764	903	1,796	1,117	949	Erreur type de revenu moyen $ (46)	503
						selon la composition du revenu total	
100.0	100.0	100.0	100.0	100.0	100.0	Total - Composition du revenu en 2000 % (47)	504
81.1	86.1	84.8	77.2	84.3	82.4	Revenu d'emploi %	505
13.1	10.9	9.0	8.2	6.3	7.8	Transferts gouvernementaux %	506
5.8	3.0	6.1	14.7	9.4	9.9	Autre %	507
						Population de 15 ans et plus ayant un revenu d'emploi en 2000 selon le sexe et le travail	
2,635	2,815	3,515	2,680	2,870	4,470	Les deux sexes ayant un revenu d'emploi (48)	508
23,982	24,280	35,018	39,087	38,561	37,363	Revenu moyen d'emploi $	509
749	737	1,574	1,888	1,745	1,030	Erreur type de revenu moyen d'emploi $	510
1,435	1,465	2,185	1,630	1,640	2,800	Ayant travaillé toute l'année à plein temps (49)	511
31,072	30,760	44,396	49,474	51,338	47,775	Revenu moyen d'emploi $	512
844	837	2,328	2,637	2,674	1,310	Erreur type de revenu moyen d'emploi $	513
1,100	1,265	1,250	1,000	1,160	1,525	Ayant travaillé une partie de l'année ou à temps partiel (50)	514
14,926	17,657	19,656	23,519	22,211	20,534	Revenu moyen d'emploi $	515
1,110	1,166	1,100	2,247	1,332	1,227	Erreur type de revenu moyen d'emploi $	516
1,435	1,500	1,855	1,380	1,480	2,330	Hommes ayant un revenu d'emploi (48)	517
28,448	27,777	40,428	45,372	44,421	43,475	Revenu moyen d'emploi $	518
1,125	1,101	2,813	3,253	3,199	1,637	Erreur type de revenu moyen d'emploi $	519
890	830	1,225	835	910	1,545	Ayant travaillé toute l'année à plein temps (49)	520
34,713	32,408	50,471	57,423	58,073	53,634	Revenu moyen d'emploi $	521
1,136	1,089	4,027	4,561	4,719	1,971	Erreur type de revenu moyen d'emploi $	522
515	630	600	515	550	685	Ayant travaillé une partie de l'année ou à temps partiel (50)	523
17,283	21,965	21,261	27,848	22,699	25,071	Revenu moyen d'emploi $	524
1,992	2,086	1,557	3,827	2,168	2,336	Erreur type de revenu moyen d'emploi $	525

Table 1. Selected Characteristics for Census Tracts, 2001 Census – 100% Data and 20% Sample Data

No.	Characteristics	Toronto 0528.31 A	Toronto 0529.01 ◆	Toronto 0529.02 ◆◇	Toronto 0530 ◆	Toronto 0531.01	Toronto 0531.02 ◆◇ A
	2000 INCOME CHARACTERISTICS						
	Population 15 years and over with employment income in 2000 by sex and work activity – concluded						
526	Females with employment income (48)	1,560	960	1,195	2,100	1,120	1,985
527	Average employment income $	21,002	20,070	19,675	20,583	18,375	22,539
528	Standard error of average employment income $	879	1,041	794	699	845	705
529	Worked full year, full time (49)	670	405	645	1,050	480	1,115
530	Average employment income $	30,409	28,446	26,185	27,474	25,812	28,819
531	Standard error of average employment income $	1,194	1,635	976	927	1,126	836
532	Worked part year or part time (50)	830	495	530	950	565	805
533	Average employment income $	14,371	14,360	11,992	14,135	13,005	15,019
534	Standard error of average employment income $	1,032	1,142	919	863	1,025	967
	Census families by structure and family income groups in 2000						
535	Total - All census families	1,725	1,215	1,455	2,405	1,155	2,015
536	Under $10,000	85	115	135	225	70	105
537	$ 10,000 - $19,999	85	140	130	180	90	80
538	$ 20,000 - $29,999	240	135	265	235	170	180
539	$ 30,000 - $39,999	245	145	215	285	225	265
540	$ 40,000 - $49,999	200	145	235	355	155	305
541	$ 50,000 - $59,999	165	95	150	335	110	205
542	$ 60,000 - $69,999	170	150	60	190	100	235
543	$ 70,000 - $79,999	155	65	80	150	50	185
544	$ 80,000 - $89,999	80	105	40	175	45	130
545	$ 90,000 - $99,999	70	40	70	110	45	95
546	$100,000 and over	225	85	60	155	85	230
547	Average family income $	57,778	49,258	43,268	50,690	49,026	59,296
548	Median family income $	50,550	44,683	38,783	47,180	41,262	53,952
549	Standard error of average family income $	1,998	1,941	1,507	1,367	2,023	1,608
550	Total - All couple census families (51)	1,470	965	1,210	1,930	865	1,745
551	Under $10,000	60	65	80	140	60	85
552	$ 10,000 - $19,999	50	80	105	90	35	55
553	$ 20,000 - $29,999	180	115	195	160	95	155
554	$ 30,000 - $39,999	200	115	200	200	165	195
555	$ 40,000 - $49,999	155	110	190	320	130	250
556	$ 50,000 - $59,999	150	80	125	320	110	175
557	$ 60,000 - $69,999	155	135	65	170	60	235
558	$ 70,000 - $79,999	145	60	80	130	50	160
559	$ 80,000 - $89,999	70	100	35	150	45	120
560	$ 90,000 - $99,999	70	40	70	105	45	100
561	$100,000 and over	225	65	65	135	75	220
562	Average family income $	61,950	53,256	46,118	54,656	53,343	61,586
563	Median family income $	54,043	49,995	40,626	51,560	47,718	58,356
564	Standard error of average family income $	2,215	2,054	1,672	1,474	2,439	1,741
	Incidence of low income in 2000						
565	Total - Economic families	1,525	1,045	1,230	2,140	995	1,715
566	Low income	255	245	290	435	195	200
567	Incidence of low income in 2000 % (52)	16.7	23.7	23.4	20.5	19.3	11.8
568	Total - Unattached individuals 15 years and over	505	260	350	565	305	215
569	Low income	250	120	200	260	100	75
570	Incidence of low income in 2000 % (52)	49.5	46.0	58.4	46.5	32.4	36.6
571	Total - Population in private households	6,435	4,170	5,065	8,795	4,235	7,300
572	Low income	1,060	990	1,225	1,890	825	865
573	Incidence of low income in 2000 % (52)	16.5	23.7	24.1	21.5	19.5	11.8
	Private households by household income groups in 2000						
574	Total - All private households	2,005	1,245	1,435	2,415	1,155	1,805
575	Under $10,000	60	95	125	120	50	65
576	$ 10,000 - $19,999	280	150	155	200	55	80
577	$ 20,000 - $29,999	295	120	135	230	90	60
578	$ 30,000 - $39,999	255	145	160	235	190	195
579	$ 40,000 - $49,999	160	125	210	325	150	210
580	$ 50,000 - $59,999	175	115	175	345	185	135
581	$ 60,000 - $69,999	170	135	90	205	95	170
582	$ 70,000 - $79,999	145	75	95	150	60	230
583	$ 80,000 - $89,999	95	110	100	150	75	155
584	$ 90,000 - $99,999	50	50	80	95	65	145
585	$100,000 and over	320	130	120	360	145	365
586	Average household income $	56,880	54,177	51,311	58,891	59,457	71,820
587	Median household income $	47,968	48,027	48,651	52,505	51,533	69,342
588	Standard error of average household income $	2,004	2,195	1,806	1,614	2,171	1,938

Tableau 1. Certaines caractéristiques des secteurs de recensement, recensement de 2001 – Données intégrales et données-échantillon (20 %)

Toronto 0532.01 ◆◇	Toronto 0532.02 ◆◇	Toronto 0540.01	Toronto 0540.02	Toronto 0550.01	Toronto 0550.02	Caractéristiques	N°
						CARACTÉRISTIQUES DU REVENU DE 2000	
						Population de 15 ans et plus ayant un revenu d'emploi en 2000 selon le sexe et le travail – fin	
1,200	1,315	1,660	1,295	1,385	2,140	Femmes ayant un revenu d'emploi (48)	526
18,640	20,295	28,959	32,395	32,297	30,717	Revenu moyen d'emploi $	527
868	896	1,113	1,700	1,198	1,125	Erreur type de revenu moyen d'emploi $	528
545	630	960	795	730	1,260	Ayant travaillé toute l'année à plein temps (49)	529
25,149	28,583	36,657	41,065	42,917	40,587	Revenu moyen d'emploi $	530
1,028	1,284	1,371	2,179	1,352	1,487	Erreur type de revenu moyen d'emploi $	531
585	635	650	490	615	840	Ayant travaillé une partie de l'année ou à temps partiel (50)	532
12,857	13,364	18,169	18,970	21,774	16,848	Revenu moyen d'emploi $	533
1,202	903	1,540	2,258	1,633	1,151	Erreur type de revenu moyen d'emploi $	534
						Familles de recensement selon la structure et les tranches de revenu de la famille en 2000	
1,365	1,410	1,395	1,210	1,370	2,075	Total - Toutes les familles de recensement	535
115	125	65	125	20	25	Moins de 10 000 $	536
80	45	55	70	35	65	10 000 $ - 19 999 $	537
210	200	155	95	50	105	20 000 $ - 29 999 $	538
160	205	160	95	125	200	30 000 $ - 39 999 $	539
180	245	115	135	80	210	40 000 $ - 49 999 $	540
170	165	160	135	165	180	50 000 $ - 59 999 $	541
120	110	165	105	150	215	60 000 $ - 69 999 $	542
90	65	160	95	150	170	70 000 $ - 79 999 $	543
75	85	80	50	150	175	80 000 $ - 89 999 $	544
60	35	95	20	80	165	90 000 $ - 99 999 $	545
110	130	180	285	370	565	100 000 $ et plus	546
50,640	50,817	68,583	77,927	81,609	80,723	Revenu moyen des familles $	547
47,514	45,864	59,065	55,205	72,718	72,155	Revenu médian des familles $	548
1,794	1,812	3,832	6,512	2,617	2,353	Erreur type de revenu moyen des familles $	549
1,140	1,125	1,100	970	1,150	1,710	Total - Toutes les familles de recensement comptant un couple (51)	550
60	105	35	90	10	-	Moins de 10 000 $	551
60	25	20	35	10	35	10 000 $ - 19 999 $	552
195	145	110	55	35	70	20 000 $ - 29 999 $	553
135	145	90	55	85	120	30 000 $ - 39 999 $	554
145	185	85	105	60	165	40 000 $ - 49 999 $	555
150	140	130	110	130	140	50 000 $ - 59 999 $	556
100	110	150	75	130	150	60 000 $ - 69 999 $	557
75	55	145	80	130	150	70 000 $ - 79 999 $	558
65	70	65	50	125	170	80 000 $ - 89 999 $	559
60	30	90	20	75	160	90 000 $ - 99 999 $	560
85	115	175	290	365	550	100 000 $ et plus	561
52,433	52,785	76,168	88,217	87,843	87,659	Revenu moyen des familles $	562
47,827	48,079	64,917	63,832	77,310	81,921	Revenu médian des familles $	563
1,903	2,126	4,654	7,998	2,851	2,601	Erreur type de revenu moyen des familles $	564
						Fréquence des unités à faible revenu en 2000	
1,155	1,220	1,380	1,225	1,350	1,980	Total - Familles économiques	565
250	260	195	235	90	105	Faible revenu	566
21.9	21.3	14.4	19.5	6.7	5.3	Fréquence des unités à faible revenu en 2000 % (52)	567
190	185	1,475	1,035	295	865	Total - Personnes hors famille économique de 15 ans et plus	568
60	110	440	275	60	235	Faible revenu	569
33.1	60.0	29.8	26.6	21.0	26.9	Fréquence des unités à faible revenu en 2000 % (52)	570
4,765	5,310	5,315	4,505	4,645	7,190	Total - Population dans les ménages privés	571
1,080	1,145	975	885	340	555	Faible revenu	572
22.7	21.5	18.3	19.7	7.3	7.7	Fréquence des unités à faible revenu en 2000 % (52)	573
						Ménages privés selon les tranches de revenu du ménage en 2000	
1,250	1,295	2,695	2,155	1,555	2,725	Total - Tous les ménages privés	574
60	105	180	175	20	55	Moins de 10 000 $	575
100	45	315	235	70	210	10 000 $ - 19 999 $	576
135	120	350	255	45	180	20 000 $ - 29 999 $	577
105	140	340	235	145	325	30 000 $ - 39 999 $	578
125	160	335	300	115	255	40 000 $ - 49 999 $	579
135	145	260	200	160	195	50 000 $ - 59 999 $	580
105	130	230	160	160	205	60 000 $ - 69 999 $	581
95	95	230	140	150	260	70 000 $ - 79 999 $	582
90	100	105	95	155	220	80 000 $ - 89 999 $	583
60	70	105	30	120	180	90 000 $ - 99 999 $	584
235	185	240	335	415	650	100 000 $ et plus	585
62,360	61,072	53,707	62,847	84,292	74,431	Revenu moyen des ménages $	586
56,918	54,503	44,225	44,413	73,250	67,026	Revenu médian des ménages $	587
2,246	2,247	2,250	3,989	3,369	2,120	Erreur type de revenu moyen des ménages $	588

Table 1. Selected Characteristics for Census Tracts, 2001 Census – 100% Data and 20% Sample Data

No.	Characteristics	Toronto 0560 A	Toronto 0561 A	Toronto 0562.01 ◆ A	Toronto 0562.02	Toronto 0562.03	Toronto 0562.04 ◇
	POPULATION CHARACTERISTICS						
1	**Population, 1996 (1)**	**6,663**	**5,296**	**7,440**	**7,193**	**5,755**	**5,133**
2	**Population, 2001 (2)**	**6,497**	**5,294**	**7,467**	**6,930**	**5,572**	**5,027**
3	Population percentage change, 1996-2001	-2.5	-	0.4	-3.7	-3.2	-2.1
4	Land area in square kilometres, 2001	4.14	4.66	6.88	2.09	1.06	1.03
5	**Total population - 100% Data (3)**	**6,495**	**5,290**	**7,470**	**6,930**	**5,575**	**5,030**
	by sex and age groups						
6	Male	3,290	2,655	3,735	3,435	2,760	2,485
7	0-4 years	230	185	260	195	210	160
8	5-9 years	220	205	210	190	250	170
9	10-14 years	240	170	220	245	260	160
10	15-19 years	220	150	205	285	225	200
11	20-24 years	215	165	320	305	210	225
12	25-29 years	230	160	375	230	195	205
13	30-34 years	275	195	390	215	195	165
14	35-39 years	310	265	370	210	235	185
15	40-44 years	275	195	315	280	225	205
16	45-49 years	220	180	245	295	180	155
17	50-54 years	205	155	215	345	215	215
18	55-59 years	200	125	170	240	155	170
19	60-64 years	155	135	140	180	95	125
20	65-69 years	130	150	115	100	55	55
21	70-74 years	80	115	75	65	30	40
22	75-79 years	45	65	55	35	10	20
23	80-84 years	20	20	50	15	5	5
24	85 years and over	10	5	10	10	5	10
25	Female	3,205	2,640	3,730	3,495	2,810	2,540
26	0-4 years	190	150	255	140	195	160
27	5-9 years	220	180	245	205	200	170
28	10-14 years	235	165	185	235	245	175
29	15-19 years	220	160	210	330	265	205
30	20-24 years	200	150	315	305	245	205
31	25-29 years	215	180	395	215	190	175
32	30-34 years	255	195	340	190	215	190
33	35-39 years	310	230	340	240	255	200
34	40-44 years	260	200	250	275	250	205
35	45-49 years	225	175	230	345	195	205
36	50-54 years	210	155	235	350	235	225
37	55-59 years	205	140	195	240	130	155
38	60-64 years	185	175	160	155	70	105
39	65-69 years	120	160	105	105	40	55
40	70-74 years	75	125	95	65	30	50
41	75-79 years	55	75	100	50	20	30
42	80-84 years	20	20	50	30	25	15
43	85 years and over	10	15	30	25	10	10
44	**Total population 15 years and over**	**5,160**	**4,240**	**6,095**	**5,720**	**4,210**	**4,025**
	by legal marital status						
45	Never married (single)	1,630	1,150	2,195	1,845	1,435	1,205
46	Legally married (and not separated)	2,770	2,420	2,730	3,205	2,255	2,390
47	Separated, but still legally married	190	150	305	145	145	90
48	Divorced	355	265	560	275	250	190
49	Widowed	205	255	305	245	120	145
	by common-law status						
50	Not in a common-law relationship	4,805	3,990	5,495	5,505	3,975	3,890
51	In a common-law relationship	355	250	600	215	230	140
52	**Total population - 20% Sample Data (4)**	**6,485**	**5,285**	**7,365**	**6,930**	**5,570**	**4,980**
	by mother tongue						
53	Single responses	6,390	5,170	7,155	6,735	5,415	4,930
54	English	4,840	3,540	4,975	4,735	4,025	3,415
55	French	125	40	95	85	65	65
56	Non-official languages (5)	1,415	1,590	2,080	1,920	1,325	1,445
57	Italian	90	50	150	245	100	255
58	Chinese, n.o.s.	10	20	55	140	15	35
59	Cantonese	30	10	10	-	15	15
60	Portuguese	65	70	70	20	65	50
61	Punjabi	330	460	150	500	495	465
62	Other languages (6)	890	975	1,645	1,015	635	630
63	Multiple responses	100	120	215	190	155	50
64	English and French	10	15	25	-	-	-
65	English and non-official language	95	105	185	85	145	45
66	French and non-official language	-	-	-	110	-	10
67	English, French and non-official language	-	-	10	-	-	-

See reference material at the end of the publication. – Voir les documents de référence à la fin de la publication.

Tableau 1. Certaines caractéristiques des secteurs de recensement, recensement de 2001 – Données intégrales et données-échantillon (20 %)

Toronto 0562.05	Toronto 0562.06	Toronto 0562.07	Toronto 0562.08	Toronto 0562.09	Toronto 0562.10	Caractéristiques	N°
						CARACTÉRISTIQUES DE LA POPULATION	
5,807	**2,891**	**5,063**	**4,841**	**4,470**	**7,891**	**Population, 1996 (1)**	1
5,638	**3,317**	**5,113**	**4,682**	**4,332**	**7,974**	**Population, 2001 (2)**	2
-2.9	14.7	1.0	-3.3	-3.1	1.1	Variation en pourcentage de la population, 1996-2001	3
1.29	0.82	1.10	1.05	1.00	1.97	Superficie des terres en kilomètres carrés, 2001	4
5,640	**3,320**	**5,110**	**4,680**	**4,330**	**7,970**	**Population totale – Données intégrales (3)**	5
						selon le sexe et les groupes d'âge	
2,755	1,655	2,580	2,375	2,175	4,055	Sexe masculin	6
205	85	175	160	140	225	0-4 ans	7
180	100	220	210	180	335	5-9 ans	8
170	125	205	200	180	390	10-14 ans	9
135	160	195	200	170	405	15-19 ans	10
160	140	190	170	180	335	20-24 ans	11
245	125	190	160	140	275	25-29 ans	12
265	85	200	170	145	240	30-34 ans	13
285	120	240	230	175	290	35-39 ans	14
215	140	190	215	185	335	40-44 ans	15
205	115	195	165	160	320	45-49 ans	16
170	155	195	160	160	350	50-54 ans	17
175	130	155	140	140	240	55-59 ans	18
130	90	85	85	105	165	60-64 ans	19
85	35	75	65	55	75	65-69 ans	20
60	25	30	35	35	50	70-74 ans	21
45	15	25	20	20	20	75-79 ans	22
25	5	10	10	5	10	80-84 ans	23
10	10	5	-	-	10	85 ans et plus	24
2,880	1,665	2,530	2,300	2,155	3,920	Sexe féminin	25
175	100	175	145	120	200	0-4 ans	26
180	95	185	180	150	300	5-9 ans	27
170	125	185	175	155	320	10-14 ans	28
165	130	195	150	145	345	15-19 ans	29
205	140	205	175	190	320	20-24 ans	30
255	100	190	160	110	285	25-29 ans	31
255	95	200	170	150	255	30-34 ans	32
240	135	230	215	175	320	35-39 ans	33
230	150	200	225	190	345	40-44 ans	34
195	155	180	185	180	380	45-49 ans	35
205	175	210	175	210	350	50-54 ans	36
170	105	140	140	170	220	55-59 ans	37
150	75	95	85	80	120	60-64 ans	38
105	35	60	45	50	65	65-69 ans	39
75	20	30	40	35	35	70-74 ans	40
50	15	25	20	35	35	75-79 ans	41
35	10	20	5	15	20	80-84 ans	42
20	10	10	10	10	10	85 ans et plus	43
4,560	**2,690**	**3,980**	**3,620**	**3,410**	**6,210**	**Population totale de 15 ans et plus**	44
						selon l'état matrimonial légal	
1,365	820	1,260	1,155	1,060	1,990	Célibataire (jamais marié(e))	45
2,330	1,650	2,310	1,960	1,905	3,730	Légalement marié(e) (et non séparé(e))	46
230	45	130	150	120	125	Séparé(e), mais toujours légalement marié(e)	47
405	95	180	215	195	210	Divorcé(e)	48
235	80	100	130	130	155	Veuf ou veuve	49
						selon l'union libre	
4,200	2,620	3,770	3,395	3,200	6,035	Ne vivant pas en union libre	50
360	70	210	225	210	170	Vivant en union libre	51
5,640	**3,315**	**5,110**	**4,670**	**4,320**	**7,975**	**Population totale – Données-échantillon (20 %) (4)**	52
						selon la langue maternelle	
5,550	3,275	5,065	4,580	4,280	7,895	Réponses uniques	53
4,140	2,195	3,345	3,655	3,310	5,230	Anglais	54
135	40	65	170	45	145	Français	55
1,275	1,040	1,660	750	930	2,525	Langues non officielles (5)	56
70	340	140	50	160	265	Italien	57
95	40	45	10	15	50	Chinois, n.d.a.	58
55	-	15	-	10	70	Cantonais	59
90	-	30	20	15	190	Portugais	60
80	215	715	115	25	1,000	Pendjabi	61
880	440	725	540	705	940	Autres langues (6)	62
85	45	45	90	40	75	Réponses multiples	63
-	-	15	15	10	20	Anglais et français	64
65	40	35	75	35	65	Anglais et langue non officielle	65
15	-	-	-	-	-	Français et langue non officielle	66
-	-	-	-	-	-	Anglais, français et langue non officielle	67

See reference material at the end of the publication. – Voir les documents de référence à la fin de la publication.

Table 1. Selected Characteristics for Census Tracts, 2001 Census – 100% Data and 20% Sample Data

No.	Characteristics	Toronto 0560 A	Toronto 0561 A	Toronto 0562.01 ◆ A	Toronto 0562.02	Toronto 0562.03	Toronto 0562.04 ◇
	POPULATION CHARACTERISTICS						
	by home language						
68	Single responses	5,650	4,380	5,845	5,690	4,600	4,215
69	English	5,110	3,725	5,355	5,155	4,185	3,560
70	French	45	-	-	25	20	10
71	Non-official languages (5)	500	660	485	500	395	650
72	Cantonese	25	15	-	-	10	15
73	Chinese, n.o.s.	-	-	-	45	20	20
74	Italian	10	15	20	55	10	60
75	Punjabi	240	225	45	170	240	365
76	Portuguese	15	20	15	10	15	-
77	Other languages (6)	205	385	410	220	100	190
78	Multiple responses	840	900	1,520	1,245	970	765
79	English and French	55	25	95	90	55	80
80	English and non-official language	775	870	1,390	1,050	910	670
81	French and non-official language	10	-	10	100	-	-
82	English, French and non-official language	-	10	30	10	10	20
	by knowledge of official languages						
83	English only	5,965	4,820	6,780	6,285	5,045	4,455
84	French only	-	-	10	-	10	-
85	English and French	420	200	425	495	385	415
86	Neither English nor French	100	265	155	140	125	110
	by knowledge of non-official languages (5) (7)						
87	Italian	140	105	185	395	175	335
88	Cantonese	35	25	10	25	25	20
89	Chinese, n.o.s.	25	35	55	255	30	20
90	Spanish	175	85	165	235	270	85
91	Portuguese	60	75	110	55	80	50
92	Punjabi	365	585	255	570	550	515
93	Tagalog (Pilipino)	165	65	290	80	110	80
	by first official language spoken						
94	English	6,270	4,960	7,070	6,685	5,365	4,750
95	French	110	40	105	80	80	70
96	English and French	10	20	40	25	-	50
97	Neither English nor French	95	260	155	140	125	110
98	Official language minority - (number) (8)	115	50	120	95	80	90
99	Official language minority - (percentage) (8)	1.8	0.9	1.6	1.4	1.4	1.8
	by ethnic origin (9)						
100	Canadian	1,850	1,625	1,550	1,450	1,490	1,015
101	English	1,355	1,110	1,590	1,415	1,165	1,075
102	Scottish	1,040	730	790	1,230	730	615
103	Irish	1,145	755	1,180	1,070	755	855
104	Chinese	95	55	110	330	100	150
105	Italian	315	150	295	660	360	530
106	East Indian	615	880	1,070	1,040	690	800
107	French	495	215	600	370	400	285
108	German	395	275	325	355	330	245
109	Portuguese	115	120	140	125	205	200
110	Polish	145	105	135	190	105	120
111	Jewish	35	15	30	-	-	-
112	Jamaican	335	80	370	185	390	240
113	Filipino	220	70	335	110	145	150
114	Ukrainian	70	60	85	165	65	100
	by Aboriginal identity						
115	Total Aboriginal identity population (10)	20	20	75	15	50	80
116	Total non-Aboriginal population	6,465	5,265	7,290	6,915	5,520	4,900
	by Aboriginal origin						
117	Total Aboriginal origins population (11)	120	40	135	30	115	105
118	Total non-Aboriginal population	6,370	5,250	7,235	6,900	5,450	4,875
	by Registered Indian status						
119	Registered Indian (12)	15	15	25	-	40	10
120	Not a Registered Indian	6,475	5,275	7,345	6,930	5,525	4,970

Tableau 1. Certaines caractéristiques des secteurs de recensement, recensement de 2001 – Données intégrales et données-échantillon (20 %)

Toronto 0562.05	Toronto 0562.06	Toronto 0562.07	Toronto 0562.08	Toronto 0562.09	Toronto 0562.10	Caractéristiques	Nº
						CARACTÉRISTIQUES DE LA POPULATION	
						selon la langue parlée à la maison	
4,865	2,750	4,130	4,065	3,645	6,445	Réponses uniques	68
4,495	2,490	3,580	3,825	3,430	5,680	Anglais	69
15	25	10	-	-	10	Français	70
360	235	540	240	215	755	Langues non officielles (5)	71
45	-	-	10	-	25	Cantonais	72
40	30	20	20	-	30	Chinois, n.d.a.	73
10	45	10	-	-	20	Italien	74
65	120	290	80	10	420	Pendjabi	75
-	-	-	-	10	30	Portugais	76
200	45	210	135	205	230	Autres langues (6)	77
770	565	980	605	675	1,525	Réponses multiples	78
75	20	30	170	55	120	Anglais et français	79
660	540	930	435	610	1,395	Anglais et langue non officielle	80
-	-	-	-	-	10	Français et langue non officielle	81
30	-	20	-	-	10	Anglais, français et langue non officielle	82
						selon la connaissance des langues officielles	
5,155	2,995	4,740	4,185	4,005	7,140	Anglais seulement	83
15	-	-	-	-	-	Français seulement	84
375	270	255	430	235	595	Anglais et français	85
90	55	110	60	85	235	Ni l'anglais ni le français	86
						selon la connaissance des langues non officielles (5) (7)	
95	440	220	100	200	375	Italien	87
115	10	15	10	10	85	Cantonais	88
65	45	45	20	10	60	Chinois, n.d.a.	89
145	180	160	145	320	135	Espagnol	90
115	20	50	20	50	195	Portugais	91
155	260	835	130	50	1,065	Pendjabi	92
170	30	100	50	50	120	Tagalog (pilipino)	93
						selon la première langue officielle parlée	
5,420	3,220	4,935	4,430	4,190	7,585	Anglais	94
135	40	60	165	35	135	Français	95
15	-	10	10	10	35	Anglais et français	96
75	55	115	60	85	225	Ni l'anglais ni le français	97
135	40	60	175	40	150	Minorité de langue officielle - (nombre) (8)	98
2.4	1.2	1.2	3.7	0.9	1.9	Minorité de langue officielle - (pourcentage) (8)	99
						selon l'origine ethnique (9)	
1,625	740	985	1,695	1,170	1,560	Canadien	100
1,195	630	1,030	1,090	1,020	1,595	Anglais	101
685	445	600	565	775	1,150	Écossais	102
800	285	545	705	675	815	Irlandais	103
290	80	110	50	55	320	Chinois	104
245	740	370	245	430	775	Italien	105
480	420	1,025	245	230	1,855	Indien de l'Inde	106
455	225	205	485	245	440	Français	107
325	230	205	275	350	325	Allemand	108
195	25	65	30	90	385	Portugais	109
120	115	250	150	105	200	Polonais	110
-	25	20	20	10	10	Juif	111
260	-	290	250	180	385	Jamaïquain	112
220	75	165	60	50	175	Philippin	113
55	70	105	35	70	195	Ukrainien	114
						selon l'identité autochtone	
60	-	15	10	25	55	Total de la population ayant une identité autochtone (10)	115
5,580	3,315	5,095	4,660	4,295	7,920	Total de la population non autochtone	116
						selon l'origine autochtone	
115	15	90	95	175	95	Total de la population ayant une origine autochtone (11)	117
5,525	3,305	5,020	4,575	4,150	7,880	Total de la population non autochtone	118
						selon le statut d'Indien inscrit	
25	-	15	-	15	45	Oui, Indien inscrit (12)	119
5,615	3,315	5,095	4,670	4,305	7,925	Non, pas un Indien inscrit	120

Table 1. Selected Characteristics for Census Tracts, 2001 Census – 100% Data and 20% Sample Data

No.	Characteristics	Toronto 0560 A	Toronto 0561 A	Toronto 0562.01 ◆ A	Toronto 0562.02	Toronto 0562.03	Toronto 0562.04 ◇
	POPULATION CHARACTERISTICS						
	by visible minority groups						
121	Total visible minority population	2,120	1,750	3,050	2,355	1,865	1,780
122	Chinese	65	60	70	315	55	80
123	South Asian	875	1,035	1,075	1,200	715	1,085
124	Black	535	210	780	370	520	385
125	Filipino	200	70	320	110	140	150
126	Latin American	125	60	75	195	150	10
127	Southeast Asian	55	55	95	10	20	25
128	Arab	30	55	65	-	10	15
129	West Asian	70	80	100	40	-	-
130	Korean	-	-	-	35	35	-
131	Japanese	20	15	35	-	15	-
132	Visible minority, n.i.e. (13)	90	120	400	35	195	40
133	Multiple visible minorities (14)	60	-	45	50	25	-
	by citizenship						
134	Canadian citizenship (15)	5,875	4,535	5,725	6,290	5,095	4,525
135	Citizenship other than Canadian	610	750	1,645	640	470	450
	by place of birth of respondent						
136	Non-immigrant population	4,180	3,230	4,030	4,255	3,680	3,190
137	Born in province of residence	3,445	2,610	2,975	3,700	3,065	2,840
138	Immigrant population (16)	2,285	2,015	3,215	2,670	1,865	1,770
139	United States	35	30	40	50	50	25
140	Central and South America	245	140	360	320	190	90
141	Caribbean and Bermuda	260	120	405	215	360	165
142	United Kingdom	400	465	360	435	255	185
143	Other Europe (17)	455	320	475	515	320	415
144	Africa	55	25	225	85	115	30
145	Asia and the Middle East	815	865	1,335	1,030	580	805
146	Oceania and other (18)	25	45	10	20	-	65
147	Non-permanent residents (19)	30	45	125	-	20	20
148	**Total immigrant population**	**2,285**	**2,015**	**3,210**	**2,670**	**1,865**	**1,770**
	by period of immigration						
149	Before 1961	235	345	255	335	145	185
150	1961-1970	460	280	340	395	240	375
151	1971-1980	355	300	480	760	450	450
152	1981-1990	510	350	515	650	415	300
153	1991-2001 (20)	720	740	1,625	530	615	470
154	1991-1995	395	315	465	320	315	225
155	1996-2001 (20)	330	430	1,160	210	300	240
	by age at immigration						
156	0-4 years	180	140	270	270	200	170
157	5-19 years	635	505	920	685	575	535
158	20 years and over	1,475	1,370	2,020	1,710	1,090	1,065
159	**Total population**	**6,490**	**5,285**	**7,370**	**6,930**	**5,565**	**4,980**
	by religion						
160	Catholic (21)	2,305	1,380	2,235	2,410	2,000	1,750
161	Protestant	2,320	1,765	2,020	2,145	1,910	1,550
162	Christian Orthodox	40	85	130	90	75	20
163	Christian, n.i.e. (22)	190	80	500	210	175	130
164	Muslim	185	155	535	225	135	185
165	Jewish	20	10	10	25	-	-
166	Buddhist	50	30	95	100	20	30
167	Hindu	275	480	725	360	95	340
168	Sikh	325	480	110	445	515	510
169	Eastern religions (23)	15	-	-	-	-	-
170	Other religions (24)	-	10	30	-	-	-
171	No religious affiliation (25)	780	815	975	915	640	465
172	**Total population 15 years and over**	**5,145**	**4,235**	**5,985**	**5,710**	**4,190**	**3,975**
	by generation status						
173	1st generation (26)	2,190	1,940	2,990	2,605	1,745	1,695
174	2nd generation (27)	870	740	1,165	1,410	910	940
175	3rd generation and over (28)	2,085	1,555	1,835	1,705	1,530	1,340
176	**Total population 1 year and over (29)**	**6,395**	**5,230**	**7,250**	**6,890**	**5,505**	**4,920**
	by place of residence 1 year ago (mobility)						
177	Non-movers	5,670	4,460	4,890	6,385	4,910	4,365
178	Movers	725	765	2,355	505	595	550
179	Non-migrants	385	460	1,155	360	320	350
180	Migrants	340	310	1,205	140	275	200
181	Internal migrants	240	165	720	125	255	155
182	Intraprovincial migrants	195	155	575	120	220	135
183	Interprovincial migrants	50	10	145	10	35	15
184	External migrants	100	145	480	15	25	45

Tableau 1. Certaines caractéristiques des secteurs de recensement, recensement de 2001 – Données intégrales et données-échantillon (20 %)

Toronto 0562.05	Toronto 0562.06	Toronto 0562.07	Toronto 0562.08	Toronto 0562.09	Toronto 0562.10	Caractéristiques	N°
						CARACTÉRISTIQUES DE LA POPULATION	
						selon les groupes de minorités visibles	
1,870	825	2,325	1,215	1,075	3,500	Total de la population des minorités visibles	121
215	45	105	25	30	240	Chinois	122
455	485	1,225	285	240	1,925	Sud-Asiatique	123
560	85	550	455	370	785	Noir	124
205	60	155	60	70	195	Philippin	125
85	85	85	115	215	65	Latino-Américain	126
110	-	15	10	15	15	Asiatique du Sud-Est	127
50	-	-	-	30	-	Arabe	128
25	-	-	35	-	35	Asiatique occidental	129
-	10	-	10	-	-	Coréen	130
-	-	45	10	10	30	Japonais	131
130	35	155	180	85	170	Minorité visible, n.i.a. (13)	132
35	10	10	35	15	35	Minorités visibles multiples (14)	133
						selon la citoyenneté	
5,035	3,055	4,620	4,285	4,040	7,260	Citoyenneté canadienne (15)	134
605	265	490	385	280	715	Citoyenneté autre que canadienne	135
						selon le lieu de naissance du répondant	
3,500	2,040	2,995	3,190	3,005	4,725	Population non immigrante	136
2,795	1,870	2,495	2,600	2,515	4,235	Née dans la province de résidence	137
2,125	1,250	2,105	1,465	1,285	3,215	Population immigrante (16)	138
55	25	15	25	10	40	États-Unis	139
155	120	175	180	230	260	Amérique centrale et du Sud	140
350	70	235	305	200	495	Caraïbes et Bermudes	141
350	140	195	350	215	340	Royaume-Uni	142
305	465	295	290	365	550	Autre Europe (17)	143
70	20	145	-	15	165	Afrique	144
820	410	1,030	305	250	1,355	Asie et Moyen-Orient	145
10	-	10	10	-	-	Océanie et autre (18)	146
15	25	10	15	30	30	Résidents non permanents (19)	147
2,120	**1,250**	**2,105**	**1,465**	**1,285**	**3,220**	**Population immigrante totale**	148
						selon la période d'immigration	
180	200	90	140	125	240	Avant 1961	149
355	300	225	290	360	430	1961-1970	150
350	320	420	230	260	1,020	1971-1980	151
445	120	625	370	400	715	1981-1990	152
790	305	745	435	140	815	1991-2001 (20)	153
420	220	440	255	85	535	1991-1995	154
370	85	300	180	55	280	1996-2001 (20)	155
						selon l'âge à l'immigration	
235	135	170	95	110	315	0-4 ans	156
540	390	540	395	370	985	5-19 ans	157
1,350	720	1,395	975	805	1,920	20 ans et plus	158
5,640	**3,315**	**5,110**	**4,670**	**4,320**	**7,970**	**Population totale**	159
						selon la religion	
1,885	1,725	1,380	1,540	1,710	2,885	Catholique (21)	160
1,800	745	1,700	1,730	1,685	2,065	Protestante	161
55	20	10	55	25	35	Orthodoxe chrétienne	162
220	85	155	100	70	415	Chrétiennes, n.i.a. (22)	163
195	120	290	65	30	310	Musulmane	164
30	20	25	10	-	-	Juive	165
55	-	35	35	45	40	Bouddhiste	166
220	40	235	145	185	510	Hindoue	167
45	270	655	100	25	1,000	Sikh	168
15	-	-	-	-	-	Religions orientales (23)	169
-	-	-	10	-	-	Autres religions (24)	170
1,125	290	615	890	540	705	Aucune appartenance religieuse (25)	171
4,560	**2,680**	**3,970**	**3,610**	**3,390**	**6,200**	**Population totale de 15 ans et plus**	172
						selon le statut des générations	
2,030	1,215	2,030	1,415	1,285	3,125	1re génération (26)	173
875	715	690	695	790	1,475	2e génération (27)	174
1,650	760	1,250	1,500	1,320	1,605	3e génération et plus (28)	175
5,530	**3,280**	**5,070**	**4,630**	**4,295**	**7,920**	**Population totale de 1 an et plus (29)**	176
						selon le lieu de résidence 1 an auparavant (mobilité)	
4,740	3,090	4,565	4,045	3,915	7,230	Personnes n'ayant pas déménagé	177
790	190	510	585	385	690	Personnes ayant déménagé	178
410	100	270	330	195	405	Non-migrants	179
375	90	240	255	190	285	Migrants	180
275	30	175	230	145	245	Migrants internes	181
220	30	150	165	125	225	Migrants infraprovinciaux	182
55	-	25	60	15	20	Migrants interprovinciaux	183
100	55	70	25	45	40	Migrants externes	184

Table 1. Selected Characteristics for Census Tracts, 2001 Census – 100% Data and 20% Sample Data

No.	Characteristics	Toronto 0560 A	Toronto 0561 A	Toronto 0562.01 ◆ A	Toronto 0562.02	Toronto 0562.03	Toronto 0562.04 ◇
	POPULATION CHARACTERISTICS						
185	**Total population 5 years and over (30)**	**6,055**	**4,945**	**6,830**	**6,585**	**5,155**	**4,640**
	by place of residence 5 years ago (mobility)						
186	Non-movers	3,710	3,090	2,025	4,630	2,875	3,085
187	Movers	2,350	1,865	4,805	1,955	2,280	1,550
188	Non-migrants	1,135	975	2,060	1,300	1,260	830
189	Migrants	1,215	885	2,745	655	1,020	725
190	Internal migrants	865	535	1,685	555	760	540
191	Intraprovincial migrants	730	420	1,250	465	700	490
192	Interprovincial migrants	135	115	435	90	60	45
193	External migrants	350	355	1,060	105	260	185
194	**Total population 15 to 24 years**	**860**	**630**	**1,005**	**1,220**	**935**	**785**
	by school attendance						
195	Not attending school	435	270	510	380	370	320
196	Attending school full time	405	305	390	795	545	430
197	Attending school part time	20	60	100	40	15	35
198	**Total population 15 years and over**	**5,145**	**4,235**	**5,990**	**5,715**	**4,190**	**3,975**
	by highest level of schooling						
199	Less than grade 9 (31)	370	340	370	325	290	260
200	Grades 9-13 without high school graduation certificate	1,295	1,205	1,375	1,170	1,170	815
201	Grades 9-13 with high school graduation certificate	915	845	1,095	1,025	655	800
202	Some postsecondary without degree, certificate or diploma (32)	550	440	755	645	395	425
203	Trades certificate or diploma (33)	490	435	565	475	380	360
204	College certificate or diploma (34)	890	505	885	1,035	760	725
205	University certificate below bachelor's degree	55	70	170	120	60	55
206	University with bachelor's degree or higher	590	395	770	915	480	525
	by combinations of unpaid work						
207	Males 15 years and over	2,580	2,100	2,970	2,810	2,040	1,975
208	Reported unpaid work (35)	2,220	1,875	2,525	2,535	1,850	1,695
209	Housework and child care and care or assistance to seniors	205	160	140	205	130	130
210	Housework and child care only	710	480	695	715	615	550
211	Housework and care or assistance to seniors only	135	110	155	225	110	125
212	Child care and care or assistance to seniors only	-	-	-	10	-	-
213	Housework only	1,135	1,055	1,445	1,365	920	875
214	Child care only	20	50	85	20	45	10
215	Care or assistance to seniors only	20	20	15	-	10	15
216	Females 15 years and over	2,565	2,140	3,020	2,900	2,145	2,000
217	Reported unpaid work (35)	2,355	1,960	2,745	2,705	1,940	1,875
218	Housework and child care and care or assistance to seniors	280	175	225	315	225	175
219	Housework and child care only	840	635	1,000	820	830	735
220	Housework and care or assistance to seniors only	130	95	245	215	95	120
221	Child care and care or assistance to seniors only	15	-	-	-	-	-
222	Housework only	1,080	995	1,260	1,340	785	835
223	Child care only	15	35	10	15	10	-
224	Care or assistance to seniors only	-	15	10	-	-	15
	by labour force activity						
225	Males 15 years and over	2,580	2,100	2,970	2,810	2,040	1,975
226	In the labour force	2,025	1,565	2,310	2,340	1,655	1,575
227	Employed	1,955	1,505	2,200	2,235	1,620	1,520
228	Unemployed	70	60	120	110	40	50
229	Not in the labour force	560	535	655	465	380	405
230	Participation rate	78.5	74.5	77.8	83.3	81.1	79.7
231	Employment rate	75.8	71.7	74.1	79.5	79.4	77.0
232	Unemployment rate	3.5	3.8	5.2	4.7	2.4	3.2
233	Females 15 years and over	2,560	2,135	3,015	2,905	2,145	2,000
234	In the labour force	1,780	1,255	1,980	1,990	1,615	1,430
235	Employed	1,650	1,200	1,840	1,900	1,520	1,355
236	Unemployed	125	55	140	90	95	75
237	Not in the labour force	780	880	1,035	910	535	575
238	Participation rate	69.5	58.8	65.7	68.5	75.3	71.5
239	Employment rate	64.5	56.2	61.0	65.4	70.9	67.8
240	Unemployment rate	7.0	4.4	7.1	4.5	5.9	5.2

Tableau 1. Certaines caractéristiques des secteurs de recensement, recensement de 2001 – Données intégrales et données-échantillon (20 %)

Toronto 0562.05	Toronto 0562.06	Toronto 0562.07	Toronto 0562.08	Toronto 0562.09	Toronto 0562.10	Caractéristiques	N°
						CARACTÉRISTIQUES DE LA POPULATION	
5,255	**3,130**	**4,770**	**4,360**	**4,125**	**7,550**	**Population totale de 5 ans et plus (30)**	185
						selon le lieu de résidence 5 ans auparavant (mobilité)	
2,725	1,885	2,830	2,820	2,590	5,010	Personnes n'ayant pas déménagé	186
2,525	1,245	1,940	1,540	1,535	2,545	Personnes ayant déménagé	187
1,235	615	1,170	795	825	1,620	Non-migrants	188
1,290	635	770	745	710	920	Migrants	189
960	515	545	630	645	770	Migrants internes	190
830	500	430	525	545	725	Migrants infraprovinciaux	191
135	20	115	105	95	35	Migrants interprovinciaux	192
325	115	220	115	65	160	Migrants externes	193
670	**580**	**775**	**700**	**670**	**1,400**	**Population totale de 15 à 24 ans**	194
						selon la fréquentation scolaire	
290	110	235	265	280	455	Ne fréquentant pas l'école	195
340	440	500	390	355	850	Fréquentant l'école à plein temps	196
40	25	35	40	30	95	Fréquentant l'école à temps partiel	197
4,560	**2,685**	**3,970**	**3,610**	**3,390**	**6,205**	**Population totale de 15 ans et plus**	198
						selon le plus haut niveau de scolarité atteint	
190	145	250	145	210	390	Niveau inférieur à la 9e année (31)	199
1,105	350	715	950	860	1,330	De la 9e à la 13e année sans certificat d'études secondaires	200
780	485	750	745	595	1,010	De la 9e à la 13e année avec certificat d'études secondaires	201
580	440	490	415	375	685	Études postsecondaires partielles sans grade, certificat ou diplôme (32)	202
390	260	500	430	330	520	Certificat ou diplôme d'une école de métiers (33)	203
775	470	580	520	705	1,040	Certificat ou diplôme collégial (34)	204
75	70	70	45	70	150	Certificat universitaire inférieur au baccalauréat	205
665	465	620	365	250	1,085	Études universitaires avec baccalauréat ou diplôme supérieur	206
						selon les combinaisons de travail non rémunéré	
2,200	1,325	2,010	1,810	1,655	3,110	Hommes de 15 ans et plus	207
1,855	1,105	1,820	1,650	1,405	2,675	Travail non rémunéré déclaré (35)	208
150	120	175	90	100	400	Travaux ménagers et soins aux enfants et soins ou aide aux personnes âgées	209
545	350	655	595	410	750	Travaux ménagers et soins aux enfants seulement	210
90	75	85	95	120	105	Travaux ménagers et soins ou aide aux personnes âgées seulement	211
-	25	-	-	-	-	Soins aux enfants et soins ou aide aux personnes âgées seulement	212
1,045	530	890	835	755	1,365	Travaux ménagers seulement	213
15	10	10	30	10	45	Soins aux enfants seulement	214
10	-	10	-	-	15	Soins ou aide aux personnes âgées seulement	215
2,355	1,355	1,960	1,805	1,735	3,090	Femmes de 15 ans et plus	216
2,145	1,190	1,805	1,705	1,560	2,805	Travail non rémunéré déclaré (35)	217
185	220	200	145	165	405	Travaux ménagers et soins aux enfants et soins ou aide aux personnes âgées	218
725	440	720	665	525	1,030	Travaux ménagers et soins aux enfants seulement	219
175	65	105	105	160	200	Travaux ménagers et soins ou aide aux personnes âgées seulement	220
-	-	-	-	-	-	Soins aux enfants et soins ou aide aux personnes âgées seulement	221
1,040	465	740	770	700	1,155	Travaux ménagers seulement	222
10	-	30	10	-	-	Soins aux enfants seulement	223
15	10	15	-	10	10	Soins ou aide aux personnes âgées seulement	224
						selon l'activité	
2,200	1,325	2,010	1,810	1,655	3,110	Hommes de 15 ans et plus	225
1,770	1,075	1,660	1,475	1,360	2,515	Population active	226
1,705	1,005	1,560	1,430	1,300	2,435	Personnes occupées	227
65	75	105	40	60	85	Chômeurs	228
430	250	350	330	295	590	Inactifs	229
80.5	81.1	82.6	81.5	82.2	80.9	Taux d'activité	230
77.5	75.8	77.6	79.0	78.5	78.3	Taux d'emploi	231
3.7	7.0	6.3	2.7	4.4	3.4	Taux de chômage	232
2,355	1,355	1,960	1,805	1,735	3,090	Femmes de 15 ans et plus	233
1,565	1,005	1,415	1,415	1,285	2,305	Population active	234
1,505	925	1,285	1,355	1,210	2,210	Personnes occupées	235
60	75	130	55	75	95	Chômeuses	236
790	350	550	390	450	785	Inactives	237
66.5	74.2	72.2	78.4	74.1	74.6	Taux d'activité	238
63.9	68.3	65.6	75.1	69.7	71.5	Taux d'emploi	239
3.8	7.5	9.2	3.9	5.8	4.1	Taux de chômage	240

Table 1. Selected Characteristics for Census Tracts, 2001 Census – 100% Data and 20% Sample Data

No.	Characteristics	Toronto 0560 A	Toronto 0561 A	Toronto 0562.01 ◆ A	Toronto 0562.02	Toronto 0562.03	Toronto 0562.04 ◇
	POPULATION CHARACTERISTICS						
	by labour force activity – concluded						
241	Both sexes - Participation rate	73.9	66.6	71.8	75.9	78.2	75.5
242	15-24 years	69.2	71.4	67.7	69.3	66.3	68.2
243	25 years and over	74.9	65.7	72.6	77.6	81.4	77.1
244	Both sexes - Employment rate	70.1	63.9	67.4	72.5	74.9	72.5
245	15-24 years	65.7	64.3	62.2	59.0	62.0	60.3
246	25 years and over	70.9	63.8	68.5	75.9	78.7	75.4
247	Both sexes - Unemployment rate	5.1	3.9	5.9	4.5	4.0	4.2
248	15-24 years	5.9	9.9	8.1	14.2	6.5	13.1
249	25 years and over	5.1	2.7	5.7	2.1	3.4	2.2
250	**Total labour force 15 years and over**	**3,805**	**2,820**	**4,290**	**4,335**	**3,275**	**3,000**
	by industry based on the 1997 NAICS						
251	Industry - Not applicable (36)	30	15	60	20	35	20
252	All industries (37)	3,775	2,810	4,240	4,310	3,240	2,980
253	11 Agriculture, forestry, fishing and hunting	-	-	15	15	10	-
254	21 Mining and oil and gas extraction	-	-	-	-	-	-
255	22 Utilities	10	-	10	-	-	25
256	23 Construction	185	130	110	155	225	100
257	31-33 Manufacturing	905	825	980	875	710	620
258	41 Wholesale trade	380	245	405	300	265	230
259	44-45 Retail trade	405	355	565	690	415	390
260	48-49 Transportation and warehousing	400	315	455	415	405	310
261	51 Information and cultural industries	40	60	120	180	45	75
262	52 Finance and insurance	120	50	200	235	115	130
263	53 Real estate and rental and leasing	75	45	80	125	65	55
264	54 Professional, scientific and technical services	150	130	220	265	170	190
265	55 Management of companies and enterprises	-	10	-	15	25	-
266	56 Administrative and support, waste management and remediation services	210	110	225	110	140	145
267	61 Educational services	145	110	145	235	125	150
268	62 Health care and social assistance	235	120	250	230	200	230
269	71 Arts, entertainment and recreation	70	40	20	60	60	40
270	72 Accommodation and food services	145	120	205	195	115	105
271	81 Other services (except public administration)	200	65	165	95	65	75
272	91 Public administration	110	70	95	120	80	100
	by class of worker						
273	Class of worker - Not applicable (36)	25	10	55	25	30	20
274	All classes of worker (37)	3,780	2,805	4,235	4,310	3,240	2,980
275	Paid workers	3,580	2,665	4,040	4,115	3,065	2,840
276	Employees	3,510	2,625	3,975	3,930	2,980	2,730
277	Self-employed (incorporated)	70	45	65	180	85	105
278	Self-employed (unincorporated)	185	140	185	195	175	145
279	Unpaid family workers	10	-	10	-	-	-
	by occupation based on the 2001 NOC-S						
280	Male labour force 15 years and over	2,025	1,565	2,315	2,345	1,655	1,575
281	Occupation - Not applicable (36)	10	15	15	15	15	15
282	All occupations (37)	2,015	1,555	2,300	2,330	1,645	1,555
283	A Management occupations	180	205	235	415	225	220
284	B Business, finance and administration occupations	235	150	350	245	170	190
285	C Natural and applied sciences and related occupations	115	110	250	185	215	135
286	D Health occupations	-	-	10	35	10	15
287	E Occupations in social science, education, government service and religion	45	50	60	60	20	30
288	F Occupations in art, culture, recreation and sport	50	20	10	55	40	35
289	G Sales and service occupations	350	220	290	530	210	235
290	H Trades, transport and equipment operators and related occupations	755	485	735	560	535	480
291	I Occupations unique to primary industry	15	30	20	20	25	30
292	J Occupations unique to processing, manufacturing and utilities	255	280	340	220	200	185
293	Female labour force 15 years and over	1,780	1,255	1,980	1,990	1,615	1,430
294	Occupation - Not applicable (36)	15	-	40	10	15	10
295	All occupations (37)	1,765	1,250	1,940	1,985	1,600	1,425
296	A Management occupations	100	50	180	155	70	100
297	B Business, finance and administration occupations	700	500	590	700	610	500
298	C Natural and applied sciences and related occupations	65	40	55	55	35	30
299	D Health occupations	60	30	80	95	85	130

Tableau 1. Certaines caractéristiques des secteurs de recensement, recensement de 2001 – Données intégrales et données-échantillon (20 %)

Toronto 0562.05	Toronto 0562.06	Toronto 0562.07	Toronto 0562.08	Toronto 0562.09	Toronto 0562.10	Caractéristiques	Nº
						CARACTÉRISTIQUES DE LA POPULATION	
						selon l'activité – fin	
73.2	77.6	77.5	79.9	78.0	77.7	Les deux sexes - Taux d'activité	241
68.4	64.3	70.3	66.4	70.9	66.2	15-24 ans	242
74.2	81.4	79.1	83.2	79.6	81.1	25 ans et plus	243
70.4	72.0	71.6	77.2	74.0	74.9	Les deux sexes - Taux d'emploi	244
61.2	53.4	58.7	61.4	64.2	60.7	15-24 ans	245
72.0	77.4	74.8	81.1	76.5	79.1	25 ans et plus	246
3.7	7.2	7.5	3.5	4.9	3.7	Les deux sexes - Taux de chômage	247
8.8	16.2	17.4	8.6	9.5	8.1	15-24 ans	248
2.9	5.0	5.5	2.3	4.1	2.7	25 ans et plus	249
3,340	**2,085**	**3,080**	**2,890**	**2,640**	**4,820**	**Population active totale de 15 ans et plus**	250
						selon l'industrie basée sur le SCIAN de 1997	
25	20	45	-	30	15	Industrie - Sans objet (36)	251
3,310	2,065	3,030	2,885	2,610	4,805	Toutes les industries (37)	252
-	10	10	-	-	30	11 Agriculture, foresterie, pêche et chasse	253
30	10	-	-	10	-	21 Extraction minière et extraction de pétrole et de gaz	254
20	10	25	-	10	20	22 Services publics	255
130	130	210	205	185	175	23 Construction	256
760	390	825	585	565	1,010	31-33 Fabrication	257
295	205	230	165	195	425	41 Commerce de gros	258
385	260	280	400	310	640	44-45 Commerce de détail	259
310	185	395	400	185	445	48-49 Transport et entreposage	260
50	70	60	45	45	115	51 Industrie de l'information et industrie culturelle	261
135	75	105	80	60	210	52 Finance et assurances	262
75	40	15	40	35	100	53 Services immobiliers et services de location et de location à bail	263
230	135	175	145	165	325	54 Services professionnels, scientifiques et techniques	264
-	-	10	-	-	10	55 Gestion de sociétés et d'entreprises	265
165	70	75	145	160	205	56 Services administratifs, services de soutien, services de gestion des déchets et services d'assainissement	266
105	170	125	145	130	255	61 Services d'enseignement	267
180	125	125	165	140	230	62 Soins de santé et assistance sociale	268
70	20	45	70	45	35	71 Arts, spectacles et loisirs	269
170	65	130	120	120	220	72 Hébergement et services de restauration	270
70	50	90	80	105	140	81 Autres services, sauf les administrations publiques	271
115	60	120	100	140	230	91 Administrations publiques	272
						selon la catégorie de travailleurs	
25	15	45	-	30	15	Catégorie de travailleurs - Sans objet (36)	273
3,315	2,065	3,030	2,890	2,615	4,805	Toutes les catégories de travailleurs (37)	274
3,140	1,940	2,915	2,735	2,475	4,645	Travailleurs rémunérés	275
3,050	1,815	2,815	2,685	2,415	4,505	Employés	276
90	120	100	50	55	140	Travailleurs autonomes (entreprise constituée en société)	277
180	130	105	155	125	150	Travailleurs autonomes (entreprise non constituée en société)	278
-	-	10	-	15	15	Travailleurs familiaux non rémunérés	279
						selon la profession basée sur la CNP-S de 2001	
1,770	1,075	1,665	1,475	1,360	2,515	Hommes actifs de 15 ans et plus	280
10	10	15	-	10	10	Profession - Sans objet (36)	281
1,760	1,065	1,650	1,480	1,350	2,515	Toutes les professions (37)	282
235	215	200	85	185	375	A Gestion	283
225	135	175	275	215	365	B Affaires, finance et administration	284
205	100	175	125	70	230	C Sciences naturelles et appliquées et professions apparentées	285
25	-	15	-	10	10	D Secteur de la santé	286
15	25	35	30	15	90	E Sciences sociales, enseignement, administration publique et religion	287
20	35	20	20	25	25	F Arts, culture, sports et loisirs	288
275	195	220	215	180	490	G Ventes et services	289
445	255	645	560	425	620	H Métiers, transport et machinerie	290
20	10	10	30	55	55	I Professions propres au secteur primaire	291
295	100	155	135	165	255	J Transformation, fabrication et services d'utilité publique	292
1,565	1,005	1,415	1,415	1,285	2,305	Femmes actives de 15 ans et plus	293
10	10	30	-	20	10	Profession - Sans objet (36)	294
1,555	1,000	1,385	1,410	1,260	2,295	Toutes les professions (37)	295
130	90	75	80	85	210	A Gestion	296
600	315	585	565	460	855	B Affaires, finance et administration	297
45	45	40	20	50	95	C Sciences naturelles et appliquées et professions apparentées	298
60	30	35	65	45	120	D Secteur de la santé	299

Table 1. Selected Characteristics for Census Tracts, 2001 Census – 100% Data and 20% Sample Data

No.	Characteristics	Toronto 0560 A	Toronto 0561 A	Toronto 0562.01 ◆ A	Toronto 0562.02	Toronto 0562.03	Toronto 0562.04 ◇
	POPULATION CHARACTERISTICS						
	by occupation based on the 2001 NOC-S – concluded						
300	E Occupations in social science, education, government service and religion	160	70	135	215	95	125
301	F Occupations in art, culture, recreation and sport	30	15	50	55	50	65
302	G Sales and service occupations	390	285	575	480	335	305
303	H Trades, transport and equipment operators and related occupations	85	40	90	70	130	90
304	I Occupations unique to primary industry	10	10	-	-	-	-
305	J Occupations unique to processing, manufacturing and utilities	170	225	190	155	195	75
306	**Total employed labour force 15 years and over**	**3,610**	**2,710**	**4,035**	**4,135**	**3,145**	**2,880**
	by place of work						
307	Males	1,955	1,510	2,200	2,240	1,620	1,525
308	Usual place of work	1,635	1,300	1,945	1,925	1,350	1,250
309	At home	65	60	65	90	65	110
310	Outside Canada	15	10	15	-	15	15
311	No fixed workplace address	240	145	165	220	190	145
312	Females	1,650	1,200	1,840	1,900	1,520	1,355
313	Usual place of work	1,480	1,095	1,755	1,755	1,405	1,270
314	At home	75	75	25	75	75	80
315	Outside Canada	15	-	-	10	10	-
316	No fixed workplace address	90	25	55	65	30	-
317	**Total employed labour force 15 years and over with usual place of work or no fixed workplace address**	**3,440**	**2,560**	**3,920**	**3,965**	**2,975**	**2,670**
	by mode of transportation						
318	Males	1,875	1,440	2,110	2,150	1,540	1,400
319	Car, truck, van, as driver	1,560	1,230	1,565	1,835	1,275	1,230
320	Car, truck, van, as passenger	115	55	140	120	110	60
321	Public transit	135	95	310	145	130	55
322	Walked	40	55	40	35	10	20
323	Other method	15	-	60	10	20	30
324	Females	1,565	1,120	1,810	1,820	1,435	1,275
325	Car, truck, van, as driver	1,150	800	1,055	1,415	1,045	985
326	Car, truck, van, as passenger	150	150	195	235	130	115
327	Public transit	140	95	425	110	215	140
328	Walked	110	35	95	40	45	35
329	Other method	20	35	50	15	10	-
330	**Total population 15 years and over who worked since January 1, 2000**	**4,015**	**3,070**	**4,535**	**4,735**	**3,500**	**3,220**
	by language used at work						
331	Single responses	3,790	2,850	4,240	4,435	3,270	3,010
332	English	3,775	2,795	4,225	4,370	3,240	3,005
333	French	-	-	-	25	-	10
334	Non-official languages (5)	10	55	15	45	35	10
335	Chinese, n.o.s.	-	-	-	-	-	-
336	Cantonese	-	-	-	-	-	-
337	Other languages (6)	-	55	15	40	35	-
338	Multiple responses	225	215	290	295	230	205
339	English and French	80	35	70	55	65	90
340	English and non-official language	140	180	215	235	160	105
341	French and non-official language	-	-	-	-	-	-
342	English, French and non-official language	-	10	10	10	10	10
	DWELLING AND HOUSEHOLD CHARACTERISTICS						
343	**Total number of occupied private dwellings**	**2,105**	**1,700**	**2,910**	**2,045**	**1,565**	**1,390**
	by tenure						
344	Owned	1,605	1,295	920	1,885	1,250	1,205
345	Rented	505	395	1,990	165	315	185
346	Band housing	-	-	-	-	-	-
	by structural type of dwelling						
347	Single-detached house	795	715	90	1,480	455	1,255
348	Semi-detached house	600	665	-	205	370	65
349	Row house	335	85	275	50	710	35
350	Apartment, detached duplex	-	10	-	15	15	-
351	Apartment, building that has five or more storeys	355	-	2,535	290	-	-
352	Apartment, building that has fewer than five storeys (38)	25	220	10	-	20	45
353	Other single-attached house	-	-	-	-	-	-
354	Movable dwelling (39)	-	-	-	-	-	-

Tableau 1. Certaines caractéristiques des secteurs de recensement, recensement de 2001 – Données intégrales et données-échantillon (20 %)

Toronto 0562.05	Toronto 0562.06	Toronto 0562.07	Toronto 0562.08	Toronto 0562.09	Toronto 0562.10	Caractéristiques	N°
						CARACTÉRISTIQUES DE LA POPULATION	
						selon la profession basée sur la CNP-S de 2001 - fin	
145	155	120	135	140	180	E Sciences sociales, enseignement, administration publique et religion	300
70	35	10	10	15	25	F Arts, culture, sports et loisirs	301
350	245	275	385	375	515	G Ventes et services	302
40	20	110	80	40	90	H Métiers, transport et machinerie	303
10	-	10	-	-	30	I Professions propres au secteur primaire	304
120	55	130	80	50	175	J Transformation, fabrication et services d'utilité publique	305
3,210	**1,935**	**2,845**	**2,790**	**2,510**	**4,645**	**Population active occupée totale de 15 ans et plus selon le lieu de travail**	306
1,705	1,005	1,555	1,435	1,300	2,430	Hommes	307
1,510	850	1,315	1,125	1,125	2,160	Lieu habituel de travail	308
55	40	60	90	45	85	À domicile	309
10	-	-	20	-	-	En dehors du Canada	310
125	115	180	195	130	195	Sans adresse de travail fixe	311
1,505	925	1,285	1,355	1,210	2,210	Femmes	312
1,440	855	1,135	1,235	1,105	2,065	Lieu habituel de travail	313
55	45	95	90	50	70	À domicile	314
10	-	-	-	-	-	En dehors du Canada	315
-	30	45	30	50	75	Sans adresse de travail fixe	316
3,090	**1,845**	**2,680**	**2,590**	**2,415**	**4,490**	**Population active occupée totale de 15 ans et plus ayant un lieu habituel de travail ou sans adresse de travail fixe selon le mode de transport**	317
1,640	960	1,495	1,320	1,255	2,350	Hommes	318
1,395	860	1,255	1,125	1,070	2,090	Automobile, camion ou fourgonnette, en tant que conducteur	319
90	50	105	75	100	120	Automobile, camion ou fourgonnette, en tant que passager	320
140	40	95	70	65	70	Transport en commun	321
-	-	10	25	10	50	À pied	322
15	15	40	20	20	25	Autre moyen	323
1,445	885	1,185	1,265	1,155	2,140	Femmes	324
975	700	890	870	855	1,615	Automobile, camion ou fourgonnette, en tant que conductrice	325
145	65	115	160	75	260	Automobile, camion ou fourgonnette, en tant que passagère	326
225	60	140	180	175	185	Transport en commun	327
95	10	10	35	15	50	À pied	328
10	55	30	25	40	30	Autre moyen	329
3,540	**2,230**	**3,320**	**3,080**	**2,810**	**5,270**	**Population totale de 15 ans et plus ayant travaillé depuis le 1er janvier 2000 selon la langue utilisée au travail**	330
3,370	2,055	3,030	2,865	2,670	4,835	Réponses uniques	331
3,350	2,035	2,990	2,830	2,645	4,810	Anglais	332
-	-	10	-	-	-	Français	333
15	20	35	25	25	20	Langues non officielles (5)	334
10	-	-	-	-	-	Chinois, n.d.a.	335
-	-	-	-	-	-	Cantonais	336
10	25	35	30	25	20	Autres langues (6)	337
170	175	295	220	145	435	Réponses multiples	338
75	40	30	125	40	125	Anglais et français	339
100	125	260	90	100	300	Anglais et langue non officielle	340
-	-	-	-	-	-	Français et langue non officielle	341
-	10	-	-	-	10	Anglais, français et langue non officielle	342
						CARACTÉRISTIQUES DES LOGEMENTS ET DES MÉNAGES	
2,165	**925**	**1,385**	**1,395**	**1,265**	**2,110**	**Nombre total de logements privés occupés selon le mode d'occupation**	343
1,395	870	1,180	1,255	1,185	1,860	Possédé	344
770	60	205	145	85	250	Loué	345
-	-	-	-	-	-	Logement de bande	346
						selon le type de construction résidentielle	
580	740	770	675	630	1,845	Maison individuelle non attenante	347
15	-	330	265	385	-	Maison jumelée	348
350	155	85	360	190	-	Maison en rangée	349
-	35	15	55	10	140	Appartement, duplex non attenant	350
1,220	-	-	-	-	-	Appartement, immeuble de cinq étages ou plus	351
-	-	190	30	55	125	Appartement, immeuble de moins de cinq étages (38)	352
-	-	-	-	-	-	Autre maison individuelle attenante	353
-	-	-	-	-	-	Logement mobile (39)	354

Table 1. Selected Characteristics for Census Tracts, 2001 Census – 100% Data and 20% Sample Data

No.	Characteristics	Toronto 0560 A	Toronto 0561 A	Toronto 0562.01 ◆ A	Toronto 0562.02	Toronto 0562.03	Toronto 0562.04 ◇
	DWELLING AND HOUSEHOLD CHARACTERISTICS						
	by condition of dwelling						
355	Regular maintenance only	1,420	1,100	2,290	1,650	1,080	890
356	Minor repairs	560	525	520	340	425	450
357	Major repairs	125	75	100	55	55	50
	by period of construction						
358	Before 1946	10	20	10	10	-	-
359	1946-1960	95	370	15	10	15	-
360	1961-1970	1,310	1,160	155	110	140	85
361	1971-1980	600	120	1,360	615	1,050	985
362	1981-1990	100	25	1,305	1,150	320	310
363	1991-2001 (20)	-	10	65	160	40	-
364	Average number of rooms per dwelling	6.8	6.6	5.1	7.8	7.1	7.6
365	Average number of bedrooms per dwelling	3.1	3.0	2.1	3.4	3.3	3.5
366	Average value of dwelling $	187,600	189,170	141,038	245,940	189,591	211,121
367	**Total number of private households**	**2,105**	**1,695**	**2,905**	**2,045**	**1,565**	**1,390**
	by household size						
368	1 person	280	215	705	220	100	80
369	2 persons	605	520	985	465	330	300
370	3 persons	440	350	565	400	310	320
371	4-5 persons	625	490	550	775	650	545
372	6 or more persons	155	125	105	185	165	150
	by household type						
373	One-family households	1,555	1,310	1,865	1,640	1,315	1,190
374	Multiple-family households	160	120	125	140	100	105
375	Non-family households	385	265	920	260	150	95
376	Number of persons in private households	6,485	5,290	7,360	6,925	5,565	4,980
377	Average number of persons in private households	3.1	3.1	2.5	3.4	3.6	3.6
378	Average number of persons per room	0.5	0.5	0.5	0.4	0.5	0.5
379	Tenant households in non-farm, non-reserve private dwellings (40)	505	390	1,980	160	310	185
380	Average gross rent $ (40)	944	921	1,073	1,004	1,096	1,148
381	Tenant households spending 30% or more of household income on gross rent (40) (41)	190	95	790	40	90	70
382	Tenant households spending from 30% to 99% of household income on gross rent (40) (41)	175	55	660	25	65	65
383	Owner households in non-farm, non-reserve private dwellings (42)	1,605	1,300	915	1,885	1,250	1,205
384	Average owner's major payments $ (42)	1,038	875	1,102	1,169	1,215	1,182
385	Owner households spending 30% or more of household income on owner's major payments (41) (42)	375	170	315	195	300	225
386	Owner households spending from 30% to 99% of household income on owner's major payments (41) (42)	305	135	295	180	285	210
	CENSUS FAMILY CHARACTERISTICS						
387	**Total number of census families in private households**	**1,890**	**1,565**	**2,105**	**1,930**	**1,520**	**1,415**
	by census family structure and size						
388	Total couple families	1,550	1,315	1,650	1,705	1,230	1,225
389	Total families of married couples	1,365	1,185	1,335	1,585	1,120	1,150
390	Without children at home	450	425	575	435	270	325
391	With children at home	910	755	755	1,155	845	820
392	1 child	380	305	340	360	270	290
393	2 children	355	320	320	490	370	360
394	3 or more children	175	130	100	305	200	175
395	Total families of common-law couples	185	135	310	120	110	75
396	Without children at home	100	75	190	60	45	50
397	With children at home	85	60	120	60	70	25
398	1 child	35	30	75	40	10	20
399	2 children	40	10	35	20	45	10
400	3 or more children	15	25	-	-	20	-
401	Total lone-parent families	345	250	460	225	290	195
402	Female parent	295	190	380	190	260	135
403	1 child	165	110	240	90	90	50
404	2 children	95	55	110	70	90	70
405	3 or more children	35	20	30	35	75	20

Tableau 1. Certaines caractéristiques des secteurs de recensement, recensement de 2001 – Données intégrales et données-échantillon (20 %)

Toronto 0562.05	Toronto 0562.06	Toronto 0562.07	Toronto 0562.08	Toronto 0562.09	Toronto 0562.10	Caractéristiques	N°
						CARACTÉRISTIQUES DES LOGEMENTS ET DES MÉNAGES	
						selon l'état du logement	
1,745	655	950	920	840	1,545	Entretien régulier seulement	355
345	240	375	415	350	545	Réparations mineures	356
85	35	55	65	80	20	Réparations majeures	357
						selon la période de construction	
-	-	-	-	-	10	Avant 1946	358
20	-	-	15	35	-	1946-1960	359
115	-	145	170	210	10	1961-1970	360
605	225	830	1,040	890	150	1971-1980	361
1,305	490	380	155	120	1,690	1981-1990	362
120	210	25	15	10	250	1991-2001 (20)	363
5.6	8.1	7.3	6.7	7.3	7.9	Nombre moyen de pièces par logement	364
2.3	3.6	3.4	3.1	3.3	3.6	Nombre moyen de chambres à coucher par logement	365
152,087	267,166	201,818	167,909	191,657	247,102	Valeur moyenne du logement $	366
2,165	**925**	**1,385**	**1,395**	**1,265**	**2,110**	**Nombre total de logements privés**	367
						selon la taille du ménage	
505	50	95	130	80	90	1 personne	368
725	195	265	300	315	360	2 personnes	369
405	190	270	290	275	400	3 personnes	370
455	420	585	590	505	1,025	4-5 personnes	371
75	70	165	85	100	245	6 personnes ou plus	372
						selon le genre de ménage	
1,430	775	1,150	1,170	1,095	1,795	Ménages unifamiliaux	373
85	85	115	85	80	190	Ménages multifamiliaux	374
655	70	120	145	95	125	Ménages non familiaux	375
5,635	3,315	5,110	4,670	4,320	7,975	Nombre de personnes dans les ménages privés	376
2.6	3.6	3.7	3.3	3.4	3.8	Nombre moyen de personnes dans les ménages privés	377
0.5	0.4	0.5	0.5	0.5	0.5	Nombre moyen de personnes par pièce	378
765	60	205	145	85	250	Ménages locataires dans les logements privés non agricoles hors réserve (40)	379
1,009	1,298	848	1,038	1,050	883	Loyer brut moyen $ (40)	380
290	15	90	45	25	85	Ménages locataires consacrant 30 % ou plus du revenu du ménage au loyer brut (40) (41)	381
245	10	65	30	25	70	Ménages locataires consacrant de 30 % à 99 % du revenu du ménage au loyer brut (40) (41)	382
1,395	865	1,175	1,255	1,185	1,860	Ménages propriétaires dans les logements privés non agricoles hors réserve (42)	383
1,059	1,187	1,236	1,045	1,083	1,380	Principales dépenses de propriété moyennes $ (42)	384
355	185	255	205	210	330	Ménages propriétaires consacrant 30 % ou plus du revenu du ménage aux principales dépenses de propriété (41) (42)	385
290	155	240	190	200	310	Ménages propriétaires consacrant de 30 % à 99 % du revenu du ménage aux principales dépenses de propriété (41) (42)	386
						CARACTÉRISTIQUES DES FAMILLES DE RECENSEMENT	
1,600	**940**	**1,410**	**1,335**	**1,250**	**2,185**	**Total des familles de recensement dans les ménages privés**	387
						selon la structure et la taille de la famille de recensement	
1,315	875	1,205	1,090	1,060	1,925	Total des familles avec conjoints	388
1,135	825	1,115	965	945	1,835	Total des familles avec couples mariés	389
480	205	285	235	285	385	Sans enfants à la maison	390
650	615	820	730	660	1,450	Avec enfants à la maison	391
305	195	280	235	205	400	1 enfant	392
235	310	365	375	305	665	2 enfants	393
115	115	175	115	155	385	3 enfants ou plus	394
185	50	90	120	115	90	Total des familles en union libre	395
115	15	45	30	60	35	Sans enfants à la maison	396
70	35	45	95	55	60	Avec enfants à la maison	397
40	15	15	35	10	35	1 enfant	398
30	10	15	40	30	15	2 enfants	399
-	20	15	10	10	10	3 enfants ou plus	400
285	65	205	250	195	265	Total des familles monoparentales	401
225	65	160	175	155	190	Parent de sexe féminin	402
125	50	70	85	70	85	1 enfant	403
75	10	55	70	65	70	2 enfants	404
25	-	30	20	15	35	3 enfants ou plus	405

Table 1. Selected Characteristics for Census Tracts, 2001 Census – 100% Data and 20% Sample Data

No.	Characteristics	Toronto 0560 A	Toronto 0561 A	Toronto 0562.01 ◆ A	Toronto 0562.02	Toronto 0562.03	Toronto 0562.04 ◇
	CENSUS FAMILY CHARACTERISTICS						
	by census family structure and size - concluded						
406	Male parent	50	60	75	30	35	55
407	1 child	25	40	65	25	10	30
408	2 children	20	15	10	-	15	15
409	3 or more children	-	-	-	-	10	10
410	**Total number of children at home**	**2,340**	**1,865**	**2,115**	**2,800**	**2,410**	**1,985**
	by age groups						
411	Under 6 years	515	465	625	420	495	365
412	6-14 years	825	585	735	800	865	610
413	15-17 years	225	190	215	360	295	195
414	18-24 years	450	325	300	810	505	510
415	25 years and over	325	300	245	415	255	295
416	Average number of children at home per census family (43)	1.2	1.2	1.0	1.5	1.6	1.4
417	**Total number of persons in private households**	**6,480**	**5,285**	**7,365**	**6,930**	**5,565**	**4,980**
	by census family status and living arrangements						
418	Number of non-family persons	705	535	1,495	500	400	350
419	Living with relatives (44)	175	160	315	190	145	180
420	Living with non-relatives only	255	165	475	85	155	90
421	Living alone	280	210	705	225	105	80
422	Number of family persons	5,775	4,750	5,865	6,430	5,160	4,630
423	Average number of persons per census family	3.1	3.0	2.8	3.3	3.4	3.3
424	**Total number of persons 65 years and over**	**565**	**745**	**680**	**520**	**230**	**295**
425	Number of non-family persons 65 years and over	75	195	250	125	90	115
426	Living with relatives (44)	35	60	30	80	70	95
427	Living with non-relatives only	-	-	30	-	-	10
428	Living alone	35	125	195	45	15	15
429	Number of family persons 65 years and over	485	555	430	390	140	180
	ECONOMIC FAMILY CHARACTERISTICS						
430	**Total number of economic families in private households**	**1,755**	**1,460**	**2,050**	**1,795**	**1,425**	**1,305**
	by size of family						
431	2 persons	580	515	905	455	330	300
432	3 persons	460	370	510	400	315	320
433	4 persons	390	315	380	515	415	375
434	5 or more persons	335	260	250	435	370	310
435	Total number of persons in economic families	5,955	4,910	6,185	6,620	5,305	4,805
436	Average number of persons per economic family	3.4	3.4	3.0	3.7	3.7	3.7
437	Total number of unattached individuals	535	375	1,175	310	260	170
	2000 INCOME CHARACTERISTICS						
	Population 15 years and over by sex and total income groups in 2000						
438	Total - Both sexes	5,145	4,235	5,985	5,715	4,190	3,975
439	Without income	230	215	385	150	295	250
440	With income	4,915	4,020	5,595	5,565	3,900	3,725
441	Under $1,000 (45)	210	220	190	225	145	180
442	$ 1,000 - $ 2,999	190	220	250	205	195	155
443	$ 3,000 - $ 4,999	200	170	140	185	60	150
444	$ 5,000 - $ 6,999	225	160	205	235	155	125
445	$ 7,000 - $ 9,999	300	175	285	235	225	195
446	$10,000 - $11,999	210	170	225	170	145	155
447	$12,000 - $14,999	210	210	290	285	140	125
448	$15,000 - $19,999	390	370	545	335	335	295
449	$20,000 - $24,999	380	275	445	415	245	200
450	$25,000 - $29,999	415	370	590	285	315	265
451	$30,000 - $34,999	520	320	645	485	410	380
452	$35,000 - $39,999	430	300	355	450	345	320
453	$40,000 - $44,999	295	300	320	260	285	295
454	$45,000 - $49,999	205	150	315	295	190	180
455	$50,000 - $59,999	295	215	420	450	265	290
456	$60,000 and over	435	400	380	1,050	440	415
457	Average income $ (46)	28,824	27,909	28,667	58,071	32,905	31,273
458	Median income $ (46)	26,191	25,635	26,449	31,014	29,370	29,980
459	Standard error of average income $ (46)	654	690	600	12,615	1,042	856

Tableau 1. Certaines caractéristiques des secteurs de recensement, recensement de 2001 – Données intégrales et données-échantillon (20 %)

Toronto 0562.05	Toronto 0562.06	Toronto 0562.07	Toronto 0562.08	Toronto 0562.09	Toronto 0562.10	Caractéristiques	N°
						CARACTÉRISTIQUES DES FAMILLES DE RECENSEMENT	
						selon la structure et la taille de la famille de recensement - fin	
65	-	45	70	40	70	Parent de sexe masculin	406
40	10	30	55	10	45	1 enfant	407
20	-	15	-	15	20	2 enfants	408
-	-	-	15	15	10	3 enfants ou plus	409
1,690	**1,335**	**2,065**	**1,925**	**1,760**	**3,480**	**Nombre total d'enfants à la maison**	410
						selon les groupes d'âge	
445	210	385	415	270	535	Moins de 6 ans	411
625	420	705	640	655	1,235	6-14 ans	412
160	225	170	225	165	410	15-17 ans	413
325	325	510	395	415	910	18-24 ans	414
140	160	290	245	260	390	25 ans et plus	415
1.1	1.4	1.5	1.4	1.4	1.6	Nombre moyen d'enfants à la maison par famille de recensement (43)	416
5,640	**3,315**	**5,110**	**4,670**	**4,320**	**7,975**	**Nombre total de personnes dans les ménages privés**	417
						selon la situation des particuliers dans la famille de recensement et des particuliers dans le ménage	
1,030	170	435	325	245	380	Nombre de personnes hors famille de recensement	418
225	60	180	140	125	170	Vivant avec des personnes apparentées (44)	419
305	55	165	55	40	125	Vivant avec des personnes non apparentées uniquement	420
505	45	90	130	80	90	Vivant seules	421
4,605	3,150	4,680	4,345	4,075	7,595	Nombre de personnes membres d'une famille	422
2.9	3.4	3.3	3.3	3.3	3.5	Nombre moyen de personnes par famille de recensement	423
505	**130**	**290**	**250**	**255**	**330**	**Nombre total de personnes de 65 ans et plus**	424
145	45	95	65	70	95	Nombre de personnes hors famille de recensement de 65 ans et plus	425
40	45	75	20	55	90	Vivant avec des personnes apparentées (44)	426
20	-	-	-	-	-	Vivant avec des personnes non apparentées uniquement	427
85	-	15	45	25	-	Vivant seules	428
360	80	195	185	180	230	Nombre de personnes membres d'une famille de 65 ans et plus	429
						CARACTÉRISTIQUES DES FAMILLES ÉCONOMIQUES	
1,555	**855**	**1,275**	**1,270**	**1,185**	**1,995**	**Nombre total de familles économiques dans les ménages privés**	430
						selon la taille de la famille	
655	175	275	315	315	360	2 personnes	431
390	185	280	280	295	390	3 personnes	432
320	285	395	425	330	660	4 personnes	433
190	205	325	245	255	585	5 personnes ou plus	434
4,830	3,210	4,855	4,480	4,195	7,765	Nombre total de personnes dans les familles économiques	435
3.1	3.8	3.8	3.5	3.5	3.9	Nombre moyen de personnes par famille économique	436
810	105	260	190	120	215	Nombre total de personnes hors famille économique	437
						CARACTÉRISTIQUES DU REVENU DE 2000	
						Population de 15 ans et plus selon le sexe et les tranches de revenu total en 2000	
4,560	2,680	3,970	3,615	3,390	6,200	Total - Les deux sexes	438
185	170	215	240	130	270	Sans revenu	439
4,370	2,510	3,755	3,370	3,255	5,935	Avec un revenu	440
165	60	190	95	145	280	Moins de 1 000 $ (45)	441
205	75	205	125	100	315	1 000 $ - 2 999 $	442
165	115	160	75	115	235	3 000 $ - 4 999 $	443
160	110	215	130	135	240	5 000 $ - 6 999 $	444
165	135	155	150	170	370	7 000 $ - 9 999 $	445
150	90	85	100	80	150	10 000 $ - 11 999 $	446
210	90	195	120	115	280	12 000 $ - 14 999 $	447
355	130	225	240	230	295	15 000 $ - 19 999 $	448
320	185	260	310	275	445	20 000 $ - 24 999 $	449
355	175	240	335	235	365	25 000 $ - 29 999 $	450
335	230	440	360	280	445	30 000 $ - 34 999 $	451
355	230	255	285	300	340	35 000 $ - 39 999 $	452
410	145	305	290	305	400	40 000 $ - 44 999 $	453
300	140	200	180	170	370	45 000 $ - 49 999 $	454
265	170	285	245	305	480	50 000 $ - 59 999 $	455
475	400	335	315	305	920	60 000 $ et plus	456
31,335	36,754	30,075	32,071	31,371	33,995	Revenu moyen $ (46)	457
28,554	30,225	27,969	29,346	30,141	29,754	Revenu médian $ (46)	458
805	1,534	853	836	798	784	Erreur type de revenu moyen $ (46)	459

Table 1. Selected Characteristics for Census Tracts, 2001 Census – 100% Data and 20% Sample Data

No.	Characteristics	Toronto 0560 A	Toronto 0561 A	Toronto 0562.01 ◆ A	Toronto 0562.02	Toronto 0562.03	Toronto 0562.04 ◇
	2000 INCOME CHARACTERISTICS						
	Population 15 years and over by sex and total income groups in 2000 – concluded						
460	Total - Males	2,580	2,100	2,965	2,810	2,040	1,980
461	Without income	100	55	150	55	135	75
462	With income	2,480	2,045	2,815	2,760	1,910	1,900
463	Under $1,000 (45)	100	125	75	90	95	70
464	$ 1,000 - $ 2,999	40	65	70	100	105	60
465	$ 3,000 - $ 4,999	50	70	50	50	15	70
466	$ 5,000 - $ 6,999	85	45	65	25	100	55
467	$ 7,000 - $ 9,999	105	60	95	85	35	65
468	$10,000 - $11,999	110	55	85	75	65	85
469	$12,000 - $14,999	80	50	75	110	35	50
470	$15,000 - $19,999	180	145	165	150	50	125
471	$20,000 - $24,999	170	110	255	165	60	70
472	$25,000 - $29,999	180	160	230	135	120	80
473	$30,000 - $34,999	250	185	390	235	200	175
474	$35,000 - $39,999	215	190	215	175	185	155
475	$40,000 - $44,999	230	200	175	95	160	195
476	$45,000 - $49,999	130	85	210	170	140	120
477	$50,000 - $59,999	210	140	340	335	195	200
478	$60,000 and over	345	345	315	750	360	335
479	Average income $ (46)	34,824	34,151	35,307	83,763	40,079	37,549
480	Median income $ (46)	31,863	33,528	32,108	39,133	36,907	36,866
481	Standard error of average income $ (46)	1,036	1,098	928	25,116	1,659	1,345
482	Total - Females	2,560	2,140	3,015	2,900	2,150	2,000
483	Without income	130	160	235	95	165	175
484	With income	2,435	1,975	2,780	2,805	1,985	1,825
485	Under $1,000 (45)	110	100	120	130	50	110
486	$ 1,000 - $ 2,999	150	155	185	105	95	95
487	$ 3,000 - $ 4,999	150	95	90	135	50	85
488	$ 5,000 - $ 6,999	140	115	145	210	55	70
489	$ 7,000 - $ 9,999	190	110	190	150	190	130
490	$10,000 - $11,999	95	115	135	90	80	75
491	$12,000 - $14,999	135	155	210	175	100	80
492	$15,000 - $19,999	215	230	380	180	280	175
493	$20,000 - $24,999	205	160	185	250	185	130
494	$25,000 - $29,999	235	210	355	145	190	185
495	$30,000 - $34,999	270	130	255	255	215	210
496	$35,000 - $39,999	215	110	140	280	160	155
497	$40,000 - $44,999	65	100	145	165	125	100
498	$45,000 - $49,999	80	65	105	120	55	65
499	$50,000 - $59,999	85	75	80	110	70	90
500	$60,000 and over	95	60	60	300	80	75
501	Average income $ (46)	22,707	21,467	21,938	32,833	26,004	24,725
502	Median income $ (46)	20,345	18,162	18,980	24,218	22,422	23,006
503	Standard error of average income $ (46)	721	738	649	2,497	1,187	933
	by composition of total income						
504	Total - Composition of income in 2000 % (47)	100.0	100.0	100.0	100.0	100.0	100.0
505	Employment income %	82.5	77.3	83.2	86.3	90.3	86.1
506	Government transfer payments %	9.0	11.9	9.4	3.1	5.6	6.8
507	Other %	8.4	10.8	7.4	10.5	4.1	7.2
	Population 15 years and over with employment income in 2000 by sex and work activity						
508	Both sexes with employment income (48)	3,960	2,960	4,395	4,730	3,360	3,130
509	Average employment income $	29,523	29,273	30,339	59,011	34,412	32,051
510	Standard error of average employment income $	737	846	687	14,718	1,131	856
511	Worked full year, full time (49)	2,405	1,765	2,730	2,710	2,160	1,970
512	Average employment income $	38,223	38,137	37,705	87,096	42,804	39,872
513	Standard error of average employment income $	945	1,023	850	25,501	1,433	1,020
514	Worked part year or part time (50)	1,430	1,155	1,550	1,880	1,165	1,090
515	Average employment income $	17,043	16,435	19,070	22,242	19,302	18,323
516	Standard error of average employment income $	847	1,068	890	1,491	1,469	1,170
517	Males with employment income (48)	2,120	1,620	2,370	2,525	1,710	1,645
518	Average employment income $	34,701	34,765	36,333	86,221	41,611	37,476
519	Standard error of average employment income $	1,134	1,286	1,017	27,661	1,753	1,273
520	Worked full year, full time (49)	1,380	1,015	1,660	1,615	1,200	1,055
521	Average employment income $	42,759	43,163	42,315	119,199	49,767	45,230
522	Standard error of average employment income $	1,415	1,533	1,186	42,706	2,154	1,438
523	Worked part year or part time (50)	680	590	670	865	485	555
524	Average employment income $	20,677	20,812	23,181	28,099	22,718	22,347
525	Standard error of average employment income $	1,341	1,740	1,497	2,941	2,191	1,963

Tableau 1. Certaines caractéristiques des secteurs de recensement, recensement de 2001 – Données intégrales et données-échantillon (20 %)

Toronto 0562.05	Toronto 0562.06	Toronto 0562.07	Toronto 0562.08	Toronto 0562.09	Toronto 0562.10	Caractéristiques	Nº
						CARACTÉRISTIQUES DU REVENU DE 2000	
						Population de 15 ans et plus selon le sexe et les tranches de revenu total en 2000 – fin	
2,205	1,325	2,010	1,805	1,650	3,110	Total - Hommes	460
50	80	85	90	80	100	Sans revenu	461
2,150	1,240	1,920	1,715	1,575	3,010	Avec un revenu	462
45	35	60	70	40	95	Moins de 1 000 $ (45)	463
55	40	90	55	40	130	1 000 $ - 2 999 $	464
35	40	45	25	40	90	3 000 $ - 4 999 $	465
65	60	100	65	60	120	5 000 $ - 6 999 $	466
50	30	70	25	40	165	7 000 $ - 9 999 $	467
60	25	40	45	35	60	10 000 $ - 11 999 $	468
90	35	90	15	35	100	12 000 $ - 14 999 $	469
115	55	65	100	95	105	15 000 $ - 19 999 $	470
125	85	105	165	75	190	20 000 $ - 24 999 $	471
170	90	120	130	90	155	25 000 $ - 29 999 $	472
145	85	235	145	125	215	30 000 $ - 34 999 $	473
175	110	140	155	185	180	35 000 $ - 39 999 $	474
270	65	155	185	170	210	40 000 $ - 44 999 $	475
200	80	120	110	95	225	45 000 $ - 49 999 $	476
195	110	195	170	215	270	50 000 $ - 59 999 $	477
365	295	295	255	230	690	60 000 $ et plus	478
38,579	44,956	36,729	37,398	37,605	41,004	Revenu moyen $ (46)	479
37,556	37,059	33,819	35,008	37,917	35,978	Revenu médian $ (46)	480
1,235	2,627	1,382	1,324	1,225	1,262	Erreur type de revenu moyen $ (46)	481
2,355	1,355	1,960	1,800	1,740	3,095	Total - Femmes	482
140	90	125	145	55	165	Sans revenu	483
2,220	1,265	1,835	1,655	1,685	2,925	Avec un revenu	484
115	25	130	25	105	180	Moins de 1 000 $ (45)	485
155	35	115	65	60	190	1 000 $ - 2 999 $	486
130	75	115	50	80	145	3 000 $ - 4 999 $	487
105	55	120	65	70	120	5 000 $ - 6 999 $	488
115	105	95	125	130	205	7 000 $ - 9 999 $	489
90	65	40	55	45	90	10 000 $ - 11 999 $	490
125	55	105	105	80	180	12 000 $ - 14 999 $	491
235	80	155	145	135	185	15 000 $ - 19 999 $	492
195	105	155	145	200	255	20 000 $ - 24 999 $	493
185	90	120	205	145	210	25 000 $ - 29 999 $	494
185	145	200	210	150	225	30 000 $ - 34 999 $	495
180	125	115	130	115	165	35 000 $ - 39 999 $	496
135	75	150	105	135	190	40 000 $ - 44 999 $	497
100	65	80	75	65	145	45 000 $ - 49 999 $	498
70	60	90	80	95	215	50 000 $ - 59 999 $	499
115	105	45	65	75	230	60 000 $ et plus	500
24,314	28,698	23,119	26,558	25,524	26,786	Revenu moyen $ (46)	501
21,297	26,091	20,574	25,760	22,599	23,475	Revenu médian $ (46)	502
938	1,424	872	939	946	837	Erreur type de revenu moyen $ (46)	503
						selon la composition du revenu total	
100.0	100.0	100.0	100.0	100.0	100.0	Total - Composition du revenu en 2000 % (47)	504
84.6	88.5	89.5	89.7	87.7	89.6	Revenu d'emploi %	505
7.3	4.4	6.3	5.8	6.4	4.6	Transferts gouvernementaux %	506
8.2	7.0	4.2	4.6	6.0	5.7	Autre %	507
						Population de 15 ans et plus ayant un revenu d'emploi en 2000 selon le sexe et le travail	
3,510	2,205	3,240	3,000	2,750	5,110	Les deux sexes ayant un revenu d'emploi (48)	508
33,011	37,059	31,166	32,366	32,509	35,380	Revenu moyen d'emploi $	509
818	1,720	917	890	825	826	Erreur type de revenu moyen d'emploi $	510
2,170	1,250	1,730	1,950	1,690	2,815	Ayant travaillé toute l'année à plein temps (49)	511
40,958	50,484	41,819	40,053	41,411	47,992	Revenu moyen d'emploi $	512
906	2,500	1,207	1,090	931	1,087	Erreur type de revenu moyen d'emploi $	513
1,215	910	1,475	1,010	1,035	2,255	Ayant travaillé une partie de l'année ou à temps partiel (50)	514
20,294	20,042	19,297	17,855	18,456	19,987	Revenu moyen d'emploi $	515
1,314	1,564	1,076	1,052	1,074	926	Erreur type de revenu moyen d'emploi $	516
1,900	1,125	1,760	1,550	1,410	2,640	Hommes ayant un revenu d'emploi (48)	517
38,397	44,560	36,814	37,717	37,805	42,244	Revenu moyen d'emploi $	518
1,120	2,902	1,433	1,391	1,202	1,301	Erreur type de revenu moyen d'emploi $	519
1,260	695	1,000	1,080	975	1,630	Ayant travaillé toute l'année à plein temps (49)	520
45,328	57,768	48,106	45,172	44,562	53,783	Revenu moyen d'emploi $	521
1,213	3,950	1,753	1,598	1,243	1,596	Erreur type de revenu moyen d'emploi $	522
570	410	755	455	430	1,000	Ayant travaillé une partie de l'année ou à temps partiel (50)	523
24,533	23,686	22,112	20,621	22,428	23,520	Revenu moyen d'emploi $	524
1,950	2,971	1,831	1,982	2,067	1,633	Erreur type de revenu moyen d'emploi $	525

Table 1. Selected Characteristics for Census Tracts, 2001 Census – 100% Data and 20% Sample Data

No.	Characteristics	Toronto 0560 A	Toronto 0561 A	Toronto 0562.01 ◆ A	Toronto 0562.02	Toronto 0562.03	Toronto 0562.04 ◇
	2000 INCOME CHARACTERISTICS						
	Population 15 years and over with employment income in 2000 by sex and work activity – concluded						
526	Females with employment income (48)	1,840	1,340	2,030	2,205	1,650	1,485
527	Average employment income $	23,557	22,630	23,337	27,947	26,936	26,053
528	Standard error of average employment income $	827	933	768	976	1,297	1,021
529	Worked full year, full time (49)	1,020	750	1,070	1,090	960	910
530	Average employment income $	32,095	31,345	30,555	39,657	34,149	33,639
531	Standard error of average employment income $	1,022	1,063	958	1,273	1,570	1,285
532	Worked part year or part time (50)	745	565	880	1,015	675	535
533	Average employment income $	13,733	11,866	15,963	17,258	16,827	14,187
534	Standard error of average employment income $	1,013	1,116	1,018	1,099	1,950	1,127
	Census families by structure and family income groups in 2000						
535	Total - All census families	1,890	1,570	2,105	1,925	1,520	1,420
536	Under $10,000	120	115	200	10	40	65
537	$ 10,000 - $19,999	75	55	185	45	55	25
538	$ 20,000 - $29,999	115	115	175	75	95	85
539	$ 30,000 - $39,999	195	125	280	85	115	115
540	$ 40,000 - $49,999	230	180	225	90	100	125
541	$ 50,000 - $59,999	215	205	210	185	205	150
542	$ 60,000 - $69,999	255	185	220	185	155	175
543	$ 70,000 - $79,999	200	180	200	235	195	110
544	$ 80,000 - $89,999	75	80	135	115	180	130
545	$ 90,000 - $99,999	105	110	140	145	110	95
546	$100,000 and over	310	215	135	755	265	345
547	Average family income $	64,095	61,589	51,729	157,191	75,032	74,589
548	Median family income $	60,066	59,406	49,389	82,071	69,101	68,380
549	Standard error of average family income $	1,742	1,728	1,487	38,519	2,901	2,339
550	Total - All couple census families (51)	1,545	1,320	1,650	1,700	1,235	1,225
551	Under $10,000	60	75	90	15	10	50
552	$ 10,000 - $19,999	40	35	110	30	25	25
553	$ 20,000 - $29,999	100	65	120	55	55	75
554	$ 30,000 - $39,999	125	110	225	65	60	70
555	$ 40,000 - $49,999	190	155	185	65	80	105
556	$ 50,000 - $59,999	180	185	200	170	160	125
557	$ 60,000 - $69,999	210	155	170	175	130	145
558	$ 70,000 - $79,999	170	165	175	200	200	100
559	$ 80,000 - $89,999	75	65	125	105	145	110
560	$ 90,000 - $99,999	85	105	125	130	115	95
561	$100,000 and over	305	200	130	710	255	330
562	Average family income $	68,608	65,034	56,294	168,421	82,696	78,099
563	Median family income $	62,265	62,855	57,087	85,681	74,794	73,114
564	Standard error of average family income $	1,960	1,899	1,666	43,687	3,352	2,543
	Incidence of low income in 2000						
565	Total - Economic families	1,760	1,460	2,050	1,795	1,430	1,305
566	Low income	165	175	385	45	135	85
567	Incidence of low income in 2000 % (52)	9.3	12.2	18.9	2.6	9.5	6.7
568	Total - Unattached individuals 15 years and over	535	375	1,175	310	245	155
569	Low income	135	125	275	60	80	30
570	Incidence of low income in 2000 % (52)	24.9	34.3	23.3	19.9	34.0	21.0
571	Total - Population in private households	6,485	5,290	7,360	6,930	5,550	4,965
572	Low income	685	765	1,475	205	575	325
573	Incidence of low income in 2000 % (52)	10.6	14.5	20.1	3.0	10.4	6.5
	Private households by household income groups in 2000						
574	Total - All private households	2,105	1,700	2,905	2,045	1,565	1,390
575	Under $10,000	80	85	140	25	30	20
576	$ 10,000 - $19,999	90	110	285	60	60	10
577	$ 20,000 - $29,999	145	90	280	25	75	50
578	$ 30,000 - $39,999	190	140	375	80	75	80
579	$ 40,000 - $49,999	230	180	285	95	100	100
580	$ 50,000 - $59,999	215	225	310	200	205	155
581	$ 60,000 - $69,999	290	165	275	160	130	185
582	$ 70,000 - $79,999	250	175	265	255	175	130
583	$ 80,000 - $89,999	100	85	260	105	185	150
584	$ 90,000 - $99,999	115	155	190	175	120	105
585	$100,000 and over	385	285	245	860	405	400
586	Average household income $	67,267	66,150	55,169	157,988	81,964	83,764
587	Median household income $	61,937	62,537	51,327	90,412	75,527	77,512
588	Standard error of average household income $	1,695	1,916	1,251	35,465	2,917	2,383

Tableau 1. Certaines caractéristiques des secteurs de recensement, recensement de 2001 – Données intégrales et données-échantillon (20 %)

Toronto 0562.05	Toronto 0562.06	Toronto 0562.07	Toronto 0562.08	Toronto 0562.09	Toronto 0562.10	Caractéristiques	N°
						CARACTÉRISTIQUES DU REVENU DE 2000	
						Population de 15 ans et plus ayant un revenu d'emploi en 2000 selon le sexe et le travail – fin	
1,610	1,080	1,485	1,440	1,345	2,470	Femmes ayant un revenu d'emploi (48)	526
26,663	29,255	24,475	26,605	26,956	28,039	Revenu moyen d'emploi $	527
1,110	1,605	955	1,002	1,039	908	Erreur type de revenu moyen d'emploi $	528
905	555	725	880	715	1,185	Ayant travaillé toute l'année à plein temps (49)	529
34,900	41,365	33,192	33,761	37,080	40,008	Revenu moyen d'emploi $	530
1,249	2,356	1,293	1,303	1,331	1,224	Erreur type de revenu moyen d'emploi $	531
640	500	720	560	605	1,255	Ayant travaillé une partie de l'année ou à temps partiel (50)	532
16,491	17,061	16,351	15,594	15,631	17,164	Revenu moyen d'emploi $	533
1,712	1,414	1,087	1,020	1,065	1,008	Erreur type de revenu moyen d'emploi $	534
						Familles de recensement selon la structure et les tranches de revenu de la famille en 2000	
1,605	945	1,410	1,335	1,255	2,190	Total - Toutes les familles de recensement	535
85	15	55	30	10	25	Moins de 10 000 $	536
60	25	70	35	30	100	10 000 $ - 19 999 $	537
115	40	60	75	50	85	20 000 $ - 29 999 $	538
160	70	120	50	35	110	30 000 $ - 39 999 $	539
190	60	145	155	155	180	40 000 $ - 49 999 $	540
165	70	145	175	170	155	50 000 $ - 59 999 $	541
185	70	100	145	180	210	60 000 $ - 69 999 $	542
215	150	135	200	150	180	70 000 $ - 79 999 $	543
140	70	120	155	130	230	80 000 $ - 89 999 $	544
90	40	110	95	85	110	90 000 $ - 99 999 $	545
185	340	345	220	250	810	100 000 $ et plus	546
62,750	93,250	72,984	72,996	75,505	86,737	Revenu moyen des familles $	547
60,387	76,920	69,908	69,970	69,754	81,529	Revenu médian des familles $	548
1,940	4,108	2,233	1,993	2,092	2,061	Erreur type de revenu moyen des familles $	549
1,315	875	1,200	1,085	1,060	1,925	Total - Toutes les familles de recensement comptant un couple (51)	550
45	-	40	15	10	20	Moins de 10 000 $	551
30	20	40	15	10	50	10 000 $ - 19 999 $	552
85	30	30	50	30	50	20 000 $ - 29 999 $	553
115	45	100	35	25	85	30 000 $ - 39 999 $	554
145	50	95	100	120	130	40 000 $ - 49 999 $	555
145	65	120	125	130	125	50 000 $ - 59 999 $	556
165	70	90	135	170	190	60 000 $ - 69 999 $	557
190	150	135	175	135	160	70 000 $ - 79 999 $	558
140	65	105	135	120	205	80 000 $ - 89 999 $	559
85	40	110	100	75	110	90 000 $ - 99 999 $	560
180	335	340	205	240	790	100 000 $ et plus	561
67,824	97,684	78,033	77,599	79,545	92,017	Revenu moyen des familles $	562
64,679	80,599	74,989	74,725	72,211	85,830	Revenu médian des familles $	563
2,145	4,210	2,408	2,063	2,287	2,168	Erreur type de revenu moyen des familles $	564
						Fréquence des unités à faible revenu en 2000	
1,555	855	1,270	1,270	1,185	1,995	Total - Familles économiques	565
165	35	120	65	35	110	Faible revenu	566
10.7	4.2	9.4	5.5	2.8	5.6	Fréquence des unités à faible revenu en 2000 % (52)	567
805	105	250	185	125	210	Total - Personnes hors famille économique de 15 ans et plus	568
170	30	55	40	35	10	Faible revenu	569
21.4	28.5	22.4	23.7	26.6	5.5	Fréquence des unités à faible revenu en 2000 % (52)	570
5,640	3,315	5,105	4,665	4,320	7,970	Total - Population dans les ménages privés	571
635	165	450	285	125	445	Faible revenu	572
11.3	4.9	8.9	6.1	3.0	5.6	Fréquence des unités à faible revenu en 2000 % (52)	573
						Ménages privés selon les tranches de revenu du ménage en 2000	
2,165	925	1,380	1,400	1,265	2,110	Total - Tous les ménages privés	574
120	10	60	20	-	20	Moins de 10 000 $	575
130	20	45	60	35	45	10 000 $ - 19 999 $	576
150	40	50	75	35	40	20 000 $ - 29 999 $	577
200	35	80	65	30	100	30 000 $ - 39 999 $	578
265	65	145	100	160	170	40 000 $ - 49 999 $	579
220	60	110	150	170	130	50 000 $ - 59 999 $	580
225	55	100	120	170	195	60 000 $ - 69 999 $	581
255	130	115	225	130	155	70 000 $ - 79 999 $	582
190	60	125	170	135	205	80 000 $ - 89 999 $	583
120	55	95	100	100	120	90 000 $ - 99 999 $	584
290	395	460	315	310	940	100 000 $ et plus	585
63,158	99,691	81,710	77,333	80,692	95,571	Revenu moyen des ménages $	586
59,603	89,172	78,542	75,707	73,292	91,651	Revenu médian des ménages $	587
1,730	4,280	2,555	2,094	2,331	2,119	Erreur type de revenu moyen des ménages $	588

Table 1. Selected Characteristics for Census Tracts, 2001 Census – 100% Data and 20% Sample Data

No.	Characteristics	Toronto 0562.11	Toronto 0563.01	Toronto 0563.02	Toronto 0564.01	Toronto 0564.02 ◆	Toronto 0570.01 ◆
	POPULATION CHARACTERISTICS						
1	**Population, 1996 (1)**	**3,432**	**6,600**	**3,179**	**2,465**	**5,303**	**3,210**
2	**Population, 2001 (2)**	**3,353**	**6,799**	**3,172**	**2,447**	**5,134**	**3,371**
3	Population percentage change, 1996-2001	-2.3	3.0	-0.2	-0.7	-3.2	5.0
4	Land area in square kilometres, 2001	0.78	0.88	1.02	0.84	0.91	8.04
5	**Total population - 100% Data (3)**	**3,355**	**6,795**	**3,175**	**2,450**	**5,135**	**3,370**
	by sex and age groups						
6	Male	1,675	3,130	1,560	1,250	2,600	1,725
7	0-4 years	105	295	105	65	175	125
8	5-9 years	130	275	110	100	240	135
9	10-14 years	145	235	90	90	240	105
10	15-19 years	125	225	110	80	205	110
11	20-24 years	125	190	95	80	195	140
12	25-29 years	105	200	110	100	170	180
13	30-34 years	135	265	120	95	190	175
14	35-39 years	165	300	155	115	270	175
15	40-44 years	150	270	110	80	255	155
16	45-49 years	110	220	95	90	175	125
17	50-54 years	130	150	80	80	150	80
18	55-59 years	75	125	85	95	120	70
19	60-64 years	60	90	90	85	90	55
20	65-69 years	45	105	75	45	85	30
21	70-74 years	30	70	70	30	35	25
22	75-79 years	10	70	25	15	15	15
23	80-84 years	10	30	10	-	5	10
24	85 years and over	5	20	5	-	-	5
25	Female	1,685	3,665	1,615	1,195	2,535	1,650
26	0-4 years	120	285	105	65	185	130
27	5-9 years	145	270	120	90	230	115
28	10-14 years	125	245	95	75	200	85
29	15-19 years	125	205	95	85	195	110
30	20-24 years	110	230	100	75	155	155
31	25-29 years	90	275	105	75	190	160
32	30-34 years	145	320	105	105	230	170
33	35-39 years	170	370	160	110	230	140
34	40-44 years	150	285	115	85	230	130
35	45-49 years	120	205	85	80	195	105
36	50-54 years	110	215	100	90	130	105
37	55-59 years	100	150	100	90	125	75
38	60-64 years	60	150	110	75	85	45
39	65-69 years	35	150	85	35	85	45
40	70-74 years	35	110	75	30	35	30
41	75-79 years	25	90	45	20	30	30
42	80-84 years	10	75	10	10	5	15
43	85 years and over	5	35	5	-	5	5
44	**Total population 15 years and over**	**2,580**	**5,185**	**2,540**	**1,960**	**3,865**	**2,670**
	by legal marital status						
45	Never married (single)	810	1,595	755	575	1,300	1,145
46	Legally married (and not separated)	1,445	2,465	1,415	1,135	2,035	955
47	Separated, but still legally married	85	305	80	65	155	185
48	Divorced	150	490	160	110	240	295
49	Widowed	85	340	135	70	135	90
	by common-law status						
50	Not in a common-law relationship	2,415	4,915	2,400	1,855	3,630	2,365
51	In a common-law relationship	165	270	140	100	240	310
52	**Total population - 20% Sample Data (4)**	**3,400**	**6,800**	**3,165**	**2,450**	**5,125**	**3,370**
	by mother tongue						
53	Single responses	3,380	6,540	3,155	2,410	5,050	3,300
54	English	2,650	3,625	2,465	1,890	3,330	2,685
55	French	25	105	15	40	85	40
56	Non-official languages (5)	705	2,810	680	475	1,630	580
57	Italian	50	50	35	65	85	10
58	Chinese, n.o.s.	20	35	10	10	-	10
59	Cantonese	-	-	95	-	45	-
60	Portuguese	25	75	70	-	40	60
61	Punjabi	65	770	35	35	335	65
62	Other languages (6)	545	1,885	435	375	1,135	440
63	Multiple responses	20	260	10	35	80	65
64	English and French	-	20	-	25	-	15
65	English and non-official language	20	230	10	10	70	50
66	French and non-official language	-	10	-	-	10	-
67	English, French and non-official language	-	-	-	-	-	-

See reference material at the end of the publication. – Voir les documents de référence à la fin de la publication.

Tableau 1. Certaines caractéristiques des secteurs de recensement, recensement de 2001 – Données intégrales et données-échantillon (20 %)

Toronto 0570.02	Toronto 0571.01	Toronto 0571.02	Toronto 0572.01	Toronto 0572.04 A	Toronto 0572.05 ◆ A	Caractéristiques	Nº
						CARACTÉRISTIQUES DE LA POPULATION	
3,757	**3,704**	**4,216**	**7,272**	**3,237**	**5,894**	**Population, 1996 (1)**	1
3,668	**3,556**	**4,184**	**7,301**	**3,083**	**5,820**	**Population, 2001 (2)**	2
-2.4	-4.0	-0.8	0.4	-4.8	-1.3	Variation en pourcentage de la population, 1996-2001	3
1.31	0.73	1.36	2.11	0.80	0.82	Superficie des terres en kilomètres carrés, 2001	4
3,665	**3,555**	**4,185**	**7,300**	**3,085**	**5,820**	**Population totale - Données intégrales (3) selon le sexe et les groupes d'âge**	5
1,840	1,780	2,060	3,535	1,510	2,930	Sexe masculin	6
90	140	140	215	75	195	0-4 ans	7
105	155	115	270	130	185	5-9 ans	8
100	125	105	275	145	165	10-14 ans	9
135	100	110	260	115	180	15-19 ans	10
110	160	115	235	130	255	20-24 ans	11
80	155	130	210	90	290	25-29 ans	12
110	175	145	230	105	270	30-34 ans	13
135	155	175	310	105	245	35-39 ans	14
120	150	165	275	140	225	40-44 ans	15
135	115	130	265	125	225	45-49 ans	16
130	85	150	225	110	210	50-54 ans	17
130	75	125	205	70	140	55-59 ans	18
135	65	105	140	65	110	60-64 ans	19
135	50	115	145	35	70	65-69 ans	20
90	30	100	120	30	65	70-74 ans	21
50	30	80	85	25	60	75-79 ans	22
30	15	25	40	10	30	80-84 ans	23
15	5	20	25	5	10	85 ans et plus	24
1,830	1,780	2,130	3,770	1,575	2,890	Sexe féminin	25
70	165	95	210	60	185	0-4 ans	26
100	135	105	250	85	165	5-9 ans	27
110	105	110	275	140	170	10-14 ans	28
115	130	75	245	140	190	15-19 ans	29
80	140	120	235	115	250	20-24 ans	30
60	175	135	220	95	295	25-29 ans	31
115	175	150	280	110	245	30-34 ans	32
120	145	170	315	135	230	35-39 ans	33
145	130	140	310	135	210	40-44 ans	34
145	95	125	270	160	205	45-49 ans	35
185	100	150	245	105	185	50-54 ans	36
135	65	135	195	95	130	55-59 ans	37
130	70	120	175	65	120	60-64 ans	38
130	45	135	155	40	85	65-69 ans	39
95	50	115	155	35	90	70-74 ans	40
65	45	95	120	35	65	75-79 ans	41
20	10	75	70	20	40	80-84 ans	42
15	10	70	40	10	25	85 ans et plus	43
3,095	**2,730**	**3,505**	**5,800**	**2,455**	**4,755**	**Population totale de 15 ans et plus selon l'état matrimonial légal**	44
730	1,010	925	1,770	810	1,610	Célibataire (jamais marié(e))	45
2,030	1,285	1,970	3,040	1,285	2,285	Légalement marié(e) (et non séparé(e))	46
50	125	105	240	60	260	Séparé(e), mais toujours légalement marié(e)	47
110	180	200	405	165	355	Divorcé(e)	48
175	130	305	345	135	250	Veuf ou veuve	49
						selon l'union libre	
3,010	2,500	3,305	5,460	2,345	4,410	Ne vivant pas en union libre	50
85	230	205	345	110	345	Vivant en union libre	51
3,670	**3,520**	**4,050**	**7,285**	**3,075**	**5,810**	**Population totale - Données-échantillon (20 %) (4) selon la langue maternelle**	52
3,590	3,425	4,025	7,095	3,040	5,680	Réponses uniques	53
3,010	1,855	3,115	5,655	2,305	3,765	Anglais	54
35	45	30	75	50	45	Français	55
545	1,525	880	1,360	690	1,865	Langues non officielles (5)	56
60	-	105	70	10	70	Italien	57
-	10	-	60	65	190	Chinois, n.d.a.	58
20	30	10	10	35	15	Cantonais	59
60	690	300	340	55	130	Portugais	60
-	145	55	130	120	295	Pendjabi	61
405	645	415	750	410	1,170	Autres langues (6)	62
80	100	25	190	35	130	Réponses multiples	63
10	-	10	10	10	15	Anglais et français	64
70	100	20	180	25	115	Anglais et langue non officielle	65
-	-	-	10	-	-	Français et langue non officielle	66
-	-	-	-	-	-	Anglais, français et langue non officielle	67

See reference material at the end of the publication. – Voir les documents de référence à la fin de la publication.

Table 1. Selected Characteristics for Census Tracts, 2001 Census – 100% Data and 20% Sample Data

No.	Characteristics	Toronto 0562.11	Toronto 0563.01	Toronto 0563.02	Toronto 0564.01	Toronto 0564.02 ◆	Toronto 0570.01 ◆
	POPULATION CHARACTERISTICS						
	by home language						
68	Single responses	2,895	5,315	2,710	2,080	4,055	2,880
69	English	2,755	3,870	2,530	1,840	3,365	2,695
70	French	-	60	-	15	55	10
71	Non-official languages (5)	145	1,380	175	225	630	180
72	Cantonese	-	-	35	-	30	-
73	Chinese, n.o.s.	15	35	-	-	-	10
74	Italian	-	10	10	10	25	-
75	Punjabi	20	435	15	60	90	10
76	Portuguese	10	20	-	-	15	15
77	Other languages (6)	100	885	120	160	465	145
78	Multiple responses	505	1,490	460	365	1,075	490
79	English and French	15	60	10	55	40	55
80	English and non-official language	475	1,430	440	220	1,035	430
81	French and non-official language	10	-	-	-	-	-
82	English, French and non-official language	10	-	10	90	-	-
	by knowledge of official languages						
83	English only	3,045	6,025	3,015	2,260	4,650	3,025
84	French only	-	15	-	-	20	-
85	English and French	335	500	120	160	335	265
86	Neither English nor French	20	260	30	25	125	80
	by knowledge of non-official languages (5) (7)						
87	Italian	65	140	35	65	195	20
88	Cantonese	-	-	100	-	45	10
89	Chinese, n.o.s.	20	45	20	20	-	10
90	Spanish	130	170	70	140	255	60
91	Portuguese	25	75	75	-	95	65
92	Punjabi	70	970	60	110	465	90
93	Tagalog (Pilipino)	135	185	130	15	290	20
	by first official language spoken						
94	English	3,340	6,340	3,125	2,355	4,870	3,245
95	French	25	125	15	50	90	35
96	English and French	15	75	10	20	45	25
97	Neither English nor French	20	260	25	25	120	65
98	Official language minority - (number) (8)	30	160	20	60	115	50
99	Official language minority - (percentage) (8)	0.9	2.4	0.6	2.5	2.2	1.5
	by ethnic origin (9)						
100	Canadian	1,105	1,035	895	585	1,165	1,160
101	English	760	810	1,050	750	915	685
102	Scottish	585	385	655	460	610	505
103	Irish	450	280	440	410	420	485
104	Chinese	30	55	115	30	90	20
105	Italian	200	190	100	115	320	100
106	East Indian	275	1,390	280	155	605	195
107	French	245	250	250	155	130	345
108	German	110	205	150	75	95	110
109	Portuguese	70	155	110	20	90	85
110	Polish	50	145	115	50	120	115
111	Jewish	-	50	15	-	-	-
112	Jamaican	40	495	165	155	360	230
113	Filipino	180	195	150	15	375	25
114	Ukrainian	40	75	60	35	60	55
	by Aboriginal identity						
115	Total Aboriginal identity population (10)	10	10	55	20	50	35
116	Total non-Aboriginal population	3,395	6,790	3,110	2,425	5,080	3,335
	by Aboriginal origin						
117	Total Aboriginal origins population (11)	20	75	65	30	65	130
118	Total non-Aboriginal population	3,375	6,720	3,105	2,415	5,060	3,240
	by Registered Indian status						
119	Registered Indian (12)	-	10	10	-	-	10
120	Not a Registered Indian	3,400	6,795	3,160	2,445	5,125	3,365

Tableau 1. Certaines caractéristiques des secteurs de recensement, recensement de 2001 – Données intégrales et données-échantillon (20 %)

Toronto 0570.02	Toronto 0571.01	Toronto 0571.02	Toronto 0572.01	Toronto 0572.04 A	Toronto 0572.05 ◆ A	Caractéristiques	N°
						CARACTÉRISTIQUES DE LA POPULATION	
						selon la langue parlée à la maison	
3,265	2,710	3,575	6,460	2,570	4,660	Réponses uniques	68
3,230	2,035	3,305	6,010	2,385	3,995	Anglais	69
-	10	-	-	-	15	Français	70
30	670	270	450	180	655	Langues non officielles (5)	71
-	-	-	-	-	15	Cantonais	72
-	20	-	-	65	20	Chinois, n.d.a.	73
-	-	-	10	10	15	Italien	74
-	55	55	105	10	215	Pendjabi	75
10	360	105	145	-	45	Portugais	76
20	230	110	175	100	350	Autres langues (6)	77
405	810	470	825	505	1,150	Réponses multiples	78
15	40	-	30	45	30	Anglais et français	79
385	760	455	785	465	1,070	Anglais et langue non officielle	80
-	-	-	-	-	20	Français et langue non officielle	81
-	-	15	10	-	35	Anglais, français et langue non officielle	82
						selon la connaissance des langues officielles	
3,435	3,050	3,740	6,765	2,885	5,385	Anglais seulement	83
-	-	-	-	-	-	Français seulement	84
225	155	195	400	190	320	Anglais et français	85
10	315	115	120	-	105	Ni l'anglais ni le français	86
						selon la connaissance des langues non officielles (5) (7)	
95	40	135	110	40	90	Italien	87
20	30	-	15	55	35	Cantonais	88
-	45	-	55	60	155	Chinois, n.d.a.	89
40	75	65	145	65	130	Espagnol	90
110	725	345	460	75	160	Portugais	91
-	165	55	265	180	405	Pendjabi	92
10	20	15	20	55	180	Tagalog (pilipino)	93
						selon la première langue officielle parlée	
3,620	3,155	3,905	7,090	3,015	5,610	Anglais	94
30	35	20	70	50	35	Français	95
-	20	10	10	10	60	Anglais et français	96
10	310	115	115	-	105	Ni l'anglais ni le français	97
35	45	25	75	50	65	Minorité de langue officielle - (nombre) (8)	98
1.0	1.3	0.6	1.0	1.6	1.1	Minorité de langue officielle - (pourcentage) (8)	99
						selon l'origine ethnique (9)	
805	760	1,370	2,345	570	1,225	Canadien	100
1,370	455	1,170	1,905	560	960	Anglais	101
975	320	695	1,135	435	575	Écossais	102
975	275	625	1,395	310	570	Irlandais	103
50	85	10	95	170	275	Chinois	104
260	95	250	360	130	255	Italien	105
40	270	30	285	405	905	Indien de l'Inde	106
180	175	290	430	235	330	Français	107
270	80	260	500	220	305	Allemand	108
105	830	385	605	135	290	Portugais	109
150	50	175	290	75	75	Polonais	110
10	15	10	30	-	10	Juif	111
10	185	-	230	95	275	Jamaïquain	112
10	60	25	25	120	220	Philippin	113
145	25	40	125	95	55	Ukrainien	114
						selon l'identité autochtone	
10	25	30	30	30	45	Total de la population ayant une identité autochtone (10)	115
3,655	3,495	4,010	7,255	3,050	5,765	Total de la population non autochtone	116
						selon l'origine autochtone	
25	55	70	125	40	65	Total de la population ayant une origine autochtone (11)	117
3,645	3,465	3,980	7,160	3,035	5,740	Total de la population non autochtone	118
						selon le statut d'Indien inscrit	
15	-	-	20	-	10	Oui, Indien inscrit (12)	119
3,655	3,520	4,040	7,265	3,075	5,795	Non, pas un Indien inscrit	120

Table 1. Selected Characteristics for Census Tracts, 2001 Census – 100% Data and 20% Sample Data

No.	Characteristics	Toronto 0562.11	Toronto 0563.01	Toronto 0563.02	Toronto 0564.01	Toronto 0564.02 ◆	Toronto 0570.01 ◆
	POPULATION CHARACTERISTICS						
	by visible minority groups						
121	Total visible minority population	1,055	4,105	850	640	2,315	875
122	Chinese	30	50	125	25	55	20
123	South Asian	330	1,830	200	200	895	215
124	Black	230	1,360	235	255	465	485
125	Filipino	180	205	150	10	345	25
126	Latin American	90	110	40	65	150	20
127	Southeast Asian	50	145	10	50	110	45
128	Arab	40	70	-	-	35	10
129	West Asian	30	70	-	-	-	-
130	Korean	-	-	-	-	-	-
131	Japanese	-	15	10	-	15	-
132	Visible minority, n.i.e. (13)	35	220	70	40	220	65
133	Multiple visible minorities (14)	25	25	20	-	20	-
	by citizenship						
134	Canadian citizenship (15)	3,250	5,270	2,860	2,260	4,135	2,955
135	Citizenship other than Canadian	150	1,530	310	185	995	410
	by place of birth of respondent						
136	Non-immigrant population	2,365	3,020	2,035	1,570	2,725	2,320
137	Born in province of residence	1,855	2,415	1,755	1,285	2,310	1,490
138	Immigrant population (16)	1,035	3,740	1,125	865	2,285	1,040
139	United States	20	20	50	20	10	-
140	Central and South America	90	305	85	95	435	55
141	Caribbean and Bermuda	115	480	145	155	300	140
142	United Kingdom	165	180	250	195	215	180
143	Other Europe (17)	200	435	250	185	305	265
144	Africa	50	505	20	25	50	220
145	Asia and the Middle East	400	1,805	315	190	975	190
146	Oceania and other (18)	-	10	10	-	-	-
147	Non-permanent residents (19)	-	35	10	15	115	10
148	**Total immigrant population**	**1,035**	**3,740**	**1,130**	**860**	**2,285**	**1,045**
	by period of immigration						
149	Before 1961	85	130	210	150	120	105
150	1961-1970	180	185	220	165	240	90
151	1971-1980	140	430	240	120	250	95
152	1981-1990	385	715	155	205	520	215
153	1991-2001 (20)	245	2,285	300	220	1,155	530
154	1991-1995	155	1,195	105	130	675	195
155	1996-2001 (20)	85	1,090	195	90	485	335
	by age at immigration						
156	0-4 years	115	280	105	75	180	45
157	5-19 years	240	845	320	285	730	350
158	20 years and over	680	2,620	700	505	1,380	645
159	**Total population**	**3,400**	**6,800**	**3,165**	**2,450**	**5,130**	**3,370**
	by religion						
160	Catholic (21)	1,100	2,085	995	770	1,650	1,145
161	Protestant	1,345	1,745	1,265	1,080	1,260	1,170
162	Christian Orthodox	130	135	20	65	40	80
163	Christian, n.i.e. (22)	125	325	50	10	285	215
164	Muslim	75	450	80	35	365	50
165	Jewish	10	35	10	-	-	-
166	Buddhist	40	55	10	10	110	15
167	Hindu	80	640	80	110	360	100
168	Sikh	80	625	35	75	305	90
169	Eastern religions (23)	15	25	-	-	20	-
170	Other religions (24)	45	-	-	-	-	-
171	No religious affiliation (25)	360	675	620	290	740	500
172	**Total population 15 years and over**	**2,615**	**5,200**	**2,515**	**1,980**	**3,860**	**2,695**
	by generation status						
173	1st generation (26)	995	3,450	1,080	870	2,150	985
174	2nd generation (27)	475	665	525	365	585	355
175	3rd generation and over (28)	1,145	1,090	905	745	1,125	1,360
176	**Total population 1 year and over (29)**	**3,360**	**6,675**	**3,110**	**2,415**	**5,100**	**3,310**
	by place of residence 1 year ago (mobility)						
177	Non-movers	3,035	5,345	2,725	2,090	4,075	2,570
178	Movers	325	1,325	385	325	1,025	740
179	Non-migrants	175	755	225	230	470	470
180	Migrants	145	575	160	95	550	275
181	Internal migrants	130	340	120	100	425	240
182	Intraprovincial migrants	80	245	115	95	415	175
183	Interprovincial migrants	45	100	10	10	10	70
184	External migrants	20	230	40	-	125	35

Tableau 1. Certaines caractéristiques des secteurs de recensement, recensement de 2001 – Données intégrales et données-échantillon (20 %)

Toronto 0570.02	Toronto 0571.01	Toronto 0571.02	Toronto 0572.01	Toronto 0572.04 A	Toronto 0572.05 ◆ A	Caractéristiques	N°
						CARACTÉRISTIQUES DE LA POPULATION	
						selon les groupes de minorités visibles	
170	1,225	250	1,235	1,185	2,685	Total de la population des minorités visibles	121
50	35	10	50	170	240	Chinois	122
45	465	145	370	515	980	Sud-Asiatique	123
20	550	40	485	170	635	Noir	124
10	30	20	20	125	210	Philippin	125
10	10	25	105	50	100	Latino-Américain	126
-	75	-	55	25	15	Asiatique du Sud-Est	127
-	-	10	25	10	100	Arabe	128
-	-	-	35	25	80	Asiatique occidental	129
-	-	-	20	-	70	Coréen	130
10	-	-	-	10	10	Japonais	131
20	15	-	60	50	205	Minorité visible, n.i.a. (13)	132
-	40	-	-	40	35	Minorités visibles multiples (14)	133
						selon la citoyenneté	
3,490	2,745	3,830	6,590	2,950	4,560	Citoyenneté canadienne (15)	134
175	775	215	700	125	1,250	Citoyenneté autre que canadienne	135
						selon le lieu de naissance du répondant	
2,800	1,810	2,920	5,295	2,010	3,020	Population non immigrante	136
2,475	1,535	2,440	4,520	1,710	2,340	Née dans la province de résidence	137
865	1,705	1,115	1,950	1,065	2,680	Population immigrante (16)	138
35	10	20	35	15	45	États-Unis	139
20	60	60	105	125	200	Amérique centrale et du Sud	140
15	170	30	220	155	325	Caraïbes et Bermudes	141
350	75	215	295	110	225	Royaume-Uni	142
355	655	660	840	195	340	Autre Europe (17)	143
10	160	15	70	25	160	Afrique	144
70	570	110	375	445	1,380	Asie et Moyen-Orient	145
10	-	-	10	10	10	Océanie et autre (18)	146
-	-	10	40	-	110	Résidents non permanents (19)	147
865	**1,705**	**1,115**	**1,945**	**1,065**	**2,680**	**Population immigrante totale**	148
						selon la période d'immigration	
250	50	365	275	65	235	Avant 1961	149
210	195	245	390	235	230	1961-1970	150
215	280	120	300	310	385	1971-1980	151
105	280	185	505	235	335	1981-1990	152
90	895	205	480	220	1,495	1991-2001 (20)	153
60	365	135	270	120	325	1991-1995	154
30	535	65	210	100	1,170	1996-2001 (20)	155
						selon l'âge à l'immigration	
105	135	100	190	60	285	0-4 ans	156
215	550	315	585	380	695	5-19 ans	157
550	1,020	695	1,175	630	1,700	20 ans et plus	158
3,665	**3,520**	**4,045**	**7,285**	**3,075**	**5,810**	**Population totale**	159
						selon la religion	
1,375	1,460	1,535	2,535	970	1,730	Catholique (21)	160
1,705	890	1,770	3,165	950	1,565	Protestante	161
30	30	15	80	20	40	Orthodoxe chrétienne	162
70	145	50	135	190	325	Chrétiennes, n.i.a. (22)	163
10	330	25	90	100	345	Musulmane	164
-	-	-	40	-	-	Juive	165
10	75	-	30	20	45	Bouddhiste	166
15	135	55	50	230	470	Hindoue	167
-	100	65	160	115	255	Sikh	168
-	-	-	-	10	-	Religions orientales (23)	169
-	-	-	-	15	10	Autres religions (24)	170
450	365	530	1,005	465	1,025	Aucune appartenance religieuse (25)	171
3,095	**2,665**	**3,370**	**5,785**	**2,395**	**4,735**	**Population totale de 15 ans et plus**	172
						selon le statut des générations	
860	1,520	1,115	1,885	1,070	2,450	1re génération (26)	173
930	355	780	1,335	445	840	2e génération (27)	174
1,305	785	1,475	2,560	875	1,455	3e génération et plus (28)	175
3,645	**3,435**	**4,025**	**7,215**	**3,045**	**5,740**	**Population totale de 1 an et plus (29)**	176
						selon le lieu de résidence 1 an auparavant (mobilité)	
3,300	2,725	3,515	6,475	2,855	4,200	Personnes n'ayant pas déménagé	177
340	715	510	740	190	1,545	Personnes ayant déménagé	178
295	455	305	470	125	710	Non-migrants	179
50	265	205	270	65	835	Migrants	180
15	195	200	235	65	540	Migrants internes	181
10	175	150	215	50	445	Migrants infraprovinciaux	182
10	20	50	15	15	85	Migrants interprovinciaux	183
35	65	-	40	-	300	Migrants externes	184

Table 1. Selected Characteristics for Census Tracts, 2001 Census – 100% Data and 20% Sample Data

No.	Characteristics	Toronto 0562.11	Toronto 0563.01	Toronto 0563.02	Toronto 0564.01	Toronto 0564.02 ◆	Toronto 0570.01 ◆
	POPULATION CHARACTERISTICS						
185	**Total population 5 years and over (30)**	**3,170**	**6,225**	**2,940**	**2,335**	**4,765**	**3,110**
	by place of residence 5 years ago (mobility)						
186	Non-movers	1,815	2,660	1,795	1,375	2,290	1,105
187	Movers	1,355	3,565	1,145	960	2,480	2,000
188	Non-migrants	660	1,755	655	510	820	890
189	Migrants	700	1,815	490	445	1,660	1,115
190	Internal migrants	610	940	345	420	1,170	890
191	Intraprovincial migrants	520	620	310	365	995	560
192	Interprovincial migrants	95	315	40	55	175	325
193	External migrants	80	870	145	25	490	225
194	**Total population 15 to 24 years**	**510**	**855**	**390**	**330**	**720**	**520**
	by school attendance						
195	Not attending school	165	345	160	155	295	295
196	Attending school full time	305	425	210	165	370	200
197	Attending school part time	40	80	20	10	50	20
198	**Total population 15 years and over**	**2,615**	**5,205**	**2,520**	**1,980**	**3,860**	**2,695**
	by highest level of schooling						
199	Less than grade 9 (31)	110	485	110	100	275	175
200	Grades 9-13 without high school graduation certificate	595	1,355	520	525	1,145	1,010
201	Grades 9-13 with high school graduation certificate	400	980	460	390	715	485
202	Some postsecondary without degree, certificate or diploma (32)	340	540	325	200	330	205
203	Trades certificate or diploma (33)	255	535	285	260	425	340
204	College certificate or diploma (34)	385	645	360	330	465	295
205	University certificate below bachelor's degree	100	95	45	40	50	25
206	University with bachelor's degree or higher	430	570	410	140	455	165
	by combinations of unpaid work						
207	Males 15 years and over	1,295	2,330	1,225	1,010	1,905	1,370
208	Reported unpaid work (35)	1,135	2,020	1,105	910	1,575	1,110
209	Housework and child care and care or assistance to seniors	70	165	90	65	160	15
210	Housework and child care only	395	575	325	280	635	345
211	Housework and care or assistance to seniors only	75	95	120	65	70	50
212	Child care and care or assistance to seniors only	-	20	-	-	-	-
213	Housework only	570	1,060	565	455	670	670
214	Child care only	15	95	-	35	35	25
215	Care or assistance to seniors only	-	15	10	10	10	-
216	Females 15 years and over	1,325	2,875	1,295	975	1,950	1,330
217	Reported unpaid work (35)	1,235	2,560	1,225	920	1,830	1,160
218	Housework and child care and care or assistance to seniors	65	345	105	65	210	95
219	Housework and child care only	550	930	435	365	775	345
220	Housework and care or assistance to seniors only	100	125	120	65	65	105
221	Child care and care or assistance to seniors only	-	-	-	-	-	-
222	Housework only	505	1,105	550	430	745	605
223	Child care only	10	50	-	-	35	-
224	Care or assistance to seniors only	-	15	10	-	-	-
	by labour force activity						
225	Males 15 years and over	1,295	2,330	1,225	1,010	1,910	1,370
226	In the labour force	1,060	1,660	970	830	1,530	1,105
227	Employed	1,025	1,535	950	785	1,460	1,060
228	Unemployed	35	125	25	45	65	40
229	Not in the labour force	230	670	255	180	380	260
230	Participation rate	81.9	71.2	79.2	82.2	80.1	80.7
231	Employment rate	79.2	65.9	77.6	77.7	76.4	77.4
232	Unemployment rate	3.3	7.5	2.6	5.4	4.2	3.6
233	Females 15 years and over	1,320	2,875	1,295	970	1,950	1,330
234	In the labour force	925	1,690	850	695	1,305	870
235	Employed	870	1,535	835	625	1,120	795
236	Unemployed	55	160	20	70	190	70
237	Not in the labour force	395	1,185	445	275	640	465
238	Participation rate	70.1	58.8	65.6	71.6	66.9	65.4
239	Employment rate	65.9	53.4	64.5	64.4	57.4	59.8
240	Unemployment rate	5.9	9.5	2.4	10.1	14.6	8.0

Tableau 1. Certaines caractéristiques des secteurs de recensement, recensement de 2001 – Données intégrales et données-échantillon (20 %)

Toronto 0570.02	Toronto 0571.01	Toronto 0571.02	Toronto 0572.01	Toronto 0572.04 A	Toronto 0572.05 ◆ A	Caractéristiques	N°
						CARACTÉRISTIQUES DE LA POPULATION	
3,510	**3,220**	**3,820**	**6,865**	**2,890**	**5,405**	**Population totale de 5 ans et plus (30) .... selon le lieu de résidence 5 ans auparavant (mobilité)**	185
2,425	1,445	2,500	4,190	2,135	1,975	Personnes n'ayant pas déménagé	186
1,090	1,780	1,320	2,680	760	3,430	Personnes ayant déménagé	187
770	900	800	1,630	395	1,360	Non-migrants	188
320	875	515	1,050	360	2,075	Migrants	189
290	540	480	845	255	1,045	Migrants internes	190
260	400	330	790	215	770	Migrants infraprovinciaux	191
25	145	145	55	35	275	Migrants interprovinciaux	192
30	335	40	205	105	1,030	Migrants externes	193
475	**530**	**425**	**970**	**510**	**850**	**Population totale de 15 à 24 ans .... selon la fréquentation scolaire**	194
145	225	165	385	140	435	Ne fréquentant pas l'école	195
310	275	245	555	350	400	Fréquentant l'école à plein temps	196
30	30	15	25	15	15	Fréquentant l'école à temps partiel	197
3,095	**2,665**	**3,370**	**5,780**	**2,395**	**4,735**	**Population totale de 15 ans et plus .... selon le plus haut niveau de scolarité atteint**	198
135	565	360	410	90	290	Niveau inférieur à la 9e année (31)	199
565	725	775	1,415	645	1,165	De la 9e à la 13e année sans certificat d'études secondaires	200
560	345	550	910	320	635	De la 9e à la 13e année avec certificat d'études secondaires	201
400	225	355	800	245	405	Études postsecondaires partielles sans grade, certificat ou diplôme (32)	202
240	235	285	400	185	470	Certificat ou diplôme d'une école de métiers (33)	203
595	310	570	1,000	410	620	Certificat ou diplôme collégial (34)	204
85	80	75	110	95	215	Certificat universitaire inférieur au baccalauréat.....	205
520	175	415	740	410	935	Études universitaires avec baccalauréat ou diplôme supérieur	206
						selon les combinaisons de travail non rémunéré	
1,540	1,320	1,665	2,770	1,125	2,375	Hommes de 15 ans et plus	207
1,385	1,040	1,475	2,420	935	2,020	Travail non rémunéré déclaré (35)	208
105	50	85	270	55	160	Travaux ménagers et soins aux enfants et soins ou aide aux personnes âgées	209
395	330	385	595	295	505	Travaux ménagers et soins aux enfants seulement	210
175	75	50	260	70	120	Travaux ménagers et soins ou aide aux personnes âgées seulement	211
10	-	10	-	-	-	Soins aux enfants et soins ou aide aux personnes âgées seulement	212
680	575	935	1,230	485	1,180	Travaux ménagers seulement	213
15	-	-	45	25	45	Soins aux enfants seulement	214
-	-	10	20	10	10	Soins ou aide aux personnes âgées seulement	215
1,550	1,340	1,705	3,015	1,275	2,365	Femmes de 15 ans et plus	216
1,465	1,220	1,605	2,760	1,160	2,205	Travail non rémunéré déclaré (35)	217
185	80	170	310	125	210	Travaux ménagers et soins aux enfants et soins ou aide aux personnes âgées	218
375	450	465	860	370	655	Travaux ménagers et soins aux enfants seulement	219
200	55	130	310	70	135	Travaux ménagers et soins ou aide aux personnes âgées seulement	220
-	-	-	-	-	-	Soins aux enfants et soins ou aide aux personnes âgées seulement	221
700	625	830	1,260	590	1,135	Travaux ménagers seulement	222
-	10	-	15	-	60	Soins aux enfants seulement	223
-	-	-	-	10	10	Soins ou aide aux personnes âgées seulement	224
						selon l'activité	
1,540	1,325	1,665	2,770	1,120	2,375	Hommes de 15 ans et plus	225
1,045	1,005	1,185	2,000	820	1,805	Population active	226
1,030	965	1,125	1,930	790	1,670	Personnes occupées	227
15	35	60	70	30	130	Chômeurs	228
495	320	485	770	300	570	Inactifs	229
67.9	75.8	71.2	72.2	73.2	76.0	Taux d'activité	230
66.9	72.8	67.6	69.7	70.5	70.3	Taux d'emploi	231
1.4	3.5	5.1	3.5	3.7	7.2	Taux de chômage	232
1,555	1,340	1,700	3,015	1,275	2,365	Femmes de 15 ans et plus	233
910	810	1,015	1,845	960	1,450	Population active	234
865	745	965	1,765	920	1,320	Personnes occupées	235
45	65	55	85	45	135	Chômeuses	236
645	535	690	1,165	315	915	Inactives	237
58.5	60.4	59.7	61.2	75.3	61.3	Taux d'activité	238
55.6	55.6	56.8	58.5	72.2	55.8	Taux d'emploi	239
4.9	8.0	5.4	4.6	4.7	9.3	Taux de chômage	240

Table 1. Selected Characteristics for Census Tracts, 2001 Census – 100% Data and 20% Sample Data

No.	Characteristics	Toronto 0562.11	Toronto 0563.01	Toronto 0563.02	Toronto 0564.01	Toronto 0564.02 ◆	Toronto 0570.01 ◆
	POPULATION CHARACTERISTICS						
	by labour force activity – concluded						
241	Both sexes - Participation rate	75.9	64.4	72.6	77.0	73.4	73.1
242	15-24 years	68.3	56.7	70.5	84.6	62.8	68.0
243	25 years and over	77.7	65.9	72.9	75.8	76.0	74.5
244	Both sexes - Employment rate	72.5	59.0	70.8	71.0	67.0	68.9
245	15-24 years	63.4	47.4	70.5	72.3	47.6	58.7
246	25 years and over	74.8	61.3	70.7	71.2	71.2	71.3
247	Both sexes - Unemployment rate	4.5	8.4	2.5	7.9	9.0	5.8
248	15-24 years	7.2	16.5	-	14.8	24.2	12.7
249	25 years and over	4.3	7.2	2.9	6.4	6.1	4.0
250	**Total labour force 15 years and over**	**1,990**	**3,350**	**1,825**	**1,525**	**2,835**	**1,970**
	by industry based on the 1997 NAICS						
251	Industry - Not applicable (36)	15	45	10	30	90	35
252	All industries (37)	1,970	3,310	1,815	1,495	2,750	1,935
253	11 Agriculture, forestry, fishing and hunting	-	10	10	-	10	20
254	21 Mining and oil and gas extraction	-	-	-	-	-	-
255	22 Utilities	10	10	10	10	-	-
256	23 Construction	60	90	95	75	130	110
257	31-33 Manufacturing	445	895	395	360	750	555
258	41 Wholesale trade	225	285	135	165	275	180
259	44-45 Retail trade	240	360	285	165	310	215
260	48-49 Transportation and warehousing	180	350	145	155	310	235
261	51 Information and cultural industries	40	40	35	25	55	35
262	52 Finance and insurance	95	40	75	25	55	30
263	53 Real estate and rental and leasing	40	55	20	30	15	70
264	54 Professional, scientific and technical services	185	95	115	90	150	60
265	55 Management of companies and enterprises	10	-	-	-	-	-
266	56 Administrative and support, waste management and remediation services	90	275	55	40	130	105
267	61 Educational services	95	100	45	55	85	50
268	62 Health care and social assistance	100	155	145	85	110	40
269	71 Arts, entertainment and recreation	30	15	60	-	45	10
270	72 Accommodation and food services	35	305	70	90	150	115
271	81 Other services (except public administration)	40	125	50	65	110	90
272	91 Public administration	55	110	75	50	55	20
	by class of worker						
273	Class of worker - Not applicable (36)	15	45	10	30	90	35
274	All classes of worker (37)	1,975	3,310	1,820	1,495	2,750	1,940
275	Paid workers	1,840	3,240	1,745	1,395	2,580	1,900
276	Employees	1,800	3,185	1,720	1,390	2,555	1,890
277	Self-employed (incorporated)	40	45	25	-	20	-
278	Self-employed (unincorporated)	130	70	70	105	155	40
279	Unpaid family workers	-	-	10	-	20	-
	by occupation based on the 2001 NOC-S						
280	Male labour force 15 years and over	1,060	1,660	975	830	1,530	1,105
281	Occupation - Not applicable (36)	15	-	10	10	10	15
282	All occupations (37)	1,045	1,660	970	820	1,520	1,090
283	A Management occupations	105	85	125	85	155	75
284	B Business, finance and administration occupations	145	230	70	140	150	145
285	C Natural and applied sciences and related occupations	135	125	75	50	110	65
286	D Health occupations	15	-	25	20	10	-
287	E Occupations in social science, education, government service and religion	25	30	10	15	10	15
288	F Occupations in art, culture, recreation and sport	30	-	15	-	20	-
289	G Sales and service occupations	195	315	140	120	245	140
290	H Trades, transport and equipment operators and related occupations	265	555	310	285	530	400
291	I Occupations unique to primary industry	15	10	15	-	25	15
292	J Occupations unique to processing, manufacturing and utilities	120	315	185	110	270	225
293	Female labour force 15 years and over	930	1,690	850	695	1,310	870
294	Occupation - Not applicable (36)	-	45	-	20	80	20
295	All occupations (37)	930	1,650	850	675	1,225	850
296	A Management occupations	70	45	85	40	70	30
297	B Business, finance and administration occupations	340	555	285	245	340	240
298	C Natural and applied sciences and related occupations	25	40	20	10	55	10
299	D Health occupations	40	65	60	40	40	15

Tableau 1. Certaines caractéristiques des secteurs de recensement, recensement de 2001 – Données intégrales et données-échantillon (20 %)

Toronto 0570.02	Toronto 0571.01	Toronto 0571.02	Toronto 0572.01	Toronto 0572.04 A	Toronto 0572.05 ◆ A	Caractéristiques	N°
						CARACTÉRISTIQUES DE LA POPULATION	
						selon l'activité – fin	
63.0	68.1	65.3	66.5	74.4	68.6	Les deux sexes - Taux d'activité	241
69.5	68.6	74.1	61.3	61.2	73.4	15-24 ans	242
61.8	68.0	63.9	67.5	77.7	67.6	25 ans et plus	243
61.2	64.4	62.0	63.9	71.2	63.0	Les deux sexes - Taux d'emploi	244
67.4	61.9	65.9	57.0	57.3	61.8	15-24 ans	245
60.1	64.9	61.3	65.2	74.6	63.2	25 ans et plus	246
3.1	5.5	5.0	3.9	4.5	8.3	Les deux sexes - Taux de chômage	247
4.5	9.7	11.1	7.6	7.9	16.0	15-24 ans	248
3.1	4.5	4.2	3.2	3.4	6.3	25 ans et plus	249
1,950	**1,810**	**2,200**	**3,840**	**1,780**	**3,255**	**Population active totale de 15 ans et plus**	250
						selon l'industrie basée sur le SCIAN de 1997	
10	10	15	30	10	95	Industrie - Sans objet (36)	251
1,940	1,810	2,185	3,815	1,770	3,160	Toutes les industries (37)	252
-	-	10	15	-	10	11 Agriculture, foresterie, pêche et chasse	253
-	-	-	-	10	-	21 Extraction minière et extraction de pétrole et de gaz	254
-	10	15	20	15	10	22 Services publics	255
130	145	160	195	60	130	23 Construction	256
245	540	435	815	370	705	31-33 Fabrication	257
120	105	170	365	130	260	41 Commerce de gros	258
225	210	195	475	190	340	44-45 Commerce de détail	259
195	135	180	325	95	380	48-49 Transport et entreposage	260
60	35	40	95	25	65	51 Industrie de l'information et industrie culturelle	261
60	15	60	145	85	135	52 Finance et assurances	262
65	15	45	65	30	15	53 Services immobiliers et services de location et de location à bail	263
160	40	110	210	120	185	54 Services professionnels, scientifiques et techniques	264
-	-	-	-	-	-	55 Gestion de sociétés et d'entreprises	265
55	80	150	140	90	185	56 Services administratifs, services de soutien, services de gestion des déchets et services d'assainissement	266
185	40	105	215	90	185	61 Services d'enseignement	267
155	125	210	215	225	150	62 Soins de santé et assistance sociale	268
35	10	35	40	15	40	71 Arts, spectacles et loisirs	269
55	130	110	175	50	140	72 Hébergement et services de restauration	270
60	110	65	145	80	150	81 Autres services, sauf les administrations publiques	271
145	60	95	160	85	60	91 Administrations publiques	272
						selon la catégorie de travailleurs	
10	10	20	30	15	90	Catégorie de travailleurs - Sans objet (36)	273
1,940	1,805	2,180	3,815	1,770	3,160	Toutes les catégories de travailleurs (37)	274
1,810	1,760	2,080	3,525	1,675	3,045	Travailleurs rémunérés	275
1,740	1,715	2,010	3,435	1,655	2,995	Employés	276
75	45	70	90	15	40	Travailleurs autonomes (entreprise constituée en société)	277
130	40	100	280	90	120	Travailleurs autonomes (entreprise non constituée en société)	278
-	10	-	15	10	-	Travailleurs familiaux non rémunérés	279
						selon la profession basée sur la CNP-S de 2001	
1,040	1,005	1,185	2,000	820	1,800	Hommes actifs de 15 ans et plus	280
-	10	10	10	-	35	Profession - Sans objet (36)	281
1,045	1,000	1,175	1,990	820	1,765	Toutes les professions (37)	282
170	70	170	260	65	175	A Gestion	283
115	70	140	225	100	185	B Affaires, finance et administration	284
115	55	100	155	85	320	C Sciences naturelles et appliquées et professions apparentées	285
25	-	20	15	35	15	D Secteur de la santé	286
65	15	75	50	35	55	E Sciences sociales, enseignement, administration publique et religion	287
25	-	25	35	20	10	F Arts, culture, sports et loisirs	288
195	165	165	345	150	275	G Ventes et services	289
280	440	360	620	190	510	H Métiers, transport et machinerie	290
20	-	40	20	20	-	I Professions propres au secteur primaire	291
40	175	90	275	125	215	J Transformation, fabrication et services d'utilité publique	292
910	810	1,020	1,845	960	1,450	Femmes actives de 15 ans et plus	293
15	-	-	20	10	60	Profession - Sans objet (36)	294
895	805	1,010	1,830	950	1,395	Toutes les professions (37)	295
80	50	65	135	45	95	A Gestion	296
355	180	340	630	350	415	B Affaires, finance et administration	297
15	10	35	20	30	70	C Sciences naturelles et appliquées et professions apparentées	298
75	50	75	60	85	100	D Secteur de la santé	299

Table 1. Selected Characteristics for Census Tracts, 2001 Census – 100% Data and 20% Sample Data

No.	Characteristics	Toronto 0562.11	Toronto 0563.01	Toronto 0563.02	Toronto 0564.01	Toronto 0564.02 ◆	Toronto 0570.01 ◆
	POPULATION CHARACTERISTICS						
	by occupation based on the 2001 NOC-S – concluded						
300	E Occupations in social science, education, government service and religion	85	85	75	45	70	40
301	F Occupations in art, culture, recreation and sport	25	10	20	10	30	15
302	G Sales and service occupations	150	520	175	190	335	275
303	H Trades, transport and equipment operators and related occupations	80	55	30	30	50	60
304	I Occupations unique to primary industry	15	-	10	10	-	10
305	J Occupations unique to processing, manufacturing and utilities	95	290	105	65	235	155
306	**Total employed labour force 15 years and over**	**1,895**	**3,070**	**1,780**	**1,410**	**2,580**	**1,860**
	by place of work						
307	Males	1,025	1,535	945	785	1,465	1,065
308	Usual place of work	845	1,380	810	685	1,255	915
309	At home	60	35	25	35	30	10
310	Outside Canada	-	10	10	-	-	10
311	No fixed workplace address	115	120	105	65	180	125
312	Females	875	1,535	830	625	1,120	795
313	Usual place of work	790	1,460	730	575	990	755
314	At home	30	20	40	20	85	20
315	Outside Canada	10	-	10	-	10	10
316	No fixed workplace address	50	50	55	35	45	20
317	**Total employed labour force 15 years and over with usual place of work or no fixed workplace address**	**1,805**	**3,005**	**1,700**	**1,355**	**2,465**	**1,815**
	by mode of transportation						
318	Males	965	1,495	915	750	1,435	1,040
319	Car, truck, van, as driver	830	1,155	740	635	1,030	785
320	Car, truck, van, as passenger	75	60	40	30	155	85
321	Public transit	50	250	95	65	215	85
322	Walked	-	10	35	10	25	55
323	Other method	15	25	10	15	10	30
324	Females	840	1,515	785	610	1,040	770
325	Car, truck, van, as driver	620	790	465	440	610	490
326	Car, truck, van, as passenger	100	130	90	60	175	90
327	Public transit	80	465	175	85	175	125
328	Walked	30	120	55	20	60	65
329	Other method	10	10	10	-	20	10
330	**Total population 15 years and over who worked since January 1, 2000**	**2,150**	**3,720**	**1,950**	**1,555**	**2,915**	**2,090**
	by language used at work						
331	Single responses	2,045	3,400	1,905	1,435	2,645	1,945
332	English	2,035	3,320	1,900	1,435	2,635	1,935
333	French	-	10	-	-	-	-
334	Non-official languages (5)	10	75	10	-	10	10
335	Chinese, n.o.s.	10	-	-	-	-	-
336	Cantonese	-	-	-	-	-	-
337	Other languages (6)	-	70	-	-	-	-
338	Multiple responses	100	320	45	115	275	145
339	English and French	40	50	20	80	80	45
340	English and non-official language	60	265	25	35	170	105
341	French and non-official language	-	-	-	-	-	-
342	English, French and non-official language	-	-	-	10	25	-
	DWELLING AND HOUSEHOLD CHARACTERISTICS						
343	**Total number of occupied private dwellings**	**995**	**2,520**	**1,025**	**745**	**1,445**	**1,345**
	by tenure						
344	Owned	900	1,005	810	680	1,085	140
345	Rented	90	1,510	215	75	360	1,205
346	Band housing	-	-	-	-	-	-
	by structural type of dwelling						
347	Single-detached house	990	-	550	385	385	80
348	Semi-detached house	-	-	175	245	320	-
349	Row house	-	-	165	80	520	360
350	Apartment, detached duplex	-	-	-	15	-	10
351	Apartment, building that has five or more storeys	-	2,390	140	-	175	890
352	Apartment, building that has fewer than five storeys (38)	-	125	-	20	40	-
353	Other single-attached house	-	-	-	-	-	-
354	Movable dwelling (39)	-	-	-	-	-	-

Tableau 1. Certaines caractéristiques des secteurs de recensement, recensement de 2001 – Données intégrales et données-échantillon (20 %)

Toronto 0570.02	Toronto 0571.01	Toronto 0571.02	Toronto 0572.01	Toronto 0572.04 A	Toronto 0572.05 ◆ A	Caractéristiques	N°
						CARACTÉRISTIQUES DE LA POPULATION	
						selon la profession basée sur la CNP-S de 2001 – fin	
115	45	85	295	95	115	E Sciences sociales, enseignement, administration publique et religion	300
25	10	25	60	20	20	F Arts, culture, sports et loisirs	301
200	265	260	410	200	390	G Ventes et services	302
15	35	35	65	35	65	H Métiers, transport et machinerie	303
-	-	-	20	-	15	I Professions propres au secteur primaire	304
15	170	95	135	100	105	J Transformation, fabrication et services d'utilité publique	305
1,895	**1,710**	**2,090**	**3,695**	**1,705**	**2,985**	**Population active occupée totale de 15 ans et plus .....**	306
						selon le lieu de travail	
1,030	970	1,125	1,930	790	1,670	Hommes	307
855	780	945	1,635	630	1,475	Lieu habituel de travail	308
80	20	15	70	40	45	À domicile	309
-	-	-	-	-	15	En dehors du Canada	310
90	170	160	220	115	130	Sans adresse de travail fixe	311
865	745	965	1,765	915	1,320	Femmes	312
760	685	870	1,595	830	1,225	Lieu habituel de travail	313
90	35	45	100	25	35	À domicile	314
-	-	-	-	-	-	En dehors du Canada	315
15	25	45	70	60	60	Sans adresse de travail fixe	316
1,720	**1,665**	**2,025**	**3,510**	**1,635**	**2,895**	**Population active occupée totale de 15 ans et plus ayant un lieu habituel de travail ou sans adresse de travail fixe..........................**	317
						selon le mode de transport	
950	950	1,105	1,850	745	1,610	Hommes	318
830	715	935	1,590	665	1,305	Automobile, camion ou fourgonnette, en tant que conducteur	319
20	85	55	95	25	70	Automobile, camion ou fourgonnette, en tant que passager	320
35	95	60	125	20	195	Transport en commun	321
35	50	45	20	10	30	À pied	322
20	-	10	20	15	20	Autre moyen	323
775	715	915	1,660	895	1,285	Femmes	324
550	390	705	1,200	685	685	Automobile, camion ou fourgonnette, en tant que conductrice	325
85	65	60	185	100	235	Automobile, camion ou fourgonnette, en tant que passagère	326
75	150	75	200	65	290	Transport en commun	327
60	105	50	55	35	65	À pied	328
10	-	25	15	10	10	Autre moyen	329
2,150	**1,990**	**2,355**	**4,250**	**1,920**	**3,465**	**Population totale de 15 ans et plus ayant travaillé depuis le 1er janvier 2000 ....**	330
						selon la langue utilisée au travail	
2,075	1,790	2,210	3,940	1,835	3,270	Réponses uniques	331
2,075	1,615	2,195	3,920	1,830	3,235	Anglais	332
-	10	-	-	-	15	Français	333
-	170	20	15	-	20	Langues non officielles (5)	334
-	10	-	-	-	-	Chinois, n.d.a.	335
-	-	-	-	-	-	Cantonais	336
-	170	20	15	-	25	Autres langues (6)	337
75	195	140	315	85	195	Réponses multiples	338
25	45	15	75	30	80	Anglais et français	339
45	150	115	225	55	115	Anglais et langue non officielle	340
-	-	-	-	-	-	Français et langue non officielle	341
-	-	10	10	-	-	Anglais, français et langue non officielle	342
						CARACTÉRISTIQUES DES LOGEMENTS ET DES MÉNAGES	
1,295	**1,125**	**1,505**	**2,615**	**995**	**2,325**	**Nombre total de logements privés occupés ....**	343
						selon le mode d'occupation	
1,265	460	1,220	1,715	725	660	Possédé	344
35	665	285	900	265	1,670	Loué	345
-	-	-	-	-	-	Logement de bande	346
						selon le type de construction résidentielle	
1,290	270	1,170	1,340	630	485	Maison individuelle non attenante	347
-	140	55	275	15	-	Maison jumelée	348
-	285	-	200	205	-	Maison en rangée	349
10	10	95	45	10	25	Appartement, duplex non attenant	350
-	270	55	575	-	1,815	Appartement, immeuble de cinq étages ou plus	351
-	150	125	175	135	10	Appartement, immeuble de moins de cinq étages (38) ...	352
-	-	-	-	-	-	Autre maison individuelle attenante	353
-	-	-	-	-	-	Logement mobile (39)	354

Table 1. Selected Characteristics for Census Tracts, 2001 Census – 100% Data and 20% Sample Data

No.	Characteristics	Toronto 0562.11	Toronto 0563.01	Toronto 0563.02	Toronto 0564.01	Toronto 0564.02 ◆	Toronto 0570.01 ◆
	DWELLING AND HOUSEHOLD CHARACTERISTICS						
	by condition of dwelling						
355	Regular maintenance only	625	2,010	725	475	785	510
356	Minor repairs	250	330	255	225	445	410
357	Major repairs	120	180	45	50	215	420
	by period of construction						
358	Before 1946	-	40	-	-	10	25
359	1946-1960	15	60	30	65	70	175
360	1961-1970	135	435	820	510	640	840
361	1971-1980	690	1,575	135	155	435	250
362	1981-1990	145	205	45	15	290	50
363	1991-2001 (20)	10	200	-	-	10	-
364	Average number of rooms per dwelling	7.3	4.3	6.8	7.2	6.5	4.8
365	Average number of bedrooms per dwelling	3.3	1.9	3.0	3.3	3.2	2.0
366	Average value of dwelling $	192,767	125,636	193,955	186,928	158,210	160,940
367	**Total number of private households**	**995**	**2,520**	**1,025**	**750**	**1,450**	**1,340**
	by household size						
368	1 person	70	640	115	60	120	395
369	2 persons	240	695	345	220	300	400
370	3 persons	210	465	195	145	295	215
371	4-5 persons	395	590	300	270	580	290
372	6 or more persons	80	125	75	55	155	45
	by household type						
373	One-family households	855	1,705	835	620	1,145	840
374	Multiple-family households	45	85	70	40	125	15
375	Non-family households	95	730	120	80	175	490
376	Number of persons in private households	3,395	6,800	3,170	2,445	5,120	3,365
377	Average number of persons in private households	3.4	2.7	3.1	3.3	3.5	2.5
378	Average number of persons per room	0.5	0.6	0.5	0.5	0.5	0.5
379	Tenant households in non-farm, non-reserve private dwellings (40)	90	1,515	210	75	360	1,200
380	Average gross rent $ (40)	1,184	827	1,057	1,031	1,141	853
381	Tenant households spending 30% or more of household income on gross rent (40) (41)	40	655	85	40	140	380
382	Tenant households spending from 30% to 99% of household income on gross rent (40) (41)	35	485	60	30	110	315
383	Owner households in non-farm, non-reserve private dwellings (42)	905	1,005	810	675	1,085	140
384	Average owner's major payments $ (42)	1,146	968	992	1,029	1,054	1,090
385	Owner households spending 30% or more of household income on owner's major payments (41) (42)	165	380	105	105	235	25
386	Owner households spending from 30% to 99% of household income on owner's major payments (41) (42)	170	320	100	95	210	20
	CENSUS FAMILY CHARACTERISTICS						
387	**Total number of census families in private households**	**940**	**1,880**	**975**	**710**	**1,395**	**870**
	by census family structure and size						
388	Total couple families	805	1,320	765	620	1,090	640
389	Total families of married couples	735	1,180	700	560	965	475
390	Without children at home	195	430	265	180	200	165
391	With children at home	540	745	435	380	765	310
392	1 child	185	295	185	140	230	110
393	2 children	240	325	160	190	325	125
394	3 or more children	115	125	90	55	205	75
395	Total families of common-law couples	70	140	65	60	125	160
396	Without children at home	40	105	40	20	50	110
397	With children at home	30	35	25	35	70	55
398	1 child	-	-	10	20	55	30
399	2 children	15	25	20	10	10	15
400	3 or more children	-	15	-	10	-	-
401	Total lone-parent families	140	560	210	90	305	230
402	Female parent	105	470	185	45	225	190
403	1 child	50	215	95	35	135	70
404	2 children	30	200	70	15	75	80
405	3 or more children	30	50	20	-	15	30

Tableau 1. Certaines caractéristiques des secteurs de recensement, recensement de 2001 – Données intégrales et données-échantillon (20 %)

Toronto 0570.02	Toronto 0571.01	Toronto 0571.02	Toronto 0572.01	Toronto 0572.04 A	Toronto 0572.05 ◆ A	Caractéristiques	Nº
						CARACTÉRISTIQUES DES LOGEMENTS ET DES MÉNAGES	
						selon l'état du logement	
895	635	950	1,660	755	1,845	Entretien régulier seulement	355
365	330	475	765	220	350	Réparations mineures	356
40	160	85	185	15	125	Réparations majeures	357
						selon la période de construction	
-	75	55	180	-	25	Avant 1946	358
70	160	695	545	10	40	1946-1960	359
1,140	430	610	890	25	185	1961-1970	360
80	380	135	490	225	905	1971-1980	361
-	75	15	345	665	1,085	1981-1990	362
-	-	-	165	70	90	1991-2001 (20)	363
7.6	6.0	7.0	6.4	7.3	4.9	Nombre moyen de pièces par logement	364
3.3	2.7	3.0	2.8	3.2	2.0	Nombre moyen de chambres à coucher par logement	365
226,212	181,195	220,528	223,878	220,171	221,944	Valeur moyenne du logement $	366
1,295	**1,125**	**1,505**	**2,615**	**990**	**2,325**	**Nombre total de logements privés**	367
						selon la taille du ménage	
145	165	275	560	165	705	1 personne	368
510	280	545	795	245	705	2 personnes	369
245	280	295	450	185	385	3 personnes	370
360	300	345	690	325	430	4-5 personnes	371
30	100	45	115	70	100	6 personnes ou plus	372
						selon le genre de ménage	
1,095	860	1,130	1,900	770	1,435	Ménages unifamiliaux	373
20	60	65	85	40	65	Ménages multifamiliaux	374
175	205	315	625	185	830	Ménages non familiaux	375
3,665	3,520	4,050	7,280	3,080	5,810	Nombre de personnes dans les ménages privés	376
2.8	3.1	2.7	2.8	3.1	2.5	Nombre moyen de personnes dans les ménages privés	377
0.4	0.5	0.4	0.4	0.4	0.5	Nombre moyen de personnes par pièce	378
30	650	290	900	270	1,660	Ménages locataires dans les logements privés non agricoles hors réserve (40)	379
1,160	972	757	733	937	956	Loyer brut moyen $ (40)	380
25	285	75	370	120	775	Ménages locataires consacrant 30 % ou plus du revenu du ménage au loyer brut (40) (41)	381
15	225	55	315	110	645	Ménages locataires consacrant de 30 % à 99 % du revenu du ménage au loyer brut (40) (41)	382
1,265	460	1,220	1,710	725	660	Ménages propriétaires dans les logements privés non agricoles hors réserve (42)	383
896	1,007	942	1,077	1,032	1,007	Principales dépenses de propriété moyennes $ (42)	384
150	120	240	255	145	135	Ménages propriétaires consacrant 30 % ou plus du revenu du ménage aux principales dépenses de propriété (41) (42)	385
130	75	215	210	110	105	Ménages propriétaires consacrant de 30 % à 99 % du revenu du ménage aux principales dépenses de propriété (41) (42)	386
						CARACTÉRISTIQUES DES FAMILLES DE RECENSEMENT	
1,140	**980**	**1,260**	**2,090**	**855**	**1,565**	**Total des familles de recensement dans les ménages privés**	387
						selon la structure et la taille de la famille de recensement	
1,055	735	1,070	1,675	690	1,290	Total des familles avec conjoints	388
1,010	615	960	1,500	615	1,110	Total des familles avec couples mariés	389
460	185	445	615	170	415	Sans enfants à la maison	390
550	425	520	885	450	695	Avec enfants à la maison	391
195	160	230	270	115	320	1 enfant	392
255	145	220	415	235	230	2 enfants	393
95	125	75	200	105	145	3 enfants ou plus	394
40	120	115	175	75	180	Total des familles en union libre	395
10	55	80	110	25	140	Sans enfants à la maison	396
25	65	30	70	45	40	Avec enfants à la maison	397
20	10	30	45	20	25	1 enfant	398
-	35	-	15	10	10	2 enfants	399
-	25	-	-	15	-	3 enfants ou plus	400
95	245	185	410	165	270	Total des familles monoparentales	401
80	185	130	360	145	230	Parent de sexe féminin	402
60	110	90	150	65	120	1 enfant	403
15	55	35	100	55	60	2 enfants	404
-	25	-	110	20	45	3 enfants ou plus	405

Table 1. Selected Characteristics for Census Tracts, 2001 Census – 100% Data and 20% Sample Data

No.	Characteristics	Toronto 0562.11	Toronto 0563.01	Toronto 0563.02	Toronto 0564.01	Toronto 0564.02 ◆	Toronto 0570.01 ◆
	CENSUS FAMILY CHARACTERISTICS						
	by census family structure and size – concluded						
406	Male parent	30	90	20	45	80	45
407	1 child	30	45	10	20	50	20
408	2 children	-	35	15	10	25	10
409	3 or more children	-	15	-	10	10	10
410	**Total number of children at home**	**1,325**	**2,410**	**1,190**	**895**	**2,135**	**1,145**
	by age groups						
411	Under 6 years	295	705	260	145	450	295
412	6-14 years	480	875	380	315	810	375
413	15-17 years	145	235	130	105	265	130
414	18-24 years	285	405	210	200	305	190
415	25 years and over	120	190	210	130	300	150
	Average number of children at home per						
416	census family (43)	1.4	1.3	1.2	1.3	1.5	1.3
417	**Total number of persons in private households**	**3,395**	**6,800**	**3,170**	**2,445**	**5,120**	**3,360**
	by census family status and living arrangements						
418	Number of non-family persons	325	1,190	240	220	510	710
419	Living with relatives (44)	110	205	65	85	185	130
420	Living with non-relatives only	150	350	65	80	210	185
421	Living alone	65	640	115	55	120	395
422	Number of family persons	3,075	5,605	2,930	2,225	4,615	2,650
423	Average number of persons per census family	3.3	3.0	3.0	3.1	3.3	3.0
424	**Total number of persons 65 years and over**	**215**	**735**	**425**	**180**	**290**	**210**
425	Number of non-family persons 65 years and over	50	310	35	65	75	90
426	Living with relatives (44)	50	60	10	55	45	25
427	Living with non-relatives only	-	20	-	-	15	-
428	Living alone	-	230	35	15	20	60
429	Number of family persons 65 years and over	160	420	390	120	220	115
	ECONOMIC FAMILY CHARACTERISTICS						
	Total number of economic families in						
430	**private households**	**900**	**1,820**	**905**	**670**	**1,290**	**880**
	by size of family						
431	2 persons	245	710	340	205	305	350
432	3 persons	200	450	220	150	285	230
433	4 persons	255	400	185	175	360	190
434	5 or more persons	195	265	160	140	340	120
435	Total number of persons in economic families	3,185	5,810	2,990	2,310	4,795	2,780
436	Average number of persons per economic family	3.5	3.2	3.3	3.4	3.7	3.2
437	Total number of unattached individuals	215	985	175	140	325	585
	2000 INCOME CHARACTERISTICS						
	Population 15 years and over by sex and total income groups in 2000						
438	Total - Both sexes	2,615	5,205	2,515	1,985	3,860	2,695
439	Without income	100	330	95	70	305	185
440	With income	2,515	4,870	2,420	1,910	3,550	2,515
441	Under $1,000 (45)	70	310	60	80	240	130
442	$ 1,000 - $ 2,999	105	230	40	55	205	100
443	$ 3,000 - $ 4,999	110	270	80	65	120	90
444	$ 5,000 - $ 6,999	105	175	85	95	195	85
445	$ 7,000 - $ 9,999	110	380	185	70	185	80
446	$10,000 - $11,999	70	230	55	80	95	135
447	$12,000 - $14,999	125	375	160	100	205	135
448	$15,000 - $19,999	220	565	205	130	310	270
449	$20,000 - $24,999	215	385	140	165	330	195
450	$25,000 - $29,999	210	480	190	155	220	220
451	$30,000 - $34,999	190	510	150	200	330	275
452	$35,000 - $39,999	185	270	190	155	190	165
453	$40,000 - $44,999	155	195	170	85	185	180
454	$45,000 - $49,999	105	160	205	100	205	150
455	$50,000 - $59,999	205	195	200	175	260	105
456	$60,000 and over	350	130	315	215	275	200
457	Average income $ (46)	37,852	22,173	33,997	30,884	27,083	27,740
458	Median income $ (46)	27,961	18,758	30,220	28,469	23,674	25,563
459	Standard error of average income $ (46)	4,084	542	1,114	1,071	797	832

Tableau 1. Certaines caractéristiques des secteurs de recensement, recensement de 2001 – Données intégrales et données-échantillon (20 %)

Toronto 0570.02	Toronto 0571.01	Toronto 0571.02	Toronto 0572.01	Toronto 0572.04 A	Toronto 0572.05 ◆ A	Caractéristiques	N°
						CARACTÉRISTIQUES DES FAMILLES DE RECENSEMENT	
						selon la structure et la taille de la famille de recensement - fin	
15	55	50	45	20	40	Parent de sexe masculin	406
15	55	25	25	20	25	1 enfant	407
-	10	30	20	-	15	2 enfants	408
-	-	-	-	-	-	3 enfants ou plus	409
1,175	**1,360**	**1,210**	**2,665**	**1,275**	**1,780**	**Nombre total d'enfants à la maison**	410
						selon les groupes d'âge	
215	365	265	500	215	490	Moins de 6 ans	411
360	480	410	995	460	575	6-14 ans	412
140	175	100	295	135	195	15-17 ans	413
315	190	245	555	355	290	18-24 ans	414
150	150	200	320	100	235	25 ans et plus	415
1.0	1.4	1.0	1.3	1.5	1.1	Nombre moyen d'enfants à la maison par famille de recensement (43)	416
3,665	**3,520**	**4,045**	**7,285**	**3,075**	**5,810**	**Nombre total de personnes dans les ménages privés**	417
						selon la situation des particuliers dans la famille de recensement et des particuliers dans le ménage	
295	445	500	855	265	1,175	Nombre de personnes hors famille de recensement	418
80	125	110	100	85	150	Vivant avec des personnes apparentées (44)	419
70	155	115	185	10	320	Vivant avec des personnes non apparentées uniquement	420
145	165	275	565	165	705	Vivant seules	421
3,370	3,075	3,545	6,430	2,815	4,635	Nombre de personnes membres d'une famille	422
3.0	3.1	2.8	3.1	3.3	3.0	Nombre moyen de personnes par famille de recensement	423
640	**270**	**700**	**945**	**200**	**560**	**Nombre total de personnes de 65 ans et plus**	424
115	75	145	265	75	225	Nombre de personnes hors famille de recensement de 65 ans et plus	425
30	30	20	20	20	30	Vivant avec des personnes apparentées (44)	426
-	10	-	10	10	10	Vivant avec des personnes non apparentées uniquement	427
85	40	125	235	45	195	Vivant seules	428
525	200	560	685	125	335	Nombre de personnes membres d'une famille de 65 ans et plus	429
						CARACTÉRISTIQUES DES FAMILLES ÉCONOMIQUES	
1,135	**930**	**1,200**	**2,000**	**825**	**1,525**	**Nombre total de familles économiques dans les ménages privés**	430
						selon la taille de la famille	
520	315	535	790	245	660	2 personnes	431
240	240	300	410	185	360	3 personnes	432
255	180	230	475	220	255	4 personnes	433
120	195	135	320	175	240	5 personnes ou plus	434
3,450	3,200	3,660	6,535	2,900	4,785	Nombre total de personnes dans les familles économiques	435
3.0	3.4	3.0	3.3	3.5	3.1	Nombre moyen de personnes par famille économique	436
220	320	390	745	175	1,025	Nombre total de personnes hors famille économique	437
						CARACTÉRISTIQUES DU REVENU DE 2000	
						Population de 15 ans et plus selon le sexe et les tranches de revenu total en 2000	
3,095	2,665	3,370	5,785	2,395	4,735	Total - Les deux sexes	438
105	205	95	285	100	260	Sans revenu	439
2,990	2,460	3,275	5,500	2,300	4,480	Avec un revenu	440
85	105	120	245	135	155	Moins de 1 000 $ (45)	441
105	175	170	210	195	180	1 000 $ - 2 999 $	442
90	65	80	250	100	245	3 000 $ - 4 999 $	443
150	130	165	220	65	160	5 000 $ - 6 999 $	444
180	200	160	290	35	295	7 000 $ - 9 999 $	445
105	85	110	155	40	170	10 000 $ - 11 999 $	446
200	120	140	335	140	365	12 000 $ - 14 999 $	447
230	245	195	385	190	300	15 000 $ - 19 999 $	448
180	170	320	485	150	305	20 000 $ - 24 999 $	449
210	305	225	350	120	445	25 000 $ - 29 999 $	450
195	265	290	440	250	370	30 000 $ - 34 999 $	451
155	160	205	445	165	240	35 000 $ - 39 999 $	452
125	205	255	240	165	250	40 000 $ - 44 999 $	453
170	65	135	210	80	270	45 000 $ - 49 999 $	454
235	115	270	415	120	355	50 000 $ - 59 999 $	455
575	60	440	835	355	375	60 000 $ et plus	456
36,036	24,342	34,203	34,637	32,898	28,781	Revenu moyen $ (46)	457
29,479	23,946	28,542	26,910	28,704	25,629	Revenu médian $ (46)	458
1,260	954	1,188	947	1,392	778	Erreur type de revenu moyen $ (46)	459

Table 1. Selected Characteristics for Census Tracts, 2001 Census – 100% Data and 20% Sample Data

No.	Characteristics	Toronto 0562.11	Toronto 0563.01	Toronto 0563.02	Toronto 0564.01	Toronto 0564.02 ◆	Toronto 0570.01 ◆
	2000 INCOME CHARACTERISTICS						
	Population 15 years and over by sex and total income groups in 2000 – concluded						
460	Total - Males	1,295	2,330	1,220	1,010	1,905	1,365
461	Without income	40	150	35	20	100	55
462	With income	1,250	2,175	1,190	990	1,810	1,310
463	Under $1,000 (45)	25	135	40	30	75	75
464	$ 1,000 - $ 2,999	30	70	15	25	85	45
465	$ 3,000 - $ 4,999	50	85	10	20	25	55
466	$ 5,000 - $ 6,999	45	50	30	35	65	15
467	$ 7,000 - $ 9,999	65	120	35	15	95	10
468	$10,000 - $11,999	30	110	15	10	40	65
469	$12,000 - $14,999	30	105	40	45	75	50
470	$15,000 - $19,999	75	260	75	60	100	135
471	$20,000 - $24,999	60	170	45	65	160	110
472	$25,000 - $29,999	95	205	90	65	95	105
473	$30,000 - $34,999	75	250	90	115	165	165
474	$35,000 - $39,999	130	170	120	90	100	105
475	$40,000 - $44,999	105	85	110	45	150	120
476	$45,000 - $49,999	50	115	135	70	140	75
477	$50,000 - $59,999	160	135	105	120	190	55
478	$60,000 and over	230	105	235	180	245	130
479	Average income $ (46)	49,212	26,129	41,887	37,971	34,228	30,456
480	Median income $ (46)	36,354	24,718	39,391	35,219	31,236	29,435
481	Standard error of average income $ (46)	8,035	859	1,765	1,596	1,231	1,199
482	Total - Females	1,325	2,875	1,290	970	1,950	1,330
483	Without income	55	180	65	50	205	125
484	With income	1,265	2,695	1,230	920	1,745	1,205
485	Under $1,000 (45)	45	185	20	50	165	50
486	$ 1,000 - $ 2,999	70	155	25	35	125	50
487	$ 3,000 - $ 4,999	60	180	70	45	90	40
488	$ 5,000 - $ 6,999	60	130	60	55	130	65
489	$ 7,000 - $ 9,999	45	265	150	55	90	70
490	$10,000 - $11,999	40	120	40	70	60	75
491	$12,000 - $14,999	90	275	120	55	130	80
492	$15,000 - $19,999	145	300	125	75	215	140
493	$20,000 - $24,999	150	215	95	100	170	85
494	$25,000 - $29,999	110	275	100	85	130	115
495	$30,000 - $34,999	115	260	60	90	160	110
496	$35,000 - $39,999	55	100	70	60	85	65
497	$40,000 - $44,999	50	115	65	40	35	60
498	$45,000 - $49,999	60	45	65	25	65	75
499	$50,000 - $59,999	40	60	95	50	70	50
500	$60,000 and over	115	25	80	35	30	75
501	Average income $ (46)	26,585	18,981	26,370	23,256	19,682	24,782
502	Median income $ (46)	21,949	15,476	20,652	21,001	17,313	20,365
503	Standard error of average income $ (46)	1,337	658	1,235	1,210	841	1,116
	by composition of total income						
504	Total - Composition of income in 2000 % (47)	100.0	100.0	100.0	100.0	100.0	100.0
505	Employment income %	87.9	78.7	80.7	85.0	88.0	86.7
506	Government transfer payments %	6.7	16.6	8.4	8.1	8.0	9.3
507	Other %	5.2	4.8	11.0	7.2	4.0	3.9
	Population 15 years and over with employment income in 2000 by sex and work activity						
508	Both sexes with employment income (48)	2,095	3,575	1,905	1,525	2,820	1,985
509	Average employment income $	40,016	23,766	34,779	32,765	30,036	30,499
510	Standard error of average employment income $	4,856	655	1,236	1,193	892	929
511	Worked full year, full time (49)	1,295	1,990	1,150	900	1,585	1,205
512	Average employment income $	54,757	31,227	44,758	40,117	40,661	36,771
513	Standard error of average employment income $	7,703	893	1,470	1,262	1,116	1,120
514	Worked part year or part time (50)	755	1,495	725	605	1,150	675
515	Average employment income $	16,218	14,653	19,219	22,877	16,444	20,957
516	Standard error of average employment income $	1,255	703	1,578	2,055	969	1,394
517	Males with employment income (48)	1,105	1,755	1,000	845	1,555	1,100
518	Average employment income $	51,365	27,098	40,813	39,195	36,112	32,754
519	Standard error of average employment income $	9,110	954	1,853	1,699	1,325	1,276
520	Worked full year, full time (49)	760	1,075	655	570	1,010	700
521	Average employment income $	66,636	33,399	49,451	43,985	45,206	39,228
522	Standard error of average employment income $	13,053	1,240	2,138	1,685	1,528	1,554
523	Worked part year or part time (50)	325	620	330	260	505	305
524	Average employment income $	17,550	17,729	23,557	30,145	19,876	21,445
525	Standard error of average employment income $	2,098	1,166	2,536	3,653	1,709	1,738

Tableau 1. Certaines caractéristiques des secteurs de recensement, recensement de 2001 – Données intégrales et données-échantillon (20 %)

Toronto 0570.02	Toronto 0571.01	Toronto 0571.02	Toronto 0572.01	Toronto 0572.04 A	Toronto 0572.05 ◆ A	Caractéristiques	N°
						CARACTÉRISTIQUES DU REVENU DE 2000	
						Population de 15 ans et plus selon le sexe et les tranches de revenu total en 2000 – fin	
1,540	1,325	1,670	2,770	1,125	2,370	Total - Hommes	460
35	85	40	90	45	80	Sans revenu	461
1,505	1,235	1,630	2,680	1,075	2,290	Avec un revenu	462
20	35	45	130	65	60	Moins de 1 000 $ (45)	463
45	60	65	100	105	70	1 000 $ - 2 999 $	464
10	25	15	80	45	80	3 000 $ - 4 999 $	465
35	75	75	75	15	70	5 000 $ - 6 999 $	466
95	70	50	95	-	95	7 000 $ - 9 999 $	467
30	40	35	65	10	55	10 000 $ - 11 999 $	468
95	55	30	115	35	135	12 000 $ - 14 999 $	469
115	75	65	90	85	110	15 000 $ - 19 999 $	470
75	75	145	210	65	145	20 000 $ - 24 999 $	471
95	130	120	140	50	185	25 000 $ - 29 999 $	472
60	140	140	190	80	210	30 000 $ - 34 999 $	473
85	90	105	250	85	145	35 000 $ - 39 999 $	474
65	165	135	150	60	170	40 000 $ - 44 999 $	475
90	60	85	190	40	205	45 000 $ - 49 999 $	476
145	95	190	240	80	255	50 000 $ - 59 999 $	477
445	45	335	580	245	285	60 000 $ et plus	478
45,008	29,636	42,710	43,437	40,397	34,847	Revenu moyen $ (46)	479
38,964	27,381	36,098	35,485	34,330	33,315	Revenu médian $ (46)	480
2,086	1,646	1,998	1,653	2,545	1,145	Erreur type de revenu moyen $ (46)	481
1,555	1,340	1,705	3,015	1,275	2,365	Total - Femmes	482
70	115	55	195	50	180	Sans revenu	483
1,485	1,225	1,650	2,820	1,225	2,185	Avec un revenu	484
60	70	75	120	75	95	Moins de 1 000 $ (45)	485
60	115	105	115	85	110	1 000 $ - 2 999 $	486
80	45	60	165	60	165	3 000 $ - 4 999 $	487
115	55	95	145	45	85	5 000 $ - 6 999 $	488
85	125	110	195	25	205	7 000 $ - 9 999 $	489
70	40	75	95	25	110	10 000 $ - 11 999 $	490
100	70	110	225	105	235	12 000 $ - 14 999 $	491
110	170	135	290	110	195	15 000 $ - 19 999 $	492
105	90	170	280	85	155	20 000 $ - 24 999 $	493
120	175	105	205	80	260	25 000 $ - 29 999 $	494
140	125	150	250	175	155	30 000 $ - 34 999 $	495
65	75	100	190	80	95	35 000 $ - 39 999 $	496
65	35	120	90	105	80	40 000 $ - 44 999 $	497
80	10	50	15	40	60	45 000 $ - 49 999 $	498
95	20	80	180	35	100	50 000 $ - 59 999 $	499
130	10	105	260	105	90	60 000 $ et plus	500
26,935	18,998	25,792	26,279	26,298	22,416	Revenu moyen $ (46)	501
23,427	17,113	21,018	20,471	25,008	16,381	Revenu médian $ (46)	502
1,233	838	1,200	864	1,234	971	Erreur type de revenu moyen $ (46)	503
						selon la composition du revenu total	
100.0	100.0	100.0	100.0	100.0	100.0	Total - Composition du revenu en 2000 % (47)	504
76.5	81.7	78.5	76.5	88.9	79.4	Revenu d'emploi %	505
10.0	12.4	9.9	8.7	6.3	10.5	Transferts gouvernementaux %	506
13.4	5.9	11.6	14.9	4.7	10.2	Autre %	507
						Population de 15 ans et plus ayant un revenu d'emploi en 2000 selon le sexe et le travail	
2,130	1,845	2,260	4,145	1,895	3,325	Les deux sexes ayant un revenu d'emploi (48)	508
38,821	26,552	38,909	35,110	35,463	30,704	Revenu moyen d'emploi $	509
1,554	1,166	1,454	1,038	1,620	924	Erreur type de revenu moyen d'emploi $	510
1,115	1,005	1,410	2,470	1,065	1,960	Ayant travaillé toute l'année à plein temps (49)	511
54,533	34,127	49,434	46,414	44,148	40,424	Revenu moyen d'emploi $	512
2,035	1,728	1,841	1,386	2,097	1,104	Erreur type de revenu moyen d'emploi $	513
985	810	820	1,560	785	1,275	Ayant travaillé une partie de l'année ou à temps partiel (50)	514
21,305	16,936	21,384	19,126	24,836	17,362	Revenu moyen d'emploi $	515
1,784	1,083	1,850	1,221	2,380	1,274	Erreur type de revenu moyen d'emploi $	516
1,145	980	1,225	2,170	925	1,845	Hommes ayant un revenu d'emploi (48)	517
46,377	32,373	45,721	41,629	43,156	36,458	Revenu moyen d'emploi $	518
2,426	1,909	2,343	1,723	2,889	1,283	Erreur type de revenu moyen d'emploi $	519
670	575	810	1,405	560	1,210	Ayant travaillé toute l'année à plein temps (49)	520
62,128	40,188	56,783	51,788	50,928	44,678	Revenu moyen d'emploi $	521
2,918	2,700	2,951	2,157	3,599	1,531	Erreur type de revenu moyen d'emploi $	522
460	400	405	720	345	615	Ayant travaillé une partie de l'année ou à temps partiel (50)	523
22,987	21,160	23,723	23,841	32,509	21,474	Revenu moyen d'emploi $	524
3,060	1,778	2,587	2,401	4,703	1,658	Erreur type de revenu moyen d'emploi $	525

Table 1. Selected Characteristics for Census Tracts, 2001 Census – 100% Data and 20% Sample Data

No.	Characteristics	Toronto 0562.11	Toronto 0563.01	Toronto 0563.02	Toronto 0564.01	Toronto 0564.02 ◆	Toronto 0570.01 ◆
	2000 INCOME CHARACTERISTICS						
	Population 15 years and over with employment income in 2000 by sex and work activity – concluded						
526	Females with employment income (48)	990	1,820	910	685	1,265	885
527	Average employment income $	27,315	20,558	28,118	24,884	22,547	27,696
528	Standard error of average employment income $	1,569	865	1,501	1,422	954	1,316
529	Worked full year, full time (49)	535	915	495	325	570	500
530	Average employment income $	37,815	28,678	38,524	33,280	32,638	33,328
531	Standard error of average employment income $	2,240	1,258	1,799	1,636	1,215	1,485
532	Worked part year or part time (50)	430	875	400	350	645	370
533	Average employment income $	15,206	12,476	15,670	17,500	13,747	20,558
534	Standard error of average employment income $	1,527	823	1,920	2,045	1,025	2,149
	Census families by structure and family income groups in 2000						
535	Total - All census families	945	1,880	975	710	1,395	870
536	Under $10,000	-	175	30	-	125	50
537	$ 10,000 - $19,999	35	190	45	30	100	90
538	$ 20,000 - $29,999	50	310	70	50	105	85
539	$ 30,000 - $39,999	90	345	70	55	140	115
540	$ 40,000 - $49,999	70	230	100	45	160	110
541	$ 50,000 - $59,999	130	200	115	60	115	120
542	$ 60,000 - $69,999	95	160	110	105	135	70
543	$ 70,000 - $79,999	115	100	90	50	130	65
544	$ 80,000 - $89,999	65	55	50	110	135	45
545	$ 90,000 - $99,999	65	45	45	75	65	35
546	$100,000 and over	220	75	255	135	185	70
547	Average family income $	90,310	42,879	75,644	75,697	59,691	53,253
548	Median family income $	68,759	37,420	65,310	71,395	54,599	47,231
549	Standard error of average family income $	10,656	1,450	3,197	2,877	2,230	2,496
550	Total - All couple census families (51)	805	1,320	765	620	1,090	640
551	Under $10,000	-	85	10	-	50	25
552	$ 10,000 - $19,999	15	95	20	10	50	35
553	$ 20,000 - $29,999	30	175	50	45	55	70
554	$ 30,000 - $39,999	80	265	35	45	120	75
555	$ 40,000 - $49,999	55	175	65	50	135	90
556	$ 50,000 - $59,999	105	150	95	55	85	95
557	$ 60,000 - $69,999	85	150	85	95	105	70
558	$ 70,000 - $79,999	115	70	75	45	115	60
559	$ 80,000 - $89,999	60	55	45	90	135	35
560	$ 90,000 - $99,999	50	45	45	60	65	35
561	$100,000 and over	215	70	245	130	170	45
562	Average family income $	84,774	48,052	83,203	77,987	66,969	56,096
563	Median family income $	72,296	41,731	74,962	72,529	63,553	53,498
564	Standard error of average family income $	4,281	1,764	3,590	3,064	2,537	2,496
	Incidence of low income in 2000						
565	Total - Economic families	900	1,820	910	670	1,290	880
566	Low income	45	560	85	25	210	185
567	Incidence of low income in 2000 % (52)	4.6	30.6	9.2	3.9	16.5	21.4
568	Total - Unattached individuals 15 years and over	205	980	165	135	320	585
569	Low income	45	435	15	50	135	130
570	Incidence of low income in 2000 % (52)	21.6	44.3	10.3	40.1	41.1	22.8
571	Total - Population in private households	3,385	6,790	3,155	2,440	5,120	3,360
572	Low income	195	2,290	285	115	995	755
573	Incidence of low income in 2000 % (52)	5.8	33.7	9.0	4.7	19.4	22.5
	Private households by household income groups in 2000						
574	Total - All private households	990	2,520	1,030	745	1,450	1,340
575	Under $10,000	-	265	30	15	45	55
576	$ 10,000 - $19,999	20	305	30	30	60	135
577	$ 20,000 - $29,999	45	340	65	35	165	160
578	$ 30,000 - $39,999	75	405	80	45	125	220
579	$ 40,000 - $49,999	95	310	90	55	125	175
580	$ 50,000 - $59,999	100	260	120	45	145	160
581	$ 60,000 - $69,999	110	240	75	135	170	130
582	$ 70,000 - $79,999	95	145	100	65	110	115
583	$ 80,000 - $89,999	95	80	55	85	165	70
584	$ 90,000 - $99,999	90	65	60	60	105	60
585	$100,000 and over	275	95	305	180	230	75
586	Average household income $	95,799	42,867	80,262	78,923	66,435	51,705
587	Median household income $	73,782	38,049	71,878	71,308	60,658	46,481
588	Standard error of average household income $	10,150	1,229	3,231	2,997	2,069	1,986

Tableau 1. Certaines caractéristiques des secteurs de recensement, recensement de 2001 – Données intégrales et données-échantillon (20 %)

Toronto 0570.02	Toronto 0571.01	Toronto 0571.02	Toronto 0572.01	Toronto 0572.04 A	Toronto 0572.05 ◆ A	Caractéristiques	N°
						CARACTÉRISTIQUES DU REVENU DE 2000	
						Population de 15 ans et plus ayant un revenu d'emploi en 2000 selon le sexe et le travail – fin	
985	860	1,035	1,970	975	1,480	Femmes ayant un revenu d'emploi (48)	526
30,074	19,913	30,865	27,945	28,125	23,532	Revenu moyen d'emploi $	527
1,660	1,027	1,504	1,010	1,385	1,219	Erreur type de revenu moyen d'emploi $	528
445	430	590	1,065	505	750	Ayant travaillé toute l'année à plein temps (49)	529
43,063	25,999	39,371	39,313	36,592	33,607	Revenu moyen d'emploi $	530
2,205	1,418	1,546	1,382	1,750	1,353	Erreur type de revenu moyen d'emploi $	531
525	410	420	835	440	665	Ayant travaillé une partie de l'année ou à temps partiel (50)	532
19,836	12,849	19,115	15,062	18,944	13,552	Revenu moyen d'emploi $	533
2,015	1,116	2,616	970	1,776	1,857	Erreur type de revenu moyen d'emploi $	534
						Familles de recensement selon la structure et les tranches de revenu de la famille en 2000	
1,145	980	1,260	2,090	850	1,565	Total - Toutes les familles de recensement	535
15	110	30	110	40	80	Moins de 10 000 $	536
20	60	50	95	30	100	10 000 $ - 19 999 $	537
80	95	105	175	20	185	20 000 $ - 29 999 $	538
85	155	95	185	90	200	30 000 $ - 39 999 $	539
65	105	145	150	75	160	40 000 $ - 49 999 $	540
120	130	145	185	100	210	50 000 $ - 59 999 $	541
115	120	110	240	95	150	60 000 $ - 69 999 $	542
85	55	105	195	65	130	70 000 $ - 79 999 $	543
105	50	135	130	40	75	80 000 $ - 89 999 $	544
95	45	40	110	65	70	90 000 $ - 99 999 $	545
365	65	300	520	215	205	100 000 $ et plus	546
85,247	50,838	75,683	76,606	78,188	59,144	Revenu moyen des familles $	547
79,337	46,082	65,501	65,697	65,220	51,825	Revenu médian des familles $	548
3,100	2,533	2,891	2,477	3,819	2,386	Erreur type de revenu moyen des familles $	549
1,050	735	1,075	1,675	690	1,290	Total - Toutes les familles de recensement comptant un couple (51)	550
10	65	25	30	30	55	Moins de 10 000 $	551
10	45	20	50	15	60	10 000 $ - 19 999 $	552
75	50	90	105	10	135	20 000 $ - 29 999 $	553
70	70	70	130	55	160	30 000 $ - 39 999 $	554
60	90	120	105	25	130	40 000 $ - 49 999 $	555
95	110	125	170	75	185	50 000 $ - 59 999 $	556
100	100	90	215	80	125	60 000 $ - 69 999 $	557
75	60	100	170	70	115	70 000 $ - 79 999 $	558
105	45	125	105	40	70	80 000 $ - 89 999 $	559
95	35	40	110	65	70	90 000 $ - 99 999 $	560
360	60	280	485	215	185	100 000 $ et plus	561
88,576	55,952	79,566	85,087	87,263	62,796	Revenu moyen des familles $	562
84,232	54,626	71,261	71,922	74,920	53,749	Revenu médian des familles $	563
3,277	3,047	3,239	2,803	4,250	2,805	Erreur type de revenu moyen des familles $	564
						Fréquence des unités à faible revenu en 2000	
1,140	930	1,205	2,000	825	1,520	Total - Familles économiques	565
80	220	105	265	85	245	Faible revenu	566
6.9	23.7	8.6	13.3	10.2	15.8	Fréquence des unités à faible revenu en 2000 % (52)	567
215	315	380	750	175	1,010	Total - Personnes hors famille économique de 15 ans et plus	568
70	105	95	250	50	340	Faible revenu	569
32.3	32.3	25.6	32.9	28.8	33.6	Fréquence des unités à faible revenu en 2000 % (52)	570
3,670	3,520	4,040	7,285	3,080	5,800	Total - Population dans les ménages privés	571
275	925	375	1,190	360	1,130	Faible revenu	572
7.6	26.2	9.3	16.3	11.6	19.5	Fréquence des unités à faible revenu en 2000 % (52)	573
						Ménages privés selon les tranches de revenu du ménage en 2000	
1,295	1,125	1,505	2,615	995	2,330	Total - Tous les ménages privés	574
15	105	40	155	45	150	Moins de 10 000 $	575
65	85	85	230	50	265	10 000 $ - 19 999 $	576
105	135	145	205	40	250	20 000 $ - 29 999 $	577
80	120	150	245	130	270	30 000 $ - 39 999 $	578
95	130	150	215	90	260	40 000 $ - 49 999 $	579
130	105	155	245	90	320	50 000 $ - 59 999 $	580
110	130	115	230	120	185	60 000 $ - 69 999 $	581
85	95	110	225	65	180	70 000 $ - 79 999 $	582
100	65	130	140	40	95	80 000 $ - 89 999 $	583
100	45	50	115	70	80	90 000 $ - 99 999 $	584
415	105	370	615	260	265	100 000 $ et plus	585
83,183	53,155	74,353	72,744	76,151	55,369	Revenu moyen des ménages $	586
76,262	47,151	61,883	60,141	64,564	47,330	Revenu médian des ménages $	587
3,033	2,361	2,892	2,358	3,455	2,014	Erreur type de revenu moyen des ménages $	588

Table 1. Selected Characteristics for Census Tracts, 2001 Census – 100% Data and 20% Sample Data

No.	Characteristics	Toronto 0572.06 A	Toronto 0572.07 A	Toronto 0572.08 A	Toronto 0573.02	Toronto 0573.03	Toronto 0573.04 A
	POPULATION CHARACTERISTICS						
1	**Population, 1996 (1)**	**2,184**	**4,776**	**4,952**	**6,612**	**6,193**	**6,087**
2	**Population, 2001 (2)**	**6,587**	**4,870**	**5,645**	**10,322**	**6,675**	**7,778**
3	Population percentage change, 1996-2001	201.6	2.0	14.0	56.1	7.8	27.8
4	Land area in square kilometres, 2001	2.18	1.19	0.86	2.36	1.40	2.88
5	**Total population - 100% Data (3)**	**6,590**	**4,870**	**5,645**	**10,325**	**6,675**	**7,780**
	by sex and age groups						
6	Male	3,335	2,465	2,875	5,080	3,300	3,825
7	0-4 years	385	175	280	465	235	390
8	5-9 years	355	200	250	445	315	350
9	10-14 years	250	210	235	365	285	305
10	15-19 years	245	260	230	325	270	250
11	20-24 years	190	195	235	310	230	205
12	25-29 years	205	160	235	430	200	370
13	30-34 years	390	175	210	560	270	450
14	35-39 years	445	200	250	540	355	400
15	40-44 years	300	200	220	395	300	320
16	45-49 years	210	190	190	335	240	215
17	50-54 years	125	190	165	300	195	180
18	55-59 years	90	115	140	235	125	145
19	60-64 years	60	80	90	145	85	95
20	65-69 years	35	40	55	85	55	75
21	70-74 years	30	25	40	85	50	40
22	75-79 years	15	15	20	40	35	25
23	80-84 years	5	10	15	10	30	10
24	85 years and over	-	10	5	10	20	-
25	Female	3,255	2,405	2,775	5,240	3,375	3,950
26	0-4 years	355	150	230	410	245	335
27	5-9 years	370	210	200	385	295	345
28	10-14 years	230	180	205	355	275	330
29	15-19 years	195	220	220	315	245	250
30	20-24 years	180	210	230	345	180	260
31	25-29 years	280	180	225	500	205	445
32	30-34 years	415	165	225	590	290	460
33	35-39 years	385	210	285	500	345	390
34	40-44 years	260	235	205	415	310	315
35	45-49 years	185	200	225	355	245	225
36	50-54 years	125	155	170	335	185	185
37	55-59 years	85	95	130	220	115	130
38	60-64 years	65	70	80	160	80	95
39	65-69 years	55	40	45	125	65	75
40	70-74 years	35	40	40	105	55	55
41	75-79 years	25	20	30	60	85	40
42	80-84 years	10	10	25	35	50	10
43	85 years and over	-	5	5	30	100	5
44	**Total population 15 years and over**	**4,650**	**3,730**	**4,240**	**7,885**	**5,025**	**5,715**
	by legal marital status						
45	Never married (single)	1,210	1,190	1,245	2,420	1,445	1,640
46	Legally married (and not separated)	2,945	2,195	2,635	4,310	2,860	3,485
47	Separated, but still legally married	150	100	100	275	155	170
48	Divorced	215	160	130	595	260	260
49	Widowed	120	95	135	290	300	155
	by common-law status						
50	Not in a common-law relationship	4,435	3,640	4,120	7,290	4,760	5,345
51	In a common-law relationship	215	90	120	590	265	375
52	**Total population - 20% Sample Data (4)**	**6,515**	**4,860**	**5,635**	**10,325**	**6,500**	**7,780**
	by mother tongue						
53	Single responses	6,400	4,720	5,415	10,125	6,380	7,675
54	English	4,040	2,770	2,740	7,375	4,595	5,605
55	French	85	50	20	155	80	135
56	Non-official languages (5)	2,275	1,895	2,650	2,600	1,705	1,935
57	Italian	145	90	100	160	105	130
58	Chinese, n.o.s.	65	200	10	65	55	30
59	Cantonese	-	10	115	-	-	10
60	Portuguese	485	110	90	735	620	355
61	Punjabi	700	1,000	1,600	210	270	515
62	Other languages (6)	890	495	745	1,425	660	895
63	Multiple responses	115	135	225	200	120	105
64	English and French	15	-	10	25	10	25
65	English and non-official language	75	125	210	155	105	60
66	French and non-official language	20	15	-	15	10	10
67	English, French and non-official language	-	-	-	-	-	-

See reference material at the end of the publication. – Voir les documents de référence à la fin de la publication.

Tableau 1. Certaines caractéristiques des secteurs de recensement, recensement de 2001 – Données intégrales et données-échantillon (20 %)

Toronto 0573.05 A	Toronto 0574	Toronto 0575.01	Toronto 0575.02	Toronto 0575.03	Toronto 0575.04	Caractéristiques	N°
						CARACTÉRISTIQUES DE LA POPULATION	
3,964	**5,086**	**6,824**	**4,655**	**7,164**	**7,005**	**Population, 1996 (1)**	1
6,010	**5,222**	**6,806**	**4,838**	**7,170**	**6,847**	**Population, 2001 (2)**	2
51.6	2.7	-0.3	3.9	0.1	-2.3	Variation en pourcentage de la population, 1996-2001	3
1.39	1.98	1.22	1.00	1.07	1.55	Superficie des terres en kilomètres carrés, 2001	4
6,010	**5,225**	**6,805**	**4,840**	**7,170**	**6,845**	**Population totale – Données intégrales (3)**	5
						selon le sexe et les groupes d'âge	
2,970	2,440	3,365	2,390	3,595	3,435	Sexe masculin	6
150	135	255	180	265	220	0-4 ans	7
210	130	265	175	315	285	5-9 ans	8
260	125	255	130	255	285	10-14 ans	9
240	130	245	115	280	275	15-19 ans	10
240	165	265	180	300	260	20-24 ans	11
190	165	270	210	280	270	25-29 ans	12
215	205	290	220	290	275	30-34 ans	13
250	255	315	275	325	350	35-39 ans	14
240	245	260	210	300	290	40-44 ans	15
240	195	195	160	220	230	45-49 ans	16
240	145	230	155	265	205	50-54 ans	17
175	135	185	105	210	195	55-59 ans	18
110	110	125	90	115	135	60-64 ans	19
90	90	95	70	80	75	65-69 ans	20
70	65	60	50	50	45	70-74 ans	21
35	70	25	40	25	20	75-79 ans	22
15	35	20	20	10	10	80-84 ans	23
5	30	15	5	10	10	85 ans et plus	24
3,040	2,780	3,445	2,445	3,570	3,410	Sexe féminin	25
165	130	230	165	295	250	0-4 ans	26
215	125	235	155	275	270	5-9 ans	27
265	120	235	115	305	240	10-14 ans	28
255	175	260	125	265	285	15-19 ans	29
190	160	290	175	265	240	20-24 ans	30
180	190	290	195	305	275	25-29 ans	31
205	225	280	255	280	275	30-34 ans	32
250	230	275	235	350	310	35-39 ans	33
285	230	245	200	275	310	40-44 ans	34
275	185	235	165	265	225	45-49 ans	35
215	180	245	135	245	230	50-54 ans	36
150	125	180	120	175	185	55-59 ans	37
100	120	135	105	95	115	60-64 ans	38
110	105	100	90	75	85	65-69 ans	39
85	145	60	70	40	45	70-74 ans	40
65	130	60	70	40	30	75-79 ans	41
25	115	50	50	15	15	80-84 ans	42
25	85	45	20	15	10	85 ans et plus	43
4,755	**4,460**	**5,330**	**3,930**	**5,455**	**5,295**	**Population totale de 15 ans et plus**	44
						selon l'état matrimonial légal	
1,485	1,490	1,775	1,370	1,740	1,820	Célibataire (jamais marié(e))	45
2,700	1,840	2,810	1,690	3,030	2,720	Légalement marié(e) (et non séparé(e))	46
130	215	170	235	220	245	Séparé(e), mais toujours légalement marié(e)	47
220	485	300	385	290	335	Divorcé(e)	48
225	430	275	250	170	175	Veuf ou veuve	49
						selon l'union libre	
4,520	4,005	5,020	3,500	5,135	4,910	Ne vivant pas en union libre	50
235	450	315	430	320	385	Vivant en union libre	51
6,000	**5,180**	**6,805**	**4,840**	**7,170**	**6,840**	**Population totale – Données-échantillon (20 %) (4)**	52
						selon la langue maternelle	
5,895	5,120	6,680	4,765	7,090	6,710	Réponses uniques	53
3,990	4,385	3,940	3,565	4,395	5,245	Anglais	54
35	80	70	65	85	195	Français	55
1,870	650	2,670	1,135	2,615	1,265	Langues non officielles (5)	56
230	75	275	90	160	90	Italien	57
45	10	30	10	10	80	Chinois, n.d.a.	58
-	-	65	20	10	15	Cantonais	59
645	160	615	310	415	175	Portugais	60
210	25	910	155	1,170	60	Pendjabi	61
740	385	770	550	855	845	Autres langues (6)	62
105	60	130	70	75	130	Réponses multiples	63
-	10	-	-	10	20	Anglais et français	64
105	40	115	50	70	115	Anglais et langue non officielle	65
-	-	15	10	-	-	Français et langue non officielle	66
-	10	-	10	-	-	Anglais, français et langue non officielle	67

See reference material at the end of the publication. – Voir les documents de référence à la fin de la publication.

Table 1. Selected Characteristics for Census Tracts, 2001 Census – 100% Data and 20% Sample Data

No.	Characteristics	Toronto 0572.06 A	Toronto 0572.07 A	Toronto 0572.08 A	Toronto 0573.02	Toronto 0573.03	Toronto 0573.04 A
	POPULATION CHARACTERISTICS						
	by home language						
68	Single responses	5,265	4,070	4,260	8,450	5,370	6,450
69	English	4,435	3,155	2,840	7,905	4,740	5,855
70	French	-	10	-	25	40	35
71	Non-official languages (5)	830	910	1,415	520	590	560
72	Cantonese	-	10	30	-	-	-
73	Chinese, n.o.s.	15	165	-	15	50	-
74	Italian	50	10	10	20	10	-
75	Punjabi	360	660	960	70	225	200
76	Portuguese	115	25	-	190	125	115
77	Other languages (6)	290	40	405	225	180	235
78	Multiple responses	1,250	790	1,380	1,875	1,130	1,325
79	English and French	70	25	45	150	75	100
80	English and non-official language	1,160	705	1,320	1,680	1,035	1,185
81	French and non-official language	10	30	-	-	-	10
82	English, French and non-official language	10	30	15	45	25	30
	by knowledge of official languages						
83	English only	5,945	4,390	4,880	9,590	5,915	6,985
84	French only	-	-	-	20	20	20
85	English and French	385	205	325	605	410	660
86	Neither English nor French	180	265	435	105	155	110
	by knowledge of non-official languages (5) (7)						
87	Italian	230	120	130	295	245	220
88	Cantonese	-	15	100	10	-	10
89	Chinese, n.o.s.	55	195	10	60	50	45
90	Spanish	100	90	125	320	165	90
91	Portuguese	585	135	95	940	685	435
92	Punjabi	795	1,150	1,920	270	375	695
93	Tagalog (Pilipino)	115	-	35	190	50	35
	by first official language spoken						
94	English	6,225	4,530	5,170	10,035	6,230	7,505
95	French	95	70	20	170	85	140
96	English and French	15	15	25	15	30	25
97	Neither English nor French	185	250	425	100	155	105
98	Official language minority - (number) (8)	105	80	30	175	95	150
99	Official language minority - (percentage) (8)	1.6	1.6	0.5	1.7	1.5	1.9
	by ethnic origin (9)						
100	Canadian	975	925	840	2,595	1,730	1,590
101	English	770	575	440	1,750	1,130	950
102	Scottish	485	375	370	1,145	730	755
103	Irish	460	470	195	990	795	770
104	Chinese	120	260	125	220	125	105
105	Italian	520	290	330	670	370	510
106	East Indian	1,155	1,495	2,145	810	540	1,305
107	French	275	145	105	665	435	685
108	German	215	165	260	605	345	375
109	Portuguese	880	230	170	1,020	880	625
110	Polish	235	60	155	295	175	270
111	Jewish	45	10	-	45	10	55
112	Jamaican	830	330	425	755	385	1,195
113	Filipino	235	20	30	290	80	95
114	Ukrainian	45	130	85	155	45	85
	by Aboriginal identity						
115	Total Aboriginal identity population (10)	15	10	60	70	25	10
116	Total non-Aboriginal population	6,500	4,850	5,580	10,250	6,480	7,765
	by Aboriginal origin						
117	Total Aboriginal origins population (11)	20	20	65	100	95	130
118	Total non-Aboriginal population	6,495	4,840	5,575	10,225	6,405	7,645
	by Registered Indian status						
119	Registered Indian (12)	15	15	-	20	25	-
120	Not a Registered Indian	6,500	4,850	5,635	10,305	6,475	7,775

Tableau 1. Certaines caractéristiques des secteurs de recensement, recensement de 2001 – Données intégrales et données-échantillon (20 %)

Toronto 0573.05 A	Toronto 0574	Toronto 0575.01	Toronto 0575.02	Toronto 0575.03	Toronto 0575.04	Caractéristiques	N°
						CARACTÉRISTIQUES DE LA POPULATION	
						selon la langue parlée à la maison	
5,020	4,925	5,255	4,190	5,890	5,825	Réponses uniques	68
4,400	4,710	4,035	3,785	4,725	5,470	Anglais	69
-	10	-	20	-	45	Français	70
625	210	1,210	390	1,165	310	Langues non officielles (5)	71
-	-	30	20	-	-	Cantonais	72
15	10	15	-	-	65	Chinois, n.d.a.	73
45	10	85	-	20	15	Italien	74
140	-	530	90	680	-	Pendjabi	75
185	45	255	70	110	50	Portugais	76
240	135	290	215	355	180	Autres langues (6)	77
980	255	1,555	645	1,285	1,020	Réponses multiples	78
20	60	65	60	75	40	Anglais et français	79
930	185	1,475	580	1,195	925	Anglais et langue non officielle	80
-	-	10	-	-	-	Français et langue non officielle	81
30	-	10	-	10	50	Anglais, français et langue non officielle	82
						selon la connaissance des langues officielles	
5,495	4,655	6,030	4,375	6,505	6,320	Anglais seulement	83
-	-	10	-	-	-	Français seulement	84
305	460	370	370	260	435	Anglais et français	85
200	60	395	95	405	90	Ni l'anglais ni le français	86
						selon la connaissance des langues non officielles (5) (7)	
375	120	350	100	210	140	Italien	87
-	10	95	20	-	15	Cantonais	88
35	-	50	10	10	95	Chinois, n.d.a.	89
105	70	100	80	220	365	Espagnol	90
870	170	720	390	450	205	Portugais	91
270	35	995	190	1,230	60	Pendjabi	92
55	25	75	50	20	110	Tagalog (pilipino)	93
						selon la première langue officielle parlée	
5,810	5,005	6,300	4,655	6,680	6,560	Anglais	94
40	95	85	65	70	190	Français	95
-	20	40	20	20	-	Anglais et français	96
155	60	375	95	410	85	Ni l'anglais ni le français	97
35	105	110	75	75	195	Minorité de langue officielle - (nombre) (8)	98
0.6	2.0	1.6	1.5	1.0	2.9	Minorité de langue officielle - (pourcentage) (8)	99
						selon l'origine ethnique (9)	
1,465	1,495	1,185	1,540	1,340	2,325	Canadien	100
1,190	1,780	1,180	995	1,060	1,370	Anglais	101
560	1,125	650	630	755	1,210	Écossais	102
695	1,280	770	530	790	1,025	Irlandais	103
90	15	165	85	50	150	Chinois	104
765	240	530	215	515	385	Italien	105
330	90	1,125	345	1,415	435	Indien de l'Inde	106
335	445	395	300	370	615	Français	107
310	515	145	310	430	345	Allemand	108
1,020	275	820	605	625	290	Portugais	109
180	100	250	170	110	225	Polonais	110
45	30	10	-	50	45	Juif	111
165	195	225	155	695	325	Jamaïquain	112
60	45	125	65	30	140	Philippin	113
35	125	55	60	45	115	Ukrainien	114
						selon l'identité autochtone	
95	90	20	70	20	80	Total de la population ayant une identité autochtone (10)	115
5,905	5,090	6,785	4,770	7,155	6,765	Total de la population non autochtone	116
						selon l'origine autochtone	
125	145	155	190	85	120	Total de la population ayant une origine autochtone (11)	117
5,875	5,030	6,650	4,650	7,085	6,725	Total de la population non autochtone	118
						selon le statut d'Indien inscrit	
40	70	10	35	-	15	Oui, Indien inscrit (12)	119
5,955	5,105	6,795	4,805	7,170	6,820	Non, pas un Indien inscrit	120

Table 1. Selected Characteristics for Census Tracts, 2001 Census – 100% Data and 20% Sample Data

No.	Characteristics	Toronto 0572.06 A	Toronto 0572.07 A	Toronto 0572.08 A	Toronto 0573.02	Toronto 0573.03	Toronto 0573.04 A
	POPULATION CHARACTERISTICS						
	by visible minority groups						
121	Total visible minority population	3,120	2,615	4,075	3,220	1,905	3,455
122	Chinese	95	120	160	125	35	140
123	South Asian	1,260	1,460	2,560	820	690	1,150
124	Black	1,070	655	930	1,265	585	1,385
125	Filipino	230	20	30	320	80	80
126	Latin American	95	60	110	210	40	95
127	Southeast Asian	105	10	95	70	70	30
128	Arab	55	45	15	110	30	-
129	West Asian	15	-	-	-	-	20
130	Korean	-	10	25	30	20	10
131	Japanese	-	-	-	25	10	-
132	Visible minority, n.i.e. (13)	170	95	120	200	295	500
133	Multiple visible minorities (14)	15	140	25	50	45	45
	by citizenship						
134	Canadian citizenship (15)	5,490	4,040	4,410	9,415	6,060	7,220
135	Citizenship other than Canadian	1,030	815	1,225	910	440	555
	by place of birth of respondent						
136	Non-immigrant population	3,555	2,740	2,545	6,800	4,375	4,760
137	Born in province of residence	3,120	2,460	2,160	5,780	3,635	4,150
138	Immigrant population (16)	2,950	2,110	3,045	3,485	2,115	2,980
139	United States	35	10	10	50	20	10
140	Central and South America	260	225	165	360	130	365
141	Caribbean and Bermuda	530	285	515	670	470	920
142	United Kingdom	220	110	120	275	135	155
143	Other Europe (17)	735	230	285	1,145	710	640
144	Africa	110	95	125	105	80	105
145	Asia and the Middle East	1,045	1,150	1,810	825	560	775
146	Oceania and other (18)	10	10	25	50	10	10
147	Non-permanent residents (19)	15	10	45	35	15	40
148	**Total immigrant population**	**2,945**	**2,115**	**3,045**	**3,485**	**2,115**	**2,980**
	by period of immigration						
149	Before 1961	100	115	160	250	70	150
150	1961-1970	320	215	220	400	355	310
151	1971-1980	550	490	590	875	655	835
152	1981-1990	905	430	755	880	560	885
153	1991-2001 (20)	1,075	865	1,325	1,070	475	810
154	1991-1995	645	315	640	520	295	470
155	1996-2001 (20)	425	550	680	555	180	340
	by age at immigration						
156	0-4 years	320	180	220	340	165	250
157	5-19 years	1,040	530	870	1,115	590	1,040
158	20 years and over	1,590	1,395	1,955	2,030	1,360	1,685
159	**Total population**	**6,515**	**4,860**	**5,640**	**10,320**	**6,500**	**7,780**
	by religion						
160	Catholic (21)	2,945	1,500	1,290	4,210	2,535	3,025
161	Protestant	1,355	1,205	1,150	3,160	2,025	2,035
162	Christian Orthodox	30	50	60	130	85	60
163	Christian, n.i.e. (22)	225	170	170	595	420	270
164	Muslim	230	55	330	220	160	230
165	Jewish	35	10	-	-	10	10
166	Buddhist	70	190	90	90	45	75
167	Hindu	305	395	395	405	140	450
168	Sikh	770	970	1,785	225	360	675
169	Eastern religions (23)	-	-	65	-	10	-
170	Other religions (24)	-	-	-	-	-	-
171	No religious affiliation (25)	555	305	295	1,285	725	945
172	**Total population 15 years and over**	**4,575**	**3,715**	**4,235**	**7,875**	**4,845**	**5,700**
	by generation status						
173	1st generation (26)	2,790	2,020	2,920	3,385	2,080	2,920
174	2nd generation (27)	985	790	705	1,870	1,105	1,280
175	3rd generation and over (28)	805	910	615	2,625	1,660	1,510
176	**Total population 1 year and over (29)**	**6,380**	**4,795**	**5,565**	**10,115**	**6,395**	**7,610**
	by place of residence 1 year ago (mobility)						
177	Non-movers	5,435	4,275	4,455	8,345	5,465	5,840
178	Movers	940	520	1,105	1,770	925	1,770
179	Non-migrants	395	205	575	1,280	630	965
180	Migrants	545	315	525	490	290	805
181	Internal migrants	480	225	380	435	235	790
182	Intraprovincial migrants	470	175	340	420	190	760
183	Interprovincial migrants	10	50	40	15	45	30
184	External migrants	70	90	140	60	50	10

Tableau 1. Certaines caractéristiques des secteurs de recensement, recensement de 2001 – Données intégrales et données-échantillon (20 %)

Toronto 0573.05 A	Toronto 0574	Toronto 0575.01	Toronto 0575.02	Toronto 0575.03	Toronto 0575.04	Caractéristiques	N°
						CARACTÉRISTIQUES DE LA POPULATION	
						selon les groupes de minorités visibles	
1,100	560	2,575	1,065	3,030	1,800	Total de la population des minorités visibles	121
85	10	130	55	25	115	Chinois	122
455	75	1,460	430	1,610	470	Sud-Asiatique	123
315	205	465	230	885	600	Noir	124
65	30	30	65	20	140	Philippin	125
55	30	85	10	165	295	Latino-Américain	126
15	20	90	40	15	70	Asiatique du Sud-Est	127
25	20	90	65	95	10	Arabe	128
10	35	-	-	20	-	Asiatique occidental	129
10	-	-	-	-	-	Coréen	130
15	15	-	-	-	-	Japonais	131
45	65	105	150	190	105	Minorité visible, n.i.a. (13)	132
-	55	120	20	10	-	Minorités visibles multiples (14)	133
						selon la citoyenneté	
5,550	4,885	5,770	4,275	6,065	6,125	Citoyenneté canadienne (15)	134
450	295	1,030	560	1,105	715	Citoyenneté autre que canadienne	135
						selon le lieu de naissance du répondant	
4,010	4,015	3,880	3,230	4,035	4,720	Population non immigrante	136
3,605	3,395	3,370	2,465	3,385	3,930	Née dans la province de résidence	137
1,970	1,140	2,780	1,545	3,050	2,110	Population immigrante (16)	138
20	60	15	15	45	15	États-Unis	139
110	90	100	75	245	355	Amérique centrale et du Sud	140
150	150	300	235	565	270	Caraïbes et Bermudes	141
250	275	285	210	265	360	Royaume-Uni	142
1,015	385	890	475	645	560	Autre Europe (17)	143
65	50	85	30	85	20	Afrique	144
350	125	1,105	490	1,200	445	Asie et Moyen-Orient	145
20	10	-	10	-	95	Océanie et autre (18)	146
20	20	145	60	85	10	Résidents non permanents (19)	147
1,970	**1,140**	**2,775**	**1,545**	**3,050**	**2,115**	**Population immigrante totale**	148
						selon la période d'immigration	
200	285	205	165	205	155	Avant 1961	149
550	175	415	180	365	355	1961-1970	150
780	280	640	335	700	375	1971-1980	151
170	235	760	365	620	580	1981-1990	152
270	170	760	500	1,160	645	1991-2001 (20)	153
155	85	420	250	590	345	1991-1995	154
115	90	340	250	565	300	1996-2001 (20)	155
						selon l'âge à l'immigration	
195	90	300	150	275	240	0-4 ans	156
695	420	735	520	935	575	5-19 ans	157
1,080	625	1,745	875	1,840	1,295	20 ans et plus	158
6,000	**5,175**	**6,805**	**4,835**	**7,170**	**6,845**	**Population totale**	159
						selon la religion	
2,925	1,560	2,440	1,910	2,415	2,610	Catholique (21)	160
1,785	2,240	1,625	1,490	1,825	2,365	Protestante	161
170	55	55	90	70	20	Orthodoxe chrétienne	162
140	200	120	120	265	255	Chrétiennes, n.i.a. (22)	163
105	45	265	170	180	140	Musulmane	164
40	10	30	-	10	20	Juive	165
20	30	145	45	20	90	Bouddhiste	166
70	55	405	155	405	170	Hindoue	167
240	20	830	140	1,100	70	Sikh	168
-	-	15	-	-	-	Religions orientales (23)	169
-	10	-	15	-	-	Autres religions (24)	170
515	950	870	705	875	1,105	Aucune appartenance religieuse (25)	171
4,735	**4,420**	**5,325**	**3,920**	**5,460**	**5,280**	**Population totale de 15 ans et plus**	172
						selon le statut des générations	
1,975	1,175	2,795	1,525	3,000	1,985	1re génération (26)	173
1,310	915	1,095	760	1,015	1,040	2e génération (27)	174
1,455	2,330	1,435	1,635	1,440	2,255	3e génération et plus (28)	175
5,950	**5,100**	**6,740**	**4,785**	**6,990**	**6,760**	**Population totale de 1 an et plus (29)**	176
						selon le lieu de résidence 1 an auparavant (mobilité)	
5,430	4,300	5,915	3,790	5,855	5,735	Personnes n'ayant pas déménagé	177
525	805	825	995	1,140	1,020	Personnes ayant déménagé	178
295	550	565	730	670	560	Non-migrants	179
225	250	260	265	465	465	Migrants	180
215	210	210	255	405	440	Migrants internes	181
180	185	180	225	325	380	Migrants infraprovinciaux	182
35	25	30	30	75	55	Migrants interprovinciaux	183
15	40	50	15	65	25	Migrants externes	184

Table 1. Selected Characteristics for Census Tracts, 2001 Census – 100% Data and 20% Sample Data

No.	Characteristics	Toronto 0572.06 A	Toronto 0572.07 A	Toronto 0572.08 A	Toronto 0573.02	Toronto 0573.03	Toronto 0573.04 A
	POPULATION CHARACTERISTICS						
185	**Total population 5 years and over (30)**	**5,775**	**4,535**	**5,140**	**9,445**	**6,030**	**7,030**
	by place of residence 5 years ago (mobility)						
186	Non-movers	1,390	2,655	2,785	3,490	3,225	2,360
187	Movers	4,380	1,880	2,350	5,960	2,800	4,675
188	Non-migrants	2,490	1,050	815	3,735	1,460	2,705
189	Migrants	1,895	830	1,540	2,225	1,340	1,970
190	Internal migrants	1,615	525	935	1,775	1,115	1,780
191	Intraprovincial migrants	1,520	415	845	1,665	885	1,600
192	Interprovincial migrants	95	115	90	105	235	185
193	External migrants	280	305	605	450	225	190
194	**Total population 15 to 24 years**	**790**	**875**	**910**	**1,305**	**935**	**960**
	by school attendance						
195	Not attending school	330	385	355	605	335	320
196	Attending school full time	430	430	510	600	555	590
197	Attending school part time	35	60	40	100	45	55
198	**Total population 15 years and over**	**4,580**	**3,715**	**4,235**	**7,875**	**4,845**	**5,705**
	by highest level of schooling						
199	Less than grade 9 (31)	360	270	450	585	430	185
200	Grades 9-13 without high school graduation certificate	880	835	805	1,880	1,170	1,210
201	Grades 9-13 with high school graduation certificate	700	495	720	1,450	825	985
202	Some postsecondary without degree, certificate or diploma (32)	635	465	490	950	685	855
203	Trades certificate or diploma (33)	425	260	375	790	385	650
204	College certificate or diploma (34)	880	710	650	1,370	780	1,090
205	University certificate below bachelor's degree	110	70	80	140	65	175
206	University with bachelor's degree or higher	585	620	665	710	515	550
	by combinations of unpaid work						
207	Males 15 years and over	2,275	1,870	2,095	3,790	2,430	2,765
208	Reported unpaid work (35)	2,045	1,700	1,920	3,425	2,110	2,500
209	Housework and child care and care or assistance to seniors	205	125	175	245	190	230
210	Housework and child care only	870	640	705	1,230	755	1,080
211	Housework and care or assistance to seniors only	65	90	120	175	105	85
212	Child care and care or assistance to seniors only	10	-	10	-	15	15
213	Housework only	870	815	845	1,710	1,000	1,045
214	Child care only	30	20	45	60	35	40
215	Care or assistance to seniors only	-	15	20	-	-	-
216	Females 15 years and over	2,300	1,845	2,140	4,090	2,415	2,935
217	Reported unpaid work (35)	2,155	1,710	2,030	3,840	2,265	2,765
218	Housework and child care and care or assistance to seniors	320	280	315	450	270	380
219	Housework and child care only	1,045	705	890	1,465	950	1,235
220	Housework and care or assistance to seniors only	90	70	130	270	125	125
221	Child care and care or assistance to seniors only	-	-	-	-	10	10
222	Housework only	675	645	640	1,595	895	985
223	Child care only	20	10	40	40	15	15
224	Care or assistance to seniors only	10	-	-	10	-	10
	by labour force activity						
225	Males 15 years and over	2,280	1,870	2,095	3,785	2,430	2,765
226	In the labour force	1,930	1,560	1,690	3,270	2,035	2,290
227	Employed	1,810	1,530	1,595	3,090	1,955	2,180
228	Unemployed	125	30	90	175	80	110
229	Not in the labour force	345	305	405	515	400	475
230	Participation rate	84.6	83.4	80.7	86.4	83.7	82.8
231	Employment rate	79.4	81.8	76.1	81.6	80.5	78.8
232	Unemployment rate	6.5	1.9	5.3	5.4	3.9	4.8
233	Females 15 years and over	2,300	1,845	2,145	4,090	2,415	2,940
234	In the labour force	1,715	1,325	1,525	2,945	1,715	2,185
235	Employed	1,635	1,265	1,425	2,810	1,625	2,050
236	Unemployed	80	65	100	135	85	135
237	Not in the labour force	585	515	615	1,145	700	750
238	Participation rate	74.6	71.8	71.1	72.0	71.0	74.3
239	Employment rate	71.1	68.6	66.4	68.7	67.3	69.7
240	Unemployment rate	4.7	4.9	6.6	4.6	5.0	6.2

Tableau 1. Certaines caractéristiques des secteurs de recensement, recensement de 2001 – Données intégrales et données-échantillon (20 %)

Toronto 0573.05 A	Toronto 0574	Toronto 0575.01	Toronto 0575.02	Toronto 0575.03	Toronto 0575.04	Caractéristiques	N°
						CARACTÉRISTIQUES DE LA POPULATION	
5,685	**4,915**	**6,345**	**4,485**	**6,630**	**6,370**	**Population totale de 5 ans et plus (30)**	185
						selon le lieu de résidence 5 ans auparavant (mobilité)	
4,295	2,650	3,990	2,390	3,455	3,510	Personnes n'ayant pas déménagé	186
1,390	2,260	2,355	2,100	3,180	2,855	Personnes ayant déménagé	187
755	1,445	1,415	1,100	1,535	1,540	Non-migrants	188
635	815	945	1,000	1,645	1,315	Migrants	189
570	710	670	775	1,195	1,115	Migrants internes	190
460	590	530	625	980	985	Migrants infraprovinciaux	191
115	125	140	150	215	130	Migrants interprovinciaux	192
65	110	275	225	450	205	Migrants externes	193
930	**625**	**1,070**	**590**	**1,115**	**1,055**	**Population totale de 15 à 24 ans**	194
						selon la fréquentation scolaire	
345	335	470	315	475	490	Ne fréquentant pas l'école	195
495	250	550	205	600	515	Fréquentant l'école à plein temps	196
85	35	45	70	45	50	Fréquentant l'école à temps partiel	197
4,735	**4,425**	**5,330**	**3,920**	**5,460**	**5,280**	**Population totale de 15 ans et plus**	198
						selon le plus haut niveau de scolarité atteint	
425	370	770	355	525	290	Niveau inférieur à la 9e année (31)	199
1,315	1,050	1,495	1,185	1,310	1,555	De la 9e à la 13e année sans certificat d'études secondaires	200
800	615	925	560	1,005	990	De la 9e à la 13e année avec certificat d'études secondaires	201
455	625	610	415	620	635	Études postsecondaires partielles sans grade, certificat ou diplôme (32)	202
525	285	390	390	550	545	Certificat ou diplôme d'une école de métiers (33)	203
635	635	680	610	820	940	Certificat ou diplôme collégial (34)	204
70	140	55	45	105	45	Certificat universitaire inférieur au baccalauréat	205
515	700	400	350	530	285	Études universitaires avec baccalauréat ou diplôme supérieur	206
						selon les combinaisons de travail non rémunéré	
2,355	2,015	2,605	1,910	2,745	2,615	Hommes de 15 ans et plus	207
2,090	1,815	2,215	1,690	2,480	2,345	Travail non rémunéré déclaré (35)	208
165	110	205	75	265	105	Travaux ménagers et soins aux enfants et soins ou aide aux personnes âgées	209
690	420	670	450	850	905	Travaux ménagers et soins aux enfants seulement	210
150	110	90	75	195	125	Travaux ménagers et soins ou aide aux personnes âgées seulement	211
-	-	10	-	10	10	Soins aux enfants et soins ou aide aux personnes âgées seulement	212
1,055	1,145	1,185	1,060	1,100	1,155	Travaux ménagers seulement	213
20	20	50	30	60	35	Soins aux enfants seulement	214
15	10	10	-	10	-	Soins ou aide aux personnes âgées seulement	215
2,380	2,410	2,725	2,010	2,715	2,665	Femmes de 15 ans et plus	216
2,195	2,215	2,470	1,915	2,600	2,465	Travail non rémunéré déclaré (35)	217
255	135	315	110	325	195	Travaux ménagers et soins aux enfants et soins ou aide aux personnes âgées	218
755	580	790	625	1,100	1,110	Travaux ménagers et soins aux enfants seulement	219
155	290	135	145	205	125	Travaux ménagers et soins ou aide aux personnes âgées seulement	220
10	-	10	-	-	-	Soins aux enfants et soins ou aide aux personnes âgées seulement	221
990	1,185	1,200	1,010	945	995	Travaux ménagers seulement	222
40	-	20	15	25	15	Soins aux enfants seulement	223
-	20	-	15	-	10	Soins ou aide aux personnes âgées seulement	224
						selon l'activité	
2,355	2,015	2,605	1,910	2,745	2,615	Hommes de 15 ans et plus	225
1,860	1,570	2,050	1,485	2,200	2,135	Population active	226
1,775	1,515	1,980	1,400	2,055	2,060	Personnes occupées	227
90	55	70	85	145	80	Chômeurs	228
495	445	550	425	545	480	Inactifs	229
79.0	77.9	78.7	77.7	80.1	81.6	Taux d'activité	230
75.4	75.2	76.0	73.3	74.9	78.8	Taux d'emploi	231
4.8	3.5	3.4	5.7	6.6	3.7	Taux de chômage	232
2,380	2,405	2,725	2,015	2,715	2,660	Femmes de 15 ans et plus	233
1,565	1,385	1,860	1,275	1,840	1,995	Population active	234
1,480	1,295	1,755	1,220	1,690	1,840	Personnes occupées	235
85	90	105	55	155	145	Chômeuses	236
815	1,020	865	735	870	670	Inactives	237
65.8	57.6	68.3	63.3	67.8	75.0	Taux d'activité	238
62.2	53.8	64.4	60.5	62.2	69.2	Taux d'emploi	239
5.4	6.5	5.6	4.3	8.4	7.3	Taux de chômage	240

Table 1. Selected Characteristics for Census Tracts, 2001 Census – 100% Data and 20% Sample Data

No.	Characteristics	Toronto 0572.06 A	Toronto 0572.07 A	Toronto 0572.08 A	Toronto 0573.02	Toronto 0573.03	Toronto 0573.04 A
	POPULATION CHARACTERISTICS						
	by labour force activity – concluded						
241	Both sexes - Participation rate	79.7	77.8	75.9	78.9	77.4	78.4
242	15-24 years	62.0	70.3	70.7	73.6	70.6	65.1
243	25 years and over	83.5	80.1	77.6	79.9	78.9	81.1
244	Both sexes - Employment rate	75.2	75.2	71.3	74.9	73.9	74.3
245	15-24 years	54.4	64.6	65.9	64.4	67.2	57.8
246	25 years and over	79.5	78.3	72.8	77.0	75.4	77.4
247	Both sexes - Unemployment rate	5.6	3.5	5.9	5.1	4.5	5.5
248	15-24 years	12.2	8.1	6.3	13.0	4.6	11.1
249	25 years and over	4.6	2.2	6.0	3.7	4.5	4.6
250	**Total labour force 15 years and over**	**3,650**	**2,895**	**3,215**	**6,220**	**3,745**	**4,475**
	by industry based on the 1997 NAICS						
251	Industry - Not applicable (36)	50	20	50	105	40	85
252	All industries (37)	3,595	2,870	3,165	6,115	3,705	4,395
253	11 Agriculture, forestry, fishing and hunting	-	-	10	25	-	15
254	21 Mining and oil and gas extraction	-	-	15	-	-	-
255	22 Utilities	15	10	10	20	10	20
256	23 Construction	220	100	85	420	185	290
257	31-33 Manufacturing	970	715	960	1,515	835	995
258	41 Wholesale trade	230	260	240	445	280	360
259	44-45 Retail trade	385	375	365	670	510	490
260	48-49 Transportation and warehousing	440	220	295	630	300	420
261	51 Information and cultural industries	75	65	75	180	145	75
262	52 Finance and insurance	210	130	165	320	175	270
263	53 Real estate and rental and leasing	70	55	65	85	55	60
264	54 Professional, scientific and technical services	195	90	200	235	175	190
265	55 Management of companies and enterprises	-	-	-	-	-	10
266	56 Administrative and support, waste management and remediation services	155	150	180	300	155	200
267	61 Educational services	130	95	70	235	145	180
268	62 Health care and social assistance	215	185	115	320	215	375
269	71 Arts, entertainment and recreation	20	40	10	45	10	55
270	72 Accommodation and food services	50	115	95	265	205	95
271	81 Other services (except public administration)	80	100	125	210	170	175
272	91 Public administration	115	165	90	200	120	115
	by class of worker						
273	Class of worker - Not applicable (36)	55	25	50	105	45	80
274	All classes of worker (37)	3,595	2,865	3,165	6,110	3,705	4,390
275	Paid workers	3,435	2,695	3,080	5,790	3,540	4,175
276	Employees	3,345	2,645	2,960	5,725	3,465	4,090
277	Self-employed (incorporated)	95	50	120	65	80	90
278	Self-employed (unincorporated)	150	155	85	320	155	205
279	Unpaid family workers	-	20	-	10	10	10
	by occupation based on the 2001 NOC-S						
280	Male labour force 15 years and over	1,930	1,565	1,690	3,275	2,035	2,285
281	Occupation - Not applicable (36)	30	-	25	65	20	50
282	All occupations (37)	1,895	1,555	1,670	3,205	2,020	2,240
283	A Management occupations	200	220	175	305	235	235
284	B Business, finance and administration occupations	230	245	200	320	225	250
285	C Natural and applied sciences and related occupations	210	150	185	330	165	205
286	D Health occupations	20	10	10	15	-	10
287	E Occupations in social science, education, government service and religion	40	40	20	30	35	35
288	F Occupations in art, culture, recreation and sport	-	65	25	50	25	20
289	G Sales and service occupations	270	255	255	545	495	380
290	H Trades, transport and equipment operators and related occupations	680	420	530	1,130	550	775
291	I Occupations unique to primary industry	-	20	25	20	-	35
292	J Occupations unique to processing, manufacturing and utilities	230	130	250	465	275	295
293	Female labour force 15 years and over	1,715	1,330	1,525	2,950	1,710	2,190
294	Occupation - Not applicable (36)	25	15	30	40	25	30
295	All occupations (37)	1,695	1,310	1,500	2,905	1,685	2,155
296	A Management occupations	110	90	105	180	145	160
297	B Business, finance and administration occupations	685	480	445	1,125	570	845
298	C Natural and applied sciences and related occupations	55	20	60	60	50	50
299	D Health occupations	75	65	45	130	100	130

Tableau 1. Certaines caractéristiques des secteurs de recensement, recensement de 2001 – Données intégrales et données-échantillon (20 %)

Toronto 0573.05 A	Toronto 0574	Toronto 0575.01	Toronto 0575.02	Toronto 0575.03	Toronto 0575.04	Caractéristiques	N°
						CARACTÉRISTIQUES DE LA POPULATION	
						selon l'activité – fin	
72.3	67.0	73.5	70.4	74.1	78.1	Les deux sexes - Taux d'activité	241
66.1	69.6	72.9	78.0	68.0	71.6	15-24 ans	242
74.0	66.5	73.6	69.2	75.7	79.9	25 ans et plus	243
68.6	63.5	70.1	66.7	68.6	74.0	Les deux sexes - Taux d'emploi	244
58.1	57.9	68.7	66.1	60.5	64.5	15-24 ans	245
71.1	64.4	70.4	66.9	70.9	76.2	25 ans et plus	246
5.0	4.9	4.6	5.3	7.3	5.5	Les deux sexes - Taux de chômage	247
12.3	16.1	5.8	15.2	10.7	9.9	15-24 ans	248
3.7	3.0	4.1	3.3	6.5	4.3	25 ans et plus	249
3,425	**2,955**	**3,910**	**2,760**	**4,040**	**4,125**	**Population active totale de 15 ans et plus**	250
						selon l'industrie basée sur le SCIAN de 1997	
55	20	35	25	65	10	Industrie - Sans objet (36)	251
3,370	2,935	3,880	2,735	3,980	4,115	Toutes les industries (37)	252
10	15	25	-	-	15	11 Agriculture, foresterie, pêche et chasse	253
-	10	-	-	10	10	21 Extraction minière et extraction de pétrole et de gaz	254
30	10	-	15	20	-	22 Services publics	255
225	190	180	160	265	220	23 Construction	256
855	535	1,010	600	1,010	870	31-33 Fabrication	257
265	200	225	235	305	375	41 Commerce de gros	258
405	310	615	310	440	480	44-45 Commerce de détail	259
280	280	500	295	420	510	48-49 Transport et entreposage	260
25	40	50	40	80	115	51 Industrie de l'information et industrie culturelle	261
105	160	115	85	115	150	52 Finance et assurances	262
40	105	50	30	50	55	53 Services immobiliers et services de location et de location à bail	263
245	190	160	115	135	185	54 Services professionnels, scientifiques et techniques	264
-	-	-	-	-	-	55 Gestion de sociétés et d'entreprises	265
155	135	165	230	260	205	56 Services administratifs, services de soutien, services de gestion des déchets et services d'assainissement	266
185	160	130	110	175	105	61 Services d'enseignement	267
210	190	160	105	190	295	62 Soins de santé et assistance sociale	268
25	25	40	20	30	30	71 Arts, spectacles et loisirs	269
130	135	170	160	195	235	72 Hébergement et services de restauration	270
130	120	150	150	150	140	81 Autres services, sauf les administrations publiques	271
80	125	130	65	115	115	91 Administrations publiques	272
						selon la catégorie de travailleurs	
55	20	35	25	65	10	Catégorie de travailleurs - Sans objet (36)	273
3,370	2,940	3,880	2,735	3,980	4,115	Toutes les catégories de travailleurs (37)	274
3,170	2,775	3,745	2,655	3,810	3,895	Travailleurs rémunérés	275
3,075	2,690	3,720	2,615	3,770	3,835	Employés	276
95	90	25	40	40	65	Travailleurs autonomes (entreprise constituée en société)	277
205	155	135	80	165	205	Travailleurs autonomes (entreprise non constituée en société)	278
10	-	-	10	-	10	Travailleurs familiaux non rémunérés	279
						selon la profession basée sur la CNP-S de 2001	
1,865	1,570	2,050	1,480	2,205	2,135	Hommes actifs de 15 ans et plus	280
35	10	10	10	55	-	Profession - Sans objet (36)	281
1,825	1,565	2,040	1,475	2,145	2,135	Toutes les professions (37)	282
215	195	185	100	160	165	A Gestion	283
135	175	200	155	255	280	B Affaires, finance et administration	284
145	155	110	75	190	140	C Sciences naturelles et appliquées et professions apparentées	285
10	10	-	-	-	20	D Secteur de la santé	286
55	80	40	20	35	20	E Sciences sociales, enseignement, administration publique et religion	287
40	25	40	10	35	50	F Arts, culture, sports et loisirs	288
330	280	325	215	325	360	G Ventes et services	289
645	475	730	635	790	790	H Métiers, transport et machinerie	290
15	20	20	45	20	35	I Professions propres au secteur primaire	291
235	145	385	215	345	280	J Transformation, fabrication et services d'utilité publique	292
1,565	1,390	1,860	1,275	1,845	1,990	Femmes actives de 15 ans et plus	293
15	20	25	10	10	-	Profession - Sans objet (36)	294
1,550	1,370	1,840	1,265	1,835	1,980	Toutes les professions (37)	295
120	155	110	65	80	95	A Gestion	296
515	445	475	420	610	800	B Affaires, finance et administration	297
40	35	80	20	20	50	C Sciences naturelles et appliquées et professions apparentées	298
100	60	65	45	85	120	D Secteur de la santé	299

Table 1. Selected Characteristics for Census Tracts, 2001 Census – 100% Data and 20% Sample Data

No.	Characteristics	Toronto 0572.06 A	Toronto 0572.07 A	Toronto 0572.08 A	Toronto 0573.02	Toronto 0573.03	Toronto 0573.04 A
	POPULATION CHARACTERISTICS						
	by occupation based on the 2001 NOC-S – concluded						
300	E Occupations in social science, education, government service and religion	160	110	80	330	125	225
301	F Occupations in art, culture, recreation and sport	10	30	30	20	15	25
302	G Sales and service occupations	320	275	350	605	420	445
303	H Trades, transport and equipment operators and related occupations	60	25	100	155	75	95
304	I Occupations unique to primary industry	10	-	-	10	-	-
305	J Occupations unique to processing, manufacturing and utilities	215	210	290	285	190	185
306	**Total employed labour force 15 years and over**	**3,440**	**2,795**	**3,020**	**5,900**	**3,580**	**4,235**
	by place of work						
307	Males	1,805	1,530	1,600	3,090	1,950	2,180
308	Usual place of work	1,470	1,290	1,335	2,650	1,770	1,875
309	At home	40	70	120	35	40	35
310	Outside Canada	10	10	20	-	10	10
311	No fixed workplace address	295	160	125	410	140	265
312	Females	1,630	1,265	1,425	2,810	1,625	2,055
313	Usual place of work	1,415	1,150	1,330	2,625	1,485	1,855
314	At home	105	70	50	85	80	115
315	Outside Canada	-	-	-	-	-	-
316	No fixed workplace address	110	50	45	105	60	80
317	**Total employed labour force 15 years and over with usual place of work or no fixed workplace address**	**3,290**	**2,645**	**2,835**	**5,780**	**3,450**	**4,075**
	by mode of transportation						
318	Males	1,765	1,450	1,460	3,060	1,905	2,140
319	Car, truck, van, as driver	1,545	1,165	1,200	2,660	1,625	1,895
320	Car, truck, van, as passenger	105	105	130	95	125	125
321	Public transit	95	130	120	240	105	110
322	Walked	-	25	10	45	35	10
323	Other method	15	30	10	15	15	-
324	Females	1,530	1,190	1,375	2,725	1,545	1,935
325	Car, truck, van, as driver	1,240	880	900	2,025	1,240	1,550
326	Car, truck, van, as passenger	125	155	195	255	140	155
327	Public transit	145	135	270	410	135	220
328	Walked	-	20	10	15	25	10
329	Other method	10	10	-	20	-	-
330	**Total population 15 years and over who worked since January 1, 2000**	**3,905**	**3,015**	**3,460**	**6,500**	**3,925**	**4,730**
	by language used at work						
331	Single responses	3,540	2,845	2,975	6,020	3,550	4,335
332	English	3,480	2,800	2,925	5,980	3,515	4,290
333	French	-	10	-	-	10	-
334	Non-official languages (5)	60	45	55	30	25	45
335	Chinese, n.o.s.	-	-	-	-	-	-
336	Cantonese	-	-	-	-	-	-
337	Other languages (6)	60	40	55	30	30	45
338	Multiple responses	365	170	480	480	375	400
339	English and French	75	35	40	145	65	155
340	English and non-official language	295	120	420	325	305	245
341	French and non-official language	-	-	-	-	-	-
342	English, French and non-official language	-	15	20	15	-	-
	DWELLING AND HOUSEHOLD CHARACTERISTICS						
343	**Total number of occupied private dwellings**	**1,770**	**1,250**	**1,390**	**3,435**	**1,895**	**2,210**
	by tenure						
344	Owned	1,660	1,015	1,100	2,480	1,580	2,015
345	Rented	110	235	285	960	315	195
346	Band housing	-	-	-	-	-	-
	by structural type of dwelling						
347	Single-detached house	1,260	1,120	1,210	1,660	1,435	1,305
348	Semi-detached house	280	-	15	330	235	465
349	Row house	225	125	155	790	50	405
350	Apartment, detached duplex	-	-	-	40	15	15
351	Apartment, building that has five or more storeys	-	-	-	600	85	20
352	Apartment, building that has fewer than five storeys (38)	-	-	-	20	75	-
353	Other single-attached house	-	-	-	-	-	-
354	Movable dwelling (39)	-	-	-	-	-	-

Tableau 1. Certaines caractéristiques des secteurs de recensement, recensement de 2001 – Données intégrales et données-échantillon (20 %)

Toronto 0573.05 A	Toronto 0574	Toronto 0575.01	Toronto 0575.02	Toronto 0575.03	Toronto 0575.04	Caractéristiques	N°
						CARACTÉRISTIQUES DE LA POPULATION	
						selon la profession basée sur la CNP-S de 2001 - fin	
195	150	125	65	140	120	E Sciences sociales, enseignement, administration publique et religion	300
30	60	20	35	55	10	F Arts, culture, sports et loisirs	301
350	360	520	355	520	525	G Ventes et services	302
80	45	135	70	95	105	H Métiers, transport et machinerie	303
-	-	15	10	-	10	I Professions propres au secteur primaire	304
120	55	290	175	225	145	J Transformation, fabrication et services d'utilité publique	305
3,255	**2,810**	**3,740**	**2,620**	**3,750**	**3,900**	**Population active occupée totale de 15 ans et plus**	306
						selon le lieu de travail	
1,780	1,515	1,985	1,395	2,055	2,060	Hommes	307
1,550	1,295	1,710	1,245	1,750	1,755	Lieu habituel de travail	308
70	40	70	-	45	115	À domicile	309
-	-	-	-	10	-	En dehors du Canada	310
155	180	205	150	245	185	Sans adresse de travail fixe	311
1,475	1,300	1,750	1,220	1,685	1,845	Femmes	312
1,380	1,135	1,665	1,125	1,610	1,695	Lieu habituel de travail	313
55	115	55	35	40	80	À domicile	314
-	10	10	10	-	-	En dehors du Canada	315
40	45	35	60	40	70	Sans adresse de travail fixe	316
3,130	**2,660**	**3,610**	**2,580**	**3,650**	**3,700**	**Population active occupée totale de 15 ans et plus ayant un lieu habituel de travail ou sans adresse de travail fixe**	317
						selon le mode de transport	
1,705	1,480	1,915	1,395	2,000	1,940	Hommes	318
1,530	1,135	1,640	1,095	1,710	1,680	Automobile, camion ou fourgonnette, en tant que conducteur	319
105	100	140	90	105	125	Automobile, camion ou fourgonnette, en tant que passager	320
55	195	80	160	120	60	Transport en commun	321
10	30	25	30	45	65	À pied	322
10	15	25	20	20	-	Autre moyen	323
1,425	1,180	1,700	1,185	1,645	1,760	Femmes	324
1,100	795	1,230	800	1,085	1,190	Automobile, camion ou fourgonnette, en tant que conductrice	325
170	105	245	115	215	215	Automobile, camion ou fourgonnette, en tant que passagère	326
110	145	185	185	310	270	Transport en commun	327
15	130	30	75	10	75	À pied	328
25	10	10	-	20	-	Autre moyen	329
3,675	**3,155**	**4,095**	**2,940**	**4,305**	**4,435**	**Population totale de 15 ans et plus ayant travaillé depuis le 1er janvier 2000**	330
						selon la langue utilisée au travail	
3,330	3,020	3,765	2,695	3,915	4,185	Réponses uniques	331
3,310	3,005	3,670	2,680	3,810	4,165	Anglais	332
10	-	10	10	-	15	Français	333
10	15	90	10	105	10	Langues non officielles (5)	334
-	-	-	-	-	-	Chinois, n.d.a.	335
-	-	-	-	-	-	Cantonais	336
15	15	95	10	105	10	Autres langues (6)	337
340	130	330	245	390	250	Réponses multiples	338
35	85	40	25	40	95	Anglais et français	339
300	40	290	220	350	150	Anglais et langue non officielle	340
-	-	-	-	-	-	Français et langue non officielle	341
10	-	-	-	-	-	Anglais, français et langue non officielle	342
						CARACTÉRISTIQUES DES LOGEMENTS ET DES MÉNAGES	
1,770	**2,395**	**1,955**	**1,935**	**1,935**	**2,045**	**Nombre total de logements privés occupés**	343
						selon le mode d'occupation	
1,585	1,140	1,460	725	1,535	1,760	Possédé	344
180	1,255	500	1,205	400	285	Loué	345
-	-	-	-	-	-	Logement de bande	346
						selon le type de construction résidentielle	
1,565	1,065	360	580	435	690	Maison individuelle non attenante	347
85	140	915	290	940	775	Maison jumelée	348
40	15	195	20	335	525	Maison en rangée	349
15	85	10	75	15	20	Appartement, duplex non attenant	350
30	755	130	760	-	-	Appartement, immeuble de cinq étages ou plus	351
30	325	355	205	220	35	Appartement, immeuble de moins de cinq étages (38)	352
-	15	-	-	-	-	Autre maison individuelle attenante	353
-	-	-	-	-	-	Logement mobile (39)	354

Table 1. Selected Characteristics for Census Tracts, 2001 Census – 100% Data and 20% Sample Data

No.	Characteristics	Toronto 0572.06 A	Toronto 0572.07 A	Toronto 0572.08 A	Toronto 0573.02	Toronto 0573.03	Toronto 0573.04 A
	DWELLING AND HOUSEHOLD CHARACTERISTICS						
	by condition of dwelling						
355	Regular maintenance only	1,600	890	1,030	2,805	1,375	1,795
356	Minor repairs	150	340	320	490	450	305
357	Major repairs	15	15	40	140	65	105
	by period of construction						
358	Before 1946	-	10	10	20	100	20
359	1946-1960	-	-	-	305	100	55
360	1961-1970	-	10	15	460	45	190
361	1971-1980	10	100	220	350	265	65
362	1981-1990	80	955	770	670	1,045	520
363	1991-2001 (20)	1,680	170	375	1,635	345	1,365
364	Average number of rooms per dwelling	6.9	7.7	7.5	6.3	7.1	7.2
365	Average number of bedrooms per dwelling	3.3	3.6	3.6	2.8	3.2	3.4
366	Average value of dwelling $	222,741	230,068	233,317	199,559	208,273	213,553
367	**Total number of private households**	**1,770**	**1,245**	**1,390**	**3,435**	**1,895**	**2,210**
	by household size						
368	1 person	90	75	80	575	230	145
369	2 persons	305	200	200	920	345	500
370	3 persons	365	210	230	655	370	480
371	4-5 persons	820	580	635	1,085	780	845
372	6 or more persons	185	185	245	200	175	235
	by household type						
373	One-family households	1,470	960	1,060	2,585	1,520	1,795
374	Multiple-family households	165	180	230	200	110	200
375	Non-family households	135	110	105	655	265	210
376	Number of persons in private households	6,515	4,855	5,640	10,320	6,500	7,770
377	Average number of persons in private households	3.7	3.9	4.1	3.0	3.4	3.5
378	Average number of persons per room	0.5	0.5	0.5	0.5	0.5	0.5
379	Tenant households in non-farm, non-reserve private dwellings (40)	110	230	275	955	305	195
380	Average gross rent $ (40)	946	1,005	826	795	950	1,077
381	Tenant households spending 30% or more of household income on gross rent (40) (41)	35	90	90	295	130	80
382	Tenant households spending from 30% to 99% of household income on gross rent (40) (41)	30	55	75	260	115	70
383	Owner households in non-farm, non-reserve private dwellings (42)	1,660	1,010	1,100	2,480	1,580	2,000
384	Average owner's major payments $ (42)	1,433	1,405	1,463	1,248	1,251	1,381
385	Owner households spending 30% or more of household income on owner's major payments (41) (42)	425	240	290	520	430	520
386	Owner households spending from 30% to 99% of household income on owner's major payments (41) (42)	375	215	260	480	370	455
	CENSUS FAMILY CHARACTERISTICS						
387	**Total number of census families in private households**	**1,810**	**1,315**	**1,560**	**3,005**	**1,745**	**2,225**
	by census family structure and size						
388	Total couple families	1,560	1,105	1,330	2,420	1,520	1,895
389	Total families of married couples	1,445	1,050	1,240	2,120	1,390	1,710
390	Without children at home	330	230	330	620	340	490
391	With children at home	1,110	820	910	1,500	1,050	1,220
392	1 child	320	200	245	515	305	410
393	2 children	540	395	450	730	505	550
394	3 or more children	260	230	205	260	235	260
395	Total families of common-law couples	115	55	90	300	130	190
396	Without children at home	55	35	50	175	60	75
397	With children at home	60	15	45	115	65	115
398	1 child	25	10	15	60	30	45
399	2 children	35	10	20	35	25	30
400	3 or more children	-	-	10	25	15	35
401	Total lone-parent families	250	210	235	585	225	325
402	Female parent	210	175	210	435	195	240
403	1 child	90	75	85	285	90	140
404	2 children	70	70	70	115	65	65
405	3 or more children	50	25	55	35	45	35

Tableau 1. Certaines caractéristiques des secteurs de recensement, recensement de 2001 – Données intégrales et données-échantillon (20 %)

Toronto 0573.05 A	Toronto 0574	Toronto 0575.01	Toronto 0575.02	Toronto 0575.03	Toronto 0575.04	Caractéristiques	N[o]
						CARACTÉRISTIQUES DES LOGEMENTS ET DES MÉNAGES	
						selon l'état du logement	
1,290	1,560	1,225	1,070	1,365	1,375	Entretien régulier seulement	355
405	620	630	620	480	555	Réparations mineures	356
75	220	105	245	90	120	Réparations majeures	357
						selon la période de construction	
35	945	-	105	10	-	Avant 1946	358
440	370	65	435	35	55	1946-1960	359
355	230	205	755	205	430	1961-1970	360
70	225	1,415	475	1,255	1,450	1971-1980	361
775	335	260	45	420	105	1981-1990	362
95	295	10	115	20	10	1991-2001 (20)	363
7.9	5.5	6.6	5.4	7.0	6.8	Nombre moyen de pièces par logement	364
3.5	2.1	3.1	2.2	3.3	3.3	Nombre moyen de chambres à coucher par logement	365
218,772	221,638	189,729	199,220	186,372	168,153	Valeur moyenne du logement $	366
1,770	**2,395**	**1,955**	**1,930**	**1,935**	**2,050**	**Nombre total de logements privés**	367
						selon la taille du ménage	
170	970	240	540	125	180	1 personne	368
440	730	370	585	400	485	2 personnes	369
320	285	410	355	375	470	3 personnes	370
695	355	730	385	785	750	4-5 personnes	371
145	55	210	70	250	155	6 personnes ou plus	372
						selon le genre de ménage	
1,445	1,290	1,530	1,275	1,555	1,630	Ménages unifamiliaux	373
95	50	155	30	220	145	Ménages multifamiliaux	374
225	1,055	275	630	160	270	Ménages non familiaux	375
6,000	5,155	6,800	4,835	7,170	6,835	Nombre de personnes dans les ménages privés	376
3.4	2.2	3.5	2.5	3.7	3.3	Nombre moyen de personnes dans les ménages privés	377
0.4	0.4	0.5	0.5	0.5	0.5	Nombre moyen de personnes par pièce	378
180	1,255	495	1,205	395	285	Ménages locataires dans les logements privés non agricoles hors réserve (40)	379
875	751	879	781	923	1,168	Loyer brut moyen $ (40)	380
25	490	215	420	165	105	Ménages locataires consacrant 30 % ou plus du revenu du ménage au loyer brut (40) (41)	381
25	420	155	315	150	90	Ménages locataires consacrant de 30 % à 99 % du revenu du ménage au loyer brut (40) (41)	382
1,580	1,145	1,460	730	1,535	1,760	Ménages propriétaires dans les logements privés non agricoles hors réserve (42)	383
1,039	1,139	1,133	981	1,202	1,116	Principales dépenses de propriété moyennes $ (42)	384
205	255	345	100	360	430	Ménages propriétaires consacrant 30 % ou plus du revenu du ménage aux principales dépenses de propriété (41) (42)	385
170	245	300	85	320	385	Ménages propriétaires consacrant de 30 % à 99 % du revenu du ménage aux principales dépenses de propriété (41) (42)	386
						CARACTÉRISTIQUES DES FAMILLES DE RECENSEMENT	
1,655	**1,390**	**1,855**	**1,335**	**2,035**	**1,920**	**Total des familles de recensement dans les ménages privés**	387
						selon la structure et la taille de la famille de recensement	
1,445	1,140	1,545	1,060	1,680	1,545	Total des familles avec conjoints	388
1,325	915	1,395	830	1,510	1,350	Total des familles avec couples mariés	389
325	450	330	300	440	385	Sans enfants à la maison	390
1,000	470	1,065	535	1,070	965	Avec enfants à la maison	391
285	155	325	210	305	340	1 enfant	392
460	200	460	215	515	390	2 enfants	393
265	115	280	110	250	235	3 enfants ou plus	394
125	225	150	225	170	200	Total des familles en union libre	395
100	160	55	155	65	75	Sans enfants à la maison	396
25	70	95	75	100	125	Avec enfants à la maison	397
-	45	35	35	65	50	1 enfant	398
-	20	35	35	30	40	2 enfants	399
15	-	25	10	10	35	3 enfants ou plus	400
205	255	305	275	355	370	Total des familles monoparentales	401
150	195	240	225	265	270	Parent de sexe féminin	402
95	150	130	120	150	135	1 enfant	403
35	30	85	80	80	110	2 enfants	404
15	10	25	15	35	30	3 enfants ou plus	405

Table 1. Selected Characteristics for Census Tracts, 2001 Census – 100% Data and 20% Sample Data

No.	Characteristics	Toronto 0572.06 A	Toronto 0572.07 A	Toronto 0572.08 A	Toronto 0573.02	Toronto 0573.03	Toronto 0573.04 A
	CENSUS FAMILY CHARACTERISTICS						
	by census family structure and size – concluded						
406	Male parent	35	35	20	150	25	85
407	1 child	30	15	20	110	10	65
408	2 children	-	15	10	25	15	25
409	3 or more children	10	-	-	15	-	-
410	**Total number of children at home**	**2,760**	**2,125**	**2,355**	**3,850**	**2,655**	**3,090**
	by age groups						
411	Under 6 years	880	410	590	1,070	630	885
412	6-14 years	1,065	730	810	1,355	1,025	1,170
413	15-17 years	255	260	220	360	345	325
414	18-24 years	415	525	525	690	465	415
415	25 years and over	145	195	200	375	190	290
416	Average number of children at home per census family (43)	1.5	1.6	1.5	1.3	1.5	1.4
417	**Total number of persons in private households**	**6,515**	**4,860**	**5,635**	**10,320**	**6,500**	**7,770**
	by census family status and living arrangements						
418	Number of non-family persons	390	310	395	1,045	585	565
419	Living with relatives (44)	185	130	250	195	205	185
420	Living with non-relatives only	110	110	60	275	150	235
421	Living alone	90	70	85	570	230	145
422	Number of family persons	6,130	4,545	5,245	9,275	5,915	7,205
423	Average number of persons per census family	3.4	3.4	3.4	3.1	3.4	3.2
424	**Total number of persons 65 years and over**	**175**	**180**	**270**	**575**	**375**	**350**
425	Number of non-family persons 65 years and over	85	55	90	200	175	130
426	Living with relatives (44)	60	55	75	95	70	90
427	Living with non-relatives only	15	-	10	10	15	15
428	Living alone	-	-	10	95	95	25
429	Number of family persons 65 years and over	90	130	175	375	195	225
	ECONOMIC FAMILY CHARACTERISTICS						
430	**Total number of economic families in private households**	**1,650**	**1,145**	**1,295**	**2,810**	**1,655**	**2,015**
	by size of family						
431	2 persons	315	200	200	925	345	495
432	3 persons	340	195	235	620	385	460
433	4 persons	550	360	390	770	540	580
434	5 or more persons	450	395	475	495	380	475
435	Total number of persons in economic families	6,315	4,675	5,500	9,470	6,125	7,390
436	Average number of persons per economic family	3.8	4.1	4.2	3.4	3.7	3.7
437	Total number of unattached individuals	200	180	145	850	380	375
	2000 INCOME CHARACTERISTICS						
	Population 15 years and over by sex and total income groups in 2000						
438	Total - Both sexes	4,575	3,715	4,235	7,880	4,845	5,705
439	Without income	250	255	255	325	230	315
440	With income	4,330	3,455	3,980	7,555	4,615	5,390
441	Under $1,000 (45)	225	190	230	250	300	225
442	$ 1,000 - $ 2,999	180	200	225	325	275	155
443	$ 3,000 - $ 4,999	235	110	125	235	115	210
444	$ 5,000 - $ 6,999	95	150	175	285	160	170
445	$ 7,000 - $ 9,999	140	160	170	265	290	300
446	$10,000 - $11,999	155	150	185	230	155	125
447	$12,000 - $14,999	205	140	170	245	270	205
448	$15,000 - $19,999	175	270	325	415	225	275
449	$20,000 - $24,999	300	290	305	660	355	370
450	$25,000 - $29,999	365	200	370	715	320	480
451	$30,000 - $34,999	425	295	380	855	435	660
452	$35,000 - $39,999	395	250	280	700	325	455
453	$40,000 - $44,999	245	140	185	610	275	345
454	$45,000 - $49,999	240	105	140	355	165	355
455	$50,000 - $59,999	345	310	315	650	400	490
456	$60,000 and over	605	490	410	760	555	570
457	Average income $ (46)	32,764	32,537	29,110	32,001	30,196	32,355
458	Median income $ (46)	30,252	25,692	25,621	30,127	26,553	31,063
459	Standard error of average income $ (46)	775	1,082	813	557	803	711

Tableau 1. Certaines caractéristiques des secteurs de recensement, recensement de 2001 – Données intégrales et données-échantillon (20 %)

Toronto 0573.05 A	Toronto 0574	Toronto 0575.01	Toronto 0575.02	Toronto 0575.03	Toronto 0575.04	Caractéristiques	N°
						CARACTÉRISTIQUES DES FAMILLES DE RECENSEMENT	
						selon la structure et la taille de la famille de recensement - fin	
55	60	60	55	95	100	Parent de sexe masculin	406
30	30	25	30	70	70	1 enfant	407
25	25	35	25	10	20	2 enfants	408
-	-	-	-	15	15	3 enfants ou plus	409
2,445	**1,335**	**2,835**	**1,540**	**2,865**	**2,730**	**Nombre total d'enfants à la maison**	410
						selon les groupes d'âge	
360	315	555	395	665	535	Moins de 6 ans	411
895	435	900	495	1,000	1,025	6-14 ans	412
305	150	330	125	320	335	15-17 ans	413
560	270	625	295	560	530	18-24 ans	414
320	165	420	230	325	305	25 ans et plus	415
1.5	1.0	1.5	1.2	1.4	1.4	Nombre moyen d'enfants à la maison par famille de recensement (43)	416
6,000	**5,155**	**6,800**	**4,835**	**7,170**	**6,835**	**Nombre total de personnes dans les ménages privés**	417
						selon la situation des particuliers dans la famille de recensement et des particuliers dans le ménage	
460	1,290	565	905	590	635	Nombre de personnes hors famille de recensement	418
125	85	160	125	230	215	Vivant avec des personnes apparentées (44)	419
160	225	165	235	235	245	Vivant avec des personnes non apparentées uniquement	420
170	970	240	540	125	185	Vivant seules	421
5,545	3,870	6,235	3,930	6,580	6,195	Nombre de personnes membres d'une famille	422
3.4	2.8	3.4	2.9	3.2	3.2	Nombre moyen de personnes par famille de recensement	423
515	**870**	**535**	**495**	**365**	**350**	**Nombre total de personnes de 65 ans et plus**	424
200	455	195	165	80	125	Nombre de personnes hors famille de recensement de 65 ans et plus	425
85	40	85	15	75	85	Vivant avec des personnes apparentées (44)	426
25	-	10	10	-	10	Vivant avec des personnes non apparentées uniquement	427
90	410	100	145	10	30	Vivant seules	428
310	410	335	330	285	220	Nombre de personnes membres d'une famille de 65 ans et plus	429
						CARACTÉRISTIQUES DES FAMILLES ÉCONOMIQUES	
1,550	**1,355**	**1,705**	**1,340**	**1,815**	**1,815**	**Nombre total de familles économiques dans les ménages privés**	430
						selon la taille de la famille	
430	700	400	600	450	505	2 personnes	431
300	280	415	325	410	460	3 personnes	432
445	230	445	265	485	445	4 personnes	433
380	145	450	145	465	405	5 personnes ou plus	434
5,665	3,960	6,390	4,055	6,810	6,410	Nombre total de personnes dans les familles économiques	435
3.7	2.9	3.7	3.0	3.8	3.5	Nombre moyen de personnes par famille économique	436
335	1,200	405	780	360	425	Nombre total de personnes hors famille économique	437
						CARACTÉRISTIQUES DU REVENU DE 2000	
						Population de 15 ans et plus selon le sexe et les tranches de revenu total en 2000	
4,735	4,420	5,330	3,915	5,460	5,280	Total - Les deux sexes	438
265	155	320	165	385	210	Sans revenu	439
4,465	4,265	5,005	3,750	5,075	5,070	Avec un revenu	440
185	195	210	145	290	160	Moins de 1 000 $ (45)	441
115	195	280	140	310	225	1 000 $ - 2 999 $	442
140	65	200	130	160	195	3 000 $ - 4 999 $	443
90	120	240	170	220	230	5 000 $ - 6 999 $	444
210	165	355	165	205	335	7 000 $ - 9 999 $	445
165	145	215	85	280	165	10 000 $ - 11 999 $	446
225	330	285	260	220	195	12 000 $ - 14 999 $	447
295	380	390	375	370	335	15 000 $ - 19 999 $	448
335	325	395	325	385	465	20 000 $ - 24 999 $	449
390	375	450	360	495	415	25 000 $ - 29 999 $	450
400	280	460	390	510	525	30 000 $ - 34 999 $	451
380	325	355	355	415	455	35 000 $ - 39 999 $	452
300	265	365	240	385	345	40 000 $ - 44 999 $	453
205	225	230	110	255	245	45 000 $ - 49 999 $	454
430	340	260	215	335	430	50 000 $ - 59 999 $	455
600	545	325	290	250	345	60 000 $ et plus	456
33,573	34,230	26,358	27,691	26,652	28,423	Revenu moyen $ (46)	457
30,261	26,887	24,329	25,618	25,603	27,924	Revenu médian $ (46)	458
796	1,302	625	672	594	583	Erreur type de revenu moyen $ (46)	459

Table 1. Selected Characteristics for Census Tracts, 2001 Census – 100% Data and 20% Sample Data

No.	Characteristics	Toronto 0572.06 A	Toronto 0572.07 A	Toronto 0572.08 A	Toronto 0573.02	Toronto 0573.03	Toronto 0573.04 A
	2000 INCOME CHARACTERISTICS						
	Population 15 years and over by sex and total income groups in 2000 – concluded						
460	Total - Males	2,275	1,870	2,095	3,785	2,430	2,765
461	Without income	110	90	80	125	85	135
462	With income	2,165	1,780	2,015	3,665	2,350	2,630
463	Under $1,000 (45)	100	70	75	135	125	100
464	$ 1,000 - $ 2,999	80	90	125	90	120	55
465	$ 3,000 - $ 4,999	95	45	60	105	40	35
466	$ 5,000 - $ 6,999	-	50	85	120	75	35
467	$ 7,000 - $ 9,999	50	65	75	100	100	110
468	$10,000 - $11,999	45	55	75	95	95	70
469	$12,000 - $14,999	55	35	60	75	110	95
470	$15,000 - $19,999	70	130	95	115	80	80
471	$20,000 - $24,999	145	130	155	240	135	115
472	$25,000 - $29,999	150	80	175	260	120	225
473	$30,000 - $34,999	145	135	205	430	225	210
474	$35,000 - $39,999	165	115	95	315	170	235
475	$40,000 - $44,999	150	100	110	360	165	185
476	$45,000 - $49,999	175	65	70	225	90	260
477	$50,000 - $59,999	275	230	225	445	280	370
478	$60,000 and over	475	385	320	565	425	455
479	Average income $ (46)	40,175	40,790	33,898	37,687	36,201	39,563
480	Median income $ (46)	39,563	34,841	30,013	35,284	33,074	38,137
481	Standard error of average income $ (46)	1,208	1,726	1,270	899	1,255	1,162
482	Total - Females	2,300	1,845	2,140	4,090	2,415	2,940
483	Without income	135	165	175	200	145	175
484	With income	2,165	1,680	1,970	3,890	2,265	2,765
485	Under $1,000 (45)	125	120	150	120	175	120
486	$ 1,000 - $ 2,999	105	105	100	235	150	100
487	$ 3,000 - $ 4,999	135	75	60	130	75	175
488	$ 5,000 - $ 6,999	95	100	85	170	90	130
489	$ 7,000 - $ 9,999	95	95	95	165	190	190
490	$10,000 - $11,999	105	90	105	140	60	50
491	$12,000 - $14,999	145	105	115	165	160	115
492	$15,000 - $19,999	105	140	230	300	150	200
493	$20,000 - $24,999	165	160	150	420	225	255
494	$25,000 - $29,999	215	120	200	455	200	260
495	$30,000 - $34,999	280	160	180	425	205	455
496	$35,000 - $39,999	235	135	185	385	155	225
497	$40,000 - $44,999	100	40	75	250	110	160
498	$45,000 - $49,999	70	40	65	135	70	95
499	$50,000 - $59,999	70	85	90	205	120	125
500	$60,000 and over	130	110	90	190	130	120
501	Average income $ (46)	25,341	23,765	24,210	26,640	23,969	25,499
502	Median income $ (46)	25,260	20,113	21,581	26,488	21,000	25,686
503	Standard error of average income $ (46)	853	1,089	948	616	919	729
	by composition of total income						
504	Total - Composition of income in 2000 % (47)	100.0	100.0	100.0	100.0	100.0	100.0
505	Employment income %	93.1	91.7	91.4	90.6	89.2	90.9
506	Government transfer payments %	4.9	5.0	5.9	6.0	7.4	5.7
507	Other %	2.0	3.3	2.7	3.4	3.4	3.4
	Population 15 years and over with employment income in 2000 by sex and work activity						
508	Both sexes with employment income (48)	3,760	2,940	3,335	6,430	3,840	4,715
509	Average employment income $	35,131	35,024	31,787	34,085	32,382	33,648
510	Standard error of average employment income $	824	1,181	872	601	904	768
511	Worked full year, full time (49)	2,465	1,840	1,920	4,055	2,325	3,105
512	Average employment income $	43,365	45,456	40,750	41,267	41,344	41,462
513	Standard error of average employment income $	986	1,504	1,079	705	1,136	922
514	Worked part year or part time (50)	1,210	1,045	1,375	2,255	1,400	1,470
515	Average employment income $	19,958	18,168	20,009	21,804	18,539	18,782
516	Standard error of average employment income $	1,062	1,293	1,135	870	1,198	978
517	Males with employment income (48)	1,995	1,620	1,760	3,260	2,110	2,420
518	Average employment income $	41,780	42,181	36,260	39,534	37,128	40,142
519	Standard error of average employment income $	1,239	1,821	1,314	954	1,337	1,218
520	Worked full year, full time (49)	1,435	1,095	1,055	2,140	1,345	1,740
521	Average employment income $	49,348	53,959	46,271	46,806	46,338	47,501
522	Standard error of average employment income $	1,362	2,140	1,567	1,115	1,581	1,398
523	Worked part year or part time (50)	520	505	695	1,085	700	610
524	Average employment income $	23,560	18,139	21,517	25,719	20,988	21,900
525	Standard error of average employment income $	1,958	1,915	1,689	1,439	1,992	1,694

Tableau 1. Certaines caractéristiques des secteurs de recensement, recensement de 2001 – Données intégrales et données-échantillon (20 %)

Toronto 0573.05 A	Toronto 0574	Toronto 0575.01	Toronto 0575.02	Toronto 0575.03	Toronto 0575.04	Caractéristiques	N°
						CARACTÉRISTIQUES DU REVENU DE 2000	
						Population de 15 ans et plus selon le sexe et les tranches de revenu total en 2000 – fin	
2,355	2,015	2,605	1,910	2,745	2,620	Total - Hommes	460
70	40	140	65	165	120	Sans revenu	461
2,290	1,975	2,460	1,845	2,580	2,505	Avec un revenu	462
70	95	125	80	120	65	Moins de 1 000 $ (45)	463
30	45	105	45	100	55	1 000 $ - 2 999 $	464
65	10	90	35	75	90	3 000 $ - 4 999 $	465
55	50	50	50	65	65	5 000 $ - 6 999 $	466
55	40	120	50	45	90	7 000 $ - 9 999 $	467
75	50	85	40	140	55	10 000 $ - 11 999 $	468
105	85	110	100	95	75	12 000 $ - 14 999 $	469
115	110	110	150	145	140	15 000 $ - 19 999 $	470
125	120	145	160	170	180	20 000 $ - 24 999 $	471
170	160	190	110	235	175	25 000 $ - 29 999 $	472
200	125	200	195	250	290	30 000 $ - 34 999 $	473
195	190	245	225	235	250	35 000 $ - 39 999 $	474
165	145	240	180	245	195	40 000 $ - 44 999 $	475
130	125	145	65	195	185	45 000 $ - 49 999 $	476
285	260	205	145	235	295	50 000 $ - 59 999 $	477
455	360	285	200	230	290	60 000 $ et plus	478
39,283	41,708	32,519	32,206	32,147	34,304	Revenu moyen $ (46)	479
36,543	36,920	30,755	32,088	31,070	34,019	Revenu médian $ (46)	480
1,214	2,317	1,030	1,003	916	851	Erreur type de revenu moyen $ (46)	481
2,380	2,410	2,725	2,010	2,710	2,665	Total - Femmes	482
200	115	180	100	220	100	Sans revenu	483
2,175	2,290	2,545	1,910	2,490	2,570	Avec un revenu	484
115	95	90	65	170	95	Moins de 1 000 $ (45)	485
90	140	175	95	210	170	1 000 $ - 2 999 $	486
70	55	105	95	85	105	3 000 $ - 4 999 $	487
35	75	190	115	155	160	5 000 $ - 6 999 $	488
160	125	230	115	165	245	7 000 $ - 9 999 $	489
85	100	125	45	140	105	10 000 $ - 11 999 $	490
120	245	170	155	125	120	12 000 $ - 14 999 $	491
175	270	280	225	220	200	15 000 $ - 19 999 $	492
210	205	250	165	215	280	20 000 $ - 24 999 $	493
225	220	260	250	260	235	25 000 $ - 29 999 $	494
205	155	255	195	260	235	30 000 $ - 34 999 $	495
185	130	110	130	175	200	35 000 $ - 39 999 $	496
145	115	130	60	140	150	40 000 $ - 44 999 $	497
70	100	85	40	55	55	45 000 $ - 49 999 $	498
140	85	55	70	100	140	50 000 $ - 59 999 $	499
145	185	30	90	25	60	60 000 $ et plus	500
27,569	27,783	20,407	23,336	20,954	22,692	Revenu moyen $ (46)	501
25,056	20,633	17,067	20,541	19,305	20,689	Revenu médian $ (46)	502
944	1,278	631	846	666	716	Erreur type de revenu moyen $ (46)	503
						selon la composition du revenu total	
100.0	100.0	100.0	100.0	100.0	100.0	Total - Composition du revenu en 2000 % (47)	504
86.5	81.8	84.7	82.9	87.7	88.2	Revenu d'emploi %	505
7.1	9.7	10.0	11.3	8.3	7.1	Transferts gouvernementaux %	506
6.5	8.4	5.3	5.7	3.9	4.8	Autre %	507
						Population de 15 ans et plus ayant un revenu d'emploi en 2000 selon le sexe et le travail	
3,635	3,060	3,935	2,805	4,190	4,350	Les deux sexes ayant un revenu d'emploi (48)	508
35,624	38,998	28,379	30,760	28,381	29,201	Revenu moyen d'emploi $	509
867	1,365	682	762	653	609	Erreur type de revenu moyen d'emploi $	510
2,315	1,980	2,175	1,730	2,495	2,800	Ayant travaillé toute l'année à plein temps (49)	511
43,599	45,599	37,674	37,195	36,747	36,960	Revenu moyen d'emploi $	512
999	1,488	885	887	767	658	Erreur type de revenu moyen d'emploi $	513
1,190	1,060	1,640	995	1,575	1,485	Ayant travaillé une partie de l'année ou à temps partiel (50)	514
22,311	26,890	17,112	19,801	16,261	15,528	Revenu moyen d'emploi $	515
1,398	2,597	726	1,170	827	837	Erreur type de revenu moyen d'emploi $	516
1,955	1,605	2,050	1,495	2,210	2,265	Hommes ayant un revenu d'emploi (48)	517
41,159	44,692	34,266	35,008	33,805	34,525	Revenu moyen d'emploi $	518
1,333	1,992	1,038	1,061	982	867	Erreur type de revenu moyen d'emploi $	519
1,280	1,150	1,245	1,015	1,455	1,575	Ayant travaillé toute l'année à plein temps (49)	520
49,021	47,912	43,096	40,431	40,897	41,752	Revenu moyen d'emploi $	521
1,480	1,688	1,228	1,249	1,115	883	Erreur type de revenu moyen d'emploi $	522
590	435	745	450	715	650	Ayant travaillé une partie de l'année ou à temps partiel (50)	523
27,711	36,576	20,740	23,830	19,915	18,878	Revenu moyen d'emploi $	524
2,459	5,556	1,258	1,614	1,435	1,379	Erreur type de revenu moyen d'emploi $	525

Table 1. Selected Characteristics for Census Tracts, 2001 Census – 100% Data and 20% Sample Data

No.	Characteristics	Toronto 0572.06 A	Toronto 0572.07 A	Toronto 0572.08 A	Toronto 0573.02	Toronto 0573.03	Toronto 0573.04 A
	2000 INCOME CHARACTERISTICS						
	Population 15 years and over with employment income in 2000 by sex and work activity – concluded						
526	Females with employment income (48)	1,765	1,320	1,575	3,170	1,735	2,295
527	Average employment income $	27,618	26,266	26,795	28,478	26,616	26,793
528	Standard error of average employment income $	927	1,198	1,051	662	1,102	801
529	Worked full year, full time (49)	1,030	750	860	1,910	980	1,365
530	Average employment income $	35,021	33,006	34,008	35,067	34,502	33,791
531	Standard error of average employment income $	1,201	1,485	1,268	690	1,483	912
532	Worked part year or part time (50)	690	535	680	1,175	700	860
533	Average employment income $	17,249	18,195	18,482	18,183	16,089	16,574
534	Standard error of average employment income $	1,107	1,747	1,506	989	1,311	1,134
	Census families by structure and family income groups in 2000						
535	Total - All census families	1,810	1,315	1,560	3,005	1,745	2,220
536	Under $10,000	55	35	110	120	75	95
537	$ 10,000 - $19,999	105	75	95	120	80	70
538	$ 20,000 - $29,999	100	120	135	145	115	80
539	$ 30,000 - $39,999	125	125	125	295	135	190
540	$ 40,000 - $49,999	110	125	130	275	115	180
541	$ 50,000 - $59,999	185	70	115	255	165	215
542	$ 60,000 - $69,999	250	110	150	400	180	310
543	$ 70,000 - $79,999	160	120	120	425	220	290
544	$ 80,000 - $89,999	225	110	120	205	180	235
545	$ 90,000 - $99,999	165	50	105	280	185	160
546	$100,000 and over	340	390	355	495	290	395
547	Average family income $	71,707	78,658	68,054	68,879	70,138	70,654
548	Median family income $	68,707	71,145	64,226	67,528	70,487	69,207
549	Standard error of average family income $	1,842	3,114	2,379	1,411	1,981	1,691
550	Total - All couple census families (51)	1,565	1,105	1,330	2,420	1,520	1,895
551	Under $10,000	35	30	65	65	65	75
552	$ 10,000 - $19,999	75	40	60	45	40	55
553	$ 20,000 - $29,999	85	100	120	80	75	45
554	$ 30,000 - $39,999	45	80	80	135	110	85
555	$ 40,000 - $49,999	100	85	105	210	85	120
556	$ 50,000 - $59,999	175	60	100	220	145	185
557	$ 60,000 - $69,999	195	90	145	345	150	280
558	$ 70,000 - $79,999	160	120	110	395	215	285
559	$ 80,000 - $89,999	220	85	115	185	175	225
560	$ 90,000 - $99,999	145	40	90	265	185	155
561	$100,000 and over	330	375	350	470	290	400
562	Average family income $	75,935	84,392	73,576	74,868	74,389	76,011
563	Median family income $	74,758	75,770	70,692	71,960	75,172	74,167
564	Standard error of average family income $	1,949	3,450	2,594	1,476	2,114	1,799
	Incidence of low income in 2000						
565	Total - Economic families	1,650	1,145	1,300	2,810	1,650	2,015
566	Low income	140	105	170	220	210	185
567	Incidence of low income in 2000 % (52)	8.3	9.3	13.1	7.8	12.9	9.2
568	Total - Unattached individuals 15 years and over	200	180	140	835	380	360
569	Low income	30	80	45	160	125	60
570	Incidence of low income in 2000 % (52)	15.0	43.2	32.7	18.8	33.1	16.8
571	Total - Population in private households	6,515	4,855	5,635	10,305	6,500	7,755
572	Low income	560	500	715	850	915	770
573	Incidence of low income in 2000 % (52)	8.6	10.3	12.7	8.2	14.1	9.9
	Private households by household income groups in 2000						
574	Total - All private households	1,770	1,245	1,390	3,435	1,895	2,210
575	Under $10,000	30	40	30	65	70	75
576	$ 10,000 - $19,999	75	40	85	155	140	40
577	$ 20,000 - $29,999	30	35	50	175	90	70
578	$ 30,000 - $39,999	85	40	90	375	120	150
579	$ 40,000 - $49,999	100	95	140	340	140	115
580	$ 50,000 - $59,999	180	130	50	340	170	210
581	$ 60,000 - $69,999	230	110	100	435	165	290
582	$ 70,000 - $79,999	175	120	115	425	195	260
583	$ 80,000 - $89,999	230	125	115	210	235	260
584	$ 90,000 - $99,999	160	50	110	290	200	195
585	$100,000 and over	465	460	495	630	380	535
586	Average household income $	80,225	90,089	83,437	70,294	73,495	78,838
587	Median household income $	78,228	81,977	82,640	66,555	73,148	75,584
588	Standard error of average household income $	1,875	3,052	2,702	1,434	2,110	1,799

Tableau 1. Certaines caractéristiques des secteurs de recensement, recensement de 2001 – Données intégrales et données-échantillon (20 %)

Toronto 0573.05 A	Toronto 0574	Toronto 0575.01	Toronto 0575.02	Toronto 0575.03	Toronto 0575.04	Caractéristiques	N°
						CARACTÉRISTIQUES DU REVENU DE 2000	
						Population de 15 ans et plus ayant un revenu d'emploi en 2000 selon le sexe et le travail - fin	
1,690	1,460	1,895	1,310	1,970	2,080	Femmes ayant un revenu d'emploi (48)	526
29,223	32,728	22,011	25,890	22,303	23,400	Revenu moyen d'emploi $	527
960	1,784	764	1,024	731	760	Erreur type de revenu moyen d'emploi $	528
1,030	825	930	710	1,040	1,225	Ayant travaillé toute l'année à plein temps (49)	529
36,826	42,387	30,428	32,602	30,957	30,810	Revenu moyen d'emploi $	530
1,119	2,652	1,088	1,117	843	849	Erreur type de revenu moyen d'emploi $	531
610	625	900	550	865	835	Ayant travaillé une partie de l'année ou à temps partiel (50)	532
17,070	20,143	14,104	16,508	13,224	12,906	Revenu moyen d'emploi $	533
1,307	1,692	757	1,617	847	966	Erreur type de revenu moyen d'emploi $	534
						Familles de recensement selon la structure et les tranches de revenu de la famille en 2000	
1,655	1,395	1,855	1,335	2,040	1,920	Total - Toutes les familles de recensement	535
25	35	90	55	85	40	Moins de 10 000 $	536
45	60	95	30	120	80	10 000 $ - 19 999 $	537
80	130	125	115	185	105	20 000 $ - 29 999 $	538
100	145	140	215	280	195	30 000 $ - 39 999 $	539
125	135	240	160	185	180	40 000 $ - 49 999 $	540
205	110	250	135	260	270	50 000 $ - 59 999 $	541
135	125	165	215	225	340	60 000 $ - 69 999 $	542
150	170	210	70	160	155	70 000 $ - 79 999 $	543
110	75	105	130	195	185	80 000 $ - 89 999 $	544
150	80	115	55	125	110	90 000 $ - 99 999 $	545
530	320	305	160	225	265	100 000 $ et plus	546
82,277	76,833	64,202	59,834	59,743	64,838	Revenu moyen des familles $	547
76,844	65,930	58,680	55,692	56,920	61,940	Revenu médian des familles $	548
2,143	3,867	1,784	1,862	1,599	1,466	Erreur type de revenu moyen des familles $	549
1,450	1,140	1,545	1,060	1,680	1,550	Total - Toutes les familles de recensement comptant un couple (51)	550
20	10	50	10	50	-	Moins de 10 000 $	551
25	25	40	10	100	40	10 000 $ - 19 999 $	552
45	85	95	85	120	60	20 000 $ - 29 999 $	553
60	105	105	155	170	95	30 000 $ - 39 999 $	554
95	100	210	120	145	145	40 000 $ - 49 999 $	555
190	95	210	100	240	235	50 000 $ - 59 999 $	556
105	110	130	200	180	300	60 000 $ - 69 999 $	557
135	150	185	65	160	145	70 000 $ - 79 999 $	558
105	70	105	120	180	160	80 000 $ - 89 999 $	559
140	75	120	45	115	105	90 000 $ - 99 999 $	560
515	310	305	145	215	250	100 000 $ et plus	561
86,837	84,347	69,409	64,992	63,955	70,167	Revenu moyen des familles $	562
83,118	71,715	63,267	61,853	60,447	65,948	Revenu médian des familles $	563
2,292	4,492	1,963	2,041	1,794	1,566	Erreur type de revenu moyen des familles $	564
						Fréquence des unités à faible revenu en 2000	
1,545	1,350	1,705	1,340	1,810	1,815	Total - Familles économiques	565
60	135	210	195	250	155	Faible revenu	566
4.1	10.2	12.1	14.3	13.7	8.5	Fréquence des unités à faible revenu en 2000 % (52)	567
330	1,200	390	760	315	425	Total - Personnes hors famille économique de 15 ans et plus	568
100	450	175	295	120	105	Faible revenu	569
31.1	37.5	44.4	38.5	37.9	24.2	Fréquence des unités à faible revenu en 2000 % (52)	570
5,995	5,155	6,780	4,820	7,125	6,835	Total - Population dans les ménages privés	571
305	775	890	920	995	610	Faible revenu	572
5.2	15.0	13.1	19.1	14.0	8.9	Fréquence des unités à faible revenu en 2000 % (52)	573
						Ménages privés selon les tranches de revenu du ménage en 2000	
1,770	2,395	1,960	1,935	1,935	2,045	Total - Tous les ménages privés	574
30	85	80	155	55	35	Moins de 10 000 $	575
70	385	155	170	100	105	10 000 $ - 19 999 $	576
80	285	105	230	150	110	20 000 $ - 29 999 $	577
120	250	155	255	165	190	30 000 $ - 39 999 $	578
100	260	185	245	165	165	40 000 $ - 49 999 $	579
180	185	230	100	195	255	50 000 $ - 59 999 $	580
145	180	180	270	200	290	60 000 $ - 69 999 $	581
155	175	185	70	190	175	70 000 $ - 79 999 $	582
125	80	120	125	185	195	80 000 $ - 89 999 $	583
165	110	180	90	175	120	90 000 $ - 99 999 $	584
605	395	380	235	355	410	100 000 $ et plus	585
84,767	60,790	67,302	53,719	69,888	70,350	Revenu moyen des ménages $	586
80,102	47,234	63,093	44,536	66,460	65,617	Revenu médian des ménages $	587
2,302	2,602	1,820	1,684	1,839	1,670	Erreur type de revenu moyen des ménages $	588

Table 1. Selected Characteristics for Census Tracts, 2001 Census – 100% Data and 20% Sample Data

No.	Characteristics	Toronto 0575.05	Toronto 0575.06	Toronto 0576.01	Toronto 0576.04	Toronto 0576.05	Toronto 0576.06
	POPULATION CHARACTERISTICS						
1	**Population, 1996 (1)**	**4,664**	**4,548**	**2,344**	**5,140**	**7,046**	**6,198**
2	**Population, 2001 (2)**	**7,377**	**4,631**	**5,869**	**5,053**	**7,405**	**6,271**
3	Population percentage change, 1996-2001	58.2	1.8	150.4	-1.7	5.1	1.2
4	Land area in square kilometres, 2001	1.56	1.59	63.56	3.23	1.54	2.21
5	**Total population – 100% Data (3)**	**7,375**	**4,635**	**5,870**	**5,055**	**7,405**	**6,270**
	by sex and age groups						
6	Male	3,620	2,280	2,960	2,480	3,685	3,145
7	0-4 years	345	155	280	135	270	215
8	5-9 years	345	195	245	200	335	300
9	10-14 years	300	225	190	240	320	325
10	15-19 years	260	225	145	240	340	270
11	20-24 years	235	180	175	210	295	235
12	25-29 years	230	160	370	110	250	170
13	30-34 years	365	165	345	125	265	215
14	35-39 years	390	210	290	215	335	290
15	40-44 years	355	220	250	210	315	295
16	45-49 years	235	190	160	245	285	275
17	50-54 years	205	145	125	245	270	220
18	55-59 years	155	100	120	145	150	145
19	60-64 years	85	45	75	65	100	80
20	65-69 years	50	30	85	40	50	55
21	70-74 years	40	15	60	30	40	30
22	75-79 years	10	5	25	10	25	25
23	80-84 years	5	10	15	5	20	5
24	85 years and over	5	5	5	5	15	-
25	Female	3,760	2,350	2,910	2,575	3,720	3,125
26	0-4 years	305	165	230	155	250	190
27	5-9 years	340	210	225	200	310	245
28	10-14 years	315	215	170	220	345	280
29	15-19 years	280	190	160	290	300	280
30	20-24 years	245	190	210	180	305	235
31	25-29 years	250	160	400	125	240	180
32	30-34 years	435	200	325	140	285	225
33	35-39 years	405	215	295	225	370	325
34	40-44 years	360	225	220	260	335	315
35	45-49 years	255	190	150	290	300	285
36	50-54 years	210	165	140	220	240	225
37	55-59 years	160	90	115	120	130	135
38	60-64 years	75	45	100	55	95	80
39	65-69 years	40	35	65	30	65	45
40	70-74 years	45	20	45	25	45	45
41	75-79 years	20	20	30	15	40	25
42	80-84 years	10	5	15	15	30	15
43	85 years and over	10	-	10	10	40	5
44	**Total population 15 years and over**	**5,435**	**3,455**	**4,535**	**3,900**	**5,570**	**4,720**
	by legal marital status						
45	Never married (single)	1,675	1,135	1,260	1,265	1,755	1,440
46	Legally married (and not separated)	2,960	1,995	2,805	2,260	3,240	2,730
47	Separated, but still legally married	235	95	135	100	155	145
48	Divorced	415	145	220	185	210	255
49	Widowed	145	85	125	90	215	150
	by common-law status						
50	Not in a common-law relationship	4,990	3,280	4,105	3,750	5,365	4,515
51	In a common-law relationship	440	180	430	150	210	205
52	**Total population – 20% Sample Data (4)**	**7,360**	**4,630**	**5,870**	**5,045**	**7,330**	**6,270**
	by mother tongue						
53	Single responses	7,210	4,450	5,760	4,990	7,225	6,170
54	English	5,365	2,955	3,830	3,990	4,540	4,760
55	French	110	70	110	90	55	45
56	Non-official languages (5)	1,740	1,425	1,820	915	2,630	1,365
57	Italian	165	125	50	170	200	140
58	Chinese, n.o.s.	50	75	30	-	50	35
59	Cantonese	15	35	35	35	35	45
60	Portuguese	305	145	175	135	190	60
61	Punjabi	205	585	450	65	975	210
62	Other languages (6)	995	460	1,085	505	1,180	870
63	Multiple responses	150	180	110	55	110	100
64	English and French	15	35	15	-	10	30
65	English and non-official language	130	100	95	30	90	75
66	French and non-official language	10	45	-	25	-	-
67	English, French and non-official language	-	-	-	-	10	-

See reference material at the end of the publication. – Voir les documents de référence à la fin de la publication.

Tableau 1. Certaines caractéristiques des secteurs de recensement, recensement de 2001 – Données intégrales et données-échantillon (20 %)

Toronto 0576.07	Toronto 0576.08 A	Toronto 0576.09 A	Toronto 0576.10 A	Toronto 0576.11 A	Toronto 0576.12 A	Caractéristiques	N°
						CARACTÉRISTIQUES DE LA POPULATION	
4,279	**4,778**	**4,396**	**89**	**6,715**	**4,780**	**Population, 1996 (1)**	1
4,599	**10,358**	**4,270**	**4,716**	**15,126**	**16,565**	**Population, 2001 (2)**	2
7.5	116.8	-2.9	5,198.9	125.3	246.5	Variation en pourcentage de la population, 1996-2001	3
3.56	6.02	1.87	5.89	5.90	11.85	Superficie des terres en kilomètres carrés, 2001	4
4,595	**10,355**	**4,270**	**4,715**	**15,125**	**16,565**	**Population totale – Données intégrales (3)**	5
						selon le sexe et les groupes d'âge	
2,320	5,215	2,130	2,320	7,510	8,230	Sexe masculin	6
170	480	105	250	830	1,015	0-4 ans	7
235	470	160	225	815	870	5-9 ans	8
210	455	185	160	640	675	10-14 ans	9
200	390	220	125	535	470	15-19 ans	10
165	315	185	125	395	425	20-24 ans	11
135	385	105	220	495	600	25-29 ans	12
185	515	115	280	775	970	30-34 ans	13
250	560	180	275	855	990	35-39 ans	14
240	460	150	190	665	720	40-44 ans	15
185	380	210	115	450	475	45-49 ans	16
150	335	215	105	355	345	50-54 ans	17
85	200	140	70	235	245	55-59 ans	18
45	110	85	60	175	170	60-64 ans	19
30	75	45	55	110	105	65-69 ans	20
15	45	15	35	90	75	70-74 ans	21
15	25	5	25	45	50	75-79 ans	22
-	5	5	15	25	15	80-84 ans	23
5	10	5	-	20	15	85 ans et plus	24
2,275	5,145	2,140	2,395	7,615	8,335	Sexe féminin	25
170	400	115	230	815	885	0-4 ans	26
200	460	135	220	735	870	5-9 ans	27
185	445	190	145	605	650	10-14 ans	28
180	375	210	135	485	460	15-19 ans	29
150	320	150	135	445	470	20-24 ans	30
150	415	135	275	570	780	25-29 ans	31
220	545	120	295	895	1,080	30-34 ans	32
275	560	175	265	885	955	35-39 ans	33
240	480	210	175	660	635	40-44 ans	34
185	370	215	135	405	405	45-49 ans	35
120	300	210	105	340	345	50-54 ans	36
80	175	140	80	240	245	55-59 ans	37
45	90	60	60	180	210	60-64 ans	38
25	80	15	55	145	135	65-69 ans	39
20	45	25	45	95	85	70-74 ans	40
15	55	30	25	70	60	75-79 ans	41
10	20	10	10	25	40	80-84 ans	42
10	15	5	-	20	30	85 ans et plus	43
3,425	**7,645**	**3,390**	**3,485**	**10,690**	**11,590**	**Population totale de 15 ans et plus**	44
						selon l'état matrimonial légal	
1,015	2,025	1,070	845	2,615	2,640	Célibataire (jamais marié(e))	45
2,090	4,900	1,930	2,275	7,135	7,890	Légalement marié(e) (et non séparé(e))	46
85	210	95	100	240	285	Séparé(e), mais toujours légalement marié(e)	47
155	330	195	155	385	395	Divorcé(e)	48
85	185	100	110	305	385	Veuf ou veuve	49
						selon l'union libre	
3,290	7,235	3,250	3,285	10,300	11,180	Ne vivant pas en union libre	50
135	410	135	195	385	410	Vivant en union libre	51
4,600	**10,360**	**4,270**	**4,720**	**15,125**	**16,565**	**Population totale – Données-échantillon (20 %) (4)**	52
						selon la langue maternelle	
4,550	10,145	4,255	4,635	14,610	16,105	Réponses uniques	53
3,345	7,605	3,670	2,750	7,795	8,685	Anglais	54
70	220	40	60	135	95	Français	55
1,135	2,325	545	1,820	6,680	7,320	Langues non officielles (5)	56
200	470	65	225	630	990	Italien	57
30	50	65	130	100	135	Chinois, n.d.a.	58
35	90	10	45	200	35	Cantonais	59
220	310	60	65	200	325	Portugais	60
210	270	20	315	3,115	3,185	Pendjabi	61
440	1,125	335	1,035	2,435	2,660	Autres langues (6)	62
50	215	15	85	515	455	Réponses multiples	63
-	15	-	-	15	-	Anglais et français	64
50	180	10	85	480	440	Anglais et langue non officielle	65
-	10	10	-	20	20	Français et langue non officielle	66
-	15	-	-	-	-	Anglais, français et langue non officielle	67

See reference material at the end of the publication. – Voir les documents de référence à la fin de la publication.

Table 1. Selected Characteristics for Census Tracts, 2001 Census – 100% Data and 20% Sample Data

No.	Characteristics	Toronto 0575.05	Toronto 0575.06	Toronto 0576.01	Toronto 0576.04	Toronto 0576.05	Toronto 0576.06
	POPULATION CHARACTERISTICS						
	by home language						
68	Single responses	6,180	3,690	4,685	4,340	5,815	5,490
69	English	5,665	3,110	4,255	4,235	4,760	5,115
70	French	-	30	60	-	-	-
71	Non-official languages (5)	510	545	370	110	1,055	375
72	Cantonese	20	15	10	-	25	40
73	Chinese, n.o.s.	25	-	-	-	15	15
74	Italian	15	25	15	10	10	-
75	Punjabi	115	410	190	45	600	95
76	Portuguese	55	-	50	25	55	10
77	Other languages (6)	285	85	110	30	350	215
78	Multiple responses	1,180	940	1,190	705	1,515	780
79	English and French	100	35	115	125	70	35
80	English and non-official language	1,055	870	1,050	535	1,415	740
81	French and non-official language	-	20	-	25	10	-
82	English, French and non-official language	15	15	25	15	35	10
	by knowledge of official languages						
83	English only	6,820	4,180	5,290	4,595	6,625	5,830
84	French only	-	-	20	-	-	-
85	English and French	405	295	500	430	410	385
86	Neither English nor French	125	150	65	20	295	45
	by knowledge of non-official languages (5) (7)						
87	Italian	195	195	160	230	295	235
88	Cantonese	40	85	30	35	100	50
89	Chinese, n.o.s.	75	90	30	-	95	75
90	Spanish	175	30	120	40	300	165
91	Portuguese	310	150	335	105	235	75
92	Punjabi	370	690	495	80	1,145	320
93	Tagalog (Pilipino)	30	85	70	-	200	110
	by first official language spoken						
94	English	7,120	4,395	5,645	4,920	6,985	6,170
95	French	110	85	145	85	45	50
96	English and French	15	10	15	20	15	-
97	Neither English nor French	115	145	65	20	290	50
98	Official language minority - (number) (8)	115	85	150	95	50	50
99	Official language minority - (percentage) (8)	1.6	1.8	2.6	1.9	0.7	0.8
	by ethnic origin (9)						
100	Canadian	1,875	990	1,435	1,535	1,275	1,625
101	English	1,320	925	980	1,375	1,125	1,495
102	Scottish	1,010	415	755	890	595	1,085
103	Irish	905	465	575	770	670	945
104	Chinese	160	230	105	50	295	175
105	Italian	460	385	360	605	435	585
106	East Indian	740	875	1,045	270	1,465	710
107	French	445	345	320	335	325	360
108	German	455	150	220	380	215	445
109	Portuguese	480	245	415	190	375	165
110	Polish	180	150	110	205	55	210
111	Jewish	-	20	35	25	-	15
112	Jamaican	575	255	275	110	620	390
113	Filipino	40	125	95	-	330	185
114	Ukrainian	115	90	100	125	70	100
	by Aboriginal identity						
115	Total Aboriginal identity population (10)	65	25	-	25	25	30
116	Total non-Aboriginal population	7,300	4,600	5,870	5,020	7,300	6,240
	by Aboriginal origin						
117	Total Aboriginal origins population (11)	105	40	20	75	45	70
118	Total non-Aboriginal population	7,255	4,585	5,855	4,970	7,285	6,200
	by Registered Indian status						
119	Registered Indian (12)	-	-	-	20	-	10
120	Not a Registered Indian	7,360	4,620	5,875	5,020	7,330	6,265

Tableau 1. Certaines caractéristiques des secteurs de recensement, recensement de 2001 – Données intégrales et données-échantillon (20 %)

Toronto 0576.07	Toronto 0576.08 A	Toronto 0576.09 A	Toronto 0576.10 A	Toronto 0576.11 A	Toronto 0576.12 A	Caractéristiques	N°
						CARACTÉRISTIQUES DE LA POPULATION	
						selon la langue parlée à la maison	
3,840	8,610	3,850	3,600	11,005	12,170	Réponses uniques	68
3,570	8,125	3,795	2,905	8,565	9,530	Anglais	69
15	30	-	10	10	40	Français	70
260	460	55	695	2,425	2,600	Langues non officielles (5)	71
10	10	-	40	50	10	Cantonais	72
-	20	-	85	50	-	Chinois, n.d.a.	73
20	65	10	35	90	115	Italien	74
105	75	-	215	1,700	1,510	Pendjabi	75
40	100	15	10	25	90	Portugais	76
80	200	30	310	515	875	Autres langues (6)	77
750	1,745	420	1,110	4,125	4,395	Réponses multiples	78
65	210	55	30	150	45	Anglais et français	79
685	1,430	360	1,070	3,905	4,255	Anglais et langue non officielle	80
-	-	-	-	-	-	Français et langue non officielle	81
-	105	-	10	60	85	Anglais, français et langue non officielle	82
						selon la connaissance des langues officielles	
4,270	9,475	3,960	4,290	13,575	15,170	Anglais seulement	83
-	10	-	-	10	-	Français seulement	84
260	770	290	215	840	795	Anglais et français	85
70	105	25	205	690	595	Ni l'anglais ni le français	86
						selon la connaissance des langues non officielles (5) (7)	
305	675	85	320	955	1,445	Italien	87
30	105	10	50	225	40	Cantonais	88
-	40	65	85	130	90	Chinois, n.d.a.	89
65	165	25	315	505	465	Espagnol	90
245	440	70	85	295	405	Portugais	91
220	315	45	410	3,580	3,710	Pendjabi	92
20	100	-	50	425	300	Tagalog (pilipino)	93
						selon la première langue officielle parlée	
4,465	10,025	4,200	4,435	14,155	15,775	Anglais	94
60	220	50	50	155	100	Français	95
-	15	-	30	145	110	Anglais et français	96
65	105	20	200	675	575	Ni l'anglais ni le français	97
65	225	50	65	225	160	Minorité de langue officielle - (nombre) (8)	98
1.4	2.2	1.2	1.4	1.5	1.0	Minorité de langue officielle - (pourcentage) (8)	99
						selon l'origine ethnique (9)	
1,105	2,525	1,065	730	1,955	2,230	Canadien	100
700	2,020	1,490	655	1,175	1,275	Anglais	101
665	1,490	915	375	945	1,020	Écossais	102
545	1,640	1,050	320	790	860	Irlandais	103
75	270	95	260	640	325	Chinois	104
610	1,315	205	565	1,695	2,425	Italien	105
575	800	145	760	4,625	4,980	Indien de l'Inde	106
305	750	310	135	590	375	Français	107
175	575	255	135	320	400	Allemand	108
330	575	180	120	490	695	Portugais	109
120	330	145	100	165	380	Polonais	110
10	-	10	15	25	120	Juif	111
345	410	120	320	1,335	1,095	Jamaïquain	112
40	180	10	80	560	495	Philippin	113
180	175	135	65	70	180	Ukrainien	114
						selon l'identité autochtone	
10	40	45	10	30	50	Total de la population ayant une identité autochtone (10)	115
4,590	10,320	4,225	4,710	15,095	16,515	Total de la population non autochtone	116
						selon l'origine autochtone	
35	80	95	35	130	100	Total de la population ayant une origine autochtone (11)	117
4,560	10,280	4,175	4,685	14,995	16,460	Total de la population non autochtone	118
						selon le statut d'Indien inscrit	
-	10	-	-	10	10	Oui, Indien inscrit (12)	119
4,600	10,350	4,270	4,715	15,115	16,560	Non, pas un Indien inscrit	120

Table 1. Selected Characteristics for Census Tracts, 2001 Census – 100% Data and 20% Sample Data

No.	Characteristics	Toronto 0575.05	Toronto 0575.06	Toronto 0576.01	Toronto 0576.04	Toronto 0576.05	Toronto 0576.06
	POPULATION CHARACTERISTICS						
	by visible minority groups						
121	Total visible minority population	2,620	1,945	1,985	725	3,990	1,965
122	Chinese	135	75	50	45	110	65
123	South Asian	855	895	1,055	315	1,925	595
124	Black	1,150	435	460	185	860	615
125	Filipino	35	130	60	-	330	145
126	Latin American	80	20	40	10	215	120
127	Southeast Asian	55	35	35	10	120	145
128	Arab	40	130	20	25	20	20
129	West Asian	50	15	10	70	-	-
130	Korean	-	-	-	20	-	25
131	Japanese	15	20	55	20	15	10
132	Visible minority, n.i.e. (13)	175	60	90	20	245	150
133	Multiple visible minorities (14)	30	130	110	10	150	70
	by citizenship						
134	Canadian citizenship (15)	6,615	3,955	5,300	4,790	6,235	5,820
135	Citizenship other than Canadian	745	675	570	260	1,095	450
	by place of birth of respondent						
136	Non-immigrant population	4,845	2,800	3,670	3,825	4,015	4,220
137	Born in province of residence	4,135	2,450	3,375	3,290	3,570	3,765
138	Immigrant population (16)	2,440	1,830	2,170	1,215	3,285	2,035
139	United States	30	30	-	60	20	75
140	Central and South America	205	90	125	25	430	280
141	Caribbean and Bermuda	675	305	265	50	560	370
142	United Kingdom	240	155	165	225	180	220
143	Other Europe (17)	555	300	535	530	455	500
144	Africa	95	110	145	45	55	55
145	Asia and the Middle East	615	820	925	270	1,585	530
146	Oceania and other (18)	20	15	-	-	10	-
147	Non-permanent residents (19)	75	-	25	10	35	20
148	**Total immigrant population**	**2,440**	**1,825**	**2,175**	**1,210**	**3,280**	**2,035**
	by period of immigration						
149	Before 1961	120	60	210	185	120	180
150	1961-1970	360	150	250	285	305	310
151	1971-1980	645	515	400	335	1,000	510
152	1981-1990	640	620	460	310	770	600
153	1991-2001 (20)	670	485	855	95	1,095	430
154	1991-1995	345	235	530	40	525	290
155	1996-2001 (20)	330	255	330	55	570	145
	by age at immigration						
156	0-4 years	210	185	190	220	275	270
157	5-19 years	795	535	695	380	945	600
158	20 years and over	1,430	1,115	1,290	610	2,065	1,165
159	**Total population**	**7,360**	**4,625**	**5,870**	**5,045**	**7,330**	**6,270**
	by religion						
160	Catholic (21)	2,805	1,810	1,860	2,210	2,435	2,420
161	Protestant	2,340	1,150	1,730	1,770	1,700	2,080
162	Christian Orthodox	80	25	135	155	105	80
163	Christian, n.i.e. (22)	325	85	180	30	240	215
164	Muslim	220	210	185	185	405	90
165	Jewish	-	60	-	10	-	25
166	Buddhist	125	100	20	-	85	125
167	Hindu	355	170	415	50	445	295
168	Sikh	265	645	410	85	980	290
169	Eastern religions (23)	20	-	30	15	-	-
170	Other religions (24)	-	-	-	-	-	-
171	No religious affiliation (25)	815	385	905	555	935	655
172	**Total population 15 years and over**	**5,410**	**3,450**	**4,525**	**3,885**	**5,495**	**4,705**
	by generation status						
173	1st generation (26)	2,425	1,715	2,090	1,210	3,150	1,905
174	2nd generation (27)	1,105	810	970	1,075	1,215	1,105
175	3rd generation and over (28)	1,885	930	1,465	1,595	1,130	1,690
176	**Total population 1 year and over (29)**	**7,290**	**4,560**	**5,760**	**5,000**	**7,235**	**6,210**
	by place of residence 1 year ago (mobility)						
177	Non-movers	6,205	4,170	1,900	4,755	6,335	5,630
178	Movers	1,080	395	3,860	245	905	580
179	Non-migrants	810	220	2,400	180	440	335
180	Migrants	270	170	1,460	70	460	240
181	Internal migrants	235	125	1,425	60	315	235
182	Intraprovincial migrants	205	115	1,415	60	300	215
183	Interprovincial migrants	30	10	-	-	15	20
184	External migrants	35	45	35	-	150	-

Tableau 1. Certaines caractéristiques des secteurs de recensement, recensement de 2001 – Données intégrales et données-échantillon (20 %)

Toronto 0576.07	Toronto 0576.08 A	Toronto 0576.09 A	Toronto 0576.10 A	Toronto 0576.11 A	Toronto 0576.12 A	Caractéristiques	N°
						CARACTÉRISTIQUES DE LA POPULATION	
						selon les groupes de minorités visibles	
1,360	2,365	545	2,530	9,395	9,860	Total de la population des minorités visibles	121
65	220	95	195	440	215	Chinois	122
500	835	180	915	5,105	5,480	Sud-Asiatique	123
440	660	200	580	1,945	1,945	Noir	124
35	170	-	80	570	450	Philippin	125
35	85	-	280	300	410	Latino-Américain	126
25	10	-	125	125	305	Asiatique du Sud-Est	127
25	25	20	90	110	80	Arabe	128
-	-	-	15	75	40	Asiatique occidental	129
45	75	15	15	15	15	Coréen	130
-	-	10	-	45	20	Japonais	131
130	235	10	215	545	805	Minorité visible, n.i.a. (13)	132
60	50	-	15	130	90	Minorités visibles multiples (14)	133
						selon la citoyenneté	
4,165	9,650	4,090	4,125	12,815	14,250	Citoyenneté canadienne (15)	134
430	710	180	585	2,315	2,315	Citoyenneté autre que canadienne	135
						selon le lieu de naissance du répondant	
3,045	7,285	3,325	2,535	7,715	8,575	Population non immigrante	136
2,675	6,415	2,895	2,270	7,120	7,920	Née dans la province de résidence	137
1,545	3,055	945	2,170	7,295	7,860	Population immigrante (16)	138
10	70	50	30	45	35	États-Unis	139
150	210	10	385	670	840	Amérique centrale et du Sud	140
290	395	165	415	1,150	1,045	Caraïbes et Bermudes	141
175	450	265	90	395	430	Royaume-Uni	142
455	1,080	320	370	955	1,275	Autre Europe (17)	143
40	210	10	85	445	340	Afrique	144
430	635	130	800	3,550	3,810	Asie et Moyen-Orient	145
-	-	-	-	75	85	Océanie et autre (18)	146
-	20	-	15	115	130	Résidents non permanents (19)	147
1,545	**3,050**	**945**	**2,170**	**7,295**	**7,865**	**Population immigrante totale**	148
						selon la période d'immigration	
75	305	245	85	185	360	Avant 1961	149
330	585	260	155	515	495	1961-1970	150
465	875	210	455	1,505	1,530	1971-1980	151
345	630	125	520	2,405	2,450	1981-1990	152
325	660	105	955	2,690	3,030	1991-2001 (20)	153
165	270	100	545	1,610	1,850	1991-1995	154
160	385	-	405	1,080	1,180	1996-2001 (20)	155
						selon l'âge à l'immigration	
180	345	90	185	525	645	0-4 ans	156
590	1,025	295	620	2,185	2,390	5-19 ans	157
770	1,685	555	1,365	4,585	4,825	20 ans et plus	158
4,595	**10,355**	**4,270**	**4,720**	**15,125**	**16,565**	**Population totale**	159
						selon la religion	
2,055	4,475	1,560	1,785	4,960	5,690	Catholique (21)	160
1,255	3,255	1,720	1,150	2,675	2,825	Protestante	161
115	230	170	70	215	295	Orthodoxe chrétienne	162
160	205	30	185	600	560	Chrétiennes, n.i.a. (22)	163
95	115	55	335	845	655	Musulmane	164
-	15	-	-	10	65	Juive	165
45	40	-	200	195	230	Bouddhiste	166
170	285	55	280	1,165	1,825	Hindoue	167
210	295	45	340	3,320	3,165	Sikh	168
-	10	-	25	165	45	Religions orientales (23)	169
-	10	-	10	10	40	Autres religions (24)	170
495	1,425	625	350	965	1,175	Aucune appartenance religieuse (25)	171
3,415	**7,655**	**3,385**	**3,490**	**10,695**	**11,575**	**Population totale de 15 ans et plus**	172
						selon le statut des générations	
1,490	2,895	930	2,080	7,170	7,605	1re génération (26)	173
825	2,105	920	825	2,135	2,445	2e génération (27)	174
1,095	2,655	1,530	585	1,390	1,525	3e génération et plus (28)	175
4,520	**10,170**	**4,240**	**4,650**	**14,855**	**16,200**	**Population totale de 1 an et plus (29)**	176
						selon le lieu de résidence 1 an auparavant (mobilité)	
4,140	7,730	3,870	2,820	11,980	13,720	Personnes n'ayant pas déménagé	177
385	2,435	370	1,830	2,875	2,475	Personnes ayant déménagé	178
215	1,605	210	1,095	1,305	1,445	Non-migrants	179
170	835	155	735	1,575	1,035	Migrants	180
110	700	145	690	1,355	905	Migrants internes	181
90	685	145	660	1,325	855	Migrants infraprovinciaux	182
20	15	-	25	25	50	Migrants interprovinciaux	183
60	135	10	40	225	130	Migrants externes	184

Table 1. Selected Characteristics for Census Tracts, 2001 Census – 100% Data and 20% Sample Data

No.	Characteristics	Toronto 0575.05	Toronto 0575.06	Toronto 0576.01	Toronto 0576.04	Toronto 0576.05	Toronto 0576.06
	POPULATION CHARACTERISTICS						
185	**Total population 5 years and over (30)**	**6,720**	**4,300**	**5,355**	**4,760**	**6,795**	**5,875**
	by place of residence 5 years ago (mobility)						
186	Non-movers	2,780	2,720	1,455	3,360	3,885	3,585
187	Movers	3,940	1,575	3,900	1,400	2,910	2,290
188	Non-migrants	2,365	865	2,275	870	1,595	1,190
189	Migrants	1,575	715	1,630	525	1,320	1,105
190	Internal migrants	1,215	580	1,375	510	870	960
191	Intraprovincial migrants	1,115	540	1,305	460	760	830
192	Interprovincial migrants	105	45	70	55	115	125
193	External migrants	360	130	255	15	450	145
194	**Total population 15 to 24 years**	**1,000**	**780**	**695**	**925**	**1,250**	**1,005**
	by school attendance						
195	Not attending school	380	275	290	285	440	295
196	Attending school full time	585	475	345	610	740	690
197	Attending school part time	30	30	55	25	70	20
198	**Total population 15 years and over**	**5,410**	**3,450**	**4,530**	**3,885**	**5,495**	**4,705**
	by highest level of schooling						
199	Less than grade 9 (31)	360	225	205	100	415	140
200	Grades 9-13 without high school graduation certificate	1,160	745	620	755	1,140	1,145
201	Grades 9-13 with high school graduation certificate	865	715	775	650	890	715
202	Some postsecondary without degree, certificate or diploma (32)	590	400	580	600	835	610
203	Trades certificate or diploma (33)	650	350	480	330	535	360
204	College certificate or diploma (34)	1,060	605	870	580	895	855
205	University certificate below bachelor's degree	115	65	125	55	80	100
206	University with bachelor's degree or higher	610	345	880	810	710	770
	by combinations of unpaid work						
207	Males 15 years and over	2,590	1,700	2,245	1,890	2,740	2,300
208	Reported unpaid work (35)	2,285	1,530	1,995	1,675	2,390	1,985
209	Housework and child care and care or assistance to seniors	175	175	200	155	210	255
210	Housework and child care only	1,025	500	675	640	965	745
211	Housework and care or assistance to seniors only	100	75	85	55	80	110
212	Child care and care or assistance to seniors only	-	10	10	-	-	10
213	Housework only	955	750	1,005	800	1,060	825
214	Child care only	20	20	30	15	55	25
215	Care or assistance to seniors only	-	-	-	10	20	15
216	Females 15 years and over	2,820	1,755	2,285	1,990	2,755	2,400
217	Reported unpaid work (35)	2,645	1,630	2,140	1,840	2,525	2,290
218	Housework and child care and care or assistance to seniors	335	215	240	195	345	345
219	Housework and child care only	1,160	600	835	725	1,055	870
220	Housework and care or assistance to seniors only	150	100	115	130	145	140
221	Child care and care or assistance to seniors only	-	10	10	-	-	10
222	Housework only	985	685	915	765	915	930
223	Child care only	10	20	25	10	45	-
224	Care or assistance to seniors only	-	10	-	10	20	-
	by labour force activity						
225	Males 15 years and over	2,590	1,700	2,240	1,890	2,740	2,300
226	In the labour force	2,195	1,505	1,890	1,655	2,345	1,950
227	Employed	2,080	1,465	1,830	1,610	2,215	1,870
228	Unemployed	115	35	60	45	135	75
229	Not in the labour force	400	195	350	235	390	355
230	Participation rate	84.7	88.5	84.4	87.6	85.6	84.8
231	Employment rate	80.3	86.2	81.7	85.2	80.8	81.3
232	Unemployment rate	5.2	2.3	3.2	2.7	5.8	3.8
233	Females 15 years and over	2,820	1,755	2,285	1,990	2,755	2,405
234	In the labour force	2,095	1,325	1,705	1,515	1,960	1,820
235	Employed	1,975	1,275	1,640	1,450	1,835	1,690
236	Unemployed	120	55	65	60	125	130
237	Not in the labour force	730	430	585	480	795	585
238	Participation rate	74.3	75.5	74.6	76.1	71.1	75.7
239	Employment rate	70.0	72.6	71.8	72.9	66.6	70.3
240	Unemployment rate	5.7	4.2	3.8	4.0	6.4	7.1

Tableau 1. Certaines caractéristiques des secteurs de recensement, recensement de 2001 – Données intégrales et données-échantillon (20 %)

Toronto 0576.07	Toronto 0576.08 A	Toronto 0576.09 A	Toronto 0576.10 A	Toronto 0576.11 A	Toronto 0576.12 A	Caractéristiques	N°
						CARACTÉRISTIQUES DE LA POPULATION	
4,250	**9,490**	**4,055**	**4,230**	**13,500**	**14,630**	**Population totale de 5 ans et plus (30)**	185
						selon le lieu de résidence 5 ans auparavant (mobilité)	
2,675	3,340	2,815	245	4,470	3,440	Personnes n'ayant pas déménagé	186
1,575	6,150	1,240	3,990	9,025	11,195	Personnes ayant déménagé	187
790	4,000	700	2,050	4,600	5,230	Non-migrants	188
785	2,150	540	1,940	4,420	5,965	Migrants	189
605	1,870	535	1,625	3,565	5,110	Migrants internes	190
555	1,755	485	1,550	3,255	4,960	Migrants infraprovinciaux	191
55	115	50	80	310	155	Migrants interprovinciaux	192
175	285	10	315	855	850	Migrants externes	193
705	**1,400**	**760**	**515**	**1,860**	**1,825**	**Population totale de 15 à 24 ans**	194
						selon la fréquentation scolaire	
280	520	195	175	585	665	Ne fréquentant pas l'école	195
380	840	535	305	1,195	1,055	Fréquentant l'école à plein temps	196
45	45	25	35	80	115	Fréquentant l'école à temps partiel	197
3,415	**7,650**	**3,385**	**3,485**	**10,690**	**11,580**	**Population totale de 15 ans et plus**	198
						selon le plus haut niveau de scolarité atteint	
190	385	85	275	960	810	Niveau inférieur à la 9e année (31)	199
880	1,340	805	645	2,110	2,055	De la 9e à la 13e année sans certificat d'études secondaires	200
560	1,330	565	560	1,915	1,985	De la 9e à la 13e année avec certificat d'études secondaires	201
470	965	405	290	1,210	1,355	Études postsecondaires partielles sans grade, certificat ou diplôme (32)	202
315	870	340	295	1,035	1,115	Certificat ou diplôme d'une école de métiers (33)	203
570	1,635	560	765	1,590	1,970	Certificat ou diplôme collégial (34)	204
65	165	115	120	240	355	Certificat universitaire inférieur au baccalauréat	205
360	965	505	550	1,640	1,930	Études universitaires avec baccalauréat ou diplôme supérieur	206
						selon les combinaisons de travail non rémunéré	
1,700	3,795	1,670	1,690	5,215	5,640	Hommes de 15 ans et plus	207
1,515	3,440	1,540	1,545	4,630	5,195	Travail non rémunéré déclaré (35)	208
70	395	135	165	625	660	Travaux ménagers et soins aux enfants et soins ou aide aux personnes âgées	209
690	1,220	485	550	2,065	2,290	Travaux ménagers et soins aux enfants seulement	210
30	180	90	135	145	150	Travaux ménagers et soins ou aide aux personnes âgées seulement	211
-	10	-	-	25	20	Soins aux enfants et soins ou aide aux personnes âgées seulement	212
720	1,590	805	650	1,695	1,940	Travaux ménagers seulement	213
-	45	20	40	75	110	Soins aux enfants seulement	214
10	-	-	-	-	15	Soins ou aide aux personnes âgées seulement	215
1,715	3,855	1,710	1,795	5,475	5,935	Femmes de 15 ans et plus	216
1,615	3,565	1,625	1,685	5,060	5,640	Travail non rémunéré déclaré (35)	217
130	495	180	220	930	915	Travaux ménagers et soins aux enfants et soins ou aide aux personnes âgées	218
730	1,425	575	700	2,325	2,740	Travaux ménagers et soins aux enfants seulement	219
85	185	80	75	205	240	Travaux ménagers et soins ou aide aux personnes âgées seulement	220
10	15	-	-	10	-	Soins aux enfants et soins ou aide aux personnes âgées seulement	221
630	1,410	765	655	1,550	1,660	Travaux ménagers seulement	222
10	30	25	20	35	65	Soins aux enfants seulement	223
25	-	-	10	10	20	Soins ou aide aux personnes âgées seulement	224
						selon l'activité	
1,700	3,800	1,670	1,690	5,220	5,640	Hommes de 15 ans et plus	225
1,450	3,250	1,320	1,330	4,365	4,815	Population active	226
1,400	3,125	1,235	1,270	4,245	4,650	Personnes occupées	227
45	125	85	60	125	160	Chômeurs	228
250	550	355	360	855	830	Inactifs	229
85.3	85.5	79.0	78.7	83.6	85.4	Taux d'activité	230
82.4	82.2	74.0	75.1	81.3	82.4	Taux d'emploi	231
3.1	3.8	6.4	4.5	2.9	3.3	Taux de chômage	232
1,715	3,855	1,710	1,795	5,475	5,940	Femmes de 15 ans et plus	233
1,265	2,890	1,325	1,300	3,925	4,385	Population active	234
1,205	2,800	1,255	1,215	3,700	4,130	Personnes occupées	235
55	90	70	85	225	260	Chômeuses	236
445	965	380	500	1,550	1,550	Inactives	237
73.8	75.0	77.5	72.4	71.7	73.8	Taux d'activité	238
70.3	72.6	73.4	67.7	67.6	69.5	Taux d'emploi	239
4.3	3.1	5.3	6.5	5.7	5.9	Taux de chômage	240

Table 1. Selected Characteristics for Census Tracts, 2001 Census – 100% Data and 20% Sample Data

No.	Characteristics	Toronto 0575.05	Toronto 0575.06	Toronto 0576.01	Toronto 0576.04	Toronto 0576.05	Toronto 0576.06
	POPULATION CHARACTERISTICS						
	by labour force activity – concluded						
241	Both sexes - Participation rate	79.2	81.9	79.3	81.7	78.4	80.2
242	15-24 years	70.0	77.4	77.5	68.6	64.5	72.8
243	25 years and over	81.3	83.6	79.8	85.5	82.3	82.0
244	Both sexes - Employment rate	74.9	79.4	76.5	78.9	73.7	75.9
245	15-24 years	65.0	71.8	74.8	63.2	56.4	65.8
246	25 years and over	77.3	81.8	76.8	83.8	78.7	78.5
247	Both sexes - Unemployment rate	5.4	3.2	3.5	3.3	6.0	5.6
248	15-24 years	7.9	6.7	2.8	7.9	13.0	9.5
249	25 years and over	4.7	2.5	3.6	2.2	4.6	4.5
250	**Total labour force 15 years and over**	**4,285**	**2,830**	**3,590**	**3,170**	**4,305**	**3,765**
	by industry based on the 1997 NAICS						
251	Industry - Not applicable (36)	45	20	25	10	50	35
252	All industries (37)	4,240	2,815	3,570	3,160	4,260	3,730
253	11 Agriculture, forestry, fishing and hunting	-	-	140	15	25	-
254	21 Mining and oil and gas extraction	-	-	10	-	-	-
255	22 Utilities	25	-	40	15	25	25
256	23 Construction	250	125	325	145	170	155
257	31-33 Manufacturing	955	640	665	520	840	805
258	41 Wholesale trade	320	250	320	400	420	295
259	44-45 Retail trade	500	495	275	360	610	495
260	48-49 Transportation and warehousing	505	255	295	220	435	375
261	51 Information and cultural industries	85	70	115	65	110	145
262	52 Finance and insurance	200	115	165	185	145	190
263	53 Real estate and rental and leasing	55	45	60	100	40	80
264	54 Professional, scientific and technical services	250	160	285	235	210	205
265	55 Management of companies and enterprises	-	-	-	-	-	-
266	56 Administrative and support, waste management and remediation services	225	120	170	45	170	125
267	61 Educational services	90	120	130	235	240	185
268	62 Health care and social assistance	290	130	225	245	235	255
269	71 Arts, entertainment and recreation	35	25	30	65	25	20
270	72 Accommodation and food services	175	160	130	100	240	210
271	81 Other services (except public administration)	165	55	95	75	205	90
272	91 Public administration	115	40	90	130	115	80
	by class of worker						
273	Class of worker - Not applicable (36)	50	20	30	-	50	40
274	All classes of worker (37)	4,240	2,815	3,565	3,165	4,255	3,730
275	Paid workers	4,020	2,760	3,300	2,950	4,055	3,515
276	Employees	3,920	2,710	3,150	2,760	3,910	3,355
277	Self-employed (incorporated)	105	50	145	185	140	165
278	Self-employed (unincorporated)	220	50	265	215	190	205
279	Unpaid family workers	-	-	-	-	20	10
	by occupation based on the 2001 NOC-S						
280	Male labour force 15 years and over	2,190	1,505	1,890	1,655	2,350	1,950
281	Occupation - Not applicable (36)	20	-	-	-	20	15
282	All occupations (37)	2,175	1,500	1,885	1,650	2,325	1,935
283	A Management occupations	275	200	215	350	325	415
284	B Business, finance and administration occupations	325	270	170	255	275	315
285	C Natural and applied sciences and related occupations	195	165	180	170	245	210
286	D Health occupations	35	10	20	35	20	15
287	E Occupations in social science, education, government service and religion	55	10	70	55	100	55
288	F Occupations in art, culture, recreation and sport	40	10	25	-	25	-
289	G Sales and service occupations	365	220	315	340	385	230
290	H Trades, transport and equipment operators and related occupations	610	450	595	360	655	480
291	I Occupations unique to primary industry	10	-	110	30	40	10
292	J Occupations unique to processing, manufacturing and utilities	270	160	180	60	250	195
293	Female labour force 15 years and over	2,095	1,330	1,700	1,515	1,960	1,825
294	Occupation - Not applicable (36)	30	15	25	-	30	25
295	All occupations (37)	2,065	1,310	1,675	1,505	1,935	1,800
296	A Management occupations	135	95	160	175	115	170
297	B Business, finance and administration occupations	780	490	600	540	580	615
298	C Natural and applied sciences and related occupations	70	15	50	45	50	50
299	D Health occupations	130	50	95	65	140	105

Tableau 1. Certaines caractéristiques des secteurs de recensement, recensement de 2001 – Données intégrales et données-échantillon (20 %)

Toronto 0576.07	Toronto 0576.08 A	Toronto 0576.09 A	Toronto 0576.10 A	Toronto 0576.11 A	Toronto 0576.12 A	Caractéristiques	N°
						CARACTÉRISTIQUES DE LA POPULATION	
						selon l'activité – fin	
79.5	80.2	78.3	75.5	77.5	79.4	Les deux sexes - Taux d'activité	241
70.9	74.6	60.5	63.1	63.2	68.5	15-24 ans	242
81.7	81.4	83.6	77.4	80.6	81.4	25 ans et plus	243
76.4	77.4	73.7	71.2	74.3	75.8	Les deux sexes - Taux d'emploi	244
64.3	67.5	54.3	52.4	55.9	60.8	15-24 ans	245
79.7	79.6	79.6	74.6	78.2	78.7	25 ans et plus	246
3.9	3.4	5.9	5.5	4.2	4.6	Les deux sexes - Taux de chômage	247
10.1	9.1	10.9	18.2	11.1	12.0	15-24 ans	248
2.5	2.2	4.6	3.7	3.0	3.4	25 ans et plus	249
2,710	**6,135**	**2,645**	**2,625**	**8,290**	**9,200**	**Population active totale de 15 ans et plus**	250
						selon l'industrie basée sur le SCIAN de 1997	
10	35	15	55	85	85	Industrie - Sans objet (36)	251
2,700	6,105	2,635	2,575	8,205	9,110	Toutes les industries (37)	252
20	25	10	15	10	-	11 Agriculture, foresterie, pêche et chasse	253
-	-	-	25	-	-	21 Extraction minière et extraction de pétrole et de gaz	254
15	55	20	10	25	15	22 Services publics	255
170	330	150	140	340	445	23 Construction	256
565	1,150	455	590	2,130	2,415	31-33 Fabrication	257
230	605	260	170	560	690	41 Commerce de gros	258
315	670	230	345	860	1,025	44-45 Commerce de détail	259
215	505	235	230	1,025	920	48-49 Transport et entreposage	260
50	185	70	60	115	240	51 Industrie de l'information et industrie culturelle	261
150	355	85	135	490	515	52 Finance et assurances	262
60	90	50	45	110	115	53 Services immobiliers et services de location et de location à bail	263
105	400	160	165	540	550	54 Services professionnels, scientifiques et techniques	264
10	-	10	-	10	15	55 Gestion de sociétés et d'entreprises	265
85	180	80	80	340	350	56 Services administratifs, services de soutien, services de gestion des déchets et services d'assainissement	266
100	315	170	115	285	225	61 Services d'enseignement	267
195	500	210	160	415	500	62 Soins de santé et assistance sociale	268
25	85	45	15	30	85	71 Arts, spectacles et loisirs	269
180	260	205	120	335	385	72 Hébergement et services de restauration	270
100	235	110	95	315	365	81 Autres services, sauf les administrations publiques	271
110	160	85	60	270	250	91 Administrations publiques	272
						selon la catégorie de travailleurs	
10	35	15	50	85	85	Catégorie de travailleurs - Sans objet (36)	273
2,705	6,100	2,630	2,570	8,210	9,110	Toutes les catégories de travailleurs (37)	274
2,615	5,685	2,505	2,465	7,760	8,640	Travailleurs rémunérés	275
2,565	5,455	2,335	2,410	7,480	8,235	Employés	276
55	230	165	55	280	405	Travailleurs autonomes (entreprise constituée en société)	277
85	415	125	105	430	450	Travailleurs autonomes (entreprise non constituée en société)	278
-	-	-	10	15	25	Travailleurs familiaux non rémunérés	279
						selon la profession basée sur la CNP-S de 2001	
1,445	3,245	1,320	1,330	4,365	4,810	Hommes actifs de 15 ans et plus	280
-	15	-	20	20	35	Profession - Sans objet (36)	281
1,445	3,235	1,320	1,310	4,350	4,780	Toutes les professions (37)	282
230	525	280	175	635	590	A Gestion	283
120	325	210	160	540	645	B Affaires, finance et administration	284
95	355	160	140	350	515	C Sciences naturelles et appliquées et professions apparentées	285
-	35	20	10	15	20	D Secteur de la santé	286
50	115	25	60	95	80	E Sciences sociales, enseignement, administration publique et religion	287
15	65	30	10	70	70	F Arts, culture, sports et loisirs	288
285	490	205	190	625	610	G Ventes et services	289
455	960	255	410	1,320	1,580	H Métiers, transport et machinerie	290
30	75	25	-	30	25	I Professions propres au secteur primaire	291
165	285	105	165	665	650	J Transformation, fabrication et services d'utilité publique	292
1,265	2,890	1,325	1,295	3,925	4,390	Femmes actives de 15 ans et plus	293
10	15	10	35	65	50	Profession - Sans objet (36)	294
1,255	2,875	1,315	1,260	3,860	4,335	Toutes les professions (37)	295
120	265	125	140	400	380	A Gestion	296
480	1,070	485	440	1,300	1,630	B Affaires, finance et administration	297
40	105	25	35	105	145	C Sciences naturelles et appliquées et professions apparentées	298
110	240	105	60	155	250	D Secteur de la santé	299

Table 1. Selected Characteristics for Census Tracts, 2001 Census – 100% Data and 20% Sample Data

No.	Characteristics	Toronto 0575.05	Toronto 0575.06	Toronto 0576.01	Toronto 0576.04	Toronto 0576.05	Toronto 0576.06
	POPULATION CHARACTERISTICS						
	by occupation based on the 2001 NOC-S – concluded						
	E Occupations in social science, education,						
300	government service and religion	135	100	155	205	210	150
301	F Occupations in art, culture, recreation and sport	10	20	40	50	30	45
302	G Sales and service occupations	510	305	310	295	465	490
	H Trades, transport and equipment						
303	operators and related occupations	95	35	90	45	75	60
304	I Occupations unique to primary industry	10	15	55	25	10	-
	J Occupations unique to processing,						
305	manufacturing and utilities	180	185	115	65	250	115
306	**Total employed labour force 15 years and over**	**4,055**	**2,740**	**3,465**	**3,065**	**4,050**	**3,565**
	by place of work						
307	Males	2,075	1,470	1,830	1,610	2,215	1,870
308	Usual place of work	1,765	1,260	1,400	1,390	1,895	1,600
309	At home	65	60	130	80	55	45
310	Outside Canada	-	-	-	-	20	15
311	No fixed workplace address	245	145	300	135	250	210
312	Females	1,975	1,275	1,640	1,450	1,835	1,690
313	Usual place of work	1,805	1,175	1,420	1,315	1,665	1,510
314	At home	70	50	120	95	95	110
315	Outside Canada	20	-	-	-	-	-
316	No fixed workplace address	85	40	100	40	70	70
	Total employed labour force 15 years and over with usual place of work or no fixed						
317	**workplace address**	**3,900**	**2,625**	**3,215**	**2,880**	**3,880**	**3,390**
	by mode of transportation						
318	Males	2,015	1,405	1,700	1,525	2,140	1,810
319	Car, truck, van, as driver	1,760	1,180	1,560	1,365	1,855	1,615
320	Car, truck, van, as passenger	50	50	55	85	125	90
321	Public transit	135	160	55	60	120	70
322	Walked	40	10	10	10	35	15
323	Other method	20	10	10	10	10	20
324	Females	1,885	1,220	1,520	1,360	1,740	1,580
325	Car, truck, van, as driver	1,350	890	1,205	1,130	1,315	1,215
326	Car, truck, van, as passenger	225	140	165	110	170	195
327	Public transit	210	165	135	70	155	135
328	Walked	90	20	10	20	75	15
329	Other method	10	10	10	30	30	15
	Total population 15 years and over who worked						
330	**since January 1, 2000**	**4,575**	**2,955**	**3,810**	**3,405**	**4,680**	**3,950**
	by language used at work						
331	Single responses	4,285	2,750	3,530	3,265	4,255	3,740
332	English	4,265	2,695	3,510	3,255	4,210	3,735
333	French	-	-	10	-	-	-
334	Non-official languages (5)	15	55	15	-	45	-
335	Chinese, n.o.s.	-	-	-	-	-	-
336	Cantonese	-	-	-	-	-	-
337	Other languages (6)	15	55	15	-	40	10
338	Multiple responses	295	200	285	140	425	215
339	English and French	80	30	90	80	50	55
340	English and non-official language	190	165	175	55	340	150
341	French and non-official language	-	-	-	-	-	-
342	English, French and non-official language	30	-	15	-	30	10
	DWELLING AND HOUSEHOLD CHARACTERISTICS						
343	**Total number of occupied private dwellings**	**2,225**	**1,225**	**1,945**	**1,395**	**1,880**	**1,715**
	by tenure						
344	Owned	2,030	1,055	1,735	1,310	1,625	1,595
345	Rented	190	170	205	90	255	120
346	Band housing	-	-	-	-	-	-
	by structural type of dwelling						
347	Single-detached house	620	770	1,335	1,230	1,300	1,110
348	Semi-detached house	400	90	420	20	160	315
349	Row house	1,170	90	145	145	240	235
350	Apartment, detached duplex	25	30	-	10	75	20
351	Apartment, building that has five or more storeys	-	-	-	-	-	-
	Apartment, building that has fewer than						
352	five storeys (38)	10	245	15	-	110	40
353	Other single-attached house	-	-	10	-	-	-
354	Movable dwelling (39)	-	-	10	-	-	-

Tableau 1. Certaines caractéristiques des secteurs de recensement, recensement de 2001 – Données intégrales et données-échantillon (20 %)

Toronto 0576.07	Toronto 0576.08 A	Toronto 0576.09 A	Toronto 0576.10 A	Toronto 0576.11 A	Toronto 0576.12 A	Caractéristiques	N°
						CARACTÉRISTIQUES DE LA POPULATION	
						selon la profession basée sur la CNP-S de 2001 - fin	
80	235	150	125	220	280	E Sciences sociales, enseignement, administration publique et religion	300
-	80	10	15	75	65	F Arts, culture, sports et loisirs	301
320	725	320	290	830	875	G Ventes et services	302
-	55	45	45	150	170	H Métiers, transport et machinerie	303
-	10	10	-	-	10	I Professions propres au secteur primaire	304
90	100	50	115	635	545	J Transformation, fabrication et services d'utilité publique	305
2,610	**5,930**	**2,490**	**2,480**	**7,945**	**8,780**	**Population active occupée totale de 15 ans et plus**	306
						selon le lieu de travail	
1,405	3,125	1,235	1,265	4,245	4,650	Hommes	307
1,210	2,580	1,055	1,110	3,585	3,950	Lieu habituel de travail	308
65	170	85	35	150	140	À domicile	309
10	30	10	10	-	30	En dehors du Canada	310
125	345	90	115	500	530	Sans adresse de travail fixe	311
1,205	2,795	1,255	1,215	3,705	4,130	Femmes	312
1,110	2,580	1,140	1,135	3,405	3,800	Lieu habituel de travail	313
55	155	60	30	160	215	À domicile	314
10	-	-	-	15	-	En dehors du Canada	315
35	60	60	40	120	115	Sans adresse de travail fixe	316
2,480	**5,565**	**2,340**	**2,400**	**7,620**	**8,395**	**Population active occupée totale de 15 ans et plus ayant un lieu habituel de travail ou sans adresse de travail fixe**	317
						selon le mode de transport	
1,335	2,925	1,140	1,220	4,090	4,480	Hommes	318
1,165	2,625	1,020	1,105	3,720	4,075	Automobile, camion ou fourgonnette, en tant que conducteur	319
95	135	55	40	175	150	Automobile, camion ou fourgonnette, en tant que passager	320
60	95	40	65	180	190	Transport en commun	321
10	35	25	-	-	30	À pied	322
10	30	10	10	15	30	Autre moyen	323
1,145	2,640	1,195	1,180	3,530	3,920	Femmes	324
840	2,175	975	910	2,695	2,975	Automobile, camion ou fourgonnette, en tant que conductrice	325
140	200	80	130	445	490	Automobile, camion ou fourgonnette, en tant que passagère	326
115	210	95	90	325	350	Transport en commun	327
50	40	35	45	40	75	À pied	328
10	15	10	-	20	30	Autre moyen	329
2,865	**6,635**	**2,870**	**2,855**	**8,815**	**9,720**	**Population totale de 15 ans et plus ayant travaillé depuis le 1er janvier 2000**	330
						selon la langue utilisée au travail	
2,670	6,220	2,785	2,585	7,795	8,555	Réponses uniques	331
2,645	6,210	2,765	2,530	7,750	8,420	Anglais	332
20	-	10	-	-	-	Français	333
-	15	-	60	40	135	Langues non officielles (5)	334
-	-	-	40	-	-	Chinois, n.d.a.	335
-	-	-	-	-	-	Cantonais	336
-	10	10	20	30	140	Autres langues (6)	337
200	415	85	265	1,020	1,165	Réponses multiples	338
45	170	25	45	185	120	Anglais et français	339
140	235	60	210	800	1,020	Anglais et langue non officielle	340
-	-	-	-	-	10	Français et langue non officielle	341
15	10	-	10	40	15	Anglais, français et langue non officielle	342
						CARACTÉRISTIQUES DES LOGEMENTS ET DES MÉNAGES	
1,260	**2,975**	**1,255**	**1,375**	**3,755**	**4,210**	**Nombre total de logements privés occupés**	343
						selon le mode d'occupation	
1,215	2,890	1,150	1,325	3,575	4,070	Possédé	344
50	90	105	50	180	135	Loué	345
-	-	-	-	-	-	Logement de bande	346
						selon le type de construction résidentielle	
1,035	2,500	765	565	2,370	2,635	Maison individuelle non attenante	347
155	205	160	645	900	1,200	Maison jumelée	348
80	255	330	165	375	300	Maison en rangée	349
-	-	-	-	95	75	Appartement, duplex non attenant	350
-	10	-	-	-	-	Appartement, immeuble de cinq étages ou plus	351
-	10	-	-	-	10	Appartement, immeuble de moins de cinq étages (38)	352
-	-	-	-	-	-	Autre maison individuelle attenante	353
-	-	-	-	15	-	Logement mobile (39)	354

Table 1. Selected Characteristics for Census Tracts, 2001 Census – 100% Data and 20% Sample Data

No.	Characteristics	Toronto 0575.05	Toronto 0575.06	Toronto 0576.01	Toronto 0576.04	Toronto 0576.05	Toronto 0576.06
	DWELLING AND HOUSEHOLD CHARACTERISTICS						
	by condition of dwelling						
355	Regular maintenance only	1,760	750	1,460	890	1,325	1,280
356	Minor repairs	410	420	400	435	500	385
357	Major repairs	50	50	85	80	55	55
	by period of construction						
358	Before 1946	-	-	225	10	-	-
359	1946-1960	10	-	185	15	-	10
360	1961-1970	60	45	90	-	30	30
361	1971-1980	690	525	120	400	385	425
362	1981-1990	555	635	115	925	1,280	895
363	1991-2001 (20)	915	10	1,210	40	180	370
364	Average number of rooms per dwelling	6.6	7.1	7.0	8.7	7.2	7.6
365	Average number of bedrooms per dwelling	3.1	3.2	3.2	3.6	3.3	3.5
366	Average value of dwelling $	177,557	190,459	260,296	277,130	218,355	234,793
367	**Total number of private households**	**2,225**	**1,220**	**1,945**	**1,400**	**1,880**	**1,720**
	by household size						
368	1 person	190	60	220	70	105	115
369	2 persons	515	210	645	260	270	290
370	3 persons	505	225	390	295	340	360
371	4-5 persons	895	575	585	670	890	785
372	6 or more persons	115	150	105	100	280	165
	by household type						
373	One-family households	1,850	1,025	1,530	1,210	1,565	1,490
374	Multiple-family households	95	125	120	75	185	90
375	Non-family households	280	75	295	115	125	140
376	Number of persons in private households	7,355	4,625	5,870	5,050	7,335	6,270
377	Average number of persons in private households	3.3	3.8	3.0	3.6	3.9	3.6
378	Average number of persons per room	0.5	0.5	0.4	0.4	0.5	0.5
379	Tenant households in non-farm, non-reserve private dwellings (40)	185	170	200	85	260	125
380	Average gross rent $ (40)	1,085	856	934	1,856	898	953
381	Tenant households spending 30% or more of household income on gross rent (40) (41)	65	45	55	35	75	40
382	Tenant households spending from 30% to 99% of household income on gross rent (40) (41)	55	30	45	35	40	25
383	Owner households in non-farm, non-reserve private dwellings (42)	2,025	1,055	1,695	1,310	1,620	1,595
384	Average owner's major payments $ (42)	1,269	1,275	1,337	1,304	1,374	1,336
385	Owner households spending 30% or more of household income on owner's major payments (41) (42)	590	270	500	120	430	320
386	Owner households spending from 30% to 99% of household income on owner's major payments (41) (42)	535	235	445	120	400	295
	CENSUS FAMILY CHARACTERISTICS						
387	**Total number of census families in private households**	**2,050**	**1,275**	**1,775**	**1,365**	**1,970**	**1,665**
	by census family structure and size						
388	Total couple families	1,685	1,075	1,605	1,200	1,705	1,465
389	Total families of married couples	1,475	980	1,395	1,115	1,595	1,355
390	Without children at home	320	225	500	245	325	285
391	With children at home	1,155	760	895	870	1,270	1,075
392	1 child	385	190	355	215	330	335
393	2 children	550	390	390	455	590	480
394	3 or more children	225	180	155	205	360	255
395	Total families of common-law couples	210	90	205	85	115	115
396	Without children at home	85	50	140	35	45	30
397	With children at home	125	45	70	50	65	80
398	1 child	40	15	50	25	35	50
399	2 children	60	-	-	15	15	25
400	3 or more children	25	25	15	10	10	10
401	Total lone-parent families	355	205	170	160	260	200
402	Female parent	310	185	135	90	205	160
403	1 child	195	105	95	45	80	55
404	2 children	65	35	20	35	85	55
405	3 or more children	50	45	15	10	35	50

Tableau 1. Certaines caractéristiques des secteurs de recensement, recensement de 2001 – Données intégrales et données-échantillon (20 %)

Toronto 0576.07	Toronto 0576.08 A	Toronto 0576.09 A	Toronto 0576.10 A	Toronto 0576.11 A	Toronto 0576.12 A	Caractéristiques	N°
						CARACTÉRISTIQUES DES LOGEMENTS ET DES MÉNAGES	
						selon l'état du logement	
895	2,500	855	1,260	3,425	3,855	Entretien régulier seulement	355
320	425	380	105	310	300	Réparations mineures	356
45	45	25	10	20	50	Réparations majeures	357
						selon la période de construction	
15	-	-	20	-	-	Avant 1946	358
20	20	-	15	-	-	1946-1960	359
10	15	20	-	10	30	1961-1970	360
55	175	680	-	10	10	1971-1980	361
880	610	550	-	75	40	1981-1990	362
285	2,150	-	1,340	3,645	4,120	1991-2001 (20)	363
7.6	7.7	8.0	6.3	7.3	7.1	Nombre moyen de pièces par logement	364
3.4	3.5	3.6	3.0	3.5	3.4	Nombre moyen de chambres à coucher par logement	365
216,329	252,926	249,705	224,101	244,426	239,103	Valeur moyenne du logement $	366
1,265	**2,980**	**1,255**	**1,380**	**3,755**	**4,210**	**Nombre total de logements privés**	367
						selon la taille du ménage	
55	145	75	90	170	170	1 personne	368
245	670	290	355	550	675	2 personnes	369
250	680	270	290	700	865	3 personnes	370
600	1,270	540	510	1,750	1,905	4-5 personnes	371
115	210	75	135	580	600	6 personnes ou plus	372
						selon le genre de ménage	
1,105	2,640	1,120	1,160	3,050	3,440	Ménages unifamiliaux	373
70	145	40	110	500	525	Ménages multifamiliaux	374
85	195	90	110	205	235	Ménages non familiaux	375
4,600	10,355	4,270	4,715	15,125	16,565	Nombre de personnes dans les ménages privés	376
3.6	3.5	3.4	3.4	4.0	3.9	Nombre moyen de personnes dans les ménages privés	377
0.5	0.4	0.4	0.5	0.6	0.6	Nombre moyen de personnes par pièce	378
50	90	105	50	180	130	Ménages locataires dans les logements privés non agricoles hors réserve (40)	379
1,094	1,337	990	1,279	1,155	1,161	Loyer brut moyen $ (40)	380
15	15	20	35	60	30	Ménages locataires consacrant 30 % ou plus du revenu du ménage au loyer brut (40) (41)	381
-	20	20	35	50	30	Ménages locataires consacrant de 30 % à 99 % du revenu du ménage au loyer brut (40) (41)	382
1,195	2,890	1,150	1,320	3,555	4,065	Ménages propriétaires dans les logements privés non agricoles hors réserve (42)	383
1,450	1,443	1,275	1,428	1,464	1,453	Principales dépenses de propriété moyennes $ (42)	384
375	565	180	390	990	1,030	Ménages propriétaires consacrant 30 % ou plus du revenu du ménage aux principales dépenses de propriété (41) (42)	385
330	500	155	340	830	920	Ménages propriétaires consacrant de 30 % à 99 % du revenu du ménage aux principales dépenses de propriété (41) (42)	386
						CARACTÉRISTIQUES DES FAMILLES DE RECENSEMENT	
1,250	**2,925**	**1,205**	**1,375**	**4,165**	**4,610**	**Total des familles de recensement dans les ménages privés**	387
						selon la structure et la taille de la famille de recensement	
1,110	2,655	1,030	1,220	3,685	4,105	Total des familles avec conjoints	388
1,020	2,440	960	1,120	3,465	3,900	Total des familles avec couples mariés	389
255	650	255	345	820	880	Sans enfants à la maison	390
765	1,790	705	770	2,650	3,025	Avec enfants à la maison	391
190	550	210	295	765	990	1 enfant	392
375	775	320	325	1,160	1,360	2 enfants	393
200	465	175	150	720	670	3 enfants ou plus	394
95	215	65	95	215	205	Total des familles en union libre	395
25	85	-	45	80	70	Sans enfants à la maison	396
65	125	65	55	135	135	Avec enfants à la maison	397
20	65	25	20	40	55	1 enfant	398
30	60	25	25	55	65	2 enfants	399
15	-	15	-	40	20	3 enfants ou plus	400
140	270	175	165	485	505	Total des familles monoparentales	401
105	210	150	140	395	405	Parent de sexe féminin	402
35	115	95	85	235	245	1 enfant	403
55	65	50	20	120	125	2 enfants	404
25	30	15	30	40	35	3 enfants ou plus	405

Table 1. Selected Characteristics for Census Tracts, 2001 Census – 100% Data and 20% Sample Data

No.	Characteristics	Toronto 0575.05	Toronto 0575.06	Toronto 0576.01	Toronto 0576.04	Toronto 0576.05	Toronto 0576.06
	CENSUS FAMILY CHARACTERISTICS						
	by census family structure and size - concluded						
406	Male parent	50	20	40	70	60	40
407	1 child	30	10	20	30	30	35
408	2 children	15	10	10	40	20	-
409	3 or more children	10	-	10	-	-	10
410	**Total number of children at home**	**3,015**	**2,040**	**1,985**	**2,155**	**3,255**	**2,660**
	by age groups						
411	Under 6 years	830	395	595	375	660	460
412	6-14 years	1,110	780	745	785	1,170	1,100
413	15-17 years	340	235	125	285	375	290
414	18-24 years	505	435	380	540	745	595
415	25 years and over	230	195	145	170	305	215
416	Average number of children at home per census family (43)	1.5	1.6	1.1	1.6	1.7	1.6
417	**Total number of persons in private households**	**7,360**	**4,625**	**5,865**	**5,045**	**7,330**	**6,270**
	by census family status and living arrangements						
418	Number of non-family persons	610	235	505	325	395	475
419	Living with relatives (44)	185	120	130	100	210	235
420	Living with non-relatives only	235	55	155	155	85	130
421	Living alone	190	60	225	70	105	115
422	Number of family persons	6,745	4,385	5,365	4,720	6,935	5,790
423	Average number of persons per census family	3.3	3.4	3.0	3.5	3.5	3.5
424	**Total number of persons 65 years and over**	**235**	**180**	**355**	**175**	**285**	**255**
425	Number of non-family persons 65 years and over	65	55	85	80	95	120
426	Living with relatives (44)	30	55	30	60	80	105
427	Living with non-relatives only	10	-	-	-	-	-
428	Living alone	25	-	55	15	10	15
429	Number of family persons 65 years and over	170	120	270	95	190	130
	ECONOMIC FAMILY CHARACTERISTICS						
430	**Total number of economic families in private households**	**1,980**	**1,155**	**1,680**	**1,310**	**1,765**	**1,585**
	by size of family						
431	2 persons	520	210	640	290	280	300
432	3 persons	475	220	365	280	340	365
433	4 persons	620	370	395	440	575	505
434	5 or more persons	370	355	280	300	575	415
435	Total number of persons in economic families	6,930	4,510	5,495	4,825	7,145	6,030
436	Average number of persons per economic family	3.5	3.9	3.3	3.7	4.0	3.8
437	Total number of unattached individuals	425	110	375	225	185	245
	2000 INCOME CHARACTERISTICS						
	Population 15 years and over by sex and total income groups in 2000						
438	Total - Both sexes	5,410	3,450	4,525	3,885	5,500	4,705
439	Without income	260	185	145	165	365	235
440	With income	5,155	3,265	4,385	3,715	5,130	4,470
441	Under $1,000 (45)	235	235	130	120	250	205
442	$ 1,000 - $ 2,999	250	185	155	140	265	145
443	$ 3,000 - $ 4,999	225	100	120	145	280	245
444	$ 5,000 - $ 6,999	180	215	110	145	190	195
445	$ 7,000 - $ 9,999	235	130	170	160	320	240
446	$10,000 - $11,999	175	105	145	85	155	125
447	$12,000 - $14,999	230	175	155	120	265	200
448	$15,000 - $19,999	280	185	320	190	430	255
449	$20,000 - $24,999	325	225	355	165	315	310
450	$25,000 - $29,999	410	210	340	225	410	315
451	$30,000 - $34,999	515	275	490	225	435	285
452	$35,000 - $39,999	430	270	355	270	410	285
453	$40,000 - $44,999	395	225	325	265	315	265
454	$45,000 - $49,999	280	110	175	230	250	305
455	$50,000 - $59,999	430	225	390	345	270	395
456	$60,000 and over	570	390	640	900	560	690
457	Average income $ (46)	32,066	29,321	36,728	46,430	29,281	37,525
458	Median income $ (46)	30,026	26,244	32,017	37,767	26,126	29,799
459	Standard error of average income $ (46)	784	863	1,214	1,963	712	1,521

Tableau 1. Certaines caractéristiques des secteurs de recensement, recensement de 2001 – Données intégrales et données-échantillon (20 %)

Toronto 0576.07	Toronto 0576.08 A	Toronto 0576.09 A	Toronto 0576.10 A	Toronto 0576.11 A	Toronto 0576.12 A	Caractéristiques	N°
						CARACTÉRISTIQUES DES FAMILLES DE RECENSEMENT	
						selon la structure et la taille de la famille de recensement – fin	
30	60	25	15	95	100	Parent de sexe masculin	406
10	20	20	-	55	55	1 enfant	407
15	40	-	10	25	15	2 enfants	408
10	-	-	-	20	25	3 enfants ou plus	409
1,955	**4,260**	**1,800**	**1,805**	**6,515**	**6,905**	**Nombre total d'enfants à la maison**	410
						selon les groupes d'âge	
415	1,025	260	575	2,010	2,290	Moins de 6 ans	411
765	1,670	620	650	2,400	2,620	6-14 ans	412
270	435	245	190	635	550	15-17 ans	413
310	840	500	265	955	950	18-24 ans	414
205	295	175	125	525	490	25 ans et plus	415
1.6	1.5	1.5	1.3	1.6	1.5	Nombre moyen d'enfants à la maison par famille de recensement (43)	416
4,600	**10,360**	**4,270**	**4,715**	**15,120**	**16,565**	**Nombre total de personnes dans les ménages privés**	417
						selon la situation des particuliers dans la famille de recensement et des particuliers dans le ménage	
280	520	230	310	755	950	Nombre de personnes hors famille de recensement	418
130	190	95	155	390	520	Vivant avec des personnes apparentées (44)	419
95	180	60	65	195	260	Vivant avec des personnes non apparentées uniquement	420
55	145	75	95	175	170	Vivant seules	421
4,320	9,840	4,040	4,395	14,370	15,620	Nombre de personnes membres d'une famille	422
3.5	3.4	3.3	3.2	3.4	3.4	Nombre moyen de personnes par famille de recensement	423
140	**370**	**160**	**270**	**640**	**595**	**Nombre total de personnes de 65 ans et plus**	424
45	115	75	85	150	225	Nombre de personnes hors famille de recensement de 65 ans et plus	425
40	90	65	70	130	215	Vivant avec des personnes apparentées (44)	426
-	10	10	-	10	-	Vivant avec des personnes non apparentées uniquement	427
-	20	-	10	-	15	Vivant seules	428
100	255	85	190	495	365	Nombre de personnes membres d'une famille de 65 ans et plus	429
						CARACTÉRISTIQUES DES FAMILLES ÉCONOMIQUES	
1,200	**2,800**	**1,175**	**1,265**	**3,570**	**4,005**	**Nombre total de familles économiques dans les ménages privés**	430
						selon la taille de la famille	
245	670	310	350	585	690	2 personnes	431
255	665	290	280	695	840	3 personnes	432
435	865	335	365	1,125	1,260	4 personnes	433
265	600	240	270	1,165	1,215	5 personnes ou plus	434
4,450	10,035	4,130	4,555	14,755	16,140	Nombre total de personnes dans les familles économiques	435
3.7	3.6	3.5	3.6	4.1	4.0	Nombre moyen de personnes par famille économique	436
150	325	140	160	365	425	Nombre total de personnes hors famille économique	437
						CARACTÉRISTIQUES DU REVENU DE 2000	
						Population de 15 ans et plus selon le sexe et les tranches de revenu total en 2000	
3,415	7,655	3,385	3,490	10,690	11,575	Total - Les deux sexes	438
210	370	205	155	795	580	Sans revenu	439
3,200	7,290	3,175	3,335	9,895	11,000	Avec un revenu	440
205	255	150	180	440	490	Moins de 1 000 $ (45)	441
160	300	205	115	510	440	1 000 $ - 2 999 $	442
155	225	80	110	375	380	3 000 $ - 4 999 $	443
80	225	85	120	345	375	5 000 $ - 6 999 $	444
170	270	175	175	570	440	7 000 $ - 9 999 $	445
90	215	90	140	290	330	10 000 $ - 11 999 $	446
120	285	105	170	390	580	12 000 $ - 14 999 $	447
130	355	105	210	665	780	15 000 $ - 19 999 $	448
180	415	195	165	790	900	20 000 $ - 24 999 $	449
230	555	280	345	795	865	25 000 $ - 29 999 $	450
260	530	230	290	780	900	30 000 $ - 34 999 $	451
200	550	225	290	685	880	35 000 $ - 39 999 $	452
260	560	245	230	520	855	40 000 $ - 44 999 $	453
125	295	125	195	545	580	45 000 $ - 49 999 $	454
365	840	325	225	910	830	50 000 $ - 59 999 $	455
465	1,410	560	390	1,295	1,375	60 000 $ et plus	456
33,762	38,603	39,312	31,514	32,479	32,555	Revenu moyen $ (46)	457
30,817	34,845	32,317	28,353	27,594	29,501	Revenu médian $ (46)	458
1,171	796	1,434	859	612	506	Erreur type de revenu moyen $ (46)	459

Table 1. Selected Characteristics for Census Tracts, 2001 Census – 100% Data and 20% Sample Data

No.	Characteristics	Toronto 0575.05	Toronto 0575.06	Toronto 0576.01	Toronto 0576.04	Toronto 0576.05	Toronto 0576.06
	2000 INCOME CHARACTERISTICS						
	Population 15 years and over by sex and total income groups in 2000 – concluded						
460	Total - Males	2,590	1,695	2,240	1,895	2,735	2,300
461	Without income	95	75	55	65	80	70
462	With income	2,500	1,620	2,185	1,830	2,655	2,235
463	Under $1,000 (45)	115	110	65	25	145	90
464	$ 1,000 - $ 2,999	105	75	30	30	130	50
465	$ 3,000 - $ 4,999	100	50	35	60	120	110
466	$ 5,000 - $ 6,999	35	55	55	50	45	65
467	$ 7,000 - $ 9,999	60	45	40	40	110	110
468	$10,000 - $11,999	75	65	55	30	45	75
469	$12,000 - $14,999	70	70	40	40	90	60
470	$15,000 - $19,999	110	80	90	80	190	95
471	$20,000 - $24,999	105	95	175	65	170	90
472	$25,000 - $29,999	160	110	105	75	180	160
473	$30,000 - $34,999	205	80	220	95	225	105
474	$35,000 - $39,999	185	125	220	125	190	140
475	$40,000 - $44,999	215	110	185	145	200	140
476	$45,000 - $49,999	180	75	115	120	165	145
477	$50,000 - $59,999	320	160	300	200	205	240
478	$60,000 and over	440	335	465	655	435	570
479	Average income $ (46)	39,530	36,214	44,981	60,900	35,157	48,533
480	Median income $ (46)	38,052	33,980	39,013	45,930	31,411	39,065
481	Standard error of average income $ (46)	1,347	1,406	2,014	3,419	1,139	2,883
482	Total - Females	2,820	1,755	2,290	1,995	2,755	2,405
483	Without income	170	115	90	110	285	170
484	With income	2,655	1,645	2,200	1,885	2,475	2,235
485	Under $1,000 (45)	120	120	70	95	105	120
486	$ 1,000 - $ 2,999	150	110	120	110	135	95
487	$ 3,000 - $ 4,999	125	55	85	85	165	135
488	$ 5,000 - $ 6,999	145	160	60	95	145	130
489	$ 7,000 - $ 9,999	170	90	135	115	210	130
490	$10,000 - $11,999	100	40	85	55	110	55
491	$12,000 - $14,999	155	105	115	80	180	145
492	$15,000 - $19,999	165	105	230	105	240	160
493	$20,000 - $24,999	225	135	180	100	140	215
494	$25,000 - $29,999	250	100	235	150	230	160
495	$30,000 - $34,999	305	195	270	125	210	185
496	$35,000 - $39,999	240	150	135	145	215	150
497	$40,000 - $44,999	180	120	140	120	120	125
498	$45,000 - $49,999	100	40	65	110	80	160
499	$50,000 - $59,999	105	65	90	145	65	150
500	$60,000 and over	125	55	175	250	125	120
501	Average income $ (46)	25,043	22,516	28,518	32,404	22,968	26,539
502	Median income $ (46)	24,492	20,081	25,237	28,686	18,970	23,099
503	Standard error of average income $ (46)	737	892	1,248	1,558	757	946
	by composition of total income						
504	Total - Composition of income in 2000 % (47)	100.0	100.0	100.0	100.0	100.0	100.0
505	Employment income %	91.9	92.5	88.4	92.6	91.2	91.5
506	Government transfer payments %	5.4	5.6	4.6	2.5	5.3	4.1
507	Other %	2.8	1.8	7.0	5.0	3.4	4.5
	Population 15 years and over with employment income in 2000 by sex and work activity						
508	Both sexes with employment income (48)	4,480	2,845	3,815	3,360	4,530	3,875
509	Average employment income $	33,855	31,137	37,315	47,553	30,259	39,575
510	Standard error of average employment income $	853	932	1,289	2,111	741	1,662
511	Worked full year, full time (49)	2,735	1,685	2,455	1,970	2,605	2,280
512	Average employment income $	43,762	39,782	45,192	63,862	40,582	51,660
513	Standard error of average employment income $	1,122	1,087	1,711	3,065	953	2,072
514	Worked part year or part time (50)	1,635	1,140	1,245	1,330	1,830	1,540
515	Average employment income $	18,598	18,670	23,184	24,992	16,267	22,452
516	Standard error of average employment income $	902	1,349	1,694	1,994	790	2,574
517	Males with employment income (48)	2,260	1,525	1,995	1,745	2,410	2,020
518	Average employment income $	41,395	36,896	44,598	60,559	36,090	49,960
519	Standard error of average employment income $	1,428	1,451	2,104	3,550	1,147	3,040
520	Worked full year, full time (49)	1,565	995	1,475	1,155	1,545	1,280
521	Average employment income $	49,791	43,416	48,732	75,482	45,931	61,612
522	Standard error of average employment income $	1,759	1,611	2,518	4,693	1,367	3,464
523	Worked part year or part time (50)	660	520	475	570	820	715
524	Average employment income $	22,210	24,997	33,451	32,240	18,518	30,351
525	Standard error of average employment income $	1,697	2,583	3,763	3,969	1,399	5,650

Tableau 1. Certaines caractéristiques des secteurs de recensement, recensement de 2001 – Données intégrales et données-échantillon (20 %)

Toronto 0576.07	Toronto 0576.08 A	Toronto 0576.09 A	Toronto 0576.10 A	Toronto 0576.11 A	Toronto 0576.12 A	Caractéristiques	N°
						CARACTÉRISTIQUES DU REVENU DE 2000	
						Population de 15 ans et plus selon le sexe et les tranches de revenu total en 2000 – fin	
1,700	3,795	1,670	1,690	5,220	5,640	Total - Hommes	460
85	130	100	90	255	195	Sans revenu	461
1,615	3,665	1,570	1,600	4,965	5,450	Avec un revenu	462
110	80	60	70	215	175	Moins de 1 000 $ (45)	463
20	100	85	45	205	150	1 000 $ - 2 999 $	464
50	110	50	25	100	135	3 000 $ - 4 999 $	465
25	75	55	55	105	120	5 000 $ - 6 999 $	466
75	85	50	55	215	150	7 000 $ - 9 999 $	467
55	80	10	50	185	125	10 000 $ - 11 999 $	468
45	95	40	75	125	220	12 000 $ - 14 999 $	469
50	125	25	70	265	305	15 000 $ - 19 999 $	470
110	220	90	50	285	315	20 000 $ - 24 999 $	471
75	190	125	130	380	340	25 000 $ - 29 999 $	472
105	150	95	90	390	345	30 000 $ - 34 999 $	473
75	245	90	140	310	465	35 000 $ - 39 999 $	474
155	320	120	130	320	495	40 000 $ - 44 999 $	475
80	140	55	135	340	400	45 000 $ - 49 999 $	476
265	510	265	195	560	570	50 000 $ - 59 999 $	477
325	1,150	360	280	960	1,135	60 000 $ et plus	478
40,930	48,130	46,397	38,601	38,884	40,406	Revenu moyen $ (46)	479
40,021	43,794	39,998	36,608	34,913	37,938	Revenu médian $ (46)	480
1,943	1,272	2,279	1,368	992	807	Erreur type de revenu moyen $ (46)	481
1,715	3,855	1,710	1,795	5,475	5,935	Total - Femmes	482
130	240	105	65	540	390	Sans revenu	483
1,585	3,620	1,600	1,730	4,935	5,550	Avec un revenu	484
90	175	85	110	225	310	Moins de 1 000 $ (45)	485
140	205	120	70	300	290	1 000 $ - 2 999 $	486
110	115	30	90	280	245	3 000 $ - 4 999 $	487
65	150	30	60	240	260	5 000 $ - 6 999 $	488
95	185	125	115	355	285	7 000 $ - 9 999 $	489
40	135	80	95	110	205	10 000 $ - 11 999 $	490
75	190	65	90	260	355	12 000 $ - 14 999 $	491
85	230	80	140	390	475	15 000 $ - 19 999 $	492
70	195	105	110	505	580	20 000 $ - 24 999 $	493
160	370	155	220	410	530	25 000 $ - 29 999 $	494
155	380	135	195	390	560	30 000 $ - 34 999 $	495
125	300	135	150	375	420	35 000 $ - 39 999 $	496
105	245	130	95	195	360	40 000 $ - 44 999 $	497
45	160	65	60	200	180	45 000 $ - 49 999 $	498
95	330	60	30	350	260	50 000 $ - 59 999 $	499
140	255	205	105	335	235	60 000 $ et plus	500
26,471	28,944	32,372	24,955	26,032	24,850	Revenu moyen $ (46)	501
25,926	27,907	27,368	24,863	22,886	22,630	Revenu médian $ (46)	502
1,146	829	1,711	960	660	538	Erreur type de revenu moyen $ (46)	503
						selon la composition du revenu total	
100.0	100.0	100.0	100.0	100.0	100.0	Total - Composition du revenu en 2000 % (47)	504
91.8	92.6	89.4	89.4	92.2	91.4	Revenu d'emploi %	505
4.2	4.1	4.9	6.4	5.2	5.5	Transferts gouvernementaux %	506
4.0	3.4	5.7	4.2	2.5	3.1	Autre %	507
						Population de 15 ans et plus ayant un revenu d'emploi en 2000 selon le sexe et le travail	
2,760	6,440	2,800	2,815	8,500	9,425	Les deux sexes ayant un revenu d'emploi (48)	508
35,876	40,430	39,875	33,337	34,906	34,722	Revenu moyen d'emploi $	509
1,329	826	1,472	903	668	534	Erreur type de revenu moyen d'emploi $	510
1,815	4,195	1,730	1,790	5,370	6,090	Ayant travaillé toute l'année à plein temps (49)	511
44,111	49,936	50,872	42,045	43,329	42,428	Revenu moyen d'emploi $	512
1,308	918	1,854	1,075	857	638	Erreur type de revenu moyen d'emploi $	513
880	2,125	1,045	910	2,960	3,160	Ayant travaillé une partie de l'année ou à temps partiel (50)	514
21,171	22,951	22,490	18,069	20,409	20,906	Revenu moyen d'emploi $	515
2,543	1,389	2,012	1,191	853	754	Erreur type de revenu moyen d'emploi $	516
1,460	3,390	1,425	1,400	4,415	4,925	Hommes ayant un revenu d'emploi (48)	517
41,977	49,156	46,052	40,118	41,382	41,869	Revenu moyen d'emploi $	518
2,200	1,318	2,294	1,427	1,049	813	Erreur type de revenu moyen d'emploi $	519
1,050	2,425	940	1,015	3,075	3,550	Ayant travaillé toute l'année à plein temps (49)	520
49,047	57,837	55,788	47,380	48,435	47,544	Revenu moyen d'emploi $	521
1,968	1,365	2,551	1,572	1,255	901	Erreur type de revenu moyen d'emploi $	522
385	905	470	365	1,290	1,305	Ayant travaillé une partie de l'année ou à temps partiel (50)	523
28,004	28,006	27,976	20,952	25,199	27,329	Revenu moyen d'emploi $	524
5,257	2,775	4,123	2,324	1,618	1,521	Erreur type de revenu moyen d'emploi $	525

Table 1. Selected Characteristics for Census Tracts, 2001 Census – 100% Data and 20% Sample Data

No.	Characteristics	Toronto 0575.05	Toronto 0575.06	Toronto 0576.01	Toronto 0576.04	Toronto 0576.05	Toronto 0576.06
	2000 INCOME CHARACTERISTICS						
	Population 15 years and over with employment income in 2000 by sex and work activity – concluded						
526	Females with employment income (48)	2,230	1,315	1,825	1,615	2,120	1,855
527	Average employment income $	26,209	24,472	29,353	33,523	23,639	28,230
528	Standard error of average employment income $	788	1,001	1,304	1,690	808	1,035
529	Worked full year, full time (49)	1,170	695	975	815	1,060	1,005
530	Average employment income $	35,682	34,596	39,834	47,466	32,798	38,952
531	Standard error of average employment income $	944	1,209	1,960	2,550	1,079	1,411
532	Worked part year or part time (50)	975	620	765	755	1,010	830
533	Average employment income $	16,144	13,345	16,767	19,540	14,434	15,657
534	Standard error of average employment income $	947	1,073	1,164	1,603	848	1,037
	Census families by structure and family income groups in 2000						
535	Total - All census families	2,050	1,280	1,775	1,365	1,965	1,665
536	Under $10,000	65	90	45	10	115	40
537	$ 10,000 - $19,999	80	55	20	15	75	60
538	$ 20,000 - $29,999	95	80	110	10	105	45
539	$ 30,000 - $39,999	180	85	140	60	170	130
540	$ 40,000 - $49,999	190	85	175	90	155	120
541	$ 50,000 - $59,999	250	140	160	80	265	110
542	$ 60,000 - $69,999	260	130	195	125	200	160
543	$ 70,000 - $79,999	240	140	240	95	215	135
544	$ 80,000 - $89,999	130	140	180	95	105	190
545	$ 90,000 - $99,999	200	85	70	110	160	105
546	$100,000 and over	365	245	440	675	395	580
547	Average family income $	72,078	69,668	79,052	117,908	69,958	93,644
548	Median family income $	66,462	68,838	71,398	98,536	63,755	81,709
549	Standard error of average family income $	1,963	2,372	2,738	4,908	1,871	3,942
550	Total - All couple census families (51)	1,690	1,070	1,605	1,205	1,705	1,465
551	Under $10,000	40	45	25	-	80	10
552	$ 10,000 - $19,999	50	25	-	-	50	45
553	$ 20,000 - $29,999	65	50	95	10	90	25
554	$ 30,000 - $39,999	85	40	110	40	135	95
555	$ 40,000 - $49,999	115	75	130	45	135	90
556	$ 50,000 - $59,999	210	130	150	65	230	75
557	$ 60,000 - $69,999	240	120	190	100	150	150
558	$ 70,000 - $79,999	220	130	225	90	195	120
559	$ 80,000 - $89,999	130	140	180	85	95	175
560	$ 90,000 - $99,999	175	80	65	100	160	100
561	$100,000 and over	360	230	425	660	390	575
562	Average family income $	77,753	76,012	82,536	125,683	73,798	100,497
563	Median family income $	70,782	71,412	73,475	102,831	68,433	86,303
564	Standard error of average family income $	2,189	2,523	2,897	5,328	2,043	4,388
	Incidence of low income in 2000						
565	Total - Economic families	1,980	1,155	1,680	1,310	1,765	1,590
566	Low income	165	150	55	20	155	120
567	Incidence of low income in 2000 % (52)	8.3	13.2	3.4	1.6	8.9	7.5
568	Total - Unattached individuals 15 years and over	420	115	370	225	185	235
569	Low income	110	15	35	40	30	70
570	Incidence of low income in 2000 % (52)	26.3	15.7	9.5	17.9	15.6	28.7
571	Total - Population in private households	7,350	4,630	5,865	5,045	7,330	6,265
572	Low income	720	745	255	115	645	515
573	Incidence of low income in 2000 % (52)	9.8	16.1	4.3	2.3	8.8	8.2
	Private households by household income groups in 2000						
574	Total - All private households	2,225	1,225	1,940	1,400	1,880	1,720
575	Under $10,000	60	50	35	-	35	20
576	$ 10,000 - $19,999	90	40	40	20	50	40
577	$ 20,000 - $29,999	85	35	110	10	80	55
578	$ 30,000 - $39,999	185	85	150	25	165	135
579	$ 40,000 - $49,999	190	100	140	50	100	115
580	$ 50,000 - $59,999	270	115	185	60	210	145
581	$ 60,000 - $69,999	290	125	215	135	200	135
582	$ 70,000 - $79,999	245	135	275	115	220	120
583	$ 80,000 - $89,999	165	135	210	90	140	185
584	$ 90,000 - $99,999	175	70	65	135	180	105
585	$100,000 and over	455	335	525	760	500	670
586	Average household income $	74,223	78,274	82,799	123,289	79,886	97,553
587	Median household income $	67,248	72,041	72,409	103,259	74,270	84,541
588	Standard error of average household income $	1,929	2,476	2,987	4,699	1,977	3,990

Tableau 1. Certaines caractéristiques des secteurs de recensement, recensement de 2001 – Données intégrales et données-échantillon (20 %)

Toronto 0576.07	Toronto 0576.08 A	Toronto 0576.09 A	Toronto 0576.10 A	Toronto 0576.11 A	Toronto 0576.12 A	Caractéristiques	N°
						CARACTÉRISTIQUES DU REVENU DE 2000	
						Population de 15 ans et plus ayant un revenu d'emploi en 2000 selon le sexe et le travail – fin	
1,305	3,045	1,375	1,415	4,085	4,505	Femmes ayant un revenu d'emploi (48)	526
29,029	30,723	33,477	26,592	27,907	26,915	Revenu moyen d'emploi $	527
1,216	802	1,788	985	733	595	Erreur type de revenu moyen d'emploi $	528
765	1,770	790	775	2,290	2,545	Ayant travaillé toute l'année à plein temps (49)	529
37,320	39,119	45,029	35,100	36,473	35,292	Revenu moyen d'emploi $	530
1,348	854	2,626	1,215	1,016	785	Erreur type de revenu moyen d'emploi $	531
500	1,220	575	545	1,665	1,855	Ayant travaillé une partie de l'année ou à temps partiel (50)	532
15,960	19,216	18,011	16,123	16,696	16,391	Revenu moyen d'emploi $	533
1,645	1,267	1,740	1,234	777	639	Erreur type de revenu moyen d'emploi $	534
						Familles de recensement selon la structure et les tranches de revenu de la famille en 2000	
1,250	2,925	1,205	1,375	4,170	4,610	Total - Toutes les familles de recensement	535
55	50	35	45	235	145	Moins de 10 000 $	536
35	50	30	60	130	225	10 000 $ - 19 999 $	537
50	90	35	40	350	230	20 000 $ - 29 999 $	538
50	140	45	115	305	335	30 000 $ - 39 999 $	539
110	130	90	110	295	370	40 000 $ - 49 999 $	540
130	170	95	170	490	500	50 000 $ - 59 999 $	541
185	325	130	205	465	525	60 000 $ - 69 999 $	542
105	370	90	190	320	550	70 000 $ - 79 999 $	543
110	330	125	125	390	465	80 000 $ - 89 999 $	544
90	305	110	115	290	375	90 000 $ - 99 999 $	545
335	975	425	200	900	905	100 000 $ et plus	546
80,198	89,934	97,007	69,428	71,832	72,164	Revenu moyen des familles $	547
71,091	84,651	85,417	64,988	65,928	69,698	Revenu médian des familles $	548
2,978	1,818	3,849	1,938	1,488	1,168	Erreur type de revenu moyen des familles $	549
1,110	2,655	1,030	1,215	3,680	4,105	Total - Toutes les familles de recensement comptant un couple (51)	550
35	35	25	40	155	100	Moins de 10 000 $	551
25	45	-	40	95	135	10 000 $ - 19 999 $	552
25	55	25	25	265	195	20 000 $ - 29 999 $	553
30	110	15	90	255	220	30 000 $ - 39 999 $	554
100	95	55	80	260	295	40 000 $ - 49 999 $	555
105	130	80	160	410	430	50 000 $ - 59 999 $	556
160	280	115	180	405	495	60 000 $ - 69 999 $	557
105	350	85	180	315	530	70 000 $ - 79 999 $	558
110	325	115	105	390	445	80 000 $ - 89 999 $	559
85	280	100	115	270	365	90 000 $ - 99 999 $	560
325	955	420	200	865	885	100 000 $ et plus	561
84,304	93,441	106,120	72,569	75,515	75,922	Revenu moyen des familles $	562
77,719	87,018	89,843	68,536	69,854	72,698	Revenu médian des familles $	563
3,207	1,889	4,212	2,046	1,586	1,228	Erreur type de revenu moyen des familles $	564
						Fréquence des unités à faible revenu en 2000	
1,205	2,795	1,175	1,270	3,565	4,010	Total - Familles économiques	565
85	145	70	90	315	285	Faible revenu	566
7.1	5.2	5.9	7.0	8.9	7.1	Fréquence des unités à faible revenu en 2000 % (52)	567
145	315	130	155	365	385	Total - Personnes hors famille économique de 15 ans et plus	568
50	75	10	25	115	80	Faible revenu	569
36.4	22.2	9.8	15.4	32.2	20.3	Fréquence des unités à faible revenu en 2000 % (52)	570
4,595	10,350	4,265	4,710	15,115	16,525	Total - Population dans les ménages privés	571
310	600	210	360	1,425	1,200	Faible revenu	572
6.8	5.8	4.9	7.7	9.4	7.3	Fréquence des unités à faible revenu en 2000 % (52)	573
						Ménages privés selon les tranches de revenu du ménage en 2000	
1,260	2,980	1,250	1,380	3,750	4,205	Total - Tous les ménages privés	574
40	25	20	35	150	70	Moins de 10 000 $	575
20	45	30	60	35	75	10 000 $ - 19 999 $	576
25	65	30	25	110	140	20 000 $ - 29 999 $	577
45	135	35	90	150	150	30 000 $ - 39 999 $	578
110	110	105	110	245	260	40 000 $ - 49 999 $	579
110	160	125	160	405	390	50 000 $ - 59 999 $	580
195	330	130	180	445	525	60 000 $ - 69 999 $	581
95	385	75	200	335	525	70 000 $ - 79 999 $	582
130	315	120	130	450	485	80 000 $ - 89 999 $	583
80	285	95	110	350	365	90 000 $ - 99 999 $	584
420	1,115	480	280	1,085	1,220	100 000 $ et plus	585
85,612	94,449	99,532	76,110	85,636	85,127	Revenu moyen des ménages $	586
79,627	87,707	87,831	71,905	79,967	78,825	Revenu médian des ménages $	587
2,900	1,815	3,809	2,200	1,646	1,314	Erreur type de revenu moyen des ménages $	588

Table 1. Selected Characteristics for Census Tracts, 2001 Census – 100% Data and 20% Sample Data

No.	Characteristics	Toronto 0576.13 A	Toronto 0585.02	Toronto 0585.03	Toronto 0585.05 A	Toronto 0585.06 A	Toronto 0585.07 A
	POPULATION CHARACTERISTICS						
1	**Population, 1996 (1)**	**3,190**	**3,612**	**3,789**	**3,953**	**4,550**	**4,844**
2	**Population, 2001 (2)**	**5,573**	**4,779**	**4,621**	**4,787**	**9,529**	**5,008**
3	Population percentage change, 1996-2001	74.7	32.3	22.0	21.1	109.4	3.4
4	Land area in square kilometres, 2001	75.16	77.34	8.19	3.56	4.44	98.66
5	**Total population - 100% Data (3)**	**5,575**	**4,780**	**4,620**	**4,790**	**9,530**	**5,005**
	by sex and age groups						
6	Male	2,850	2,400	2,230	2,360	4,755	2,550
7	0-4 years	195	165	180	155	605	110
8	5-9 years	215	210	190	205	455	190
9	10-14 years	180	165	175	240	330	225
10	15-19 years	185	150	150	160	250	210
11	20-24 years	215	130	115	150	180	140
12	25-29 years	240	185	130	120	325	90
13	30-34 years	195	205	180	185	660	100
14	35-39 years	235	230	245	245	605	195
15	40-44 years	230	235	225	235	395	230
16	45-49 years	165	130	165	205	225	255
17	50-54 years	200	160	125	160	190	225
18	55-59 years	200	110	95	130	175	180
19	60-64 years	150	120	75	80	150	145
20	65-69 years	110	85	50	40	90	90
21	70-74 years	60	65	60	35	70	65
22	75-79 years	45	35	40	10	40	40
23	80-84 years	15	10	20	10	5	25
24	85 years and over	10	5	20	5	10	25
25	Female	2,725	2,385	2,395	2,430	4,770	2,460
26	0-4 years	160	185	150	165	555	105
27	5-9 years	175	180	200	180	420	150
28	10-14 years	195	160	170	215	320	235
29	15-19 years	160	140	150	195	200	195
30	20-24 years	210	155	115	175	190	120
31	25-29 years	250	165	130	155	390	75
32	30-34 years	265	220	210	205	705	120
33	35-39 years	200	255	245	250	625	215
34	40-44 years	195	205	215	225	365	260
35	45-49 years	215	135	160	195	210	250
36	50-54 years	195	155	130	170	235	225
37	55-59 years	165	125	100	115	140	165
38	60-64 years	120	90	85	55	135	110
39	65-69 years	90	75	85	40	85	90
40	70-74 years	60	55	60	30	60	65
41	75-79 years	40	40	60	20	55	40
42	80-84 years	15	15	60	15	25	25
43	85 years and over	15	20	75	5	50	20
44	**Total population 15 years and over**	**4,445**	**3,705**	**3,560**	**3,625**	**6,845**	**3,995**
	by legal marital status						
45	Never married (single)	1,320	995	885	970	1,380	1,040
46	Legally married (and not separated)	2,755	2,295	2,050	2,325	4,765	2,530
47	Separated, but still legally married	75	95	110	80	165	80
48	Divorced	140	180	240	160	305	185
49	Widowed	160	140	270	90	230	165
	by common-law status						
50	Not in a common-law relationship	4,320	3,515	3,340	3,450	6,515	3,805
51	In a common-law relationship	125	190	220	175	330	195
52	**Total population - 20% Sample Data (4)**	**5,555**	**4,790**	**4,540**	**4,790**	**9,465**	**4,995**
	by mother tongue						
53	Single responses	5,410	4,670	4,510	4,760	9,320	4,950
54	English	2,485	3,165	3,780	4,020	6,560	4,110
55	French	40	50	30	55	110	80
56	Non-official languages (5)	2,890	1,455	700	685	2,650	765
57	Italian	1,145	980	330	320	1,635	265
58	Chinese, n.o.s.	-	-	-	20	40	-
59	Cantonese	-	10	-	-	45	-
60	Portuguese	45	60	60	60	90	-
61	Punjabi	1,020	40	30	-	30	10
62	Other languages (6)	675	360	275	285	810	495
63	Multiple responses	145	125	25	30	145	45
64	English and French	10	-	-	-	10	-
65	English and non-official language	130	120	15	30	135	45
66	French and non-official language	-	-	10	-	-	-
67	English, French and non-official language	-	-	-	-	-	-

See reference material at the end of the publication. – Voir les documents de référence à la fin de la publication.

Tableau 1. Certaines caractéristiques des secteurs de recensement, recensement de 2001 – Données intégrales et données-échantillon (20 %)

Toronto 0585.08 A	Toronto 0586 A	Toronto 0587.01	Toronto 0587.02	Toronto 0590	Toronto 0591	Caractéristiques	N°
						CARACTÉRISTIQUES DE LA POPULATION	
2,798	**6,352**	**5,000**	**4,995**	**5,322**	**5,390**	**Population, 1996 (1)**	1
3,052	**8,105**	**5,413**	**5,301**	**5,273**	**7,958**	**Population, 2001 (2)**	2
9.1	27.6	8.3	6.1	-0.9	47.6	Variation en pourcentage de la population, 1996-2001	3
42.77	169.58	130.92	151.57	1.88	6.10	Superficie des terres en kilomètres carrés, 2001	4
3,055	**8,100**	**5,415**	**5,300**	**5,275**	**7,960**	**Population totale – Données intégrales (3) selon le sexe et les groupes d'âge**	5
1,515	4,060	2,760	2,650	2,540	4,005	Sexe masculin	6
80	240	165	150	175	385	0-4 ans	7
105	275	190	185	175	400	5-9 ans	8
120	320	270	230	195	380	10-14 ans	9
125	315	225	195	155	285	15-19 ans	10
125	240	125	140	175	220	20-24 ans	11
55	210	85	90	200	325	25-29 ans	12
75	220	125	145	195	405	30-34 ans	13
115	375	240	230	225	410	35-39 ans	14
130	375	270	245	220	350	40-44 ans	15
135	345	245	225	185	250	45-49 ans	16
135	345	265	220	160	215	50-54 ans	17
110	260	190	210	125	165	55-59 ans	18
80	180	140	140	110	85	60-64 ans	19
55	150	90	95	100	75	65-69 ans	20
35	90	75	75	55	40	70-74 ans	21
25	50	30	30	45	10	75-79 ans	22
10	30	20	25	30	10	80-84 ans	23
5	15	5	15	10	5	85 ans et plus	24
1,540	4,045	2,655	2,655	2,740	3,955	Sexe féminin	25
70	240	135	175	175	360	0-4 ans	26
125	290	210	185	180	385	5-9 ans	27
125	300	215	205	185	360	10-14 ans	28
135	320	195	205	180	255	15-19 ans	29
80	225	140	115	170	235	20-24 ans	30
50	205	70	105	200	330	25-29 ans	31
80	265	150	180	195	385	30-34 ans	32
110	350	265	215	255	455	35-39 ans	33
165	410	285	270	205	345	40-44 ans	34
135	340	240	260	200	255	45-49 ans	35
170	350	240	220	175	210	50-54 ans	36
105	245	170	180	140	150	55-59 ans	37
65	155	105	100	105	80	60-64 ans	38
50	130	75	75	95	55	65-69 ans	39
25	85	55	70	100	40	70-74 ans	40
25	75	60	50	80	35	75-79 ans	41
10	40	20	35	45	20	80-84 ans	42
10	35	20	20	55	10	85 ans et plus	43
2,420	**6,440**	**4,225**	**4,170**	**4,185**	**5,700**	**Population totale de 15 ans et plus selon l'état matrimonial légal**	44
660	1,745	1,095	1,065	1,280	1,500	Célibataire (jamais marié(e))	45
1,515	3,970	2,650	2,545	2,035	3,460	Légalement marié(e) (et non séparé(e))	46
55	170	110	120	200	220	Séparé(e), mais toujours légalement marié(e)	47
95	350	220	255	390	390	Divorcé(e)	48
90	215	155	195	280	130	Veuf ou veuve	49
						selon l'union libre	
2,330	6,095	4,000	3,875	3,795	5,195	Ne vivant pas en union libre	50
90	345	230	300	390	500	Vivant en union libre	51
3,040	**8,090**	**5,340**	**5,300**	**5,230**	**7,955**	**Population totale – Données-échantillon (20 %) (4) selon la langue maternelle**	52
3,030	8,060	5,315	5,290	5,215	7,895	Réponses uniques	53
2,595	6,530	4,675	4,850	4,795	7,470	Anglais	54
25	60	55	45	65	90	Français	55
405	1,470	585	400	360	330	Langues non officielles (5)	56
180	330	120	75	10	45	Italien	57
-	-	-	10	-	15	Chinois, n.d.a.	58
-	-	-	-	20	-	Cantonais	59
-	235	70	15	10	20	Portugais	60
-	185	-	20	10	10	Pendjabi	61
225	715	395	285	320	245	Autres langues (6)	62
15	35	25	10	15	60	Réponses multiples	63
-	-	10	-	-	30	Anglais et français	64
10	25	10	10	10	25	Anglais et langue non officielle	65
-	10	-	-	10	-	Français et langue non officielle	66
-	-	10	-	-	-	Anglais, français et langue non officielle	67

See reference material at the end of the publication. – Voir les documents de référence à la fin de la publication.

Table 1. Selected Characteristics for Census Tracts, 2001 Census – 100% Data and 20% Sample Data

No.	Characteristics	Toronto 0576.13 A	Toronto 0585.02	Toronto 0585.03	Toronto 0585.05 A	Toronto 0585.06 A	Toronto 0585.07 A
	POPULATION CHARACTERISTICS						
	by home language						
68	Single responses	3,490	3,805	4,165	4,520	7,910	4,570
69	English	2,780	3,615	4,035	4,430	7,470	4,520
70	French	10	10	-	-	-	-
71	Non-official languages (5)	705	175	130	95	435	55
72	Cantonese	-	-	-	-	-	-
73	Chinese, n.o.s.	-	-	-	10	35	-
74	Italian	170	130	45	10	185	20
75	Punjabi	420	-	40	-	35	-
76	Portuguese	10	30	10	35	-	-
77	Other languages (6)	105	15	35	40	175	35
78	Multiple responses	2,065	990	375	270	1,560	425
79	English and French	30	50	35	35	70	70
80	English and non-official language	2,015	930	320	225	1,450	325
81	French and non-official language	-	-	-	-	-	-
82	English, French and non-official language	20	10	20	-	35	30
	by knowledge of official languages						
83	English only	5,030	4,480	4,210	4,375	8,785	4,620
84	French only	-	-	-	-	-	-
85	English and French	340	265	285	400	525	360
86	Neither English nor French	180	50	45	15	150	20
	by knowledge of non-official languages (5) (7)						
87	Italian	1,545	1,220	475	495	2,345	365
88	Cantonese	10	15	-	-	30	-
89	Chinese, n.o.s.	-	-	-	15	40	10
90	Spanish	30	65	50	45	190	65
91	Portuguese	65	90	70	70	120	-
92	Punjabi	1,165	40	50	-	45	10
93	Tagalog (Pilipino)	50	10	10	-	20	10
	by first official language spoken						
94	English	5,315	4,675	4,460	4,720	9,190	4,890
95	French	25	50	35	50	115	75
96	English and French	50	20	10	-	10	10
97	Neither English nor French	160	50	45	15	150	20
98	Official language minority - (number) (8)	50	60	40	55	120	80
99	Official language minority - (percentage) (8)	0.9	1.3	0.9	1.1	1.3	1.6
	by ethnic origin (9)						
100	Canadian	530	1,345	1,525	1,165	2,115	1,380
101	English	405	765	1,515	1,610	1,810	1,605
102	Scottish	365	610	1,040	1,060	1,135	1,145
103	Irish	350	545	865	865	1,105	1,090
104	Chinese	20	30	-	25	140	15
105	Italian	2,155	2,050	970	1,075	4,030	855
106	East Indian	1,290	75	75	-	130	25
107	French	185	270	355	350	450	310
108	German	180	370	350	435	455	605
109	Portuguese	135	105	140	120	280	-
110	Polish	90	130	180	165	405	150
111	Jewish	15	-	20	15	10	15
112	Jamaican	95	20	25	-	95	25
113	Filipino	55	15	10	-	20	-
114	Ukrainian	85	160	110	125	295	220
	by Aboriginal identity						
115	Total Aboriginal identity population (10)	-	15	10	25	30	-
116	Total non-Aboriginal population	5,545	4,780	4,525	4,760	9,430	4,990
	by Aboriginal origin						
117	Total Aboriginal origins population (11)	-	35	45	110	90	40
118	Total non-Aboriginal population	5,540	4,755	4,495	4,680	9,375	4,950
	by Registered Indian status						
119	Registered Indian (12)	-	10	-	-	10	10
120	Not a Registered Indian	5,555	4,790	4,535	4,780	9,455	4,990

Tableau 1. Certaines caractéristiques des secteurs de recensement, recensement de 2001 – Données intégrales et données-échantillon (20 %)

Toronto 0585.08 A	Toronto 0586 A	Toronto 0587.01	Toronto 0587.02	Toronto 0590	Toronto 0591	Caractéristiques	N°
						CARACTÉRISTIQUES DE LA POPULATION	
						selon la langue parlée à la maison	
2,885	7,260	5,080	5,110	5,090	7,640	Réponses uniques	68
2,850	7,050	5,045	5,095	4,980	7,615	Anglais	69
-	-	-	-	30	-	Français	70
35	210	40	15	80	15	Langues non officielles (5)	71
-	-	-	-	-	-	Cantonais	72
-	-	-	-	-	-	Chinois, n.d.a.	73
30	35	-	15	-	-	Italien	74
-	60	-	-	15	10	Pendjabi	75
-	35	-	-	-	-	Portugais	76
-	75	30	-	65	10	Autres langues (6)	77
155	835	265	190	140	315	Réponses multiples	78
10	75	50	30	30	170	Anglais et français	79
145	720	185	165	110	145	Anglais et langue non officielle	80
-	15	-	-	-	-	Français et langue non officielle	81
-	25	25	-	-	-	Anglais, français et langue non officielle	82
						selon la connaissance des langues officielles	
2,765	7,525	4,925	4,805	5,035	7,420	Anglais seulement	83
-	-	-	-	10	-	Français seulement	84
270	535	415	500	185	535	Anglais et français	85
-	35	10	-	-	-	Ni l'anglais ni le français	86
						selon la connaissance des langues non officielles (5) (7)	
230	535	155	130	25	85	Italien	87
-	-	-	-	10	-	Cantonais	88
-	-	-	-	-	15	Chinois, n.d.a.	89
15	70	30	80	20	40	Espagnol	90
20	265	80	35	10	35	Portugais	91
-	225	-	25	15	10	Pendjabi	92
-	-	-	10	-	10	Tagalog (pilipino)	93
						selon la première langue officielle parlée	
3,005	7,980	5,280	5,260	5,170	7,845	Anglais	94
30	60	55	45	55	75	Français	95
-	15	-	-	10	25	Anglais et français	96
10	35	-	-	-	-	Ni l'anglais ni le français	97
25	70	60	45	60	90	Minorité de langue officielle - (nombre) (8)	98
0.8	0.9	1.1	0.8	1.1	1.1	Minorité de langue officielle - (pourcentage) (8)	99
						selon l'origine ethnique (9)	
930	2,360	1,850	2,050	2,280	3,440	Canadien	100
1,210	2,425	1,875	1,975	1,930	2,795	Anglais	101
785	1,545	1,150	1,385	1,305	2,175	Écossais	102
620	1,370	1,180	1,355	1,220	1,775	Irlandais	103
20	20	15	10	25	35	Chinois	104
410	1,060	435	320	150	485	Italien	105
10	280	-	20	35	45	Indien de l'Inde	106
240	355	390	440	590	820	Français	107
385	865	590	615	645	755	Allemand	108
10	500	125	30	30	115	Portugais	109
70	365	160	160	155	200	Polonais	110
-	15	40	45	35	15	Juif	111
20	155	15	25	65	80	Jamaïquain	112
-	-	-	-	-	15	Philippin	113
75	300	140	190	140	250	Ukrainien	114
						selon l'identité autochtone	
-	30	15	10	45	65	Total de la population ayant une identité autochtone (10)	115
3,040	8,065	5,325	5,295	5,185	7,890	Total de la population non autochtone	116
						selon l'origine autochtone	
-	120	35	50	155	190	Total de la population ayant une origine autochtone (11)	117
3,035	7,970	5,305	5,250	5,075	7,760	Total de la population non autochtone	118
						selon le statut d'Indien inscrit	
-	15	15	-	15	35	Oui, Indien inscrit (12)	119
3,040	8,080	5,330	5,300	5,210	7,920	Non, pas un Indien inscrit	120

Table 1. Selected Characteristics for Census Tracts, 2001 Census – 100% Data and 20% Sample Data

No.	Characteristics	Toronto 0576.13 A	Toronto 0585.02	Toronto 0585.03	Toronto 0585.05 A	Toronto 0585.06 A	Toronto 0585.07 A
	POPULATION CHARACTERISTICS						
	by visible minority groups						
121	Total visible minority population	2,040	210	225	110	760	110
122	Chinese	15	30	10	15	115	10
123	South Asian	1,545	70	115	-	145	20
124	Black	195	25	45	15	185	40
125	Filipino	60	10	-	-	20	-
126	Latin American	10	55	-	25	50	10
127	Southeast Asian	-	-	-	-	-	-
128	Arab	30	-	10	-	60	-
129	West Asian	25	-	15	-	100	10
130	Korean	30	-	-	15	30	-
131	Japanese	-	-	-	-	10	-
132	Visible minority, n.i.e. (13)	135	10	35	25	35	10
133	Multiple visible minorities (14)	-	-	-	-	-	15
	by citizenship						
134	Canadian citizenship (15)	5,155	4,530	4,365	4,680	8,970	4,815
135	Citizenship other than Canadian	405	260	175	110	490	180
	by place of birth of respondent						
136	Non-immigrant population	3,060	3,600	3,700	3,945	7,290	4,060
137	Born in province of residence	2,895	3,365	3,275	3,495	6,780	3,560
138	Immigrant population (16)	2,490	1,170	835	845	2,145	925
139	United States	60	-	20	35	35	25
140	Central and South America	130	35	60	60	150	10
141	Caribbean and Bermuda	95	30	10	25	75	20
142	United Kingdom	45	80	220	270	250	320
143	Other Europe (17)	1,200	970	455	400	1,335	485
144	Africa	75	-	-	10	10	15
145	Asia and the Middle East	885	50	65	55	290	35
146	Oceania and other (18)	-	-	-	-	10	10
147	Non-permanent residents (19)	-	20	-	-	35	15
148	**Total immigrant population**	**2,490**	**1,170**	**835**	**845**	**2,140**	**925**
	by period of immigration						
149	Before 1961	530	425	260	180	440	305
150	1961-1970	525	450	220	180	670	305
151	1971-1980	495	210	115	290	345	155
152	1981-1990	490	55	110	80	305	100
153	1991-2001 (20)	450	35	135	115	375	65
154	1991-1995	250	20	65	95	280	45
155	1996-2001 (20)	200	10	65	20	100	20
	by age at immigration						
156	0-4 years	210	160	85	110	280	75
157	5-19 years	935	475	315	315	860	320
158	20 years and over	1,350	540	435	420	1,000	530
159	**Total population**	**5,550**	**4,795**	**4,540**	**4,790**	**9,465**	**4,995**
	by religion						
160	Catholic (21)	2,825	2,850	1,825	1,920	6,140	1,840
161	Protestant	620	1,185	1,775	1,940	1,910	2,110
162	Christian Orthodox	95	85	75	120	170	50
163	Christian, n.i.e. (22)	170	10	85	105	45	65
164	Muslim	90	35	30	20	60	15
165	Jewish	10	-	10	35	15	10
166	Buddhist	-	15	-	-	10	-
167	Hindu	200	10	20	10	85	-
168	Sikh	1,235	35	40	-	35	10
169	Eastern religions (23)	35	-	-	-	15	10
170	Other religions (24)	10	-	-	-	-	-
171	No religious affiliation (25)	265	570	675	635	985	885
172	**Total population 15 years and over**	**4,430**	**3,710**	**3,480**	**3,625**	**6,780**	**3,980**
	by generation status						
173	1st generation (26)	2,450	1,195	810	845	2,145	955
174	2nd generation (27)	1,500	1,340	1,005	1,105	2,560	1,185
175	3rd generation and over (28)	480	1,175	1,665	1,670	2,080	1,840
176	**Total population 1 year and over (29)**	**5,495**	**4,735**	**4,485**	**4,755**	**9,210**	**4,950**
	by place of residence 1 year ago (mobility)						
177	Non-movers	3,050	4,115	3,770	3,710	8,010	4,575
178	Movers	2,450	625	710	1,045	1,205	370
179	Non-migrants	1,290	230	300	345	345	110
180	Migrants	1,155	390	410	705	855	260
181	Internal migrants	1,130	370	370	700	820	245
182	Intraprovincial migrants	1,120	370	315	700	815	225
183	Interprovincial migrants	10	-	50	-	-	20
184	External migrants	25	15	45	-	40	20

Tableau 1. Certaines caractéristiques des secteurs de recensement, recensement de 2001 – Données intégrales et données-échantillon (20 %)

Toronto 0585.08 A	Toronto 0586 A	Toronto 0587.01	Toronto 0587.02	Toronto 0590	Toronto 0591	Caractéristiques	N°
						CARACTÉRISTIQUES DE LA POPULATION	
						selon les groupes de minorités visibles	
65	755	130	140	165	230	Total de la population des minorités visibles	121
-	10	15	15	20	30	Chinois	122
15	290	10	30	30	25	Sud-Asiatique	123
35	305	30	80	75	95	Noir	124
-	-	-	-	10	15	Philippin	125
-	10	-	10	-	10	Latino-Américain	126
-	20	-	-	-	-	Asiatique du Sud-Est	127
-	10	10	-	25	-	Arabe	128
-	45	-	-	-	-	Asiatique occidental	129
-	-	-	-	-	-	Coréen	130
10	35	40	10	10	15	Japonais	131
-	-	20	-	-	15	Minorité visible, n.i.a. (13)	132
-	25	-	-	10	15	Minorités visibles multiples (14)	133
						selon la citoyenneté	
2,950	7,760	5,205	5,140	5,070	7,735	Citoyenneté canadienne (15)	134
90	340	140	160	160	220	Citoyenneté autre que canadienne	135
						selon le lieu de naissance du répondant	
2,515	6,295	4,470	4,490	4,615	7,060	Population non immigrante	136
2,215	5,700	3,980	3,985	4,055	6,120	Née dans la province de résidence	137
525	1,770	875	810	615	885	Population immigrante (16)	138
25	60	75	95	10	30	États-Unis	139
10	50	20	25	10	30	Amérique centrale et du Sud	140
-	205	-	30	20	40	Caraïbes et Bermudes	141
225	380	295	310	300	420	Royaume-Uni	142
245	805	420	295	230	320	Autre Europe (17)	143
10	65	15	20	30	-	Afrique	144
-	205	20	20	20	40	Asie et Moyen-Orient	145
-	-	20	-	-	-	Océanie et autre (18)	146
-	35	-	-	-	10	Résidents non permanents (19)	147
525	**1,770**	**875**	**810**	**615**	**890**	**Population immigrante totale**	148
						selon la période d'immigration	
185	355	320	280	220	190	Avant 1961	149
210	460	185	205	175	275	1961-1970	150
90	590	210	195	95	195	1971-1980	151
35	230	120	90	45	135	1981-1990	152
15	130	35	40	75	90	1991-2001 (20)	153
10	65	-	25	40	60	1991-1995	154
10	65	40	15	35	25	1996-2001 (20)	155
						selon l'âge à l'immigration	
55	250	120	110	80	190	0-4 ans	156
195	565	305	280	210	320	5-19 ans	157
270	955	445	425	330	380	20 ans et plus	158
3,040	**8,090**	**5,340**	**5,300**	**5,230**	**7,955**	**Population totale**	159
						selon la religion	
1,005	2,790	1,665	1,255	1,185	1,955	Catholique (21)	160
1,465	3,675	2,480	2,490	2,650	4,010	Protestante	161
-	65	25	25	35	15	Orthodoxe chrétienne	162
35	170	70	180	140	375	Chrétiennes, n.i.a. (22)	163
-	-	-	-	-	10	Musulmane	164
10	-	10	30	35	-	Juive	165
-	-	10	10	-	-	Bouddhiste	166
10	40	10	-	15	-	Hindoue	167
-	235	-	20	-	15	Sikh	168
-	50	-	-	45	10	Religions orientales (23)	169
-	25	-	20	10	-	Autres religions (24)	170
520	1,040	1,070	1,275	1,125	1,570	Aucune appartenance religieuse (25)	171
2,425	**6,430**	**4,160**	**4,170**	**4,140**	**5,680**	**Population totale de 15 ans et plus**	172
						selon le statut des générations	
525	1,760	870	845	605	875	1re génération (26)	173
690	1,685	1,125	940	700	1,250	2e génération (27)	174
1,210	2,985	2,170	2,385	2,840	3,550	3e génération et plus (28)	175
3,020	**7,955**	**5,275**	**5,250**	**5,180**	**7,780**	**Population totale de 1 an et plus (29)**	176
						selon le lieu de résidence 1 an auparavant (mobilité)	
2,825	7,100	4,945	5,020	4,495	6,120	Personnes n'ayant pas déménagé	177
195	855	330	230	685	1,660	Personnes ayant déménagé	178
90	190	80	70	250	600	Non-migrants	179
110	665	255	160	435	1,060	Migrants	180
95	610	245	155	435	1,035	Migrants internes	181
65	605	215	145	420	985	Migrants infraprovinciaux	182
40	-	25	-	15	50	Migrants interprovinciaux	183
10	55	10	10	-	25	Migrants externes	184

Table 1. Selected Characteristics for Census Tracts, 2001 Census – 100% Data and 20% Sample Data

No.	Characteristics	Toronto 0576.13 A	Toronto 0585.02	Toronto 0585.03	Toronto 0585.05 A	Toronto 0585.06 A	Toronto 0585.07 A
	POPULATION CHARACTERISTICS						
185	**Total population 5 years and over (30)**	**5,180**	**4,420**	**4,215**	**4,465**	**8,295**	**4,785**
	by place of residence 5 years ago (mobility)						
186	Non-movers	2,230	2,745	2,305	2,690	2,955	3,200
187	Movers	2,945	1,675	1,905	1,775	5,345	1,580
188	Non-migrants	1,560	525	690	590	1,570	375
189	Migrants	1,390	1,145	1,215	1,190	3,770	1,205
190	Internal migrants	1,210	1,115	1,130	1,115	3,650	1,175
191	Intraprovincial migrants	1,150	1,065	1,015	1,065	3,595	1,100
192	Interprovincial migrants	60	55	115	50	60	80
193	External migrants	185	25	85	75	115	30
194	**Total population 15 to 24 years**	**820**	**590**	**535**	**685**	**820**	**660**
	by school attendance						
195	Not attending school	290	305	170	225	305	170
196	Attending school full time	485	275	335	405	495	475
197	Attending school part time	40	10	25	50	25	15
198	**Total population 15 years and over**	**4,430**	**3,705**	**3,480**	**3,620**	**6,780**	**3,980**
	by highest level of schooling						
199	Less than grade 9 (31)	695	440	195	90	490	145
200	Grades 9-13 without high school graduation certificate	655	710	840	635	1,295	745
201	Grades 9-13 with high school graduation certificate	685	640	485	505	1,105	620
202	Some postsecondary without degree, certificate or diploma (32)	540	455	410	515	735	470
203	Trades certificate or diploma (33)	450	425	390	440	750	390
204	College certificate or diploma (34)	560	620	720	725	1,235	740
205	University certificate below bachelor's degree	95	50	40	80	130	115
206	University with bachelor's degree or higher	755	365	395	635	1,040	755
	by combinations of unpaid work						
207	Males 15 years ahd over	2,285	1,830	1,675	1,760	3,355	2,005
208	Reported unpaid work (35)	1,955	1,645	1,500	1,590	3,020	1,770
209	Housework and child care and care or assistance to seniors	165	105	115	115	240	95
210	Housework and child care only	540	525	520	615	1,255	560
211	Housework and care or assistance to seniors only	140	95	95	110	130	130
212	Child care and care or assistance to seniors only	-	-	-	-	-	-
213	Housework only	1,030	890	745	725	1,375	975
214	Child care only	55	-	10	25	25	10
215	Care or assistance to seniors only	20	10	15	-	-	10
216	Females 15 years and over	2,140	1,870	1,810	1,860	3,425	1,980
217	Reported unpaid work (35)	1,950	1,760	1,660	1,730	3,240	1,855
218	Housework and child care and care or assistance to seniors	250	205	200	235	330	250
219	Housework and child care only	725	625	595	655	1,455	570
220	Housework and care or assistance to seniors only	195	70	120	115	200	160
221	Child care and care or assistance to seniors only	-	-	-	-	-	-
222	Housework only	745	845	720	730	1,235	870
223	Child care only	25	15	15	-	20	-
224	Care or assistance to seniors only	15	-	15	-	-	-
	by labour force activity						
225	Males 15 years and over	2,290	1,835	1,670	1,765	3,355	2,005
226	In the labour force	1,835	1,485	1,345	1,575	2,845	1,630
227	Employed	1,775	1,410	1,310	1,520	2,775	1,555
228	Unemployed	55	70	35	50	70	75
229	Not in the labour force	450	350	325	185	510	370
230	Participation rate	80.1	80.9	80.5	89.2	84.8	81.3
231	Employment rate	77.5	76.8	78.4	86.1	82.7	77.6
232	Unemployment rate	3.0	4.7	2.6	3.2	2.5	4.6
233	Females 15 years and over	2,140	1,875	1,805	1,860	3,425	1,975
234	In the labour force	1,400	1,325	1,220	1,460	2,545	1,385
235	Employed	1,375	1,290	1,190	1,400	2,450	1,340
236	Unemployed	30	35	30	60	95	45
237	Not in the labour force	740	550	590	400	880	590
238	Participation rate	65.4	70.7	67.6	78.5	74.3	70.1
239	Employment rate	64.3	68.8	65.9	75.3	71.5	67.8
240	Unemployment rate	2.1	2.6	2.5	4.1	3.7	3.2

Tableau 1. Certaines caractéristiques des secteurs de recensement, recensement de 2001 – Données intégrales et données-échantillon (20 %)

Toronto 0585.08 A	Toronto 0586 A	Toronto 0587.01	Toronto 0587.02	Toronto 0590	Toronto 0591	Caractéristiques	N°
						CARACTÉRISTIQUES DE LA POPULATION	
2,900	**7,610**	**5,050**	**4,985**	**4,875**	**7,185**	**Population totale de 5 ans et plus (30)**	185
						selon le lieu de résidence 5 ans auparavant (mobilité)	
1,950	4,340	3,435	3,075	2,715	2,815	Personnes n'ayant pas déménagé	186
955	3,270	1,610	1,915	2,160	4,375	Personnes ayant déménagé	187
375	775	360	515	955	1,685	Non-migrants	188
580	2,495	1,255	1,405	1,205	2,690	Migrants	189
565	2,380	1,240	1,360	1,140	2,635	Migrants internes	190
505	2,325	1,050	1,300	995	2,450	Migrants infraprovinciaux	191
60	55	185	60	140	185	Migrants interprovinciaux	192
15	110	15	45	60	50	Migrants externes	193
460	**1,105**	**665**	**645**	**665**	**980**	**Population totale de 15 à 24 ans**	194
						selon la fréquentation scolaire	
135	340	240	190	380	455	Ne fréquentant pas l'école	195
305	705	415	435	255	475	Fréquentant l'école à plein temps	196
20	60	15	20	35	45	Fréquentant l'école à temps partiel	197
2,425	**6,425**	**4,160**	**4,165**	**4,145**	**5,680**	**Population totale de 15 ans et plus**	198
						selon le plus haut niveau de scolarité atteint	
95	365	120	120	285	150	Niveau inférieur à la 9e année (31)	199
445	1,475	895	895	1,260	1,380	De la 9e à la 13e année sans certificat d'études secondaires	200
305	1,040	690	615	695	1,180	De la 9e à la 13e année avec certificat d'études secondaires	201
300	785	515	465	400	730	Études postsecondaires partielles sans grade, certificat ou diplôme (32)	202
185	635	415	415	450	605	Certificat ou diplôme d'une école de métiers (33)	203
490	1,110	760	785	700	1,105	Certificat ou diplôme collégial (34)	204
55	135	115	70	70	20	Certificat universitaire inférieur au baccalauréat.....	205
560	890	650	795	285	510	Études universitaires avec baccalauréat ou diplôme supérieur	206
						selon les combinaisons de travail non rémunéré	
1,235	3,240	2,100	2,080	1,975	2,830	Hommes de 15 ans et plus	207
1,100	3,000	1,975	1,905	1,780	2,625	Travail non rémunéré déclaré (35)	208
105	240	185	175	135	215	Travaux ménagers et soins aux enfants et soins ou aide aux personnes âgées	209
340	815	610	570	495	1,155	Travaux ménagers et soins aux enfants seulement	210
95	210	90	125	170	100	Travaux ménagers et soins ou aide aux personnes âgées seulement	211
10	-	-	-	10	10	Soins aux enfants et soins ou aide aux personnes âgées seulement	212
540	1,700	1,075	1,020	960	1,110	Travaux ménagers seulement	213
10	25	10	10	10	25	Soins aux enfants seulement	214
10	10	10	10	10	15	Soins ou aide aux personnes âgées seulement	215
1,190	3,185	2,060	2,090	2,170	2,850	Femmes de 15 ans et plus	216
1,120	3,005	1,990	1,950	1,995	2,745	Travail non rémunéré déclaré (35)	217
220	355	240	250	280	360	Travaux ménagers et soins aux enfants et soins ou aide aux personnes âgées	218
320	1,010	665	665	645	1,285	Travaux ménagers et soins aux enfants seulement	219
120	255	130	160	200	155	Travaux ménagers et soins ou aide aux personnes âgées seulement	220
-	-	-	-	-	-	Soins aux enfants et soins ou aide aux personnes âgées seulement	221
445	1,370	950	865	855	925	Travaux ménagers seulement	222
-	-	-	10	-	15	Soins aux enfants seulement	223
-	-	-	-	-	-	Soins ou aide aux personnes âgées seulement	224
						selon l'activité	
1,235	3,240	2,095	2,080	1,975	2,825	Hommes de 15 ans et plus	225
1,025	2,660	1,670	1,740	1,510	2,470	Population active	226
1,000	2,605	1,610	1,705	1,440	2,430	Personnes occupées	227
25	60	65	40	65	45	Chômeurs	228
210	580	430	335	465	355	Inactifs	229
83.0	82.1	79.7	83.7	76.5	87.4	Taux d'activité	230
81.0	80.4	76.8	82.0	72.9	86.0	Taux d'emploi	231
2.4	2.3	3.9	2.3	4.3	1.8	Taux de chômage	232
1,195	3,185	2,060	2,090	2,165	2,850	Femmes de 15 ans et plus	233
835	2,270	1,385	1,405	1,325	2,115	Population active	234
775	2,195	1,320	1,360	1,205	2,020	Personnes occupées	235
65	70	60	35	120	95	Chômeuses	236
360	915	680	690	845	735	Inactives	237
69.9	71.3	67.2	67.2	61.2	74.2	Taux d'activité	238
64.9	68.9	64.1	65.1	55.7	70.9	Taux d'emploi	239
7.8	3.1	4.3	2.5	9.1	4.5	Taux de chômage	240

Table 1. Selected Characteristics for Census Tracts, 2001 Census – 100% Data and 20% Sample Data

No.	Characteristics	Toronto 0576.13 A	Toronto 0585.02	Toronto 0585.03	Toronto 0585.05 A	Toronto 0585.06 A	Toronto 0585.07 A
	POPULATION CHARACTERISTICS						
	by labour force activity – concluded						
241	Both sexes - Participation rate	73.0	75.8	73.6	83.7	79.4	75.9
242	15-24 years	68.9	73.7	72.0	84.7	69.1	75.0
243	25 years and over	74.0	76.1	74.0	83.6	80.8	75.9
244	Both sexes - Employment rate	71.1	73.0	72.0	80.7	77.1	72.7
245	15-24 years	64.6	67.2	68.2	77.5	67.3	65.9
246	25 years and over	72.7	73.8	72.7	81.3	78.4	74.1
247	Both sexes - Unemployment rate	2.6	3.6	2.3	3.8	3.1	4.1
248	15-24 years	7.1	8.0	3.9	6.9	3.5	12.2
249	25 years and over	1.7	3.0	1.8	2.9	3.1	2.8
250	**Total labour force 15 years and over**	**3,235**	**2,805**	**2,565**	**3,035**	**5,390**	**3,015**
	by industry based on the 1997 NAICS						
251	Industry - Not applicable (36)	-	30	10	15	15	-
252	All industries (37)	3,235	2,780	2,555	3,020	5,375	3,020
253	11 Agriculture, forestry, fishing and hunting	45	30	20	45	30	90
254	21 Mining and oil and gas extraction	-	10	-	-	-	30
255	22 Utilities	30	45	40	10	15	25
256	23 Construction	515	310	250	265	600	215
257	31-33 Manufacturing	590	555	585	455	995	500
258	41 Wholesale trade	215	205	190	255	490	275
259	44-45 Retail trade	395	340	250	360	665	240
260	48-49 Transportation and warehousing	285	230	155	160	350	205
261	51 Information and cultural industries	85	45	55	60	80	45
262	52 Finance and insurance	100	115	90	120	310	105
263	53 Real estate and rental and leasing	70	55	35	50	130	50
264	54 Professional, scientific and technical services	95	155	150	280	370	235
265	55 Management of companies and enterprises	-	10	-	-	-	-
266	56 Administrative and support, waste management and remediation services	120	155	135	120	190	130
267	61 Educational services	145	110	125	245	280	150
268	62 Health care and social assistance	165	100	135	205	290	215
269	71 Arts, entertainment and recreation	55	50	35	70	75	115
270	72 Accommodation and food services	115	110	165	175	135	165
271	81 Other services (except public administration)	115	105	60	60	190	115
272	91 Public administration	105	60	100	95	175	110
	by class of worker						
273	Class of worker - Not applicable (36)	-	30	10	15	15	-
274	All classes of worker (37)	3,235	2,785	2,555	3,020	5,375	3,015
275	Paid workers	2,965	2,500	2,380	2,870	4,915	2,640
276	Employees	2,635	2,340	2,265	2,750	4,690	2,410
277	Self-employed (incorporated)	335	155	115	125	225	230
278	Self-employed (unincorporated)	245	270	180	150	450	370
279	Unpaid family workers	20	-	-	-	15	-
	by occupation based on the 2001 NOC-S						
280	Male labour force 15 years and over	1,835	1,485	1,345	1,575	2,845	1,635
281	Occupation - Not applicable (36)	-	20	10	-	10	-
282	All occupations (37)	1,835	1,465	1,335	1,575	2,840	1,635
283	A Management occupations	345	275	230	350	515	460
284	B Business, finance and administration occupations	135	150	115	185	270	125
285	C Natural and applied sciences and related occupations	140	110	110	125	230	110
286	D Health occupations	55	-	10	15	10	35
287	E Occupations in social science, education, government service and religion	40	25	25	55	100	100
288	F Occupations in art, culture, recreation and sport	40	30	40	10	60	40
289	G Sales and service occupations	305	195	245	235	515	235
290	H Trades, transport and equipment operators and related occupations	575	540	405	490	875	315
291	I Occupations unique to primary industry	45	50	30	45	50	100
292	J Occupations unique to processing, manufacturing and utilities	160	85	115	60	220	100
293	Female labour force 15 years and over	1,400	1,325	1,220	1,460	2,540	1,390
294	Occupation - Not applicable (36)	-	10	-	15	10	-
295	All occupations (37)	1,400	1,320	1,220	1,450	2,530	1,385
296	A Management occupations	165	210	135	195	245	205
297	B Business, finance and administration occupations	530	525	420	450	1,075	405
298	C Natural and applied sciences and related occupations	35	10	35	65	80	40
299	D Health occupations	85	65	75	105	130	95

Tableau 1. Certaines caractéristiques des secteurs de recensement, recensement de 2001 – Données intégrales et données-échantillon (20 %)

Toronto 0585.08 A	Toronto 0586 A	Toronto 0587.01	Toronto 0587.02	Toronto 0590	Toronto 0591	Caractéristiques	N°
						CARACTÉRISTIQUES DE LA POPULATION	
						selon l'activité – fin	
76.7	76.7	73.4	75.4	68.5	80.9	Les deux sexes - Taux d'activité	241
76.1	69.2	63.4	72.1	77.4	78.6	15-24 ans	242
76.8	78.3	75.2	76.1	66.8	81.3	25 ans et plus	243
73.2	74.7	70.4	73.7	63.9	78.4	Les deux sexes - Taux d'emploi	244
65.2	64.5	58.6	66.2	65.4	72.4	15-24 ans	245
74.8	76.7	72.8	75.1	63.6	79.6	25 ans et plus	246
4.6	2.7	3.9	2.4	6.5	3.1	Les deux sexes - Taux de chômage	247
12.9	7.2	10.5	7.5	15.5	7.8	15-24 ans	248
2.6	1.8	3.0	1.3	4.7	2.0	25 ans et plus	249
1,860	**4,930**	**3,055**	**3,145**	**2,835**	**4,590**	**Population active totale de 15 ans et plus**	250
						selon l'industrie basée sur le SCIAN de 1997	
15	25	20	10	55	25	Industrie - Sans objet (36)	251
1,845	4,910	3,030	3,140	2,780	4,560	Toutes les industries (37)	252
55	345	55	115	35	10	11 Agriculture, foresterie, pêche et chasse	253
-	-	-	-	10	10	21 Extraction minière et extraction de pétrole et de gaz	254
-	35	25	10	10	30	22 Services publics	255
135	360	200	245	160	225	23 Construction	256
330	760	560	495	675	1,060	31-33 Fabrication	257
165	345	255	210	215	365	41 Commerce de gros	258
175	420	280	300	290	500	44-45 Commerce de détail	259
130	345	250	220	180	320	48-49 Transport et entreposage	260
25	75	80	40	70	80	51 Industrie de l'information et industrie culturelle	261
50	200	85	140	50	135	52 Finance et assurances	262
40	105	40	95	55	30	53 Services immobiliers et services de location et de location à bail	263
160	365	250	295	90	215	54 Services professionnels, scientifiques et techniques	264
-	-	-	10	-	10	55 Gestion de sociétés et d'entreprises	265
125	305	95	170	115	230	56 Services administratifs, services de soutien, services de gestion des déchets et services d'assainissement	266
125	325	250	235	145	185	61 Services d'enseignement	267
115	215	155	235	180	395	62 Soins de santé et assistance sociale	268
65	130	65	55	90	50	71 Arts, spectacles et loisirs	269
85	130	135	100	230	330	72 Hébergement et services de restauration	270
35	205	115	80	105	175	81 Autres services, sauf les administrations publiques	271
25	240	150	100	90	225	91 Administrations publiques	272
						selon la catégorie de travailleurs	
15	25	20	-	50	25	Catégorie de travailleurs - Sans objet (36)	273
1,845	4,905	3,035	3,135	2,785	4,560	Toutes les catégories de travailleurs (37)	274
1,640	4,330	2,720	2,715	2,610	4,275	Travailleurs rémunérés	275
1,490	3,990	2,525	2,445	2,550	4,175	Employés	276
150	330	195	270	65	100	Travailleurs autonomes (entreprise constituée en société)	277
200	545	310	405	170	275	Travailleurs autonomes (entreprise non constituée en société)	278
-	35	-	15	-	15	Travailleurs familiaux non rémunérés	279
						selon la profession basée sur la CNP-S de 2001	
1,025	2,660	1,670	1,740	1,510	2,475	Hommes actifs de 15 ans et plus	280
-	15	10	-	10	10	Profession - Sans objet (36)	281
1,020	2,645	1,660	1,735	1,505	2,465	Toutes les professions (37)	282
315	520	440	375	145	310	A Gestion	283
100	235	100	160	90	240	B Affaires, finance et administration	284
110	205	135	190	100	210	C Sciences naturelles et appliquées et professions apparentées	285
-	10	10	35	-	20	D Secteur de la santé	286
45	70	115	65	55	55	E Sciences sociales, enseignement, administration publique et religion	287
20	70	40	20	25	-	F Arts, culture, sports et loisirs	288
130	360	265	240	215	375	G Ventes et services	289
165	765	390	385	570	805	H Métiers, transport et machinerie	290
95	315	70	160	30	40	I Professions propres au secteur primaire	291
25	95	95	105	265	405	J Transformation, fabrication et services d'utilité publique	292
840	2,265	1,380	1,400	1,325	2,110	Femmes actives de 15 ans et plus	293
-	10	10	-	45	20	Profession - Sans objet (36)	294
825	2,265	1,370	1,400	1,280	2,095	Toutes les professions (37)	295
80	280	225	145	95	190	A Gestion	296
310	735	470	365	305	585	B Affaires, finance et administration	297
15	40	35	35	15	50	C Sciences naturelles et appliquées et professions apparentées	298
40	85	45	90	75	205	D Secteur de la santé	299

Table 1. Selected Characteristics for Census Tracts, 2001 Census – 100% Data and 20% Sample Data

No.	Characteristics	Toronto 0576.13 A	Toronto 0585.02	Toronto 0585.03	Toronto 0585.05 A	Toronto 0585.06 A	Toronto 0585.07 A
	POPULATION CHARACTERISTICS						
	by occupation based on the 2001 NOC-S – concluded						
300	E Occupations in social science, education, government service and religion	130	100	100	220	205	110
301	F Occupations in art, culture, recreation and sport	35	25	40	25	45	75
302	G Sales and service occupations	260	275	290	350	550	370
303	H Trades, transport and equipment operators and related occupations	25	40	35	15	90	15
304	I Occupations unique to primary industry	-	25	10	10	15	35
305	J Occupations unique to processing, manufacturing and utilities	135	50	85	10	100	45
306	**Total employed labour force 15 years and over**	**3,150**	**2,705**	**2,505**	**2,920**	**5,225**	**2,895**
	by place of work						
307	Males	1,780	1,415	1,310	1,520	2,775	1,555
308	Usual place of work	1,330	1,075	1,025	1,275	2,125	1,145
309	At home	100	100	70	65	110	220
310	Outside Canada	-	-	10	10	10	15
311	No fixed workplace address	350	235	210	170	535	180
312	Females	1,370	1,295	1,195	1,405	2,445	1,340
313	Usual place of work	1,235	1,130	1,075	1,260	2,235	1,115
314	At home	100	90	85	100	145	175
315	Outside Canada	10	-	-	-	-	-
316	No fixed workplace address	25	70	25	40	75	45
317	**Total employed labour force 15 years and over with usual place of work or no fixed workplace address**	**2,940**	**2,515**	**2,340**	**2,740**	**4,970**	**2,485**
	by mode of transportation						
318	Males	1,680	1,310	1,235	1,445	2,660	1,320
319	Car, truck, van, as driver	1,515	1,240	1,100	1,370	2,440	1,220
320	Car, truck, van, as passenger	95	30	65	65	150	50
321	Public transit	35	-	25	-	-	10
322	Walked	25	20	45	-	45	30
323	Other method	10	25	-	-	30	15
324	Females	1,265	1,205	1,105	1,295	2,305	1,165
325	Car, truck, van, as driver	1,090	1,015	890	1,150	2,010	985
326	Car, truck, van, as passenger	80	115	130	70	145	130
327	Public transit	85	25	10	15	45	-
328	Walked	10	25	55	50	95	40
329	Other method	10	25	15	15	10	15
330	**Total population 15 years and over who worked since January 1, 2000**	**3,555**	**2,980**	**2,745**	**3,225**	**5,840**	**3,280**
	by language used at work						
331	Single responses	2,980	2,725	2,600	3,090	5,300	3,115
332	English	2,940	2,715	2,595	3,085	5,280	3,105
333	French	-	-	-	-	-	-
334	Non-official languages (5)	40	10	10	-	25	-
335	Chinese, n.o.s.	-	-	-	-	-	-
336	Cantonese	-	-	-	-	-	-
337	Other languages (6)	40	10	10	-	15	-
338	Multiple responses	580	255	145	140	540	170
339	English and French	40	65	10	30	100	60
340	English and non-official language	530	190	115	110	435	100
341	French and non-official language	-	-	-	-	-	-
342	English, French and non-official language	15	-	20	-	10	15
	DWELLING AND HOUSEHOLD CHARACTERISTICS						
343	**Total number of occupied private dwellings**	**1,425**	**1,480**	**1,560**	**1,465**	**2,965**	**1,630**
	by tenure						
344	Owned	1,335	1,350	1,200	1,390	2,830	1,495
345	Rented	90	125	360	70	140	135
346	Band housing	-	-	-	-	-	-
	by structural type of dwelling						
347	Single-detached house	1,345	1,190	1,175	1,355	2,345	1,540
348	Semi-detached house	70	95	105	60	225	-
349	Row house	-	165	70	25	365	25
350	Apartment, detached duplex	15	-	25	10	20	25
351	Apartment, building that has five or more storeys	-	-	-	-	-	-
352	Apartment, building that has fewer than five storeys (38)	-	25	180	15	15	40
353	Other single-attached house	-	-	-	-	-	-
354	Movable dwelling (39)	-	-	-	-	-	-

Tableau 1. Certaines caractéristiques des secteurs de recensement, recensement de 2001 – Données intégrales et données-échantillon (20 %)

Toronto 0585.08 A	Toronto 0586 A	Toronto 0587.01	Toronto 0587.02	Toronto 0590	Toronto 0591	Caractéristiques	N°
						CARACTÉRISTIQUES DE LA POPULATION	
						selon la profession basée sur la CNP-S de 2001 - fin	
						E Sciences sociales, enseignement,	
135	245	200	220	100	190	administration publique et religion	300
20	90	60	85	70	50	F Arts, culture, sports et loisirs	301
200	485	245	325	460	640	G Ventes et services	302
-	90	20	45	60	45	H Métiers, transport et machinerie	303
20	130	30	50	10	15	I Professions propres au secteur primaire	304
						J Transformation, fabrication et	
10	85	30	35	100	120	services d'utilité publique	305
1,775	**4,795**	**2,930**	**3,070**	**2,650**	**4,450**	**Population active occupée totale de 15 ans et plus**	306
						selon le lieu de travail	
1,000	2,605	1,610	1,710	1,445	2,425	Hommes	307
700	1,900	1,295	1,265	1,190	2,045	Lieu habituel de travail	308
165	320	145	185	45	90	À domicile	309
10	15	10	-	-	-	En dehors du Canada	310
120	365	165	255	205	285	Sans adresse de travail fixe	311
775	2,200	1,325	1,365	1,205	2,020	Femmes	312
625	1,770	1,090	1,080	1,070	1,800	Lieu habituel de travail	313
115	325	160	205	90	130	À domicile	314
10	10	10	-	10	-	En dehors du Canada	315
40	100	65	75	35	95	Sans adresse de travail fixe	316
						Population active occupée totale de 15 ans et plus ayant un lieu habituel de travail ou	
1,480	**4,135**	**2,615**	**2,680**	**2,500**	**4,230**	**sans adresse de travail fixe**	317
						selon le mode de transport	
820	2,265	1,460	1,525	1,395	2,335	Hommes	318
						Automobile, camion ou fourgonnette, en tant	
755	2,060	1,340	1,435	1,205	2,035	que conducteur	319
						Automobile, camion ou fourgonnette, en tant	
40	105	80	50	85	130	que passager	320
-	50	10	15	-	10	Transport en commun	321
-	45	15	25	80	105	À pied	322
15	-	15	10	30	55	Autre moyen	323
660	1,870	1,155	1,155	1,105	1,895	Femmes	324
						Automobile, camion ou fourgonnette, en tant	
585	1,610	1,020	945	900	1,530	que conductrice	325
						Automobile, camion ou fourgonnette, en tant	
55	145	70	95	50	240	que passagère	326
15	60	15	25	-	15	Transport en commun	327
-	25	45	50	120	95	À pied	328
-	25	10	40	35	20	Autre moyen	329
						Population totale de 15 ans et plus ayant travaillé	
1,985	**5,220**	**3,325**	**3,370**	**3,045**	**4,855**	**depuis le 1er janvier 2000**	330
						selon la langue utilisée au travail	
1,860	5,005	3,220	3,280	2,985	4,705	Réponses uniques	331
1,860	4,990	3,215	3,280	2,980	4,705	Anglais	332
-	-	10	-	-	-	Français	333
-	20	-	-	-	-	Langues non officielles (5)	334
-	-	-	-	-	-	Chinois, n.d.a.	335
-	-	-	-	-	-	Cantonais	336
-	15	-	-	-	-	Autres langues (6)	337
120	220	105	90	60	150	Réponses multiples	338
45	85	35	55	45	110	Anglais et français	339
70	135	65	30	10	40	Anglais et langue non officielle	340
-	-	-	10	-	-	Français et langue non officielle	341
10	-	-	-	-	-	Anglais, français et langue non officielle	342
						CARACTÉRISTIQUES DES LOGEMENTS ET DES MÉNAGES	
935	**2,565**	**1,715**	**1,800**	**2,055**	**2,500**	**Nombre total de logements privés occupés**	343
						selon le mode d'occupation	
890	2,195	1,525	1,610	1,335	2,335	Possédé	344
45	370	185	190	720	160	Loué	345
-	-	-	-	-	-	Logement de bande	346
						selon le type de construction résidentielle	
910	2,330	1,650	1,750	905	1,535	Maison individuelle non attenante	347
-	55	10	-	480	520	Maison jumelée	348
-	55	-	-	120	420	Maison en rangée	349
10	20	-	10	35	10	Appartement, duplex non attenant	350
-	-	25	20	185	-	Appartement, immeuble de cinq étages ou plus	351
-	75	20	10	325	-	Appartement, immeuble de moins de cinq étages (38)	352
10	15	-	-	-	10	Autre maison individuelle attenante	353
-	15	-	-	-	-	Logement mobile (39)	354

Table 1. Selected Characteristics for Census Tracts, 2001 Census – 100% Data and 20% Sample Data

No.	Characteristics	Toronto 0576.13 A	Toronto 0585.02	Toronto 0585.03	Toronto 0585.05 A	Toronto 0585.06 A	Toronto 0585.07 A
	DWELLING AND HOUSEHOLD CHARACTERISTICS						
	by condition of dwelling						
355	Regular maintenance only	1,080	1,070	1,170	1,060	2,425	1,115
356	Minor repairs	330	310	345	365	470	430
357	Major repairs	20	100	45	40	70	90
	by period of construction						
358	Before 1946	70	95	110	30	60	140
359	1946-1960	85	85	270	15	110	115
360	1961-1970	55	200	125	140	140	220
361	1971-1980	175	255	325	510	320	495
362	1981-1990	365	205	345	465	240	495
363	1991-2001 (20)	675	635	380	305	2,100	160
364	Average number of rooms per dwelling	8.4	7.7	7.1	8.0	7.3	8.1
365	Average number of bedrooms per dwelling	3.8	3.5	3.1	3.5	3.3	3.3
366	Average value of dwelling $	391,375	292,299	258,420	241,793	240,834	342,313
367	**Total number of private households**	**1,425**	**1,480**	**1,560**	**1,465**	**2,965**	**1,630**
	by household size						
368	1 person	60	130	270	85	205	180
369	2 persons	290	435	410	400	820	510
370	3 persons	255	285	305	300	705	305
371	4-5 persons	595	540	520	610	1,135	565
372	6 or more persons	225	85	50	65	105	75
	by household type						
373	One-family households	1,190	1,280	1,230	1,335	2,615	1,395
374	Multiple-family households	150	55	25	10	95	35
375	Non-family households	85	150	310	120	260	200
376	Number of persons in private households	5,440	4,795	4,540	4,785	9,460	4,995
377	Average number of persons in private households	3.8	3.2	2.9	3.3	3.2	3.1
378	Average number of persons per room	0.5	0.4	0.4	0.4	0.4	0.4
379	Tenant households in non-farm, non-reserve private dwellings (40)	85	130	355	75	140	130
380	Average gross rent $ (40)	1,090	1,126	786	875	923	699
381	Tenant households spending 30% or more of household income on gross rent (40) (41)	35	35	175	25	25	10
382	Tenant households spending from 30% to 99% of household income on gross rent (40) (41)	30	35	150	20	25	10
383	Owner households in non-farm, non-reserve private dwellings (42)	1,315	1,330	1,195	1,395	2,830	1,465
384	Average owner's major payments $ (42)	1,486	1,214	1,112	1,187	1,256	1,282
385	Owner households spending 30% or more of household income on owner's major payments (41) (42)	290	270	225	205	665	205
386	Owner households spending from 30% to 99% of household income on owner's major payments (41) (42)	270	225	200	165	605	190
	CENSUS FAMILY CHARACTERISTICS						
387	**Total number of census families in private households**	**1,500**	**1,395**	**1,270**	**1,350**	**2,805**	**1,465**
	by census family structure and size						
388	Total couple families	1,410	1,250	1,125	1,245	2,535	1,380
389	Total families of married couples	1,355	1,155	1,010	1,165	2,360	1,255
390	Without children at home	350	355	290	300	705	450
391	With children at home	1,005	805	720	860	1,655	800
392	1 child	275	255	240	240	590	260
393	2 children	445	360	345	430	760	355
394	3 or more children	285	185	140	185	305	190
395	Total families of common-law couples	60	100	115	85	180	130
396	Without children at home	40	75	80	45	95	70
397	With children at home	20	25	35	40	85	60
398	1 child	10	15	10	30	30	30
399	2 children	10	10	15	10	45	20
400	3 or more children	-	-	10	-	10	-
401	Total lone-parent families	90	145	150	105	270	80
402	Female parent	55	110	120	90	250	60
403	1 child	25	40	60	40	130	25
404	2 children	25	60	50	10	80	30
405	3 or more children	10	10	10	40	35	10

Tableau 1. Certaines caractéristiques des secteurs de recensement, recensement de 2001 – Données intégrales et données-échantillon (20 %)

Toronto 0585.08 A	Toronto 0586 A	Toronto 0587.01	Toronto 0587.02	Toronto 0590	Toronto 0591	Caractéristiques	N°
						CARACTÉRISTIQUES DES LOGEMENTS ET DES MÉNAGES	
						selon l'état du logement	
615	1,870	1,010	1,030	1,225	1,915	Entretien régulier seulement	355
260	520	570	625	635	490	Réparations mineures	356
60	175	130	140	195	95	Réparations majeures	357
						selon la période de construction	
65	375	295	450	460	15	Avant 1946	358
50	210	120	200	275	15	1946-1960	359
115	375	205	170	615	215	1961-1970	360
350	375	315	235	330	985	1971-1980	361
225	325	520	530	235	280	1981-1990	362
130	900	255	220	135	985	1991-2001 (20)	363
8.6	7.6	8.2	7.8	6.2	7.1	Nombre moyen de pièces par logement	364
3.6	3.2	3.4	3.2	2.6	3.2	Nombre moyen de chambres à coucher par logement	365
376,370	311,847	331,874	327,708	170,392	171,438	Valeur moyenne du logement $	366
935	**2,565**	**1,715**	**1,800**	**2,055**	**2,500**	**Nombre total de logements privés**	367
						selon la taille du ménage	
80	255	185	260	535	235	1 personne	368
285	755	520	595	625	675	2 personnes	369
175	500	300	310	375	555	3 personnes	370
320	900	635	555	465	920	4-5 personnes	371
75	155	80	85	55	115	6 personnes ou plus	372
						selon le genre de ménage	
815	2,105	1,470	1,465	1,440	2,185	Ménages unifamiliaux	373
40	150	50	35	35	55	Ménages multifamiliaux	374
85	305	195	300	580	260	Ménages non familiaux	375
3,035	8,090	5,340	5,285	5,230	7,955	Nombre de personnes dans les ménages privés	376
3.3	3.2	3.1	2.9	2.5	3.2	Nombre moyen de personnes dans les ménages privés	377
0.4	0.4	0.4	0.4	0.4	0.4	Nombre moyen de personnes par pièce	378
45	350	180	180	720	160	Ménages locataires dans les logements privés non agricoles hors réserve (40)	379
834	795	910	858	657	967	Loyer brut moyen $ (40)	380
20	80	70	40	345	65	Ménages locataires consacrant 30 % ou plus du revenu du ménage au loyer brut (40) (41)	381
20	55	65	35	295	50	Ménages locataires consacrant de 30 % à 99 % du revenu du ménage au loyer brut (40) (41)	382
880	2,090	1,510	1,550	1,335	2,335	Ménages propriétaires dans les logements privés non agricoles hors réserve (42)	383
1,396	1,244	1,237	1,249	948	1,195	Principales dépenses de propriété moyennes $ (42)	384
185	345	220	280	285	485	Ménages propriétaires consacrant 30 % ou plus du revenu du ménage aux principales dépenses de propriété (41) (42)	385
175	295	195	260	245	420	Ménages propriétaires consacrant de 30 % à 99 % du revenu du ménage aux principales dépenses de propriété (41) (42)	386
						CARACTÉRISTIQUES DES FAMILLES DE RECENSEMENT	
895	**2,410**	**1,575**	**1,535**	**1,510**	**2,295**	**Total des familles de recensement dans les ménages privés**	387
						selon la structure et la taille de la famille de recensement	
800	2,150	1,430	1,415	1,230	1,975	Total des familles avec conjoints	388
735	1,965	1,315	1,270	1,020	1,725	Total des familles avec couples mariés	389
240	710	465	485	415	495	Sans enfants à la maison	390
490	1,255	850	785	605	1,225	Avec enfants à la maison	391
150	430	245	265	220	390	1 enfant	392
205	565	415	335	275	575	2 enfants	393
135	265	195	185	110	270	3 enfants ou plus	394
65	185	115	145	210	255	Total des familles en union libre	395
35	110	60	80	105	145	Sans enfants à la maison	396
35	75	50	60	110	110	Avec enfants à la maison	397
15	40	20	15	50	35	1 enfant	398
10	20	30	15	40	55	2 enfants	399
-	15	-	30	15	15	3 enfants ou plus	400
95	255	150	125	285	320	Total des familles monoparentales	401
80	180	105	90	235	245	Parent de sexe féminin	402
55	100	60	45	130	115	1 enfant	403
15	55	35	20	85	85	2 enfants	404
10	25	15	25	20	40	3 enfants ou plus	405

Table 1. Selected Characteristics for Census Tracts, 2001 Census – 100% Data and 20% Sample Data

No.	Characteristics	Toronto 0576.13 A	Toronto 0585.02	Toronto 0585.03	Toronto 0585.05 A	Toronto 0585.06 A	Toronto 0585.07 A
	CENSUS FAMILY CHARACTERISTICS						
	by census family structure and size – concluded						
406	Male parent	35	35	25	15	20	20
407	1 child	35	25	20	10	15	20
408	2 children	-	10	10	-	10	-
409	3 or more children	-	10	-	-	-	-
410	**Total number of children at home**	**2,275**	**1,860**	**1,665**	**1,965**	**3,665**	**1,820**
	by age groups						
411	Under 6 years	445	465	435	400	1,320	280
412	6-14 years	675	620	615	755	1,355	730
413	15-17 years	155	150	195	215	290	240
414	18-24 years	565	380	310	420	415	390
415	25 years and over	450	245	115	165	280	180
416	Average number of children at home per census family (43)	1.5	1.3	1.3	1.5	1.3	1.2
417	**Total number of persons in private households**	**5,445**	**4,795**	**4,535**	**4,785**	**9,460**	**4,990**
	by census family status and living arrangements						
418	Number of non-family persons	250	285	475	225	450	320
419	Living with relatives (44)	145	85	70	80	125	55
420	Living with non-relatives only	45	75	135	60	120	90
421	Living alone	65	130	270	90	205	180
422	Number of family persons	5,190	4,510	4,065	4,555	9,005	4,670
423	Average number of persons per census family	3.5	3.2	3.2	3.4	3.2	3.2
424	**Total number of persons 65 years and over**	**450**	**405**	**450**	**220**	**440**	**470**
425	Number of non-family persons 65 years and over	125	90	175	60	110	120
426	Living with relatives (44)	95	55	20	15	60	40
427	Living with non-relatives only	-	-	-	-	-	-
428	Living alone	25	35	150	40	50	75
429	Number of family persons 65 years and over	325	320	275	160	330	350
	ECONOMIC FAMILY CHARACTERISTICS						
430	**Total number of economic families in private households**	**1,350**	**1,330**	**1,255**	**1,360**	**2,725**	**1,430**
	by size of family						
431	2 persons	285	425	410	390	810	510
432	3 persons	255	280	290	300	685	300
433	4 persons	390	375	380	445	820	375
434	5 or more persons	430	250	170	225	405	245
435	Total number of persons in economic families	5,335	4,590	4,130	4,640	9,135	4,725
436	Average number of persons per economic family	4.0	3.5	3.3	3.4	3.4	3.3
437	Total number of unattached individuals	105	205	405	145	330	270
	2000 INCOME CHARACTERISTICS						
	Population 15 years and over by sex and total income groups in 2000						
438	Total - Both sexes	4,430	3,705	3,480	3,625	6,780	3,980
439	Without income	240	195	125	120	220	175
440	With income	4,190	3,510	3,355	3,500	6,565	3,805
441	Under $1,000 (45)	170	180	125	100	155	150
442	$ 1,000 - $ 2,999	215	145	180	145	140	130
443	$ 3,000 - $ 4,999	85	120	115	140	210	155
444	$ 5,000 - $ 6,999	150	140	110	100	205	105
445	$ 7,000 - $ 9,999	145	135	135	180	275	145
446	$10,000 - $11,999	230	115	110	70	180	110
447	$12,000 - $14,999	190	130	185	155	270	185
448	$15,000 - $19,999	300	345	235	195	320	250
449	$20,000 - $24,999	325	205	160	230	505	185
450	$25,000 - $29,999	320	185	260	165	445	275
451	$30,000 - $34,999	300	300	225	220	690	185
452	$35,000 - $39,999	285	175	210	220	495	175
453	$40,000 - $44,999	265	195	270	230	520	240
454	$45,000 - $49,999	120	260	150	225	350	150
455	$50,000 - $59,999	370	330	305	310	645	330
456	$60,000 and over	715	545	570	825	1,155	1,040
457	Average income $ (46)	40,364	35,747	36,049	45,575	37,601	50,874
458	Median income $ (46)	29,004	30,060	30,491	35,502	33,148	34,975
459	Standard error of average income $ (46)	1,857	1,253	1,143	2,790	718	3,583

Tableau 1. Certaines caractéristiques des secteurs de recensement, recensement de 2001 – Données intégrales et données-échantillon (20 %)

Toronto 0585.08 A	Toronto 0586 A	Toronto 0587.01	Toronto 0587.02	Toronto 0590	Toronto 0591	Caractéristiques	N°
						CARACTÉRISTIQUES DES FAMILLES DE RECENSEMENT	
						selon la structure et la taille de la famille de recensement - fin	
20	75	45	30	45	75	Parent de sexe masculin	406
15	55	30	15	35	40	1 enfant	407
10	20	15	20	-	25	2 enfants	408
-	-	-	-	10	10	3 enfants ou plus	409
1,205	**2,970**	**2,025**	**1,870**	**1,745**	**3,180**	**Nombre total d'enfants à la maison**	410
						selon les groupes d'âge	
165	600	375	405	440	900	Moins de 6 ans	411
450	1,055	810	720	645	1,350	6-14 ans	412
180	340	265	245	225	300	15-17 ans	413
260	650	380	360	265	495	18-24 ans	414
150	320	195	145	175	145	25 ans et plus	415
1.3	1.2	1.3	1.2	1.2	1.4	Nombre moyen d'enfants à la maison par famille de recensement (43)	416
3,040	**8,085**	**5,340**	**5,280**	**5,230**	**7,955**	**Nombre total de personnes dans les ménages privés**	417
						selon la situation des particuliers dans la famille de recensement et des particuliers dans le ménage	
135	560	310	465	745	495	Nombre de personnes hors famille de recensement	418
10	105	105	95	75	125	Vivant avec des personnes apparentées (44)	419
40	200	20	110	135	145	Vivant avec des personnes non apparentées uniquement	420
80	260	185	255	535	230	Vivant seules	421
2,905	7,530	5,025	4,825	4,485	7,460	Nombre de personnes membres d'une famille	422
3.2	3.1	3.2	3.1	3.0	3.2	Nombre moyen de personnes par famille de recensement	423
245	**695**	**440**	**490**	**600**	**265**	**Nombre total de personnes de 65 ans et plus**	424
50	165	100	150	260	75	Nombre de personnes hors famille de recensement de 65 ans et plus	425
15	85	55	30	20	15	Vivant avec des personnes apparentées (44)	426
10	-	-	15	-	20	Vivant avec des personnes non apparentées uniquement	427
25	70	40	100	240	40	Vivant seules	428
195	535	340	340	340	185	Nombre de personnes membres d'une famille de 65 ans et plus	429
						CARACTÉRISTIQUES DES FAMILLES ÉCONOMIQUES	
850	**2,265**	**1,530**	**1,510**	**1,485**	**2,270**	**Nombre total de familles économiques dans les ménages privés**	430
						selon la taille de la famille	
295	750	520	570	615	725	2 personnes	431
160	480	295	315	360	535	3 personnes	432
225	635	450	385	350	665	4 personnes	433
170	400	260	235	160	340	5 personnes ou plus	434
2,915	7,635	5,140	4,915	4,560	7,580	Nombre total de personnes dans les familles économiques	435
3.4	3.4	3.4	3.2	3.1	3.3	Nombre moyen de personnes par famille économique	436
120	450	205	370	665	375	Nombre total de personnes hors famille économique	437
						CARACTÉRISTIQUES DU REVENU DE 2000	
						Population de 15 ans et plus selon le sexe et les tranches de revenu total en 2000	
2,425	6,430	4,160	4,170	4,140	5,680	Total - Les deux sexes	438
110	330	210	130	160	175	Sans revenu	439
2,315	6,095	3,950	4,040	3,980	5,505	Avec un revenu	440
115	300	165	110	205	190	Moins de 1 000 $ (45)	441
95	205	205	175	135	335	1 000 $ - 2 999 $	442
35	205	90	200	195	240	3 000 $ - 4 999 $	443
80	155	130	165	140	160	5 000 $ - 6 999 $	444
140	325	165	210	325	255	7 000 $ - 9 999 $	445
35	105	135	130	180	165	10 000 $ - 11 999 $	446
180	310	145	170	350	315	12 000 $ - 14 999 $	447
150	345	210	260	360	370	15 000 $ - 19 999 $	448
135	395	210	205	340	375	20 000 $ - 24 999 $	449
70	460	220	165	265	350	25 000 $ - 29 999 $	450
115	520	280	265	335	430	30 000 $ - 34 999 $	451
145	370	265	180	220	390	35 000 $ - 39 999 $	452
100	365	150	215	230	410	40 000 $ - 44 999 $	453
80	290	135	250	165	295	45 000 $ - 49 999 $	454
175	540	440	320	215	495	50 000 $ - 59 999 $	455
660	1,215	995	1,025	335	725	60 000 $ et plus	456
51,895	39,070	47,512	46,639	26,275	32,178	Revenu moyen $ (46)	457
34,867	31,234	34,929	34,048	21,556	29,957	Revenu médian $ (46)	458
2,840	1,020	1,741	2,295	746	689	Erreur type de revenu moyen $ (46)	459

Table 1. Selected Characteristics for Census Tracts, 2001 Census – 100% Data and 20% Sample Data

No.	Characteristics	Toronto 0576.13 A	Toronto 0585.02	Toronto 0585.03	Toronto 0585.05 A	Toronto 0585.06 A	Toronto 0585.07 A
	2000 INCOME CHARACTERISTICS						
	Population 15 years and over by sex and total income groups in 2000 – concluded						
460	Total - Males	2,290	1,830	1,675	1,765	3,355	2,000
461	Without income	100	70	40	30	75	60
462	With income	2,195	1,770	1,635	1,730	3,275	1,945
463	Under $1,000 (45)	100	125	55	45	60	70
464	$ 1,000 - $ 2,999	110	45	30	40	50	45
465	$ 3,000 - $ 4,999	25	55	65	55	60	55
466	$ 5,000 - $ 6,999	65	35	50	35	70	25
467	$ 7,000 - $ 9,999	30	50	30	90	85	55
468	$10,000 - $11,999	155	25	15	10	95	55
469	$12,000 - $14,999	75	50	60	25	110	50
470	$15,000 - $19,999	105	115	95	75	100	100
471	$20,000 - $24,999	150	95	60	80	200	90
472	$25,000 - $29,999	135	70	105	105	150	120
473	$30,000 - $34,999	120	175	100	85	210	70
474	$35,000 - $39,999	120	75	100	130	250	85
475	$40,000 - $44,999	155	140	145	120	310	130
476	$45,000 - $49,999	40	120	115	105	205	85
477	$50,000 - $59,999	235	190	180	170	445	215
478	$60,000 and over	565	405	440	555	875	710
479	Average income $ (46)	48,612	40,919	46,327	58,628	46,255	66,857
480	Median income $ (46)	35,012	35,975	40,162	40,360	42,170	45,304
481	Standard error of average income $ (46)	2,880	1,701	1,941	5,249	1,182	6,626
482	Total - Females	2,145	1,875	1,810	1,860	3,425	1,975
483	Without income	145	125	90	90	135	125
484	With income	2,000	1,750	1,720	1,775	3,285	1,860
485	Under $1,000 (45)	75	60	70	55	95	80
486	$ 1,000 - $ 2,999	105	95	150	105	95	90
487	$ 3,000 - $ 4,999	60	60	55	85	145	105
488	$ 5,000 - $ 6,999	80	110	60	65	135	75
489	$ 7,000 - $ 9,999	110	90	110	90	200	90
490	$10,000 - $11,999	75	95	95	55	90	55
491	$12,000 - $14,999	115	85	125	125	160	135
492	$15,000 - $19,999	195	230	135	115	225	150
493	$20,000 - $24,999	180	110	100	150	300	95
494	$25,000 - $29,999	185	115	160	60	300	155
495	$30,000 - $34,999	180	125	125	135	475	115
496	$35,000 - $39,999	165	100	110	90	235	90
497	$40,000 - $44,999	110	55	125	100	215	110
498	$45,000 - $49,999	85	140	40	120	145	65
499	$50,000 - $59,999	130	135	130	145	200	115
500	$60,000 and over	150	145	125	275	280	330
501	Average income $ (46)	31,316	30,512	26,269	32,819	28,969	34,118
502	Median income $ (46)	25,360	22,571	22,893	28,562	27,374	26,068
503	Standard error of average income $ (46)	2,157	1,806	1,046	1,429	700	1,570
	by composition of total income						
504	Total - Composition of income in 2000 % (47)	100.0	100.0	100.0	100.0	100.0	100.0
505	Employment income %	89.3	86.3	86.8	93.1	91.8	83.3
506	Government transfer payments %	5.2	6.4	6.9	2.9	4.8	4.0
507	Other %	5.4	7.3	6.4	4.1	3.3	12.8
	Population 15 years and over with employment income in 2000 by sex and work activity						
508	Both sexes with employment income (48)	3,410	2,865	2,665	3,155	5,760	3,220
509	Average employment income $	44,325	37,776	39,321	47,010	39,326	50,009
510	Standard error of average employment income $	2,211	1,405	1,335	2,993	775	3,531
511	Worked full year, full time (49)	2,140	1,825	1,600	1,905	3,835	1,935
512	Average employment income $	56,895	47,900	49,856	62,361	47,088	67,380
513	Standard error of average employment income $	3,272	1,948	1,687	4,497	898	5,637
514	Worked part year or part time (50)	1,215	965	1,025	1,225	1,795	1,215
515	Average employment income $	23,661	20,603	23,416	23,503	24,061	24,107
516	Standard error of average employment income $	1,652	1,252	1,795	2,480	1,250	2,206
517	Males with employment income (48)	1,910	1,470	1,410	1,600	2,965	1,730
518	Average employment income $	51,224	43,000	48,126	60,103	47,755	63,746
519	Standard error of average employment income $	3,228	1,860	2,169	5,511	1,257	6,195
520	Worked full year, full time (49)	1,305	1,050	945	1,090	2,180	1,170
521	Average employment income $	64,175	50,215	57,007	74,996	54,553	78,212
522	Standard error of average employment income $	4,410	2,316	2,528	7,691	1,338	9,007
523	Worked part year or part time (50)	595	405	455	490	775	525
524	Average employment income $	23,924	25,249	30,683	28,037	28,832	34,387
525	Standard error of average employment income $	2,366	2,245	3,639	4,867	2,519	4,379

Tableau 1. Certaines caractéristiques des secteurs de recensement, recensement de 2001 – Données intégrales et données-échantillon (20 %)

Toronto 0585.08 A	Toronto 0586 A	Toronto 0587.01	Toronto 0587.02	Toronto 0590	Toronto 0591	Caractéristiques	N°
						CARACTÉRISTIQUES DU REVENU DE 2000	
						Population de 15 ans et plus selon le sexe et les tranches de revenu total en 2000 – fin	
1,235	3,240	2,100	2,075	1,975	2,825	Total - Hommes	460
35	135	95	55	40	55	Sans revenu	461
1,195	3,105	2,005	2,020	1,940	2,770	Avec un revenu	462
30	130	60	20	90	55	Moins de 1 000 $ (45)	463
25	60	80	40	85	105	1 000 $ - 2 999 $	464
15	95	50	40	40	55	3 000 $ - 4 999 $	465
30	35	50	55	45	55	5 000 $ - 6 999 $	466
65	95	20	55	100	70	7 000 $ - 9 999 $	467
10	55	55	85	40	45	10 000 $ - 11 999 $	468
80	110	70	70	95	70	12 000 $ - 14 999 $	469
65	125	75	95	125	115	15 000 $ - 19 999 $	470
60	190	80	110	125	105	20 000 $ - 24 999 $	471
35	180	95	70	130	125	25 000 $ - 29 999 $	472
70	225	95	110	180	190	30 000 $ - 34 999 $	473
85	195	115	105	150	235	35 000 $ - 39 999 $	474
40	190	60	110	150	310	40 000 $ - 44 999 $	475
65	170	90	115	135	235	45 000 $ - 49 999 $	476
70	355	245	220	185	400	50 000 $ - 59 999 $	477
470	895	755	730	265	590	60 000 $ et plus	478
68,979	48,820	61,052	61,296	33,675	42,417	Revenu moyen $ (46)	479
44,989	40,115	49,373	47,140	31,674	42,107	Revenu médian $ (46)	480
4,764	1,697	2,690	4,232	1,218	1,039	Erreur type de revenu moyen $ (46)	481
1,190	3,185	2,060	2,090	2,165	2,850	Total - Femmes	482
70	190	115	75	120	120	Sans revenu	483
1,115	2,995	1,940	2,015	2,045	2,730	Avec un revenu	484
85	170	105	85	110	135	Moins de 1 000 $ (45)	485
70	150	120	135	55	230	1 000 $ - 2 999 $	486
10	105	45	155	155	180	3 000 $ - 4 999 $	487
55	120	80	115	90	110	5 000 $ - 6 999 $	488
75	230	145	155	220	185	7 000 $ - 9 999 $	489
35	50	75	45	135	125	10 000 $ - 11 999 $	490
105	200	80	100	255	245	12 000 $ - 14 999 $	491
80	225	135	165	235	250	15 000 $ - 19 999 $	492
80	205	125	95	215	265	20 000 $ - 24 999 $	493
35	275	125	95	135	215	25 000 $ - 29 999 $	494
50	295	185	155	155	240	30 000 $ - 34 999 $	495
55	175	150	80	70	155	35 000 $ - 39 999 $	496
60	180	95	110	80	105	40 000 $ - 44 999 $	497
20	125	45	135	30	60	45 000 $ - 49 999 $	498
105	185	195	105	30	100	50 000 $ - 59 999 $	499
185	315	240	290	65	130	60 000 $ et plus	500
33,553	28,952	33,555	31,918	19,272	21,797	Revenu moyen $ (46)	501
23,607	25,295	27,621	23,324	14,898	17,411	Revenu médian $ (46)	502
2,399	942	2,009	1,666	740	708	Erreur type de revenu moyen $ (46)	503
						selon la composition du revenu total	
100.0	100.0	100.0	100.0	100.0	100.0	Total - Composition du revenu en 2000 % (47)	504
86.6	86.2	87.7	80.7	80.2	90.9	Revenu d'emploi %	505
3.8	5.7	4.2	4.3	12.2	5.2	Transferts gouvernementaux %	506
9.6	8.1	8.1	15.0	7.4	3.8	Autre %	507
						Population de 15 ans et plus ayant un revenu d'emploi en 2000 selon le sexe et le travail	
1,940	5,085	3,290	3,295	2,950	4,785	Les deux sexes ayant un revenu d'emploi (48)	508
53,563	40,394	49,937	46,144	28,495	33,642	Revenu moyen d'emploi $	509
3,257	1,134	2,000	2,107	918	756	Erreur type de revenu moyen d'emploi $	510
1,060	3,135	1,945	1,935	1,670	2,900	Ayant travaillé toute l'année à plein temps (49)	511
77,163	51,904	65,159	58,792	39,107	43,793	Revenu moyen d'emploi $	512
4,785	1,517	2,869	2,222	1,158	915	Erreur type de revenu moyen d'emploi $	513
855	1,790	1,290	1,315	1,195	1,765	Ayant travaillé une partie de l'année ou à temps partiel (50)	514
25,882	22,357	28,121	29,005	14,970	18,229	Revenu moyen d'emploi $	515
3,249	1,332	2,121	3,936	1,070	938	Erreur type de revenu moyen d'emploi $	516
1,090	2,735	1,790	1,805	1,535	2,585	Hommes ayant un revenu d'emploi (48)	517
67,862	48,535	61,934	57,056	36,514	42,630	Revenu moyen d'emploi $	518
5,163	1,816	2,901	3,476	1,379	1,113	Erreur type de revenu moyen d'emploi $	519
715	1,870	1,215	1,250	1,015	1,815	Ayant travaillé toute l'année à plein temps (49)	520
86,462	58,369	72,907	63,688	44,537	50,285	Revenu moyen d'emploi $	521
6,513	2,286	3,625	3,067	1,603	1,215	Erreur type de revenu moyen d'emploi $	522
365	770	555	515	500	730	Ayant travaillé une partie de l'année ou à temps partiel (50)	523
33,359	27,869	38,565	44,688	20,917	24,312	Revenu moyen d'emploi $	524
6,997	2,519	4,249	9,495	1,937	1,861	Erreur type de revenu moyen d'emploi $	525

Table 1. Selected Characteristics for Census Tracts, 2001 Census – 100% Data and 20% Sample Data

No.	Characteristics	Toronto 0576.13 A	Toronto 0585.02	Toronto 0585.03	Toronto 0585.05 A	Toronto 0585.06 A	Toronto 0585.07 A
	2000 INCOME CHARACTERISTICS						
	Population 15 years and over with employment income in 2000 by sex and work activity – concluded						
526	Females with employment income (48)	1,500	1,395	1,260	1,560	2,800	1,490
527	Average employment income $	35,534	32,269	29,435	33,558	30,389	34,053
528	Standard error of average employment income $	2,771	2,077	1,224	1,527	737	1,701
529	Worked full year, full time (49)	840	775	655	820	1,655	770
530	Average employment income $	45,617	44,773	39,573	45,533	37,245	50,930
531	Standard error of average employment income $	4,585	3,341	1,507	1,684	892	2,376
532	Worked part year or part time (50)	620	565	565	730	1,020	685
533	Average employment income $	23,409	17,282	17,551	20,450	20,435	16,207
534	Standard error of average employment income $	2,308	1,361	1,335	2,279	1,047	1,461
	Census families by structure and family income groups in 2000						
535	Total - All census families	1,500	1,400	1,275	1,350	2,805	1,465
536	Under $10,000	60	35	45	20	40	15
537	$ 10,000 - $19,999	40	35	10	15	55	10
538	$ 20,000 - $29,999	40	60	60	30	145	80
539	$ 30,000 - $39,999	135	90	90	40	140	55
540	$ 40,000 - $49,999	60	145	80	75	175	110
541	$ 50,000 - $59,999	100	135	140	90	335	75
542	$ 60,000 - $69,999	75	140	135	160	265	100
543	$ 70,000 - $79,999	145	140	90	105	350	90
544	$ 80,000 - $89,999	135	130	135	130	305	150
545	$ 90,000 - $99,999	70	125	95	110	245	115
546	$100,000 and over	635	360	390	580	755	675
547	Average family income $	108,088	84,011	82,047	111,482	81,160	118,893
548	Median family income $	86,068	73,016	78,188	91,366	77,290	94,732
549	Standard error of average family income $	6,550	3,486	2,490	7,445	1,611	9,185
550	Total - All couple census families (51)	1,410	1,255	1,125	1,245	2,540	1,380
551	Under $10,000	45	20	20	20	25	10
552	$ 10,000 - $19,999	25	25	10	10	35	10
553	$ 20,000 - $29,999	30	50	45	25	110	65
554	$ 30,000 - $39,999	120	85	80	25	95	50
555	$ 40,000 - $49,999	45	120	65	70	150	105
556	$ 50,000 - $59,999	90	110	115	75	290	65
557	$ 60,000 - $69,999	70	125	110	140	240	95
558	$ 70,000 - $79,999	145	125	85	95	330	90
559	$ 80,000 - $89,999	140	110	125	115	285	130
560	$ 90,000 - $99,999	70	125	90	110	230	115
561	$100,000 and over	630	350	385	550	750	655
562	Average family income $	112,581	86,915	86,755	114,925	84,608	121,768
563	Median family income $	88,931	75,616	82,520	93,303	79,815	96,101
564	Standard error of average family income $	6,906	3,723	2,605	8,185	1,681	9,622
	Incidence of low income in 2000						
565	Total - Economic families	1,345	1,330	1,255	1,360	2,725	1,430
566	Low income	45	60	60	45	115	20
567	Incidence of low income in 2000 % (52)	3.5	4.3	4.8	3.3	4.2	1.1
568	Total - Unattached individuals 15 years and over	105	200	395	140	330	270
569	Low income	40	45	105	20	50	15
570	Incidence of low income in 2000 % (52)	41.1	23.2	27.0	13.6	15.2	5.2
571	Total - Population in private households	5,440	4,790	4,525	4,780	9,460	4,990
572	Low income	225	270	300	210	395	70
573	Incidence of low income in 2000 % (52)	4.2	5.6	6.7	4.3	4.2	1.4
	Private households by household income groups in 2000						
574	Total - All private households	1,425	1,480	1,560	1,465	2,970	1,625
575	Under $10,000	45	35	60	35	45	10
576	$ 10,000 - $19,999	30	55	120	20	60	40
577	$ 20,000 - $29,999	35	90	90	55	155	80
578	$ 30,000 - $39,999	110	75	140	55	120	70
579	$ 40,000 - $49,999	60	140	115	85	180	115
580	$ 50,000 - $59,999	80	150	120	80	360	100
581	$ 60,000 - $69,999	75	140	130	135	280	95
582	$ 70,000 - $79,999	90	145	85	105	355	80
583	$ 80,000 - $89,999	135	135	135	155	315	140
584	$ 90,000 - $99,999	60	120	110	110	240	135
585	$100,000 and over	715	395	450	620	860	760
586	Average household income $	117,119	84,893	77,524	109,140	83,077	118,790
587	Median household income $	99,879	72,670	70,668	90,729	77,837	95,141
588	Standard error of average household income $	6,826	3,506	2,638	6,925	1,626	8,509

Tableau 1. Certaines caractéristiques des secteurs de recensement, recensement de 2001 – Données intégrales et données-échantillon (20 %)

Toronto 0585.08 A	Toronto 0586 A	Toronto 0587.01	Toronto 0587.02	Toronto 0590	Toronto 0591	Caractéristiques	N°
						CARACTÉRISTIQUES DU REVENU DE 2000	
						Population de 15 ans et plus ayant un revenu d'emploi en 2000 selon le sexe et le travail – fin	
855	2,350	1,505	1,490	1,415	2,205	Femmes ayant un revenu d'emploi (48)	526
35,308	30,910	35,669	32,915	19,848	23,122	Revenu moyen d'emploi $	527
2,902	1,096	2,505	1,919	980	784	Erreur type de revenu moyen d'emploi $	528
345	1,265	735	680	655	1,085	Ayant travaillé toute l'année à plein temps (49)	529
57,857	42,364	52,321	49,786	30,647	32,955	Revenu moyen d'emploi $	530
5,462	1,481	4,536	2,813	1,301	1,073	Erreur type de revenu moyen d'emploi $	531
490	1,015	735	795	690	1,030	Ayant travaillé une partie de l'année ou à temps partiel (50)	532
20,335	18,172	20,221	18,865	10,707	13,922	Revenu moyen d'emploi $	533
2,026	1,221	1,649	2,211	1,074	813	Erreur type de revenu moyen d'emploi $	534
						Familles de recensement selon la structure et les tranches de revenu de la famille en 2000	
895	2,410	1,580	1,535	1,510	2,295	Total - Toutes les familles de recensement	535
-	100	35	10	40	55	Moins de 10 000 $	536
25	40	55	35	60	60	10 000 $ - 19 999 $	537
30	95	50	75	165	120	20 000 $ - 29 999 $	538
55	175	65	85	200	130	30 000 $ - 39 999 $	539
105	195	65	105	210	255	40 000 $ - 49 999 $	540
35	150	115	100	170	300	50 000 $ - 59 999 $	541
75	205	115	150	185	345	60 000 $ - 69 999 $	542
20	190	80	125	135	270	70 000 $ - 79 999 $	543
50	190	95	100	110	225	80 000 $ - 89 999 $	544
40	175	100	160	85	150	90 000 $ - 99 999 $	545
455	895	795	600	145	375	100 000 $ et plus	546
125,780	90,810	110,422	108,280	57,986	70,268	Revenu moyen des familles $	547
100,157	82,824	99,911	89,115	54,843	66,806	Revenu médian des familles $	548
6,654	2,530	4,350	5,628	1,672	1,472	Erreur type de revenu moyen des familles $	549
800	2,150	1,425	1,415	1,225	1,975	Total - Toutes les familles de recensement comptant un couple (51)	550
-	65	15	-	25	30	Moins de 10 000 $	551
15	30	40	30	40	20	10 000 $ - 19 999 $	552
30	80	40	50	90	55	20 000 $ - 29 999 $	553
40	145	45	70	135	100	30 000 $ - 39 999 $	554
95	150	50	85	180	220	40 000 $ - 49 999 $	555
30	125	90	90	160	265	50 000 $ - 59 999 $	556
40	190	110	145	165	320	60 000 $ - 69 999 $	557
25	160	80	110	115	270	70 000 $ - 79 999 $	558
45	170	90	100	85	205	80 000 $ - 89 999 $	559
40	170	90	150	85	155	90 000 $ - 99 999 $	560
435	865	770	575	145	345	100 000 $ et plus	561
133,570	95,170	116,966	110,980	62,495	74,298	Revenu moyen des familles $	562
101,846	86,653	102,034	90,317	59,004	69,589	Revenu médian des familles $	563
7,167	2,746	4,652	6,020	1,848	1,505	Erreur type de revenu moyen des familles $	564
						Fréquence des unités à faible revenu en 2000	
850	2,265	1,530	1,510	1,485	2,270	Total - Familles économiques	565
25	125	55	35	125	100	Faible revenu	566
3.1	5.6	3.7	2.6	8.4	4.6	Fréquence des unités à faible revenu en 2000 % (52)	567
125	440	205	355	670	345	Total - Personnes hors famille économique de 15 ans et plus	568
10	80	35	65	300	55	Faible revenu	569
8.3	19.0	15.1	18.5	44.5	17.4	Fréquence des unités à faible revenu en 2000 % (52)	570
3,040	8,070	5,340	5,275	5,230	7,920	Total - Population dans les ménages privés	571
95	520	240	205	635	380	Faible revenu	572
3.1	6.5	4.5	3.9	12.2	4.8	Fréquence des unités à faible revenu en 2000 % (52)	573
						Ménages privés selon les tranches de revenu du ménage en 2000	
935	2,565	1,715	1,800	2,055	2,495	Total - Tous les ménages privés	574
-	90	25	15	120	60	Moins de 10 000 $	575
50	85	75	105	310	75	10 000 $ - 19 999 $	576
35	115	85	85	195	130	20 000 $ - 29 999 $	577
45	135	55	105	235	120	30 000 $ - 39 999 $	578
105	200	75	125	235	285	40 000 $ - 49 999 $	579
25	165	110	95	185	315	50 000 $ - 59 999 $	580
70	170	140	170	240	370	60 000 $ - 69 999 $	581
35	200	75	140	155	280	70 000 $ - 79 999 $	582
45	225	105	90	120	235	80 000 $ - 89 999 $	583
60	200	125	160	70	180	90 000 $ - 99 999 $	584
475	990	840	705	190	445	100 000 $ et plus	585
128,313	92,841	109,349	104,447	50,953	70,852	Revenu moyen des ménages $	586
100,057	85,123	97,448	84,920	45,954	67,812	Revenu médian des ménages $	587
7,103	2,477	4,126	5,199	1,575	1,421	Erreur type de revenu moyen des ménages $	588

Table 1. Selected Characteristics for Census Tracts, 2001 Census – 100% Data and 20% Sample Data

No.	Characteristics	Toronto 0592.01 A	Toronto 0592.02 A	Toronto 0593	Toronto 0600.01	Toronto 0600.02	Toronto 0601
	POPULATION CHARACTERISTICS						
1	**Population, 1996 (1)**	**4,771**	**6,015**	**6,552**	**6,783**	**7,465**	**4,008**
2	**Population, 2001 (2)**	**5,946**	**6,071**	**6,922**	**6,566**	**7,438**	**3,949**
3	Population percentage change, 1996-2001	24.6	0.9	5.6	-3.2	-0.4	-1.5
4	Land area in square kilometres, 2001	3.84	3.76	277.77	4.95	5.30	3.23
5	**Total population - 100% Data (3)**	**5,945**	**6,070**	**6,920**	**6,565**	**7,440**	**3,945**
	by sex and age groups						
6	Male	2,815	2,990	3,540	3,245	3,655	1,930
7	0-4 years	260	220	180	145	220	95
8	5-9 years	275	300	280	260	345	145
9	10-14 years	210	305	305	285	370	170
10	15-19 years	160	275	265	280	345	165
11	20-24 years	170	130	210	230	240	105
12	25-29 years	215	100	110	100	165	65
13	30-34 years	265	175	160	95	175	55
14	35-39 years	270	365	280	150	280	100
15	40-44 years	220	335	300	265	425	165
16	45-49 years	160	210	345	270	340	165
17	50-54 years	155	175	285	310	285	155
18	55-59 years	120	115	270	300	195	140
19	60-64 years	75	85	190	210	105	115
20	65-69 years	60	65	155	125	85	90
21	70-74 years	70	55	100	110	45	80
22	75-79 years	50	35	70	65	20	70
23	80-84 years	45	25	35	25	10	25
24	85 years and over	35	30	15	10	5	20
25	Female	3,125	3,080	3,385	3,320	3,780	2,020
26	0-4 years	220	190	150	140	225	95
27	5-9 years	260	310	240	230	365	155
28	10-14 years	200	305	325	285	375	180
29	15-19 years	160	245	250	285	330	155
30	20-24 years	155	135	165	230	215	100
31	25-29 years	250	95	105	80	160	55
32	30-34 years	270	220	180	115	205	70
33	35-39 years	320	350	290	215	360	125
34	40-44 years	210	320	330	300	480	180
35	45-49 years	170	210	325	330	365	175
36	50-54 years	170	170	315	335	270	160
37	55-59 years	125	95	225	290	165	155
38	60-64 years	95	85	165	170	100	105
39	65-69 years	90	60	115	120	65	110
40	70-74 years	115	60	80	95	45	95
41	75-79 years	110	65	75	60	35	60
42	80-84 years	95	60	30	35	10	30
43	85 years and over	95	95	25	15	15	20
44	**Total population 15 years and over**	**4,515**	**4,445**	**5,450**	**5,225**	**5,540**	**3,115**
	by legal marital status						
45	Never married (single)	1,255	1,090	1,395	1,345	1,590	730
46	Legally married (and not separated)	2,165	2,775	3,440	3,520	3,525	2,090
47	Separated, but still legally married	265	105	135	65	110	50
48	Divorced	410	195	280	135	195	95
49	Widowed	415	280	200	155	125	140
	by common-law status						
50	Not in a common-law relationship	4,045	4,225	5,105	5,155	5,410	3,055
51	In a common-law relationship	470	220	350	70	130	55
52	**Total population - 20% Sample Data (4)**	**5,865**	**5,855**	**6,900**	**6,565**	**7,435**	**3,945**
	by mother tongue						
53	Single responses	5,835	5,835	6,870	6,510	7,290	3,930
54	English	5,445	5,380	6,300	5,570	4,965	3,380
55	French	70	125	65	125	80	75
56	Non-official languages (5)	320	330	510	820	2,240	480
57	Italian	25	65	40	65	205	45
58	Chinese, n.o.s.	10	-	15	25	225	10
59	Cantonese	-	-	-	10	25	-
60	Portuguese	25	10	-	35	310	-
61	Punjabi	-	10	25	50	60	20
62	Other languages (6)	265	245	430	635	1,420	405
63	Multiple responses	25	25	35	55	145	10
64	English and French	-	-	10	25	20	10
65	English and non-official language	20	20	30	20	95	-
66	French and non-official language	-	-	-	-	30	-
67	English, French and non-official language	-	-	-	-	-	-

See reference material at the end of the publication. – Voir les documents de référence à la fin de la publication.

Tableau 1. Certaines caractéristiques des secteurs de recensement, recensement de 2001 – Données intégrales et données-échantillon (20 %)

Toronto 0602	Toronto 0603	Toronto 0604	Toronto 0605	Toronto 0606	Toronto 0607	Caractéristiques	N°
						CARACTÉRISTIQUES DE LA POPULATION	
4,448	**4,814**	**2,361**	**2,107**	**5,675**	**3,152**	**Population, 1996 (1)**	1
4,651	**4,823**	**2,407**	**2,162**	**5,618**	**3,076**	**Population, 2001 (2)**	2
4.6	0.2	1.9	2.6	-1.0	-2.4	Variation en pourcentage de la population, 1996-2001	3
3.94	1.15	0.86	1.53	3.36	3.21	Superficie des terres en kilomètres carrés, 2001	4
4,655	**4,820**	**2,410**	**2,160**	**5,615**	**3,075**	**Population totale – Données intégrales (3)**	5
						selon le sexe et les groupes d'âge	
2,155	2,255	1,055	1,020	2,750	1,505	Sexe masculin	6
105	130	30	50	145	85	0-4 ans	7
155	110	45	55	165	90	5-9 ans	8
185	90	35	60	175	95	10-14 ans	9
175	105	55	45	160	85	15-19 ans	10
110	150	50	60	190	65	20-24 ans	11
70	225	65	70	175	65	25-29 ans	12
70	230	55	65	225	80	30-34 ans	13
135	230	65	75	245	130	35-39 ans	14
180	195	65	80	245	150	40-44 ans	15
190	150	75	75	185	95	45-49 ans	16
155	115	95	75	150	95	50-54 ans	17
155	100	80	85	145	80	55-59 ans	18
105	90	70	50	125	70	60-64 ans	19
115	75	70	50	130	95	65-69 ans	20
85	110	75	30	125	110	70-74 ans	21
80	75	40	40	95	70	75-79 ans	22
45	55	35	30	65	20	80-84 ans	23
45	30	45	35	25	15	85 ans et plus	24
2,500	2,565	1,355	1,135	2,865	1,570	Sexe féminin	25
115	115	30	45	125	85	0-4 ans	26
165	105	30	50	180	115	5-9 ans	27
175	75	40	55	160	85	10-14 ans	28
155	80	50	50	140	90	15-19 ans	29
120	150	55	80	165	65	20-24 ans	30
80	225	75	60	175	75	25-29 ans	31
115	250	75	55	220	120	30-34 ans	32
140	220	65	75	255	120	35-39 ans	33
215	170	80	75	215	140	40-44 ans	34
205	160	90	80	185	90	45-49 ans	35
195	115	115	105	185	95	50-54 ans	36
165	120	95	90	165	90	55-59 ans	37
110	125	95	40	175	90	60-64 ans	38
115	160	90	45	160	125	65-69 ans	39
105	160	95	35	150	90	70-74 ans	40
95	145	80	55	120	50	75-79 ans	41
75	110	100	50	65	30	80-84 ans	42
145	75	105	75	30	15	85 ans et plus	43
3,750	**4,200**	**2,195**	**1,840**	**4,665**	**2,515**	**Population totale de 15 ans et plus**	44
						selon l'état matrimonial légal	
880	1,400	550	490	1,350	575	Célibataire (jamais marié(e))	45
2,325	1,760	1,045	975	2,535	1,595	Légalement marié(e) (et non séparé(e))	46
70	175	90	65	150	65	Séparé(e), mais toujours légalement marié(e)	47
165	440	180	125	300	115	Divorcé(e)	48
310	425	330	185	330	165	Veuf ou veuve	49
						selon l'union libre	
3,645	3,830	2,085	1,720	4,415	2,420	Ne vivant pas en union libre	50
110	370	110	125	250	100	Vivant en union libre	51
4,385	**4,740**	**2,280**	**2,040**	**5,615**	**3,065**	**Population totale – Données-échantillon (20 %) (4)**	52
						selon la langue maternelle	
4,370	4,630	2,275	2,035	5,550	3,050	Réponses uniques	53
3,970	3,415	2,035	1,685	3,140	2,340	Anglais	54
50	70	25	60	125	55	Français	55
345	1,140	210	285	2,285	660	Langues non officielles (5)	56
10	215	-	30	350	80	Italien	57
25	15	-	10	-	-	Chinois, n.d.a.	58
-	-	-	10	10	-	Cantonais	59
10	100	10	45	905	125	Portugais	60
10	45	-	-	20	70	Pendjabi	61
290	770	200	205	1,000	390	Autres langues (6)	62
20	115	10	10	65	15	Réponses multiples	63
10	-	10	-	15	-	Anglais et français	64
-	105	-	10	45	10	Anglais et langue non officielle	65
-	10	-	-	-	-	Français et langue non officielle	66
-	-	-	-	10	-	Anglais, français et langue non officielle	67

See reference material at the end of the publication. – Voir les documents de référence à la fin de la publication.

Table 1. Selected Characteristics for Census Tracts, 2001 Census – 100% Data and 20% Sample Data

No.	Characteristics	Toronto 0592.01 A	Toronto 0592.02 A	Toronto 0593	Toronto 0600.01	Toronto 0600.02	Toronto 0601
	POPULATION CHARACTERISTICS						
	by home language						
68	Single responses	5,685	5,615	6,685	5,975	6,000	3,570
69	English	5,610	5,545	6,620	5,870	5,490	3,550
70	French	20	15	-	40	-	-
71	Non-official languages (5)	50	60	70	70	510	15
72	Cantonese	-	-	-	-	-	-
73	Chinese, n.o.s.	-	-	-	-	135	-
74	Italian	-	20	-	-	10	-
75	Punjabi	-	-	10	30	20	-
76	Portuguese	-	-	-	10	55	-
77	Other languages (6)	45	30	55	25	295	15
78	Multiple responses	180	245	215	585	1,435	375
79	English and French	30	85	40	175	60	155
80	English and non-official language	120	155	175	385	1,280	215
81	French and non-official language	-	-	-	10	-	-
82	English, French and non-official language	30	-	-	25	90	-
	by knowledge of official languages						
83	English only	5,605	5,480	6,490	5,345	6,610	3,200
84	French only	10	-	-	20	10	-
85	English and French	250	380	410	1,175	725	740
86	Neither English nor French	10	-	-	25	85	-
	by knowledge of non-official languages (5) (7)						
87	Italian	35	85	75	135	315	65
88	Cantonese	-	-	-	10	80	-
89	Chinese, n.o.s.	15	15	15	20	215	10
90	Spanish	50	35	40	120	155	40
91	Portuguese	25	10	15	45	350	10
92	Punjabi	10	-	30	65	160	25
93	Tagalog (Pilipino)	25	10	15	35	160	-
	by first official language spoken						
94	English	5,795	5,745	6,845	6,360	7,215	3,840
95	French	60	115	60	130	120	75
96	English and French	10	-	-	50	10	25
97	Neither English nor French	10	-	-	25	85	-
98	Official language minority - (number) (8)	60	115	55	155	130	90
99	Official language minority - (percentage) (8)	1.0	2.0	0.8	2.4	1.7	2.3
	by ethnic origin (9)						
100	Canadian	2,265	2,290	2,625	2,090	1,405	1,135
101	English	1,995	2,570	2,590	2,710	1,280	1,560
102	Scottish	1,330	1,590	1,870	1,840	825	860
103	Irish	1,535	1,445	1,615	1,385	940	980
104	Chinese	40	20	60	110	450	-
105	Italian	295	275	230	405	860	255
106	East Indian	35	25	80	30	625	30
107	French	575	525	660	650	255	120
108	German	485	485	740	615	395	390
109	Portuguese	55	60	70	120	575	-
110	Polish	240	150	205	240	465	95
111	Jewish	35	15	45	75	20	60
112	Jamaican	180	50	40	10	150	-
113	Filipino	65	10	15	35	235	-
114	Ukrainian	175	185	200	300	130	95
	by Aboriginal identity						
115	Total Aboriginal identity population (10)	75	15	100	10	30	-
116	Total non-Aboriginal population	5,790	5,845	6,805	6,555	7,405	3,940
	by Aboriginal origin						
117	Total Aboriginal origins population (11)	245	35	190	55	30	15
118	Total non-Aboriginal population	5,615	5,825	6,715	6,510	7,405	3,930
	by Registered Indian status						
119	Registered Indian (12)	15	-	50	-	35	-
120	Not a Registered Indian	5,850	5,855	6,855	6,560	7,405	3,940

Tableau 1. Certaines caractéristiques des secteurs de recensement, recensement de 2001 – Données intégrales et données-échantillon (20 %)

Toronto 0602	Toronto 0603	Toronto 0604	Toronto 0605	Toronto 0606	Toronto 0607	Caractéristiques	N°
						CARACTÉRISTIQUES DE LA POPULATION	
						selon la langue parlée à la maison	
4,195	4,005	2,175	1,835	4,275	2,710	Réponses uniques	68
4,170	3,680	2,165	1,795	3,465	2,545	Anglais	69
-	10	-	-	20	-	Français	70
25	320	-	35	790	165	Langues non officielles (5)	71
-	-	-	-	-	-	Cantonais	72
-	-	-	-	-	-	Chinois, n.d.a.	73
-	75	-	-	140	-	Italien	74
-	40	-	-	-	40	Pendjabi	75
-	15	-	10	440	50	Portugais	76
20	190	10	25	215	75	Autres langues (6)	77
190	740	100	200	1,340	360	Réponses multiples	78
60	50	35	40	100	60	Anglais et français	79
100	680	65	155	1,225	300	Anglais et langue non officielle	80
-	-	-	-	-	-	Français et langue non officielle	81
25	-	10	10	20	-	Anglais, français et langue non officielle	82
						selon la connaissance des langues officielles	
3,680	4,165	1,960	1,680	4,895	2,715	Anglais seulement	83
-	-	-	-	10	-	Français seulement	84
695	530	310	350	465	325	Anglais et français	85
10	45	-	10	250	25	Ni l'anglais ni le français	86
						selon la connaissance des langues non officielles (5) (7)	
60	260	10	45	465	105	Italien	87
-	-	-	10	10	-	Cantonais	88
30	30	-	-	-	-	Chinois, n.d.a.	89
80	60	50	75	70	10	Espagnol	90
10	120	-	50	970	140	Portugais	91
15	60	-	-	50	90	Pendjabi	92
-	115	15	-	35	15	Tagalog (pilipino)	93
						selon la première langue officielle parlée	
4,310	4,575	2,220	1,960	5,190	2,980	Anglais	94
40	80	30	60	125	50	Français	95
25	30	20	10	60	15	Anglais et français	96
10	50	-	10	240	25	Ni l'anglais ni le français	97
55	100	40	60	155	55	Minorité de langue officielle - (nombre) (8)	98
1.3	2.1	1.8	2.9	2.8	1.8	Minorité de langue officielle - (pourcentage) (8)	99
						selon l'origine ethnique (9)	
1,315	1,240	570	595	1,390	920	Canadien	100
2,040	1,330	870	765	1,110	1,000	Anglais	101
1,190	850	590	440	770	675	Écossais	102
1,065	680	435	430	635	575	Irlandais	103
75	40	10	25	40	10	Chinois	104
335	390	30	200	670	230	Italien	105
35	135	15	10	120	90	Indien de l'Inde	106
340	335	200	150	350	220	Français	107
370	340	275	255	340	345	Allemand	108
-	160	10	50	1,095	180	Portugais	109
155	200	50	100	335	85	Polonais	110
60	10	25	40	10	-	Juif	111
30	60	-	-	10	20	Jamaïquain	112
-	130	20	-	85	30	Philippin	113
205	80	55	70	140	85	Ukrainien	114
						selon l'identité autochtone	
-	60	10	10	65	15	Total de la population ayant une identité autochtone (10)	115
4,385	4,685	2,270	2,035	5,550	3,055	Total de la population non autochtone	116
						selon l'origine autochtone	
15	100	20	15	110	50	Total de la population ayant une origine autochtone (11)	117
4,370	4,645	2,255	2,020	5,510	3,020	Total de la population non autochtone	118
						selon le statut d'Indien inscrit	
-	45	-	-	-	10	Oui, Indien inscrit (12)	119
4,385	4,700	2,275	2,035	5,610	3,065	Non, pas un Indien inscrit	120

Table 1. Selected Characteristics for Census Tracts, 2001 Census – 100% Data and 20% Sample Data

No.	Characteristics	Toronto 0592.01 A	Toronto 0592.02 A	Toronto 0593	Toronto 0600.01	Toronto 0600.02	Toronto 0601
	POPULATION CHARACTERISTICS						
	by visible minority groups						
121	Total visible minority population	480	185	220	380	1,965	160
122	Chinese	35	20	65	85	420	10
123	South Asian	45	25	55	90	735	135
124	Black	305	65	30	35	275	-
125	Filipino	40	10	15	35	215	-
126	Latin American	10	20	20	15	15	15
127	Southeast Asian	-	30	-	15	15	-
128	Arab	-	-	-	30	75	-
129	West Asian	-	-	-	10	15	-
130	Korean	20	-	-	35	100	-
131	Japanese	-	25	10	-	20	-
132	Visible minority, n.i.e. (13)	-	-	10	10	40	-
133	Multiple visible minorities (14)	25	-	15	20	45	-
	by citizenship						
134	Canadian citizenship (15)	5,595	5,645	6,545	6,215	7,010	3,640
135	Citizenship other than Canadian	265	215	360	350	425	305
	by place of birth of respondent						
136	Non-immigrant population	5,000	5,125	5,815	4,965	4,855	3,090
137	Born in province of residence	4,380	4,690	5,055	3,705	4,245	2,535
138	Immigrant population (16)	855	730	1,055	1,455	2,545	740
139	United States	70	25	60	195	45	65
140	Central and South America	25	30	45	50	105	20
141	Caribbean and Bermuda	125	25	25	40	200	10
142	United Kingdom	300	400	390	375	230	240
143	Other Europe (17)	220	170	400	465	945	300
144	Africa	20	10	25	150	125	45
145	Asia and the Middle East	80	70	80	160	890	45
146	Oceania and other (18)	20	-	30	25	10	15
147	Non-permanent residents (19)	10	10	35	145	35	115
148	**Total immigrant population**	**850**	**730**	**1,055**	**1,460**	**2,545**	**740**
	by period of immigration						
149	Before 1961	195	155	295	355	235	195
150	1961-1970	150	230	320	310	580	195
151	1971-1980	155	150	165	325	635	175
152	1981-1990	110	55	105	195	620	80
153	1991-2001 (20)	245	130	170	275	475	85
154	1991-1995	120	30	65	140	275	50
155	1996-2001 (20)	130	100	100	130	200	45
	by age at immigration						
156	0-4 years	155	110	170	135	280	70
157	5-19 years	290	245	380	375	815	175
158	20 years and over	405	375	510	950	1,450	490
159	**Total population**	**5,860**	**5,855**	**6,905**	**6,565**	**7,435**	**3,940**
	by religion						
160	Catholic (21)	1,565	1,565	1,530	2,170	3,785	945
161	Protestant	2,695	2,995	3,420	3,150	1,900	2,110
162	Christian Orthodox	25	-	55	15	165	80
163	Christian, n.i.e. (22)	195	140	135	60	170	10
164	Muslim	10	10	10	45	370	35
165	Jewish	10	10	30	75	15	70
166	Buddhist	20	-	10	10	30	-
167	Hindu	-	-	10	65	165	30
168	Sikh	10	-	25	-	130	-
169	Eastern religions (23)	-	-	-	-	15	70
170	Other religions (24)	-	-	10	-	-	-
171	No religious affiliation (25)	1,335	1,140	1,670	970	680	585
172	**Total population 15 years and over**	**4,440**	**4,230**	**5,435**	**5,215**	**5,535**	**3,110**
	by generation status						
173	1st generation (26)	820	700	1,025	1,520	2,475	830
174	2nd generation (27)	1,045	860	1,260	1,110	1,620	825
175	3rd generation and over (28)	2,575	2,675	3,150	2,590	1,435	1,455
176	**Total population 1 year and over (29)**	**5,775**	**5,810**	**6,850**	**6,525**	**7,380**	**3,925**
	by place of residence 1 year ago (mobility)						
177	Non-movers	4,905	5,480	6,075	6,015	6,990	3,595
178	Movers	870	325	775	510	390	330
179	Non-migrants	315	105	325	255	195	155
180	Migrants	555	215	455	255	195	175
181	Internal migrants	555	205	410	225	175	120
182	Intraprovincial migrants	490	190	390	145	130	120
183	Interprovincial migrants	65	25	15	75	45	-
184	External migrants	-	10	45	35	25	60

Tableau 1. Certaines caractéristiques des secteurs de recensement, recensement de 2001 – Données intégrales et données-échantillon (20 %)

Toronto 0602	Toronto 0603	Toronto 0604	Toronto 0605	Toronto 0606	Toronto 0607	Caractéristiques	N°
						CARACTÉRISTIQUES DE LA POPULATION	
						selon les groupes de minorités visibles	
170	510	70	60	605	215	Total de la population des minorités visibles	121
75	10	-	20	15	-	Chinois	122
35	150	25	10	160	90	Sud-Asiatique	123
10	115	25	-	105	30	Noir	124
-	120	15	-	75	15	Philippin	125
-	15	10	20	10	-	Latino-Américain	126
-	10	-	-	25	35	Asiatique du Sud-Est	127
10	45	-	-	25	-	Arabe	128
-	-	-	-	170	-	Asiatique occidental	129
20	15	-	-	-	-	Coréen	130
15	10	-	-	-	20	Japonais	131
-	10	-	-	20	15	Minorité visible, n.i.a. (13)	132
-	15	-	-	-	10	Minorités visibles multiples (14)	133
						selon la citoyenneté	
4,120	4,160	2,115	1,865	4,800	2,950	Citoyenneté canadienne (15)	134
265	580	165	175	810	120	Citoyenneté autre que canadienne	135
						selon le lieu de naissance du répondant	
3,345	3,095	1,630	1,475	3,195	2,265	Population non immigrante	136
2,595	2,490	1,210	1,190	2,735	1,930	Née dans la province de résidence	137
1,000	1,590	615	530	2,375	800	Population immigrante (16)	138
80	90	80	60	30	25	États-Unis	139
10	15	10	30	50	10	Amérique centrale et du Sud	140
35	65	15	-	20	30	Caraïbes et Bermudes	141
465	390	310	200	320	200	Royaume-Uni	142
235	660	130	185	1,545	430	Autre Europe (17)	143
50	75	40	10	40	10	Afrique	144
95	285	30	40	330	95	Asie et Moyen-Orient	145
40	-	-	10	30	10	Océanie et autre (18)	146
35	55	35	30	50	-	Résidents non permanents (19)	147
1,005	**1,590**	**615**	**535**	**2,375**	**800**	**Population immigrante totale**	148
						selon la période d'immigration	
220	400	205	180	575	285	Avant 1961	149
280	205	155	105	365	255	1961-1970	150
230	195	130	100	475	70	1971-1980	151
180	245	65	50	430	90	1981-1990	152
95	545	60	100	520	100	1991-2001 (20)	153
35	205	15	20	240	15	1991-1995	154
65	335	40	80	280	90	1996-2001 (20)	155
						selon l'âge à l'immigration	
125	150	40	45	165	75	0-4 ans	156
230	325	145	80	685	250	5-19 ans	157
650	1,115	425	405	1,530	480	20 ans et plus	158
4,385	**4,745**	**2,275**	**2,035**	**5,615**	**3,065**	**Population totale**	159
						selon la religion	
1,290	1,705	455	750	2,845	1,110	Catholique (21)	160
2,165	1,695	1,215	835	1,490	1,240	Protestante	161
10	90	25	30	75	55	Orthodoxe chrétienne	162
95	80	40	20	65	85	Chrétiennes, n.i.a. (22)	163
55	75	15	-	240	-	Musulmane	164
35	10	30	20	10	-	Juive	165
10	10	-	10	35	-	Bouddhiste	166
15	80	-	10	65	20	Hindoue	167
15	45	-	-	15	70	Sikh	168
10	-	-	-	-	-	Religions orientales (23)	169
10	-	-	-	20	-	Autres religions (24)	170
680	965	490	365	750	490	Aucune appartenance religieuse (25)	171
3,480	**4,105**	**2,070**	**1,715**	**4,670**	**2,545**	**Population totale de 15 ans et plus**	172
						selon le statut des générations	
995	1,570	635	540	2,305	770	1re génération (26)	173
900	925	560	395	1,010	735	2e génération (27)	174
1,585	1,620	870	780	1,355	1,040	3e génération et plus (28)	175
4,355	**4,680**	**2,265**	**2,020**	**5,570**	**3,050**	**Population totale de 1 an et plus (29)**	176
						selon le lieu de résidence 1 an auparavant (mobilité)	
3,675	3,745	1,995	1,665	4,970	2,865	Personnes n'ayant pas déménagé	177
680	940	275	355	600	190	Personnes ayant déménagé	178
365	400	145	160	245	95	Non-migrants	179
315	535	130	195	355	95	Migrants	180
270	340	100	140	285	75	Migrants internes	181
250	315	75	90	240	70	Migrants infraprovinciaux	182
20	25	25	50	50	-	Migrants interprovinciaux	183
45	195	25	55	70	15	Migrants externes	184

Table 1. Selected Characteristics for Census Tracts, 2001 Census – 100% Data and 20% Sample Data

No.	Characteristics	Toronto 0592.01 A	Toronto 0592.02 A	Toronto 0593	Toronto 0600.01	Toronto 0600.02	Toronto 0601
	POPULATION CHARACTERISTICS						
185	**Total population 5 years and over (30)**	**5,395**	**5,445**	**6,570**	**6,275**	**6,990**	**3,760**
	by place of residence 5 years ago (mobility)						
186	Non-movers	2,320	3,690	4,155	4,420	5,055	2,490
187	Movers	3,075	1,755	2,415	1,860	1,935	1,270
188	Non-migrants	1,095	635	775	730	500	645
189	Migrants	1,980	1,120	1,635	1,125	1,435	625
190	Internal migrants	1,840	1,010	1,520	805	1,235	445
191	Intraprovincial migrants	1,715	895	1,420	570	1,075	395
192	Interprovincial migrants	120	115	100	235	155	50
193	External migrants	140	110	120	320	205	175
194	**Total population 15 to 24 years**	**655**	**780**	**875**	**1,025**	**1,135**	**540**
	by school attendance						
195	Not attending school	315	240	370	205	340	65
196	Attending school full time	310	510	470	805	760	440
197	Attending school part time	35	35	35	20	30	30
198	**Total population 15 years and over**	**4,440**	**4,230**	**5,440**	**5,220**	**5,535**	**3,105**
	by highest level of schooling						
199	Less than grade 9 (31)	220	110	180	45	235	45
200	Grades 9-13 without high school graduation certificate	1,120	1,030	980	590	975	360
201	Grades 9-13 with high school graduation certificate	710	575	895	445	635	230
202	Some postsecondary without degree, certificate or diploma (32)	530	475	515	690	700	365
203	Trades certificate or diploma (33)	480	495	595	260	320	135
204	College certificate or diploma (34)	790	970	1,035	680	1,000	535
205	University certificate below bachelor's degree	70	40	125	155	195	70
206	University with bachelor's degree or higher	525	535	1,110	2,360	1,470	1,355
	by combinations of unpaid work						
207	Males 15 years and over	2,060	2,105	2,765	2,550	2,715	1,520
208	Reported unpaid work (35)	1,815	1,890	2,500	2,280	2,430	1,340
209	Housework and child care and care or assistance to seniors	110	205	190	245	260	100
210	Housework and child care only	680	780	800	710	980	395
211	Housework and care or assistance to seniors only	110	90	180	165	170	140
212	Child care and care or assistance to seniors only	-	-	-	-	-	-
213	Housework only	870	755	1,310	1,140	990	695
214	Child care only	35	30	10	15	15	-
215	Care or assistance to seniors only	-	20	-	-	10	10
216	Females 15 years and over	2,380	2,125	2,670	2,665	2,815	1,585
217	Reported unpaid work (35)	2,235	2,025	2,520	2,470	2,585	1,485
218	Housework and child care and care or assistance to seniors	210	270	310	355	395	175
219	Housework and child care only	800	915	850	825	985	460
220	Housework and care or assistance to seniors only	125	115	240	225	210	165
221	Child care and care or assistance to seniors only	-	-	10	-	-	-
222	Housework only	1,085	680	1,100	1,025	965	690
223	Child care only	-	15	-	10	25	-
224	Care or assistance to seniors only	10	15	10	30	10	-
	by labour force activity						
225	Males 15 years and over	2,055	2,105	2,765	2,555	2,715	1,525
226	In the labour force	1,635	1,770	2,230	1,925	2,210	1,085
227	Employed	1,545	1,685	2,150	1,860	2,080	1,035
228	Unemployed	90	80	80	60	130	50
229	Not in the labour force	420	340	540	625	505	435
230	Participation rate	79.6	84.1	80.7	75.3	81.4	71.1
231	Employment rate	75.2	80.0	77.8	72.8	76.6	67.9
232	Unemployment rate	5.5	4.5	3.6	3.1	5.9	4.6
233	Females 15 years and over	2,385	2,120	2,670	2,665	2,815	1,585
234	In the labour force	1,510	1,480	1,845	1,675	2,025	860
235	Employed	1,430	1,385	1,785	1,590	2,000	810
236	Unemployed	75	95	60	80	30	50
237	Not in the labour force	875	640	825	995	790	730
238	Participation rate	63.3	69.8	69.1	62.9	71.9	54.3
239	Employment rate	60.0	65.3	66.9	59.7	71.0	51.1
240	Unemployment rate	5.0	6.4	3.3	4.8	1.5	5.8

Tableau 1. Certaines caractéristiques des secteurs de recensement, recensement de 2001 – Données intégrales et données-échantillon (20 %)

Toronto 0602	Toronto 0603	Toronto 0604	Toronto 0605	Toronto 0606	Toronto 0607	Caractéristiques	N°
						CARACTÉRISTIQUES DE LA POPULATION	
4,170	**4,490**	**2,190**	**1,960**	**5,350**	**2,975**	**Population totale de 5 ans et plus (30)**	185
						selon le lieu de résidence 5 ans auparavant (mobilité)	
2,600	2,065	1,080	925	3,240	2,185	Personnes n'ayant pas déménagé	186
1,565	2,425	1,110	1,040	2,110	795	Personnes ayant déménagé	187
905	885	510	565	870	375	Non-migrants	188
660	1,535	600	470	1,235	415	Migrants	189
530	1,195	510	345	935	365	Migrants internes	190
430	1,060	390	275	760	320	Migrants infraprovinciaux	191
100	135	120	65	170	50	Migrants interprovinciaux	192
130	340	90	130	305	45	Migrants externes	193
550	**445**	**200**	**250**	**665**	**320**	**Population totale de 15 à 24 ans**	194
						selon la fréquentation scolaire	
125	160	65	95	245	130	Ne fréquentant pas l'école	195
400	240	130	150	355	180	Fréquentant l'école à plein temps	196
25	40	-	10	60	10	Fréquentant l'école à temps partiel	197
3,480	**4,105**	**2,070**	**1,715**	**4,675**	**2,540**	**Population totale de 15 ans et plus**	198
						selon le plus haut niveau de scolarité atteint	
45	325	25	45	805	220	Niveau inférieur à la 9e année (31)	199
470	695	210	245	1,045	470	De la 9e à la 13e année sans certificat d'études secondaires	200
325	495	225	130	625	295	De la 9e à la 13e année avec certificat d'études secondaires	201
440	525	275	235	540	305	Études postsecondaires partielles sans grade, certificat ou diplôme (32)	202
135	360	125	100	300	245	Certificat ou diplôme d'une école de métiers (33)	203
470	710	425	345	675	560	Certificat ou diplôme collégial (34)	204
145	155	115	85	80	55	Certificat universitaire inférieur au baccalauréat	205
1,440	840	670	525	600	405	Études universitaires avec baccalauréat ou diplôme supérieur	206
						selon les combinaisons de travail non rémunéré	
1,645	1,885	915	830	2,275	1,265	Hommes de 15 ans et plus	207
1,490	1,650	755	740	1,990	1,120	Travail non rémunéré déclaré (35)	208
135	80	25	85	95	65	Travaux ménagers et soins aux enfants et soins ou aide aux personnes âgées	209
480	335	155	200	550	410	Travaux ménagers et soins aux enfants seulement	210
140	120	80	55	115	100	Travaux ménagers et soins ou aide aux personnes âgées seulement	211
-	-	-	-	-	-	Soins aux enfants et soins ou aide aux personnes âgées seulement	212
715	1,080	475	370	1,220	525	Travaux ménagers seulement	213
25	30	10	10	10	10	Soins aux enfants seulement	214
-	10	-	30	10	10	Soins ou aide aux personnes âgées seulement	215
1,840	2,225	1,150	885	2,395	1,275	Femmes de 15 ans et plus	216
1,765	2,055	1,060	840	2,255	1,225	Travail non rémunéré déclaré (35)	217
220	180	75	130	180	100	Travaux ménagers et soins aux enfants et soins ou aide aux personnes âgées	218
530	450	160	220	640	415	Travaux ménagers et soins aux enfants seulement	219
215	260	170	105	205	160	Travaux ménagers et soins ou aide aux personnes âgées seulement	220
-	-	-	-	10	-	Soins aux enfants et soins ou aide aux personnes âgées seulement	221
785	1,145	635	370	1,180	535	Travaux ménagers seulement	222
10	10	15	-	-	10	Soins aux enfants seulement	223
-	15	-	10	30	-	Soins ou aide aux personnes âgées seulement	224
						selon l'activité	
1,640	1,880	910	830	2,275	1,270	Hommes de 15 ans et plus	225
1,240	1,365	690	605	1,610	855	Population active	226
1,170	1,275	645	565	1,515	810	Personnes occupées	227
65	85	45	30	90	45	Chômeurs	228
405	520	225	225	675	405	Inactifs	229
75.6	72.6	75.8	72.9	70.8	67.3	Taux d'activité	230
71.3	67.8	70.9	68.1	66.6	63.8	Taux d'emploi	231
5.2	6.2	6.5	5.0	5.6	5.3	Taux de chômage	232
1,840	2,225	1,150	885	2,395	1,280	Femmes de 15 ans et plus	233
1,075	1,255	600	580	1,395	675	Population active	234
1,020	1,195	565	580	1,320	655	Personnes occupées	235
55	65	35	10	70	25	Chômeuses	236
765	970	550	305	1,000	600	Inactives	237
58.4	56.4	52.2	65.5	58.2	52.7	Taux d'activité	238
55.4	53.7	49.1	65.5	55.1	51.2	Taux d'emploi	239
5.1	5.2	5.8	1.7	5.0	3.7	Taux de chômage	240

Table 1. Selected Characteristics for Census Tracts, 2001 Census – 100% Data and 20% Sample Data

No.	Characteristics	Toronto 0592.01 A	Toronto 0592.02 A	Toronto 0593	Toronto 0600.01	Toronto 0600.02	Toronto 0601
	POPULATION CHARACTERISTICS						
	by labour force activity – concluded						
241	Both sexes - Participation rate	70.8	76.7	74.9	68.9	76.5	62.6
242	15-24 years	80.2	67.3	73.1	56.6	61.5	62.6
243	25 years and over	69.2	78.8	75.2	72.0	80.4	62.8
244	Both sexes - Employment rate	67.0	72.7	72.5	66.2	73.7	59.3
245	15-24 years	71.0	54.1	67.4	51.5	53.3	51.9
246	25 years and over	66.5	76.7	73.5	69.8	78.9	60.8
247	Both sexes - Unemployment rate	5.4	5.4	3.3	4.0	3.8	5.1
248	15-24 years	11.4	18.1	7.8	9.5	13.7	15.2
249	25 years and over	4.0	2.9	2.5	3.0	1.8	3.4
250	**Total labour force 15 years and over**	**3,140**	**3,250**	**4,075**	**3,600**	**4,240**	**1,945**
	by industry based on the 1997 NAICS						
251	Industry - Not applicable (36)	20	35	35	25	35	40
252	All industries (37)	3,125	3,210	4,040	3,570	4,200	1,910
253	11 Agriculture, forestry, fishing and hunting	20	15	265	15	-	-
254	21 Mining and oil and gas extraction	15	-	20	45	-	25
255	22 Utilities	20	35	35	50	35	25
256	23 Construction	145	140	290	20	100	40
257	31-33 Manufacturing	640	585	595	225	585	145
258	41 Wholesale trade	200	180	170	285	250	190
259	44-45 Retail trade	440	485	350	285	525	90
260	48-49 Transportation and warehousing	170	235	260	150	190	70
261	51 Information and cultural industries	115	45	155	165	120	55
262	52 Finance and insurance	85	85	90	470	450	200
263	53 Real estate and rental and leasing	65	30	115	75	90	110
264	54 Professional, scientific and technical services	135	140	240	560	465	325
265	55 Management of companies and enterprises	-	10	-	10	-	-
266	56 Administrative and support, waste management and remediation services	85	170	215	160	140	75
267	61 Educational services	135	280	340	240	285	145
268	62 Health care and social assistance	205	255	280	380	305	145
269	71 Arts, entertainment and recreation	30	75	105	80	50	90
270	72 Accommodation and food services	195	170	275	100	260	45
271	81 Other services (except public administration)	235	115	140	145	185	40
272	91 Public administration	175	160	100	115	150	60
	by class of worker						
273	Class of worker - Not applicable (36)	20	35	30	25	40	40
274	All classes of worker (37)	3,125	3,210	4,045	3,570	4,200	1,910
275	Paid workers	2,890	2,920	3,385	3,190	3,945	1,670
276	Employees	2,800	2,810	3,105	2,925	3,765	1,490
277	Self-employed (incorporated)	95	105	285	265	185	185
278	Self-employed (unincorporated)	215	280	615	355	250	230
279	Unpaid family workers	15	10	40	25	-	-
	by occupation based on the 2001 NOC-S						
280	Male labour force 15 years and over	1,635	1,770	2,230	1,920	2,210	1,085
281	Occupation - Not applicable (36)	-	-	15	15	30	30
282	All occupations (37)	1,635	1,765	2,215	1,910	2,180	1,055
283	A Management occupations	255	415	465	800	525	310
284	B Business, finance and administration occupations	150	155	90	325	370	160
285	C Natural and applied sciences and related occupations	130	130	190	270	250	155
286	D Health occupations	20	20	25	45	30	35
287	E Occupations in social science, education, government service and religion	25	80	145	120	100	65
288	F Occupations in art, culture, recreation and sport	35	20	80	30	20	45
289	G Sales and service occupations	325	330	425	245	455	180
290	H Trades, transport and equipment operators and related occupations	500	465	535	70	290	45
291	I Occupations unique to primary industry	25	40	185	10	15	25
292	J Occupations unique to processing, manufacturing and utilities	160	115	80	-	130	40
293	Female labour force 15 years and over	1,510	1,480	1,845	1,675	2,025	860
294	Occupation - Not applicable (36)	20	35	15	10	-	10
295	All occupations (37)	1,490	1,445	1,830	1,660	2,020	850
296	A Management occupations	180	150	215	275	250	125
297	B Business, finance and administration occupations	375	420	475	455	625	235
298	C Natural and applied sciences and related occupations	25	15	40	55	65	40
299	D Health occupations	110	115	140	140	125	85

Tableau 1. Certaines caractéristiques des secteurs de recensement, recensement de 2001 – Données intégrales et données-échantillon (20 %)

Toronto 0602	Toronto 0603	Toronto 0604	Toronto 0605	Toronto 0606	Toronto 0607	Caractéristiques	Nº
						CARACTÉRISTIQUES DE LA POPULATION	
						selon l'activité – fin	
66.4	63.8	62.3	69.1	64.2	60.3	Les deux sexes - Taux d'activité	241
68.2	86.5	77.5	63.3	82.0	74.6	15-24 ans	242
66.4	61.2	60.6	70.3	61.2	58.5	25 ans et plus	243
63.0	60.3	58.6	66.8	60.6	57.6	Les deux sexes - Taux d'emploi	244
57.3	76.4	47.5	53.1	71.4	66.7	15-24 ans	245
64.2	58.3	59.4	69.4	59.0	56.3	25 ans et plus	246
5.4	5.7	6.2	3.4	5.5	4.9	Les deux sexes - Taux de chômage	247
16.0	11.7	38.7	19.4	13.0	8.5	15-24 ans	248
3.3	4.5	2.2	1.0	3.9	3.8	25 ans et plus	249
2,315	**2,625**	**1,285**	**1,185**	**3,000**	**1,535**	**Population active totale de 15 ans et plus**	250
						selon l'industrie basée sur le SCIAN de 1997	
15	65	20	10	45	10	Industrie - Sans objet (36)	251
2,300	2,555	1,270	1,175	2,960	1,520	Toutes les industries (37)	252
-	-	15	-	-	-	11 Agriculture, foresterie, pêche et chasse	253
-	15	15	10	10	-	21 Extraction minière et extraction de pétrole et de gaz	254
15	-	-	-	20	10	22 Services publics	255
115	200	25	50	215	65	23 Construction	256
150	390	105	110	445	285	31-33 Fabrication	257
175	160	50	70	195	80	41 Commerce de gros	258
180	215	70	95	330	120	44-45 Commerce de détail	259
55	130	60	35	225	100	48-49 Transport et entreposage	260
100	85	45	45	95	70	51 Industrie de l'information et industrie culturelle	261
270	125	100	115	145	95	52 Finance et assurances	262
95	100	85	65	40	20	53 Services immobiliers et services de location et de location à bail	263
375	260	260	185	240	125	54 Services professionnels, scientifiques et techniques	264
15	-	-	-	-	-	55 Gestion de sociétés et d'entreprises	265
75	155	40	30	160	65	56 Services administratifs, services de soutien, services de gestion des déchets et services d'assainissement	266
215	105	80	90	85	105	61 Services d'enseignement	267
185	180	120	115	165	100	62 Soins de santé et assistance sociale	268
95	70	15	40	55	50	71 Arts, spectacles et loisirs	269
85	175	105	50	215	80	72 Hébergement et services de restauration	270
50	125	55	45	175	95	81 Autres services, sauf les administrations publiques	271
50	75	25	20	125	45	91 Administrations publiques	272
						selon la catégorie de travailleurs	
15	65	20	10	40	10	Catégorie de travailleurs - Sans objet (36)	273
2,300	2,555	1,270	1,175	2,960	1,525	Toutes les catégories de travailleurs (37)	274
1,950	2,335	1,130	1,035	2,735	1,425	Travailleurs rémunérés	275
1,760	2,280	1,035	950	2,670	1,360	Employés	276
190	55	100	90	70	60	Travailleurs autonomes (entreprise constituée en société)	277
325	210	130	135	205	100	Travailleurs autonomes (entreprise non constituée en société)	278
30	10	10	-	15	-	Travailleurs familiaux non rémunérés	279
						selon la profession basée sur la CNP-S de 2001	
1,240	1,365	685	600	1,605	855	Hommes actifs de 15 ans et plus	280
10	25	15	10	25	10	Profession - Sans objet (36)	281
1,235	1,335	670	595	1,585	850	Toutes les professions (37)	282
455	195	210	155	170	135	A Gestion	283
155	100	75	50	180	120	B Affaires, finance et administration	284
110	180	50	95	145	65	C Sciences naturelles et appliquées et professions apparentées	285
45	25	35	20	10	15	D Secteur de la santé	286
85	65	55	65	40	-	E Sciences sociales, enseignement, administration publique et religion	287
55	35	40	15	45	15	F Arts, culture, sports et loisirs	288
175	215	115	135	340	200	G Ventes et services	289
130	315	65	15	495	190	H Métiers, transport et machinerie	290
10	15	15	15	20	10	I Professions propres au secteur primaire	291
20	180	-	35	135	105	J Transformation, fabrication et services d'utilité publique	292
1,080	1,260	600	580	1,395	680	Femmes actives de 15 ans et plus	293
15	35	-	-	15	-	Profession - Sans objet (36)	294
1,065	1,220	595	585	1,375	675	Toutes les professions (37)	295
130	100	135	90	80	75	A Gestion	296
315	340	135	165	335	225	B Affaires, finance et administration	297
40	85	15	15	50	20	C Sciences naturelles et appliquées et professions apparentées	298
85	75	35	60	60	35	D Secteur de la santé	299

Table 1. Selected Characteristics for Census Tracts, 2001 Census – 100% Data and 20% Sample Data

No.	Characteristics	Toronto 0592.01 A	Toronto 0592.02 A	Toronto 0593	Toronto 0600.01	Toronto 0600.02	Toronto 0601
	POPULATION CHARACTERISTICS						
	by occupation based on the 2001 NOC-S – concluded						
	E Occupations in social science, education,						
300	government service and religion	150	175	235	275	230	125
301	F Occupations in art, culture, recreation and sport	40	65	45	80	65	60
302	G Sales and service occupations	440	385	480	335	570	150
	H Trades, transport and equipment						
303	operators and related occupations	40	40	20	10	15	-
304	I Occupations unique to primary industry	10	-	135	10	-	-
	J Occupations unique to processing,						
305	manufacturing and utilities	130	80	50	20	75	15
306	**Total employed labour force 15 years and over**	**2,980**	**3,070**	**3,940**	**3,455**	**4,075**	**1,845**
	by place of work						
307	Males	1,545	1,685	2,150	1,865	2,080	1,035
308	Usual place of work	1,305	1,390	1,515	1,570	1,835	805
309	At home	50	75	330	225	110	155
310	Outside Canada	-	10	50	25	-	10
311	No fixed workplace address	190	210	260	45	130	70
312	Females	1,430	1,385	1,785	1,590	1,995	810
313	Usual place of work	1,315	1,185	1,275	1,300	1,775	665
314	At home	65	150	410	215	175	120
315	Outside Canada	10	-	10	10	15	-
316	No fixed workplace address	50	50	100	75	30	25
	Total employed labour force 15 years and over with usual place of work or no fixed						
317	**workplace address**	**2,850**	**2,835**	**3,145**	**2,985**	**3,770**	**1,565**
	by mode of transportation						
318	Males	1,495	1,600	1,775	1,615	1,960	875
319	Car, truck, van, as driver	1,280	1,440	1,625	1,230	1,630	645
320	Car, truck, van, as passenger	65	115	80	60	100	25
321	Public transit	20	-	10	290	180	165
322	Walked	105	35	40	25	40	25
323	Other method	15	10	20	10	10	15
324	Females	1,360	1,235	1,375	1,370	1,805	685
325	Car, truck, van, as driver	965	1,030	1,175	1,015	1,255	515
326	Car, truck, van, as passenger	115	105	135	120	185	40
327	Public transit	45	10	15	160	345	100
328	Walked	230	70	20	55	15	20
329	Other method	-	20	30	20	15	10
	Total population 15 years and over who worked						
330	**since January 1, 2000**	**3,360**	**3,495**	**4,345**	**4,035**	**4,500**	**2,065**
	by language used at work						
331	Single responses	3,260	3,390	4,275	3,825	4,250	1,965
332	English	3,250	3,390	4,270	3,815	4,210	1,965
333	French	10	-	-	15	10	-
334	Non-official languages (5)	10	-	-	-	30	-
335	Chinese, n.o.s.	-	-	-	-	10	-
336	Cantonese	-	-	-	-	-	-
337	Other languages (6)	-	-	-	-	20	-
338	Multiple responses	100	100	70	210	250	105
339	English and French	65	65	55	165	70	65
340	English and non-official language	30	30	15	30	185	25
341	French and non-official language	-	-	-	-	-	-
342	English, French and non-official language	-	10	-	15	-	15
	DWELLING AND HOUSEHOLD CHARACTERISTICS						
343	**Total number of occupied private dwellings**	**2,315**	**1,735**	**2,285**	**2,040**	**2,055**	**1,295**
	by tenure						
344	Owned	1,395	1,690	2,035	1,995	1,895	1,235
345	Rented	915	45	245	45	155	55
346	Band housing	-	-	-	-	-	-
	by structural type of dwelling						
347	Single-detached house	1,025	1,675	2,115	2,035	1,780	1,280
348	Semi-detached house	205	40	35	-	65	-
349	Row house	200	10	10	-	115	-
350	Apartment, detached duplex	15	10	60	-	20	-
351	Apartment, building that has five or more storeys	410	-	-	-	25	-
	Apartment, building that has fewer than						
352	five storeys (38)	395	10	35	-	50	-
353	Other single-attached house	60	-	30	-	-	-
354	Movable dwelling (39)	-	-	-	-	-	-

Tableau 1. Certaines caractéristiques des secteurs de recensement, recensement de 2001 – Données intégrales et données-échantillon (20 %)

Toronto 0602	Toronto 0603	Toronto 0604	Toronto 0605	Toronto 0606	Toronto 0607	Caractéristiques	N°
						CARACTÉRISTIQUES DE LA POPULATION	
						selon la profession basée sur la CNP-S de 2001 - fin	
200	105	85	70	105	95	E Sciences sociales, enseignement, administration publique et religion	300
75	35	25	40	60	15	F Arts, culture, sports et loisirs	301
185	385	160	140	570	170	G Ventes et services	302
10	20	-	10	40	-	H Métiers, transport et machinerie	303
-	10	-	-	-	-	I Professions propres au secteur primaire	304
25	60	-	-	70	40	J Transformation, fabrication et services d'utilité publique	305
2,195	**2,470**	**1,205**	**1,145**	**2,840**	**1,465**	**Population active occupée totale de 15 ans et plus**	306
						selon le lieu de travail	
1,175	1,280	640	570	1,515	815	Hommes	307
955	1,040	495	495	1,245	670	Lieu habituel de travail	308
140	85	80	45	55	60	À domicile	309
10	10	15	-	15	-	En dehors du Canada	310
65	140	45	35	195	80	Sans adresse de travail fixe	311
1,020	1,200	565	575	1,320	655	Femmes	312
805	1,060	475	480	1,145	580	Lieu habituel de travail	313
170	70	75	75	110	45	À domicile	314
15	-	10	-	-	-	En dehors du Canada	315
35	65	15	20	70	25	Sans adresse de travail fixe	316
1,855	**2,305**	**1,025**	**1,030**	**2,655**	**1,355**	**Population active occupée totale de 15 ans et plus ayant un lieu habituel de travail ou sans adresse de travail fixe**	317
						selon le mode de transport	
1,020	1,180	540	525	1,440	750	Hommes	318
625	830	430	380	1,180	625	Automobile, camion ou fourgonnette, en tant que conducteur	319
70	60	-	15	120	50	Automobile, camion ou fourgonnette, en tant que passager	320
240	145	60	60	70	35	Transport en commun	321
50	125	45	40	50	20	À pied	322
40	20	-	25	20	10	Autre moyen	323
835	1,125	485	500	1,215	605	Femmes	324
580	725	305	365	740	445	Automobile, camion ou fourgonnette, en tant que conductrice	325
60	45	30	10	195	25	Automobile, camion ou fourgonnette, en tant que passagère	326
110	215	70	65	165	95	Transport en commun	327
45	135	65	45	100	35	À pied	328
40	10	15	15	10	-	Autre moyen	329
2,540	**2,745**	**1,370**	**1,250**	**3,175**	**1,695**	**Population totale de 15 ans et plus ayant travaillé depuis le 1er janvier 2000**	330
						selon la langue utilisée au travail	
2,425	2,670	1,320	1,150	2,875	1,630	Réponses uniques	331
2,425	2,655	1,320	1,150	2,805	1,630	Anglais	332
10	-	-	-	-	-	Français	333
-	15	-	-	65	-	Langues non officielles (5)	334
-	-	-	-	-	-	Chinois, n.d.a.	335
-	-	-	-	-	-	Cantonais	336
-	15	-	-	70	-	Autres langues (6)	337
115	75	50	100	300	65	Réponses multiples	338
80	35	25	70	75	25	Anglais et français	339
35	35	25	35	220	40	Anglais et langue non officielle	340
-	-	-	-	-	-	Français et langue non officielle	341
-	-	-	-	10	-	Anglais, français et langue non officielle	342
						CARACTÉRISTIQUES DES LOGEMENTS ET DES MÉNAGES	
1,590	**2,415**	**1,210**	**805**	**2,155**	**1,085**	**Nombre total de logements privés occupés**	343
						selon le mode d'occupation	
1,385	660	590	545	1,305	1,020	Possédé	344
200	1,755	615	255	850	65	Loué	345
-	-	-	-	-	-	Logement de bande	346
						selon le type de construction résidentielle	
1,315	600	355	475	1,405	1,050	Maison individuelle non attenante	347
-	30	40	10	45	-	Maison jumelée	348
-	35	90	190	125	10	Maison en rangée	349
10	10	10	10	15	30	Appartement, duplex non attenant	350
200	1,515	470	75	255	-	Appartement, immeuble de cinq étages ou plus	351
70	220	250	55	315	-	Appartement, immeuble de moins de cinq étages (38)	352
-	-	-	-	-	-	Autre maison individuelle attenante	353
-	-	-	-	-	-	Logement mobile (39)	354

Table 1. Selected Characteristics for Census Tracts, 2001 Census – 100% Data and 20% Sample Data

No.	Characteristics	Toronto 0592.01 A	Toronto 0592.02 A	Toronto 0593	Toronto 0600.01	Toronto 0600.02	Toronto 0601
	DWELLING AND HOUSEHOLD CHARACTERISTICS						
	by condition of dwelling						
355	Regular maintenance only	1,690	1,370	1,385	1,615	1,575	960
356	Minor repairs	465	330	755	370	455	295
357	Major repairs	160	40	140	55	20	40
	by period of construction						
358	Before 1946	395	40	390	50	-	60
359	1946-1960	290	90	170	245	-	670
360	1961-1970	225	100	255	175	25	265
361	1971-1980	465	160	515	1,085	30	225
362	1981-1990	355	565	590	430	1,515	55
363	1991-2001 (20)	585	775	360	60	475	15
364	Average number of rooms per dwelling	5.9	7.8	8.0	9.2	8.4	8.7
365	Average number of bedrooms per dwelling	2.5	3.3	3.3	3.9	3.8	3.5
366	Average value of dwelling $	181,674	198,796	304,827	440,245	301,615	480,953
367	**Total number of private households**	**2,315**	**1,735**	**2,280**	**2,040**	**2,055**	**1,290**
	by household size						
368	1 person	675	140	275	120	90	120
369	2 persons	660	415	795	625	375	425
370	3 persons	370	310	375	380	415	230
371	4-5 persons	545	780	710	845	1,035	490
372	6 or more persons	60	90	125	70	135	25
	by household type						
373	One-family households	1,515	1,525	1,895	1,870	1,885	1,135
374	Multiple-family households	45	50	60	35	65	15
375	Non-family households	750	155	330	135	105	140
376	Number of persons in private households	5,865	5,855	6,890	6,560	7,430	3,940
377	Average number of persons in private households	2.5	3.4	3.0	3.2	3.6	3.1
378	Average number of persons per room	0.4	0.4	0.4	0.4	0.4	0.4
379	Tenant households in non-farm, non-reserve private dwellings (40)	920	45	220	45	155	55
380	Average gross rent $ (40)	766	719	948	1,761	1,376	1,742
381	Tenant households spending 30% or more of household income on gross rent (40) (41)	430	20	70	25	70	20
382	Tenant households spending from 30% to 99% of household income on gross rent (40) (41)	385	20	55	25	65	10
383	Owner households in non-farm, non-reserve private dwellings (42)	1,400	1,695	1,955	1,990	1,895	1,235
384	Average owner's major payments $ (42)	1,118	1,190	1,213	1,394	1,378	1,283
385	Owner households spending 30% or more of household income on owner's major payments (41) (42)	260	245	320	205	270	85
386	Owner households spending from 30% to 99% of household income on owner's major payments (41) (42)	245	205	275	175	245	65
	CENSUS FAMILY CHARACTERISTICS						
387	**Total number of census families in private households**	**1,610**	**1,630**	**2,010**	**1,940**	**2,015**	**1,160**
	by census family structure and size						
388	Total couple families	1,310	1,470	1,885	1,795	1,810	1,075
389	Total families of married couples	1,070	1,360	1,705	1,760	1,745	1,040
390	Without children at home	380	325	650	600	355	420
391	With children at home	695	1,035	1,060	1,160	1,395	620
392	1 child	235	265	310	305	335	135
393	2 children	300	495	470	630	755	295
394	3 or more children	160	270	275	225	300	185
395	Total families of common-law couples	240	110	180	35	65	30
396	Without children at home	135	40	100	30	40	10
397	With children at home	105	70	80	10	25	20
398	1 child	70	40	40	-	-	10
399	2 children	20	20	35	-	10	-
400	3 or more children	-	15	-	-	10	-
401	Total lone-parent families	295	155	125	140	210	90
402	Female parent	225	125	100	105	180	50
403	1 child	150	85	65	55	60	-
404	2 children	45	35	35	50	75	40
405	3 or more children	30	-	-	-	40	10

Tableau 1. Certaines caractéristiques des secteurs de recensement, recensement de 2001 – Données intégrales et données-échantillon (20 %)

Toronto 0602	Toronto 0603	Toronto 0604	Toronto 0605	Toronto 0606	Toronto 0607	Caractéristiques	N°
						CARACTÉRISTIQUES DES LOGEMENTS ET DES MÉNAGES	
						selon l'état du logement	
1,145	1,500	835	565	1,390	720	Entretien régulier seulement	355
365	660	270	200	520	335	Réparations mineures	356
80	260	105	35	245	30	Réparations majeures	357
						selon la période de construction	
400	200	255	65	110	25	Avant 1946	358
545	650	135	235	1,040	810	1946-1960	359
240	745	305	85	465	185	1961-1970	360
125	590	80	155	275	40	1971-1980	361
70	220	255	155	100	10	1981-1990	362
210	10	180	105	165	10	1991-2001 (20)	363
7.9	4.7	5.8	7.3	6.3	7.4	Nombre moyen de pièces par logement	364
3.2	1.8	2.2	2.8	2.6	3.3	Nombre moyen de chambres à coucher par logement	365
553,209	231,908	549,485	467,738	203,272	228,427	Valeur moyenne du logement $	366
1,590	**2,415**	**1,210**	**805**	**2,155**	**1,085**	**Nombre total de logements privés**	367
						selon la taille du ménage	
300	1,055	525	185	510	160	1 personne	368
540	795	460	300	755	405	2 personnes	369
245	265	105	130	345	175	3 personnes	370
460	285	110	175	450	305	4-5 personnes	371
40	10	10	10	100	45	6 personnes ou plus	372
						selon le genre de ménage	
1,235	1,225	660	570	1,490	880	Ménages unifamiliaux	373
30	25	-	10	95	30	Ménages multifamiliaux	374
330	1,165	550	235	570	180	Ménages non familiaux	375
4,385	4,735	2,275	2,000	5,615	3,065	Nombre de personnes dans les ménages privés	376
2.8	2.0	1.9	2.5	2.6	2.8	Nombre moyen de personnes dans les ménages privés	377
0.4	0.4	0.3	0.3	0.4	0.4	Nombre moyen de personnes par pièce	378
200	1,735	615	255	845	65	Ménages locataires dans les logements privés non agricoles hors réserve (40)	379
941	796	1,057	1,097	821	1,159	Loyer brut moyen $ (40)	380
80	810	270	80	265	-	Ménages locataires consacrant 30 % ou plus du revenu du ménage au loyer brut (40) (41)	381
55	715	240	65	225	10	Ménages locataires consacrant de 30 % à 99 % du revenu du ménage au loyer brut (40) (41)	382
1,375	655	590	550	1,300	1,015	Ménages propriétaires dans les logements privés non agricoles hors réserve (42)	383
1,434	870	1,396	1,456	852	960	Principales dépenses de propriété moyennes $ (42)	384
170	110	130	70	175	165	Ménages propriétaires consacrant 30 % ou plus du revenu du ménage aux principales dépenses de propriété (41) (42)	385
160	85	115	75	165	155	Ménages propriétaires consacrant de 30 % à 99 % du revenu du ménage aux principales dépenses de propriété (41) (42)	386
						CARACTÉRISTIQUES DES FAMILLES DE RECENSEMENT	
1,290	**1,275**	**660**	**580**	**1,685**	**935**	**Total des familles de recensement dans les ménages privés**	387
						selon la structure et la taille de la famille de recensement	
1,175	1,050	580	520	1,390	830	Total des familles avec conjoints	388
1,120	860	515	470	1,255	780	Total des familles avec couples mariés	389
475	435	345	215	550	370	Sans enfants à la maison	390
640	425	175	255	705	410	Avec enfants à la maison	391
175	205	85	100	285	130	1 enfant	392
305	185	60	105	305	195	2 enfants	393
160	40	30	50	120	85	3 enfants ou plus	394
50	185	65	50	135	50	Total des familles en union libre	395
50	165	55	30	80	20	Sans enfants à la maison	396
-	20	15	25	50	30	Avec enfants à la maison	397
10	15	10	20	35	10	1 enfant	398
-	-	-	-	15	15	2 enfants	399
-	-	-	-	-	10	3 enfants ou plus	400
115	225	75	55	295	110	Total des familles monoparentales	401
75	170	60	55	235	85	Parent de sexe féminin	402
50	110	40	35	155	75	1 enfant	403
25	35	10	-	45	15	2 enfants	404
-	20	10	10	40	-	3 enfants ou plus	405

Table 1. Selected Characteristics for Census Tracts, 2001 Census – 100% Data and 20% Sample Data

No.	Characteristics	Toronto 0592.01 A	Toronto 0592.02 A	Toronto 0593	Toronto 0600.01	Toronto 0600.02	Toronto 0601
	CENSUS FAMILY CHARACTERISTICS						
	by census family structure and size - concluded						
406	Male parent	80	30	25	35	30	40
407	1 child	55	20	15	10	15	-
408	2 children	15	-	10	10	10	30
409	3 or more children	10	-	-	25	-	-
410	**Total number of children at home**	**1,965**	**2,465**	**2,455**	**2,545**	**3,255**	**1,530**
	by age groups						
411	Under 6 years	580	480	465	390	560	220
412	6-14 years	820	1,140	995	950	1,330	620
413	15-17 years	165	330	315	285	480	200
414	18-24 years	305	385	480	695	565	315
415	25 years and over	95	130	195	225	325	180
416	Average number of children at home per census family (43)	1.2	1.5	1.2	1.3	1.6	1.3
417	**Total number of persons in private households**	**5,865**	**5,855**	**6,885**	**6,560**	**7,430**	**3,945**
	by census family status and living arrangements						
418	Number of non-family persons	970	295	540	285	350	175
419	Living with relatives (44)	140	90	90	50	155	10
420	Living with non-relatives only	150	65	175	115	105	45
421	Living alone	680	140	275	120	90	125
422	Number of family persons	4,890	5,565	6,345	6,280	7,085	3,765
423	Average number of persons per census family	3.0	3.4	3.2	3.2	3.5	3.2
424	**Total number of persons 65 years and over**	**705**	**365**	**680**	**680**	**335**	**605**
425	Number of non-family persons 65 years and over	355	130	155	120	120	95
426	Living with relatives (44)	25	75	45	40	95	10
427	Living with non-relatives only	10	-	25	25	10	10
428	Living alone	320	50	90	60	15	80
429	Number of family persons 65 years and over	350	235	530	560	220	510
	ECONOMIC FAMILY CHARACTERISTICS						
430	**Total number of economic families in private households**	**1,605**	**1,580**	**1,960**	**1,905**	**1,955**	**1,145**
	by size of family						
431	2 persons	660	400	770	625	370	410
432	3 persons	345	320	370	375	415	220
433	4 persons	395	525	490	625	740	315
434	5 or more persons	205	330	330	280	430	205
435	Total number of persons in economic families	5,030	5,655	6,435	6,330	7,240	3,775
436	Average number of persons per economic family	3.1	3.6	3.3	3.3	3.7	3.3
437	Total number of unattached individuals	830	205	450	230	195	165
	2000 INCOME CHARACTERISTICS						
	Population 15 years and over by sex and total income groups in 2000						
438	Total - Both sexes	4,440	4,230	5,435	5,215	5,535	3,110
439	Without income	100	235	190	385	375	245
440	With income	4,340	3,995	5,250	4,835	5,155	2,870
441	Under $1,000 (45)	195	105	205	190	250	95
442	$ 1,000 - $ 2,999	190	235	275	190	290	120
443	$ 3,000 - $ 4,999	100	195	175	180	125	95
444	$ 5,000 - $ 6,999	150	155	220	170	250	105
445	$ 7,000 - $ 9,999	220	200	280	180	195	140
446	$10,000 - $11,999	165	145	165	150	95	45
447	$12,000 - $14,999	305	125	235	190	170	140
448	$15,000 - $19,999	375	275	395	275	250	105
449	$20,000 - $24,999	310	200	275	265	270	145
450	$25,000 - $29,999	335	235	250	230	300	190
451	$30,000 - $34,999	365	285	455	220	300	155
452	$35,000 - $39,999	270	290	275	195	310	120
453	$40,000 - $44,999	280	250	305	150	280	130
454	$45,000 - $49,999	215	185	185	70	245	70
455	$50,000 - $59,999	230	315	495	285	405	160
456	$60,000 and over	630	795	1,065	1,905	1,415	1,045
457	Average income $ (46)	32,065	36,166	43,431	80,565	48,895	72,577
458	Median income $ (46)	27,232	31,627	30,463	38,966	35,908	39,082
459	Standard error of average income $ (46)	893	970	1,873	3,953	1,887	4,254

Tableau 1. Certaines caractéristiques des secteurs de recensement, recensement de 2001 – Données intégrales et données-échantillon (20 %)

Toronto 0602	Toronto 0603	Toronto 0604	Toronto 0605	Toronto 0606	Toronto 0607	Caractéristiques	N°
						CARACTÉRISTIQUES DES FAMILLES DE RECENSEMENT	
						selon la structure et la taille de la famille de recensement – fin	
40	55	15	-	60	20	Parent de sexe masculin	406
15	50	10	-	50	15	1 enfant	407
20	-	-	-	15	-	2 enfants	408
10	-	-	-	-	-	3 enfants ou plus	409
1,505	**1,025**	**430**	**595**	**1,790**	**980**	**Nombre total d'enfants à la maison**	410
						selon les groupes d'âge	
255	320	95	70	345	175	Moins de 6 ans	411
650	310	115	240	590	340	6-14 ans	412
190	60	50	80	175	110	15-17 ans	413
315	145	100	140	370	200	18-24 ans	414
95	190	65	65	315	160	25 ans et plus	415
1.2	0.8	0.6	1.0	1.1	1.0	Nombre moyen d'enfants à la maison par famille de recensement (43)	416
4,385	**4,730**	**2,275**	**2,005**	**5,610**	**3,065**	**Nombre total de personnes dans les ménages privés**	417
						selon la situation des particuliers dans la famille de recensement et des particuliers dans le ménage	
415	1,390	605	305	750	320	Nombre de personnes hors famille de recensement	418
30	55	15	50	80	85	Vivant avec des personnes apparentées (44)	419
85	275	70	70	160	75	Vivant avec des personnes non apparentées uniquement	420
300	1,055	520	190	510	160	Vivant seules	421
3,970	3,345	1,670	1,695	4,865	2,745	Nombre de personnes membres d'une famille	422
3.1	2.6	2.5	2.9	2.9	2.9	Nombre moyen de personnes par famille de recensement	423
650	**1,005**	**620**	**310**	**950**	**615**	**Nombre total de personnes de 65 ans et plus**	424
170	510	250	105	265	130	Nombre de personnes hors famille de recensement de 65 ans et plus	425
20	10	-	25	60	40	Vivant avec des personnes apparentées (44)	426
-	10	-	-	15	10	Vivant avec des personnes non apparentées uniquement	427
145	490	240	80	200	80	Vivant seules	428
480	495	375	205	685	485	Nombre de personnes membres d'une famille de 65 ans et plus	429
						CARACTÉRISTIQUES DES FAMILLES ÉCONOMIQUES	
1,260	**1,260**	**660**	**585**	**1,610**	**915**	**Nombre total de familles économiques dans les ménages privés**	430
						selon la taille de la famille	
535	740	440	280	755	410	2 personnes	431
235	245	110	120	320	160	3 personnes	432
315	215	80	120	305	205	4 personnes	433
180	65	30	70	235	135	5 personnes ou plus	434
4,000	3,405	1,680	1,745	4,945	2,830	Nombre total de personnes dans les familles économiques	435
3.2	2.7	2.5	3.0	3.1	3.1	Nombre moyen de personnes par famille économique	436
390	1,330	590	255	670	235	Nombre total de personnes hors famille économique	437
						CARACTÉRISTIQUES DU REVENU DE 2000	
						Population de 15 ans et plus selon le sexe et les tranches de revenu total en 2000	
3,485	4,105	2,065	1,715	4,670	2,545	Total - Les deux sexes	438
205	165	80	90	250	125	Sans revenu	439
3,280	3,940	1,990	1,625	4,425	2,415	Avec un revenu	440
145	80	50	20	120	70	Moins de 1 000 $ (45)	441
145	150	60	20	215	70	1 000 $ - 2 999 $	442
75	115	25	20	145	75	3 000 $ - 4 999 $	443
145	115	50	45	240	70	5 000 $ - 6 999 $	444
140	250	75	60	170	170	7 000 $ - 9 999 $	445
70	170	75	60	150	105	10 000 $ - 11 999 $	446
165	440	100	80	290	125	12 000 $ - 14 999 $	447
220	305	145	85	440	150	15 000 $ - 19 999 $	448
130	310	120	145	385	140	20 000 $ - 24 999 $	449
135	305	115	125	355	245	25 000 $ - 29 999 $	450
160	325	160	80	310	175	30 000 $ - 34 999 $	451
150	250	120	80	275	185	35 000 $ - 39 999 $	452
180	265	90	110	345	105	40 000 $ - 44 999 $	453
90	130	60	85	230	100	45 000 $ - 49 999 $	454
165	240	155	105	255	230	50 000 $ - 59 999 $	455
1,170	495	575	510	495	395	60 000 $ et plus	456
75,281	31,885	64,915	64,835	31,506	35,816	Revenu moyen $ (46)	457
37,820	25,586	34,917	39,422	25,928	29,691	Revenu médian $ (46)	458
4,859	985	6,027	5,184	959	1,364	Erreur type de revenu moyen $ (46)	459

Table 1. Selected Characteristics for Census Tracts, 2001 Census – 100% Data and 20% Sample Data

No.	Characteristics	Toronto 0592.01 A	Toronto 0592.02 A	Toronto 0593	Toronto 0600.01	Toronto 0600.02	Toronto 0601
	2000 INCOME CHARACTERISTICS						
	Population 15 years and over by sex and total income groups in 2000 – concluded						
460	Total - Males	2,055	2,105	2,770	2,550	2,720	1,525
461	Without income	20	80	40	70	180	55
462	With income	2,035	2,030	2,725	2,485	2,535	1,465
463	Under $1,000 (45)	55	25	45	50	105	45
464	$ 1,000 - $ 2,999	50	80	120	70	100	55
465	$ 3,000 - $ 4,999	35	85	40	70	50	25
466	$ 5,000 - $ 6,999	55	70	80	90	90	25
467	$ 7,000 - $ 9,999	75	55	110	70	75	70
468	$10,000 - $11,999	80	50	65	60	40	10
469	$12,000 - $14,999	85	25	85	60	45	65
470	$15,000 - $19,999	120	75	175	70	85	20
471	$20,000 - $24,999	75	90	100	75	150	55
472	$25,000 - $29,999	125	80	90	90	80	75
473	$30,000 - $34,999	140	140	255	65	105	75
474	$35,000 - $39,999	165	130	145	40	105	40
475	$40,000 - $44,999	180	145	170	60	135	70
476	$45,000 - $49,999	130	120	70	30	135	30
477	$50,000 - $59,999	160	240	335	170	260	85
478	$60,000 and over	510	635	830	1,415	980	735
479	Average income $ (46)	42,033	46,709	57,235	116,481	63,245	104,210
480	Median income $ (46)	38,085	42,946	40,141	70,007	48,419	59,914
481	Standard error of average income $ (46)	1,599	1,474	3,083	7,004	3,225	7,730
482	Total - Females	2,380	2,125	2,670	2,665	2,820	1,585
483	Without income	80	155	150	310	200	190
484	With income	2,305	1,970	2,520	2,355	2,620	1,400
485	Under $1,000 (45)	135	80	155	140	140	55
486	$ 1,000 - $ 2,999	135	155	160	120	190	70
487	$ 3,000 - $ 4,999	70	110	135	110	75	75
488	$ 5,000 - $ 6,999	95	85	140	75	160	80
489	$ 7,000 - $ 9,999	150	145	170	110	120	75
490	$10,000 - $11,999	85	100	105	90	55	35
491	$12,000 - $14,999	220	100	150	125	125	80
492	$15,000 - $19,999	250	205	220	205	165	85
493	$20,000 - $24,999	230	115	170	195	120	90
494	$25,000 - $29,999	210	150	155	135	225	115
495	$30,000 - $34,999	225	145	200	160	195	80
496	$35,000 - $39,999	105	165	130	155	205	80
497	$40,000 - $44,999	105	105	135	95	145	55
498	$45,000 - $49,999	90	70	115	40	110	45
499	$50,000 - $59,999	70	75	160	115	145	80
500	$60,000 and over	120	155	235	485	440	310
501	Average income $ (46)	23,270	25,295	28,496	42,703	34,984	39,393
502	Median income $ (46)	20,053	19,793	20,497	25,042	28,640	27,963
503	Standard error of average income $ (46)	782	1,020	1,858	2,552	1,796	2,302
	by composition of total income						
504	Total - Composition of income in 2000 % (47)	100.0	100.0	100.0	100.0	100.0	100.0
505	Employment income %	79.9	88.8	81.1	84.2	91.9	75.3
506	Government transfer payments %	9.8	5.0	5.4	2.4	3.0	3.7
507	Other %	10.4	6.2	13.5	13.3	5.1	20.9
	Population 15 years and over with employment income in 2000 by sex and work activity						
508	Both sexes with employment income (48)	3,280	3,390	4,225	3,980	4,385	2,050
509	Average employment income $	33,885	37,843	43,744	82,577	52,807	76,669
510	Standard error of average employment income $	1,071	1,063	2,126	4,519	2,143	5,086
511	Worked full year, full time (49)	2,045	2,020	2,335	2,125	2,640	1,030
512	Average employment income $	43,065	50,604	58,110	121,989	68,878	120,333
513	Standard error of average employment income $	1,329	1,284	2,641	7,408	3,029	8,921
514	Worked part year or part time (50)	1,210	1,360	1,775	1,800	1,710	955
515	Average employment income $	18,939	19,047	26,300	37,537	29,091	33,300
516	Standard error of average employment income $	1,390	1,271	3,474	3,787	2,373	3,397
517	Males with employment income (48)	1,710	1,830	2,345	2,115	2,295	1,140
518	Average employment income $	43,261	47,575	54,958	118,370	65,454	106,198
519	Standard error of average employment income $	1,772	1,579	3,365	7,774	3,512	8,517
520	Worked full year, full time (49)	1,190	1,290	1,425	1,410	1,515	680
521	Average employment income $	51,306	57,414	67,910	148,644	80,944	146,927
522	Standard error of average employment income $	2,033	1,689	3,282	10,548	4,531	12,933
523	Worked part year or part time (50)	520	530	850	675	755	410
524	Average employment income $	24,823	23,872	35,431	58,231	36,342	49,298
525	Standard error of average employment income $	2,798	2,597	7,228	8,629	4,737	7,026

Tableau 1. Certaines caractéristiques des secteurs de recensement, recensement de 2001 – Données intégrales et données-échantillon (20 %)

Toronto 0602	Toronto 0603	Toronto 0604	Toronto 0605	Toronto 0606	Toronto 0607	Caractéristiques	N°
						CARACTÉRISTIQUES DU REVENU DE 2000	
						Population de 15 ans et plus selon le sexe et les tranches de revenu total en 2000 – fin	
1,640	1,885	915	825	2,275	1,270	Total - Hommes	460
40	60	25	40	75	20	Sans revenu	461
1,605	1,820	885	785	2,200	1,250	Avec un revenu	462
40	35	30	-	50	40	Moins de 1 000 $ (45)	463
85	55	30	10	65	50	1 000 $ - 2 999 $	464
40	50	-	10	55	35	3 000 $ - 4 999 $	465
55	30	10	20	80	20	5 000 $ - 6 999 $	466
35	80	35	15	55	40	7 000 $ - 9 999 $	467
25	60	20	25	65	40	10 000 $ - 11 999 $	468
55	135	30	35	95	55	12 000 $ - 14 999 $	469
60	95	25	20	185	70	15 000 $ - 19 999 $	470
65	160	35	55	155	55	20 000 $ - 24 999 $	471
45	150	45	70	165	120	25 000 $ - 29 999 $	472
70	125	65	40	150	105	30 000 $ - 34 999 $	473
15	140	45	45	160	80	35 000 $ - 39 999 $	474
80	145	30	25	170	65	40 000 $ - 44 999 $	475
45	80	30	10	150	75	45 000 $ - 49 999 $	476
85	135	70	60	200	115	50 000 $ - 59 999 $	477
805	335	380	335	405	295	60 000 $ et plus	478
110,045	38,570	98,777	87,130	40,171	42,547	Revenu moyen $ (46)	479
59,930	30,335	50,066	49,148	32,723	34,900	Revenu médian $ (46)	480
8,827	1,750	12,740	9,940	1,673	2,289	Erreur type de revenu moyen $ (46)	481
1,840	2,225	1,150	885	2,400	1,275	Total - Femmes	482
165	100	55	40	170	110	Sans revenu	483
1,675	2,120	1,100	845	2,225	1,165	Avec un revenu	484
105	40	20	15	70	35	Moins de 1 000 $ (45)	485
60	95	30	10	145	20	1 000 $ - 2 999 $	486
40	65	20	15	85	40	3 000 $ - 4 999 $	487
90	80	40	25	160	50	5 000 $ - 6 999 $	488
105	165	40	45	120	130	7 000 $ - 9 999 $	489
45	110	60	35	85	65	10 000 $ - 11 999 $	490
110	305	75	50	195	65	12 000 $ - 14 999 $	491
160	205	125	65	255	85	15 000 $ - 19 999 $	492
65	150	85	90	230	80	20 000 $ - 24 999 $	493
90	155	75	60	195	125	25 000 $ - 29 999 $	494
85	205	90	45	160	70	30 000 $ - 34 999 $	495
140	110	75	35	110	105	35 000 $ - 39 999 $	496
100	115	60	80	175	40	40 000 $ - 44 999 $	497
45	55	25	70	80	30	45 000 $ - 49 999 $	498
80	100	85	45	55	115	50 000 $ - 59 999 $	499
365	155	200	175	95	100	60 000 $ et plus	500
42,007	26,146	37,668	44,044	22,929	28,611	Revenu moyen $ (46)	501
28,848	19,578	28,725	32,045	19,904	25,382	Revenu médian $ (46)	502
3,868	979	2,334	3,351	754	1,299	Erreur type de revenu moyen $ (46)	503
						selon la composition du revenu total	
100.0	100.0	100.0	100.0	100.0	100.0	Total - Composition du revenu en 2000 % (47)	504
77.4	75.0	71.3	76.2	72.7	74.6	Revenu d'emploi %	505
3.5	13.9	6.4	4.3	12.0	11.5	Transferts gouvernementaux %	506
19.1	11.0	22.4	19.6	15.2	13.9	Autre %	507
						Population de 15 ans et plus ayant un revenu d'emploi en 2000 selon le sexe et le travail	
2,460	2,705	1,325	1,260	3,090	1,655	Les deux sexes ayant un revenu d'emploi (48)	508
77,619	34,862	69,536	63,496	32,852	38,978	Revenu moyen d'emploi $	509
5,695	1,294	8,171	5,629	1,076	1,919	Erreur type de revenu moyen d'emploi $	510
1,255	1,495	705	635	1,725	970	Ayant travaillé toute l'année à plein temps (49)	511
123,734	46,081	95,664	84,815	43,830	51,356	Revenu moyen d'emploi $	512
10,201	1,528	13,929	9,326	1,262	2,604	Erreur type de revenu moyen d'emploi $	513
1,125	1,130	595	590	1,295	640	Ayant travaillé une partie de l'année ou à temps partiel (50)	514
30,441	20,541	40,916	43,859	19,107	22,560	Revenu moyen d'emploi $	515
3,304	1,971	6,888	6,047	1,569	2,255	Erreur type de revenu moyen d'emploi $	516
1,320	1,395	680	630	1,655	925	Hommes ayant un revenu d'emploi (48)	517
110,346	41,107	97,130	88,430	40,548	44,579	Revenu moyen d'emploi $	518
9,792	2,139	15,276	10,662	1,704	3,104	Erreur type de revenu moyen d'emploi $	519
810	845	420	400	1,000	560	Ayant travaillé toute l'année à plein temps (49)	520
154,774	50,111	123,766	101,558	50,457	57,316	Revenu moyen d'emploi $	521
14,533	2,283	22,842	14,151	1,833	4,152	Erreur type de revenu moyen d'emploi $	522
490	500	250	220	625	345	Ayant travaillé une partie de l'année ou à temps partiel (50)	523
41,566	27,401	54,478	66,516	25,749	26,345	Revenu moyen d'emploi $	524
7,169	4,132	14,613	15,209	3,023	3,844	Erreur type de revenu moyen d'emploi $	525

Table 1. Selected Characteristics for Census Tracts, 2001 Census – 100% Data and 20% Sample Data

No.	Characteristics	Toronto 0592.01 A	Toronto 0592.02 A	Toronto 0593	Toronto 0600.01	Toronto 0600.02	Toronto 0601
	2000 INCOME CHARACTERISTICS						
	Population 15 years and over with employment income in 2000 by sex and work activity – concluded						
526	Females with employment income (48)	1,565	1,560	1,885	1,865	2,095	910
527	Average employment income $	23,623	26,431	29,805	41,927	38,958	39,670
528	Standard error of average employment income $	947	1,120	2,178	2,841	2,102	2,880
529	Worked full year, full time (49)	850	725	905	715	1,125	350
530	Average employment income $	31,550	38,476	42,657	69,045	52,602	68,282
531	Standard error of average employment income $	1,159	1,565	4,226	5,425	3,318	5,539
532	Worked part year or part time (50)	690	825	925	1,125	960	550
533	Average employment income $	14,510	15,949	17,894	25,132	23,402	21,315
534	Standard error of average employment income $	1,214	1,174	1,143	2,726	1,929	1,927
	Census families by structure and family income groups in 2000						
535	Total - All census families	1,610	1,625	2,010	1,935	2,015	1,160
536	Under $10,000	55	25	40	10	15	10
537	$ 10,000 - $19,999	55	25	40	10	20	25
538	$ 20,000 - $29,999	125	45	90	40	65	30
539	$ 30,000 - $39,999	150	90	120	90	65	25
540	$ 40,000 - $49,999	170	170	105	90	80	35
541	$ 50,000 - $59,999	155	130	175	30	155	35
542	$ 60,000 - $69,999	185	135	210	65	170	75
543	$ 70,000 - $79,999	170	195	180	60	195	65
544	$ 80,000 - $89,999	125	210	125	105	165	35
545	$ 90,000 - $99,999	130	140	125	50	145	45
546	$100,000 and over	295	465	795	1,375	950	790
547	Average family income $	69,417	83,351	102,506	195,630	119,751	171,021
548	Median family income $	65,568	79,951	83,354	145,696	95,334	127,061
549	Standard error of average family income $	2,136	2,034	4,818	9,342	4,820	9,380
550	Total - All couple census families (51)	1,310	1,470	1,885	1,795	1,810	1,075
551	Under $10,000	40	20	20	15	-	10
552	$ 10,000 - $19,999	10	10	20	-	-	20
553	$ 20,000 - $29,999	90	20	70	40	35	25
554	$ 30,000 - $39,999	95	75	90	70	35	15
555	$ 40,000 - $49,999	115	135	95	55	50	30
556	$ 50,000 - $59,999	120	90	175	20	145	35
557	$ 60,000 - $69,999	170	130	195	60	140	50
558	$ 70,000 - $79,999	145	185	180	60	195	65
559	$ 80,000 - $89,999	125	210	125	95	150	40
560	$ 90,000 - $99,999	110	140	125	45	145	45
561	$100,000 and over	295	460	800	1,325	905	745
562	Average family income $	75,506	87,617	107,336	203,060	126,420	178,113
563	Median family income $	71,366	84,085	87,112	150,842	99,933	133,866
564	Standard error of average family income $	2,425	2,094	5,018	9,830	5,192	9,821
	Incidence of low income in 2000						
565	Total - Economic families	1,600	1,580	1,960	1,905	1,955	1,150
566	Low income	100	30	85	45	50	45
567	Incidence of low income in 2000 % (52)	6.2	2.0	4.4	2.5	2.5	4.0
568	Total - Unattached individuals 15 years and over	810	195	445	230	185	165
569	Low income	175	50	95	80	65	30
570	Incidence of low income in 2000 % (52)	21.8	27.7	21.8	34.6	34.1	18.7
571	Total - Population in private households	5,840	5,850	6,885	6,560	7,425	3,945
572	Low income	440	180	330	230	285	180
573	Incidence of low income in 2000 % (52)	7.6	3.1	4.8	3.5	3.8	4.6
	Private households by household income groups in 2000						
574	Total - All private households	2,315	1,735	2,285	2,035	2,050	1,290
575	Under $10,000	85	40	45	10	10	15
576	$ 10,000 - $19,999	285	40	105	45	25	40
577	$ 20,000 - $29,999	295	40	120	50	35	40
578	$ 30,000 - $39,999	225	100	135	85	65	40
579	$ 40,000 - $49,999	230	175	135	85	100	40
580	$ 50,000 - $59,999	205	120	210	40	140	45
581	$ 60,000 - $69,999	175	145	215	80	150	80
582	$ 70,000 - $79,999	170	200	185	65	240	80
583	$ 80,000 - $89,999	130	205	135	115	145	40
584	$ 90,000 - $99,999	165	140	130	60	155	55
585	$100,000 and over	350	525	860	1,395	990	810
586	Average household income $	60,081	83,257	99,748	191,010	122,731	161,212
587	Median household income $	51,910	79,922	78,172	143,159	97,189	116,139
588	Standard error of average household income $	1,848	2,041	4,504	8,918	4,794	8,610

Tableau 1. Certaines caractéristiques des secteurs de recensement, recensement de 2001 – Données intégrales et données-échantillon (20 %)

Toronto 0602	Toronto 0603	Toronto 0604	Toronto 0605	Toronto 0606	Toronto 0607	Caractéristiques	N°
						CARACTÉRISTIQUES DU REVENU DE 2000	
						Population de 15 ans et plus ayant un revenu d'emploi en 2000 selon le sexe et le travail - fin	
1,140	1,315	640	635	1,435	725	Femmes ayant un revenu d'emploi (48)	526
39,865	28,226	40,369	38,741	23,958	31,842	Revenu moyen d'emploi $	527
4,039	1,322	3,354	2,907	1,007	1,778	Erreur type de revenu moyen d'emploi $	528
450	660	285	230	730	410	Ayant travaillé toute l'année à plein temps (49)	529
67,631	40,920	53,948	56,070	34,739	43,217	Revenu moyen d'emploi $	530
9,495	1,854	4,879	5,770	1,306	2,238	Erreur type de revenu moyen d'emploi $	531
635	635	340	365	665	295	Ayant travaillé une partie de l'année ou à temps partiel (50)	532
21,902	15,167	30,896	29,971	12,920	18,150	Revenu moyen d'emploi $	533
1,958	1,164	4,459	2,882	918	1,896	Erreur type de revenu moyen d'emploi $	534
						Familles de recensement selon la structure et les tranches de revenu de la famille en 2000	
1,290	1,270	660	580	1,685	935	Total - Toutes les familles de recensement	535
25	65	15	-	60	15	Moins de 10 000 $	536
15	110	15	20	110	15	10 000 $ - 19 999 $	537
40	135	35	10	165	50	20 000 $ - 29 999 $	538
70	130	30	45	145	70	30 000 $ - 39 999 $	539
60	150	50	25	210	85	40 000 $ - 49 999 $	540
50	105	35	50	90	110	50 000 $ - 59 999 $	541
105	100	30	45	140	75	60 000 $ - 69 999 $	542
65	85	65	35	210	95	70 000 $ - 79 999 $	543
65	100	30	30	120	95	80 000 $ - 89 999 $	544
40	55	15	15	135	100	90 000 $ - 99 999 $	545
755	240	340	305	305	225	100 000 $ et plus	546
174,335	67,008	159,237	150,893	69,441	79,829	Revenu moyen des familles $	547
114,887	54,453	106,004	104,429	63,424	75,670	Revenu médian des familles $	548
11,443	3,165	17,463	14,443	2,496	3,016	Erreur type de revenu moyen des familles $	549
1,175	1,050	585	525	1,385	830	Total - Toutes les familles de recensement comptant un couple (51)	550
20	45	15	-	35	10	Moins de 10 000 $	551
10	70	15	10	60	-	10 000 $ - 19 999 $	552
40	110	25	10	110	50	20 000 $ - 29 999 $	553
45	115	30	35	130	55	30 000 $ - 39 999 $	554
60	115	30	15	175	70	40 000 $ - 49 999 $	555
40	70	20	45	75	85	50 000 $ - 59 999 $	556
100	90	25	40	110	75	60 000 $ - 69 999 $	557
50	75	45	35	155	90	70 000 $ - 79 999 $	558
55	80	30	20	120	80	80 000 $ - 89 999 $	559
40	50	15	20	125	95	90 000 $ - 99 999 $	560
720	235	340	295	290	220	100 000 $ et plus	561
181,407	72,616	173,128	160,304	74,377	82,589	Revenu moyen des familles $	562
118,546	60,057	121,356	108,718	69,077	77,708	Revenu médian des familles $	563
12,290	3,658	19,126	15,410	2,761	3,306	Erreur type de revenu moyen des familles $	564
						Fréquence des unités à faible revenu en 2000	
1,260	1,260	660	590	1,610	915	Total - Familles économiques	565
55	250	50	30	220	35	Faible revenu	566
4.3	19.8	7.1	4.6	13.6	3.8	Fréquence des unités à faible revenu en 2000 % (52)	567
390	1,330	590	255	660	220	Total - Personnes hors famille économique de 15 ans et plus	568
95	535	175	35	170	40	Faible revenu	569
24.7	40.5	29.6	12.3	25.7	18.0	Fréquence des unités à faible revenu en 2000 % (52)	570
4,385	4,735	2,275	2,005	5,605	3,055	Total - Population dans les ménages privés	571
240	1,215	300	90	985	125	Faible revenu	572
5.5	25.6	13.2	4.6	17.5	4.0	Fréquence des unités à faible revenu en 2000 % (52)	573
						Ménages privés selon les tranches de revenu du ménage en 2000	
1,585	2,415	1,205	805	2,155	1,085	Total - Tous les ménages privés	574
30	135	50	-	80	15	Moins de 10 000 $	575
80	460	145	55	185	50	10 000 $ - 19 999 $	576
80	385	125	35	265	50	20 000 $ - 29 999 $	577
100	285	100	30	250	90	30 000 $ - 39 999 $	578
85	260	95	65	245	110	40 000 $ - 49 999 $	579
65	170	90	90	140	110	50 000 $ - 59 999 $	580
155	150	55	55	175	75	60 000 $ - 69 999 $	581
100	105	95	60	195	105	70 000 $ - 79 999 $	582
65	120	40	45	145	90	80 000 $ - 89 999 $	583
40	60	30	15	130	120	90 000 $ - 99 999 $	584
795	290	370	355	350	280	100 000 $ et plus	585
155,407	51,976	106,930	129,756	64,716	79,641	Revenu moyen des ménages $	586
99,926	38,244	59,157	81,134	53,522	73,873	Revenu médian des ménages $	587
9,863	2,048	10,334	11,269	2,236	2,983	Erreur type de revenu moyen des ménages $	588

Table 1. Selected Characteristics for Census Tracts, 2001 Census – 100% Data and 20% Sample Data

No.	Characteristics	Toronto 0608	Toronto 0609	Toronto 0610.02	Toronto 0610.03 A	Toronto 0610.04 A	Toronto 0611
	POPULATION CHARACTERISTICS						
1	**Population, 1996 (1)**	**2,759**	**2,616**	**4,246**	**3,559**	**4,083**	**5,338**
2	**Population, 2001 (2)**	**2,647**	**2,692**	**4,498**	**3,202**	**3,986**	**5,069**
3	Population percentage change, 1996-2001	-4.1	2.9	5.9	-10.0	-2.4	-5.0
4	Land area in square kilometres, 2001	1.40	2.14	3.22	1.07	1.01	4.92
5	**Total population – 100% Data (3)**	**2,650**	**2,695**	**4,500**	**3,205**	**3,990**	**5,070**
	by sex and age groups						
6	Male	1,310	1,320	2,200	1,505	1,775	2,560
7	0-4 years	70	70	135	65	70	145
8	5-9 years	85	95	165	60	85	150
9	10-14 years	90	95	210	65	75	180
10	15-19 years	85	90	160	75	80	190
11	20-24 years	80	55	105	75	80	155
12	25-29 years	80	35	75	115	70	130
13	30-34 years	110	40	125	125	70	150
14	35-39 years	100	80	165	140	95	195
15	40-44 years	115	105	240	150	120	230
16	45-49 years	75	120	195	110	110	180
17	50-54 years	80	75	185	100	115	175
18	55-59 years	65	85	140	105	120	170
19	60-64 years	65	80	90	85	95	160
20	65-69 years	70	100	85	80	140	140
21	70-74 years	65	80	60	70	160	105
22	75-79 years	40	65	45	55	150	75
23	80-84 years	25	30	20	25	105	25
24	85 years and over	20	5	10	15	50	10
25	Female	1,340	1,375	2,300	1,695	2,210	2,505
26	0-4 years	65	65	135	50	55	125
27	5-9 years	80	85	175	70	65	145
28	10-14 years	65	105	175	70	85	145
29	15-19 years	75	85	155	70	80	145
30	20-24 years	75	60	115	70	75	125
31	25-29 years	65	30	75	130	60	130
32	30-34 years	100	60	140	120	75	145
33	35-39 years	110	90	210	160	100	215
34	40-44 years	100	125	225	125	125	215
35	45-49 years	90	115	210	125	100	205
36	50-54 years	80	90	190	135	160	215
37	55-59 years	65	95	145	110	135	180
38	60-64 years	70	80	85	105	140	155
39	65-69 years	80	95	80	80	180	135
40	70-74 years	60	90	90	110	210	120
41	75-79 years	65	75	55	85	255	60
42	80-84 years	45	25	30	50	165	25
43	85 years and over	50	20	15	40	145	15
44	**Total population 15 years and over**	**2,195**	**2,180**	**3,505**	**2,830**	**3,550**	**4,180**
	by legal marital status						
45	Never married (single)	620	415	780	790	630	1,040
46	Legally married (and not separated)	1,145	1,525	2,300	1,300	2,020	2,680
47	Separated, but still legally married	70	35	85	150	100	95
48	Divorced	145	75	195	355	235	180
49	Widowed	220	125	145	230	565	180
	by common-law status						
50	Not in a common-law relationship	2,080	2,135	3,375	2,555	3,435	4,025
51	In a common-law relationship	115	50	130	275	115	155
52	**Total population – 20% Sample Data (4)**	**2,535**	**2,675**	**4,505**	**3,185**	**3,810**	**5,070**
	by mother tongue						
53	Single responses	2,515	2,675	4,425	3,170	3,790	5,030
54	English	1,975	2,185	3,745	2,730	3,225	4,250
55	French	40	70	140	50	70	50
56	Non-official languages (5)	500	415	545	390	495	725
57	Italian	35	50	45	40	30	100
58	Chinese, n.o.s.	45	30	20	40	10	-
59	Cantonese	-	-	-	-	-	-
60	Portuguese	60	10	25	15	95	110
61	Punjabi	130	45	-	-	-	30
62	Other languages (6)	230	290	455	285	360	485
63	Multiple responses	15	10	80	15	20	40
64	English and French	10	10	45	-	10	-
65	English and non-official language	10	-	25	10	10	35
66	French and non-official language	-	-	10	-	-	10
67	English, French and non-official language	-	-	-	-	-	-

See reference material at the end of the publication. – Voir les documents de référence à la fin de la publication.

Tableau 1. Certaines caractéristiques des secteurs de recensement, recensement de 2001 – Données intégrales et données-échantillon (20 %)

Toronto 0612.01	Toronto 0612.02	Toronto 0612.03	Toronto 0612.05	Toronto 0612.07	Toronto 0612.08	Caractéristiques	N°
						CARACTÉRISTIQUES DE LA POPULATION	
58	**2,324**	**5,966**	**5,830**	**4,110**	**3,022**	**Population, 1996 (1)**	1
47	**11,761**	**6,043**	**5,844**	**6,459**	**4,403**	**Population, 2001 (2)**	2
-19.0	406.1	1.3	0.2	57.2	45.7	Variation en pourcentage de la population, 1996-2001	3
7.98	11.88	4.20	3.28	2.69	1.66	Superficie des terres en kilomètres carrés, 2001	4
50	**11,760**	**6,045**	**5,840**	**6,460**	**4,405**	**Population totale – Données intégrales (3)**	5
						selon le sexe et les groupes d'âge	
20	5,810	2,945	2,825	3,080	2,155	Sexe masculin	6
-	695	220	170	275	175	0-4 ans	7
-	525	345	270	320	175	5-9 ans	8
5	390	355	265	235	215	10-14 ans	9
-	290	245	240	200	175	15-19 ans	10
-	250	145	210	135	135	20-24 ans	11
5	435	90	135	170	140	25-29 ans	12
-	835	145	115	290	155	30-34 ans	13
-	825	265	215	365	170	35-39 ans	14
5	535	335	290	350	190	40-44 ans	15
5	335	275	265	215	190	45-49 ans	16
5	235	195	245	160	135	50-54 ans	17
-	195	120	170	130	110	55-59 ans	18
-	95	75	100	65	80	60-64 ans	19
-	95	55	60	40	55	65-69 ans	20
5	55	30	40	45	30	70-74 ans	21
-	25	15	20	45	15	75-79 ans	22
-	10	10	15	15	5	80-84 ans	23
-	5	5	5	15	5	85 ans et plus	24
25	5,950	3,100	3,020	3,380	2,245	Sexe féminin	25
-	685	205	180	280	140	0-4 ans	26
-	510	370	225	275	190	5-9 ans	27
5	370	320	285	230	225	10-14 ans	28
-	270	245	245	215	160	15-19 ans	29
5	225	150	205	135	150	20-24 ans	30
-	565	125	145	205	155	25-29 ans	31
-	900	195	160	330	185	30-34 ans	32
5	820	340	255	405	185	35-39 ans	33
-	555	385	335	390	225	40-44 ans	34
-	305	305	315	255	205	45-49 ans	35
-	250	180	245	185	150	50-54 ans	36
-	180	95	160	125	95	55-59 ans	37
-	120	65	100	65	65	60-64 ans	38
-	75	50	55	70	45	65-69 ans	39
5	55	35	40	75	25	70-74 ans	40
-	40	25	30	60	15	75-79 ans	41
-	15	10	25	45	15	80-84 ans	42
-	10	10	15	30	10	85 ans et plus	43
40	**8,590**	**4,225**	**4,440**	**4,840**	**3,280**	**Population totale de 15 ans et plus**	44
						selon l'état matrimonial légal	
10	1,810	1,130	1,270	1,205	945	Célibataire (jamais marié(e))	45
30	6,010	2,710	2,730	2,995	2,060	Légalement marié(e) (et non séparé(e))	46
-	235	105	115	150	65	Séparé(e), mais toujours légalement marié(e)	47
-	370	190	205	270	120	Divorcé(e)	48
-	165	95	130	210	85	Veuf ou veuve	49
						selon l'union libre	
45	8,135	4,115	4,315	4,575	3,165	Ne vivant pas en union libre	50
-	450	110	125	255	120	Vivant en union libre	51
45	**11,760**	**6,040**	**5,845**	**6,365**	**4,415**	**Population totale – Données-échantillon (20 %) (4)**	52
						selon la langue maternelle	
40	11,550	5,930	5,825	6,285	4,345	Réponses uniques	53
35	8,170	4,440	4,685	4,880	2,685	Anglais	54
-	270	130	95	105	35	Français	55
-	3,110	1,360	1,050	1,300	1,625	Langues non officielles (5)	56
-	330	170	165	125	135	Italien	57
-	80	100	70	70	100	Chinois, n.d.a.	58
-	35	25	-	115	40	Cantonais	59
-	295	140	45	95	100	Portugais	60
-	240	95	35	30	400	Pendjabi	61
-	2,125	835	735	865	850	Autres langues (6)	62
-	210	115	20	80	70	Réponses multiples	63
-	30	15	-	35	-	Anglais et français	64
-	160	85	15	45	65	Anglais et langue non officielle	65
-	10	15	-	-	10	Français et langue non officielle	66
-	15	-	-	10	-	Anglais, français et langue non officielle	67

See reference material at the end of the publication. – Voir les documents de référence à la fin de la publication.

Table 1. Selected Characteristics for Census Tracts, 2001 Census – 100% Data and 20% Sample Data

No.	Characteristics	Toronto 0608	Toronto 0609	Toronto 0610.02	Toronto 0610.03 A	Toronto 0610.04 A	Toronto 0611
	POPULATION CHARACTERISTICS						
	by home language						
68	Single responses	2,235	2,300	4,140	2,925	3,435	4,625
69	English	2,090	2,255	3,990	2,890	3,360	4,465
70	French	-	-	40	20	-	10
71	Non-official languages (5)	145	50	110	15	70	150
72	Cantonese	-	-	-	-	-	-
73	Chinese, n.o.s.	35	15	15	-	10	-
74	Italian	-	10	-	-	10	10
75	Punjabi	40	10	-	-	-	10
76	Portuguese	25	-	-	-	10	60
77	Other languages (6)	45	10	95	10	45	75
78	Multiple responses	300	380	370	260	375	445
79	English and French	40	110	150	20	85	65
80	English and non-official language	255	240	210	240	285	360
81	French and non-official language	-	-	-	-	-	-
82	English, French and non-official language	-	30	10	-	-	15
	by knowledge of official languages						
83	English only	2,130	2,170	3,935	2,920	3,355	4,595
84	French only	-	-	-	-	-	-
85	English and French	355	500	560	265	440	415
86	Neither English nor French	50	10	-	-	10	55
	by knowledge of non-official languages (5) (7)						
87	Italian	55	55	105	90	40	150
88	Cantonese	-	-	10	-	-	-
89	Chinese, n.o.s.	45	25	15	40	10	-
90	Spanish	35	55	30	85	55	90
91	Portuguese	70	10	35	40	100	110
92	Punjabi	145	45	-	-	10	30
93	Tagalog (Pilipino)	25	10	25	10	10	25
	by first official language spoken						
94	English	2,450	2,590	4,330	3,130	3,715	4,945
95	French	40	65	160	60	75	50
96	English and French	-	20	10	-	10	20
97	Neither English nor French	45	10	-	-	10	50
98	Official language minority - (number) (8)	40	75	165	60	80	60
99	Official language minority - (percentage) (8)	1.6	2.8	3.7	1.9	2.1	1.2
	by ethnic origin (9)						
100	Canadian	780	900	1,560	895	1,130	1,520
101	English	760	1,015	1,485	1,240	1,595	1,830
102	Scottish	580	530	960	835	1,125	1,155
103	Irish	445	650	1,090	585	800	990
104	Chinese	65	25	75	40	15	10
105	Italian	115	100	310	180	150	430
106	East Indian	135	75	15	35	50	65
107	French	230	295	350	210	255	460
108	German	270	225	360	315	390	485
109	Portuguese	105	25	115	40	130	170
110	Polish	90	85	190	75	160	205
111	Jewish	10	15	25	20	60	50
112	Jamaican	-	-	45	15	10	35
113	Filipino	35	25	30	10	10	45
114	Ukrainian	170	130	150	120	140	145
	by Aboriginal identity						
115	Total Aboriginal identity population (10)	25	-	10	10	15	20
116	Total non-Aboriginal population	2,505	2,670	4,500	3,180	3,790	5,050
	by Aboriginal origin						
117	Total Aboriginal origins population (11)	100	10	50	80	15	105
118	Total non-Aboriginal population	2,430	2,675	4,460	3,105	3,795	4,960
	by Registered Indian status						
119	Registered Indian (12)	-	-	-	-	10	10
120	Not a Registered Indian	2,530	2,680	4,505	3,185	3,800	5,060

Tableau 1. Certaines caractéristiques des secteurs de recensement, recensement de 2001 – Données intégrales et données-échantillon (20 %)

Toronto 0612.01	Toronto 0612.02	Toronto 0612.03	Toronto 0612.05	Toronto 0612.07	Toronto 0612.08	Caractéristiques	N°
						CARACTÉRISTIQUES DE LA POPULATION	
						selon la langue parlée à la maison	
40	9,680	5,120	5,095	5,420	3,315	Réponses uniques	68
45	8,900	4,835	4,805	5,150	2,865	Anglais	69
-	50	10	-	15	-	Français	70
-	725	265	290	250	445	Langues non officielles (5)	71
-	10	-	-	30	30	Cantonais	72
-	-	40	10	45	40	Chinois, n.d.a.	73
-	35	55	-	10	20	Italien	74
-	150	15	35	-	210	Pendjabi	75
-	60	-	-	15	10	Portugais	76
-	470	160	255	150	135	Autres langues (6)	77
-	2,080	920	745	945	1,100	Réponses multiples	78
-	260	110	105	150	30	Anglais et français	79
-	1,780	735	605	780	1,005	Anglais et langue non officielle	80
-	-	-	10	-	-	Français et langue non officielle	81
-	35	80	30	25	60	Anglais, français et langue non officielle	82
						selon la connaissance des langues officielles	
35	10,145	5,245	5,070	5,550	3,845	Anglais seulement	83
-	10	10	-	-	10	Français seulement	84
10	1,495	760	740	755	505	Anglais et français	85
-	105	25	30	60	65	Ni l'anglais ni le français	86
						selon la connaissance des langues non officielles (5) (7)	
-	540	250	275	170	145	Italien	87
-	60	25	-	125	70	Cantonais	88
-	110	115	65	90	85	Chinois, n.d.a.	89
-	320	190	165	105	80	Espagnol	90
-	405	175	60	115	125	Portugais	91
-	290	160	65	60	495	Pendjabi	92
-	230	30	45	65	30	Tagalog (pilipino)	93
						selon la première langue officielle parlée	
40	11,215	5,865	5,670	6,145	4,220	Anglais	94
-	280	130	85	105	50	Français	95
-	165	20	60	60	100	Anglais et français	96
-	100	20	35	60	50	Ni l'anglais ni le français	97
-	365	140	115	135	95	Minorité de langue officielle - (nombre) (8)	98
-	3.1	2.3	2.0	2.1	2.1	Minorité de langue officielle - (pourcentage) (8)	99
						selon l'origine ethnique (9)	
10	2,590	1,590	1,675	1,705	870	Canadien	100
-	2,635	1,515	1,930	1,760	755	Anglais	101
-	1,880	1,165	1,105	1,310	515	Écossais	102
-	1,660	975	1,110	1,045	520	Irlandais	103
-	385	185	150	395	245	Chinois	104
15	1,425	535	605	500	355	Italien	105
-	665	355	240	305	600	Indien de l'Inde	106
-	1,035	395	580	395	295	Français	107
-	975	380	620	595	265	Allemand	108
-	610	265	125	230	220	Portugais	109
10	640	225	330	365	335	Polonais	110
-	50	100	90	35	15	Juif	111
-	135	75	140	95	85	Jamaïquain	112
-	440	75	65	130	40	Philippin	113
-	510	205	205	245	120	Ukrainien	114
						selon l'identité autochtone	
-	15	-	10	50	10	Total de la population ayant une identité autochtone (10)	115
40	11,745	6,035	5,840	6,320	4,400	Total de la population non autochtone	116
						selon l'origine autochtone	
-	75	-	20	95	25	Total de la population ayant une origine autochtone (11)	117
45	11,685	6,030	5,825	6,270	4,390	Total de la population non autochtone	118
						selon le statut d'Indien inscrit	
-	15	-	-	25	10	Oui, Indien inscrit (12)	119
40	11,740	6,035	5,845	6,340	4,405	Non, pas un Indien inscrit	120

Table 1. Selected Characteristics for Census Tracts, 2001 Census – 100% Data and 20% Sample Data

No.	Characteristics	Toronto 0608	Toronto 0609	Toronto 0610.02	Toronto 0610.03 A	Toronto 0610.04 A	Toronto 0611
	POPULATION CHARACTERISTICS						
	by visible minority groups						
121	Total visible minority population	295	150	205	185	90	220
122	Chinese	60	30	45	40	10	-
123	South Asian	155	75	25	65	35	60
124	Black	10	-	55	30	15	50
125	Filipino	30	25	30	-	10	45
126	Latin American	15	10	-	15	-	-
127	Southeast Asian	-	-	-	-	-	-
128	Arab	-	10	-	-	-	10
129	West Asian	-	-	-	-	-	-
130	Korean	10	-	-	15	-	-
131	Japanese	-	10	40	-	-	15
132	Visible minority, n.i.e. (13)	-	-	-	-	10	30
133	Multiple visible minorities (14)	15	10	-	15	15	-
	by citizenship						
134	Canadian citizenship (15)	2,370	2,530	4,200	3,000	3,655	4,800
135	Citizenship other than Canadian	165	150	305	190	155	275
	by place of birth of respondent						
136	Non-immigrant population	1,840	1,950	3,380	2,385	2,840	3,750
137	Born in province of residence	1,515	1,545	2,730	1,845	2,000	3,160
138	Immigrant population (16)	690	690	1,100	750	970	1,315
139	United States	20	25	55	30	65	35
140	Central and South America	20	-	30	40	-	70
141	Caribbean and Bermuda	10	-	40	20	35	45
142	United Kingdom	180	290	405	290	415	430
143	Other Europe (17)	250	250	385	275	375	530
144	Africa	30	25	80	25	10	110
145	Asia and the Middle East	165	90	100	70	45	90
146	Oceania and other (18)	-	10	-	-	20	10
147	Non-permanent residents (19)	10	45	25	55	-	10
148	**Total immigrant population**	**690**	**690**	**1,105**	**750**	**970**	**1,315**
	by period of immigration						
149	Before 1961	150	225	320	265	460	445
150	1961-1970	160	195	225	175	200	285
151	1971-1980	95	90	180	95	90	200
152	1981-1990	110	160	155	85	100	225
153	1991-2001 (20)	170	25	210	125	120	160
154	1991-1995	80	25	60	80	85	60
155	1996-2001 (20)	90	-	155	40	35	100
	by age at immigration						
156	0-4 years	35	35	120	40	145	130
157	5-19 years	145	130	290	190	185	370
158	20 years and over	505	520	685	520	645	810
159	**Total population**	**2,530**	**2,680**	**4,505**	**3,190**	**3,805**	**5,070**
	by religion						
160	Catholic (21)	840	785	1,790	715	1,305	2,065
161	Protestant	1,000	1,345	1,820	1,670	1,915	2,165
162	Christian Orthodox	45	25	60	30	75	70
163	Christian, n.i.e. (22)	35	85	55	70	45	20
164	Muslim	15	-	25	35	30	85
165	Jewish	-	30	30	15	30	20
166	Buddhist	-	25	-	-	-	-
167	Hindu	-	65	-	-	-	-
168	Sikh	120	-	-	-	10	30
169	Eastern religions (23)	-	-	10	-	-	-
170	Other religions (24)	-	-	-	15	-	-
171	No religious affiliation (25)	470	330	710	630	390	615
172	**Total population 15 years and over**	**2,045**	**2,190**	**3,520**	**2,815**	**3,350**	**4,175**
	by generation status						
173	1st generation (26)	680	745	1,095	790	945	1,275
174	2nd generation (27)	385	490	850	715	880	1,160
175	3rd generation and over (28)	975	950	1,575	1,310	1,525	1,745
176	**Total population 1 year and over (29)**	**2,495**	**2,665**	**4,435**	**3,165**	**3,790**	**5,010**
	by place of residence 1 year ago (mobility)						
177	Non-movers	2,180	2,475	3,895	2,630	3,515	4,635
178	Movers	315	190	550	535	275	380
179	Non-migrants	160	60	280	200	135	160
180	Migrants	155	135	260	335	135	220
181	Internal migrants	115	80	215	245	125	200
182	Intraprovincial migrants	105	65	185	220	125	205
183	Interprovincial migrants	10	20	35	30	-	-
184	External migrants	40	50	45	90	10	15

Tableau 1. Certaines caractéristiques des secteurs de recensement, recensement de 2001 – Données intégrales et données-échantillon (20 %)

Toronto 0612.01	Toronto 0612.02	Toronto 0612.03	Toronto 0612.05	Toronto 0612.07	Toronto 0612.08	Caractéristiques	N°
						CARACTÉRISTIQUES DE LA POPULATION	
						selon les groupes de minorités visibles	
-	2,555	1,290	880	1,200	1,310	Total de la population des minorités visibles	121
-	285	145	110	355	255	Chinois	122
-	765	470	255	275	665	Sud-Asiatique	123
-	360	200	140	190	180	Noir	124
-	390	55	65	120	35	Philippin	125
-	180	90	10	-	-	Latino-Américain	126
-	145	45	35	30	20	Asiatique du Sud-Est	127
-	155	130	65	40	30	Arabe	128
-	90	15	35	80	10	Asiatique occidental	129
-	95	25	20	30	15	Coréen	130
-	-	10	55	10	50	Japonais	131
-	30	50	70	25	45	Minorité visible, n.i.a. (13)	132
-	60	50	20	40	-	Minorités visibles multiples (14)	133
						selon la citoyenneté	
35	10,565	5,665	5,255	5,955	4,110	Citoyenneté canadienne (15)	134
10	1,195	375	595	415	305	Citoyenneté autre que canadienne	135
						selon le lieu de naissance du répondant	
40	8,085	4,190	4,070	4,590	2,775	Population non immigrante	136
35	6,350	3,465	3,155	3,785	2,350	Née dans la province de résidence	137
10	3,550	1,705	1,670	1,765	1,575	Population immigrante (16)	138
-	100	55	100	105	55	États-Unis	139
-	290	90	65	35	25	Amérique centrale et du Sud	140
-	170	120	115	125	95	Caraïbes et Bermudes	141
-	525	235	380	315	195	Royaume-Uni	142
-	1,105	485	465	410	600	Autre Europe (17)	143
-	265	165	130	180	50	Afrique	144
-	1,085	530	410	595	555	Asie et Moyen-Orient	145
-	15	20	10	10	-	Océanie et autre (18)	146
-	120	145	95	15	65	Résidents non permanents (19)	147
10	**3,550**	**1,705**	**1,675**	**1,765**	**1,575**	**Population immigrante totale**	148
						selon la période d'immigration	
-	225	230	230	155	140	Avant 1961	149
-	425	325	325	235	335	1961-1970	150
-	660	330	255	395	345	1971-1980	151
-	890	410	285	400	415	1981-1990	152
-	1,360	415	580	575	330	1991-2001 (20)	153
-	655	165	205	310	200	1991-1995	154
-	705	245	375	265	130	1996-2001 (20)	155
						selon l'âge à l'immigration	
-	400	215	205	155	155	0-4 ans	156
-	1,110	525	570	575	390	5-19 ans	157
-	2,045	955	895	1,030	1,025	20 ans et plus	158
40	**11,760**	**6,035**	**5,845**	**6,365**	**4,415**	**Population totale**	159
						selon la religion	
20	5,500	2,710	2,425	2,300	2,075	Catholique (21)	160
10	3,205	1,600	2,105	2,225	930	Protestante	161
-	450	170	85	135	50	Orthodoxe chrétienne	162
-	140	130	65	155	95	Chrétiennes, n.i.a. (22)	163
-	385	215	200	150	190	Musulmane	164
-	70	125	20	25	25	Juive	165
-	85	15	65	70	50	Bouddhiste	166
-	145	125	45	185	220	Hindoue	167
-	255	70	30	25	355	Sikh	168
-	40	105	10	30	15	Religions orientales (23)	169
-	10	-	-	10	-	Autres religions (24)	170
15	1,480	770	790	1,065	415	Aucune appartenance religieuse (25)	171
25	**8,590**	**4,220**	**4,440**	**4,735**	**3,315**	**Population totale de 15 ans et plus**	172
						selon le statut des générations	
-	3,410	1,765	1,610	1,660	1,555	1re génération (26)	173
10	2,150	955	1,005	1,305	875	2e génération (27)	174
15	3,025	1,500	1,825	1,770	885	3e génération et plus (28)	175
40	**11,395**	**5,960**	**5,775**	**6,245**	**4,370**	**Population totale de 1 an et plus (29)**	176
						selon le lieu de résidence 1 an auparavant (mobilité)	
30	8,230	5,255	5,080	5,500	3,610	Personnes n'ayant pas déménagé	177
-	3,170	700	695	740	765	Personnes ayant déménagé	178
-	1,475	240	280	250	380	Non-migrants	179
10	1,695	455	420	495	390	Migrants	180
-	1,415	425	330	430	370	Migrants internes	181
10	1,240	255	300	405	305	Migrants infraprovinciaux	182
-	175	165	25	25	70	Migrants interprovinciaux	183
-	280	35	85	60	20	Migrants externes	184

Table 1. Selected Characteristics for Census Tracts, 2001 Census – 100% Data and 20% Sample Data

No.	Characteristics	Toronto 0608	Toronto 0609	Toronto 0610.02	Toronto 0610.03 A	Toronto 0610.04 A	Toronto 0611
	POPULATION CHARACTERISTICS						
185	**Total population 5 years and over (30)**	**2,435**	**2,565**	**4,230**	**3,075**	**3,670**	**4,795**
	by place of residence 5 years ago (mobility)						
186	Non-movers	1,590	1,975	2,725	1,440	2,440	3,435
187	Movers	840	585	1,500	1,630	1,230	1,370
188	Non-migrants	390	350	605	720	575	615
189	Migrants	450	235	895	910	655	755
190	Internal migrants	370	180	705	770	605	665
191	Intraprovincial migrants	330	160	510	605	505	600
192	Interprovincial migrants	40	20	190	165	105	65
193	External migrants	80	50	195	135	50	90
194	**Total population 15 to 24 years**	**305**	**290**	**540**	**285**	**300**	**620**
	by school attendance						
195	Not attending school	120	40	155	120	120	205
196	Attending school full time	145	235	375	135	155	400
197	Attending school part time	50	15	15	30	30	10
198	**Total population 15 years and over**	**2,045**	**2,185**	**3,520**	**2,815**	**3,350**	**4,180**
	by highest level of schooling						
199	Less than grade 9 (31)	110	65	125	155	85	135
200	Grades 9-13 without high school graduation certificate	455	310	490	550	570	765
201	Grades 9-13 with high school graduation certificate	290	245	360	260	455	710
202	Some postsecondary without degree, certificate or diploma (32)	320	235	470	315	365	510
203	Trades certificate or diploma (33)	250	130	390	270	300	375
204	College certificate or diploma (34)	340	395	790	570	625	805
205	University certificate below bachelor's degree	20	70	75	115	75	100
206	University with bachelor's degree or higher	260	725	820	575	870	770
	by combinations of unpaid work						
207	Males 15 years and over	1,000	1,070	1,700	1,310	1,485	2,085
208	Reported unpaid work (35)	870	980	1,540	1,155	1,290	1,845
209	Housework and child care and care or assistance to seniors	110	90	95	85	80	120
210	Housework and child care only	240	290	520	235	335	645
211	Housework and care or assistance to seniors only	60	70	150	160	150	115
212	Child care and care or assistance to seniors only	-	-	-	-	-	-
213	Housework only	460	520	755	675	710	940
214	Child care only	10	10	10	10	-	15
215	Care or assistance to seniors only	10	-	-	-	10	15
216	Females 15 years and over	1,045	1,115	1,820	1,505	1,860	2,090
217	Reported unpaid work (35)	990	1,060	1,710	1,405	1,680	1,945
218	Housework and child care and care or assistance to seniors	145	160	130	100	125	185
219	Housework and child care only	310	280	655	270	395	675
220	Housework and care or assistance to seniors only	90	100	230	230	235	175
221	Child care and care or assistance to seniors only	-	-	-	-	-	-
222	Housework only	425	505	690	810	920	890
223	Child care only	10	-	10	-	-	15
224	Care or assistance to seniors only	10	10	-	-	-	-
	by labour force activity						
225	Males 15 years and over	1,000	1,070	1,705	1,310	1,485	2,085
226	In the labour force	730	690	1,320	990	920	1,545
227	Employed	700	655	1,305	955	855	1,465
228	Unemployed	30	35	20	40	60	80
229	Not in the labour force	265	380	380	315	560	545
230	Participation rate	73.0	64.5	77.4	75.6	62.0	74.1
231	Employment rate	70.0	61.2	76.5	72.9	57.6	70.3
232	Unemployment rate	4.1	5.1	1.5	4.0	6.5	5.2
233	Females 15 years and over	1,050	1,115	1,820	1,510	1,865	2,090
234	In the labour force	650	605	1,160	925	780	1,355
235	Employed	595	585	1,100	890	750	1,320
236	Unemployed	60	20	55	35	30	35
237	Not in the labour force	400	510	660	580	1,085	740
238	Participation rate	61.9	54.3	63.7	61.3	41.8	64.8
239	Employment rate	56.7	52.5	60.4	58.9	40.2	63.2
240	Unemployment rate	9.2	3.3	4.7	3.8	3.8	2.6

Tableau 1. Certaines caractéristiques des secteurs de recensement, recensement de 2001 – Données intégrales et données-échantillon (20 %)

Toronto 0612.01	Toronto 0612.02	Toronto 0612.03	Toronto 0612.05	Toronto 0612.07	Toronto 0612.08	Caractéristiques	N°
						CARACTÉRISTIQUES DE LA POPULATION	
40	**10,370**	**5,610**	**5,490**	**5,810**	**4,100**	**Population totale de 5 ans et plus (30)**	185
						selon le lieu de résidence 5 ans auparavant (mobilité)	
10	1,205	3,465	2,835	2,540	2,210	Personnes n'ayant pas déménagé	186
30	9,170	2,145	2,655	3,270	1,890	Personnes ayant déménagé	187
15	3,760	905	1,010	905	835	Non-migrants	188
15	5,410	1,240	1,645	2,360	1,055	Migrants	189
15	4,630	920	1,180	2,070	970	Migrants internes	190
15	3,905	645	865	1,785	865	Migrants infraprovinciaux	191
-	725	275	320	280	105	Migrants interprovinciaux	192
-	780	315	465	290	85	Migrants externes	193
-	**1,035**	**790**	**900**	**685**	**620**	**Population totale de 15 à 24 ans**	194
						selon la fréquentation scolaire	
-	345	300	260	185	165	Ne fréquentant pas l'école	195
-	650	480	590	480	425	Fréquentant l'école à plein temps	196
-	45	10	60	30	25	Fréquentant l'école à temps partiel	197
30	**8,590**	**4,225**	**4,435**	**4,735**	**3,315**	**Population totale de 15 ans et plus**	198
						selon le plus haut niveau de scolarité atteint	
-	230	135	115	180	240	Niveau inférieur à la 9e année (31)	199
10	865	640	850	585	630	De la 9e à la 13e année sans certificat d'études secondaires	200
-	935	340	480	500	375	De la 9e à la 13e année avec certificat d'études secondaires	201
10	1,035	535	455	590	420	Études postsecondaires partielles sans grade, certificat ou diplôme (32)	202
-	535	295	235	350	210	Certificat ou diplôme d'une école de métiers (33)	203
10	1,615	745	640	855	540	Certificat ou diplôme collégial (34)	204
-	275	80	215	145	45	Certificat universitaire inférieur au baccalauréat	205
10	3,095	1,450	1,445	1,535	860	Études universitaires avec baccalauréat ou diplôme supérieur	206
						selon les combinaisons de travail non rémunéré	
10	4,200	2,020	2,115	2,210	1,610	Hommes de 15 ans et plus	207
10	3,915	1,805	1,950	2,050	1,425	Travail non rémunéré déclaré (35)	208
-	350	160	160	150	110	Travaux ménagers et soins aux enfants et soins ou aide aux personnes âgées	209
-	1,625	765	730	795	505	Travaux ménagers et soins aux enfants seulement	210
-	175	75	160	135	80	Travaux ménagers et soins ou aide aux personnes âgées seulement	211
-	-	-	-	-	-	Soins aux enfants et soins ou aide aux personnes âgées seulement	212
10	1,740	775	855	945	720	Travaux ménagers seulement	213
-	25	10	35	25	10	Soins aux enfants seulement	214
-	-	15	-	-	-	Soins ou aide aux personnes âgées seulement	215
20	4,385	2,200	2,320	2,525	1,700	Femmes de 15 ans et plus	216
15	4,210	2,050	2,160	2,375	1,520	Travail non rémunéré déclaré (35)	217
-	425	255	270	250	155	Travaux ménagers et soins aux enfants et soins ou aide aux personnes âgées	218
10	1,910	880	900	980	610	Travaux ménagers et soins aux enfants seulement	219
-	260	80	235	210	95	Travaux ménagers et soins ou aide aux personnes âgées seulement	220
-	-	-	-	10	10	Soins aux enfants et soins ou aide aux personnes âgées seulement	221
-	1,590	790	750	935	645	Travaux ménagers seulement	222
-	35	40	10	-	15	Soins aux enfants seulement	223
-	-	-	-	-	-	Soins ou aide aux personnes âgées seulement	224
						selon l'activité	
10	4,205	2,025	2,115	2,210	1,610	Hommes de 15 ans et plus	225
10	3,725	1,630	1,690	1,790	1,335	Population active	226
10	3,665	1,540	1,600	1,680	1,285	Personnes occupées	227
-	65	85	90	110	50	Chômeurs	228
-	475	395	425	415	285	Inactifs	229
-	88.6	80.5	79.9	81.0	82.9	Taux d'activité	230
-	87.2	76.0	75.7	76.0	79.8	Taux d'emploi	231
-	1.7	5.2	5.3	6.1	3.7	Taux de chômage	232
20	4,385	2,205	2,320	2,530	1,705	Femmes de 15 ans et plus	233
15	3,190	1,575	1,560	1,845	1,220	Population active	234
15	3,030	1,470	1,480	1,775	1,135	Personnes occupées	235
-	155	100	80	70	90	Chômeuses	236
-	1,200	630	760	680	480	Inactives	237
75.0	72.7	71.4	67.2	72.9	71.6	Taux d'activité	238
75.0	69.1	66.7	63.8	70.2	66.6	Taux d'emploi	239
-	4.9	6.3	5.1	3.8	7.4	Taux de chômage	240

Table 1. Selected Characteristics for Census Tracts, 2001 Census – 100% Data and 20% Sample Data

No.	Characteristics	Toronto 0608	Toronto 0609	Toronto 0610.02	Toronto 0610.03 A	Toronto 0610.04 A	Toronto 0611
	POPULATION CHARACTERISTICS						
	by labour force activity – concluded						
241	Both sexes - Participation rate	67.5	59.3	70.5	68.0	50.8	69.4
242	15-24 years	79.0	56.9	71.6	77.2	83.3	71.8
243	25 years and over	65.7	59.9	70.1	67.2	47.5	69.1
244	Both sexes - Employment rate	63.3	56.8	68.3	65.4	48.1	66.6
245	15-24 years	65.6	46.6	65.1	75.4	68.3	66.9
246	25 years and over	62.9	58.3	68.7	64.2	46.1	66.4
247	Both sexes - Unemployment rate	6.2	4.2	3.0	3.9	5.3	4.1
248	15-24 years	16.7	15.6	7.7	-	16.0	6.7
249	25 years and over	3.9	2.6	2.2	4.4	3.1	3.5
250	**Total labour force 15 years and over**	**1,385**	**1,295**	**2,480**	**1,915**	**1,700**	**2,900**
	by industry based on the 1997 NAICS						
251	Industry - Not applicable (36)	15	-	15	20	-	20
252	All industries (37)	1,365	1,290	2,465	1,900	1,695	2,880
253	11 Agriculture, forestry, fishing and hunting	15	-	10	-	-	-
254	21 Mining and oil and gas extraction	10	-	-	-	-	-
255	22 Utilities	10	10	10	-	-	15
256	23 Construction	90	30	90	75	50	170
257	31-33 Manufacturing	225	165	340	285	175	350
258	41 Wholesale trade	130	130	165	110	135	205
259	44-45 Retail trade	125	85	255	225	215	320
260	48-49 Transportation and warehousing	120	70	160	80	75	210
261	51 Information and cultural industries	45	35	75	60	85	65
262	52 Finance and insurance	25	85	235	80	165	305
263	53 Real estate and rental and leasing	15	40	40	40	45	55
264	54 Professional, scientific and technical services	155	265	245	195	185	260
265	55 Management of companies and enterprises	-	-	-	-	-	10
266	56 Administrative and support, waste management and remediation services	75	25	55	30	60	110
267	61 Educational services	90	110	170	190	125	135
268	62 Health care and social assistance	70	80	185	145	140	200
269	71 Arts, entertainment and recreation	10	10	65	50	40	70
270	72 Accommodation and food services	100	40	160	120	55	175
271	81 Other services (except public administration)	55	20	95	140	70	70
272	91 Public administration	20	80	105	60	75	140
	by class of worker						
273	Class of worker - Not applicable (36)	20	10	15	20	10	25
274	All classes of worker (37)	1,365	1,290	2,465	1,895	1,695	2,880
275	Paid workers	1,250	1,125	2,230	1,725	1,500	2,685
276	Employees	1,240	990	2,125	1,685	1,405	2,545
277	Self-employed (incorporated)	15	135	105	35	95	140
278	Self-employed (unincorporated)	105	165	230	170	185	190
279	Unpaid family workers	10	-	10	10	10	10
	by occupation based on the 2001 NOC-S						
280	Male labour force 15 years and over	730	690	1,325	995	920	1,545
281	Occupation - Not applicable (36)	-	-	-	-	10	10
282	All occupations (37)	730	685	1,320	985	915	1,535
283	A Management occupations	65	170	390	185	145	350
284	B Business, finance and administration occupations	60	95	160	80	130	150
285	C Natural and applied sciences and related occupations	110	125	150	100	120	140
286	D Health occupations	-	10	10	10	15	15
287	E Occupations in social science, education, government service and religion	25	50	55	85	60	20
288	F Occupations in art, culture, recreation and sport	-	55	60	60	45	40
289	G Sales and service occupations	170	130	235	205	200	385
290	H Trades, transport and equipment operators and related occupations	200	35	175	200	175	280
291	I Occupations unique to primary industry	15	10	15	10	10	35
292	J Occupations unique to processing, manufacturing and utilities	85	15	80	50	25	115
293	Female labour force 15 years and over	650	605	1,155	925	780	1,355
294	Occupation - Not applicable (36)	15	-	15	15	-	15
295	All occupations (37)	635	605	1,140	910	780	1,340
296	A Management occupations	90	65	180	110	75	160
297	B Business, finance and administration occupations	180	200	360	305	210	420
298	C Natural and applied sciences and related occupations	25	20	40	40	30	55
299	D Health occupations	35	40	80	65	65	75

Tableau 1. Certaines caractéristiques des secteurs de recensement, recensement de 2001 – Données intégrales et données-échantillon (20 %)

Toronto 0612.01	Toronto 0612.02	Toronto 0612.03	Toronto 0612.05	Toronto 0612.07	Toronto 0612.08	Caractéristiques	Nº
						CARACTÉRISTIQUES DE LA POPULATION	
						selon l'activité – fin	
66.7	80.5	75.8	73.1	76.8	77.1	Les deux sexes - Taux d'activité	241
-	69.1	61.8	67.8	64.5	72.6	15-24 ans	242
66.7	82.0	78.9	74.5	78.9	78.1	25 ans et plus	243
66.7	77.9	71.2	69.3	73.0	72.9	Les deux sexes - Taux d'emploi	244
-	61.1	52.2	59.7	54.7	64.5	15-24 ans	245
66.7	80.3	75.7	71.9	76.3	74.6	25 ans et plus	246
-	3.3	5.9	5.2	5.0	5.3	Les deux sexes - Taux de chômage	247
-	11.8	15.3	10.7	15.7	10.0	15-24 ans	248
-	2.3	4.2	4.0	3.4	4.3	25 ans et plus	249
25	**6,915**	**3,200**	**3,245**	**3,635**	**2,555**	**Population active totale de 15 ans et plus**	250
						selon l'industrie basée sur le SCIAN de 1997	
-	45	35	25	25	20	Industrie - Sans objet (36)	251
25	6,870	3,165	3,220	3,610	2,530	Toutes les industries (37)	252
-	25	-	-	30	-	11 Agriculture, foresterie, pêche et chasse	253
-	15	15	35	25	-	21 Extraction minière et extraction de pétrole et de gaz	254
-	20	75	15	30	15	22 Services publics	255
-	300	95	65	130	95	23 Construction	256
10	1,025	325	360	390	420	31-33 Fabrication	257
-	465	215	230	285	190	41 Commerce de gros	258
-	525	380	315	405	345	44-45 Commerce de détail	259
-	295	100	155	195	100	48-49 Transport et entreposage	260
-	260	65	120	100	65	51 Industrie de l'information et industrie culturelle	261
-	940	365	395	405	255	52 Finance et assurances	262
-	160	70	70	95	50	53 Services immobiliers et services de location et de location à bail	263
10	870	430	395	520	270	54 Services professionnels, scientifiques et techniques	264
-	15	15	10	10	-	55 Gestion de sociétés et d'entreprises	265
-	260	160	100	130	75	56 Services administratifs, services de soutien, services de gestion des déchets et services d'assainissement	266
-	400	215	255	220	130	61 Services d'enseignement	267
-	490	220	255	260	195	62 Soins de santé et assistance sociale	268
-	100	30	45	40	10	71 Arts, spectacles et loisirs	269
-	265	185	195	130	115	72 Hébergement et services de restauration	270
-	175	85	110	105	95	81 Autres services, sauf les administrations publiques	271
10	270	125	120	100	85	91 Administrations publiques	272
						selon la catégorie de travailleurs	
-	45	35	30	30	25	Catégorie de travailleurs - Sans objet (36)	273
20	6,865	3,165	3,220	3,610	2,535	Toutes les catégories de travailleurs (37)	274
20	6,425	2,945	3,050	3,400	2,385	Travailleurs rémunérés	275
20	6,210	2,810	2,920	3,285	2,335	Employés	276
-	215	125	130	115	50	Travailleurs autonomes (entreprise constituée en société)	277
-	435	215	165	195	140	Travailleurs autonomes (entreprise non constituée en société)	278
-	15	10	-	15	-	Travailleurs familiaux non rémunérés	279
						selon la profession basée sur la CNP-S de 2001	
-	3,725	1,625	1,690	1,795	1,330	Hommes actifs de 15 ans et plus	280
-	20	25	-	25	-	Profession - Sans objet (36)	281
10	3,705	1,605	1,685	1,765	1,330	Toutes les professions (37)	282
-	970	460	555	460	220	A Gestion	283
-	580	225	255	255	160	B Affaires, finance et administration	284
-	495	240	180	250	105	C Sciences naturelles et appliquées et professions apparentées	285
-	55	45	25	15	40	D Secteur de la santé	286
-	180	100	70	110	70	E Sciences sociales, enseignement, administration publique et religion	287
-	75	25	15	55	30	F Arts, culture, sports et loisirs	288
-	615	250	305	310	385	G Ventes et services	289
-	485	170	190	210	175	H Métiers, transport et machinerie	290
-	35	15	25	10	10	I Professions propres au secteur primaire	291
-	210	85	60	95	140	J Transformation, fabrication et services d'utilité publique	292
15	3,185	1,575	1,555	1,845	1,220	Femmes actives de 15 ans et plus	293
-	30	10	20	-	20	Profession - Sans objet (36)	294
10	3,160	1,560	1,530	1,845	1,200	Toutes les professions (37)	295
-	460	220	200	385	130	A Gestion	296
10	1,125	450	490	525	345	B Affaires, finance et administration	297
10	165	50	60	110	80	C Sciences naturelles et appliquées et professions apparentées	298
-	255	115	120	105	95	D Secteur de la santé	299

Table 1. Selected Characteristics for Census Tracts, 2001 Census – 100% Data and 20% Sample Data

No.	Characteristics	Toronto 0608	Toronto 0609	Toronto 0610.02	Toronto 0610.03 A	Toronto 0610.04 A	Toronto 0611
	POPULATION CHARACTERISTICS						
	by occupation based on the 2001 NOC-S – concluded						
300	E Occupations in social science, education, government service and religion	40	95	125	105	105	180
301	F Occupations in art, culture, recreation and sport	40	40	50	40	75	30
302	G Sales and service occupations	185	120	275	225	215	360
303	H Trades, transport and equipment operators and related occupations	15	10	15	-	15	20
304	I Occupations unique to primary industry	-	-	10	-	-	15
305	J Occupations unique to processing, manufacturing and utilities	30	-	15	15	10	30
306	**Total employed labour force 15 years and over by place of work**	**1,300**	**1,240**	**2,400**	**1,840**	**1,615**	**2,780**
307	Males	705	655	1,305	955	860	1,465
308	Usual place of work	575	505	1,070	750	675	1,155
309	At home	45	110	90	75	80	125
310	Outside Canada	10	-	15	25	10	20
311	No fixed workplace address	75	40	125	100	105	165
312	Females	595	585	1,100	885	755	1,315
313	Usual place of work	525	475	980	825	590	1,165
314	At home	45	105	85	20	110	75
315	Outside Canada	-	-	-	-	-	-
316	No fixed workplace address	15	-	35	45	45	70
317	**Total employed labour force 15 years and over with usual place of work or no fixed workplace address by mode of transportation**	**1,195**	**1,025**	**2,210**	**1,720**	**1,415**	**2,555**
318	Males	650	545	1,195	850	775	1,320
319	Car, truck, van, as driver	560	420	950	730	630	1,045
320	Car, truck, van, as passenger	15	25	95	25	50	80
321	Public transit	50	80	105	45	85	150
322	Walked	25	-	30	45	10	30
323	Other method	-	15	15	10	-	25
324	Females	545	480	1,020	870	640	1,235
325	Car, truck, van, as driver	400	355	780	620	460	940
326	Car, truck, van, as passenger	45	35	90	60	60	85
327	Public transit	80	75	100	110	90	180
328	Walked	20	15	30	60	20	20
329	Other method	-	10	15	15	10	10
330	**Total population 15 years and over who worked since January 1, 2000 by language used at work**	**1,455**	**1,430**	**2,615**	**2,045**	**1,820**	**3,150**
331	Single responses	1,355	1,330	2,480	1,925	1,690	3,030
332	English	1,355	1,330	2,460	1,920	1,685	3,005
333	French	-	-	10	-	-	-
334	Non-official languages (5)	10	-	10	-	10	15
335	Chinese, n.o.s.	-	-	-	10	-	-
336	Cantonese	-	-	-	-	-	-
337	Other languages (6)	-	-	-	-	10	20
338	Multiple responses	100	105	135	125	125	125
339	English and French	35	50	100	60	95	55
340	English and non-official language	65	35	30	60	35	55
341	French and non-official language	-	-	-	-	-	-
342	English, French and non-official language	-	15	-	-	-	20
	DWELLING AND HOUSEHOLD CHARACTERISTICS						
343	**Total number of occupied private dwellings by tenure**	**890**	**945**	**1,545**	**1,605**	**1,770**	**1,695**
344	Owned	740	865	1,470	675	1,480	1,660
345	Rented	150	85	75	930	295	35
346	Band housing	-	-	-	-	-	-
	by structural type of dwelling						
347	Single-detached house	775	900	1,295	450	650	1,695
348	Semi-detached house	-	-	-	50	15	-
349	Row house	110	30	35	185	265	-
350	Apartment, detached duplex	-	15	10	55	-	-
351	Apartment, building that has five or more storeys	-	-	205	605	840	-
352	Apartment, building that has fewer than five storeys (38)	10	-	-	260	-	-
353	Other single-attached house	-	-	-	-	-	-
354	Movable dwelling (39)	-	-	-	-	-	-

Tableau 1. Certaines caractéristiques des secteurs de recensement, recensement de 2001 – Données intégrales et données-échantillon (20 %)

Toronto 0612.01	Toronto 0612.02	Toronto 0612.03	Toronto 0612.05	Toronto 0612.07	Toronto 0612.08	Caractéristiques	N°
						CARACTÉRISTIQUES DE LA POPULATION	
						selon la profession basée sur la CNP-S de 2001 - fin	
-	350	205	165	170	115	E Sciences sociales, enseignement, administration publique et religion	300
-	85	65	80	65	20	F Arts, culture, sports et loisirs	301
-	605	400	360	415	310	G Ventes et services	302
-	25	10	25	25	35	H Métiers, transport et machinerie	303
-	20	-	-	15	-	I Professions propres au secteur primaire	304
-	80	40	35	30	75	J Transformation, fabrication et services d'utilité publique	305
20	**6,690**	**3,015**	**3,075**	**3,455**	**2,415**	**Population active occupée totale de 15 ans et plus**	306
						selon le lieu de travail	
10	3,660	1,545	1,600	1,685	1,285	Hommes	307
10	3,035	1,295	1,400	1,390	1,100	Lieu habituel de travail	308
-	230	140	85	125	50	À domicile	309
-	30	10	30	40	10	En dehors du Canada	310
-	365	95	75	125	125	Sans adresse de travail fixe	311
10	3,030	1,470	1,475	1,775	1,130	Femmes	312
15	2,660	1,195	1,240	1,550	1,045	Lieu habituel de travail	313
-	215	205	180	115	75	À domicile	314
-	10	10	15	-	-	En dehors du Canada	315
-	140	70	45	105	15	Sans adresse de travail fixe	316
20	**6,195**	**2,650**	**2,765**	**3,175**	**2,285**	**Population active occupée totale de 15 ans et plus ayant un lieu habituel de travail ou sans adresse de travail fixe**	317
						selon le mode de transport	
-	3,395	1,390	1,475	1,515	1,220	Hommes	318
10	2,800	1,135	1,130	1,190	1,045	Automobile, camion ou fourgonnette, en tant que conducteur	319
-	95	40	50	60	35	Automobile, camion ou fourgonnette, en tant que passager	320
-	450	180	225	230	115	Transport en commun	321
-	50	25	65	15	25	À pied	322
-	10	15	10	20	-	Autre moyen	323
15	2,800	1,260	1,285	1,655	1,060	Femmes	324
10	2,060	930	880	1,190	715	Automobile, camion ou fourgonnette, en tant que conductrice	325
-	185	110	90	125	120	Automobile, camion ou fourgonnette, en tant que passagère	326
-	500	175	205	290	165	Transport en commun	327
-	35	40	90	40	55	À pied	328
-	15	-	15	10	10	Autre moyen	329
25	**7,375**	**3,435**	**3,525**	**3,865**	**2,655**	**Population totale de 15 ans et plus ayant travaillé depuis le 1er janvier 2000**	330
						selon la langue utilisée au travail	
25	6,745	3,190	3,250	3,560	2,515	Réponses uniques	331
25	6,725	3,150	3,235	3,560	2,490	Anglais	332
-	10	10	10	-	-	Français	333
-	15	30	15	-	25	Langues non officielles (5)	334
-	-	35	-	-	-	Chinois, n.d.a.	335
-	-	-	-	-	-	Cantonais	336
-	15	-	15	-	25	Autres langues (6)	337
-	630	250	275	305	140	Réponses multiples	338
-	325	125	160	145	35	Anglais et français	339
-	280	125	100	155	100	Anglais et langue non officielle	340
-	-	-	-	-	-	Français et langue non officielle	341
-	25	-	15	-	10	Anglais, français et langue non officielle	342
						CARACTÉRISTIQUES DES LOGEMENTS ET DES MÉNAGES	
15	**3,865**	**1,725**	**1,865**	**2,095**	**1,245**	**Nombre total de logements privés occupés**	343
						selon le mode d'occupation	
15	3,690	1,430	1,375	1,920	1,120	Possédé	344
-	170	295	490	170	120	Loué	345
-	-	-	-	-	-	Logement de bande	346
						selon le type de construction résidentielle	
15	2,700	1,190	1,070	975	920	Maison individuelle non attenante	347
-	345	75	105	250	-	Maison jumelée	348
-	815	315	370	740	325	Maison en rangée	349
-	-	-	-	10	10	Appartement, duplex non attenant	350
-	-	145	325	-	-	Appartement, immeuble de cinq étages ou plus	351
-	-	-	-	120	-	Appartement, immeuble de moins de cinq étages (38)	352
-	-	-	-	-	-	Autre maison individuelle attenante	353
-	-	-	-	-	-	Logement mobile (39)	354

Table 1. Selected Characteristics for Census Tracts, 2001 Census – 100% Data and 20% Sample Data

No.	Characteristics	Toronto 0608	Toronto 0609	Toronto 0610.02	Toronto 0610.03 A	Toronto 0610.04 A	Toronto 0611
	DWELLING AND HOUSEHOLD CHARACTERISTICS						
	by condition of dwelling						
355	Regular maintenance only	590	715	1,100	1,010	1,345	1,110
356	Minor repairs	260	210	355	395	335	505
357	Major repairs	40	10	85	195	95	85
	by period of construction						
358	Before 1946	35	25	35	75	15	10
359	1946-1960	600	425	70	365	195	250
360	1961-1970	170	340	25	535	465	730
361	1971-1980	55	100	240	315	640	600
362	1981-1990	25	15	1,055	240	440	85
363	1991-2001 (20)	-	30	115	70	20	20
364	Average number of rooms per dwelling	7.4	8.4	7.6	5.4	6.5	8.3
365	Average number of bedrooms per dwelling	3.2	3.4	3.2	2.1	2.5	3.5
366	Average value of dwelling $	219,312	411,660	280,433	231,103	256,695	237,540
367	**Total number of private households**	**890**	**945**	**1,545**	**1,605**	**1,775**	**1,695**
	by household size						
368	1 person	130	115	215	630	585	150
369	2 persons	305	385	505	615	715	585
370	3 persons	170	135	255	180	210	345
371	4-5 persons	245	290	525	160	240	570
372	6 or more persons	40	25	45	15	25	45
	by household type						
373	One-family households	685	820	1,280	885	1,165	1,480
374	Multiple-family households	25	-	25	10	10	50
375	Non-family households	175	115	245	715	600	170
376	Number of persons in private households	2,530	2,680	4,505	3,190	3,810	5,070
377	Average number of persons in private households	2.8	2.8	2.9	2.0	2.1	3.0
378	Average number of persons per room	0.4	0.3	0.4	0.4	0.3	0.4
379	Tenant households in non-farm, non-reserve private dwellings (40)	150	85	75	930	295	35
380	Average gross rent $ (40)	1,243	1,307	1,433	930	773	1,180
381	Tenant households spending 30% or more of household income on gross rent (40) (41)	75	15	40	370	180	10
382	Tenant households spending from 30% to 99% of household income on gross rent (40) (41)	65	15	35	340	165	10
383	Owner households in non-farm, non-reserve private dwellings (42)	740	865	1,460	675	1,480	1,665
384	Average owner's major payments $ (42)	967	1,265	1,228	974	916	1,054
385	Owner households spending 30% or more of household income on owner's major payments (41) (42)	130	90	190	100	210	190
386	Owner households spending from 30% to 99% of household income on owner's major payments (41) (42)	125	65	175	80	195	185
	CENSUS FAMILY CHARACTERISTICS						
387	**Total number of census families in private households**	**740**	**835**	**1,320**	**890**	**1,180**	**1,580**
	by census family structure and size						
388	Total couple families	635	780	1,225	775	1,065	1,425
389	Total families of married couples	570	760	1,155	640	1,000	1,335
390	Without children at home	260	355	420	360	610	520
391	With children at home	310	400	735	285	385	815
392	1 child	100	130	210	155	170	290
393	2 children	160	200	375	95	165	400
394	3 or more children	45	75	150	35	50	125
395	Total families of common-law couples	65	20	70	130	65	85
396	Without children at home	25	20	60	120	35	20
397	With children at home	40	-	10	15	35	60
398	1 child	10	-	10	-	10	30
399	2 children	30	-	-	10	10	30
400	3 or more children	-	-	-	-	10	10
401	Total lone-parent families	105	55	100	115	120	155
402	Female parent	100	50	65	65	80	110
403	1 child	45	25	25	40	45	80
404	2 children	45	10	20	20	20	30
405	3 or more children	10	20	20	-	10	-

Tableau 1. Certaines caractéristiques des secteurs de recensement, recensement de 2001 – Données intégrales et données-échantillon (20 %)

Toronto 0612.01	Toronto 0612.02	Toronto 0612.03	Toronto 0612.05	Toronto 0612.07	Toronto 0612.08	Caractéristiques	N°
						CARACTÉRISTIQUES DES LOGEMENTS ET DES MÉNAGES	
						selon l'état du logement	
10	3,620	1,385	1,425	1,880	995	Entretien régulier seulement	355
-	225	325	415	185	220	Réparations mineures	356
10	20	20	25	25	25	Réparations majeures	357
						selon la période de construction	
-	15	10	10	-	-	Avant 1946	358
10	15	-	-	10	-	1946-1960	359
-	10	-	-	-	10	1961-1970	360
-	10	-	60	35	15	1971-1980	361
-	15	975	1,345	670	675	1981-1990	362
-	3,805	745	445	1,385	555	1991-2001 (20)	363
7.3	7.1	8.3	7.8	7.4	7.6	Nombre moyen de pièces par logement	364
2.7	3.3	3.6	3.3	3.3	3.6	Nombre moyen de chambres à coucher par logement	365
340,699	282,425	321,251	328,002	266,273	283,872	Valeur moyenne du logement $	366
15	**3,860**	**1,725**	**1,865**	**2,095**	**1,245**	**Nombre total de logements privés**	367
						selon la taille du ménage	
-	345	140	195	290	95	1 personne	368
-	1,185	355	510	580	255	2 personnes	369
-	895	310	370	390	270	3 personnes	370
10	1,340	815	740	755	530	4-5 personnes	371
-	105	115	55	75	100	6 personnes ou plus	372
						selon le genre de ménage	
10	3,385	1,515	1,595	1,715	1,050	Ménages unifamiliaux	373
-	80	45	10	45	75	Ménages multifamiliaux	374
10	405	165	260	330	120	Ménages non familiaux	375
40	11,750	6,040	5,845	6,365	4,415	Nombre de personnes dans les ménages privés	376
2.7	3.0	3.5	3.1	3.0	3.6	Nombre moyen de personnes dans les ménages privés	377
0.4	0.4	0.4	0.4	0.4	0.5	Nombre moyen de personnes par pièce	378
-	175	295	490	170	120	Ménages locataires dans les logements privés non agricoles hors réserve (40)	379
-	1,397	1,037	940	1,212	1,145	Loyer brut moyen $ (40)	380
-	65	75	200	70	30	Ménages locataires consacrant 30 % ou plus du revenu du ménage au loyer brut (40) (41)	381
-	45	75	155	50	30	Ménages locataires consacrant de 30 % à 99 % du revenu du ménage au loyer brut (40) (41)	382
-	3,685	1,435	1,370	1,915	1,125	Ménages propriétaires dans les logements privés non agricoles hors réserve (42)	383
-	1,499	1,604	1,358	1,403	1,358	Principales dépenses de propriété moyennes $ (42)	384
-	690	250	175	265	140	Ménages propriétaires consacrant 30 % ou plus du revenu du ménage aux principales dépenses de propriété (41) (42)	385
-	605	200	155	245	130	Ménages propriétaires consacrant de 30 % à 99 % du revenu du ménage aux principales dépenses de propriété (41) (42)	386
						CARACTÉRISTIQUES DES FAMILLES DE RECENSEMENT	
-	**3,545**	**1,610**	**1,620**	**1,805**	**1,215**	**Total des familles de recensement dans les ménages privés**	387
						selon la structure et la taille de la famille de recensement	
-	3,225	1,405	1,410	1,595	1,070	Total des familles avec conjoints	388
10	2,995	1,345	1,345	1,460	1,005	Total des familles avec couples mariés	389
-	985	270	335	475	255	Sans enfants à la maison	390
10	2,005	1,075	1,005	985	750	Avec enfants à la maison	391
-	750	220	265	295	255	1 enfant	392
10	985	535	500	480	280	2 enfants	393
-	275	320	245	205	215	3 enfants ou plus	394
-	235	65	65	130	60	Total des familles en union libre	395
-	130	40	40	85	30	Sans enfants à la maison	396
-	105	20	30	45	30	Avec enfants à la maison	397
-	50	10	15	10	-	1 enfant	398
-	35	20	10	15	20	2 enfants	399
-	20	-	10	20	-	3 enfants ou plus	400
-	320	205	205	210	150	Total des familles monoparentales	401
-	245	180	180	190	115	Parent de sexe féminin	402
-	130	95	95	115	75	1 enfant	403
-	110	60	65	35	35	2 enfants	404
-	10	30	10	50	-	3 enfants ou plus	405

Table 1. Selected Characteristics for Census Tracts, 2001 Census – 100% Data and 20% Sample Data

No.	Characteristics	Toronto 0608	Toronto 0609	Toronto 0610.02	Toronto 0610.03 A	Toronto 0610.04 A	Toronto 0611
	CENSUS FAMILY CHARACTERISTICS						
	by census family structure and size – concluded						
406	Male parent	10	10	35	50	40	45
407	1 child	-	-	25	25	35	35
408	2 children	-	10	10	10	-	10
409	3 or more children	-	-	-	10	-	-
410	**Total number of children at home**	**820**	**895**	**1,635**	**675**	**900**	**1,780**
	by age groups						
411	Under 6 years	120	145	320	155	170	340
412	6-14 years	365	350	665	220	295	545
413	15-17 years	75	140	205	90	80	215
414	18-24 years	165	155	325	115	205	390
415	25 years and over	90	110	115	100	150	300
416	Average number of children at home per census family (43)	1.1	1.1	1.2	0.8	0.8	1.1
417	**Total number of persons in private households**	**2,530**	**2,680**	**4,505**	**3,190**	**3,810**	**5,070**
	by census family status and living arrangements						
418	Number of non-family persons	340	170	330	845	665	290
419	Living with relatives (44)	60	55	35	65	40	90
420	Living with non-relatives only	145	-	75	150	40	45
421	Living alone	135	115	215	630	585	155
422	Number of family persons	2,195	2,510	4,175	2,340	3,145	4,780
423	Average number of persons per census family	3.0	3.0	3.2	2.6	2.7	3.0
424	**Total number of persons 65 years and over**	**420**	**595**	**490**	**615**	**1,385**	**715**
425	Number of non-family persons 65 years and over	145	125	115	250	445	85
426	Living with relatives (44)	40	45	15	25	15	40
427	Living with non-relatives only	10	-	20	10	10	-
428	Living alone	95	85	75	225	430	50
429	Number of family persons 65 years and over	280	465	375	360	935	630
	ECONOMIC FAMILY CHARACTERISTICS						
430	**Total number of economic families in private households**	**720**	**830**	**1,300**	**910**	**1,175**	**1,540**
	by size of family						
431	2 persons	295	385	485	560	715	595
432	3 persons	155	135	250	190	200	340
433	4 persons	190	205	395	115	180	405
434	5 or more persons	80	105	170	50	85	195
435	Total number of persons in economic families	2,255	2,565	4,215	2,405	3,180	4,870
436	Average number of persons per economic family	3.2	3.1	3.2	2.6	2.7	3.2
437	Total number of unattached individuals	275	115	290	780	625	195
	2000 INCOME CHARACTERISTICS						
	Population 15 years and over by sex and total income groups in 2000						
438	Total - Both sexes	2,045	2,185	3,520	2,815	3,350	4,180
439	Without income	105	80	160	130	85	210
440	With income	1,935	2,105	3,360	2,685	3,260	3,970
441	Under $1,000 (45)	70	75	195	40	80	120
442	$ 1,000 - $ 2,999	40	50	165	40	85	160
443	$ 3,000 - $ 4,999	50	95	135	70	140	120
444	$ 5,000 - $ 6,999	60	90	65	85	55	160
445	$ 7,000 - $ 9,999	90	105	125	90	110	225
446	$10,000 - $11,999	50	55	100	95	90	130
447	$12,000 - $14,999	125	105	165	180	200	180
448	$15,000 - $19,999	215	95	155	265	285	290
449	$20,000 - $24,999	220	135	190	170	210	130
450	$25,000 - $29,999	155	80	195	215	215	245
451	$30,000 - $34,999	135	110	180	250	250	305
452	$35,000 - $39,999	150	105	150	190	205	215
453	$40,000 - $44,999	90	130	220	200	160	275
454	$45,000 - $49,999	120	85	150	145	135	195
455	$50,000 - $59,999	110	150	225	195	275	355
456	$60,000 and over	265	645	945	455	765	860
457	Average income $ (46)	32,683	56,224	52,477	38,984	42,628	41,236
458	Median income $ (46)	25,948	37,820	34,964	30,995	32,778	32,859
459	Standard error of average income $ (46)	1,325	3,443	2,817	1,441	1,519	1,475

Tableau 1. Certaines caractéristiques des secteurs de recensement, recensement de 2001 – Données intégrales et données-échantillon (20 %)

Toronto 0612.01	Toronto 0612.02	Toronto 0612.03	Toronto 0612.05	Toronto 0612.07	Toronto 0612.08	Caractéristiques	Nº
						CARACTÉRISTIQUES DES FAMILLES DE RECENSEMENT	
						selon la structure et la taille de la famille de recensement – fin	
-	70	25	30	15	30	Parent de sexe masculin	406
-	40	20	10	15	10	1 enfant	407
-	15	10	20	-	15	2 enfants	408
-	10	-	-	-	10	3 enfants ou plus	409
15	**4,250**	**2,695**	**2,405**	**2,405**	**1,820**	**Nombre total d'enfants à la maison selon les groupes d'âge**	410
-	1,620	545	435	690	390	Moins de 6 ans	411
10	1,545	1,270	970	940	670	6-14 ans	412
-	320	310	315	260	205	15-17 ans	413
-	555	380	515	365	370	18-24 ans	414
-	205	185	175	145	175	25 ans et plus	415
-	1.2	1.7	1.5	1.3	1.5	Nombre moyen d'enfants à la maison par famille de recensement (43)	416
35	**11,750**	**6,035**	**5,845**	**6,365**	**4,420**	**Nombre total de personnes dans les ménages privés selon la situation des particuliers dans la famille de recensement et des particuliers dans le ménage**	417
10	725	325	415	565	315	Nombre de personnes hors famille de recensement	418
-	225	95	75	130	100	Vivant avec des personnes apparentées (44)	419
-	155	95	145	145	120	Vivant avec des personnes non apparentées uniquement	420
10	345	140	195	290	90	Vivant seules	421
30	11,025	5,710	5,430	5,800	4,095	Nombre de personnes membres d'une famille	422
-	3.1	3.5	3.4	3.2	3.4	Nombre moyen de personnes par famille de recensement	423
-	**375**	**240**	**290**	**355**	**215**	**Nombre total de personnes de 65 ans et plus**	424
10	130	70	80	165	75	Nombre de personnes hors famille de recensement de 65 ans et plus	425
-	85	40	45	90	55	Vivant avec des personnes apparentées (44)	426
-	-	-	-	10	-	Vivant avec des personnes non apparentées uniquement	427
10	40	20	35	60	25	Vivant seules	428
-	245	170	210	190	140	Nombre de personnes membres d'une famille de 65 ans et plus	429
						CARACTÉRISTIQUES DES FAMILLES ÉCONOMIQUES	
10	**3,475**	**1,570**	**1,610**	**1,760**	**1,130**	**Nombre total de familles économiques dans les ménages privés selon la taille de la famille**	430
-	1,165	345	455	560	250	2 personnes	431
-	890	300	360	370	270	3 personnes	432
10	1,015	545	515	550	330	4 personnes	433
-	405	375	280	280	280	5 personnes ou plus	434
30	11,255	5,800	5,510	5,930	4,205	Nombre total de personnes dans les familles économiques	435
-	3.2	3.7	3.4	3.4	3.7	Nombre moyen de personnes par famille économique	436
10	500	230	335	435	215	Nombre total de personnes hors famille économique	437
						CARACTÉRISTIQUES DU REVENU DE 2000	
						Population de 15 ans et plus selon le sexe et les tranches de revenu total en 2000	
XXX	8,590	4,225	4,435	4,735	3,315	Total - Les deux sexes	438
	425	270	310	240	220	Sans revenu	439
	8,165	3,955	4,130	4,495	3,095	Avec un revenu	440
	320	155	160	155	145	Moins de 1 000 $ (45)	441
	315	190	185	205	145	1 000 $ - 2 999 $	442
	225	155	165	165	120	3 000 $ - 4 999 $	443
	260	115	190	110	85	5 000 $ - 6 999 $	444
	260	280	240	195	150	7 000 $ - 9 999 $	445
	145	165	130	75	105	10 000 $ - 11 999 $	446
	305	115	125	180	140	12 000 $ - 14 999 $	447
	355	250	245	185	145	15 000 $ - 19 999 $	448
	350	205	255	210	155	20 000 $ - 24 999 $	449
	365	215	240	220	190	25 000 $ - 29 999 $	450
	530	200	215	255	170	30 000 $ - 34 999 $	451
	490	140	240	215	215	35 000 $ - 39 999 $	452
	570	200	180	235	170	40 000 $ - 44 999 $	453
	475	120	185	205	180	45 000 $ - 49 999 $	454
	880	285	190	415	260	50 000 $ - 59 999 $	455
	2,320	1,160	1,190	1,465	720	60 000 $ et plus	456
	48,377	52,901	55,585	52,443	41,913	Revenu moyen $ (46)	457
	40,170	32,417	32,810	40,169	34,909	Revenu médian $ (46)	458
	1,054	2,526	2,912	1,856	1,627	Erreur type de revenu moyen $ (46)	459

Table 1. Selected Characteristics for Census Tracts, 2001 Census – 100% Data and 20% Sample Data

No.	Characteristics	Toronto 0608	Toronto 0609	Toronto 0610.02	Toronto 0610.03 A	Toronto 0610.04 A	Toronto 0611
	2000 INCOME CHARACTERISTICS						
	Population 15 years and over by sex and total income groups in 2000 – concluded						
460	Total - Males	1,000	1,075	1,700	1,310	1,485	2,085
461	Without income	45	10	40	45	10	60
462	With income	950	1,055	1,660	1,265	1,470	2,025
463	Under $1,000 (45)	35	50	80	10	50	60
464	$ 1,000 - $ 2,999	15	30	50	30	30	85
465	$ 3,000 - $ 4,999	15	50	75	30	50	45
466	$ 5,000 - $ 6,999	10	20	30	55	20	60
467	$ 7,000 - $ 9,999	25	40	35	45	30	80
468	$10,000 - $11,999	10	15	35	25	20	45
469	$12,000 - $14,999	50	50	35	40	35	50
470	$15,000 - $19,999	80	20	70	95	75	65
471	$20,000 - $24,999	90	35	80	55	60	60
472	$25,000 - $29,999	80	25	60	90	90	90
473	$30,000 - $34,999	65	40	85	100	125	145
474	$35,000 - $39,999	65	30	45	85	75	60
475	$40,000 - $44,999	45	55	90	75	60	145
476	$45,000 - $49,999	110	60	65	80	60	135
477	$50,000 - $59,999	65	80	120	135	170	235
478	$60,000 and over	200	445	705	325	515	665
479	Average income $ (46)	40,421	77,283	71,807	49,192	54,160	52,913
480	Median income $ (46)	35,203	49,247	49,135	38,326	44,974	44,998
481	Standard error of average income $ (46)	2,303	6,254	5,092	2,714	2,671	2,592
482	Total - Females	1,045	1,110	1,820	1,505	1,865	2,090
483	Without income	65	65	120	85	75	150
484	With income	985	1,045	1,700	1,420	1,795	1,940
485	Under $1,000 (45)	35	25	110	35	25	55
486	$ 1,000 - $ 2,999	25	25	110	15	55	80
487	$ 3,000 - $ 4,999	40	45	60	40	90	75
488	$ 5,000 - $ 6,999	45	70	35	30	40	100
489	$ 7,000 - $ 9,999	60	65	90	45	75	145
490	$10,000 - $11,999	35	40	60	65	75	85
491	$12,000 - $14,999	75	60	130	145	165	125
492	$15,000 - $19,999	135	70	90	175	210	230
493	$20,000 - $24,999	125	100	110	115	150	70
494	$25,000 - $29,999	80	55	135	125	125	155
495	$30,000 - $34,999	70	70	95	150	125	155
496	$35,000 - $39,999	90	70	100	105	130	155
497	$40,000 - $44,999	45	75	135	130	95	130
498	$45,000 - $49,999	10	20	90	65	75	65
499	$50,000 - $59,999	45	65	105	60	110	115
500	$60,000 and over	65	195	245	130	245	195
501	Average income $ (46)	25,204	34,947	33,611	29,907	33,153	29,060
502	Median income $ (46)	22,552	28,223	26,003	27,659	25,313	24,988
503	Standard error of average income $ (46)	1,212	1,889	2,056	1,129	1,573	1,163
	by composition of total income						
504	Total - Composition of income in 2000 % (47)	100.0	100.0	100.0	100.0	100.0	100.0
505	Employment income %	79.3	74.2	84.0	80.7	55.2	80.4
506	Government transfer payments %	10.7	6.4	4.5	8.6	12.7	6.3
507	Other %	10.0	19.2	11.5	10.7	32.0	13.2
	Population 15 years and over with employment income in 2000 by sex and work activity						
508	Both sexes with employment income (48)	1,420	1,430	2,630	1,990	1,790	3,105
509	Average employment income $	35,291	61,623	56,349	42,427	42,947	42,422
510	Standard error of average employment income $	1,694	4,631	3,317	1,843	2,312	1,749
511	Worked full year, full time (49)	850	720	1,560	1,275	920	1,825
512	Average employment income $	45,590	93,057	74,033	52,089	64,461	55,381
513	Standard error of average employment income $	2,395	7,178	4,033	2,518	3,564	2,183
514	Worked part year or part time (50)	575	655	985	710	800	1,220
515	Average employment income $	20,050	30,347	31,108	25,403	20,936	23,683
516	Standard error of average employment income $	1,479	4,814	5,662	1,916	1,868	2,531
517	Males with employment income (48)	755	765	1,370	1,030	915	1,625
518	Average employment income $	42,302	83,631	76,105	51,089	53,984	52,685
519	Standard error of average employment income $	2,777	7,972	5,670	3,272	3,930	3,053
520	Worked full year, full time (49)	500	420	915	675	540	980
521	Average employment income $	52,632	120,666	89,213	63,614	74,527	66,401
522	Standard error of average employment income $	3,728	11,354	6,054	4,299	5,281	3,659
523	Worked part year or part time (50)	255	320	435	350	345	615
524	Average employment income $	22,196	39,938	51,096	27,321	25,475	31,470
525	Standard error of average employment income $	2,287	9,180	12,236	3,330	3,803	4,901

Tableau 1. Certaines caractéristiques des secteurs de recensement, recensement de 2001 – Données intégrales et données-échantillon (20 %)

Toronto 0612.01	Toronto 0612.02	Toronto 0612.03	Toronto 0612.05	Toronto 0612.07	Toronto 0612.08	Caractéristiques	N°
						CARACTÉRISTIQUES DU REVENU DE 2000	
						Population de 15 ans et plus selon le sexe et les tranches de revenu total en 2000 – fin	
XXX	4,200	2,020	2,115	2,210	1,610	Total - Hommes	460
	105	95	115	110	40	Sans revenu	461
	4,100	1,925	2,005	2,100	1,570	Avec un revenu	462
	125	55	40	80	40	Moins de 1 000 $ (45)	463
	130	90	105	45	60	1 000 $ - 2 999 $	464
	90	60	40	70	50	3 000 $ - 4 999 $	465
	90	30	65	30	15	5 000 $ - 6 999 $	466
	75	70	65	55	90	7 000 $ - 9 999 $	467
	50	75	50	10	35	10 000 $ - 11 999 $	468
	70	45	60	45	60	12 000 $ - 14 999 $	469
	115	110	75	45	45	15 000 $ - 19 999 $	470
	80	30	70	75	65	20 000 $ - 24 999 $	471
	140	45	90	100	75	25 000 $ - 29 999 $	472
	230	40	85	75	75	30 000 $ - 34 999 $	473
	210	35	95	85	80	35 000 $ - 39 999 $	474
	230	135	105	80	65	40 000 $ - 44 999 $	475
	250	55	70	105	80	45 000 $ - 49 999 $	476
	515	155	100	180	190	50 000 $ - 59 999 $	477
	1,700	895	880	1,010	540	60 000 $ et plus	478
	61,890	76,709	79,413	69,637	53,700	Revenu moyen $ (46)	479
	51,087	54,954	45,876	57,025	45,160	Revenu médian $ (46)	480
	1,746	4,562	4,966	3,378	2,797	Erreur type de revenu moyen $ (46)	481
	4,385	2,200	2,320	2,525	1,700	Total - Femmes	482
	325	180	195	130	175	Sans revenu	483
	4,070	2,020	2,125	2,395	1,525	Avec un revenu	484
	195	105	120	75	105	Moins de 1 000 $ (45)	485
	190	100	85	165	90	1 000 $ - 2 999 $	486
	135	105	125	90	65	3 000 $ - 4 999 $	487
	170	80	125	80	65	5 000 $ - 6 999 $	488
	185	205	175	140	60	7 000 $ - 9 999 $	489
	90	90	75	65	70	10 000 $ - 11 999 $	490
	235	70	60	135	80	12 000 $ - 14 999 $	491
	240	145	165	135	105	15 000 $ - 19 999 $	492
	270	180	185	135	95	20 000 $ - 24 999 $	493
	225	165	150	125	115	25 000 $ - 29 999 $	494
	305	160	125	185	95	30 000 $ - 34 999 $	495
	280	105	150	130	135	35 000 $ - 39 999 $	496
	340	65	75	160	105	40 000 $ - 44 999 $	497
	225	65	110	100	100	45 000 $ - 49 999 $	498
	365	130	90	230	70	50 000 $ - 59 999 $	499
	615	265	300	450	185	60 000 $ et plus	500
	34,745	30,236	33,160	37,365	29,757	Revenu moyen $ (46)	501
	31,036	23,755	22,687	30,786	25,282	Revenu médian $ (46)	502
	958	1,527	2,867	1,510	1,361	Erreur type de revenu moyen $ (46)	503
						selon la composition du revenu total	
	100.0	100.0	100.0	100.0	100.0	Total - Composition du revenu en 2000 % (47)	504
	93.2	92.9	88.3	91.1	88.4	Revenu d'emploi %	505
	2.6	3.2	3.3	2.9	4.8	Transferts gouvernementaux %	506
	4.2	4.0	8.5	5.9	6.7	Autre %	507
						Population de 15 ans et plus ayant un revenu d'emploi en 2000 selon le sexe et le travail	
	7,255	3,380	3,460	3,810	2,570	Les deux sexes ayant un revenu d'emploi (48)	508
	50,767	57,441	58,532	56,403	44,694	Revenu moyen d'emploi $	509
	1,128	2,859	3,355	2,048	1,739	Erreur type de revenu moyen d'emploi $	510
	4,825	1,945	1,955	2,490	1,550	Ayant travaillé toute l'année à plein temps (49)	511
	61,261	80,604	80,414	70,317	59,735	Revenu moyen d'emploi $	512
	1,282	4,321	5,094	2,768	2,349	Erreur type de revenu moyen d'emploi $	513
	2,315	1,350	1,445	1,240	995	Ayant travaillé une partie de l'année ou à temps partiel (50)	514
	30,685	25,890	30,661	30,031	22,087	Revenu moyen d'emploi $	515
	2,024	2,377	3,456	2,172	1,763	Erreur type de revenu moyen d'emploi $	516
	3,815	1,720	1,805	1,870	1,325	Hommes ayant un revenu d'emploi (48)	517
	63,666	81,558	80,498	71,978	57,187	Revenu moyen d'emploi $	518
	1,809	4,962	5,318	3,560	2,904	Erreur type de revenu moyen d'emploi $	519
	2,890	1,145	1,220	1,365	895	Ayant travaillé toute l'année à plein temps (49)	520
	72,384	104,174	98,151	84,591	70,938	Revenu moyen d'emploi $	521
	1,875	6,698	6,561	4,459	3,641	Erreur type de revenu moyen d'emploi $	522
	885	540	560	470	420	Ayant travaillé une partie de l'année ou à temps partiel (50)	523
	37,418	37,454	44,713	36,853	28,386	Revenu moyen d'emploi $	524
	4,280	5,090	8,559	4,335	3,264	Erreur type de revenu moyen d'emploi $	525

Table 1. Selected Characteristics for Census Tracts, 2001 Census – 100% Data and 20% Sample Data

No.	Characteristics	Toronto 0608	Toronto 0609	Toronto 0610.02	Toronto 0610.03 A	Toronto 0610.04 A	Toronto 0611
	2000 INCOME CHARACTERISTICS						
	Population 15 years and over with employment income in 2000 by sex and work activity – concluded						
526	Females with employment income (48)	670	665	1,255	960	875	1,475
527	Average employment income $	27,412	36,197	34,846	33,194	31,444	31,089
528	Standard error of average employment income $	1,594	2,388	2,494	1,430	2,158	1,337
529	Worked full year, full time (49)	355	300	650	600	380	845
530	Average employment income $	35,612	54,474	52,696	39,094	50,032	42,626
531	Standard error of average employment income $	2,127	2,820	4,036	1,755	3,700	1,663
532	Worked part year or part time (50)	320	335	555	360	450	605
533	Average employment income $	18,346	21,208	15,521	23,559	17,459	15,791
534	Standard error of average employment income $	1,905	2,860	1,519	2,111	1,639	1,459
	Census families by structure and family income groups in 2000						
535	Total - All census families	745	835	1,320	890	1,180	1,580
536	Under $10,000	30	-	15	10	30	-
537	$ 10,000 - $19,999	10	25	15	20	15	25
538	$ 20,000 - $29,999	80	25	70	60	30	80
539	$ 30,000 - $39,999	75	30	50	95	85	85
540	$ 40,000 - $49,999	55	50	110	85	65	85
541	$ 50,000 - $59,999	85	25	85	105	80	135
542	$ 60,000 - $69,999	65	65	90	100	115	130
543	$ 70,000 - $79,999	85	55	60	75	115	200
544	$ 80,000 - $89,999	70	80	125	45	115	100
545	$ 90,000 - $99,999	45	40	110	70	125	145
546	$100,000 and over	140	425	590	220	410	595
547	Average family income $	72,103	132,724	120,313	83,221	93,987	95,774
548	Median family income $	66,337	99,969	92,215	65,310	82,988	84,578
549	Standard error of average family income $	3,410	7,668	6,598	4,246	3,565	3,316
550	Total - All couple census families (51)	635	780	1,225	780	1,065	1,420
551	Under $10,000	15	10	15	-	10	-
552	$ 10,000 - $19,999	-	10	10	15	10	10
553	$ 20,000 - $29,999	55	25	55	50	25	70
554	$ 30,000 - $39,999	60	20	45	80	75	75
555	$ 40,000 - $49,999	40	45	60	60	55	70
556	$ 50,000 - $59,999	80	20	70	95	75	105
557	$ 60,000 - $69,999	55	65	85	95	95	110
558	$ 70,000 - $79,999	85	55	65	55	115	175
559	$ 80,000 - $89,999	70	80	125	45	105	85
560	$ 90,000 - $99,999	35	40	115	60	115	135
561	$100,000 and over	140	410	580	220	385	580
562	Average family income $	77,324	137,873	124,189	88,151	97,281	99,186
563	Median family income $	75,401	101,495	94,375	68,754	89,221	89,709
564	Standard error of average family income $	3,781	8,065	6,862	4,672	3,756	3,604
	Incidence of low income in 2000						
565	Total - Economic families	720	830	1,300	910	1,180	1,540
566	Low income	75	30	70	75	70	60
567	Incidence of low income in 2000 % (52)	10.8	3.3	5.5	8.2	5.8	4.0
568	Total - Unattached individuals 15 years and over	275	115	290	780	625	185
569	Low income	100	30	55	170	195	40
570	Incidence of low income in 2000 % (52)	35.9	26.3	20.1	21.9	31.7	22.0
571	Total - Population in private households	2,535	2,680	4,505	3,190	3,810	5,060
572	Low income	370	160	315	380	380	220
573	Incidence of low income in 2000 % (52)	14.5	5.9	7.0	11.8	10.0	4.4
	Private households by household income groups in 2000						
574	Total - All private households	890	945	1,545	1,605	1,775	1,700
575	Under $10,000	15	10	30	40	40	10
576	$ 10,000 - $19,999	60	45	30	155	205	30
577	$ 20,000 - $29,999	100	60	105	175	135	80
578	$ 30,000 - $39,999	85	40	60	195	185	90
579	$ 40,000 - $49,999	65	50	125	185	105	120
580	$ 50,000 - $59,999	95	30	120	180	115	155
581	$ 60,000 - $69,999	80	65	130	155	130	115
582	$ 70,000 - $79,999	95	60	65	115	150	160
583	$ 80,000 - $89,999	70	80	135	70	125	130
584	$ 90,000 - $99,999	60	45	120	85	140	125
585	$100,000 and over	170	460	625	245	455	685
586	Average household income $	71,223	125,439	114,107	65,231	78,398	96,404
587	Median household income $	65,301	96,775	87,172	51,906	65,755	86,233
588	Standard error of average household income $	3,290	7,057	5,984	2,771	3,060	3,220

Tableau 1. Certaines caractéristiques des secteurs de recensement, recensement de 2001 – Données intégrales et données-échantillon (20 %)

Toronto 0612.01	Toronto 0612.02	Toronto 0612.03	Toronto 0612.05	Toronto 0612.07	Toronto 0612.08	Caractéristiques	N°
						CARACTÉRISTIQUES DU REVENU DE 2000	
						Population de 15 ans et plus ayant un revenu d'emploi en 2000 selon le sexe et le travail – fin	
XXX	3,440	1,660	1,655	1,940	1,240	Femmes ayant un revenu d'emploi (48)	526
	36,460	32,464	34,593	41,352	31,394	Revenu moyen d'emploi $	527
	1,021	1,685	3,555	1,739	1,493	Erreur type de revenu moyen d'emploi $	528
	1,940	805	740	1,130	650	Ayant travaillé toute l'année à plein temps (49)	529
	44,710	47,206	51,153	53,040	44,203	Revenu moyen d'emploi $	530
	1,112	2,619	7,521	2,329	1,824	Erreur type de revenu moyen d'emploi $	531
	1,430	805	885	770	580	Ayant travaillé une partie de l'année ou à temps partiel (50)	532
	26,529	18,080	21,714	25,844	17,530	Revenu moyen d'emploi $	533
	1,746	1,385	1,854	2,175	1,823	Erreur type de revenu moyen d'emploi $	534
						Familles de recensement selon la structure et les tranches de revenu de la famille en 2000	
	3,540	1,605	1,615	1,805	1,215	Total - Toutes les familles de recensement	535
	105	45	30	45	15	Moins de 10 000 $	536
	45	75	50	20	25	10 000 $ - 19 999 $	537
	80	130	85	30	60	20 000 $ - 29 999 $	538
	130	30	100	90	60	30 000 $ - 39 999 $	539
	165	80	95	55	110	40 000 $ - 49 999 $	540
	240	35	65	130	50	50 000 $ - 59 999 $	541
	370	100	85	135	95	60 000 $ - 69 999 $	542
	260	110	70	100	110	70 000 $ - 79 999 $	543
	375	95	95	130	110	80 000 $ - 89 999 $	544
	305	60	55	140	115	90 000 $ - 99 999 $	545
	1,480	850	885	945	460	100 000 $ et plus	546
	102,109	120,737	133,549	117,926	96,533	Revenu moyen des familles $	547
	89,982	103,642	110,178	103,251	88,142	Revenu médian des familles $	548
	2,306	5,718	7,508	4,143	3,694	Erreur type de revenu moyen des familles $	549
	3,230	1,405	1,415	1,595	1,065	Total - Toutes les familles de recensement comptant un couple (51)	550
	85	40	10	30	10	Moins de 10 000 $	551
	20	20	20	10	15	10 000 $ - 19 999 $	552
	60	75	35	20	40	20 000 $ - 29 999 $	553
	85	20	65	45	45	30 000 $ - 39 999 $	554
	125	60	80	45	55	40 000 $ - 49 999 $	555
	185	30	40	90	40	50 000 $ - 59 999 $	556
	295	90	80	110	85	60 000 $ - 69 999 $	557
	265	100	75	80	110	70 000 $ - 79 999 $	558
	365	95	85	135	95	80 000 $ - 89 999 $	559
	290	55	50	140	115	90 000 $ - 99 999 $	560
	1,445	820	875	890	455	100 000 $ et plus	561
	106,178	131,611	147,751	124,780	103,447	Revenu moyen des familles $	562
	93,974	113,452	119,097	107,805	94,241	Revenu médian des familles $	563
	2,427	6,234	8,265	4,446	3,971	Erreur type de revenu moyen des familles $	564
						Fréquence des unités à faible revenu en 2000	
	3,475	1,565	1,610	1,760	1,130	Total - Familles économiques	565
	160	215	175	55	55	Faible revenu	566
	4.6	13.6	10.8	3.3	4.9	Fréquence des unités à faible revenu en 2000 % (52)	567
	500	230	335	435	175	Total - Personnes hors famille économique de 15 ans et plus	568
	80	65	160	110	15	Faible revenu	569
	15.7	27.7	48.1	25.0	7.2	Fréquence des unités à faible revenu en 2000 % (52)	570
	11,750	6,035	5,845	6,370	4,380	Total - Population dans les ménages privés	571
	670	750	725	360	225	Faible revenu	572
	5.7	12.5	12.4	5.6	5.2	Fréquence des unités à faible revenu en 2000 % (52)	573
						Ménages privés selon les tranches de revenu du ménage en 2000	
	3,865	1,725	1,865	2,090	1,250	Total - Tous les ménages privés	574
	100	45	85	40	20	Moins de 10 000 $	575
	60	85	100	65	15	10 000 $ - 19 999 $	576
	100	120	110	50	45	20 000 $ - 29 999 $	577
	140	50	110	115	55	30 000 $ - 39 999 $	578
	185	80	110	80	65	40 000 $ - 49 999 $	579
	250	50	65	135	40	50 000 $ - 59 999 $	580
	400	115	95	140	115	60 000 $ - 69 999 $	581
	270	105	75	140	135	70 000 $ - 79 999 $	582
	410	90	110	155	100	80 000 $ - 89 999 $	583
	305	90	65	150	120	90 000 $ - 99 999 $	584
	1,645	895	935	1,020	540	100 000 $ et plus	585
	102,225	120,833	123,061	112,591	104,078	Revenu moyen des ménages $	586
	90,024	102,708	99,898	97,876	92,433	Revenu médian des ménages $	587
	2,196	5,464	6,829	3,814	3,733	Erreur type de revenu moyen des ménages $	588

Table 1. Selected Characteristics for Census Tracts, 2001 Census – 100% Data and 20% Sample Data

No.	Characteristics	Toronto 0612.09	Toronto 0612.10 ◆	Toronto 0612.11 A	Toronto 0612.12 A	Toronto 0612.13 A	Toronto 0612.14 A
	POPULATION CHARACTERISTICS						
1	**Population, 1996 (1)**	**4,217**	**71**	**3,031**	**5,504**	**3,813**	**4,700**
2	**Population, 2001 (2)**	**5,471**	**58**	**4,962**	**6,956**	**3,713**	**4,643**
3	Population percentage change, 1996-2001	29.7	-18.3	63.7	26.4	-2.6	-1.2
4	Land area in square kilometres, 2001	4.20	4.17	2.43	1.85	1.20	2.13
5	**Total population - 100% Data (3)**	**5,475**	**55**	**4,965**	**6,960**	**3,715**	**4,645**
	by sex and age groups						
6	Male	2,630	30	2,460	3,420	1,870	2,310
7	0-4 years	195	-	225	345	70	130
8	5-9 years	280	-	275	395	165	215
9	10-14 years	300	-	255	335	220	255
10	15-19 years	225	-	160	220	205	220
11	20-24 years	120	-	105	160	135	150
12	25-29 years	80	5	100	110	60	120
13	30-34 years	100	-	230	270	35	130
14	35-39 years	225	-	290	445	105	180
15	40-44 years	310	-	280	370	175	225
16	45-49 years	310	-	190	305	200	230
17	50-54 years	200	5	150	200	175	195
18	55-59 years	105	-	85	105	105	105
19	60-64 years	80	-	40	75	75	50
20	65-69 years	50	-	30	40	50	40
21	70-74 years	30	-	10	30	40	30
22	75-79 years	15	5	10	20	25	15
23	80-84 years	5	-	5	-	15	10
24	85 years and over	5	-	-	-	5	5
25	Female	2,840	25	2,495	3,535	1,845	2,335
26	0-4 years	190	-	230	350	70	120
27	5-9 years	280	-	260	375	145	185
28	10-14 years	310	-	235	295	205	220
29	15-19 years	245	5	150	245	200	235
30	20-24 years	145	-	125	175	105	135
31	25-29 years	75	5	130	145	40	125
32	30-34 years	145	-	235	340	45	130
33	35-39 years	300	-	335	480	135	230
34	40-44 years	365	5	285	380	225	275
35	45-49 years	290	5	190	290	210	275
36	50-54 years	200	-	140	170	155	135
37	55-59 years	105	5	70	110	85	100
38	60-64 years	55	-	35	75	50	60
39	65-69 years	60	5	30	40	55	35
40	70-74 years	30	-	15	25	50	40
41	75-79 years	25	5	15	20	30	25
42	80-84 years	20	-	10	10	25	10
43	85 years and over	10	-	5	10	15	5
44	**Total population 15 years and over**	**3,930**	**50**	**3,475**	**4,860**	**2,830**	**3,525**
	by legal marital status						
45	Never married (single)	950	20	795	1,130	765	1,075
46	Legally married (and not separated)	2,665	30	2,405	3,375	1,890	2,075
47	Separated, but still legally married	75	-	80	90	40	115
48	Divorced	140	-	120	170	50	180
49	Widowed	100	-	75	95	90	85
	by common-law status						
50	Not in a common-law relationship	3,825	55	3,345	4,715	2,795	3,385
51	In a common-law relationship	105	-	130	150	30	135
52	**Total population - 20% Sample Data (4)**	**5,470**	**95**	**4,960**	**6,955**	**3,715**	**4,640**
	by mother tongue						
53	Single responses	5,430	95	4,940	6,845	3,620	4,605
54	English	4,165	85	3,970	5,350	2,800	3,615
55	French	60	-	50	140	85	135
56	Non-official languages (5)	1,200	10	925	1,355	735	860
57	Italian	100	10	120	195	155	145
58	Chinese, n.o.s.	130	-	190	10	55	25
59	Cantonese	95	-	20	80	10	25
60	Portuguese	55	-	55	195	65	55
61	Punjabi	30	-	20	60	20	45
62	Other languages (6)	780	-	530	815	435	565
63	Multiple responses	45	-	20	110	90	40
64	English and French	10	-	-	10	10	15
65	English and non-official language	35	-	10	90	60	25
66	French and non-official language	10	-	10	10	20	-
67	English, French and non-official language	-	-	-	-	-	-

See reference material at the end of the publication. – Voir les documents de référence à la fin de la publication.

Tableau 1. Certaines caractéristiques des secteurs de recensement, recensement de 2001 – Données intégrales et données-échantillon (20 %)

Toronto 0613.01	Toronto 0613.03 A	Toronto 0613.04 A	Toronto 0614.01 A	Toronto 0614.02 A	Toronto 0615	Caractéristiques	N°
						CARACTÉRISTIQUES DE LA POPULATION	
4,642	**4,279**	**4,778**	**3,693**	**4,399**	**554**	**Population, 1996 (1)**	1
4,537	**4,188**	**4,589**	**3,499**	**4,226**	**555**	**Population, 2001 (2)**	2
-2.3	-2.1	-4.0	-5.3	-3.9	0.2	Variation en pourcentage de la population, 1996-2001	3
1.88	1.75	1.34	1.61	3.11	39.86	Superficie des terres en kilomètres carrés, 2001	4
4,540	**4,190**	**4,590**	**3,500**	**4,225**	**555**	**Population totale – Données intégrales (3)**	5
						selon le sexe et les groupes d'âge	
2,275	2,115	2,220	1,705	2,105	300	Sexe masculin	6
145	105	90	95	115	20	0-4 ans	7
170	125	110	135	125	20	5-9 ans	8
175	145	125	150	160	30	10-14 ans	9
145	165	125	165	130	20	15-19 ans	10
165	190	235	115	175	10	20-24 ans	11
135	160	210	55	140	15	25-29 ans	12
145	135	175	80	145	25	30-34 ans	13
190	175	195	135	140	25	35-39 ans	14
195	195	165	180	180	35	40-44 ans	15
180	145	140	150	155	25	45-49 ans	16
165	150	125	160	170	15	50-54 ans	17
155	110	145	110	140	15	55-59 ans	18
125	85	85	70	125	15	60-64 ans	19
75	85	95	55	80	10	65-69 ans	20
60	75	65	40	75	10	70-74 ans	21
35	40	70	20	25	5	75-79 ans	22
15	20	45	5	10	5	80-84 ans	23
5	20	15	-	10	-	85 ans et plus	24
2,265	2,070	2,370	1,795	2,120	255	Sexe féminin	25
140	100	80	105	100	15	0-4 ans	26
140	115	75	135	115	15	5-9 ans	27
145	125	120	150	140	25	10-14 ans	28
150	110	130	155	175	20	15-19 ans	29
145	140	205	110	125	10	20-24 ans	30
135	150	205	70	120	15	25-29 ans	31
160	145	200	90	130	15	30-34 ans	32
220	180	155	160	170	25	35-39 ans	33
205	195	170	190	175	20	40-44 ans	34
190	175	175	185	190	25	45-49 ans	35
180	140	160	155	205	10	50-54 ans	36
160	125	140	100	165	15	55-59 ans	37
90	95	115	70	115	15	60-64 ans	38
85	95	105	45	80	10	65-69 ans	39
50	70	115	25	60	10	70-74 ans	40
40	60	110	30	35	5	75-79 ans	41
20	35	80	15	15	5	80-84 ans	42
15	20	30	10	5	-	85 ans et plus	43
3,620	**3,475**	**4,000**	**2,730**	**3,465**	**435**	**Population totale de 15 ans et plus**	44
						selon l'état matrimonial légal	
1,005	1,105	1,380	775	1,025	135	Célibataire (jamais marié(e))	45
2,200	1,815	1,890	1,665	2,035	230	Légalement marié(e) (et non séparé(e))	46
110	135	140	80	100	20	Séparé(e), mais toujours légalement marié(e)	47
195	250	300	145	195	35	Divorcé(e)	48
115	175	290	70	110	15	Veuf ou veuve	49
						selon l'union libre	
3,455	3,260	3,715	2,625	3,325	400	Ne vivant pas en union libre	50
160	220	280	105	140	30	Vivant en union libre	51
4,540	**4,190**	**4,590**	**3,480**	**4,185**	**555**	**Population totale – Données-échantillon (20 %) (4)**	52
						selon la langue maternelle	
4,460	4,170	4,450	3,455	4,180	555	Réponses uniques	53
3,705	3,295	3,340	2,775	3,360	450	Anglais	54
75	35	105	55	55	-	Français	55
680	840	1,010	625	765	105	Langues non officielles (5)	56
105	70	85	20	30	-	Italien	57
15	15	70	35	-	-	Chinois, n.d.a.	58
40	-	-	-	-	-	Cantonais	59
65	90	80	80	100	15	Portugais	60
20	30	35	50	-	15	Pendjabi	61
435	620	740	440	625	80	Autres langues (6)	62
80	20	135	25	10	-	Réponses multiples	63
45	10	20	20	-	-	Anglais et français	64
25	15	70	10	10	-	Anglais et langue non officielle	65
10	-	30	-	-	-	Français et langue non officielle	66
-	-	10	-	-	-	Anglais, français et langue non officielle	67

See reference material at the end of the publication. – Voir les documents de référence à la fin de la publication.

Table 1. Selected Characteristics for Census Tracts, 2001 Census – 100% Data and 20% Sample Data

No.	Characteristics	Toronto 0612.09	Toronto 0612.10 ◆	Toronto 0612.11 A	Toronto 0612.12 A	Toronto 0612.13 A	Toronto 0612.14 A
	POPULATION CHARACTERISTICS						
	by home language						
68	Single responses	4,735	90	4,400	5,975	3,230	3,905
69	English	4,590	90	4,130	5,745	3,090	3,635
70	French	25	-	-	20	-	35
71	Non-official languages (5)	120	-	265	210	140	235
72	Cantonese	25	-	-	25	-	25
73	Chinese, n.o.s.	-	-	110	-	-	-
74	Italian	-	-	35	25	20	10
75	Punjabi	45	-	10	25	-	45
76	Portuguese	-	-	-	35	10	15
77	Other languages (6)	50	-	115	100	105	150
78	Multiple responses	735	10	560	980	480	735
79	English and French	35	-	20	150	65	155
80	English and non-official language	695	10	485	805	415	545
81	French and non-official language	-	-	20	-	-	-
82	English, French and non-official language	10	-	35	25	-	35
	by knowledge of official languages						
83	English only	4,850	95	4,440	6,160	3,155	3,785
84	French only	-	-	-	-	-	-
85	English and French	570	-	475	775	510	820
86	Neither English nor French	45	-	50	20	45	35
	by knowledge of non-official languages (5) (7)						
87	Italian	145	10	160	275	205	235
88	Cantonese	100	-	25	95	10	20
89	Chinese, n.o.s.	205	-	180	10	55	25
90	Spanish	110	-	80	175	75	75
91	Portuguese	75	-	50	235	75	70
92	Punjabi	90	-	30	80	10	105
93	Tagalog (Pilipino)	25	-	45	20	10	25
	by first official language spoken						
94	English	5,330	90	4,850	6,790	3,545	4,440
95	French	60	-	60	135	105	125
96	English and French	30	-	-	15	20	50
97	Neither English nor French	45	-	55	15	45	25
98	Official language minority - (number) (8)	75	-	60	145	115	155
99	Official language minority - (percentage) (8)	1.4	-	1.2	2.1	3.1	3.3
	by ethnic origin (9)						
100	Canadian	1,275	70	1,310	1,775	875	1,390
101	English	1,295	20	1,610	2,145	1,245	1,235
102	Scottish	920	10	1,050	1,355	700	835
103	Irish	1,145	-	870	1,130	865	800
104	Chinese	430	-	245	280	100	70
105	Italian	590	10	510	895	460	470
106	East Indian	285	-	180	215	100	385
107	French	355	-	370	580	340	425
108	German	580	-	530	650	315	405
109	Portuguese	205	-	105	345	105	120
110	Polish	300	-	250	425	210	260
111	Jewish	40	-	40	110	10	20
112	Jamaican	35	-	60	70	20	45
113	Filipino	50	-	130	55	10	40
114	Ukrainian	235	-	250	460	175	255
	by Aboriginal identity						
115	Total Aboriginal identity population (10)	-	-	10	50	10	10
116	Total non-Aboriginal population	5,470	95	4,955	6,905	3,710	4,640
	by Aboriginal origin						
117	Total Aboriginal origins population (11)	10	-	40	90	-	40
118	Total non-Aboriginal population	5,465	90	4,925	6,865	3,710	4,600
	by Registered Indian status						
119	Registered Indian (12)	-	-	-	25	-	10
120	Not a Registered Indian	5,470	95	4,960	6,930	3,710	4,635

Tableau 1. Certaines caractéristiques des secteurs de recensement, recensement de 2001 – Données intégrales et données-échantillon (20 %)

Toronto 0613.01	Toronto 0613.03 A	Toronto 0613.04 A	Toronto 0614.01 A	Toronto 0614.02 A	Toronto 0615	Caractéristiques	N°
						CARACTÉRISTIQUES DE LA POPULATION	
						selon la langue parlée à la maison	
4,000	3,675	3,945	3,110	3,775	465	Réponses uniques	68
3,855	3,530	3,595	2,990	3,550	435	Anglais	69
15	-	-	-	10	-	Français	70
125	145	350	120	220	30	Langues non officielles (5)	71
30	-	-	-	-	-	Cantonais	72
15	-	40	15	-	-	Chinois, n.d.a.	73
10	10	15	-	-	-	Italien	74
-	-	20	35	-	-	Pendjabi	75
10	20	30	15	-	10	Portugaïs	76
65	120	235	60	215	15	Autres langues (6)	77
535	515	645	370	415	90	Réponses multiples	78
85	25	95	60	45	-	Anglais et français	79
445	485	490	290	365	90	Anglais et langue non officielle	80
-	-	20	-	-	-	Français et langue non officielle	81
-	-	45	25	-	-	Anglais, français et langue non officielle	82
						selon la connaissance des langues officielles	
3,925	3,890	3,735	3,045	3,745	510	Anglais seulement	83
-	-	-	-	-	-	Français seulement	84
600	270	760	405	415	40	Anglais et français	85
20	30	95	30	25	10	Ni l'anglais ni le français	86
						selon la connaissance des langues non officielles (5) (7)	
135	90	145	25	35	-	Italien	87
40	-	-	-	-	-	Cantonais	88
15	20	55	25	-	-	Chinois, n.d.a.	89
95	60	95	90	55	-	Espagnol	90
90	100	90	90	105	45	Portugais	91
20	30	50	60	-	15	Pendjabi	92
-	15	-	10	-	-	Tagalog (pilipino)	93
						selon la première langue officielle parlée	
4,395	4,115	4,305	3,360	4,055	555	Anglais	94
70	35	135	50	70	-	Français	95
50	15	55	40	35	-	Anglais et français	96
20	25	90	35	25	-	Ni l'anglais ni le français	97
90	45	160	70	85	-	Minorité de langue officielle - (nombre) (8)	98
2.0	1.1	3.5	2.0	2.0	-	Minorité de langue officielle - (pourcentage) (8)	99
						selon l'origine ethnique (9)	
1,510	1,240	1,090	1,150	1,140	220	Canadien	100
1,510	1,150	1,310	1,155	1,375	130	Anglais	101
885	890	995	715	780	85	Écossais	102
705	905	830	635	770	40	Irlandais	103
115	25	110	55	10	-	Chinois	104
325	250	285	140	235	10	Italien	105
15	95	185	135	100	35	Indien de l'Inde	106
330	320	380	400	345	10	Français	107
350	290	315	325	265	50	Allemand	108
160	140	125	170	160	50	Portugais	109
120	215	165	260	415	20	Polonais	110
65	35	60	40	50	-	Juif	111
55	40	60	65	10	-	Jamaïquain	112
-	30	15	20	20	-	Philippin	113
185	85	120	155	135	-	Ukrainien	114
						selon l'identité autochtone	
-	60	15	15	-	-	Total de la population ayant une identité autochtone (10)	115
4,540	4,130	4,575	3,465	4,185	555	Total de la population non autochtone	116
						selon l'origine autochtone	
10	115	80	25	20	-	Total de la population ayant une origine autochtone (11)	117
4,525	4,075	4,510	3,455	4,170	550	Total de la population non autochtone	118
						selon le statut d'Indien inscrit	
-	30	-	15	-	-	Oui, Indien inscrit (12)	119
4,535	4,155	4,585	3,460	4,185	555	Non, pas un Indien inscrit	120

Table 1. Selected Characteristics for Census Tracts, 2001 Census – 100% Data and 20% Sample Data

No.	Characteristics	Toronto 0612.09	Toronto 0612.10 ◆	Toronto 0612.11 A	Toronto 0612.12 A	Toronto 0612.13 A	Toronto 0612.14 A
	POPULATION CHARACTERISTICS						
	by visible minority groups						
121	Total visible minority population	1,075	10	820	905	305	645
122	Chinese	415	-	235	240	105	50
123	South Asian	305	-	190	325	100	385
124	Black	55	-	155	145	25	60
125	Filipino	55	-	130	35	10	40
126	Latin American	45	-	30	25	15	10
127	Southeast Asian	-	-	-	20	-	-
128	Arab	-	-	10	-	45	-
129	West Asian	25	-	20	-	-	45
130	Korean	60	-	35	35	-	-
131	Japanese	30	-	-	-	-	15
132	Visible minority, n.i.e. (13)	75	-	-	45	10	-
133	Multiple visible minorities (14)	10	-	10	35	-	30
	by citizenship						
134	Canadian citizenship (15)	5,250	95	4,715	6,590	3,515	4,215
135	Citizenship other than Canadian	220	-	245	370	200	430
	by place of birth of respondent						
136	Non-immigrant population	4,070	70	3,795	5,210	2,775	3,305
137	Born in province of residence	3,505	75	3,120	4,340	2,025	2,455
138	Immigrant population (16)	1,375	20	1,150	1,650	870	1,275
139	United States	30	-	80	105	45	85
140	Central and South America	45	-	50	70	15	65
141	Caribbean and Bermuda	110	-	95	125	35	65
142	United Kingdom	265	10	245	325	140	205
143	Other Europe (17)	395	10	300	580	380	450
144	Africa	65	-	55	115	70	75
145	Asia and the Middle East	440	-	325	340	185	325
146	Oceania and other (18)	25	-	-	10	10	-
147	Non-permanent residents (19)	25	-	20	95	70	65
148	**Total immigrant population**	**1,375**	**25**	**1,145**	**1,655**	**870**	**1,270**
	by period of immigration						
149	Before 1961	190	10	85	240	190	140
150	1961-1970	265	10	260	295	185	205
151	1971-1980	430	-	250	360	165	245
152	1981-1990	315	-	240	325	215	265
153	1991-2001 (20)	180	-	315	440	110	410
154	1991-1995	90	-	200	170	15	200
155	1996-2001 (20)	85	-	115	270	100	215
	by age at immigration						
156	0-4 years	205	15	170	285	125	145
157	5-19 years	390	-	260	435	275	435
158	20 years and over	775	10	710	930	470	690
159	**Total population**	**5,470**	**95**	**4,965**	**6,955**	**3,715**	**4,645**
	by religion						
160	Catholic (21)	2,425	20	2,295	3,085	1,635	1,720
161	Protestant	1,765	80	1,750	2,025	1,445	1,785
162	Christian Orthodox	105	-	60	100	85	120
163	Christian, n.i.e. (22)	165	-	55	210	55	65
164	Muslim	100	-	50	195	-	100
165	Jewish	35	-	10	80	25	30
166	Buddhist	65	-	30	10	-	15
167	Hindu	85	-	65	80	65	125
168	Sikh	85	-	35	70	-	95
169	Eastern religions (23)	-	-	35	-	-	25
170	Other religions (24)	20	-	-	-	-	-
171	No religious affiliation (25)	605	-	580	1,095	400	575
172	**Total population 15 years and over**	**3,925**	**75**	**3,475**	**4,855**	**2,880**	**3,455**
	by generation status						
173	1st generation (26)	1,345	25	1,140	1,605	855	1,200
174	2nd generation (27)	1,245	35	995	1,315	880	725
175	3rd generation and over (28)	1,340	10	1,340	1,935	1,140	1,525
176	**Total population 1 year and over (29)**	**5,425**	**90**	**4,900**	**6,830**	**3,685**	**4,625**
	by place of residence 1 year ago (mobility)						
177	Non-movers	5,070	95	3,985	6,310	3,475	4,100
178	Movers	365	-	910	520	210	525
179	Non-migrants	140	-	440	155	60	150
180	Migrants	220	-	470	360	155	370
181	Internal migrants	200	-	425	305	125	255
182	Intraprovincial migrants	165	-	355	220	95	210
183	Interprovincial migrants	30	-	75	80	30	40
184	External migrants	20	-	40	60	35	120

Tableau 1. Certaines caractéristiques des secteurs de recensement, recensement de 2001 – Données intégrales et données-échantillon (20 %)

Toronto 0613.01	Toronto 0613.03 A	Toronto 0613.04 A	Toronto 0614.01 A	Toronto 0614.02 A	Toronto 0615	Caractéristiques	N°
						CARACTÉRISTIQUES DE LA POPULATION	
						selon les groupes de minorités visibles	
440	375	805	405	300	60	Total de la population des minorités visibles	121
80	10	110	60	-	-	Chinois	122
30	175	275	130	45	35	Sud-Asiatique	123
85	60	120	170	65	-	Noir	124
-	20	15	10	10	-	Philippin	125
90	10	45	25	15	10	Latino-Américain	126
-	10	-	-	40	-	Asiatique du Sud-Est	127
25	45	35	-	-	-	Arabe	128
10	20	50	-	15	-	Asiatique occidental	129
20	-	75	-	20	10	Coréen	130
65	-	45	-	20	-	Japonais	131
10	10	10	10	10	-	Minorité visible, n.i.a. (13)	132
20	15	10	-	60	-	Minorités visibles multiples (14)	133
						selon la citoyenneté	
4,230	3,930	4,010	3,305	4,020	530	Citoyenneté canadienne (15)	134
305	255	580	175	175	30	Citoyenneté autre que canadienne	135
						selon le lieu de naissance du répondant	
3,325	3,120	3,005	2,650	3,070	410	Population non immigrante	136
2,880	2,560	2,335	2,260	2,505	390	Née dans la province de résidence	137
1,195	1,050	1,535	815	1,115	130	Population immigrante (16)	138
15	40	40	40	40	10	États-Unis	139
55	20	70	55	30	-	Amérique centrale et du Sud	140
135	45	60	85	75	-	Caraïbes et Bermudes	141
355	270	275	150	270	20	Royaume-Uni	142
435	450	535	345	455	75	Autre Europe (17)	143
35	55	120	40	85	-	Afrique	144
165	155	425	60	140	35	Asie et Moyen-Orient	145
-	10	10	35	-	-	Océanie et autre (18)	146
20	20	45	20	-	10	Résidents non permanents (19)	147
1,195	**1,050**	**1,535**	**810**	**1,110**	**135**	**Population immigrante totale**	148
						selon la période d'immigration	
205	320	360	175	160	25	Avant 1961	149
335	165	320	200	180	50	1961-1970	150
170	130	175	90	290	30	1971-1980	151
265	190	205	130	205	15	1981-1990	152
225	240	475	210	265	-	1991-2001 (20)	153
100	95	90	140	140	-	1991-1995	154
125	145	385	70	125	-	1996-2001 (20)	155
						selon l'âge à l'immigration	
115	100	100	115	135	15	0-4 ans	156
380	315	455	180	330	40	5-19 ans	157
695	645	975	515	645	80	20 ans et plus	158
4,535	**4,185**	**4,590**	**3,480**	**4,190**	**555**	**Population totale**	159
						selon la religion	
1,455	1,530	1,625	1,350	1,535	175	Catholique (21)	160
1,615	1,545	1,415	1,225	1,655	265	Protestante	161
90	30	160	65	125	-	Orthodoxe chrétienne	162
200	100	145	130	65	40	Chrétiennes, n.i.a. (22)	163
40	95	180	10	-	-	Musulmane	164
50	25	70	20	45	-	Juive	165
15	25	25	-	10	10	Bouddhiste	166
-	35	85	90	30	-	Hindoue	167
20	35	35	35	-	40	Sikh	168
15	15	15	-	20	-	Religions orientales (23)	169
-	-	15	-	-	-	Autres religions (24)	170
1,045	745	820	560	705	30	Aucune appartenance religieuse (25)	171
3,610	**3,480**	**4,000**	**2,680**	**3,450**	**435**	**Population totale de 15 ans et plus**	172
						selon le statut des générations	
1,150	1,030	1,465	765	1,055	140	1re génération (26)	173
775	920	880	625	805	70	2e génération (27)	174
1,685	1,535	1,650	1,295	1,585	230	3e génération et plus (28)	175
4,465	**4,165**	**4,560**	**3,455**	**4,140**	**555**	**Population totale de 1 an et plus (29)**	176
						selon le lieu de résidence 1 an auparavant (mobilité)	
4,075	3,580	3,410	3,200	3,845	490	Personnes n'ayant pas déménagé	177
390	580	1,150	255	295	60	Personnes ayant déménagé	178
110	215	395	75	135	10	Non-migrants	179
280	365	755	175	160	55	Migrants	180
235	295	610	135	135	50	Migrants internes	181
210	285	525	125	120	55	Migrants infraprovinciaux	182
25	15	80	15	15	-	Migrants interprovinciaux	183
40	75	150	40	25	-	Migrants externes	184

Table 1. Selected Characteristics for Census Tracts, 2001 Census – 100% Data and 20% Sample Data

No.	Characteristics	Toronto 0612.09	Toronto 0612.10 ◆	Toronto 0612.11 A	Toronto 0612.12 A	Toronto 0612.13 A	Toronto 0612.14 A
	POPULATION CHARACTERISTICS						
185	**Total population 5 years and over (30)**	**5,095**	**95**	**4,490**	**6,260**	**3,595**	**4,370**
	by place of residence 5 years ago (mobility)						
186	Non-movers	2,750	95	1,995	3,580	2,480	2,515
187	Movers	2,350	-	2,500	2,675	1,115	1,850
188	Non-migrants	900	-	900	855	420	645
189	Migrants	1,450	-	1,600	1,820	695	1,210
190	Internal migrants	1,350	-	1,485	1,540	535	910
191	Intraprovincial migrants	1,090	-	1,205	1,370	320	545
192	Interprovincial migrants	255	-	280	170	210	365
193	External migrants	105	-	115	280	160	295
194	**Total population 15 to 24 years**	**735**	**40**	**535**	**800**	**710**	**660**
	by school attendance						
195	Not attending school	160	-	115	270	170	150
196	Attending school full time	555	40	395	500	495	470
197	Attending school part time	15	-	30	30	40	35
198	**Total population 15 years and over**	**3,920**	**75**	**3,475**	**4,860**	**2,880**	**3,455**
	by highest level of schooling						
199	Less than grade 9 (31)	80	-	50	140	160	115
200	Grades 9-13 without high school graduation certificate	530	15	390	630	460	510
201	Grades 9-13 with high school graduation certificate	420	20	395	595	305	420
202	Some postsecondary without degree, certificate or diploma (32)	430	10	445	640	355	400
203	Trades certificate or diploma (33)	220	-	225	360	145	235
204	College certificate or diploma (34)	730	25	755	980	355	690
205	University certificate below bachelor's degree	115	-	110	110	50	110
206	University with bachelor's degree or higher	1,405	-	1,095	1,400	1,045	970
	by combinations of unpaid work						
207	Males 15 years and over	1,860	20	1,695	2,355	1,425	1,675
208	Reported unpaid work (35)	1,790	25	1,550	2,170	1,305	1,510
209	Housework and child care and care or assistance to seniors	250	-	155	180	115	150
210	Housework and child care only	670	10	725	1,025	465	560
211	Housework and care or assistance to seniors only	120	-	55	115	35	150
212	Child care and care or assistance to seniors only	10	-	10	10	-	-
213	Housework only	705	10	565	825	670	615
214	Child care only	35	-	40	15	10	25
215	Care or assistance to seniors only	10	-	-	10	10	10
216	Females 15 years and over	2,060	50	1,785	2,505	1,450	1,785
217	Reported unpaid work (35)	1,960	50	1,720	2,340	1,280	1,700
218	Housework and child care and care or assistance to seniors	385	10	255	285	205	215
219	Housework and child care only	815	-	820	1,140	460	645
220	Housework and care or assistance to seniors only	115	15	55	160	60	185
221	Child care and care or assistance to seniors only	-	-	-	-	-	10
222	Housework only	635	25	585	720	540	630
223	Child care only	15	-	-	30	20	15
224	Care or assistance to seniors only	-	-	-	-	10	-
	by labour force activity						
225	Males 15 years and over	1,860	20	1,695	2,355	1,425	1,670
226	In the labour force	1,625	20	1,485	2,090	1,125	1,405
227	Employed	1,560	25	1,460	2,030	1,090	1,335
228	Unemployed	65	-	25	65	40	70
229	Not in the labour force	235	-	205	265	300	265
230	Participation rate	87.4	100.0	87.6	88.7	78.9	84.1
231	Employment rate	83.9	100.0	86.1	86.2	76.5	79.9
232	Unemployment rate	4.0	-	1.7	3.1	3.6	5.0
233	Females 15 years and over	2,065	45	1,785	2,500	1,450	1,785
234	In the labour force	1,455	20	1,295	1,850	850	1,300
235	Employed	1,415	10	1,265	1,730	820	1,270
236	Unemployed	40	10	30	125	25	30
237	Not in the labour force	610	25	485	650	605	485
238	Participation rate	70.5	44.4	72.5	74.0	58.6	72.8
239	Employment rate	68.5	22.2	70.9	69.2	56.6	71.1
240	Unemployment rate	2.7	50.0	2.3	6.8	2.9	2.3

Tableau 1. Certaines caractéristiques des secteurs de recensement, recensement de 2001 – Données intégrales et données-échantillon (20 %)

Toronto 0613.01	Toronto 0613.03 A	Toronto 0613.04 A	Toronto 0614.01 A	Toronto 0614.02 A	Toronto 0615	Caractéristiques	N°
						CARACTÉRISTIQUES DE LA POPULATION	
4,245	**3,985**	**4,420**	**3,295**	**3,980**	**530**	**Population totale de 5 ans et plus (30)**	185
						selon le lieu de résidence 5 ans auparavant (mobilité)	
2,960	2,325	2,125	2,260	2,640	290	Personnes n'ayant pas déménagé	186
1,280	1,660	2,300	1,035	1,345	240	Personnes ayant déménagé	187
510	630	825	375	525	115	Non-migrants	188
775	1,025	1,470	660	820	125	Migrants	189
660	845	1,055	610	705	110	Migrants internes	190
560	790	890	580	640	110	Migrants infraprovinciaux	191
100	50	160	30	65	-	Migrants interprovinciaux	192
120	185	420	50	115	15	Migrants externes	193
600	**610**	**695**	**535**	**580**	**70**	**Population totale de 15 à 24 ans**	194
						selon la fréquentation scolaire	
230	265	210	155	185	10	Ne fréquentant pas l'école	195
320	325	440	370	370	55	Fréquentant l'école à plein temps	196
55	20	45	15	20	-	Fréquentant l'école à temps partiel	197
3,610	**3,480**	**4,000**	**2,680**	**3,450**	**440**	**Population totale de 15 ans et plus**	198
						selon le plus haut niveau de scolarité atteint	
135	155	105	70	70	10	Niveau inférieur à la 9e année (31)	199
600	795	530	545	490	135	De la 9e à la 13e année sans certificat d'études secondaires	200
580	550	565	340	515	45	De la 9e à la 13e année avec certificat d'études secondaires	201
420	395	680	350	445	55	Études postsecondaires partielles sans grade, certificat ou diplôme (32)	202
290	295	250	155	220	35	Certificat ou diplôme d'une école de métiers (33)	203
800	560	865	510	795	55	Certificat ou diplôme collégial (34)	204
90	70	190	55	145	10	Certificat universitaire inférieur au baccalauréat	205
705	655	820	655	775	90	Études universitaires avec baccalauréat ou diplôme supérieur	206
						selon les combinaisons de travail non rémunéré	
1,765	1,735	1,885	1,300	1,710	240	Hommes de 15 ans et plus	207
1,590	1,540	1,665	1,170	1,485	225	Travail non rémunéré déclaré (35)	208
110	65	80	130	80	25	Travaux ménagers et soins aux enfants et soins ou aide aux personnes âgées	209
485	370	355	390	410	45	Travaux ménagers et soins aux enfants seulement	210
85	120	135	65	120	-	Travaux ménagers et soins ou aide aux personnes âgées seulement	211
-	-	-	-	15	-	Soins aux enfants et soins ou aide aux personnes âgées seulement	212
900	955	1,050	560	845	140	Travaux ménagers seulement	213
10	10	35	20	10	-	Soins aux enfants seulement	214
-	15	-	-	15	-	Soins ou aide aux personnes âgées seulement	215
1,850	1,740	2,110	1,380	1,745	200	Femmes de 15 ans et plus	216
1,710	1,655	1,980	1,285	1,615	185	Travail non rémunéré déclaré (35)	217
170	135	180	185	225	35	Travaux ménagers et soins aux enfants et soins ou aide aux personnes âgées	218
535	515	425	500	490	60	Travaux ménagers et soins aux enfants seulement	219
180	130	245	90	175	20	Travaux ménagers et soins ou aide aux personnes âgées seulement	220
-	-	-	-	-	-	Soins aux enfants et soins ou aide aux personnes âgées seulement	221
805	860	1,130	500	725	75	Travaux ménagers seulement	222
10	-	10	-	-	-	Soins aux enfants seulement	223
15	10	-	-	-	-	Soins ou aide aux personnes âgées seulement	224
						selon l'activité	
1,765	1,740	1,890	1,300	1,710	240	Hommes de 15 ans et plus	225
1,485	1,390	1,415	1,060	1,410	225	Population active	226
1,420	1,265	1,340	1,015	1,330	225	Personnes occupées	227
65	125	80	45	80	-	Chômeurs	228
280	345	470	235	300	15	Inactifs	229
84.1	79.9	74.9	81.5	82.5	93.8	Taux d'activité	230
80.5	72.7	70.9	78.1	77.8	93.8	Taux d'emploi	231
4.4	9.0	5.7	4.2	5.7	-	Taux de chômage	232
1,845	1,740	2,110	1,380	1,745	200	Femmes de 15 ans et plus	233
1,315	1,070	1,365	1,065	1,265	150	Population active	234
1,290	1,020	1,265	1,020	1,185	145	Personnes occupées	235
25	50	100	45	85	10	Chômeuses	236
535	675	745	320	475	45	Inactives	237
71.3	61.5	64.7	77.2	72.5	75.0	Taux d'activité	238
69.9	58.6	60.0	73.9	67.9	72.5	Taux d'emploi	239
1.9	4.7	7.3	4.2	6.7	6.7	Taux de chômage	240

Table 1. Selected Characteristics for Census Tracts, 2001 Census – 100% Data and 20% Sample Data

No.	Characteristics	Toronto 0612.09	Toronto 0612.10 ◆	Toronto 0612.11 A	Toronto 0612.12 A	Toronto 0612.13 A	Toronto 0612.14 A
	POPULATION CHARACTERISTICS						
	by labour force activity – concluded						
241	Both sexes - Participation rate	78.5	64.3	80.0	81.2	68.6	78.3
242	15-24 years	68.0	75.0	72.9	73.0	68.3	68.7
243	25 years and over	81.0	66.7	81.3	82.9	68.7	80.5
244	Both sexes - Employment rate	75.9	50.0	78.6	77.3	66.1	75.4
245	15-24 years	60.5	50.0	69.2	65.6	62.7	59.8
246	25 years and over	79.3	50.0	80.0	79.6	67.3	78.9
247	Both sexes - Unemployment rate	3.4	33.3	2.2	4.7	3.5	3.7
248	15-24 years	11.0	50.0	5.1	8.7	7.2	12.2
249	25 years and over	2.1	-	1.5	4.0	2.3	2.0
250	**Total labour force 15 years and over**	**3,085**	**45**	**2,785**	**3,945**	**1,975**	**2,705**
	by industry based on the 1997 NAICS						
251	Industry - Not applicable (36)	35	-	-	60	-	20
252	All industries (37)	3,050	50	2,780	3,885	1,975	2,680
253	11 Agriculture, forestry, fishing and hunting	-	-	-	-	-	-
254	21 Mining and oil and gas extraction	20	-	-	10	-	-
255	22 Utilities	20	-	20	25	10	15
256	23 Construction	75	10	115	165	40	85
257	31-33 Manufacturing	300	-	385	490	320	400
258	41 Wholesale trade	195	-	200	305	70	160
259	44-45 Retail trade	450	15	315	525	295	275
260	48-49 Transportation and warehousing	125	-	120	190	55	100
261	51 Information and cultural industries	130	-	120	125	55	70
262	52 Finance and insurance	275	-	325	430	260	320
263	53 Real estate and rental and leasing	60	-	65	80	75	45
264	54 Professional, scientific and technical services	510	15	385	465	210	335
265	55 Management of companies and enterprises	-	-	-	10	-	15
266	56 Administrative and support, waste management and remediation services	130	-	75	120	65	55
267	61 Educational services	215	-	130	205	170	160
268	62 Health care and social assistance	205	-	195	230	100	270
269	71 Arts, entertainment and recreation	40	-	55	60	40	30
270	72 Accommodation and food services	80	10	50	220	160	60
271	81 Other services (except public administration)	90	-	95	95	15	175
272	91 Public administration	115	-	125	145	45	115
	by class of worker						
273	Class of worker - Not applicable (36)	35	-	-	65	10	25
274	All classes of worker (37)	3,050	45	2,775	3,880	1,975	2,675
275	Paid workers	2,800	45	2,600	3,630	1,850	2,440
276	Employees	2,620	45	2,355	3,430	1,785	2,365
277	Self-employed (incorporated)	175	10	245	200	75	75
278	Self-employed (unincorporated)	250	-	170	250	125	230
279	Unpaid family workers	-	-	-	-	-	10
	by occupation based on the 2001 NOC-S						
280	Male labour force 15 years and over	1,625	20	1,485	2,090	1,130	1,405
281	Occupation - Not applicable (36)	20	-	10	25	-	10
282	All occupations (37)	1,610	20	1,480	2,070	1,130	1,395
283	A Management occupations	495	-	415	585	375	360
284	B Business, finance and administration occupations	245	10	185	245	120	230
285	C Natural and applied sciences and related occupations	310	-	185	315	160	155
286	D Health occupations	20	-	25	-	10	55
287	E Occupations in social science, education, government service and religion	60	-	60	75	55	60
288	F Occupations in art, culture, recreation and sport	35	10	35	55	20	30
289	G Sales and service occupations	235	-	260	425	240	235
290	H Trades, transport and equipment operators and related occupations	165	-	185	250	95	185
291	I Occupations unique to primary industry	10	-	15	25	-	10
292	J Occupations unique to processing, manufacturing and utilities	40	-	115	100	50	75
293	Female labour force 15 years and over	1,455	25	1,295	1,850	850	1,295
294	Occupation - Not applicable (36)	15	-	-	40	-	15
295	All occupations (37)	1,440	25	1,295	1,815	845	1,285
296	A Management occupations	250	-	180	285	95	180
297	B Business, finance and administration occupations	460	-	530	550	265	415
298	C Natural and applied sciences and related occupations	75	-	45	90	55	55
299	D Health occupations	100	-	90	145	30	105

Tableau 1. Certaines caractéristiques des secteurs de recensement, recensement de 2001 – Données intégrales et données-échantillon (20 %)

Toronto 0613.01	Toronto 0613.03 A	Toronto 0613.04 A	Toronto 0614.01 A	Toronto 0614.02 A	Toronto 0615	Caractéristiques	N°
						CARACTÉRISTIQUES DE LA POPULATION	
						selon l'activité – fin	
77.4	70.8	69.7	79.3	77.5	86.4	Les deux sexes - Taux d'activité	241
80.8	77.7	75.0	74.1	77.6	64.3	15-24 ans	242
76.9	69.3	68.3	80.2	77.4	89.2	25 ans et plus	243
75.2	65.8	65.1	75.9	72.9	85.2	Les deux sexes - Taux d'emploi	244
75.8	66.1	68.3	69.2	62.9	57.1	15-24 ans	245
75.1	65.6	64.5	78.0	74.6	89.3	25 ans et plus	246
3.0	7.3	6.3	4.2	5.8	2.7	Les deux sexes - Taux de chômage	247
6.2	15.8	9.4	8.8	18.7	-	15-24 ans	248
2.4	5.3	5.5	3.2	3.4	-	25 ans et plus	249
2,795	**2,465**	**2,780**	**2,125**	**2,675**	**375**	**Population active totale de 15 ans et plus**	250
						selon l'industrie basée sur le SCIAN de 1997	
-	45	35	25	20	10	Industrie - Sans objet (36)	251
2,795	2,420	2,745	2,100	2,655	370	Toutes les industries (37)	252
-	10	-	10	-	30	11 Agriculture, foresterie, pêche et chasse	253
-	10	10	10	10	-	21 Extraction minière et extraction de pétrole et de gaz	254
25	35	-	10	25	15	22 Services publics	255
125	165	125	80	110	50	23 Construction	256
380	400	380	245	350	15	31-33 Fabrication	257
165	110	165	105	180	10	41 Commerce de gros	258
325	255	345	245	295	35	44-45 Commerce de détail	259
105	160	80	110	150	10	48-49 Transport et entreposage	260
80	90	90	130	105	-	51 Industrie de l'information et industrie culturelle	261
190	95	250	140	185	-	52 Finance et assurances	262
60	55	50	60	55	15	53 Services immobiliers et services de location et de location à bail	263
315	235	300	245	345	35	54 Services professionnels, scientifiques et techniques	264
-	-	-	-	-	-	55 Gestion de sociétés et d'entreprises	265
125	70	95	70	115	20	56 Services administratifs, services de soutien, services de gestion des déchets et services d'assainissement	266
145	170	175	160	175	40	61 Services d'enseignement	267
240	150	180	155	195	20	62 Soins de santé et assistance sociale	268
75	30	60	20	75	10	71 Arts, spectacles et loisirs	269
135	210	210	135	85	25	72 Hébergement et services de restauration	270
170	85	135	65	120	30	81 Autres services, sauf les administrations publiques	271
130	90	85	100	90	15	91 Administrations publiques	272
						selon la catégorie de travailleurs	
-	45	35	25	20	-	Catégorie de travailleurs - Sans objet (36)	273
2,795	2,420	2,750	2,095	2,650	375	Toutes les catégories de travailleurs (37)	274
2,580	2,280	2,565	1,940	2,410	280	Travailleurs rémunérés	275
2,495	2,195	2,485	1,870	2,325	240	Employés	276
85	85	75	70	85	35	Travailleurs autonomes (entreprise constituée en société)	277
205	145	175	165	225	90	Travailleurs autonomes (entreprise non constituée en société)	278
10	-	-	-	15	-	Travailleurs familiaux non rémunérés	279
						selon la profession basée sur la CNP-S de 2001	
1,485	1,395	1,415	1,060	1,410	225	Hommes actifs de 15 ans et plus	280
-	35	15	10	10	-	Profession - Sans objet (36)	281
1,485	1,355	1,405	1,055	1,395	225	Toutes les professions (37)	282
245	165	280	225	235	30	A Gestion	283
180	180	165	145	155	-	B Affaires, finance et administration	284
170	180	225	155	160	15	C Sciences naturelles et appliquées et professions apparentées	285
25	-	20	10	15	10	D Secteur de la santé	286
60	40	75	60	30	10	E Sciences sociales, enseignement, administration publique et religion	287
30	40	60	40	35	10	F Arts, culture, sports et loisirs	288
350	320	295	195	390	30	G Ventes et services	289
315	330	175	165	260	65	H Métiers, transport et machinerie	290
20	-	-	10	10	45	I Professions propres au secteur primaire	291
95	100	105	45	105	-	J Transformation, fabrication et services d'utilité publique	292
1,315	1,070	1,365	1,065	1,270	150	Femmes actives de 15 ans et plus	293
-	-	20	15	10	10	Profession - Sans objet (36)	294
1,310	1,065	1,345	1,045	1,255	145	Toutes les professions (37)	295
130	100	210	115	115	-	A Gestion	296
495	260	380	340	435	45	B Affaires, finance et administration	297
45	25	60	40	45	-	C Sciences naturelles et appliquées et professions apparentées	298
85	70	80	95	100	10	D Secteur de la santé	299

Table 1. Selected Characteristics for Census Tracts, 2001 Census – 100% Data and 20% Sample Data

No.	Characteristics	Toronto 0612.09	Toronto 0612.10 ◆	Toronto 0612.11 A	Toronto 0612.12 A	Toronto 0612.13 A	Toronto 0612.14 A
	POPULATION CHARACTERISTICS						
	by occupation based on the 2001 NOC-S – concluded						
	E Occupations in social science, education,						
300	government service and religion	175	-	190	155	105	140
301	F Occupations in art, culture, recreation and sport	60	-	10	70	30	45
302	G Sales and service occupations	320	20	215	460	225	270
	H Trades, transport and equipment						
303	operators and related occupations	-	-	15	15	10	20
304	I Occupations unique to primary industry	-	-	-	-	-	-
	J Occupations unique to processing,						
305	manufacturing and utilities	-	-	15	45	30	50
306	**Total employed labour force 15 years and over**	**2,975**	**30**	**2,725**	**3,760**	**1,910**	**2,600**
	by place of work						
307	Males	1,565	20	1,460	2,025	1,085	1,335
308	Usual place of work	1,260	20	1,180	1,705	925	1,180
309	At home	165	-	140	150	70	70
310	Outside Canada	15	-	-	25	15	15
311	No fixed workplace address	125	-	145	155	75	75
312	Females	1,415	10	1,265	1,730	820	1,265
313	Usual place of work	1,210	10	1,075	1,435	735	1,070
314	At home	165	-	145	220	75	125
315	Outside Canada	-	-	-	10	-	10
316	No fixed workplace address	40	-	50	65	15	65
	Total employed labour force 15 years and over with usual place of work or no fixed						
317	**workplace address**	**2,635**	**35**	**2,445**	**3,355**	**1,750**	**2,385**
	by mode of transportation						
318	Males	1,385	20	1,320	1,855	1,000	1,255
319	Car, truck, van, as driver	1,145	25	1,085	1,465	695	1,005
320	Car, truck, van, as passenger	45	-	60	75	110	50
321	Public transit	180	-	130	270	155	180
322	Walked	15	-	-	15	25	10
323	Other method	-	-	40	30	15	10
324	Females	1,255	10	1,125	1,500	750	1,130
325	Car, truck, van, as driver	910	-	865	1,100	535	885
326	Car, truck, van, as passenger	120	10	80	110	145	55
327	Public transit	185	-	155	235	60	155
328	Walked	30	-	10	25	15	20
329	Other method	10	-	-	25	-	15
	Total population 15 years and over who worked						
330	**since January 1, 2000**	**3,290**	**45**	**2,950**	**4,145**	**2,220**	**2,880**
	by language used at work						
331	Single responses	3,135	45	2,770	3,925	2,115	2,725
332	English	3,125	45	2,765	3,915	2,115	2,700
333	French	-	-	-	10	-	10
334	Non-official languages (5)	10	-	-	-	-	15
335	Chinese, n.o.s.	-	-	-	-	-	-
336	Cantonese	-	-	-	-	-	-
337	Other languages (6)	-	-	10	10	-	10
338	Multiple responses	155	10	180	220	105	155
339	English and French	40	-	125	145	60	85
340	English and non-official language	115	10	55	65	45	60
341	French and non-official language	-	-	-	-	-	-
342	English, French and non-official language	10	-	-	15	-	10
	DWELLING AND HOUSEHOLD CHARACTERISTICS						
343	**Total number of occupied private dwellings**	**1,555**	**15**	**1,445**	**1,990**	**1,060**	**1,445**
	by tenure						
344	Owned	1,470	-	1,410	1,895	1,010	1,225
345	Rented	90	15	35	100	55	215
346	Band housing	-	-	-	-	-	-
	by structural type of dwelling						
347	Single-detached house	1,270	20	1,130	1,450	850	835
348	Semi-detached house	45	-	85	340	-	10
349	Row house	235	-	225	190	75	280
350	Apartment, detached duplex	-	-	-	10	-	-
351	Apartment, building that has five or more storeys	-	-	-	-	135	10
	Apartment, building that has fewer than						
352	five storeys (38)	-	-	-	-	-	310
353	Other single-attached house	-	-	-	-	-	-
354	Movable dwelling (39)	-	-	-	-	-	-

Tableau 1. Certaines caractéristiques des secteurs de recensement, recensement de 2001 – Données intégrales et données-échantillon (20 %)

Toronto 0613.01	Toronto 0613.03 A	Toronto 0613.04 A	Toronto 0614.01 A	Toronto 0614.02 A	Toronto 0615	Caractéristiques	N°
						CARACTÉRISTIQUES DE LA POPULATION	
						selon la profession basée sur la CNP-S de 2001 – fin	
140	115	160	125	165	15	E Sciences sociales, enseignement, administration publique et religion	300
15	65	55	45	65	25	F Arts, culture, sports et loisirs	301
350	335	355	255	285	35	G Ventes et services	302
10	20	10	-	-	10	H Métiers, transport et machinerie	303
-	10	-	15	-	10	I Professions propres au secteur primaire	304
45	75	35	20	55	-	J Transformation, fabrication et services d'utilité publique	305
2,715	**2,285**	**2,605**	**2,030**	**2,515**	**370**	**Population active occupée totale de 15 ans et plus**	306
						selon le lieu de travail	
1,425	1,265	1,335	1,020	1,330	225	Hommes	307
1,200	1,050	1,090	885	1,055	135	Lieu habituel de travail	308
65	65	100	50	80	30	À domicile	309
10	15	-	10	-	-	En dehors du Canada	310
150	140	140	75	190	60	Sans adresse de travail fixe	311
1,290	1,020	1,270	1,020	1,185	145	Femmes	312
1,085	930	1,135	915	960	110	Lieu habituel de travail	313
150	40	100	60	120	35	À domicile	314
-	-	10	-	10	-	En dehors du Canada	315
60	55	25	40	95	-	Sans adresse de travail fixe	316
2,490	**2,170**	**2,395**	**1,915**	**2,300**	**300**	**Population active occupée totale de 15 ans et plus ayant un lieu habituel de travail ou sans adresse de travail fixe**	317
						selon le mode de transport	
1,350	1,190	1,235	960	1,245	195	Hommes	318
1,170	905	965	805	995	165	Automobile, camion ou fourgonnette, en tant que conducteur	319
55	80	25	40	105	20	Automobile, camion ou fourgonnette, en tant que passager	320
110	130	95	95	100	-	Transport en commun	321
10	50	105	-	30	15	À pied	322
-	20	40	15	15	-	Autre moyen	323
1,140	980	1,155	955	1,050	110	Femmes	324
805	675	785	730	795	90	Automobile, camion ou fourgonnette, en tant que conductrice	325
105	70	105	70	65	15	Automobile, camion ou fourgonnette, en tant que passagère	326
190	160	160	120	165	-	Transport en commun	327
25	65	100	25	10	10	À pied	328
25	10	-	10	20	-	Autre moyen	329
3,030	**2,655**	**2,905**	**2,250**	**2,800**	**380**	**Population totale de 15 ans et plus ayant travaillé depuis le 1er janvier 2000**	330
						selon la langue utilisée au travail	
2,875	2,530	2,720	2,125	2,695	365	Réponses uniques	331
2,860	2,515	2,715	2,125	2,685	365	Anglais	332
10	-	-	-	-	-	Français	333
-	10	-	-	10	-	Langues non officielles (5)	334
-	-	-	-	-	-	Chinois, n.d.a.	335
-	-	-	-	-	-	Cantonais	336
10	-	-	-	10	-	Autres langues (6)	337
150	130	180	125	105	15	Réponses multiples	338
75	35	75	55	45	-	Anglais et français	339
80	90	95	65	60	15	Anglais et langue non officielle	340
-	-	-	-	-	-	Français et langue non officielle	341
-	-	15	-	-	-	Anglais, français et langue non officielle	342
						CARACTÉRISTIQUES DES LOGEMENTS ET DES MÉNAGES	
1,500	**1,600**	**2,040**	**1,095**	**1,415**	**190**	**Nombre total de logements privés occupés**	343
						selon le mode d'occupation	
1,345	965	1,035	1,005	1,355	100	Possédé	344
155	635	1,000	90	60	90	Loué	345
-	-	-	-	-	-	Logement de bande	346
						selon le type de construction résidentielle	
1,000	630	405	785	1,025	145	Maison individuelle non attenante	347
245	115	60	90	35	-	Maison jumelée	348
255	395	160	195	215	-	Maison en rangée	349
-	10	125	10	-	-	Appartement, duplex non attenant	350
-	385	1,290	-	-	-	Appartement, immeuble de cinq étages ou plus	351
-	55	-	20	135	30	Appartement, immeuble de moins de cinq étages (38)	352
-	15	-	-	-	-	Autre maison individuelle attenante	353
-	-	-	-	-	-	Logement mobile (39)	354

Table 1. Selected Characteristics for Census Tracts, 2001 Census – 100% Data and 20% Sample Data

No.	Characteristics	Toronto 0612.09	Toronto 0612.10 ◆	Toronto 0612.11 A	Toronto 0612.12 A	Toronto 0612.13 A	Toronto 0612.14 A
	DWELLING AND HOUSEHOLD CHARACTERISTICS						
	by condition of dwelling						
355	Regular maintenance only	1,295	-	1,250	1,640	785	1,150
356	Minor repairs	245	15	190	325	270	280
357	Major repairs	10	-	10	30	-	15
	by period of construction						
358	Before 1946	10	-	-	-	-	10
359	1946-1960	10	-	-	-	-	-
360	1961-1970	10	-	-	15	-	15
361	1971-1980	10	10	10	35	20	35
362	1981-1990	845	-	485	845	970	1,180
363	1991-2001 (20)	680	-	955	1,105	65	205
364	Average number of rooms per dwelling	8.8	6.8	8.3	8.2	9.0	7.6
365	Average number of bedrooms per dwelling	3.8	4.0	3.7	3.6	3.7	3.3
366	Average value of dwelling $	369,428	-	308,563	275,028	333,469	282,326
367	**Total number of private households**	**1,555**	**20**	**1,445**	**1,995**	**1,060**	**1,440**
	by household size						
368	1 person	90	-	70	110	75	195
369	2 persons	290	-	310	385	220	320
370	3 persons	310	-	315	415	165	275
371	4-5 persons	785	-	685	1,000	550	555
372	6 or more persons	80	10	70	85	45	90
	by household type						
373	One-family households	1,425	15	1,310	1,790	955	1,160
374	Multiple-family households	40	-	35	55	20	40
375	Non-family households	100	-	105	150	85	250
376	Number of persons in private households	5,470	95	4,960	6,955	3,715	4,640
377	Average number of persons in private households	3.5	4.8	3.4	3.5	3.5	3.2
378	Average number of persons per room	0.4	0.7	0.4	0.4	0.4	0.4
379	Tenant households in non-farm, non-reserve private dwellings (40)	90	-	40	95	55	210
380	Average gross rent $ (40)	1,370	-	1,562	1,307	1,979	1,428
381	Tenant households spending 30% or more of household income on gross rent (40) (41)	25	-	10	35	15	50
382	Tenant households spending from 30% to 99% of household income on gross rent (40) (41)	15	-	10	35	20	40
383	Owner households in non-farm, non-reserve private dwellings (42)	1,455	-	1,410	1,895	1,005	1,230
384	Average owner's major payments $ (42)	1,537	-	1,511	1,497	1,272	1,331
385	Owner households spending 30% or more of household income on owner's major payments (41) (42)	195	-	215	320	110	190
386	Owner households spending from 30% to 99% of household income on owner's major payments (41) (42)	180	-	205	295	85	190
	CENSUS FAMILY CHARACTERISTICS						
387	**Total number of census families in private households**	**1,500**	**15**	**1,380**	**1,910**	**990**	**1,230**
	by census family structure and size						
388	Total couple families	1,355	15	1,275	1,740	950	1,100
389	Total families of married couples	1,330	10	1,220	1,670	925	1,035
390	Without children at home	265	-	245	320	210	245
391	With children at home	1,065	15	970	1,345	715	785
392	1 child	275	-	280	360	155	230
393	2 children	550	-	505	745	335	365
394	3 or more children	235	10	185	240	225	200
395	Total families of common-law couples	30	-	60	75	25	70
396	Without children at home	15	-	30	55	10	30
397	With children at home	15	-	30	25	20	35
398	1 child	10	-	25	10	10	-
399	2 children	-	-	-	10	10	30
400	3 or more children	10	-	-	15	10	10
401	Total lone-parent families	150	-	100	170	45	130
402	Female parent	125	-	95	135	30	110
403	1 child	50	-	45	55	-	65
404	2 children	45	-	40	65	20	40
405	3 or more children	30	-	-	10	-	10

Tableau 1. Certaines caractéristiques des secteurs de recensement, recensement de 2001 – Données intégrales et données-échantillon (20 %)

Toronto 0613.01	Toronto 0613.03 A	Toronto 0613.04 A	Toronto 0614.01 A	Toronto 0614.02 A	Toronto 0615	Caractéristiques	N°
						CARACTÉRISTIQUES DES LOGEMENTS ET DES MÉNAGES	
						selon l'état du logement	
870	975	1,400	665	975	110	Entretien régulier seulement	355
510	500	460	365	395	55	Réparations mineures	356
125	125	180	60	40	25	Réparations majeures	357
						selon la période de construction	
15	55	20	-	20	65	Avant 1946	358
255	290	30	15	55	35	1946-1960	359
415	555	265	240	370	40	1961-1970	360
700	210	815	475	790	25	1971-1980	361
100	370	890	345	140	20	1981-1990	362
10	105	20	15	35	10	1991-2001 (20)	363
7.5	6.6	6.0	8.2	8.0	7.1	Nombre moyen de pièces par logement	364
3.4	2.7	2.4	3.5	3.4	3.1	Nombre moyen de chambres à coucher par logement	365
218,842	218,925	203,134	254,035	239,889	460,379	Valeur moyenne du logement $	366
1,500	**1,600**	**2,035**	**1,095**	**1,415**	**190**	**Nombre total de logements privés**	367
						selon la taille du ménage	
150	335	660	70	150	35	1 personne	368
495	570	725	330	455	60	2 personnes	369
310	285	295	220	325	35	3 personnes	370
490	365	305	445	450	30	4-5 personnes	371
55	45	45	30	35	25	6 personnes ou plus	372
						selon le genre de ménage	
1,255	1,145	1,220	960	1,180	135	Ménages unifamiliaux	373
40	40	10	20	35	-	Ménages multifamiliaux	374
200	415	810	115	200	55	Ménages non familiaux	375
4,540	4,190	4,565	3,480	4,190	555	Nombre de personnes dans les ménages privés	376
3.0	2.6	2.2	3.2	3.0	2.9	Nombre moyen de personnes dans les ménages privés	377
0.4	0.4	0.4	0.4	0.4	0.4	Nombre moyen de personnes par pièce	378
155	630	985	95	65	90	Ménages locataires dans les logements privés non agricoles hors réserve (40)	379
879	1,076	1,114	1,276	1,279	1,018	Loyer brut moyen $ (40)	380
55	275	440	40	35	30	Ménages locataires consacrant 30 % ou plus du revenu du ménage au loyer brut (40) (41)	381
50	230	350	45	30	25	Ménages locataires consacrant de 30 % à 99 % du revenu du ménage au loyer brut (40) (41)	382
1,340	960	1,035	995	1,350	90	Ménages propriétaires dans les logements privés non agricoles hors réserve (42)	383
1,050	1,039	1,030	1,123	1,055	1,191	Principales dépenses de propriété moyennes $ (42)	384
155	200	180	155	195	15	Ménages propriétaires consacrant 30 % ou plus du revenu du ménage aux principales dépenses de propriété (41) (42)	385
140	175	165	145	165	15	Ménages propriétaires consacrant de 30 % à 99 % du revenu du ménage aux principales dépenses de propriété (41) (42)	386
						CARACTÉRISTIQUES DES FAMILLES DE RECENSEMENT	
1,345	**1,230**	**1,235**	**1,005**	**1,260**	**140**	**Total des familles de recensement dans les ménages privés**	387
						selon la structure et la taille de la famille de recensement	
1,180	1,010	1,070	905	1,090	115	Total des familles avec conjoints	388
1,090	905	935	850	1,015	95	Total des familles avec couples mariés	389
400	410	430	235	330	35	Sans enfants à la maison	390
690	495	505	610	690	60	Avec enfants à la maison	391
225	165	230	190	250	20	1 enfant	392
320	225	190	315	340	15	2 enfants	393
145	105	80	105	95	30	3 enfants ou plus	394
95	105	140	60	75	20	Total des familles en union libre	395
40	75	120	35	45	10	Sans enfants à la maison	396
55	30	20	30	30	15	Avec enfants à la maison	397
40	20	10	15	15	10	1 enfant	398
10	10	15	-	10	10	2 enfants	399
10	10	-	10	10	10	3 enfants ou plus	400
160	220	160	100	165	25	Total des familles monoparentales	401
130	180	120	85	150	15	Parent de sexe féminin	402
85	110	90	55	105	15	1 enfant	403
35	65	15	30	40	-	2 enfants	404
15	10	20	10	-	-	3 enfants ou plus	405

Table 1. Selected Characteristics for Census Tracts, 2001 Census – 100% Data and 20% Sample Data

No.	Characteristics	Toronto 0612.09	Toronto 0612.10 ◆	Toronto 0612.11 A	Toronto 0612.12 A	Toronto 0612.13 A	Toronto 0612.14 A
	CENSUS FAMILY CHARACTERISTICS						
	by census family structure and size – concluded						
406	Male parent	20	-	10	35	15	20
407	1 child	25	-	-	20	-	-
408	2 children	-	-	10	15	10	20
409	3 or more children	-	-	-	10	10	-
410	**Total number of children at home**	**2,420**	**65**	**2,085**	**2,955**	**1,640**	**1,880**
	by age groups						
411	Under 6 years	460	-	595	905	165	335
412	6-14 years	1,085	20	895	1,190	670	850
413	15-17 years	320	15	220	320	310	240
414	18-24 years	395	25	290	400	390	365
415	25 years and over	165	-	90	135	115	95
416	Average number of children at home per census family (43)	1.6	-	1.5	1.5	1.7	1.5
417	**Total number of persons in private households**	**5,470**	**95**	**4,965**	**6,960**	**3,710**	**4,640**
	by census family status and living arrangements						
418	Number of non-family persons	190	-	225	350	130	425
419	Living with relatives (44)	65	-	85	130	35	80
420	Living with non-relatives only	30	-	65	110	20	155
421	Living alone	95	-	70	105	70	195
422	Number of family persons	5,280	95	4,735	6,610	3,585	4,215
423	Average number of persons per census family	3.5	-	3.4	3.5	3.6	3.4
424	**Total number of persons 65 years and over**	**270**	**-**	**160**	**185**	**285**	**235**
425	Number of non-family persons 65 years and over	60	-	60	40	55	55
426	Living with relatives (44)	55	-	55	40	25	15
427	Living with non-relatives only	-	-	-	-	-	-
428	Living alone	10	-	-	-	30	40
429	Number of family persons 65 years and over	210	-	100	140	230	185
	ECONOMIC FAMILY CHARACTERISTICS						
430	**Total number of economic families in private households**	**1,460**	**15**	**1,350**	**1,860**	**985**	**1,195**
	by size of family						
431	2 persons	290	-	290	365	220	275
432	3 persons	310	-	310	425	175	280
433	4 persons	575	10	490	735	340	375
434	5 or more persons	285	10	260	335	250	255
435	Total number of persons in economic families	5,345	90	4,825	6,740	3,620	4,295
436	Average number of persons per economic family	3.6	-	3.6	3.6	3.7	3.6
437	Total number of unattached individuals	125	10	135	220	95	345
	2000 INCOME CHARACTERISTICS						
	Population 15 years and over by sex and total income groups in 2000						
438	Total - Both sexes	3,925	XXX	3,475	4,860	2,880	3,455
439	Without income	170		150	260	225	200
440	With income	3,760		3,325	4,595	2,660	3,255
441	Under $1,000 (45)	210		145	190	90	80
442	$ 1,000 - $ 2,999	240		150	215	155	165
443	$ 3,000 - $ 4,999	105		95	190	110	120
444	$ 5,000 - $ 6,999	135		105	130	135	135
445	$ 7,000 - $ 9,999	130		85	205	180	105
446	$10,000 - $11,999	120		75	115	160	115
447	$12,000 - $14,999	115		75	175	100	145
448	$15,000 - $19,999	120		145	215	125	175
449	$20,000 - $24,999	120		110	195	90	130
450	$25,000 - $29,999	120		220	210	110	185
451	$30,000 - $34,999	185		185	215	115	255
452	$35,000 - $39,999	220		220	245	55	180
453	$40,000 - $44,999	135		190	265	115	150
454	$45,000 - $49,999	175		205	215	85	90
455	$50,000 - $59,999	360		230	415	100	240
456	$60,000 and over	1,265		1,085	1,400	940	980
457	Average income $ (46)	56,142		54,304	49,792	62,501	50,919
458	Median income $ (46)	40,301		40,154	39,759	32,105	34,997
459	Standard error of average income $ (46)	2,417		2,244	1,474	4,177	2,379

Tableau 1. Certaines caractéristiques des secteurs de recensement, recensement de 2001 – Données intégrales et données-échantillon (20 %)

Toronto 0613.01	Toronto 0613.03 A	Toronto 0613.04 A	Toronto 0614.01 A	Toronto 0614.02 A	Toronto 0615	Caractéristiques	N°
						CARACTÉRISTIQUES DES FAMILLES DE RECENSEMENT	
						selon la structure et la taille de la famille de recensement – fin	
35	35	40	10	20	-	Parent de sexe masculin	406
10	15	40	10	10	-	1 enfant	407
25	20	-	-	10	-	2 enfants	408
-	-	-	10	-	-	3 enfants ou plus	409
1,665	**1,340**	**1,155**	**1,360**	**1,510**	**215**	**Nombre total d'enfants à la maison**	410
						selon les groupes d'âge	
340	250	205	220	245	25	Moins de 6 ans	411
585	460	385	580	495	85	6-14 ans	412
125	145	120	210	165	30	15-17 ans	413
405	315	290	285	365	30	18-24 ans	414
210	170	150	65	240	35	25 ans et plus	415
1.2	1.1	0.9	1.4	1.2	1.6	Nombre moyen d'enfants à la maison par famille de recensement (43)	416
4,540	**4,185**	**4,565**	**3,480**	**4,190**	**555**	**Nombre total de personnes dans les ménages privés**	417
						selon la situation des particuliers dans la famille de recensement et des particuliers dans le ménage	
345	610	1,105	210	330	85	Nombre de personnes hors famille de recensement	418
55	75	85	90	60	-	Vivant avec des personnes apparentées (44)	419
150	205	360	55	125	55	Vivant avec des personnes non apparentées uniquement	420
150	335	665	70	150	35	Vivant seules	421
4,190	3,575	3,455	3,270	3,860	470	Nombre de personnes membres d'une famille	422
3.1	2.9	2.8	3.2	3.1	3.4	Nombre moyen de personnes par famille de recensement	423
395	**515**	**720**	**230**	**400**	**45**	**Nombre total de personnes de 65 ans et plus**	424
105	155	340	45	70	10	Nombre de personnes hors famille de recensement de 65 ans et plus	425
25	25	30	25	45	-	Vivant avec des personnes apparentées (44)	426
15	10	10	-	-	-	Vivant avec des personnes non apparentées uniquement	427
70	125	300	15	25	10	Vivant seules	428
285	360	380	190	325	40	Nombre de personnes membres d'une famille de 65 ans et plus	429
						CARACTÉRISTIQUES DES FAMILLES ÉCONOMIQUES	
1,305	**1,200**	**1,245**	**1,010**	**1,225**	**135**	**Nombre total de familles économiques dans les ménages privés**	430
						selon la taille de la famille	
455	550	670	325	420	55	2 personnes	431
305	260	245	225	320	35	3 personnes	432
360	250	245	320	340	15	4 personnes	433
180	140	85	135	145	35	5 personnes ou plus	434
4,240	3,650	3,540	3,360	3,915	470	Nombre total de personnes dans les familles économiques	435
3.3	3.0	2.8	3.3	3.2	3.4	Nombre moyen de personnes par famille économique	436
290	535	1,025	120	270	85	Nombre total de personnes hors famille économique	437
						CARACTÉRISTIQUES DU REVENU DE 2000	
						Population de 15 ans et plus selon le sexe et les tranches de revenu total en 2000	
3,610	3,480	3,995	2,680	3,450	440	Total - Les deux sexes	438
115	160	165	90	150	30	Sans revenu	439
3,495	3,325	3,830	2,590	3,305	410	Avec un revenu	440
80	155	110	125	115	15	Moins de 1 000 $ (45)	441
145	65	75	120	130	10	1 000 $ - 2 999 $	442
185	135	115	95	155	20	3 000 $ - 4 999 $	443
135	210	175	105	125	10	5 000 $ - 6 999 $	444
155	140	180	105	170	30	7 000 $ - 9 999 $	445
130	65	185	85	120	-	10 000 $ - 11 999 $	446
175	190	255	120	155	15	12 000 $ - 14 999 $	447
295	260	285	140	195	-	15 000 $ - 19 999 $	448
230	280	285	180	180	50	20 000 $ - 24 999 $	449
215	240	285	115	235	45	25 000 $ - 29 999 $	450
195	240	320	160	205	40	30 000 $ - 34 999 $	451
235	260	275	150	190	55	35 000 $ - 39 999 $	452
165	240	215	150	130	20	40 000 $ - 44 999 $	453
245	165	225	90	145	25	45 000 $ - 49 999 $	454
295	205	245	170	320	30	50 000 $ - 59 999 $	455
615	470	590	680	730	40	60 000 $ et plus	456
37,536	33,373	37,429	41,842	41,306	38,098	Revenu moyen $ (46)	457
30,000	28,293	28,346	32,789	30,469	30,279	Revenu médian $ (46)	458
1,393	1,083	1,399	1,638	1,684	4,691	Erreur type de revenu moyen $ (46)	459

Table 1. Selected Characteristics for Census Tracts, 2001 Census – 100% Data and 20% Sample Data

No.	Characteristics	Toronto 0612.09	Toronto 0612.10 ◆	Toronto 0612.11 A	Toronto 0612.12 A	Toronto 0612.13 A	Toronto 0612.14 A
	2000 INCOME CHARACTERISTICS						
	Population 15 years and over by sex and total income groups in 2000 – concluded						
460	Total - Males	1,860	XXX	1,695	2,355	1,430	1,670
461	Without income	25		25	45	55	70
462	With income	1,835		1,670	2,310	1,375	1,595
463	Under $1,000 (45)	50		75	55	40	25
464	$ 1,000 - $ 2,999	90		50	75	70	60
465	$ 3,000 - $ 4,999	40		50	45	60	30
466	$ 5,000 - $ 6,999	30		45	45	40	65
467	$ 7,000 - $ 9,999	40		25	85	105	50
468	$10,000 - $11,999	35		35	45	45	50
469	$12,000 - $14,999	40		25	25	25	45
470	$15,000 - $19,999	50		45	55	30	30
471	$20,000 - $24,999	55		45	95	40	25
472	$25,000 - $29,999	40		70	90	35	90
473	$30,000 - $34,999	75		60	100	30	95
474	$35,000 - $39,999	85		80	30	30	55
475	$40,000 - $44,999	50		65	115	45	70
476	$45,000 - $49,999	90		80	120	35	60
477	$50,000 - $59,999	190		75	260	65	125
478	$60,000 and over	880		845	1,065	670	725
479	Average income $ (46)	76,039		71,092	66,352	87,000	70,581
480	Median income $ (46)	57,044		60,004	53,220	54,990	52,017
481	Standard error of average income $ (46)	4,264		3,997	2,373	7,111	4,389
482	Total - Females	2,065		1,785	2,505	1,450	1,785
483	Without income	145		125	220	170	125
484	With income	1,915		1,655	2,285	1,285	1,660
485	Under $1,000 (45)	160		65	130	55	55
486	$ 1,000 - $ 2,999	155		105	140	85	105
487	$ 3,000 - $ 4,999	60		50	140	50	85
488	$ 5,000 - $ 6,999	105		60	85	95	75
489	$ 7,000 - $ 9,999	90		65	120	70	55
490	$10,000 - $11,999	90		40	70	120	65
491	$12,000 - $14,999	85		50	150	80	100
492	$15,000 - $19,999	70		105	160	95	150
493	$20,000 - $24,999	65		65	95	50	100
494	$25,000 - $29,999	80		145	120	75	90
495	$30,000 - $34,999	110		115	120	80	160
496	$35,000 - $39,999	135		145	215	25	125
497	$40,000 - $44,999	85		125	145	65	80
498	$45,000 - $49,999	80		130	95	45	35
499	$50,000 - $59,999	170		150	155	30	115
500	$60,000 and over	385		240	330	265	260
501	Average income $ (46)	37,078		37,384	33,050	36,280	31,980
502	Median income $ (46)	30,958		32,686	26,037	19,893	26,526
503	Standard error of average income $ (46)	2,001		1,728	1,432	3,442	1,450
	by composition of total income						
504	Total - Composition of income in 2000 % (47)	100.0		100.0	100.0	100.0	100.0
505	Employment income %	90.8		91.1	93.4	89.0	91.3
506	Government transfer payments %	2.4		2.1	2.5	2.7	3.0
507	Other %	6.8		6.8	4.0	8.5	5.7
	Population 15 years and over with employment income in 2000 by sex and work activity						
508	Both sexes with employment income (48)	3,275		2,900	4,035	2,140	2,850
509	Average employment income $	58,417		56,668	52,977	69,041	53,055
510	Standard error of average employment income $	2,606		2,395	1,558	4,872	2,600
511	Worked full year, full time (49)	1,915		1,930	2,550	1,175	1,715
512	Average employment income $	83,134		72,399	68,758	103,976	73,231
513	Standard error of average employment income $	3,825		3,172	1,988	7,592	3,694
514	Worked part year or part time (50)	1,320		945	1,480	960	1,075
515	Average employment income $	24,158		26,230	26,211	26,703	21,888
516	Standard error of average employment income $	1,799		2,175	1,833	4,271	2,224
517	Males with employment income (48)	1,695		1,515	2,125	1,190	1,455
518	Average employment income $	77,547		73,816	68,657	90,800	72,910
519	Standard error of average employment income $	4,383		4,116	2,408	7,744	4,610
520	Worked full year, full time (49)	1,210		1,145	1,595	715	1,030
521	Average employment income $	96,867		87,164	81,211	126,407	89,889
522	Standard error of average employment income $	5,588		4,858	2,782	10,841	5,698
523	Worked part year or part time (50)	465		360	530	470	385
524	Average employment income $	30,725		33,279	30,829	36,442	29,575
525	Standard error of average employment income $	3,447		5,184	3,055	8,314	5,770

Tableau 1. Certaines caractéristiques des secteurs de recensement, recensement de 2001 – Données intégrales et données-échantillon (20 %)

Toronto 0613.01	Toronto 0613.03 A	Toronto 0613.04 A	Toronto 0614.01 A	Toronto 0614.02 A	Toronto 0615	Caractéristiques	N°
						CARACTÉRISTIQUES DU REVENU DE 2000	
						Population de 15 ans et plus selon le sexe et les tranches de revenu total en 2000 – fin	
1,765	1,740	1,885	1,300	1,705	240	Total - Hommes	460
25	70	40	45	45	10	Sans revenu	461
1,735	1,670	1,845	1,255	1,660	235	Avec un revenu	462
15	80	50	65	55	-	Moins de 1 000 $ (45)	463
25	30	40	60	60	-	1 000 $ - 2 999 $	464
85	55	35	30	50	-	3 000 $ - 4 999 $	465
55	65	85	50	45	-	5 000 $ - 6 999 $	466
55	55	75	35	65	15	7 000 $ - 9 999 $	467
30	20	65	30	45	-	10 000 $ - 11 999 $	468
50	70	95	20	45	-	12 000 $ - 14 999 $	469
115	90	80	45	60	-	15 000 $ - 19 999 $	470
95	145	160	50	100	35	20 000 $ - 24 999 $	471
75	100	120	30	110	25	25 000 $ - 29 999 $	472
100	95	135	40	90	40	30 000 $ - 34 999 $	473
120	115	115	60	95	35	35 000 $ - 39 999 $	474
95	145	135	50	60	15	40 000 $ - 44 999 $	475
130	105	115	45	70	10	45 000 $ - 49 999 $	476
210	125	115	90	175	25	50 000 $ - 59 999 $	477
465	370	430	555	535	40	60 000 $ et plus	478
48,587	40,554	47,036	55,844	51,893	50,828	Revenu moyen $ (46)	479
40,315	35,311	33,978	50,034	40,270	35,846	Revenu médian $ (46)	480
2,425	1,757	2,593	2,818	2,941	7,483	Erreur type de revenu moyen $ (46)	481
1,845	1,745	2,110	1,385	1,745	200	Total - Femmes	482
90	90	125	45	100	25	Sans revenu	483
1,755	1,650	1,985	1,335	1,640	175	Avec un revenu	484
65	75	60	60	55	10	Moins de 1 000 $ (45)	485
115	35	35	55	65	10	1 000 $ - 2 999 $	486
100	80	80	65	100	15	3 000 $ - 4 999 $	487
80	145	90	55	85	10	5 000 $ - 6 999 $	488
100	85	105	70	105	20	7 000 $ - 9 999 $	489
95	45	120	55	75	-	10 000 $ - 11 999 $	490
125	120	165	100	110	15	12 000 $ - 14 999 $	491
180	175	205	95	135	-	15 000 $ - 19 999 $	492
135	140	125	135	85	20	20 000 $ - 24 999 $	493
135	140	170	85	130	25	25 000 $ - 29 999 $	494
90	140	190	120	115	-	30 000 $ - 34 999 $	495
115	145	160	85	95	25	35 000 $ - 39 999 $	496
75	95	75	100	70	-	40 000 $ - 44 999 $	497
115	65	105	50	75	15	45 000 $ - 49 999 $	498
85	75	130	85	145	-	50 000 $ - 59 999 $	499
155	100	160	125	190	-	60 000 $ et plus	500
26,597	26,123	28,476	28,705	30,587	21,178	Revenu moyen $ (46)	501
20,074	21,822	24,654	23,545	25,153	20,066	Revenu médian $ (46)	502
1,190	1,135	1,075	1,402	1,442	2,538	Erreur type de revenu moyen $ (46)	503
						selon la composition du revenu total	
100.0	100.0	100.0	100.0	100.0	100.0	Total - Composition du revenu en 2000 % (47)	504
86.1	80.9	81.1	86.8	83.2	86.6	Revenu d'emploi %	505
6.0	8.1	8.5	4.1	5.3	5.6	Transferts gouvernementaux %	506
7.9	11.0	10.3	9.2	11.6	8.7	Autre %	507
						Population de 15 ans et plus ayant un revenu d'emploi en 2000 selon le sexe et le travail	
2,940	2,605	2,860	2,220	2,705	350	Les deux sexes ayant un revenu d'emploi (48)	508
38,415	34,429	40,664	42,375	41,950	37,582	Revenu moyen d'emploi $	509
1,537	1,235	1,685	1,670	1,900	5,315	Erreur type de revenu moyen d'emploi $	510
1,675	1,435	1,625	1,240	1,490	215	Ayant travaillé toute l'année à plein temps (49)	511
51,562	45,259	55,154	60,510	60,169	48,108	Revenu moyen d'emploi $	512
1,804	1,647	2,299	2,196	2,938	7,753	Erreur type de revenu moyen d'emploi $	513
1,225	1,075	1,125	945	1,200	140	Ayant travaillé une partie de l'année ou à temps partiel (50)	514
20,819	21,495	22,520	19,928	19,771	21,036	Revenu moyen d'emploi $	515
2,325	1,597	2,056	1,752	1,305	3,602	Erreur type de revenu moyen d'emploi $	516
1,540	1,395	1,470	1,095	1,385	215	Hommes ayant un revenu d'emploi (48)	517
47,766	40,785	50,926	55,239	53,257	48,451	Revenu moyen d'emploi $	518
2,566	1,971	2,939	2,728	3,365	8,075	Erreur type de revenu moyen d'emploi $	519
985	840	905	710	880	155	Ayant travaillé toute l'année à plein temps (49)	520
58,895	50,448	66,608	73,424	70,734	55,356	Revenu moyen d'emploi $	521
2,611	2,432	3,739	3,007	4,570	10,368	Erreur type de revenu moyen d'emploi $	522
525	495	525	380	500	60	Ayant travaillé une partie de l'année ou à temps partiel (50)	523
27,702	26,671	26,157	22,548	22,826	30,840	Revenu moyen d'emploi $	524
5,150	3,109	3,927	3,605	2,652	6,065	Erreur type de revenu moyen d'emploi $	525

Table 1. Selected Characteristics for Census Tracts, 2001 Census – 100% Data and 20% Sample Data

No.	Characteristics	Toronto 0612.09	Toronto 0612.10 ◆	Toronto 0612.11 A	Toronto 0612.12 A	Toronto 0612.13 A	Toronto 0612.14 A
	2000 INCOME CHARACTERISTICS						
	Population 15 years and over with employment income in 2000 by sex and work activity – concluded						
526	Females with employment income (48)	1,585	XXX	1,385	1,905	950	1,395
527	Average employment income $	37,948		37,926	35,505	41,779	32,431
528	Standard error of average employment income $	2,181		1,815	1,579	4,437	1,612
529	Worked full year, full time (49)	710		780	950	455	690
530	Average employment income $	59,666		50,727	47,801	68,564	48,356
531	Standard error of average employment income $	3,489		2,588	1,904	8,365	2,450
532	Worked part year or part time (50)	845		590	950	485	685
533	Average employment income $	20,524		21,965	23,625	17,304	17,561
534	Standard error of average employment income $	1,979		1,657	2,274	1,805	1,237
	Census families by structure and family income groups in 2000						
535	Total - All census families	1,500		1,375	1,910	990	1,235
536	Under $10,000	10		20	20	15	20
537	$ 10,000 - $19,999	-		15	40	10	25
538	$ 20,000 - $29,999	30		30	15	45	30
539	$ 30,000 - $39,999	20		20	95	25	65
540	$ 40,000 - $49,999	50		70	95	45	60
541	$ 50,000 - $59,999	30		110	135	50	70
542	$ 60,000 - $69,999	120		75	100	60	50
543	$ 70,000 - $79,999	75		95	140	20	120
544	$ 80,000 - $89,999	120		145	145	60	80
545	$ 90,000 - $99,999	100		85	90	40	95
546	$100,000 and over	945		720	1,035	635	620
547	Average family income $	133,790		123,159	113,075	157,560	118,833
548	Median family income $	118,008		103,103	102,208	122,923	100,260
549	Standard error of average family income $	4,991		4,863	3,152	9,508	5,328
550	Total - All couple census families (51)	1,355		1,275	1,745	950	1,100
551	Under $10,000	-		15	-	15	15
552	$ 10,000 - $19,999	-		15	15	10	10
553	$ 20,000 - $29,999	30		15	10	40	25
554	$ 30,000 - $39,999	15		10	85	25	35
555	$ 40,000 - $49,999	35		55	80	40	40
556	$ 50,000 - $59,999	20		90	115	35	65
557	$ 60,000 - $69,999	95		60	80	60	35
558	$ 70,000 - $79,999	65		85	135	20	105
559	$ 80,000 - $89,999	115		130	135	60	80
560	$ 90,000 - $99,999	80		75	65	30	95
561	$100,000 and over	900		720	1,010	630	595
562	Average family income $	139,864		128,210	117,909	161,448	125,300
563	Median family income $	122,838		111,449	106,792	125,223	106,005
564	Standard error of average family income $	5,364		5,186	3,348	9,850	5,690
	Incidence of low income in 2000						
565	Total - Economic families	1,460		1,350	1,855	985	1,195
566	Low income	25		40	60	35	35
567	Incidence of low income in 2000 % (52)	1.9		2.9	3.3	3.9	3.0
568	Total - Unattached individuals 15 years and over	120		140	215	90	335
569	Low income	20		30	80	30	70
570	Incidence of low income in 2000 % (52)	16.4		20.1	36.9	27.1	21.0
571	Total - Population in private households	5,470		4,960	6,955	3,710	4,635
572	Low income	90		155	335	115	200
573	Incidence of low income in 2000 % (52)	1.6		3.1	4.8	3.2	4.3
	Private households by household income groups in 2000						
574	Total - All private households	1,555		1,450	1,995	1,060	1,445
575	Under $10,000	15		20	20	20	20
576	$ 10,000 - $19,999	-		20	40	20	35
577	$ 20,000 - $29,999	30		10	20	25	40
578	$ 30,000 - $39,999	20		15	80	35	50
579	$ 40,000 - $49,999	40		70	90	45	95
580	$ 50,000 - $59,999	60		100	150	65	110
581	$ 60,000 - $69,999	105		75	100	60	100
582	$ 70,000 - $79,999	70		115	155	35	125
583	$ 80,000 - $89,999	115		130	150	70	85
584	$ 90,000 - $99,999	100		85	100	25	100
585	$100,000 and over	1,000		805	1,090	665	690
586	Average household income $	135,318		124,948	114,796	156,676	114,835
587	Median household income $	120,189		106,931	103,220	121,249	96,039
588	Standard error of average household income $	4,871		4,633	3,089	9,421	4,994

Tableau 1. Certaines caractéristiques des secteurs de recensement, recensement de 2001 – Données intégrales et données-échantillon (20 %)

Toronto 0613.01	Toronto 0613.03 A	Toronto 0613.04 A	Toronto 0614.01 A	Toronto 0614.02 A	Toronto 0615	Caractéristiques	N°
						CARACTÉRISTIQUES DU REVENU DE 2000	
						Population de 15 ans et plus ayant un revenu d'emploi en 2000 selon le sexe et le travail – fin	
1,405	1,210	1,390	1,125	1,320	140	Femmes ayant un revenu d'emploi (48)	526
28,157	27,107	29,791	29,852	30,094	20,770	Revenu moyen d'emploi $	527
1,390	1,257	1,322	1,604	1,372	2,894	Erreur type de revenu moyen d'emploi $	528
690	595	715	535	605	60	Ayant travaillé toute l'année à plein temps (49)	529
41,062	37,904	40,614	43,372	44,824	30,026	Revenu moyen d'emploi $	530
1,999	1,818	1,600	2,449	2,031	3,707	Erreur type de revenu moyen d'emploi $	531
700	580	600	565	705	75	Ayant travaillé une partie de l'année ou à temps partiel (50)	532
15,626	17,082	19,364	18,167	17,618	13,336	Revenu moyen d'emploi $	533
1,381	1,278	1,884	1,605	1,250	3,260	Erreur type de revenu moyen d'emploi $	534
						Familles de recensement selon la structure et les tranches de revenu de la famille en 2000	
1,345	1,225	1,235	1,005	1,260	135	Total - Toutes les familles de recensement	535
25	25	30	20	15	-	Moins de 10 000 $	536
40	55	45	20	40	10	10 000 $ - 19 999 $	537
50	120	90	20	45	-	20 000 $ - 29 999 $	538
75	110	75	60	100	10	30 000 $ - 39 999 $	539
115	130	120	50	50	10	40 000 $ - 49 999 $	540
140	130	145	75	75	45	50 000 $ - 59 999 $	541
110	90	105	95	125	35	60 000 $ - 69 999 $	542
150	120	95	70	105	10	70 000 $ - 79 999 $	543
75	105	95	80	90	-	80 000 $ - 89 999 $	544
80	60	60	110	75	-	90 000 $ - 99 999 $	545
480	290	380	400	535	40	100 000 $ et plus	546
88,400	74,268	85,653	100,102	98,496	92,028	Revenu moyen des familles $	547
78,591	63,669	72,509	90,681	87,688	63,804	Revenu médian des familles $	548
3,280	2,916	3,544	3,777	4,011	12,877	Erreur type de revenu moyen des familles $	549
1,185	1,005	1,075	905	1,095	115	Total - Toutes les familles de recensement comptant un couple (51)	550
25	20	10	25	-	-	Moins de 10 000 $	551
10	25	25	15	25	-	10 000 $ - 19 999 $	552
35	55	65	20	45	-	20 000 $ - 29 999 $	553
55	115	65	40	100	-	30 000 $ - 39 999 $	554
105	70	75	35	30	-	40 000 $ - 49 999 $	555
100	105	120	45	60	45	50 000 $ - 59 999 $	556
95	80	95	75	110	30	60 000 $ - 69 999 $	557
140	100	90	75	90	10	70 000 $ - 79 999 $	558
75	90	85	75	80	-	80 000 $ - 89 999 $	559
75	60	60	105	65	10	90 000 $ - 99 999 $	560
470	280	375	400	485	30	100 000 $ et plus	561
93,822	80,169	92,373	105,367	100,761	83,182	Revenu moyen des familles $	562
82,931	72,385	78,565	94,116	90,175	63,771	Revenu médian des familles $	563
3,549	3,301	3,859	4,020	4,363	9,729	Erreur type de revenu moyen des familles $	564
						Fréquence des unités à faible revenu en 2000	
1,300	1,200	1,250	1,010	1,220	140	Total - Familles économiques	565
80	105	115	40	70	-	Faible revenu	566
6.2	8.7	9.2	3.6	5.5	2.1	Fréquence des unités à faible revenu en 2000 % (52)	567
290	540	1,025	125	270	85	Total - Personnes hors famille économique de 15 ans et plus	568
95	175	315	45	65	10	Faible revenu	569
30.9	32.2	30.4	36.7	22.9	13.4	Fréquence des unités à faible revenu en 2000 % (52)	570
4,540	4,185	4,565	3,480	4,190	555	Total - Population dans les ménages privés	571
360	515	745	175	300	20	Faible revenu	572
8.0	12.3	16.3	5.0	7.1	3.1	Fréquence des unités à faible revenu en 2000 % (52)	573
						Ménages privés selon les tranches de revenu du ménage en 2000	
1,505	1,600	2,040	1,095	1,415	190	Total - Tous les ménages privés	574
15	35	75	20	40	10	Moins de 10 000 $	575
80	130	205	25	30	-	10 000 $ - 19 999 $	576
100	145	215	20	65	25	20 000 $ - 29 999 $	577
80	200	190	55	90	-	30 000 $ - 39 999 $	578
105	170	225	60	90	15	40 000 $ - 49 999 $	579
150	150	215	115	105	55	50 000 $ - 59 999 $	580
120	90	150	105	130	25	60 000 $ - 69 999 $	581
145	115	145	85	125	10	70 000 $ - 79 999 $	582
75	100	105	85	95	-	80 000 $ - 89 999 $	583
70	85	75	110	75	-	90 000 $ - 99 999 $	584
555	360	425	420	570	50	100 000 $ et plus	585
87,423	69,340	70,243	99,121	96,365	82,345	Revenu moyen des ménages $	586
77,272	57,938	53,478	86,004	86,561	56,734	Revenu médian des ménages $	587
3,118	2,580	2,836	3,678	3,869	10,658	Erreur type de revenu moyen des ménages $	588

Table 1. Selected Characteristics for Census Tracts, 2001 Census – 100% Data and 20% Sample Data

No.	Characteristics	Toronto 0620	Toronto 0621	Toronto 0622	Toronto 0623	Toronto 0624	Toronto 0625
	POPULATION CHARACTERISTICS						
1	**Population, 1996 (1)**	**3,212**	**6,235**	**6,545**	**3,497**	**6,172**	**712**
2	**Population, 2001 (2)**	**3,181**	**5,919**	**6,480**	**3,594**	**5,900**	**627**
3	Population percentage change, 1996-2001	-1.0	-5.1	-1.0	2.8	-4.4	-11.9
4	Land area in square kilometres, 2001	153.51	2.54	2.63	1.48	1.72	15.04
5	**Total population - 100% Data (3)**	**3,180**	**5,920**	**6,480**	**3,590**	**5,900**	**625**
	by sex and age groups						
6	Male	1,670	2,895	3,210	1,700	2,960	395
7	0-4 years	60	140	220	85	155	15
8	5-9 years	85	165	250	100	220	20
9	10-14 years	90	255	235	70	235	15
10	15-19 years	120	345	280	85	260	35
11	20-24 years	105	265	215	90	255	60
12	25-29 years	85	135	205	140	190	40
13	30-34 years	95	135	240	120	185	20
14	35-39 years	135	200	260	150	220	30
15	40-44 years	165	235	290	150	250	35
16	45-49 years	125	265	245	110	255	30
17	50-54 years	140	330	250	120	280	25
18	55-59 years	105	165	155	95	205	20
19	60-64 years	105	85	105	90	110	15
20	65-69 years	80	40	95	80	60	10
21	70-74 years	80	35	70	75	40	10
22	75-79 years	50	40	55	75	30	10
23	80-84 years	25	15	25	40	15	5
24	85 years and over	15	30	20	25	5	-
25	Female	1,510	3,025	3,270	1,895	2,940	235
26	0-4 years	45	135	165	70	145	5
27	5-9 years	90	185	240	90	180	15
28	10-14 years	95	235	240	85	225	15
29	15-19 years	90	295	255	95	240	20
30	20-24 years	90	230	215	105	240	10
31	25-29 years	90	130	215	130	160	10
32	30-34 years	70	135	235	100	165	15
33	35-39 years	130	215	310	135	265	20
34	40-44 years	135	285	295	130	280	25
35	45-49 years	130	325	290	120	290	20
36	50-54 years	125	305	235	125	305	25
37	55-59 years	100	155	145	105	150	15
38	60-64 years	105	75	105	70	105	15
39	65-69 years	65	30	90	105	50	5
40	70-74 years	70	40	85	125	55	10
41	75-79 years	35	65	80	130	40	5
42	80-84 years	25	55	50	85	30	5
43	85 years and over	15	130	35	85	10	5
44	**Total population 15 years and over**	**2,715**	**4,805**	**5,130**	**3,090**	**4,740**	**540**
	by legal marital status						
45	Never married (single)	755	1,490	1,570	880	1,510	220
46	Legally married (and not separated)	1,585	2,690	2,795	1,415	2,640	245
47	Separated, but still legally married	85	105	195	170	175	15
48	Divorced	160	215	325	290	275	40
49	Widowed	125	295	240	355	140	15
	by common-law status						
50	Not in a common-law relationship	2,525	4,635	4,770	2,820	4,475	510
51	In a common-law relationship	190	160	360	275	265	25
52	**Total population - 20% Sample Data (4)**	**3,180**	**5,625**	**6,460**	**3,575**	**5,890**	**500**
	by mother tongue						
53	Single responses	3,135	5,615	6,410	3,540	5,800	500
54	English	2,575	5,220	5,855	3,125	5,325	410
55	French	35	40	65	100	45	15
56	Non-official languages (5)	520	355	490	320	430	80
57	Italian	75	75	180	110	85	30
58	Chinese, n.o.s.	10	-	-	-	25	-
59	Cantonese	-	-	-	-	-	-
60	Portuguese	10	10	20	-	45	-
61	Punjabi	-	-	-	30	-	-
62	Other languages (6)	425	265	280	175	270	50
63	Multiple responses	45	15	50	35	95	-
64	English and French	40	10	15	20	15	-
65	English and non-official language	-	10	25	15	80	10
66	French and non-official language	-	-	10	-	-	-
67	English, French and non-official language	-	-	-	-	-	-

See reference material at the end of the publication. – Voir les documents de référence à la fin de la publication.

Tableau 1. Certaines caractéristiques des secteurs de recensement, recensement de 2001 – Données intégrales et données-échantillon (20 %)

Toronto 0626	Toronto 0630	Toronto 0631	Toronto 0632	Toronto 0633	Toronto 0634	Caractéristiques	Nº
						CARACTÉRISTIQUES DE LA POPULATION	
5,731	**3,541**	**4,685**	**4,243**	**2,558**	**5,584**	**Population, 1996 (1)**	1
5,770	**3,501**	**8,493**	**4,430**	**2,639**	**6,243**	**Population, 2001 (2)**	2
0.7	-1.1	81.3	4.4	3.2	11.8	Variation en pourcentage de la population, 1996-2001	3
189.54	110.44	5.66	2.06	3.65	4.39	Superficie des terres en kilomètres carrés, 2001	4
5,770	**3,500**	**8,495**	**4,425**	**2,640**	**6,245**	**Population totale – Données intégrales (3)**	5
						selon le sexe et les groupes d'âge	
2,970	1,805	4,250	2,175	1,250	3,135	Sexe masculin	6
165	85	480	135	110	205	0-4 ans	7
190	105	570	150	95	245	5-9 ans	8
245	110	430	145	90	255	10-14 ans	9
230	140	240	155	80	205	15-19 ans	10
150	125	125	120	70	170	20-24 ans	11
125	95	130	115	105	190	25-29 ans	12
140	90	370	140	125	245	30-34 ans	13
230	155	635	225	130	290	35-39 ans	14
245	155	520	195	115	275	40-44 ans	15
265	120	295	160	85	200	45-49 ans	16
300	155	185	145	70	195	50-54 ans	17
230	150	105	120	40	195	55-59 ans	18
160	110	70	120	35	145	60-64 ans	19
135	75	40	85	30	110	65-69 ans	20
90	70	30	75	25	100	70-74 ans	21
45	35	10	50	20	70	75-79 ans	22
25	20	-	30	10	30	80-84 ans	23
10	10	5	10	15	10	85 ans et plus	24
2,795	1,695	4,245	2,260	1,385	3,105	Sexe féminin	25
115	90	490	140	70	180	0-4 ans	26
175	100	570	155	85	220	5-9 ans	27
205	105	365	145	90	215	10-14 ans	28
185	85	250	145	85	180	15-19 ans	29
135	100	115	105	65	140	20-24 ans	30
130	85	145	105	115	175	25-29 ans	31
165	115	515	155	135	250	30-34 ans	32
260	135	670	225	140	315	35-39 ans	33
265	130	465	185	140	270	40-44 ans	34
295	140	235	160	95	200	45-49 ans	35
265	180	150	150	80	225	50-54 ans	36
210	120	95	155	55	210	55-59 ans	37
140	100	70	130	50	130	60-64 ans	38
95	75	50	95	45	135	65-69 ans	39
60	65	35	95	45	100	70-74 ans	40
55	40	20	65	30	95	75-79 ans	41
30	10	15	30	35	50	80-84 ans	42
25	15	5	15	25	20	85 ans et plus	43
4,675	**2,910**	**5,590**	**3,550**	**2,100**	**4,920**	**Population totale de 15 ans et plus**	44
						selon l'état matrimonial légal	
1,255	810	1,025	870	635	1,245	Célibataire (jamais marié(e))	45
2,860	1,750	4,220	2,185	945	3,045	Légalement marié(e) (et non séparé(e))	46
120	75	85	100	120	130	Séparé(e), mais toujours légalement marié(e)	47
270	165	165	210	250	250	Divorcé(e)	48
175	120	100	185	155	250	Veuf ou veuve	49
						selon l'union libre	
4,325	2,730	5,375	3,355	1,860	4,630	Ne vivant pas en union libre	50
350	185	220	200	240	295	Vivant en union libre	51
5,770	**3,480**	**8,490**	**4,425**	**2,595**	**6,235**	**Population totale – Données-échantillon (20 %) (4)**	52
						selon la langue maternelle	
5,740	3,450	8,430	4,405	2,570	6,225	Réponses uniques	53
5,165	2,955	7,280	3,940	2,275	5,570	Anglais	54
65	65	175	110	95	70	Français	55
505	435	975	355	195	595	Langues non officielles (5)	56
75	85	185	15	-	10	Italien	57
-	-	-	-	10	-	Chinois, n.d.a.	58
-	-	35	-	-	35	Cantonais	59
30	10	150	85	30	105	Portugais	60
-	20	15	-	-	-	Pendjabi	61
400	320	580	250	160	445	Autres langues (6)	62
35	35	60	20	30	10	Réponses multiples	63
20	-	10	10	20	-	Anglais et français	64
10	25	40	15	15	10	Anglais et langue non officielle	65
10	-	10	-	-	-	Français et langue non officielle	66
-	10	-	-	-	-	Anglais, français et langue non officielle	67

See reference material at the end of the publication. – Voir les documents de référence à la fin de la publication.

Table 1. Selected Characteristics for Census Tracts, 2001 Census – 100% Data and 20% Sample Data

No.	Characteristics	Toronto 0620	Toronto 0621	Toronto 0622	Toronto 0623	Toronto 0624	Toronto 0625
	POPULATION CHARACTERISTICS						
	by home language						
68	Single responses	2,655	5,510	6,165	3,365	5,590	475
69	English	2,625	5,485	6,055	3,260	5,520	475
70	French	-	-	10	-	-	-
71	Non-official languages (5)	35	25	95	100	75	-
72	Cantonese	-	-	-	-	-	-
73	Chinese, n.o.s.	-	-	-	-	10	-
74	Italian	-	20	80	30	-	-
75	Punjabi	-	-	-	30	-	-
76	Portuguese	-	-	-	-	-	-
77	Other languages (6)	25	10	20	30	60	-
78	Multiple responses	525	115	290	210	300	30
79	English and French	30	10	45	95	55	-
80	English and non-official language	490	105	230	115	235	25
81	French and non-official language	-	-	10	-	-	-
82	English, French and non-official language	-	-	-	-	10	-
	by knowledge of official languages						
83	English only	2,860	5,140	5,935	3,200	5,310	465
84	French only	-	-	-	-	-	-
85	English and French	300	485	475	370	560	35
86	Neither English nor French	20	-	45	10	20	-
	by knowledge of non-official languages (5) (7)						
87	Italian	170	105	280	155	140	40
88	Cantonese	-	-	-	-	-	-
89	Chinese, n.o.s.	10	-	10	10	40	-
90	Spanish	50	40	50	60	20	15
91	Portuguese	10	25	30	-	40	-
92	Punjabi	-	-	10	30	20	-
93	Tagalog (Pilipino)	-	-	40	-	20	-
	by first official language spoken						
94	English	3,115	5,595	6,325	3,460	5,835	490
95	French	35	25	85	105	40	10
96	English and French	-	-	10	-	-	-
97	Neither English nor French	20	-	50	10	20	-
98	Official language minority - (number) (8)	40	30	85	110	40	15
99	Official language minority - (percentage) (8)	1.3	0.5	1.3	3.1	0.7	3.0
	by ethnic origin (9)						
100	Canadian	910	2,610	2,585	1,450	2,100	155
101	English	905	2,000	2,335	1,240	2,030	155
102	Scottish	650	1,410	1,630	800	1,720	125
103	Irish	475	1,280	1,380	800	1,400	85
104	Chinese	10	10	50	10	95	-
105	Italian	300	375	560	225	520	110
106	East Indian	15	-	65	60	-	25
107	French	200	630	665	480	510	30
108	German	300	695	745	300	450	20
109	Portuguese	15	20	95	-	85	-
110	Polish	125	155	165	50	120	-
111	Jewish	-	70	-	-	-	-
112	Jamaican	10	15	35	10	90	-
113	Filipino	10	-	35	-	40	-
114	Ukrainian	95	155	170	80	265	-
	by Aboriginal identity						
115	Total Aboriginal identity population (10)	10	35	20	45	30	10
116	Total non-Aboriginal population	3,165	5,590	6,435	3,525	5,860	495
	by Aboriginal origin						
117	Total Aboriginal origins population (11)	25	55	130	105	80	-
118	Total non-Aboriginal population	3,150	5,575	6,330	3,475	5,810	500
	by Registered Indian status						
119	Registered Indian (12)	15	-	10	10	10	-
120	Not a Registered Indian	3,170	5,625	6,445	3,570	5,880	500

Tableau 1. Certaines caractéristiques des secteurs de recensement, recensement de 2001 – Données intégrales et données-échantillon (20 %)

Toronto 0626	Toronto 0630	Toronto 0631	Toronto 0632	Toronto 0633	Toronto 0634	Caractéristiques	N°
						CARACTÉRISTIQUES DE LA POPULATION	
						selon la langue parlée à la maison	
5,495	3,220	7,775	4,140	2,410	5,900	Réponses uniques	68
5,475	3,110	7,590	4,090	2,365	5,800	Anglais	69
10	25	30	30	20	20	Français	70
10	90	160	25	35	85	Langues non officielles (5)	71
-	-	25	-	-	25	Cantonais	72
-	-	-	-	-	-	Chinois, n.d.a.	73
10	20	10	-	-	-	Italien	74
-	-	-	-	-	-	Pendjabi	75
-	-	25	20	-	-	Portugais	76
-	70	95	-	30	55	Autres langues (6)	77
275	260	715	285	185	335	Réponses multiples	78
45	15	250	125	50	45	Anglais et français	79
215	245	445	145	140	295	Anglais et langue non officielle	80
-	-	-	-	-	-	Français et langue non officielle	81
20	-	20	10	-	-	Anglais, français et langue non officielle	82
						selon la connaissance des langues officielles	
5,250	3,200	7,640	3,965	2,310	5,875	Anglais seulement	83
10	-	-	-	-	-	Français seulement	84
515	275	810	445	275	330	Anglais et français	85
-	-	40	20	-	35	Ni l'anglais ni le français	86
						selon la connaissance des langues non officielles (5) (7)	
120	105	250	15	20	35	Italien	87
-	-	35	-	-	45	Cantonais	88
-	-	-	-	-	-	Chinois, n.d.a.	89
55	25	55	40	40	15	Espagnol	90
50	20	155	90	40	140	Portugais	91
15	25	10	-	-	-	Pendjabi	92
-	-	10	15	-	10	Tagalog (pilipino)	93
						selon la première langue officielle parlée	
5,705	3,410	8,270	4,300	2,500	6,145	Anglais	94
70	60	180	105	90	60	Français	95
-	-	-	10	-	-	Anglais et français	96
-	10	35	15	10	30	Ni l'anglais ni le français	97
70	60	185	105	95	65	Minorité de langue officielle - (nombre) (8)	98
1.2	1.7	2.2	2.4	3.7	1.0	Minorité de langue officielle - (pourcentage) (8)	99
						selon l'origine ethnique (9)	
2,310	1,195	3,100	1,755	995	2,510	Canadien	100
2,245	1,195	2,820	1,755	885	2,230	Anglais	101
1,280	830	1,960	1,135	540	1,465	Écossais	102
945	665	1,820	1,025	615	1,200	Irlandais	103
20	15	135	-	-	50	Chinois	104
265	190	850	125	95	225	Italien	105
65	50	105	-	30	75	Indien de l'Inde	106
500	265	865	585	245	405	Français	107
650	425	890	395	270	605	Allemand	108
65	20	300	100	90	205	Portugais	109
225	105	435	100	105	200	Polonais	110
70	-	35	-	20	-	Juif	111
30	10	-	-	10	-	Jamaïquain	112
-	-	20	40	-	45	Philippin	113
185	115	290	90	115	85	Ukrainien	114
						selon l'identité autochtone	
20	30	-	-	40	15	Total de la population ayant une identité autochtone (10)	115
5,750	3,455	8,485	4,420	2,560	6,225	Total de la population non autochtone	116
						selon l'origine autochtone	
85	55	120	20	70	115	Total de la population ayant une origine autochtone (11)	117
5,685	3,425	8,370	4,405	2,520	6,125	Total de la population non autochtone	118
						selon le statut d'Indien inscrit	
-	-	10	-	20	10	Oui, Indien inscrit (12)	119
5,765	3,475	8,485	4,425	2,585	6,230	Non, pas un Indien inscrit	120

Table 1. Selected Characteristics for Census Tracts, 2001 Census – 100% Data and 20% Sample Data

No.	Characteristics	Toronto 0620	Toronto 0621	Toronto 0622	Toronto 0623	Toronto 0624	Toronto 0625
	POPULATION CHARACTERISTICS						
	by visible minority groups						
121	Total visible minority population	90	110	285	100	295	35
122	Chinese	10	25	35	10	65	-
123	South Asian	15	-	70	55	15	25
124	Black	20	35	105	10	110	-
125	Filipino	-	-	35	-	40	10
126	Latin American	20	-	10	15	-	-
127	Southeast Asian	-	-	-	-	-	-
128	Arab	-	-	-	-	10	10
129	West Asian	-	-	-	-	10	-
130	Korean	-	-	-	-	-	-
131	Japanese	10	40	10	-	15	-
132	Visible minority, n.i.e. (13)	15	10	-	10	30	-
133	Multiple visible minorities (14)	-	-	30	-	-	-
	by citizenship						
134	Canadian citizenship (15)	3,055	5,450	6,255	3,455	5,560	465
135	Citizenship other than Canadian	125	180	205	120	330	35
	by place of birth of respondent						
136	Non-immigrant population	2,475	4,870	5,565	3,025	4,820	400
137	Born in province of residence	2,210	4,315	4,965	2,525	4,065	385
138	Immigrant population (16)	660	750	890	540	1,060	100
139	United States	20	70	25	35	35	10
140	Central and South America	10	10	30	15	15	-
141	Caribbean and Bermuda	15	35	60	25	85	-
142	United Kingdom	150	325	330	265	465	25
143	Other Europe (17)	425	210	340	160	350	35
144	Africa	30	95	30	-	15	10
145	Asia and the Middle East	10	15	60	40	85	15
146	Oceania and other (18)	10	-	15	-	10	-
147	Non-permanent residents (19)	45	10	10	10	10	-
148	**Total immigrant population**	**660**	**750**	**890**	**535**	**1,060**	**100**
	by period of immigration						
149	Before 1961	240	255	240	240	215	25
150	1961-1970	165	145	160	105	250	25
151	1971-1980	100	210	230	100	235	30
152	1981-1990	55	40	145	55	90	10
153	1991-2001 (20)	95	110	115	40	270	10
154	1991-1995	95	30	65	25	155	10
155	1996-2001 (20)	-	75	50	15	110	-
	by age at immigration						
156	0-4 years	65	100	125	80	120	25
157	5-19 years	260	275	215	150	335	30
158	20 years and over	330	375	545	310	610	45
159	**Total population**	**3,180**	**5,625**	**6,455**	**3,575**	**5,890**	**505**
	by religion						
160	Catholic (21)	760	1,450	2,125	1,095	2,330	190
161	Protestant	1,725	2,785	3,030	1,735	2,445	225
162	Christian Orthodox	200	15	10	-	25	-
163	Christian, n.i.e. (22)	45	175	105	90	50	10
164	Muslim	10	15	20	25	30	35
165	Jewish	-	35	-	-	-	-
166	Buddhist	10	-	-	10	15	-
167	Hindu	10	-	20	-	15	-
168	Sikh	-	-	-	35	-	-
169	Eastern religions (23)	-	-	-	-	-	-
170	Other religions (24)	-	-	-	10	-	-
171	No religious affiliation (25)	435	1,150	1,150	590	985	40
172	**Total population 15 years and over**	**2,695**	**4,505**	**5,105**	**3,085**	**4,725**	**415**
	by generation status						
173	1st generation (26)	685	730	875	550	1,025	100
174	2nd generation (27)	580	1,115	1,145	640	1,070	80
175	3rd generation and over (28)	1,430	2,655	3,090	1,895	2,625	235
176	**Total population 1 year and over (29)**	**3,160**	**5,580**	**6,355**	**3,560**	**5,845**	**505**
	by place of residence 1 year ago (mobility)						
177	Non-movers	2,865	5,115	5,715	3,100	5,230	450
178	Movers	295	460	645	460	615	55
179	Non-migrants	55	265	295	235	290	25
180	Migrants	240	195	355	220	325	30
181	Internal migrants	235	190	335	210	315	30
182	Intraprovincial migrants	215	160	320	180	315	35
183	Interprovincial migrants	20	25	20	35	10	-
184	External migrants	10	-	15	-	10	-

Tableau 1. Certaines caractéristiques des secteurs de recensement, recensement de 2001 – Données intégrales et données-échantillon (20 %)

Toronto 0626	Toronto 0630	Toronto 0631	Toronto 0632	Toronto 0633	Toronto 0634	Caractéristiques	N°
						CARACTÉRISTIQUES DE LA POPULATION	
						selon les groupes de minorités visibles	
125	130	400	45	60	215	Total de la population des minorités visibles	121
15	15	95	-	-	50	Chinois	122
30	50	95	-	10	85	Sud-Asiatique	123
30	-	40	-	-	-	Noir	124
-	-	10	15	-	45	Philippin	125
-	-	20	-	15	-	Latino-Américain	126
10	15	30	-	-	-	Asiatique du Sud-Est	127
20	15	-	-	-	-	Arabe	128
-	-	25	-	10	-	Asiatique occidental	129
-	10	15	-	15	-	Coréen	130
10	25	15	-	-	20	Japonais	131
15	-	35	20	-	10	Minorité visible, n.i.a. (13)	132
-	-	20	-	-	-	Minorités visibles multiples (14)	133
						selon la citoyenneté	
5,590	3,375	8,170	4,225	2,470	6,045	Citoyenneté canadienne (15)	134
185	110	325	200	125	185	Citoyenneté autre que canadienne	135
						selon le lieu de naissance du répondant	
4,820	2,845	7,110	3,755	2,205	5,160	Population non immigrante	136
4,235	2,485	6,065	3,075	1,805	4,475	Née dans la province de résidence	137
950	645	1,335	650	395	1,065	Population immigrante (16)	138
75	45	40	15	20	60	États-Unis	139
20	-	35	-	30	15	Amérique centrale et du Sud	140
15	-	25	10	-	20	Caraïbes et Bermudes	141
370	210	405	345	160	425	Royaume-Uni	142
410	345	590	260	145	435	Autre Europe (17)	143
15	-	20	-	-	15	Afrique	144
40	35	170	15	30	90	Asie et Moyen-Orient	145
10	-	35	10	-	-	Océanie et autre (18)	146
-	-	50	15	-	10	Résidents non permanents (19)	147
945	**640**	**1,335**	**650**	**395**	**1,065**	**Population immigrante totale**	148
						selon la période d'immigration	
365	265	150	260	125	365	Avant 1961	149
215	165	360	145	75	315	1961-1970	150
200	60	300	105	70	180	1971-1980	151
90	115	260	85	55	120	1981-1990	152
80	40	260	65	55	85	1991-2001 (20)	153
50	15	145	10	15	75	1991-1995	154
35	30	115	55	40	15	1996-2001 (20)	155
						selon l'âge à l'immigration	
175	70	220	75	55	140	0-4 ans	156
235	175	510	200	125	310	5-19 ans	157
535	395	605	370	215	615	20 ans et plus	158
5,770	**3,480**	**8,490**	**4,425**	**2,600**	**6,240**	**Population totale**	159
						selon la religion	
1,565	1,055	3,705	1,295	915	1,650	Catholique (21)	160
2,775	1,590	3,135	2,125	910	3,130	Protestante	161
70	-	110	25	50	75	Orthodoxe chrétienne	162
130	150	110	190	55	140	Chrétiennes, n.i.a. (22)	163
-	15	45	-	10	10	Musulmane	164
35	-	25	-	-	-	Juive	165
-	-	-	-	-	-	Bouddhiste	166
20	-	15	-	-	45	Hindoue	167
10	45	15	-	-	-	Sikh	168
-	-	65	-	-	10	Religions orientales (23)	169
-	-	-	20	-	-	Autres religions (24)	170
1,165	620	1,270	765	655	1,185	Aucune appartenance religieuse (25)	171
4,670	**2,905**	**5,580**	**3,560**	**2,055**	**4,915**	**Population totale de 15 ans et plus**	172
						selon le statut des générations	
940	630	1,295	655	380	1,085	1re génération (26)	173
1,160	670	1,540	835	375	1,225	2e génération (27)	174
2,575	1,605	2,745	2,060	1,300	2,600	3e génération et plus (28)	175
5,725	**3,465**	**8,350**	**4,405**	**2,570**	**6,170**	**Population totale de 1 an et plus (29)**	176
						selon le lieu de résidence 1 an auparavant (mobilité)	
5,330	3,085	7,535	3,845	2,140	5,005	Personnes n'ayant pas déménagé	177
390	375	815	560	425	1,165	Personnes ayant déménagé	178
105	145	305	240	310	575	Non-migrants	179
290	230	510	315	115	585	Migrants	180
240	230	470	285	100	570	Migrants internes	181
225	215	370	255	95	515	Migrants infraprovinciaux	182
15	10	100	30	10	50	Migrants interprovinciaux	183
45	-	40	30	15	25	Migrants externes	184

Table 1. Selected Characteristics for Census Tracts, 2001 Census – 100% Data and 20% Sample Data

No.	Characteristics	Toronto 0620	Toronto 0621	Toronto 0622	Toronto 0623	Toronto 0624	Toronto 0625
	POPULATION CHARACTERISTICS						
185	**Total population 5 years and over (30)**	**3,110**	**5,345**	**6,065**	**3,425**	**5,590**	**475**
	by place of residence 5 years ago (mobility)						
186	Non-movers	2,225	4,025	3,535	1,975	3,750	335
187	Movers	885	1,320	2,525	1,450	1,840	140
188	Non-migrants	280	845	1,355	730	1,010	100
189	Migrants	605	475	1,170	720	830	40
190	Internal migrants	565	390	1,115	695	715	40
191	Intraprovincial migrants	525	355	1,065	570	655	40
192	Interprovincial migrants	35	35	55	125	65	-
193	External migrants	45	90	55	25	105	-
194	**Total population 15 to 24 years**	**410**	**1,135**	**950**	**375**	**980**	**80**
	by school attendance						
195	Not attending school	140	355	370	190	375	35
196	Attending school full time	260	710	540	170	565	45
197	Attending school part time	10	70	40	10	45	10
198	**Total population 15 years and over**	**2,700**	**4,510**	**5,105**	**3,085**	**4,725**	**420**
	by highest level of schooling						
199	Less than grade 9 (31)	145	95	240	270	110	40
200	Grades 9-13 without high school graduation certificate	625	885	1,110	805	1,210	115
201	Grades 9-13 with high school graduation certificate	370	860	795	500	770	45
202	Some postsecondary without degree, certificate or diploma (32)	330	690	675	325	565	55
203	Trades certificate or diploma (33)	295	350	465	290	420	55
204	College certificate or diploma (34)	475	810	1,155	545	960	40
205	University certificate below bachelor's degree	75	75	65	50	110	10
206	University with bachelor's degree or higher	390	745	600	305	570	65
	by combinations of unpaid work						
207	Males 15 years and over	1,425	2,250	2,495	1,435	2,355	220
208	Reported unpaid work (35)	1,265	2,085	2,250	1,250	2,165	185
209	Housework and child care and care or assistance to seniors	60	160	240	70	180	-
210	Housework and child care only	265	620	730	370	590	55
211	Housework and care or assistance to seniors only	115	145	190	90	140	15
212	Child care and care or assistance to seniors only	-	-	-	-	-	-
213	Housework only	805	1,130	1,060	700	1,205	120
214	Child care only	15	20	20	25	25	-
215	Care or assistance to seniors only	10	-	10	-	30	-
216	Females 15 years and over	1,275	2,260	2,610	1,650	2,370	200
217	Reported unpaid work (35)	1,215	2,155	2,440	1,500	2,230	185
218	Housework and child care and care or assistance to seniors	105	230	345	125	240	10
219	Housework and child care only	340	730	850	445	700	70
220	Housework and care or assistance to seniors only	185	235	255	195	230	35
221	Child care and care or assistance to seniors only	-	-	-	-	-	-
222	Housework only	590	935	975	740	1,045	65
223	Child care only	-	-	-	-	10	-
224	Care or assistance to seniors only	-	10	20	-	-	-
	by labour force activity						
225	Males 15 years and over	1,425	2,250	2,495	1,435	2,355	215
226	In the labour force	1,095	1,945	2,025	1,025	2,035	150
227	Employed	1,055	1,835	1,940	990	1,990	155
228	Unemployed	45	105	80	35	45	-
229	Not in the labour force	330	305	475	415	315	65
230	Participation rate	76.8	86.4	81.2	71.4	86.4	69.8
231	Employment rate	74.0	81.6	77.8	69.0	84.5	72.1
232	Unemployment rate	4.1	5.4	4.0	3.4	2.2	-
233	Females 15 years and over	1,270	2,260	2,610	1,645	2,370	200
234	In the labour force	885	1,740	1,855	955	1,670	155
235	Employed	855	1,700	1,780	895	1,625	155
236	Unemployed	30	40	70	60	45	-
237	Not in the labour force	385	520	755	695	695	45
238	Participation rate	69.7	77.0	71.1	58.1	70.5	77.5
239	Employment rate	67.3	75.2	68.2	54.4	68.6	77.5
240	Unemployment rate	3.4	2.3	3.8	6.3	2.7	-

Tableau 1. Certaines caractéristiques des secteurs de recensement, recensement de 2001 – Données intégrales et données-échantillon (20 %)

Toronto 0626	Toronto 0630	Toronto 0631	Toronto 0632	Toronto 0633	Toronto 0634	Caractéristiques	N^{o}
						CARACTÉRISTIQUES DE LA POPULATION	
5,480	**3,315**	**7,520**	**4,150**	**2,420**	**5,845**	**Population totale de 5 ans et plus (30)**	185
						selon le lieu de résidence 5 ans auparavant (mobilité)	
3,735	2,225	3,205	2,535	1,110	3,700	Personnes n'ayant pas déménagé	186
1,745	1,085	4,315	1,615	1,310	2,150	Personnes ayant déménagé	187
610	460	1,185	775	705	1,040	Non-migrants	188
1,135	625	3,135	835	605	1,105	Migrants	189
1,095	615	2,970	770	560	1,055	Migrants internes	190
950	595	2,670	735	455	930	Migrants infraprovinciaux	191
140	25	300	35	110	120	Migrants interprovinciaux	192
40	10	165	65	40	55	Migrants externes	193
695	**445**	**720**	**510**	**310**	**700**	**Population totale de 15 à 24 ans**	194
						selon la fréquentation scolaire	
170	110	250	245	165	310	Ne fréquentant pas l'école	195
495	325	445	220	135	380	Fréquentant l'école à plein temps	196
35	10	25	50	10	15	Fréquentant l'école à temps partiel	197
4,675	**2,905**	**5,580**	**3,560**	**2,055**	**4,915**	**Population totale de 15 ans et plus**	198
						selon le plus haut niveau de scolarité atteint	
105	115	140	170	80	260	Niveau inférieur à la 9e année (31)	199
855	750	795	720	490	1,060	De la 9e à la 13e année sans certificat d'études secondaires	200
575	350	825	470	345	940	De la 9e à la 13e année avec certificat d'études secondaires	201
420	365	690	495	225	480	Études postsecondaires partielles sans grade, certificat ou diplôme (32)	202
585	320	475	325	200	455	Certificat ou diplôme d'une école de métiers (33)	203
690	495	1,275	725	445	1,025	Certificat ou diplôme collégial (34)	204
140	70	100	70	40	80	Certificat universitaire inférieur au baccalauréat	205
1,305	430	1,290	575	225	600	Études universitaires avec baccalauréat ou diplôme supérieur	206
						selon les combinaisons de travail non rémunéré	
2,370	1,520	2,760	1,735	905	2,425	Hommes de 15 ans et plus	207
2,145	1,325	2,600	1,580	835	2,200	Travail non rémunéré déclaré (35)	208
145	105	255	145	55	165	Travaux ménagers et soins aux enfants et soins ou aide aux personnes âgées	209
640	390	1,445	530	335	790	Travaux ménagers et soins aux enfants seulement	210
265	115	130	145	30	155	Travaux ménagers et soins ou aide aux personnes âgées seulement	211
15	-	10	-	-	-	Soins aux enfants et soins ou aide aux personnes âgées seulement	212
1,060	715	725	740	390	1,040	Travaux ménagers seulement	213
25	10	20	15	20	10	Soins aux enfants seulement	214
-	-	20	10	10	40	Soins ou aide aux personnes âgées seulement	215
2,300	1,385	2,820	1,820	1,150	2,490	Femmes de 15 ans et plus	216
2,210	1,320	2,695	1,750	1,060	2,360	Travail non rémunéré déclaré (35)	217
280	190	370	235	95	235	Travaux ménagers et soins aux enfants et soins ou aide aux personnes âgées	218
610	360	1,450	620	410	820	Travaux ménagers et soins aux enfants seulement	219
230	220	135	165	65	210	Travaux ménagers et soins ou aide aux personnes âgées seulement	220
-	-	-	-	-	-	Soins aux enfants et soins ou aide aux personnes âgées seulement	221
1,070	545	730	730	475	1,075	Travaux ménagers seulement	222
10	-	-	-	15	10	Soins aux enfants seulement	223
-	10	10	10	-	-	Soins ou aide aux personnes âgées seulement	224
						selon l'activité	
2,370	1,515	2,765	1,735	910	2,425	Hommes de 15 ans et plus	225
1,955	1,230	2,420	1,325	765	1,950	Population active	226
1,905	1,205	2,385	1,305	740	1,875	Personnes occupées	227
50	25	25	15	25	75	Chômeurs	228
410	290	345	405	135	475	Inactifs	229
82.5	81.2	87.5	76.4	84.1	80.4	Taux d'activité	230
80.4	79.5	86.3	75.2	81.3	77.3	Taux d'emploi	231
2.6	2.0	1.0	1.1	3.3	3.8	Taux de chômage	232
2,305	1,385	2,815	1,820	1,145	2,490	Femmes de 15 ans et plus	233
1,575	935	2,130	1,200	830	1,715	Population active	234
1,520	905	2,070	1,150	800	1,650	Personnes occupées	235
55	30	60	50	35	65	Chômeuses	236
725	450	695	620	315	775	Inactives	237
68.3	67.5	75.7	65.9	72.5	68.9	Taux d'activité	238
65.9	65.3	73.5	63.2	69.9	66.3	Taux d'emploi	239
3.5	3.2	2.8	4.2	4.2	3.8	Taux de chômage	240

Table 1. Selected Characteristics for Census Tracts, 2001 Census – 100% Data and 20% Sample Data

No.	Characteristics	Toronto 0620	Toronto 0621	Toronto 0622	Toronto 0623	Toronto 0624	Toronto 0625
	POPULATION CHARACTERISTICS						
	by labour force activity – concluded						
241	Both sexes - Participation rate	73.5	81.8	75.9	64.0	78.5	73.8
242	15-24 years	74.1	73.6	80.1	73.3	79.7	68.8
243	25 years and over	73.4	84.4	75.1	62.9	78.1	74.6
244	Both sexes - Employment rate	70.7	78.5	73.0	60.9	76.5	74.7
245	15-24 years	64.6	64.8	72.6	62.2	74.6	68.8
246	25 years and over	72.1	83.1	73.0	60.8	77.1	72.1
247	Both sexes - Unemployment rate	3.5	3.9	3.9	5.1	2.4	-
248	15-24 years	13.1	12.0	10.5	16.4	5.8	-
249	25 years and over	2.1	1.6	2.4	3.2	1.5	-
250	**Total labour force 15 years and over**	**1,985**	**3,685**	**3,880**	**1,980**	**3,710**	**305**
	by industry based on the 1997 NAICS						
251	Industry - Not applicable (36)	20	15	20	10	10	-
252	All industries (37)	1,960	3,670	3,860	1,975	3,695	305
253	11 Agriculture, forestry, fishing and hunting	260	10	45	15	10	-
254	21 Mining and oil and gas extraction	-	10	10	15	10	-
255	22 Utilities	15	45	35	-	35	-
256	23 Construction	115	100	190	110	155	20
257	31-33 Manufacturing	245	690	640	360	685	45
258	41 Wholesale trade	235	360	305	160	265	25
259	44-45 Retail trade	155	365	420	130	370	25
260	48-49 Transportation and warehousing	75	190	255	160	330	20
261	51 Information and cultural industries	75	60	60	35	110	15
262	52 Finance and insurance	70	165	155	60	135	10
263	53 Real estate and rental and leasing	20	55	70	35	25	15
264	54 Professional, scientific and technical services	110	230	240	125	245	25
265	55 Management of companies and enterprises	10	-	10	-	-	-
266	56 Administrative and support, waste management and remediation services	105	140	100	50	105	10
267	61 Educational services	70	315	215	85	240	10
268	62 Health care and social assistance	150	290	380	190	370	15
269	71 Arts, entertainment and recreation	10	80	105	75	125	-
270	72 Accommodation and food services	75	230	260	100	260	25
271	81 Other services (except public administration)	120	145	180	160	110	40
272	91 Public administration	60	200	190	105	105	-
	by class of worker						
273	Class of worker - Not applicable (36)	20	15	20	10	10	-
274	All classes of worker (37)	1,965	3,670	3,860	1,975	3,695	305
275	Paid workers	1,670	3,490	3,660	1,795	3,535	265
276	Employees	1,465	3,355	3,550	1,710	3,460	260
277	Self-employed (incorporated)	205	130	110	90	65	-
278	Self-employed (unincorporated)	235	160	190	170	155	40
279	Unpaid family workers	50	20	10	-	10	-
	by occupation based on the 2001 NOC-S						
280	Male labour force 15 years and over	1,095	1,940	2,025	1,020	2,035	150
281	Occupation - Not applicable (36)	15	10	10	-	-	-
282	All occupations (37)	1,080	1,935	2,015	1,020	2,025	150
283	A Management occupations	225	325	270	145	320	15
284	B Business, finance and administration occupations	75	210	105	85	230	25
285	C Natural and applied sciences and related occupations	45	205	215	95	220	20
286	D Health occupations	15	15	40	20	25	-
287	E Occupations in social science, education, government service and religion	20	95	120	25	65	-
288	F Occupations in art, culture, recreation and sport	25	20	50	-	30	10
289	G Sales and service occupations	170	470	445	200	510	10
290	H Trades, transport and equipment operators and related occupations	250	330	550	320	420	55
291	I Occupations unique to primary industry	225	25	60	30	35	-
292	J Occupations unique to processing, manufacturing and utilities	30	235	170	105	170	25
293	Female labour force 15 years and over	890	1,740	1,855	960	1,675	155
294	Occupation - Not applicable (36)	10	10	10	10	-	-
295	All occupations (37)	885	1,735	1,845	950	1,670	155
296	A Management occupations	85	150	130	125	110	15
297	B Business, finance and administration occupations	300	580	575	210	555	60
298	C Natural and applied sciences and related occupations	20	15	50	35	65	-
299	D Health occupations	60	105	185	95	155	10

Tableau 1. Certaines caractéristiques des secteurs de recensement, recensement de 2001 – Données intégrales et données-échantillon (20 %)

Toronto 0626	Toronto 0630	Toronto 0631	Toronto 0632	Toronto 0633	Toronto 0634	Caractéristiques	N°
						CARACTÉRISTIQUES DE LA POPULATION	
						selon l'activité – fin	
75.6	74.4	81.3	71.1	77.9	74.6	Les deux sexes - Taux d'activité	241
69.1	71.1	68.8	75.7	81.0	77.1	15-24 ans	242
76.9	74.8	83.2	70.1	77.6	74.3	25 ans et plus	243
73.3	72.6	79.9	69.2	74.9	71.6	Les deux sexes - Taux d'emploi	244
61.9	65.6	63.9	73.8	73.0	65.7	15-24 ans	245
75.5	73.9	82.2	68.3	75.3	72.6	25 ans et plus	246
3.1	2.5	1.9	2.8	3.8	3.8	Les deux sexes - Taux de chômage	247
11.5	7.8	7.1	3.8	7.8	14.0	15-24 ans	248
1.8	1.4	1.2	2.6	3.0	2.1	25 ans et plus	249
3,535	**2,160**	**4,540**	**2,530**	**1,600**	**3,665**	**Population active totale de 15 ans et plus**	250
						selon l'industrie basée sur le SCIAN de 1997	
-	10	10	15	20	15	Industrie - Sans objet (36)	251
3,530	2,155	4,535	2,515	1,580	3,645	Toutes les industries (37)	252
145	300	25	-	10	60	11 Agriculture, foresterie, pêche et chasse	253
30	-	-	-	-	-	21 Extraction minière et extraction de pétrole et de gaz	254
40	20	65	10	30	15	22 Services publics	255
195	155	160	110	60	190	23 Construction	256
520	345	700	440	380	820	31-33 Fabrication	257
300	155	640	285	160	285	41 Commerce de gros	258
220	80	460	275	120	365	44-45 Commerce de détail	259
165	120	420	185	155	235	48-49 Transport et entreposage	260
60	25	180	75	30	60	51 Industrie de l'information et industrie culturelle	261
115	50	260	105	40	110	52 Finance et assurances	262
55	50	65	25	30	95	53 Services immobiliers et services de location et de location à bail	263
375	185	385	170	70	255	54 Services professionnels, scientifiques et techniques	264
20	-	15	10	-	-	55 Gestion de sociétés et d'entreprises	265
195	50	110	85	50	195	56 Services administratifs, services de soutien, services de gestion des déchets et services d'assainissement	266
260	165	275	210	95	195	61 Services d'enseignement	267
175	115	270	185	140	235	62 Soins de santé et assistance sociale	268
265	10	45	60	20	40	71 Arts, spectacles et loisirs	269
140	130	120	90	80	250	72 Hébergement et services de restauration	270
110	120	120	125	75	105	81 Autres services, sauf les administrations publiques	271
135	75	215	70	50	130	91 Administrations publiques	272
						selon la catégorie de travailleurs	
10	10	-	10	20	15	Catégorie de travailleurs - Sans objet (36)	273
3,535	2,155	4,535	2,520	1,585	3,645	Toutes les catégories de travailleurs (37)	274
3,080	1,865	4,315	2,345	1,455	3,375	Travailleurs rémunérés	275
2,780	1,700	4,135	2,230	1,395	3,280	Employés	276
295	170	180	115	60	95	Travailleurs autonomes (entreprise constituée en société)	277
420	285	220	165	130	260	Travailleurs autonomes (entreprise non constituée en société)	278
35	-	10	10	-	10	Travailleurs familiaux non rémunérés	279
						selon la profession basée sur la CNP-S de 2001	
1,960	1,225	2,415	1,330	770	1,950	Hommes actifs de 15 ans et plus	280
10	-	-	-	10	-	Profession - Sans objet (36)	281
1,955	1,225	2,410	1,325	765	1,945	Toutes les professions (37)	282
470	215	845	245	90	415	A Gestion	283
155	60	210	160	115	200	B Affaires, finance et administration	284
220	115	280	125	65	125	C Sciences naturelles et appliquées et professions apparentées	285
40	10	20	10	15	25	D Secteur de la santé	286
110	50	75	35	15	25	E Sciences sociales, enseignement, administration publique et religion	287
35	15	35	45	10	15	F Arts, culture, sports et loisirs	288
255	195	445	260	145	400	G Ventes et services	289
385	325	395	340	205	390	H Métiers, transport et machinerie	290
175	175	-	20	-	50	I Professions propres au secteur primaire	291
100	70	95	90	110	300	J Transformation, fabrication et services d'utilité publique	292
1,580	930	2,130	1,200	835	1,715	Femmes actives de 15 ans et plus	293
-	-	-	10	15	10	Profession - Sans objet (36)	294
1,580	930	2,125	1,190	820	1,700	Toutes les professions (37)	295
235	135	330	120	60	220	A Gestion	296
470	280	685	295	310	490	B Affaires, finance et administration	297
60	20	85	55	10	40	C Sciences naturelles et appliquées et professions apparentées	298
105	70	115	90	45	145	D Secteur de la santé	299

Table 1. Selected Characteristics for Census Tracts, 2001 Census – 100% Data and 20% Sample Data

No.	Characteristics	Toronto 0620	Toronto 0621	Toronto 0622	Toronto 0623	Toronto 0624	Toronto 0625
	POPULATION CHARACTERISTICS						
	by occupation based on the 2001 NOC-S – concluded						
300	E Occupations in social science, education, government service and religion	70	230	180	110	190	20
301	F Occupations in art, culture, recreation and sport	30	50	35	35	35	-
302	G Sales and service occupations	180	560	555	260	445	20
303	H Trades, transport and equipment operators and related occupations	30	-	30	25	20	-
304	I Occupations unique to primary industry	90	-	20	10	10	-
305	J Occupations unique to processing, manufacturing and utilities	25	35	90	45	90	25
306	**Total employed labour force 15 years and over by place of work**	**1,910**	**3,540**	**3,725**	**1,880**	**3,620**	**305**
307	Males	1,055	1,840	1,940	990	1,990	150
308	Usual place of work	725	1,560	1,640	825	1,760	125
309	At home	185	85	60	90	50	15
310	Outside Canada	10	-	-	-	15	-
311	No fixed workplace address	135	190	240	65	175	10
312	Females	855	1,700	1,780	895	1,625	150
313	Usual place of work	620	1,570	1,625	785	1,510	140
314	At home	195	70	90	80	80	10
315	Outside Canada	-	-	-	-	-	-
316	No fixed workplace address	40	65	65	30	35	-
317	**Total employed labour force 15 years and over with usual place of work or no fixed workplace address by mode of transportation**	**1,520**	**3,390**	**3,570**	**1,705**	**3,480**	**285**
318	Males	860	1,750	1,880	895	1,930	135
319	Car, truck, van, as driver	770	1,485	1,610	715	1,650	120
320	Car, truck, van, as passenger	10	135	120	75	140	-
321	Public transit	10	40	85	10	25	-
322	Walked	70	65	30	65	75	15
323	Other method	-	20	35	25	40	-
324	Females	660	1,635	1,685	815	1,550	145
325	Car, truck, van, as driver	580	1,340	1,345	580	1,280	110
326	Car, truck, van, as passenger	50	125	175	40	115	-
327	Public transit	10	60	70	50	55	-
328	Walked	20	100	95	125	90	15
329	Other method	10	10	10	25	-	-
330	**Total population 15 years and over who worked since January 1, 2000 by language used at work**	**2,100**	**3,925**	**4,145**	**2,165**	**3,995**	**330**
331	Single responses	1,870	3,810	4,020	2,075	3,860	330
332	English	1,855	3,810	4,015	2,070	3,860	325
333	French	-	-	-	-	-	-
334	Non-official languages (5)	15	-	-	-	-	-
335	Chinese, n.o.s.	-	-	-	-	-	-
336	Cantonese	-	-	-	-	-	-
337	Other languages (6)	-	-	-	-	-	-
338	Multiple responses	235	115	125	90	130	-
339	English and French	85	65	75	65	75	-
340	English and non-official language	150	55	50	25	50	-
341	French and non-official language	-	-	-	-	-	-
342	English, French and non-official language	-	-	-	-	10	-
	DWELLING AND HOUSEHOLD CHARACTERISTICS						
343	**Total number of occupied private dwellings by tenure**	**1,100**	**1,655**	**2,225**	**1,660**	**1,965**	**180**
344	Owned	925	1,620	1,680	840	1,590	130
345	Rented	175	35	545	820	380	45
346	Band housing	-	-	-	-	-	-
	by structural type of dwelling						
347	Single-detached house	1,020	1,105	1,415	620	1,340	160
348	Semi-detached house	20	265	35	45	-	-
349	Row house	10	275	490	10	305	-
350	Apartment, detached duplex	20	-	25	125	10	10
351	Apartment, building that has five or more storeys	-	-	170	635	215	-
352	Apartment, building that has fewer than five storeys (38)	-	10	95	230	90	-
353	Other single-attached house	10	-	-	-	-	-
354	Movable dwelling (39)	25	-	-	-	-	-

Tableau 1. Certaines caractéristiques des secteurs de recensement, recensement de 2001 – Données intégrales et données-échantillon (20 %)

Toronto 0626	Toronto 0630	Toronto 0631	Toronto 0632	Toronto 0633	Toronto 0634	Caractéristiques	N°
						CARACTÉRISTIQUES DE LA POPULATION	
						selon la profession basée sur la CNP-S de 2001 - fin	
220	90	280	160	115	180	E Sciences sociales, enseignement, administration publique et religion	300
50	20	80	55	10	75	F Arts, culture, sports et loisirs	301
300	155	445	325	185	345	G Ventes et services	302
30	20	60	30	15	30	H Métiers, transport et machinerie	303
70	130	20	-	10	30	I Professions propres au secteur primaire	304
30	-	30	65	75	140	J Transformation, fabrication et services d'utilité publique	305
3,425	**2,105**	**4,455**	**2,460**	**1,540**	**3,525**	**Population active occupée totale de 15 ans et plus**	306
						selon le lieu de travail	
1,905	1,205	2,385	1,310	740	1,875	Hommes	307
1,400	880	2,035	1,115	575	1,575	Lieu habituel de travail	308
260	220	115	40	15	90	À domicile	309
15	10	-	-	-	10	En dehors du Canada	310
230	105	225	150	145	200	Sans adresse de travail fixe	311
1,520	905	2,075	1,150	800	1,650	Femmes	312
1,210	670	1,800	1,025	715	1,490	Lieu habituel de travail	313
230	185	190	80	45	75	À domicile	314
-	-	10	-	-	10	En dehors du Canada	315
80	35	70	45	35	75	Sans adresse de travail fixe	316
2,920	**1,695**	**4,135**	**2,330**	**1,475**	**3,335**	**Population active occupée totale de 15 ans et plus ayant un lieu habituel de travail ou sans adresse de travail fixe**	317
						selon le mode de transport	
1,630	985	2,265	1,260	720	1,775	Hommes	318
1,500	875	2,085	1,095	580	1,595	Automobile, camion ou fourgonnette, en tant que conducteur	319
60	40	70	60	45	85	Automobile, camion ou fourgonnette, en tant que passager	320
35	15	75	25	25	20	Transport en commun	321
25	25	10	85	45	65	À pied	322
15	35	25	-	25	15	Autre moyen	323
1,290	710	1,870	1,070	755	1,565	Femmes	324
1,035	605	1,595	830	625	1,250	Automobile, camion ou fourgonnette, en tant que conductrice	325
140	35	155	130	25	110	Automobile, camion ou fourgonnette, en tant que passagère	326
50	30	50	40	35	55	Transport en commun	327
50	25	45	50	60	130	À pied	328
10	10	20	20	10	25	Autre moyen	329
3,890	**2,335**	**4,895**	**2,665**	**1,645**	**3,905**	**Population totale de 15 ans et plus ayant travaillé depuis le 1er janvier 2000**	330
						selon la langue utilisée au travail	
3,785	2,255	4,555	2,535	1,560	3,825	Réponses uniques	331
3,780	2,250	4,555	2,530	1,550	3,830	Anglais	332
10	-	-	-	10	-	Français	333
-	15	-	-	-	-	Langues non officielles (5)	334
-	-	-	-	-	-	Chinois, n.d.a.	335
-	-	-	-	-	-	Cantonais	336
-	15	-	-	-	-	Autres langues (6)	337
105	75	340	130	80	75	Réponses multiples	338
90	40	210	90	50	40	Anglais et français	339
10	30	105	35	20	35	Anglais et langue non officielle	340
-	-	-	-	-	-	Français et langue non officielle	341
-	10	25	-	10	10	Anglais, français et langue non officielle	342
						CARACTÉRISTIQUES DES LOGEMENTS ET DES MÉNAGES	
1,890	**1,175**	**2,380**	**1,565**	**1,090**	**2,140**	**Nombre total de logements privés occupés**	343
						selon le mode d'occupation	
1,690	985	2,355	1,380	860	1,935	Possédé	344
200	195	20	185	230	205	Loué	345
-	-	-	-	-	-	Logement de bande	346
						selon le type de construction résidentielle	
1,780	1,145	2,175	1,250	195	1,780	Maison individuelle non attenante	347
20	10	95	110	15	40	Maison jumelée	348
-	10	100	25	465	215	Maison en rangée	349
25	15	10	-	10	25	Appartement, duplex non attenant	350
-	-	-	80	205	-	Appartement, immeuble de cinq étages ou plus	351
20	-	-	95	200	80	Appartement, immeuble de moins de cinq étages (38)	352
30	10	-	-	-	-	Autre maison individuelle attenante	353
20	-	-	-	-	-	Logement mobile (39)	354

Table 1. Selected Characteristics for Census Tracts, 2001 Census – 100% Data and 20% Sample Data

No.	Characteristics	Toronto 0620	Toronto 0621	Toronto 0622	Toronto 0623	Toronto 0624	Toronto 0625
	DWELLING AND HOUSEHOLD CHARACTERISTICS						
	by condition of dwelling						
355	Regular maintenance only	630	1,270	1,510	1,135	1,415	100
356	Minor repairs	380	350	570	330	415	60
357	Major repairs	90	40	150	200	140	15
	by period of construction						
358	Before 1946	260	-	175	370	-	35
359	1946-1960	160	20	435	385	35	55
360	1961-1970	300	65	385	150	340	40
361	1971-1980	175	970	675	385	1,455	35
362	1981-1990	135	590	495	195	140	20
363	1991-2001 (20)	75	15	60	180	-	-
364	Average number of rooms per dwelling	7.8	8.0	7.1	5.5	7.1	7.8
365	Average number of bedrooms per dwelling	3.2	3.5	3.0	2.2	3.1	3.3
366	Average value of dwelling $	369,147	215,729	203,988	199,849	203,178	295,687
367	**Total number of private households**	**1,100**	**1,655**	**2,230**	**1,665**	**1,970**	**180**
	by household size						
368	1 person	145	105	340	620	265	30
369	2 persons	415	340	655	570	560	65
370	3 persons	205	390	440	215	390	25
371	4-5 persons	265	745	725	230	705	60
372	6 or more persons	65	80	60	30	50	-
	by household type						
373	One-family households	880	1,485	1,785	915	1,620	150
374	Multiple-family households	35	45	50	50	35	10
375	Non-family households	180	125	390	700	310	30
376	Number of persons in private households	3,155	5,630	6,455	3,560	5,890	500
377	Average number of persons in private households	2.9	3.4	2.9	2.1	3.0	2.8
378	Average number of persons per room	0.4	0.4	0.4	0.4	0.4	0.4
379	Tenant households in non-farm, non-reserve private dwellings (40)	170	35	545	820	380	45
380	Average gross rent $ (40)	843	1,336	979	773	825	853
381	Tenant households spending 30% or more of household income on gross rent (40) (41)	35	20	195	350	140	10
382	Tenant households spending from 30% to 99% of household income on gross rent (40) (41)	35	20	180	325	130	10
383	Owner households in non-farm, non-reserve private dwellings (42)	850	1,620	1,685	840	1,585	130
384	Average owner's major payments $ (42)	1,078	1,135	985	777	1,111	877
385	Owner households spending 30% or more of household income on owner's major payments (41) (42)	110	215	285	130	225	25
386	Owner households spending from 30% to 99% of household income on owner's major payments (41) (42)	100	195	265	105	175	25
	CENSUS FAMILY CHARACTERISTICS						
387	**Total number of census families in private households**	**950**	**1,575**	**1,880**	**1,015**	**1,695**	**155**
	by census family structure and size						
388	Total couple families	885	1,360	1,580	840	1,470	130
389	Total families of married couples	780	1,300	1,395	695	1,325	120
390	Without children at home	355	260	440	395	410	60
391	With children at home	425	1,040	960	300	915	60
392	1 child	155	310	370	115	300	10
393	2 children	160	495	450	140	435	25
394	3 or more children	105	235	140	50	180	20
395	Total families of common-law couples	100	65	190	140	145	15
396	Without children at home	75	20	75	65	60	10
397	With children at home	30	45	110	80	80	10
398	1 child	15	25	35	70	35	10
399	2 children	10	10	35	10	40	-
400	3 or more children	-	10	35	-	10	-
401	Total lone-parent families	70	210	305	180	225	20
402	Female parent	50	190	245	150	170	20
403	1 child	25	115	155	105	115	10
404	2 children	20	70	80	45	25	10
405	3 or more children	10	-	10	-	30	-

Tableau 1. Certaines caractéristiques des secteurs de recensement, recensement de 2001 – Données intégrales et données-échantillon (20 %)

Toronto 0626	Toronto 0630	Toronto 0631	Toronto 0632	Toronto 0633	Toronto 0634	Caractéristiques	N°
						CARACTÉRISTIQUES DES LOGEMENTS ET DES MÉNAGES	
						selon l'état du logement	
1,170	760	2,185	1,140	810	1,550	Entretien régulier seulement	355
570	290	170	365	225	500	Réparations mineures	356
150	130	25	60	60	85	Réparations majeures	357
						selon la période de construction	
410	230	10	25	40	75	Avant 1946	358
160	180	20	360	60	735	1946-1960	359
260	295	-	790	75	565	1961-1970	360
425	270	15	120	190	405	1971-1980	361
410	120	255	100	385	100	1981-1990	362
220	85	2,085	165	345	260	1991-2001 (20)	363
8.0	8.1	8.5	7.8	5.9	7.5	Nombre moyen de pièces par logement	364
3.4	3.3	3.6	3.2	2.6	3.2	Nombre moyen de chambres à coucher par logement	365
370,857	317,571	274,342	211,483	174,821	220,519	Valeur moyenne du logement $	366
1,890	**1,180**	**2,380**	**1,565**	**1,090**	**2,140**	**Nombre total de logements privés**	367
						selon la taille du ménage	
205	145	85	235	305	280	1 personne	368
660	415	455	520	370	695	2 personnes	369
335	230	460	325	200	420	3 personnes	370
610	310	1,265	445	205	675	4-5 personnes	371
75	75	115	45	10	65	6 personnes ou plus	372
						selon le genre de ménage	
1,575	985	2,215	1,275	685	1,775	Ménages unifamiliaux	373
70	35	60	45	15	35	Ménages multifamiliaux	374
245	160	110	250	390	325	Ménages non familiaux	375
5,680	3,480	8,490	4,420	2,590	6,235	Nombre de personnes dans les ménages privés	376
3.0	2.9	3.6	2.8	2.4	2.9	Nombre moyen de personnes dans les ménages privés	377
0.4	0.4	0.4	0.4	0.4	0.4	Nombre moyen de personnes par pièce	378
190	175	25	180	230	200	Ménages locataires dans les logements privés non agricoles hors réserve (40)	379
833	1,187	1,217	882	906	788	Loyer brut moyen $ (40)	380
60	55	10	55	60	85	Ménages locataires consacrant 30 % ou plus du revenu du ménage au loyer brut (40) (41)	381
55	45	15	50	60	80	Ménages locataires consacrant de 30 % à 99 % du revenu du ménage au loyer brut (40) (41)	382
1,585	895	2,360	1,375	860	1,935	Ménages propriétaires dans les logements privés non agricoles hors réserve (42)	383
1,267	1,121	1,553	1,038	1,062	1,066	Principales dépenses de propriété moyennes $ (42)	384
300	185	310	190	240	245	Ménages propriétaires consacrant 30 % ou plus du revenu du ménage aux principales dépenses de propriété (41) (42)	385
270	170	250	180	215	215	Ménages propriétaires consacrant de 30 % à 99 % du revenu du ménage aux principales dépenses de propriété (41) (42)	386
						CARACTÉRISTIQUES DES FAMILLES DE RECENSEMENT	
1,720	**1,050**	**2,330**	**1,360**	**715**	**1,855**	**Total des familles de recensement dans les ménages privés**	387
						selon la structure et la taille de la famille de recensement	
1,590	965	2,220	1,200	595	1,650	Total des familles avec conjoints	388
1,410	875	2,105	1,085	470	1,515	Total des familles avec couples mariés	389
595	380	425	455	205	555	Sans enfants à la maison	390
810	505	1,685	630	270	960	Avec enfants à la maison	391
265	160	395	235	105	320	1 enfant	392
360	215	920	280	115	440	2 enfants	393
185	120	365	110	50	200	3 enfants ou plus	394
180	90	115	115	125	140	Total des familles en union libre	395
110	50	55	60	70	65	Sans enfants à la maison	396
75	40	60	50	50	80	Avec enfants à la maison	397
30	25	30	35	25	55	1 enfant	398
30	10	20	15	10	20	2 enfants	399
15	10	10	-	15	-	3 enfants ou plus	400
130	90	105	160	120	205	Total des familles monoparentales	401
80	70	70	120	110	165	Parent de sexe féminin	402
50	40	45	65	35	110	1 enfant	403
30	20	20	40	70	45	2 enfants	404
-	10	-	15	-	15	3 enfants ou plus	405

Table 1. Selected Characteristics for Census Tracts, 2001 Census – 100% Data and 20% Sample Data

No.	Characteristics	Toronto 0620	Toronto 0621	Toronto 0622	Toronto 0623	Toronto 0624	Toronto 0625
	CENSUS FAMILY CHARACTERISTICS						
	by census family structure and size – concluded						
406	Male parent	20	20	55	25	60	-
407	1 child	-	15	40	30	35	-
408	2 children	20	10	15	-	-	-
409	3 or more children	-	-	10	-	10	-
410	**Total number of children at home**	**1,025**	**2,415**	**2,375**	**865**	**2,240**	**175**
	by age groups						
411	Under 6 years	110	310	475	195	370	35
412	6-14 years	355	775	865	300	785	55
413	15-17 years	145	365	305	75	275	25
414	18-24 years	235	735	515	150	615	40
415	25 years and over	180	225	215	145	200	25
416	Average number of children at home per census family (43)	1.1	1.5	1.3	0.8	1.3	1.2
417	**Total number of persons in private households**	**3,160**	**5,625**	**6,455**	**3,565**	**5,890**	**500**
	by census family status and living arrangements						
418	Number of non-family persons	300	280	620	845	485	45
419	Living with relatives (44)	30	70	115	65	85	-
420	Living with non-relatives only	125	105	160	155	140	10
421	Living alone	150	110	340	620	265	30
422	Number of family persons	2,860	5,345	5,840	2,720	5,405	455
423	Average number of persons per census family	3.0	3.4	3.1	2.7	3.2	2.9
424	**Total number of persons 65 years and over**	**455**	**200**	**595**	**830**	**345**	**55**
425	Number of non-family persons 65 years and over	95	55	180	350	110	20
426	Living with relatives (44)	15	15	25	10	20	-
427	Living with non-relatives only	15	-	-	-	10	-
428	Living alone	70	40	155	335	90	20
429	Number of family persons 65 years and over	360	145	415	485	235	40
	ECONOMIC FAMILY CHARACTERISTICS						
430	**Total number of economic families in private households**	**915**	**1,540**	**1,870**	**985**	**1,665**	**150**
	by size of family						
431	2 persons	390	350	680	525	555	70
432	3 persons	215	385	450	215	375	25
433	4 persons	165	540	510	165	490	35
434	5 or more persons	140	270	230	85	250	20
435	Total number of persons in economic families	2,885	5,420	5,955	2,790	5,485	455
436	Average number of persons per economic family	3.2	3.5	3.2	2.8	3.3	3.1
437	Total number of unattached individuals	270	210	500	775	410	45
	2000 INCOME CHARACTERISTICS						
	Population 15 years and over by sex and total income groups in 2000						
438	Total - Both sexes	2,700	4,510	5,110	3,085	4,725	420
439	Without income	115	225	165	55	190	10
440	With income	2,585	4,280	4,945	3,030	4,530	405
441	Under $1,000 (45)	75	205	105	85	105	20
442	$ 1,000 - $ 2,999	95	195	220	125	205	35
443	$ 3,000 - $ 4,999	60	190	250	65	220	-
444	$ 5,000 - $ 6,999	100	180	215	115	165	-
445	$ 7,000 - $ 9,999	170	195	240	120	325	20
446	$10,000 - $11,999	85	175	135	135	135	20
447	$12,000 - $14,999	155	110	235	225	210	15
448	$15,000 - $19,999	140	235	360	270	350	50
449	$20,000 - $24,999	155	240	325	315	250	55
450	$25,000 - $29,999	170	265	375	205	315	20
451	$30,000 - $34,999	190	290	380	285	345	45
452	$35,000 - $39,999	175	250	395	215	335	25
453	$40,000 - $44,999	200	235	290	190	265	15
454	$45,000 - $49,999	125	195	245	145	190	15
455	$50,000 - $59,999	175	355	475	175	370	15
456	$60,000 and over	505	985	700	365	765	55
457	Average income $ (46)	42,565	40,226	34,223	30,636	34,125	31,792
458	Median income $ (46)	32,127	32,075	29,986	26,325	29,555	22,258
459	Standard error of average income $ (46)	2,424	1,244	989	843	852	3,011

Tableau 1. Certaines caractéristiques des secteurs de recensement, recensement de 2001 – Données intégrales et données-échantillon (20 %)

Toronto 0626	Toronto 0630	Toronto 0631	Toronto 0632	Toronto 0633	Toronto 0634	Caractéristiques	N°
						CARACTÉRISTIQUES DES FAMILLES DE RECENSEMENT	
						selon la structure et la taille de la famille de recensement - fin	
45	15	35	35	15	40	Parent de sexe masculin	406
25	15	25	15	10	25	1 enfant	407
25	-	15	15	10	15	2 enfants	408
-	-	-	10	-	-	3 enfants ou plus	409
1,900	**1,185**	**3,645**	**1,495**	**785**	**2,220**	**Nombre total d'enfants à la maison**	410
						selon les groupes d'âge	
315	205	1,180	305	215	495	Moins de 6 ans	411
765	360	1,725	540	325	830	6-14 ans	412
210	160	300	195	80	240	15-17 ans	413
400	245	360	255	125	380	18-24 ans	414
205	215	75	205	30	275	25 ans et plus	415
1.1	1.1	1.6	1.1	1.1	1.2	Nombre moyen d'enfants à la maison par famille de recensement (43)	416
5,680	**3,480**	**8,490**	**4,425**	**2,595**	**6,240**	**Nombre total de personnes dans les ménages privés**	417
						selon la situation des particuliers dans la famille de recensement et des particuliers dans le ménage	
475	270	300	375	495	510	Nombre de personnes hors famille de recensement	418
80	70	160	55	40	125	Vivant avec des personnes apparentées (44)	419
190	55	55	85	150	100	Vivant avec des personnes non apparentées uniquement	420
210	145	85	235	305	280	Vivant seules	421
5,205	3,210	8,190	4,055	2,095	5,730	Nombre de personnes membres d'une famille	422
3.0	3.0	3.5	3.0	2.9	3.1	Nombre moyen de personnes par famille de recensement	423
545	**390**	**205**	**545**	**230**	**710**	**Nombre total de personnes de 65 ans et plus**	424
115	65	85	125	140	195	Nombre de personnes hors famille de recensement de 65 ans et plus	425
60	30	70	20	-	55	Vivant avec des personnes apparentées (44)	426
10	-	-	-	-	-	Vivant avec des personnes non apparentées uniquement	427
45	35	15	105	130	135	Vivant seules	428
425	325	120	420	85	515	Nombre de personnes membres d'une famille de 65 ans et plus	429
						CARACTÉRISTIQUES DES FAMILLES ÉCONOMIQUES	
1,650	**1,030**	**2,295**	**1,335**	**715**	**1,830**	**Nombre total de familles économiques dans les ménages privés**	430
						selon la taille de la famille	
665	420	460	555	300	685	2 personnes	431
330	225	460	315	210	430	3 personnes	432
405	230	925	330	125	455	4 personnes	433
250	150	445	140	75	255	5 personnes ou plus	434
5,285	3,275	8,350	4,105	2,135	5,855	Nombre total de personnes dans les familles économiques	435
3.2	3.2	3.6	3.1	3.0	3.2	Nombre moyen de personnes par famille économique	436
400	200	140	320	455	380	Nombre total de personnes hors famille économique	437
						CARACTÉRISTIQUES DU REVENU DE 2000	
						Population de 15 ans et plus selon le sexe et les tranches de revenu total en 2000	
4,670	2,905	5,580	3,560	2,055	4,915	Total - Les deux sexes	438
155	85	200	150	80	140	Sans revenu	439
4,520	2,815	5,385	3,415	1,980	4,775	Avec un revenu	440
110	70	150	75	35	135	Moins de 1 000 $ (45)	441
190	70	160	115	45	230	1 000 $ - 2 999 $	442
240	145	145	115	60	125	3 000 $ - 4 999 $	443
110	115	210	90	70	205	5 000 $ - 6 999 $	444
220	130	150	140	95	215	7 000 $ - 9 999 $	445
110	125	125	110	50	165	10 000 $ - 11 999 $	446
240	110	155	240	80	275	12 000 $ - 14 999 $	447
315	215	210	185	210	310	15 000 $ - 19 999 $	448
265	230	195	280	80	340	20 000 $ - 24 999 $	449
235	145	230	280	140	235	25 000 $ - 29 999 $	450
250	195	295	270	180	300	30 000 $ - 34 999 $	451
240	240	340	255	190	350	35 000 $ - 39 999 $	452
325	185	415	240	160	345	40 000 $ - 44 999 $	453
230	85	335	190	120	265	45 000 $ - 49 999 $	454
245	205	525	255	280	480	50 000 $ - 59 999 $	455
1,185	540	1,745	590	190	810	60 000 $ et plus	456
47,323	42,279	50,276	36,547	34,278	36,349	Revenu moyen $ (46)	457
33,828	30,240	43,850	31,744	32,084	32,119	Revenu médian $ (46)	458
1,745	5,316	1,289	1,001	1,062	922	Erreur type de revenu moyen $ (46)	459

Table 1. Selected Characteristics for Census Tracts, 2001 Census – 100% Data and 20% Sample Data

No.	Characteristics	Toronto 0620	Toronto 0621	Toronto 0622	Toronto 0623	Toronto 0624	Toronto 0625
	2000 INCOME CHARACTERISTICS						
	Population 15 years and over by sex and total income groups in 2000 – concluded						
460	Total - Males	1,425	2,255	2,495	1,435	2,355	215
461	Without income	40	85	60	10	40	-
462	With income	1,385	2,160	2,435	1,430	2,315	210
463	Under $1,000 (45)	30	105	30	30	50	20
464	$ 1,000 - $ 2,999	55	50	105	50	70	10
465	$ 3,000 - $ 4,999	10	100	95	25	105	-
466	$ 5,000 - $ 6,999	45	110	80	35	75	-
467	$ 7,000 - $ 9,999	25	35	65	20	135	10
468	$10,000 - $11,999	20	65	55	45	45	-
469	$12,000 - $14,999	65	35	60	40	75	10
470	$15,000 - $19,999	70	60	145	105	95	30
471	$20,000 - $24,999	80	105	120	160	95	25
472	$25,000 - $29,999	100	85	170	125	120	15
473	$30,000 - $34,999	125	115	155	125	140	10
474	$35,000 - $39,999	100	85	205	125	175	10
475	$40,000 - $44,999	110	55	155	110	150	20
476	$45,000 - $49,999	85	115	145	105	135	10
477	$50,000 - $59,999	85	250	295	95	265	10
478	$60,000 and over	385	790	555	240	590	40
479	Average income $ (46)	54,280	51,553	42,735	36,755	42,449	37,651
480	Median income $ (46)	37,853	47,951	38,179	32,749	39,315	28,024
481	Standard error of average income $ (46)	4,157	2,036	1,729	1,336	1,338	5,122
482	Total - Females	1,270	2,260	2,610	1,650	2,370	200
483	Without income	70	145	105	50	160	-
484	With income	1,200	2,115	2,505	1,600	2,215	200
485	Under $1,000 (45)	45	100	75	50	60	10
486	$ 1,000 - $ 2,999	45	145	115	75	135	20
487	$ 3,000 - $ 4,999	50	90	155	40	110	-
488	$ 5,000 - $ 6,999	60	65	130	80	95	-
489	$ 7,000 - $ 9,999	145	160	175	95	185	10
490	$10,000 - $11,999	65	110	80	95	95	20
491	$12,000 - $14,999	90	75	175	180	140	-
492	$15,000 - $19,999	65	175	215	165	255	20
493	$20,000 - $24,999	75	135	205	160	155	30
494	$25,000 - $29,999	70	175	205	75	200	-
495	$30,000 - $34,999	65	175	225	160	205	30
496	$35,000 - $39,999	80	160	185	90	155	20
497	$40,000 - $44,999	90	180	135	80	110	-
498	$45,000 - $49,999	45	75	100	40	55	-
499	$50,000 - $59,999	95	105	180	80	105	10
500	$60,000 and over	120	195	145	125	170	10
501	Average income $ (46)	29,070	28,656	25,943	25,159	25,405	25,483
502	Median income $ (46)	22,211	25,034	23,620	20,011	21,608	21,405
503	Standard error of average income $ (46)	1,563	1,198	851	987	874	2,850
	by composition of total income						
504	Total - Composition of income in 2000 % (47)	100.0	100.0	100.0	100.0	100.0	100.0
505	Employment income %	75.0	90.7	84.2	73.7	88.3	76.2
506	Government transfer payments %	7.2	3.3	7.3	13.2	5.2	7.3
507	Other %	17.9	6.0	8.3	13.2	6.5	16.0
	Population 15 years and over with employment income in 2000 by sex and work activity						
508	Both sexes with employment income (48)	2,040	3,840	4,060	2,115	3,885	320
509	Average employment income $	40,407	40,687	35,131	32,278	35,159	31,215
510	Standard error of average employment income $	2,076	1,336	1,121	1,069	935	2,812
511	Worked full year, full time (49)	1,225	2,255	2,535	1,235	2,135	180
512	Average employment income $	53,385	55,206	45,813	41,725	47,895	45,020
513	Standard error of average employment income $	3,166	1,756	1,464	1,300	1,212	3,623
514	Worked part year or part time (50)	800	1,520	1,440	820	1,670	135
515	Average employment income $	21,104	20,179	18,231	19,221	19,675	13,984
516	Standard error of average employment income $	1,373	1,602	1,347	1,405	1,072	2,013
517	Males with employment income (48)	1,105	2,010	2,110	1,110	2,100	165
518	Average employment income $	49,652	51,475	43,551	36,576	42,186	34,416
519	Standard error of average employment income $	3,342	2,143	1,902	1,589	1,436	4,530
520	Worked full year, full time (49)	760	1,320	1,455	660	1,290	110
521	Average employment income $	60,426	65,117	53,149	47,507	55,325	46,478
522	Standard error of average employment income $	4,645	2,535	2,322	1,849	1,718	4,900
523	Worked part year or part time (50)	340	670	630	420	770	50
524	Average employment income $	26,244	25,154	22,869	20,083	21,243	9,459
525	Standard error of average employment income $	2,242	3,129	2,719	2,023	1,767	3,830

Tableau 1. Certaines caractéristiques des secteurs de recensement, recensement de 2001 – Données intégrales et données-échantillon (20 %)

Toronto 0626	Toronto 0630	Toronto 0631	Toronto 0632	Toronto 0633	Toronto 0634	Caractéristiques	N°
						CARACTÉRISTIQUES DU REVENU DE 2000	
						Population de 15 ans et plus selon le sexe et les tranches de revenu total en 2000 – fin	
2,370	1,520	2,765	1,735	905	2,425	Total - Hommes	460
40	30	60	70	25	55	Sans revenu	461
2,330	1,490	2,705	1,665	880	2,365	Avec un revenu	462
45	30	25	25	10	25	Moins de 1 000 $ (45)	463
70	45	60	45	20	80	1 000 $ - 2 999 $	464
90	45	25	15	10	45	3 000 $ - 4 999 $	465
50	65	40	30	30	85	5 000 $ - 6 999 $	466
95	20	45	50	40	60	7 000 $ - 9 999 $	467
25	60	30	15	35	50	10 000 $ - 11 999 $	468
80	25	25	45	20	50	12 000 $ - 14 999 $	469
145	105	60	35	55	120	15 000 $ - 19 999 $	470
125	100	80	130	15	185	20 000 $ - 24 999 $	471
110	75	90	135	40	95	25 000 $ - 29 999 $	472
135	85	105	145	80	130	30 000 $ - 34 999 $	473
100	125	160	105	50	185	35 000 $ - 39 999 $	474
145	125	185	145	75	170	40 000 $ - 44 999 $	475
165	55	140	115	70	125	45 000 $ - 49 999 $	476
185	135	270	140	215	335	50 000 $ - 59 999 $	477
770	400	1,370	495	125	620	60 000 $ et plus	478
58,234	55,256	66,197	47,597	41,464	46,041	Revenu moyen $ (46)	479
42,740	38,349	59,984	40,689	40,662	41,532	Revenu médian $ (46)	480
2,815	9,900	2,090	1,602	1,803	1,500	Erreur type de revenu moyen $ (46)	481
2,300	1,385	2,820	1,820	1,145	2,490	Total - Femmes	482
120	55	135	75	50	80	Sans revenu	483
2,190	1,325	2,680	1,745	1,100	2,410	Avec un revenu	484
65	40	125	45	30	110	Moins de 1 000 $ (45)	485
120	30	100	75	25	150	1 000 $ - 2 999 $	486
150	100	120	100	55	70	3 000 $ - 4 999 $	487
65	55	170	60	45	120	5 000 $ - 6 999 $	488
125	110	100	85	60	155	7 000 $ - 9 999 $	489
85	60	95	95	15	115	10 000 $ - 11 999 $	490
165	90	130	190	55	220	12 000 $ - 14 999 $	491
170	110	145	150	155	190	15 000 $ - 19 999 $	492
140	130	115	145	70	150	20 000 $ - 24 999 $	493
120	75	145	145	100	135	25 000 $ - 29 999 $	494
120	110	195	125	100	175	30 000 $ - 34 999 $	495
145	115	180	145	140	165	35 000 $ - 39 999 $	496
175	65	235	95	85	175	40 000 $ - 44 999 $	497
65	30	190	80	50	135	45 000 $ - 49 999 $	498
60	65	255	115	65	145	50 000 $ - 59 999 $	499
415	140	370	95	65	185	60 000 $ et plus	500
35,695	27,682	34,221	25,991	28,521	26,812	Revenu moyen $ (46)	501
24,986	21,097	30,797	21,727	28,320	22,342	Revenu médian $ (46)	502
1,808	1,328	1,180	963	1,154	920	Erreur type de revenu moyen $ (46)	503
						selon la composition du revenu total	
100.0	100.0	100.0	100.0	100.0	100.0	Total - Composition du revenu en 2000 % (47)	504
86.3	80.5	94.0	81.7	85.7	85.3	Revenu d'emploi %	505
4.2	7.2	2.4	7.1	7.4	6.9	Transferts gouvernementaux %	506
9.6	12.1	3.6	11.0	6.9	7.8	Autre %	507
						Population de 15 ans et plus ayant un revenu d'emploi en 2000 selon le sexe et le travail	
3,775	2,230	4,855	2,630	1,620	3,820	Les deux sexes ayant un revenu d'emploi (48)	508
48,846	43,039	52,368	38,774	35,816	38,766	Revenu moyen d'emploi $	509
1,966	6,080	1,397	1,192	1,228	1,072	Erreur type de revenu moyen d'emploi $	510
2,220	1,350	3,300	1,630	1,075	2,450	Ayant travaillé toute l'année à plein temps (49)	511
66,007	48,284	64,961	49,419	44,459	49,260	Revenu moyen d'emploi $	512
2,950	2,075	1,567	1,465	1,411	1,357	Erreur type de revenu moyen d'emploi $	513
1,505	845	1,520	970	520	1,290	Ayant travaillé une partie de l'année ou à temps partiel (50)	514
24,375	35,899	26,129	21,480	18,583	20,695	Revenu moyen d'emploi $	515
1,563	15,549	2,306	1,460	1,455	1,262	Erreur type de revenu moyen d'emploi $	516
2,035	1,245	2,555	1,375	790	2,030	Hommes ayant un revenu d'emploi (48)	517
58,106	55,215	67,318	48,659	42,163	47,865	Revenu moyen d'emploi $	518
3,029	10,711	2,229	1,844	1,964	1,668	Erreur type de revenu moyen d'emploi $	519
1,310	850	2,040	980	535	1,470	Ayant travaillé toute l'année à plein temps (49)	520
74,597	53,259	75,131	57,498	51,026	56,990	Revenu moyen d'emploi $	521
4,238	2,980	2,217	2,041	2,186	1,936	Erreur type de revenu moyen d'emploi $	522
705	385	510	385	250	520	Ayant travaillé une partie de l'année ou à temps partiel (50)	523
28,303	60,827	37,412	26,748	23,270	24,620	Revenu moyen d'emploi $	524
2,516	33,322	6,028	2,927	2,572	2,374	Erreur type de revenu moyen d'emploi $	525

Table 1. Selected Characteristics for Census Tracts, 2001 Census – 100% Data and 20% Sample Data

No.	Characteristics	Toronto 0620	Toronto 0621	Toronto 0622	Toronto 0623	Toronto 0624	Toronto 0625
	2000 INCOME CHARACTERISTICS						
	Population 15 years and over with employment income in 2000 by sex and work activity – concluded						
526	Females with employment income (48)	935	1,830	1,950	1,005	1,785	155
527	Average employment income $	29,475	28,852	26,025	27,537	26,889	27,739
528	Standard error of average employment income $	1,856	1,291	921	1,348	974	3,206
529	Worked full year, full time (49)	465	930	1,080	575	845	65
530	Average employment income $	41,880	41,105	35,945	35,118	36,538	42,521
531	Standard error of average employment income $	2,956	1,916	1,150	1,646	1,233	5,097
532	Worked part year or part time (50)	465	845	805	400	900	90
533	Average employment income $	17,327	16,214	14,618	18,303	18,337	16,536
534	Standard error of average employment income $	1,604	1,266	1,005	1,946	1,260	2,188
	Census families by structure and family income groups in 2000						
535	Total - All census families	950	1,575	1,880	1,020	1,695	150
536	Under $10,000	10	25	30	30	40	-
537	$ 10,000 - $19,999	10	10	45	35	40	-
538	$ 20,000 - $29,999	80	45	130	110	55	25
539	$ 30,000 - $39,999	50	40	130	100	100	15
540	$ 40,000 - $49,999	75	100	140	105	120	10
541	$ 50,000 - $59,999	55	105	175	90	165	10
542	$ 60,000 - $69,999	105	130	225	115	140	20
543	$ 70,000 - $79,999	55	135	235	85	195	10
544	$ 80,000 - $89,999	65	135	175	100	180	20
545	$ 90,000 - $99,999	45	135	135	35	115	-
546	$100,000 and over	390	715	465	200	535	30
547	Average family income $	105,527	103,980	79,007	67,830	82,633	70,564
548	Median family income $	83,440	94,103	71,494	62,505	78,207	67,230
549	Standard error of average family income $	6,528	3,019	2,530	2,488	2,069	6,616
550	Total - All couple census families (51)	880	1,365	1,580	835	1,470	130
551	Under $10,000	10	-	25	10	-	-
552	$ 10,000 - $19,999	10	-	25	10	25	-
553	$ 20,000 - $29,999	70	25	90	85	25	20
554	$ 30,000 - $39,999	50	15	80	80	80	15
555	$ 40,000 - $49,999	65	40	110	90	100	10
556	$ 50,000 - $59,999	55	85	120	70	135	10
557	$ 60,000 - $69,999	110	100	210	95	115	15
558	$ 70,000 - $79,999	50	125	200	70	180	10
559	$ 80,000 - $89,999	65	130	130	100	165	15
560	$ 90,000 - $99,999	50	125	135	35	110	-
561	$100,000 and over	345	715	450	190	530	35
562	Average family income $	106,107	112,817	84,327	73,179	88,137	73,184
563	Median family income $	82,242	101,731	76,296	65,632	84,495	67,080
564	Standard error of average family income $	6,823	3,129	2,859	2,724	2,162	7,253
	Incidence of low income in 2000						
565	Total - Economic families	915	1,540	1,870	985	1,665	150
566	Low income	15	-	90	45	70	-
567	Incidence of low income in 2000 % (52)	1.5	0.6	4.7	4.6	4.0	2.7
568	Total - Unattached individuals 15 years and over	255	180	490	775	400	45
569	Low income	30	25	70	175	80	-
570	Incidence of low income in 2000 % (52)	11.6	14.1	13.5	22.6	20.2	13.1
571	Total - Population in private households	3,145	5,600	6,445	3,565	5,885	500
572	Low income	60	45	345	275	280	15
573	Incidence of low income in 2000 % (52)	1.8	0.8	5.3	7.7	4.8	2.8
	Private households by household income groups in 2000						
574	Total - All private households	1,100	1,660	2,225	1,665	1,970	180
575	Under $10,000	10	15	50	55	30	10
576	$ 10,000 - $19,999	60	25	115	270	125	10
577	$ 20,000 - $29,999	95	50	195	230	95	20
578	$ 30,000 - $39,999	80	35	145	160	125	15
579	$ 40,000 - $49,999	55	120	185	155	145	25
580	$ 50,000 - $59,999	70	105	190	145	190	10
581	$ 60,000 - $69,999	110	140	260	140	160	30
582	$ 70,000 - $79,999	55	130	240	130	225	10
583	$ 80,000 - $89,999	85	135	180	100	200	15
584	$ 90,000 - $99,999	70	160	140	50	115	10
585	$100,000 and over	415	740	520	230	560	40
586	Average household income $	100,038	103,991	75,918	55,680	78,568	71,980
587	Median household income $	82,954	93,793	68,818	47,514	73,588	66,655
588	Standard error of average household income $	5,932	3,038	2,364	2,015	2,044	6,805

Tableau 1. Certaines caractéristiques des secteurs de recensement, recensement de 2001 – Données intégrales et données-échantillon (20 %)

Toronto 0626	Toronto 0630	Toronto 0631	Toronto 0632	Toronto 0633	Toronto 0634	Caractéristiques	N°
						CARACTÉRISTIQUES DU REVENU DE 2000	
						Population de 15 ans et plus ayant un revenu d'emploi en 2000 selon le sexe et le travail – fin	
1,735	980	2,300	1,260	835	1,785	Femmes ayant un revenu d'emploi (48)	526
37,985	27,614	35,759	27,956	29,804	28,434	Revenu moyen d'emploi $	527
2,187	1,565	1,233	1,157	1,394	1,090	Erreur type de revenu moyen d'emploi $	528
910	505	1,260	645	540	975	Ayant travaillé toute l'année à plein temps (49)	529
53,647	39,846	48,571	37,131	38,007	37,573	Revenu moyen d'emploi $	530
3,530	2,205	1,596	1,486	1,601	1,449	Erreur type de revenu moyen d'emploi $	531
800	460	1,010	585	270	770	Ayant travaillé une partie de l'année ou à temps partiel (50)	532
20,905	15,117	20,464	18,013	14,208	18,051	Revenu moyen d'emploi $	533
1,872	1,501	1,358	1,396	1,425	1,325	Erreur type de revenu moyen d'emploi $	534
						Familles de recensement selon la structure et les tranches de revenu de la famille en 2000	
1,715	1,050	2,325	1,360	715	1,855	Total - Toutes les familles de recensement	535
20	15	40	10	15	10	Moins de 10 000 $	536
-	25	-	10	15	45	10 000 $ - 19 999 $	537
50	75	30	40	55	80	20 000 $ - 29 999 $	538
165	80	100	120	75	140	30 000 $ - 39 999 $	539
120	75	70	195	60	140	40 000 $ - 49 999 $	540
110	110	85	70	100	150	50 000 $ - 59 999 $	541
145	75	120	145	75	185	60 000 $ - 69 999 $	542
115	65	175	125	85	170	70 000 $ - 79 999 $	543
110	75	220	115	60	225	80 000 $ - 89 999 $	544
175	115	230	110	70	130	90 000 $ - 99 999 $	545
705	355	1,245	415	105	580	100 000 $ et plus	546
113,591	104,376	111,823	83,382	68,986	84,072	Revenu moyen des familles $	547
92,213	80,474	101,894	76,788	67,685	80,064	Revenu médian des familles $	548
4,789	14,078	2,763	2,291	2,439	2,117	Erreur type de revenu moyen des familles $	549
1,590	965	2,220	1,195	595	1,655	Total - Toutes les familles de recensement comptant un couple (51)	550
10	15	25	10	15	-	Moins de 10 000 $	551
10	10	-	-	10	35	10 000 $ - 19 999 $	552
50	75	25	30	35	60	20 000 $ - 29 999 $	553
130	60	85	95	55	125	30 000 $ - 39 999 $	554
95	60	55	120	30	105	40 000 $ - 49 999 $	555
110	95	75	65	85	130	50 000 $ - 59 999 $	556
135	70	105	145	65	145	60 000 $ - 69 999 $	557
95	60	180	120	75	145	70 000 $ - 79 999 $	558
105	75	220	105	60	210	80 000 $ - 89 999 $	559
175	115	210	110	70	130	90 000 $ - 99 999 $	560
675	335	1,235	395	105	565	100 000 $ et plus	561
116,658	107,872	114,514	87,297	73,216	87,181	Revenu moyen des familles $	562
94,628	85,016	104,093	80,443	73,538	83,305	Revenu médian des familles $	563
5,005	15,422	2,806	2,452	2,745	2,277	Erreur type de revenu moyen des familles $	564
						Fréquence des unités à faible revenu en 2000	
1,655	1,030	2,295	1,340	715	1,830	Total - Familles économiques	565
30	35	50	15	40	55	Faible revenu	566
1.9	3.4	2.1	1.3	5.3	3.0	Fréquence des unités à faible revenu en 2000 % (52)	567
380	190	140	295	460	385	Total - Personnes hors famille économique de 15 ans et plus	568
85	45	25	80	55	125	Faible revenu	569
23.2	23.8	15.5	27.4	12.6	32.2	Fréquence des unités à faible revenu en 2000 % (52)	570
5,665	3,465	8,490	4,400	2,590	6,240	Total - Population dans les ménages privés	571
185	185	185	135	185	270	Faible revenu	572
3.2	5.4	2.2	3.1	7.1	4.3	Fréquence des unités à faible revenu en 2000 % (52)	573
						Ménages privés selon les tranches de revenu du ménage en 2000	
1,890	1,180	2,380	1,560	1,090	2,140	Total - Tous les ménages privés	574
50	25	45	10	30	25	Moins de 10 000 $	575
40	30	15	90	105	140	10 000 $ - 19 999 $	576
55	60	20	80	75	105	20 000 $ - 29 999 $	577
145	90	75	125	140	170	30 000 $ - 39 999 $	578
135	85	90	200	85	155	40 000 $ - 49 999 $	579
105	145	80	95	145	200	50 000 $ - 59 999 $	580
145	95	105	165	110	185	60 000 $ - 69 999 $	581
140	65	185	100	95	170	70 000 $ - 79 999 $	582
115	80	215	120	65	205	80 000 $ - 89 999 $	583
175	120	225	105	85	145	90 000 $ - 99 999 $	584
795	385	1,320	485	150	650	100 000 $ et plus	585
112,131	100,951	113,700	79,722	61,859	81,162	Revenu moyen des ménages $	586
92,037	78,841	104,893	72,556	58,303	75,781	Revenu médian des ménages $	587
4,541	12,725	2,768	2,308	2,212	2,156	Erreur type de revenu moyen des ménages $	588

Table 1. Selected Characteristics for Census Tracts, 2001 Census – 100% Data and 20% Sample Data

No.	Characteristics	Toronto 0635	Toronto 0636	Toronto 0637	Toronto 0638	Toronto 0639	Toronto 0800.01
	POPULATION CHARACTERISTICS						
1	**Population, 1996 (1)**	**4,545**	**2,970**	**6,334**	**5,153**	**2,777**	**2,454**
2	**Population, 2001 (2)**	**5,215**	**2,872**	**6,755**	**4,996**	**3,040**	**2,431**
3	Population percentage change, 1996-2001	14.7	-3.3	6.6	-3.0	9.5	-0.9
4	Land area in square kilometres, 2001	2.88	1.57	128.93	6.43	10.34	1.06
5	**Total population – 100% Data (3)**	**5,220**	**2,870**	**6,755**	**4,995**	**3,040**	**2,430**
	by sex and age groups						
6	Male	2,535	1,415	3,545	2,440	1,535	1,155
7	0-4 years	155	90	170	180	100	60
8	5-9 years	205	120	245	185	125	70
9	10-14 years	165	115	285	180	115	85
10	15-19 years	155	110	250	150	115	85
11	20-24 years	145	70	195	130	95	55
12	25-29 years	190	65	170	140	85	75
13	30-34 years	200	105	200	185	140	85
14	35-39 years	240	145	330	260	150	110
15	40-44 years	230	120	355	235	155	115
16	45-49 years	205	120	310	180	135	85
17	50-54 years	175	100	260	175	90	90
18	55-59 years	135	95	255	120	80	65
19	60-64 years	100	70	190	85	45	50
20	65-69 years	65	40	135	65	30	45
21	70-74 years	70	35	90	75	25	40
22	75-79 years	50	15	50	55	25	25
23	80-84 years	25	5	30	25	10	15
24	85 years and over	20	5	25	15	5	5
25	Female	2,685	1,455	3,215	2,555	1,505	1,275
26	0-4 years	155	100	180	140	115	65
27	5-9 years	160	115	200	200	135	80
28	10-14 years	180	110	240	190	115	80
29	15-19 years	185	95	195	160	105	85
30	20-24 years	155	80	170	120	75	60
31	25-29 years	185	65	135	150	95	70
32	30-34 years	200	120	200	215	135	85
33	35-39 years	240	145	320	255	150	135
34	40-44 years	225	150	340	225	140	110
35	45-49 years	185	110	275	180	125	100
36	50-54 years	185	105	255	190	95	90
37	55-59 years	130	85	205	100	55	65
38	60-64 years	100	55	170	80	45	55
39	65-69 years	70	40	115	90	25	55
40	70-74 years	110	30	75	85	25	65
41	75-79 years	90	30	60	80	30	35
42	80-84 years	55	15	40	55	15	30
43	85 years and over	65	10	40	30	10	15
44	**Total population 15 years and over**	**4,205**	**2,220**	**5,440**	**3,925**	**2,330**	**1,995**
	by legal marital status						
45	Never married (single)	1,215	550	1,370	1,065	640	595
46	Legally married (and not separated)	2,155	1,355	3,440	2,170	1,370	920
47	Separated, but still legally married	180	70	125	165	95	110
48	Divorced	360	160	280	265	135	235
49	Widowed	300	90	220	255	90	140
	by common-law status						
50	Not in a common-law relationship	3,805	2,065	5,105	3,595	2,140	1,820
51	In a common-law relationship	405	155	340	330	190	175
52	**Total population – 20% Sample Data (4)**	**5,205**	**2,870**	**6,685**	**4,950**	**3,035**	**2,430**
	by mother tongue						
53	Single responses	5,180	2,850	6,665	4,935	3,015	2,420
54	English	4,665	2,605	5,695	4,600	2,720	2,015
55	French	160	65	155	120	30	20
56	Non-official languages (5)	355	180	815	210	265	395
57	Italian	-	10	25	30	20	10
58	Chinese, n.o.s.	30	-	20	20	15	-
59	Cantonese	-	-	-	-	-	15
60	Portuguese	30	15	50	10	15	15
61	Punjabi	-	-	-	15	-	10
62	Other languages (6)	285	165	715	140	215	350
63	Multiple responses	20	20	20	15	25	10
64	English and French	-	-	-	-	10	10
65	English and non-official language	20	10	20	10	20	10
66	French and non-official language	-	10	-	-	-	-
67	English, French and non-official language	-	-	-	-	-	-

See reference material at the end of the publication. – Voir les documents de référence à la fin de la publication.

Tableau 1. Certaines caractéristiques des secteurs de recensement, recensement de 2001 – Données intégrales et données-échantillon (20 %)

Toronto 0800.02	Toronto 0801.01	Toronto 0801.02	Toronto 0802.01 A	Toronto 0802.02 A	Toronto 0803.03 A	Caractéristiques	N°
						CARACTÉRISTIQUES DE LA POPULATION	
5,155	**4,166**	**5,854**	**3,050**	**4,872**	**4,916**	**Population, 1996 (1)**	1
5,018	**4,006**	**6,092**	**4,014**	**5,424**	**5,298**	**Population, 2001 (2)**	2
-2.7	-3.8	4.1	31.6	11.3	7.8	Variation en pourcentage de la population, 1996-2001	3
10.52	1.43	3.84	2.19	2.26	2.97	Superficie des terres en kilomètres carrés, 2001	4
5,015	**4,005**	**6,095**	**4,015**	**5,425**	**5,295**	**Population totale – Données intégrales (3)**	5
						selon le sexe et les groupes d'âge	
2,485	1,985	2,990	1,925	2,695	2,580	Sexe masculin	6
150	115	175	135	140	135	0-4 ans	7
175	145	260	135	210	220	5-9 ans	8
190	150	260	150	220	240	10-14 ans	9
180	145	245	125	270	235	15-19 ans	10
160	135	200	150	180	190	20-24 ans	11
145	120	110	105	130	130	25-29 ans	12
150	140	165	155	105	135	30-34 ans	13
230	200	265	165	195	195	35-39 ans	14
235	170	305	165	270	230	40-44 ans	15
190	140	265	175	255	235	45-49 ans	16
175	140	230	165	245	245	50-54 ans	17
150	120	190	95	185	150	55-59 ans	18
125	95	110	65	100	85	60-64 ans	19
105	80	70	55	75	65	65-69 ans	20
75	40	65	25	65	50	70-74 ans	21
40	30	45	25	40	25	75-79 ans	22
10	10	25	15	15	10	80-84 ans	23
5	5	15	10	-	5	85 ans et plus	24
2,525	2,015	3,105	2,090	2,725	2,720	Sexe féminin	25
135	130	195	115	155	150	0-4 ans	26
160	110	245	135	200	190	5-9 ans	27
175	150	235	135	205	245	10-14 ans	28
160	135	230	170	190	220	15-19 ans	29
135	110	170	115	170	180	20-24 ans	30
140	100	120	105	110	145	25-29 ans	31
185	150	185	165	135	155	30-34 ans	32
225	180	325	180	230	235	35-39 ans	33
245	170	325	215	290	295	40-44 ans	34
195	175	270	175	285	255	45-49 ans	35
160	165	250	175	265	225	50-54 ans	36
165	120	170	90	160	155	55-59 ans	37
135	110	120	65	85	95	60-64 ans	38
120	80	75	55	95	70	65-69 ans	39
95	60	60	50	75	45	70-74 ans	40
55	40	55	35	45	35	75-79 ans	41
20	30	35	40	20	15	80-84 ans	42
20	15	30	75	15	25	85 ans et plus	43
4,020	**3,210**	**4,730**	**3,215**	**4,290**	**4,125**	**Population totale de 15 ans et plus**	44
						selon l'état matrimonial légal	
1,220	975	1,335	905	1,215	1,255	Célibataire (jamais marié(e))	45
2,080	1,695	2,755	1,830	2,590	2,425	Légalement marié(e) (et non séparé(e))	46
170	135	145	95	110	130	Séparé(e), mais toujours légalement marié(e)	47
350	245	280	150	205	180	Divorcé(e)	48
205	165	215	230	165	140	Veuf ou veuve	49
						selon l'union libre	
3,675	2,980	4,480	3,075	4,125	3,935	Ne vivant pas en union libre	50
350	230	250	135	165	185	Vivant en union libre	51
5,015	**4,005**	**6,035**	**3,855**	**5,425**	**5,270**	**Population totale – Données-échantillon (20 %) (4)**	52
						selon la langue maternelle	
5,000	3,980	6,015	3,770	5,315	5,230	Réponses uniques	53
4,555	3,555	5,240	2,815	4,220	4,185	Anglais	54
35	80	70	45	10	35	Français	55
410	345	710	915	1,080	1,010	Langues non officielles (5)	56
60	30	180	95	70	150	Italien	57
-	-	55	50	115	50	Chinois, n.d.a.	58
-	-	30	35	100	20	Cantonais	59
25	-	-	10	15	30	Portugais	60
50	10	10	30	55	50	Pendjabi	61
265	300	435	695	730	715	Autres langues (6)	62
15	30	20	80	105	35	Réponses multiples	63
-	-	10	10	25	10	Anglais et français	64
10	25	10	75	80	25	Anglais et langue non officielle	65
-	-	-	-	10	-	Français et langue non officielle	66
-	-	-	-	-	10	Anglais, français et langue non officielle	67

See reference material at the end of the publication. – Voir les documents de référence à la fin de la publication.

Table 1. Selected Characteristics for Census Tracts, 2001 Census – 100% Data and 20% Sample Data

No.	Characteristics	Toronto 0635	Toronto 0636	Toronto 0637	Toronto 0638	Toronto 0639	Toronto 0800.01
	POPULATION CHARACTERISTICS						
	by home language						
68	Single responses	4,880	2,715	6,155	4,830	2,900	2,235
69	English	4,760	2,715	6,060	4,795	2,815	2,115
70	French	45	-	15	-	15	-
71	Non-official languages (5)	75	-	75	35	70	120
72	Cantonese	-	-	-	-	10	-
73	Chinese, n.o.s.	20	-	-	20	-	-
74	Italian	-	-	-	-	-	-
75	Punjabi	-	-	-	-	-	-
76	Portuguese	10	-	10	-	-	-
77	Other languages (6)	55	-	65	20	60	120
78	Multiple responses	325	155	530	120	140	200
79	English and French	125	55	125	55	25	25
80	English and non-official language	190	105	400	65	115	175
81	French and non-official language	-	-	-	-	-	-
82	English, French and non-official language	10	-	10	-	-	-
	by knowledge of official languages						
83	English only	4,695	2,605	6,120	4,525	2,820	2,310
84	French only	20	-	15	-	10	-
85	English and French	455	270	550	415	190	120
86	Neither English nor French	40	-	-	-	20	-
	by knowledge of non-official languages (5) (7)						
87	Italian	25	-	75	25	15	45
88	Cantonese	-	-	10	-	25	15
89	Chinese, n.o.s.	30	-	15	20	-	-
90	Spanish	70	10	95	10	35	25
91	Portuguese	55	25	125	35	15	15
92	Punjabi	-	-	-	15	-	20
93	Tagalog (Pilipino)	-	-	-	-	-	15
	by first official language spoken						
94	English	5,010	2,805	6,525	4,845	2,985	2,410
95	French	155	70	155	95	35	20
96	English and French	-	-	10	-	-	10
97	Neither English nor French	45	-	-	10	15	-
98	Official language minority - (number) (8)	160	70	160	95	30	20
99	Official language minority - (percentage) (8)	3.1	2.4	2.4	1.9	1.0	0.8
	by ethnic origin (9)						
100	Canadian	1,820	960	2,365	2,045	1,425	700
101	English	2,300	1,165	2,485	1,730	1,215	650
102	Scottish	1,270	660	1,265	1,180	910	445
103	Irish	1,165	555	970	1,090	655	535
104	Chinese	55	-	50	20	25	55
105	Italian	95	35	290	200	95	75
106	East Indian	30	-	70	-	-	55
107	French	540	255	590	595	285	135
108	German	435	225	720	545	305	245
109	Portuguese	100	40	155	55	20	50
110	Polish	100	150	240	110	55	40
111	Jewish	45	10	50	20	15	-
112	Jamaican	40	10	20	15	-	110
113	Filipino	10	-	-	-	-	25
114	Ukrainian	150	70	275	105	50	55
	by Aboriginal identity						
115	Total Aboriginal identity population (10)	20	10	10	65	20	10
116	Total non-Aboriginal population	5,185	2,865	6,675	4,890	3,020	2,425
	by Aboriginal origin						
117	Total Aboriginal origins population (11)	110	50	45	115	55	55
118	Total non-Aboriginal population	5,090	2,820	6,645	4,835	2,985	2,380
	by Registered Indian status						
119	Registered Indian (12)	10	-	-	20	15	10
120	Not a Registered Indian	5,195	2,870	6,685	4,930	3,025	2,430

Tableau 1. Certaines caractéristiques des secteurs de recensement, recensement de 2001 – Données intégrales et données-échantillon (20 %)

Toronto 0800.02	Toronto 0801.01	Toronto 0801.02	Toronto 0802.01 A	Toronto 0802.02 A	Toronto 0803.03 A	Caractéristiques	N°
						CARACTÉRISTIQUES DE LA POPULATION	
						selon la langue parlée à la maison	
4,695	3,700	5,725	3,125	4,745	4,555	Réponses uniques	68
4,640	3,690	5,620	2,960	4,480	4,440	Anglais	69
10	15	15	-	-	10	Français	70
50	-	90	170	265	95	Langues non officielles (5)	71
-	-	30	20	90	-	Cantonais	72
-	-	-	-	15	30	Chinois, n.d.a.	73
-	-	25	-	-	40	Italien	74
-	-	-	15	15	-	Pendjabi	75
10	-	-	-	-	-	Portugais	76
35	-	30	135	145	30	Autres langues (6)	77
320	300	305	725	675	715	Réponses multiples	78
30	50	45	50	20	25	Anglais et français	79
285	245	255	660	650	690	Anglais et langue non officielle	80
-	-	-	15	-	-	Français et langue non officielle	81
-	10	-	-	10	-	Anglais, français et langue non officielle	82
						selon la connaissance des langues officielles	
4,670	3,635	5,470	3,515	4,980	4,880	Anglais seulement	83
-	-	-	-	-	-	Français seulement	84
330	375	540	340	420	360	Anglais et français	85
-	-	15	10	25	20	Ni l'anglais ni le français	86
						selon la connaissance des langues non officielles (5) (7)	
65	35	220	105	90	195	Italien	87
-	-	40	40	160	30	Cantonais	88
-	-	50	40	65	80	Chinois, n.d.a.	89
75	10	70	40	75	130	Espagnol	90
25	20	10	15	15	30	Portugais	91
105	10	20	80	65	55	Pendjabi	92
10	55	120	55	45	45	Tagalog (pilipino)	93
						selon la première langue officielle parlée	
4,970	3,925	5,955	3,765	5,365	5,215	Anglais	94
30	75	65	55	20	30	Français	95
10	10	-	30	25	-	Anglais et français	96
10	-	10	10	15	25	Ni l'anglais ni le français	97
40	80	65	70	35	30	Minorité de langue officielle - (nombre) (8)	98
0.8	2.0	1.1	1.8	0.6	0.6	Minorité de langue officielle - (pourcentage) (8)	99
						selon l'origine ethnique (9)	
1,885	1,370	1,810	910	1,405	1,195	Canadien	100
1,810	1,525	2,185	940	1,590	1,235	Anglais	101
1,020	920	1,400	775	1,100	650	Écossais	102
1,085	925	1,180	490	970	530	Irlandais	103
15	30	245	210	320	250	Chinois	104
210	140	440	240	220	545	Italien	105
210	75	180	510	655	535	Indien de l'Inde	106
465	300	600	280	460	390	Français	107
465	230	585	185	425	315	Allemand	108
80	65	90	60	105	90	Portugais	109
90	30	105	120	165	100	Polonais	110
40	10	40	-	30	10	Juif	111
145	70	110	125	65	375	Jamaïquain	112
20	80	205	80	70	105	Philippin	113
155	110	120	45	120	60	Ukrainien	114
						selon l'identité autochtone	
45	15	50	10	25	10	Total de la population ayant une identité autochtone (10)	115
4,970	3,990	5,985	3,845	5,395	5,265	Total de la population non autochtone	116
						selon l'origine autochtone	
70	55	105	45	75	25	Total de la population ayant une origine autochtone (11)	117
4,940	3,950	5,925	3,810	5,350	5,245	Total de la population non autochtone	118
						selon le statut d'Indien inscrit	
10	20	25	10	10	-	Oui, Indien inscrit (12)	119
5,005	3,990	6,005	3,845	5,415	5,265	Non, pas un Indien inscrit	120

Table 1. Selected Characteristics for Census Tracts, 2001 Census – 100% Data and 20% Sample Data

No.	Characteristics	Toronto 0635	Toronto 0636	Toronto 0637	Toronto 0638	Toronto 0639	Toronto 0800.01
	POPULATION CHARACTERISTICS						
	by visible minority groups						
121	Total visible minority population	295	125	170	100	85	560
122	Chinese	55	-	30	25	25	35
123	South Asian	30	55	55	15	-	75
124	Black	40	70	60	45	-	230
125	Filipino	10	-	-	-	-	15
126	Latin American	55	-	10	-	-	10
127	Southeast Asian	-	-	10	-	-	-
128	Arab	-	-	-	-	-	120
129	West Asian	45	-	-	-	-	20
130	Korean	20	-	-	-	55	-
131	Japanese	35	-	-	-	-	-
132	Visible minority, n.i.e. (13)	-	-	-	-	-	45
133	Multiple visible minorities (14)	-	-	-	-	-	15
	by citizenship						
134	Canadian citizenship (15)	4,980	2,755	6,470	4,875	2,885	2,285
135	Citizenship other than Canadian	225	115	215	70	155	145
	by place of birth of respondent						
136	Non-immigrant population	4,435	2,410	5,435	4,450	2,640	1,665
137	Born in province of residence	3,795	2,105	4,700	3,765	2,265	1,425
138	Immigrant population (16)	720	465	1,255	495	385	750
139	United States	65	20	70	35	20	30
140	Central and South America	20	10	30	10	-	25
141	Caribbean and Bermuda	40	20	35	30	-	200
142	United Kingdom	325	200	400	190	135	135
143	Other Europe (17)	165	150	615	185	135	155
144	Africa	10	10	30	20	15	-
145	Asia and the Middle East	90	60	70	30	80	205
146	Oceania and other (18)	15	-	-	-	10	-
147	Non-permanent residents (19)	50	-	10	10	15	20
148	**Total immigrant population**	**720**	**465**	**1,250**	**495**	**385**	**750**
	by period of immigration						
149	Before 1961	180	145	455	225	90	115
150	1961-1970	110	100	275	100	80	160
151	1971-1980	200	75	275	65	60	115
152	1981-1990	120	145	165	15	35	85
153	1991-2001 (20)	115	-	85	90	110	280
154	1991-1995	40	-	15	55	60	185
155	1996-2001 (20)	70	-	70	30	50	90
	by age at immigration						
156	0-4 years	115	40	170	50	55	55
157	5-19 years	205	180	430	175	120	225
158	20 years and over	405	245	655	270	210	475
159	**Total population**	**5,205**	**2,870**	**6,690**	**4,950**	**3,040**	**2,435**
	by religion						
160	Catholic (21)	1,340	780	2,040	1,285	555	555
161	Protestant	2,435	1,535	3,420	2,555	1,720	960
162	Christian Orthodox	45	10	10	-	45	35
163	Christian, n.i.e. (22)	200	30	125	125	105	30
164	Muslim	45	-	30	-	-	230
165	Jewish	25	-	10	-	-	-
166	Buddhist	-	-	-	-	-	-
167	Hindu	15	-	-	-	-	-
168	Sikh	-	-	10	15	-	10
169	Eastern religions (23)	-	-	10	-	-	-
170	Other religions (24)	25	-	-	10	-	-
171	No religious affiliation (25)	1,075	520	1,035	945	610	605
172	**Total population 15 years and over**	**4,180**	**2,205**	**5,370**	**3,885**	**2,320**	**2,015**
	by generation status						
173	1st generation (26)	765	450	1,230	485	375	720
174	2nd generation (27)	915	585	1,595	805	475	430
175	3rd generation and over (28)	2,500	1,175	2,545	2,600	1,475	860
176	**Total population 1 year and over (29)**	**5,145**	**2,850**	**6,625**	**4,875**	**2,990**	**2,395**
	by place of residence 1 year ago (mobility)						
177	Non-movers	3,715	2,530	6,050	4,235	2,630	2,140
178	Movers	1,425	325	575	640	360	260
179	Non-migrants	570	175	205	315	160	120
180	Migrants	860	150	365	320	205	140
181	Internal migrants	830	150	355	315	205	110
182	Intraprovincial migrants	740	140	340	280	180	105
183	Interprovincial migrants	90	15	15	40	20	-
184	External migrants	35	-	10	10	-	30

Tableau 1. Certaines caractéristiques des secteurs de recensement, recensement de 2001 – Données intégrales et données-échantillon (20 %)

Toronto 0800.02	Toronto 0801.01	Toronto 0801.02	Toronto 0802.01 A	Toronto 0802.02 A	Toronto 0803.03 A	Caractéristiques	N^o
						CARACTÉRISTIQUES DE LA POPULATION	
						selon les groupes de minorités visibles	
610	470	960	1,405	1,530	1,705	Total de la population des minorités visibles	121
20	10	190	170	325	175	Chinois	122
155	110	190	525	770	430	Sud-Asiatique	123
190	200	195	335	155	585	Noir	124
20	75	145	75	65	85	Philippin	125
30	-	85	15	30	60	Latino-Américain	126
10	10	-	55	-	-	Asiatique du Sud-Est	127
15	-	20	-	-	35	Arabe	128
-	-	-	65	20	20	Asiatique occidental	129
-	10	-	10	50	15	Coréen	130
20	25	20	10	30	45	Japonais	131
110	10	40	140	40	210	Minorité visible, n.i.a. (13)	132
45	30	70	20	45	50	Minorités visibles multiples (14)	133
						selon la citoyenneté	
4,745	3,825	5,870	3,560	5,020	5,045	Citoyenneté canadienne (15)	134
270	180	160	295	400	225	Citoyenneté autre que canadienne	135
						selon le lieu de naissance du répondant	
3,915	3,065	4,640	2,415	3,590	3,555	Population non immigrante	136
3,400	2,630	4,250	2,180	3,235	3,285	Née dans la province de résidence	137
1,080	925	1,390	1,425	1,830	1,705	Population immigrante (16)	138
15	30	30	40	25	30	États-Unis	139
60	10	80	195	115	210	Amérique centrale et du Sud	140
170	155	200	145	135	375	Caraïbes et Bermudes	141
435	345	460	220	335	195	Royaume-Uni	142
305	260	315	230	320	455	Autre Europe (17)	143
40	15	55	40	145	135	Afrique	144
65	105	245	540	755	300	Asie et Moyen-Orient	145
-	10	-	-	-	-	Océanie et autre (18)	146
15	15	-	15	-	10	Résidents non permanents (19)	147
1,085	**925**	**1,390**	**1,420**	**1,835**	**1,705**	**Population immigrante totale**	148
						selon la période d'immigration	
315	195	285	95	260	295	Avant 1961	149
290	325	490	165	250	340	1961-1970	150
220	200	345	330	515	630	1971-1980	151
125	155	190	400	325	280	1981-1990	152
130	50	75	435	485	155	1991-2001 (20)	153
95	40	65	210	305	110	1991-1995	154
30	-	10	225	180	45	1996-2001 (20)	155
						selon l'âge à l'immigration	
140	140	115	140	135	160	0-4 ans	156
335	285	490	390	600	610	5-19 ans	157
610	510	785	895	1,100	935	20 ans et plus	158
5,015	**4,005**	**6,030**	**3,860**	**5,420**	**5,270**	**Population totale**	159
						selon la religion	
1,475	1,145	2,145	1,200	1,570	1,830	Catholique (21)	160
2,130	1,740	2,395	1,260	1,945	1,910	Protestante	161
60	85	110	90	160	330	Orthodoxe chrétienne	162
160	210	195	40	195	135	Chrétiennes, n.i.a. (22)	163
15	15	65	210	165	290	Musulmane	164
-	10	15	-	-	-	Juive	165
-	10	-	35	105	15	Bouddhiste	166
25	60	55	200	155	100	Hindoue	167
110	-	-	-	65	55	Sikh	168
-	-	-	20	30	-	Religions orientales (23)	169
10	-	10	-	-	-	Autres religions (24)	170
1,040	740	1,045	810	1,030	610	Aucune appartenance religieuse (25)	171
4,020	**3,200**	**4,680**	**3,070**	**4,265**	**4,125**	**Population totale de 15 ans et plus**	172
						selon le statut des générations	
1,085	920	1,400	1,380	1,750	1,705	1re génération (26)	173
880	835	1,320	720	1,065	1,155	2e génération (27)	174
2,050	1,440	1,965	975	1,455	1,260	3e génération et plus (28)	175
4,985	**3,940**	**5,940**	**3,785**	**5,380**	**5,215**	**Population totale de 1 an et plus (29)**	176
						selon le lieu de résidence 1 an auparavant (mobilité)	
4,445	3,555	5,495	3,415	4,835	4,720	Personnes n'ayant pas déménagé	177
540	385	445	370	545	490	Personnes ayant déménagé	178
285	165	170	220	410	210	Non-migrants	179
255	220	275	150	130	280	Migrants	180
250	210	275	110	80	260	Migrants internes	181
225	190	265	105	60	210	Migrants infraprovinciaux	182
20	20	10	10	15	45	Migrants interprovinciaux	183
-	10	-	40	60	20	Migrants externes	184

Table 1. Selected Characteristics for Census Tracts, 2001 Census – 100% Data and 20% Sample Data

No.	Characteristics	Toronto 0635	Toronto 0636	Toronto 0637	Toronto 0638	Toronto 0639	Toronto 0800.01
	POPULATION CHARACTERISTICS						
185	**Total population 5 years and over (30)**	**4,895**	**2,675**	**6,340**	**4,650**	**2,795**	**2,315**
	by place of residence 5 years ago (mobility)						
186	Non-movers	2,345	1,740	4,305	2,535	1,445	1,205
187	Movers	2,555	940	2,035	2,115	1,350	1,110
188	Non-migrants	970	470	625	950	655	470
189	Migrants	1,585	465	1,410	1,165	690	640
190	Internal migrants	1,450	465	1,330	1,150	630	540
191	Intraprovincial migrants	1,290	395	1,205	915	520	495
192	Interprovincial migrants	160	75	130	235	115	50
193	External migrants	135	-	80	20	60	95
194	**Total population 15 to 24 years**	**620**	**340**	**815**	**580**	**385**	**345**
	by school attendance						
195	Not attending school	295	130	300	220	195	100
196	Attending school full time	300	200	455	330	170	240
197	Attending school part time	25	15	60	25	20	10
198	**Total population 15 years and over**	**4,180**	**2,205**	**5,375**	**3,885**	**2,325**	**2,010**
	by highest level of schooling						
199	Less than grade 9 (31)	180	75	270	340	130	90
200	Grades 9-13 without high school graduation certificate	1,060	510	1,090	1,100	630	520
201	Grades 9-13 with high school graduation certificate	570	350	965	685	320	305
202	Some postsecondary without degree, certificate or diploma (32)	495	185	505	375	320	215
203	Trades certificate or diploma (33)	315	275	575	455	235	195
204	College certificate or diploma (34)	685	435	1,080	615	415	415
205	University certificate below bachelor's degree	105	55	100	30	35	45
206	University with bachelor's degree or higher	770	330	780	280	240	235
	by combinations of unpaid work						
207	Males 15 years and over	2,000	1,105	2,785	1,850	1,205	950
208	Reported unpaid work (35)	1,735	980	2,635	1,605	1,075	825
209	Housework and child care and care or assistance to seniors	135	125	275	115	110	35
210	Housework and child care only	560	360	695	555	330	205
211	Housework and care or assistance to seniors only	135	80	305	95	90	65
212	Child care and care or assistance to seniors only	-	-	-	-	-	-
213	Housework only	835	405	1,330	775	535	505
214	Child care only	50	10	20	30	10	10
215	Care or assistance to seniors only	15	-	-	40	-	-
216	Females 15 years and over	2,175	1,100	2,590	2,035	1,115	1,055
217	Reported unpaid work (35)	2,075	1,075	2,480	1,895	1,075	1,015
218	Housework and child care and care or assistance to seniors	255	165	365	225	185	105
219	Housework and child care only	660	370	760	675	330	360
220	Housework and care or assistance to seniors only	220	60	315	120	105	100
221	Child care and care or assistance to seniors only	-	-	-	-	-	-
222	Housework only	935	475	1,030	860	450	445
223	Child care only	10	-	-	10	15	10
224	Care or assistance to seniors only	-	-	10	10	-	10
	by labour force activity						
225	Males 15 years and over	2,000	1,105	2,780	1,850	1,205	955
226	In the labour force	1,600	850	2,080	1,545	1,000	745
227	Employed	1,570	815	2,055	1,445	950	725
228	Unemployed	30	35	35	100	55	20
229	Not in the labour force	405	260	700	310	210	215
230	Participation rate	80.0	76.9	74.8	83.5	83.0	78.0
231	Employment rate	78.5	73.8	73.9	78.1	78.8	75.9
232	Unemployment rate	1.9	4.1	1.7	6.5	5.5	2.7
233	Females 15 years and over	2,180	1,100	2,590	2,035	1,115	1,055
234	In the labour force	1,475	775	1,715	1,340	830	680
235	Employed	1,445	740	1,675	1,275	780	620
236	Unemployed	30	35	40	65	45	60
237	Not in the labour force	705	330	870	695	285	375
238	Participation rate	67.7	70.5	66.2	65.8	74.4	64.5
239	Employment rate	66.3	67.3	64.7	62.7	70.0	58.8
240	Unemployment rate	2.0	4.5	2.3	4.9	5.4	8.8

Tableau 1. Certaines caractéristiques des secteurs de recensement, recensement de 2001 – Données intégrales et données-échantillon (20 %)

Toronto 0800.02	Toronto 0801.01	Toronto 0801.02	Toronto 0802.01 A	Toronto 0802.02 A	Toronto 0803.03 A	Caractéristiques	N°
						CARACTÉRISTIQUES DE LA POPULATION	
4,720	**3,750**	**5,665**	**3,620**	**5,105**	**4,995**	**Population totale de 5 ans et plus (30)**	185
						selon le lieu de résidence 5 ans auparavant (mobilité)	
3,045	2,330	3,810	1,845	3,575	3,375	Personnes n'ayant pas déménagé	186
1,680	1,420	1,855	1,775	1,535	1,620	Personnes ayant déménagé	187
665	640	705	1,335	1,170	635	Non-migrants	188
1,010	780	1,150	445	365	985	Migrants	189
990	765	1,120	310	230	880	Migrants internes	190
950	725	1,100	275	195	835	Migrants infraprovinciaux	191
35	35	20	40	35	45	Migrants interprovinciaux	192
20	15	25	135	135	110	Migrants externes	193
630	**470**	**855**	**585**	**810**	**820**	**Population totale de 15 à 24 ans**	194
						selon la fréquentation scolaire	
265	185	300	110	205	265	Ne fréquentant pas l'école	195
335	255	515	420	550	510	Fréquentant l'école à plein temps	196
30	30	35	55	55	45	Fréquentant l'école à temps partiel	197
4,020	**3,195**	**4,680**	**3,070**	**4,260**	**4,120**	**Population totale de 15 ans et plus**	198
						selon le plus haut niveau de scolarité atteint	
180	105	215	35	85	160	Niveau inférieur à la 9e année (31)	199
995	735	845	480	685	780	De la 9e à la 13e année sans certificat d'études secondaires	200
845	550	745	410	510	520	De la 9e à la 13e année avec certificat d'études secondaires	201
560	365	630	430	560	445	Études postsecondaires partielles sans grade, certificat ou diplôme (32)	202
465	400	395	250	355	500	Certificat ou diplôme d'une école de métiers (33)	203
645	645	945	600	885	840	Certificat ou diplôme collégial (34)	204
60	60	105	90	90	170	Certificat universitaire inférieur au baccalauréat	205
280	350	805	770	1,110	710	Études universitaires avec baccalauréat ou diplôme supérieur	206
						selon les combinaisons de travail non rémunéré	
1,970	1,575	2,295	1,495	2,105	1,990	Hommes de 15 ans et plus	207
1,815	1,405	2,095	1,315	1,915	1,795	Travail non rémunéré déclaré (35)	208
190	140	175	110	225	170	Travaux ménagers et soins aux enfants et soins ou aide aux personnes âgées	209
485	420	660	330	605	620	Travaux ménagers et soins aux enfants seulement	210
130	145	145	110	115	110	Travaux ménagers et soins ou aide aux personnes âgées seulement	211
-	-	-	-	-	-	Soins aux enfants et soins ou aide aux personnes âgées seulement	212
990	650	1,095	725	940	880	Travaux ménagers seulement	213
15	35	15	20	10	15	Soins aux enfants seulement	214
-	15	-	15	20	-	Soins ou aide aux personnes âgées seulement	215
2,045	1,630	2,390	1,580	2,165	2,135	Femmes de 15 ans et plus	216
1,915	1,555	2,285	1,520	2,025	2,030	Travail non rémunéré déclaré (35)	217
260	220	310	170	300	265	Travaux ménagers et soins aux enfants et soins ou aide aux personnes âgées	218
585	520	775	510	665	705	Travaux ménagers et soins aux enfants seulement	219
195	185	215	115	205	150	Travaux ménagers et soins ou aide aux personnes âgées seulement	220
-	-	-	-	-	-	Soins aux enfants et soins ou aide aux personnes âgées seulement	221
840	610	970	730	835	890	Travaux ménagers seulement	222
25	10	10	-	15	10	Soins aux enfants seulement	223
10	10	10	-	-	10	Soins ou aide aux personnes âgées seulement	224
						selon l'activité	
1,970	1,575	2,290	1,495	2,100	1,990	Hommes de 15 ans et plus	225
1,570	1,210	1,865	1,270	1,535	1,635	Population active	226
1,480	1,155	1,790	1,195	1,465	1,570	Personnes occupées	227
95	50	75	80	70	65	Chômeurs	228
400	365	425	220	570	350	Inactifs	229
79.7	76.8	81.4	84.9	73.1	82.2	Taux d'activité	230
75.1	73.3	78.2	79.9	69.8	78.9	Taux d'emploi	231
6.1	4.1	4.0	6.3	4.6	4.0	Taux de chômage	232
2,045	1,630	2,390	1,580	2,160	2,135	Femmes de 15 ans et plus	233
1,315	1,130	1,735	1,130	1,460	1,560	Population active	234
1,230	1,030	1,625	1,100	1,420	1,455	Personnes occupées	235
85	95	105	30	40	105	Chômeuses	236
730	500	655	450	705	575	Inactives	237
64.3	69.3	72.6	71.5	67.6	73.1	Taux d'activité	238
60.1	63.2	68.0	69.6	65.7	68.1	Taux d'emploi	239
6.5	8.4	6.1	2.7	2.7	6.7	Taux de chômage	240

Table 1. Selected Characteristics for Census Tracts, 2001 Census – 100% Data and 20% Sample Data

No.	Characteristics	Toronto 0635	Toronto 0636	Toronto 0637	Toronto 0638	Toronto 0639	Toronto 0800.01
	POPULATION CHARACTERISTICS						
	by labour force activity – concluded						
241	Both sexes - Participation rate	73.6	73.5	70.6	74.1	78.7	70.6
242	15-24 years	75.0	75.0	63.2	81.7	76.6	65.2
243	25 years and over	73.3	73.2	72.2	73.1	79.1	71.8
244	Both sexes - Employment rate	72.1	70.4	69.3	70.0	74.4	66.7
245	15-24 years	74.2	69.6	61.3	73.0	65.4	56.5
246	25 years and over	71.9	70.5	70.8	69.6	76.0	69.4
247	Both sexes - Unemployment rate	2.0	4.0	2.0	5.5	5.2	5.3
248	15-24 years	2.2	5.9	2.0	9.7	15.3	15.6
249	25 years and over	1.9	3.7	1.8	5.0	3.6	3.3
250	**Total labour force 15 years and over**	**3,075**	**1,620**	**3,800**	**2,880**	**1,830**	**1,420**
	by industry based on the 1997 NAICS						
251	Industry - Not applicable (36)	-	15	-	40	10	10
252	All industries (37)	3,075	1,605	3,795	2,845	1,820	1,405
253	11 Agriculture, forestry, fishing and hunting	20	50	170	15	10	-
254	21 Mining and oil and gas extraction	10	-	25	30	15	-
255	22 Utilities	10	-	10	25	10	15
256	23 Construction	170	100	275	225	85	70
257	31-33 Manufacturing	565	420	725	675	395	195
258	41 Wholesale trade	190	100	300	250	120	70
259	44-45 Retail trade	265	140	365	255	180	155
260	48-49 Transportation and warehousing	265	90	160	220	150	110
261	51 Information and cultural industries	35	30	95	35	85	20
262	52 Finance and insurance	125	80	135	50	55	85
263	53 Real estate and rental and leasing	95	20	25	25	25	40
264	54 Professional, scientific and technical services	280	140	285	85	95	90
265	55 Management of companies and enterprises	-	-	10	10	20	10
266	56 Administrative and support, waste management and remediation services	135	50	195	130	50	110
267	61 Educational services	175	60	205	125	85	80
268	62 Health care and social assistance	240	105	165	180	65	100
269	71 Arts, entertainment and recreation	125	25	50	70	30	25
270	72 Accommodation and food services	205	55	205	175	150	60
271	81 Other services (except public administration)	90	90	295	145	140	55
272	91 Public administration	70	50	90	115	50	110
	by class of worker						
273	Class of worker - Not applicable (36)	-	15	10	35	10	15
274	All classes of worker (37)	3,075	1,605	3,795	2,845	1,820	1,405
275	Paid workers	2,790	1,495	3,250	2,630	1,645	1,265
276	Employees	2,645	1,440	2,970	2,570	1,620	1,210
277	Self-employed (incorporated)	150	55	280	65	25	50
278	Self-employed (unincorporated)	285	105	515	210	175	140
279	Unpaid family workers	-	10	25	-	-	-
	by occupation based on the 2001 NOC-S						
280	Male labour force 15 years and over	1,600	850	2,085	1,540	995	740
281	Occupation - Not applicable (36)	-	10	-	30	-	-
282	All occupations (37)	1,595	845	2,085	1,510	1,000	735
283	A Management occupations	255	170	450	215	85	100
284	B Business, finance and administration occupations	125	90	135	115	60	80
285	C Natural and applied sciences and related occupations	210	70	180	75	80	80
286	D Health occupations	25	-	30	10	10	10
287	E Occupations in social science, education, government service and religion	60	15	70	50	30	40
288	F Occupations in art, culture, recreation and sport	35	20	35	10	30	10
289	G Sales and service occupations	280	145	355	245	185	150
290	H Trades, transport and equipment operators and related occupations	370	145	550	535	325	210
291	I Occupations unique to primary industry	45	25	170	35	-	20
292	J Occupations unique to processing, manufacturing and utilities	180	165	115	220	185	40
293	Female labour force 15 years and over	1,475	770	1,715	1,335	830	680
294	Occupation - Not applicable (36)	-	10	-	10	10	15
295	All occupations (37)	1,480	760	1,710	1,330	825	670
296	A Management occupations	155	75	235	170	65	85
297	B Business, finance and administration occupations	430	250	590	350	245	255
298	C Natural and applied sciences and related occupations	45	35	70	20	20	20
299	D Health occupations	100	60	95	60	30	20

Tableau 1. Certaines caractéristiques des secteurs de recensement, recensement de 2001 – Données intégrales et données-échantillon (20 %)

Toronto 0800.02	Toronto 0801.01	Toronto 0801.02	Toronto 0802.01 A	Toronto 0802.02 A	Toronto 0803.03 A	Caractéristiques	N°
						CARACTÉRISTIQUES DE LA POPULATION	
						selon l'activité – fin	
71.8	72.8	76.8	78.3	70.2	77.4	Les deux sexes - Taux d'activité	241
77.8	75.5	74.9	72.6	55.6	72.0	15-24 ans	242
70.6	72.3	77.4	79.5	73.8	78.8	25 ans et plus	243
67.4	68.4	73.0	74.6	67.7	73.3	Les deux sexes - Taux d'emploi	244
63.5	61.7	61.4	64.1	47.5	60.4	15-24 ans	245
68.0	69.4	75.6	77.3	72.5	76.7	25 ans et plus	246
6.2	6.2	5.0	4.6	3.7	5.3	Les deux sexes - Taux de chômage	247
19.4	16.7	17.1	12.9	15.6	16.2	15-24 ans	248
3.8	4.0	2.4	2.8	1.8	2.9	25 ans et plus	249
2,890	**2,335**	**3,595**	**2,400**	**2,995**	**3,190**	**Population active totale de 15 ans et plus**	250
						selon l'industrie basée sur le SCIAN de 1997	
20	35	80	40	20	50	Industrie - Sans objet (36)	251
2,865	2,305	3,520	2,365	2,970	3,140	Toutes les industries (37)	252
20	-	10	-	10	-	11 Agriculture, foresterie, pêche et chasse	253
-	-	-	-	-	-	21 Extraction minière et extraction de pétrole et de gaz	254
70	40	45	60	50	80	22 Services publics	255
230	120	315	135	125	170	23 Construction	256
455	325	400	215	255	330	31-33 Fabrication	257
160	165	185	75	110	130	41 Commerce de gros	258
425	260	325	315	280	370	44-45 Commerce de détail	259
185	155	130	70	120	135	48-49 Transport et entreposage	260
95	105	175	100	210	160	51 Industrie de l'information et industrie culturelle	261
210	160	315	265	345	360	52 Finance et assurances	262
60	40	65	20	65	100	53 Services immobiliers et services de location et de location à bail	263
175	195	275	155	350	220	54 Services professionnels, scientifiques et techniques	264
-	15	25	15	10	10	55 Gestion de sociétés et d'entreprises	265
175	125	220	110	75	150	56 Services administratifs, services de soutien, services de gestion des déchets et services d'assainissement	266
90	85	310	185	265	175	61 Services d'enseignement	267
170	205	290	245	250	290	62 Soins de santé et assistance sociale	268
15	25	50	25	35	45	71 Arts, spectacles et loisirs	269
100	85	95	80	110	135	72 Hébergement et services de restauration	270
115	85	105	110	75	120	81 Autres services, sauf les administrations publiques	271
105	140	190	185	235	150	91 Administrations publiques	272
						selon la catégorie de travailleurs	
20	30	80	40	20	55	Catégorie de travailleurs - Sans objet (36)	273
2,870	2,300	3,525	2,365	2,975	3,140	Toutes les catégories de travailleurs (37)	274
2,715	2,175	3,280	2,180	2,770	2,895	Travailleurs rémunérés	275
2,635	2,105	3,115	2,115	2,665	2,750	Employés	276
80	70	165	70	105	145	Travailleurs autonomes (entreprise constituée en société)	277
145	130	240	165	200	240	Travailleurs autonomes (entreprise non constituée en société)	278
10	-	-	20	-	-	Travailleurs familiaux non rémunérés	279
						selon la profession basée sur la CNP-S de 2001	
1,575	1,210	1,865	1,270	1,530	1,635	Hommes actifs de 15 ans et plus	280
10	10	30	30	15	20	Profession - Sans objet (36)	281
1,565	1,200	1,830	1,240	1,525	1,615	Toutes les professions (37)	282
145	200	335	190	280	320	A Gestion	283
155	130	255	165	255	205	B Affaires, finance et administration	284
140	170	235	210	250	135	C Sciences naturelles et appliquées et professions apparentées	285
10	20	20	15	25	55	D Secteur de la santé	286
40	25	80	80	75	40	E Sciences sociales, enseignement, administration publique et religion	287
20	-	45	25	45	35	F Arts, culture, sports et loisirs	288
305	240	370	240	290	375	G Ventes et services	289
560	325	420	240	225	365	H Métiers, transport et machinerie	290
40	10	20	10	30	30	I Professions propres au secteur primaire	291
160	70	55	60	50	55	J Transformation, fabrication et services d'utilité publique	292
1,315	1,125	1,735	1,130	1,460	1,560	Femmes actives de 15 ans et plus	293
10	25	40	-	10	40	Profession - Sans objet (36)	294
1,305	1,100	1,695	1,125	1,450	1,520	Toutes les professions (37)	295
135	120	180	125	155	160	A Gestion	296
505	435	595	360	535	515	B Affaires, finance et administration	297
30	20	65	45	60	70	C Sciences naturelles et appliquées et professions apparentées	298
85	75	100	125	85	140	D Secteur de la santé	299

Table 1. Selected Characteristics for Census Tracts, 2001 Census – 100% Data and 20% Sample Data

No.	Characteristics	Toronto 0635	Toronto 0636	Toronto 0637	Toronto 0638	Toronto 0639	Toronto 0800.01
	POPULATION CHARACTERISTICS						
	by occupation based on the 2001 NOC-S – concluded						
300	E Occupations in social science, education, government service and religion	140	45	145	115	90	90
301	F Occupations in art, culture, recreation and sport	20	25	75	20	10	-
302	G Sales and service occupations	455	200	340	405	250	160
303	H Trades, transport and equipment operators and related occupations	40	15	55	30	50	15
304	I Occupations unique to primary industry	15	25	35	20	-	-
305	J Occupations unique to processing, manufacturing and utilities	75	50	75	135	60	20
306	**Total employed labour force 15 years and over**	**3,020**	**1,555**	**3,725**	**2,720**	**1,730**	**1,345**
	by place of work						
307	Males	1,570	815	2,050	1,450	945	725
308	Usual place of work	1,310	680	1,585	1,205	775	600
309	At home	85	45	215	70	30	20
310	Outside Canada	10	10	10	10	10	10
311	No fixed workplace address	175	75	245	165	125	85
312	Females	1,445	740	1,675	1,275	780	620
313	Usual place of work	1,295	675	1,280	1,125	710	565
314	At home	110	55	315	75	30	30
315	Outside Canada	-	10	-	-	10	10
316	No fixed workplace address	40	15	75	65	40	20
317	**Total employed labour force 15 years and over with usual place of work or no fixed workplace address**	**2,815**	**1,440**	**3,180**	**2,565**	**1,650**	**1,275**
	by mode of transportation						
318	Males	1,480	755	1,825	1,375	900	690
319	Car, truck, van, as driver	1,150	670	1,655	1,195	785	545
320	Car, truck, van, as passenger	65	35	75	80	70	50
321	Public transit	80	25	50	15	10	65
322	Walked	110	25	35	70	35	25
323	Other method	65	10	10	-	-	10
324	Females	1,335	680	1,360	1,190	750	585
325	Car, truck, van, as driver	910	530	1,075	920	595	355
326	Car, truck, van, as passenger	145	75	170	150	60	95
327	Public transit	100	30	75	20	15	115
328	Walked	150	25	30	100	65	10
329	Other method	30	15	15	-	10	-
330	**Total population 15 years and over who worked since January 1, 2000**	**3,310**	**1,745**	**4,175**	**3,040**	**1,930**	**1,490**
	by language used at work						
331	Single responses	3,180	1,680	4,070	2,985	1,895	1,470
332	English	3,165	1,680	4,065	2,975	1,865	1,475
333	French	15	-	-	-	-	-
334	Non-official languages (5)	-	-	-	10	30	-
335	Chinese, n.o.s.	-	-	-	10	-	-
336	Cantonese	-	-	-	-	-	-
337	Other languages (6)	-	-	-	-	30	-
338	Multiple responses	135	60	110	60	35	20
339	English and French	100	40	55	45	15	15
340	English and non-official language	25	15	45	10	20	-
341	French and non-official language	-	-	-	-	-	-
342	English, French and non-official language	10	10	10	-	-	-
	DWELLING AND HOUSEHOLD CHARACTERISTICS						
343	**Total number of occupied private dwellings**	**2,065**	**985**	**2,085**	**1,865**	**1,030**	**925**
	by tenure						
344	Owned	1,240	800	1,895	1,320	835	770
345	Rented	820	190	190	550	190	160
346	Band housing	-	-	-	-	-	-
	by structural type of dwelling						
347	Single-detached house	1,120	805	1,965	1,080	845	480
348	Semi-detached house	95	15	45	145	20	50
349	Row house	95	-	-	190	30	155
350	Apartment, detached duplex	65	90	40	20	45	15
351	Apartment, building that has five or more storeys	305	-	-	140	-	180
352	Apartment, building that has fewer than five storeys (38)	390	75	10	290	75	50
353	Other single-attached house	-	-	-	-	15	-
354	Movable dwelling (39)	-	-	25	-	-	-

Tableau 1. Certaines caractéristiques des secteurs de recensement, recensement de 2001 – Données intégrales et données-échantillon (20 %)

Toronto 0800.02	Toronto 0801.01	Toronto 0801.02	Toronto 0802.01 A	Toronto 0802.02 A	Toronto 0803.03 A	Caractéristiques	N°
						CARACTÉRISTIQUES DE LA POPULATION	
						selon la profession basée sur la CNP-S de 2001 – fin	
70	110	240	130	220	115	E Sciences sociales, enseignement, administration publique et religion	300
20	30	45	25	90	60	F Arts, culture, sports et loisirs	301
340	270	425	255	265	410	G Ventes et services	302
45	10	10	15	-	15	H Métiers, transport et machinerie	303
-	-	10	-	-	15	I Professions propres au secteur primaire	304
75	35	35	50	30	35	J Transformation, fabrication et services d'utilité publique	305
2,705	**2,190**	**3,420**	**2,290**	**2,890**	**3,025**	**Population active occupée totale de 15 ans et plus selon le lieu de travail**	306
1,480	1,160	1,790	1,190	1,470	1,575	Hommes	307
1,175	945	1,470	1,065	1,250	1,280	Lieu habituel de travail	308
35	75	95	20	90	50	À domicile	309
-	-	10	-	-	20	En dehors du Canada	310
265	140	220	105	125	220	Sans adresse de travail fixe	311
1,230	1,030	1,630	1,100	1,420	1,455	Femmes	312
1,135	950	1,440	985	1,245	1,265	Lieu habituel de travail	313
35	45	140	75	125	120	À domicile	314
-	-	-	-	-	-	En dehors du Canada	315
60	35	45	40	45	75	Sans adresse de travail fixe	316
2,630	**2,075**	**3,180**	**2,190**	**2,670**	**2,840**	**Population active occupée totale de 15 ans et plus ayant un lieu habituel de travail ou sans adresse de travail fixe selon le mode de transport**	317
1,435	1,085	1,695	1,170	1,370	1,500	Hommes	318
1,110	875	1,420	855	1,000	1,250	Automobile, camion ou fourgonnette, en tant que conducteur	319
135	60	90	20	25	75	Automobile, camion ou fourgonnette, en tant que passager	320
120	90	160	260	300	150	Transport en commun	321
40	30	20	30	35	20	À pied	322
35	30	-	-	10	-	Autre moyen	323
1,195	990	1,490	1,020	1,295	1,335	Femmes	324
730	770	1,185	615	795	975	Automobile, camion ou fourgonnette, en tant que conductrice	325
125	70	80	65	80	105	Automobile, camion ou fourgonnette, en tant que passagère	326
240	135	200	305	395	210	Transport en commun	327
60	10	10	45	10	35	À pied	328
40	-	10	-	15	10	Autre moyen	329
3,065	**2,480**	**3,775**	**2,535**	**3,295**	**3,345**	**Population totale de 15 ans et plus ayant travaillé depuis le 1er janvier 2000 selon la langue utilisée au travail**	330
3,010	2,400	3,700	2,390	3,190	3,255	Réponses uniques	331
3,005	2,400	3,685	2,385	3,175	3,230	Anglais	332
10	-	10	-	10	-	Français	333
-	-	-	-	-	20	Langues non officielles (5)	334
-	-	-	-	10	20	Chinois, n.d.a.	335
-	-	-	-	-	-	Cantonais	336
-	-	-	-	-	-	Autres langues (6)	337
60	80	80	150	100	90	Réponses multiples	338
20	65	50	50	45	40	Anglais et français	339
35	-	25	100	60	55	Anglais et langue non officielle	340
-	-	-	-	-	-	Français et langue non officielle	341
-	10	10	-	-	-	Anglais, français et langue non officielle	342
						CARACTÉRISTIQUES DES LOGEMENTS ET DES MÉNAGES	
1,710	**1,335**	**1,885**	**1,180**	**1,670**	**1,590**	**Nombre total de logements privés occupés selon le mode d'occupation**	343
1,455	1,225	1,820	1,140	1,570	1,385	Possédé	344
245	110	65	35	100	205	Loué	345
-	-	-	-	-	-	Logement de bande	346
						selon le type de construction résidentielle	
1,365	955	1,700	830	1,550	1,310	Maison individuelle non attenante	347
245	245	-	190	15	-	Maison jumelée	348
60	135	170	160	105	120	Maison en rangée	349
10	-	10	-	-	45	Appartement, duplex non attenant	350
-	-	10	-	-	120	Appartement, immeuble de cinq étages ou plus	351
30	-	-	-	-	-	Appartement, immeuble de moins de cinq étages (38)	352
-	-	-	-	-	10	Autre maison individuelle attenante	353
-	-	-	-	-	-	Logement mobile (39)	354

Table 1. Selected Characteristics for Census Tracts, 2001 Census – 100% Data and 20% Sample Data

No.	Characteristics	Toronto 0635	Toronto 0636	Toronto 0637	Toronto 0638	Toronto 0639	Toronto 0800.01
	DWELLING AND HOUSEHOLD CHARACTERISTICS						
	by condition of dwelling						
355	Regular maintenance only	1,290	620	1,280	1,235	650	590
356	Minor repairs	630	300	630	475	300	230
357	Major repairs	140	75	180	155	75	115
	by period of construction						
358	Before 1946	540	160	345	305	235	50
359	1946-1960	330	235	360	340	185	75
360	1961-1970	215	260	490	400	115	280
361	1971-1980	295	110	395	540	235	305
362	1981-1990	305	95	230	130	85	160
363	1991-2001 (20)	380	125	265	150	170	55
364	Average number of rooms per dwelling	6.2	7.0	7.6	6.5	6.8	6.4
365	Average number of bedrooms per dwelling	2.5	3.0	3.2	2.8	2.9	2.9
366	Average value of dwelling $	231,879	217,967	324,235	189,239	197,333	164,798
367	**Total number of private households**	**2,065**	**985**	**2,090**	**1,865**	**1,025**	**925**
	by household size						
368	1 person	570	130	225	380	165	230
369	2 persons	655	325	725	595	290	255
370	3 persons	320	180	370	385	200	185
371	4-5 persons	470	320	665	475	335	235
372	6 or more persons	50	30	100	40	35	20
	by household type						
373	One-family households	1,370	825	1,815	1,445	805	660
374	Multiple-family households	30	20	25	15	30	-
375	Non-family households	660	145	250	405	185	265
376	Number of persons in private households	5,185	2,870	6,300	4,950	3,030	2,405
377	Average number of persons in private households	2.5	2.9	3.0	2.6	2.9	2.6
378	Average number of persons per room	0.4	0.4	0.4	0.4	0.4	0.4
379	Tenant households in non-farm, non-reserve private dwellings (40)	815	190	190	550	190	160
380	Average gross rent $ (40)	736	775	890	672	807	753
381	Tenant households spending 30% or more of household income on gross rent (40) (41)	265	55	50	170	50	65
382	Tenant households spending from 30% to 99% of household income on gross rent (40) (41)	240	50	55	155	35	70
383	Owner households in non-farm, non-reserve private dwellings (42)	1,245	800	1,835	1,320	830	770
384	Average owner's major payments $ (42)	1,187	1,094	1,162	1,066	1,133	1,163
385	Owner households spending 30% or more of household income on owner's major payments (41) (42)	200	75	280	220	125	215
386	Owner households spending from 30% to 99% of household income on owner's major payments (41) (42)	205	75	265	195	105	195
	CENSUS FAMILY CHARACTERISTICS						
387	**Total number of census families in private households**	**1,440**	**860**	**1,865**	**1,475**	**875**	**670**
	by census family structure and size						
388	Total couple families	1,280	755	1,760	1,265	770	530
389	Total families of married couples	1,075	665	1,575	1,100	665	465
390	Without children at home	420	235	585	390	200	155
391	With children at home	655	430	990	710	465	310
392	1 child	240	145	340	255	195	140
393	2 children	310	195	365	325	185	130
394	3 or more children	105	85	280	125	85	35
395	Total families of common-law couples	205	90	190	160	110	60
396	Without children at home	90	45	100	90	40	30
397	With children at home	115	45	90	70	65	30
398	1 child	85	20	25	35	-	-
399	2 children	25	20	60	30	50	10
400	3 or more children	10	-	-	-	20	20
401	Total lone-parent families	160	105	105	215	105	135
402	Female parent	95	80	55	185	65	130
403	1 child	50	35	45	140	50	80
404	2 children	30	30	10	40	15	40
405	3 or more children	15	15	-	10	-	15

Tableau 1. Certaines caractéristiques des secteurs de recensement, recensement de 2001 – Données intégrales et données-échantillon (20 %)

Toronto 0800.02	Toronto 0801.01	Toronto 0801.02	Toronto 0802.01 A	Toronto 0802.02 A	Toronto 0803.03 A	Caractéristiques	N°
						CARACTÉRISTIQUES DES LOGEMENTS ET DES MÉNAGES	
						selon l'état du logement	
1,015	890	1,300	865	1,175	1,170	Entretien régulier seulement	355
540	360	470	245	415	350	Réparations mineures	356
150	85	110	75	80	70	Réparations majeures	357
						selon la période de construction	
55	30	100	-	70	35	Avant 1946	358
355	145	175	90	360	105	1946-1960	359
1,145	860	140	180	150	50	1961-1970	360
110	230	605	105	100	45	1971-1980	361
25	30	625	385	820	870	1981-1990	362
15	45	245	415	170	480	1991-2001 (20)	363
7.1	7.5	8.2	7.4	8.1	8.0	Nombre moyen de pièces par logement	364
3.2	3.4	3.5	3.4	3.5	3.4	Nombre moyen de chambres à coucher par logement	365
187,700	192,470	244,774	230,669	262,869	289,121	Valeur moyenne du logement $	366
1,710	**1,335**	**1,885**	**1,180**	**1,675**	**1,590**	**Nombre total de logements privés**	367
						selon la taille du ménage	
260	165	185	75	150	160	1 personne	368
540	450	495	305	460	385	2 personnes	369
325	260	360	270	305	300	3 personnes	370
510	405	745	480	675	650	4-5 personnes	371
80	60	95	45	85	95	6 personnes ou plus	372
						selon le genre de ménage	
1,330	1,080	1,610	1,025	1,430	1,365	Ménages unifamiliaux	373
75	45	55	30	60	60	Ménages multifamiliaux	374
300	205	220	120	180	160	Ménages non familiaux	375
5,015	4,005	6,035	3,855	5,425	5,270	Nombre de personnes dans les ménages privés	376
2.9	3.0	3.2	3.3	3.2	3.3	Nombre moyen de personnes dans les ménages privés	377
0.4	0.4	0.4	0.4	0.4	0.4	Nombre moyen de personnes par pièce	378
250	110	65	40	100	200	Ménages locataires dans les logements privés non agricoles hors réserve (40)	379
826	795	1,267	1,077	1,152	835	Loyer brut moyen $ (40)	380
70	30	25	10	35	65	Ménages locataires consacrant 30 % ou plus du revenu du ménage au loyer brut (40) (41)	381
55	30	30	10	20	60	Ménages locataires consacrant de 30 % à 99 % du revenu du ménage au loyer brut (40) (41)	382
1,460	1,225	1,820	1,140	1,570	1,385	Ménages propriétaires dans les logements privés non agricoles hors réserve (42)	383
1,087	1,061	1,231	1,265	1,172	1,343	Principales dépenses de propriété moyennes $ (42)	384
315	230	250	185	225	230	Ménages propriétaires consacrant 30 % ou plus du revenu du ménage aux principales dépenses de propriété (41) (42)	385
295	205	235	155	200	190	Ménages propriétaires consacrant de 30 % à 99 % du revenu du ménage aux principales dépenses de propriété (41) (42)	386
						CARACTÉRISTIQUES DES FAMILLES DE RECENSEMENT	
1,490	**1,180**	**1,720**	**1,100**	**1,545**	**1,495**	**Total des familles de recensement dans les ménages privés**	387
						selon la structure et la taille de la famille de recensement	
1,215	965	1,495	955	1,360	1,310	Total des familles avec conjoints	388
1,040	825	1,375	880	1,285	1,205	Total des familles avec couples mariés	389
420	285	410	235	355	330	Sans enfants à la maison	390
620	540	960	645	930	875	Avec enfants à la maison	391
225	220	275	230	260	250	1 enfant	392
250	225	490	300	515	485	2 enfants	393
140	100	200	115	155	145	3 enfants ou plus	394
175	145	125	75	80	105	Total des familles en union libre	395
90	80	75	45	45	60	Sans enfants à la maison	396
85	60	50	25	35	45	Avec enfants à la maison	397
40	25	25	10	-	25	1 enfant	398
40	20	10	10	30	20	2 enfants	399
15	15	10	10	-	-	3 enfants ou plus	400
280	210	225	145	190	185	Total des familles monoparentales	401
230	180	185	125	155	175	Parent de sexe féminin	402
135	100	70	60	95	65	1 enfant	403
70	70	85	60	50	80	2 enfants	404
25	15	35	-	15	30	3 enfants ou plus	405

Table 1. Selected Characteristics for Census Tracts, 2001 Census – 100% Data and 20% Sample Data

No.	Characteristics	Toronto 0635	Toronto 0636	Toronto 0637	Toronto 0638	Toronto 0639	Toronto 0800.01
	CENSUS FAMILY CHARACTERISTICS						
	by census family structure and size - concluded						
406	Male parent	65	25	45	30	40	10
407	1 child	50	15	35	20	30	-
408	2 children	15	10	10	10	15	-
409	3 or more children	-	-	-	-	-	-
410	**Total number of children at home**	**1,600**	**1,070**	**2,305**	**1,700**	**1,145**	**825**
	by age groups						
411	Under 6 years	375	250	445	375	320	145
412	6-14 years	650	415	835	690	395	280
413	15-17 years	195	135	285	190	125	130
414	18-24 years	250	185	455	295	225	175
415	25 years and over	130	90	280	155	75	100
416	Average number of children at home per census family (43)	1.1	1.2	1.2	1.2	1.3	1.2
417	**Total number of persons in private households**	**5,180**	**2,870**	**6,300**	**4,950**	**3,035**	**2,410**
	by census family status and living arrangements						
418	Number of non-family persons	865	185	365	515	245	380
419	Living with relatives (44)	85	15	70	25	10	90
420	Living with non-relatives only	210	40	75	110	70	55
421	Living alone	565	130	225	375	160	230
422	Number of family persons	4,320	2,690	5,930	4,440	2,785	2,030
423	Average number of persons per census family	3.0	3.1	3.2	3.0	3.2	3.1
424	**Total number of persons 65 years and over**	**620**	**260**	**605**	**580**	**220**	**280**
425	Number of non-family persons 65 years and over	310	35	145	230	65	85
426	Living with relatives (44)	35	10	25	10	10	15
427	Living with non-relatives only	-	-	10	10	15	-
428	Living alone	280	25	110	220	45	75
429	Number of family persons 65 years and over	305	225	465	350	145	190
	ECONOMIC FAMILY CHARACTERISTICS						
430	**Total number of economic families in private households**	**1,440**	**840**	**1,855**	**1,465**	**840**	**680**
	by size of family						
431	2 persons	620	315	735	610	285	250
432	3 persons	320	180	380	360	190	175
433	4 persons	350	245	430	360	220	190
434	5 or more persons	155	100	310	145	145	60
435	Total number of persons in economic families	4,405	2,700	6,000	4,465	2,800	2,115
436	Average number of persons per economic family	3.1	3.2	3.2	3.1	3.3	3.1
437	Total number of unattached individuals	775	165	300	485	235	290
	2000 INCOME CHARACTERISTICS						
	Population 15 years and over by sex and total income groups in 2000						
438	Total - Both sexes	4,180	2,210	5,375	3,885	2,320	2,010
439	Without income	140	50	240	130	60	55
440	With income	4,045	2,160	5,130	3,755	2,260	1,955
441	Under $1,000 (45)	125	65	335	135	95	35
442	$ 1,000 - $ 2,999	175	65	200	125	60	140
443	$ 3,000 - $ 4,999	160	75	190	125	95	70
444	$ 5,000 - $ 6,999	130	110	150	140	80	105
445	$ 7,000 - $ 9,999	180	120	220	205	90	110
446	$10,000 - $11,999	80	75	120	115	130	45
447	$12,000 - $14,999	250	65	265	165	105	120
448	$15,000 - $19,999	290	130	325	335	170	125
449	$20,000 - $24,999	365	170	400	300	150	140
450	$25,000 - $29,999	325	150	360	335	160	145
451	$30,000 - $34,999	290	175	385	290	165	190
452	$35,000 - $39,999	230	150	230	255	175	105
453	$40,000 - $44,999	260	145	340	290	130	150
454	$45,000 - $49,999	190	125	215	235	115	110
455	$50,000 - $59,999	270	205	400	305	200	175
456	$60,000 and over	705	350	985	400	340	190
457	Average income $ (46)	36,737	36,780	42,885	31,358	34,892	30,232
458	Median income $ (46)	28,415	30,467	29,645	28,013	28,367	27,559
459	Standard error of average income $ (46)	1,118	1,415	1,536	795	1,858	1,114

Tableau 1. Certaines caractéristiques des secteurs de recensement, recensement de 2001 – Données intégrales et données-échantillon (20 %)

Toronto 0800.02	Toronto 0801.01	Toronto 0801.02	Toronto 0802.01 A	Toronto 0802.02 A	Toronto 0803.03 A	Caractéristiques	N°
						CARACTÉRISTIQUES DES FAMILLES DE RECENSEMENT	
						selon la structure et la taille de la famille de recensement - fin	
50	30	40	25	30	15	Parent de sexe masculin	406
35	15	20	25	15	15	1 enfant	407
15	10	10	-	15	-	2 enfants	408
-	-	10	-	-	-	3 enfants ou plus	409
1,760	**1,440**	**2,385**	**1,475**	**2,160**	**2,115**	**Nombre total d'enfants à la maison**	410
						selon les groupes d'âge	
355	300	465	300	380	375	Moins de 6 ans	411
605	470	875	480	780	770	6-14 ans	412
185	135	275	160	275	270	15-17 ans	413
395	300	525	340	515	495	18-24 ans	414
220	240	245	195	215	200	25 ans et plus	415
1.2	1.2	1.4	1.3	1.4	1.4	Nombre moyen d'enfants à la maison par famille de recensement (43)	416
5,015	**4,005**	**6,035**	**3,855**	**5,425**	**5,265**	**Nombre total de personnes dans les ménages privés**	417
						selon la situation des particuliers dans la famille de recensement et des particuliers dans le ménage	
545	415	435	325	355	345	Nombre de personnes hors famille de recensement	418
155	135	100	135	110	135	Vivant avec des personnes apparentées (44)	419
135	115	150	110	90	50	Vivant avec des personnes non apparentées uniquement	420
260	165	185	80	155	155	Vivant seules	421
4,465	3,590	5,600	3,535	5,070	4,920	Nombre de personnes membres d'une famille	422
3.0	3.0	3.3	3.2	3.3	3.3	Nombre moyen de personnes par famille de recensement	423
540	**430**	**420**	**215**	**455**	**340**	**Nombre total de personnes de 65 ans et plus**	424
140	120	115	50	120	105	Nombre de personnes hors famille de recensement de 65 ans et plus	425
45	60	55	15	70	65	Vivant avec des personnes apparentées (44)	426
10	-	-	10	20	-	Vivant avec des personnes non apparentées uniquement	427
85	60	55	25	35	35	Vivant seules	428
400	310	300	165	335	235	Nombre de personnes membres d'une famille de 65 ans et plus	429
						CARACTÉRISTIQUES DES FAMILLES ÉCONOMIQUES	
1,445	**1,150**	**1,665**	**1,080**	**1,505**	**1,435**	**Nombre total de familles économiques dans les ménages privés**	430
						selon la taille de la famille	
570	440	480	310	460	380	2 personnes	431
320	265	385	275	310	315	3 personnes	432
330	265	525	325	480	445	4 personnes	433
225	180	285	170	255	285	5 personnes ou plus	434
4,620	3,720	5,700	3,670	5,185	5,060	Nombre total de personnes dans les familles économiques	435
3.2	3.3	3.4	3.4	3.4	3.5	Nombre moyen de personnes par famille économique	436
395	285	335	185	245	210	Nombre total de personnes hors famille économique	437
						CARACTÉRISTIQUES DU REVENU DE 2000	
						Population de 15 ans et plus selon le sexe et les tranches de revenu total en 2000	
4,020	3,200	4,680	3,075	4,265	4,120	Total - Les deux sexes	438
175	85	185	85	245	290	Sans revenu	439
3,840	3,115	4,495	2,990	4,025	3,835	Avec un revenu	440
95	175	125	135	230	180	Moins de 1 000 $ (45)	441
200	105	200	140	205	200	1 000 $ - 2 999 $	442
145	80	195	100	165	115	3 000 $ - 4 999 $	443
105	110	135	180	130	95	5 000 $ - 6 999 $	444
165	115	140	125	195	155	7 000 $ - 9 999 $	445
115	90	95	100	100	155	10 000 $ - 11 999 $	446
250	175	230	150	145	185	12 000 $ - 14 999 $	447
380	260	295	155	195	255	15 000 $ - 19 999 $	448
325	260	235	150	195	330	20 000 $ - 24 999 $	449
250	210	270	195	185	185	25 000 $ - 29 999 $	450
355	320	275	235	270	180	30 000 $ - 34 999 $	451
265	225	220	195	210	215	35 000 $ - 39 999 $	452
265	190	280	175	230	255	40 000 $ - 44 999 $	453
205	155	245	140	235	175	45 000 $ - 49 999 $	454
265	255	420	240	395	305	50 000 $ - 59 999 $	455
460	390	1,125	575	940	855	60 000 $ et plus	456
30,934	37,490	46,928	35,230	40,282	41,423	Revenu moyen $ (46)	457
27,122	29,483	35,319	30,061	34,836	30,580	Revenu médian $ (46)	458
775	4,479	2,187	1,114	1,304	1,438	Erreur type de revenu moyen $ (46)	459

Table 1. Selected Characteristics for Census Tracts, 2001 Census – 100% Data and 20% Sample Data

No.	Characteristics	Toronto 0635	Toronto 0636	Toronto 0637	Toronto 0638	Toronto 0639	Toronto 0800.01
	2000 INCOME CHARACTERISTICS						
	Population 15 years and over by sex and total income groups in 2000 – concluded						
460	Total - Males	2,000	1,110	2,785	1,850	1,205	955
461	Without income	25	35	80	35	30	30
462	With income	1,975	1,075	2,700	1,810	1,180	925
463	Under $1,000 (45)	65	25	180	40	35	10
464	$ 1,000 - $ 2,999	40	25	70	20	-	60
465	$ 3,000 - $ 4,999	55	25	80	30	35	15
466	$ 5,000 - $ 6,999	60	15	45	60	25	50
467	$ 7,000 - $ 9,999	90	50	65	50	25	30
468	$10,000 - $11,999	25	15	35	50	75	15
469	$12,000 - $14,999	90	30	110	30	10	25
470	$15,000 - $19,999	105	40	155	125	85	50
471	$20,000 - $24,999	145	20	195	100	75	75
472	$25,000 - $29,999	160	40	115	135	55	50
473	$30,000 - $34,999	120	85	210	180	85	110
474	$35,000 - $39,999	85	90	95	145	105	50
475	$40,000 - $44,999	155	100	185	145	65	75
476	$45,000 - $49,999	105	90	115	130	80	65
477	$50,000 - $59,999	155	135	255	240	155	115
478	$60,000 and over	530	295	795	325	265	130
479	Average income $ (46)	46,263	49,153	55,923	39,617	43,730	36,501
480	Median income $ (46)	36,306	44,366	39,507	38,219	39,050	32,956
481	Standard error of average income $ (46)	1,894	2,348	2,588	1,237	3,241	1,818
482	Total - Females	2,180	1,100	2,590	2,035	1,115	1,060
483	Without income	115	15	160	95	35	30
484	With income	2,070	1,080	2,430	1,940	1,080	1,030
485	Under $1,000 (45)	70	40	165	95	60	30
486	$ 1,000 - $ 2,999	135	35	130	110	50	85
487	$ 3,000 - $ 4,999	105	50	105	95	60	55
488	$ 5,000 - $ 6,999	70	95	105	75	55	55
489	$ 7,000 - $ 9,999	95	65	155	155	65	80
490	$10,000 - $11,999	50	60	85	70	55	20
491	$12,000 - $14,999	165	40	160	130	95	90
492	$15,000 - $19,999	185	95	170	215	90	75
493	$20,000 - $24,999	220	150	200	200	75	65
494	$25,000 - $29,999	175	110	245	195	100	95
495	$30,000 - $34,999	165	90	180	105	85	75
496	$35,000 - $39,999	140	55	135	105	70	55
497	$40,000 - $44,999	100	45	150	145	60	70
498	$45,000 - $49,999	85	40	100	105	30	40
499	$50,000 - $59,999	120	70	145	60	45	65
500	$60,000 and over	175	55	195	75	80	60
501	Average income $ (46)	27,628	24,500	28,405	23,640	25,225	24,592
502	Median income $ (46)	22,811	22,034	23,861	20,072	20,503	22,401
503	Standard error of average income $ (46)	1,046	1,143	1,185	880	1,422	1,226
	by composition of total income						
504	Total - Composition of income in 2000 % (47)	100.0	100.0	100.0	100.0	100.0	100.0
505	Employment income %	83.7	80.8	84.9	82.6	87.7	84.7
506	Government transfer payments %	7.5	6.4	5.0	9.4	6.9	8.7
507	Other %	8.9	12.6	10.0	8.0	5.6	6.6
	Population 15 years and over with employment income in 2000 by sex and work activity						
508	Both sexes with employment income (48)	3,190	1,690	4,095	2,985	1,900	1,500
509	Average employment income $	38,924	38,083	45,684	32,583	36,312	33,338
510	Standard error of average employment income $	1,326	1,619	1,949	898	2,086	1,325
511	Worked full year, full time (49)	1,895	1,080	2,340	1,775	1,155	820
512	Average employment income $	51,433	48,986	61,644	41,053	49,066	44,208
513	Standard error of average employment income $	1,705	2,125	3,257	877	3,107	1,713
514	Worked part year or part time (50)	1,235	590	1,645	1,165	730	625
515	Average employment income $	20,040	18,750	25,935	20,773	17,053	21,425
516	Standard error of average employment income $	1,648	1,565	1,591	1,572	1,329	1,516
517	Males with employment income (48)	1,655	880	2,280	1,550	1,055	780
518	Average employment income $	48,702	49,732	57,925	39,919	43,813	38,109
519	Standard error of average employment income $	2,136	2,614	3,095	1,326	3,482	2,114
520	Worked full year, full time (49)	1,140	635	1,435	1,075	705	435
521	Average employment income $	59,085	59,551	74,359	45,938	55,331	49,391
522	Standard error of average employment income $	2,499	3,159	4,809	1,179	4,813	2,799
523	Worked part year or part time (50)	480	245	760	460	345	320
524	Average employment income $	26,489	24,038	33,182	27,397	20,284	25,074
525	Standard error of average employment income $	3,440	2,877	2,852	3,112	1,977	2,392

Tableau 1. Certaines caractéristiques des secteurs de recensement, recensement de 2001 – Données intégrales et données-échantillon (20 %)

Toronto 0800.02	Toronto 0801.01	Toronto 0801.02	Toronto 0802.01 A	Toronto 0802.02 A	Toronto 0803.03 A	Caractéristiques	N°
						CARACTÉRISTIQUES DU REVENU DE 2000	
						Population de 15 ans et plus selon le sexe et les tranches de revenu total en 2000 – fin	
1,975	1,570	2,290	1,495	2,100	1,985	Total - Hommes	460
50	55	55	30	95	125	Sans revenu	461
1,925	1,520	2,235	1,465	2,005	1,865	Avec un revenu	462
55	75	55	55	110	100	Moins de 1 000 $ (45)	463
70	40	80	70	115	65	1 000 $ - 2 999 $	464
50	10	85	45	65	65	3 000 $ - 4 999 $	465
35	50	60	50	55	35	5 000 $ - 6 999 $	466
55	65	30	35	70	50	7 000 $ - 9 999 $	467
30	30	65	30	40	40	10 000 $ - 11 999 $	468
90	30	60	55	50	70	12 000 $ - 14 999 $	469
180	90	90	65	80	95	15 000 $ - 19 999 $	470
130	125	90	95	95	135	20 000 $ - 24 999 $	471
110	90	150	90	75	50	25 000 $ - 29 999 $	472
180	135	105	140	120	65	30 000 $ - 34 999 $	473
165	130	105	65	70	100	35 000 $ - 39 999 $	474
120	105	110	95	90	125	40 000 $ - 44 999 $	475
115	80	125	55	105	85	45 000 $ - 49 999 $	476
165	165	230	145	215	170	50 000 $ - 59 999 $	477
365	295	790	380	660	600	60 000 $ et plus	478
37,040	49,686	61,102	41,703	48,256	52,275	Revenu moyen $ (46)	479
34,048	35,777	46,133	34,979	42,570	40,429	Revenu médian $ (46)	480
1,230	9,041	4,197	1,768	2,251	2,410	Erreur type de revenu moyen $ (46)	481
2,045	1,630	2,390	1,585	2,165	2,135	Total - Femmes	482
130	35	135	60	145	160	Sans revenu	483
1,920	1,595	2,260	1,520	2,015	1,970	Avec un revenu	484
35	100	70	80	125	85	Moins de 1 000 $ (45)	485
130	65	125	65	85	135	1 000 $ - 2 999 $	486
95	70	105	60	100	45	3 000 $ - 4 999 $	487
75	60	80	135	75	55	5 000 $ - 6 999 $	488
110	55	110	95	125	105	7 000 $ - 9 999 $	489
80	65	30	65	60	115	10 000 $ - 11 999 $	490
155	140	165	90	100	110	12 000 $ - 14 999 $	491
200	170	205	85	115	160	15 000 $ - 19 999 $	492
195	135	140	60	100	195	20 000 $ - 24 999 $	493
140	120	120	110	115	140	25 000 $ - 29 999 $	494
180	180	170	100	155	115	30 000 $ - 34 999 $	495
100	95	120	130	135	110	35 000 $ - 39 999 $	496
145	80	170	80	140	130	40 000 $ - 44 999 $	497
90	75	120	85	130	90	45 000 $ - 49 999 $	498
100	85	190	90	185	135	50 000 $ - 59 999 $	499
95	95	330	200	280	250	60 000 $ et plus	500
24,818	25,887	32,887	28,995	32,341	31,161	Revenu moyen $ (46)	501
21,140	21,973	28,754	26,314	29,994	24,397	Revenu médian $ (46)	502
842	1,016	1,164	1,284	1,247	1,436	Erreur type de revenu moyen $ (46)	503
						selon la composition du revenu total	
100.0	100.0	100.0	100.0	100.0	100.0	Total - Composition du revenu en 2000 % (47)	504
81.8	84.6	87.3	89.0	85.3	87.9	Revenu d'emploi %	505
9.9	6.6	4.3	4.9	4.6	4.6	Transferts gouvernementaux %	506
8.2	8.9	8.4	6.0	10.2	7.7	Autre %	507
						Population de 15 ans et plus ayant un revenu d'emploi en 2000 selon le sexe et le travail	
2,970	2,450	3,790	2,490	3,300	3,220	Les deux sexes ayant un revenu d'emploi (48)	508
32,767	40,284	48,616	37,695	41,876	43,297	Revenu moyen d'emploi $	509
907	5,701	2,383	1,217	1,473	1,596	Erreur type de revenu moyen d'emploi $	510
1,745	1,575	2,345	1,475	1,835	1,765	Ayant travaillé toute l'année à plein temps (49)	511
41,972	41,877	63,878	51,070	57,803	56,580	Revenu moyen d'emploi $	512
1,044	1,274	3,492	1,478	2,122	2,050	Erreur type de revenu moyen d'emploi $	513
1,190	815	1,325	975	1,385	1,440	Ayant travaillé une partie de l'année ou à temps partiel (50)	514
19,814	39,648	22,471	18,816	22,624	27,482	Revenu moyen d'emploi $	515
1,284	16,296	1,632	1,263	1,426	2,231	Erreur type de revenu moyen d'emploi $	516
1,595	1,275	1,940	1,275	1,680	1,600	Hommes ayant un revenu d'emploi (48)	517
38,047	50,933	62,109	43,884	48,838	54,313	Revenu moyen d'emploi $	518
1,387	10,819	4,430	1,870	2,545	2,606	Erreur type de revenu moyen d'emploi $	519
1,020	890	1,335	835	1,000	1,025	Ayant travaillé toute l'année à plein temps (49)	520
45,329	46,195	78,492	55,774	66,273	66,150	Revenu moyen d'emploi $	521
1,539	1,883	6,038	2,175	3,497	3,161	Erreur type de revenu moyen d'emploi $	522
560	345	560	425	645	565	Ayant travaillé une partie de l'année ou à temps partiel (50)	523
24,895	68,815	24,383	21,663	24,253	33,758	Revenu moyen d'emploi $	524
2,348	38,283	2,765	2,086	2,441	4,033	Erreur type de revenu moyen d'emploi $	525

Table 1. Selected Characteristics for Census Tracts, 2001 Census – 100% Data and 20% Sample Data

No.	Characteristics	Toronto 0635	Toronto 0636	Toronto 0637	Toronto 0638	Toronto 0639	Toronto 0800.01
	2000 INCOME CHARACTERISTICS						
	Population 15 years and over with employment income in 2000 by sex and work activity – concluded						
526	Females with employment income (48)	1,535	805	1,820	1,430	850	725
527	Average employment income $	28,363	25,330	30,356	24,628	26,964	28,211
528	Standard error of average employment income $	1,255	1,334	1,611	1,042	1,666	1,437
529	Worked full year, full time (49)	750	445	905	700	445	385
530	Average employment income $	39,754	33,904	41,595	33,557	39,091	38,313
531	Standard error of average employment income $	1,648	1,668	2,905	1,065	2,272	1,663
532	Worked part year or part time (50)	760	350	880	710	385	305
533	Average employment income $	15,982	15,052	19,672	16,490	14,121	17,566
534	Standard error of average employment income $	1,366	1,616	1,273	1,548	1,744	1,640
	Census families by structure and family income groups in 2000						
535	Total - All census families	1,440	860	1,865	1,475	875	665
536	Under $10,000	-	-	15	35	25	-
537	$ 10,000 - $19,999	40	10	40	50	20	10
538	$ 20,000 - $29,999	110	35	75	85	25	25
539	$ 30,000 - $39,999	70	75	130	140	65	80
540	$ 40,000 - $49,999	150	25	90	135	85	75
541	$ 50,000 - $59,999	135	100	105	140	95	90
542	$ 60,000 - $69,999	110	110	185	180	115	100
543	$ 70,000 - $79,999	150	120	180	210	95	80
544	$ 80,000 - $89,999	120	60	190	120	90	65
545	$ 90,000 - $99,999	85	55	155	150	70	55
546	$100,000 and over	460	265	700	225	190	100
547	Average family income $	86,543	85,381	110,642	69,242	79,471	70,852
548	Median family income $	77,013	74,273	84,200	68,644	70,785	65,435
549	Standard error of average family income $	2,853	3,391	5,001	1,869	4,888	2,738
550	Total - All couple census families (51)	1,280	755	1,765	1,265	765	530
551	Under $10,000	-	-	10	15	-	-
552	$ 10,000 - $19,999	35	-	20	35	10	-
553	$ 20,000 - $29,999	115	10	70	75	10	20
554	$ 30,000 - $39,999	40	65	120	100	50	60
555	$ 40,000 - $49,999	115	20	75	80	70	60
556	$ 50,000 - $59,999	115	90	95	110	90	50
557	$ 60,000 - $69,999	100	95	175	175	95	70
558	$ 70,000 - $79,999	140	115	175	190	85	60
559	$ 80,000 - $89,999	120	55	190	120	90	55
560	$ 90,000 - $99,999	85	45	140	150	70	45
561	$100,000 and over	430	255	695	220	195	100
562	Average family income $	89,155	90,385	114,052	73,842	84,924	74,209
563	Median family income $	79,541	79,022	86,760	71,992	74,060	69,723
564	Standard error of average family income $	3,068	3,617	5,269	1,985	5,285	3,256
	Incidence of low income in 2000						
565	Total - Economic families	1,440	845	1,855	1,465	840	680
566	Low income	60	15	50	75	45	10
567	Incidence of low income in 2000 % (52)	4.4	1.8	2.6	5.0	5.5	1.2
568	Total - Unattached individuals 15 years and over	775	170	285	485	235	290
569	Low income	220	35	45	95	30	80
570	Incidence of low income in 2000 % (52)	28.1	20.6	17.1	19.4	13.0	27.6
571	Total - Population in private households	5,185	2,870	6,290	4,945	3,030	2,405
572	Low income	405	85	155	265	150	95
573	Incidence of low income in 2000 % (52)	7.8	3.1	2.5	5.4	4.8	4.0
	Private households by household income groups in 2000						
574	Total - All private households	2,065	990	2,090	1,865	1,025	930
575	Under $10,000	55	10	15	50	45	15
576	$ 10,000 - $19,999	220	40	100	180	50	55
577	$ 20,000 - $29,999	230	55	80	150	40	80
578	$ 30,000 - $39,999	170	80	175	190	50	90
579	$ 40,000 - $49,999	160	50	115	180	120	105
580	$ 50,000 - $59,999	160	130	110	175	110	110
581	$ 60,000 - $69,999	125	105	205	200	105	120
582	$ 70,000 - $79,999	195	125	200	215	110	85
583	$ 80,000 - $89,999	150	55	175	125	85	75
584	$ 90,000 - $99,999	120	65	150	160	70	65
585	$100,000 and over	475	270	745	240	240	115
586	Average household income $	71,805	80,309	104,485	63,048	76,615	62,972
587	Median household income $	63,539	70,599	81,473	60,185	68,741	60,475
588	Standard error of average household income $	2,431	3,182	4,539	1,772	4,463	2,359

Tableau 1. Certaines caractéristiques des secteurs de recensement, recensement de 2001 – Données intégrales et données-échantillon (20 %)

Toronto 0800.02	Toronto 0801.01	Toronto 0801.02	Toronto 0802.01 A	Toronto 0802.02 A	Toronto 0803.03 A	Caractéristiques	N°
						CARACTÉRISTIQUES DU REVENU DE 2000	
						Population de 15 ans et plus ayant un revenu d'emploi en 2000 selon le sexe et le travail – fin	
1,375	1,175	1,850	1,210	1,615	1,620	Femmes ayant un revenu d'emploi (48)	526
26,649	28,719	34,460	31,201	34,626	32,399	Revenu moyen d'emploi $	527
1,016	1,193	1,272	1,449	1,374	1,632	Erreur type de revenu moyen d'emploi $	528
720	680	1,015	635	835	740	Ayant travaillé toute l'année à plein temps (49)	529
37,229	36,264	44,637	44,912	47,679	43,307	Revenu moyen d'emploi $	530
1,179	1,481	1,282	1,782	1,761	1,788	Erreur type de revenu moyen d'emploi $	531
630	475	760	545	740	870	Ayant travaillé une partie de l'année ou à temps partiel (50)	532
15,285	18,383	21,055	16,579	21,203	23,419	Revenu moyen d'emploi $	533
1,110	1,526	1,961	1,524	1,656	2,502	Erreur type de revenu moyen d'emploi $	534
						Familles de recensement selon la structure et les tranches de revenu de la famille en 2000	
1,490	1,175	1,720	1,100	1,550	1,495	Total - Toutes les familles de recensement	535
20	35	25	10	30	50	Moins de 10 000 $	536
60	35	45	30	30	45	10 000 $ - 19 999 $	537
85	45	20	35	45	50	20 000 $ - 29 999 $	538
150	140	70	45	60	85	30 000 $ - 39 999 $	539
165	100	90	75	130	85	40 000 $ - 49 999 $	540
145	105	155	120	130	60	50 000 $ - 59 999 $	541
200	135	130	80	135	110	60 000 $ - 69 999 $	542
145	105	165	115	110	160	70 000 $ - 79 999 $	543
105	95	120	140	130	130	80 000 $ - 89 999 $	544
165	100	125	95	145	145	90 000 $ - 99 999 $	545
250	285	775	355	605	570	100 000 $ et plus	546
68,572	89,014	112,872	85,178	95,437	99,239	Revenu moyen des familles $	547
65,532	69,667	92,559	80,869	88,124	87,347	Revenu médian des familles $	548
1,800	11,929	5,567	2,618	3,196	3,708	Erreur type de revenu moyen des familles $	549
1,210	970	1,495	955	1,360	1,310	Total - Toutes les familles de recensement comptant un couple (51)	550
-	20	-	10	15	40	Moins de 10 000 $	551
15	25	20	10	15	30	10 000 $ - 19 999 $	552
60	30	20	25	35	40	20 000 $ - 29 999 $	553
110	90	50	40	50	50	30 000 $ - 39 999 $	554
115	70	80	50	70	45	40 000 $ - 49 999 $	555
120	85	110	85	110	55	50 000 $ - 59 999 $	556
175	110	90	70	110	95	60 000 $ - 69 999 $	557
140	80	140	100	105	140	70 000 $ - 79 999 $	558
95	95	115	140	120	125	80 000 $ - 89 999 $	559
155	100	110	90	130	140	90 000 $ - 99 999 $	560
225	265	765	340	595	545	100 000 $ et plus	561
73,420	97,972	121,648	90,030	101,014	105,835	Revenu moyen des familles $	562
69,872	76,196	100,865	84,501	92,162	90,520	Revenu médian des familles $	563
1,931	14,514	6,286	2,780	3,392	4,074	Erreur type de revenu moyen des familles $	564
						Fréquence des unités à faible revenu en 2000	
1,445	1,145	1,665	1,080	1,505	1,430	Total - Familles économiques	565
100	90	50	50	65	110	Faible revenu	566
7.0	7.6	3.0	4.7	4.4	7.5	Fréquence des unités à faible revenu en 2000 % (52)	567
370	250	330	180	240	205	Total - Personnes hors famille économique de 15 ans et plus	568
90	60	50	25	35	70	Faible revenu	569
23.5	25.0	15.3	15.6	15.5	33.6	Fréquence des unités à faible revenu en 2000 % (52)	570
4,990	3,970	6,025	3,850	5,420	5,265	Total - Population dans les ménages privés	571
390	310	240	195	250	495	Faible revenu	572
7.8	7.7	4.0	5.1	4.7	9.4	Fréquence des unités à faible revenu en 2000 % (52)	573
						Ménages privés selon les tranches de revenu du ménage en 2000	
1,705	1,340	1,885	1,180	1,675	1,590	Total - Tous les ménages privés	574
25	30	20	10	30	50	Moins de 10 000 $	575
100	75	40	20	35	65	10 000 $ - 19 999 $	576
80	80	40	35	85	65	20 000 $ - 29 999 $	577
155	135	85	25	50	90	30 000 $ - 39 999 $	578
215	95	105	70	120	95	40 000 $ - 49 999 $	579
135	130	180	110	140	85	50 000 $ - 59 999 $	580
220	120	145	105	125	105	60 000 $ - 69 999 $	581
175	95	185	160	130	115	70 000 $ - 79 999 $	582
95	120	125	150	125	145	80 000 $ - 89 999 $	583
170	115	130	95	150	130	90 000 $ - 99 999 $	584
330	345	830	400	675	645	100 000 $ et plus	585
69,540	87,296	111,888	89,172	96,888	99,758	Revenu moyen des ménages $	586
65,913	70,219	90,884	82,307	88,883	88,223	Revenu médian des ménages $	587
1,805	10,643	5,194	2,491	3,157	3,748	Erreur type de revenu moyen des ménages $	588

Table 1. Selected Characteristics for Census Tracts, 2001 Census – 100% Data and 20% Sample Data

No.	Characteristics	Toronto 0803.04 A	Toronto 0803.05 A	Toronto 0803.06 A	Toronto 0804.01	Toronto 0804.02 A	Toronto 0804.05
	POPULATION CHARACTERISTICS						
1	**Population, 1996 (1)**	**3,715**	**2,961**	**4,959**	**6,844**	**8,919**	**5,823**
2	**Population, 2001 (2)**	**5,200**	**5,735**	**5,443**	**7,178**	**10,027**	**6,467**
3	Population percentage change, 1996-2001	40.0	93.7	9.8	4.9	12.4	11.1
4	Land area in square kilometres, 2001	2.77	2.45	1.57	3.08	3.21	3.07
5	**Total population - 100% Data (3)**	**5,200**	**5,735**	**5,445**	**7,180**	**10,030**	**6,465**
	by sex and age groups						
6	Male	2,545	2,870	2,655	3,520	4,665	3,175
7	0-4 years	310	280	205	220	290	175
8	5-9 years	280	235	250	315	375	260
9	10-14 years	195	240	280	350	300	300
10	15-19 years	140	220	245	310	320	305
11	20-24 years	115	155	170	225	280	220
12	25-29 years	100	165	115	135	320	165
13	30-34 years	225	290	150	175	350	180
14	35-39 years	355	335	255	305	420	265
15	40-44 years	245	260	265	360	395	310
16	45-49 years	180	235	245	375	305	285
17	50-54 years	155	190	210	290	330	285
18	55-59 years	85	100	100	190	225	190
19	60-64 years	70	60	60	90	180	95
20	65-69 years	35	45	45	70	185	55
21	70-74 years	30	40	30	65	160	50
22	75-79 years	20	20	15	35	115	35
23	80-84 years	10	10	5	10	75	10
24	85 years and over	5	-	-	5	30	5
25	Female	2,650	2,865	2,790	3,655	5,360	3,290
26	0-4 years	245	265	180	200	300	160
27	5-9 years	280	220	235	305	330	235
28	10-14 years	195	210	270	365	300	310
29	15-19 years	170	220	255	300	375	265
30	20-24 years	130	145	160	200	310	235
31	25-29 years	135	215	130	160	310	180
32	30-34 years	285	310	200	220	420	205
33	35-39 years	375	320	305	345	475	310
34	40-44 years	235	280	315	430	430	335
35	45-49 years	195	235	260	390	385	330
36	50-54 years	150	175	175	285	360	285
37	55-59 years	75	100	85	150	275	160
38	60-64 years	60	55	70	80	220	80
39	65-69 years	50	55	35	90	250	50
40	70-74 years	25	40	40	70	245	65
41	75-79 years	20	20	35	40	225	45
42	80-84 years	5	5	10	20	95	20
43	85 years and over	10	5	15	10	60	10
44	**Total population 15 years and over**	**3,695**	**4,285**	**4,010**	**5,430**	**8,135**	**5,025**
	by legal marital status						
45	Never married (single)	895	1,145	1,155	1,465	2,435	1,500
46	Legally married (and not separated)	2,425	2,745	2,445	3,475	4,120	2,975
47	Separated, but still legally married	95	105	105	105	355	145
48	Divorced	175	190	180	230	625	245
49	Widowed	100	95	125	155	605	155
	by common-law status						
50	Not in a common-law relationship	3,515	4,040	3,865	5,200	7,615	4,780
51	In a common-law relationship	185	245	150	230	520	245
52	**Total population - 20% Sample Data (4)**	**5,195**	**5,730**	**5,445**	**7,180**	**9,975**	**6,460**
	by mother tongue						
53	Single responses	5,040	5,575	5,400	7,155	9,880	6,410
54	English	3,995	4,285	4,500	6,155	8,185	5,495
55	French	50	85	35	80	110	55
56	Non-official languages (5)	990	1,210	870	920	1,580	860
57	Italian	140	190	165	155	100	55
58	Chinese, n.o.s.	-	15	35	45	50	15
59	Cantonese	20	-	10	15	95	60
60	Portuguese	10	45	-	15	50	35
61	Punjabi	50	-	-	35	10	55
62	Other languages (6)	765	950	660	650	1,275	635
63	Multiple responses	165	155	45	25	100	55
64	English and French	-	10	-	-	-	15
65	English and non-official language	155	145	40	15	60	40
66	French and non-official language	10	-	-	10	-	-
67	English, French and non-official language	-	-	-	-	30	-

See reference material at the end of the publication. – Voir les documents de référence à la fin de la publication.

Tableau 1. Certaines caractéristiques des secteurs de recensement, recensement de 2001 – Données intégrales et données-échantillon (20 %)

Toronto 0804.06 A	Toronto 0804.07 A	Toronto 0804.08 A	Toronto 0804.09 A	Toronto 0805.02	Toronto 0805.03 A	Caractéristiques	N°
						CARACTÉRISTIQUES DE LA POPULATION	
3,499	**4,055**	**3,995**	**7,089**	**5,043**	**7,527**	**Population, 1996 (1)**	1
3,450	**4,049**	**4,188**	**8,081**	**5,060**	**8,549**	**Population, 2001 (2)**	2
-1.4	-0.1	4.8	14.0	0.3	13.6	Variation en pourcentage de la population, 1996-2001	3
0.82	0.90	2.48	9.46	1.05	17.21	Superficie des terres en kilomètres carrés, 2001	4
3,450	**4,050**	**4,185**	**8,080**	**5,060**	**8,550**	**Population totale – Données intégrales (3)**	5
						selon le sexe et les groupes d'âge	
1,685	1,935	2,095	4,000	2,470	4,255	Sexe masculin	6
95	125	115	310	180	380	0-4 ans	7
130	165	155	390	220	410	5-9 ans	8
135	205	190	390	245	465	10-14 ans	9
180	180	220	330	220	345	15-19 ans	10
120	150	180	250	150	195	20-24 ans	11
95	115	80	225	115	220	25-29 ans	12
100	125	95	300	175	360	30-34 ans	13
140	160	165	380	255	470	35-39 ans	14
155	155	175	370	265	490	40-44 ans	15
145	140	215	340	230	345	45-49 ans	16
175	135	210	280	180	225	50-54 ans	17
95	75	120	165	115	125	55-59 ans	18
50	55	60	100	50	70	60-64 ans	19
30	40	45	65	45	65	65-69 ans	20
20	30	30	55	25	50	70-74 ans	21
15	30	15	30	10	20	75-79 ans	22
-	20	10	15	10	10	80-84 ans	23
10	25	15	5	5	5	85 ans et plus	24
1,765	2,110	2,090	4,080	2,585	4,295	Sexe féminin	25
115	100	110	285	180	350	0-4 ans	26
110	185	160	335	240	410	5-9 ans	27
155	185	185	370	250	415	10-14 ans	28
150	155	205	370	190	320	15-19 ans	29
135	130	175	260	155	210	20-24 ans	30
75	110	95	230	125	260	25-29 ans	31
110	160	100	325	215	410	30-34 ans	32
170	175	205	445	280	530	35-39 ans	33
175	205	220	415	300	490	40-44 ans	34
180	140	220	315	225	325	45-49 ans	35
165	145	175	265	145	195	50-54 ans	36
70	90	100	125	100	105	55-59 ans	37
45	65	50	105	60	80	60-64 ans	38
40	40	35	55	45	75	65-69 ans	39
20	35	20	80	35	55	70-74 ans	40
20	60	20	40	30	20	75-79 ans	41
20	45	10	25	15	10	80-84 ans	42
10	95	10	20	5	15	85 ans et plus	43
2,700	**3,085**	**3,270**	**5,995**	**3,750**	**6,115**	**Population totale de 15 ans et plus**	44
						selon l'état matrimonial légal	
850	1,000	1,030	1,830	1,100	1,710	Célibataire (jamais marié(e))	45
1,500	1,415	1,980	3,595	2,220	3,775	Légalement marié(e) (et non séparé(e))	46
90	170	70	155	105	175	Séparé(e), mais toujours légalement marié(e)	47
170	265	110	235	215	310	Divorcé(e)	48
90	230	80	180	105	145	Veuf ou veuve	49
						selon l'union libre	
2,540	2,845	3,155	5,755	3,545	5,710	Ne vivant pas en union libre	50
155	240	115	245	205	405	Vivant en union libre	51
3,450	**3,795**	**4,165**	**8,075**	**5,055**	**8,530**	**Population totale – Données-échantillon (20 %) (4)**	52
						selon la langue maternelle	
3,415	3,640	4,125	7,910	5,015	8,430	Réponses uniques	53
2,960	3,185	3,495	5,980	4,160	7,165	Anglais	54
30	70	60	105	115	145	Français	55
425	390	565	1,830	740	1,125	Langues non officielles (5)	56
20	10	55	235	80	115	Italien	57
25	-	70	85	20	10	Chinois, n.d.a.	58
10	15	15	85	-	60	Cantonais	59
40	25	15	30	20	75	Portugais	60
-	45	70	30	10	80	Pendjabi	61
335	290	340	1,360	610	785	Autres langues (6)	62
40	155	40	165	45	100	Réponses multiples	63
-	20	20	30	15	40	Anglais et français	64
35	55	20	135	25	60	Anglais et langue non officielle	65
-	80	-	-	-	-	Français et langue non officielle	66
-	-	-	-	-	-	Anglais, français et langue non officielle	67

See reference material at the end of the publication. – Voir les documents de référence à la fin de la publication.

Table 1. Selected Characteristics for Census Tracts, 2001 Census – 100% Data and 20% Sample Data

No.	Characteristics	Toronto 0803.04 A	Toronto 0803.05 A	Toronto 0803.06 A	Toronto 0804.01	Toronto 0804.02 A	Toronto 0804.05
	POPULATION CHARACTERISTICS						
	by home language						
68	Single responses	4,540	4,975	4,875	6,685	8,840	6,020
69	English	4,365	4,760	4,740	6,555	8,430	5,865
70	French	-	10	10	-	10	-
71	Non-official languages (5)	175	205	120	130	390	155
72	Cantonese	-	-	10	-	30	30
73	Chinese, n.o.s.	10	-	20	-	15	-
74	Italian	15	15	-	10	10	-
75	Punjabi	10	-	-	10	-	40
76	Portuguese	-	-	-	-	-	-
77	Other languages (6)	150	190	95	110	335	95
78	Multiple responses	650	755	575	490	1,140	445
79	English and French	20	45	15	80	110	45
80	English and non-official language	625	695	550	375	1,020	390
81	French and non-official language	-	-	10	-	-	-
82	English, French and non-official language	10	15	-	35	-	10
	by knowledge of official languages						
83	English only	4,810	5,360	5,075	6,630	9,225	6,055
84	French only	-	-	-	-	-	-
85	English and French	350	345	360	530	665	400
86	Neither English nor French	35	25	10	20	80	10
	by knowledge of non-official languages (5) (7)						
87	Italian	230	260	190	185	150	85
88	Cantonese	20	-	10	25	120	60
89	Chinese, n.o.s.	-	10	60	50	35	20
90	Spanish	65	100	135	60	170	75
91	Portuguese	15	45	10	25	55	70
92	Punjabi	85	10	-	40	55	65
93	Tagalog (Pilipino)	140	130	55	85	215	90
	by first official language spoken						
94	English	5,090	5,620	5,385	7,050	9,750	6,370
95	French	55	70	35	75	115	55
96	English and French	15	20	15	35	35	30
97	Neither English nor French	35	20	-	20	75	-
98	Official language minority - (number) (8)	65	85	40	95	130	75
99	Official language minority - (percentage) (8)	1.3	1.5	0.7	1.3	1.3	1.2
	by ethnic origin (9)						
100	Canadian	1,010	1,095	1,330	2,365	2,680	2,035
101	English	955	1,095	1,325	2,050	2,380	1,985
102	Scottish	750	900	930	1,560	1,660	1,365
103	Irish	725	750	950	1,340	1,465	1,380
104	Chinese	125	155	215	240	280	170
105	Italian	580	730	570	540	370	310
106	East Indian	625	620	455	415	710	475
107	French	385	335	445	545	640	490
108	German	195	305	305	365	415	455
109	Portuguese	75	285	90	250	345	215
110	Polish	160	140	120	160	345	205
111	Jewish	50	35	15	20	45	20
112	Jamaican	465	355	595	270	675	265
113	Filipino	205	275	85	120	235	125
114	Ukrainian	90	180	255	130	150	75
	by Aboriginal identity						
115	Total Aboriginal identity population (10)	10	-	20	55	25	25
116	Total non-Aboriginal population	5,190	5,730	5,425	7,125	9,950	6,440
	by Aboriginal origin						
117	Total Aboriginal origins population (11)	45	-	100	95	150	115
118	Total non-Aboriginal population	5,150	5,730	5,345	7,080	9,825	6,350
	by Registered Indian status						
119	Registered Indian (12)	10	-	-	10	10	15
120	Not a Registered Indian	5,190	5,730	5,445	7,165	9,970	6,450

Tableau 1. Certaines caractéristiques des secteurs de recensement, recensement de 2001 – Données intégrales et données-échantillon (20 %)

Toronto 0804.06 A	Toronto 0804.07 A	Toronto 0804.08 A	Toronto 0804.09 A	Toronto 0805.02	Toronto 0805.03 A	Caractéristiques	N°
						CARACTÉRISTIQUES DE LA POPULATION	
						selon la langue parlée à la maison	
3,095	3,395	3,900	6,775	4,405	7,825	Réponses uniques	68
3,055	3,315	3,705	6,380	4,305	7,560	Anglais	69
10	-	-	15	15	25	Français	70
35	80	195	390	85	245	Langues non officielles (5)	71
-	-	10	30	-	20	Cantonais	72
-	-	40	30	-	-	Chinois, n.d.a.	73
-	-	-	35	-	-	Italien	74
-	15	70	30	10	40	Pendjabi	75
10	-	10	-	-	-	Portugais	76
25	60	75	265	75	180	Autres langues (6)	77
355	400	265	1,295	655	705	Réponses multiples	78
20	40	65	100	125	150	Anglais et français	79
340	250	200	1,175	495	525	Anglais et langue non officielle	80
-	-	-	-	35	20	Français et langue non officielle	81
-	105	-	20	-	10	Anglais, français et langue non officielle	82
						selon la connaissance des langues officielles	
3,265	3,455	3,850	7,365	4,690	7,920	Anglais seulement	83
-	-	-	-	-	10	Français seulement	84
170	335	285	610	345	575	Anglais et français	85
15	10	25	95	25	35	Ni l'anglais ni le français	86
						selon la connaissance des langues non officielles (5) (7)	
50	20	65	300	90	185	Italien	87
15	10	35	95	15	60	Cantonais	88
25	-	35	90	10	10	Chinois, n.d.a.	89
150	50	55	115	65	55	Espagnol	90
40	25	25	45	15	85	Portugais	91
-	60	70	55	15	80	Pendjabi	92
20	70	40	315	30	135	Tagalog (pilipino)	93
						selon la première langue officielle parlée	
3,410	3,705	4,070	7,845	4,875	8,320	Anglais	94
20	80	70	80	120	150	Français	95
10	-	10	50	55	35	Anglais et français	96
10	10	20	95	15	35	Ni l'anglais ni le français	97
30	80	75	105	145	165	Minorité de langue officielle - (nombre) (8)	98
0.9	2.1	1.8	1.3	2.9	1.9	Minorité de langue officielle - (pourcentage) (8)	99
						selon l'origine ethnique (9)	
1,185	1,365	1,560	1,845	1,405	2,535	Canadien	100
1,090	990	1,120	1,470	1,250	2,375	Anglais	101
755	660	895	860	915	1,630	Écossais	102
640	595	695	695	640	1,720	Irlandais	103
65	120	250	435	235	300	Chinois	104
160	90	130	635	310	530	Italien	105
220	190	215	1,000	395	595	Indien de l'Inde	106
290	310	300	455	410	620	Français	107
295	320	360	300	270	625	Allemand	108
55	105	60	265	245	265	Portugais	109
35	55	145	145	140	195	Polonais	110
35	95	40	115	40	20	Juif	111
180	345	115	725	390	405	Jamaïquain	112
30	75	75	415	65	225	Philippin	113
100	25	55	105	90	230	Ukrainien	114
						selon l'identité autochtone	
15	65	20	10	15	25	Total de la population ayant une identité autochtone (10)	115
3,435	3,730	4,150	8,070	5,045	8,510	Total de la population non autochtone	116
						selon l'origine autochtone	
25	90	30	45	60	75	Total de la population ayant une origine autochtone (11)	117
3,430	3,705	4,135	8,035	5,000	8,460	Total de la population non autochtone	118
						selon le statut d'Indien inscrit	
10	65	10	10	-	15	Oui, Indien inscrit (12)	119
3,445	3,730	4,160	8,070	5,060	8,520	Non, pas un Indien inscrit	120

Table 1. Selected Characteristics for Census Tracts, 2001 Census – 100% Data and 20% Sample Data

No.	Characteristics	Toronto 0803.04 A	Toronto 0803.05 A	Toronto 0803.06 A	Toronto 0804.01	Toronto 0804.02 A	Toronto 0804.05
	POPULATION CHARACTERISTICS						
	by visible minority groups						
121	Total visible minority population	1,890	1,960	1,725	1,390	3,130	1,415
122	Chinese	80	85	175	155	220	135
123	South Asian	720	605	415	365	905	290
124	Black	590	550	810	490	1,250	470
125	Filipino	205	225	80	105	235	125
126	Latin American	-	15	60	15	155	15
127	Southeast Asian	-	45	-	35	10	-
128	Arab	95	55	65	20	30	-
129	West Asian	10	25	15	45	50	-
130	Korean	10	40	10	-	25	30
131	Japanese	45	45	-	70	10	40
132	Visible minority, n.i.e. (13)	85	245	70	60	185	280
133	Multiple visible minorities (14)	55	30	25	30	60	25
	by citizenship						
134	Canadian citizenship (15)	4,890	5,370	5,195	6,900	9,200	6,235
135	Citizenship other than Canadian	305	360	250	280	775	225
	by place of birth of respondent						
136	Non-immigrant population	3,425	3,820	3,750	5,325	6,525	4,840
137	Born in province of residence	3,120	3,530	3,510	4,870	5,635	4,335
138	Immigrant population (16)	1,765	1,910	1,675	1,855	3,395	1,615
139	United States	30	45	30	40	50	20
140	Central and South America	195	260	205	210	435	240
141	Caribbean and Bermuda	315	360	515	255	670	250
142	United Kingdom	210	145	215	510	675	410
143	Other Europe (17)	360	450	300	380	520	325
144	Africa	115	95	110	45	140	30
145	Asia and the Middle East	530	545	300	395	890	335
146	Oceania and other (18)	-	10	10	15	15	-
147	Non-permanent residents (19)	-	-	15	10	50	10
148	**Total immigrant population**	**1,765**	**1,910**	**1,680**	**1,855**	**3,395**	**1,615**
	by period of immigration						
149	Before 1961	135	160	110	295	395	270
150	1961-1970	305	325	360	395	470	385
151	1971-1980	610	625	625	595	760	470
152	1981-1990	365	340	325	290	890	320
153	1991-2001 (20)	345	460	260	275	880	175
154	1991-1995	230	200	110	125	485	105
155	1996-2001 (20)	110	260	150	150	395	70
	by age at immigration						
156	0-4 years	225	295	165	210	290	180
157	5-19 years	620	645	580	600	1,000	590
158	20 years and over	925	970	930	1,040	2,105	845
159	**Total population**	**5,195**	**5,730**	**5,445**	**7,180**	**9,975**	**6,460**
	by religion						
160	Catholic (21)	2,035	2,400	2,115	2,455	3,130	2,300
161	Protestant	1,485	1,425	2,160	2,875	3,945	2,335
162	Christian Orthodox	450	205	180	295	180	190
163	Christian, n.i.e. (22)	255	140	70	275	375	130
164	Muslim	325	460	330	100	590	100
165	Jewish	35	20	-	25	45	15
166	Buddhist	10	-	10	30	40	30
167	Hindu	230	225	45	100	375	180
168	Sikh	40	-	-	35	10	50
169	Eastern religions (23)	-	-	-	-	40	-
170	Other religions (24)	-	15	-	-	-	-
171	No religious affiliation (25)	335	825	530	990	1,250	1,140
172	**Total population 15 years and over**	**3,695**	**4,280**	**4,015**	**5,430**	**8,065**	**5,010**
	by generation status						
173	1st generation (26)	1,680	1,775	1,645	1,835	3,280	1,605
174	2nd generation (27)	1,025	1,135	1,090	1,380	1,850	1,280
175	3rd generation and over (28)	990	1,365	1,280	2,210	2,935	2,130
176	**Total population 1 year and over (29)**	**5,085**	**5,615**	**5,370**	**7,120**	**9,875**	**6,400**
	by place of residence 1 year ago (mobility)						
177	Non-movers	4,580	5,165	4,945	6,560	8,445	5,285
178	Movers	505	450	425	555	1,430	1,115
179	Non-migrants	185	145	185	235	510	655
180	Migrants	320	300	240	325	920	460
181	Internal migrants	270	260	230	265	795	455
182	Intraprovincial migrants	250	255	220	255	740	440
183	Interprovincial migrants	20	10	10	10	55	15
184	External migrants	45	45	15	55	120	-

Tableau 1. Certaines caractéristiques des secteurs de recensement, recensement de 2001 – Données intégrales et données-échantillon (20 %)

Toronto 0804.06 A	Toronto 0804.07 A	Toronto 0804.08 A	Toronto 0804.09 A	Toronto 0805.02	Toronto 0805.03 A	Caractéristiques	N°
						CARACTÉRISTIQUES DE LA POPULATION	
						selon les groupes de minorités visibles	
765	1,330	865	3,975	1,635	2,260	Total de la population des minorités visibles	121
55	30	250	355	130	160	Chinois	122
220	275	205	1,115	370	580	Sud-Asiatique	123
280	585	270	1,315	660	830	Noir	124
25	75	60	400	60	190	Philippin	125
80	-	10	90	50	35	Latino-Américain	126
10	-	-	45	-	10	Asiatique du Sud-Est	127
-	100	35	110	35	65	Arabe	128
-	30	10	65	130	55	Asiatique occidental	129
15	-	-	10	-	10	Coréen	130
10	10	-	-	25	-	Japonais	131
65	75	25	365	135	235	Minorité visible, n.i.a. (13)	132
-	140	-	105	50	85	Minorités visibles multiples (14)	133
						selon la citoyenneté	
3,320	3,425	4,060	7,390	4,870	8,130	Citoyenneté canadienne (15)	134
130	375	100	685	190	400	Citoyenneté autre que canadienne	135
						selon le lieu de naissance du répondant	
2,595	2,595	3,125	4,765	3,625	6,420	Population non immigrante	136
2,365	2,170	2,790	4,380	3,245	5,790	Née dans la province de résidence	137
850	1,170	1,005	3,265	1,425	2,100	Population immigrante (16)	138
55	20	10	35	20	50	États-Unis	139
225	135	215	490	190	315	Amérique centrale et du Sud	140
125	440	185	795	420	435	Caraïbes et Bermudes	141
150	130	140	260	225	320	Royaume-Uni	142
145	165	195	475	140	340	Autre Europe (17)	143
50	25	40	175	40	105	Afrique	144
115	250	215	1,025	385	525	Asie et Moyen-Orient	145
-	10	-	15	-	10	Océanie et autre (18)	146
10	25	40	45	-	10	Résidents non permanents (19)	147
850	**1,170**	**1,005**	**3,265**	**1,425**	**2,105**	**Population immigrante totale**	148
						selon la période d'immigration	
95	120	110	160	80	175	Avant 1961	149
90	80	190	395	220	335	1961-1970	150
280	190	390	1,035	475	595	1971-1980	151
250	255	185	980	365	585	1981-1990	152
130	530	140	690	290	410	1991-2001 (20)	153
100	345	115	350	220	270	1991-1995	154
30	190	25	340	65	140	1996-2001 (20)	155
						selon l'âge à l'immigration	
80	95	105	370	170	295	0-4 ans	156
270	370	370	1,025	405	695	5-19 ans	157
500	715	535	1,870	855	1,110	20 ans et plus	158
3,455	**3,795**	**4,165**	**8,075**	**5,060**	**8,530**	**Population totale**	159
						selon la religion	
1,115	1,065	1,225	2,830	1,700	3,000	Catholique (21)	160
1,495	1,590	1,695	2,350	1,965	3,220	Protestante	161
60	105	185	425	80	180	Orthodoxe chrétienne	162
115	155	105	335	250	295	Chrétiennes, n.i.a. (22)	163
35	60	130	640	175	130	Musulmane	164
20	25	10	30	10	30	Juive	165
35	10	15	50	-	-	Bouddhiste	166
120	30	75	410	195	260	Hindoue	167
-	60	-	25	10	105	Sikh	168
-	-	-	-	-	-	Religions orientales (23)	169
25	10	-	10	-	-	Autres religions (24)	170
435	680	720	955	665	1,300	Aucune appartenance religieuse (25)	171
2,730	**2,860**	**3,210**	**5,995**	**3,750**	**6,110**	**Population totale de 15 ans et plus**	172
						selon le statut des générations	
845	1,150	1,040	3,090	1,380	2,040	1re génération (26)	173
640	600	720	1,540	900	1,505	2e génération (27)	174
1,250	1,115	1,455	1,365	1,470	2,565	3e génération et plus (28)	175
3,415	**3,760**	**4,125**	**7,975**	**4,970**	**8,385**	**Population totale de 1 an et plus (29)**	176
						selon le lieu de résidence 1 an auparavant (mobilité)	
3,180	3,230	3,830	7,200	4,490	7,230	Personnes n'ayant pas déménagé	177
230	530	295	770	480	1,160	Personnes ayant déménagé	178
100	105	165	270	170	405	Non-migrants	179
135	420	130	505	310	755	Migrants	180
130	380	125	420	295	720	Migrants internes	181
130	370	125	405	225	675	Migrants infraprovinciaux	182
-	-	-	15	70	45	Migrants interprovinciaux	183
-	45	10	85	15	35	Migrants externes	184

Table 1. Selected Characteristics for Census Tracts, 2001 Census – 100% Data and 20% Sample Data

No.	Characteristics	Toronto 0803.04 A	Toronto 0803.05 A	Toronto 0803.06 A	Toronto 0804.01	Toronto 0804.02 A	Toronto 0804.05
	POPULATION CHARACTERISTICS						
185	**Total population 5 years and over (30)**	**4,635**	**5,180**	**5,055**	**6,760**	**9,375**	**6,125**
	by place of residence 5 years ago (mobility)						
186	Non-movers	2,450	2,200	3,515	4,620	4,595	3,880
187	Movers	2,185	2,985	1,540	2,140	4,780	2,245
188	Non-migrants	740	905	675	895	1,980	1,155
189	Migrants	1,440	2,075	865	1,240	2,800	1,090
190	Internal migrants	1,360	1,890	745	1,145	2,460	1,000
191	Intraprovincial migrants	1,305	1,865	705	1,075	2,340	915
192	Interprovincial migrants	55	30	35	70	120	85
193	External migrants	75	190	125	95	340	85
194	**Total population 15 to 24 years**	**555**	**735**	**840**	**1,045**	**1,230**	**1,020**
	by school attendance						
195	Not attending school	175	150	270	270	415	315
196	Attending school full time	330	560	490	720	750	645
197	Attending school part time	45	20	75	45	60	65
198	**Total population 15 years and over**	**3,700**	**4,280**	**4,020**	**5,430**	**8,065**	**5,010**
	by highest level of schooling						
199	Less than grade 9 (31)	140	55	100	90	365	115
200	Grades 9-13 without high school graduation certificate	565	700	635	940	1,800	880
201	Grades 9-13 with high school graduation certificate	405	625	560	825	1,220	945
202	Some postsecondary without degree, certificate or diploma (32)	555	510	600	730	1,075	675
203	Trades certificate or diploma (33)	340	270	385	525	800	410
204	College certificate or diploma (34)	810	960	820	1,070	1,560	1,010
205	University certificate below bachelor's degree	65	120	110	135	240	95
206	University with bachelor's degree or higher	810	1,040	800	1,110	1,005	875
	by combinations of unpaid work						
207	Males 15 years and over	1,760	2,110	1,895	2,640	3,675	2,435
208	Reported unpaid work (35)	1,635	1,925	1,740	2,435	3,285	2,255
209	Housework and child care and care or assistance to seniors	155	180	215	220	200	305
210	Housework and child care only	720	820	680	910	1,040	805
211	Housework and care or assistance to seniors only	60	70	95	200	200	150
212	Child care and care or assistance to seniors only	-	-	-	-	10	20
213	Housework only	670	840	730	1,070	1,760	935
214	Child care only	35	15	20	20	70	40
215	Care or assistance to seniors only	-	-	-	15	10	-
216	Females 15 years and over	1,935	2,165	2,120	2,795	4,390	2,575
217	Reported unpaid work (35)	1,800	2,005	1,980	2,675	4,065	2,445
218	Housework and child care and care or assistance to seniors	235	250	355	350	425	315
219	Housework and child care only	805	955	800	1,010	1,355	875
220	Housework and care or assistance to seniors only	95	120	115	235	315	170
221	Child care and care or assistance to seniors only	-	-	-	-	25	-
222	Housework only	650	665	690	1,055	1,895	1,065
223	Child care only	15	-	20	25	45	10
224	Care or assistance to seniors only	10	15	-	-	10	15
	by labour force activity						
225	Males 15 years and over	1,760	2,115	1,895	2,640	3,675	2,435
226	In the labour force	1,485	1,750	1,600	2,195	2,760	2,000
227	Employed	1,455	1,685	1,525	2,115	2,600	1,945
228	Unemployed	25	65	75	80	165	55
229	Not in the labour force	275	365	290	440	915	430
230	Participation rate	84.4	82.7	84.4	83.1	75.1	82.1
231	Employment rate	82.7	79.7	80.5	80.1	70.7	79.9
232	Unemployment rate	1.7	3.7	4.7	3.6	6.0	2.8
233	Females 15 years and over	1,935	2,165	2,125	2,795	4,390	2,575
234	In the labour force	1,465	1,510	1,585	2,015	2,810	1,820
235	Employed	1,410	1,460	1,485	1,900	2,635	1,745
236	Unemployed	55	50	100	120	180	80
237	Not in the labour force	470	655	540	775	1,580	755
238	Participation rate	75.7	69.7	74.6	72.1	64.0	70.7
239	Employment rate	72.9	67.4	69.9	68.0	60.0	67.8
240	Unemployment rate	3.8	3.3	6.3	6.0	6.4	4.4

Tableau 1. Certaines caractéristiques des secteurs de recensement, recensement de 2001 – Données intégrales et données-échantillon (20 %)

Toronto 0804.06 A	Toronto 0804.07 A	Toronto 0804.08 A	Toronto 0804.09 A	Toronto 0805.02	Toronto 0805.03 A	Caractéristiques	N°
						CARACTÉRISTIQUES DE LA POPULATION	
3,205	**3,575**	**3,970**	**7,480**	**4,700**	**7,790**	**Population totale de 5 ans et plus (30)**	185
						selon le lieu de résidence 5 ans auparavant (mobilité)	
2,345	1,620	2,240	4,610	2,990	4,700	Personnes n'ayant pas déménagé	186
855	1,955	1,730	2,865	1,710	3,085	Personnes ayant déménagé	187
385	700	825	925	535	1,025	Non-migrants	188
470	1,255	900	1,945	1,170	2,060	Migrants	189
440	1,070	865	1,695	1,110	1,910	Migrants internes	190
435	1,050	780	1,565	1,005	1,825	Migrants infraprovinciaux	191
-	25	85	130	105	85	Migrants interprovinciaux	192
30	185	40	250	60	150	Migrants externes	193
610	**640**	**750**	**1,215**	**700**	**1,080**	**Population totale de 15 à 24 ans**	194
						selon la fréquentation scolaire	
155	190	170	325	190	360	Ne fréquentant pas l'école	195
425	425	550	785	465	670	Fréquentant l'école à plein temps	196
35	25	30	100	50	50	Fréquentant l'école à temps partiel	197
2,730	**2,865**	**3,205**	**5,990**	**3,750**	**6,110**	**Population totale de 15 ans et plus**	198
						selon le plus haut niveau de scolarité atteint	
105	85	90	280	100	155	Niveau inférieur à la 9e année (31)	199
495	645	605	1,030	805	1,210	De la 9e à la 13e année sans certificat d'études secondaires	200
510	450	570	1,010	635	1,085	De la 9e à la 13e année avec certificat d'études secondaires	201
425	460	490	785	450	715	Études postsecondaires partielles sans grade, certificat ou diplôme (32)	202
280	245	260	625	340	715	Certificat ou diplôme d'une école de métiers (33)	203
560	565	535	1,235	845	1,260	Certificat ou diplôme collégial (34)	204
65	60	75	150	105	125	Certificat universitaire inférieur au baccalauréat	205
300	345	590	885	460	840	Études universitaires avec baccalauréat ou diplôme supérieur	206
						selon les combinaisons de travail non rémunéré	
1,350	1,370	1,580	2,910	1,835	2,990	Hommes de 15 ans et plus	207
1,195	1,170	1,375	2,550	1,650	2,715	Travail non rémunéré déclaré (35)	208
130	55	180	325	190	315	Travaux ménagers et soins aux enfants et soins ou aide aux personnes âgées	209
415	515	430	1,035	615	1,030	Travaux ménagers et soins aux enfants seulement	210
85	70	85	175	75	145	Travaux ménagers et soins ou aide aux personnes âgées seulement	211
-	10	-	-	-	-	Soins aux enfants et soins ou aide aux personnes âgées seulement	212
565	495	665	1,000	750	1,150	Travaux ménagers seulement	213
-	30	10	20	20	50	Soins aux enfants seulement	214
10	-	10	10	-	20	Soins ou aide aux personnes âgées seulement	215
1,385	1,485	1,630	3,080	1,915	3,115	Femmes de 15 ans et plus	216
1,280	1,390	1,520	2,905	1,840	2,940	Travail non rémunéré déclaré (35)	217
195	195	230	430	250	405	Travaux ménagers et soins aux enfants et soins ou aide aux personnes âgées	218
450	595	500	1,230	810	1,280	Travaux ménagers et soins aux enfants seulement	219
90	45	95	145	80	180	Travaux ménagers et soins ou aide aux personnes âgées seulement	220
-	10	-	-	-	-	Soins aux enfants et soins ou aide aux personnes âgées seulement	221
530	540	685	1,065	695	1,065	Travaux ménagers seulement	222
-	-	-	25	-	15	Soins aux enfants seulement	223
-	-	-	10	-	-	Soins ou aide aux personnes âgées seulement	224
						selon l'activité	
1,350	1,370	1,580	2,915	1,835	2,995	Hommes de 15 ans et plus	225
1,145	1,100	1,335	2,380	1,515	2,560	Population active	226
1,095	1,040	1,270	2,295	1,465	2,440	Personnes occupées	227
55	55	60	90	50	115	Chômeurs	228
200	275	245	535	320	435	Inactifs	229
84.8	80.3	84.5	81.6	82.6	85.5	Taux d'activité	230
81.1	75.9	80.4	78.7	79.8	81.5	Taux d'emploi	231
4.8	5.0	4.5	3.8	3.3	4.5	Taux de chômage	232
1,385	1,490	1,630	3,085	1,920	3,115	Femmes de 15 ans et plus	233
1,075	1,110	1,215	2,270	1,465	2,425	Population active	234
1,040	1,085	1,150	2,060	1,425	2,285	Personnes occupées	235
35	25	60	215	45	145	Chômeuses	236
305	380	415	810	455	690	Inactives	237
77.6	74.5	74.5	73.6	76.3	77.8	Taux d'activité	238
75.1	72.8	70.6	66.8	74.2	73.4	Taux d'emploi	239
3.3	2.3	4.9	9.5	3.1	6.0	Taux de chômage	240

Table 1. Selected Characteristics for Census Tracts, 2001 Census – 100% Data and 20% Sample Data

No.	Characteristics	Toronto 0803.04 A	Toronto 0803.05 A	Toronto 0803.06 A	Toronto 0804.01	Toronto 0804.02 A	Toronto 0804.05
	POPULATION CHARACTERISTICS						
	by labour force activity – concluded						
241	Both sexes - Participation rate	80.0	76.2	79.3	77.5	69.1	76.3
242	15-24 years	62.7	55.8	65.5	71.2	67.8	63.4
243	25 years and over	83.0	80.4	83.0	79.1	69.3	79.4
244	Both sexes - Employment rate	77.6	73.5	74.9	73.9	64.8	73.7
245	15-24 years	54.1	48.3	54.8	62.5	55.7	56.6
246	25 years and over	81.9	78.8	80.3	76.7	66.5	78.0
247	Both sexes - Unemployment rate	2.9	3.5	5.5	4.6	6.1	3.5
248	15-24 years	13.2	13.4	16.4	11.6	17.5	10.8
249	25 years and over	1.3	1.9	3.2	3.2	4.0	2.0
250	**Total labour force 15 years and over**	**2,955**	**3,260**	**3,185**	**4,210**	**5,565**	**3,825**
	by industry based on the 1997 NAICS						
251	Industry - Not applicable (36)	15	25	60	55	85	25
252	All industries (37)	2,940	3,230	3,130	4,160	5,480	3,800
253	11 Agriculture, forestry, fishing and hunting	-	-	-	10	10	-
254	21 Mining and oil and gas extraction	10	-	10	-	-	-
255	22 Utilities	25	120	45	80	115	40
256	23 Construction	160	140	115	220	255	145
257	31-33 Manufacturing	345	390	395	435	815	525
258	41 Wholesale trade	210	165	180	325	245	245
259	44-45 Retail trade	355	350	345	500	725	505
260	48-49 Transportation and warehousing	120	120	125	115	315	145
261	51 Information and cultural industries	140	140	160	285	300	210
262	52 Finance and insurance	295	460	375	345	515	360
263	53 Real estate and rental and leasing	45	75	60	80	95	55
264	54 Professional, scientific and technical services	265	330	330	350	410	345
265	55 Management of companies and enterprises	-	-	-	30	15	15
266	56 Administrative and support, waste management and remediation services	150	150	100	155	290	155
267	61 Educational services	175	165	200	275	215	240
268	62 Health care and social assistance	215	260	295	325	420	295
269	71 Arts, entertainment and recreation	25	55	40	95	75	80
270	72 Accommodation and food services	125	80	70	175	235	210
271	81 Other services (except public administration)	140	130	115	100	210	115
272	91 Public administration	140	100	175	250	220	115
	by class of worker						
273	Class of worker - Not applicable (36)	20	25	60	55	85	25
274	All classes of worker (37)	2,935	3,235	3,125	4,155	5,485	3,800
275	Paid workers	2,690	3,025	2,955	3,950	5,150	3,520
276	Employees	2,565	2,890	2,870	3,865	5,055	3,265
277	Self-employed (incorporated)	125	135	85	85	90	250
278	Self-employed (unincorporated)	225	210	170	205	330	285
279	Unpaid family workers	20	-	-	-	-	-
	by occupation based on the 2001 NOC-S						
280	Male labour force 15 years and over	1,485	1,750	1,605	2,195	2,760	2,005
281	Occupation - Not applicable (36)	-	15	15	10	40	10
282	All occupations (37)	1,485	1,735	1,585	2,180	2,720	1,990
283	A Management occupations	325	340	330	485	335	505
284	B Business, finance and administration occupations	160	290	225	310	340	230
285	C Natural and applied sciences and related occupations	215	255	220	250	330	215
286	D Health occupations	45	10	60	40	30	25
287	E Occupations in social science, education, government service and religion	65	70	55	135	120	85
288	F Occupations in art, culture, recreation and sport	35	40	30	60	75	55
289	G Sales and service occupations	255	340	295	485	540	425
290	H Trades, transport and equipment operators and related occupations	320	295	245	320	640	355
291	I Occupations unique to primary industry	10	20	30	15	40	10
292	J Occupations unique to processing, manufacturing and utilities	55	80	95	85	265	85
293	Female labour force 15 years and over	1,465	1,510	1,580	2,015	2,805	1,820
294	Occupation - Not applicable (36)	20	15	45	40	40	15
295	All occupations (37)	1,455	1,495	1,540	1,975	2,765	1,810
296	A Management occupations	190	250	200	325	320	175
297	B Business, finance and administration occupations	530	490	555	690	1,090	540
298	C Natural and applied sciences and related occupations	95	110	75	50	75	70
299	D Health occupations	100	125	135	125	165	140

Tableau 1. Certaines caractéristiques des secteurs de recensement, recensement de 2001 – Données intégrales et données-échantillon (20 %)

Toronto 0804.06 A	Toronto 0804.07 A	Toronto 0804.08 A	Toronto 0804.09 A	Toronto 0805.02	Toronto 0805.03 A	Caractéristiques	Nº
						CARACTÉRISTIQUES DE LA POPULATION	
						selon l'activité – fin	
81.5	77.0	79.4	77.7	79.5	81.6	Les deux sexes - Taux d'activité	241
73.8	62.5	70.5	67.9	67.9	70.8	15-24 ans	242
83.7	81.3	82.2	80.2	82.3	84.0	25 ans et plus	243
78.2	74.3	75.7	72.5	77.1	77.4	Les deux sexes - Taux d'emploi	244
62.3	55.5	61.1	57.2	60.7	61.1	15-24 ans	245
82.6	79.6	80.1	76.5	80.7	80.8	25 ans et plus	246
3.8	3.6	4.7	6.5	3.2	5.2	Les deux sexes - Taux de chômage	247
14.4	12.5	12.4	15.8	9.6	13.1	15-24 ans	248
1.1	1.9	2.7	4.6	1.8	3.8	25 ans et plus	249
2,225	**2,210**	**2,550**	**4,655**	**2,980**	**4,990**	**Population active totale de 15 ans et plus**	250
						selon l'industrie basée sur le SCIAN de 1997	
15	15	20	110	15	40	Industrie - Sans objet (36)	251
2,210	2,190	2,535	4,545	2,960	4,955	Toutes les industries (37)	252
-	-	-	10	-	25	11 Agriculture, foresterie, pêche et chasse	253
-	-	-	10	-	-	21 Extraction minière et extraction de pétrole et de gaz	254
40	25	35	95	95	130	22 Services publics	255
120	85	125	295	120	290	23 Construction	256
270	215	200	665	450	715	31-33 Fabrication	257
90	205	160	235	190	340	41 Commerce de gros	258
310	290	310	570	340	595	44-45 Commerce de détail	259
120	95	150	140	200	250	48-49 Transport et entreposage	260
100	105	95	170	155	195	51 Industrie de l'information et industrie culturelle	261
195	195	360	535	210	460	52 Finance et assurances	262
50	70	60	90	70	75	53 Services immobiliers et services de location et de location à bail	263
150	120	215	310	155	390	54 Services professionnels, scientifiques et techniques	264
-	-	10	-	10	15	55 Gestion de sociétés et d'entreprises	265
120	150	70	235	110	185	56 Services administratifs, services de soutien, services de gestion des déchets et services d'assainissement	266
115	90	150	140	135	200	61 Services d'enseignement	267
140	230	175	365	205	405	62 Soins de santé et assistance sociale	268
30	25	35	90	25	45	71 Arts, spectacles et loisirs	269
160	155	125	195	145	215	72 Hébergement et services de restauration	270
95	60	120	200	150	140	81 Autres services, sauf les administrations publiques	271
85	90	145	200	190	285	91 Administrations publiques	272
						selon la catégorie de travailleurs	
10	15	15	110	15	40	Catégorie de travailleurs - Sans objet (36)	273
2,210	2,190	2,530	4,545	2,960	4,950	Toutes les catégories de travailleurs (37)	274
2,095	2,095	2,415	4,270	2,855	4,685	Travailleurs rémunérés	275
2,045	2,085	2,310	4,170	2,780	4,520	Employés	276
50	10	105	100	75	165	Travailleurs autonomes (entreprise constituée en société)	277
105	85	120	270	105	270	Travailleurs autonomes (entreprise non constituée en société)	278
10	10	-	10	10	-	Travailleurs familiaux non rémunérés	279
						selon la profession basée sur la CNP-S de 2001	
1,145	1,100	1,335	2,380	1,515	2,560	Hommes actifs de 15 ans et plus	280
10	15	10	25	-	20	Profession - Sans objet (36)	281
1,145	1,085	1,325	2,355	1,520	2,540	Toutes les professions (37)	282
190	125	320	390	205	350	A Gestion	283
200	175	170	380	175	395	B Affaires, finance et administration	284
85	100	185	300	190	295	C Sciences naturelles et appliquées et professions apparentées	285
10	10	35	45	-	40	D Secteur de la santé	286
35	35	80	40	30	100	E Sciences sociales, enseignement, administration publique et religion	287
30	10	35	65	20	25	F Arts, culture, sports et loisirs	288
250	260	250	440	390	435	G Ventes et services	289
255	245	160	510	400	640	H Métiers, transport et machinerie	290
10	15	55	65	-	50	I Professions propres au secteur primaire	291
80	115	30	125	90	210	J Transformation, fabrication et services d'utilité publique	292
1,080	1,110	1,215	2,275	1,465	2,430	Femmes actives de 15 ans et plus	293
10	-	10	80	20	15	Profession - Sans objet (36)	294
1,065	1,110	1,210	2,190	1,445	2,410	Toutes les professions (37)	295
130	90	130	175	135	205	A Gestion	296
350	425	440	785	555	1,030	B Affaires, finance et administration	297
25	20	60	120	50	130	C Sciences naturelles et appliquées et professions apparentées	298
90	80	70	195	100	170	D Secteur de la santé	299

Table 1. Selected Characteristics for Census Tracts, 2001 Census – 100% Data and 20% Sample Data

No.	Characteristics	Toronto 0803.04 A	Toronto 0803.05 A	Toronto 0803.06 A	Toronto 0804.01	Toronto 0804.02 A	Toronto 0804.05
	POPULATION CHARACTERISTICS						
	by occupation based on the 2001 NOC-S – concluded						
300	E Occupations in social science, education, government service and religion	165	185	205	235	230	210
301	F Occupations in art, culture, recreation and sport	45	35	15	75	55	60
302	G Sales and service occupations	260	235	295	410	685	505
303	H Trades, transport and equipment operators and related occupations	20	10	25	25	40	-
304	I Occupations unique to primary industry	-	10	-	-	-	10
305	J Occupations unique to processing, manufacturing and utilities	50	45	50	30	100	105
306	**Total employed labour force 15 years and over**	**2,870**	**3,150**	**3,010**	**4,015**	**5,230**	**3,690**
	by place of work						
307	Males	1,455	1,685	1,525	2,115	2,600	1,945
308	Usual place of work	1,205	1,385	1,295	1,795	2,130	1,530
309	At home	85	85	85	80	85	160
310	Outside Canada	-	10	15	-	25	20
311	No fixed workplace address	165	210	130	235	355	235
312	Females	1,410	1,460	1,485	1,900	2,630	1,740
313	Usual place of work	1,265	1,335	1,320	1,765	2,445	1,475
314	At home	120	80	100	100	125	180
315	Outside Canada	-	-	-	-	-	-
316	No fixed workplace address	30	45	60	35	60	85
317	**Total employed labour force 15 years and over with usual place of work or no fixed workplace address**	**2,665**	**2,980**	**2,810**	**3,830**	**4,990**	**3,330**
	by mode of transportation						
318	Males	1,375	1,600	1,425	2,030	2,485	1,765
319	Car, truck, van, as driver	1,250	1,325	1,225	1,685	2,045	1,475
320	Car, truck, van, as passenger	40	60	55	75	105	130
321	Public transit	90	210	135	190	215	130
322	Walked	-	-	10	55	110	25
323	Other method	-	-	-	20	10	-
324	Females	1,295	1,380	1,385	1,800	2,505	1,560
325	Car, truck, van, as driver	970	1,015	1,010	1,415	1,570	1,120
326	Car, truck, van, as passenger	100	95	160	140	210	140
327	Public transit	180	240	175	200	485	240
328	Walked	25	25	20	45	215	30
329	Other method	15	-	15	10	25	25
330	**Total population 15 years and over who worked since January 1, 2000**	**3,155**	**3,525**	**3,405**	**4,505**	**5,950**	**4,200**
	by language used at work						
331	Single responses	2,990	3,405	3,280	4,400	5,780	4,075
332	English	2,985	3,405	3,275	4,400	5,730	4,065
333	French	-	-	-	-	10	10
334	Non-official languages (5)	-	-	10	-	35	-
335	Chinese, n.o.s.	10	-	-	-	-	-
336	Cantonese	-	-	-	-	-	-
337	Other languages (6)	-	-	-	-	40	-
338	Multiple responses	165	120	125	105	170	125
339	English and French	50	70	25	75	70	70
340	English and non-official language	95	50	100	25	85	60
341	French and non-official language	-	-	-	-	-	-
342	English, French and non-official language	15	-	-	-	15	-
	DWELLING AND HOUSEHOLD CHARACTERISTICS						
343	**Total number of occupied private dwellings**	**1,495**	**1,670**	**1,535**	**2,065**	**3,770**	**1,940**
	by tenure						
344	Owned	1,345	1,650	1,365	2,035	3,185	1,815
345	Rented	150	20	170	30	585	125
346	Band housing	-	-	-	-	-	-
	by structural type of dwelling						
347	Single-detached house	1,190	1,485	1,225	1,995	940	1,605
348	Semi-detached house	135	40	90	45	225	280
349	Row house	160	115	160	25	790	-
350	Apartment, detached duplex	-	-	10	-	15	-
351	Apartment, building that has five or more storeys	-	-	-	-	1,655	60
352	Apartment, building that has fewer than five storeys (38)	-	-	45	-	145	-
353	Other single-attached house	-	30	-	-	-	-
354	Movable dwelling (39)	-	-	-	-	-	-

Tableau 1. Certaines caractéristiques des secteurs de recensement, recensement de 2001 – Données intégrales et données-échantillon (20 %)

Toronto 0804.06 A	Toronto 0804.07 A	Toronto 0804.08 A	Toronto 0804.09 A	Toronto 0805.02	Toronto 0805.03 A	Caractéristiques	N°
						CARACTÉRISTIQUES DE LA POPULATION	
						selon la profession basée sur la CNP-S de 2001 - fin	
110	125	120	140	145	175	E Sciences sociales, enseignement, administration publique et religion	300
35	20	55	35	20	40	F Arts, culture, sports et loisirs	301
270	300	260	530	335	525	G Ventes et services	302
30	20	15	70	55	50	H Métiers, transport et machinerie	303
-	-	10	-	-	10	I Professions propres au secteur primaire	304
20	35	55	135	50	70	J Transformation, fabrication et services d'utilité publique	305
2,135	**2,130**	**2,425**	**4,350**	**2,890**	**4,725**	**Population active occupée totale de 15 ans et plus**	306
						selon le lieu de travail	
1,090	1,040	1,275	2,290	1,465	2,440	Hommes	307
950	885	1,095	1,930	1,290	1,980	Lieu habituel de travail	308
40	50	65	130	20	155	À domicile	309
-	-	-	-	-	10	En dehors du Canada	310
105	105	110	235	155	310	Sans adresse de travail fixe	311
1,040	1,085	1,150	2,055	1,425	2,285	Femmes	312
950	1,035	1,050	1,835	1,315	2,065	Lieu habituel de travail	313
60	35	50	120	65	135	À domicile	314
-	-	10	10	10	-	En dehors du Canada	315
35	25	50	95	40	80	Sans adresse de travail fixe	316
2,040	**2,040**	**2,300**	**4,095**	**2,795**	**4,430**	**Population active occupée totale de 15 ans et plus ayant un lieu habituel de travail ou sans adresse de travail fixe**	317
						selon le mode de transport	
1,055	990	1,205	2,165	1,445	2,285	Hommes	318
820	740	995	1,760	1,180	1,890	Automobile, camion ou fourgonnette, en tant que conducteur	319
60	65	40	100	65	145	Automobile, camion ou fourgonnette, en tant que passager	320
130	145	125	235	125	185	Transport en commun	321
30	30	45	45	50	20	À pied	322
10	15	-	30	20	45	Autre moyen	323
985	1,050	1,095	1,930	1,355	2,145	Femmes	324
625	630	750	1,350	950	1,470	Automobile, camion ou fourgonnette, en tant que conductrice	325
105	145	120	245	165	280	Automobile, camion ou fourgonnette, en tant que passagère	326
195	195	185	305	200	330	Transport en commun	327
50	55	25	10	35	50	À pied	328
10	25	15	30	10	10	Autre moyen	329
2,355	**2,370**	**2,750**	**4,860**	**3,215**	**5,255**	**Population totale de 15 ans et plus ayant travaillé depuis le 1er janvier 2000**	330
						selon la langue utilisée au travail	
2,275	2,285	2,650	4,730	3,075	5,085	Réponses uniques	331
2,260	2,280	2,640	4,725	3,070	5,085	Anglais	332
-	10	-	-	-	-	Français	333
-	-	10	10	-	-	Langues non officielles (5)	334
-	-	-	-	-	-	Chinois, n.d.a.	335
-	-	15	-	-	-	Cantonais	336
10	-	-	10	-	-	Autres langues (6)	337
80	85	100	130	140	165	Réponses multiples	338
10	55	40	40	80	135	Anglais et français	339
75	15	50	75	65	25	Anglais et langue non officielle	340
-	-	-	-	-	-	Français et langue non officielle	341
-	-	10	15	-	-	Anglais, français et langue non officielle	342
						CARACTÉRISTIQUES DES LOGEMENTS ET DES MÉNAGES	
1,065	**1,170**	**1,140**	**2,170**	**1,525**	**2,520**	**Nombre total de logements privés occupés**	343
						selon le mode d'occupation	
990	800	1,090	2,010	1,325	2,285	Possédé	344
70	370	50	160	200	235	Loué	345
-	-	-	-	-	-	Logement de bande	346
						selon le type de construction résidentielle	
670	295	1,075	1,875	1,170	2,280	Maison individuelle non attenante	347
250	155	45	45	-	-	Maison jumelée	348
110	660	-	100	140	145	Maison en rangée	349
-	10	10	155	55	20	Appartement, duplex non attenant	350
-	-	-	-	160	-	Appartement, immeuble de cinq étages ou plus	351
35	50	-	-	-	70	Appartement, immeuble de moins de cinq étages (38)	352
-	-	10	-	-	-	Autre maison individuelle attenante	353
-	-	-	-	-	-	Logement mobile (39)	354

Table 1. Selected Characteristics for Census Tracts, 2001 Census – 100% Data and 20% Sample Data

No.	Characteristics	Toronto 0803.04 A	Toronto 0803.05 A	Toronto 0803.06 A	Toronto 0804.01	Toronto 0804.02 A	Toronto 0804.05
	DWELLING AND HOUSEHOLD CHARACTERISTICS						
	by condition of dwelling						
355	Regular maintenance only	1,290	1,420	1,215	1,505	3,020	1,525
356	Minor repairs	175	205	295	500	610	375
357	Major repairs	30	40	25	60	140	40
	by period of construction						
358	Before 1946	10	10	-	40	30	30
359	1946-1960	55	40	-	45	50	85
360	1961-1970	25	-	-	15	65	65
361	1971-1980	25	20	-	85	1,045	680
362	1981-1990	170	595	990	1,580	1,515	595
363	1991-2001 (20)	1,215	995	540	305	1,060	485
364	Average number of rooms per dwelling	7.9	7.8	8.1	8.4	6.2	8.0
365	Average number of bedrooms per dwelling	3.5	3.5	3.6	3.6	2.6	3.5
366	Average value of dwelling $	269,006	251,062	245,456	261,274	175,179	256,983
367	**Total number of private households**	**1,495**	**1,670**	**1,540**	**2,065**	**3,765**	**1,940**
	by household size						
368	1 person	85	100	80	100	905	130
369	2 persons	305	385	305	500	1,210	490
370	3 persons	340	360	320	385	615	405
371	4-5 persons	670	715	725	965	870	825
372	6 or more persons	100	100	105	120	175	90
	by household type						
373	One-family households	1,275	1,490	1,400	1,830	2,590	1,730
374	Multiple-family households	85	65	40	115	135	55
375	Non-family households	130	115	100	120	1,035	155
376	Number of persons in private households	5,195	5,730	5,445	7,175	9,970	6,455
377	Average number of persons in private households	3.5	3.4	3.5	3.5	2.6	3.3
378	Average number of persons per room	0.4	0.4	0.4	0.4	0.4	0.4
379	Tenant households in non-farm, non-reserve private dwellings (40)	155	20	170	30	585	125
380	Average gross rent $ (40)	972	794	934	988	1,073	712
381	Tenant households spending 30% or more of household income on gross rent (40) (41)	35	20	70	10	205	25
382	Tenant households spending from 30% to 99% of household income on gross rent (40) (41)	35	10	55	10	175	15
383	Owner households in non-farm, non-reserve private dwellings (42)	1,345	1,650	1,365	2,040	3,185	1,815
384	Average owner's major payments $ (42)	1,521	1,422	1,361	1,376	1,087	1,309
385	Owner households spending 30% or more of household income on owner's major payments (41) (42)	270	295	170	250	800	300
386	Owner households spending from 30% to 99% of household income on owner's major payments (41) (42)	255	265	155	230	710	285
	CENSUS FAMILY CHARACTERISTICS						
387	**Total number of census families in private households**	**1,455**	**1,630**	**1,480**	**2,060**	**2,875**	**1,850**
	by census family structure and size						
388	Total couple families	1,300	1,495	1,280	1,850	2,315	1,605
389	Total families of married couples	1,205	1,365	1,200	1,725	2,030	1,475
390	Without children at home	255	355	230	490	870	400
391	With children at home	950	1,010	970	1,230	1,160	1,075
392	1 child	320	305	275	315	380	365
393	2 children	455	495	435	650	540	475
394	3 or more children	175	215	265	270	235	235
395	Total families of common-law couples	100	130	80	125	280	135
396	Without children at home	50	80	25	60	155	70
397	With children at home	45	55	55	60	130	60
398	1 child	20	35	20	35	50	25
399	2 children	30	20	35	15	50	15
400	3 or more children	-	-	-	10	30	25
401	Total lone-parent families	155	135	195	215	560	245
402	Female parent	130	90	170	165	470	175
403	1 child	70	45	90	90	255	95
404	2 children	35	30	50	55	190	50
405	3 or more children	25	15	30	25	35	30

Tableau 1. Certaines caractéristiques des secteurs de recensement, recensement de 2001 – Données intégrales et données-échantillon (20 %)

Toronto 0804.06 A	Toronto 0804.07 A	Toronto 0804.08 A	Toronto 0804.09 A	Toronto 0805.02	Toronto 0805.03 A	Caractéristiques	N°
						CARACTÉRISTIQUES DES LOGEMENTS ET DES MÉNAGES	
						selon l'état du logement	
695	760	900	1,725	1,190	1,920	Entretien régulier seulement	355
320	365	205	385	305	540	Réparations mineures	356
50	45	30	60	30	55	Réparations majeures	357
						selon la période de construction	
10	10	-	35	-	60	Avant 1946	358
85	80	-	20	-	30	1946-1960	359
50	60	-	-	15	40	1961-1970	360
605	575	65	40	90	120	1971-1980	361
295	315	795	1,540	1,365	1,785	1981-1990	362
25	130	275	535	50	490	1991-2001 (20)	363
7.4	6.9	8.6	7.6	7.5	7.3	Nombre moyen de pièces par logement	364
3.1	3.2	3.7	3.5	3.1	3.2	Nombre moyen de chambres à coucher par logement	365
195,177	169,835	258,783	233,022	213,150	217,256	Valeur moyenne du logement $	366
1,065	**1,170**	**1,140**	**2,170**	**1,525**	**2,520**	**Nombre total de logements privés**	367
						selon la taille du ménage	
115	110	50	110	155	205	1 personne	368
235	320	205	400	340	540	2 personnes	369
215	245	220	430	305	530	3 personnes	370
450	415	585	995	655	1,105	4-5 personnes	371
45	75	80	235	75	145	6 personnes ou plus	372
						selon le genre de ménage	
900	955	1,030	1,845	1,285	2,190	Ménages unifamiliaux	373
30	45	50	165	65	95	Ménages multifamiliaux	374
135	175	55	155	180	235	Ménages non familiaux	375
3,450	3,795	4,150	8,075	5,060	8,525	Nombre de personnes dans les ménages privés	376
3.2	3.2	3.6	3.7	3.3	3.4	Nombre moyen de personnes dans les ménages privés	377
0.4	0.5	0.4	0.5	0.4	0.5	Nombre moyen de personnes par pièce	378
70	365	50	160	200	235	Ménages locataires dans les logements privés non agricoles hors réserve (40)	379
730	950	1,037	868	891	956	Loyer brut moyen $ (40)	380
50	130	25	85	50	110	Ménages locataires consacrant 30 % ou plus du revenu du ménage au loyer brut (40) (41)	381
35	110	15	70	35	90	Ménages locataires consacrant de 30 % à 99 % du revenu du ménage au loyer brut (40) (41)	382
990	805	1,090	2,005	1,325	2,280	Ménages propriétaires dans les logements privés non agricoles hors réserve (42)	383
1,160	1,198	1,351	1,429	1,343	1,417	Principales dépenses de propriété moyennes $ (42)	384
145	200	105	490	320	510	Ménages propriétaires consacrant 30 % ou plus du revenu du ménage aux principales dépenses de propriété (41) (42)	385
140	185	85	430	275	435	Ménages propriétaires consacrant de 30 % à 99 % du revenu du ménage aux principales dépenses de propriété (41) (42)	386
						CARACTÉRISTIQUES DES FAMILLES DE RECENSEMENT	
975	**1,035**	**1,145**	**2,190**	**1,410**	**2,385**	**Total des familles de recensement dans les ménages privés**	387
						selon la structure et la taille de la famille de recensement	
815	765	1,045	1,915	1,215	2,100	Total des familles avec conjoints	388
725	665	990	1,785	1,110	1,875	Total des familles avec couples mariés	389
190	185	205	315	240	420	Sans enfants à la maison	390
535	475	785	1,470	870	1,455	Avec enfants à la maison	391
145	135	200	415	250	395	1 enfant	392
320	220	420	655	450	735	2 enfants	393
70	125	165	400	165	325	3 enfants ou plus	394
90	95	55	130	105	225	Total des familles en union libre	395
25	45	10	95	45	105	Sans enfants à la maison	396
70	55	45	35	60	115	Avec enfants à la maison	397
35	20	10	25	35	70	1 enfant	398
20	20	15	10	15	30	2 enfants	399
20	10	15	10	10	20	3 enfants ou plus	400
160	275	100	275	195	285	Total des familles monoparentales	401
140	215	65	220	175	270	Parent de sexe féminin	402
55	100	40	115	100	115	1 enfant	403
70	65	20	65	65	110	2 enfants	404
15	45	-	35	15	45	3 enfants ou plus	405

Table 1. Selected Characteristics for Census Tracts, 2001 Census – 100% Data and 20% Sample Data

No.	Characteristics	Toronto 0803.04 A	Toronto 0803.05 A	Toronto 0803.06 A	Toronto 0804.01	Toronto 0804.02 A	Toronto 0804.05
	CENSUS FAMILY CHARACTERISTICS						
	by census family structure and size – concluded						
406	Male parent	20	45	25	50	85	70
407	1 child	20	10	20	25	60	45
408	2 children	-	25	10	10	15	15
409	3 or more children	-	10	-	25	10	15
410	**Total number of children at home**	**2,150**	**2,305**	**2,410**	**2,955**	**3,350**	**2,600**
	by age groups						
411	Under 6 years	670	635	475	560	745	430
412	6-14 years	820	815	945	1,180	1,140	1,010
413	15-17 years	210	295	340	400	380	350
414	18-24 years	315	410	455	595	685	590
415	25 years and over	140	150	200	220	400	220
416	Average number of children at home per census family (43)	1.5	1.4	1.6	1.4	1.2	1.4
417	**Total number of persons in private households**	**5,195**	**5,725**	**5,440**	**7,175**	**9,970**	**6,455**
	by census family status and living arrangements						
418	Number of non-family persons	285	300	270	310	1,435	405
419	Living with relatives (44)	105	145	95	125	295	190
420	Living with non-relatives only	100	55	95	85	230	80
421	Living alone	85	100	80	100	905	130
422	Number of family persons	4,905	5,430	5,175	6,865	8,535	6,055
423	Average number of persons per census family	3.4	3.3	3.5	3.3	3.0	3.3
424	**Total number of persons 65 years and over**	**210**	**240**	**150**	**425**	**1,415**	**355**
425	Number of non-family persons 65 years and over	40	70	55	125	445	145
426	Living with relatives (44)	25	65	35	85	95	105
427	Living with non-relatives only	-	-	-	-	20	-
428	Living alone	10	-	20	35	335	45
429	Number of family persons 65 years and over	165	170	90	300	975	210
	ECONOMIC FAMILY CHARACTERISTICS						
430	**Total number of economic families in private households**	**1,385**	**1,560**	**1,445**	**1,965**	**2,820**	**1,790**
	by size of family						
431	2 persons	295	385	300	515	1,220	480
432	3 persons	345	380	335	375	600	430
433	4 persons	470	505	500	690	610	540
434	5 or more persons	275	295	310	375	395	350
435	Total number of persons in economic families	5,015	5,570	5,270	6,990	8,835	6,245
436	Average number of persons per economic family	3.6	3.6	3.7	3.6	3.1	3.5
437	Total number of unattached individuals	180	155	175	185	1,135	210
	2000 INCOME CHARACTERISTICS						
	Population 15 years and over by sex and total income groups in 2000						
438	Total - Both sexes	3,700	4,280	4,020	5,430	8,060	5,010
439	Without income	170	260	195	305	345	250
440	With income	3,525	4,020	3,820	5,125	7,720	4,760
441	Under $1,000 (45)	125	150	155	185	265	165
442	$ 1,000 - $ 2,999	95	155	145	250	300	230
443	$ 3,000 - $ 4,999	75	110	145	185	275	135
444	$ 5,000 - $ 6,999	170	235	80	170	280	155
445	$ 7,000 - $ 9,999	115	110	200	230	275	280
446	$10,000 - $11,999	125	130	95	100	270	150
447	$12,000 - $14,999	170	130	140	220	605	190
448	$15,000 - $19,999	175	195	205	270	670	255
449	$20,000 - $24,999	180	210	255	215	445	325
450	$25,000 - $29,999	165	190	185	215	510	240
451	$30,000 - $34,999	255	275	325	330	655	305
452	$35,000 - $39,999	205	255	260	265	545	310
453	$40,000 - $44,999	280	320	265	370	570	355
454	$45,000 - $49,999	140	290	190	250	365	225
455	$50,000 - $59,999	390	390	345	495	615	425
456	$60,000 and over	860	885	830	1,385	1,085	1,015
457	Average income $ (46)	53,483	42,300	42,911	44,808	33,687	40,831
458	Median income $ (46)	37,923	37,291	34,335	38,739	29,876	33,888
459	Standard error of average income $ (46)	7,890	1,364	2,042	1,290	776	1,224

Tableau 1. Certaines caractéristiques des secteurs de recensement, recensement de 2001 – Données intégrales et données-échantillon (20 %)

Toronto 0804.06 A	Toronto 0804.07 A	Toronto 0804.08 A	Toronto 0804.09 A	Toronto 0805.02	Toronto 0805.03 A	Caractéristiques	N°
						CARACTÉRISTIQUES DES FAMILLES DE RECENSEMENT	
						selon la structure et la taille de la famille de recensement – fin	
15	60	30	55	20	15	Parent de sexe masculin	406
10	30	25	10	-	10	1 enfant	407
-	15	10	20	10	-	2 enfants	408
-	10	-	25	10	-	3 enfants ou plus	409
1,380	**1,575**	**1,815**	**3,530**	**2,110**	**3,600**	**Nombre total d'enfants à la maison**	410
						selon les groupes d'âge	
315	255	240	735	445	875	Moins de 6 ans	411
375	660	710	1,335	865	1,530	6-14 ans	412
185	210	250	440	265	445	15-17 ans	413
395	345	480	675	385	550	18-24 ans	414
110	100	135	355	140	205	25 ans et plus	415
1.4	1.5	1.6	1.6	1.5	1.5	Nombre moyen d'enfants à la maison par famille de recensement (43)	416
3,450	**3,795**	**4,155**	**8,075**	**5,055**	**8,530**	**Nombre total de personnes dans les ménages privés**	417
						selon la situation des particuliers dans la famille de recensement et des particuliers dans le ménage	
290	415	145	440	330	445	Nombre de personnes hors famille de recensement	418
95	125	80	170	140	120	Vivant avec des personnes apparentées (44)	419
75	180	20	160	35	120	Vivant avec des personnes non apparentées uniquement	420
115	115	50	115	150	205	Vivant seules	421
3,165	3,375	4,005	7,635	4,730	8,080	Nombre de personnes membres d'une famille	422
3.3	3.2	3.5	3.5	3.4	3.4	Nombre moyen de personnes par famille de recensement	423
160	**185**	**200**	**390**	**240**	**325**	**Nombre total de personnes de 65 ans et plus**	424
85	80	60	105	75	105	Nombre de personnes hors famille de recensement de 65 ans et plus	425
30	50	50	85	55	60	Vivant avec des personnes apparentées (44)	426
10	-	-	15	-	-	Vivant avec des personnes non apparentées uniquement	427
55	30	10	10	10	45	Vivant seules	428
70	100	140	285	165	225	Nombre de personnes membres d'une famille de 65 ans et plus	429
						CARACTÉRISTIQUES DES FAMILLES ÉCONOMIQUES	
930	**1,010**	**1,090**	**2,040**	**1,370**	**2,285**	**Nombre total de familles économiques dans les ménages privés**	430
						selon la taille de la famille	
225	315	220	375	330	560	2 personnes	431
225	225	215	465	305	495	3 personnes	432
325	280	400	655	450	785	4 personnes	433
155	200	255	540	275	445	5 personnes ou plus	434
3,260	3,500	4,090	7,805	4,870	8,200	Nombre total de personnes dans les familles économiques	435
3.5	3.5	3.7	3.8	3.6	3.6	Nombre moyen de personnes par famille économique	436
195	290	70	270	190	325	Nombre total de personnes hors famille économique	437
						CARACTÉRISTIQUES DU REVENU DE 2000	
						Population de 15 ans et plus selon le sexe et les tranches de revenu total en 2000	
2,735	2,860	3,210	5,990	3,750	6,105	Total - Les deux sexes	438
110	205	125	395	140	220	Sans revenu	439
2,620	2,655	3,090	5,600	3,605	5,885	Avec un revenu	440
115	190	105	270	220	250	Moins de 1 000 $ (45)	441
195	130	140	340	120	350	1 000 $ - 2 999 $	442
90	140	135	175	165	195	3 000 $ - 4 999 $	443
80	100	125	210	95	155	5 000 $ - 6 999 $	444
165	120	190	240	115	280	7 000 $ - 9 999 $	445
70	100	130	210	120	200	10 000 $ - 11 999 $	446
125	100	110	295	130	225	12 000 $ - 14 999 $	447
105	165	135	340	180	320	15 000 $ - 19 999 $	448
130	220	135	335	230	345	20 000 $ - 24 999 $	449
195	170	185	425	250	335	25 000 $ - 29 999 $	450
170	225	175	400	340	575	30 000 $ - 34 999 $	451
205	205	225	440	315	420	35 000 $ - 39 999 $	452
185	225	230	365	265	435	40 000 $ - 44 999 $	453
115	80	170	210	195	435	45 000 $ - 49 999 $	454
225	145	270	410	315	485	50 000 $ - 59 999 $	455
450	345	635	935	540	900	60 000 $ et plus	456
37,478	30,933	40,445	33,552	34,845	34,582	Revenu moyen $ (46)	457
30,258	26,984	34,375	28,976	32,041	32,046	Revenu médian $ (46)	458
1,777	1,210	1,639	811	1,021	739	Erreur type de revenu moyen $ (46)	459

Table 1. Selected Characteristics for Census Tracts, 2001 Census – 100% Data and 20% Sample Data

No.	Characteristics	Toronto 0803.04 A	Toronto 0803.05 A	Toronto 0803.06 A	Toronto 0804.01	Toronto 0804.02 A	Toronto 0804.05
	2000 INCOME CHARACTERISTICS						
	Population 15 years and over by sex and total income groups in 2000 – concluded						
460	Total - Males	1,760	2,115	1,895	2,635	3,675	2,435
461	Without income	60	125	75	130	110	90
462	With income	1,695	1,990	1,820	2,505	3,570	2,345
463	Under $1,000 (45)	50	50	55	60	90	95
464	$ 1,000 - $ 2,999	35	65	50	100	130	45
465	$ 3,000 - $ 4,999	25	55	30	70	80	65
466	$ 5,000 - $ 6,999	60	70	20	60	70	60
467	$ 7,000 - $ 9,999	15	30	85	80	70	80
468	$10,000 - $11,999	40	50	45	30	105	65
469	$12,000 - $14,999	50	45	35	85	220	45
470	$15,000 - $19,999	70	65	65	95	300	50
471	$20,000 - $24,999	80	95	105	90	155	140
472	$25,000 - $29,999	60	65	90	80	185	110
473	$30,000 - $34,999	85	130	110	110	310	150
474	$35,000 - $39,999	105	95	95	130	205	140
475	$40,000 - $44,999	125	160	105	140	315	170
476	$45,000 - $49,999	50	140	70	130	230	115
477	$50,000 - $59,999	215	215	205	270	340	280
478	$60,000 and over	620	665	660	990	760	740
479	Average income $ (46)	75,226	52,652	57,502	55,683	41,047	52,142
480	Median income $ (46)	47,249	44,966	44,931	49,979	35,740	42,184
481	Standard error of average income $ (46)	16,061	2,326	4,047	2,018	1,387	2,091
482	Total - Females	1,940	2,165	2,125	2,790	4,390	2,575
483	Without income	110	135	125	175	235	160
484	With income	1,830	2,030	2,000	2,620	4,155	2,415
485	Under $1,000 (45)	80	100	100	125	165	70
486	$ 1,000 - $ 2,999	55	85	100	155	165	185
487	$ 3,000 - $ 4,999	50	55	110	110	200	75
488	$ 5,000 - $ 6,999	105	165	65	105	210	95
489	$ 7,000 - $ 9,999	95	75	110	155	205	205
490	$10,000 - $11,999	85	80	50	75	165	85
491	$12,000 - $14,999	120	85	110	135	380	145
492	$15,000 - $19,999	105	130	140	175	365	200
493	$20,000 - $24,999	100	115	150	125	285	185
494	$25,000 - $29,999	100	130	100	135	325	130
495	$30,000 - $34,999	170	145	220	225	345	155
496	$35,000 - $39,999	105	160	160	135	340	170
497	$40,000 - $44,999	150	160	155	235	260	185
498	$45,000 - $49,999	90	150	120	115	140	115
499	$50,000 - $59,999	175	180	135	220	275	145
500	$60,000 and over	240	220	175	400	330	275
501	Average income $ (46)	33,305	32,138	29,601	34,398	27,365	29,840
502	Median income $ (46)	30,051	29,654	28,529	30,017	24,117	23,110
503	Standard error of average income $ (46)	1,473	1,286	1,070	1,535	777	1,123
	by composition of total income						
504	Total - Composition of income in 2000 % (47)	100.0	100.0	100.0	100.0	100.0	100.0
505	Employment income %	93.4	92.0	93.2	90.4	78.7	89.0
506	Government transfer payments %	3.4	3.5	3.4	3.3	9.0	4.2
507	Other %	3.2	4.4	3.3	6.3	12.3	6.8
	Population 15 years and over with employment income in 2000 by sex and work activity						
508	Both sexes with employment income (48)	3,075	3,445	3,410	4,415	5,805	4,110
509	Average employment income $	57,356	45,522	44,873	46,995	35,268	42,109
510	Standard error of average employment income $	8,934	1,468	2,272	1,284	904	1,321
511	Worked full year, full time (49)	1,885	2,290	2,065	2,830	3,585	2,415
512	Average employment income $	77,870	54,690	55,408	60,317	43,427	56,923
513	Standard error of average employment income $	14,282	1,754	2,038	1,639	835	1,813
514	Worked part year or part time (50)	1,120	1,090	1,260	1,500	2,160	1,640
515	Average employment income $	25,627	27,626	30,183	24,228	21,833	21,477
516	Standard error of average employment income $	1,509	2,339	4,922	1,555	1,825	1,287
517	Males with employment income (48)	1,535	1,780	1,705	2,280	2,875	2,125
518	Average employment income $	79,524	55,117	58,565	56,838	41,095	52,188
519	Standard error of average employment income $	17,557	2,426	4,317	2,118	1,511	2,179
520	Worked full year, full time (49)	1,095	1,280	1,135	1,620	1,860	1,445
521	Average employment income $	99,616	62,499	66,331	68,069	49,593	63,984
522	Standard error of average employment income $	24,241	2,752	3,362	2,494	1,290	2,737
523	Worked part year or part time (50)	400	475	530	630	980	670
524	Average employment income $	31,531	36,136	46,025	30,645	24,637	27,322
525	Standard error of average employment income $	2,825	4,615	11,629	3,247	3,496	2,634

Tableau 1. Certaines caractéristiques des secteurs de recensement, recensement de 2001 – Données intégrales et données-échantillon (20 %)

Toronto 0804.06 A	Toronto 0804.07 A	Toronto 0804.08 A	Toronto 0804.09 A	Toronto 0805.02	Toronto 0805.03 A	Caractéristiques	N°
						CARACTÉRISTIQUES DU REVENU DE 2000	
						Population de 15 ans et plus selon le sexe et les tranches de revenu total en 2000 – fin	
1,350	1,375	1,575	2,915	1,835	2,995	Total - Hommes	460
50	95	55	205	55	115	Sans revenu	461
1,300	1,275	1,525	2,705	1,775	2,875	Avec un revenu	462
60	85	45	70	100	95	Moins de 1 000 $ (45)	463
90	40	85	120	60	155	1 000 $ - 2 999 $	464
25	60	30	45	70	60	3 000 $ - 4 999 $	465
30	40	50	115	35	70	5 000 $ - 6 999 $	466
65	40	45	90	50	100	7 000 $ - 9 999 $	467
20	60	65	95	60	95	10 000 $ - 11 999 $	468
40	40	40	55	55	105	12 000 $ - 14 999 $	469
35	65	45	110	70	40	15 000 $ - 19 999 $	470
45	95	55	185	100	135	20 000 $ - 24 999 $	471
80	50	45	200	80	130	25 000 $ - 29 999 $	472
70	115	40	155	115	255	30 000 $ - 34 999 $	473
100	95	125	125	125	135	35 000 $ - 39 999 $	474
100	100	115	205	145	260	40 000 $ - 44 999 $	475
75	30	90	125	90	285	45 000 $ - 49 999 $	476
110	80	125	320	220	305	50 000 $ - 59 999 $	477
345	280	515	700	390	660	60 000 $ et plus	478
47,667	37,626	53,382	42,438	41,205	41,958	Revenu moyen $ (46)	479
38,540	31,249	42,796	39,492	38,412	40,167	Revenu médian $ (46)	480
3,234	2,211	2,928	1,364	1,728	1,222	Erreur type de revenu moyen $ (46)	481
1,385	1,490	1,630	3,085	1,915	3,115	Total - Femmes	482
60	105	70	185	85	105	Sans revenu	483
1,320	1,380	1,560	2,895	1,835	3,010	Avec un revenu	484
55	100	65	195	125	160	Moins de 1 000 $ (45)	485
105	90	50	220	65	190	1 000 $ - 2 999 $	486
65	80	105	125	95	135	3 000 $ - 4 999 $	487
55	55	70	100	55	85	5 000 $ - 6 999 $	488
100	75	140	155	60	180	7 000 $ - 9 999 $	489
55	45	60	115	55	105	10 000 $ - 11 999 $	490
80	65	70	245	75	115	12 000 $ - 14 999 $	491
70	100	90	235	105	280	15 000 $ - 19 999 $	492
80	120	75	150	130	210	20 000 $ - 24 999 $	493
115	120	140	225	170	205	25 000 $ - 29 999 $	494
105	115	135	250	220	315	30 000 $ - 34 999 $	495
105	115	95	310	190	285	35 000 $ - 39 999 $	496
90	125	115	160	125	175	40 000 $ - 44 999 $	497
35	50	75	85	110	150	45 000 $ - 49 999 $	498
110	65	145	95	95	175	50 000 $ - 59 999 $	499
110	70	130	235	150	245	60 000 $ et plus	500
27,458	24,747	27,838	25,232	28,685	27,535	Revenu moyen $ (46)	501
25,018	23,380	26,930	21,017	28,730	26,021	Revenu médian $ (46)	502
1,294	1,062	1,103	808	1,019	768	Erreur type de revenu moyen $ (46)	503
						selon la composition du revenu total	
100.0	100.0	100.0	100.0	100.0	100.0	Total - Composition du revenu en 2000 % (47)	504
91.6	85.5	89.8	91.1	92.1	92.0	Revenu d'emploi %	505
3.5	7.0	3.7	5.5	5.1	5.3	Transferts gouvernementaux %	506
5.1	7.4	6.4	3.4	2.7	2.7	Autre %	507
						Population de 15 ans et plus ayant un revenu d'emploi en 2000 selon le sexe et le travail	
2,310	2,290	2,720	4,735	3,145	5,190	Les deux sexes ayant un revenu d'emploi (48)	508
38,851	30,698	41,209	36,135	36,864	36,106	Revenu moyen d'emploi $	509
1,954	1,332	1,753	903	1,129	800	Erreur type de revenu moyen d'emploi $	510
1,385	1,180	1,505	2,890	1,980	3,120	Ayant travaillé toute l'année à plein temps (49)	511
54,898	43,299	56,595	46,172	47,145	46,386	Revenu moyen d'emploi $	512
2,813	1,552	2,596	1,053	1,417	979	Erreur type de revenu moyen d'emploi $	513
895	1,090	1,180	1,735	1,125	1,995	Ayant travaillé une partie de l'année ou à temps partiel (50)	514
15,382	17,683	22,646	20,673	19,645	21,152	Revenu moyen d'emploi $	515
1,231	1,910	1,594	1,346	1,343	1,047	Erreur type de revenu moyen d'emploi $	516
1,210	1,130	1,400	2,435	1,605	2,650	Hommes ayant un revenu d'emploi (48)	517
48,150	37,332	52,552	44,098	43,211	43,257	Revenu moyen d'emploi $	518
3,395	2,406	3,081	1,461	1,863	1,284	Erreur type de revenu moyen d'emploi $	519
825	610	910	1,730	1,050	1,760	Ayant travaillé toute l'année à plein temps (49)	520
64,049	51,977	68,481	52,276	54,438	52,801	Revenu moyen d'emploi $	521
4,439	2,530	3,929	1,550	2,277	1,445	Erreur type de revenu moyen d'emploi $	522
375	505	485	645	555	855	Ayant travaillé une partie de l'année ou à temps partiel (50)	523
14,470	20,512	23,629	25,133	22,170	25,459	Revenu moyen d'emploi $	524
1,818	3,843	3,291	2,906	2,310	2,019	Erreur type de revenu moyen d'emploi $	525

Table 1. Selected Characteristics for Census Tracts, 2001 Census – 100% Data and 20% Sample Data

No.	Characteristics	Toronto 0803.04 A	Toronto 0803.05 A	Toronto 0803.06 A	Toronto 0804.01	Toronto 0804.02 A	Toronto 0804.05
	2000 INCOME CHARACTERISTICS						
	Population 15 years and over with employment income in 2000 by sex and work activity – concluded						
526	Females with employment income (48)	1,535	1,660	1,700	2,140	2,930	1,985
527	Average employment income $	35,208	35,255	31,141	36,512	29,556	31,300
528	Standard error of average employment income $	1,627	1,428	1,176	1,295	971	1,253
529	Worked full year, full time (49)	790	1,010	925	1,210	1,725	970
530	Average employment income $	47,536	44,786	42,023	49,966	36,768	46,399
531	Standard error of average employment income $	2,408	1,780	1,388	1,751	919	1,784
532	Worked part year or part time (50)	725	615	730	870	1,185	970
533	Average employment income $	22,379	21,125	18,746	19,579	19,517	17,473
534	Standard error of average employment income $	1,692	1,900	1,586	1,329	1,794	1,138
	Census families by structure and family income groups in 2000						
535	Total - All census families	1,455	1,630	1,480	2,060	2,870	1,850
536	Under $10,000	15	20	20	40	70	45
537	$ 10,000 - $19,999	30	25	25	30	95	20
538	$ 20,000 - $29,999	75	60	60	55	205	80
539	$ 30,000 - $39,999	70	55	55	80	300	120
540	$ 40,000 - $49,999	85	115	65	90	265	100
541	$ 50,000 - $59,999	100	95	85	110	300	125
542	$ 60,000 - $69,999	130	125	110	175	345	155
543	$ 70,000 - $79,999	110	200	130	175	305	125
544	$ 80,000 - $89,999	95	160	175	120	225	205
545	$ 90,000 - $99,999	130	115	100	185	160	160
546	$100,000 and over	615	655	660	1,000	605	725
547	Average family income $	122,471	97,163	104,391	105,417	72,596	98,059
548	Median family income $	90,231	87,259	92,084	98,612	65,329	89,292
549	Standard error of average family income $	19,200	3,071	4,834	3,210	2,038	2,985
550	Total - All couple census families (51)	1,300	1,495	1,285	1,845	2,315	1,605
551	Under $10,000	-	15	10	15	35	10
552	$ 10,000 - $19,999	20	15	-	20	55	10
553	$ 20,000 - $29,999	50	45	35	45	140	50
554	$ 30,000 - $39,999	50	40	25	40	235	70
555	$ 40,000 - $49,999	55	80	55	80	195	70
556	$ 50,000 - $59,999	70	70	60	95	215	105
557	$ 60,000 - $69,999	110	120	85	140	280	135
558	$ 70,000 - $79,999	105	200	125	155	270	115
559	$ 80,000 - $89,999	90	150	160	115	200	180
560	$ 90,000 - $99,999	130	100	95	155	125	155
561	$100,000 and over	610	655	640	975	560	705
562	Average family income $	131,685	101,498	112,384	110,843	77,266	105,780
563	Median family income $	94,938	91,924	99,317	101,331	69,714	94,043
564	Standard error of average family income $	21,123	3,197	5,476	3,463	2,373	3,184
	Incidence of low income in 2000						
565	Total - Economic families	1,390	1,560	1,445	1,965	2,820	1,795
566	Low income	90	70	80	60	210	100
567	Incidence of low income in 2000 % (52)	6.4	4.7	5.5	3.0	7.4	5.7
568	Total - Unattached individuals 15 years and over	180	155	170	185	1,125	210
569	Low income	50	20	55	40	280	65
570	Incidence of low income in 2000 % (52)	26.6	15.3	35.4	20.5	24.7	30.0
571	Total - Population in private households	5,190	5,725	5,435	7,175	9,960	6,455
572	Low income	385	295	315	230	1,050	415
573	Incidence of low income in 2000 % (52)	7.4	5.2	5.8	3.2	10.5	6.4
	Private households by household income groups in 2000						
574	Total - All private households	1,495	1,670	1,535	2,065	3,770	1,940
575	Under $10,000	10	20	35	20	75	25
576	$ 10,000 - $19,999	35	30	40	30	235	55
577	$ 20,000 - $29,999	55	25	50	60	280	80
578	$ 30,000 - $39,999	50	25	55	60	400	85
579	$ 40,000 - $49,999	70	100	65	90	390	115
580	$ 50,000 - $59,999	105	130	95	85	385	135
581	$ 60,000 - $69,999	135	145	95	160	435	150
582	$ 70,000 - $79,999	120	170	110	150	420	120
583	$ 80,000 - $89,999	100	165	165	130	250	170
584	$ 90,000 - $99,999	140	130	115	175	190	175
585	$100,000 and over	670	725	710	1,100	710	830
586	Average household income $	125,990	101,797	106,686	111,229	69,003	100,083
587	Median household income $	93,085	91,857	94,250	101,394	61,779	92,920
588	Standard error of average household income $	18,413	3,088	4,895	3,409	1,694	2,903

Tableau 1. Certaines caractéristiques des secteurs de recensement, recensement de 2001 – Données intégrales et données-échantillon (20 %)

Toronto 0804.06 A	Toronto 0804.07 A	Toronto 0804.08 A	Toronto 0804.09 A	Toronto 0805.02	Toronto 0805.03 A	Caractéristiques	N°
						CARACTÉRISTIQUES DU REVENU DE 2000	
						Population de 15 ans et plus ayant un revenu d'emploi en 2000 selon le sexe et le travail - fin	
1,105	1,165	1,325	2,295	1,540	2,540	Femmes ayant un revenu d'emploi (48)	526
28,637	24,272	29,204	27,692	30,253	28,630	Revenu moyen d'emploi $	527
1,446	1,137	1,158	916	1,130	841	Erreur type de revenu moyen d'emploi $	528
560	570	600	1,165	935	1,360	Ayant travaillé toute l'année à plein temps (49)	529
41,380	33,983	38,568	37,095	38,990	38,102	Revenu moyen d'emploi $	530
1,767	1,394	1,463	1,087	1,373	1,063	Erreur type de revenu moyen d'emploi $	531
520	585	695	1,090	570	1,135	Ayant travaillé une partie de l'année ou à temps partiel (50)	532
16,043	15,254	21,966	18,026	17,168	17,901	Revenu moyen d'emploi $	533
1,661	1,409	1,519	1,261	1,344	1,025	Erreur type de revenu moyen d'emploi $	534
						Familles de recensement selon la structure et les tranches de revenu de la famille en 2000	
970	1,035	1,145	2,190	1,410	2,380	Total - Toutes les familles de recensement	535
30	50	15	55	40	55	Moins de 10 000 $	536
15	45	25	55	30	15	10 000 $ - 19 999 $	537
25	60	40	140	55	95	20 000 $ - 29 999 $	538
60	105	30	145	90	115	30 000 $ - 39 999 $	539
80	130	50	165	85	165	40 000 $ - 49 999 $	540
80	80	40	180	130	245	50 000 $ - 59 999 $	541
125	150	115	190	160	325	60 000 $ - 69 999 $	542
65	80	110	230	165	315	70 000 $ - 79 999 $	543
145	65	110	165	150	270	80 000 $ - 89 999 $	544
55	110	125	200	155	205	90 000 $ - 99 999 $	545
300	155	495	665	350	575	100 000 $ et plus	546
92,593	67,273	104,468	81,259	79,767	80,368	Revenu moyen des familles $	547
81,609	61,175	93,802	77,055	75,394	75,130	Revenu médian des familles $	548
4,521	2,753	3,915	1,984	2,289	1,686	Erreur type de revenu moyen des familles $	549
815	765	1,050	1,915	1,215	2,095	Total - Toutes les familles de recensement comptant un couple (51)	550
10	25	15	35	30	30	Moins de 10 000 $	551
10	25	25	30	25	-	10 000 $ - 19 999 $	552
20	20	20	100	25	80	20 000 $ - 29 999 $	553
45	50	20	95	45	65	30 000 $ - 39 999 $	554
60	90	30	135	60	125	40 000 $ - 49 999 $	555
60	50	30	145	95	195	50 000 $ - 59 999 $	556
105	145	110	155	145	260	60 000 $ - 69 999 $	557
35	80	105	230	145	300	70 000 $ - 79 999 $	558
145	55	110	165	150	270	80 000 $ - 89 999 $	559
50	75	100	190	150	205	90 000 $ - 99 999 $	560
285	155	480	635	345	575	100 000 $ et plus	561
100,618	75,544	106,885	86,068	85,489	85,166	Revenu moyen des familles $	562
86,128	68,837	96,001	81,192	81,384	80,086	Revenu médian des familles $	563
5,123	3,326	4,030	2,085	2,446	1,762	Erreur type de revenu moyen des familles $	564
						Fréquence des unités à faible revenu en 2000	
935	1,015	1,090	2,040	1,370	2,285	Total - Familles économiques	565
50	135	50	145	110	110	Faible revenu	566
5.2	13.5	4.6	7.1	8.0	4.8	Fréquence des unités à faible revenu en 2000 % (52)	567
180	285	65	255	190	310	Total - Personnes hors famille économique de 15 ans et plus	568
55	75	15	125	30	120	Faible revenu	569
31.7	26.3	24.0	47.5	15.6	38.3	Fréquence des unités à faible revenu en 2000 % (52)	570
3,435	3,790	4,155	8,060	5,055	8,515	Total - Population dans les ménages privés	571
230	530	200	615	420	510	Faible revenu	572
6.6	13.9	4.8	7.6	8.3	6.0	Fréquence des unités à faible revenu en 2000 % (52)	573
						Ménages privés selon les tranches de revenu du ménage en 2000	
1,060	1,170	1,140	2,165	1,525	2,520	Total - Tous les ménages privés	574
25	60	15	25	40	65	Moins de 10 000 $	575
55	45	20	80	25	75	10 000 $ - 19 999 $	576
40	60	25	90	40	85	20 000 $ - 29 999 $	577
50	125	25	145	105	100	30 000 $ - 39 999 $	578
80	150	50	130	115	200	40 000 $ - 49 999 $	579
90	105	35	205	130	240	50 000 $ - 59 999 $	580
110	120	85	155	130	315	60 000 $ - 69 999 $	581
50	70	130	245	165	315	70 000 $ - 79 999 $	582
165	90	115	150	170	295	80 000 $ - 89 999 $	583
45	115	120	215	145	200	90 000 $ - 99 999 $	584
350	230	525	725	450	640	100 000 $ et plus	585
92,312	70,103	109,408	86,618	82,347	80,657	Revenu moyen des ménages $	586
82,109	61,614	95,722	80,192	79,909	75,195	Revenu médian des ménages $	587
4,473	2,717	4,019	2,195	2,255	1,736	Erreur type de revenu moyen des ménages $	588

Table 1. Selected Characteristics for Census Tracts, 2001 Census – 100% Data and 20% Sample Data

No.	Characteristics	Toronto 0805.04 A	Toronto 0805.05 A	Toronto 0805.06 A	Toronto 0805.07 A	Toronto 0806 A	Toronto 0807
	POPULATION CHARACTERISTICS						
1	**Population, 1996 (1)**	**1,417**	**3,045**	**4,911**	**2,404**	**1,844**	**2,741**
2	**Population, 2001 (2)**	**2,549**	**3,267**	**5,055**	**5,777**	**1,697**	**2,779**
3	Population percentage change, 1996-2001	79.9	7.3	2.9	140.3	-8.0	1.4
4	Land area in square kilometres, 2001	6.96	4.09	1.50	17.20	62.46	119.51
5	**Total population - 100% Data (3)**	**2,550**	**3,265**	**5,055**	**5,775**	**1,695**	**2,780**
	by sex and age groups						
6	Male	1,275	1,590	2,450	2,840	870	1,425
7	0-4 years	105	135	180	310	45	55
8	5-9 years	110	155	245	345	45	100
9	10-14 years	110	170	305	260	65	120
10	15-19 years	85	130	225	185	55	105
11	20-24 years	60	85	160	115	45	85
12	25-29 years	75	90	105	160	60	85
13	30-34 years	110	120	160	270	50	80
14	35-39 years	120	175	215	380	65	120
15	40-44 years	160	205	260	285	90	135
16	45-49 years	100	135	205	170	80	130
17	50-54 years	75	85	155	135	90	130
18	55-59 years	60	35	90	75	65	75
19	60-64 years	45	30	50	45	40	60
20	65-69 years	20	15	35	50	35	60
21	70-74 years	20	10	25	25	25	40
22	75-79 years	10	5	10	15	15	35
23	80-84 years	5	5	5	5	5	10
24	85 years and over	-	-	5	10	5	15
25	Female	1,275	1,675	2,610	2,940	830	1,355
26	0-4 years	100	115	185	300	40	60
27	5-9 years	100	190	305	330	60	90
28	10-14 years	110	175	295	235	60	130
29	15-19 years	85	145	200	185	55	110
30	20-24 years	45	85	130	130	55	75
31	25-29 years	100	75	130	190	40	65
32	30-34 years	120	150	180	350	60	80
33	35-39 years	125	205	320	405	60	130
34	40-44 years	155	200	275	280	75	135
35	45-49 years	100	130	200	175	90	110
36	50-54 years	75	85	165	120	80	115
37	55-59 years	60	35	65	65	55	75
38	60-64 years	30	30	45	55	40	60
39	65-69 years	35	20	45	35	35	45
40	70-74 years	15	15	35	30	20	25
41	75-79 years	20	10	25	25	15	30
42	80-84 years	5	5	10	10	10	15
43	85 years and over	5	-	10	10	5	20
44	**Total population 15 years and over**	**1,920**	**2,325**	**3,545**	**3,995**	**1,380**	**2,225**
	by legal marital status						
45	Never married (single)	465	710	1,070	1,025	430	675
46	Legally married (and not separated)	1,265	1,380	2,035	2,535	755	1,235
47	Separated, but still legally married	50	75	140	105	45	80
48	Divorced	90	105	190	230	95	140
49	Widowed	55	50	115	100	55	90
	by common-law status						
50	Not in a common-law relationship	1,795	2,185	3,375	3,735	1,260	2,075
51	In a common-law relationship	125	140	175	255	120	150
52	**Total population - 20% Sample Data (4)**	**2,550**	**3,275**	**5,055**	**5,775**	**1,690**	**2,765**
	by mother tongue						
53	Single responses	2,525	3,210	5,000	5,635	1,685	2,750
54	English	2,230	2,785	3,710	4,615	1,415	2,565
55	French	45	30	145	110	20	20
56	Non-official languages (5)	250	395	1,145	900	250	170
57	Italian	25	40	70	60	85	20
58	Chinese, n.o.s.	15	-	20	-	-	-
59	Cantonese	10	30	110	30	-	15
60	Portuguese	30	10	65	60	30	-
61	Punjabi	-	20	100	10	-	-
62	Other languages (6)	180	295	790	745	135	130
63	Multiple responses	25	60	60	140	10	15
64	English and French	-	10	20	15	-	10
65	English and non-official language	25	55	30	125	-	10
66	French and non-official language	-	-	-	-	-	-
67	English, French and non-official language	-	-	-	-	-	-

See reference material at the end of the publication. – Voir les documents de référence à la fin de la publication.

Tableau 1. Certaines caractéristiques des secteurs de recensement, recensement de 2001 – Données intégrales et données-échantillon (20 %)

Toronto 0810.01	Toronto 0810.02	Toronto 0810.03	Toronto 0810.04	Toronto 0810.05	Toronto 0811	Caractéristiques	N°
						CARACTÉRISTIQUES DE LA POPULATION	
4,022	**2,666**	**3,689**	**6,457**	**4,190**	**2,878**	**Population, 1996 (1)**	1
4,034	**2,570**	**3,500**	**6,223**	**4,061**	**2,833**	**Population, 2001 (2)**	2
0.3	-3.6	-5.1	-3.6	-3.1	-1.6	Variation en pourcentage de la population, 1996-2001	3
0.61	0.79	1.08	2.52	3.39	3.47	Superficie des terres en kilomètres carrés, 2001	4
4,035	**2,570**	**3,500**	**6,225**	**4,065**	**2,835**	**Population totale – Données intégrales (3)**	5
						selon le sexe et les groupes d'âge	
1,920	1,235	1,760	3,035	2,015	1,305	Sexe masculin	6
135	55	85	145	140	75	0-4 ans	7
170	80	135	255	155	75	5-9 ans	8
120	80	125	285	190	80	10-14 ans	9
115	105	145	320	195	60	15-19 ans	10
125	80	130	220	120	60	20-24 ans	11
145	65	90	155	100	80	25-29 ans	12
145	65	95	165	115	100	30-34 ans	13
175	85	120	240	155	130	35-39 ans	14
165	105	165	255	220	130	40-44 ans	15
100	85	145	275	185	90	45-49 ans	16
110	80	120	240	170	90	50-54 ans	17
65	80	140	155	120	55	55-59 ans	18
75	75	105	115	55	55	60-64 ans	19
80	70	65	95	35	50	65-69 ans	20
80	55	40	65	40	45	70-74 ans	21
65	35	45	30	20	60	75-79 ans	22
35	10	15	20	5	35	80-84 ans	23
20	10	10	10	5	30	85 ans et plus	24
2,115	1,330	1,735	3,190	2,045	1,525	Sexe féminin	25
135	55	100	175	90	70	0-4 ans	26
135	65	115	215	145	60	5-9 ans	27
125	80	95	265	170	85	10-14 ans	28
115	90	120	260	210	80	15-19 ans	29
130	70	95	190	120	70	20-24 ans	30
165	50	65	155	100	80	25-29 ans	31
175	50	95	185	125	100	30-34 ans	32
170	110	165	295	210	120	35-39 ans	33
165	125	150	310	220	125	40-44 ans	34
115	95	150	310	200	105	45-49 ans	35
115	100	160	235	170	90	50-54 ans	36
100	80	145	150	105	55	55-59 ans	37
80	90	95	110	60	55	60-64 ans	38
95	105	60	110	40	70	65-69 ans	39
115	75	55	90	35	75	70-74 ans	40
110	50	40	80	25	120	75-79 ans	41
45	25	20	35	15	75	80-84 ans	42
20	20	10	25	10	100	85 ans et plus	43
3,215	**2,160**	**2,845**	**4,890**	**3,170**	**2,395**	**Population totale de 15 ans et plus**	44
						selon l'état matrimonial légal	
1,015	570	740	1,495	940	680	Célibataire (jamais marié(e))	45
1,470	1,180	1,750	2,620	1,885	1,005	Légalement marié(e) (et non séparé(e))	46
195	85	85	180	105	140	Séparé(e), mais toujours légalement marié(e)	47
285	170	155	380	140	255	Divorcé(e)	48
250	150	125	220	100	310	Veuf ou veuve	49
						selon l'union libre	
2,910	2,055	2,720	4,530	3,020	2,120	Ne vivant pas en union libre	50
310	110	125	360	155	275	Vivant en union libre	51
4,030	**2,555**	**3,505**	**6,215**	**4,045**	**2,665**	**Population totale – Données-échantillon (20 %) (4)**	52
						selon la langue maternelle	
3,995	2,555	3,505	6,195	4,000	2,635	Réponses uniques	53
3,315	2,320	3,175	5,660	3,625	2,380	Anglais	54
55	40	40	100	35	25	Français	55
625	195	285	435	345	235	Langues non officielles (5)	56
10	20	50	40	10	20	Italien	57
15	-	-	10	-	-	Chinois, n.d.a.	58
-	-	10	-	-	-	Cantonais	59
-	20	-	25	115	15	Portugais	60
-	-	10	-	10	-	Pendjabi	61
595	155	220	355	205	195	Autres langues (6)	62
35	-	-	20	40	25	Réponses multiples	63
10	10	-	10	-	10	Anglais et français	64
15	-	-	10	45	20	Anglais et langue non officielle	65
-	-	-	-	-	-	Français et langue non officielle	66
-	-	-	-	10	-	Anglais, français et langue non officielle	67

See reference material at the end of the publication. – Voir les documents de référence à la fin de la publication.

Table 1. Selected Characteristics for Census Tracts, 2001 Census – 100% Data and 20% Sample Data

No.	Characteristics	Toronto 0805.04 A	Toronto 0805.05 A	Toronto 0805.06 A	Toronto 0805.07 A	Toronto 0806 A	Toronto 0807
	POPULATION CHARACTERISTICS						
	by home language						
68	Single responses	2,380	2,870	4,320	5,145	1,580	2,705
69	English	2,360	2,775	3,990	4,965	1,550	2,690
70	French	10	-	20	-	-	-
71	Non-official languages (5)	15	95	315	175	25	15
72	Cantonese	-	-	50	15	-	-
73	Chinese, n.o.s.	-	-	-	-	-	-
74	Italian	-	15	-	-	15	-
75	Punjabi	-	10	30	-	-	-
76	Portuguese	-	-	15	-	-	-
77	Other languages (6)	15	65	220	155	10	10
78	Multiple responses	175	405	735	625	110	65
79	English and French	45	20	90	100	-	-
80	English and non-official language	95	375	620	515	110	65
81	French and non-official language	-	-	-	10	-	-
82	English, French and non-official language	30	10	25	-	-	-
	by knowledge of official languages						
83	English only	2,320	2,940	4,600	5,345	1,590	2,645
84	French only	-	-	10	10	-	-
85	English and French	220	320	375	410	85	125
86	Neither English nor French	-	10	65	10	15	-
	by knowledge of non-official languages (5) (7)						
87	Italian	35	55	120	75	120	20
88	Cantonese	-	30	115	35	-	15
89	Chinese, n.o.s.	15	-	20	10	-	-
90	Spanish	25	90	70	85	35	25
91	Portuguese	35	15	55	65	30	-
92	Punjabi	10	35	110	20	-	-
93	Tagalog (Pilipino)	20	130	90	175	-	15
	by first official language spoken						
94	English	2,495	3,220	4,840	5,615	1,650	2,755
95	French	45	35	150	115	20	15
96	English and French	-	10	-	35	-	-
97	Neither English nor French	10	15	60	-	15	-
98	Official language minority - (number) (8)	45	35	150	130	20	15
99	Official language minority - (percentage) (8)	1.8	1.1	3.0	2.3	1.2	0.5
	by ethnic origin (9)						
100	Canadian	965	995	1,555	1,530	325	1,070
101	English	825	1,095	990	1,065	560	1,255
102	Scottish	685	585	595	860	380	705
103	Irish	530	510	760	890	310	585
104	Chinese	20	165	260	100	-	15
105	Italian	110	220	315	280	195	100
106	East Indian	100	325	330	520	15	-
107	French	220	275	515	505	245	190
108	German	275	205	260	195	185	345
109	Portuguese	60	135	170	260	15	-
110	Polish	90	80	155	130	30	40
111	Jewish	10	20	50	15	-	15
112	Jamaican	20	120	420	620	-	10
113	Filipino	45	165	155	255	-	30
114	Ukrainian	165	35	105	65	40	55
	by Aboriginal identity						
115	Total Aboriginal identity population (10)	-	10	15	20	20	65
116	Total non-Aboriginal population	2,550	3,260	5,040	5,750	1,670	2,705
	by Aboriginal origin						
117	Total Aboriginal origins population (11)	15	10	45	60	80	140
118	Total non-Aboriginal population	2,535	3,265	5,010	5,715	1,610	2,630
	by Registered Indian status						
119	Registered Indian (12)	-	10	-	15	10	30
120	Not a Registered Indian	2,550	3,265	5,055	5,760	1,685	2,740

Tableau 1. Certaines caractéristiques des secteurs de recensement, recensement de 2001 – Données intégrales et données-échantillon (20 %)

Toronto 0810.01	Toronto 0810.02	Toronto 0810.03	Toronto 0810.04	Toronto 0810.05	Toronto 0811	Caractéristiques	N°
						CARACTÉRISTIQUES DE LA POPULATION	
						selon la langue parlée à la maison	
3,625	2,415	3,340	5,875	3,825	2,600	Réponses uniques	68
3,410	2,395	3,300	5,800	3,805	2,560	Anglais	69
-	-	15	10	-	-	Français	70
210	15	25	60	20	35	Langues non officielles (5)	71
-	-	10	-	-	-	Cantonais	72
15	-	-	-	-	-	Chinois, n.d.a.	73
-	10	-	10	-	-	Italien	74
-	-	-	-	10	-	Pendjabi	75
-	-	-	-	10	-	Portugais	76
195	10	15	45	10	35	Autres langues (6)	77
405	145	170	340	215	65	Réponses multiples	78
75	15	20	65	30	15	Anglais et français	79
300	125	140	255	180	50	Anglais et langue non officielle	80
10	-	-	-	-	-	Français et langue non officielle	81
15	-	-	20	-	-	Anglais, français et langue non officielle	82
						selon la connaissance des langues officielles	
3,680	2,340	3,310	5,740	3,740	2,485	Anglais seulement	83
10	-	-	10	-	-	Français seulement	84
295	215	175	455	295	185	Anglais et français	85
45	10	15	10	10	-	Ni l'anglais ni le français	86
						selon la connaissance des langues non officielles (5) (7)	
10	25	70	65	20	15	Italien	87
-	-	10	-	10	-	Cantonais	88
15	-	-	10	-	-	Chinois, n.d.a.	89
60	45	15	60	70	-	Espagnol	90
10	20	-	30	115	15	Portugais	91
10	-	10	-	10	-	Pendjabi	92
55	-	-	40	-	-	Tagalog (pilipino)	93
						selon la première langue officielle parlée	
3,905	2,515	3,450	6,090	4,005	2,640	Anglais	94
65	35	35	90	20	25	Français	95
20	-	-	20	10	10	Anglais et français	96
35	-	15	15	10	-	Ni l'anglais ni le français	97
75	35	35	105	25	25	Minorité de langue officielle - (nombre) (8)	98
1.9	1.4	1.0	1.7	0.6	0.9	Minorité de langue officielle - (pourcentage) (8)	99
						selon l'origine ethnique (9)	
1,340	945	1,320	2,565	1,285	1,115	Canadien	100
1,130	1,050	1,550	2,175	1,585	930	Anglais	101
650	675	1,075	1,645	910	645	Écossais	102
740	425	820	1,310	895	685	Irlandais	103
25	30	10	115	25	15	Chinois	104
85	60	135	190	280	135	Italien	105
120	20	65	110	60	20	Indien de l'Inde	106
310	185	225	560	340	290	Français	107
240	290	315	630	320	145	Allemand	108
25	40	40	95	130	55	Portugais	109
45	115	120	75	95	35	Polonais	110
10	25	25	50	15	10	Juif	111
105	65	60	140	45	25	Jamaïquain	112
75	-	-	55	-	10	Philippin	113
125	60	115	115	165	25	Ukrainien	114
						selon l'identité autochtone	
30	10	45	45	15	60	Total de la population ayant une identité autochtone (10)	115
4,000	2,550	3,460	6,170	4,030	2,605	Total de la population non autochtone	116
						selon l'origine autochtone	
65	80	80	120	30	100	Total de la population ayant une origine autochtone (11)	117
3,970	2,485	3,420	6,090	4,015	2,565	Total de la population non autochtone	118
						selon le statut d'Indien inscrit	
25	10	15	20	10	15	Oui, Indien inscrit (12)	119
4,005	2,550	3,490	6,200	4,040	2,655	Non, pas un Indien inscrit	120

Table 1. Selected Characteristics for Census Tracts, 2001 Census – 100% Data and 20% Sample Data

No.	Characteristics	Toronto 0805.04 A	Toronto 0805.05 A	Toronto 0805.06 A	Toronto 0805.07 A	Toronto 0806 A	Toronto 0807
	POPULATION CHARACTERISTICS						
	by visible minority groups						
121	Total visible minority population	305	955	2,065	2,450	65	70
122	Chinese	30	50	180	95	-	15
123	South Asian	40	265	480	415	-	-
124	Black	65	245	730	1,125	30	40
125	Filipino	45	150	175	240	-	20
126	Latin American	-	10	15	125	20	-
127	Southeast Asian	-	-	15	25	-	-
128	Arab	20	-	30	170	-	-
129	West Asian	55	40	100	35	-	-
130	Korean	10	-	15	40	-	-
131	Japanese	-	-	60	10	-	-
132	Visible minority, n.i.e. (13)	30	155	205	130	10	-
133	Multiple visible minorities (14)	10	35	70	40	-	-
	by citizenship						
134	Canadian citizenship (15)	2,455	3,150	4,735	5,375	1,665	2,660
135	Citizenship other than Canadian	90	120	320	400	20	110
	by place of birth of respondent						
136	Non-immigrant population	2,080	2,495	3,310	3,790	1,300	2,405
137	Born in province of residence	1,805	2,225	2,950	3,440	1,190	2,140
138	Immigrant population (16)	470	780	1,720	1,950	390	355
139	United States	50	10	10	10	-	20
140	Central and South America	20	45	260	285	35	-
141	Caribbean and Bermuda	25	240	400	635	35	-
142	United Kingdom	145	65	130	200	165	155
143	Other Europe (17)	95	130	275	200	145	80
144	Africa	15	20	70	175	-	10
145	Asia and the Middle East	115	270	570	435	-	40
146	Oceania and other (18)	10	-	-	-	-	45
147	Non-permanent residents (19)	-	-	25	35	-	10
148	**Total immigrant population**	**470**	**780**	**1,720**	**1,950**	**390**	**355**
	by period of immigration						
149	Before 1961	90	50	65	50	160	85
150	1961-1970	100	75	280	240	120	110
151	1971-1980	90	205	480	560	70	65
152	1981-1990	110	280	490	515	15	55
153	1991-2001 (20)	75	170	405	585	25	45
154	1991-1995	55	120	235	335	20	30
155	1996-2001 (20)	20	50	175	250	10	10
	by age at immigration						
156	0-4 years	100	90	155	210	60	60
157	5-19 years	150	225	570	695	95	105
158	20 years and over	220	465	990	1,045	235	185
159	**Total population**	**2,550**	**3,275**	**5,055**	**5,775**	**1,690**	**2,770**
	by religion						
160	Catholic (21)	710	1,125	1,670	1,970	590	520
161	Protestant	1,135	1,265	1,725	1,885	670	1,325
162	Christian Orthodox	25	80	195	215	90	15
163	Christian, n.i.e. (22)	145	95	215	325	65	135
164	Muslim	30	105	325	285	-	15
165	Jewish	10	20	-	-	-	-
166	Buddhist	-	-	45	-	20	-
167	Hindu	20	175	130	230	15	-
168	Sikh	-	-	110	-	-	-
169	Eastern religions (23)	30	-	-	40	-	-
170	Other religions (24)	10	10	-	-	-	15
171	No religious affiliation (25)	440	405	645	820	245	745
172	**Total population 15 years and over**	**1,915**	**2,285**	**3,540**	**3,985**	**1,385**	**2,205**
	by generation status						
173	1st generation (26)	455	755	1,625	1,835	395	390
174	2nd generation (27)	460	645	710	840	385	540
175	3rd generation and over (28)	1,000	885	1,210	1,320	615	1,275
176	**Total population 1 year and over (29)**	**2,525**	**3,210**	**4,980**	**5,630**	**1,655**	**2,745**
	by place of residence 1 year ago (mobility)						
177	Non-movers	2,045	2,745	4,255	4,715	1,490	2,460
178	Movers	485	470	730	920	170	290
179	Non-migrants	215	265	360	345	60	105
180	Migrants	265	210	365	575	105	180
181	Internal migrants	265	185	345	505	105	180
182	Intraprovincial migrants	265	185	320	500	110	175
183	Interprovincial migrants	-	-	25	-	-	-
184	External migrants	-	25	15	70	-	-

Tableau 1. Certaines caractéristiques des secteurs de recensement, recensement de 2001 – Données intégrales et données-échantillon (20 %)

Toronto 0810.01	Toronto 0810.02	Toronto 0810.03	Toronto 0810.04	Toronto 0810.05	Toronto 0811	Caractéristiques	N°
						CARACTÉRISTIQUES DE LA POPULATION	
						selon les groupes de minorités visibles	
755	160	150	610	280	170	Total de la population des minorités visibles	121
15	15	10	55	15	10	Chinois	122
175	10	25	90	75	-	Sud-Asiatique	123
185	115	75	265	140	80	Noir	124
70	-	-	50	-	-	Philippin	125
15	-	-	20	20	-	Latino-Américain	126
-	-	-	25	-	-	Asiatique du Sud-Est	127
75	-	10	15	-	30	Arabe	128
165	-	-	25	-	-	Asiatique occidental	129
20	-	-	-	15	-	Coréen	130
-	-	-	10	-	-	Japonais	131
35	-	25	45	15	40	Minorité visible, n.i.a. (13)	132
-	15	-	15	-	-	Minorités visibles multiples (14)	133
						selon la citoyenneté	
3,685	2,475	3,395	6,045	3,870	2,575	Citoyenneté canadienne (15)	134
345	80	110	170	175	90	Citoyenneté autre que canadienne	135
						selon le lieu de naissance du répondant	
2,925	2,100	2,855	5,095	3,405	2,180	Population non immigrante	136
2,495	1,735	2,440	4,545	3,010	1,885	Née dans la province de résidence	137
1,100	460	645	1,115	625	490	Population immigrante (16)	138
55	20	15	40	20	25	États-Unis	139
60	10	10	50	40	20	Amérique centrale et du Sud	140
105	30	60	155	40	90	Caraïbes et Bermudes	141
260	210	280	440	295	190	Royaume-Uni	142
160	185	230	245	160	120	Autre Europe (17)	143
25	10	15	30	30	-	Afrique	144
445	-	25	145	40	40	Asie et Moyen-Orient	145
-	-	15	-	-	-	Océanie et autre (18)	146
10	-	-	-	10	10	Résidents non permanents (19)	147
1,100	**460**	**640**	**1,110**	**630**	**490**	**Population immigrante totale**	148
						selon la période d'immigration	
225	170	190	220	130	215	Avant 1961	149
175	140	220	265	210	85	1961-1970	150
80	80	75	325	160	100	1971-1980	151
130	20	90	195	75	50	1981-1990	152
490	50	65	105	50	40	1991-2001 (20)	153
195	40	50	95	35	10	1991-1995	154
295	10	15	10	10	25	1996-2001 (20)	155
						selon l'âge à l'immigration	
110	25	55	130	75	50	0-4 ans	156
275	110	150	315	185	120	5-19 ans	157
715	325	440	660	365	315	20 ans et plus	158
4,030	**2,560**	**3,500**	**6,215**	**4,045**	**2,670**	**Population totale**	159
						selon la religion	
1,175	695	900	2,010	1,310	765	Catholique (21)	160
1,490	1,300	1,820	2,845	1,855	1,250	Protestante	161
100	-	40	55	10	20	Orthodoxe chrétienne	162
175	45	80	80	165	85	Chrétiennes, n.i.a. (22)	163
345	-	30	50	-	70	Musulmane	164
-	30	-	20	15	10	Juive	165
-	-	-	20	10	-	Bouddhiste	166
50	-	10	20	45	-	Hindoue	167
-	-	-	-	10	-	Sikh	168
15	-	-	-	-	-	Religions orientales (23)	169
10	-	10	-	-	-	Autres religions (24)	170
675	490	620	1,120	640	470	Aucune appartenance religieuse (25)	171
3,210	**2,135**	**2,860**	**4,865**	**3,155**	**2,280**	**Population totale de 15 ans et plus**	172
						selon le statut des générations	
980	460	650	1,115	680	490	1re génération (26)	173
610	440	590	1,115	790	535	2e génération (27)	174
1,620	1,235	1,625	2,635	1,690	1,255	3e génération et plus (28)	175
3,960	**2,540**	**3,465**	**6,165**	**3,995**	**2,650**	**Population totale de 1 an et plus (29)**	176
						selon le lieu de résidence 1 an auparavant (mobilité)	
3,400	2,260	3,200	5,595	3,625	2,350	Personnes n'ayant pas déménagé	177
555	285	265	570	370	305	Personnes ayant déménagé	178
240	215	105	310	110	130	Non-migrants	179
315	70	160	260	265	175	Migrants	180
255	65	150	250	245	170	Migrants internes	181
225	60	120	250	230	170	Migrants infraprovinciaux	182
30	-	30	-	15	-	Migrants interprovinciaux	183
55	10	10	10	20	-	Migrants externes	184

Table 1. Selected Characteristics for Census Tracts, 2001 Census – 100% Data and 20% Sample Data

No.	Characteristics	Toronto 0805.04 A	Toronto 0805.05 A	Toronto 0805.06 A	Toronto 0805.07 A	Toronto 0806 A	Toronto 0807
	POPULATION CHARACTERISTICS						
185	**Total population 5 years and over (30)**	**2,350**	**2,960**	**4,685**	**5,155**	**1,605**	**2,655**
	by place of residence 5 years ago (mobility)						
186	Non-movers	950	1,760	2,760	1,420	1,235	1,780
187	Movers	1,400	1,200	1,925	3,730	370	875
188	Non-migrants	610	475	640	1,095	65	450
189	Migrants	790	730	1,285	2,635	300	420
190	Internal migrants	775	670	1,155	2,410	280	410
191	Intraprovincial migrants	735	640	1,095	2,355	265	390
192	Interprovincial migrants	35	30	60	55	10	15
193	External migrants	15	60	130	230	20	10
194	**Total population 15 to 24 years**	**300**	**450**	**725**	**615**	**210**	**375**
	by school attendance						
195	Not attending school	100	180	265	180	55	115
196	Attending school full time	185	255	425	405	140	250
197	Attending school part time	15	25	30	30	20	10
198	**Total population 15 years and over**	**1,915**	**2,285**	**3,540**	**3,990**	**1,385**	**2,210**
	by highest level of schooling						
199	Less than grade 9 (31)	35	65	170	85	80	75
200	Grades 9-13 without high school graduation certificate	395	400	820	725	340	575
201	Grades 9-13 with high school graduation certificate	260	375	605	675	95	285
202	Some postsecondary without degree, certificate or diploma (32)	215	340	415	465	210	280
203	Trades certificate or diploma (33)	195	210	280	480	205	255
204	College certificate or diploma (34)	450	520	680	900	225	320
205	University certificate below bachelor's degree	45	80	65	90	10	15
206	University with bachelor's degree or higher	330	300	510	565	225	405
	by combinations of unpaid work						
207	Males 15 years and over	945	1,105	1,715	1,915	705	1,150
208	Reported unpaid work (35)	860	995	1,580	1,765	610	1,085
209	Housework and child care and care or assistance to seniors	80	125	190	175	60	80
210	Housework and child care only	295	475	690	890	140	345
211	Housework and care or assistance to seniors only	75	20	95	65	40	80
212	Child care and care or assistance to seniors only	-	-	15	-	10	-
213	Housework only	395	355	545	620	355	575
214	Child care only	10	10	40	-	15	-
215	Care or assistance to seniors only	15	10	-	-	10	-
216	Females 15 years and over	975	1,175	1,830	2,070	685	1,055
217	Reported unpaid work (35)	925	1,110	1,720	2,020	630	1,030
218	Housework and child care and care or assistance to seniors	110	205	300	225	80	145
219	Housework and child care only	350	520	850	1,050	195	385
220	Housework and care or assistance to seniors only	100	80	100	65	30	80
221	Child care and care or assistance to seniors only	-	-	-	-	-	-
222	Housework only	360	300	475	680	330	425
223	Child care only	10	-	10	-	-	10
224	Care or assistance to seniors only	-	10	-	-	-	-
	by labour force activity						
225	Males 15 years and over	940	1,105	1,715	1,915	710	1,150
226	In the labour force	800	970	1,400	1,675	530	910
227	Employed	775	915	1,300	1,595	520	850
228	Unemployed	30	50	100	80	10	65
229	Not in the labour force	145	140	315	240	180	240
230	Participation rate	85.1	87.8	81.6	87.5	74.6	79.1
231	Employment rate	82.4	82.8	75.8	83.3	73.2	73.9
232	Unemployment rate	3.8	5.2	7.1	4.8	1.9	7.1
233	Females 15 years and over	975	1,175	1,830	2,070	680	1,060
234	In the labour force	750	905	1,320	1,640	420	690
235	Employed	715	790	1,225	1,510	410	665
236	Unemployed	35	115	95	125	15	25
237	Not in the labour force	220	270	510	430	260	370
238	Participation rate	76.9	77.0	72.1	79.2	61.8	65.1
239	Employment rate	73.3	67.2	66.9	72.9	60.3	62.7
240	Unemployment rate	4.7	12.7	7.2	7.6	3.6	3.6

Tableau 1. Certaines caractéristiques des secteurs de recensement, recensement de 2001 – Données intégrales et données-échantillon (20 %)

Toronto 0810.01	Toronto 0810.02	Toronto 0810.03	Toronto 0810.04	Toronto 0810.05	Toronto 0811	Caractéristiques	N°
						CARACTÉRISTIQUES DE LA POPULATION	
3,765	**2,440**	**3,335**	**5,905**	**3,815**	**2,580**	**Population totale de 5 ans et plus (30)**	185
						selon le lieu de résidence 5 ans auparavant (mobilité)	
1,890	1,635	2,460	4,050	2,640	1,565	Personnes n'ayant pas déménagé	186
1,875	800	870	1,855	1,170	1,015	Personnes ayant déménagé	187
675	500	565	800	530	435	Non-migrants	188
1,200	305	310	1,055	645	580	Migrants	189
990	290	295	1,035	605	575	Migrants internes	190
855	265	265	970	555	555	Migrants infraprovinciaux	191
130	15	30	70	45	20	Migrants interprovinciaux	192
205	20	10	15	40	-	Migrants externes	193
480	**345**	**480**	**980**	**630**	**265**	**Population totale de 15 à 24 ans**	194
						selon la fréquentation scolaire	
200	115	195	395	135	130	Ne fréquentant pas l'école	195
215	205	260	560	475	125	Fréquentant l'école à plein temps	196
65	25	25	30	25	10	Fréquentant l'école à temps partiel	197
3,210	**2,140**	**2,865**	**4,865**	**3,160**	**2,280**	**Population totale de 15 ans et plus**	198
						selon le plus haut niveau de scolarité atteint	
205	125	120	120	80	200	Niveau inférieur à la 9e année (31)	199
935	490	475	1,015	615	715	De la 9e à la 13e année sans certificat d'études secondaires	200
520	330	580	950	470	390	De la 9e à la 13e année avec certificat d'études secondaires	201
280	265	410	690	315	215	Études postsecondaires partielles sans grade, certificat ou diplôme (32)	202
280	295	260	445	350	245	Certificat ou diplôme d'une école de métiers (33)	203
630	405	565	985	665	295	Certificat ou diplôme collégial (34)	204
50	40	70	75	100	10	Certificat universitaire inférieur au baccalauréat.....	205
310	185	380	580	565	210	Études universitaires avec baccalauréat ou diplôme supérieur	206
						selon les combinaisons de travail non rémunéré	
1,485	1,010	1,435	2,360	1,515	1,075	Hommes de 15 ans et plus	207
1,350	865	1,245	2,085	1,385	960	Travail non rémunéré déclaré (35)	208
85	55	95	170	130	40	Travaux ménagers et soins aux enfants et soins ou aide aux personnes âgées	209
350	265	370	765	480	230	Travaux ménagers et soins aux enfants seulement	210
110	50	90	100	85	140	Travaux ménagers et soins ou aide aux personnes âgées seulement	211
10	-	-	-	-	10	Soins aux enfants et soins ou aide aux personnes âgées seulement	212
755	490	655	1,005	670	520	Travaux ménagers seulement	213
40	-	25	35	15	15	Soins aux enfants seulement	214
10	10	10	-	-	10	Soins ou aide aux personnes âgées seulement	215
1,720	1,130	1,435	2,500	1,640	1,205	Femmes de 15 ans et plus	216
1,560	1,000	1,400	2,395	1,550	1,105	Travail non rémunéré déclaré (35)	217
100	110	170	270	220	75	Travaux ménagers et soins aux enfants et soins ou aide aux personnes âgées	218
470	335	445	1,000	510	345	Travaux ménagers et soins aux enfants seulement	219
230	95	135	155	110	110	Travaux ménagers et soins ou aide aux personnes âgées seulement	220
-	-	-	-	-	-	Soins aux enfants et soins ou aide aux personnes âgées seulement	221
740	455	640	925	690	570	Travaux ménagers seulement	222
10	10	10	30	15	-	Soins aux enfants seulement	223
10	-	-	-	-	-	Soins ou aide aux personnes âgées seulement	224
						selon l'activité	
1,485	1,010	1,435	2,360	1,515	1,070	Hommes de 15 ans et plus	225
1,060	670	1,120	1,925	1,210	765	Population active	226
1,000	635	1,025	1,815	1,175	730	Personnes occupées	227
65	30	95	110	30	35	Chômeurs	228
425	340	310	435	310	310	Inactifs	229
71.4	66.3	78.0	81.6	79.9	71.5	Taux d'activité	230
67.3	62.9	71.4	76.9	77.6	68.2	Taux d'emploi	231
6.1	4.5	8.5	5.7	2.5	4.6	Taux de chômage	232
1,725	1,130	1,430	2,500	1,640	1,210	Femmes de 15 ans et plus	233
965	660	925	1,665	1,235	725	Population active	234
885	645	870	1,605	1,190	690	Personnes occupées	235
80	10	60	65	45	40	Chômeuses	236
760	470	510	840	410	480	Inactives	237
55.9	58.4	64.7	66.6	75.3	59.9	Taux d'activité	238
51.3	57.1	60.8	64.2	72.6	57.0	Taux d'emploi	239
8.3	1.5	6.5	3.9	3.6	5.5	Taux de chômage	240

Table 1. Selected Characteristics for Census Tracts, 2001 Census – 100% Data and 20% Sample Data

No.	Characteristics	Toronto 0805.04 A	Toronto 0805.05 A	Toronto 0805.06 A	Toronto 0805.07 A	Toronto 0806 A	Toronto 0807
	POPULATION CHARACTERISTICS						
	by labour force activity – concluded						
241	Both sexes - Participation rate	81.2	82.1	76.7	83.3	68.3	72.6
242	15-24 years	73.3	69.2	64.8	64.2	42.9	60.0
243	25 years and over	83.0	85.0	80.0	86.5	73.2	75.1
244	Both sexes - Employment rate	77.8	74.6	71.2	77.8	67.1	68.5
245	15-24 years	56.7	46.7	54.9	53.7	35.7	50.7
246	25 years and over	81.2	81.4	75.6	82.4	72.3	72.1
247	Both sexes - Unemployment rate	3.9	8.8	7.2	6.3	2.1	5.6
248	15-24 years	20.9	32.8	16.0	17.5	11.1	13.6
249	25 years and over	1.5	4.2	5.3	4.6	1.2	4.0
250	**Total labour force 15 years and over**	**1,555**	**1,875**	**2,720**	**3,315**	**950**	**1,600**
	by industry based on the 1997 NAICS						
251	Industry - Not applicable (36)	10	20	70	60	-	30
252	All industries (37)	1,545	1,850	2,650	3,260	955	1,565
253	11 Agriculture, forestry, fishing and hunting	30	15	25	10	-	55
254	21 Mining and oil and gas extraction	-	-	10	-	-	10
255	22 Utilities	95	55	35	45	-	15
256	23 Construction	65	90	145	160	135	200
257	31-33 Manufacturing	160	225	335	390	90	150
258	41 Wholesale trade	65	95	165	205	45	155
259	44-45 Retail trade	165	290	320	365	80	160
260	48-49 Transportation and warehousing	50	35	135	170	30	70
261	51 Information and cultural industries	50	70	125	170	25	70
262	52 Finance and insurance	140	170	240	325	55	45
263	53 Real estate and rental and leasing	45	25	35	60	15	25
264	54 Professional, scientific and technical services	245	185	235	250	95	140
265	55 Management of companies and enterprises	-	-	-	-	10	-
266	56 Administrative and support, waste management and remediation services	80	80	105	155	65	100
267	61 Educational services	45	60	80	170	60	100
268	62 Health care and social assistance	85	160	185	310	90	115
269	71 Arts, entertainment and recreation	25	10	50	50	25	45
270	72 Accommodation and food services	30	110	150	145	25	50
271	81 Other services (except public administration)	85	85	120	135	50	50
272	91 Public administration	100	95	160	155	40	25
	by class of worker						
273	Class of worker - Not applicable (36)	10	25	65	60	-	30
274	All classes of worker (37)	1,545	1,855	2,650	3,260	950	1,565
275	Paid workers	1,405	1,740	2,480	2,980	800	1,365
276	Employees	1,335	1,710	2,375	2,945	715	1,250
277	Self-employed (incorporated)	75	30	110	40	80	105
278	Self-employed (unincorporated)	135	100	165	270	140	190
279	Unpaid family workers	-	-	10	10	10	15
	by occupation based on the 2001 NOC-S						
280	Male labour force 15 years and over	805	970	1,405	1,675	530	910
281	Occupation - Not applicable (36)	-	-	35	25	-	15
282	All occupations (37)	800	970	1,370	1,655	530	895
283	A Management occupations	190	155	205	260	75	175
284	B Business, finance and administration occupations	95	145	150	245	40	55
285	C Natural and applied sciences and related occupations	85	115	130	185	60	45
286	D Health occupations	-	10	10	15	10	10
287	E Occupations in social science, education, government service and religion	15	30	45	40	15	70
288	F Occupations in art, culture, recreation and sport	15	45	35	50	35	35
289	G Sales and service occupations	135	200	370	295	75	115
290	H Trades, transport and equipment operators and related occupations	165	210	325	400	150	270
291	I Occupations unique to primary industry	30	15	20	35	30	85
292	J Occupations unique to processing, manufacturing and utilities	55	55	70	125	40	30
293	Female labour force 15 years and over	750	905	1,320	1,645	420	690
294	Occupation - Not applicable (36)	-	20	35	35	-	15
295	All occupations (37)	750	885	1,285	1,605	420	675
296	A Management occupations	90	85	120	185	80	65
297	B Business, finance and administration occupations	230	305	465	635	140	185
298	C Natural and applied sciences and related occupations	30	10	40	30	15	15
299	D Health occupations	60	65	105	150	65	50

Tableau 1. Certaines caractéristiques des secteurs de recensement, recensement de 2001 – Données intégrales et données-échantillon (20 %)

Toronto 0810.01	Toronto 0810.02	Toronto 0810.03	Toronto 0810.04	Toronto 0810.05	Toronto 0811	Caractéristiques	N°
						CARACTÉRISTIQUES DE LA POPULATION	
						selon l'activité – fin	
63.1	61.9	71.6	73.8	77.2	65.6	Les deux sexes - Taux d'activité	241
68.8	72.5	76.3	73.5	64.3	73.6	15-24 ans	242
62.1	60.3	70.4	73.9	80.4	64.4	25 ans et plus	243
58.6	60.0	66.1	70.3	75.0	62.3	Les deux sexes - Taux d'emploi	244
58.3	65.2	68.0	66.8	59.5	58.5	15-24 ans	245
58.6	59.1	65.5	71.0	78.7	63.0	25 ans et plus	246
7.1	3.4	7.6	5.0	3.1	5.0	Les deux sexes - Taux de chômage	247
15.2	10.2	10.7	9.7	7.4	20.5	15-24 ans	248
5.6	2.3	6.9	3.7	2.2	2.7	25 ans et plus	249
2,025	**1,330**	**2,045**	**3,595**	**2,440**	**1,495**	**Population active totale de 15 ans et plus**	250
						selon l'industrie basée sur le SCIAN de 1997	
45	-	30	35	15	20	Industrie - Sans objet (36)	251
1,985	1,330	2,015	3,555	2,430	1,470	Toutes les industries (37)	252
-	-	15	15	-	-	11 Agriculture, foresterie, pêche et chasse	253
-	-	-	-	-	-	21 Extraction minière et extraction de pétrole et de gaz	254
30	40	75	45	125	30	22 Services publics	255
145	75	90	255	160	80	23 Construction	256
305	205	250	545	270	365	31-33 Fabrication	257
105	90	110	170	140	75	41 Commerce de gros	258
310	110	235	425	255	160	44-45 Commerce de détail	259
110	75	110	175	105	80	48-49 Transport et entreposage	260
35	40	80	155	90	10	51 Industrie de l'information et industrie culturelle	261
85	60	155	145	240	40	52 Finance et assurances	262
25	15	45	105	50	35	53 Services immobiliers et services de location et de location à bail	263
160	40	100	285	150	100	54 Services professionnels, scientifiques et techniques	264
-	-	10	-	-	-	55 Gestion de sociétés et d'entreprises	265
115	50	70	145	80	85	56 Services administratifs, services de soutien, services de gestion des déchets et services d'assainissement	266
115	65	130	215	140	70	61 Services d'enseignement	267
165	145	175	325	190	120	62 Soins de santé et assistance sociale	268
30	15	25	20	15	-	71 Arts, spectacles et loisirs	269
115	100	120	275	100	55	72 Hébergement et services de restauration	270
85	105	45	85	75	80	81 Autres services, sauf les administrations publiques	271
40	95	180	165	225	70	91 Administrations publiques	272
						selon la catégorie de travailleurs	
45	-	30	35	10	20	Catégorie de travailleurs - Sans objet (36)	273
1,980	1,330	2,020	3,555	2,430	1,475	Toutes les catégories de travailleurs (37)	274
1,905	1,265	1,885	3,325	2,300	1,415	Travailleurs rémunérés	275
1,880	1,235	1,840	3,220	2,230	1,375	Employés	276
20	30	45	105	70	35	Travailleurs autonomes (entreprise constituée en société)	277
75	60	130	225	130	60	Travailleurs autonomes (entreprise non constituée en société)	278
-	-	-	-	-	-	Travailleurs familiaux non rémunérés	279
						selon la profession basée sur la CNP-S de 2001	
1,065	670	1,120	1,930	1,210	765	Hommes actifs de 15 ans et plus	280
30	-	15	25	10	10	Profession - Sans objet (36)	281
1,030	665	1,105	1,900	1,200	765	Toutes les professions (37)	282
140	75	150	270	275	70	A Gestion	283
110	35	140	235	130	70	B Affaires, finance et administration	284
95	55	85	160	100	60	C Sciences naturelles et appliquées et professions apparentées	285
-	10	15	10	20	-	D Secteur de la santé	286
50	30	60	95	50	30	E Sciences sociales, enseignement, administration publique et religion	287
40	25	55	25	20	10	F Arts, culture, sports et loisirs	288
180	140	230	410	255	150	G Ventes et services	289
275	215	250	465	260	215	H Métiers, transport et machinerie	290
-	10	25	40	25	20	I Professions propres au secteur primaire	291
145	85	95	200	60	135	J Transformation, fabrication et services d'utilité publique	292
965	660	925	1,665	1,230	730	Femmes actives de 15 ans et plus	293
15	-	15	10	-	20	Profession - Sans objet (36)	294
950	660	910	1,650	1,230	710	Toutes les professions (37)	295
85	40	80	130	105	70	A Gestion	296
275	190	320	485	485	190	B Affaires, finance et administration	297
-	20	20	45	60	20	C Sciences naturelles et appliquées et professions apparentées	298
75	45	55	110	85	60	D Secteur de la santé	299

Table 1. Selected Characteristics for Census Tracts, 2001 Census – 100% Data and 20% Sample Data

No.	Characteristics	Toronto 0805.04 A	Toronto 0805.05 A	Toronto 0805.06 A	Toronto 0805.07 A	Toronto 0806 A	Toronto 0807
	POPULATION CHARACTERISTICS						
	by occupation based on the 2001 NOC-S – concluded						
300	E Occupations in social science, education, government service and religion	75	80	105	170	15	70
301	F Occupations in art, culture, recreation and sport	20	15	10	35	25	30
302	G Sales and service occupations	170	225	365	310	55	145
303	H Trades, transport and equipment operators and related occupations	25	35	20	30	10	55
304	I Occupations unique to primary industry	15	-	15	-	-	35
305	J Occupations unique to processing, manufacturing and utilities	25	55	45	65	20	25
306	**Total employed labour force 15 years and over**	**1,490**	**1,710**	**2,525**	**3,110**	**930**	**1,510**
	by place of work						
307	Males	775	920	1,295	1,595	520	845
308	Usual place of work	640	795	1,085	1,280	345	580
309	At home	35	25	60	80	50	90
310	Outside Canada	10	-	-	-	-	-
311	No fixed workplace address	100	95	150	240	120	180
312	Females	715	790	1,230	1,515	410	660
313	Usual place of work	565	685	1,125	1,360	360	530
314	At home	125	95	50	115	30	100
315	Outside Canada	-	-	10	-	-	-
316	No fixed workplace address	30	-	35	35	25	35
317	**Total employed labour force 15 years and over with usual place of work or no fixed workplace address**	**1,330**	**1,580**	**2,390**	**2,915**	**850**	**1,325**
	by mode of transportation						
318	Males	740	890	1,230	1,515	465	760
319	Car, truck, van, as driver	620	745	1,005	1,300	410	700
320	Car, truck, van, as passenger	20	55	50	40	20	35
321	Public transit	75	75	110	135	20	10
322	Walked	15	15	50	20	10	-
323	Other method	10	-	15	15	10	10
324	Females	595	690	1,160	1,395	380	565
325	Car, truck, van, as driver	410	455	700	880	340	485
326	Car, truck, van, as passenger	35	80	120	140	15	35
327	Public transit	135	145	250	330	10	15
328	Walked	10	10	70	35	10	20
329	Other method	-	-	15	10	-	-
330	**Total population 15 years and over who worked since January 1, 2000**	**1,630**	**1,955**	**2,845**	**3,425**	**1,025**	**1,715**
	by language used at work						
331	Single responses	1,575	1,885	2,710	3,265	980	1,670
332	English	1,570	1,885	2,690	3,255	975	1,665
333	French	-	-	15	-	-	-
334	Non-official languages (5)	-	-	10	-	-	-
335	Chinese, n.o.s.	-	-	-	-	-	-
336	Cantonese	-	-	10	-	-	-
337	Other languages (6)	-	10	10	-	-	-
338	Multiple responses	50	65	130	160	50	45
339	English and French	20	35	55	105	15	30
340	English and non-official language	25	25	65	55	25	15
341	French and non-official language	-	-	-	-	-	-
342	English, French and non-official language	10	-	10	-	-	-
	DWELLING AND HOUSEHOLD CHARACTERISTICS						
343	**Total number of occupied private dwellings**	**805**	**910**	**1,390**	**1,635**	**570**	**900**
	by tenure						
344	Owned	745	855	1,140	1,555	425	540
345	Rented	65	55	255	75	150	360
346	Band housing	-	-	-	-	-	-
	by structural type of dwelling						
347	Single-detached house	765	465	1,075	1,230	560	865
348	Semi-detached house	-	340	20	40	-	-
349	Row house	30	105	170	355	-	-
350	Apartment, detached duplex	20	-	55	10	10	10
351	Apartment, building that has five or more storeys	-	-	75	-	-	-
352	Apartment, building that has fewer than five storeys (38)	-	-	-	-	-	20
353	Other single-attached house	-	-	-	-	-	-
354	Movable dwelling (39)	-	-	-	-	-	-

Tableau 1. Certaines caractéristiques des secteurs de recensement, recensement de 2001 – Données intégrales et données-échantillon (20 %)

Toronto 0810.01	Toronto 0810.02	Toronto 0810.03	Toronto 0810.04	Toronto 0810.05	Toronto 0811	Caractéristiques	N°
						CARACTÉRISTIQUES DE LA POPULATION	
						selon la profession basée sur la CNP-S de 2001 – fin	
110	65	115	170	95	70	E Sciences sociales, enseignement, administration publique et religion	300
25	15	15	50	30	35	F Arts, culture, sports et loisirs	301
290	270	250	500	310	205	G Ventes et services	302
25	-	25	55	35	25	H Métiers, transport et machinerie	303
-	10	-	10	-	-	I Professions propres au secteur primaire	304
55	15	25	90	25	45	J Transformation, fabrication et services d'utilité publique	305
1,880	**1,280**	**1,890**	**3,415**	**2,365**	**1,420**	**Population active occupée totale de 15 ans et plus**	306
						selon le lieu de travail	
1,000	635	1,025	1,815	1,175	730	Hommes	307
870	515	870	1,540	990	610	Lieu habituel de travail	308
40	25	55	75	65	35	À domicile	309
-	-	-	-	-	10	En dehors du Canada	310
90	90	105	200	120	80	Sans adresse de travail fixe	311
885	645	865	1,605	1,190	690	Femmes	312
835	595	785	1,450	1,090	605	Lieu habituel de travail	313
15	40	55	115	45	30	À domicile	314
-	-	-	-	-	-	En dehors du Canada	315
30	10	30	35	55	55	Sans adresse de travail fixe	316
1,825	**1,210**	**1,785**	**3,230**	**2,260**	**1,355**	**Population active occupée totale de 15 ans et plus ayant un lieu habituel de travail ou sans adresse de travail fixe**	317
						selon le mode de transport	
960	605	970	1,740	1,115	690	Hommes	318
765	485	830	1,400	1,005	565	Automobile, camion ou fourgonnette, en tant que conducteur	319
20	30	20	95	40	30	Automobile, camion ou fourgonnette, en tant que passager	320
110	45	95	200	60	45	Transport en commun	321
30	35	25	20	-	35	À pied	322
25	10	10	25	-	20	Autre moyen	323
870	605	815	1,485	1,150	660	Femmes	324
515	445	585	1,005	765	410	Automobile, camion ou fourgonnette, en tant que conductrice	325
90	30	85	180	110	30	Automobile, camion ou fourgonnette, en tant que passagère	326
175	60	90	205	220	95	Transport en commun	327
80	60	50	90	25	115	À pied	328
-	10	10	-	30	10	Autre moyen	329
2,120	**1,445**	**2,175**	**3,875**	**2,605**	**1,560**	**Population totale de 15 ans et plus ayant travaillé depuis le 1er janvier 2000**	330
						selon la langue utilisée au travail	
2,025	1,420	2,120	3,765	2,520	1,505	Réponses uniques	331
2,015	1,420	2,110	3,765	2,520	1,505	Anglais	332
-	-	-	-	-	-	Français	333
-	-	-	-	-	-	Langues non officielles (5)	334
-	-	-	-	-	-	Chinois, n.d.a.	335
-	-	-	-	-	-	Cantonais	336
-	-	-	-	-	-	Autres langues (6)	337
100	30	55	105	85	60	Réponses multiples	338
50	-	30	50	30	30	Anglais et français	339
50	30	20	40	50	30	Anglais et langue non officielle	340
-	-	-	-	10	-	Français et langue non officielle	341
-	-	-	10	-	-	Anglais, français et langue non officielle	342
						CARACTÉRISTIQUES DES LOGEMENTS ET DES MÉNAGES	
1,600	**980**	**1,180**	**2,095**	**1,335**	**1,180**	**Nombre total de logements privés occupés**	343
						selon le mode d'occupation	
845	785	1,125	1,650	1,280	535	Possédé	344
755	195	55	445	55	640	Loué	345
-	-	-	-	-	-	Logement de bande	346
						selon le type de construction résidentielle	
160	620	960	1,340	890	585	Maison individuelle non attenante	347
335	15	10	10	130	-	Maison jumelée	348
-	135	205	395	25	-	Maison en rangée	349
-	50	-	15	60	-	Appartement, duplex non attenant	350
980	-	10	240	-	380	Appartement, immeuble de cinq étages ou plus	351
120	165	-	95	235	215	Appartement, immeuble de moins de cinq étages (38)	352
-	-	-	-	-	-	Autre maison individuelle attenante	353
-	-	-	-	-	-	Logement mobile (39)	354

Table 1. Selected Characteristics for Census Tracts, 2001 Census – 100% Data and 20% Sample Data

No.	Characteristics	Toronto 0805.04 A	Toronto 0805.05 A	Toronto 0805.06 A	Toronto 0805.07 A	Toronto 0806 A	Toronto 0807
	DWELLING AND HOUSEHOLD CHARACTERISTICS						
	by condition of dwelling						
355	Regular maintenance only	675	705	1,160	1,445	350	490
356	Minor repairs	115	195	205	160	145	315
357	Major repairs	20	10	20	35	80	95
	by period of construction						
358	Before 1946	35	-	-	15	240	390
359	1946-1960	65	10	10	25	100	130
360	1961-1970	15	-	15	10	80	110
361	1971-1980	10	20	20	30	70	45
362	1981-1990	240	750	1,085	250	80	135
363	1991-2001 (20)	440	130	260	1,295	-	85
364	Average number of rooms per dwelling	7.9	7.5	7.4	7.2	7.8	7.3
365	Average number of bedrooms per dwelling	3.5	3.3	3.4	3.4	3.1	3.2
366	Average value of dwelling $	262,170	201,293	217,571	234,597	333,755	333,510
367	**Total number of private households**	**805**	**910**	**1,390**	**1,635**	**575**	**905**
	by household size						
368	1 person	65	70	100	95	75	135
369	2 persons	265	160	265	350	165	270
370	3 persons	125	165	260	320	140	140
371	4-5 persons	315	445	630	720	175	285
372	6 or more persons	40	65	145	150	15	70
	by household type						
373	One-family households	665	790	1,175	1,415	475	705
374	Multiple-family households	50	25	75	120	15	35
375	Non-family households	95	90	140	100	85	165
376	Number of persons in private households	2,555	3,270	5,055	5,775	1,690	2,770
377	Average number of persons in private households	3.2	3.6	3.6	3.5	2.9	3.1
378	Average number of persons per room	0.4	0.5	0.5	0.5	0.4	0.4
379	Tenant households in non-farm, non-reserve private dwellings (40)	60	50	255	75	145	355
380	Average gross rent $ (40)	767	1,139	714	1,139	1,041	929
381	Tenant households spending 30% or more of household income on gross rent (40) (41)	-	10	95	20	65	105
382	Tenant households spending from 30% to 99% of household income on gross rent (40) (41)	-	10	95	25	60	75
383	Owner households in non-farm, non-reserve private dwellings (42)	740	850	1,135	1,555	425	535
384	Average owner's major payments $ (42)	1,489	1,460	1,425	1,545	1,345	1,296
385	Owner households spending 30% or more of household income on owner's major payments (41) (42)	120	200	330	465	90	95
386	Owner households spending from 30% to 99% of household income on owner's major payments (41) (42)	115	175	285	415	90	95
	CENSUS FAMILY CHARACTERISTICS						
387	**Total number of census families in private households**	**765**	**865**	**1,320**	**1,655**	**505**	**780**
	by census family structure and size						
388	Total couple families	690	730	1,095	1,395	435	685
389	Total families of married couples	615	650	1,000	1,265	370	620
390	Without children at home	235	95	195	330	125	210
391	With children at home	375	555	800	930	250	415
392	1 child	95	120	150	275	85	125
393	2 children	210	265	400	455	120	155
394	3 or more children	75	165	250	205	50	130
395	Total families of common-law couples	75	75	95	135	65	65
396	Without children at home	35	25	45	50	55	45
397	With children at home	40	55	50	90	10	15
398	1 child	10	25	20	25	10	10
399	2 children	20	15	15	25	-	10
400	3 or more children	-	15	10	30	-	-
401	Total lone-parent families	80	135	225	260	65	90
402	Female parent	65	115	205	185	45	60
403	1 child	25	70	95	115	35	50
404	2 children	35	20	70	55	10	-
405	3 or more children	10	20	45	10	-	10

Tableau 1. Certaines caractéristiques des secteurs de recensement, recensement de 2001 – Données intégrales et données-échantillon (20 %)

Toronto 0810.01	Toronto 0810.02	Toronto 0810.03	Toronto 0810.04	Toronto 0810.05	Toronto 0811	Caractéristiques	N°
						CARACTÉRISTIQUES DES LOGEMENTS ET DES MÉNAGES	
						selon l'état du logement	
1,050	640	890	1,460	940	710	Entretien régulier seulement	355
420	280	260	540	375	315	Réparations mineures	356
130	60	30	95	20	145	Réparations majeures	357
						selon la période de construction	
30	15	-	10	-	125	Avant 1946	358
385	110	15	10	-	660	1946-1960	359
210	555	560	180	10	235	1961-1970	360
760	280	555	1,020	100	135	1971-1980	361
200	25	50	725	1,140	20	1981-1990	362
-	-	-	160	85	-	1991-2001 (20)	363
5.6	6.7	8.0	6.8	7.7	5.5	Nombre moyen de pièces par logement	364
2.5	2.8	3.4	3.0	3.3	2.3	Nombre moyen de chambres à coucher par logement	365
142,213	191,386	200,867	193,334	225,257	162,621	Valeur moyenne du logement $	366
1,600	**980**	**1,180**	**2,090**	**1,335**	**1,180**	**Nombre total de logements privés**	367
						selon la taille du ménage	
380	240	120	320	205	345	1 personne	368
560	315	380	565	340	455	2 personnes	369
325	155	280	395	230	180	3 personnes	370
280	245	370	745	520	185	4-5 personnes	371
55	30	35	65	40	15	6 personnes ou plus	372
						selon le genre de ménage	
1,080	675	1,035	1,695	1,070	760	Ménages unifamiliaux	373
55	30	15	55	20	20	Ménages multifamiliaux	374
465	280	130	345	230	400	Ménages non familiaux	375
4,025	2,555	3,495	6,215	4,045	2,670	Nombre de personnes dans les ménages privés	376
2.5	2.6	3.0	3.0	3.0	2.3	Nombre moyen de personnes dans les ménages privés	377
0.5	0.4	0.4	0.4	0.4	0.4	Nombre moyen de personnes par pièce	378
760	195	55	445	55	640	Ménages locataires dans les logements privés non agricoles hors réserve (40)	379
882	484	1,015	735	1,125	824	Loyer brut moyen $ (40)	380
290	85	30	190	10	285	Ménages locataires consacrant 30 % ou plus du revenu du ménage au loyer brut (40) (41)	381
235	80	20	170	10	260	Ménages locataires consacrant de 30 % à 99 % du revenu du ménage au loyer brut (40) (41)	382
845	785	1,130	1,650	1,280	540	Ménages propriétaires dans les logements privés non agricoles hors réserve (42)	383
885	1,055	1,058	1,138	1,184	938	Principales dépenses de propriété moyennes $ (42)	384
265	130	165	285	170	85	Ménages propriétaires consacrant 30 % ou plus du revenu du ménage aux principales dépenses de propriété (41) (42)	385
230	105	155	265	160	85	Ménages propriétaires consacrant de 30 % à 99 % du revenu du ménage aux principales dépenses de propriété (41) (42)	386
						CARACTÉRISTIQUES DES FAMILLES DE RECENSEMENT	
1,190	**735**	**1,065**	**1,805**	**1,120**	**795**	**Total des familles de recensement dans les ménages privés**	387
						selon la structure et la taille de la famille de recensement	
880	630	965	1,475	1,010	655	Total des familles avec conjoints	388
725	595	885	1,295	940	515	Total des familles avec couples mariés	389
340	270	330	380	240	265	Sans enfants à la maison	390
385	325	550	915	695	250	Avec enfants à la maison	391
170	110	220	290	195	125	1 enfant	392
140	155	235	440	350	85	2 enfants	393
80	55	95	185	150	40	3 enfants ou plus	394
155	35	80	180	70	135	Total des familles en union libre	395
85	15	30	65	45	80	Sans enfants à la maison	396
70	20	50	110	30	55	Avec enfants à la maison	397
35	10	25	35	10	30	1 enfant	398
35	15	15	60	20	20	2 enfants	399
-	-	10	10	-	-	3 enfants ou plus	400
305	100	100	330	110	140	Total des familles monoparentales	401
230	100	80	255	85	120	Parent de sexe féminin	402
170	65	50	135	35	95	1 enfant	403
50	25	30	110	35	25	2 enfants	404
10	10	10	10	15	-	3 enfants ou plus	405

Table 1. Selected Characteristics for Census Tracts, 2001 Census – 100% Data and 20% Sample Data

No.	Characteristics	Toronto 0805.04 A	Toronto 0805.05 A	Toronto 0805.06 A	Toronto 0805.07 A	Toronto 0806 A	Toronto 0807
	CENSUS FAMILY CHARACTERISTICS						
	by census family structure and size – concluded						
406	Male parent	15	30	20	75	25	25
407	1 child	10	25	10	45	15	25
408	2 children	10	10	10	35	-	-
409	3 or more children	-	-	-	-	-	-
410	**Total number of children at home**	**955**	**1,475**	**2,260**	**2,425**	**585**	**1,020**
	by age groups						
411	Under 6 years	220	365	455	770	115	130
412	6-14 years	405	615	1,040	1,015	180	435
413	15-17 years	110	165	285	205	75	155
414	18-24 years	175	255	330	330	120	205
415	25 years and over	40	75	140	110	100	100
416	Average number of children at home per census family (43)	1.2	1.7	1.7	1.5	1.2	1.3
417	**Total number of persons in private households**	**2,550**	**3,270**	**5,055**	**5,770**	**1,690**	**2,770**
	by census family status and living arrangements						
418	Number of non-family persons	145	200	385	295	150	285
419	Living with relatives (44)	15	75	100	135	15	80
420	Living with non-relatives only	55	60	190	65	65	70
421	Living alone	70	65	100	95	75	130
422	Number of family persons	2,410	3,070	4,675	5,475	1,530	2,485
423	Average number of persons per census family	3.1	3.5	3.5	3.3	3.0	3.2
424	**Total number of persons 65 years and over**	**95**	**90**	**215**	**210**	**200**	**240**
425	Number of non-family persons 65 years and over	15	45	90	70	35	90
426	Living with relatives (44)	10	40	65	55	-	40
427	Living with non-relatives only	-	-	-	-	10	-
428	Living alone	10	-	25	15	30	50
429	Number of family persons 65 years and over	75	45	125	140	160	150
	ECONOMIC FAMILY CHARACTERISTICS						
430	**Total number of economic families in private households**	**725**	**820**	**1,255**	**1,565**	**490**	**755**
	by size of family						
431	2 persons	250	155	265	395	190	280
432	3 persons	125	160	235	340	115	130
433	4 persons	240	285	405	470	125	180
434	5 or more persons	115	225	355	350	60	160
435	Total number of persons in economic families	2,425	3,145	4,765	5,610	1,550	2,565
436	Average number of persons per economic family	3.4	3.8	3.8	3.6	3.2	3.4
437	Total number of unattached individuals	120	130	290	160	140	205
	2000 INCOME CHARACTERISTICS						
	Population 15 years and over by sex and total income groups in 2000						
438	Total - Both sexes	1,915	2,280	3,540	3,990	1,390	2,210
439	Without income	75	95	200	185	110	105
440	With income	1,845	2,190	3,345	3,805	1,280	2,100
441	Under $1,000 (45)	70	120	155	180	40	115
442	$ 1,000 - $ 2,999	45	115	265	165	40	80
443	$ 3,000 - $ 4,999	55	125	100	105	45	65
444	$ 5,000 - $ 6,999	45	110	105	110	95	105
445	$ 7,000 - $ 9,999	105	65	195	140	50	95
446	$10,000 - $11,999	40	40	115	125	55	95
447	$12,000 - $14,999	65	85	180	105	65	135
448	$15,000 - $19,999	90	110	185	200	110	130
449	$20,000 - $24,999	85	110	260	210	75	60
450	$25,000 - $29,999	80	120	185	290	110	165
451	$30,000 - $34,999	130	195	260	320	55	115
452	$35,000 - $39,999	140	140	180	325	60	140
453	$40,000 - $44,999	175	85	210	365	85	140
454	$45,000 - $49,999	85	145	210	230	45	80
455	$50,000 - $59,999	175	255	205	335	95	185
456	$60,000 and over	465	360	535	600	260	390
457	Average income $ (46)	43,830	34,051	32,424	37,369	40,148	40,393
458	Median income $ (46)	39,072	31,954	27,187	34,037	28,192	29,997
459	Standard error of average income $ (46)	1,994	1,202	1,022	1,153	3,255	2,232

Tableau 1. Certaines caractéristiques des secteurs de recensement, recensement de 2001 – Données intégrales et données-échantillon (20 %)

Toronto 0810.01	Toronto 0810.02	Toronto 0810.03	Toronto 0810.04	Toronto 0810.05	Toronto 0811	Caractéristiques	Nº
						CARACTÉRISTIQUES DES FAMILLES DE RECENSEMENT	
						selon la structure et la taille de la famille de recensement - fin	
80	10	20	80	25	20	Parent de sexe masculin	406
50	10	-	50	25	20	1 enfant	407
25	-	-	25	-	-	2 enfants	408
10	-	10	-	-	-	3 enfants ou plus	409
1,245	**800**	**1,230**	**2,450**	**1,595**	**670**	**Nombre total d'enfants à la maison**	410
						selon les groupes d'âge	
330	145	215	425	280	140	Moins de 6 ans	411
455	270	410	920	610	245	6-14 ans	412
160	105	120	305	250	85	15-17 ans	413
165	170	310	570	355	110	18-24 ans	414
135	105	170	225	110	90	25 ans et plus	415
1.1	1.1	1.2	1.4	1.4	0.8	Nombre moyen d'enfants à la maison par famille de recensement (43)	416
4,030	**2,560**	**3,500**	**6,215**	**4,040**	**2,665**	**Nombre total de personnes dans les ménages privés**	417
						selon la situation des particuliers dans la famille de recensement et des particuliers dans le ménage	
715	395	245	490	310	545	Nombre de personnes hors famille de recensement	418
175	45	60	60	35	65	Vivant avec des personnes apparentées (44)	419
165	110	60	105	75	140	Vivant avec des personnes non apparentées uniquement	420
380	240	120	320	205	345	Vivant seules	421
3,310	2,160	3,255	5,730	3,730	2,125	Nombre de personnes membres d'une famille	422
2.8	3.0	3.1	3.2	3.3	2.7	Nombre moyen de personnes par famille de recensement	423
665	**450**	**410**	**545**	**195**	**520**	**Nombre total de personnes de 65 ans et plus**	424
205	195	90	205	60	185	Nombre de personnes hors famille de recensement de 65 ans et plus	425
35	25	30	30	20	20	Vivant avec des personnes apparentées (44)	426
10	-	10	-	-	-	Vivant avec des personnes non apparentées uniquement	427
155	170	50	170	35	155	Vivant seules	428
460	255	325	345	130	340	Nombre de personnes membres d'une famille de 65 ans et plus	429
						CARACTÉRISTIQUES DES FAMILLES ÉCONOMIQUES	
1,165	**725**	**1,050**	**1,750**	**1,100**	**785**	**Nombre total de familles économiques dans les ménages privés**	430
						selon la taille de la famille	
530	325	375	570	320	425	2 personnes	431
305	145	280	410	225	175	3 personnes	432
210	180	270	525	360	120	4 personnes	433
125	75	125	245	190	60	5 personnes ou plus	434
3,485	2,205	3,320	5,790	3,760	2,185	Nombre total de personnes dans les familles économiques	435
3.0	3.0	3.2	3.3	3.4	2.8	Nombre moyen de personnes par famille économique	436
540	350	185	430	280	480	Nombre total de personnes hors famille économique	437
						CARACTÉRISTIQUES DU REVENU DE 2000	
						Population de 15 ans et plus selon le sexe et les tranches de revenu total en 2000	
3,210	2,135	2,860	4,860	3,155	2,285	Total - Les deux sexes	438
205	120	90	200	190	45	Sans revenu	439
3,000	2,020	2,775	4,665	2,965	2,235	Avec un revenu	440
165	85	110	160	115	55	Moins de 1 000 $ (45)	441
105	90	130	220	135	95	1 000 $ - 2 999 $	442
140	55	105	220	105	70	3 000 $ - 4 999 $	443
125	90	60	185	60	95	5 000 $ - 6 999 $	444
165	115	140	235	135	90	7 000 $ - 9 999 $	445
160	75	105	165	65	95	10 000 $ - 11 999 $	446
185	105	120	210	105	135	12 000 $ - 14 999 $	447
320	170	225	395	165	215	15 000 $ - 19 999 $	448
235	150	195	405	145	220	20 000 $ - 24 999 $	449
235	150	170	215	170	210	25 000 $ - 29 999 $	450
210	155	295	335	185	170	30 000 $ - 34 999 $	451
235	130	130	340	160	165	35 000 $ - 39 999 $	452
160	115	155	185	160	95	40 000 $ - 44 999 $	453
50	90	95	150	175	100	45 000 $ - 49 999 $	454
295	180	290	415	260	195	50 000 $ - 59 999 $	455
215	270	450	835	830	230	60 000 $ et plus	456
27,114	31,685	34,456	34,541	42,476	30,580	Revenu moyen $ (46)	457
22,157	27,514	30,031	28,307	38,115	25,321	Revenu médian $ (46)	458
856	1,157	1,076	952	1,349	1,414	Erreur type de revenu moyen $ (46)	459

Table 1. Selected Characteristics for Census Tracts, 2001 Census – 100% Data and 20% Sample Data

No.	Characteristics	Toronto 0805.04 A	Toronto 0805.05 A	Toronto 0805.06 A	Toronto 0805.07 A	Toronto 0806 A	Toronto 0807
	2000 INCOME CHARACTERISTICS						
	Population 15 years and over by sex and total income groups in 2000 – concluded						
460	Total - Males	945	1,110	1,715	1,915	710	1,150
461	Without income	40	25	90	90	35	30
462	With income	905	1,080	1,625	1,825	670	1,115
463	Under $1,000 (45)	25	50	45	80	20	50
464	$ 1,000 - $ 2,999	15	50	120	40	10	25
465	$ 3,000 - $ 4,999	10	40	45	30	10	15
466	$ 5,000 - $ 6,999	10	50	45	45	35	55
467	$ 7,000 - $ 9,999	25	20	70	30	30	35
468	$10,000 - $11,999	15	25	55	45	10	55
469	$12,000 - $14,999	30	40	95	25	30	50
470	$15,000 - $19,999	20	20	40	55	60	60
471	$20,000 - $24,999	35	50	90	75	35	25
472	$25,000 - $29,999	25	65	100	115	70	100
473	$30,000 - $34,999	60	80	145	120	15	50
474	$35,000 - $39,999	65	50	60	160	35	100
475	$40,000 - $44,999	75	50	110	180	35	85
476	$45,000 - $49,999	60	90	85	155	25	45
477	$50,000 - $59,999	90	135	130	225	75	100
478	$60,000 and over	360	255	385	440	180	290
479	Average income $ (46)	57,508	40,550	38,890	45,568	50,016	49,943
480	Median income $ (46)	49,569	37,564	31,720	42,027	37,217	37,071
481	Standard error of average income $ (46)	3,481	1,919	1,706	1,865	5,594	3,818
482	Total - Females	975	1,175	1,830	2,075	685	1,060
483	Without income	35	65	110	95	75	75
484	With income	940	1,110	1,720	1,975	605	980
485	Under $1,000 (45)	45	65	110	100	15	65
486	$ 1,000 - $ 2,999	30	70	140	120	40	55
487	$ 3,000 - $ 4,999	45	85	60	75	30	45
488	$ 5,000 - $ 6,999	40	65	60	70	60	50
489	$ 7,000 - $ 9,999	85	45	125	115	20	65
490	$10,000 - $11,999	25	15	60	80	40	40
491	$12,000 - $14,999	35	45	90	80	40	85
492	$15,000 - $19,999	70	95	145	140	50	70
493	$20,000 - $24,999	50	60	165	135	40	40
494	$25,000 - $29,999	55	50	85	170	40	65
495	$30,000 - $34,999	70	115	110	205	40	70
496	$35,000 - $39,999	70	90	120	165	25	45
497	$40,000 - $44,999	100	35	110	190	40	55
498	$45,000 - $49,999	30	55	125	75	20	40
499	$50,000 - $59,999	85	125	70	105	25	85
500	$60,000 and over	105	100	150	160	80	95
501	Average income $ (46)	30,646	27,693	26,317	29,808	29,169	29,540
502	Median income $ (46)	28,347	25,576	21,295	26,720	22,384	22,381
503	Standard error of average income $ (46)	1,627	1,345	1,082	1,300	2,427	1,874
	by composition of total income						
504	Total - Composition of income in 2000 % (47)	100.0	100.0	100.0	100.0	100.0	100.0
505	Employment income %	88.3	92.6	88.0	92.0	87.1	80.3
506	Government transfer payments %	3.3	4.6	6.8	4.6	7.6	6.2
507	Other %	8.3	2.7	5.2	3.4	5.5	13.7
	Population 15 years and over with employment income in 2000 by sex and work activity						
508	Both sexes with employment income (48)	1,610	1,945	2,795	3,360	1,000	1,650
509	Average employment income $	44,475	35,578	34,109	38,945	44,807	41,196
510	Standard error of average employment income $	1,717	1,268	1,136	1,227	3,927	2,537
511	Worked full year, full time (49)	1,010	1,155	1,660	2,190	600	845
512	Average employment income $	55,186	45,978	44,930	49,240	57,916	56,107
513	Standard error of average employment income $	2,149	1,557	1,407	1,572	6,036	3,558
514	Worked part year or part time (50)	570	715	1,080	1,140	385	785
515	Average employment income $	27,231	21,637	18,723	20,214	25,417	26,182
516	Standard error of average employment income $	2,132	1,598	1,473	1,334	2,933	3,359
517	Males with employment income (48)	830	1,005	1,415	1,695	550	935
518	Average employment income $	54,645	41,546	41,316	46,629	54,399	49,541
519	Standard error of average employment income $	2,674	1,991	1,826	1,959	6,544	4,127
520	Worked full year, full time (49)	565	655	920	1,225	390	545
521	Average employment income $	64,691	53,263	51,610	56,686	63,822	61,179
522	Standard error of average employment income $	3,165	2,241	2,127	2,303	9,070	5,032
523	Worked part year or part time (50)	265	320	470	465	155	380
524	Average employment income $	33,946	21,494	22,610	20,570	31,773	34,373
525	Standard error of average employment income $	3,697	2,511	2,684	2,334	5,618	6,807

Tableau 1. Certaines caractéristiques des secteurs de recensement, recensement de 2001 – Données intégrales et données-échantillon (20 %)

Toronto 0810.01	Toronto 0810.02	Toronto 0810.03	Toronto 0810.04	Toronto 0810.05	Toronto 0811	Caractéristiques	N°
						CARACTÉRISTIQUES DU REVENU DE 2000	
						Population de 15 ans et plus selon le sexe et les tranches de revenu total en 2000 – fin	
1,485	1,005	1,435	2,365	1,515	1,075	Total - Hommes	460
65	50	15	55	90	-	Sans revenu	461
1,415	960	1,420	2,300	1,430	1,070	Avec un revenu	462
70	55	60	60	20	30	Moins de 1 000 $ (45)	463
35	45	55	75	45	40	1 000 $ - 2 999 $	464
45	25	35	85	30	15	3 000 $ - 4 999 $	465
40	25	25	95	15	10	5 000 $ - 6 999 $	466
50	40	50	55	70	30	7 000 $ - 9 999 $	467
60	25	45	60	10	25	10 000 $ - 11 999 $	468
85	20	45	75	25	35	12 000 $ - 14 999 $	469
100	35	70	120	70	75	15 000 $ - 19 999 $	470
125	30	75	185	40	135	20 000 $ - 24 999 $	471
115	65	80	120	80	105	25 000 $ - 29 999 $	472
85	85	155	120	35	80	30 000 $ - 34 999 $	473
135	50	60	155	60	95	35 000 $ - 39 999 $	474
90	65	65	95	55	75	40 000 $ - 44 999 $	475
35	50	50	95	90	40	45 000 $ - 49 999 $	476
200	135	215	285	150	120	50 000 $ - 59 999 $	477
150	210	320	625	635	150	60 000 $ et plus	478
31,789	39,904	41,259	43,222	55,216	33,905	Revenu moyen $ (46)	479
28,466	37,817	36,170	38,441	51,529	30,325	Revenu médian $ (46)	480
1,191	1,950	1,713	1,606	2,225	1,301	Erreur type de revenu moyen $ (46)	481
1,725	1,130	1,435	2,505	1,645	1,205	Total - Femmes	482
140	70	75	140	100	45	Sans revenu	483
1,580	1,060	1,355	2,360	1,540	1,165	Avec un revenu	484
95	35	40	100	90	25	Moins de 1 000 $ (45)	485
70	45	75	140	90	55	1 000 $ - 2 999 $	486
100	30	70	135	70	50	3 000 $ - 4 999 $	487
85	60	35	95	45	85	5 000 $ - 6 999 $	488
110	75	90	180	65	60	7 000 $ - 9 999 $	489
100	45	65	95	60	70	10 000 $ - 11 999 $	490
100	85	75	135	75	95	12 000 $ - 14 999 $	491
220	130	155	270	90	135	15 000 $ - 19 999 $	492
115	120	125	215	105	80	20 000 $ - 24 999 $	493
120	90	95	95	90	105	25 000 $ - 29 999 $	494
125	65	145	215	150	85	30 000 $ - 34 999 $	495
95	80	70	185	100	70	35 000 $ - 39 999 $	496
70	55	85	90	105	15	40 000 $ - 44 999 $	497
10	40	40	60	90	60	45 000 $ - 49 999 $	498
95	45	75	130	110	75	50 000 $ - 59 999 $	499
70	55	125	200	200	80	60 000 $ et plus	500
22,925	24,253	27,352	26,065	30,673	27,511	Revenu moyen $ (46)	501
17,733	20,459	23,556	20,307	29,473	19,826	Revenu médian $ (46)	502
1,182	1,117	1,166	938	1,269	2,452	Erreur type de revenu moyen $ (46)	503
						selon la composition du revenu total	
100.0	100.0	100.0	100.0	100.0	100.0	Total - Composition du revenu en 2000 % (47)	504
74.5	74.3	82.2	84.8	90.3	72.5	Revenu d'emploi %	505
15.7	12.8	7.6	7.5	3.7	13.3	Transferts gouvernementaux %	506
9.7	13.0	10.2	7.7	5.9	14.3	Autre %	507
						Population de 15 ans et plus ayant un revenu d'emploi en 2000 selon le sexe et le travail	
1,990	1,355	2,185	3,770	2,565	1,550	Les deux sexes ayant un revenu d'emploi (48)	508
30,506	35,096	35,928	36,243	44,431	31,973	Revenu moyen d'emploi $	509
1,142	1,429	1,247	1,060	1,469	1,095	Erreur type de revenu moyen d'emploi $	510
1,215	880	1,245	2,155	1,580	955	Ayant travaillé toute l'année à plein temps (49)	511
38,994	44,545	46,041	49,588	57,474	40,362	Revenu moyen d'emploi $	512
1,529	1,767	1,411	1,323	1,630	1,182	Erreur type de revenu moyen d'emploi $	513
775	450	890	1,550	950	540	Ayant travaillé une partie de l'année ou à temps partiel (50)	514
17,212	18,287	22,155	19,065	22,657	17,996	Revenu moyen d'emploi $	515
1,185	1,625	1,921	1,296	2,181	1,685	Erreur type de revenu moyen d'emploi $	516
1,010	680	1,185	1,995	1,295	785	Hommes ayant un revenu d'emploi (48)	517
34,618	43,333	41,708	43,885	56,510	37,326	Revenu moyen d'emploi $	518
1,498	2,237	1,964	1,682	2,369	1,547	Erreur type de revenu moyen d'emploi $	519
690	495	740	1,270	890	545	Ayant travaillé toute l'année à plein temps (49)	520
40,980	52,446	50,638	55,650	67,385	43,091	Revenu moyen d'emploi $	521
1,771	2,446	2,049	1,909	2,436	1,625	Erreur type de revenu moyen d'emploi $	522
325	160	430	720	385	215	Ayant travaillé une partie de l'année ou à temps partiel (50)	523
21,057	20,735	26,663	23,437	32,069	24,099	Revenu moyen d'emploi $	524
2,097	3,352	3,517	2,518	4,560	3,023	Erreur type de revenu moyen d'emploi $	525

Table 1. Selected Characteristics for Census Tracts, 2001 Census – 100% Data and 20% Sample Data

No.	Characteristics	Toronto 0805.04 A	Toronto 0805.05 A	Toronto 0805.06 A	Toronto 0805.07 A	Toronto 0806 A	Toronto 0807
	2000 INCOME CHARACTERISTICS						
	Population 15 years and over with employment income in 2000 by sex and work activity – concluded						
526	Females with employment income (48)	775	940	1,385	1,660	450	715
527	Average employment income $	33,528	29,176	26,780	31,102	33,129	30,319
528	Standard error of average employment income $	1,797	1,420	1,213	1,351	2,958	2,238
529	Worked full year, full time (49)	450	505	740	960	210	300
530	Average employment income $	43,158	36,571	36,627	39,715	47,207	47,014
531	Standard error of average employment income $	2,255	1,775	1,494	1,850	4,640	4,079
532	Worked part year or part time (50)	305	390	615	675	230	400
533	Average employment income $	21,459	21,753	15,761	19,970	21,037	18,370
534	Standard error of average employment income $	2,248	2,058	1,555	1,579	2,654	1,747
	Census families by structure and family income groups in 2000						
535	Total - All census families	765	870	1,315	1,655	505	780
536	Under $10,000	-	20	55	50	15	15
537	$ 10,000 - $19,999	25	15	65	35	20	25
538	$ 20,000 - $29,999	-	15	90	35	40	45
539	$ 30,000 - $39,999	30	85	125	110	10	45
540	$ 40,000 - $49,999	75	85	130	200	55	45
541	$ 50,000 - $59,999	40	90	80	175	55	85
542	$ 60,000 - $69,999	45	110	105	150	40	50
543	$ 70,000 - $79,999	90	40	140	210	35	90
544	$ 80,000 - $89,999	75	120	115	170	65	40
545	$ 90,000 - $99,999	105	40	95	105	15	85
546	$100,000 and over	280	245	320	415	155	250
547	Average family income $	96,887	78,585	74,115	80,746	90,313	94,501
548	Median family income $	89,730	72,111	70,418	72,921	71,582	77,246
549	Standard error of average family income $	4,485	2,731	2,559	2,670	8,003	5,266
550	Total - All couple census families (51)	685	730	1,095	1,395	440	690
551	Under $10,000	-	20	35	10	10	-
552	$ 10,000 - $19,999	10	15	35	30	-	15
553	$ 20,000 - $29,999	-	10	65	20	35	25
554	$ 30,000 - $39,999	20	25	100	60	10	35
555	$ 40,000 - $49,999	60	70	80	145	45	35
556	$ 50,000 - $59,999	40	75	70	140	50	85
557	$ 60,000 - $69,999	45	95	90	130	45	50
558	$ 70,000 - $79,999	90	35	115	200	20	90
559	$ 80,000 - $89,999	60	105	115	165	60	40
560	$ 90,000 - $99,999	90	45	90	105	15	70
561	$100,000 and over	280	250	315	395	145	250
562	Average family income $	101,847	84,899	80,079	87,330	97,224	102,046
563	Median family income $	93,046	81,641	77,180	77,054	80,236	81,834
564	Standard error of average family income $	4,762	2,870	2,828	2,884	8,875	5,547
	Incidence of low income in 2000						
565	Total - Economic families	730	825	1,250	1,560	490	755
566	Low income	25	20	160	75	15	20
567	Incidence of low income in 2000 % (52)	3.5	2.5	12.6	5.1	3.1	3.0
568	Total - Unattached individuals 15 years and over	115	120	275	165	130	205
569	Low income	10	30	90	40	10	45
570	Incidence of low income in 2000 % (52)	7.8	26.6	32.8	24.0	5.8	21.4
571	Total - Population in private households	2,550	3,265	5,040	5,770	1,680	2,770
572	Low income	65	110	685	365	45	120
573	Incidence of low income in 2000 % (52)	2.5	3.3	13.6	6.3	2.6	4.4
	Private households by household income groups in 2000						
574	Total - All private households	810	910	1,385	1,635	575	905
575	Under $10,000	-	15	60	20	10	15
576	$ 10,000 - $19,999	20	15	80	50	35	50
577	$ 20,000 - $29,999	10	10	55	15	35	70
578	$ 30,000 - $39,999	35	60	100	85	40	40
579	$ 40,000 - $49,999	60	75	145	135	50	50
580	$ 50,000 - $59,999	30	110	105	195	70	110
581	$ 60,000 - $69,999	75	130	95	160	35	45
582	$ 70,000 - $79,999	80	50	135	215	45	80
583	$ 80,000 - $89,999	75	105	95	160	70	40
584	$ 90,000 - $99,999	120	50	130	125	20	70
585	$100,000 and over	300	295	395	475	160	320
586	Average household income $	100,052	81,876	78,085	86,901	89,744	94,081
587	Median household income $	90,928	79,175	74,533	76,876	71,224	77,852
588	Standard error of average household income $	4,431	2,543	2,549	2,737	7,565	5,075

Tableau 1. Certaines caractéristiques des secteurs de recensement, recensement de 2001 – Données intégrales et données-échantillon (20 %)

Toronto 0810.01	Toronto 0810.02	Toronto 0810.03	Toronto 0810.04	Toronto 0810.05	Toronto 0811	Caractéristiques	N°
						CARACTÉRISTIQUES DU REVENU DE 2000	
						Population de 15 ans et plus ayant un revenu d'emploi en 2000 selon le sexe et le travail - fin	
980	670	1,000	1,780	1,270	765	Femmes ayant un revenu d'emploi (48)	526
26,251	26,761	29,092	27,662	32,103	26,455	Revenu moyen d'emploi $	527
1,685	1,508	1,308	1,116	1,375	1,442	Erreur type de revenu moyen d'emploi $	528
525	385	510	885	690	415	Ayant travaillé toute l'année à plein temps (49)	529
36,392	34,244	39,336	40,870	44,657	36,756	Revenu moyen d'emploi $	530
2,632	2,078	1,609	1,535	1,518	1,645	Erreur type de revenu moyen d'emploi $	531
450	290	460	835	565	325	Ayant travaillé une partie de l'année ou à temps partiel (50)	532
14,465	16,919	17,935	15,309	16,266	13,945	Revenu moyen d'emploi $	533
1,306	1,643	1,601	1,091	1,506	1,769	Erreur type de revenu moyen d'emploi $	534
						Familles de recensement selon la structure et les tranches de revenu de la famille en 2000	
1,190	730	1,060	1,805	1,120	795	Total - Toutes les familles de recensement	535
70	15	15	45	-	20	Moins de 10 000 $	536
85	15	15	60	10	40	10 000 $ - 19 999 $	537
140	60	55	125	75	100	20 000 $ - 29 999 $	538
155	55	75	150	60	115	30 000 $ - 39 999 $	539
170	105	75	110	55	95	40 000 $ - 49 999 $	540
170	50	115	185	45	65	50 000 $ - 59 999 $	541
95	70	130	125	90	65	60 000 $ - 69 999 $	542
75	80	90	165	95	70	70 000 $ - 79 999 $	543
95	50	95	190	130	75	80 000 $ - 89 999 $	544
55	110	85	115	120	45	90 000 $ - 99 999 $	545
55	135	315	530	450	105	100 000 $ et plus	546
51,830	73,846	82,261	79,699	100,160	61,563	Revenu moyen des familles $	547
44,978	71,091	75,355	75,067	90,521	53,440	Revenu médian des familles $	548
2,105	2,885	2,676	2,270	3,443	2,646	Erreur type de revenu moyen des familles $	549
880	630	960	1,475	1,015	655	Total - Toutes les familles de recensement comptant un couple (51)	550
25	10	10	10	-	-	Moins de 10 000 $	551
65	10	15	35	-	25	10 000 $ - 19 999 $	552
130	30	50	85	40	80	20 000 $ - 29 999 $	553
120	40	55	75	55	95	30 000 $ - 39 999 $	554
90	80	75	95	40	75	40 000 $ - 49 999 $	555
105	45	105	140	40	55	50 000 $ - 59 999 $	556
75	50	115	100	75	55	60 000 $ - 69 999 $	557
75	80	80	150	80	60	70 000 $ - 79 999 $	558
85	40	70	145	120	70	80 000 $ - 89 999 $	559
55	115	85	115	115	35	90 000 $ - 99 999 $	560
45	130	305	515	450	100	100 000 $ et plus	561
55,493	78,472	84,348	87,297	105,877	65,690	Revenu moyen des familles $	562
50,087	75,490	78,960	82,116	95,536	59,234	Revenu médian des familles $	563
2,635	3,100	2,882	2,461	3,645	2,897	Erreur type de revenu moyen des familles $	564
						Fréquence des unités à faible revenu en 2000	
1,165	720	1,050	1,755	1,100	780	Total - Familles économiques	565
225	45	45	165	40	105	Faible revenu	566
19.4	6.2	4.5	9.4	4.1	13.5	Fréquence des unités à faible revenu en 2000 % (52)	567
525	350	170	420	275	485	Total - Personnes hors famille économique de 15 ans et plus	568
140	155	50	120	20	125	Faible revenu	569
26.2	43.5	29.9	28.0	7.3	26.4	Fréquence des unités à faible revenu en 2000 % (52)	570
4,015	2,560	3,485	6,210	4,040	2,665	Total - Population dans les ménages privés	571
920	285	215	650	160	410	Faible revenu	572
22.9	11.2	6.1	10.5	4.0	15.4	Fréquence des unités à faible revenu en 2000 % (52)	573
						Ménages privés selon les tranches de revenu du ménage en 2000	
1,600	980	1,180	2,090	1,330	1,180	Total - Tous les ménages privés	574
95	40	10	30	-	25	Moins de 10 000 $	575
135	120	35	160	15	130	10 000 $ - 19 999 $	576
245	85	80	160	70	175	20 000 $ - 29 999 $	577
205	85	85	190	90	165	30 000 $ - 39 999 $	578
175	95	75	80	90	100	40 000 $ - 49 999 $	579
235	65	115	210	85	155	50 000 $ - 59 999 $	580
125	85	140	160	115	85	60 000 $ - 69 999 $	581
140	70	95	185	125	75	70 000 $ - 79 999 $	582
105	55	110	185	125	85	80 000 $ - 89 999 $	583
75	125	100	140	130	50	90 000 $ - 99 999 $	584
75	160	330	585	475	140	100 000 $ et plus	585
50,851	65,220	80,863	77,015	94,635	58,077	Revenu moyen des ménages $	586
45,286	60,002	74,779	73,202	85,178	48,923	Revenu médian des ménages $	587
1,760	2,843	2,589	2,132	3,029	2,909	Erreur type de revenu moyen des ménages $	588

Table 1. Selected Characteristics for Census Tracts, 2001 Census – 100% Data and 20% Sample Data

No.	Characteristics	Toronto 0812	Toronto 0820.01 ◆ A	Toronto 0820.02 A	Toronto 0820.03 A	Toronto 0830	Toronto 0831.01 A
	POPULATION CHARACTERISTICS						
1	**Population, 1996 (1)**	**6,146**	**2,321**	**3,820**	**3,894**	**4,116**	**3,561**
2	**Population, 2001 (2)**	**6,209**	**4,081**	**5,800**	**4,185**	**4,165**	**4,505**
3	Population percentage change, 1996-2001	1.0	75.8	51.8	7.5	1.2	26.5
4	Land area in square kilometres, 2001	1.59	1.46	3.02	1.15	186.30	12.15
5	**Total population – 100% Data (3)**	**6,210**	**4,085**	**5,805**	**4,185**	**4,165**	**4,505**
	by sex and age groups						
6	Male	3,075	2,040	2,865	2,060	2,095	2,190
7	0-4 years	205	190	235	125	115	155
8	5-9 years	280	260	280	215	140	230
9	10-14 years	285	240	200	235	150	230
10	15-19 years	275	130	210	180	170	165
11	20-24 years	180	115	150	150	105	110
12	25-29 years	165	80	115	75	70	80
13	30-34 years	230	155	185	90	105	115
14	35-39 years	325	295	310	200	160	215
15	40-44 years	350	205	315	225	195	245
16	45-49 years	265	140	205	185	195	190
17	50-54 years	215	105	175	140	175	115
18	55-59 years	120	40	150	100	165	90
19	60-64 years	55	45	90	50	120	65
20	65-69 years	50	15	75	35	115	65
21	70-74 years	35	15	80	20	60	50
22	75-79 years	25	5	40	20	35	25
23	80-84 years	25	5	25	5	15	25
24	85 years and over	5	5	15	5	15	15
25	Female	3,130	2,045	2,940	2,125	2,065	2,320
26	0-4 years	200	195	215	145	85	170
27	5-9 years	290	265	210	205	130	225
28	10-14 years	300	170	240	220	170	215
29	15-19 years	230	140	190	185	155	185
30	20-24 years	170	65	145	125	100	95
31	25-29 years	170	100	135	85	75	90
32	30-34 years	250	185	225	110	125	140
33	35-39 years	350	295	355	255	160	245
34	40-44 years	355	215	295	240	205	240
35	45-49 years	250	145	215	185	200	160
36	50-54 years	195	85	175	130	170	120
37	55-59 years	105	40	140	70	155	100
38	60-64 years	70	50	100	50	115	80
39	65-69 years	65	25	95	35	90	60
40	70-74 years	55	20	100	30	65	65
41	75-79 years	45	20	70	30	40	60
42	80-84 years	20	10	35	15	25	35
43	85 years and over	20	5	20	15	15	35
44	**Total population 15 years and over**	**4,650**	**2,765**	**4,425**	**3,040**	**3,375**	**3,280**
	by legal marital status						
45	Never married (single)	1,425	725	1,185	890	870	810
46	Legally married (and not separated)	2,555	1,765	2,610	1,885	2,080	2,030
47	Separated, but still legally married	180	65	160	70	90	110
48	Divorced	315	130	260	105	200	165
49	Widowed	180	75	210	90	140	170
	by common-law status						
50	Not in a common-law relationship	4,285	2,625	4,160	2,935	3,170	3,105
51	In a common-law relationship	365	140	260	100	210	175
52	**Total population – 20% Sample Data (4)**	**6,205**	**4,010**	**5,790**	**4,260**	**4,165**	**4,505**
	by mother tongue						
53	Single responses	6,125	3,955	5,760	4,235	4,145	4,495
54	English	5,320	3,300	4,835	3,530	3,615	4,190
55	French	85	45	40	25	45	55
56	Non-official languages (5)	715	610	885	685	490	250
57	Italian	70	85	105	135	95	30
58	Chinese, n.o.s.	25	45	10	70	-	-
59	Cantonese	55	10	95	10	-	-
60	Portuguese	50	40	40	35	-	-
61	Punjabi	-	25	25	25	-	-
62	Other languages (6)	515	410	620	400	395	210
63	Multiple responses	80	55	25	25	20	10
64	English and French	10	10	10	10	-	-
65	English and non-official language	65	45	20	10	20	-
66	French and non-official language	-	-	-	-	-	-
67	English, French and non-official language	-	-	-	-	-	-

See reference material at the end of the publication. – Voir les documents de référence à la fin de la publication.

Tableau 1. Certaines caractéristiques des secteurs de recensement, recensement de 2001 – Données intégrales et données-échantillon (20 %)

Toronto 0831.02 A	Toronto 0832					Caractéristiques	N°
						CARACTÉRISTIQUES DE LA POPULATION	
4,460	**3,745**					**Population, 1996 (1)**	1
4,670	**4,037**					**Population, 2001 (2)**	2
4.7	7.8					Variation en pourcentage de la population, 1996-2001	3
17.56	204.65					Superficie des terres en kilomètres carrés, 2001	4
4,670	**4,035**					**Population totale – Données intégrales (3)**	5
						selon le sexe et les groupes d'âge	
2,220	2,060					Sexe masculin	6
135	130					0-4 ans	7
170	185					5-9 ans	8
170	180					10-14 ans	9
175	150					15-19 ans	10
110	95					20-24 ans	11
80	70					25-29 ans	12
130	125					30-34 ans	13
185	185					35-39 ans	14
220	200					40-44 ans	15
160	195					45-49 ans	16
165	165					50-54 ans	17
100	110					55-59 ans	18
85	90					60-64 ans	19
85	70					65-69 ans	20
95	55					70-74 ans	21
75	40					75-79 ans	22
65	25					80-84 ans	23
30	5					85 ans et plus	24
2,445	1,975					Sexe féminin	25
120	120					0-4 ans	26
155	175					5-9 ans	27
200	155					10-14 ans	28
140	150					15-19 ans	29
90	75					20-24 ans	30
85	60					25-29 ans	31
145	145					30-34 ans	32
220	200					35-39 ans	33
240	220					40-44 ans	34
195	145					45-49 ans	35
150	150					50-54 ans	36
105	105					55-59 ans	37
110	85					60-64 ans	38
95	65					65-69 ans	39
120	60					70-74 ans	40
105	35					75-79 ans	41
90	25					80-84 ans	42
90	10					85 ans et plus	43
3,720	**3,095**					**Population totale de 15 ans et plus**	44
						selon l'état matrimonial légal	
885	780					Célibataire (jamais marié(e))	45
2,100	1,970					Légalement marié(e) (et non séparé(e))	46
150	75					Séparé(e), mais toujours légalement marié(e)	47
250	155					Divorcé(e)	48
340	110					Veuf ou veuve	49
						selon l'union libre	
3,480	2,900					Ne vivant pas en union libre	50
240	195					Vivant en union libre	51
4,565	**4,035**					**Population totale – Données-échantillon (20 %) (4)**	52
						selon la langue maternelle	
4,560	4,010					Réponses uniques	53
4,340	3,705					Anglais	54
40	40					Français	55
185	265					Langues non officielles (5)	56
10	25					Italien	57
-	35					Chinois, n.d.a.	58
10	15					Cantonais	59
-	-					Portugais	60
-	-					Pendjabi	61
165	190					Autres langues (6)	62
10	30					Réponses multiples	63
10	-					Anglais et français	64
-	25					Anglais et langue non officielle	65
-	-					Français et langue non officielle	66
-	-					Anglais, français et langue non officielle	67

See reference material at the end of the publication. – Voir les documents de référence à la fin de la publication.

Table 1. Selected Characteristics for Census Tracts, 2001 Census – 100% Data and 20% Sample Data

No.	Characteristics	Toronto 0812	Toronto 0820.01 ◆ A	Toronto 0820.02 A	Toronto 0820.03 A	Toronto 0830	Toronto 0831.01 A
	POPULATION CHARACTERISTICS						
	by home language						
68	Single responses	5,755	3,485	5,300	3,835	3,935	4,380
69	English	5,605	3,390	5,170	3,770	3,855	4,330
70	French	30	-	-	-	15	-
71	Non-official languages (5)	120	95	130	70	65	50
72	Cantonese	40	-	35	-	-	-
73	Chinese, n.o.s.	-	20	-	25	-	-
74	Italian	15	-	10	15	45	-
75	Punjabi	-	-	-	10	-	-
76	Portuguese	10	-	10	-	-	-
77	Other languages (6)	60	70	80	20	20	50
78	Multiple responses	450	525	490	415	230	120
79	English and French	50	80	65	15	60	30
80	English and non-official language	365	405	410	385	150	90
81	French and non-official language	-	-	-	-	10	-
82	English, French and non-official language	35	45	15	20	15	-
	by knowledge of official languages						
83	English only	5,755	3,635	5,450	3,955	3,815	4,090
84	French only	-	-	-	-	10	-
85	English and French	425	345	335	295	335	400
86	Neither English nor French	20	30	10	10	-	10
	by knowledge of non-official languages (5) (7)						
87	Italian	120	90	125	135	115	55
88	Cantonese	60	10	105	10	-	-
89	Chinese, n.o.s.	30	50	10	80	10	10
90	Spanish	80	75	140	60	55	60
91	Portuguese	60	35	65	35	15	-
92	Punjabi	15	40	25	55	-	-
93	Tagalog (Pilipino)	140	65	35	20	-	-
	by first official language spoken						
94	English	6,090	3,915	5,730	4,220	4,110	4,445
95	French	80	45	40	25	45	50
96	English and French	10	20	15	10	-	-
97	Neither English nor French	20	30	10	10	10	-
98	Official language minority - (number) (8)	85	55	45	30	45	45
99	Official language minority - (percentage) (8)	1.4	1.4	0.8	0.7	1.1	1.0
	by ethnic origin (9)						
100	Canadian	2,245	1,195	1,775	1,255	1,515	1,865
101	English	1,740	700	1,725	1,165	1,555	2,015
102	Scottish	1,200	515	1,200	615	1,005	1,295
103	Irish	1,035	650	1,025	570	710	1,030
104	Chinese	230	110	200	210	20	30
105	Italian	360	330	325	325	320	165
106	East Indian	215	575	385	505	-	10
107	French	415	275	440	235	245	230
108	German	345	205	375	215	445	415
109	Portuguese	155	80	140	130	25	15
110	Polish	130	30	165	105	110	80
111	Jewish	45	15	30	40	55	55
112	Jamaican	455	495	300	200	75	10
113	Filipino	160	165	55	30	-	-
114	Ukrainian	130	30	200	90	190	150
	by Aboriginal identity						
115	Total Aboriginal identity population (10)	20	15	25	30	55	15
116	Total non-Aboriginal population	6,190	3,995	5,760	4,230	4,110	4,485
	by Aboriginal origin						
117	Total Aboriginal origins population (11)	135	75	120	30	150	80
118	Total non-Aboriginal population	6,075	3,940	5,665	4,225	4,020	4,425
	by Registered Indian status						
119	Registered Indian (12)	-	-	-	-	10	-
120	Not a Registered Indian	6,205	4,010	5,790	4,255	4,155	4,500

Tableau 1. Certaines caractéristiques des secteurs de recensement, recensement de 2001 – Données intégrales et données-échantillon (20 %)

Toronto 0831.02 A	Toronto 0832				Caractéristiques	N°
					CARACTÉRISTIQUES DE LA POPULATION	
					selon la langue parlée à la maison	
4,470	3,880				Réponses uniques	68
4,450	3,875				Anglais	69
10	-				Français	70
-	-				Langues non officielles (5)	71
-	-				Cantonais	72
-	-				Chinois, n.d.a.	73
-	-				Italien	74
-	-				Pendjabi	75
-	-				Portugais	76
10	-				Autres langues (6)	77
95	160				Réponses multiples	78
25	35				Anglais et français	79
75	125				Anglais et langue non officielle	80
-	-				Français et langue non officielle	81
-	-				Anglais, français et langue non officielle	82
					selon la connaissance des langues officielles	
4,195	3,815				Anglais seulement	83
-	-				Français seulement	84
370	220				Anglais et français	85
-	-				Ni l'anglais ni le français	86
					selon la connaissance des langues non officielles (5) (7)	
10	45				Italien	87
-	15				Cantonais	88
-	30				Chinois, n.d.a.	89
35	30				Espagnol	90
-	10				Portugais	91
-	-				Pendjabi	92
-	20				Tagalog (pilipino)	93
					selon la première langue officielle parlée	
4,525	3,995				Anglais	94
40	40				Français	95
-	-				Anglais et français	96
-	-				Ni l'anglais ni le français	97
40	45				Minorité de langue officielle - (nombre) (8)	98
0.9	1.1				Minorité de langue officielle - (pourcentage) (8)	99
					selon l'origine ethnique (9)	
1,965	1,815				Canadien	100
2,240	1,690				Anglais	101
1,295	1,035				Écossais	102
1,065	750				Irlandais	103
15	85				Chinois	104
75	95				Italien	105
35	-				Indien de l'Inde	106
370	410				Français	107
390	435				Allemand	108
-	10				Portugais	109
75	140				Polonais	110
20	10				Juif	111
10	25				Jamaïquain	112
-	20				Philippin	113
115	75				Ukrainien	114
					selon l'identité autochtone	
15	25				Total de la population ayant une identité autochtone (10)	115
4,545	4,010				Total de la population non autochtone	116
					selon l'origine autochtone	
75	105				Total de la population ayant une origine autochtone (11)	117
4,495	3,935				Total de la population non autochtone	118
					selon le statut d'Indien inscrit	
10	-				Oui, Indien inscrit (12)	119
4,560	4,040				Non, pas un Indien inscrit	120

Table 1. Selected Characteristics for Census Tracts, 2001 Census – 100% Data and 20% Sample Data

No.	Characteristics	Toronto 0812	Toronto 0820.01 ◆ A	Toronto 0820.02 A	Toronto 0820.03 A	Toronto 0830	Toronto 0831.01 A
	POPULATION CHARACTERISTICS						
	by visible minority groups						
121	Total visible minority population	1,580	1,845	1,165	1,490	85	195
122	Chinese	115	95	145	155	15	10
123	South Asian	245	550	370	340	-	10
124	Black	785	770	395	620	25	-
125	Filipino	150	155	55	30	10	-
126	Latin American	45	15	35	25	15	10
127	Southeast Asian	35	-	20	-	-	-
128	Arab	15	-	-	65	-	10
129	West Asian	-	15	40	-	10	55
130	Korean	10	-	30	-	-	50
131	Japanese	20	25	-	-	10	35
132	Visible minority, n.i.e. (13)	65	195	30	190	10	-
133	Multiple visible minorities (14)	90	15	30	55	-	-
	by citizenship						
134	Canadian citizenship (15)	6,010	3,675	5,470	4,015	4,045	4,365
135	Citizenship other than Canadian	195	335	315	235	115	135
	by place of birth of respondent						
136	Non-immigrant population	4,745	2,580	4,290	2,935	3,465	3,940
137	Born in province of residence	4,155	2,315	3,950	2,605	3,160	3,605
138	Immigrant population (16)	1,450	1,410	1,450	1,330	690	555
139	United States	50	30	75	15	55	20
140	Central and South America	115	190	155	285	15	45
141	Caribbean and Bermuda	450	530	185	335	25	-
142	United Kingdom	210	85	385	165	170	260
143	Other Europe (17)	225	165	350	185	380	130
144	Africa	50	65	50	50	10	-
145	Asia and the Middle East	345	325	215	290	30	90
146	Oceania and other (18)	-	15	40	-	10	-
147	Non-permanent residents (19)	20	25	55	-	10	10
148	**Total immigrant population**	**1,450**	**1,405**	**1,450**	**1,325**	**690**	**555**
	by period of immigration						
149	Before 1961	165	65	310	70	335	150
150	1961-1970	230	150	245	255	185	130
151	1971-1980	440	365	380	340	80	130
152	1981-1990	365	410	260	335	70	80
153	1991-2001 (20)	250	420	250	320	20	70
154	1991-1995	185	315	140	255	15	10
155	1996-2001 (20)	65	100	115	70	10	60
	by age at immigration						
156	0-4 years	105	95	130	125	120	65
157	5-19 years	535	520	520	410	195	170
158	20 years and over	810	785	800	795	370	320
159	**Total population**	**6,205**	**4,010**	**5,790**	**4,260**	**4,165**	**4,500**
	by religion						
160	Catholic (21)	1,950	1,445	1,855	1,730	970	870
161	Protestant	2,625	1,305	2,465	1,380	2,145	2,220
162	Christian Orthodox	125	175	70	140	40	35
163	Christian, n.i.e. (22)	275	140	150	180	130	55
164	Muslim	105	190	55	155	30	10
165	Jewish	20	-	40	30	15	10
166	Buddhist	125	25	40	10	-	60
167	Hindu	40	295	175	165	-	-
168	Sikh	-	50	30	25	-	-
169	Eastern religions (23)	-	-	10	-	-	10
170	Other religions (24)	-	-	25	15	-	-
171	No religious affiliation (25)	940	380	885	440	830	1,230
172	**Total population 15 years and over**	**4,640**	**2,695**	**4,415**	**3,100**	**3,370**	**3,285**
	by generation status						
173	1st generation (26)	1,440	1,380	1,455	1,270	700	530
174	2nd generation (27)	1,010	585	1,030	840	915	650
175	3rd generation and over (28)	2,195	735	1,930	990	1,760	2,105
176	**Total population 1 year and over (29)**	**6,140**	**3,880**	**5,715**	**4,220**	**4,130**	**4,435**
	by place of residence 1 year ago (mobility)						
177	Non-movers	5,240	3,500	4,910	3,955	3,900	3,960
178	Movers	905	380	800	260	230	475
179	Non-migrants	400	155	360	10	85	175
180	Migrants	505	220	440	250	145	300
181	Internal migrants	470	220	400	245	130	285
182	Intraprovincial migrants	395	180	390	245	130	210
183	Interprovincial migrants	75	35	10	-	-	80
184	External migrants	35	10	40	10	15	15

Tableau 1. Certaines caractéristiques des secteurs de recensement, recensement de 2001 – Données intégrales et données-échantillon (20 %)

Toronto 0831.02 A	Toronto 0832					Caractéristiques	N°
						CARACTÉRISTIQUES DE LA POPULATION	
						selon les groupes de minorités visibles	
75	150					Total de la population des minorités visibles	121
15	80					Chinois	122
20	-					Sud-Asiatique	123
-	45					Noir	124
-	25					Philippin	125
10	-					Latino-Américain	126
10	-					Asiatique du Sud-Est	127
-	-					Arabe	128
-	-					Asiatique occidental	129
-	-					Coréen	130
15	-					Japonais	131
-	-					Minorité visible, n.i.a. (13)	132
-	-					Minorités visibles multiples (14)	133
						selon la citoyenneté	
4,475	3,935					Citoyenneté canadienne (15)	134
90	100					Citoyenneté autre que canadienne	135
						selon le lieu de naissance du répondant	
4,060	3,610					Population non immigrante	136
3,660	3,420					Née dans la province de résidence	137
500	430					Population immigrante (16)	138
45	30					États-Unis	139
25	-					Amérique centrale et du Sud	140
-	20					Caraïbes et Bermudes	141
280	145					Royaume-Uni	142
120	165					Autre Europe (17)	143
10	-					Afrique	144
20	60					Asie et Moyen-Orient	145
-	-					Océanie et autre (18)	146
-	-					Résidents non permanents (19)	147
500	**430**					**Population immigrante totale**	148
						selon la période d'immigration	
215	160					Avant 1961	149
150	65					1961-1970	150
60	75					1971-1980	151
30	70					1981-1990	152
40	55					1991-2001 (20)	153
25	10					1991-1995	154
15	45					1996-2001 (20)	155
						selon l'âge à l'immigration	
120	25					0-4 ans	156
135	155					5-19 ans	157
240	245					20 ans et plus	158
4,565	**4,035**					**Population totale**	159
						selon la religion	
650	595					Catholique (21)	160
2,770	2,220					Protestante	161
10	25					Orthodoxe chrétienne	162
120	105					Chrétiennes, n.i.a. (22)	163
-	-					Musulmane	164
10	-					Juive	165
-	10					Bouddhiste	166
20	-					Hindoue	167
-	-					Sikh	168
-	-					Religions orientales (23)	169
-	-					Autres religions (24)	170
990	1,075					Aucune appartenance religieuse (25)	171
3,615	**3,090**					**Population totale de 15 ans et plus**	172
						selon le statut des générations	
520	415					1re génération (26)	173
700	575					2e génération (27)	174
2,400	2,100					3e génération et plus (28)	175
4,540	**3,995**					**Population totale de 1 an et plus (29)**	176
						selon le lieu de résidence 1 an auparavant (mobilité)	
4,205	3,620					Personnes n'ayant pas déménagé	177
335	375					Personnes ayant déménagé	178
135	155					Non-migrants	179
200	215					Migrants	180
200	210					Migrants internes	181
190	210					Migrants infraprovinciaux	182
10	-					Migrants interprovinciaux	183
-	-					Migrants externes	184

Table 1. Selected Characteristics for Census Tracts, 2001 Census – 100% Data and 20% Sample Data

No.	Characteristics	Toronto 0812	Toronto 0820.01 ◆ A	Toronto 0820.02 A	Toronto 0820.03 A	Toronto 0830	Toronto 0831.01 A
	POPULATION CHARACTERISTICS						
185	**Total population 5 years and over (30)**	**5,800**	**3,630**	**5,330**	**3,980**	**3,950**	**4,175**
	by place of residence 5 years ago (mobility)						
186	Non-movers	3,485	1,550	2,600	2,855	2,870	2,470
187	Movers	2,310	2,080	2,730	1,125	1,080	1,700
188	Non-migrants	890	640	1,085	250	380	665
189	Migrants	1,425	1,440	1,640	870	705	1,035
190	Internal migrants	1,375	1,335	1,505	770	690	950
191	Intraprovincial migrants	1,265	1,240	1,500	745	690	860
192	Interprovincial migrants	115	100	10	35	-	95
193	External migrants	50	105	135	100	10	85
194	**Total population 15 to 24 years**	**855**	**415**	**700**	**665**	**525**	**560**
	by school attendance						
195	Not attending school	295	140	235	205	160	170
196	Attending school full time	520	250	430	430	360	375
197	Attending school part time	35	25	25	30	10	15
198	**Total population 15 years and over**	**4,645**	**2,700**	**4,410**	**3,095**	**3,370**	**3,285**
	by highest level of schooling						
199	Less than grade 9 (31)	210	45	175	90	200	135
200	Grades 9-13 without high school graduation certificate	1,170	480	945	545	810	685
201	Grades 9-13 with high school graduation certificate	860	360	695	585	570	650
202	Some postsecondary without degree, certificate or diploma (32)	525	285	480	460	385	350
203	Trades certificate or diploma (33)	545	210	435	220	410	260
204	College certificate or diploma (34)	945	630	905	555	490	605
205	University certificate below bachelor's degree	55	90	105	40	60	95
206	University with bachelor's degree or higher	350	590	675	610	445	510
	by combinations of unpaid work						
207	Males 15 years and over	2,300	1,310	2,135	1,520	1,685	1,580
208	Reported unpaid work (35)	2,105	1,215	1,965	1,375	1,480	1,435
209	Housework and child care and care or assistance to seniors	170	125	155	180	110	130
210	Housework and child care only	805	645	685	575	450	610
211	Housework and care or assistance to seniors only	145	40	190	90	100	90
212	Child care and care or assistance to seniors only	-	-	10	-	-	-
213	Housework only	935	385	870	520	815	570
214	Child care only	45	15	45	-	-	35
215	Care or assistance to seniors only	-	10	10	10	10	10
216	Females 15 years and over	2,340	1,385	2,275	1,575	1,685	1,705
217	Reported unpaid work (35)	2,200	1,295	2,105	1,445	1,580	1,575
218	Housework and child care and care or assistance to seniors	275	175	285	220	170	245
219	Housework and child care only	985	755	810	620	570	585
220	Housework and care or assistance to seniors only	105	55	200	105	155	165
221	Child care and care or assistance to seniors only	10	-	10	-	-	-
222	Housework only	795	315	790	500	690	540
223	Child care only	35	-	10	-	-	30
224	Care or assistance to seniors only	-	-	-	-	-	-
	by labour force activity						
225	Males 15 years and over	2,300	1,305	2,135	1,520	1,690	1,580
226	In the labour force	1,975	1,115	1,635	1,245	1,300	1,310
227	Employed	1,905	1,080	1,525	1,170	1,250	1,245
228	Unemployed	70	35	105	75	45	65
229	Not in the labour force	330	190	505	280	390	270
230	Participation rate	85.9	85.4	76.6	81.9	76.9	82.9
231	Employment rate	82.8	82.8	71.4	77.0	74.0	78.8
232	Unemployment rate	3.5	3.1	6.4	6.0	3.5	5.0
233	Females 15 years and over	2,340	1,385	2,280	1,575	1,685	1,705
234	In the labour force	1,680	1,005	1,540	1,040	1,095	1,110
235	Employed	1,615	920	1,455	980	1,045	1,075
236	Unemployed	65	80	85	60	50	30
237	Not in the labour force	660	380	740	530	590	595
238	Participation rate	71.8	72.6	67.5	66.0	65.0	65.1
239	Employment rate	69.0	66.4	63.8	62.2	62.0	63.0
240	Unemployment rate	3.9	8.0	5.5	5.8	4.6	2.7

Tableau 1. Certaines caractéristiques des secteurs de recensement, recensement de 2001 – Données intégrales et données-échantillon (20 %)

Toronto 0831.02 A	Toronto 0832					Caractéristiques	N°
						CARACTÉRISTIQUES DE LA POPULATION	
4,305	**3,780**					**Population totale de 5 ans et plus (30)**	185
						selon le lieu de résidence 5 ans auparavant (mobilité)	
2,375	2,645					Personnes n'ayant pas déménagé	186
1,930	1,140					Personnes ayant déménagé	187
910	300					Non-migrants	188
1,020	840					Migrants	189
975	790					Migrants internes	190
930	740					Migrants infraprovinciaux	191
45	50					Migrants interprovinciaux	192
40	50					Migrants externes	193
510	**470**					**Population totale de 15 à 24 ans**	194
						selon la fréquentation scolaire	
195	180					Ne fréquentant pas l'école	195
290	285					Fréquentant l'école à plein temps	196
20	10					Fréquentant l'école à temps partiel	197
3,615	**3,090**					**Population totale de 15 ans et plus**	198
						selon le plus haut niveau de scolarité atteint	
170	90					Niveau inférieur à la 9e année (31)	199
880	695					De la 9e à la 13e année sans certificat d'études secondaires	200
605	615					De la 9e à la 13e année avec certificat d'études secondaires	201
445	340					Études postsecondaires partielles sans grade, certificat ou diplôme (32)	202
325	335					Certificat ou diplôme d'une école de métiers (33)	203
635	570					Certificat ou diplôme collégial (34)	204
75	110					Certificat universitaire inférieur au baccalauréat	205
480	335					Études universitaires avec baccalauréat ou diplôme supérieur	206
						selon les combinaisons de travail non rémunéré	
1,710	1,565					Hommes de 15 ans et plus	207
1,555	1,465					Travail non rémunéré déclaré (35)	208
160	140					Travaux ménagers et soins aux enfants et soins ou aide aux personnes âgées	209
480	415					Travaux ménagers et soins aux enfants seulement	210
165	120					Travaux ménagers et soins ou aide aux personnes âgées seulement	211
10	10					Soins aux enfants et soins ou aide aux personnes âgées seulement	212
740	750					Travaux ménagers seulement	213
10	40					Soins aux enfants seulement	214
-	-					Soins ou aide aux personnes âgées seulement	215
1,900	1,525					Femmes de 15 ans et plus	216
1,805	1,430					Travail non rémunéré déclaré (35)	217
255	255					Travaux ménagers et soins aux enfants et soins ou aide aux personnes âgées	218
555	470					Travaux ménagers et soins aux enfants seulement	219
220	130					Travaux ménagers et soins ou aide aux personnes âgées seulement	220
-	-					Soins aux enfants et soins ou aide aux personnes âgées seulement	221
755	565					Travaux ménagers seulement	222
10	-					Soins aux enfants seulement	223
-	10					Soins ou aide aux personnes âgées seulement	224
						selon l'activité	
1,715	1,565					Hommes de 15 ans et plus	225
1,305	1,270					Population active	226
1,240	1,250					Personnes occupées	227
65	20					Chômeurs	228
405	295					Inactifs	229
76.1	81.2					Taux d'activité	230
72.3	79.9					Taux d'emploi	231
5.0	1.6					Taux de chômage	232
1,900	1,525					Femmes de 15 ans et plus	233
1,160	1,075					Population active	234
1,085	1,040					Personnes occupées	235
80	35					Chômeuses	236
740	450					Inactives	237
61.1	70.5					Taux d'activité	238
57.1	68.2					Taux d'emploi	239
6.9	3.3					Taux de chômage	240

Table 1. Selected Characteristics for Census Tracts, 2001 Census – 100% Data and 20% Sample Data

No.	Characteristics	Toronto 0812	Toronto 0820.01 ◆ A	Toronto 0820.02 A	Toronto 0820.03 A	Toronto 0830	Toronto 0831.01 A
	POPULATION CHARACTERISTICS						
	by labour force activity - concluded						
241	Both sexes - Participation rate	78.7	78.7	71.8	73.5	70.9	73.7
242	15-24 years	71.8	63.9	59.7	61.2	71.4	70.5
243	25 years and over	80.4	81.2	74.3	77.0	71.0	74.3
244	Both sexes - Employment rate	75.8	74.4	67.6	69.5	68.1	70.7
245	15-24 years	63.5	56.6	47.1	54.1	64.2	65.2
246	25 years and over	78.6	77.6	71.3	73.7	68.7	71.7
247	Both sexes - Unemployment rate	3.7	5.4	6.0	5.7	4.2	4.1
248	15-24 years	12.3	9.6	18.3	12.2	9.3	6.4
249	25 years and over	2.0	4.6	4.0	4.5	3.0	3.7
250	**Total labour force 15 years and over**	**3,655**	**2,120**	**3,175**	**2,285**	**2,390**	**2,420**
	by industry based on the 1997 NAICS						
251	Industry - Not applicable (36)	25	45	40	25	20	25
252	All industries (37)	3,630	2,075	3,135	2,255	2,370	2,390
253	11 Agriculture, forestry, fishing and hunting	10	-	-	-	130	15
254	21 Mining and oil and gas extraction	-	-	15	10	15	-
255	22 Utilities	60	20	95	65	25	10
256	23 Construction	250	75	115	110	270	170
257	31-33 Manufacturing	715	335	420	365	230	240
258	41 Wholesale trade	170	90	150	160	160	165
259	44-45 Retail trade	550	225	405	280	255	370
260	48-49 Transportation and warehousing	195	90	130	90	130	65
261	51 Information and cultural industries	130	55	150	100	45	110
262	52 Finance and insurance	240	280	220	200	125	100
263	53 Real estate and rental and leasing	50	25	110	45	95	65
264	54 Professional, scientific and technical services	135	225	345	250	180	200
265	55 Management of companies and enterprises	-	10	15	15	-	-
266	56 Administrative and support, waste management and remediation services	160	60	110	60	100	85
267	61 Educational services	110	115	160	120	120	180
268	62 Health care and social assistance	270	170	165	155	155	255
269	71 Arts, entertainment and recreation	15	25	60	35	75	65
270	72 Accommodation and food services	200	80	150	50	85	85
271	81 Other services (except public administration)	150	75	145	75	115	45
272	91 Public administration	210	95	160	60	65	160
	by class of worker						
273	Class of worker - Not applicable (36)	30	45	40	30	20	25
274	All classes of worker (37)	3,630	2,075	3,135	2,255	2,370	2,395
275	Paid workers	3,470	1,935	2,880	2,100	2,005	2,090
276	Employees	3,415	1,915	2,705	1,960	1,845	2,005
277	Self-employed (incorporated)	55	15	170	145	160	80
278	Self-employed (unincorporated)	155	145	250	150	340	305
279	Unpaid family workers	-	-	-	10	30	10
	by occupation based on the 2001 NOC-S						
280	Male labour force 15 years and over	1,975	1,115	1,635	1,245	1,300	1,310
281	Occupation - Not applicable (36)	10	25	25	15	15	15
282	All occupations (37)	1,965	1,090	1,610	1,230	1,285	1,295
283	A Management occupations	250	190	305	280	295	285
284	B Business, finance and administration occupations	210	175	205	155	95	85
285	C Natural and applied sciences and related occupations	140	140	225	180	105	95
286	D Health occupations	15	30	15	20	30	30
287	E Occupations in social science, education, government service and religion	40	40	45	30	30	75
288	F Occupations in art, culture, recreation and sport	25	15	55	40	20	15
289	G Sales and service occupations	450	225	270	195	210	295
290	H Trades, transport and equipment operators and related occupations	570	180	345	215	325	280
291	I Occupations unique to primary industry	15	25	15	10	110	45
292	J Occupations unique to processing, manufacturing and utilities	250	75	120	110	55	75
293	Female labour force 15 years and over	1,680	1,005	1,540	1,045	1,095	1,110
294	Occupation - Not applicable (36)	15	25	20	20	10	10
295	All occupations (37)	1,665	980	1,525	1,025	1,085	1,100
296	A Management occupations	160	120	215	130	160	90
297	B Business, finance and administration occupations	505	320	520	370	315	305
298	C Natural and applied sciences and related occupations	60	60	30	40	15	30
299	D Health occupations	110	90	70	75	75	65

Tableau 1. Certaines caractéristiques des secteurs de recensement, recensement de 2001 – Données intégrales et données-échantillon (20 %)

Toronto 0831.02 A	Toronto 0832				Caractéristiques	N°
					CARACTÉRISTIQUES DE LA POPULATION	
					selon l'activité – fin	
68.1	76.1				Les deux sexes - Taux d'activité	241
78.2	62.8				15-24 ans	242
66.8	78.1				25 ans et plus	243
64.4	74.0				Les deux sexes - Taux d'emploi	244
65.7	55.3				15-24 ans	245
63.9	77.3				25 ans et plus	246
5.9	2.6				Les deux sexes - Taux de chômage	247
13.9	11.9				15-24 ans	248
4.1	1.2				25 ans et plus	249
2,460	**2,350**				**Population active totale de 15 ans et plus**	250
					selon l'industrie basée sur le SCIAN de 1997	
60	10				Industrie - Sans objet (36)	251
2,410	2,340				Toutes les industries (37)	252
60	315				11 Agriculture, foresterie, pêche et chasse	253
30	15				21 Extraction minière et extraction de pétrole et de gaz	254
20	30				22 Services publics	255
195	155				23 Construction	256
250	235				31-33 Fabrication	257
190	140				41 Commerce de gros	258
270	255				44-45 Commerce de détail	259
45	85				48-49 Transport et entreposage	260
80	50				51 Industrie de l'information et industrie culturelle	261
125	85				52 Finance et assurances	262
80	30				53 Services immobiliers et services de location et de location à bail	263
180	175				54 Services professionnels, scientifiques et techniques	264
-	-				55 Gestion de sociétés et d'entreprises	265
80	80				56 Services administratifs, services de soutien, services de gestion des déchets et services d'assainissement	266
145	115				61 Services d'enseignement	267
165	165				62 Soins de santé et assistance sociale	268
110	90				71 Arts, spectacles et loisirs	269
90	95				72 Hébergement et services de restauration	270
120	145				81 Autres services, sauf les administrations publiques	271
150	70				91 Administrations publiques	272
					selon la catégorie de travailleurs	
60	10				Catégorie de travailleurs - Sans objet (36)	273
2,405	2,340				Toutes les catégories de travailleurs (37)	274
2,205	1,845				Travailleurs rémunérés	275
2,035	1,715				Employés	276
175	125				Travailleurs autonomes (entreprise constituée en société)	277
200	430				Travailleurs autonomes (entreprise non constituée en société)	278
-	70				Travailleurs familiaux non rémunérés	279
					selon la profession basée sur la CNP-S de 2001	
1,305	1,270				Hommes actifs de 15 ans et plus	280
20	-				Profession - Sans objet (36)	281
1,285	1,265				Toutes les professions (37)	282
235	200				A Gestion	283
155	35				B Affaires, finance et administration	284
70	120				C Sciences naturelles et appliquées et professions apparentées	285
-	30				D Secteur de la santé	286
60	70				E Sciences sociales, enseignement, administration publique et religion	287
35	-				F Arts, culture, sports et loisirs	288
280	185				G Ventes et services	289
295	310				H Métiers, transport et machinerie	290
125	275				I Professions propres au secteur primaire	291
35	35				J Transformation, fabrication et services d'utilité publique	292
1,160	1,075				Femmes actives de 15 ans et plus	293
35	-				Profession - Sans objet (36)	294
1,125	1,075				Toutes les professions (37)	295
125	100				A Gestion	296
390	375				B Affaires, finance et administration	297
25	40				C Sciences naturelles et appliquées et professions apparentées	298
65	70				D Secteur de la santé	299

Table 1. Selected Characteristics for Census Tracts, 2001 Census – 100% Data and 20% Sample Data

No.	Characteristics	Toronto 0812	Toronto 0820.01 ◆ A	Toronto 0820.02 A	Toronto 0820.03 A	Toronto 0830	Toronto 0831.01 A
	POPULATION CHARACTERISTICS						
	by occupation based on the 2001 NOC-S – concluded						
	E Occupations in social science, education,						
300	government service and religion	155	95	115	105	125	210
301	F Occupations in art, culture, recreation and sport	25	10	30	25	35	40
302	G Sales and service occupations	440	225	470	190	235	325
	H Trades, transport and equipment						
303	operators and related occupations	75	20	40	35	45	15
304	I Occupations unique to primary industry	10	-	10	-	55	15
	J Occupations unique to processing,						
305	manufacturing and utilities	120	35	35	35	25	10
306	**Total employed labour force 15 years and over**	**3,520**	**2,005**	**2,985**	**2,150**	**2,295**	**2,320**
	by place of work						
307	Males	1,900	1,080	1,525	1,170	1,250	1,240
308	Usual place of work	1,590	925	1,305	975	870	1,010
309	At home	40	70	85	65	145	105
310	Outside Canada	-	-	-	10	10	10
311	No fixed workplace address	275	85	140	125	225	125
312	Females	1,620	925	1,455	980	1,045	1,075
313	Usual place of work	1,485	820	1,275	885	785	905
314	At home	95	80	145	95	185	110
315	Outside Canada	-	-	-	-	-	-
316	No fixed workplace address	35	25	30	-	75	55
	Total employed labour force 15 years and						
	over with usual place of work or no fixed						
317	**workplace address**	**3,380**	**1,860**	**2,750**	**1,990**	**1,950**	**2,100**
	by mode of transportation						
318	Males	1,865	1,010	1,440	1,100	1,095	1,135
319	Car, truck, van, as driver	1,490	850	1,160	945	1,025	995
320	Car, truck, van, as passenger	135	30	85	45	35	75
321	Public transit	165	115	145	90	10	10
322	Walked	40	10	25	-	15	40
323	Other method	35	-	35	10	20	20
324	Females	1,520	845	1,305	885	855	960
325	Car, truck, van, as driver	1,020	555	890	615	715	785
326	Car, truck, van, as passenger	120	40	115	105	85	75
327	Public transit	280	235	250	160	15	10
328	Walked	65	-	25	-	30	80
329	Other method	35	-	30	10	-	15
	Total population 15 years and over who worked						
330	**since January 1, 2000**	**3,825**	**2,260**	**3,505**	**2,465**	**2,570**	**2,600**
	by language used at work						
331	Single responses	3,680	2,175	3,370	2,335	2,500	2,545
332	English	3,665	2,165	3,370	2,330	2,500	2,545
333	French	10	10	-	-	10	-
334	Non-official languages (5)	-	10	-	-	-	-
335	Chinese, n.o.s.	-	10	-	-	-	-
336	Cantonese	-	-	-	-	-	-
337	Other languages (6)	10	-	-	-	-	-
338	Multiple responses	150	85	130	125	65	55
339	English and French	35	15	50	65	30	40
340	English and non-official language	110	60	80	60	35	15
341	French and non-official language	-	-	-	-	-	-
342	English, French and non-official language	-	10	-	10	-	-
	DWELLING AND HOUSEHOLD CHARACTERISTICS						
343	**Total number of occupied private dwellings**	**1,930**	**1,075**	**1,930**	**1,095**	**1,375**	**1,470**
	by tenure						
344	Owned	1,740	1,030	1,630	1,040	1,160	1,260
345	Rented	190	45	300	55	215	210
346	Band housing	-	-	-	-	-	-
	by structural type of dwelling						
347	Single-detached house	1,690	850	1,335	995	1,350	1,185
348	Semi-detached house	60	15	30	35	-	-
349	Row house	135	210	175	45	-	50
350	Apartment, detached duplex	35	-	20	20	10	10
351	Apartment, building that has five or more storeys	-	-	195	-	-	-
	Apartment, building that has fewer than						
352	five storeys (38)	-	-	170	-	-	220
353	Other single-attached house	-	-	-	-	10	10
354	Movable dwelling (39)	-	-	-	-	-	-

Tableau 1. Certaines caractéristiques des secteurs de recensement, recensement de 2001 – Données intégrales et données-échantillon (20 %)

Toronto 0831.02 A	Toronto 0832					Caractéristiques	N°
						CARACTÉRISTIQUES DE LA POPULATION	
						selon la profession basée sur la CNP-S de 2001 - fin	
105	70					E Sciences sociales, enseignement, administration publique et religion	300
40	30					F Arts, culture, sports et loisirs	301
270	230					G Ventes et services	302
25	30					H Métiers, transport et machinerie	303
45	95					I Professions propres au secteur primaire	304
25	25					J Transformation, fabrication et services d'utilité publique	305
2,320	**2,285**					**Population active occupée totale de 15 ans et plus**	306
						selon le lieu de travail	
1,240	1,245					Hommes	307
955	825					Lieu habituel de travail	308
70	255					À domicile	309
-	-					En dehors du Canada	310
210	170					Sans adresse de travail fixe	311
1,080	1,040					Femmes	312
830	770					Lieu habituel de travail	313
180	200					À domicile	314
-	-					En dehors du Canada	315
70	70					Sans adresse de travail fixe	316
2,075	**1,830**					**Population active occupée totale de 15 ans et plus ayant un lieu habituel de travail ou sans adresse de travail fixe**	317
						selon le mode de transport	
1,165	995					Hommes	318
990	900					Automobile, camion ou fourgonnette, en tant que conducteur	319
90	80					Automobile, camion ou fourgonnette, en tant que passager	320
20	-					Transport en commun	321
55	10					À pied	322
15	10					Autre moyen	323
905	840					Femmes	324
715	750					Automobile, camion ou fourgonnette, en tant que conductrice	325
70	45					Automobile, camion ou fourgonnette, en tant que passagère	326
35	-					Transport en commun	327
85	35					À pied	328
-	10					Autre moyen	329
2,545	**2,550**					**Population totale de 15 ans et plus ayant travaillé depuis le 1er janvier 2000**	330
						selon la langue utilisée au travail	
2,515	2,500					Réponses uniques	331
2,510	2,500					Anglais	332
-	-					Français	333
-	-					Langues non officielles (5)	334
-	-					Chinois, n.d.a.	335
-	-					Cantonais	336
-	-					Autres langues (6)	337
30	55					Réponses multiples	338
20	15					Anglais et français	339
10	30					Anglais et langue non officielle	340
-	-					Français et langue non officielle	341
-	-					Anglais, français et langue non officielle	342
						CARACTÉRISTIQUES DES LOGEMENTS ET DES MÉNAGES	
1,740	**1,315**					**Nombre total de logements privés occupés**	343
						selon le mode d'occupation	
1,310	1,190					Possédé	344
430	125					Loué	345
-	-					Logement de bande	346
						selon le type de construction résidentielle	
1,195	1,300					Maison individuelle non attenante	347
65	-					Maison jumelée	348
200	-					Maison en rangée	349
20	-					Appartement, duplex non attenant	350
-	-					Appartement, immeuble de cinq étages ou plus	351
260	10					Appartement, immeuble de moins de cinq étages (38)	352
-	-					Autre maison individuelle attenante	353
-	-					Logement mobile (39)	354

Table 1. Selected Characteristics for Census Tracts, 2001 Census – 100% Data and 20% Sample Data

No.	Characteristics	Toronto 0812	Toronto 0820.01 ◆ A	Toronto 0820.02 A	Toronto 0820.03 A	Toronto 0830	Toronto 0831.01 A
	DWELLING AND HOUSEHOLD CHARACTERISTICS						
	by condition of dwelling						
355	Regular maintenance only	1,235	940	1,495	895	790	1,065
356	Minor repairs	585	135	340	180	490	330
357	Major repairs	105	-	100	20	90	80
	by period of construction						
358	Before 1946	375	-	80	15	300	210
359	1946-1960	275	10	245	20	155	100
360	1961-1970	25	-	205	25	260	230
361	1971-1980	75	15	355	10	300	155
362	1981-1990	1,010	100	240	675	180	320
363	1991-2001 (20)	160	950	800	355	180	455
364	Average number of rooms per dwelling	7.0	8.0	7.2	9.1	8.0	7.5
365	Average number of bedrooms per dwelling	3.1	3.6	3.1	3.9	3.4	3.1
366	Average value of dwelling $	177,714	248,649	247,811	266,988	324,432	241,086
367	**Total number of private households**	**1,930**	**1,075**	**1,930**	**1,095**	**1,375**	**1,470**
	by household size						
368	1 person	230	35	295	55	140	245
369	2 persons	445	175	535	165	485	390
370	3 persons	405	210	355	165	245	205
371	4-5 persons	750	575	660	580	420	565
372	6 or more persons	100	80	85	135	80	70
	by household type						
373	One-family households	1,560	975	1,535	945	1,155	1,180
374	Multiple-family households	75	55	80	80	40	30
375	Non-family households	290	40	315	70	185	255
376	Number of persons in private households	6,205	4,010	5,770	4,260	4,160	4,500
377	Average number of persons in private households	3.2	3.7	3.0	3.9	3.0	3.1
378	Average number of persons per room	0.5	0.5	0.4	0.4	0.4	0.4
379	Tenant households in non-farm, non-reserve private dwellings (40)	190	45	300	55	220	210
380	Average gross rent $ (40)	863	1,356	796	970	935	707
381	Tenant households spending 30% or more of household income on gross rent (40) (41)	35	20	100	20	50	130
382	Tenant households spending from 30% to 99% of household income on gross rent (40) (41)	35	10	85	20	50	115
383	Owner households in non-farm, non-reserve private dwellings (42)	1,740	1,025	1,630	1,040	1,085	1,260
384	Average owner's major payments $ (42)	1,243	1,614	1,368	1,476	1,133	1,250
385	Owner households spending 30% or more of household income on owner's major payments (41) (42)	415	245	400	140	190	250
386	Owner households spending from 30% to 99% of household income on owner's major payments (41) (42)	375	225	360	125	185	215
	CENSUS FAMILY CHARACTERISTICS						
387	**Total number of census families in private households**	**1,710**	**1,090**	**1,685**	**1,115**	**1,230**	**1,245**
	by census family structure and size						
388	Total couple families	1,445	950	1,430	980	1,145	1,090
389	Total families of married couples	1,255	870	1,300	935	1,035	1,015
390	Without children at home	280	140	390	170	435	320
391	With children at home	980	735	915	770	605	695
392	1 child	310	185	300	170	190	125
393	2 children	465	365	445	380	240	390
394	3 or more children	205	175	165	225	175	180
395	Total families of common-law couples	190	80	130	50	110	70
396	Without children at home	90	30	90	20	55	25
397	With children at home	100	50	45	20	55	45
398	1 child	40	30	30	10	10	15
399	2 children	55	15	10	10	25	25
400	3 or more children	-	-	15	10	20	-
401	Total lone-parent families	265	135	255	130	85	155
402	Female parent	235	135	205	110	70	130
403	1 child	105	90	125	25	45	80
404	2 children	110	30	55	60	10	35
405	3 or more children	15	20	20	20	15	20

Tableau 1. Certaines caractéristiques des secteurs de recensement, recensement de 2001 – Données intégrales et données-échantillon (20 %)

Toronto 0831.02 A	Toronto 0832				Caractéristiques	N°
					CARACTÉRISTIQUES DES LOGEMENTS ET DES MÉNAGES	
					selon l'état du logement	
1,140	730				Entretien régulier seulement	355
480	520				Réparations mineures	356
125	65				Réparations majeures	357
					selon la période de construction	
415	335				Avant 1946	358
165	125				1946-1960	359
150	200				1961-1970	360
160	215				1971-1980	361
425	290				1981-1990	362
430	155				1991-2001 (20)	363
6.9	7.6				Nombre moyen de pièces par logement	364
2.9	3.3				Nombre moyen de chambres à coucher par logement	365
239,031	256,062				Valeur moyenne du logement $	366
1,745	**1,315**				**Nombre total de logements privés**	367
					selon la taille du ménage	
390	155				1 personne	368
590	430				2 personnes	369
290	230				3 personnes	370
420	435				4-5 personnes	371
50	65				6 personnes ou plus	372
					selon le genre de ménage	
1,310	1,100				Ménages unifamiliaux	373
15	40				Ménages multifamiliaux	374
415	175				Ménages non familiaux	375
4,560	4,030				Nombre de personnes dans les ménages privés	376
2.6	3.1				Nombre moyen de personnes dans les ménages privés	377
0.4	0.4				Nombre moyen de personnes par pièce	378
435	110				Ménages locataires dans les logements privés non agricoles hors réserve (40)	379
762	786				Loyer brut moyen $ (40)	380
235	40				Ménages locataires consacrant 30 % ou plus du revenu du ménage au loyer brut (40) (41)	381
215	20				Ménages locataires consacrant de 30 % à 99 % du revenu du ménage au loyer brut (40) (41)	382
1,290	1,065				Ménages propriétaires dans les logements privés non agricoles hors réserve (42)	383
1,062	1,173				Principales dépenses de propriété moyennes $ (42)	384
235	230				Ménages propriétaires consacrant 30 % ou plus du revenu du ménage aux principales dépenses de propriété (41) (42)	385
215	175				Ménages propriétaires consacrant de 30 % à 99 % du revenu du ménage aux principales dépenses de propriété (41) (42)	386
					CARACTÉRISTIQUES DES FAMILLES DE RECENSEMENT	
1,345	**1,180**				**Total des familles de recensement dans les ménages privés**	387
					selon la structure et la taille de la famille de recensement	
1,150	1,085				Total des familles avec conjoints	388
1,035	985				Total des familles avec couples mariés	389
450	365				Sans enfants à la maison	390
590	620				Avec enfants à la maison	391
170	190				1 enfant	392
290	255				2 enfants	393
125	170				3 enfants ou plus	394
120	100				Total des familles en union libre	395
65	55				Sans enfants à la maison	396
55	50				Avec enfants à la maison	397
50	10				1 enfant	398
10	35				2 enfants	399
-	10				3 enfants ou plus	400
190	95				Total des familles monoparentales	401
165	80				Parent de sexe féminin	402
100	45				1 enfant	403
50	35				2 enfants	404
15	10				3 enfants ou plus	405

Table 1. Selected Characteristics for Census Tracts, 2001 Census – 100% Data and 20% Sample Data

No.	Characteristics	Toronto 0812	Toronto 0820.01 ◆ A	Toronto 0820.02 A	Toronto 0820.03 A	Toronto 0830	Toronto 0831.01 A
	CENSUS FAMILY CHARACTERISTICS						
	by census family structure and size – concluded						
406	Male parent	35	-	50	25	10	25
407	1 child	-	-	30	10	10	10
408	2 children	25	-	25	-	-	-
409	3 or more children	-	-	-	10	-	-
410	**Total number of children at home**	**2,505**	**1,775**	**2,185**	**1,965**	**1,475**	**1,815**
	by age groups						
411	Under 6 years	515	505	550	335	245	435
412	6-14 years	1,035	810	825	815	550	780
413	15-17 years	295	130	260	210	210	240
414	18-24 years	455	240	380	425	300	260
415	25 years and over	205	95	170	180	175	95
416	Average number of children at home per census family (43)	1.5	1.6	1.3	1.8	1.2	1.5
417	**Total number of persons in private households**	**6,205**	**4,010**	**5,770**	**4,260**	**4,155**	**4,500**
	by census family status and living arrangements						
418	Number of non-family persons	540	195	465	200	310	355
419	Living with relatives (44)	145	115	105	75	70	90
420	Living with non-relatives only	170	45	75	75	95	20
421	Living alone	230	40	295	55	140	240
422	Number of family persons	5,665	3,810	5,305	4,060	3,850	4,140
423	Average number of persons per census family	3.3	3.5	3.1	3.7	3.1	3.3
424	**Total number of persons 65 years and over**	**340**	**110**	**565**	**230**	**460**	**430**
425	Number of non-family persons 65 years and over	135	50	195	50	120	175
426	Living with relatives (44)	65	50	40	40	50	40
427	Living with non-relatives only	15	-	-	-	25	-
428	Living alone	55	-	150	10	50	135
429	Number of family persons 65 years and over	210	60	370	180	340	255
	ECONOMIC FAMILY CHARACTERISTICS						
430	**Total number of economic families in private households**	**1,660**	**1,030**	**1,620**	**1,025**	**1,200**	**1,235**
	by size of family						
431	2 persons	420	190	525	165	475	395
432	3 persons	430	195	385	165	230	210
433	4 persons	520	350	480	385	290	400
434	5 or more persons	295	290	235	315	210	235
435	Total number of persons in economic families	5,810	3,925	5,405	4,130	3,925	4,235
436	Average number of persons per economic family	3.5	3.8	3.3	4.0	3.3	3.4
437	Total number of unattached individuals	395	85	365	130	240	265
	2000 INCOME CHARACTERISTICS						
	Population 15 years and over by sex and total income groups in 2000						
438	Total - Both sexes	4,645	2,695	4,410	3,095	3,370	3,285
439	Without income	230	150	150	250	135	145
440	With income	4,420	2,550	4,265	2,850	3,235	3,145
441	Under $1,000 (45)	130	110	170	135	100	60
442	$ 1,000 - $ 2,999	205	105	110	65	145	155
443	$ 3,000 - $ 4,999	145	120	175	130	65	185
444	$ 5,000 - $ 6,999	165	65	150	115	125	125
445	$ 7,000 - $ 9,999	235	105	190	150	135	170
446	$10,000 - $11,999	150	55	150	85	145	85
447	$12,000 - $14,999	160	85	200	110	140	175
448	$15,000 - $19,999	295	110	295	155	290	175
449	$20,000 - $24,999	390	115	335	155	200	160
450	$25,000 - $29,999	245	90	295	140	255	180
451	$30,000 - $34,999	445	200	250	160	255	230
452	$35,000 - $39,999	335	225	255	230	185	210
453	$40,000 - $44,999	260	270	285	170	115	165
454	$45,000 - $49,999	255	125	230	145	230	135
455	$50,000 - $59,999	410	235	330	235	230	265
456	$60,000 and over	590	530	855	680	605	675
457	Average income $ (46)	33,274	41,410	38,236	47,208	38,450	38,304
458	Median income $ (46)	30,291	36,571	30,243	34,987	29,993	31,146
459	Standard error of average income $ (46)	779	1,999	1,125	3,244	1,387	1,281

Tableau 1. Certaines caractéristiques des secteurs de recensement, recensement de 2001 – Données intégrales et données-échantillon (20 %)

Toronto 0831.02 A	Toronto 0832	Caractéristiques	N°
		CARACTÉRISTIQUES DES FAMILLES DE RECENSEMENT	
		selon la structure et la taille de la famille de recensement - fin	
25	15	Parent de sexe masculin	406
15	10	1 enfant	407
10	-	2 enfants	408
-	-	3 enfants ou plus	409
1,510	**1,515**	**Nombre total d'enfants à la maison**	410
		selon les groupes d'âge	
280	310	Moins de 6 ans	411
650	630	6-14 ans	412
200	205	15-17 ans	413
245	245	18-24 ans	414
145	130	25 ans et plus	415
1.1	1.3	Nombre moyen d'enfants à la maison par famille de recensement (43)	416
4,565	**4,030**	**Nombre total de personnes dans les ménages privés**	417
		selon la situation des particuliers dans la famille de recensement et des particuliers dans le ménage	
550	255	Nombre de personnes hors famille de recensement	418
85	65	Vivant avec des personnes apparentées (44)	419
75	40	Vivant avec des personnes non apparentées uniquement	420
390	155	Vivant seules	421
4,010	3,775	Nombre de personnes membres d'une famille	422
3.0	3.2	Nombre moyen de personnes par famille de recensement	423
765	**390**	**Nombre total de personnes de 65 ans et plus**	424
235	50	Nombre de personnes hors famille de recensement de 65 ans et plus	425
40	10	Vivant avec des personnes apparentées (44)	426
-	-	Vivant avec des personnes non apparentées uniquement	427
200	40	Vivant seules	428
535	345	Nombre de personnes membres d'une famille de 65 ans et plus	429
		CARACTÉRISTIQUES DES FAMILLES ÉCONOMIQUES	
1,340	**1,160**	**Nombre total de familles économiques dans les ménages privés**	430
		selon la taille de la famille	
610	440	2 personnes	431
270	240	3 personnes	432
305	285	4 personnes	433
160	200	5 personnes ou plus	434
4,095	3,840	Nombre total de personnes dans les familles économiques	435
3.1	3.3	Nombre moyen de personnes par famille économique	436
465	190	Nombre total de personnes hors famille économique	437
		CARACTÉRISTIQUES DU REVENU DE 2000	
		Population de 15 ans et plus selon le sexe et les tranches de revenu total en 2000	
3,615	3,095	Total - Les deux sexes	438
110	75	Sans revenu	439
3,505	3,015	Avec un revenu	440
90	160	Moins de 1 000 $ (45)	441
175	145	1 000 $ - 2 999 $	442
95	145	3 000 $ - 4 999 $	443
125	115	5 000 $ - 6 999 $	444
220	130	7 000 $ - 9 999 $	445
110	100	10 000 $ - 11 999 $	446
190	190	12 000 $ - 14 999 $	447
360	230	15 000 $ - 19 999 $	448
230	235	20 000 $ - 24 999 $	449
195	225	25 000 $ - 29 999 $	450
355	135	30 000 $ - 34 999 $	451
295	200	35 000 $ - 39 999 $	452
155	200	40 000 $ - 44 999 $	453
155	110	45 000 $ - 49 999 $	454
225	200	50 000 $ - 59 999 $	455
525	510	60 000 $ et plus	456
32,842	34,471	Revenu moyen $ (46)	457
29,101	26,899	Revenu médian $ (46)	458
959	1,425	Erreur type de revenu moyen $ (46)	459

Table 1. Selected Characteristics for Census Tracts, 2001 Census – 100% Data and 20% Sample Data

No.	Characteristics	Toronto 0812	Toronto 0820.01 ◆ A	Toronto 0820.02 A	Toronto 0820.03 A	Toronto 0830	Toronto 0831.01 A
	2000 INCOME CHARACTERISTICS						
	Population 15 years and over by sex and total income groups in 2000 – concluded						
460	Total - Males	2,305	1,310	2,135	1,525	1,685	1,580
461	Without income	70	50	55	95	45	35
462	With income	2,235	1,255	2,080	1,430	1,640	1,540
463	Under $1,000 (45)	65	35	60	50	65	15
464	$ 1,000 - $ 2,999	75	35	25	25	80	50
465	$ 3,000 - $ 4,999	70	50	40	70	-	85
466	$ 5,000 - $ 6,999	35	15	20	30	60	45
467	$ 7,000 - $ 9,999	90	35	95	50	35	45
468	$10,000 - $11,999	65	25	85	30	65	30
469	$12,000 - $14,999	20	15	70	10	35	55
470	$15,000 - $19,999	115	45	100	60	145	60
471	$20,000 - $24,999	215	50	160	50	75	70
472	$25,000 - $29,999	85	40	85	70	95	50
473	$30,000 - $34,999	240	55	105	55	105	95
474	$35,000 - $39,999	155	85	150	100	85	100
475	$40,000 - $44,999	140	140	165	95	80	90
476	$45,000 - $49,999	130	65	80	70	115	90
477	$50,000 - $59,999	285	185	170	115	150	185
478	$60,000 and over	450	385	660	550	440	485
479	Average income $ (46)	39,328	53,204	48,132	64,657	46,644	49,740
480	Median income $ (46)	35,957	44,900	40,285	45,038	38,243	44,722
481	Standard error of average income $ (46)	1,181	3,599	1,855	6,071	2,395	2,171
482	Total - Females	2,340	1,385	2,280	1,575	1,685	1,705
483	Without income	160	95	95	155	85	105
484	With income	2,185	1,295	2,190	1,425	1,595	1,600
485	Under $1,000 (45)	65	70	105	80	35	45
486	$ 1,000 - $ 2,999	135	70	85	40	65	110
487	$ 3,000 - $ 4,999	75	70	135	55	70	105
488	$ 5,000 - $ 6,999	130	50	130	85	60	75
489	$ 7,000 - $ 9,999	140	65	95	100	100	125
490	$10,000 - $11,999	85	40	65	55	80	60
491	$12,000 - $14,999	145	70	135	105	110	120
492	$15,000 - $19,999	180	60	190	100	145	115
493	$20,000 - $24,999	170	65	175	105	125	85
494	$25,000 - $29,999	165	55	210	65	155	130
495	$30,000 - $34,999	210	145	145	100	150	135
496	$35,000 - $39,999	180	145	100	125	100	110
497	$40,000 - $44,999	115	130	120	70	35	75
498	$45,000 - $49,999	125	60	145	75	115	45
499	$50,000 - $59,999	120	55	155	125	80	80
500	$60,000 and over	150	150	195	135	170	190
501	Average income $ (46)	27,078	29,965	28,819	29,656	30,026	27,298
502	Median income $ (46)	24,012	30,180	24,259	24,209	24,989	23,476
503	Standard error of average income $ (46)	945	1,419	1,158	1,721	1,318	1,171
	by composition of total income						
504	Total - Composition of income in 2000 % (47)	100.0	100.0	100.0	100.0	100.0	100.0
505	Employment income %	89.6	93.1	85.6	92.7	81.6	85.5
506	Government transfer payments %	6.7	3.8	6.8	3.7	7.0	7.1
507	Other %	3.8	3.1	7.7	3.5	11.4	7.3
	Population 15 years and over with employment income in 2000 by sex and work activity						
508	Both sexes with employment income (48)	3,795	2,245	3,455	2,395	2,570	2,560
509	Average employment income $	34,702	43,807	40,440	52,128	39,502	40,223
510	Standard error of average employment income $	848	2,006	1,242	3,779	1,643	1,476
511	Worked full year, full time (49)	2,330	1,400	2,150	1,420	1,520	1,495
512	Average employment income $	43,925	55,252	54,088	59,838	54,045	54,421
513	Standard error of average employment income $	1,020	2,770	1,633	3,154	2,372	1,842
514	Worked part year or part time (50)	1,385	795	1,275	940	940	1,035
515	Average employment income $	20,137	24,027	17,761	42,117	19,534	20,443
516	Standard error of average employment income $	1,147	1,998	1,000	8,360	1,360	1,856
517	Males with employment income (48)	2,035	1,175	1,735	1,300	1,360	1,365
518	Average employment income $	39,858	54,051	50,270	67,710	48,179	50,132
519	Standard error of average employment income $	1,239	3,388	1,939	6,613	2,717	2,365
520	Worked full year, full time (49)	1,365	805	1,240	870	910	920
521	Average employment income $	47,630	64,613	61,280	69,072	61,114	62,459
522	Standard error of average employment income $	1,413	4,422	2,308	4,652	3,496	2,544
523	Worked part year or part time (50)	640	355	480	415	390	425
524	Average employment income $	23,665	28,549	22,455	66,557	23,587	24,803
525	Standard error of average employment income $	1,937	3,703	1,973	18,392	2,831	4,118

Tableau 1. Certaines caractéristiques des secteurs de recensement, recensement de 2001 – Données intégrales et données-échantillon (20 %)

Toronto 0831.02 A	Toronto 0832	Caractéristiques	N°
		CARACTÉRISTIQUES DU REVENU DE 2000	
		Population de 15 ans et plus selon le sexe et les tranches de revenu total en 2000 – fin	
1,715	1,565	Total - Hommes	460
35	40	Sans revenu	461
1,675	1,520	Avec un revenu	462
50	70	Moins de 1 000 $ (45)	463
30	25	1 000 $ - 2 999 $	464
60	60	3 000 $ - 4 999 $	465
60	50	5 000 $ - 6 999 $	466
40	85	7 000 $ - 9 999 $	467
25	60	10 000 $ - 11 999 $	468
50	40	12 000 $ - 14 999 $	469
155	105	15 000 $ - 19 999 $	470
105	75	20 000 $ - 24 999 $	471
70	90	25 000 $ - 29 999 $	472
155	60	30 000 $ - 34 999 $	473
145	110	35 000 $ - 39 999 $	474
105	120	40 000 $ - 44 999 $	475
95	75	45 000 $ - 49 999 $	476
160	120	50 000 $ - 59 999 $	477
370	370	60 000 $ et plus	478
40,829	42,098	Revenu moyen $ (46)	479
36,843	35,847	Revenu médian $ (46)	480
1,591	2,434	Erreur type de revenu moyen $ (46)	481
1,900	1,525	Total - Femmes	482
75	35	Sans revenu	483
1,830	1,495	Avec un revenu	484
45	90	Moins de 1 000 $ (45)	485
145	120	1 000 $ - 2 999 $	486
40	85	3 000 $ - 4 999 $	487
65	65	5 000 $ - 6 999 $	488
185	40	7 000 $ - 9 999 $	489
80	35	10 000 $ - 11 999 $	490
140	145	12 000 $ - 14 999 $	491
205	125	15 000 $ - 19 999 $	492
120	160	20 000 $ - 24 999 $	493
130	135	25 000 $ - 29 999 $	494
200	75	30 000 $ - 34 999 $	495
155	85	35 000 $ - 39 999 $	496
45	80	40 000 $ - 44 999 $	497
60	35	45 000 $ - 49 999 $	498
60	85	50 000 $ - 59 999 $	499
160	135	60 000 $ et plus	500
25,514	26,689	Revenu moyen $ (46)	501
20,287	20,550	Revenu médian $ (46)	502
1,007	1,367	Erreur type de revenu moyen $ (46)	503
		selon la composition du revenu total	
100.0	100.0	Total - Composition du revenu en 2000 % (47)	504
76.7	82.4	Revenu d'emploi %	505
10.5	7.1	Transferts gouvernementaux %	506
12.9	10.4	Autre %	507
		Population de 15 ans et plus ayant un revenu d'emploi en 2000 selon le sexe et le travail	
2,510	2,510	Les deux sexes ayant un revenu d'emploi (48)	508
35,158	34,145	Revenu moyen d'emploi $	509
1,213	1,612	Erreur type de revenu moyen d'emploi $	510
1,410	1,475	Ayant travaillé toute l'année à plein temps (49)	511
46,759	43,052	Revenu moyen d'emploi $	512
1,606	1,690	Erreur type de revenu moyen d'emploi $	513
1,060	980	Ayant travaillé une partie de l'année ou à temps partiel (50)	514
20,486	22,497	Revenu moyen d'emploi $	515
1,430	3,070	Erreur type de revenu moyen d'emploi $	516
1,345	1,335	Hommes ayant un revenu d'emploi (48)	517
40,969	40,851	Revenu moyen d'emploi $	518
1,906	2,652	Erreur type de revenu moyen d'emploi $	519
805	915	Ayant travaillé toute l'année à plein temps (49)	520
52,974	46,386	Revenu moyen d'emploi $	521
2,373	2,347	Erreur type de revenu moyen d'emploi $	522
530	405	Ayant travaillé une partie de l'année ou à temps partiel (50)	523
23,159	29,503	Revenu moyen d'emploi $	524
2,436	7,029	Erreur type de revenu moyen d'emploi $	525

Table 1. Selected Characteristics for Census Tracts, 2001 Census – 100% Data and 20% Sample Data

No.	Characteristics	Toronto 0812	Toronto 0820.01 ◆ A	Toronto 0820.02 A	Toronto 0820.03 A	Toronto 0830	Toronto 0831.01 A
	2000 INCOME CHARACTERISTICS						
	Population 15 years and over with employment income in 2000 by sex and work activity – concluded						
526	Females with employment income (48)	1,760	1,065	1,715	1,095	1,210	1,195
527	Average employment income $	28,741	32,512	30,493	33,681	29,744	28,903
528	Standard error of average employment income $	1,079	1,537	1,371	2,105	1,603	1,414
529	Worked full year, full time (49)	965	600	910	550	605	575
530	Average employment income $	38,693	42,688	44,264	45,211	43,437	41,449
531	Standard error of average employment income $	1,379	1,935	2,023	3,113	2,562	2,057
532	Worked part year or part time (50)	745	440	795	525	550	615
533	Average employment income $	17,105	20,378	14,926	22,679	16,693	17,435
534	Standard error of average employment income $	1,316	1,860	1,025	2,521	1,281	1,464
	Census families by structure and family income groups in 2000						
535	Total - All census families	1,710	1,090	1,685	1,115	1,225	1,245
536	Under $10,000	40	25	30	20	10	35
537	$ 10,000 - $19,999	45	30	60	10	30	50
538	$ 20,000 - $29,999	90	20	100	55	70	70
539	$ 30,000 - $39,999	95	40	90	40	40	75
540	$ 40,000 - $49,999	185	95	165	60	115	95
541	$ 50,000 - $59,999	190	75	130	115	120	80
542	$ 60,000 - $69,999	180	105	110	75	135	80
543	$ 70,000 - $79,999	150	130	190	65	95	135
544	$ 80,000 - $89,999	160	165	170	90	95	85
545	$ 90,000 - $99,999	175	105	90	105	95	80
546	$100,000 and over	405	310	560	470	420	455
547	Average family income $	75,884	91,587	88,156	113,864	93,070	88,369
548	Median family income $	71,091	80,732	78,563	91,227	79,175	80,165
549	Standard error of average family income $	1,957	4,451	2,820	7,890	3,623	3,130
550	Total - All couple census families (51)	1,450	950	1,435	985	1,145	1,090
551	Under $10,000	10	15	10	15	10	-
552	$ 10,000 - $19,999	20	10	30	10	20	15
553	$ 20,000 - $29,999	65	15	70	35	60	30
554	$ 30,000 - $39,999	55	20	55	30	40	50
555	$ 40,000 - $49,999	130	80	80	45	110	95
556	$ 50,000 - $59,999	160	60	105	75	115	60
557	$ 60,000 - $69,999	160	90	105	80	135	75
558	$ 70,000 - $79,999	135	110	180	60	90	130
559	$ 80,000 - $89,999	160	155	160	85	100	90
560	$ 90,000 - $99,999	160	105	90	100	95	80
561	$100,000 and over	395	295	550	455	395	455
562	Average family income $	81,486	96,774	96,373	121,381	95,147	96,767
563	Median family income $	78,966	85,073	84,875	95,074	80,985	88,093
564	Standard error of average family income $	2,085	4,744	3,051	8,675	3,742	3,206
	Incidence of low income in 2000						
565	Total - Economic families	1,660	1,030	1,620	1,025	1,205	1,235
566	Low income	125	35	95	35	45	65
567	Incidence of low income in 2000 % (52)	7.5	3.5	6.0	3.3	3.5	5.2
568	Total - Unattached individuals 15 years and over	390	85	365	115	235	265
569	Low income	120	10	115	15	15	65
570	Incidence of low income in 2000 % (52)	30.2	11.5	30.9	12.7	5.4	23.6
571	Total - Population in private households	6,200	4,010	5,775	4,245	4,155	4,500
572	Low income	545	130	415	125	160	220
573	Incidence of low income in 2000 % (52)	8.8	3.3	7.2	2.9	3.9	4.9
	Private households by household income groups in 2000						
574	Total - All private households	1,925	1,075	1,930	1,095	1,375	1,470
575	Under $10,000	40	10	35	15	-	45
576	$ 10,000 - $19,999	60	25	115	10	45	110
577	$ 20,000 - $29,999	125	10	140	30	70	105
578	$ 30,000 - $39,999	130	30	135	20	90	95
579	$ 40,000 - $49,999	175	65	150	50	135	125
580	$ 50,000 - $59,999	205	60	160	80	140	90
581	$ 60,000 - $69,999	210	105	140	75	145	100
582	$ 70,000 - $79,999	175	135	175	70	105	155
583	$ 80,000 - $89,999	160	155	170	75	95	105
584	$ 90,000 - $99,999	155	120	100	135	95	75
585	$100,000 and over	485	355	610	530	445	465
586	Average household income $	76,177	98,354	84,263	122,914	90,441	81,798
587	Median household income $	70,745	85,379	74,152	97,973	72,778	72,733
588	Standard error of average household income $	1,931	4,510	2,753	8,003	3,503	2,963

Tableau 1. Certaines caractéristiques des secteurs de recensement, recensement de 2001 – Données intégrales et données-échantillon (20 %)

Toronto 0831.02 A	Toronto 0832					Caractéristiques	N°
						CARACTÉRISTIQUES DU REVENU DE 2000	
						Population de 15 ans et plus ayant un revenu d'emploi en 2000 selon le sexe et le travail - fin	
1,165	1,180					Femmes ayant un revenu d'emploi (48)	526
28,437	26,550					Revenu moyen d'emploi $	527
1,334	1,589					Erreur type de revenu moyen d'emploi $	528
605	560					Ayant travaillé toute l'année à plein temps (49)	529
38,496	37,581					Revenu moyen d'emploi $	530
1,822	2,209					Erreur type de revenu moyen d'emploi $	531
530	570					Ayant travaillé une partie de l'année ou à temps partiel (50)	532
17,787	17,541					Revenu moyen d'emploi $	533
1,526	2,018					Erreur type de revenu moyen d'emploi $	534
						Familles de recensement selon la structure et les tranches de revenu de la famille en 2000	
1,345	1,175					Total - Toutes les familles de recensement	535
20	25					Moins de 10 000 $	536
35	35					10 000 $ - 19 999 $	537
105	90					20 000 $ - 29 999 $	538
95	70					30 000 $ - 39 999 $	539
200	80					40 000 $ - 49 999 $	540
135	125					50 000 $ - 59 999 $	541
105	130					60 000 $ - 69 999 $	542
155	105					70 000 $ - 79 999 $	543
105	135					80 000 $ - 89 999 $	544
130	110					90 000 $ - 99 999 $	545
245	285					100 000 $ et plus	546
74,154	81,085					Revenu moyen des familles $	547
67,008	74,118					Revenu médian des familles $	548
2,455	3,455					Erreur type de revenu moyen des familles $	549
1,155	1,085					Total - Toutes les familles de recensement comptant un couple (51)	550
15	20					Moins de 10 000 $	551
25	35					10 000 $ - 19 999 $	552
70	55					20 000 $ - 29 999 $	553
70	65					30 000 $ - 39 999 $	554
160	75					40 000 $ - 49 999 $	555
105	115					50 000 $ - 59 999 $	556
90	125					60 000 $ - 69 999 $	557
145	95					70 000 $ - 79 999 $	558
105	130					80 000 $ - 89 999 $	559
135	100					90 000 $ - 99 999 $	560
235	275					100 000 $ et plus	561
79,051	83,999					Revenu moyen des familles $	562
72,758	77,241					Revenu médian des familles $	563
2,722	3,674					Erreur type de revenu moyen des familles $	564
						Fréquence des unités à faible revenu en 2000	
1,340	1,165					Total - Familles économiques	565
55	65					Faible revenu	566
3.9	5.5					Fréquence des unités à faible revenu en 2000 % (52)	567
445	185					Total - Personnes hors famille économique de 15 ans et plus	568
110	35					Faible revenu	569
24.3	18.6					Fréquence des unités à faible revenu en 2000 % (52)	570
4,540	4,020					Total - Population dans les ménages privés	571
270	215					Faible revenu	572
5.9	5.4					Fréquence des unités à faible revenu en 2000 % (52)	573
						Ménages privés selon les tranches de revenu du ménage en 2000	
1,745	1,315					Total - Tous les ménages privés	574
50	50					Moins de 10 000 $	575
175	70					10 000 $ - 19 999 $	576
155	70					20 000 $ - 29 999 $	577
145	90					30 000 $ - 39 999 $	578
240	85					40 000 $ - 49 999 $	579
145	125					50 000 $ - 59 999 $	580
115	155					60 000 $ - 69 999 $	581
175	135					70 000 $ - 79 999 $	582
120	135					80 000 $ - 89 999 $	583
150	95					90 000 $ - 99 999 $	584
270	305					100 000 $ et plus	585
66,076	78,863					Revenu moyen des ménages $	586
55,769	71,533					Revenu médian des ménages $	587
2,213	3,317					Erreur type de revenu moyen des ménages $	588

Footnotes

(1) Based on 2001 area. These figures have not been subjected to random rounding.

(2) These figures have not been subjected to random rounding.

(3) Includes institutional residents.

(4) Excludes institutional residents. These data are based on weighted sample data (20%). In some instances, due to weighting factors, it is possible for small areas to have an "estimated population excluding institutional residents" higher than the "population including institutional residents".

(5) Non-official language categories are based on the most frequently reported responses in the census metropolitan area or census agglomeration. When zero values are obtained for most of the non-official languages in some geographic areas, the number of non-official languages shown is less.

(6) This is a subtotal of all non-official languages collected by the census that are not displayed separately here.

(7) Indicates the number of respondents reporting knowledge of each of these non-official languages.

(8) The official language minority is English in Quebec and French in all other provinces and territories.

(9) This table shows total response counts for the 15 most frequently reported ethnic origins in the census metropolitan area or census agglomeration. Total responses indicate the number of respondents who reported each ethnic origin, either as their only response or in addition to one or more other ethnic origins. Total responses represent the sum of single ethnic origin responses and multiple ethnic origin responses received in the census.

(10) Refers to those persons identifying with at least one Aboriginal group, i.e. North American Indian, Métis or Inuit (Eskimo), and/or those who reported being a Treaty Indian or a Registered Indian as defined by the *Indian Act* of Canada and/or who were members of an Indian Band or First Nation.

Renvois

(1) Selon la superficie de 2001. Ces chiffres n'ont pas fait l'objet d'un arrondissement aléatoire.

(2) Ces chiffres n'ont pas fait l'objet d'un arrondissement aléatoire.

(3) Comprend les pensionnaires d'un établissement institutionnel.

(4) Ne comprend pas les pensionnaires d'un établissement institutionnel. Ces données sont basées sur les données-échantillon pondérées (20 %). Dans certains cas, en raison des coefficients de pondération, il est possible que, dans les petites régions, « l'estimation de la population ne comprenant pas les pensionnaires d'un établissement institutionnel » soit plus élevée que « la population comprenant les pensionnaires d'un établissement institutionnel ».

(5) Les catégories de langues non officielles sont basées sur les réponses le plus souvent déclarées dans la région métropolitaine de recensement ou l'agglomération de recensement. Le nombre de langues non officielles présentées est moindre lorsque des valeurs égales à zéro sont obtenues pour la plupart des langues non officielles dans certaines régions géographiques.

(6) Ceci est un sous-total de toutes les langues non officielles recueillies par le recensement qui ne sont pas affichées séparément ici.

(7) Indique le nombre de répondants qui ont indiqué avoir une connaissance de chacune de ces langues non officielles.

(8) Au Québec, la langue officielle minoritaire est l'anglais, et dans les autres provinces et territoires, la langue officielle minoritaire est le français.

(9) Ce tableau présente les chiffres des réponses totales des 15 origines ethniques le plus souvent déclarées dans la région métropolitaine de recensement ou l'agglomération de recensement. Le total des réponses correspond au nombre de recensés ayant indiqué chaque origine ethnique, soit comme étant leur seule réponse ou comme étant associée à une autre origine ethnique ou plus. Le total des réponses représente la somme des réponses uniques portant sur l'origine ethnique et des réponses multiples portant sur l'origine ethnique déclarées dans le cadre du recensement.

(10) S'entend des personnes ayant déclaré appartenir à au moins un groupe autochtone, c'est-à-dire Indien de l'Amérique du Nord, Métis, ou Inuit (Esquimau) et/ou ayant déclaré être un Indien des traités ou un Indien inscrit aux termes de la *Loi sur les Indiens* du Canada et/ou ayant déclaré être membre d'une bande indienne ou d'une première nation.

(11) Refers to those persons who reported at least one Aboriginal origin (North American Indian, Métis or Inuit) to the ethnic origin question. Ethnic origin refers to the ethnic or cultural group(s) to which the respondent's ancestors belong. Additional information on ethnic origin can be obtained from the 2001 Census Dictionary.

(12) Registered or Treaty Indian: The expression "Registered Indian" refers to those persons who reported they were registered under the *Indian Act* of Canada. Treaty Indians are persons who are registered under the *Indian Act* and can prove descent from a Band that signed a treaty.

The Registered Indian counts in this table may differ from the administrative counts maintained by the Department of Indian Affairs and Northern Development, with the most important causes of these differences being the incompletely enumerated Indian reserves and Indian settlements as well as methodological and conceptual differences between the two sources.

(13) Includes respondents who reported a write-in response classified as a visible minority such as "Polynesian", "Guyanese", "Mauritian", etc.

(14) Includes respondents who reported more than one visible minority group by checking two or more mark-in circles, e.g. "Black" and "South Asian".

(15) Includes those who reported dual citizenship including Canadian.

(16) Refers to people who are, or have been, landed immigrants in Canada. A landed immigrant is a person who has been granted the right to live in Canada permanently by immigration authorities. Some immigrants have resided in Canada for a number of years, while others are recent arrivals. Most immigrants are born outside Canada, but a small number were born in Canada.

(17) "Other Europe" includes Southern Europe, Eastern Europe, Northern and Western Europe, excluding the United Kingdom. Data not directly comparable to censuses prior to 1996, where Europe included Cyprus and the U.S.S.R. In 1996 and 2001, Cyprus and the former Soviet republics of Armenia, Azerbaijan, Georgia, Kazakhstan, Kyrgyzstan, Tajikistan, Turkmenistan and Uzbekistan are included in Asia.

(11) Personne ayant indiqué appartenir à au moins un groupe autochtone à la question sur l'origine ethnique, c'est-à-dire Indien de l'Amérique du Nord, Métis ou Inuit. L'origine ethnique se rapporte au(x) groupe(s) ethnique(s) ou culturel(s) auquel (auxquels) appartenaient les ancêtres du recensé. Pour de plus amples renseignements au sujet de l'origine ethnique, veuillez consulter le Dictionnaire du recensement de 2001.

(12) Indien inscrit ou Indien des traités : Les Indiens inscrits sont des personnes ayant déclaré être inscrites en vertu de la *Loi sur les Indiens* du Canada. Les Indiens des traités sont des personnes qui sont inscrites en vertu de la *Loi sur les Indiens* et qui peuvent démontrer qu'elles descendent d'une bande qui a signé un traité.

Il est possible que les nombres d'Indiens inscrits qui figurent dans le présent tableau ne concordent pas avec les chiffres du ministère des Affaires indiennes et du Nord canadien, les divergences étant surtout attribuables au dénombrement partiel des réserves indiennes et des établissements indiens et à la diversité des méthodes et concepts adoptés.

(13) Comprend les répondants ayant fourni une réponse écrite classifiée comme faisant partie des minorités visibles, p. ex. « Polynésien », « Guyanais », « Mauricien », etc.

(14) Comprend les répondants ayant déclaré plus d'un groupe de minorités visibles en cochant au moins deux cercles, p. ex. « Noir » et « Sud-Asiatique ».

(15) Comprend les personnes qui ont indiqué une double citoyenneté, y compris « Canadien ».

(16) Personnes ayant le statut d'immigrant reçu au Canada, ou l'ayant déjà eu. Un immigrant reçu est une personne à qui les autorités de l'immigration ont accordé le droit de résider au Canada en permanence. Certains immigrants résident au Canada depuis un certain nombre d'années, alors que d'autres sont arrivés récemment. La plupart des immigrants sont nés à l'extérieur du Canada, mais un petit nombre d'entre eux sont nés ici.

(17) « Autre Europe » comprend l'Europe méridionale, l'Europe orientale, l'Europe septentrionale et l'Europe occidentale excluant le Royaume-Uni. Les données ne sont pas directement comparables avec celles des recensements antérieurs à celui de 1996, alors que l'Europe comprenait Chypre et l'URSS. En 1996 et en 2001, Chypre et les anciennes républiques soviétiques d'Arménie, d'Azerbaïdjan, de Géorgie, du Kazakhstan, du Kirghizistan, d'Ouzbékistan, du Tadjikistan et du Turkménistan sont comprises dans l'Asie.

(18) "Other" includes Greenland, Saint Pierre and Miquelon, the category "Other country", as well as immigrants born in Canada.

(19) Refers to persons who, at the time of the census, held a student or employment authorization, Minister's permit or who were refugee claimants, as well as family members living with them.

(20) Includes data up to May 15, 2001.

(21) Includes Roman Catholic, Eastern Catholic, Polish National Catholic Church, Old Catholic.

(22) Includes mostly answers of "Christian", not otherwise stated.

(23) Includes Baha'i, Eckankar, Jains, Shinto, Taoist, Zoroastrian and Eastern religions, not identified elsewhere.

(24) Includes Aboriginal spirituality, Pagan, Wicca, Unity - New Thought - Pantheist, Scientology, Rastafarian, New Age, Gnostic, Satanist, etc.

(25) Includes Agnostic, Atheist, Humanist, and No religion, and other responses, such as Darwinism, etc.

(26) Refers to persons born outside Canada.

(27) Refers to persons born inside Canada with at least one parent born outside Canada.

(28) Refers to persons born inside Canada with both parents born inside Canada.

(29) Population 1 year of age and over residing in Canada, excluding institutional residents and Canadians (military and government personnel) in households outside Canada.

The concept of "migrants" is defined at the Census Subdivision (CSD) level. For geographic levels below the CSD, such as census tracts (CTs), the distinction between the migrant and non-migrant population refers to the corresponding CSD of the CT. For example, migrants within a CT are those persons who moved from a different CSD, while non-migrants are those who moved within the same CSD, although they moved in from a different CT in the same CSD or moved within the same CT.

(18) « Autre » comprend le Groenland, Saint-Pierre-et-Miquelon, la catégorie « Autre pays » ainsi que les immigrants nés au Canada.

(19) Personnes qui, au moment du recensement, étaient titulaires d'un permis de séjour pour étudiants, d'un permis de travail ou d'un permis ministériel, ou qui revendiquaient le statut de réfugié, ainsi que les membres de leur famille vivant avec elles.

(20) Comprend les données jusqu'au 15 mai 2001.

(21) Comprend Catholique romaine, Catholique orientale, Église catholique nationale polonaise, Vieille-catholique.

(22) Comprend la plupart des réponses « Chrétienne » non déterminées autrement.

(23) Comprend Baha'i, Eckankar, Djaïn, Shintoïste, Taoïste, Zoroastrienne et les religions orientales, non incluses ailleurs.

(24) Comprend Spiritualité autochtone, Païenne, Wicca, Unité - Nouvelle Pensée - Panthéiste, Scientologie, Rasta, Nouvel Âge, Gnostique, Satanique, etc.

(25) Comprend Agnostique, Athée, Humaniste et Aucune religion, et autres réponses, telles que darwiniste, etc.

(26) Comprend les personnes nées à l'extérieur du Canada.

(27) Comprend les personnes nées au Canada avec au moins un parent né à l'extérieur du Canada.

(28) Comprend les personnes nées au Canada de parents qui sont nés au Canada.

(29) Population de 1 an et plus résidant au Canada, à l'exclusion des pensionnaires d'un établissement institutionnel et des Canadiens (militaires et fonctionnaires) appartenant à un ménage à l'extérieur du Canada.

Le concept de « migrants » est défini au niveau des subdivisions de recensement (SDR). Pour les niveaux géographiques inférieurs aux SDR, comme les secteurs de recensement (SR), la distinction entre la population des migrants et des non-migrants est faite au niveau de la SDR correspondant au SR. Par exemple, les migrants au sein d'un SR sont les personnes qui sont originaires d'une SDR différente, alors que les non-migrants sont celles qui ont déménagé à l'intérieur de la même SDR, même s'ils sont passés d'un SR à un autre à l'intérieur de la même SDR ou ont déménagé à l'intérieur du même SR.

(30) Population 5 years of age and over residing in Canada, excluding institutional residents and Canadians (military and government personnel) in households outside Canada.

The concept of "migrants" is defined at the Census Subdivision (CSD) level. For geographic levels below the CSD, such as census tracts (CTs), the distinction between the migrant and non-migrant population refers to the corresponding CSD of the CT. For example, migrants within a CT are those persons who moved from a different CSD, while non-migrants are those who moved within the same CSD, although they moved in from a different CT in the same CSD or moved within the same CT.

(31) Includes "Never attended school or attended kindergarten only".

(32) Excludes persons with a postsecondary certificate, diploma or degree. Refers to courses completed at postsecondary institutions (university or college) which normally require a high school graduation certificate or equivalent for entrance, as well as to other courses in related or similar institutions which may not require a high school graduation certificate for entrance.

(33) Includes persons who may or may not have, in addition to a Trades certificate or diploma, some postsecondary courses without any degree, certificate or diploma.

(34) Referred to as "Other **non-university** certificate or diploma" in previous censuses, this sector includes non-degree-granting institutions such as community colleges, CEGEPs, private business colleges and technical institutes.

(35) Refers to persons who reported time spent doing one or more of the following unpaid work activities: (a) unpaid housework; (b) unpaid child care; (c) unpaid care or assistance to seniors. For example, a respondent who reported 5 to 14 hours of housework, 30 to 59 hours of child care and no hours of care or assistance to seniors would fall into the category "Housework and child care only".

(36) Unemployed persons 15 years and over who have never worked for pay or in self-employment or who had last worked prior to January 1, 2000.

(30) Population de 5 ans et plus résidant au Canada, à l'exclusion des pensionnaires d'un établissement institutionnel et des Canadiens (militaires et fonctionnaires) appartenant à un ménage à l'extérieur du Canada.

Le concept de « migrants » est défini au niveau des subdivisions de recensement (SDR). Pour les niveaux géographiques inférieurs aux SDR, comme les secteurs de recensement (SR), la distinction entre la population des migrants et des non-migrants est faite au niveau de la SDR correspondant au SR. Par exemple, les migrants au sein d'un SR sont les personnes qui sont originaires d'une SDR différente, alors que les non-migrants sont celles qui ont déménagé à l'intérieur de la même SDR, même s'ils sont passés d'un SR à un autre à l'intérieur de la même SDR ou ont déménagé à l'intérieur du même SR.

(31) Comprend la catégorie « Aucune scolarité ou uniquement l'école maternelle ».

(32) Ne comprend pas les personnes ayant un certificat, un diplôme ou un grade postsecondaire. Désigne les cours terminés dans un établissement postsecondaire (université ou collège) qui exige habituellement comme condition d'admission un certificat d'études secondaires ou l'équivalent; il peut aussi s'agir d'autres cours dans des établissements similaires ou connexes qui ne demandent pas nécessairement comme condition d'admission un certificat d'études secondaires.

(33) Comprend les personnes pouvant avoir ou ne pas avoir des études postsecondaires partielles sans aucun grade, certificat ou diplôme, en plus d'un certificat ou un diplôme d'une école de métiers.

(34) Désigné par l'expression « Certificat ou diplôme d'autres études **non universitaires** » dans les recensements précédents, ce secteur comprend tous les autres établissements ne décernant pas de grade, tels que les collèges communautaires, les cégeps, les collèges commerciaux privés et les instituts techniques.

(35) Personnes qui ont déclaré du temps consacré à une ou plusieurs des activités de travail non rémunéré suivantes : a) travaux ménagers, sans paye ou sans salaire; b) soins aux enfants, sans paye ou sans salaire; c) soins ou aide aux personnes âgées, sans paye ou sans salaire. Par exemple, un répondant qui a déclaré 5 à 14 heures de travaux ménagers, 30 à 59 heures de soins aux enfants et aucune heure de soins ou d'aide aux personnes âgées serait classé dans la catégorie « Travaux ménagers et soins aux enfants seulement ».

(36) Chômeurs de 15 ans et plus qui n'ont jamais travaillé à un emploi salarié ou à leur compte ou qui ont travaillé la dernière fois avant le 1er janvier 2000.

(37) Refers to the experienced labour force: persons who, during the week prior to Census Day, were employed or unemployed who worked for pay or in self-employment since January 1, 2000.

(38) Includes apartments without direct ground access in buildings that have fewer than five storeys and apartments with direct ground access in buildings that have fewer than five storeys.

(39) Includes mobile homes and other movable dwellings such as houseboats and railroad cars.

(40) Includes households in tenant-occupied, non-farm, non-reserve dwellings with household income greater than $0 in 2000 (i.e. excludes negative or zero household income).

(41) It should be noted that not all households spending 30% or more of incomes on shelter costs are necessarily experiencing housing affordability problems. This is particularly true of households with high incomes. There are also other households who choose to spend more on shelter than on other goods. Nevertheless, the allocation of 30% or more of a household's income to housing expenses provides a useful benchmark for assessing trends in housing affordability.

The relatively high shelter cost to household income ratios for some households may have resulted from the difference in the reference period for shelter cost and household income data. The reference period for shelter cost data (gross rent for tenants, and owner's major payments for owners) is 2001, while household income is reported for the year 2000. As well, for some households the 2000 household income may represent income for only part of a year.

(42) Includes households in owner-occupied, non-farm, non-reserve dwellings with household income greater than $0 in 2000 (i.e. excludes negative or zero household income).

(43) The average number of children at home per family is calculated using the total number of children at home and the total number of families.

(44) Non-relatives may be present.

(45) Including loss.

(37) S'entend de la population active expérimentée : les personnes qui, pendant la semaine ayant précédé le jour du recensement, étaient occupées ou en chômage et qui avaient travaillé à un emploi salarié ou à leur compte depuis le 1er janvier 2000.

(38) Comprend les appartements sans accès direct au niveau du sol dans les immeubles de moins de cinq étages et les appartements avec accès direct au niveau du sol dans les immeubles de moins de cinq étages.

(39) Comprend les maisons mobiles et les autres logements mobiles tels que les bateaux-maisons et les wagons de chemin de fer.

(40) Comprend les ménages ayant un revenu supérieur à 0 $ en 2000 dans les logements non agricoles hors réserve occupés par un locataire (sont exclus les ménages ayant un revenu négatif ou nul).

(41) Il convient de souligner que les ménages qui consacrent 30 % ou plus de leur revenu aux coûts d'habitation n'éprouvent pas nécessairement des problèmes d'abordabilité du logement. C'est notamment le cas des ménages ayant un revenu élevé. D'autres ménages choisissent de consacrer une plus grande part de leur revenu aux coûts d'habitation qu'à d'autres biens. Néanmoins, ce seuil (30 % ou plus du revenu du ménage consacré aux coûts d'habitation) constitue un repère utile pour l'évaluation des tendances en matière d'abordabilité du logement.

Les rapports entre les coûts d'habitation et le revenu du ménage relativement élevés pour certains ménages s'expliquent du fait que les périodes de référence utilisées pour les données sur les coûts d'habitation et pour les données sur le revenu du ménage ne sont pas les mêmes. En effet, la période de référence est l'année 2001 dans le cas des données sur les coûts d'habitation (loyer brut pour les locataires et principales dépenses de propriété pour les propriétaires), et l'année 2000 dans le cas des données sur le revenu du ménage. En outre, pour certains ménages, le revenu du ménage déclaré ne correspond qu'à une partie de l'année 2000.

(42) Comprend les ménages ayant un revenu supérieur à 0 $ en 2000 dans les logements non agricoles hors réserve occupés par le propriétaire (sont exclus les ménages ayant un revenu négatif ou nul).

(43) Le nombre moyen d'enfants à la maison par famille est calculé à partir du nombre total d'enfants à la maison et du nombre total de familles.

(44) Il peut y avoir des personnes non apparentées.

(45) Comprend les pertes.

(46) For persons with income.

(47) Percentages may not add to 100% due to rounding of the data.

(48) Includes persons who did not work in 2000 but reported employment income.

(49) Worked 49-52 weeks in 2000, mostly full time.

(50) Worked less than 49 weeks or worked mostly part time in 2000.

(51) Refers to married, opposite-sex and same-sex common-law couple families.

(52) Incidence of low income rates are calculated from rounded counts of low-income persons or families and the total number of persons or families. These counts have been rounded independently of the rounded counts shown in the table; thus, there may be a small difference between the rate shown and the one derived from the counts shown. Users are advised to interpret incidence of low income rates based upon small counts with caution.

(46) S'applique aux personnes ayant un revenu.

(47) Il est possible que la somme des pourcentages ne soit pas de 100 % en raison de l'arrondissement des données.

(48) Comprend les personnes qui n'ont pas travaillé en 2000 mais qui ont déclaré un revenu d'emploi.

(49) A travaillé 49-52 semaines en 2000, surtout à plein temps.

(50) A travaillé moins de 49 semaines ou a travaillé surtout à temps partiel en 2000.

(51) Comprend les familles comptant un couple marié et les familles comptant un couple en union libre formé de partenaires de sexe opposé ou de même sexe.

(52) Les taux de fréquence des unités à faible revenu sont calculés à partir des chiffres arrondis des personnes ou des familles à faible revenu et du nombre total de personnes ou de familles. Ces chiffres ont été arrondis séparément des chiffres arrondis figurant dans le tableau; par conséquent, il peut y avoir une légère différence entre la fréquence indiquée et une fréquence calculée à partir des chiffres figurant dans le tableau. Les utilisateurs doivent faire preuve de circonspection lorsqu'ils interprètent les fréquences des unités à faible revenu fondées sur des chiffres peu élevés.

Definitions

For further information on definitions and special notes, refer to the 2001 Census Dictionary, Catalogue No. 92-378-XIE or 92-378-XPE.

Aboriginal Identity

Refers to those persons who reported identifying with at least one Aboriginal group, i.e. North American Indian, Métis or Inuit (Eskimo), and/or those who reported being a Treaty Indian or a Registered Indian as defined by the *Indian Act* of Canada and/or who were members of an Indian Band or First Nation. In 1991 and previous censuses, Aboriginal persons were determined using the ethnic origin question (ancestry). The 1996 Census included a question on the individual's own perception of his/her Aboriginal identity. The 2001 Census question is the same as the one used in 1996.

Aboriginal Origin

Refers to those persons who reported at least one Aboriginal origin to the ethnic origin question (North American Indian, Métis or Inuit). Ethnic origin refers to the ethnic or cultural group(s) to which the respondent's ancestors belong. See Ethnic Origin.

Age

Refers to the age at last birthday (as of the census reference date, May 15, 2001). This variable is derived from date of birth.

Age at Immigration

Refers to the age at which the respondent first obtained landed immigrant status. A landed immigrant is a person who has been granted the right to live in Canada permanently by immigration authorities.

Bedrooms

Refers to all rooms designed and furnished as bedrooms and used mainly for sleeping purposes, even though the use may be occasional (e.g. spare bedroom).

Census Agglomeration (CA)

See the definition of Census Metropolitan Area (CMA) and Census Agglomeration (CA).

Census Division (CD)

Census division (CD) is the general term for provincially legislated areas (such as county, municipalité régionale de comté and regional district) or their equivalents. Census divisions are intermediate geographic areas between the province level and the municipality (census subdivision).

Census Family

Refers to a married couple (with or without children of either or both spouses), a couple living common-law (with or without children of either or both partners) or a lone parent of any marital status, with at least one child living in the same dwelling. A couple living common-law may be of opposite or same sex. "Children" in a census family include grandchildren living with their grandparent(s) but with no parents present.

Census Family Status

Refers to the classification of the population according to whether or not the persons are members of a census family.

Family persons refer to household members who belong to a census family. They, in turn, are further classified as follows:

Spouses refer to persons of opposite sex who are legally married to each other and living in the same dwelling.

Common-law partners are two persons of opposite sex or of the same sex who are not legally married to each other, but live together as a couple in the same dwelling.

Lone parent refers to a mother or a father, with no spouse or common-law partner present, living in a dwelling with one or more children.

Children refer to blood, step- or adopted sons and daughters (regardless of age or marital status) who are living in the same dwelling as their parent(s), as well as grandchildren in households where there are no parents present. Sons and daughters who are living with their spouse or common-law partner, or with one or more of their own children, are not considered to be members of the census family of their parent(s), even if they are living in the same dwelling. In addition, those sons and daughters who do not live in the same dwelling as their parent(s) are not considered members of the census family of their parent(s). The category of children can be further distinguished as follows:

Never-married sons and/or daughters in a census family, as used in censuses prior to 2001.

Other sons and/or daughters in a census family who would not have been included in the census family of their parents according to the previous concept.

Grandchildren living in the same household as their grandparent(s), with no parents present.

Non-family persons refer to household members who do not belong to a census family. They may be related to Person 1 (e.g. Person 1's sister, brother-in-law, cousin, grandparent), or unrelated to Person 1 (e.g. lodger, room-mate, employee). A person living alone is always a non-family person.

Census Family Structure

Refers to the classification of census families into married couples (with or without children of either or both spouses), common-law couples (with or without children of either or both partners), and lone-parent families by sex of parent. A couple living common-law may be of opposite or same sex. "Children" in a census family include grandchildren living with their grandparent(s) but with no parents present.

Census Metropolitan Area (CMA) and Census Agglomeration (CA)

A census metropolitan area (CMA) or a census agglomeration (CA) is formed by one or more adjacent municipalities centred on a large urban area (known as the urban core). The census population count of the urban core is at least 10,000 to form a census agglomeration and at least 100,000 to form a census metropolitan area. To be included in the CMA or CA, other adjacent municipalities must have a high degree of integration with the central urban area, as measured by commuting flows derived from census place of work data.

If the population of the urban core of a CA declines below 10,000, the CA is retired. However, once an area becomes a CMA, it is retained as a CMA even if the population of its urban core declines below 100,000. The urban areas in the CMA or CA that are not contiguous to the urban core are called the urban fringe. Rural areas in the CMA or CA are called the rural fringe.

When a CA has an urban core of at least 50,000 based on census counts, it is subdivided into census tracts. Census tracts are maintained for the CA even if the population of the urban core subsequently falls below 50,000. All CMAs are subdivided into census tracts.

Census Subdivision (CSD)

Census subdivision (CSD) is the general term for municipalities (as determined by provincial legislation) or areas treated as municipal equivalents for statistical purposes (for example, Indian reserves, Indian settlements and unorganized territories).

Census Subdivision Type

Census subdivisions (CSDs) are classified into 46 types according to official designations adopted by provincial or federal authorities. Two exceptions are "Subdivision of Unorganized" in Newfoundland and Labrador, and "Subdivision of County Municipality" in Nova Scotia, which are geographic areas created as equivalents for municipalities by Statistics Canada, in cooperation with those provinces, for the purpose of disseminating statistical data.

The **census subdivision type** accompanies the census subdivision name in order to distinguish CSDs from each other, for example, Granby, V (for the *ville* of Granby) and Granby, CT (for the *municipalité de canton* of Granby).

Census Tract (CT)

Census tracts (CTs) are small, relatively stable geographic areas that usually have a population of 2,500 to 8,000. They are located in census metropolitan areas and in census agglomerations with an urban core population of 50,000 or more in the previous census.

A committee of local specialists (for example, planners, health and social workers and educators) initially delineates CTs in conjunction with Statistics Canada. Once a census metropolitan area (CMA) or census agglomeration (CA) has been subdivided into census tracts, the census tracts are maintained even if the urban core population subsequently declines below 50,000.

Citizenship

Refers to the legal citizenship status of the respondent. Persons who are citizens of more than one country were instructed to provide the name of the other country(ies).

Class of Worker

This variable classifies persons who reported a job into the following categories:

(a) persons who worked mainly for wages, salaries, commissions, tips, piece-rates, or payments "in kind" (payments in goods or services rather than money);

(b) persons who worked mainly for themselves, with or without paid help, operating a business, farm or professional practice, alone or in partnership;

(c) persons who worked without pay in a family business, farm or professional practice owned or operated by a related household member; unpaid family work does not include unpaid housework, unpaid childcare, unpaid care to seniors and volunteer work.

The job reported was the one held in the week (Sunday to Saturday) prior to enumeration (May 15, 2001) if the person was employed, or the job of longest duration since January 1, 2000, if the person was not employed during the reference week. Persons with two or more jobs in the reference week were asked to provide information for the job at which they worked the most hours.

Incorporation Status

Refers to the legal status of a business, farm or professional practice. It is directed at persons who were mainly self-employed, either with or without paid help in the job reported (i.e. their job in the week [Sunday to Saturday] prior to enumeration [May 15, 2001] or the one of longest duration since January 1, 2000). An **incorporated business** is a business, farm or professional practice that has been formed into a legal corporation, thus constituting a legal entity under either federal or provincial laws. An **unincorporated business**, farm or professional practice is not a separate legal entity, but may be a partnership, family business or owner-operated business.

Common-law Status

Refers to two people of the opposite sex or of the same sex who live together as a couple, but who are not legally married to each other.

Condition of Dwelling

Refers to whether, in the judgement of the respondent, the dwelling requires any repairs (excluding desirable remodelling or additions).

Dwelling, Occupied Private

Refers to a private dwelling in which a person or a group of persons is permanently residing. Also included are private dwellings whose usual residents are temporarily absent on Census Day. Unless otherwise specified, all data in housing products are for occupied private dwellings, rather than for unoccupied private dwellings or dwellings occupied solely by foreign and/or temporary residents.

Dwelling, Private

Refers to a separate set of living quarters with a private entrance either from outside or from a common hall, lobby, vestibule or stairway inside the building. The entrance to the dwelling must be one that can be used without passing through the living quarters of someone else. The dwelling must meet the two conditions necessary for year-round occupancy:

(a) a source of heat or power (as evidenced by chimneys, power lines, oil or gas pipes or meters, generators, woodpiles, electric lights, heating pumps, solar heating panels, etc.);

(b) an enclosed space that provides shelter from the elements (as evidenced by complete and enclosed walls and roof, and by doors and windows that provide protection from wind, rain and snow).

The census classifies private dwellings into **regular private dwellings** and **occupied marginal dwellings**. Regular private dwellings are further classified into three major groups: **occupied dwellings** (occupied by usual residents), **dwellings occupied by foreign and/or temporary residents** and **unoccupied dwellings**. Marginal dwellings are classified as occupied by usual residents or by foreign and/or temporary residents. Marginal dwellings that were unoccupied on Census Day are not counted in the housing stock.

Earner or Employment Income Recipient

Refers to a person 15 years of age and over who received wages and salaries, net income from a non-farm unincorporated business and/or professional practice, and/or net farm self-employment income during calendar year 2000.

Economic Family

Refers to a group of two or more persons who live in the same dwelling and are related to each other by blood, marriage, common-law or adoption.

Ethnic Origin

Refers to the ethnic or cultural group(s) to which the respondent's ancestors belong.

First Official Language Spoken

Refers to a variable specified within the framework of the *Official Languages Act.*

Generation Status

Generation status of the respondent, i.e. "1st", "2nd" or "3rd +" generation, refers to whether the respondent or the respondent's parents were born in or outside Canada.

Highest Level of Schooling

Refers to the highest grade or year of elementary or secondary (high) school attended, or to the highest year of university or college education completed. University education is considered to be a higher level of schooling than college education. Also, the attainment of a degree, certificate or diploma is considered to be at a higher level than years completed or attended without an educational qualification.

Home Language

Refers to the language spoken most often or on a regular basis at home by the individual at the time of the census.

Hours Spent Doing Unpaid Housework

Refers to the number of hours persons spent doing unpaid housework, yard work or home maintenance in the week (Sunday to Saturday) prior to Census Day (May 15, 2001). It includes hours spent doing unpaid housework for members of one's own household, for other family members outside the household, and for friends or neighbours.

Unpaid housework does not include volunteer work for a non-profit organization, a religious organization, a charity or community group, or work without pay in the operation of a family farm, business or professional practice.

Hours Spent Looking After Children, Without Pay

Refers to the number of hours persons spent looking after children without pay. It includes hours spent providing unpaid child care for members of one's own household, for other family members outside the household, for friends or neighbours or for other family members outside the household in the week (Sunday to Saturday) prior to Census Day (May 15, 2001).

Unpaid child care does not include volunteer work for a non-profit organization, a religious organization, a charity or community group, or work without pay in the operation of a family farm, business or professional practice.

Hours Spent Providing Unpaid Care or Assistance to Seniors

Refers to the number of hours persons spent providing unpaid care or assistance to seniors of one's own household, to other senior family members outside the household, and to friends or neighbours in the week (Sunday to Saturday) prior to Census Day (May 15, 2001).

Unpaid care or assistance to seniors does not include volunteer work for a non-profit organization, religious organization, charity or community group, or work without pay in the operation of a family farm, business or professional practice.

Household Living Arrangements

Refers to the classification of persons in terms of whether they are members of a family household or of a non-family household, and whether they are family or non-family persons.

Household, Private

Refers to a person or a group of persons (other than foreign residents) who occupy a private dwelling and do not have a usual place of residence elsewhere in Canada.

Household Size

Refers to the number of persons in a private household.

Household Type

Refers to the basic division of private households into family and non-family households. Family household refers to a household that contains at least one census family, that is, a married couple with or without children, or a couple living common-law with or without children, or a lone parent living with one or more children (lone-parent family). One-family household refers to a single census family (with or without other non-family persons) that occupies a private dwelling. Multiple-family household refers to a household in which two or more census families (with or without additional non-family persons) occupy the same private dwelling.

Non-family household refers to either one person living alone in a private dwelling or to a group of two or more people who share a private dwelling, but who do not constitute a census family.

Immigrant Population

Refers to people who are, or have been, landed immigrants in Canada. A landed immigrant is a person who has been granted the right to live in Canada permanently by immigration authorities. Some immigrants have resided in Canada for a number of years, while others have arrived recently. Most immigrants are born outside Canada, but a small number were born in Canada.

Incidence of Low Income

The incidence of low income is the proportion or percentage of economic families or unattached individuals in a given classification below the low income cut-offs. These incidence rates are calculated from unrounded estimates of economic families and unattached individuals 15 years of age and over.

Income Status

Refers to the position of an economic family or an unattached individual 15 years of age and over in relation to Statistics Canada's low income cut-offs (LICOs).

Industry (Based on the 1997 North American Industry Classification System [NAICS])

Refers to the general nature of the business carried out in the establishment where the person worked. If the person did not have a job during the week (Sunday to Saturday) prior to enumeration (May 15, 2001), the data relate to the job of longest duration since January 1, 2000. Persons with two or more jobs were required to report the information for the job at which they worked the most hours.

The 2001 industry data are produced according to the 1997 NAICS. The NAICS provides enhanced industry comparability among the three North American Free Trade Agreement (NAFTA) trading partners (Canada, United States and Mexico). This classification consists of a systematic and comprehensive arrangement of industries structured into 20 sectors, 99 subsectors and 300 industry groups. The criteria used to create these categories are similarity of input structures, labour skills or production processes used by the establishment. For further information on the classification, see *North American Industry Classification System, Canada, 1997*, Catalogue No. 12-501-XPE.

The variable "Industry (based on the 1997 NAICS)" does not permit direct comparison to any previous census industry data. The 1980 Standard Industrial Classification should be used for comparisons between the 1986, 1991, 1996 and 2001 Censuses.

Knowledge of Non-official Languages

Refers to languages, other than English or French, in which the respondent can conduct a conversation.

Knowledge of Official Languages

Refers to the ability to conduct a conversation in English only, in French only, in both English and French, or in neither of the official languages of Canada.

Labour Force Activity (in Reference Week)

Refers to the labour market activity of the population 15 years of age and over in the week (Sunday to Saturday) prior to Census Day (May 15, 2001). Respondents were classified as either employed, or unemployed, or as not in the labour force. The labour force includes the employed and the unemployed.

Employed (in Reference Week)
Refers to persons 15 years of age and over, excluding institutional residents, who, during the week (Sunday to Saturday) prior to Census Day (May 15, 2001):

(a) did any work at all for pay or in self-employment or without pay in a family farm, business or professional practice;

(b) were absent from their job or business, with or without pay, for the entire week because of a vacation, an illness, a labour dispute at their place of work, or any other reasons.

Unemployed (in Reference Week)
Refers to persons 15 years of age and over, excluding institutional residents, who, during the week (Sunday to Saturday) prior to Census Day (May 15, 2001), were without paid work or without self-employment work and were available for work and either:

(a) had actively looked for paid work in the past four weeks; or

(b) were on temporary lay-off and expected to return to their job; or

(c) had definite arrangements to start a new job in four weeks or less.

Not in the Labour Force (in Reference Week)
Refers to persons 15 years of age and over, excluding institutional residents, who, in the week (Sunday to Saturday) prior to Census Day (May 15, 2001), were neither employed nor unemployed. It includes students, homemakers, retired workers, seasonal workers in an "off" season who were not looking for work, and persons who could not work because of a long-term illness or disability.

Labour Force (in Reference Week)
Refers to persons who were either employed or unemployed during the week (Sunday to Saturday) prior to Census Day (May 15, 2001).

In past censuses, this was called "Total Labour Force".

Participation Rate (in Reference Week)
Refers to the labour force in the week (Sunday to Saturday) prior to Census Day (May 15, 2001), expressed as a percentage of the population 15 years of age and over excluding institutional residents.

The participation rate for a particular group (age, sex, marital status, geographic area, etc.) is the total labour force in that group, expressed as a percentage of the population 15 years of age and over, in that group.

Employment Rate (in Reference Week)
Refers to the number of persons employed in the week (Sunday to Saturday) prior to Census Day (May 15, 2001), expressed as a percentage of the total population 15 years of age and over excluding institutional residents.

The employment rate for a particular group (age, sex, marital status, geographic area, etc.) is the number of employed in that group, expressed as a percentage of the population 15 years of age and over in that group.

In past censuses, this was called the Employment-population Ratio.

Unemployment Rate (in Reference Week)
Refers to the unemployed expressed as a percentage of the labour force in the week (Sunday to Saturday) prior to Census Day (May 15, 2001).

The unemployment rate for a particular group (age, sex, marital status, geographic area, etc.) is the unemployed in that group, expressed as a percentage of the labour force in that group, in the week prior to enumeration.

Land Area

Land area is the area in square kilometres of the land-based portions of standard geographic areas.

The land area measurements are unofficial, and are provided for the sole purpose of calculating population density.

Landed Immigrant Status

Refers to people who have been granted the right to live in Canada permanently by immigration authorities.

Language Used at Work

Refers to the language used most often at work by the individual at the time of the census. Other languages used at work on a regular basis are also collected.

Legal Marital Status

Refers to the legal conjugal status of a person.

The various responses are defined as follows:

Never legally married (single) – Persons who have never married (including all persons less than 15 years of age) and persons whose marriage has been annulled and who have not remarried.

Legally married (and not separated) – Persons whose husband or wife is living, unless the couple is separated or a divorce has been obtained.

Separated, but still legally married – Persons currently married, but who are no longer living with their spouse (for any reason other than illness or work) and have not obtained a divorce.

Divorced – Persons who have obtained a legal divorce and who have not remarried.

Widowed – Persons who have lost their spouse through death and who have not remarried.

Low Income Cut-offs (LICOs)

Measures of low income known as low income cut-offs (LICOs) were first introduced in Canada in 1968 based on 1961 Census income data and 1959 family expenditure patterns. At that time, expenditure patterns indicated that Canadian families spent about 50% of their total income on food, shelter and clothing. It was arbitrarily estimated that families spending 70% or more of their income (20 percentage points more than the average) on these basic necessities would be in "straitened" circumstances. With this assumption, low income cut-off points were set for five different sizes of families.

Subsequent to these initial cut-offs, revised low income cut-offs were established based on national family expenditure data from 1969, 1978, 1986 and 1992. These data indicated that Canadian families spent, on average, 42% in 1969, 38.5% in 1978, 36.2% in 1986 and 34.7% in 1992 of their total income on basic necessities. Since 1992, data from the expenditure survey have indicated that this proportion has remained fairly stable. By adding the original difference of 20 percentage points to the basic level of expenditure on necessities, new low income cut-offs were set at income levels differentiated by family size and degree of urbanization. Since 1992, these cut-offs have been updated yearly by changes in the consumer price index.

Mode of Transportation

Refers to the mode of transportation to work of non-institutional residents 15 years of age and over who worked at some time since January 1, 2000. Persons who indicate in the place of work question that they either had no fixed workplace address, or specified a usual workplace address, are asked to identify the mode of transportation they most frequently use to commute from home to work. The variable usually relates to the individual's job in the week prior to enumeration. However, if the person did not work during that week but had worked at some time since January 1, 2000, the information relates to the job held longest during that period.

Persons who use more than one mode of transportation are asked to identify the single mode they use for most of the travel distance. As a result, the question provides data on the primary mode of transportation to work. The question does not measure multiple modes of transportation, nor does it measure the seasonal variation in mode of transportation or trips made for purposes other than the commute from home to work.

Mother Tongue

Refers to the first language learned at home in childhood and still understood by the individual at the time of the census.

Non-immigrant Population

Refers to people who are Canadian citizens by birth. Although most were born in Canada, a small number of them were born outside Canada to Canadian parents.

Occupation (Based on the 2001 National Occupational Classification for Statistics [2001 NOC–S])

Refers to the kind of work persons were doing during the reference week, as determined by their kind of work and the description of the main activities in their job. If the person did not have a job during the week (Sunday to Saturday) prior to enumeration (May 15, 2001), the data relate to the job of longest duration since January 1, 2000. Persons with two or more jobs were to report the information for the job at which they worked the most hours.

The 2001 occupation data are classified according to the 2001 National Occupational Classification for Statistics (2001 NOC–S). This classification is composed of four levels of aggregation. There are 10 broad occupational categories containing 47 major groups that are further subdivided into 140 minor groups. At the most detailed level, there are 520 occupation unit groups. Occupation unit groups are formed on the basis of the education, training, or skill level required to enter the job, as well as the kind of work performed, as determined by the tasks, duties and responsibilities of the occupation.

For information on the 2001 NOC–S, see the *National Occupational Classification for Statistics, 2001*, Catalogue No. 12-583-XPE.

Owner's Major Payments or Gross Rent as a Percentage of Household Income

Refers to the proportion of average monthly 2000 total household income which is spent on owner's major payments (in the case of owner-occupied dwellings) or on gross rent (in the case of tenant-occupied dwellings). This concept is illustrated below:

(a) **Owner-occupied non-farm dwellings:**

$$\frac{\text{Owner's major payments}}{\text{(2000 total annual household income) /12}} \times 100 = \_\_\_\%$$

(b) **Tenant-occupied non-farm dwellings:**

$$\frac{\text{Gross rent}}{\text{(2000 total annual household income) /12}} \times 100 = \_\_\_\%$$

Period of Construction

Refers to the period in time during which the building or dwelling was originally constructed.

Period of Immigration

Refers to ranges of years based on the year of immigration question. Year of immigration refers to the year in which landed immigrant status was first obtained.

Place of Birth of Respondent

Refers to specific provinces or territories for respondents who were born in Canada, or to specific countries if born outside Canada.

Place of Residence 1 Year Ago (Mobility)

Refers to the relationship between a person's usual place of residence on Census Day and his or her usual place of residence one year earlier. A person is classified as a non-mover if no difference exists. Otherwise, a person is classified as a mover and this categorization is called Mobility Status (1 Year Ago). Within the category of movers, a further distinction is made between non-migrants and migrants; this difference is called migration status.

Non-movers are persons who, on Census Day, were living at the same address as the one at which they resided one year earlier.

Movers are persons who, on Census Day, were living at a different address than the one at which they resided one year earlier.

Non-migrants are movers who, on Census Day, were living at a different address, but in the same census subdivision (CSD) as the one they lived in one year earlier.

Migrants are movers who, on Census Day, were residing in a different CSD one year earlier (internal migrants) or who were living outside Canada one year earlier (external migrants).

Intraprovincial migrants are movers who, on Census Day, were living in a different census subdivision than the one at which they resided one year earlier, in the same province.

Interprovincial migrants are movers who, on Census Day, were living in a different census subdivision than the one at which they resided one year earlier, in a different province.

Place of Residence 5 Years Ago (Mobility)

Refers to the relationship between a person's usual place of residence on Census Day and his or her usual place of residence five years earlier. A person is classified as a non-mover if no difference exists. Otherwise, a person is classified as a mover and this categorization is called Mobility Status (5 Years Ago). Within the movers category, a further distinction is made between non-migrants and migrants; this difference is called migration status.

Non-movers are persons who, on Census Day, were living at the same address as the one at which they resided five years earlier.

Movers are persons who, on Census Day, were living at a different address than the one at which they resided five years earlier.

Non-migrants are movers who, on Census Day, were living at a different address, but in the same census subdivision (CSD) as the one they lived in five years earlier.

Migrants are movers who, on Census Day, were residing in a different CSD five years earlier (internal migrants) or who were living outside Canada five years earlier (external migrants).

Intraprovincial migrants are movers who, on Census Day, were living in a different census subdivision than the one in which they resided five years earlier, in the same province.

Interprovincial migrants are movers who, on Census Day, were living in a different census subdivision than the one in which they resided five years earlier, in a different province.

Place of Work Status

Refers to the place of work of non-institutional residents 15 years of age and over who worked at some time since January 1, 2000. The variable usually relates to the individual's job held in the week prior to enumeration. However, if the person did not work during that week but had worked at some time since January 1, 2000, the information relates to the job held longest during that period.

Worked at home – Persons whose job is located in the same building as their place of residence, persons who live and work on the same farm, building superintendents and teleworkers who spend most of their work week working at home.

Worked outside Canada – Persons who work at a location outside Canada. This can include diplomats, Armed Forces personnel and other persons enumerated abroad. This category also includes recent immigrants who may not currently be employed, but whose job of longest duration since January 1, 2000 was held outside Canada.

No fixed workplace address – Persons who do not go from home to the same workplace location at the beginning of each shift. Such persons include building and landscape contractors, travelling salespersons, independent truck drivers, etc.

Worked at the address specified below – Persons who are not included in the categories described above and who report to the same (usual) workplace location at the beginning of each shift are included here. Respondents are asked to provide the street address, city, town, village, township, municipality or Indian reserve, province/territory and postal code of their workplace. If the full street address was not known, the name of the building or nearest street intersection could be substituted.

Teleworkers who spend less than one-half of their workweek working at their home office are asked to report the full address of their employer. Persons whose workplace location varied, but who reported regularly to an employer's address at the beginning of each shift, are asked to report the full address of the employer.

Population Universe

The Population Universe of the 2001 Census includes the following groups:

- Canadian citizens (by birth or by naturalization) and landed immigrants with a usual place of residence in Canada;
- Canadian citizens (by birth or by naturalization) and landed immigrants who are abroad, either on a military base or attached to a diplomatic mission;
- Canadian citizens (by birth or by naturalization) and landed immigrants at sea or in port aboard merchant vessels under Canadian registry;
- persons with a usual place of residence in Canada who are claiming refugee status and members of their families living with them;
- persons with a usual place of residence in Canada who hold student authorizations (student visas or student permits) and members of their families living with them;
- persons with a usual place of residence in Canada who hold employment authorizations (or work permits) and members of their families living with them;
- persons with a usual place of residence in Canada who hold Minister's permits (including extensions) and members of their families living with them.

For census purposes, the last four groups in this list are referred to as "non-permanent residents".

Presence of Children

Refers to the number of children in private households by age groups.

Province or Territory

Province and territory refer to the major political units of Canada. From a statistical point of view, province and territory are basic areas for which data are tabulated. Canada is divided into ten provinces and three territories.

Registered or Treaty Indian

Refers to those persons who reported they were registered under the *Indian Act* of Canada. Treaty Indians are persons who are registered under the *Indian Act* and can prove descent from a Band that signed a treaty. Although there was a question in the 1991 Census on registration status, the layout of the 1996 question was somewhat different. In 1991, registration status was a subcomponent of Question 16 on Registered Indians. In the first part of the question, respondents were asked about their registration status, while the second part of the question dealt with Band membership. In 1996, one direct question was developed to collect data on registration or treaty status.

The wording of the 1996 question differed slightly from the one in previous years. Prior to 1996, the term "treaty" was excluded from the question. It was added in 1996 at the request of individuals from the Western provinces, where the term is more widely used.

Religion

Refers to specific religious denominations, groups or bodies, as well as to sects, cults, or other religiously defined communities or systems of belief.

Rent, Gross

Refers to the total average monthly payments paid by tenant households to secure shelter.

Rooms

Refers to the number of rooms in a dwelling. A room is an enclosed area within a dwelling which is finished and suitable for year-round living.

School Attendance

Refers to either full-time or part-time (day or evening) attendance at school, college or university during the nine-month period between September 2000 and May 15, 2001. Attendance is counted only for courses which could be used as credits towards a certificate, diploma or degree.

Sex

Refers to the gender of the respondent.

Structural Type of Dwelling

Refers to the structural characteristics and/or dwelling configuration, that is, whether the dwelling is a single-detached house, an apartment in a high-rise building, a row house, a mobile home, etc.

Tenure

Refers to whether some member of the household owns or rents the dwelling, or whether the dwelling is Band housing (on an Indian reserve or settlement).

Total Income

Refers to the total money income received from the following sources during calendar year 2000 by persons 15 years of age and over:

- wages and salaries (total);
- net farm income;
- net non-farm income from unincorporated business and/or professional practice;
- Canada Child Tax Benefits;
- Old Age Security pension and Guaranteed Income Supplement;
- benefits from Canada or Quebec Pension Plan;
- benefits from Employment Insurance;
- other income from government sources;
- dividends, interest on bonds, deposits and savings certificates, and other investment income;
- retirement pensions, superannuation and annuities, including those from RRSPs and RRIFs;
- other money income.

Receipts Not Counted as Income – The income concept excluded gambling gains and losses, lottery prizes, money inherited during the year in a lump sum, capital gains or losses, receipts from the sale of property, income tax refunds, loan payments received, lump-sum settlements of insurance policies, rebates received on property taxes, refunds of pension contributions, as well as all income "in kind", such as free meals, living accommodations, or agricultural products produced and consumed on the farm.

Average Income of Individuals – Average income of individuals refers to the weighted mean total income of individuals 15 years of age and over who reported income for 2000. Average income is calculated from unrounded data by dividing the aggregate income of a specified group of individuals (e.g. males 45 to 54 years of age) by the number of individuals with income in that group.

Average and median incomes and standard errors for average income of individuals will be calculated for those individuals who are at least 15 years of age and who have an income (positive or negative). For all other universes (e.g. census families or private households), these statistics will be calculated over all units, whether or not they reported any income.

Median Income of Individuals – The median income of a specified group of income recipients is that amount which divides their income size distribution into two halves, i.e. the incomes of the first half of individuals are below the median, while those of the second half are above the median. Median income is calculated from the unrounded number of individuals (e.g. males 45 to 54 years of age) with income in that group.

Average and median incomes and standard errors for average income of individuals will be calculated for those individuals who are at least 15 years of age and who have an income (positive or negative). For all other universes (e.g. census families or private households), these statistics will be calculated over all units, whether or not they reported any income.

Standard Error of Average Income – Refers to the estimated standard error of average income for an income size distribution. If interpreted as shown below, it serves as a rough indicator of the precision of the corresponding estimate of average income. For about 68% of the samples which could be selected from the sample frame, the difference between the sample estimate of average income and the corresponding figure based on complete enumeration would be less than one standard error. For about 95% of the possible samples, the difference would be less than two standard errors and, in about 99% of the samples, the difference would be approximately two and one half standard errors.

Unattached Individuals

Refers to household members who are not members of an economic family. Persons living alone are included in this category.

Value of Dwelling

Refers to the dollar amount expected by the owner if the dwelling were to be sold.

Visible Minorities

Refers to the visible minority group to which the respondent belongs. The *Employment Equity Act* defines visible minorities as "persons, other than Aboriginal peoples, who are non-Caucasian in race or non-white in colour".

The visible minority population includes the following groups: Chinese, South Asian, Black, Filipino, Latin American, Southeast Asian, Arab, West Asian, Korean, Japanese, Visible Minority, n.i.e. and Multiple Visible Minorities.

Data Quality

General

The 2001 Census was a large and complex undertaking and, while considerable effort was taken to ensure high standards throughout all collection and processing operations, the resulting estimates are inevitably subject to a certain degree of error. Users of census data should be aware that such error exists, and should have some appreciation of its main components, so that they can assess the usefulness of census data for their purposes and the risks involved in basing conclusions or decisions on these data.

Errors can arise at virtually every stage of the census process, from the preparation of materials through data processing, including the listing of dwellings and the collection of data. Some errors occur at random, and when the individual responses are aggregated for a sufficiently large group, such errors tend to cancel out. For errors of this nature, the larger the group, the more accurate the corresponding estimate. It is for this reason that users are advised to be cautious when using small estimates. There are some errors, however, which might occur more systematically, and which result in "biased" estimates. Because the bias from such errors is persistent no matter how large the group for which responses are aggregated, and because bias is particularly difficult to measure, systematic errors are a more serious problem for most data users than the random errors referred to previously.

For census data in general, the principal types of error are as follows:

- **coverage errors**, which occur when dwellings or individuals are missed, incorrectly enumerated or counted more than once;

- **non-response errors**, which result when responses cannot be obtained from a certain number of households and/or individuals, because of extended absence or some other reason;

- **response errors**, which occur when the respondent, or sometimes the Census Representative, misunderstands a census question, and records an incorrect response or simply uses the wrong response box;

- **processing errors**, which can occur at various steps including **coding**, when "write-in" responses are transformed into numerical codes; **data capture**, when responses are transferred from the census questionnaire in an electronic format, by key-entry operators; and **imputation**, when a "valid", but not necessarily correct, response is inserted into a record by the computer to replace missing or "invalid" data ("valid" and "invalid" referring to whether or not the response is consistent with other information on the record);

- **sampling errors**, which apply only to the supplementary questions on the "long form" asked of a one-fifth sample of households, and which arise from the fact that the responses to these questions, when weighted up to represent the whole population, inevitably differ somewhat from the responses which would have been obtained if these questions had been asked of all households.

The above types of error each have both random and systematic components. Usually, however, the systematic component of sampling error is very small in relation to its random component. For the other non sampling errors, both random and systematic components may be significant.

Coverage Errors

Coverage errors affect the accuracy of the census counts, that is, the sizes of the various census universes: population, families, households and dwellings. While steps have been taken to correct certain identifiable errors, the final counts are still subject to some degree of error because persons or dwellings have been missed, incorrectly enumerated in the census or counted more than once.

Missed dwellings or persons result in **undercoverage**. Dwellings can be missed because of the misunderstanding of enumeration area (EA) boundaries, or because either they do not look like dwellings or they appear uninhabitable. Persons can be missed when their dwelling is missed or is classified as vacant, or because the respondent misinterprets the instructions on whom to include on the questionnaire. Some individuals may be missed because they have no usual residence and did not spend census night in a dwelling.

Dwellings or persons incorrectly enumerated or double counted result in **overcoverage**. Overcoverage of dwellings can occur when structures unfit for habitation are listed as dwellings (incorrectly enumerated), when there is a certain ambiguity regarding the EA boundaries or when units (for example, rooms) are listed separately instead of being treated as part of one dwelling (double counted). Persons can be counted more than once because their dwelling is double counted or because the guidelines on whom to include on the questionnaire have been misunderstood. Occasionally, someone who is not in the census population universe, such as a foreign resident or a fictitious person, may, incorrectly, be enumerated in the census. On average, overcoverage is less likely to occur than undercoverage and, as a result, counts of dwellings and persons are likely to be slightly underestimated.

For the 2001 Census, three studies are used to measure coverage error. In the Dwelling Classification Study, dwellings listed as vacant were revisited to verify that they were vacant on Census Day, and dwellings whose households were listed as non-respondent were revisited to determine the number of usual residents and their characteristics. Adjustments have been made to the final census counts for households and persons missed because their dwelling was incorrectly classified as vacant. The census counts may also have been adjusted for dwellings whose households were classified as non-respondent. Despite these adjustments, the final counts are still subject to some undercoverage. Undercoverage tends to be higher for certain segments of the population, such as young adults (especially young adult males) and recent immigrants. The Reverse Record Check Study is used to measure the residual undercoverage for Canada, and each province and territory. The Overcoverage Study is designed to investigate overcoverage errors. The results of the Reverse Record Check and the Overcoverage Study, when taken together, furnish an estimate of net undercoverage.

Other Non-sampling Errors

While coverage errors affect the number of units in the various census universes, other errors affect the characteristics of those units.

Sometimes it is not possible to obtain a complete response from a household, even though the dwelling was identified as occupied and a questionnaire was dropped off. The household members may have been away throughout the census period or, in rare instances, the householder may have refused to complete the form. More frequently, the questionnaire is returned but no response is provided to certain questions. Effort is devoted to ensure as complete a questionnaire as possible. Census representatives edit the questionnaires and follow up on missing information. Their work is then checked by a supervisor and a quality control technician. Despite this, at the end of the collection stage, a small number of responses are still missing, i.e. **non-response errors**. Although missing responses are eliminated during processing by replacing each one of them by the corresponding response for a "similar" record, there remain some potential imputation errors. This is particularly serious if the non-respondents differ in some respects from the respondents; this procedure will then introduce a **non-response bias**.

Even when a response is obtained, it may not be entirely accurate. The respondent may have misinterpreted the question or may have guessed the answer, especially when answering on behalf of another, possibly absent, household member. The respondent may also have entered the answer in the wrong place on the questionnaire. Such errors are referred to as **response errors**. While response errors usually arise from inaccurate information provided by respondents, they can also result from mistakes by the Census Representative who completed certain parts of the questionnaire, such as the structural type of dwelling, or who followed up to obtain a missing response.

Some of the census questions require a written response. During processing, these "write-in" entries are given a numeric code. **Coding errors** can occur when the written response is ambiguous, incomplete, difficult to read or when the code list is extensive (e.g. major field of study, place of work). A formal Quality Control (QC) operation is used to detect, rectify and reduce coding errors. Within each work unit, a sample of responses is independently coded a second time. The resolution of discrepancies between the first and second codings determines whether recoding of the work unit is necessary. Except for the Industry and Occupation variables, much of the census coding is now automated, resulting in a reduction of coding errors.

The information on the questionnaires is typed into a computer file. Two procedures are used to control the number of **data capture errors**. First, certain edits (such as range checks) are performed as the data are keyed in. Second, a sample from each batch of documents is retyped and compared with the original entries. Unsatisfactory work is identified and corrected, and the remainder of the batch is captured as needed.

Once captured, the data are edited where they undergo a series of computer checks to identify missing or inconsistent responses. These are replaced during the imputation stage of processing where either a response consistent with the other respondents' data is inferred or a response from a similar donor is substituted. Imputation ensures a complete database where the data correspond to the census counts and facilitate multivariate analyses. Although errors may have been introduced during **imputation**, the methods used have been rigorously tested to minimize systematic errors.

Various studies are being carried out to evaluate the quality of the responses obtained in the 2001 Census. For each question, non-response rates and edit failure rates have been calculated. These can be useful in identifying the potential for non-response errors and other types of errors. Also, tabulations from the 2001 Census have been or will be compared with corresponding estimates from previous censuses, from sample surveys (such as the Labour Force Survey) and from various administrative records (such as birth registrations and municipal assessment records). Such comparisons can indicate potential quality problems or at least discrepancies between the sources.

In addition to these aggregate-level comparisons, there are some micro-match studies in progress, in which census responses are compared with another source of information at the individual record level. For certain "stable" characteristics (such as age, sex, mother tongue and place of birth), the responses obtained in the 2001 Census, for a sample of individuals, are being compared with those for the same individuals in the 1996 Census.

Sampling Errors

Estimates obtained by weighting up responses collected on a sample basis are subject to error due to the fact that the distribution of characteristics within the sample will not usually be identical to the distribution of characteristics within the population from which the sample has been selected.

The potential error introduced by sampling will vary according to the relative scarcity of the characteristics in the population. For large cell values, the potential error due to sampling, as a proportion of the cell value, will be relatively small. For small cell values, this potential error, as a proportion of the cell value, will be relatively large.

The potential error due to sampling is usually expressed in terms of the so-called "standard error". This is the square root of the average, taken over all possible samples of the same size and design, of the squared deviation of the sample estimate from the value for the total population.

The following table provides approximate measures of the standard error due to sampling. These measures are intended as a general guide only.

Approximate Standard Error Due to Sampling for 2001 Census Sample Data

Cell Value	Approximate Standard Error
50 or less	15
100	20
200	30
500	45
1,000	65
2,000	90
5,000	140
10,000	200
20,000	280
50,000	450
100,000	630
500,000	1,400

Users wishing to determine the approximate error due to sampling for any given cell of data, based upon the 20% sample, should choose the standard error value corresponding to the cell value that is closest to the value of the given cell in the census tabulation. When using the obtained standard error value, the user, in general, can be reasonably certain that, for the enumerated population, the true value (discounting all forms of error other than sampling) lies within plus or minus three times the standard error (e.g. for a cell value of 1,000, the range would be 1,000 ± [3 x 65] or 1,000 ± 195).

The standard errors given in the table above will not apply to population, household, dwelling or family counts for the geographic area under consideration (see Sampling and Weighting below). The effect of sampling for these cells can be determined by a comparison with a corresponding 100% data product.

The effect of the particular sample design and weighting procedure used in the 2001 Census will vary, however, from one characteristic to another and from one geographic area to another. The standard error values in the table may, therefore, understate or overstate the error due to sampling.

Sampling and Weighting

The 2001 Census data were collected either from 100% of the households or on a sample basis (i.e. from a random sample of one in five households) with the data weighted up to provide estimates for the entire population. The information was collected on a 20% sample basis and weighted up to compensate for sampling. All table headings are noted accordingly. Note that, on Indian reserves and in remote areas, all data were collected on a 100% basis.

For any given geographic area, the weighted population, household, dwelling or family total or subtotal may differ from that shown in reports containing data collected on a 100% basis. Such variations are due to sampling and to the fact that, unlike sample data, 100% data do not exclude institutional residents.

Confidentiality and Random Rounding

The figures shown in the tables have been subjected to a confidentiality procedure known as **random rounding** to prevent the possibility of associating statistical data with any identifiable individual. Under this method, all figures, including totals and margins, are randomly rounded either up or down to a multiple of "5", and in some cases "10". While providing strong protection against disclosure, this technique does not add significant error to the census data. The user should be aware that totals and margins are rounded independently of the cell data so that some differences between these and the sum of rounded cell data may exist. Also, minor differences can be expected in corresponding totals and cell values among various census tabulations. Similarly, percentages, which are calculated on rounded figures, do not necessarily add up to 100%. Order statistics (median, quartiles, percentiles, etc.) and measures of dispersion such as the standard error are computed in the usual manner. When a statistic is defined as the quotient of two numbers (which is the case for averages, percentages, and proportions), the two numbers are rounded before the division is performed. For income, owner's payments, value of dwelling, hours worked, weeks worked and age, the sum is defined as the product of the average and the rounded weighted frequency. Otherwise, it is the weighted sum that is rounded. It should also be noted that small cell counts may suffer a significant distortion as a result of random rounding. Individual data cells containing small numbers may lose their precision as a result. Also, a statistic is suppressed if the number of actual records used in the calculation is less than 4 or if the sum of the weight of these records is less than 10. In addition, for values expressed in dollar units, other rules are applied. For standard products, if all the values are the same, the statistic is suppressed. For all other products, the statistic is suppressed if the range of the values is too narrow or if all values are less than, in absolute value, to a specified threshold.

Users should be aware of possible data distortions when they are aggregating these rounded data. Imprecisions as a result of rounding tend to cancel each other out when data cells are re-aggregated. However, users can minimize these distortions by using, whenever possible, the appropriate subtotals when aggregating.

For those requiring maximum precision, the option exists to use custom tabulations. With custom products, aggregation is done using individual census database records. Random rounding occurs only after the data cells have been aggregated, thus minimizing any distortion.

In addition to random rounding, **area suppression** has been adopted to further protect the confidentiality of individual responses.

Area suppression is the deletion of all characteristic data for geographic areas with populations below a specified size. The extent to which data are suppressed depends upon the following factors:

- If the data are tabulated from the 100% database, they are suppressed if the total population in the area is less than 40.

- If the data are tabulated from the 20% sample database, they are suppressed if the total non-institutional population in the area from either the 100% or 20% database is less than 40.

There are some exceptions to these rules:

- Income distributions and related statistics are suppressed if the population in the area, excluding institutional residents, is less than 250 from either the 100% or the 20% database, or if the number of private households is less than 40 from the 20% database.

- Place-of-work distributions and related statistics are suppressed if the total number of employed persons in the area is less than 40, according to the sample database. If the data also include an income distribution, the threshold is raised to 250, again according to the sample database.

- Tabulations covering both place of work and place of residence along with related statistics are suppressed, if the total number of employed persons in the area is less than 40 according to the sample database, or if the area's total population, excluding institutional residents, according to either the 100% or the sample database, is less than 40. If the tabulations also include an income distribution, the threshold is raised to 250 in all cases and the tabulations are suppressed if the number of private dwellings in the place of residence area is less than 40.

- Same-sex couples distributions and related statistics are suppressed if the population in private households in the area is less than 5,000, according to the 20% sample database.

- If the data are tabulated from the 100% database and refer to six-character postal codes or to groups of either blocks or block-faces, they are suppressed if the total population in the area is less than 100.

- If the data are tabulated from the 20% sample database and refer to six-character postal codes or to groups of either blocks or block-faces, they are suppressed if the total non-institutional population in the area from either the 100% or 20% database is less than 100.

- If the data refer to groups of either blocks or block-faces, and cover place of work, they are suppressed if the total number of employed persons in the area is less than 100, according to the sample database.

- If the data refer to groups of either blocks or block-faces, and cover both place of work and place of residence, they are suppressed if the total number of employed persons in the area is less than 100, according to the sample database, or if the area's total population, excluding institutional residents, according to either 100% or the sample database, is less than 100.

In all cases, suppressed data are included in the appropriate higher aggregate subtotals and totals.

The suppression technique is being implemented for all products involving subprovincial data (i.e. Profile series, basic cross-tabulations, semi-custom and custom data products) collected on a 100% or 20% sample basis.

For further information on the quality of census data, contact the Social Survey Methods Division at Statistics Canada, Ottawa, Ontario, Canada K1A 0T6, or by calling (613) 951-4783.

Special Notes

Aboriginal Identity

Users should be aware that the population counts associated with this variable are more affected than most by the incomplete enumeration of certain Indian reserves and Indian settlements. The extent of the impact will depend on the geographical area under study. In 2001, a total of 30 Indian reserves and Indian settlements were incompletely enumerated by the census. The population of these 30 communities are not included in the census counts.

Changes to Family Concepts for the 2001 Census

For the 1996 Census, the definition of census family was as follows:

Refers to a now-married couple (with or without never-married sons and/or daughters of either or both spouses), a couple living common-law (with or without never-married sons and/or daughters of either or both partners) or a lone-parent of any marital status, with at least one never-married son or daughter living in the same dwelling.

This reflected a concept that had not changed since 1976. However, during the planning for the 2001 Census, it was decided that some changes were required, due to the following factors: (1) changes to federal and provincial legislation putting same-sex couples on an equal footing with opposite-sex common-law couples (most notably Bill C-23, the *Modernization of Benefits and Obligations Act*, which was passed by the Government of Canada in 2000); (2) recommendations by the United Nations as part of a process of standardization of concepts for the 2000-2001 round of censuses in member countries; and (3) a significant number of persons less than 15 years of age classified as "non-family persons" in previous censuses.

As a result, the census family concept for the 2001 Census reflects the following changes:

- Two persons living in a same-sex common-law relationship, along with any of their children residing in the household, are considered a census family.
- Children in a census family can have been previously married (as long as they are not currently living with a spouse or common-law partner). Previously, they had to be "never-married".
- A grandchild living in a three-generation household where the parent (middle generation) is never-married is, contrary to previous censuses, now considered as a child in the census family of his or her parent, provided the grandchild is not living with his or her own spouse, common-law partner, or child. Traditionally, the census family usually consisted of the two older generations.
- A grandchild of another household member, where a middle-generation parent is not present, is now considered as a child in the census family of his or her grandparent, provided the grandchild is not living with his or her own spouse, common-law partner, or child. Traditionally, such a grandchild would not be considered as a member of a census family.

The last three changes listed (definition of "child"), together, result in a 1.5% increase in the total number of census families, and in a 10.1% increase in the number of lone-parent families. The inclusion of same-sex couples results in a 0.4% increase in the number of census families at the national level.

The term economic family refers to a group of two or more persons who live in the same dwelling and are related to each other by blood, marriage, common-law or adoption. This definition has not changed for 2001. The only effect of conceptual changes on economic families is that same-sex partners are now considered to be common-law partners. Thus they are considered related and members of the same economic family.

Outside of the "family universe", there are two related concepts that are affected by the change in the census family definition: common-law status and household type. Prior to 2001, two people living together as husband and wife without being legally married to each other were considered to be living common-law. For 2001, this has been expanded to include persons living in a same-sex partnership. The concept of household type refers to the basic division of private households into family and non-family households. Since it is based on the census family concept, the household type (whether a household is "family" or "non-family") is affected by the change. Also, the detailed classification of this variable is affected, since married couples and common-law couples were broken down into those "without never-married sons or daughters" and "with never-married sons or daughters". For 2001 this reads "without children" and "with children", with the attendant change in meaning.

Comparability of 2001 Place of Work Data

Working at home can be measured in different ways. In the census, the "Worked at home" category includes persons who live and work at the same physical location, such as farmers, teleworkers and work camp workers. In addition, the 2001 Census Guide instructed persons who worked part of the time at home and part of the time at an employer's address to indicate that they "Worked at home" if most of their time was spent working at home (e.g. three days out of five).

Other Statistics Canada surveys such as the General Social Survey, the Survey of Labour and Income Dynamics, and the Workplace and Employee Survey also collect information on working at home. However, the survey data are not directly comparable to the census data since the surveys ask respondents whether they did some or all of their paid work at home, whereas the census asks them where they usually worked most of the time. Consequently, census estimates on work at home are lower than survey estimates.

The place-of-work question has remained in virtually the same format in each census since 1971. However, in 1996, the category "No fixed workplace address" replaced "No usual place of work". In 1996, the census questionnaire was modified by adding a check box for the "No fixed workplace" response category. In previous censuses, respondents were asked to write "No usual place of work" in the address fields. It is believed that previous censuses have undercounted the number of persons with "No fixed workplace address".

Annexations, incorporations and amalgamations of municipalities could create some difficulties when comparing spatial units and structures which change over time.

Data Quality for School Attendance

The overall quality of the education variables from the 2001 Census is acceptable. However, users of the 2001 Census data on school attendance are cautioned that the counts for the 15 to 19 year olds not attending school category may be too high. The proportion of persons aged 15 to 19 who indicated they had not attended school in the school year prior to the census increased from 18% in 1996 to 23% in 2001. This variable requires further research.

Data Quality – Relationship of Census Income Estimates to the National Accounts and Survey of Labour and Income Dynamics

Census income estimates of aggregate income in 2000 were compared to similar personal income estimates from the national accounts. After adjustments to the personal income estimates for differences in concepts and coverage, the census estimate of aggregate income in 2000 from comparable sources was 4.1% lower than the national accounts estimate. As in the past, census estimates for some income components and for some provinces compared more favourably than for others.

Census estimates of aggregate wages and salaries, the largest component of income, were almost identical to the national accounts estimates. Although there was a large difference between the two estimates of net income from farm self-employment (the smallest component of individual earnings), census estimates of aggregate income from both farm and non-farm self-employment were lower by 1%. Overall, estimates of total income from employment were nearly identical.

Census estimates of Old Age Security pensions and the Guaranteed Income Supplement were about 5% higher, while those for Canada/Quebec Pension Plan benefits were about 9% lower, than adjusted national accounts estimates. Employment Insurance benefits reported in the census were smaller by about 6%. Estimates of aggregate Canada Child Tax benefits were nearly identical in both estimates. Census estimates of other government transfer payments, which include such items as social welfare benefits, provincial income supplements to seniors, veterans' pensions and GST/HST/QST refunds, were significantly below the estimates from the national accounts. Overall, census estimates of aggregate income from all government transfer payments were lower by about 13%. As in previous census-year comparisons, the census estimate of investment income was significantly lower, by 32% in 2000, than the national accounts estimate.

Census income statistics were also compared with similar statistics from the annual Survey of Labour and Income Dynamics (SLID). SLID estimates reflect adjustments made for population undercoverage, while census estimates do not include such an adjustment. This adjustment contributes to census estimates showing fewer income recipients (by 3.4%) and earners (by 7.2%) than SLID estimates. Consequently, census estimates of aggregate earnings are 4% lower than the SLID estimate, while the census estimate of aggregate total income of individuals is lower by 3%. Most of the observed provincial differences were considered acceptable in the light of sampling errors in the Survey.

Immigration and Citizenship Data

Persons living on Indian reserves and Indian settlements, who were enumerated with the 2001 Census Form 2D questionnaire, were not asked the citizenship and immigration questions. Consequently, data are not shown for Indian reserves and Indian settlements at the lower geographic levels. These data, however, are included in the totals for larger geographic areas, such as census divisions and provinces.

Impact of Municipal Restructuring

The boundaries and names of municipalities (census subdivisions) can change from one census to the next because of annexations, dissolutions and incorporations. However, since the 1996 Census, the changes are more numerous and more dramatic, especially in the provinces of Quebec, Ontario and British Columbia. In general, data from the 2001 Census are available for fewer and larger census subdivisions, and historical analyses are more complex. To bridge the impact of these municipal changes on data dissemination, the 2001 Census is producing a profile for dissolved census subdivisions.

Income Reference Period

Canadian censuses were conducted in 1996 and 2001. Income data from these censuses relate to the calendar year prior to the census year, i.e. 1995 and 2000 respectively.

Income Suppression

Area suppression is the deletion of all characteristic data for geographic areas with populations below a specified size. Income distributions and related statistics are suppressed if the population in the area, excluding institutional residents, is less than 250 from either the 100% or the 20% database, or if the number of private households is less than 40 from the 20% database.

Migration Data for Small Geographic Areas

Estimates of internal migration may be less accurate for small geographic areas, areas with a place name which is duplicated elsewhere, and for some Census Subdivisions (CSD) where previous residents may have provided the name of the Census Metropolitan Area or Census Agglomeration instead of the specific name of the component CSD from which they migrated.

Non-permanent Residents

In 1991, 1996 and 2001, the Census of Population enumerated both permanent and non-permanent residents of Canada. Non-permanent residents are persons who held a student or employment authorization, Minister's permit, or who were refugee claimants, at the time of the census. Family members living with these persons are also classified as non-permanent residents.

Prior to 1991, only permanent residents of Canada were included in the census. (The only exception to this occurred in 1941.) Non-permanent residents were considered foreign residents and were not enumerated.

Today in Canada, non-permanent residents make up a significant segment of the population, especially in several census metropolitan areas. Their presence can affect the demand for such government services as health care, schooling, employment programs and language training. The inclusion of non-permanent residents in the census facilitates comparisons with provincial and territorial statistics (marriages, divorces, births and deaths) which include this population. In addition, this inclusion of non-permanent residents brings Canadian practice closer to the UN recommendation that long-term residents (persons living in a country for one year or longer) be enumerated in the census.

According to the 1996 Census, there were 166,715 non-permanent residents in Canada, representing 0.6% of the total population. There were slightly more non-permanent residents in Canada at the time of the 2001 Census: 198,645 non-permanent residents, or 0.7% of the total population.

Total population counts, as well as counts for all variables, are affected by this change in the census universe. Users should be especially careful when comparing data from 1991, 1996 or 2001 with data from previous censuses in geographic areas where there is a concentration of non-permanent residents. Such areas include the major metropolitan areas in Ontario, Quebec and British Columbia.

Although every attempt has been made to enumerate non-permanent residents, factors such as language difficulties, the reluctance to complete a government form or to understand the need to participate may have affected the enumeration of this population.

Nunavut

Data from the 2001 Census are available for Nunavut, the new territory that came into effect on April 1, 1999.

Standard data products released only at the Canada/Province/Territory geographic levels will not contain data for Nunavut for the census years prior to 2001.

Standard data products released at the Census Metropolitan Area (CMA) and Census Agglomeration (CA) geographic levels will contain data for Nunavut for the 2001, 1996 and/or 1991 Censuses.

The 1996 and 1991 CMA/CA data have been adjusted to reflect as closely as possible the 2001 CMA/CA geographic boundaries. This has been done to facilitate data comparisons using the 2001 geographic boundaries.

Ontario Census Tracts

A database error affected the presentation of the 1996 population counts for two census tracts (CTs), namely CTs 0520.05 and 0520.06, in the Census Metropolitan Area (CMA) of Toronto. The data for these CTs are correct but inverted: 0520.05 contains the data for 0520.06, and 0520.06 contains the data for 0520.05. Because of operational constraints, it was not possible to make adjustments to the 1996 database (adjusted counts) for these two CTs. Care should therefore be exercised when using these data.

Population 15 Years and Over Who Worked Since 2000

Refers to those who have worked since January 1, 2000, regardless of whether or not they were in the labour force in the reference week.

Population and Dwelling Count Amendments

After the release of the population and dwelling counts, errors are occasionally uncovered in the data. It is not possible to make changes to the 2001 Census data presented in these tables. Users can, however, obtain the population and dwelling count amendments listed by census subdivisions and other levels of geography by visiting the 2001 Census portion of the Statistics Canada Web site at www.statcan.ca. In addition, users can contact the nearest Statistics Canada regional reference centre by telephone at 1 800 263-1136 or by e-mail at infostats@statcan.ca.

Population Counts

The 2001 Census population counts for a particular area represent the number of Canadians whose usual place of residence is in that area, regardless of where they happened to be on Census Day. Also included are any Canadians who were staying in that area on Census Day and who had no usual place of residence elsewhere in Canada, as well as those considered to be "non-permanent residents" (see the Special Notes). For most areas, there is little difference between the number of usual residents and the number of people staying in the area on Census Day. For certain places, however, such as tourist or vacation areas, or those including large work camps, the number of people staying in that area at any particular time could significantly exceed the number of usual residents shown here. The population counts include Canadians living in other countries, but do not include foreign residents living in Canada (the "foreign residents" category does not include "non-permanent residents" - see the Special Notes). Given these differences, users are advised not to interpret population counts as being the number of people living in the reported dwellings.

Structural Type of Dwelling

The 2001 Census collected data for two new categories for structural type of dwelling:

Apartment with direct ground access in a building that has fewer than five storeys; and Apartment without direct ground access in a building that has fewer than five storeys.

Postcensal data evaluation has revealed a serious misclassification problem with these dwellings. As a result, the data will not be released.

Data for "Apartment in a building that has fewer than five storeys" have been released in 2001 products. This category is an aggregate of the two new previously mentioned categories, and is directly comparable with the same category from previous censuses. It presents no data problems.

Appendix 1. Incompletely Enumerated Indian Reserves and Indian Settlements, 1996 and 1991 Population Counts

Province	Incompletely enumerated Indian reserves and Indian settlements, 2001	Population	
		1996	1991
Quebec	Akwesasne (Partie)	¶	¶
	Doncaster 17	0	4
	Kahnawake 14	¶	¶
	Kanesatake	¶	¶
	Lac-Rapide	228	¶
Ontario	Akwesasne (Part) 59 (formerly Akwesasne [Part])	¶	¶
	Bear Island 1	153	¶
	Chippewas of the Thames First Nation 42 (formerly Chippewa of the Thames First Nation)	¶	¶
	Goulais Bay 15A	¶	¶
	Marten Falls 65	204	187
	Moose Factory 68	0	0
	Munsee-Delaware Nation 1	¶	¶
	Ojibway Nation of Saugeen (Savant Lake) (formerly Savant Lake)	¶	171
	Oneida 41	¶	¶
	Pikangikum 14	1,170	1,303
	Rankin Location 15D	¶	¶
	Six Nations (Part) 40 (Brant County)	¶	¶
	Six Nations (Part) 40 (Haldimand-Norfolk Regional Municipality)	¶	¶
	Tyendinaga Mohawk Territory (formerly Tyendinaga 38)	¶	¶
	Wahta Mohawk Territory (formerly Gibson 31)	¶	130
	Whitefish Bay 32A	¶	¶
	Whitesand	115	0
Manitoba	Dakota Tipi 1	¶	72
Saskatchewan	Big Head 124	¶	¶
Alberta	Ermineskin 138	¶	¶
	Little Buffalo	¶	186
	Saddle Lake 125	¶	1,893
British Columbia	Esquimalt	¶	¶
	Marble Canyon 3	67	¶
	Pavilion 1	76	73

Appendix 2. Suppressed Census Tracts Showing Population Counts by Census Metropolitan Area and Census Agglomeration, 2001 Census

Suppressed Census Tracts	Population Counts (100% Data)	Population Counts (20% Sample Data)
Belleville CA		
0010	35	34
0013 **A**	10	4
0014 **A**	33	33
0405	-	-
0407	-	-
Edmonton CMA		
0015.01	5	4
0016.01	-	-
0019.01	-	-
0052.01	-	-
0064.02	-	-
0065.03	-	-
0090.07	-	-
Granby CA		
0003 **A**	38	38
Greater Sudbury CMA		
0013	-	-
Halifax CMA		
0155 ◆◆◆◇◇◇ **A**	15	14
Kitchener CMA		
0106.03 ◆◆◆◇◇◇	5	2
Lethbridge CA		
0010	25	15
London CMA		
0035	-	-
Montréal CMA		
0014.02	23	23
0040	-	-
0071	-	-
0091	-	-
0094.02	-	-
0127.02	17	17
0145	-	-
0189	-	-
0229	-	-
0268.03	-	-
0440	-	-
0832 ¶		-
Ottawa - Hull CMA		
0140.01	20	16
Saint John CMA		
0005	15	6
Saint-Jean-sur-Richelieu CA		
0006	5	-
0010	-	-
0303	-	-
Toronto CMA		
0003	-	-
0376.06 ◇	35	20
0401.05	5	5
Trois-Rivières CMA		
0301	39	38
Vancouver CMA		
0270	-	-
Winnipeg CMA		
0052	-	-

Note:

For more information on the 2001 suppression rules, please see the Data Quality section in the Reference Material of this publication.

Regional Reference Centres

The Advisory Services Division of Statistics Canada provides an information dissemination network across the country through eight regional reference centres. Each reference centre has a collection of current publications and reference documents that can be consulted or purchased, along with diskettes, CD-ROMs, maps, and other products. Copying facilities for printed materials are available on site.

Each reference centre provides a wide range of additional services. Advisory Services can provide assistance in helping you identify your informational needs, establish sources of available data, consolidate and integrate data from different sources, develop profiles, provide analysis of highlights or tendencies and, finally, provide training on products, services, Statistics Canada concepts and the use of statistical data.

For more information, call the National Toll-free Enquiries Line listed below or send an e-mail to infostats@statcan.ca.

Contact Us

National Toll-free **Enquiries** Line
(Canada and United States):
1 800 263-1136

TTY: 1 800 363-7629

Toll-free **Order Only** Line (Canada and United States): 1 800 267-6677

National Toll-free **Fax Order** Line
(Canada and United States):
1 877 287-4369

E-mail: infostats@statcan.ca

Atlantic Region

Serving the provinces of Newfoundland and Labrador, Nova Scotia, Prince Edward Island and New Brunswick.

Advisory Services
Statistics Canada
2nd Floor, Box 11
1741 Brunswick Street
Halifax, Nova Scotia
B3J 3X8

Toll-free number: 1 800 263-1136
Local calls: (902) 426-5331
Fax number: (902) 426-9538
E-mail: infostats@statcan.ca

Quebec Region

Serving the province of Quebec and the territory of Nunavut except the National Capital Region.

Advisory Services
Statistics Canada
4th Floor, East Tower
Guy Favreau Complex
200 René Lévesque Blvd. W
Montréal, Quebec
H2Z 1X4

Toll-free number: 1 800 263-1136
Local calls: (514) 283-5725
Fax number: (514) 283-9350
E-mail: infostats@statcan.ca

National Capital Region

Serving the National Capital Region.

Statistical Reference Centre
(National Capital Region)
Statistics Canada
Main Building, Room 1500
120 Parkdale Avenue
Ottawa, Ontario
K1A 0T6

Toll-free number: 1 800 263-1136
Local calls: (613) 951-8116
Fax number: (613) 951-0581
E-mail: infostats@statcan.ca

Ontario Region

Serving the province of Ontario except the National Capital Region.

Advisory Services
Statistics Canada
Arthur Meighen Building, 10th Floor
25 St. Clair Avenue E
Toronto, Ontario
M4T 1M4

Toll-free number: 1 800 263-1136
Local calls: (416) 973-6586
Fax number: (416) 973-7475
E-mail: infostats@statcan.ca

Prairie Region

This region has three reference centres serving the provinces of Manitoba, Saskatchewan, Alberta and the Northwest Territories.

Serving the province of Manitoba:

Advisory Services
Statistics Canada
Via Rail Building, Suite 200
123 Main Street
Winnipeg, Manitoba
R3C 4V9

Toll-free number: 1 800 263-1136
Local calls: (204) 983-4020
Fax number: (204) 983-7543
E-mail: infostats@statcan.ca

Prairie Region – concluded

Serving the province of Saskatchewan:

Advisory Services
Statistics Canada
Park Plaza, Suite 440
2365 Albert Street
Regina, Saskatchewan
S4P 4K1

Toll-free number: 1 800 263-1136
Local calls: (306) 780-5405
Fax number: (306) 780-5403
E-mail: infostats@statcan.ca

Serving Alberta and the Northwest Territories:

Advisory Services
Statistics Canada
Pacific Plaza, Suite 900
10909 Jasper Avenue NW
Edmonton, Alberta
T5J 4J3

Toll-free number: 1 800 263-1136
Local calls: (780) 495-3027
Fax number: (780) 495-5318
E-mail: infostats@statcan.ca

Pacific Region

Serving the province of British Columbia and the Yukon Territory.

Advisory Services
Statistics Canada
Library Square Tower
600-300 West Georgia Street
Vancouver, British Columbia
V6B 6C7

Toll-free number: 1 800 263-1136
Local calls: (604) 666-3691
Fax number: (604) 666-4863
E-mail: infostats@statcan.ca

Définitions

Pour de plus amples renseignements sur les définitions et les notes spéciales, veuillez consultez le Dictionnaire du recensement de 2001, n° 92-378-XIF ou 92-378-XPF au catalogue.

Activité (pendant la semaine de référence)

Activité sur le marché du travail des personnes âgées de 15 ans et plus au cours de la semaine (du dimanche au samedi) ayant précédé le jour du recensement (le 15 mai 2001). Les recensés sont classés dans les catégories « Personnes occupées », « Chômeurs » ou « Inactifs ». La population active comprend les personnes occupées et les chômeurs.

Personnes occupées (pendant la semaine de référence)
Personnes âgées de 15 ans et plus, à l'exclusion des pensionnaires d'un établissement institutionnel, qui, au cours de la semaine (du dimanche au samedi) ayant précédé le jour du recensement (le 15 mai 2001) :

a) avaient fait un travail quelconque à un emploi salarié ou à leur compte ou sans rémunération dans une ferme ou une entreprise familiale ou dans l'exercice d'une profession;

b) étaient temporairement absentes de leur travail ou de l'entreprise, avec ou sans rémunération, toute la semaine à cause de vacances, d'une maladie, d'un conflit de travail à leur lieu de travail, ou encore pour d'autres raisons.

Chômeurs (pendant la semaine de référence)
Personnes âgées de 15 ans et plus, à l'exclusion des pensionnaires d'un établissement institutionnel, qui, pendant la semaine (du dimanche au samedi) ayant précédé le jour du recensement (le 15 mai 2001), étaient sans emploi salarié et sans travail à leur compte, étaient prêtes à travailler et :

a) avaient activement cherché un emploi salarié au cours des quatre semaines précédentes; ou

b) avaient été mises à pied mais prévoyaient reprendre leur emploi; ou

c) avaient pris des arrangements définis en vue de se présenter à un nouvel emploi dans les quatre semaines suivantes.

Inactifs (pendant la semaine de référence)
Personnes âgées de 15 ans et plus, à l'exclusion des pensionnaires d'un établissement institutionnel, qui, pendant la semaine (du dimanche au samedi) ayant précédé le jour du recensement (le 15 mai 2001), n'étaient ni occupées ni en chômage. Les inactifs comprennent les étudiants, les personnes au foyer, les retraités, les travailleurs saisonniers en période de relâche qui ne cherchaient pas un travail et les personnes qui ne pouvaient travailler en raison d'une maladie chronique ou d'une incapacité à long terme.

Population active (pendant la semaine de référence)
Personnes qui étaient soit occupées, soit en chômage pendant la semaine (du dimanche au samedi) ayant précédé le jour du recensement (le 15 mai 2001).

Au cours des recensements précédents, cette variable était appelée « Population active totale ».

Taux d'activité (pendant la semaine de référence)
Pourcentage de la population active pendant la semaine (du dimanche au samedi) ayant précédé le jour du recensement (le 15 mai 2001) par rapport aux personnes âgées de 15 ans et plus à l'exclusion des pensionnaires d'un établissement institutionnel.

Le taux d'activité d'un groupe donné (âge, sexe, état matrimonial, région géographique, etc.) correspond au nombre total d'actifs dans ce groupe, exprimé en pourcentage des personnes âgées de 15 ans et plus, de ce groupe.

Taux d'emploi (pendant la semaine de référence)
Pourcentage de la population occupée au cours de la semaine (du dimanche au samedi) ayant précédé le jour du recensement (le 15 mai 2001), par rapport au pourcentage de la population de 15 ans et plus à l'exclusion des pensionnaires d'un établissement institutionnel.

Le taux d'emploi pour un groupe donné (âge, sexe, état matrimonial, région géographique, etc.) correspond au nombre de personnes occupées dans ce groupe, exprimé en pourcentage des personnes âgées de 15 ans et plus, de ce groupe.

Au cours des recensements antérieurs, cette variable était appelée « Rapport emploi-population ».

Taux de chômage (pendant la semaine de référence)
Pourcentage de la population en chômage par rapport à la population active pendant la semaine (du dimanche au samedi) ayant précédé le jour du recensement (le 15 mai 2001).

Le taux de chômage d'un groupe donné (âge, sexe, état matrimonial, région géographique, etc.) correspond au nombre de chômeurs dans ce groupe exprimé en pourcentage de la population active dans ce groupe pendant la semaine ayant précédé le recensement.

Âge

Âge au dernier anniversaire de naissance (à la date de référence du recensement, soit le 15 mai 2001). Cette variable est établie d'après la réponse à la question sur la date de naissance.

Âge à l'immigration

Âge du recensé lorsqu'il a obtenu pour la première fois le statut d'immigrant reçu. Un immigrant reçu est une personne à qui les autorités de l'immigration ont accordé le droit de résider au Canada en permanence.

Agglomération de recensement (AR)

Se reporter à la définition de Région métropolitaine de recensement (RMR) et agglomération de recensement (AR).

Catégorie de lieu de travail

Lieu de travail des personnes âgées de 15 ans et plus, à l'exclusion des pensionnaires d'un établissement institutionnel, qui ont travaillé depuis le 1er janvier 2000. La variable se rapporte habituellement à l'emploi occupé par les recensés au cours de la semaine ayant précédé le recensement. Toutefois, dans le cas des personnes qui n'ont pas travaillé cette semaine-là, mais qui avaient travaillé à un moment quelconque depuis le 1er janvier 2000, les données portent sur l'emploi occupé le plus longtemps au cours de cette période.

À domicile – Les personnes dont le lieu de travail et la résidence se trouvaient dans le même immeuble, celles qui habitaient la ferme où elles travaillaient, les concierges d'immeuble et les télétravailleurs qui travaillaient à domicile pendant la plus grande partie de leur semaine de travail.

En dehors du Canada – Personnes dont le lieu de travail est à l'extérieur du Canada. Les diplomates, les membres des Forces armées et les autres personnes dénombrées à l'étranger, de même que les nouveaux immigrants ne travaillant pas en ce moment, mais dont l'emploi de plus longue durée depuis le 1er janvier 2000 avait été exercé à l'extérieur du Canada.

Sans adresse de travail fixe – Les personnes qui ne se rendaient pas au même lieu de travail au début de chaque quart, notamment les entrepreneurs en bâtiments, les entrepreneurs paysagistes, les représentants de commerce, les chauffeurs de camion indépendants, etc.

À l'adresse précisée ci-dessous – Les personnes qui ne sont pas incluses dans les catégories ci-dessus et qui se rendent au même lieu de travail (habituel) au début de chaque quart sont incluses ici. Les recensés devaient inscrire le numéro de voirie, la ville, le village, le canton, la municipalité ou la réserve indienne, la province ou le territoire et le code postal de leur lieu de travail. Ceux qui ne connaissaient pas l'adresse complète pouvaient donner uniquement le nom de l'immeuble ou de l'intersection la plus proche.

Les télétravailleurs qui passaient moins que la moitié de la semaine de travail à leur bureau à domicile devaient donner l'adresse complète de leur employeur. Les personnes qui travaillaient à des endroits différents, mais se présentaient à un siège social au début de chaque quart devaient donner l'adresse complète du siège social.

Catégorie de revenu

Situation de la famille économique ou de la personne hors famille économique de 15 ans et plus par rapport aux seuils de faible revenu (SFR) de Statistique Canada.

Catégorie de travailleurs

Variable permettant de classer les personnes qui ont déclaré un emploi selon les catégories suivantes :

a) personnes qui ont travaillé principalement pour un salaire, pour un traitement, à commission, pour des pourboires, à la pièce ou contre rémunération « en nature » (paiements sous forme de biens ou de services, plutôt qu'en espèces);

b) personnes qui ont travaillé surtout à leur compte, avec ou sans aide rémunérée dans une entreprise, une ferme ou à exercer une profession, seules ou avec des associés;

c) personnes qui ont travaillé sans rémunération à exercer une profession ou dans une entreprise ou une ferme familiale appartenant à un parent du même ménage ou exploitée par celui-ci; le travail familial non rémunéré ne comprend pas les travaux ménagers non rémunérés, les soins aux enfants non rémunérés, les soins ou l'aide aux personnes âgées non rémunérés, ni le travail bénévole.

L'emploi déclaré désigne l'emploi que la personne occupait au cours de la semaine (du dimanche au samedi) ayant précédé le recensement (le 15 mai 2001) si elle avait travaillé, l'emploi qu'elle a occupé le plus longtemps depuis le 1er janvier 2000, si la personne n'avait pas travaillé au cours de la semaine de référence. Les personnes ayant occupé deux emplois ou plus cette semaine-là devaient donner des renseignements sur celui auquel elles avaient consacré le plus grand nombre d'heures.

Forme juridique

Forme juridique des entreprises commerciales ou agricoles ou dans l'exercice d'une profession. Cette variable s'applique aux personnes qui travaillaient surtout à leur compte, avec ou sans aide rémunérée, dans l'emploi déclaré, c'est-à-dire l'emploi qu'elles avaient pendant la semaine (du dimanche au samedi) ayant précédé le recensement (le 15 mai 2001) ou l'emploi qu'elles ont occupé le plus longtemps depuis le 1er janvier 2000. Une **entreprise constituée en société** est une entreprise ou une ferme ou l'exercice d'une profession ayant une entité juridique constituée sous le régime de lois provinciales ou fédérales. Une **entreprise** ou une ferme ou l'exercice d'une profession **non constituée en société** ne représente pas une entité juridique distincte; il peut toutefois s'agir d'une société en nom collectif, d'une entreprise familiale ou d'une entreprise exploitée par le propriétaire.

Chambres à coucher

Pièces conçues et meublées pour servir de chambres à coucher et utilisées principalement pour y dormir, même si ce n'est qu'à l'occasion (une chambre d'ami par exemple).

Citoyenneté

Statut légal de citoyenneté du recensé. Les personnes ayant plus d'une citoyenneté devaient indiquer le nom du ou des autres pays dont ils étaient citoyens.

Connaissance des langues non officielles

Indique les langues autres que le français ou l'anglais dans lesquelles le recensé peut soutenir une conversation.

Connaissance des langues officielles

Indique si le recensé peut soutenir une conversation en français seulement, en anglais seulement, en français et en anglais, ou dans aucune des deux langues officielles du Canada.

Division de recensement (DR)

Division de recensement (DR) est le terme général de régions créées en vertu des lois provinciales (comme les comtés, les municipalités régionales de comté et les regional districts) ou d'autres genres de régions. Les divisions de recensement sont des régions géographiques intermédiaires entre la municipalité (subdivision de recensement) et la province.

État du logement

Variable indiquant si, selon le répondant, le logement nécessite des réparations (à l'exception des rénovations ou ajouts souhaités).

État matrimonial légal

Situation conjugale légale d'une personne.

Voici la définition des diverses catégories de réponse :

Jamais légalement marié (célibataire) – Personne qui n'a jamais été mariée (y compris toute personne de moins de 15 ans) ou personne dont le mariage a été annulé et qui ne s'est pas remariée.

Légalement marié (et non séparé) – Personne mariée dont le conjoint est vivant, à moins que le couple ne soit séparé ou divorcé.

Séparé, mais toujours légalement marié – Personne actuellement mariée, mais qui ne vit plus avec son conjoint (pour quelque raison que ce soit autre que la maladie ou le travail) et qui n'a pas obtenu de divorce.

Divorcé – Personne qui a obtenu un divorce et qui ne s'est pas remariée.

Veuf ou veuve – Personne dont le conjoint est décédé et qui ne s'est pas remariée.

Famille de recensement

Couple marié (avec ou sans enfants des deux conjoints ou de l'un d'eux), couple vivant en union libre (avec ou sans enfants des deux partenaires ou de l'un d'eux) ou parent seul (peu importe son état matrimonial) demeurant avec au moins un enfant dans le même logement. Un couple vivant en union libre peut être de sexe opposé ou de même sexe. Les « enfants » dans une famille de recensement incluent les petits-enfants vivant dans le même ménage que leurs grands-parents, en l'absence des parents.

Famille économique

Groupe de deux personnes ou plus qui vivent dans le même logement et qui sont apparentées par le sang, par alliance, par union libre ou par adoption.

Fréquence des unités à faible revenu

Proportion ou pourcentage de familles économiques ou de personnes hors famille économique dans une catégorie donnée dont le revenu est inférieur aux seuils de faible revenu. Ces taux de fréquence sont calculés d'après des estimations non arrondies des familles économiques et des personnes hors famille économique âgées de 15 ans et plus.

Fréquentation scolaire

Fréquentation à plein temps ou à temps partiel (le jour ou le soir) d'une école, d'un collège ou d'une université au cours de la période de neuf mois allant de septembre 2000 au 15 mai 2001. La fréquentation est comptée seulement pour les cours permettant d'accumuler des crédits en vue de l'obtention d'un certificat, d'un diplôme ou d'un grade.

Genre de ménage

Répartition fondamentale des ménages privés en ménages familiaux et en ménages non familiaux. Un ménage familial est un ménage qui comprend au moins une famille de recensement, c'est-à-dire un couple marié avec ou sans enfants, ou un couple vivant en union libre avec ou sans enfants, ou un parent seul avec un ou plusieurs enfants (famille monoparentale). Un ménage unifamilial se compose d'une seule famille de recensement (avec ou sans autres personnes hors famille) qui occupe un logement privé. Un ménage multifamilial se compose de deux familles de recensement ou plus (avec ou sans autres personnes hors famille de recensement) qui occupent le même logement privé.

Un ménage non familial est constitué soit d'une personne vivant seule dans un logement privé, soit d'un groupe de deux personnes ou plus qui partagent un logement privé, mais qui ne forment pas une famille de recensement.

Genre de subdivision de recensement

Les subdivisions de recensement (SDR) sont classées en 46 genres, selon les appellations officielles adoptées par les autorités provinciales ou fédérales. Il y a toutefois deux exceptions, soit la *Subdivision of Unorganized* à Terre-Neuve-et-Labrador et la *Subdivision of County Municipality* en Nouvelle-Écosse, qui constituent des régions géographiques équivalant aux municipalités et qui ont été créées par Statistique Canada et ces provinces pour la diffusion de données statistiques.

Afin de mieux distinguer les SDR les unes des autres, le nom de chaque subdivision de recensement est généralement accompagné d'une indication du **genre de subdivision de recensement**, par exemple, Granby, V (pour la « ville » de Granby) et Granby, CT (pour la « municipalité de canton » de Granby).

Heures consacrées à offrir des soins ou de l'aide aux personnes âgées, sans paye ou sans salaire

Nombre d'heures que la personne a consacrées à offrir des soins ou de l'aide aux personnes âgées, sans salaire, pour des membres du ménage du recensé, pour d'autres membres âgés de la famille ne faisant pas partie du ménage, pour des amis ou des voisins pendant la semaine (du dimanche au samedi) ayant précédé le jour du recensement (le 15 mai 2001).

Les soins ou l'aide aux personnes âgées sans paye ou sans salaire ne comprennent pas le travail bénévole pour un organisme à but non lucratif, un organisme religieux, une oeuvre de charité ou un groupe communautaire ni le travail sans paye dans une ferme ou une entreprise familiale ou dans l'exercice d'une profession.

Heures consacrées aux soins des enfants, sans paye ou sans salaire

Nombre d'heures que la personne a consacrées à donner des soins aux enfants, sans paye ou sans salaire. Sont incluses les heures consacrées à donner des soins aux enfants, sans paye ou sans salaire, pour des membres du ménage du recensé, pour d'autres membres de la famille ne faisant pas partie du ménage, pour des amis ou des voisins ou d'autres membres de la famille à l'extérieur du ménage pendant la semaine (du dimanche au samedi) ayant précédé le jour du recensement (le 15 mai 2001).

Les soins aux enfants sans paye ou sans salaire ne comprennent pas le travail bénévole pour un organisme à but non lucratif, un organisme religieux, une oeuvre de charité ou un groupe communautaire ni le travail sans paye dans une ferme ou une entreprise familiale ou dans l'exercice d'une profession.

Heures consacrées aux travaux ménagers, sans paye ou sans salaire

Nombre d'heures que la personne a consacrées aux travaux ménagers, à l'entretien de la maison ou du jardin, sans paye ou sans salaire, pendant la semaine (du dimanche au samedi) ayant précédé le jour du recensement (le 15 mai 2001). Sont incluses les heures consacrées aux travaux ménagers, sans paye ou sans salaire, pour des membres du ménage du recensé, pour d'autres membres de la famille ne faisant pas partie du ménage, pour des amis ou des voisins.

Les travaux ménagers sans paye ou sans salaire ne comprennent pas le travail bénévole pour un organisme à but non lucratif, un organisme religieux, une oeuvre de charité ou un groupe communautaire ni le travail sans paye dans une ferme ou une entreprise familiale ou dans l'exercice d'une profession.

Identité autochtone

Personne ayant déclaré appartenir à au moins un groupe autochtone, c'est-à-dire Indien de l'Amérique du Nord, Métis ou Inuit (Esquimau) et/ou personne ayant déclaré être un Indien des traités ou un Indien inscrit tel que défini par la *Loi sur les Indiens* du Canada et/ou personne ayant déclaré appartenir à une bande indienne ou à une première nation. Lors du recensement de 1991 et des recensements antérieurs, la population autochtone était déterminée au moyen de la question sur l'origine ethnique (ancêtres). Au recensement de 1996, on a ajouté une question sur la propre perception du recensé face à son identité autochtone. La question du recensement de 2001 est la même que celle de 1996.

Indien inscrit ou Indien des traités

Personnes ayant déclaré être inscrites en vertu de la *Loi sur les Indiens* du Canada. Les Indiens des traités sont des personnes qui sont inscrites en vertu de la *Loi sur les Indiens* et qui peuvent démontrer qu'elles descendent d'une bande qui a signé un traité. La question sur le statut d'Indien inscrit a été posée en 1991; toutefois, la présentation de la question posée au recensement de 1996 était quelque peu différente. En 1991, l'appartenance à une bande indienne était un sous élément de la question 16 portant sur les Indiens inscrits. Le recensé devait indiquer s'il était un Indien inscrit dans la première partie de la question, puis préciser la bande indienne ou la première nation à laquelle il appartenait dans la deuxième partie de la question. En 1996, une question directe a été élaborée en vue de recueillir des données sur le statut d'Indien inscrit ou d'Indien des traités.

Le libellé de la question de 1996 différait légèrement de celui des questions posées aux recensements précédents. Avant 1996, le terme « Indien des traités » n'était pas utilisé dans la question. Il a été ajouté en 1996 à la demande des personnes des provinces de l'Ouest où ce terme est davantage utilisé.

Industrie (basée sur le Système de classification des industries de l'Amérique du Nord de 1997 [SCIAN])

Nature générale de l'activité de l'établissement où travaille la personne. Si la personne n'avait pas d'emploi au cours de la semaine (du dimanche au samedi) ayant précédé le recensement (le 15 mai 2001), elle devait donner des renseignements sur l'emploi qu'elle avait occupé le plus longtemps depuis le 1er janvier 2000. Les personnes qui avaient deux emplois ou plus devaient fournir des renseignements sur celui auquel elles avaient consacré le plus grand nombre d'heures de travail.

Les données sur l'industrie du recensement de 2001 sont produites en fonction du Système de classification des industries de l'Amérique du Nord (SCIAN) de 1997. Ce dernier, qui assure une meilleure comparabilité entre les données sur l'industrie des trois partenaires de l'Accord de libre-échange nord-américain (ALENA) (Canada, États-Unis et Mexique), consiste en un répertoire systématique et détaillé des industries regroupées en 20 secteurs, 99 sous-secteurs et 300 groupes. Les critères utilisés pour créer ces catégories sont la similitude des structures d'intrants, des qualifications de la main-d'oeuvre ou des processus de production utilisés par l'établissement. Pour obtenir plus de renseignements au sujet de cette classification, reportez-vous au *Système de classification des industries de l'Amérique du Nord, Canada, 1997*, n° 12-501-XPF au catalogue.

La variable Industrie (selon le SCIAN de 1997) ne permet pas d'établir de comparaisons directes avec les données sur l'industrie des recensements antérieurs. Il faut utiliser la Classification type des industries de 1980 pour effectuer des comparaisons entre les données des recensements de 1986, 1991, 1996 et 2001.

Langue maternelle

Première langue apprise à la maison dans l'enfance et encore comprise par le recensé au moment du recensement.

Langue parlée à la maison

Langue que le recensé parlait le plus souvent à la maison ou de façon régulière au moment du recensement.

Langue utilisée au travail

Cette question portait sur la langue le plus souvent utilisée au travail par le recensé au moment du recensement. Des données sur les autres langues utilisées au travail de façon régulière ont aussi été recueillies.

Lieu de naissance du répondant

Provinces ou territoires de naissance pour les répondants nés au Canada ou pays de naissance pour les répondants nés à l'extérieur du Canada.

Lieu de résidence 1 an auparavant (mobilité)

La mobilité est déterminée d'après le lien entre le domicile habituel d'une personne le jour du recensement et son domicile habituel un an plus tôt. Il s'agit d'une personne n'ayant pas déménagé si son domicile n'a pas changé dans l'intervalle; sinon, il s'agit d'une personne ayant déménagé. Cette catégorisation correspond à la mobilité (1 an auparavant). Dans la catégorie des personnes ayant déménagé, on peut également distinguer les non-migrants et les migrants; cette distinction correspond au statut migratoire.

Les **personnes n'ayant pas déménagé** sont celles qui, le jour du recensement, demeuraient à la même adresse que celle où elles résidaient un an plus tôt.

Les **personnes ayant déménagé** sont celles qui, le jour du recensement, demeuraient à une autre adresse que celle où elles résidaient un an plus tôt.

Les **non-migrants** sont des personnes ayant déménagé qui, le jour du recensement, demeuraient à une autre adresse mais dans la même subdivision de recensement (SDR) que celle où elles résidaient un an plus tôt.

Les **migrants** sont des personnes ayant déménagé qui, le jour du recensement, demeuraient dans une SDR autre que celle où elles résidaient un an plus tôt (migrants internes) ou qui résidaient à l'extérieur du Canada un an plus tôt (migrants externes).

Les **migrants infraprovinciaux** sont des personnes ayant déménagé qui, le jour du recensement, demeuraient dans une subdivision de recensement autre que celle où elles résidaient un an plus tôt, dans la même province.

Les **migrants interprovinciaux** sont des personnes ayant déménagé qui, le jour du recensement, demeuraient dans une subdivision de recensement autre que celle où elles résidaient un an plus tôt, dans une province différente.

Lieu de résidence 5 ans auparavant (mobilité)

La mobilité est déterminée d'après le lien entre le domicile habituel d'une personne le jour du recensement et son domicile habituel cinq ans plus tôt. Il s'agit d'une personne n'ayant pas déménagé si son domicile n'a pas changé dans l'intervalle; sinon, il s'agit d'une personne ayant déménagé. Cette catégorisation correspond à la mobilité (5 ans auparavant). Dans la catégorie des personnes ayant déménagé, on peut également distinguer les non-migrants et les migrants; cette distinction correspond au statut migratoire.

Les **personnes n'ayant pas déménagé** sont celles qui, le jour du recensement, demeuraient à la même adresse que celle où elles résidaient cinq ans plus tôt.

Les **personnes ayant déménagé** sont celles qui, le jour du recensement, demeuraient à une autre adresse que celle où elles résidaient cinq ans plus tôt.

Les **non-migrants** sont des personnes ayant déménagé qui, le jour du recensement, demeuraient à une autre adresse mais dans la même subdivision de recensement (SDR) que celle où elles résidaient cinq ans plus tôt.

Les **migrants** sont des personnes ayant déménagé qui, le jour du recensement, demeuraient dans une SDR autre que celle où elles résidaient cinq ans plus tôt (migrants internes) ou qui résidaient à l'extérieur du Canada cinq ans plus tôt (migrants externes).

Les **migrants infraprovinciaux** sont des personnes ayant déménagé qui, le jour du recensement, demeuraient dans une subdivision de recensement autre que celle où elles résidaient cinq ans plus tôt, dans la même province.

Les **migrants interprovinciaux** sont des personnes ayant déménagé qui, le jour du recensement, demeuraient dans une subdivision de recensement autre que celle où elles résidaient cinq ans plus tôt, dans une province différente.

Logement privé

Ensemble distinct de pièces d'habitation ayant une entrée privée donnant sur l'extérieur ou sur un corridor, un hall, un vestibule ou un escalier commun à l'intérieur. L'entrée doit donner accès au logement sans que l'on ait à passer par les pièces d'habitation de quelqu'un d'autre. Le logement doit répondre aux deux conditions qui le rendent propre à l'habitation durant toute l'année :

a) avoir une source de chauffage ou d'énergie (comme en atteste la présence d'une cheminée, de fils électriques, de tuyaux ou compteurs pour l'huile [mazout] ou le gaz, d'une génératrice, de bois de chauffage, d'ampoules électriques, d'une thermopompe, de panneaux solaires, etc.);

b) fournir un espace clos permettant de s'abriter des intempéries (comme en atteste la présence de murs d'enceinte et d'un toit ainsi que de portes et fenêtres offrant une protection contre le vent, la pluie et la neige).

Pour les besoins du recensement, on classe les logements privés comme **logements privés ordinaires** et **logements marginaux occupés**. Les logements privés ordinaires se subdivisent en trois grandes catégories : les **logements occupés** (par des résidents habituels), les **logements occupés par des résidents étrangers et/ou temporaires** et les **logements inoccupés**. Les logements marginaux sont classés comme logements occupés par des résidents habituels ou comme logements occupés par des résidents étrangers et/ou temporaires. Les logements marginaux inoccupés le jour du recensement ne font pas partie du parc immobilier.

Logement privé occupé

Logement privé occupé de façon permanente par une personne ou un groupe de personnes. Sont également inclus dans cette catégorie les logements privés dont les résidents habituels sont temporairement absents le jour du recensement. Sauf indication contraire, toutes les données présentées dans les produits sur le logement ont trait aux logements privés occupés et non aux logements privés inoccupés ou aux logements occupés par des résidents étrangers et/ou temporaires uniquement.

Loyer brut

Total des montants mensuels moyens versés par les ménages locataires au titre de l'habitation.

Ménage privé

Personne ou groupe de personnes (autres que des résidents étrangers) occupant un logement privé et n'ayant pas de domicile habituel ailleurs au Canada.

Minorités visibles

Groupe de minorités visibles auquel le recensé appartient. Selon la *Loi sur l'équité en matière d'emploi*, font partie des minorités visibles « les personnes, autres que les Autochtones, qui ne sont pas de race blanche ou qui n'ont pas la peau blanche ».

La population des minorités visibles comprend les groupes suivants : Chinois, Sud-Asiatique, Noir, Philippin, Latino-Américain, Asiatique du Sud-Est, Arabe, Asiatique occidental, Coréen, Japonais, Minorité visible, n.i.a. et Minorités visibles multiples.

Mode d'occupation

Indique si le logement est possédé ou loué par un membre du ménage, ou s'il s'agit d'un logement de bande (dans une réserve ou un établissement indien).

Mode de transport

Mode de transport utilisé pour se rendre au travail par les personnes âgées de 15 ans et plus, à l'exclusion des pensionnaires d'un établissement institutionnel, qui ont travaillé depuis le 1er janvier 2000. Les personnes qui ont indiqué qu'elles n'avaient pas d'adresse de travail fixe, ou ont précisé l'adresse d'un lieu habituel de travail, devaient inscrire le moyen de transport utilisé le plus souvent pour faire la navette entre le domicile et le travail. La variable se rapporte habituellement à l'emploi occupé par les recensés au cours de la semaine ayant précédé le recensement. Toutefois, dans le cas des personnes qui n'ont pas travaillé cette semaine-là, mais qui avaient travaillé à un moment quelconque depuis le 1er janvier 2000, les données portent sur l'emploi occupé le plus longtemps au cours de cette période.

Les personnes qui utilisaient plus d'un moyen de transport devaient indiquer seulement celui qu'elles utilisaient pour faire la plus grande partie du trajet. En conséquence, la question a permis de recueillir des données sur le principal mode de transport utilisé pour se rendre au travail. Elle ne permet toutefois pas d'obtenir des données sur l'utilisation de plusieurs modes de transport, la variation saisonnière dans le choix du mode de transport, ni sur les déplacements faits à d'autres fins que pour faire la navette entre le domicile et le travail.

Origine autochtone

Personne ayant indiqué appartenir à au moins un groupe autochtone à la question sur l'origine ethnique, c'est-à-dire Indien de l'Amérique du Nord, Métis ou Inuit (Esquimau). L'origine ethnique se rapporte au(x) groupe(s) ethnique(s) ou culturel(s) auquel (auxquels) appartenaient les ancêtres du recensé. (Voir Origine ethnique.)

Origine ethnique

Groupe(s) ethnique(s) ou culturel(s) auquel (auxquels) appartenaient les ancêtres du recensé.

Période d'immigration

Tranches d'années établies d'après les réponses à la question sur l'année d'immigration. Par année d'immigration, on entend l'année au cours de laquelle la personne a obtenu le statut d'immigrant reçu pour la première fois.

Période de construction

Période au cours de laquelle l'immeuble ou le logement a été construit.

Personnes hors famille économique

Membres d'un ménage qui ne sont pas membres d'une famille économique. Les personnes qui vivent seules sont toujours comprises dans cette catégorie.

Pièces

Nombre de pièces dans un logement. Une pièce est un espace fermé à l'intérieur d'un logement, fini et habitable toute l'année.

Plus haut niveau de scolarité atteint

Dernière année d'études primaires ou secondaires, terminée ou non, ou dernière année universitaire ou collégiale terminée. Dans la hiérarchie de la scolarité, les études universitaires sont classées au-dessus des études collégiales. En outre, la personne qui a obtenu un grade, certificat ou diplôme se trouve classée à un échelon au-dessus de celle qui a un nombre d'années de scolarité plus élevé, terminées ou non, mais qui n'a pas de titre scolaire.

Population des immigrants

Personnes ayant le statut d'immigrant reçu au Canada, ou l'ayant déjà eu. Un immigrant reçu est une personne à qui les autorités de l'immigration ont accordé le droit de résider au Canada en permanence. Certains immigrants résident au Canada depuis un certain nombre d'années, alors que d'autres sont arrivés récemment. La plupart des immigrants sont nés à l'extérieur du Canada, mais un petit nombre d'entre eux sont nés au Canada.

Population des non-immigrants

Personnes qui sont des citoyens canadiens de naissance. Bien que la plupart de ces personnes soient nées au Canada, un petit nombre d'entre elles sont nées à l'étranger de parents canadiens.

Première langue officielle parlée

Variable élaborée pour l'application de la *Loi sur les langues officielles*.

Présence d'enfants

Nombre d'enfants dans les ménages privés selon le groupe d'âge.

Principales dépenses de propriété ou loyer brut, sous forme de pourcentage du revenu du ménage

Proportion du revenu mensuel total moyen du ménage en 2000 consacrée aux principales dépenses de propriété (dans le cas des logements occupés par leur propriétaire) ou au loyer brut (dans le cas des logements occupés par un locataire). Voici comment ces résultats sont obtenus :

a) **Logements non agricoles occupés par leur propriétaire :**

$$\frac{\text{Principales dépenses de propriété}}{\text{(Revenu annuel total du ménage en 2000) /12}} \times 100 = \_\_\_ \%$$

b) **Logements non agricoles occupés par un locataire :**

$$\frac{\text{Loyer brut}}{\text{(Revenu annuel total du ménage en 2000) /12}} \times 100 = \_\_\_ \%$$

Profession (basée sur la Classification nationale des professions pour statistiques de 2001 [CNP–S de 2001])

Genre de travail que faisaient les personnes pendant la semaine de référence, défini d'après le type d'emploi occupé par le recensé et la description des tâches les plus importantes qui s'y rattachent. Si le recensé n'avait pas d'emploi au cours de la semaine (du dimanche au samedi) ayant précédé le recensement (le 15 mai 2001), les données portent sur l'emploi qu'il avait occupé le plus longtemps depuis le 1er janvier 2000. Les personnes qui avaient deux emplois ou plus devaient donner des renseignements sur l'emploi auquel elles avaient consacré le plus d'heures de travail.

Les données sur la profession du recensement de 2001 sont produites selon la Classification nationale des professions pour statistiques de 2001 (CNP–S de 2001). Cette classification comprend quatre niveaux d'agrégation. Elle comprend 10 grandes catégories professionnelles englobant 47 grands groupes, lesquels comprennent à leur tour 140 sous-groupes. Ces sous-groupes renferment 520 groupes de base. Les titres de profession sont classés selon le niveau de scolarité, de formation ou de compétence nécessaire pour exercer cette profession, ainsi que le genre de travail exécuté, déterminé d'après les tâches, les fonctions et les responsabilités reliées au poste.

Pour plus de renseignements sur la CNP–S de 2001, se reporter à la *Classification nationale des professions pour statistiques 2001*, n° 12-583-XPF au catalogue.

Province ou territoire

Les termes « province » et « territoire » désignent les principales unités politiques du Canada. Du point de vue statistique, les provinces et les territoires sont des régions de base selon lesquelles les données du recensement sont totalisées et recoupées. Le Canada est divisé en dix provinces et trois territoires.

Région métropolitaine de recensement (RMR) et agglomération de recensement (AR)

Une région métropolitaine de recensement (RMR) ou une agglomération de recensement (AR) est formée d'une ou de plusieurs municipalités adjacentes situées autour d'une grande région urbaine (appelée noyau urbain). Un noyau urbain doit compter au moins 10 000 habitants pour former une agglomération de recensement et au moins 100 000 habitants pour former une région métropolitaine de recensement. Pour être incluses dans une RMR ou une AR, les autres municipalités adjacentes doivent avoir un degré d'intégration élevé avec la région urbaine centrale, lequel est déterminé par le pourcentage de navetteurs établi d'après les données du recensement sur le lieu de travail.

Si la population du noyau urbain d'une AR devient inférieure à 10 000 habitants, l'AR est retirée du programme. Cependant, une RMR restera une RMR même si la population de son noyau urbain devient inférieure à 100 000 habitants. Les régions urbaines comprises dans une RMR ou une AR qui ne sont pas contiguës à un noyau urbain sont appelées banlieues urbaines, tandis que les régions rurales sont appelées banlieues rurales.

Lorsque le noyau urbain d'une AR compte au moins 50 000 habitants d'après les chiffres du recensement, il est subdivisé en secteurs de recensement. Les secteurs de recensement de l'AR sont maintenus même si, ultérieurement, la population de son noyau urbain devient inférieure à 50 000 habitants. Toutes les RMR sont subdivisées en secteurs de recensement.

Religion

Confession religieuse précise ou appartenance à un groupe ou à un organisme religieux, à une secte, à un culte ou à toute autre collectivité ayant adopté une religion ou un système de croyances quelconque.

Revenu total

Revenu total en espèces, reçu par les personnes âgées de 15 ans et plus durant l'année civile 2000, provenant des sources suivantes :

- salaires et traitements (total);
- revenu agricole net;
- revenu non agricole net de l'exploitation d'une entreprise non constituée en société et/ou de l'exercice d'une profession;
- prestations fiscales canadiennes pour enfants;
- pension de sécurité de la vieillesse et supplément de revenu garanti;
- prestations du Régime de rentes du Québec ou du Régime de pensions du Canada;
- prestations d'assurance-emploi;
- autre revenu provenant de sources publiques;
- dividendes, intérêts d'obligations, de dépôts et de certificats d'épargne, et autre revenu de placements;
- pensions de retraite et rentes, y compris les rentes de REÉR et de FERR;
- autre revenu en espèces.

Recettes non comptées comme revenu – Le concept du revenu excluait les gains et les pertes au jeu, les prix gagnés à la loterie, les sommes forfaitaires reçues en héritage au cours de l'année, les gains et les pertes en capital, le produit de la vente d'une propriété, les remboursements d'impôt sur le revenu, les remboursements de prêts reçus, les règlements monétaires forfaitaires d'assurance, les remboursements d'impôt foncier, les remboursements de cotisations à un régime de pensions ainsi que les revenus en nature tels que les repas et l'hébergement gratuits ou les produits agricoles cultivés et consommés à la ferme.

Revenu moyen des particuliers – Revenu total moyen pondéré des personnes âgées de 15 ans et plus qui ont déclaré un revenu en 2000. Pour établir le revenu moyen à partir des données non arrondies, il faut diviser le revenu agrégé d'un groupe de particuliers (par exemple, les hommes de 45 à 54 ans) par le nombre de personnes qui ont déclaré un revenu dans ce groupe.

Les revenus moyen et médian des particuliers, ainsi que les erreurs types de revenu moyen correspondantes, sont calculés pour les personnes qui sont âgées d'au moins 15 ans et qui ont un revenu (positif ou négatif). En ce qui concerne tous les autres univers (p. ex. les familles de recensement ou les ménages privés), ces statistiques sont calculées pour toutes les unités, qu'un revenu ait été déclaré ou non.

Revenu médian des particuliers – Valeur centrale séparant en deux parties égales la répartition par tranches de revenu d'un groupe donné de personnes ayant un revenu; la première partie regroupe les personnes ayant un revenu inférieur à la médiane, et la seconde, les personnes ayant un revenu supérieur à la médiane. Le revenu médian pour un groupe de personnes est calculé à partir des données non arrondies pour les membres de ce groupe (par exemple, les hommes de 45 à 54 ans) qui ont déclaré un revenu.

Les revenus moyen et médian des particuliers, ainsi que les erreurs types de revenu moyen correspondantes, sont calculés pour les personnes qui sont âgées d'au moins 15 ans et qui ont un revenu (positif ou négatif). En ce qui concerne tous les autres univers (p. ex. familles de recensement ou ménages privés), ces statistiques sont calculées pour toutes les unités, qu'un revenu ait été déclaré ou non.

Erreur type de revenu moyen – Estimation de l'erreur type de revenu moyen pour une répartition par tranches de revenu. Si elle est interprétée de la façon décrite ci-après, elle sert d'indicateur brut de la précision avec laquelle le revenu moyen a été estimé. Pour environ 68 % des échantillons qui peuvent être tirés de la base de sondage, la différence entre l'estimation du revenu moyen calculée pour un échantillon et le chiffre correspondant obtenu par un dénombrement exhaustif est inférieure à une erreur type. Pour près de 95 % des échantillons possibles, la différence est de moins de deux erreurs types et, dans environ 99 % des échantillons, elle est inférieure à environ deux erreurs types et demie.

Salarié ou bénéficiaire d'un revenu d'emploi

Revenu total des personnes âgées de 15 ans et plus ayant reçu un revenu au cours de l'année civile 2000 sous forme de salaires et traitements, de revenu net de l'exploitation d'une entreprise non agricole non constituée en société et/ou dans l'exercice d'une profession et de revenu net provenant d'un travail autonome agricole.

Secteur de recensement (SR)

Les secteurs de recensement (SR) sont de petites régions géographiques relativement stables qui comptent habituellement entre 2 500 et 8 000 habitants. Ils sont créés au sein de régions métropolitaines de recensement et d'agglomérations de recensement dont le noyau urbain compte 50 000 habitants ou plus d'après le recensement précédent.

Un comité de spécialistes locaux (par exemple, des planificateurs, des travailleurs sociaux, des travailleurs du secteur de la santé et des éducateurs) délimitent initialement les SR de concert avec Statistique Canada. Une fois qu'une région métropolitaine de recensement (RMR) ou qu'une agglomération de recensement (AR) a été divisée en secteurs de recensement, les secteurs de recensement sont maintenus même si, ultérieurement, la population du noyau urbain de la RMR ou de l'AR devient inférieure à 50 000 habitants.

Seuils de faible revenu (SFR)

Les mesures du faible revenu appelées seuils de faible revenu (SFR) ont été établies pour la première fois au Canada en 1968, d'après les données sur le revenu du recensement de 1961 et les régimes de dépenses des familles en 1959. À cette époque, les régimes de dépenses indiquaient que les familles canadiennes consacraient environ 50 % de leur revenu total à la nourriture, au logement et à l'habillement. On a arbitrairement estimé que les familles consacrant 70 % ou plus de leur revenu (soit 20 points de pourcentage de plus que la moyenne) à ces biens de première nécessité sont « dans le besoin ». À partir de cette hypothèse, des seuils de faible revenu ont été établis pour cinq différentes tailles de famille.

Par la suite, les seuils de faible revenu ont été révisés d'après les données nationales sur les dépenses des familles pour 1969, 1978, 1986 et 1992. Selon ces données, les familles canadiennes consacraient en moyenne 42 % de leur revenu total aux biens de première nécessité en 1969, contre 38,5 % en 1978, 36,2 % en 1986 et 34,7 % en 1992. Depuis 1992, les données de l'enquête sur les dépenses des familles indiquent que cette proportion est demeurée relativement stable. En ajoutant la différence initiale de 20 points au niveau de base des dépenses au titre des biens de première nécessité, de nouveaux seuils de faible revenu ont été fixés selon la taille de la famille et le degré d'urbanisation. Depuis 1992, ces seuils de faible revenu ont été mis à jour chaque année d'après les changements subis par l'indice des prix à la consommation.

Sexe

Qualité d'homme ou de femme.

Situation des particuliers dans la famille de recensement

Classement des personnes selon qu'elles appartiennent ou non à une famille de recensement.

Membres d'une famille de recensement – Membres d'un ménage qui appartiennent à une famille de recensement. Ces personnes se répartissent dans les catégories suivantes :

Époux et épouses – Personnes de sexe opposé qui sont légalement mariées l'une à l'autre et qui habitent le même logement.

Partenaires en union libre – Personnes de sexe opposé ou de même sexe qui ne sont pas légalement mariées l'une à l'autre, mais qui vivent comme couple dans le même logement.

Parent seul – Mère ou père, sans époux(se) ni partenaire en union libre, qui habite un logement avec au moins un de ses enfants.

Enfants – Fils ou filles apparentés par le sang, par alliance ou par adoption, peu importe leur âge ou leur état matrimonial, qui vivent dans le même logement que leur(s) parent(s), ainsi que les petits-enfants des ménages où les parents sont absents. Les fils et les filles qui vivent avec leur conjoint(e), ou avec un(e) partenaire en union libre ou avec un ou plusieurs de leurs propres enfants, ne sont pas considérés comme des membres de la famille de recensement de leur(s) parent(s), même s'ils vivent dans le même logement. En outre, les fils et les filles qui n'habitent pas dans le même logement que leur(s) parent(s) ne sont pas considérés comme des membres de la famille de ce(s) dernier(s). Les personnes suivantes font donc partie de la catégorie « enfants » :

Fils et/ou filles jamais mariés faisant partie d'une famille de recensement, comme dans le cas des recensements précédant celui de 2001.

Autres fils et/ou filles faisant partie d'une famille de recensement qui n'auraient pas été inclus dans la famille de recensement de leurs parents selon le concept précédent.

Petits-enfants vivant dans le même ménage que leurs grands-parents, en l'absence des parents.

Personnes hors famille de recensement – Membres d'un ménage qui ne font pas partie d'une famille de recensement. Ils peuvent être apparentés à la Personne 1 (p. ex. soeur, beau-frère, cousine ou grand-père de la Personne 1), ou non apparentés (p. ex. chambreur, colocataire ou employé). Les personnes qui vivent seules sont toujours considérées comme des personnes hors famille de recensement.

Situation des particuliers dans le ménage

Classement des personnes selon qu'elles sont des membres d'un ménage familial ou non familial et selon qu'elles sont des membres d'une famille de recensement ou des personnes hors famille de recensement.

Statut d'immigrant reçu

Personne à qui les autorités de l'immigration ont accordé le droit de résider au Canada en permanence.

Statut des générations

Le « statut des générations » du répondant (c.-à-d. « 1re », « 2e » ou « 3e ou plus » des générations) indique si le répondant ou ses parents sont nés au Canada ou à l'extérieur du Canada.

Structure de la famille de recensement

Classement des familles de recensement en couples mariés (avec ou sans enfants des deux conjoints ou de l'un d'eux), en couples en union libre (avec ou sans enfants des deux partenaires ou de l'un deux) et en familles monoparentales selon le sexe du parent. Un couple vivant en union libre peut être de sexe opposé ou de même sexe. Les « enfants » dans une famille de recensement incluent les petits-enfants vivant dans le même ménage que leurs grands-parents, en l'absence des parents.

Subdivision de recensement (SDR)

Subdivision de recensement (SDR) est un terme générique qui désigne les municipalités (telles que définies par les lois provinciales) ou les territoires considérés comme étant des équivalents municipaux à des fins statistiques (par exemple, les réserves indiennes, les établissements indiens et les territoires non organisés).

Superficie des terres

La superficie des terres correspond à la surface en kilomètres carrés des parties des terres des régions géographiques normalisées.

Les données sur les superficies des terres ne sont pas officielles et servent uniquement à calculer la densité de la population.

Taille du ménage

Nombre de personnes dans un ménage privé.

Type de construction résidentielle

Type de construction et/ou caractéristiques du logement (maison individuelle non attenante, appartement dans une tour d'habitation, maison en rangée, habitation mobile, etc.).

Union libre

Par union libre, on entend deux personnes de sexe opposé ou de même sexe qui vivent ensemble en tant que couple sans être légalement mariées l'une à l'autre.

Univers de la population

L'univers de la population du recensement de 2001 comprend les groupes suivants :

- les citoyens canadiens (par naissance ou par naturalisation) et les immigrants reçus ayant un lieu habituel de résidence au Canada;
- les citoyens canadiens (par naissance ou par naturalisation) et les immigrants reçus qui sont à l'étranger, dans une base militaire ou en mission diplomatique;
- les citoyens canadiens (par naissance ou par naturalisation) et les immigrants reçus qui sont en mer ou dans des ports à bord de navires marchands battant pavillon canadien;
- les personnes ayant un lieu habituel de résidence au Canada qui demandent le statut de réfugié et les membres de leur famille vivant avec elles;
- les personnes ayant un lieu habituel de résidence au Canada, qui sont titulaires d'un permis de séjour pour étudiants (visas pour étudiants, permis pour étudiants) et les membres de leur famille vivant avec elles;

- les personnes ayant un lieu habituel de résidence au Canada, qui sont titulaires d'un permis de travail et les membres de leur famille vivant avec elles;
- les personnes ayant un lieu habituel de résidence au Canada, qui sont titulaires d'un permis ministériel (y compris les prolongements) et les membres de leur famille vivant avec elles.

Aux fins du recensement, les personnes des quatre derniers groupes de la liste sont des « résidents non permanents ».

Valeur du logement

Montant en dollars que s'attendrait à recevoir le propriétaire s'il vendait son logement.

Qualité des données

Généralités

Le recensement de 2001 a été une entreprise complexe et de grande envergure. Bien que l'on ait déployé des efforts considérables pour assurer le respect de normes élevées au cours des opérations de la collecte et du traitement, il est inévitable que les estimations résultantes soient entachées d'erreurs. Les utilisateurs des données du recensement doivent savoir que ces erreurs existent et doivent avoir une idée générale de leurs principales composantes afin d'être en mesure de déterminer l'utilité des données produites et d'évaluer les risques qu'ils courent en tirant des conclusions ou en prenant des décisions à partir de ces données.

Des erreurs peuvent se produire pratiquement à toutes les étapes du recensement, depuis la préparation des documents jusqu'au traitement des données, en passant par l'établissement des listes de logements et la collecte des données. Certaines erreurs, qui surviennent par hasard, ont tendance à s'annuler lorsque les réponses fournies par les divers répondants sont agrégées pour un groupe assez important. Dans le cas d'erreurs de cette nature, l'estimation correspondante sera d'autant plus précise que le groupe visé sera grand. C'est pourquoi on conseille aux utilisateurs de faire preuve de prudence lorsqu'ils utilisent des estimations relatives à de petits groupes. Toutefois, certaines erreurs peuvent survenir de façon plus systématique et introduire un « biais » dans les estimations. Comme ce biais persiste quelle que soit la taille du groupe pour lequel les réponses sont agrégées et comme il est particulièrement difficile d'en mesurer l'importance, les erreurs systématiques posent pour la plupart des utilisateurs de données des problèmes plus graves que les erreurs aléatoires mentionnées plus haut.

En ce qui concerne les données du recensement en général, les principaux types d'erreurs sont les suivants :

- les **erreurs de couverture** qui se produisent lorsqu'on oublie des logements ou des personnes, qu'on les dénombre à tort ou qu'on les compte plus d'une fois;
- les **erreurs dues à la non-réponse** qui surviennent lorsqu'on n'a pu obtenir de réponses d'un certain nombre de ménages ou de personnes en raison d'une absence prolongée ou pour toute autre raison;
- les **erreurs de réponse** qui surviennent lorsque le répondant, ou parfois le recenseur, a mal interprété une question du recensement et a inscrit une mauvaise réponse ou s'est tout simplement trompé de case de réponse;
- les **erreurs de traitement** qui peuvent se produire à diverses étapes, notamment lors du **codage**, lorsque les réponses en lettres sont converties en codes numériques; lors de la **saisie des données**, lorsque les préposés à l'entrée des données transfèrent dans un format électronique les réponses figurant au questionnaire du recensement; lors de l'**imputation**, lorsqu'une réponse « valide », mais pas nécessairement exacte, est insérée dans un enregistrement par l'ordinateur pour remplacer une réponse manquante ou « invalide » (« valide » et « invalide » renvoient à la cohérence de la réponse, compte tenu des autres renseignements compris dans l'enregistrement);
- les **erreurs d'échantillonnage** qui s'appliquent uniquement aux questions supplémentaires figurant dans le questionnaire complet distribué à un échantillon de un cinquième des ménages. Ces erreurs résultent du fait que les réponses à ces questions supplémentaires, une fois pondérées pour représenter l'ensemble de la population, diffèrent inévitablement des réponses qu'on aurait obtenues si l'on avait posé ces questions à tous les ménages.

Les types d'erreur mentionnés plus haut ont tous une composante aléatoire et une composante systématique. Toutefois, la composante systématique de l'erreur d'échantillonnage est d'ordinaire très petite comparativement à sa composante aléatoire. Dans le cas des autres erreurs non dues à l'échantillonnage, tant la composante aléatoire que la composante systématique peuvent être importantes.

Erreurs de couverture

Les erreurs de couverture ont une incidence directe sur la précision des chiffres du recensement, c'est-à-dire sur la taille des divers univers du recensement : la population, les familles, les ménages et les logements. Bien que des mesures aient été prises pour corriger certaines erreurs identifiables, les chiffres définitifs sont toujours entachés d'une certaine erreur parce que des personnes ou des logements ont été oubliés, dénombrés à tort ou comptés plus d'une fois.

L'oubli de logements ou de personnes se traduit par un **sous-dénombrement**. Des logements peuvent être oubliés en raison soit d'une mauvaise interprétation des limites du secteur de dénombrement (SD), soit qu'ils n'ont pas l'apparence de logements ou soit qu'ils semblent inhabitables. Des personnes peuvent être oubliées parce que leur logement est oublié ou classé comme inoccupé, ou parce que le répondant a mal interprété les instructions concernant les personnes à inclure sur le questionnaire. Enfin, certaines personnes peuvent être oubliées parce qu'elles n'ont pas de domicile habituel et qu'elles n'ont pas passé la nuit du recensement dans un logement.

Le dénombrement à tort ou le double compte de logements ou de personnes se traduit par un **surdénombrement**. Il peut y avoir surdénombrement de logements lorsque des constructions impropres à l'habitation sont classées comme logements (dénombrement à tort), lorsqu'il existe une certaine ambiguïté au sujet des limites des SD ou lorsque des unités d'habitation (par exemple, des chambres) sont comptées séparément plutôt que d'être considérées comme faisant partie d'un seul logement (double compte). Les personnes peuvent être comptées plus d'une fois parce que leur logement a été compté deux fois ou parce que les lignes directrices concernant les personnes à inscrire dans le questionnaire ont été mal interprétées. À l'occasion, il arrive qu'une personne ne faisant pas partie de l'univers de la population du recensement, comme un résident étranger ou une personne fictive, soit dénombrée à tort. En moyenne, le surdénombrement est moins susceptible de se produire que le sous-dénombrement; les chiffres des logements et des personnes sont donc probablement légèrement sous-estimés.

Pour le recensement de 2001, trois études permettent de mesurer l'erreur de couverture. Dans le contexte de l'Étude sur la classification des logements, on a de nouveau visité des logements classés comme inoccupés afin de vérifier s'ils étaient réellement inoccupés le jour du recensement, et des logements dont le ménage a été classé comme non répondant afin de déterminer le nombre de résidents habituels et leurs caractéristiques. Les chiffres définitifs du recensement ont ensuite été corrigés pour tenir compte des personnes ou des ménages oubliés parce que leur logement avait été classé par erreur comme inoccupé. Il est aussi possible que les chiffres du recensement aient été corrigés pour tenir compte des logements dont le ménage a été classé comme non répondant. En dépit de ces ajustements, les chiffres définitifs peuvent tout de même être entachés d'un certain sous-dénombrement. Le sous-dénombrement tend à être plus élevé pour certains segments de la population comme les jeunes adultes (plus particulièrement ceux de sexe masculin) et les personnes récemment immigrées. L'Étude de la contre-vérification des dossiers permet de mesurer le sous-dénombrement résiduel pour le Canada, de même que pour chaque province et chaque territoire. L'Étude sur le surdénombrement a pour objet d'étudier les erreurs de surdénombrement. Ensemble, les résultats de l'Étude de la contre-vérification des dossiers et de l'Étude sur le surdénombrement fournissent une estimation du sous-dénombrement net.

Autres erreurs non dues à l'échantillonnage

Alors que les erreurs de couverture ont une incidence sur le nombre d'unités comprises dans les divers univers du recensement, d'autres erreurs influent sur les caractéristiques de ces unités.

Il est parfois impossible d'obtenir une réponse complète d'un ménage, même si le logement a été classé comme étant occupé et un questionnaire y a été livré. Il se peut que les membres du ménage aient été absents pendant toute la période du recensement ou, en de rares occasions, que le membre responsable du ménage ait refusé de remplir le questionnaire. Il arrive plus souvent que le questionnaire soit retourné, mais qu'il y ait des questions laissées sans réponse. Des efforts sont déployés afin d'obtenir un questionnaire le plus complet possible. Les recenseurs contrôlent les questionnaires et assurent un suivi à l'égard de l'information manquante. Le travail du recenseur est ensuite vérifié par un surveillant et par un technicien du contrôle qualitatif. Malgré tout, il existe toujours un petit nombre de réponses manquantes à la fin de l'étape de la collecte, c'est-à-dire d'**erreurs dues à la non-réponse**. Bien que les réponses manquantes soient éliminées en cours de traitement en remplaçant chacune d'elles par la réponse correspondante figurant dans un enregistrement « similaire », il est possible que certaines erreurs d'imputation s'y glissent. Cela est particulièrement grave lorsque les personnes non répondantes diffèrent des répondants sous certains aspects; en effet, cette procédure introduit un **biais dû à la non-réponse**.

Même lorsqu'une réponse est obtenue, il se peut qu'elle ne soit pas tout à fait exacte. Il est possible que le répondant ait mal interprété la question ou ait donné une réponse au jugé, surtout lorsqu'il répondait pour le compte d'un autre membre du ménage, qui était peut-être absent. Il est aussi possible que le répondant ait inscrit sa réponse au mauvais endroit sur le questionnaire. Ces erreurs sont désignées sous le nom d'**erreurs de réponse**. Bien que ces erreurs surviennent d'ordinaire parce que les répondants ont fourni des renseignements inexacts, elles peuvent aussi résulter d'erreurs commises par les recenseurs qui ont rempli certaines parties du questionnaire, comme le type de construction résidentielle, ou qui ont effectué le suivi pour obtenir une réponse manquante.

Certaines questions du recensement nécessitent une réponse en lettres. Pendant le traitement, on attribue un code numérique à ces réponses. Il est possible que des **erreurs de codage** se produisent lorsque la réponse écrite est ambiguë, incomplète ou difficile à lire, ou lorsque la liste des codes est longue (p. ex. principal domaine d'études, lieu de travail). L'étape formelle du contrôle qualitatif (CQ) permet de cerner et de rectifier les erreurs de codage et d'en réduire le nombre. À l'intérieur de chaque unité de travail, un échantillon des réponses est codé indépendamment une deuxième fois. La résolution des incohérences entre les premier et deuxième codages détermine la nécessité, s'il y a lieu, de coder à nouveau l'unité de travail. Exception faite pour le codage des variables de l'industrie et de la profession, la plupart des tâches de codage du recensement sont maintenant automatisées, ce qui a pour conséquence de réduire le nombre d'erreurs de codage.

Les renseignements figurant dans les questionnaires sont tapés dans un fichier informatique. Deux méthodes de résolution ordonnée sont utilisées pour limiter le nombre d'**erreurs à la saisie des données**. Dans un premier temps, certains contrôles (comme des vérifications d'étendue) sont effectués à mesure que les données sont entrées. Dans un second temps, on tape de nouveau à l'ordinateur un échantillon tiré de chaque lot de documents, puis on compare les entrées résultantes aux entrées initiales. Le travail non satisfaisant est ainsi circonscrit et corrigé et, si cela est nécessaire, le reste du lot est de nouveau saisi.

Une fois saisies, les données font l'objet de vérifications qui consistent à les soumettre à une série de contrôles informatiques visant à relever les réponses manquantes ou incohérentes. À l'étape de l'imputation, on substitue à ces dernières des réponses déduites à partir des autres données de l'enregistrement ou des réponses tirées d'un enregistrement donneur similaire. L'imputation permet d'obtenir une base de données complète dont les données correspondent aux chiffres du recensement et facilitent les analyses multidimensionnelles. Même si des erreurs peuvent être introduites à l'**étape de l'imputation**, les méthodes utilisées ont fait l'objet de tests rigoureux visant à réduire au minimum les erreurs systématiques.

Diverses études sont réalisées afin d'évaluer la qualité des réponses obtenues dans le cadre du recensement de 2001. Ainsi, on a calculé les taux de non-réponse et les taux de rejet au contrôle pour chaque question. Ces taux peuvent permettre de déterminer le potentiel d'erreurs dues à la non-réponse et d'autres types d'erreurs. De même, les totalisations établies à partir des données du recensement de 2001 ont été ou seront comparées avec les estimations correspondantes obtenues à partir des données des recensements précédents, des enquêtes-échantillon (comme l'Enquête sur la population active) et de divers dossiers administratifs (comme les registres des naissances et le cadastre municipal). Ces comparaisons peuvent permettre de cerner les problèmes de qualité éventuels ou, à tout le moins, de relever les divergences entre les sources.

Outre ces comparaisons entre données agrégées, certaines études de couplage de microdonnées sont actuellement menées afin de comparer les réponses de certains particuliers obtenues au recensement à celles d'une autre source de renseignements. Pour un certain nombre de caractéristiques « stables » (comme l'âge, le sexe, la langue maternelle et le lieu de naissance), on compare les réponses obtenues auprès d'un échantillon de personnes à l'occasion du recensement de 2001 aux réponses obtenues des mêmes personnes à l'occasion du recensement de 1996.

Erreurs d'échantillonnage

Les estimations obtenues en pondérant les réponses recueillies auprès d'un échantillon sont susceptibles d'être entachées d'erreurs en raison de la répartition des caractéristiques au sein de l'échantillon, qui n'est généralement pas identique à la répartition correspondante au sein de la population dans laquelle l'échantillon a été prélevé.

L'erreur susceptible d'être introduite par l'échantillonnage variera en fonction de la rareté relative de la caractéristique étudiée au sein de la population. Lorsque la valeur contenue dans la case est élevée, cette erreur sera relativement faible proportionnellement à cette valeur. Lorsque la valeur contenue dans la case est faible, cette erreur sera relativement importante proportionnellement à cette valeur.

L'erreur susceptible d'être introduite par l'échantillonnage est d'ordinaire exprimée sous forme d'« erreur type ». Il s'agit de la racine carrée de la moyenne, calculée pour l'ensemble des échantillons de même taille prélevés selon le même plan d'échantillonnage, des carrés de l'écart de l'estimation obtenue à partir de l'échantillon par rapport à la valeur pour l'ensemble de la population.

Le tableau ci-dessous fournit des mesures approximatives de l'erreur type due à l'échantillonnage. Ces mesures sont données uniquement à titre indicatif.

Erreur type approximative due à l'échantillonnage pour les données-échantillon du recensement de 2001

Valeur contenue dans la case	Erreur type approximative
50 ou moins	15
100	20
200	30
500	45
1 000	65
2 000	90
5 000	140
10 000	200
20 000	280
50 000	450
100 000	630
500 000	1 400

Les utilisateurs souhaitant déterminer l'erreur d'échantillonnage approximative pour une case de données dont la valeur a été obtenue à partir de l'échantillon de 20 % doivent choisir l'erreur type correspondant à l'entrée dans la colonne « Valeur contenue dans la case » ci dessus qui se rapproche le plus de celle qui figure dans la case de données de la totalisation en cause. En utilisant la valeur ainsi obtenue pour l'erreur type, l'utilisateur peut, en général et à juste titre, être certain que la valeur réelle pour la population dénombrée (ne tenant pas compte des formes d'erreurs autres que l'erreur d'échantillonnage) ne s'écarte pas de la valeur contenue dans la case dans une proportion supérieure ou inférieure à trois fois l'erreur type (p. ex. si la valeur contenue dans la case est 1 000, la fourchette à l'intérieur de laquelle se situe la valeur réelle serait de 1 000 ± [3 x 65] ou de 1 000 ± 195).

Les erreurs types données dans le tableau ci-dessus ne s'appliquent pas aux chiffres de population, de logements, de ménages ou de familles pour la région géographique étudiée (voir Échantillonnage et pondération ci-dessous). On peut déterminer l'effet de l'échantillonnage pour ces valeurs en les comparant à celles des produits correspondants contenant des données intégrales.

Il est à noter que l'effet du plan d'échantillonnage et de la méthode de pondération utilisés dans le cadre du recensement de 2001 variera d'une caractéristique à l'autre et d'une région géographique à l'autre. Il est donc possible que les valeurs de l'erreur type données dans le tableau ci-dessus sous-estiment ou surestiment l'erreur attribuable à l'échantillonnage.

Échantillonnage et pondération

Les données du recensement de 2001 sont soit des données intégrales (c'est-à-dire recueillies auprès de l'ensemble des ménages), soit des données-échantillon (c'est-à-dire recueillies auprès d'un échantillon aléatoire comprenant un ménage sur cinq) que l'on a pondérées pour obtenir des estimations pour l'ensemble de la population. Les données ont été recueillies auprès d'un échantillon de 20 % et pondérées pour compenser pour l'échantillonnage. Tous les en-têtes de tableaux sont annotés en conséquence. On notera que, dans les réserves indiennes et les régions éloignées, toutes les données ont été recueillies auprès de l'ensemble de la population.

Il est possible que, pour une région géographique donnée, le total ou le total partiel pondéré de la population, des ménages, des logements ou des familles diffère du chiffre correspondant figurant dans les publications contenant des données intégrales. Ces variations sont attribuables à l'échantillonnage et au fait que les données intégrales n'excluent pas les pensionnaires d'établissements institutionnels, contrairement aux données-échantillon.

Confidentialité et arrondissement aléatoire

Afin de protéger le caractère confidentiel des renseignements fournis, les chiffres indiqués aux tableaux ont fait l'objet d'un **arrondissement aléatoire** qui supprime toute possibilité d'associer des données statistiques à une personne facilement reconnaissable. Selon cette méthode, tous les chiffres, y compris les totaux et les marges, sont arrondis de façon aléatoire (vers le haut ou vers le bas) jusqu'à un multiple de « 5 » et, dans certains cas, de « 10 ». Cette technique assure une protection efficace contre la divulgation sans ajouter d'erreur significative dans les données du recensement. Les utilisateurs doivent savoir que les totaux et les marges sont arrondis séparément et qu'ils ne correspondent pas nécessairement à la somme des chiffres arrondis séparément dans les répartitions. De plus, il faut s'attendre à ce que les totaux et les autres chiffres correspondants dans diverses totalisations du recensement présentent quelques légères différences. De même, la somme des pourcentages, qui sont calculés à partir de chiffres arrondis, ne correspond pas forcément à 100 %. Les statistiques d'ordre (médiane, quartiles, percentiles, etc.) ainsi que les mesures de dispersion comme l'erreur type sont calculées de la façon habituelle. Lorsqu'une statistique est définie comme le quotient de deux nombres (c'est le cas pour des moyennes, des pourcentages et des proportions), les deux nombres sont arrondis avant d'effectuer la division. S'il s'agit de revenu, de dépenses de propriété, de valeur du logement, d'heures travaillées, de semaines travaillées ou d'âge, la somme est définie comme le produit de la moyenne par la fréquence pondérée arrondie. Sinon, c'est la somme pondérée qui est arrondie. La distorsion importante pouvant résulter de l'arrondissement aléatoire dans le cas des cases de faible valeur mérite aussi d'être signalée. Cette distorsion peut entraîner une perte de précision pour les cases de données renfermant des chiffres peu élevés. De plus, une statistique est supprimée si le nombre actuel d'enregistrements ayant servi au calcul est inférieur à 4 ou si la somme du poids de ces enregistrements est inférieure à 10. En outre, dans le cas de valeurs exprimées en dollars, d'autres règles s'ajoutent. Ainsi, pour les produits normalisés, si toutes les valeurs sont égales, la statistique est supprimée. Pour tous les autres produits, la statistique est supprimée si l'étendue des valeurs est trop petite ou si toutes les valeurs sont inférieures, en valeur absolue, à un certain seuil.

Les utilisateurs devraient, lors de l'agrégation des données arrondies, être conscients de cette distorsion. Les erreurs dues à l'arrondissement ont tendance à s'annuler lorsque les chiffres contenus dans les cases sont agrégés de nouveau. Cependant, il est possible de réduire les distorsions en intégrant dans la mesure du possible les totaux partiels appropriés dans les totalisations.

Les utilisateurs désirant obtenir un maximum de précision peuvent aussi choisir de demander des totalisations personnalisées. Dans le cas de produits personnalisés, l'agrégation se fait à partir des enregistrements dans la base de données du recensement se rapportant aux particuliers. L'arrondissement aléatoire a lieu uniquement après que les cases de données ont été agrégées, ce qui réduit la distorsion au minimum.

Outre l'arrondissement aléatoire, on a adopté la technique de la **suppression des régions**, afin d'assurer encore mieux la confidentialité des réponses des particuliers.

Dans le cadre de la **suppression des régions**, toutes les données caractéristiques se rapportant aux régions géographiques dont la population est inférieure à une taille donnée sont supprimées. L'importance de la suppression est fonction des facteurs suivants :

- Si les données sont totalisées à partir de la base de données intégrales, elles sont supprimées si la population totale de la région est inférieure à 40 personnes.

- Si les données sont totalisées à partir de la base de données-échantillon, elles sont supprimées si la population totale de la région, à l'exclusion des pensionnaires d'un établissement institutionnel, est inférieure à 40 personnes, selon la base de données intégrales ou la base de données-échantillon.

Il y a quelques exceptions à ces règles :

- Les données renfermant une répartition du revenu et les statistiques connexes sont supprimées si la population de la région, à l'exclusion des pensionnaires d'un établissement institutionnel, est inférieure à 250 personnes selon la base de données intégrales ou la base de données-échantillon, ou encore si le nombre de ménages privés est inférieur à 40, selon la base de données-échantillon.

- Les données renfermant une répartition du lieu du travail et les statistiques connexes sont supprimées si le nombre de personnes occupées dans la région est inférieur à 40, selon la base de données-échantillon. Si ces données incluent, en plus, une répartition du revenu, le seuil est changé à 250 personnes, toujours selon la base de données-échantillon.

- Les totalisations traitant à la fois du lieu de travail et du lieu de résidence ainsi que les statistiques connexes sont supprimées si le nombre de personnes occupées dans la région est inférieur à 40 selon la base de données-échantillon ou si la population totale de la région, à l'exclusion des pensionnaires d'un établissement institutionnel, selon la base de données intégrales ou la base de données-échantillon est inférieure à 40 personnes. Si ces totalisations incluent, en plus, une répartition du revenu, le seuil est changé à 250 personnes dans tous les cas et les totalisations sont supprimées si le nombre de ménages privés dans la région du lieu de résidence est inférieur à 40.

- Les données renfermant une répartition sur les couples de même sexe et les statistiques connexes sont supprimées si la population de la région dans les ménages privés est inférieure à 5 000 personnes, selon la base de données-échantillon.

- Si les données sont totalisées à partir de la base de données intégrales et se réfèrent aux codes postaux de six caractères ou encore à des regroupements d'îlots ou de côtés d'îlots, elles sont supprimées si la population totale de la région est inférieure à 100 personnes.

- Si les données sont totalisées à partir de la base de données-échantillon et se réfèrent aux codes postaux de six caractères ou encore à des regroupements d'îlots ou de côtés d'îlots, elles sont supprimées si la population totale de la région, à l'exclusion des pensionnaires d'un établissement institutionnel, et selon la base de données intégrales ou la base de données-échantillon, est inférieure à 100 personnes.

- Si les données se réfèrent à des regroupements d'îlots ou de côtés d'îlots, et renferment une répartition du lieu de travail, elles sont supprimées si le nombre de personnes occupées dans la région est inférieur à 100 selon la base de données-échantillon.

- Si les données se réfèrent à des regroupements d'îlots ou de côtés d'îlots, et renferment, à la fois, une répartition du lieu de travail et du lieu de résidence, elles sont supprimées si le nombre total de personnes occupées dans la région est inférieur à 100 selon la base de données-échantillon ou si la population totale de la région, à l'exclusion des pensionnaires d'un établissement institutionnel, selon la base de données intégrales ou la base de données-échantillon, est inférieure à 100 personnes.

Dans tous les cas, les données supprimées sont incluses dans les totaux ou totaux partiels du niveau d'agrégation supérieur approprié.

La technique de suppression est appliquée à tous les produits renfermant des données infraprovinciales (c'est-à-dire la série des Profils, les tableaux croisés de base, les produits personnalisés et semi personnalisés), qu'il s'agisse de données intégrales ou de données-échantillon.

Pour obtenir de plus amples renseignements sur la qualité des données du recensement, veuillez communiquer avec la Division des méthodes d'enquêtes sociales, Statistique Canada, Ottawa (Ontario), Canada K1A 0T6, ou en composant le (613) 951-4783.

Notes spéciales

Chiffres de population

Les chiffres de population du recensement de 2001 pour une région particulière représentent le nombre de Canadiens dont le domicile habituel est dans cette région, quel que soit l'endroit où ils se trouvent le jour du recensement. Sont également compris dans ces chiffres tous les Canadiens qui demeurent dans un logement de cette région le jour du recensement qui n'ont pas de domicile habituel ailleurs au Canada, de même que ceux qui sont considérés comme des « résidents non permanents » (voir les Notes spéciales). Dans la plupart des régions, la différence entre le nombre de résidents habituels et le nombre de résidents qui demeurent dans cette région le jour du recensement est minime. Toutefois, à certains endroits, notamment dans des régions touristiques ou de villégiature, ou dans celles où l'on trouve d'importants camps de travail, le nombre de personnes qui demeurent dans la région à n'importe quel moment pourrait être bien supérieur au nombre de résidents habituels dont il est ici fait mention. Les chiffres de population tiennent compte des Canadiens qui habitent dans d'autres pays, mais non pas des résidents étrangers qui habitent au Canada (la catégorie des « résidents étrangers » ne comprend pas les « résidents non permanents » [voir les Notes spéciales]). Compte tenu de ces divergences, les utilisateurs ne doivent pas déduire que les chiffres de population correspondent au nombre de personnes qui habitent dans les logements déclarés.

Comparabilité des données de 2001 sur le lieu de travail

Le travail à domicile peut être mesuré de différentes façons. Dans le cadre du recensement, la catégorie des personnes travaillant à domicile comprend les personnes qui résident et travaillent au même endroit, comme les agriculteurs, les télétravailleurs et les travailleurs d'un camp de chantier. Par ailleurs, selon les instructions données dans le Guide du recensement de 2001, les personnes ayant travaillé à domicile une partie du temps et à l'adresse d'un employeur le reste du temps devaient indiquer qu'elles avaient travaillé à domicile si elles avaient travaillé la majeure partie du temps chez elles (par exemple trois jours sur cinq).

D'autres enquêtes de Statistique Canada, telles que l'Enquête sociale générale, l'Enquête sur la dynamique du travail et du revenu et l'Enquête sur le milieu de travail et les employés, recueillent également des données sur les personnes travaillant à domicile. Toutefois, les données de ces enquêtes ne sont pas directement comparables à celles du recensement, étant donné que dans le cadre des enquêtes, les répondants doivent indiquer s'ils font une partie ou la totalité de leur travail rémunéré à domicile, alors qu'au recensement, ils doivent indiquer où ils travaillent habituellement la plupart du temps. Par conséquent, les estimations du travail à domicile tirées du recensement sont inférieures à celles tirées des enquêtes.

La présentation de la question sur le lieu de travail est demeurée à peu près la même pour chaque recensement depuis 1971. Cependant, en 1996, la catégorie « Sans adresse de travail fixe » a remplacé la catégorie « Sans lieu habituel de travail ». Sur le questionnaire du recensement de 1996, une case à cocher a été ajoutée pour la catégorie de réponse « Sans adresse de travail fixe ». Lors des recensements antérieurs, les répondants devaient inscrire « Sans lieu habituel de travail » dans les zones réservées à l'adresse. Il semble y avoir eu un sous-dénombrement des personnes sans lieu de travail fixe lors des recensements antérieurs.

Les annexions, les incorporations et les fusions de municipalités pourraient rendre difficile l'établissement de comparaisons entre des unités et des structures spatiales qui changent dans le temps.

Données sur l'immigration et la citoyenneté

Les questions sur la citoyenneté et l'immigration n'ont pas été posées aux personnes qui vivent sur des réserves indiennes et dans des établissements indiens et qui ont été dénombrées à l'aide du questionnaire 2D du recensement de 2001. Par conséquent, les données ne sont pas affichées pour les réserves indiennes et les établissements indiens aux niveaux géographiques inférieurs. Toutefois, ces données sont comprises dans les totaux pour les plus grandes régions géographiques, telles que les divisions de recensement et les provinces.

Données sur la migration pour les petites régions géographiques

Les chiffres estimatifs sur la migration interne peuvent manquer d'exactitude pour les petites régions géographiques, pour les localités ayant le même nom que d'autres localités situées ailleurs et pour certaines subdivisions de recensement (SDR) dans les cas où des résidents, au lieu d'indiquer le nom de la composante SDR dans laquelle ils résidaient auparavant, ont fourni le nom de la région métropolitaine de recensement ou de l'agglomération de recensement.

Identité autochtone

Les utilisateurs doivent prendre note du fait que le dénombrement partiel de certaines réserves indiennes ou de certains établissements indiens a une plus grande incidence sur les chiffres de population associés à la présente variable que sur la plupart des autres chiffres. L'ampleur de cette incidence sera fonction de la région géographique à l'étude. En 2001, un total de 30 réserves indiennes et établissements indiens ont été partiellement dénombrés dans le contexte du recensement. Les chiffres du recensement ne tiennent pas compte des populations de ces 30 collectivités.

Incidence de la restructuration municipale

Il est possible que les limites et les noms des municipalités (subdivisions de recensement) soient modifiés d'un recensement à un autre par suite d'annexions, de dissolutions et d'incorporations. Le nombre et l'importance de ces modifications ont toutefois augmenté depuis le recensement de 1996, surtout au Québec, en Ontario et en Colombie-Britannique. En général, les données du recensement de 2001 sont diffusées pour un plus petit nombre de subdivisions de recensement de plus grande taille, ce qui a pour effet de compliquer les analyses historiques. Afin d'atténuer l'impact de ces modifications sur la diffusion des données, l'équipe du recensement de 2001 entend produire un profil pour les subdivisions de recensement dissoutes.

Modifications apportées aux concepts relatifs à la famille pour le recensement de 2001

Au recensement de 1996, la définition du concept de famille de recensement était la suivante :

Couple actuellement marié (avec ou sans fils et/ou filles jamais mariés des deux conjoints ou de l'un d'eux), couple vivant en union libre (avec ou sans fils et/ou filles jamais mariés des deux partenaires ou de l'un d'eux) ou parent seul (peu importe son état matrimonial) demeurant avec au moins un fils ou une fille jamais marié(e).

La définition de ce concept n'avait pas été modifiée depuis 1976. Toutefois, au cours de la planification du recensement de 2001, il a été décidé qu'il était nécessaire de le modifier compte tenu des facteurs suivants : 1) les changements apportés aux lois fédérales et provinciales afin que les couples formés de partenaires de même sexe soient considérés sur un pied d'égalité avec les couples formés de partenaires de sexe opposé vivant en union libre, plus particulièrement le Projet de loi C-23, *Loi sur la modernisation de certains régimes d'avantages et d'obligations*, qui a été adopté par le gouvernement du Canada en 2000; 2) les recommandations des Nations Unies dans le cadre d'un processus de normalisation des concepts pour les recensements qui devaient être réalisés en 2000 et en 2001 dans les pays membres; 3) le fait qu'aux recensements précédents un nombre important de personnes âgées de moins de 15 ans aient été classées comme personnes hors famille.

Par conséquent, les changements suivants ont été apportés au concept de famille de recensement pour le recensement de 2001 :

- Deux personnes constituant un couple en union libre formé de partenaires de même sexe et tous les enfants faisant partie de leur ménage sont considérés comme une famille de recensement.

- Les enfants compris dans une famille de recensement peuvent avoir déjà été mariés (pourvu qu'ils n'habitent actuellement pas avec leur époux(se) ou partenaire en union libre). Auparavant, il fallait qu'ils n'aient jamais été mariés.

- Un petit-fils ou une petite-fille vivant dans un ménage à trois générations où le parent (deuxième génération) n'a jamais été marié est, contrairement aux recensements précédents, maintenant considéré(e) comme faisant partie de la famille de recensement du parent, à condition de ne pas habiter avec son époux(se), son/sa partenaire en union libre ou son enfant. Auparavant, la famille de recensement était ordinairement constituée des deux générations les plus anciennes.

- Un petit-fils ou une petite-fille d'un autre membre du ménage où le parent (deuxième génération) n'est pas présent est maintenant considéré(e) comme faisant partie de la famille de recensement du grand-père ou de la grand-mère, à condition que le petit-fils ou la petite-fille n'habite pas avec son époux(se), son/sa partenaire en union libre ou son enfant. Auparavant, un tel petit-fils ou une telle petite-fille n'aurait pas été considéré(e) comme faisant partie de la famille de recensement.

Les trois dernières modifications apportées (définition du terme « enfant ») se traduisent par une augmentation de 1,5 % du nombre total de familles de recensement, et une augmentation de 10,1 % du nombre de familles monoparentales. L'inclusion de couples formés de partenaires de même sexe se traduit par une augmentation de 0,4 % du nombre de familles de recensement à l'échelle nationale.

Le terme famille économique désigne un groupe de deux personnes ou plus qui vivent dans le même logement et qui sont apparentées par le sang, par alliance, par union libre ou par adoption. Cette définition n'a pas été modifiée pour le recensement de 2001. La seule incidence des changements sur le concept de famille économique est que les couples formés de partenaires de même sexe sont maintenant considérés comme étant des partenaires en union libre et donc considérés comme étant apparentés et membres de la même famille économique.

Deux concepts connexes ne faisant pas partie de l'univers des familles sont touchés par la modification apportée à la définition du concept de famille de recensement : union libre et genre de ménage. Avant 2001, deux personnes vivant ensemble comme mari et femme sans être mariées étaient considérées comme formant un couple en union libre. Pour 2001, l'expression « comme mari et femme » a été remplacée par « comme couple » de sorte que les partenaires de même sexe sont maintenant inclus. Le concept de genre de ménage renvoie à la répartition fondamentale des ménages privés en ménages familiaux et en ménages non familiaux. Comme il est fondé sur le concept de famille de recensement, la modification apportée à ce dernier concept a une incidence sur le classement des ménages en ménages familiaux ou non familiaux. La classification détaillée de cette variable est également touchée puisque les couples mariés et les couples en union libre étaient répartis auparavant entre les catégories « sans fils ou filles jamais mariés » et « avec fils ou filles jamais mariés ». En 2001, ces expressions sont remplacées par les termes « sans enfant » et « avec enfants » conformément à la nouvelle définition.

Modifications aux chiffres de population et des logements

Suite à la diffusion des chiffres de population et des logements, des erreurs sont occasionnellement relevées dans les données. Il est impossible d'apporter des changements aux données du recensement de 2001 qui sont présentées dans ces tableaux. Toutefois, les utilisateurs peuvent obtenir les modifications aux chiffres de population et des logements touchant les subdivisions de recensement et d'autres niveaux géographiques en visitant la section consacrée au recensement de 2001 dans le site Web de Statistique Canada à l'adresse suivante : www.statcan.ca. Ils peuvent également communiquer avec le centre régional de consultation de Statistique Canada le plus près au numéro 1 800 263-1136 ou par courriel à infostats@statcan.ca.

Nunavut

Des données du recensement de 2001 sont disponibles pour le Nunavut, nouveau territoire reconnu officiellement le 1er avril 1999.

Les produits de données normalisés diffusés seulement pour le Canada, les provinces et les territoires n'afficheront pas de données pour le Nunavut pour les années de recensement antérieures à 2001.

Les produits de données normalisés diffusés pour les régions métropolitaines de recensement (RMR) et les agglomérations de recensement (AR) afficheront des données pour le Nunavut pour les recensements de 2001, 1996 ou 1991.

Les données de 1996 et de 1991 pour les RMR/AR ont été ajustées le plus possible selon les limites des RMR et des AR de 2001 afin de faciliter les comparaisons de données selon les limites géographiques de 2001.

Période de référence du revenu

Des recensements canadiens ont eu lieu en 1996 et en 2001. Les données de ces recensements portant sur le revenu correspondent à l'année civile précédant l'année du recensement, c.-à-d. 1995 et 2000 respectivement.

Population de 15 ans et plus ayant travaillé depuis 2000

Ce sont les personnes ayant travaillé depuis le 1er janvier 2000, qu'elles aient fait partie ou non de la population active pendant la semaine de référence.

Qualité des données – Comparaison des estimations du revenu tirées du recensement avec des estimations établies à partir des comptes nationaux et de l'Enquête sur la dynamique du travail et du revenu

Les estimations du revenu agrégé en 2000 qui ont été tirées du recensement ont été comparées à des estimations semblables du revenu des particuliers établies à partir des comptes nationaux. Une fois que les estimations du revenu des particuliers ont été ajustées pour tenir compte des différences touchant les concepts et la couverture, on a observé que les estimations du revenu agrégé en 2000 qui sont tirées du recensement sont inférieures de 4,1 % à celles qui sont établies à partir des comptes nationaux. Comme par le passé, les estimations tirées du recensement soutiennent davantage la comparaison pour certaines composantes du revenu et pour certaines provinces que pour d'autres.

Dans le cas des salaires et traitements agrégés, qui constituent la plus grande composante du revenu, les estimations tirées du recensement et celles établies à partir des comptes nationaux sont presque identiques. Bien qu'il y ait une grande différence entre les deux estimations du revenu net provenant d'un travail autonome agricole (la plus petite composante du revenu des particuliers), dans le cas du revenu agrégé provenant d'un travail autonome agricole et d'un travail non agricole, les estimations du recensement ne sont inférieures que de 1 %. Dans l'ensemble, les estimations du revenu d'emploi total tirées du recensement et celles établies à partir des comptes nationaux sont quasi identiques.

Les estimations des prestations de la sécurité de la vieillesse et du supplément de revenu garanti qui sont tirées du recensement sont supérieures d'environ 5 % aux estimations ajustées établies à partir des comptes nationaux. En revanche, les estimations tirées du recensement leur sont inférieures d'environ 9 % dans le cas des prestations du Régime de rentes du Québec ou du Régime de pensions du Canada, et d'environ 6 % dans le cas des prestations d'assurance-emploi. Pour ce qui est des prestations fiscales canadiennes pour enfants, les deux estimations sont quasi identiques. Les estimations des autres transferts gouvernementaux tirées du recensement, qui incluent notamment les allocations sociales, les prestations provinciales de supplément du revenu aux personnes âgées, les pensions d'ancien combattant et les remboursements de la TPS/TVH/TVQ, sont plus faibles que les estimations tirées des comptes nationaux. Dans l'ensemble, les estimations du revenu agrégé tirées du recensement, qui proviennent de tous les transferts gouvernementaux, sont inférieures d'environ 13 %. Comme aux recensements antérieurs, l'estimation du revenu de placement tirée du recensement est de beaucoup inférieure, soit de 32 % en 2000, à l'estimation tirée des comptes nationaux.

Les statistiques du recensement sur le revenu ont également été comparées à des statistiques similaires tirées de l'Enquête sur la dynamique du travail et du revenu (EDTR), qui est tenue chaque année. Les estimations tirées de l'EDTR ont été ajustées pour tenir compte du sous-dénombrement de la population, alors que ce n'est pas le cas pour les estimations du recensement. Cette correction contribue à faire en sorte que les estimations tirées du recensement affichent, par rapport à celles de l'EDTR, un nombre moins élevé de bénéficiaires d'un revenu et de soutiens économiques, qui présente un écart de 3,4 % et de 7,2 % respectivement. Par conséquent, les estimations tirées du recensement sont inférieures à celles de l'EDTR, de 4 % dans le cas des gains agrégés et de 3 % dans le cas du revenu total agrégé des particuliers. À la lumière des erreurs d'échantillonnage dans l'EDTR, la plupart des différences observées entre les provinces ont été jugées acceptables.

Qualité des données concernant la fréquentation scolaire

La qualité générale des variables de l'éducation du recensement de 2001 est acceptable. Toutefois, il importe aux usagers des données du recensement de 2001 sur la fréquentation scolaire de savoir que les chiffres pour la catégorie des 15 à 19 ans qui ne fréquentent pas l'école sont peut-être trop élevés. La proportion de personnes âgées entre 15 et 19 ans qui ont répondu qu'elles n'avaient pas fréquenté l'école au cours de l'année scolaire avant le recensement est passée de 18 % en 1996 à 23 % en 2001. Il est nécessaire d'effectuer de plus amples recherches à cet effet.

Résidents non permanents

En 1991, 1996 et 2001, le Recensement de la population a dénombré à la fois les résidents permanents et non permanents au Canada. Les résidents non permanents sont les personnes qui, au moment du recensement, étaient titulaires d'un permis de séjour pour étudiants, d'un permis de travail ou d'un permis ministériel, ou qui revendiquaient le statut de réfugié. Les membres de leur famille vivant avec elles sont aussi considérés comme des résidents non permanents.

Avant 1991, seuls les résidents permanents du Canada étaient inclus dans le recensement (exception faite pour 1941). Les résidents non permanents étaient considérés comme des résidents étrangers et n'étaient pas dénombrés.

Présentement au Canada, les résidents non permanents forment un segment important de la population, en particulier dans plusieurs régions métropolitaines de recensement. Leur présence peut influer sur la demande de services gouvernementaux tels que les soins de santé, l'éducation, les programmes d'emploi et la formation linguistique. L'inclusion des résidents non permanents au recensement facilite la comparaison avec les statistiques provinciales et territoriales (mariages, divorces, naissances et décès) qui incluent cette population. En outre, l'inclusion des résidents non permanents permet au Canada de mieux refléter la recommandation de l'ONU, à savoir que les résidents à long terme (personnes demeurant dans un pays pour un an ou plus) soient dénombrés au recensement.

Le recensement de 1996 a dénombré 166 715 résidents non permanents au Canada, soit 0,6 % de la population totale. Le nombre avait augmenté quelque peu au recensement de 2001 : 198 645 résidents non permanents, soit 0,7 % de la population totale.

Le total des chiffres de population, de même que ceux de toutes les variables, sont touchés par ce changement apporté à l'univers du recensement. Les utilisateurs doivent faire preuve d'une très grande prudence lorsqu'ils comparent des données de 1991, de 1996 ou de 2001 avec celles de recensements antérieurs pour des régions géographiques où la concentration de résidents non permanents est importante. Celles-ci comprennent les principales régions métropolitaines de recensement de l'Ontario, du Québec et de la Colombie-Britannique.

Même si tous les efforts possibles ont été déployés pour dénombrer les résidents non permanents, des facteurs tels que les problèmes linguistiques, la réticence à remplir un formulaire du gouvernement ou à comprendre l'importance de participer peuvent avoir influé sur le dénombrement de cette population.

Secteurs de recensement en Ontario

On a décelé, dans la base de données, une erreur qui touche la présentation des chiffres de population de 1996 pour deux secteurs de recensement (SR), c'est-à-dire les SR 0520.05 et 0520.06, dans la région métropolitaine de recensement (RMR) de Toronto. Les données pour ces SR sont correctes, mais elles ont été inversées : 0520.05 contient les données de 0520.06 et 0520.06 contient les données de 0520.05. En raison de contraintes opérationnelles, il n'a pas été possible d'effectuer des ajustements à la base de données de 1996 (chiffres ajustés) pour ces deux SR. Il importe de faire preuve de prudence dans l'utilisation de ces données.

Suppression des données sur le revenu

Dans le cadre de la suppression des régions, toutes les données caractéristiques se rapportant aux régions géographiques dont la population est inférieure à une taille donnée sont supprimées. Les données renfermant une répartition du revenu et les statistiques connexes sont supprimées si la population de la région, à l'exclusion des pensionnaires d'un établissement institutionnel, est inférieure à 250 personnes selon la base de données intégrales ou la base de données-échantillon, ou encore si le nombre de ménages privés est inférieur à 40, selon la base de données-échantillon.

Type de construction résidentielle

Au recensement de 2001, on a recueilli des données sur deux nouvelles catégories de la variable Type de construction résidentielle :

Appartement avec accès direct au niveau du sol dans un immeuble de moins de cinq étages et appartement sans accès direct au niveau du sol dans un immeuble de moins de cinq étages.

L'évaluation postcensitaire des données a révélé un problème grave d'erreur de classement pour ces types de logements. Par conséquent, les données ne seront pas diffusées.

Les données sur le type « Appartement dans un immeuble de moins de cinq étages » sont diffusées dans les produits du recensement de 2001. Cette catégorie constitue un regroupement des deux nouvelles catégories susmentionnées, et les données correspondantes sont directement comparables avec celles de la même catégorie utilisée aux recensements précédents et ne posent en outre aucun problème.

Annexe 1. Réserves indiennes et établissements indiens partiellement dénombrés, chiffres de population de 1996 et de 1991

Province	Réserves indiennes et établissements indiens partiellement dénombrés, 2001	Population	
		1996	1991
Québec	Akwesasne (Partie)	¶	¶
	Doncaster 17	0	4
	Kahnawake 14	¶	¶
	Kanesatake	¶	¶
	Lac-Rapide	228	¶
Ontario	Akwesasne (Part) 59 (formerly Akwesasne [Part])	¶	¶
	Bear Island 1	153	¶
	Chippewas of the Thames First Nation 42 (formerly Chippewa of the Thames First Nation)	¶	¶
	Goulais Bay 15A	¶	¶
	Marten Falls 65	204	187
	Moose Factory 68	0	0
	Munsee-Delaware Nation 1	¶	¶
	Ojibway Nation of Saugeen (Savant Lake) (formerly Savant Lake)	¶	171
	Oneida 41	¶	¶
	Pikangikum 14	1 170	1 303
	Rankin Location 15D	¶	¶
	Six Nations (Part) 40 (Brant County)	¶	¶
	Six Nations (Part) 40 (Haldimand-Norfolk Regional Municipality)	¶	¶
	Tyendinaga Mohawk Territory (formerly Tyendinaga 38)	¶	¶
	Wahta Mohawk Territory (formerly Gibson 31)	¶	130
	Whitefish Bay 32A	¶	¶
	Whitesand	115	0
Manitoba	Dakota Tipi 1	¶	72
Saskatchewan	Big Head 124	¶	¶
Alberta	Ermineskin 138	¶	¶
	Little Buffalo	¶	186
	Saddle Lake 125	¶	1 893
Colombie-Britannique	Esquimalt	¶	¶
	Marble Canyon 3	67	¶
	Pavilion 1	76	73

Annexe 2. Secteurs de recensement supprimés par chiffres de population selon la région métropolitaine de recensement et l'agglomération de recensement, recensement de 2001

Secteurs de recensement supprimés	Chiffres de population (données intégrales)	Chiffres de population (données-échantillon (20 %))
Belleville AR		
0010	35	34
0013 **A**	10	4
0014 **A**	33	33
0405	-	-
0407	-	-
Edmonton RMR		
0015.01	5	4
0016.01	-	-
0019.01	-	-
0052.01	-	-
0064.02	-	-
0065.03	-	-
0090.07	-	-
Granby AR		
0003 **A**	38	38
Greater Sudbury RMR		
0013	-	-
Halifax RMR		
0155 ◆◆◆◇◇◇ **A**	15	14
Kitchener RMR		
0106.03 ◆◆◆◇◇◇	5	2
Lethbridge AR		
0010	25	15
London RMR		
0035	-	-
Montréal RMR		
0014.02	23	23
0040	-	-
0071	-	-
0091	-	-
0094.02	-	-
0127.02	17	17
0145	-	-
0189	-	-
0229	-	-
0268.03	-	-
0440	-	-
0832 ¶		-
Ottawa - Hull RMR		
0140.01	20	16
Saint John RMR		
0005	15	6
Saint-Jean-sur-Richelieu AR		
0006	5	-
0010	-	-
0303	-	-
Toronto RMR		
0003	-	-
0376.06 ◇	35	20
0401.05	5	5
Trois-Rivières RMR		
0301	39	38
Vancouver RMR		
0270	-	-
Winnipeg RMR		
0052	-	-

Nota :

Pour obtenir de plus amples renseignements sur les règles de suppression du recensement de 2001, se reporter à « Qualité des données » de la section « Documents de référence » de cette publication.

Centres régionaux de consultation

La Division des services consultatifs de Statistique Canada vous offre un réseau de diffusion de l'information qui couvre tout le Canada au moyen de huit centres régionaux de consultation. Chaque centre de consultation possède une série de publications courantes et des documents de référence qui peuvent être consultés ou achetés, de même que des disquettes, des CD-ROM, des cartes et d'autres produits. On peut photocopier sur place les documents imprimés.

Chaque centre de consultation vous offre un vaste éventail de services additionnels. Les services consultatifs peuvent vous aider à identifier vos besoins en information, établir des sources de données disponibles, consolider et intégrer des données de différentes sources, élaborer des profils, analyser les faits saillants et les tendances, et finalement, offrir de la formation sur les produits, les services, les concepts de Statistique Canada et l'utilisation de données statistiques.

Pour de plus amples renseignements, veuillez composer le numéro sans frais ci-dessous ou envoyer un courriel à infostats@statcan.ca.

Contactez-nous

Numéro sans frais pour les **demandes de renseignements** (Canada et les États-Unis) : 1 800 263-1136

ATS : 1 800 363-7629

Numéro sans frais **pour commander seulement** (Canada et les États-Unis) : 1 800 267-6677

Numéro sans frais **pour commander par télécopieur** (Canada et les États-Unis) : 1 877 287-4369

Courriel : infostats@statcan.ca

Région de l'atlantique

Couvre les provinces suivantes : Terre-Neuve-et-Labrador, la Nouvelle-Écosse, l'Île-du-Prince-Édouard et le Nouveau-Brunswick.

Services consultatifs
Statistique Canada
2e étage, boîte 11
1741, rue Brunswick
Halifax (Nouvelle-Écosse)
B3J 3X8

Téléphone : (902) 426-5331 ou,
sans frais, 1 800 263-1136
Télécopieur : (902) 426-9538
Courriel : infostats@statcan.ca

Région du Québec

Couvre tout le Québec et le Nunavut sauf la région de la Capitale nationale.

Services consultatifs
Statistique Canada
Complexe Guy-Favreau, tour Est,
4e étage
200, boulevard René-Lévesque Ouest
Montréal (Québec)
H2Z 1X4

Téléphone : (514) 283-5725 ou,
sans frais, 1 800 263-1136
Télécopieur : (514) 283-9350
Courriel : infostats@statcan.ca

Région de la Capitale nationale

Couvre la région de la Capitale nationale.

Centre de consultation statistique
(région de la Capitale nationale)
Statistique Canada
Immeuble Principal, pièce 1500
120, avenue Parkdale
Ottawa (Ontario)
K1A 0T6

Téléphone : (613) 951-8116 ou,
sans frais, 1 800 263-1136
Télécopieur : (613) 951-0581
Courriel : infostats@statcan.ca

Région de l'Ontario

Couvre tout l'Ontario sauf la région de la Capitale nationale.

Services consultatifs
Statistique Canada
Immeuble Arthur-Meighen, 10e étage
25, avenue St. Clair Est
Toronto (Ontario)
M4T 1M4

Téléphone : (416) 973-6586 ou,
sans frais, 1 800 263-1136
Télécopieur : (416) 973-7475
Courriel : infostats@statcan.ca

Région des prairies

Il y a trois centres de consultation dans cette région qui couvre le Manitoba, la Saskatchewan, l'Alberta et les Territoires du Nord-Ouest.

Pour le Manitoba :

Services consultatifs
Statistique Canada
Immeuble Via Rail, bureau 200
123, rue Main
Winnipeg (Manitoba)
R3C 4V9

Téléphone : (204) 983-4020 ou,
sans frais, 1 800 263-1136
Télécopieur : (204) 983-7543
Courriel : infostats@statcan.ca

Région des prairies – fin

Pour la Saskatchewan :

Services consultatifs
Statistique Canada
Immeuble Park Plaza, bureau 440
2365, rue Albert
Regina (Saskatchewan)
S4P 4K1

Téléphone : (306) 780-5405 ou,
sans frais, 1 800 263-1136
Télécopieur : (306) 780-5403
Courriel : infostats@statcan.ca

Pour l'Alberta et les Territoires du Nord-Ouest :

Services consultatifs
Statistique Canada
Immeuble Pacific Plaza, bureau 900
10909, avenue Jasper Nord-Ouest
Edmonton (Alberta)
T5J 4J3

Téléphone : (780) 495-3027 ou,
sans frais, 1 800 263-1136
Télécopieur : (780) 495-5318
Courriel : infostats@statcan.ca

Région du pacifique

Couvre la Colombie-Britannique et le territoire du Yukon.

Services consultatifs
Statistique Canada
Library Square Tower, bureau 600
300, rue West Georgia
Vancouver (Colombie-Britannique)
V6B 6C7

Téléphone : (604) 666-3691 ou,
sans frais, 1 800 263-1136
Télécopieur : (604) 666-4863
Courriel : infostats@statcan.ca

BON DE COMMANDE

Statistique Canada

POUR COMMANDER :

COURRIER
Statistique Canada
Opérations et intégration
Gestion de la circulation
120, avenue Parkdale
Ottawa (Ontario) K1A 0T6
CANADA

TÉLÉPHONE 1 800 267-6677

TÉLÉCOPIEUR 1 877 287-4369

COURRIEL order@statcan.ca

ATM 1 800 363-7629

(Veuillez écrire en majuscules)

Compagnie ____________

Service ____________

À l'attention de ____________ Titre ____________

Adresse ____________

Ville ____________ Province ____________

Code postal ____ Téléphone ( ) ____ Télécopieur ( ) ____

Courriel : ____________

Vos renseignements personnels sont protégés par la *Loi sur la protection des renseignements personnels*.**

MODALITÉS DE PAIEMENT :

(Cochez une seule case)

☐ **Veuillez débiter mon compte** ☐ VISA ☐ Master Card ☐ American Express

Numéro de carte ____________

Date d'expiration ____________

Détenteur de carte (en majuscules s.v.p.) ____________

Signature ____________

☐ **Paiement inclus $** ____________
(à l'ordre du Receveur général du Canada)

☐ **Numéro du bon de commande** ____________
(Veuillez joindre le bon)

Signature de la personne autorisée ____________

Numéro au catalogue	Titre	Édition(s) demandée(s) ou inscrire « A » pour les abonnements	Prix (Les prix n'incluent pas la taxe de vente)	*Frais de port (Pour les envois à l'extérieur du Canada)	Quantité	Total $

*Frais de port : Aucuns frais pour les envois au Canada. Pour les envois à destination des États-Unis, veuillez ajouter 6 $ pour chaque numéro ou article commandé. Pour les envois à destination des autres pays, veuillez ajouter 10 $ pour chaque numéro ou article commandé. Fréquence des parutions : publication annuelle = 1; publication trimestrielle = 4; publication mensuelle = 12.	**TOTAL**	
Les clients canadiens ajoutent **soit** la TPS de 7 % et la TVP en vigueur, **soit** la TVH (TPS n° R121491807).	**TPS (7 %)**	
Les clients de l'étranger paient en dollars canadiens tirés sur une banque canadienne **ou** en dollars US tirés sur une banque américaine selon le taux de change quotidien en vigueur.	**TVP en vigueur**	
Statistique Canada utilise la SIF. Les ministères et les organismes du gouvernement fédéral doivent indiquer sur toutes les commandes leur code d'organisme RI ____________ et leur code de référence RI ____________.	**TVH en vigueur (N.-É., N.-B., T.-N.L.)**	
****Statistique Canada utilisera les renseignements qui vous concernent seulement pour effectuer la présente transaction, livrer votre (vos) produit(s), annoncer les mises à jour de ce(s) produit(s) et gérer votre compte. Nous pourrions de temps à autre vous informer au sujet d'autres produits et services de Statistique Canada ou vous demander de participer à nos études de marché.** Si vous ne voulez pas qu'on communique avec vous de nouveau pour des promotions ☐ ou des études de marché ☐, cochez la case correspondante et faites-nous parvenir cette page par télécopieur ou par la poste, téléphonez-nous au **1 800 700-1033** ou envoyez un courriel à **order@statcan.ca.**	**TOTAL GÉNÉRAL**	
	PF021207	

MERCI POUR VOTRE COMMANDE!

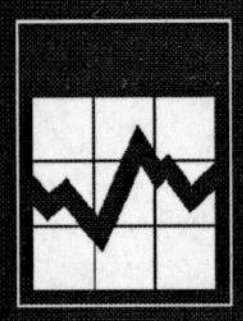

ORDER FORM

Statistics Canada

TO ORDER:	METHOD OF PAYMENT:

TO ORDER:

MAIL — **TELEPHONE** 1 800 267- 6677 — **FAX** 1 877 287- 4369

Statistics Canada
Operations and Integration
Circulation Management
120 Parkdale Avenue
Ottawa, Ontario K1A 0T6
CANADA

E-MAIL order@statcan.ca — **TTY** 1 800 363-7629

(Please print)

Company ______________________

Department ______________________

Attention ______________ Title ______________

Address ______________________

City ______________ Province ______________

Postal Code ______________ Telephone ( ) ______________ Fax ( ) ______________

E-mail Address: ______________________

Your personal information is protected by the Privacy Act.**

METHOD OF PAYMENT:

(Check only one)

☐ **Please charge my:** ☐ VISA ☐ Master Card ☐ American Express

Card Number ______________________

Expiry Date ______________________

Cardholder *(please print)* ______________________

Signature ______________________

☐ **Payment enclosed $** ______________________ *(payable to the Receiver General for Canada)*

☐ **Purchase Order Number** ______________________ *(please enclose)*

Authorized Signature ______________________

Catalogue Number	Title	Date of issue(s) or indicate an "S" for subscription(s)	Price (All prices exclude sales tax)	*Shipping Charges (Applicable to shipments sent outside Canada)	Quantity	Total $

*Shipping charges: No shipping charges for delivery in Canada. For shipments to the United States, please add $6 per issue or item ordered. For shipments to other countries, please add $10 per issue or item ordered. Annual frequency = 1. Quarterly frequency = 4. Monthly frequency = 12.	**SUBTOTAL**	
Canadian clients add **either** 7% GST and applicable PST **or** HST (GST Registration No. R121491807).	**GST (7%)**	
Clients outside Canada pay in Canadian dollars drawn on a Canadian bank **or** pay in equivalent US dollars, converted at the prevailing daily exchange rate, drawn on a US bank.	**Applicable PST**	
Statistics Canada is FIS-ready. Federal government departments and agencies must include with all orders their IS Organization Code ______________ and IS Reference Code ______________.	**Applicable HST (N.S., N.B., Nfld.Lab.)**	
**** Statistics Canada will only use your information to complete this sales transaction, deliver your product(s), announce product updates and administer your account. From time to time, we may also offer you other Statistics Canada products and services or ask you to participate in our market research.** If you do not wish to be contacted again for promotional purposes ☐ and/or market research ☐, check as appropriate and fax or mail this page to us, call **1 800 700-1033** or e-mail **order@statcan.ca.**	**GRAND TOTAL**	
	PF021207	

THANK YOU FOR YOUR ORDER!